THE OXFORD HA

OPERA

THE OXFORD HANDBOOK OF

OPERA

Edited by

HELEN M. GREENWALD

OXFORD
UNIVERSITY PRESS

OXFORD
UNIVERSITY PRESS

Oxford University Press is a department of the University of Oxford.
It furthers the University's objective of excellence in research, scholarship,
and education by publishing worldwide.

Oxford New York
Auckland Cape Town Dar es Salaam Hong Kong Karachi
Kuala Lumpur Madrid Melbourne Mexico City Nairobi
New Delhi Shanghai Taipei Toronto

With offices in
Argentina Austria Brazil Chile Czech Republic France Greece
Guatemala Hungary Italy Japan Poland Portugal Singapore
South Korea Switzerland Thailand Turkey Ukraine Vietnam

Published in the United States of America by
Oxford University Press
198 Madison Avenue, New York, NY 10016

First issued as an Oxford University Press paperback, 2022

Library of Congress Cataloging-in-Publication Data

The Oxford handbook of opera / edited by Helen M. Greenwald.
pages cm
Includes bibliographical references and index.
ISBN 978-0-19-533553-8 (hardcover : alk. paper); 978-0-19-762545-3 (paperback)
1. Opera.
I. Greenwald, Helen M., editor.
ML1700.O916 2014
782.1—dc23
2013028673

1 3 5 7 9 8 6 4 2

Printed by Integrated Books International, United States of America

Contents

PART V TRANSMISSION AND RECEPTION

PART VI OPERA ON THE EDGE

EPILOGUE

List of Figures

List of Music Examples

List of Tables

List of Contributors

Marianne Betz is Professor of Musicology at the Hochschule für Musik und Theater "Felix Mendelssohn Bartholdy" Leipzig. Her research explores transatlantic relations, focusing on American music of the generation of George W. Chadwick. Her publications include articles for the *Handwörterbuch der musikalischen Terminologie, Archiv für Musikwissenschaft, Die Musikforschung, Musical Quarterly, Zibaldone*, and the *Yearbook of the American Music Research Centre* (Boulder, CO). She is editor of the critical editions of Chadwick's *String Quartets* (A-R, 2007) and his opera *The Padrone*, and is currently preparing a monograph on Chadwick.

Thomas Betzwieser is Chair of Historical Musicology at the Goethe-Universität in Frankfurt. He was Assistant Professor at the Freie Universität Berlin (1990–1995), DAAD Research Fellow at the Maison des Sciences de l'Homme, Paris (1995–1996), and Lecturer in Music at the University of Southampton (1999–2001). From 2001–2012 he held the Professorship of Musicology at the University of Bayreuth. He is a member of several musicological advisory boards (Heidelberger Akademie der Wissenschaften, Akademie der Wissenschaften und der Literatur Mainz), and since 2009 head of the project *OPERA—Spektrum des europäischen Musiktheaters in Einzeleditionen* (funded by the Union of German Academies of Sciences).

Charles S. Brauner is Professor Emeritus of Music History and Literature at Roosevelt University. He is editor of the critical edition of Rossini's *Mosè in Egitto*, which was a finalist for the Claude V. Palisca Prize of the American Musicological Society, and co-editor of the critical edition of Rossini's *Armida*. He has published articles on Rossini, Bellini, Monteverdi, German Lieder, and a study of libretti on the story of Armida from 1639 to 1817. His critical edition of Rossini's *Moïse* is in preparation.

Patricia B. Brauner was until 2011 Managing Editor of *Works of Gioachino Rossini* (Bärenreiter) and Coordinator of the Center for Italian Opera Studies at the University of Chicago. She is editor of critical editions of Rossini's *Il barbiere di Siviglia* and the cantatas *La riconoscenza / Il vero omaggio* and co-editor of four other volumes of Rossini's works, including the *Petite Messe solennelle* (with Philip Gossett), which received the 2010 Claude Palisca Award of the American Musicological Society for a scholarly edition or translation. She has taught music history at Connecticut College, Loyola University of Chicago, and Roosevelt University, as well as seminars in music editing for the Fondazione Rossini (Pesaro, Italy), and the Université François-Rabelais (Tours, France).

Joy H. Calico is Associate Professor of Musicology and Director of the Max Kade Center for European and German Studies at Vanderbilt University. She is the author of *Brecht at the Opera* (California, 2008), *Arnold Schoenberg's 'A Survivor from Warsaw' in Postwar Europe* (California, 2014), and numerous other publications on opera and on Cold War cultural politics. She has received fellowships and grants from the Howard Foundation, the American Academy in Berlin, the National Endowment for the Humanities, the Berlin Program for Advanced German and European Studies, and the German Academic Exchange Service.

Tim Carter is the author of books on opera and musical theater ranging from the early Baroque to the mid-twentieth century, including *W. A. Mozart: 'Le nozze di Figaro'* (Cambridge, 1987), *Monteverdi's Musical Theatre* (Yale, 2002), and *'Oklahoma!' The Making of an American Musical* (Yale, 2007), and (with Richard Goldthwaite), *Orpheus in the Marketplace: Jacopo Peri and the Economy of Late Renaissance Florence* (Harvard, 2013). His critical edition of Kurt Weill and Paul Green's 1936 musical play *Johnny Johnson* (Kurt Weill Foundation, 2012) won the 2013 Claude V. Palisca Prize awarded from the American Musicological Society; his work on Monteverdi was similarly recognized by the society's H. Colin Slim Award that same year. He is currently David G. Frey Distinguished Professor of Music at the University of North Carolina at Chapel Hill.

Thomas Christensen is the Avalon Foundation Professor of Music and the Humanities at the University of Chicago. He has published on a wide variety of topics, including the history of music theory, four-hand piano arrangements, and on eighteenth-century musical aesthetics. His books include *Aesthetics and the Art of Musical Composition in the German Enlightenment: Selected Writings of Johann Georg Sulzer and Heinrich Koch* (co-authored and translated with Nancy Baker; Cambridge, 1995), *Rameau and Musical Thought in the Enlightenment* (Cambridge, 1993), and (as editor), the *Cambridge History of Western Music Theory* (Cambridge, 2002). He is currently finishing a book concerning discourses of tonality in nineteenth-century France.

Marcia J. Citron is Lovett Distinguished Service Professor of Musicology at Rice University. She is the author of *When Opera Meets Film* (Cambridge, 2010) and *Opera on Screen* (Yale, 2000), and the award-winning *Gender and the Musical Canon* (reprint Illinois, 2000). In 2012 she was awarded Honorary Membership by the American Musicological Society.

Damien Colas is Director of Research at CNRS (Research Institute of Musical Heritage in Paris, France). His research focuses on Italian opera of the eighteenth and nineteenth centuries, especially performance practice (vocals, orchestra) and Franco-Italian cultural exchange and misunderstandings. For several years, Dr. Colas has been teaching a seminar on musical dramaturgy at the Université François-Rabelais (Tours). He is co-editor (with Alessandro Di Profio) of *D'une scène à l'autre. L'opéra italien en Europe* (Mardaga, 2009) and editor of the critical edition of Rossini's *Le comte Ory* for *Works of Gioachino Rossini* (Bärenreiter, 2013).

Georgia Cowart is Professor of Music at Case Western Reserve University. She has published three books and a number of articles on music, art, and cultural politics in early modern France. Her most recent book, *The Triumph of Pleasure: Louis XIV and the Politics of Spectacle* (Chicago, 2008) focuses on the shifting intersections of the arts, ideology, and aesthetics at the court of Louis XIV and in Paris ca. 1650–1720. She has received a number of research grants and awards, including fellowships from the American Council of Learned Societies, the National Endowment for the Humanities, the Metropolitan Museum of Art in New York, and the Stanford Center for the Humanities. In 2009 she served as Guest Curator for the exhibition *Watteau, Music, and Theater* at the Metropolitan Museum of Art, and is currently completing a book on Watteau and musical theater.

Valeria De Lucca is a Lecturer in Music at the University of Southampton. Her work concentrates on patronage of music and aristocratic culture in early modern Italy, with a particular emphasis on the ways in which gender and class shaped motives, goals, and strategies of women patrons and on the role that visual aspects of operatic performance played in the construction of the patron's identity. Recent publications include "Strategies of Women Patrons of Music and Theatre in Rome: Maria Mancini Colonna, Queen Christina of Sweden, and Women of their Circles" in *Renaissance Studies* 25/3 (2011) and "*L'Alcasta* and the Emergence of Collective Patronage in Mid-Seventeenth-Century Rome" in *The Journal of Musicology* 28/2 (2011). Dr. De Lucca has received grants and fellowships from the Andrew W. Mellon Foundation, American Council of Learned Societies, the British Academy, and the Metropolitan Museum of Art, New York.

Alessandro Di Profio is Professor at the Université Sorbonne Nouvelle Paris 3. He is the author of *La révolution des Bouffons: L'opéra italien au Théâtre de Monsieur, 1789–1792* (Paris, 2003), and co-editor (with Maria Grazia Melucci) of *Piccinni, un musicista europeo* (Adda, 2004) and (with Damien Colas) *D'une scène à l'autre. L'opéra italien en Europe* (Mardaga, 2009). He is the recipient of many prestigious awards and fellowships, including the Villa Medici in Rome (1999–2000), Beinecke Library (Yale University, 2003), and the Alexander von Humboldt Foundation (Berlin, 2013–2014).

William Drabkin is Professor of Music at the University of Southampton. He has published books on Haydn's quartets (Greenwood, 2000) and Beethoven's *Missa solemnis* (Cambridge, 1991), and an edition of Beethoven's sketchbook Artaria 197 (Beethoven-Haus, 2011). His editions, in English translation, of Heinrich Schenker's analytical writings from the 1920s won a Citation of Special Merit from the Society for Music Theory (2005). He has since published translations of Schenker's writings from the early 1900s, including *The Decline of the Art of Composition* (2005) and is co-recipient of a second Citation of Special Merit for work on Schenker Documents Online, a website devoted to the transmission of the theorist's correspondence and dairies. His analytical work on opera has appeared in *Music and Analysis* and the Cambridge Opera Handbook of *La bohème* (1986). He is currently Editor of the journal *Music Analysis*.

Mark Everist is Professor of Music, Associate Dean (Research) in the Faculty of Humanities, and Director of the Humanities Graduate School at the University of Southampton. His research focuses on the music of Western Europe in the period 1150–1330, French opera in the first half of the nineteenth century, Mozart, reception theory, and historiography. He is the author of *Mozart's Ghosts: Reception and Renown, 1791 to the Present* (Oxford, 2012), *Giacomo Meyerbeer and Music Drama in Nineteenth-Century Paris* (Ashgate, 2005), *Music Drama at the Paris Odéon, 1824–1828* (California, 2002), *French Motets in the Thirteenth Century* (Cambridge, 1994), and *Polyphonic Music in Thirteenth-Century France* (Garland, 1989), as well as editor of three volumes of the *Magnus Liber Organi* for Editions de l'Oiseau-Lyre (2001–2003). The recipient of the Solie (2010) and Slim (2011) awards of the American Musicological Association, he is President of the Royal Musical Association.

Linda B. Fairtile is the Head of Parsons Music Library at the University of Richmond. She is the author of *Giacomo Puccini: A Guide to Research* (Garland, 1999) and her articles on Italian opera have appeared in *19th-Century Music, Cambridge Opera Journal*, and *Studi pucciniani*. In 2008 her reconstruction of the four-act version of Puccini's *Edgar* was premiered at the Teatro Regio in Turin, and she is currently preparing the critical edition of that opera for Ricordi. Fairtile is Co-Director of the American Institute for Verdi Studies, and she has appeared as a panelist on the Texaco Metropolitan Opera Quiz radio broadcasts.

Martha Feldman is the Mabel Greene Myers Professor of Music and the Humanities at the University of Chicago. She is the author of *The Castrato: Reflections on Natures and Kinds* (California, 2014), *Opera and Sovereignty: Transforming Myths in Eighteenth-Century Italy* (Chicago, 2007), and *City Culture and the Madrigal at Venice* (California, 1995). Her book (co-edited with Bonnie Gordon), *The Courtesan's Arts: Cross-Cultural Perspectives* (Oxford, 2006) won the 2007 Ruth A. Solie Award of the American Musicological Society).

Robert Fink is Professor of Musicology at the University of California, Los Angeles. He has published widely on contemporary music (both art and popular), most notably *Repeating Ourselves: American Minimal Music as Cultural Practice* (California, 2005). His current projects include an edited collection on tone and timbre in popular music, and *Declassified*, a study of the politics of art music in a post-classical world. He currently serves on the steering committee of the Society for Minimalist Music.

Marina Frolova-Walker is Reader in Music History at the Faculty of Music, University of Cambridge, and Fellow of Clare College. She received her Ph.D. from Moscow Conservatoire before moving to the UK. She is the author of *Russian Music and Nationalism from Glinka to Stalin* (Yale, 2007) and co-author (with Jonathan Walker) of *Music and Soviet Power, 1917–32* (Boydell, 2012), and has written numerous scholarly articles and popular essays on Russian and Soviet music and culture.

Andreas Giger is the Louise and Kenneth L. Kinney Professor of Music at Louisiana State University. His research interests have concentrated on nineteenth-century Italian opera and the work of Leonard Bernstein. He is author of *Verdi and the French Aesthetic: Verse, Stanza, and Melody in Nineteenth-Century Opera* (Cambridge, 2008), editor of the critical edition of Verdi's *I due Foscari* for *The Works of Giuseppe Verdi* (Chicago/Milan, forthcoming), co-editor (with Thomas J. Mathiesen) of *Music in the Mirror: Reflections on the History of Music Theory and Literature for the Twenty-First Century* (Nebraska, 2002), and founder of the Internet database *Saggi musicali italiani*.

Vincent Giroud is Professor of Comparative Literature at the University of Franche-Comté in Besançon. An École normale supérieure and Oxford graduate, he has previously taught at the Sorbonne, Johns Hopkins, Vassar, Bard, and Yale, where he also served for many years as curator of modern books and manuscripts at the Beinecke Library. Among his most recent publications are *The World of Witold Gombrowicz* (Yale University Library, 2004), *Picasso and Gertrude Stein* (Metropolitan Museum of Art, 2007), and *French Opera: A Short History* (Yale, 2010). He is an associate editor of *The Oxford Companion to the Book* (Oxford, 2010), and is currently completing a biography of the American composer Nicolas Nabokov for Oxford University Press.

Lydia Goehr is Professor of Philosophy at Columbia University. She is the author of *The Imaginary Museum of Musical Works: An Essay in the Philosophy of Music* (Oxford, 1992; second edition with a new essay, 2007), *The Quest for Voice: Music, Politics, and the Limits of Philosophy* [essays on Richard Wagner] (Oxford, 1998), *Elective Affinities: Musical Essays on the History of Aesthetic Theory* [essays on Adorno and Danto] (Columbia University, 2008), and co-editor (with Daniel Herwitz) of *The Don Giovanni Moment: Essays on the Legacy of an Opera* (Columbia University, 2006).

Philip Gossett is the Robert W. Reneker Distinguished Service Professor Emeritus at The University of Chicago. He is General Editor of *The Works of Giuseppe Verdi* (a joint publication of The University of Chicago Press and Ricordi-Universal Music of Milan) and of *Works of Gioachino Rossini* (Bärenreiter). His 2006 book, *Divas and Scholars: Performing Italian Opera* (Chicago), was awarded the Kinkeldey Prize of the American Musicological Society as the best book about music published that year. For his contributions to Italian opera, he was awarded the Cavaliere di Gran Croce, Italy's highest civilian honor, by the President of Italy in 1999. He works extensively with opera houses and singers in mounting operas whose critical editions he has been responsible for publishing.

John Graziano is Director of *Music in Gotham*, a database project (generously funded by the National Endowment for the Humanities), which documents musical events in New York City from September 1862 through August 1875. His recent publications include *European Music and Musicians in New York City, 1840–1900* (Rochester, 2006), and articles on John Phillip Sousa, Harry Burleigh, and the "Black Patti." He is Professor Emeritus of Music at the City College and Graduate Center, City University of New York.

Helen M. Greenwald has taught at the New England Conservatory of Music since 1991, and was Visiting Professor in the Music Department at the University of Chicago in 2008. Her numerous articles on vocal music of the eighteenth through twentieth centuries have appeared in *19th-Century Music, Acta Musicologica, Journal of the American Musicological Society, the Mozart-Jahrbuch, Cambridge Opera Journal*, and the *Salzburger Akademische Beiträge*. She is the editor of the critical edition of Verdi's *Attila* (Chicago/Milan, 2012), which was premiered in 2010 by Riccardo Muti in his debut at the Metropolitan Opera, and the co-editor (with Kathleen Kuzmick Hansell) of the critical edition of Rossini's *Zelmira* (Pesaro, 2005), premiered (2009) by Robert Abbado at the Rossini Opera Festival in Pesaro, Italy, with Juan Diego Flórez in the role of Ilo, and recently released on DVD (Decca, 2012). She writes frequently for the Boston Symphony Orchestra, the Royal Opera at Covent Garden, and the Metropolitan Opera.

Michal Grover-Friedlander teaches in the Musicology program at the Buchmann-Mehta School of Music at Tel Aviv University. She has written two books, *Vocal Apparitions: The Attraction of Cinema to Opera* (Princeton, 2005), which was named one of Choice's outstanding academic titles for 2005, *Operatic Afterlives* (Zone, 2011), and co-edited an interdisciplinary book about the voice and the gaze (Resling, 2002, in Hebrew). She has written numerous articles and received several grants (*Yad Hanandiv*, Institute for Advanced Studies, Princeton, the Israel Science Foundation, and the Kurt Weill Foundation). Since 2005, Grover-Friedlander has been directing opera in Italy, Germany, and Israel, and in 2011 she founded the opera group Ta Opera Zuta.

Jake Heggie is an American composer of the operas *Moby-Dick* (libretto, Gene Scheer), *Dead Man Walking* (libretto, Terrence McNally), *To Hell and Back* (Scheer), *Three Decembers* (Scheer), *For a Look or a Touch* (Scheer), more than two hundred art songs, and orchestral and chamber music. As pianist and composer, he collaborates regularly with many of the world's most beloved singers, and his songs, song cycles, and operas are programmed and produced internationally. Upcoming projects include *Great Scott*, a new opera for Joyce DiDonato with a libretto by Terrence McNally, commissioned by the Dallas Opera for its 2015 season. He lives in San Francisco.

Wendy Heller is Professor of Music and Director of the Program in Italian Studies at Princeton University. She is a specialist in seventeenth- and eighteenth-century opera from interdisciplinary perspectives, with particular emphasis on gender and sexuality, art history, and the classical tradition. Author of *Emblems of Eloquence: Opera and Women's Voices in Seventeenth-Century Venice* (California, 2004), Heller has been a Fellow of the American Academy in Rome, of the Villa I Tatti (Harvard University Center for Renaissance Studies), and the Sylvan C. and Pamela Coleman Fellow at the Metropolitan Museum of Art. She is also the author of *Music in the Baroque* and *Anthology of Music in the Baroque* (both for W. W. Norton, 2013), and is completing a book entitled *Animating Ovid: Opera and the Metamorphoses of Antiquity in Early Modern Italy*.

Monika Hennemann's research interests center on the music and literature of the "long nineteenth century" in German- and English-speaking countries. Her work has appeared in the Cambridge Companions to Mendelssohn and Liszt, and she has prepared the first edition of Anton Webern's play "Tot." Her monograph *Mendelssohns Opernprojekte* *in ihrem kulturellen Kontext: Ein Beitrag zur deutschen Opern- und Librettogeschichte zwischen 1820 und 1850* will appear in 2014. She is presently a Lecturer in German Studies at Cardiff University, the Program Director of the University of Rhode Island's "Deutsche Sommerschule am Atlantik," and an Honorary Research Fellow in Musicology at the University of Birmingham.

Mary Hunter is A. LeRoy Greason Professor of Music at Bowdoin College. She is the author of *The Culture of Opera Buffa in Mozart's Vienna: A Poetics of Entertainment* (Princeton, 1999), for which she won the Kinkeldey Prize of the American Musicological Society, *Mozart's Operas: A Companion* (Yale, 2008), and co-editor (with James Webster) of *The Opera Buffa in Mozart's Vienna* (Cambridge, 1997) and (with Richard Will) *Engaging Haydn: Culture, Content and Context* (Cambridge, 2012). She was the editor of *Cambridge Opera Journal* 1997–2002, and has written articles on many aspects of late-eighteenth-century music. She is currently at work on a project on the ideology of performance in classical music culture.

Veronica Isaac is Assistant Curator in the Department of Theatre and Performance at the Victoria & Albert Museum, London. She was formerly Keeper of Costume for the Chertsey Museum and has carried out a number of freelance projects for other museums and institutions, including "Starstruck," an exhibition of film, television, and theatrical costumes (Worcester Cathedral, 2009) and, most recently, an exhibition of 1930s dress entitled "Day and Night: From the Bedroom to the Ballroom 1929–1939" (Chertsey Museum). Her recent publications include "Presuming Too Far 'above his very base and low degree'?: Thomas Cromwell's Use of Textiles in his Schemes for Social and Political Success (1527–1540)," *Costume* 45 (2011) and "The Art of Costume: Highlights from the Wardrobe of the Painter's Actress," *Nineteenth Century Theatre and Film* 39/2 (2012).

Francesco Izzo is Senior Lecturer in Music at the University of Southampton. His research focuses on nineteenth-century opera and culture. He has published articles in *Acta Musicologica, Cambridge Opera Journal, Journal of the American Musicological Society, Journal of Musicology, Nineteenth-Century Music Review, Studi musicali*, and in numerous books and congress proceedings. He is Co-Director of the American Institute for Verdi Studies at New York University, the author of *Laughter Between Two Revolutions: Opera Buffa in Italy, 1831–1848* (Rochester, 2013), and the editor of Giuseppe Verdi's *Un giorno di regno* for *The Works of Giuseppe Verdi* (Chicago/ Milan, forthcoming).

Lawrence Kramer is Distinguished Professor of English and Music at Fordham University. He is the author of numerous books, most recently including *Expression and Truth: On the Music of Knowledge* and *Interpreting Music*, both (like most of his others) from the University of California Press; he has held numerous visiting professorships in North America, Europe, and Asia; he is the long-time editor of the journal *19th-Century Music*; and he is a composer whose music has been performed internationally.

Daniela Macchione is Managing Editor of *Works of Gioachino Rossini* (WGR) for Bärenreiter Verlag (Kassel, Germany), for which she co-authored (with Martina Grempler) the inaugural volume of the series, *Chamber Music without Piano* (2007) and editor of the Bärenreiter critical edition of *Paganini, Niccolò: 24 Capricci op. 1 / 24 Contradanze Inglesi for Violin solo* (2013). She has taught at the University of Rome, La Sapienza, where she earned her doctorate in the History and Analysis of Musical Cultures (2004), and was *assegnista di ricerca* (research associate) at the University of Pavia/Cremona. She is consultant for the Center for Italian Opera Studies at the University of Chicago, where her work is devoted mainly to the *OperaCat* project. Dr. Macchione has received many prestigious awards and grants, including the Houghton Library Fellowship at Harvard University.

Ryan Minor is Associate Professor of Music History and Theory at the State University of New York at Stony Brook. He is the author of *Choral Fantasies: Music, Festivity, and Nationhood in 19th-Century Germany* (Cambridge, 2012), in addition to articles on Wagner and the historiography of music and nationalism. His current projects focus on dramaturgy and the politics of musical spectatorship in German opera. His work has been supported by the Alexander von Humboldt Foundation and the Radcliffe Institute for Advanced Study at Harvard University, and he currently serves as Co-Executive Editor of *The Opera Quarterly*.

Ulrich Müller (†2012) was Professor Emeritus (medieval German literature) at the University of Salzburg and published and edited numerous books and articles about European literature, musical theater (above all Mozart, Wagner, Kurt Weill, and musical comedy) and medieval music and modern performances (including LPs and CDs). For over fifteen years he served (with Oswald Panagl) as Dramaturg at the Landestheater Salzburg, and co-organized (until 2012) symposia about "Musiktheater" together with the Salzburg Festival and the Osterfestspiele Salzburg. Professor Müller contributed to numerous program books of the Salzburg Festival, the Bayreuth Festival, the Vienna Staatsoper and Volksoper, and other opera houses.

James Parakilas is the James L. Moody, Jr., Family Professor of Performing Arts at Bates College, where his teaching includes a course on Music and Drama. He is the author of *Ballads Without Words: Chopin and the Tradition of the Instrumental Ballade* (Amadeus, 1992), *Piano Roles: 300 Years of Life with the Piano* (Yale, 2000), and the textbook *The Story of Opera* (W. W. Norton, 2012), as well as articles on canon formation in Western music, grand opera, the opera chorus, exoticism in opera, and operas of Mozart, Tchaikovsky, and Gershwin.

Hilary Poriss is Associate Professor of Music History at Northeastern University, Boston. Her research interests focus on Italian and French opera, performance practice, and diva studies. She is the author of *Changing the Score: Arias, Prima Donnas, and the Authority of Performance* (Oxford, 2009), and co-editor (with Roberta Montemorra Marvin) of *Fashions and Legacies of Nineteenth-Century Italian Opera* (Cambridge, 2010) and (with Rachel Cowgill) of *The Arts of the Prima Donna in the Long Nineteenth Century* (Oxford, 2012). In addition, she has published articles and reviews in *19th-Century Music, Cambridge Opera Journal, Verdi Forum*, and *Nineteenth-Century Music Review*.

Jesse Rosenberg is Associate Professor of Music at Northwestern University. He received his Ph.D. from New York University, where he worked as archivist for the American Institute for Verdi Studies and received the Outstanding Dissertation Award and Excellence in Teaching Award. His published research includes studies on Rossini, Bellini, Donizetti, Verdi, and the Italian critic and theorist Abramo Basevi.

Julian Rushton taught at the Universities of East Anglia and Cambridge before becoming West Riding Professor of Music at the University of Leeds in 1982; he is now Professor Emeritus. His publications have centered on Berlioz, including two books—*The Musical Language of Berlioz* (Cambridge, 1983) and *The Music of Berlioz* (Oxford, 2001)—in addition to a number of articles and four volumes edited for the *New Berlioz Edition*. He has also published short studies of Mozart, including Cambridge Opera Handbooks on *Don Giovanni* (1981) and *Idomeneo* (1993), *Mozart* (The Master Musicians, 2006), and the *New Grove Guide to Mozart and His Operas* (2006). He was general editor of Cambridge Music Handbooks, contributing two volumes: *Berlioz: 'Roméo et Juliette'* (1994) and *Elgar: 'Enigma Variations'* (1999); he is now joint editor with J. P. E. Harper-Scott of the Cambridge series *Music in Context*. Professor Rushton was President of the Royal Musical Association (1994–1999), and has been Chairman of the Editorial Committee of *Musica Britannica* since 1993. He is a Corresponding Member of the American Musicological Society and a Director of the International Musicological Society (from 2007).

Derek B. Scott is Professor of Critical Musicology and former Head of the School of Music at the University of Leeds. He has a special interest in the historical sociology of popular music and music for the stage, and is also a composer of theater music, symphonies for brass band, and a concerto for Highland Bagpipe. He has worked professionally as a singer and pianist on radio and TV, and in concert hall and theater. His books include *The Singing Bourgeois* (Ashgate 1989, 2001), *From the Erotic to the Demonic: On Critical Musicology* (Oxford, 2003), *Sounds of the Metropolis: The 19th-Century Popular Music Revolution in London, New York, Paris, and Vienna* (Oxford, 2008), and *Musical Style and Social Meaning* (Ashgate, 2010). He is the editor of *Music, Culture, and Society: A Reader* (Oxford, 2000) and *The Ashgate Research Companion to Popular Musicology* (2009), General Editor of Ashgate's Popular and Folk Music Series, and Associate Editor of *Popular Musicology Online*.

Emanuele Senici is Professor of Music History at the University of Rome, La Sapienza. His publications include *'La clemenza di Tito' di Mozart: I primi trent'anni (1791–1821)* (Brepols, 1997), *The Cambridge Companion to Rossini* (Cambridge, 2004, as editor) and *Landscape and Gender in Italian Opera: The Alpine Virgin from Bellini to Puccini* (Cambridge, 2005). Between 2003 and 2008 he was co-editor of the *Cambridge Opera Journal*.

W. Anthony Sheppard is Professor of Music at Williams College where he teaches courses in opera, twentieth-century music, popular music, and Asian music. His research interests include twentieth-century opera and music theater, cross-cultural influence and Orientalism, and film music. His first book, *Revealing Masks: Exotic Influences* *and Ritualized Performance in Modernist Music Theater* (California, 2001) received the Kurt Weill Prize, his article on *Madama Butterfly* and film earned the ASCAP Deems Taylor Award, and his article in the *Journal of the American Musicological Society* on World War II film music was honored with the Alfred Einstein Award by the American Musicological Society. His research has been supported by grants from the NEH, the American Philosophical Society, and the Institute for Advanced Study, Princeton, and he is currently completing a book entitled *Extreme Exoticism: Japan in the American Musical Imagination.* Sheppard frequently delivers lectures for the Metropolitan Opera Guild and is Editor-in-Chief of the *Journal of the American Musicological Society.*

Louise K. Stein is Professor of Musicology at the University of Michigan. She held visiting appointments at University of North Carolina, Chapel Hill, Universidad Complutense in Madrid, and the University of Chicago, and fellowships from the Fulbright Foundation, ACLS, NEH, the American Philosophical Society, the Gladys Krieble Delmas Foundation, Spain's Ministry of Culture, and the Institute for the Humanities at Michigan. Her research concerns early modern music and theater, patronage, the history of singing, and the politics and economics of opera production. Her book *Songs of Mortals, Dialogues of the Gods: Music and Theatre in 17th-Century Spain* (Oxford, 1993) received the First Book Prize from the Society for Spanish and Portuguese Historical Studies, and her collaborations have resulted in prize-winning recordings, such as *¡Ay amor!* (Harmonia Mundi; Mary Springfels and the Newberry Consort), and Jordi Savall's performances of the first extant Spanish opera, *Celos aun del aire matan* by Juan Hidalgo (Recent Researches in the Music of the Baroque Era, A-R Editions, 2014). She was artistic advisor to the BMG recording of the first New World opera, *La púrpura de la rosa* (her critical edition, Madrid, 1999). In 1996 the American Musicological Society recognized her with the Noah Greenberg Award for "distinguished contributions to the study and performance of early music."

Katherine Syer is Associate Professor of Musicology and Theatre History at the University of Illinois at Urbana-Champaign. Her writings on opera production history and Wagner have appeared in the revised English National Opera Guide to *Der fliegende Holländer* (2012), *Musical Quarterly* (2011), *Wagner and His World* (Princeton, 2009) edited by Thomas Grey, and *The Wagner Journal.* She co-edited, with William Kinderman, *A Companion to Wagner's 'Parsifal'* (Camden House, 2005), to which she contributed two chapters. Syer's book *Wagner's Visions: Poetry, Politics, and the Psyche in the Operas through 'Die Walküre'* (Rochester, 2014) explores the historical/political basis of the psychological dimension of his operas.

Linda J. Tomko is a historian, dancer, and embodier of dances past. She earned the Ph.D. in History at UCLA and conducts research in two areas: dance in the early twentieth-century United States and theater and court dance in early eighteenth-century France and England. Her book *Dancing Class: Gender, Ethnicity, and Social Divides in American Dance, 1890–1920* was published by Indiana University Press (1999). She was a founding member of Les Menus Plaisirs, a Baroque dance troupe, and she led a group of dancers in performance with the early music band Musica Pacifica at the 2012 Berkeley

Festival and Exhibition. Tomko is Associate Professor of Dance at the University of California, Riverside, where she chaired the Department of Dance for two different periods during the past decade. She is a Past President of the Society for Dance History Scholars, and she is Dance & Music series editor for Pendragon Press.

John Warrack was formerly Lecturer in Music at Oxford University. His books include *Carl Maria von Weber* and an edition of *Weber's Writings on Music* (Cambridge, 1981), *German Opera: from the Beginnings to Wagner* (Cambridge, 2001), and the Cambridge Opera Handbook to Wagner's *Die Meistersinger von Nürnberg* (1994). He is also co-author of the *Oxford Dictionary of Opera*, and has edited Weber's *Piano Concerto N. 1 in C Major* (WeV N.9) for the *Neue Weber Gesamtausgabe* and co-edited (with Richard Macnutt) Gunther Braam's *The Portraits of Berlioz* (NBE 26) for the *New Berlioz Edition*.

Paul Watt is Lecturer in Musicology at Monash University, Australia. With Patrick Spedding, he is editor of *Bawdy Songbooks of the Romantic Period* (Pickering & Chatto, 2011), and his studies of nineteenth-century music have been published in *Music & Letters*, the *Royal Musical Association Research Chronicle*, and *Nineteenth-Century Music Review*. Dr. Watt earned his Ph.D. from the University of Sydney, and has held visiting fellowships at the School of Advanced Studies of the University of London, and the Humanities Research Center, University of Texas, Austin. He is currently writing a critical biography of Ernest Newman and a history of music criticism in nineteenth-century England.

Marc A. Weiner is Professor of Germanic Studies and Adjunct Professor of Comparative Literature, Communication and Culture, and Culture Studies at Indiana University, Bloomington. He is the author of *Undertones of Insurrection: Music and Cultural Politics in the Modern German Narrative* (Transaction, 2009), *Richard Wagner and the Anti-Semitic Imagination* (Nebraska, 1995, 1997), which won the Eugene M. Kayden National University Press Book Award for best book in the Humanities, and *Arthur Schnitzler and the Crisis of Musical Culture* (Carl Winter, 1986). He has received fellowships from the German Academic Exchange Service, the Andrew W. Mellon Foundation, the Alexander von Humboldt Foundation, and the Richard Wagner Gedenkstätte in Bayreuth. He writes regularly for the Lyric Opera of Chicago.

Simon Williams is Professor of Theater and Dance at the University of California, Santa Barbara. He has published widely on the history of acting, Shakespearean performance, opera as drama, and the history of operatic staging, including two books on Wagner, including *Wagner and the Romantic Hero* (Cambridge, 2004, 2010). He has served for several years as *Opera News* critic for Los Angeles and Santa Fe. He is co-editor of the first *History of German Theatre* (Cambridge, 2008), and is chief editor of the forthcoming *Cambridge World Encyclopedia of Stage Actors and Acting*. He is a director of opera and spoken drama.

Alexandra Wilson is Reader in Musicology at Oxford Brookes University, where she co-directs the OBERTO opera research unit. Her research focuses on late-nineteenth- and early-twentieth-century opera and operatic culture, and on postmodern interpretations and appropriations of opera. She has published her work in *Cambridge Opera Journal*, *Music & Letters*, and *The Opera Quarterly*, and is author of *The Puccini Problem: Opera, Nationalism, and Modernity* (Cambridge, 2007), for which she earned the American Musicological Society's Lewis Lockwood Award. Her latest book is *Opera: A Beginner's Guide* (Oneworld, 2010).

Acknowledgments

I would like to thank, first of all, the contributors to the volume for their wonderful work, patience, and collegiality. The volume could not have been completed without the sabbatical leave granted in spring 2012 by New England Conservatory President Tony Woodcock and Provost and Dean of the College Thomas Novak. Jean Morrow, Director of Libraries at New England Conservatory, provided materials, patience, and superb advice. I thank also members of the NEC library staff for their unflagging professionalism and generous assistance: Richard Vallone, Wallace Corey-Dunbar, Maria Jane Loizou, Patrick Maxfield, Maryalyce Perrin-Mohr, Jason Coleman, and Suzanne Jalbert. I am also deeply grateful to Cristiano Ostinelli, General Manager of the Classical Division, Universal Music Publishing Ricordi, Dr. Arnold Nesselrath and Paola Salvieri of the Vatican Museums, Anna Sheppard, Imogen Plouviez, and Amy Prescott of the Victoria & Albert Museum, and photographer Karen Almond of the Dallas Opera. Many friends and colleagues assisted with the realization of the *Oxford Handbook of Opera*, and I offer them my deep appreciation for sharing their time and resources so generously: Evan Baker, Charles Brauner, Patricia Brauner, Marcia Citron, Valeria De Lucca, Dexter Edge, Katharine Ellis, Linda Fairtile, Andreas Giger, Ellen Harris, Francesco Izzo, Orly Krasner, Ralph P. Locke, Lewis Lockwood, Michael Loo, Albert Oppenheimer, Hilary Poriss, Derek B. Scott, Daniel Snowman, and Ruth Solie. I am indebted to Bridget Haile and Gabriel Alfieri for close readings, critical eyes, and great company. Translators Julia Grella O'Connell, Edward Schneider, and Jeff Tapia did a superb job of probing and challenging their subjects. Jake Heggie shared generously of his time and his musical autographs and vast operatic experience.

This volume would not be possible without the support of Oxford University Press. I wish to offer my heartfelt gratitude to Editor in Chief of Humanities and Executive Editor of Music Suzanne Ryan for lighting the spark and keeping it going, and to Assistant Editor Lisbeth Redfield for her wisdom and good will. The team at Oxford University Press all offered their considerable expertise and gracious assistance: Saranya Prabuthass, Sreejith Viswanathan, Pilar Wyman, Kristen Holt-Browning, Rick Stinson, Thomas Finnegan, Dorothy Bauhoff, Adam Cohen, and Norm Hirschy.

Steven, Julia, Sashi, Frankie, Hitch, and Kipling offered encouragement, criticism, smiles, and frowns as needed.

A Note about Translations and Music Examples

Unless otherwise indicated, authors have made their own translations. In such cases, the original texts are included in footnotes or in the main text. Where contributors quote published translations by others, the translator is credited and the original text provided only when context requires it or when the text may not be easily accessed through print and electronic sources.

Albert Oppenheimer prepared the music examples for Chapters 10, 32, and 50. All other music examples were prepared by individual contributors.

THE OXFORD HANDBOOK OF

OPERA

INTRODUCTION

HELEN M. GREENWALD

Arguing about Opera

Opera was born into the aristocratic courts, but that didn't prevent it from becoming one of the first of the performing arts to cultivate and maintain a devoted audience among the public at large. With the opening of the first opera house to a paying audience in Venice (1637), opera soon acquired some of the characteristics of such modern sporting entertainments as baseball and soccer: star players, home runs, errors, and, throughout its history, additional innings and penalty kicks. And here is where the viscera come in: as opera lovers of all stripes know well, it doesn't take a college degree to experience the sheer thrill of the singing voice. It is precisely this "spectator sport" aspect of opera, its penchant for dramatic extremes—in essence, what we love most about it—that contributed to the rather late acceptance of opera as a legitimate topic of discourse in the scholarly arena. That is not to say that there were no opera critics until modern times—hardly the case. Opera became a topic for debate even as it was being "invented" by a late-sixteenth-century "think tank" looking to promote an agenda about words and music. But the issues that vexed the Florentine *Camerata* only set the fuse on an argument that continued for centuries as opera lovers and opera loathers found more things to argue about. Early theorists, composers, and librettists thought deeply about the relationship between words and music, how text should be set, whether their ideas conformed to classical ideals (see Chapter 12, "Opera between the Ancients and the Moderns," by Wendy Heller), and still more important, whether or not a story that was sung could be accepted as at all plausible. Opera *had* to contain some aspect of truth (Chapter 13 by Thomas Betzwieser, "Verisimilitude," and Chapter 1 by Tim Carter, "What Is Opera?"): What kinds of characters could or would sing such truths and in what manner (Chapter 15, "Characterization," by Julian Rushton)? For the contemporary scholar, the problem of words and music is equally challenging. A central issue, debated at length in the second half of Part II of the *Oxford Handbook of*

Opera, is the concept of "voice" (see Chapters 13, 14, 15, and 16 by Thomas Betzwieser, Michal Grover-Friedlander, Julian Rushton, and Lawrence Kramer, respectively). What do we mean by "voice"? The obvious response is: the sound that comes out of singers' mouths. But opera contains other "voices"—the composer's voice, heavenly voices, voices living and dead, multiple levels of vocal discourse—the voice that sings arias, but also that "other" voice that sings dialogue. There is also the choral voice (Chapter 21, by Ryan Minor, "The Chorus"), reflecting group sentiments as well as political and national ones, while raising questions about the verisimilitude of crowd-speak. And there is the orchestral voice, which, as Alessandro Di Profio observes in Chapter 22 ("The Orchestra"), evolved over time from a local phenomenon to an international body that could accommodate continuously expanding repertoires, adapt to new instrumentation, and thereby enhance its role in governing movement on stage, from acting (Chapter 20 by Simon Williams) to both the decorative and dramatic roles of dance (Chapter 23 by Linda Tomko). Documents have a voice as well. Katherine Syer, in Chapter 24 ("Production Aesthetics and Materials"), demonstrates that surviving records not only reveal how an opera was mounted, but also mirror the artistic and cultural context of a work. Mark Everist, in Chapter 19 ("Rehearsal Practices"), uncovers a whole world of documents that reveal some of the ways that singers in nineteenth-century Paris prepared for and were coached in their roles. And what of the musical score? William Drabkin (Chapter 11, "Analysis") and the many other scholars in this volume who refer generously to opera scores offer multifaceted views of these primary documents, concluding that beyond their function as a set of instructions *for* performance and a record *of* rehearsal and performance, scores also transmit a type of social history-in-code that reveals much about taste, composers, singers, conductors, commerce, and even politics (see, for example, Chapter 32, "Politics," by Marc A. Weiner).

If we speak of operatic strategies, that is, how composers and librettists fit words to music (or the other way around) in order to tell a story, must we always presume that the words have the last word, or does the music have an equally forceful and independent life (see Chapter 8, "Musical Dramaturgy," by Damien Colas)? Moreover, as Marina Frolova-Walker shows in Chapter 7 ("The Language of National Style"), language is at the very core of collective expression on the opera stage. The idea of a correct and essential mode of verbal communication raises other questions about language, not least: Does opera in translation really work, or is the relationship between verbal and musical cadence and message so closely knit as to be disrupted in a text other than the original one (see Chapter 9, "Versification," by Andreas Giger)? But what constitutes a good text for opera? Traditionally, that would be a story unfolded in verses intended to be sung. Those verses could support conventional musical forms, as was the practice of the Italian *primo ottocento*, or imply new, more open structures, as was Wagner's intention. Opera's near past finds composers and librettists experimenting with all kinds of texts, setting to music, for example, original (and hence, "un-librettized") versions of spoken drama. These so-called *Literaturopern* include Debussy's *Pelléas et Mélisande* (after Maurice Maeterlinck), Strauss's *Salome* (after Oscar Wilde), and Berg's *Wozzeck* (after Georg Büchner). In Chapter 49 ("After the Canon"), Robert Fink takes the issue of composers' and librettists' textual choices into the present day with a close look at John Adams's *Doctor Atomic*.

All of these topics have remained on the table in a continuous cycle of reforms that have frequently addressed and continue to address many of the same problems that chafed at opera's originators (see Chapter 1, "What Is Opera?" by Tim Carter), including the relationship between words and music: Are there too many syllables, not enough notes? Too many notes, not enough syllables? *Prima la musica e poi le parole* (as Antonio Salieri put it in the title of his 1786 opera and which Richard Strauss later debated in his 1942 *Capriccio*)? What are the consequences of one way or the other? If there are too many notes and not enough syllables, then words are obscured, and emphasis is redirected to the singing voice and ultimately to the singer. A new can of worms is opened: the cult of celebrity. Singers inspire composers and audiences, but they also enrage, well, composers and audiences, elevating or cheapening the art form, as critics complain about it or praise it. Growing technologies of stagecraft also intruded on the high-minded ideals that drove opera in its first decades (and forever after, it would seem), inviting negative critical commentary on the ways that sheer spectacle overwhelmed performance. Outstanding in the pantheon of polemicists is eighteenth-century critic Benedetto Marcello (1686–1739), whose often hilarious *Il teatro alla moda* (1720) offers a litany of sarcastic "dos" (most of which mock artistic priorities) to composers, librettists, impresarios, and just about every individual associated with opera production. Here's one telling example: "The librettist should not worry about the ability of the performers, but so much more about whether the impresario has at his disposal a good bear or lion, an able nightingale, genuine-looking bolts of lightning, earthquakes, storms, etc." (Marcello [1720] 1948/1949: 373, trans. Pauly).

Most influential among so-called reformers were composer Christoph Willibald Gluck (1714–1787) and critic Francesco Algarotti (1712–1764), who argued for a return to the simplicity of earlier opera, which, viewed from the eighteenth-century perspective, was the guardian of an ideal form in which words, music, and all aspects of production would serve the drama. Remarkably, from that very ideal arose the "Beast in the Room," who has loomed large from the middle of the nineteenth century until the present day: Wagner. No composer before or after Wagner wrote as much or more *about* opera, and whether or not he actually practiced what he preached fades into the background, as his music exerted game-changing influence on the very sonority of opera. Wagner altered poetic forms, large-scale musical structures, relationships between singers, singers and orchestra, and production elements from lighting to the buildings that house performance. Joy H. Calico, in Chapter 48 ("1900–1945"), shows that Wagner's continued influence has shaped scholarly discourse on opera well into the twentieth century.

But we shouldn't give Wagner too much credit. He was not solely responsible for the major changes that overtook opera in the nineteenth century and spilled into the next. Rather, Wagner entered a musical game-in-progress that was kneading such global issues as genre classification, emotional expression, realism (a relative term), and the possibilities for staging that technical advances in lighting and machines had to offer. The consequences were profound, leading to new narrative modes that eschewed arias and ensembles for continuity, closed musical forms for open ones. Open forms, moreover, required that dissonance, the fundamental tool that governs musical motion, also had a new role to play that would ultimately impinge on the most essential ingredients of opera, melody and "vocality," or *vocalità*, the bedrock of *bel canto*.

Despite the seriousness of reform, however, the one thing that opera has always done is laugh at itself, as evidenced by works that feature mute actors, cross-dressing singers, gender-bending vocal casting, and plots that heap scorn on egotistical performers and impresarios, and even opera's own performance practices. Comedy, more than other genres, relies on context, recognition of the target and all of its absurdities, and, hence, resisted for much longer the musical changes that affected more serious works (see Hunter 1999). In some ways it is this very conservativeness that precipitated the decline of comic opera, as it became increasingly associated with more popular forms that retained the older styles, and in particular the closed musical numbers that continued to flourish in Italian strongholds such as Naples (see Izzo 2013). The few major works that did enter the canon, say, post-*Don Pasquale* (1843)—*Die Meistersinger, Falstaff, Ariadne auf Naxos*—consider as plot and/or musical points the dilemmas of operatic composition and, again, performance practice.

Performance Practice, *Werk-Treue*, or: What Is an Opera, Anyway?

Performance practice, meaning everything that affects the execution and presentation of a work—voices, instruments, pitch, venue, acting, and even *what* is being performed—is an issue deeply connected to the definition of the work itself (see Gossett 2006, especially chapters 7 and 8). If modern productions don't follow the practices of the era in which an opera was composed (at least insofar as they are known), does that make a performance something less than authentic (see Chapter 27, "Historically Informed Performance," by Mary Hunter)?

The *Oxford Handbook of Opera* begins with what would seem to be an easy question: What is opera? *Everyone* knows what opera is, right? The five scholars who address this apparently simple matter make clear enough that definitions can't be so readily offered up or left un-parsed, especially since that very question was at the heart of opera's "planning" stage. In short, the issues are nomenclature (Chapter 1, "What Is Opera?" by Tim Carter), the apparent disjuncture between the idea of invention and the prescription for convention (Chapter 2, "Genre," by Emanuele Senici), the slippery distinction(s) between the traditions of popular musical theater and opera (Chapter 3, "Musical Theater[s]," by Derek B. Scott), the question of whether performance practice can obscure the lines between received definitions, say, of opera versus oratorio (Chapter 4, "Operatorio?" by Monika Hennemann), and finally opera as a *contested* art form that actually arose from acts of argument or competition (Chapter 5, "The Concept of Opera," by Lydia Goehr).

As many of the chapters of this handbook reiterate, opera remains, as it was for much of its history, a fluid entity. Philosophically, that much could be said about many different kinds of musical works whose composers tinkered endlessly with them (Liszt comes to mind here). But opera is a special case where changes can be more extreme, major revisions notwithstanding (consider, for example, three Verdian operatic complexes: *I Lombardi alla prima crociata/Jérusalem* and *Stiffelio/Aroldo*, much less the fraught journey of *Un ballo in maschera* [see Gossett 2006]). Particular to opera is that its "fluidity" is played out in public, as singers substituted arias (see Poriss 2009), music was and still is transposed (Greenwald 1998), pieces cut and added (Gossett 2006, chapter 8), and even endings changed (as in the case of Mozart's *Don Giovanni*; see Parakilas 1990). Are all revisions of equal weight (Lawton and Rosen 1974), and is there a "final" version of an opera, not subject to constant adaptation to its environment (see Chapter 38, "How Opera Traveled," by Louise K. Stein; von Dadelsen 1961; and Greenwald 1998)? How much gets lost in transmission, is just "lost," or is never completed (Chapter 45, "Reconstructions," by Charles S. Brauner), requiring an editor's intervention (Chapter 46, "Editing Opera," by Patricia B. Brauner)? What kinds of sources remain to testify to opera's past (Chapter 44, "Sources," by Linda B. Fairtile)? Operatic "environments" are by definition chameleon-like, subject to singers' availability and ability, audience demand, composers' revisions, concert practice, and above all, taste (see Chapter 30, "Audiences," by Georgia Cowart; Poriss 2009). Moreover, as Philip Gossett (Chapter 47, "Writing the History of Opera"), Charles S. Brauner, Patricia B. Brauner, and Linda B. Fairtile collectively make clear in Part V of this handbook, the reality of the operatic work, at least insofar as scholars can ascertain it, lies buried somewhere in the vast amount of material that composers leave behind: sketches, revisions, new pieces, discarded pieces, the collective detritus of a life (the work's, that is) lived long and hard.

As any editor of an operatic critical edition knows, autograph scores, perhaps more than any other kind of musical document, travel great distances, pass through many hands, suffer cuts, pin-prickings, invasions by foreign inks, and multilingual additions. These personal "touches" constitute the inherent humanity of the scientific and intellectual processes of editorial work of this kind. Handlers—meaning conductors, copyists, singers, orchestra musicians—sometimes imprint their personalities on composers' autographs with a doodle or a ditty as they study or rehearse from a score or a part. Here are some amusing examples: one previous owner of Verdi's *Attila* autograph added cardboard covers to bind each act, decorating the Act I cover with an amateurish sketch of what might be an opera character, while users of one of the many copyists' manuscripts for the same work added all kinds of marginalia, including cartoons (New York Public Libraries, the Research Libraries JOF 80-41; see Greenwald 2012b). But even composers often see fit to comment on their own work through non-musical additions to their scores: consider Puccini, who drew a skull and crossbones next to the point in his *La bohème* autograph where Mimì dies (Greenwald 2012a), or Rossini, who scribbled a somewhat cryptic remark at the end of his *Zelmira* manuscript: "Scusate se vi sbruffo." The essence of it is: "pardon me if I give you the raspberries" (Greenwald 2005a; Reto Müller believes the meaning is a bit more akin to an expression in Wienerisch: "Tuat ma läid, i schäiss ouf aich" [2006: 31]). Whether Rossini intended raspberries or worse is beside the point: it's not an entirely farfetched exit line for the work that marked the end of Rossini's career in Naples. He packed up, left for Vienna, got married to soprano Isabella Colbran along the way, and didn't look back (see Greenwald 2005b: xxi–xxvii). Rossini's second wife and widow Olympe Pélissier eventually passed along the *Zelmira* autograph to her personal physician—Dr. Frémy—in exchange for medical services, and that doctor ceded it to a Mr. Donmartin, who then sold it to the Bibliothèque du Conservatoire de Musique (the holdings of which are now part of the Bibliothèque Nationale de France; see Greenwald 2005a: 15).

Rarely, however, do we know exactly how many hands a composer's autograph may have passed through, as is the case with Verdi's *Attila*; it's impossible to pinpoint exactly when or to whom Verdi ceded his manuscript for this work. Somewhere along the way it became the property of "F. Goring," who lived in Florence and might have been the exuberant artist who added the cardboard covers to the autograph. Later on, the elusive Josef Coen acquired it and then sold it to the British Library (Museum). The British Library, near the end of its fiscal cycle in January 1898, had a few pounds left in its budget, and possibly invoking the principle of "use it or lose it," spent £50 to have in its collection the only Verdi opera manuscript ever to leave the Continent (Greenwald 2012). Such dealings are common practice in the antiquarian marketplace, as Daniela Macchione explains in Chapter 31 ("Autographs, Memorabilia, and the Aesthetics of Collecting"). While the second Madame Rossini might not have placed such a high price on her late husband's material legacy, the vast number of collectors and traders of opera relics who operate beneath the radar attests to both the human and commercial value of such objects.

A work's ownership and performance history can reveal the most human side of the operatic cosmos. As Louise K. Stein shows in Chapter 38 ("How Opera Traveled"), early operatic travels were often politically motivated; a work would adapt and re-adapt to each new environment, and not least if its patron imagined the work of art to be a personal legacy (see Chapter 29, "Patronage," by Valeria De Lucca). It is thus possible to justify the interventions of modern performance as an extension of a historically legitimate process. But audiences of the past did not have as much information or the same kind of information about works that modern record keeping of every variety has offered to fans and scholars. A well-transmitted version of an opera thus stands as a challenge to the idea of "adaptation" and can become obscured in modern performance, as Ulrich Müller discusses in Chapter 26 ("*Regietheater*/Director's Theater"). Are all the components of an opera legitimately "subject to change," or are they as inviolable as the notes in a Beethoven symphony? (See Latham and Parker 2001.) How and when did the producers of opera gain such power—or did they always have it? Is it all right if Tosca doesn't put the candelabra beside Scarpia's corpse (as in the current Metropolitan Opera production)? Can we "read" Mozart's *Don Giovanni* in a way in which it makes any sense at all if Don Giovanni sings Leporello's opening lines and Leporello does not (as in the 2006 Salzburg production)? Perhaps no other issue has raised as much spleen in the discussion of contemporary opera production as *Werktreue*.

Recurring Motives and a Few Statistics

As the *Oxford Handbook of Opera* reveals, contemporary opera scholars relish the sociological and popular aspects of opera: the topics of finance and reception resonate throughout the volume alongside such classically important areas for study as genre (Chapter 2 by Emanuele Senici), source studies (Chapter 44 by Linda B. Fairtile), editions (Chapter 46 by Patricia B. Brauner), and music analysis (Chapter 11 by William Drabkin). Recurring themes include identity and money, and connected to both of these, power: who sings, who composes and in what style, how opera has addressed ethnicity (Chapter 7 by Marina Frolova-Walker), politics (Chapter 32 by Marc A. Weiner), religion (Chapter 33 by Jesse Rosenberg), race and racism (Chapter 34 by John Graziano), gender (Chapter 35 by Alexandra Wilson), and anybody who might be "different" from "us," and hence "exotic" (Chapter 36 by W. Anthony Sheppard) or, perhaps even "irrational," as Tim Carter puts it (Chapter 1, "What Is Opera?"). Even the visual aspects of opera—staging manuals (Chapter 24 by Katherine Syer), costumes (Chapter 25 by Veronica Isaac), staging (Chapter 26 by Ulrich Müller), and public image (Chapter 43 by Helen M. Greenwald)—are shown to be extensions of the human condition. What does opera cost, who pays for it, how much, and does financial backing extend rights over content to the backer (Chapters 1, 29, and 50 by Tim Carter, Valeria De Lucca, and Jake Heggie)? How is opera advertised and marketed (Chapter 43 by Helen M. Greenwald)? What role does government play (Chapter 37 by Francesco Izzo)? Does opera take a political stance, teach a lesson, preach ideology, conform to rules, make moral and ethical judgments, speak for a nation? Essays about visual media (Chapter 42 by Marcia J. Citron), commerce and patronage (Chapter 29 by Valeria De Lucca), singers (Chapter 17 by Hilary Poriss and Chapter 18 by Martha Feldman), criticism (Chapter 40 by Paul Watt), and the many transcriptions and arrangements that inundate the marketplace (Chapter 41, "Soundings Offstage," by Thomas Christensen), moreover, bring the subject of opera into the mainstream conversation about the performing arts and claim a rare opportunity to make an accessible and intelligent link between the ivory tower and the opera house. Contemporary opera weaves in and out of the volume, as authors reconfirm the continued relevance of opera's own history.

Contributors to *The Oxford Handbook of Opera* were given a keyword and instructed, more or less, to build their own sandboxes and have some fun. They were asked to define issues, discuss important research, and then focus on a problem in some detail. The yield from this mandate includes many surprises, not least the vast range of composers and works that have been indexed at the back of this volume. Here are some observations:

with twenty-eight works cited (about 50 percent of his output), Handel is the statistical winner by sheer numbers, while Wagner, with all of his operatic works (fourteen) referenced, wins by percentage. Numbers become fuzzy when the question of genre is argued, but here are the runners-up: Verdi—twenty-seven (practically all), Mozart—fourteen (about three-quarters), Strauss—ten (two-thirds), Puccini—nine (two-thirds), Lully—nine (more than half), Rossini—twenty (about half), Cavalli—seventeen (less than half), Donizetti—seventeen (a little less than 25 percent). The least familiar works in the list? For me, any number of the numerous "Ariadne" operas (Chapter 6, "Oft-Told Tales," by Vincent Giroud), all of the works of Poissl (now much less foreign, thanks to John Warrack's discussion in Chapter 10 of the German libretto), and Samuel Coleridge-Taylor's cantata trilogy *Hiawatha's Wedding Feast* (see Chapter 4, "Operatorio?" and Chapter 34, "Race and Racism"). These numbers don't mean much on their own—they are raw data. But they do reveal that Italian opera is still foremost in the minds of a slice of the scholarly community, and not just those scholars whose specialty is Italian opera. Efforts to hold the number of Italianists in this volume in check did not prevent (nor should they) scholars of every aspect of opera from turning to Italian opera and its conventions over and again. Italian opera has infiltrated every corner of the world, and repertoire in all the major opera houses today reveals a distinct resistance to unseat that domination. Italy produced more operas than any other country, and that has to do with a number of factors, not least a constant demand for the new—first at court and later in the theater—and an operatic industry that dominated all of Europe. The system of transmission in Italy in the nineteenth century, wherein copyists would work furiously to produce scores that could be used elsewhere, insured timely dissemination of new operas, while piano-vocal scores reached the market soon after the last echo died out in the opera house. No surprise, as James Parakilas points out in Chapter 39, "The Operatic Canon," that the audience, in its desire for repetition—of something pleasurable—will keep works alive and profitable.

What's missing from the index of works at the end of this volume? Every reader will have a different response to this question. Still, it was a bit surprising not to see any mention of Samuel Barber (now added because of this discussion), especially since his *Antony and Cleopatra* opened the new Metropolitan Opera House at Lincoln Center on September 16, 1966, and we observed his centenary in 2010. But *Antony and Cleopatra* was not well received at its premiere, and, according to Barber biographer Barbara Heyman, "The commission that was one of the greatest tributes to Barber's whole career turned out, ironically, to be his nemesis" (Heyman 1992: 428). The opera was, apparently, a victim of disagreement between composer and librettist/production designer/director Franco Zeffirelli, and, despite a revision with the help of Gian Carlo Menotti and re-launch in 1975 at the Juilliard Opera Theater, it never entered "the repertory." Heyman suggests that *Antony and Cleopatra* became lost in emerging interest in music that explored more diverse compositional techniques, against which Barber's music must have seemed "ultraconservative" (1992: 455). Barber, who had enjoyed moderate success with *Vanessa* (1956–1957), became with *Antony and Cleopatra* a member of a different kind of club—successful composers who tried and failed at opera, Schumann and Liszt, for example—or managed a single success, as did Otto Nicolai, who never caught the brass ring on the operatic carousel (despite much effort), and died soon after his single "hit," *Die lustigen Weiber von Windsor* (see Greenwald 2005c). As Marianne Betz observes in Chapter 28 ("Opera Composition and Cultural Environment"), outside factors have exerted tremendous influence on composers, and some social domains are not culturally attuned to opera, including Boston, the "Athens of America," which has to date been unable to sustain a major opera company.

The idea of recurring motives leads us to yet another distinctly human phenomenon, which is that people like to hear, read, and see the same stories told over and again. Repetition is comforting, as is experiencing the satisfaction of justice served, or perhaps even the hope that somehow—"this time"—tragedy will be averted. John Russell (1993: 445–491) reports over two hundred performances of numerous operatic versions of the Don Juan story between 1669 and 1800. But Mozart didn't enter the Don Juan opera sweepstakes until 1787, and the record of performances from that year to 1800 reveals that his take on this overwhelmingly popular story was actually not repeated very often in that time period. The composer whose name appears most frequently in Russell's post-1787 list is someone credited with around fifty operas, Giuseppe Gazzaniga (1743–1818), who, with prolific librettist Giovanni Bertati (1735–1815; best known for the libretto of Cimarosa's 1792 *Il matrimonio segreto*), composed *Don Giovanni Tenorio, o sia il convitato di pietra*, which premiered at the Teatro San Moisè in Venice on February 5, 1787, just months before Mozart and Da Ponte's version appeared on October 29 in Prague. Given the number of performances that Gazzaniga and Bertati's *Don Giovanni* enjoyed, its makers undoubtedly went to their just rewards believing they had finally landed a place in posterity. Gazzaniga's opera, however tuneful and often adroit, is studied more often today for its libretto, which Lorenzo Da Ponte surely followed (perhaps too closely), most conspicuously in the opening scene. We wouldn't have to look very hard to find numerous renderings of the story of Orfeo either, and it is not difficult to see why a tale of tragic love featuring the character of a musician would attract so many opera composers. Moreover, as Vincent Giroud shows in Chapter 6 ("Oft-Told Tales"), one of the most revisited stories on the opera stage has been that of Ariadne, surely for her most human plight. But *Artaserse*? Metastasio's (b. Pietro Antonio Domenico Trapassi, 1698–1782) libretto for *Artaserse* inspired at least eighty different versions, solid testimony to the popularity of violent subjects on the premodern stage.

The Opera of the Future (Meaning Now, after the So-Called Golden Age, and Beyond)

Most music history texts report a catastrophe that took place around 1900: the tonal system "dissolved," the dissonance "emancipated"—old news, but news, nonetheless, and very important for opera. With compositional experimentation that encroached upon the most basic components of opera—melody and voice—where was opera to turn? In the middle of this crisis, Richard Strauss composed *Salome* (1905) and *Elektra* (1909), both of which captured the modern essentials of continuous drama, large orchestra, and vocal writing that extended the Wagnerian idea and successfully challenged the notion of vocal melody. But even Strauss was not able to maintain his modernistic flush, and the stubborn question, "What is opera?" began to reassert itself.

Only two chapters in *The Oxford Handbook of Opera* address opera in a chronological framework: Chapter 48, "1900–1945," by Joy H. Calico, and Chapter 49, "After the Canon," by Robert Fink. The reason for this exception in a volume that generally avoids "period" essays is that the extreme diversity of post-tonal operatic production cannot be assessed through "schools" of composition, national style, or the work of a single trend-setting composer. Together, Calico's and Fink's chapters constitute Part VI, "Opera on the Edge." The meaning of the word "edge" in the section title is deliberately ambiguous: Does it refer to the edge of a precipice and hence a catastrophe (see the final chapter of Abbate and Parker 2012)? Or could "edge" be, to borrow a familiar phrase, "the start of something new"? The turn of the twentieth century and the end of World War II have served too long and too well as historical signposts to be overlooked; it's useful to get a global view of that half century and how scholars have thought about it. Calico identifies three interrelated themes for this era that engage Wagner, Hitler, and the ongoing question of genre. In Chapter 49 ("After the Canon"), Robert Fink revives and explores an old question—*prima la musica e poi le parole?*—on new terms. Through a detailed case study of John Adams's *Doctor Atomic*, Fink shows that while historical texts and important *documents* may record a real dramatic event and provide vivid source material for operatic storytelling (consider *Boris Godunov, Don Carlos*, and a host of other historically based operas), their actual words are not only by definition un-dramatic, but also unsuitable "poetry" for a libretto. Composer Jake Heggie has the final word in Chapter 50, providing us with the opportunity to be a fly on the wall in his studio as he offers a candid view of his work process in lively response to the question that opens this collection, revised here for contemporary users: "Now, what is opera?"

Bibliography

Abbate, Carolyn, and Roger Parker. 2012. *A History of Opera*. New York: W.W. Norton.

Dadelsen, Georg von. 1961. "Die 'Fassung letzter Hand' in der Musik." *Acta Musicologica* 33/1: 1–14.

Gossett, Philip. 2006. *Divas and Scholars: Performing Italian Opera*. Chicago: University of Chicago Press.

Greenwald, Helen M. 2012a. "*Ars moriendi*: Reflections on the Death of Mimì." In *The Arts of the Prima Donna in the Long Nineteenth Century*, edited by Rachel Cowgill and Hilary Poriss, 167–185. New York: Oxford University Press.

——. 2012b. "Introduction" to Giuseppe Verdi, *Attila*, edited by Helen M. Greenwald. *The Works of Giuseppe Verdi*. Ser. I: 9, xi–xxviii. Chicago: University of Chicago Press; Milan: Ricordi.

——. 2005a. "Fonti autografe." *Commento Critico* to Gioachino Rossini, *Zelmira*, 4 vols., edited by Helen M. Greenwald and Kathleen Kuzmick Hansell, *Edizione Critica delle Opere di Gioachino Rossini*. Sez I: 33, 15–20. Pesaro: Fondazione Rossini.

——. 2005b. "Notizie Storiche." Gioachino Rossini, *Zelmira*. 4 vols., edited by Helen M. Greenwald and Kathleen Kuzmick Hansell, *Edizione Critica delle Opere di Gioachino Rossini*. Sez. I: 33, xxi–xliv. Pesaro: Fondazione Rossini.

——. 2005c. "Otto Nicolais italienische Reise: A Diary in Exile." *Das (Musik-) Theater in Exil und Diktatur*. Vorträge und Gespräche des Salzburger Symposions 2003. Wort und Musik: Salzburger Akademische Beiträge 58, edited by Peter Csobádi, Gernot Gruber, Jürgen Kühnel, Ulrich Müller, et al., 225–238. Salzburg: Verlag Mueller-Speiser.

——. 1998. "Puccini, *Il tabarro*, and the Dilemma of Operatic Transposition." *Journal of the American Musicological Society* 51/3: 521–558.

Heyman, Barbara. 1992. *Samuel Barber: The Composer and His Music*. New York: Oxford University Press.

Hunter, Mary. 1999. *The Culture of Opera Buffa in Mozart's Vienna: A Poetics of Entertainment*. Princeton, NJ: Princeton University Press.

Izzo, Francesco. 2013. *Laughter between Two Revolutions: Opera Buffa in Italy, 1831–1848*. Eastman Studies in Music. Rochester, NY: University of Rochester Press.

Lawton, David, and David Rosen. 1974."Verdi's Non-definitive Revisions: The Early Operas." In *Atti del III° congresso internazionale di studi verdiani (Milano, Piccola Scala, 12–17 giugno 1972)*, 189–237. Parma: Istituto nazionale di studi verdiani.

Marcello, Benedetto. [1720] 1948/1949. *Il teatro alla moda*, translated by Reinhard Pauly. *Musical Quarterly* 34/3: 371–403 and 35/1: 85–105.

Müller, Reto. 2006. Review of Gioachino Rossini, *Zelmira*, edited by Helen M. Greenwald and Kathleen Kuzmick Hansell. 3 vols. *Edizione critica delle opere di Gioachino Rossini*. Sez. I: 33 (Pesaro: Fondazione Rossini 2005). *La gazzetta* [Zeitschrift der Deutschen Rossini Gesellschaft] 16: 27–31.

Parakilas, James. 1990. "The Afterlife of *Don Giovanni*: Turning Production History into Criticism." *Journal of Musicology* 8/2: 251–265.

Poriss, Hilary. 2009. *Changing the Score: Arias, Prima Donnas, and the Authority of Performance*. AMS Studies in Music. New York: Oxford University Press.

Russell, John. 1993. *The Don Juan Legend before Mozart with a Collection of Eighteenth-Century Opera Librettos*. Ann Arbor: University of Michigan Press.

PART I

WHAT IS OPERA?

CHAPTER 1

WHAT IS OPERA?

TIM CARTER

It was a sad day for opera aficionados when the great Italian tenor Luciano Pavarotti died (on September 6, 2007). It was also headline news. In scenes reminiscent of another great singer's funeral—Nelly Melba's in Melbourne, Australia, on February 26, 1931—the cameras showed the crowds outside Modena cathedral applauding Pavarotti's coffin as it was carried into the nave: thousands then passed through the church to pay their respects. The eulogies on US and UK television covered his career: an Italian baker's son who found a voice at the age of four, sang in a church choir, starred at a Welsh Eisteddfod, then hit the operatic stage for an illustrious career that spanned several decades and included most of the great tenor roles of Italian opera (but never Wagner) with all the eminent divas. These eulogies each reached their climax at precisely the same point: that breathtaking moment when Pavarotti sang "Nessun dorma" from Puccini's *Turandot* as part of the "Three Tenors" concert (with José Carreras and Plácido Domingo), first on the eve of the final soccer match of the 1990 World Cup in Rome, then for the finals in Los Angeles (1994), Paris (1998), and Yokohama (2002). His audiences went wild. What is opera?—one might ask. Surely not this; but then again...

Great singers have always been celebrated as larger-than-life individuals (often quite literally) with seemingly superhuman powers, doing gladiatorial battle with themselves, and with each other, on the stage. *Vincerò—Vin-CE...-rò* ("I will be victorious"): Puccini's music sets the personal challenges that singers must overcome if they are not to be booed off the stage in ignominy. Operatic characters and the performers who bring them to life become conflated in complex metonymies: we set a premium on, and have paid through the nose for, Plácido Domingo's Rodolfo, Renée Fleming's Lucia, or Jon Vickers's Peter Grimes, although we then argue his pros and cons versus the singer for whom Benjamin Britten originally wrote that last role: Peter Pears. For many, these warbling throats are indeed what opera is all about.

Composers and librettists might not agree: after all, without their music and words, singers would have no stage to display their vocal prowess. Of course, many composers have had close connections with singers for whom they have wisely crafted their music: there is scant point in writing something that a singer cannot, or will not, sing. Mozart was by no means alone in being very reluctant to write an aria until he knew the voice that would perform it—he temporized by writing recitatives and ensembles—and in exploiting the best characteristics of that voice when doing so: just trace the path of the young Anna Gottlieb from Barbarina in *Le nozze di Figaro* (1786; Gottlieb was twelve) to Pamina in *Die Zauberflöte* (1791). Likewise, there is some merit in recognizing the voice of baritone Felice Varesi in Donizetti's music for Antonio in *Linda di Chamounix* (1842) and in Verdi's for the title roles in *Macbeth* (1847) and *Rigoletto* (1851), and for Giorgio Germont in *La traviata* (1853). The corollary—that singers taking on a role not written for them can plausibly expect some accommodation within it either by the original composer, by some other composer, or just by importing their favorite arias—had significant force through the seventeenth, eighteenth, and early nineteenth centuries; it also leads to some curious quandaries (should we prefer Mozart's 1786 *Le nozze di Figaro* or his 1789 one?). The counterargument is the well-known story of Handel threatening to throw a recalcitrant soprano, Francesca Cuzzoni, out of a window for refusing to sing her first aria as Teofane in his *Ottone* (1723)—though Handel learned his lesson and went on to write a series of major roles for her.

Many scholars also have problems with singers. At least until recently, we have preferred to study works, not their performances, and works are fixed in texts both verbal (librettos) and musical (scores). For example, analyzing the treatment of leitmotifs in Wagner's *Ring*, or the handling of serial techniques in Berg's *Lulu*, focuses the attention on the printed page, and on compositional process, which therefore forces a consequent downplaying of performative contingencies. Thus we have tended to worry more about, say, Monteverdi's musical symbolism in *Orfeo* than what it took to get that work on the stage. This has the advantage of being straightforward and even comfortable; it also runs the risk of perceived irrelevance to the operatic enterprise, and also to its experience. Even here, however, we cannot always decide where to start: should it be from the libretto (where most composers began) or from the music (where they ended up)? Treating an opera as, in effect, a symphony with words may seem to have impeccable Wagnerian credentials, but it forces a formalist approach that ignores, or conflicts with, the theatrical world (Abbate and Parker 1989); it also marginalizes the much larger number of works that seemingly fail to meet the high standards of formalism by being either too conventional, and therefore uninteresting, or too wayward, and therefore unmanageable.

Opera is by definition messy, both for those producing and experiencing it, and for the critic observing it from a scholarly distance: not for nothing did musicology once privilege other, more "abstract" genres. But the discipline has shifted in the past decades as canonic operas have found their place in the scholarly canon, embracing the gamut from much-needed critical editions (Gossett 2006) to no-less-needed critical theory (Koestenbaum 1993). Messiness—or if you prefer, plural multiplicities—has become the liberating norm in this postmodern age, and as has always been the case with opera, it might even be viewed as cause for celebration.

What's in a Word?

The entry "Opera" in the *New Grove Dictionary of Music and Musicians* also directs the reader to a bewilderingly large number of other subject entries by genre: *azione teatrale*, ballad opera, *ballet de cour*, *ballet-héroïque*, burlesque, *burletta*, chamber opera, *comédie-ballet*, *divertissement*, *drame lyrique*, *dramma giocoso*, *dramma per musica*, *entrée*, *extravaganza*, *farsa*, *favola in musica*, *festa teatrale*, film musical, *grand opéra*, *intermède*, *intermedio*, *intermezzo*, *Lehrstück*, libretto, *Liederspiel*, madrigal comedy, *Märchenoper*, masque, medieval drama, melodrama, *melodramma*, monodrama, musical, music drama, music theatre, number opera, *opéra-ballet*, *opéra bouffon*, *opera buffa*, *opéra comique*, *opéra-féerie*, *opera semiseria*, *opera seria*, operetta, pantomime, *pasticcio*, pastoral, *pastorale-héroïque*, *Posse*, puppet opera, puppet theatre, *rappresentazione sacra*, rescue opera, *sainete*, *Schuldrama*, *Schuloper*, semi-opera, *sepolcro*, *serenata*, *Singspiel*, *Spieloper*, *tonadilla*, tourney, *tragédie en musique*, *vaudeville*, *verismo*, *zarzuela*, *Zauberoper*, *Zeitoper*. Of these sixty-nine entries, nineteen use Italian words, fifteen French, ten German, three Spanish—which is a fairly representative distribution of the genre itself, save for eastern Europe—and twenty-two English (*New Grove* is, after all, an Anglo-Saxon encyclopedia), although most of the last are not necessarily English-specific and have their foreign-language equivalents. Only twenty of these terms have "opera" (*opera*, *opéra*, *Oper*, or their cognates) in the heading (three Italian, five French, five German, seven English). Some identify national genres (*zarzuela*) or subgenres (*opera seria*, *opéra comique*, *Märchenoper*); some suggest generic mixtures (*comédie-ballet*, masque); some are function-specific (*entrée*, *Lehrstück*, *Schuloper*); and a significant number place more emphasis on the theater than does the simple word "opera" (*azione* or *festa teatrale*, *rappresentazione sacra*, music theatre), or on drama (*dramma giocoso*, *dramma per musica*, *favola in musica*, *melodramma*, *drame lyrique*, *tragédie en musique*, *Singspiel*, music drama, and others). Clearly, we are in a terminological minefield. Even the *New Grove*'s opening definition of "opera" ("Most narrowly conceived, the word 'opera' signifies a drama in which the actors sing throughout...") admits "so many" exceptions—Mozart's *Die Zauberflöte* and Beethoven's *Fidelio* would not be operas by this reckoning—as to force revision ("...the word should be more generically defined as a drama in which the actors sing some or all of their parts"). But even this broader definition still remains problematic: So Rodgers and Hammerstein's *Oklahoma!* is an opera?

Anglo-Saxon usage is, as usual, imprecise and confusing. In Paris one might just as well see *drames lyriques* or *opéras comiques*, while the statutes of the Teatro alla Scala in Milan refer to its mission to perform *spettacoli lirici* (although the preferred Italian term for opera is *melodramma*). If one goes to the "opera" in France or Germany, one goes to a place such as the Paris Opéra (whether at the Palais Garnier or the Bastille) or the Deutsche Staatsoper, unless one is a Wagner fanatic lucky enough to procure tickets to the Bayreuth Festspielhaus. At the opera house, one attends a performance by a resident or visiting opera company, but in Continental Europe what one sees there can have, at least for an educated audience, a number of more nuanced generic labels that would be resisted at, say, the Royal Opera House or the Met. However, the apparent absurdity caused by elliptical English (and still more, American) usage—one goes to the opera to see the opera perform an opera—does serve one useful purpose in terms of revealing the complex intermingling of space, agency, and outcome embedded within the term. Even its etymology (the plural of the Latin *opus* taken over as a singular noun) carries a suggestion of multiple "works" while also exposing a dual meaning: work as action and the "work" as its result. Opera is essentially a collaborative venture that focuses in the end on the event of performance; this is what makes it so intriguing—and so difficult—to study. Moreover, what defines an opera as "opera" can sometimes be as much about where it is done, and by and for whom, as its generic proprieties or innate qualities. This is particularly true of works that cross between the worlds of opera and of musical theater. While the Met is unlikely to perform Jonathan Larson's *Rent* (which opened on Broadway in 1996) alongside its model, Puccini's *La bohème*, or Elton John and Tim Rice's *Aida* (2000) alongside Verdi, Leonard Bernstein nevertheless recorded (1985) his *West Side Story* (1957) with a set of opera stars including Kiri Te Kanawa, José Carreras, Tatiana Troyanos, and Marilyn Horne—with somewhat unfortunate results, it must be said. More experimental approaches to the musical stage have always produced still more problems of definition, as in the case of Debussy's *Le martyre de St. Sébastien* and the Brecht-Weill collaborations of the late 1920s, while Gershwin's *Porgy and Bess* has always posed special challenges since its premiere on Broadway (at the Alvin Theatre) in 1935.

Operatic Operations

One place to start untangling this operatic messiness might well be the business of opera (Agid and Tarondeau 2010). According to its 2007–2008 *Annual Review*, London's Royal Opera House (ROH), Covent Garden, more or less broke even, with a total expenditure that year of £90.1 million against an income of £90.4 million provided by government grants (£26.3 million), box-office receipts (£35.6 million), donations, legacies and the like (£15.3 million), and other income from commercial operations, touring, and so on (£13.2 million). The New York Metropolitan Opera's 2006–2007 *Annual Report* lists much higher operating expenses at $239.6 million against revenues of $138.5 million (with $90.5 million from box office receipts), the "loss" being covered by contributions and bequests ($133.8 million) and investment returns ($24 million), such that net assets increased over the year from $378.9 million to $410.4 million. In both cases, the proportion of expenditure covered by box office receipts—39.5 percent for the ROH and 37.8 percent for the Met—was close to the rule-of-thumb 40 percent for high-end arts-promoting organizations, which usually need to find at least three-fifths of their annual budgets from other sources. The striking differences between the ROH and the

Met are, of course, the ROH's reliance on government grants (mostly from Arts Council England), covering 29.2 percent of total expenditure, and the relative importance of their donor income and investment returns (for the ROH, covering 17 percent of expenditure; for the Met, 65.9 percent). This reflects different funding regimes on the one hand (with government subsidies for the arts being more common in Europe), and on the other, the importance in the United States of philanthropy, encouraged by an enabling tax system. The ROH seems to be running chiefly on a year-to-year basis; the Met appears to have healthier reserves, although it is worth noting that its endowment investment valued at $336.2 million as of July 31, 2007 (again, according to the 2006–2007 report) would normally be expected to generate (at a 5 percent return, by another rule of thumb) an annual income of only $16.8 million, which will, of course, decrease in lean economic times. From that point of view, both the ROH and the Met seem to live precariously.

Comparison with the spoken theater is also instructive. For 2007–2008 (the period discussed for the ROH, above), the *Annual Report* of London's Royal National Theatre (RNT) notes an income of £49 million against expenditures of £47.5 million, that is, just over half of the ROH, a difference that is all the more striking given that the RNT ran productions in three house theaters (if with a total seating capacity, at 2,450, only some 200 more than the ROH, at 2,256). Box-office receipts were £15.4 million (31.4 percent of income); government grants amounted to £18.4 million (covering 38.7 percent of expenditure); and £4.9 million was gained by fundraising (10.3 percent of expenditure). At the risk of crass generalization, the RNT made proportionally less money from selling tickets (top-price tickets at its main stage cost about one-fifth of those at the ROH); it gained more in UK government grants (opera is widely regarded as elitist and therefore less worthy of state support); and it had a harder time fundraising (rich donors are more willing to give to opera).

Opera costs money, and it cannot normally be expected to generate a profit. The earliest court operas were essentially paid from princely coffers with little or no regard for any return on large expenditures: Jacopo Peri's *Euridice* (widely regarded as the first "opera" to survive complete) and Giulio Caccini's *Il rapimento di Cefalo* were both performed during the festivities in Florence celebrating the wedding of Maria de' Medici to King Henri IV of France in October 1600 (though this was not the first staging of *Euridice*), and save where Grand Duke Ferdinando de' Medici persuaded others to pick up at least part of the tab (as seems to have occurred in part with *Euridice*, sponsored by the Florentine patron Jacopo Corsi), he would have regarded their cost simply as the price of entertaining his guests in an appropriately sumptuous manner. Later in the seventeenth century, some Italian courts operated what one might call a "mixed-mode" system for opera, contracting with impresarios who could charge for tickets but would also receive guarantees against loss (Duke Francesco II d'Este in Modena is a good example). Other monarchs, princes, and prelates could regularly be accused—at least when times were bad—of squandering their treasury on frivolous entertainment: the charge was leveled against the Barberini family in Rome in the early 1640s (immediately after the death of Maffeo Barberini, Pope Urban VIII), and periodically against King Louis XIV of France, although it was usually answered by some combination of *noblesse oblige*, on the one hand, and the necessary prestige to be granted by conspicuous consumption, on the other.

A different model was established in Venice in 1637 with "public" or "commercial" opera, as it is often called. This necessarily lacked princely support—Venice was a proud republic—marking a fundamental shift in the mechanisms of opera production in favor of market forces and a ticket-buying public (Glixon and Glixon 2006). But it still benefited from financial backing by individual or collective patrons, whether or not as investors hoping to turn a profit. The pattern also held true for opera in Handel's London in the 1720s (with support from one or other member of the extended British royal family) or in Mozart's Vienna in the 1780s (from Habsburg Emperor Joseph II). In the nineteenth century, princely patronage gradually changed in favor of state funding—what in one context has been called the "urbanization of opera" (Gerhard 1998)—although more slowly than some might expect: even Wagner was beholden to King Ludwig II of Bavaria, who from 1864 paid him a large annual stipend of 4,000 *gulden*, and who made possible the construction of the Bayreuth theater. The Paris Opéra has in effect received national funding (from royal, republican, or imperial coffers, depending on the regime in place at the time) from its founding in 1671, while the shift from German court theaters (Hoftheater) to civic ones supported by the local or regional tax base depended on changing political circumstances, and even Covent Garden still retains a vestige of its status as one of London's "royal" theaters. In most European or European-influenced countries (including North and South America), an opera house and the company associated with it have come to be seen as a matter of civic pride and responsibility, although arguments inevitably persist over the prices worth paying for it, and the compromises needed to assure them.

The Venetian model was brought into action remarkably quickly, presumably because it drew at least in part on mechanisms already in place for the spoken theater. It also established models for what soon became an opera industry supported by complex interactions between theater owners, impresarios, and independent entrepreneurs (poets, composers, singers, instrumentalists, dancing masters, stage designers, costume manufacturers, and so on and so forth down the line) selling their services at a price. The impact was immediate. In the Italian courts, opera had been relatively infrequent, and not always popular. In Venice, however, five new operas appeared in the three seasons following the opening of the Teatro San Cassiano in 1637 (soon followed by three other opera houses in the city), and by the end of the 1646–1647 season, some thirty-three new works and six revivals had been staged there. Regardless of profit or loss, output was enormous. To judge by Claudio Sartori's catalogue of printed Italian librettos to 1800, the number of seventeenth-century operas stretches into four figures, even accepting that not every surviving libretto represents a different opera. In effect, composers operated on a production line. There are thirty operas securely attributed to Francesco Cavalli (1602–1676), and perhaps another ten by him, while Alessandro Scarlatti (1660–1725) wrote some thirty-five operas before 1700, and another thirty or so after. Lully's output of *tragédies en musique*, protected as he was by a court position, pales in comparison (fourteen, at a rather leisurely rate of one per year from 1673 to 1687). These numbers are not unusual for later periods: Handel wrote forty-six operas, Mozart twenty, Cimarosa almost sixty, Paisiello eighty or so, Rossini thirty-nine, Donizetti some sixty-five, and Verdi twenty-eight. Add to those the countless works by lesser (we assume) composers and it becomes clear that with only a few obvious exceptions, opera was very largely a disposable commodity. A huge number of works lie unperformed, unstudied, and therefore unknown.

Although the Venetian model favored constant innovation in order not to jade the palate, it also fostered the notion of a repertory, something hitherto lacking within the genre wherein operas were essentially one-off events. Tried-and-tested operas could be revived in successive seasons in order to mitigate the risk of new works becoming flops, and could also be taken on tour by independent companies operating on the model of the *commedia dell'arte*. One early example is the rather amorphous group known as the Febiarmonici, with performances of operas such as Francesco Sacrati's *La finta pazza* and Cavalli's *Didone*, *Egisto*, and *Giasone* in smaller centers across northern Italy before members associated with the troupe settled in Naples, where they revived works by Cavalli and also Monteverdi's *L'incoronazione di Poppea*. In the United States in the nineteenth and early twentieth centuries, independent touring companies provided the main access to opera in significant urban centers, as with Manuel García's company that brought Italian operas to New York City in the 1820s, and Fortune T. Gallo's San Carlo Opera Company that toured from 1913 to 1951. Even now, in the UK and elsewhere, regional opera companies will often have some touring obligations as part of their grant-earning requirements.

Like any industry, opera needs both to cultivate a market and to find the skilled personnel needed to sustain its output. The most obvious are the singers, who inevitably come at a premium—they are often paid very well indeed—and can make or break a performance. As opera burgeoned in the seventeenth century, the infrastructure to train its prized workers was fairly quickly put into place, as music conservatoires were established, particularly in Venice and Naples, and curricula were created to identify and nurture the talent demanded by the genre (Rosselli 1992). Even more special treatment was offered to the type of singer most in demand until the early nineteenth century—the castrato—because of the sacrifices required to achieve that exalted, and relatively rare, status. These conservatoires quickly achieved a hegemony over Europe—matching the hegemony of Italian opera in general, save in certain specific countries (notably, France)—also creating myths that still endure today about what it takes to be an opera star. As is typical of any industry, too, its chief workers became highly specialized in terms both of voice types and their subdivisions (viz., the German *Fächer*) and, at least at the highest level, of repertory, although there have always been exceptions (i.e., singers able and willing to take on a wide variety of roles), and the profession is changing in part in response to new aesthetic preferences (singers who can also act) and economic circumstances.

As for the market, it may seem small and relatively narrow, but it exists and, contrary to popular belief, may even be expanding. Ticket prices may seem exorbitantly high in most Western houses (they are often much less so in former Communist Europe, for obvious reasons), but in New York City, at least, their range is not so different from a Broadway musical save perhaps at the top end (often aimed at corporate entertainment), and claims that opera is elitist do not square with the fact that on a good day one can buy three cheap tickets for the Metropolitan Opera for the cost of one for *Wicked* or *The Lion King*. The Met's 2006–2007 report records playing to 84 percent capacity—which is on a par with the more successful commercial theaters—and sold-out performances are a norm, at least in the first-class houses: try getting a ticket for the Wiener Staatsoper sometime, although one can queue to stand at the back of the stalls for next to nothing. Opera's reach was broadened by way of publishing (printed collections of favorite arias for domestic consumption), radio (the Met's legendary Saturday afternoon broadcasts from 1933 on), and then, if less successfully, television, and it has gained significant new energies from film and DVD releases (Citron 2000), and still more from live broadcasts to cinemas, stadiums, and other outdoor locations; these have also garnered younger audiences that have surprisingly little resistance to the genre's rather fantastical mixing of the audio and the visual, perhaps because of their exposure to music videos. Yet opera houses have also had to adjust to global economies of scale, for example by way of the increasingly common practice of sharing product lines (i.e., productions). Save the relative rarities produced by enterprising opera festivals, on the one hand, and record labels, on the other, choices of repertory also tend to play on the side of safety: innovation is usually achieved within the context of the familiar rather than the new, save for the occasional token commission, or the unknown old.

There is a strong tendency for the major houses to favor Italian opera, then German, then French, then opera from other countries (Russian, Czech, etc.). If one can trust the endlessly fascinating online *Operabase*, from January 1 to December 31, 2008, there were 524 performances of Puccini's *Tosca* in eighty-seven cities worldwide from Albuquerque to Zürich, with thirteen new productions (other top favorites included Verdi's *La traviata* with 516 performances and Puccini's *La bohème* with 512, each in eighty-two cities), and only seven of Berg's *Lulu* in one. The statistics of 2008 performances by a relatively haphazard selection of composers still reveal clearly the opera industry's fairly narrow orientation: Verdi (2,373), Puccini (2,108), Mozart (1,760), Rossini (805), Wagner (721), Richard Strauss (508), Handel (342), Tchaikovsky (329), Janáček (184), Gounod (162), Massenet (159), and Monteverdi (111). Our modernist friend Berg had 58 performances and our Baroque one Cavalli had 42, which beats Lully (23) and at least competes well enough with Hans Werner Henze (44), John Adams (37), Philip Glass (34), Kaija Saariaho (19), and Helmut Lachenmann (1).*

A more recent set of *Operabase* statistics might prompt a less jaded picture over the longer term. Over the five seasons from 2005–2006 to 2009–2010, there were more than 100,000 performances of 2,156 different operas by just over a thousand composers, over

* These figures were available on the public version of the *Operabase* site when accessed on May 14, 2009, but have since been removed and replaced by more generic statistics (accessed January 16, 2012) that cannot always be reconciled with the ones given above given that the parameters appear to have changed.

half of whom were still living. Of the total number of performances by country in the 2009–2010 season (about 23,000), almost a third occurred in Germany (7,315)—reflecting the importance of civic opera houses there—followed a long way behind by the United States (1,979), Austria (1,361), France (1,275), Italy (1,182), and the UK (1,076). In terms of the number of performances of individual operas from 2005–2006 to 2009–2010, however, the canon continued to rule the roost (and those living composers came way down the list): the top four were Mozart's *Die Zauberflöte* (a surprise), Verdi's *La traviata*, Bizet's *Carmen*, and Puccini's *La bohème*, with Wagner only making an entrance (with *Der fliegende Holländer*) at place twenty-five.

The conservatism and biases of the repertory are probably not so different from other spheres of so-called classical music. However, over the past half century they have encouraged the phenomenon of so-called *Regietheater* and its Anglo-American equivalents, with star directors and designers achieving their own cult status, and with familiar works needing to be done in new ways (Levin 2007). As with spoken theater, opera productions must negotiate a path between "traditional" stagings and those "updated" in pursuit of relevance, in some cases motivated also by Brechtian notions of alienation. Well-known controversial examples include, among many others, Patrice Chéreau's centennial *Ring* cycle at Bayreuth in 1976 (an anti-capitalist, Marxist reading, with the Rhinemaidens as whores and the gods as industrialist oppressors), Jonathan Miller's *Rigoletto* in the mafia underworld of 1950s New York (English National Opera, 1982), Peter Sellars's Mozart trilogy at the PepsiCo Summerfare in Purchase, NY, in 1989 (with *Le nozze di Figaro*, for example, set in Trump Tower), and Calixto Bieito's toilet-themed *Un ballo in maschera* (Barcelona, 2001). The willingness of audiences to accept such interpretations will vary from country to country, and house to house, but they often provoke some kind of scandal.

Despite periodic attempts to remove opera from the pantheons of high art and into more experimental theatrical (and even non-theatrical) performance spaces, it remains a highly specialized activity limited to specific performance environments. But while its patrons may be open to ridicule, the genre itself is often treated with respect and even affection, as the Marx Brothers' hilarious movie *A Night at the Opera* (1935) reveals. Other Hollywood films that bring operatic performances squarely into their frame also suggest how they can offer a key to social mobility (*Moonstruck*), to self-awareness (*Pretty Woman*), to spiritual transformation (*The Shawshank Redemption*), and even to transcendent consolation (*Philadelphia*). These are powerful moments that reveal an endless fascination with what opera as drama, or even opera as not-drama, can do.

Dramma per Musica

The tendency of non-English operatic terms to introduce some notion of drama into the reckoning (*melodramma, tragédie lyrique, Singspiel*) poses aesthetic dilemmas as well as historiographical ones. Although the libretto tends to come first when composing an opera, it tends to diminish thereafter within the operatic reckoning. *Prima la musica e poi le parole* (first the music, and then the words) was a catchphrase enshrined in the title of a satirical *divertimento teatrale* by Antonio Salieri (1786)—it was also addressed by Richard Strauss in *Capriccio* (1942)—but it finds its resonances within opera audiences, on the one hand, and in the scholarly literature, on the other.

One problem for English-speaking audiences is, of course, the simple fact that opera is often in languages that they do not readily understand (Robinson 2002): a Russian listening to Tchaikovsky, or a Spanish-speaker to de Falla, will have a far richer time of it. Surtitles help but in the end are fairly crude, and singing opera in translation raises difficulties not just in terms of perceived "dumbing down" but also because a composer's musical accents will often be language specific—Mozart writes very differently when setting Italian texts compared with German ones—such that the "wrong" language can often seem, well, wrong. Nor are singers always prized for their diction, especially when they have learned their parts phonetically, while musical setting can tend to interfere with verbal understanding. The resulting difficulties have led even to the oddity of opera in English for English-speaking audiences with English surtitles. On the whole, however, the presumption with opera has often been that once one has the gist of the plot (usually from a prior reading of a synopsis), one can just leave the melody to carry things along. For that matter, one hardly goes to the opera house expecting to see Shakespeare, Corneille, Goethe, or Ibsen, or if one does, it will be radically shortened: in the case of Verdi's *Otello*, to a libretto by Arrigo Boito, Act IV, scene 3 (where Desdemona dies), takes up forty lines in total, whereas Shakespeare has twenty-two lines of wonderful iambic pentameters ("It is the cause, it is the cause, my soul...") just to get to the point where Desdemona first speaks to her husband. Boito and Verdi cut those lines completely in favor of a long orchestral introduction to the scene, with a very detailed stage direction, where the music and action are presumed to stand in for the speech.

In fact, many librettos of *Otello* published for Anglo-Saxon readers will make those forty lines appear almost double in number because their editors are unaware of, or disregard, one simple fact: at least until the late nineteenth century, and often beyond, texts for opera in almost all languages are written in some kind of poetry, not in prose. In the case of Boito's *Otello*, for example, Act IV, scene 3, is in free-rhymed eleven-syllable lines (in Italian the eleven-syllable line has a similar classical status to the iambic pentameter in English, or the alexandrine in French, and its characteristic stress patterns are readily identifiable). The principle that texts for musical setting must be in verse extends back long before the beginnings of opera: on the one hand, it reflects the notion that poetry is itself "musical" by virtue of its meter and rhyme, as well as its elevated language; on the other, poetic meters have strong musical implications in terms of melodic patterns and phrase structures, further influenced by whether line-endings are feminine (ending on a weak syllable) or masculine (on a strong one).

In effect, the librettist's poetry directs the composer in terms of what should happen musically at any given moment in terms of form and articulation. The very first Italian opera librettos by Ottavio Rinuccini (*Dafne*, first performed in 1598, and *Euridice* of 1600) followed the precedent of plays in verse: Rinuccini has the action take place in *versi sciolti*, that is, free-rhyming seven- and eleven-syllable lines (*settenari* and *endecasillabi*); such lines can also be divided between two or more characters in order to create a sense of flow. Formal moments of lyrical expression for one or more characters, or for a chorus, will be distinguished from the *versi sciolti* by one or more of regular rhymes, stanzaic structures, and other line-lengths (e.g., four-, five-, and eight-syllable lines; in Italian, six-, nine-, and ten-syllable lines are also possible). This creates a clear poetic distinction between musical "speech" and song. Very roughly speaking, the "speech" is where action occurs (things happen, characters interact, etc.) and the song is where characters fix the circumstances or consequences of that action, reflect upon it, or establish a position that will determine the action to come. This distinction was very soon formalized in musical terms as one between recitative and aria, which in turn has become characterized (though somewhat wrongly) as a contrast between dramatic action and emotional expression. Thus a typical Handel opera, say, will have passages in *recitativo semplice* (sometimes called *secco*—"dry"—recitative) in a fast-flowing speech-like style for voice and continuo accompaniment, and more elaborate arias for voice and orchestra, with the occasional use of *recitativo stromentato* (a more intense form of recitative with orchestral accompaniment) at moments of high drama, somewhat in the manner of the soliloquy. As was established by Rinuccini, Handel's recitative texts will be in seven- and eleven-syllable *versi sciolti*. On the other hand, arias will usually have texts in two stanzas, the second of which mirrors the first in terms of the number of lines (usually four), their meter, and their rhyme scheme. Aria texts will often, but not always, be in single line-length other than the mixed *settenari* and *endecasillabi* used for recitative (*quinari*, *senari*, and *ottonari* are common), and this two-stanza format becomes set musically in the ternary form typical of the "da capo" aria, that is, A (stanza 1)–B (stanza 2)–A (stanza 1).

Similar poetic principles apply in later eighteenth- and nineteenth-century Italian librettos that introduce action-ensembles (duets, trios, quartets, etc.) and two- or three-tempo numbers that seek to encapsulate some kind of dramatic progression (as in the *cantabile–tempo di mezzo–cabaletta* sequence), as well as in operas where the orchestra plays throughout and therefore seemingly softens any clear textural distinction between recitative and aria. These principles also apply, *mutatis mutandis*, to librettos in other languages: their verse will exploit different types and degrees of poetic formality in terms of meter, rhyme, and stanzaic organization so as to shift the dramatic focus to, from, or within a given combination of action and expression. Reading an opera libretto on its own—and in its original language—can be very instructive indeed, not just for its content, but also for the way in which it maps out the musical design of the work.

Does this matter? Certainly yes, if one wants to understand why opera composers do what they do when they do it. The issue becomes still more important when a composer seemingly contradicts a librettist's instruction. Take, for example, the rare cases where Mozart goes against Lorenzo Da Ponte's poetic choices, as at Donna Elvira's first entrance in *Don Giovanni* ("Ah chi mi dice mai," which Da Ponte cast as an aria but which Mozart turned into a trio by bringing Don Giovanni and Leporello's succeeding recitative into the musical number); another case is the "letter" quintet in Act I of *Così fan tutte* ("Di scrivermi ogni giorno"), which Da Ponte designed as recitative. These are very revealing of Mozart's handling of a character (Why is Donna Elvira denied a proper entrance aria?) or of a situation (Is he taking the "letter" quintet too seriously, or is he overexaggerating the moment for ironic effect?). Likewise, presumably it is worth knowing that in Act II, scene 6, of *La traviata*, Verdi took a line of verse that his librettist, Francesco Maria Piave, simply intended as the first of a closing rhyming couplet in *endecasillabi* (Violetta's "Amami, Alfredo, quant'io t'amo! Addio!"—"Love me, Alfredo, as much as I love you! Farewell!") and turned it into a moment of glorious lyrical expansion that also became thematic for the opera as a whole (Violetta's melody dominates the opera's orchestral prelude).

Toward the end of the nineteenth century, these standard poetic structures within opera librettos started to break down in the search for a more naturalistic verbal, and therefore musical, expression. However, the connection is not quite as direct as one might think. While Mascagni's *Cavalleria rusticana* and Leoncavallo's *I Pagliacci* are usually hailed as masterpieces of the new *verismo*—opera that was somehow "true" to life—in poetic terms their librettos differ little, if at all, from their predecessors. The trend in the early twentieth century in favor of so-called *Literaturoper* (using a spoken play directly as an opera's text) necessarily forced a different approach depending on the source-play's use of language, ranging from Maeterlinck's prose-like but elevated *vers libres* (in Debussy's *Pelléas et Mélisande*) through Oscar Wilde's prose-based *Salome* (Richard Strauss) to Georg Büchner's wholly prosaic *Woyzeck* (set by Berg). The impulse also derived from Wagner, whose arguments in favor of a free-flowing musical drama gained significant influence, even if his self-authored librettos are still in verse, and indeed still often fall into sections with identifiable beginnings and endings. However, the loss of poetry was not necessarily music's gain, and even Berg, in his *Wozzeck*, seeks to find a range of musical means to restore a sense of form and balance denied him by Büchner's forceful but unstructured text.

It is commonly argued that "great" poetry is too powerful to be set to music but must be left to stand alone. However, there is no logic to the corollary, that poetry for music must, by definition, be second-rate, even if it usually must, in the end, be different, and although there are good librettists and bad, their work usually deserves greater recognition than is often the case. Lully's librettist Philippe Quinault may not have been a Racine or Molière, but he certainly knew what he was doing and did it well; Lorenzo Da Ponte, Francesco Maria Piave, and Hugo von Hofmannsthal are worthy of similar credit. A significant number of opera librettos merit high literary status, and some certainly gained it within the canon: Pietro Metastasio's *Artaserse* was set either in its original or in some revised form by eighty composers, ranging from Leonardo Vinci's opera of 1730 to Charles Lucas's of 1840, and his *Didone abbandonata* by sixty between 1724 (Domenico Sarro) and 1824 (Karl Gottlieb Reissiger). Whether or not in collaboration with a composer, a librettist will identify or create a plot, pace the drama within (or sometimes outside) the genre-based conventions of the day, accommodate the requirements of staging, decide who sings what and where, and even, if the composer is lucky, come up with words worthy of taking wings of song.

Dramma in Musica

The term *dramma per musica* places the emphasis not just on drama, but also on what exists prior to the composer's handling of it. But a drama "for" music will not necessarily produce a drama "in" music, unless one uses the term just to signify an object and not some kind of action or result. While the terms *dramma per musica* and *dramma in musica* were more or less interchangeable in Italian opera in the later seventeenth and eighteenth centuries—save where they served to distinguish a libretto from its particular setting—they open up a debate that has recurred constantly in operatic history. Although that debate has usually been cast in terms of the relative priorities of word and music, the more fundamental question is whether opera can or should be dramatic in the first place. It may seem an odd one to ask, given that the genre has often sought to vindicate itself by some appeal to its dramatic pretensions. However, it has not always been thus: there are plenty of accounts of eighteenth-century onlookers yawning (talking, drinking, gambling, flirting...) through the recitatives of an *opera seria*, returning their attention to the stage only when their favorite singer began an aria. And while some patterns of audience behavior may have changed since then, those operatic moments that focus the attention may not. The notion that opera indissolubly melds music and drama in some superior heightened experience has often been a convenient fiction for the genre, its protagonists, and its advocates, but it is a dangerous strategy for works that inevitably, and perhaps even necessarily, fail to meet such elevated expectations (Kivy 1988).

It depends, of course, on how one defines "drama." If one is talking about larger-than-life characters and situations engaging monumental existential issues, or about grand settings and pageantry, then a good many operas fit one or other bill. Cozier domestic comedies would seem, on the face of it, less well suited to the operatic stage, although they were a trend in the *opera buffa*, *opéra comique*, and *Singspiel* traditions of the second half of the eighteenth century, and one that regained some favor during the neoclassical revival in the mid-twentieth. It would probably be unreasonable to expect operas to have complex plots—although some can certainly appear confusing—working their way to subtle conclusions, and their pacing will usually be more variable than in spoken plays, with greater pause for reflection and commentary. Operas that aspire to naturalism or realism have a harder time of it than those that do not, at least without some redefinition of what might be "natural" or "real": the genre handles Stanislavski's theories less well than it does Brecht's.

A sure sign of the tensions within and between these different notions of what might constitute the "drama" in opera is the periodic call for reform, based on the claim that a supposedly "pure" art form has become corrupted by forces working from within but essentially out of control, be they empty-headed librettists, foolish composers, or vainglorious singers. Purge the genre of these contaminations, so the argument goes, and all will be right with the world. Gluck made the point in and through his "reform" operas of the 1760s and 1770s, with the preface to his *Alceste* (1767), written by librettist Ranieri de' Calzabigi but signed by the composer, serving as his manifesto. Wagner did much the same thing: his manifesto was *Oper und Drama* (1850–1851). It is revealing that neither Gluck nor Wagner were Italians—Italian opera being, of course, one *bête noire*—although Wagner had not much good to say about earlier German opera, while his view of the French soured still more after the disastrous reception accorded his *Tannhäuser* in Paris in 1861. It is also revealing that both were, of course, composers: even when the argument was in favor of drama gaining the upper hand, the musician needed to stay in charge. These and other reform movements often harked back to the Utopian age when opera emerged from the pure, literary ideals of the Florentines who invented the genre, and further still to the roots that they also claimed as their own: ancient Greece. For the late eighteenth and nineteenth centuries, Hellenism had its own special resonances in terms of nobility, severity, and purity, as well—for Wagner, at least—as republicanism. In the early twentieth century, the thrust could be against Wagner, against Puccini, or against Romantic opera in general. The main point, however, was to restore a degenerate art to one or other kind of former glory, an issue that often went beyond the aesthetic to the political.

What composers say and what they do need not always be the same thing; for that matter, if composers always did what they said, the musical results might not be very successful. Gluck's preface to *Alceste* and Wagner's *Oper und Drama* are powerful documents, albeit a bit muddleheaded in places, and reading these and similar polemics promulgated throughout the history of opera forces the consideration of issues that may not be uppermost in one's mind during the immediate operatic experience. These issues also direct—some might claim, divert—the discussion of opera in the scholarly literature, whether that discussion involves attempts to rescue late Baroque opera from the accusation of being merely a concert in costume; to demonstrate how Mozart exploits the potentials of contemporary musical forms and syntaxes to establish dramatic conflict and resolution; to argue that Rossinian coloratura serves also to illustrate character and purpose; to show that in Wagner's music dramas the orchestra can, by way of its leitmotifs, present a complex narrative independent of, and supplemental to, what is in fact happening on the stage; or even to defend a seemingly outmoded genre in these modernist and postmodernist times.

While music can delineate characters both separately and, within limits, simultaneously, it cannot fairly represent their interactions, save in the broadest terms. Even in the best-written ensembles—as, for example, the Act III sextet from Mozart's *Le nozze di Figaro*—characters tend to polarize in musical groups, albeit in shifting alliances (which is in part the point), and dramatic tensions get played out in a fairly obvious manner. For all its subtlety in other ways, music tends to paint emotions with a broad brush, even if its very wordlessness offers the sense that it is plumbing pre-rational, and therefore more intense, emotional depths. And whatever music can reveal about a character's inner feelings—allowing the expression of what cannot be said—it would probably be foolish to claim that the result smacks of any psychological sophistication. Indeed, what more often grabs the attention in the opera house is precisely the lack of any such sophistication when a raw emotion delivers a punch to the stomach. Add to that one's innate pleasure in the visual and aural spectacle of performance, plus the aesthetic contemplation of the musically beautiful, and drama, as it were, tends to go out the window. At that point, opera needs neither defense nor apology, save an appeal to accept it for what it is, rather than what we might wish it to be.

Exotic and Irrational?

A drama "in music" would seem to be an odd concept anyway. In principle, it is no stranger than a drama in iambic pentameters (unless you happen to believe that Julius Caesar did indeed address Mark Antony in five-feet lines), or for that matter, one in Elizabethan English purporting to represent life in ancient Rome. Of course, Shakespeare has conditioned most of us to accept the convention with nary a question, and a willing "suspension of disbelief" is part of the contract required to gain admission to the theater. But while we can believe—or at least, temporarily agree not to disbelieve—in pentameters, music may seem one step too far.

The issue hinges on verisimilitude, which is one subtext of Dr. Johnson's well-known characterization of opera as "an exotic and irrational entertainment." This was a somewhat throwaway, and anti-Italian, remark in Johnson's *Life of Hughes* (one of his set of biographical sketches of English poets written between 1777 and 1781); for his famous dictionary, Johnson instead borrowed the more reasonable definition of the genre from Dryden's preface to *Albion and Albanus* (1685) as "a poetical tale or fiction, represented by vocal and instrumental musick, adorned with scenes, machines, and dancing." Suspicion of, yet delight in, the exotic and the irrational have always animated the history of opera since it emerged in Florence at the end of the sixteenth century (Tomlinson 1999). Jacopo Peri and Ottavio Rinuccini sought to solve the problem in two ways. They deliberately placed their *favole in musica* in the context of a revival of the putative performance practices of ancient drama, a matter of some debate in the course of the Renaissance but which provided a hallowed precedent. Their choice of subject matter was also significant. The hero of *Euridice* is, of course, Orpheus, the greatest musician of classical myth; the work is also set in a pastoral Arcadia, a land of milk and honey where shepherds and shepherdesses could plausibly carry out their day-to-day lives in song. Likewise, in Monteverdi's *Orfeo* (1607), Orpheus sings a highly virtuosic aria to charm the powers of Hades to grant him access to rescue his beloved Eurydice from death. Earlier in the same opera, he also performs songs about his joy on his wedding day, while his pastoral companions sing and dance in praise of the happy couple. These songs are inherently lifelike (some would call them diegetic, although the term is problematic): People sing at weddings, and by report, Orpheus sang at the gates of the Inferno, so such songs can plausibly be heard as onstage performances. The same would apply to other non-deities who use the voice by profession, be it a troubadour, a would-be Meistersinger, or even a singing barber. In other words, operas commonly veer between two types of music—with complex shades between—one presented as verisimilar in the narrow sense of the term, and the other not.

Opera has customarily attempted to meet at least some principles of verisimilitude by providing occasions for music that is, to use Carolyn Abbate's term, phenomenal, as distinct from the noumenal music to which operatic characters usually appear deaf (Abbate 1991: 119). (A third possible category—where the music invokes natural sounds audible to those onstage such as birdsong or a storm—is a very special case.) The use of "real" music on the stage—that is, performances that characters can themselves be reckoned to hear—usually provides an excuse for a lyric interlude that may or may not have a dramatic point (Cherubino's "Voi che sapete" in Act II of *Le nozze di Figaro*, with Susanna "playing" her guitar to accompany him; Alfredo's *brindisi* toward the beginning of *La traviata*; Musetta's waltz in Act II of *La bohème*; the tenor who suddenly appears in Act I of *Der Rosenkavalier*). Likewise, representing actual music-making and dancing with or without onstage musicians has become a virtuoso (for the composer) cliché, and Mozart's ingenious dance music in the Act I finale of *Don Giovanni*—providing a background to onstage action—had a strong influence on the opening of Verdi's *Rigoletto*, also fixing a trope that echoes through Act III, scene 3 of his *Un ballo in maschera*, the tavern scene in Berg's *Wozzeck* (II.4), and even the "Jazzbo Brown" opening to Gershwin's *Porgy and Bess*. Similar motives underpin hunters' or sailors' songs, military marches, spinning songs, and lullabies, for which excuses can usually readily be found, assuming the right subject matter.

Moving away from the phenomenal, but still plausibly within its boundaries, are standard set-pieces with which "real" music conventionally becomes associated, such as prayer-scenes (Micaëla in Bizet's *Carmen*, Act III, scene 5; Desdemona in Verdi's *Otello*, Act IV, scene 2) on the one hand, and magical incantations on the other (Alcina's "Ombre pallide" in Handel's eponymous opera; the "Wolf's Glen" scene in Weber's *Der Freischütz*), given that music is often associated with heightened invocation. The principle may extend to exhortations, whether in person (the choruses of prisoners in Beethoven's *Fidelio* or Verdi's *Nabucco*) or by letter (Tatyana in Tchaikovsky's *Yevgeny Onegin* is the obvious example), and also to "mad"-scenes (Donizetti's *Lucia di Lammermoor*) where the recourse to music further gains verisimilitude by virtue of the situation (sane people do not normally hear flutes twittering in the air around them). Exhortation and madness usually also combine in another typical set-piece, the lament, although there was some debate, at least in the seventeenth century, over whether laments are better framed as musical speeches (so, in an impassioned recitative, as in the only surviving part of Monteverdi's *Arianna*) or as formal arias (the heroine in Purcell's *Dido and Aeneas*, over her famous ground bass).

These tropes or their derivatives can usually be found to some degree woven by librettists and composers in any opera, even those that seemingly eschew conventional set-pieces to seek a more "natural" form of musical drama. Other conventions include the "I"-songs in which characters introduce or explain themselves to each other or to the audience (Leporello's "Notte e giorno faticar" at the beginning of *Don Giovanni*; "A Wand'ring Minstrel I" in Gilbert and Sullivan's *The Mikado*; Rodolfo's "Chi son?

Sono un poeta" in *La bohème*); narrative songs in which a character offers an account of prior events that provide the backstory necessary to understand the action (Senta's ballad in Act II of Wagner's *Der fliegende Holländer*); or songs that simply set a time and a place (Clara's "Summertime" in *Porgy and Bess*). A special form of the "I"-song is the monologue where the character alone on stage muses on matters of life or death, somewhat in the manner of the formal soliloquy in spoken plays. One might also add other song-types to this list, such as the revenge aria, love duet, and so forth. While all such settings are rarely phenomenal, strictly speaking, they tend to have a formality that makes them appear nearly so, while also setting them somehow apart from the other dramatic and musical action.

Of course, this leaves a great deal of operatic music unexplained, at which point the argument tends to return once more to notions of emotional truth or psychological penetration. But how a given opera moves between episodes of greater or lesser verisimilitude—or if you prefer, different versions of verisimilitude—can be very revealing. So, too, is the tendency to play on whether the characters hear only each others' words or also their music. Much depends on the subject matter: mythical deities (whether Greek, Roman, or Norse), Arcadian shepherds and shepherdesses, ancient Egyptian rulers, and exotic non-Western Others pose fewer problems than characters from European history (whether Julius Caesar or Richard Nixon) or from "real life" contemporary to the opera. Much also depends on the period in terms of whether opera is just accepted as a theatrical norm (as it was for the most part in the seventeenth, eighteenth, and nineteenth centuries) or requires some manner of special pleading. However, the genre can often appear skittish about its *raison d'être*. Early operas often had prologues to justify their aesthetic premises, and the technique returned in the late nineteenth and early twentieth centuries as the genre once more came under suspicion: thus Leoncavallo's *I Pagliacci* has the protagonist Tonio first appear as the "Prologo" to emphasize the claims of *verismo*, and Busoni's *Doktor Faustus* uses a spoken prologue to explain the composer's choice of subject. Similar is the use of other framing devices that somehow distance the plot from the lives it represents: whether by establishing it as a lesson-bearing exemplar (the power of Amor in Monteverdi's *L'incoronazione di Poppea*; the "school for lovers" in Mozart's *Così fan tutte*), as the telling of a "story" (Offenbach's *Les contes d'Hoffmann*, Rimsky-Korsakov's *The Golden Cockerel*, Benjamin Britten's *The Turn of the Screw* and *Billy Budd*), or as part of an overtly theatrical exercise (the circus-master in Berg's *Lulu*, the theater director in Poulenc's *Les mamelles de Tirésias*, and the Choregos in Birtwistle's *Punch and Judy*) or debate (the beginning of Prokofiev's *The Love for Three Oranges*).

The technique has been extended still further to the rather self-conscious trick of making an opera be "about" opera: Richard Strauss's *Ariadne auf Naxos* and *Capriccio*, and Berio's *Un re in ascolto*, are different cases in point. Such narrower self-reflexivity, which can also extend to a rather knowing self-parody, seemingly stands in contrast to more grandiose claims for opera's universality embodied in Wagnerian music drama and its modernist successors (such as Prokofiev's *War and Peace* and Stockhausen's *Licht* cycle), although they are, in the end, two sides of the same coin. Opera composers may have variously sought in different ways, times, and places to prove the eminent Dr. Johnson wholly wrong, but we all know, deep down, that he was exactly right.

See also: Genre, Musical Theater(s), Operatorio? The Concept of Opera, Verisimilitude

Bibliography

Abbate, Carolyn. 1991. *Unsung Voices: Opera and Musical Narrative in the Nineteenth Century.* Princeton, NJ: Princeton University Press.

Abbate, Carolyn, and Roger Parker, eds. 1989. *Analyzing Opera: Verdi and Wagner.* Berkeley and Los Angeles: University of California Press.

Agid, Philippe, and Jean-Claude Tarondeau. 2010. *The Management of Opera: An International Comparative Study.* Basingstoke, UK, and New York: Palgrave Macmillan.

Citron, Marcia J. 2000. *Opera on Screen.* New Haven: Yale University Press.

Gerhard, Anselm. 1998. *The Urbanization of Opera: Music Theater in Paris in the Nineteenth Century,* translated by Mary Whittall. Chicago: University of Chicago Press.

Glixon, Beth L., and Jonathan E. Glixon. 2006. *Inventing the Business of Opera: The Impresario and His World in Seventeenth-Century Venice.* New York: Oxford University Press.

Gossett, Philip. 2006. *Divas and Scholars: Performing Italian Opera.* Chicago: University of Chicago Press.

Groos, Arthur, and Roger Parker, eds. 1988. *Reading Opera.* Princeton, NJ: Princeton University Press.

Kivy, Peter. 1988. *Osmin's Rage: Philosophical Reflections on Opera, Drama, and Text.* Princeton, NJ: Princeton University Press.

Koestenbaum, Wayne. 1993. *The Queen's Throat: Opera, Homosexuality, and the Mystery of Desire.* New York: Poseidon Press.

Levin, David J. 2007. *Unsettling Opera: Staging Mozart, Verdi, Wagner, and Zemlinsky.* Chicago: University of Chicago Press.

Lindenberger, Herbert. 1998. *Opera in History: From Monteverdi to Cage.* Stanford: Stanford University Press.

Metropolitan Opera. *Annual Report 2006–07.* Online. Available: http://www.metoperafamily.org/metopera/about/report.aspx (accessed May 14, 2009).

Operabase. Online. Available: http://operabase.com (accessed January 16, 2012).

Robinson, Paul. 2002. "A Deconstructive Postscript: Reading Libretti and Misreading Opera." In *Opera, Sex, and Other Vital Matters,* 30–51. Chicago: University of Chicago Press. Originally published in Groos and Parker 1988, 328–346.

Rosselli, John. 1992. *Singers of Italian Opera: The History of a Profession.* Cambridge: Cambridge University Press.

Royal National Theatre. *Annual Report and Financial Statements 2007–2008.* Online. Available: http://www.nationaltheatre.org.uk/41321/annual-reportreview/annual-report-0708.html (accessed May 14, 2009).

Royal Opera House, Covent Garden (London, UK). *Annual Review 2007/08.* Online. Available: http://www.roh.org.uk/about/annualreview/index.aspx (accessed May 14, 2009).

Sartori, Claudio. 1990–1994. *I libretti italiani a stampa dalle origini al 1800: Catalogo analitico con 16 indici.* 7 vols. Cuneo: Bertola & Locatelli.

Tomlinson, Gary. 1999. *Metaphysical Song: An Essay on Opera.* Princeton: Princeton, NJ: Princeton University Press.

CHAPTER 2

GENRE

EMANUELE SENICI

WHEN considered from the point of view of genre, opera's reputation for improbability and paradox seems spectacularly confirmed. On the one hand, opera counts among the very few genres in the history of artistic creation in which theory came before practice: rather than being recognized as a genre after it had been in existence for some time, as usually happens, opera was famously "invented." On the other hand, perhaps no other genre relies on convention as heavily as opera: its production involves so many individuals with such a diverse array of abilities and duties that the repetition of many different kinds of actions constitutes a fundamental requirement for its existence. If what is necessary for the successful realization of an opera were not highly predictable, it would be impossible to go beyond a few extremely labor-intensive and prohibitively expensive occasional performances. This applies to all sorts of different roles, from theatrical architect to urban planner, from librettist to composer, from impresario to singer, from orchestral player to costume maker, from financial manager to usher, and from spectator to critic. In other words, in the world of opera convention reigns supreme. But convention also lies at the very core of genre. Generic features and considerations, therefore, have played a more relevant part in the composition, performance, fruition, and discussion of opera than is the case for most other genres, be they theatrical, musical, or more generally artistic. How could such a complex genre be "invented," then?

Attempting to answer this question helps bring into focus a few issues crucial for understanding opera as a genre, and therefore the first part of this chapter is devoted to such an attempt. The second part concentrates instead on the ways in which the category of genre has been employed in the aesthetic and historiographical discourse on opera. More specifically, it investigates how the relationship between a given opera and its possible generic contexts has been conceived in the last two centuries, given that current understandings of this relationship began to emerge around 1800.

The Genrification of Opera

Much recent genre theory, while insisting on the communicative and rhetorical aspects of genre, tends to maintain a separation, often implicit but no less deep-rooted, between works, on the one hand, and discourses—authorial, critical, spectatorial, and so on—on the other (for an application of this theoretical orientation to the study of opera, see Senici 2004: 625). Some theorists, however, have argued in favor of obliterating this distinction altogether, and seeing genres as discursive fields shaped by different kinds of utterances, regardless of whether they emanate from works, authors, critics, or audiences broadly meant. According to literary critic Adena Rosmarin, a radical proponent of this position, "genre is not, as is commonly thought, a class, but, rather, a classifying statement. It is therefore itself a text" (Rosmarin 1985: 46). This theory has emerged most forcefully in the context of literary studies, has been conceived for literary genres, and is therefore predicated on the fact that works of literature and works of literary criticism share the same communicative mode, verbal language. A more flexible version, one perhaps more useful for our purposes, has been elaborated by film theorists and historians. Discussing *film noir*, James Naremore has recently stated: "If we want to understand it, or to make sense of genres or art-historical categories in general, we need to recognize that [it] belongs to the history of ideas as much as to the history of cinema; it has less to do with a group of artifacts than with a discourse—a loose, evolving system of arguments and readings, helping to shape commercial strategies and aesthetic ideologies" (Naremore 2008: 10–11).

An approach to genres that focuses on discourse, process, and ideology, and that sidelines, at least at a theoretical level, any distinction between works and the words surrounding them, seems better suited to the case of opera. In particular, it has the notable advantage of offering a more convincing perspective on the thorny question of the "invention" of the genre than has hitherto been the case (for a critique of current historiographical positions on the "birth" of opera, see Leopold 2003). When artifacts are kept at the center of generic thinking, the coming into being of a new artistic genre is always conceptualized theoretically and narrated historically as the retrospective naming of a group of works as belonging to a new genre. But this model does not function well for opera, which was discussed, imagined, and invoked well before works recognized as eventually instantiating the genre were actually performed. The inevitable question arises of how opera could be conceived of—even if not explicitly named as such—in the absence of actual works whose generic allegiance could be reconfigured in terms of the newly emerging genre.

A thoroughly discursive perspective on the "birth" of opera helps circumvent this theoretical impasse, changing the terms in which the question has traditionally been cast. If, from a production-centered point of view, "either one says that opera began in Florence in 1600, or one says that operatic theatre began in Venice in 1637" (Bianconi 1987: 162), from a discourse-oriented position one will probably say that opera first appeared in Italian intellectual and courtly circles in the final third of the sixteenth century, slowly gained ground over the course of the following decades, and finally found a stable generic identity in the mid-seventeenth century. Far from suddenly appearing in a specific year, then, opera took almost a century to emerge, as seems to befit such a complex artistic manifestation.

Such a long process of genrification necessarily entailed a multiplication of overlapping but also at times contrasting discursive positions, which highlight different aspects of the process itself, and therefore of the genre in the making. It seems worth emphasizing that, in the words of film theorist Rick Altman, "no isolated part of this process actually *is* the genre; instead, the genre lies somewhere in the overall circulation of meaning constitutive of the process." Equally crucial, however, is acknowledging "the extent to which genres appear to be initiated, stabilized and protected by a series of institutions essential to the very existence of genres" (Altman 1999: 84–85). Identifying different discursive positions is not enough; they should also be placed within the institutions—meant in the broadest sense of the term—that make them possible. Moreover, account should be taken of the roles played within such institutions by individuals or groups from which the positions themselves originate.

Institutional Discourses

In the case of opera, the institutions that made crucial contributions to its genrification include academies and groups of intellectuals, courts and aristocratic circles, networks of musicians, theaters and their promoters, and different types of audiences. Obviously, different people could participate in more than one kind of institution, and therefore the discourses that originated from them could respond to multiple strategic positions. Librettists, for example, could, and in fact normally would, be associated with intellectual groups as well as courtly circles, and therefore their role in the process of opera's genrification would depend on their position within both institutions. What is more, their contributions could take different textual forms, from the actual libretto of an opera to its paratexts (generic indicator, for example, or prefatory letter, if in fact penned by librettists), and from correspondence with a composer or courtly official to theoretical tracts. Finally, each text enacts specific rhetorical strategies, which have an impact not only on the formulation of generic discourse, but also on its content, and therefore on the ways in which it participates in the process of genrification.

The numerous treatises from the final decades of the sixteenth century that performed a role in the process of opera's genrification, for example, belong to several different disciplinary discourses, and originated in different institutional spaces. To focus on one case, Angelo Ingegneri's *Della poesia rappresentativa o del modo di rappresentare le favole sceniche* (1598) resonantly endorsed pastoral drama over tragedy and comedy, and therefore contributed to creating a favorable climate for this "third genre," whose proximity to opera is well known. Ingegneri's extended discussion of theatrical genres places his treatise in the context of sixteenth-century debates on literary genres, which had flourished since Aristotle's *Poetics* had become more widely available and sparked the first commentaries in the 1540s. Thus, *Della poesia rappresentativa* conforms to a set of assumptions and positions specific to sixteenth-century literary theory, building on previous suggestions such as Giovanni Battista Giraldi Cinzio's defense of the "tragedy with a happy ending" (for the relevance of this defense to opera, see Gerbino and Fenlon 2006: 477). Ingegneri dedicated his treatise, published in Ferrara, to Cesare d'Este, duke of Modena. Although the author was not directly dependent on the Estes, his endorsement of pastoral drama also belongs to the institutional space of the Este court (recently forced to cede Ferrara to the Pope and retreat to Modena), since it was precisely in this space that the genre had long been favored—one of its foremost representatives, Torquato Tasso's *Aminta* (performed 1573, published 1580) was promoted, set, and performed there. Finally, Ingegneri was also a theatrical practitioner, famously in charge of staging Sophocles' *Edipo re* (with Andrea Gabrieli's musical setting of the choruses) for the inauguration of Vicenza's Teatro Olimpico in 1585, and *Della poesia rappresentativa* stems in no small part from its author's direct experience of theatrical performance. The theater constitutes therefore a third institutional space to which Ingegneri's treatise belongs, and from which, with its emphasis on generic mixture and the affective power of performance, it contributes to a discursive climate in which opera could grow.

After having identified the main institutional spaces in which and through which opera became a genre, the next question that a discursive approach foregrounds is "for what purpose?" This is not the place to attempt even a cursory answer, given the complexity of the issue. What is more immediately relevant is to observe how the "why" influenced the "how." The struggle on the part of intellectuals to find satisfactory and broadly shared solutions to the blatant contrast between "classic" literary theory (i.e., mainly Aristotle), generally perceived as rule-binding, and unruly contemporary theatrical practices highlighted issues of verisimilitude on the one hand, and spectatorial pleasure and emotional involvement on the other. According to this discourse—which would accompany opera all along its history up to the present—opera was the genre of pleasurable and emotional artificiality, to be praised or, more frequently, bemoaned.

Conversely, what sixteenth-century courts needed and cared about was an ever more magnificent theatricalization of their rituals, made necessary by the challenges of the gradual but inexorable transition from feudal to early modern models of princely authority and, more generally, political power (see Adamson 1999 and, for a recent musical perspective, Borghetti 2008). In this context, the discourse of opera revolved around the unprecedented and awe-inspiring wonder afforded by the genre, or, better, afforded by the prince for the entertainment of courtiers and the renown of himself and his family. It should be noted that opera was by no means the only kind of theatrical entertainment devoted to this purpose, with or without music, and therefore the contribution of courtly discourse to its genrification focused not on what has traditionally been taken as its most genre-defining characteristic, that is, the musical setting of dialogue and action. If music is mentioned at all, it is in order to highlight the added dimension of splendor and pleasure brought about by its continuous presence. In this sense, it is instructive to compare contemporary official descriptions of the musical *intermedi* performed between the acts of a play as part of wedding festivities at the court of Florence in 1589, and of the performance of Rinuccini's and Peri's *Euridice*, which we now consider the first extant opera, for a similar occasion and for the same court in 1600: they hardly differ (Weiss 2002: 1–7, 11–12).

Different still are the concerns exhibited in the institutional space of the musicians' network, which emerge most clearly in the prefaces to the published scores of the earliest operas, signed—if perhaps not always actually written—by composers. While these texts do not belong exclusively to such a space—both intellectual and courtly interests are also evident—they contribute in specific ways to opera's genrification, focusing as they do on the technical novelty of solo singing and *stile recitativo*, and on the crucial importance of skilled performers to its execution. Singer Vittoria Archilei, for example, receives effusive praise from all three composers whose "musical tales" were published in the year 1600, Peri's and Caccini's *Euridice*s and Cavalieri's *Rappresentazione di Anima e di Corpo* (Weiss 2002: 12–23).

Singing Genre, Naming Opera

Individual works naturally contributed in crucial ways to the process of opera's genrification, especially given the heightened generic self-consciousness that characterizes them—as tends to be the case for all early representatives of a genre in the making. Their texts abound in cues alerting readers/listeners to their new generic dimensions. Since, in John Frow's words, these cues are "the ways in which texts seek to situate themselves rhetorically, to define and delimit their uptake by a reader," such "aspects of the text which ... stand out as being also, reflexively, *about* the text and how to use it" are crucial for texts whose conventions of usage have not yet been established, and whose uptake therefore needs explicit definition and delimitation (Frow 2006: 115). The earliest operas are famously introduced by prologues sung by such characters as the poets Ovid (*Dafne*, 1598) and Ariosto (*L'isola di Alcina*, 1626), the personifications of Tragedy (*Euridice*, 1600) and Music (*Orfeo*, 1607), the god Apollo (*Arianna*, 1608), and so on. Their function is typically both to make explicit the celebratory occasion of the performance, and to direct the audience's reception of the work about to be performed in terms of genre, typically by claiming, with varying degrees of emphasis, that the work itself is not a tragedy but a mixed kind of entertainment with a happy ending, set in a mythological and pastoral ambience, and in which music plays a crucial part.

Music also participates in this self-reflective discourse, starting precisely with the prologues. Their strophic form, with each stanza connected by a ritornello, can be heard as spotlighting music as a rhetorically powerful structural device, one that makes possible the sort of pleasurable emotional intensification about to be experienced in the main body of the opera, to which the words of such prologues usually call attention. Moreover, early opera's well-known penchant for characters who are renowned musicians (Orpheus, Apollo) and who perform superior feats of musical prowess, usually taken to be a ploy to avert charges of lack of verisimilitude from the new genre, can be understood, from a generic point of view, as a way of pointing toward the crucial role played by music in opera—a way of emphasizing the novelty of music's presence and its rhetorical and affective power, rather than apologizing for it. In this sense, librettist Alessandro Striggio's choice to assign the prologue of his *Orfeo* to the personification of Music seems to acknowledge, or anticipate, the fundamental function of Monteverdi's music for the overall effect of the performance. The contribution of this prologue to the genrification of opera is therefore rather different from that of Rinuccini's *Euridice*, with which *Orfeo* shares the same subject matter. Whereas *Euridice*'s Tragedy proclaims "this is not a tragedy as you, ladies and gentlemen, normally know it, but a new kind of play," *Orfeo*'s Music sings "I, Music, am the crucial factor in the intense emotional impact that the forthcoming play about Orpheus, a famous singer, is going to have on you, dear public. Listen out!"

Perhaps the weakest contribution to the genrification of opera comes from the discursive space where genre is normally explicitly named, that is, the generic indicator on published librettos or scores. We find neither any agreement on one or few locutions, nor any significant discontinuity between what we now call operas and earlier forms of entertainment such as *intermedi*, pastoral plays, and so on. A plethora of terms circulated freely, from *favola* to *rappresentazione*, from *dramma* to *tragedia*, and from *azione* to *opera*, each term often followed by such qualifiers as *pastorale*, *in musica*, *rappresentata in musica*, *musicale*, *regia*, and so on. This is far from surprising: Generic indicators functioning as, in Gérard Genette's word, "paratexts" (that is, actually appearing on the same object where the texts are "contained," be they librettos, scores, audio or video recordings, and so on) are generally the discursive space most resistant to a process of genrification. More interesting are the rhetorical strategies of such acts of naming, and the kinds of transactions that such terms are meant to accomplish (Genette 1997). Calling a work "tragedy" means placing it squarely in the context of Aristotelian theory and its controversial sixteenth-century reception, and claiming for it arguably the most elevated position in the hierarchy of theatrical genres—despite the many challenges thrown at such hierarchy by theorists. But it also means immediately needing help from a fictional authority in the prologue to qualify that eye-catching term: Apollo in Rinuccini's *Arianna* saying that the play is going to be about love rather than war and death, but that, even so, perhaps it will revive the glories of ancient drama; or Ariosto in Testi's *L'isola di Alcina* reassuring everybody that no-one is going to die, but hopefully love's sorrows will be equally moving.

Paratextual indicators of genre stabilized only after the process of opera's genrification had come to some sort of completion, which it famously did first in Venice in the second quarter of the seventeenth century. From the abundance of terms mentioned above, *dramma*, in turn *per musica*, *musicale*, *rappresentato in musica*, and so on, emerged as by far the most popular generic subtitle. It is interesting in this respect to compare Venice with Rome, another city that saw a sustained activity of a kind that we would now call "operatic" throughout the seventeenth century. In Venice, between 1637, the year when the first public opera theater opened, and 1650, 44 percent of libretti were designated with any one version of the locution *dramma per musica*; between 1651 and 1675, this percentage had risen to 90. In the papal capital, however, the same percentage stood at 42 between 1626 and 1650, but in the following quarter-century had climbed only to 58 (Di Giuseppe 1996). The difference between Venice and Rome is that, whereas in the former opera had become a public spectacle frequently repeated in purpose-built theaters for a paying audience, in the latter it was still tied to the courtly-academic model.

Why Venice?

The commercialization of opera in Venice has generally been seen as the crucial final step in the process of its genrification. In the words of Ellen Rosand, "opera essentially defined itself as a genre in Venice. There, and only there, three conditions existed that proved crucial for its permanent establishment: regular demand, dependable financial backing, and a broad and predictable audience" (Rosand 1991: 1). But what were the profound reasons for such regularity of demand, dependability of financial backing, and breadth and predictability of audiences? Historians have invoked, with differing emphasis, rivalry among Venetian aristocratic families; competition on the part of Venice, a "republican" state, with the princely courts of Italy; the need to give ever more magnificent, and therefore musical, representation to the self-aggrandizing ideology of the "Most Serene Republic" of Venice; an intellectual politics of subversion that found in opera's carnivalesque aesthetics an ideal artistic ground (operas were performed during the Venetian carnival, already a tourist attraction); and the desire on the part of the Venetian aristocracy—the class for which opera was performed in the first place, and that backed it financially—to see and hear represented on stage "a new, more reflective, interior sense of self" generated by the profound changes undergone by this social group at the time, one that music was particularly suited to express (Romano 2006: 407; see also, among others, Bianconi 1987; Rosand 1991; Heller 2003; Muir 2007).

For our purposes, these complementary rather than contrasting hypotheses are remarkable because they invoke a wide spectrum of institutions, and therefore discursive spaces. In a specific sense, all these spaces were peculiar to mid-seventeenth-century Venice. From a more general perspective, however, at least some of the ideologies articulated here were common to other sociopolitical contexts, or would become so over the course of the following century. It could be said, then, that it was the richness of intersecting discourses in favor of opera in mid-seventeenth-century Venice that gave it the final genrifying push it needed, and at the same time guaranteed that at least some of this force would be present somewhere else. The ground was prepared for opera's dissemination to other cities and states.

Finally, to return to Rosand's words, speaking of "regular demand, dependable financial backing, and a broad and predictable audience" means acknowledging the fundamental role of repetition in the process of genrification. This is especially the case for such a complex artistic manifestation as opera, since, as mentioned above, its production is so complex that repeatability constitutes a fundamental requirement for it to have any hope of ever becoming a genre. This need for repetition was eventually met by a modern system of commercial production, a mechanism that, in its turn, demanded repetition at all levels in order to function. The modern market can exist only through repetition, and the same is particularly true of opera, more so than in the case of most other artistic genres. It was only when opera and the market met in Venice in the 1630s that the former found the institution fully capable of meeting its specific generic needs. At the same time, perhaps the market bound opera to repetition, and therefore convention, for the centuries to come, even more durably than the genre demanded. As early as 1650, a librettist complained that the Venetian public, having seen more than fifty operas in the span of only a few years, was "nauseated," and the desire for novelty was intense (cited in Rosand 1991: 155). In the centuries to come, opera would be characterized by a constant tension between convention and innovation, unique in its complexity as well as its self-consciousness.

Beyond Venice

Over the course of the seventeenth century, opera spread to many Italian cities and traveled further abroad. Changed contexts meant evolving generic discourses and practices, with some centers adapting the Venetian model, others welcoming the genre but changing it in order to suit local circumstances better, and others rejecting it altogether. Generally speaking, however, in the second half of the seventeenth century, each center where opera was performed knew only one kind of it. While paratextual generic indicators could be varied, broader discursive practices testify to awareness of a single genre. Outside Italy, its Italian origins were part of its identity, as the spread of terms derived from the Italian word "opera" proves: *opera* in English, *opéra* in French, *Oper* in German. Conversely, "opera" appeared infrequently in Italian, probably because it was considered too generic and imprecise (Trovato 1994: 22–29; LESMU 2007: entry "opera"). It was only over the course of the following century that this single genre splintered into sub-genres.

This statement immediately needs to be qualified in institutional and geographical terms. Intellectuals who wrote on opera were perfectly well aware already at the beginning of the eighteenth century of the existence of several different "national" traditions; the French in particular kept comparing their own to the Italian. But in the 1680s, for example, opera goers in Venice or Vienna knew only the Italian kind, *dramma per musica*; in Paris only the French one, *tragédie en musique*; and in Hamburg only the German one, *Oper* or *Singspiel*. A century later, however, in Venice they could choose between *opera seria*, *opera buffa*, and a third incipient genre sometimes called *dramma eroicomico*; in Vienna between Italian *seria* and *buffa*, and German *Singspiel*; in Paris between *tragédie en musique*, *opéra comique*, and the occasional performance of Italian works; in London between the Italian genres and opera (mostly comic) in English; in Madrid between, again, the Italian genres and Spanish *tonadillas*; and so on.

The reasons for the emergence of different operatic genres in the eighteenth century are varied and complex, and cannot be discussed here. For the serious genres, especially *opera seria*, intellectuals tended to couch them in terms of "reform," while for the comic or "vernacular" ones (*opera buffa, opéra comique, Singspiel*) the link with evolving social structures was more readily acknowledged. In any case, the category of genre itself was not questioned, even by reform-minded intellectuals. This does not mean that novelty was not praised, nor that what were considered the more deleterious consequences of convention, such as the lowering of creative and performative standards into routine, were not bemoaned. But the relationship between individual works and their genre was not generally construed in oppositional terms. The closing decades of the eighteenth century and the initial ones of the nineteenth, however, brought about a fundamental shift in the idea of genre as theorized and practiced in opera, a shift whose legacy is still strongly felt.

The Modern Rhetoric of Genre

It will not come as a surprise that the voice that has expressed most eloquently the new conception of genre in opera is Richard Wagner's. His short essay "Über die Benennung 'Musikdrama' (On the Term 'Music Drama')," first published in 1872, is devoted to the task of rejecting the generic descriptor that was beginning to be attached to his most recent operas, precisely that of "music drama," on both critical-aesthetic and historical grounds. The critical-aesthetic argument rests on the claim that his operas were totally and irreconcilably different from the rest of contemporary operatic production, and leads to an openly acknowledged fear of domestication and colonization of this utterly "other" terrain on the part of the operatic world. "The less I have felt disposed to accept [this term], the more have I perceived an inclination in other quarters to adopt the name for a presumably new art-genre, which would appear to have been bound to evolve in answer to the temper and tendencies of the day, even without my intervention, and now to lie ready as a cozy nest for everyone to hatch his musical eggs in"—hence Wagner's strongly worded suggestion that his "professional competitors" stick to the word "opera" for their works "intended for the present theatre" (Wagner [1872] 1896: 299, 302).

From a historical point of view, Wagner observes that works going "beyond their kind and custom" have retained their exceptional status across the ages: "Never has a *genre* arisen thence, a genre in which, once given its proper name, the extra-ordinary lay ready for the common use of every fumbler" (Wagner [1872] 1896: 303; original emphasis). Wagner's strategy, therefore, could not be other than "handing [my works] to the theatres without any designation of their genre at all; by this device I also think of abiding for just as long as I have to do with our theatres, which rightly recognize no other genre than 'Opera', and, let one give them . . . a 'music-drama', would make of it an 'opera' notwithstanding." Only Bayreuth will bring salvation from "our theatres," but "the thing" shall remain, in Wagner's concluding words, "an unnamed deed of art" (Wagner [1872] 1896: 304).

The Wagnerian genealogy of modern historiographical and critical attitudes toward opera has been repeatedly remarked upon, more often than not in order to decry its pernicious influence, especially on critical assessments of non-Germanic operatic traditions. This does not mean, however, that Wagnerian undertones have completely disappeared from current discourse. This is nowhere more evident than in the treatment of the relationship between famous works and their generic contexts, where the standard maneuver consists of arguing that these works went against or at least beyond the genres in which they were initially located. This is Wagner's strategy in "Über die Benennung 'Musikdrama,'" where the rejection of the term "music drama" voices resistance to a generic definition for works supposed to go beyond the very notion of genre. This attitude does not begin with Wagner, however, even if he expressed it in characteristically strong terms, not only in the essay on the term "music drama," but throughout his writings. Rather, as I have mentioned above, it slowly emerged between the late eighteenth and the early nineteenth centuries as part of a much larger shift in attitudes toward the notion of genre, most frequently explored in connection with literary Romanticism.

Romanticizing Genre

Romantic aesthetic theory introduced a historicist view of literary genres, promoting as a goal of contemporary literature the creation of works beyond traditional genres, often by means of some sort of fusion among them. Among the champions of this conception were the brothers Friedrich and August Wilhelm Schlegel (especially in August Wilhelm's *Lectures on Dramatic Art and Literature*, 1809–1811, translated into French in 1813, into English in 1815, and into Italian in 1817), Friedrich Schiller (*On Naïve and Sentimental Poetry*, 1800), Stendhal (*Racine and Shakespeare*, 1823), Victor Hugo (preface to *Cromwell*, 1827; preface to *Odes et Ballades*, 1828), the Milanese intellectuals gathered around the journal *Il conciliatore*, and Alessandro Manzoni (*Letter to M. Chauvet*, 1823) (see respectively Schlegel [1809–1811] 1879; Schiller [1800] 1966; Stendhal [1823] 2006; Hugo [1827] 1971; Hugo [1828] 1980; *Manifesti* 1968; Manzoni [1823] 2008). The literature of the past was re-conceived in terms of the new aesthetic, promoting writers whose works seemed to correspond to its tenets, such as Cervantes, Calderón, Corneille, and above all Shakespeare, while demoting those who appeared blindingly to obey what were increasingly considered the shackles of literary genres. What made a literary text worthy of aesthetic appreciation and critical attention was its individuality, its uniqueness: in the words of Friedrich Schlegel, "every work is its own genre" (Schlegel 1957: 116, cited in Frow 2006: 26).

The resistance to genre that emerged with Romantic literary theory intersected with a number of interrelated discourses that gathered force or underwent profound changes at around the same time. Among the most important is nationalism: Romantic ideas of genre were crucially, if often implicitly, inflected by ideas of the nation; specifically, each text was meant to contribute in its unique way to the "progress" of a national literature that found its *raison d'être* in its supposedly direct links with the nation's "spirit" or "essence." Awareness of the continuous expansion of literary and artistic markets also shaped Romantic genre theory. The eighteenth century saw the rise of what Jürgen Habermas ([1962] 1989) has famously called "the public sphere," the site where, among other things, the middle classes could acquire generalized aesthetic tastes. This sociocultural entity was an important factor in the formation of the Romantic anti-generic stance, which reacted precisely against such generalized, widely shared, and therefore supposedly devalued tastes. The eighteenth-century middle-class "public sphere" would then give way to the nineteenth- and twentieth-century lower-class "mass," in the process ensuring the survival of Romantic ideas of art, which not only were to contribute crucially to various twentieth-century modernisms, but would in fact come to stand for cultural modernity *tout court*.

In this sense, it is interesting to note that in English the word "genre" has been widely used to indicate kinds of artifacts, and most specifically literary texts, only from the nineteenth century. In the words of Steve Neale, the term "emerges with industrialization, mass production, new technologies, new capital, new means of distribution...the formation of a relatively large literate (or semi-literate) population—and hence a potential market—at a point of profound transformation in the conditions governing cultural production and the discourses and debates with which it was accompanied" (Neale 2000: 22–23). It is in this context that the adjective "generic" acquired the negative connotations that it still retains in most cases (but not in the present chapter, needless to say). If, as Terry Threadgold has put it, "before Romanticism what was Generic was Literature" (with a capital "L," that is to say, "high" literary activity), afterward "Literature" was characterized precisely by its supposed rejection of genre, which became instead a defining and negative attribute of "low," "popular" texts and other kinds of cultural products (Threadgold 1989: 121).

The Romantic aesthetics of genre, although primarily elaborated in the field of literature, had a significant impact on opera; indeed, opera contributed to it in important ways. This encounter rests on an essential contradiction, however, seldom acknowledged explicitly yet a source of endless tension. As I have said above, in the world of opera convention reigns supreme, and convention lies at the very core of the idea of genre. How could an anti-generic aesthetic such as the Romantic one be applied to an arch-generic art form such as opera? As Wagner sourly realized, one could well give theaters "music dramas," and they would turn them into "operas" no matter what. His solution was to have the *Festspielhaus* at Bayreuth built. Over the course of the past two centuries, many opera composers have indeed expressed a desire for their own theater, over which to exercise total control. Since only Wagner has succeeded thus far, however, the history of opera from the early nineteenth century has often been told as a story of uneasy tension between centripetal generic forces and centrifugal authorial opposition to them.

This tale, rhetorically satisfying as it may sound, tends to sideline that the discourse of opera had become highly composite and multivoiced, certainly much more so than at the genre's inception. Perhaps the main change is to be located in the rise of the periodical press—both general newspapers and specialized music journals and magazines—which brought about the figure of the professional critic. On one hand, journalists contributed crucially to the formation of those generalized, widely shared aesthetic tastes mentioned above, against which the Romantics reacted. On the other, many critical voices worked hard to propagate the Romantic idea of genre—which we should call simply "modern" from now on—or at least a watered-down version of it. This situation, whose paradoxical character should not go unnoticed, was among the causes of the recurring trope of "the artwork of the future," an artwork that was supposed to go against the conventions of its genre and the expectations of the public with such force that its time was not the present, but the future, when its "timeless," or at least "prophetic" qualities would eventually be recognized.

That "the artwork of the future" is Wagner's expression suggests the importance newly accorded to another discursive position, that of the composer. Composers contributed ever more substantially to opera's generic discourse, for two main reasons. First, they could now take advantage of the periodical press as a forum to present their ideas and from which to shape the reception of their own works as well as others'. Second, great attention was paid to their voices because they had become the authors of operas, which were now "theirs"—as opposed to librettists' works for which they had supplied the music. Given the widely shared orientation toward resistance to genre, more often than not composers tried to direct the reception of their operas precisely in these terms. Wagner's "artwork of the future" is only the most quoted among many different pronouncements by composers trying to place their works within the rhetoric of the resistance to genre.

National Service

The trope of "the artwork of the future" generated its own share of problems, however, among them its uneasy interaction with the nation-building work to which all the arts, including opera, were supposed to contribute. The nation needed to be built in the present, or at the very least in the near future, but the future of the modern artwork often looked rather distant. Moreover, the artwork itself was supposed to be not only unique, but also a challenge to the generalized tastes of that most nation-building of classes, the bourgeoisie. While the resulting tension emerges in all national discourses on operas, it is particularly acute in the case of the German-speaking lands, for at least five reasons. First, the drive to build a nation was stronger there than in France, Great Britain, Spain, or Russia, where a nation already existed. Second, an operatic tradition that could be constructed as national, that is to say, a tradition of opera in German, was considerably weaker and younger than in Italy and France. Third, Italian operas performed in Italian constituted a prominent presence in the operatic landscape of several German-speaking cities. Fourth, many of the works performed in German in the late eighteenth and early nineteenth centuries were translations and adaptations of Italian and especially French titles. Fifth, the Romantic conception of genre was elaborated and disseminated in the German-speaking lands particularly early and forcefully.

One of the ways in which German critics tried to come to terms with such a multi-layered network of potentially contradictory forces was by emphasizing the virtues of generic mixture. Fusing current genres, especially those of Italian and French opera, into a higher synthesis that would be new (since it left convention behind) and at the same time not *too* new (since it took from Italian and French opera what was supposed best to suit the "German spirit") became the most widely acknowledged way in which operas in German could become true "German operas." This fusion had to be continually renewed, however, in order to avoid its ossification into yet another genre—a tall order indeed for authors and audiences alike, who struggled with it throughout the nineteenth century and beyond (for recent discussions of the various aspects of the German discourse on opera as genre and genres in opera at the turn of the nineteenth century, see the essays in Lippe 2007).

Generic mixture was by no means exclusive to the German discourse on opera, however. The idea of a convergence or fusion of genres was common to other national operatic traditions, notably the French and Italian ones, from the late eighteenth century onward. A distinction must be made, however, between the notion of a convergence of genres as a process of genrification, and a fusion of genres understood as the aesthetic goal of a single composer or even a single opera. The former was at work in both the Italian and French contexts. South of the Alps it presided over the emergence of late eighteenth-century "sentimental" opera and early nineteenth-century *opera semiseria*, both closely tied to developments in the generic landscape of French spoken theatre and *mélodrame* (Castelvecchi 2013; Jacobshagen 2005). In France it resounded in the discourse on the genrification of *grand opéra* in the second quarter of the nineteenth century (De Van 1996; Lacombe 2001: 226–251). The idea of a fusion of genres as a composer's aesthetic goal has been forcefully explored in the case of Verdi, for example, most often in terms of a gradual approximation to the Shakespearean dramatic ideal, as divulged particularly by the Schlegels, Stendhal, and Hugo, and best represented by *Macbeth* and especially *Rigoletto* (Weiss 1982). This said, the discourses of convergence and fusion of genres often overlap both historically and critically, and, despite the genrifying role of the former, rhetorically belong to the modern resistance to genre.

The Times of Genre

Besides nation-building and the expansion of artistic markets, this resistance also intersected with other developments specific to music and opera but general to all centers of operatic activity, those of repertory and canon. It seems difficult to ascertain any kind of direct causal connection between the evolution of genre discourse, on the one hand, and the development of repertory and canon on the other, or vice versa. There is no doubt, however, that a link can be established between the dramatic increase in the life span of a number of operas, the claim of superior artistic quality for several among them (plus others that were canonized even if they were not part of the repertory), and the idea that they had gone against or beyond the genre into which they were originally located. As I have argued above, this idea contributed to the trope of the artwork of the future, a "timeless" entity. Thus, operas were acclaimed as timeless precisely as they entered time—performative, critical, and historiographical.

The discursive codification of the resistance to genre happened in different ways and at different times in different operatic centers and cultures, but over the course of the nineteenth century it slowly yet powerfully solidified into a trope common to all such centers and cultures. Its force was such that its influence is still strongly felt: As I have suggested above, saying that an opera went against or at least beyond the genre in which it initially participated remains the standard maneuver to promote its critical shares. The continuing currency of this trope should not come as a surprise, given that the social conditions, cultural formations, and ideological orientations that favored its spread are still at work. To mention only some of those more specific to opera, since the forces of repertory and canon still powerfully shape its production and consumption, the modern rhetoric of genre, which accompanied the formation of an operatic repertory and canon, lives on with them. A brief exploration of the modern critical traditions of a few operas of particular historiographical significance from the viewpoint of their treatment of genre demonstrates that, while the recurring theme of the breaking free from generic shackles is modulated in different tones and serves a variety of specific purposes, it ultimately both shapes and serves critical and aesthetic judgment.

Don Giovanni, *Carmen*, *Fidelio*

The first and perhaps most obvious case is that of Mozart's *Don Giovanni*. The generic discourse surrounding this opera in the last two centuries constitutes a striking example of the promotion of a work perceived as masterpiece in terms of its supposed stance beyond generic conventions. This trend started very early: According to the critic Friedrich Rochlitz, writing in the *Allgemeine musikalische Zeitung* in 1799, *Don Giovanni* was the example to follow for German operas in its innovative mixture of comic and serious, since this brought it closer to reality (Betzwieser 2007: 30–31; see also Henze-Döhring 1986). What is of interest here is not whether *Don Giovanni* does indeed go beyond its genre, but the critical commonplace that considers it as an operatic masterpiece *because* it does so. This maneuver emerges most obviously in the debate about its generic definition. The libretto's generic descriptor, "dramma giocoso per musica," has often been taken as an indication of the unusually "dramatic," that is to say, serious, character of the plot. Exceptional status has been granted to a term that is simply one of the "official" names of comic opera, a paratextual indicator for the object that was commonly known as *opera buffa*. Perhaps paradoxically, this critical claim can be related to the uninterrupted presence of *Don Giovanni* in the repertory of opera houses since its premiere. The generic definition became a problem in the first half of the nineteenth century, once the original generic context had been lost. Witness, for example, the standard term for *Don Giovanni* in nineteenth-century Italy, *opera semiseria*: this term evidently tries to account for what may have seemed an unusual degree of "seriousness" from a nineteenth-century point of view, one that *dramma giocoso* no longer covered. In short, claiming that in 1787 *dramma giocoso* meant something unusual and innovative is a critical move that belongs squarely to the modern rhetoric of the resistance to genre.

The case of Bizet's *Carmen* brings to the fore another aspect of this rhetoric. The supposed fiasco of the opera's premiere at the Opéra-Comique in 1875 (in reality, more a lukewarm reception than an outright failure) has been repeatedly attributed to the gap between, on one hand, the expectations of that theater's audience and the coordinates of the genre of *opéra comique* and, on the other, the serious, dramatic character of the work, especially its tragic ending. Therefore, *Carmen* initially failed because it went beyond the boundaries of the genre to which it officially belongs. The success that soon came, not by chance initially outside Paris, was due at least in part to the opera's removal from its original generic context and its transformation into an unambiguously tragic work, thanks also to the substitution of sung recitatives for spoken dialogues. From this point of view, the trend of the last few decades to restore *Carmen* to its "authentic" text, with spoken dialogues, could be implicated in an attempt to recuperate its generic originality, presumably evident from the clash between its serious tone and style (for example, in its use of recurring themes) and the interruption of musical continuity by the spoken parts. Moreover, it seems justified to suspect that in this case the rhetoric of generic subversion has also served a further ideological purpose: to keep in the background some of the other possible reasons that *Carmen* was initially unsuccessful, namely its treatment of gender, race, and class (McClary 1992).

An interesting comparison can be made between *Carmen* and Beethoven's *Fidelio*. In the German-language operatic landscape of the early nineteenth century, genre was a less stable category than in mid- to late-century France. In other words, *Carmen*'s immediate generic context is unarguably that of *opéra comique*, while *Fidelio*'s is less easily identified. This creates a potential problem from the point of view of the modern aesthetic of genre. Beethoven's opera must be a masterpiece, since it is by the most famous composer of Western music. What is more, this opera failed not once, but at least twice, and was not exactly an overwhelming success in its third version. There must be no question, then, that this masterpiece went against or beyond its genre. The problem is that this genre seems rather hard to define. What to do? I would suggest that the currency gained by the notion of "rescue opera" over the course of the twentieth century is due in significant part to the need to have a genre for *Fidelio* to transcend. In 1810s Vienna, the term *Befreieungsgeschichte* (story of liberation) was often used to indicate a type of plot, culminating with the rescue of one of the protagonists, common to various types of theatrical entertainments popular at the time, and of which *Fidelio* was considered a prime example (Rice 2007: 318–319). The concept, however, seems not to have entered operatic historiography for about a century, apparently reappearing as *Rettungs- oder Befreiungstück* (play of rescue or liberation) in Karl Maria Klob's *Die Oper von Gluck bis Wagner*, published in 1913; although the immediate context is a discussion of Cherubini's *Lodoïska*, the sentence in which the term appears includes references to *Fidelio* (Klob 1913: 281; Longyear 1959: 49). *Rettungsstück* was then translated into English as "rescue opera," and French as *pièce à sauvetage* (it is worth noting how in Italian the French term is invariably used, no doubt because it sounds so "authentic"). As David Charlton and Sieghart Döhring have demonstrated, "rescue opera" has been most often invoked, directly or indirectly, in the context of discussions of *Fidelio*, generally in order to point out how Beethoven's work transcends the traditional elements of this genre (Döhring 1989; Charlton 1992). The strategy at work here is the reverse of Wagner's discussed above. Whereas for him it was the rejection of a generic definition that supported his claim to generic subversion, in *Fidelio*'s case it is the invention of a new genre that allows us to bestow extraordinary status on the masterpiece in question.

Wagnerian Genealogies

Despite this fundamental difference, *Fidelio* performs a crucial role in the imposing genealogy that Wagner constructed for his own music drama. Wagner's strategy, especially evident in the first part of *Opera and Drama* (1851), consisted in writing a history of opera that promoted composers and works that could be drafted into the chosen group of fighters against genre, especially Gluck, Mozart, and Weber (not by chance all "Germans") among the former, and *Don Giovanni* among the latter. Wagner wrote not only the history of opera, but also his own artistic biography, in order to prove that he was able to draw inspiration from *all* operatic genres, that music drama represented a move beyond the *entirety* of nineteenth-century musical theater. *Die Feen* became a first attempt at fantastic German romantic opera. *Das Liebesverbot* followed as an ingenious fusion of serious and comic Italian style, a pleasurable excursion south of the Alps. *Rienzi* was then French *grand opéra*, thus suitably completing Wagner's initial survey of Europe's operatic landscape. Back to the fatherland, in his so-called Romantic operas, the composer put on stage allegorically the tension among the various generic tendencies of German opera, for example in *The Flying Dutchman*, a fusion as well as an overcoming of *Fidelio* and Weber's *Der Freischütz* (Wagner [1851] 1893: 12–115; see also Groos 1995–1996).

In the context of this Wagnerian rhetoric, the music drama that had to be created is *Die Meistersinger von Nürnberg*. This opera stages the battle of genres no longer in allegorical terms, but in literal ones. In this sense, not only the comic moments of the plot, but also the very wide stylistic variety that characterizes the score represented by synecdoche operatic traditions and genres. In other words, *Die Meistersinger* promotes itself as the apex of the history and practice of operatic genres, reaffirming explicitly that music drama comprehends and at the same goes beyond all operatic schools and genres. The essay "On the Term 'Music Drama'" appeared three years after the premiere of *Die Meistersinger*, acting as a literary postlude to the meta-operatic debate staged in this work.

The construction of music drama as a "non-genre," as going beyond the very notion of genre, resonated throughout the twentieth century, contributing to the widespread notion of Wagner as the progenitor of modernism in music. As mentioned above, resistance to genre, which originated at the turn of the nineteenth century, constituted one of the central tenets of twentieth-century modernisms, but with one crucial difference in the case of opera. Whereas in the nineteenth century resistance was to operatic sub-genres (*seria* and *buffa*, *grand* and *comique*, and so on) and national traditions, in the twentieth the genre to be resisted was opera itself (including Wagnerian music drama). This shift is connected to the progressive aging of both repertory and canon, with the vast majority of new works failing to get a foot in the former and to be admitted to the latter. In this context, opera resembled ever more a Fafner-like giant, guarding the entrance to the riches of music-theatrical resources. A reaction against this situation led to the rise of "music theater," generally defined not by what it is, but by what it is not, namely opera: in W. Anthony Sheppard's words, "music theater" is "a loosely defined definition for a genre of staged works developed in opposition to the styles, structures, and social functions of nineteenth-century opera" (Sheppard 2001: xi).

New or Old?

"Music theater" offers a revealing final perspective on the idea of genre in opera in the twentieth and early twenty-first centuries. Music-theatrical works that explicitly posited themselves in opposition to opera appeared with considerable frequency in the 1910s and 1920s, from Schoenberg's *Pierrot Lunaire* to Stravinsky's *Histoire du soldat* and *Oedipus Rex*, and from Falla's *El retablo de maese Pedro* to Walton's *Façade*. A significant number of common traits soon emerged, well beyond these works' initial oppositional stance. This stance was perceived as the defining characteristic of the emerging genre to such a degree, however, that all the discursive components of "music theater" rallied together to preserve it and avoid any talk of genrification. The 1960s and 1970s saw this happen all over again, only even more markedly, given the much greater number of "music theater" works composed and performed. Nor does this trend show any sign of abating, if a recent book, tellingly titled *The* New *Music Theater* (emphasis added), purports to treat this by now long-emerged genre as a "still-emerging art form" (Salzman and Desi 2008: dust jacket description).

As the case of "music theater" shows, present-day discourse on genre in and around opera is still by and large dominated by the rhetoric of the resistance to genre. In the case of nineteenth- and twentieth-century operas, it could be claimed that this rhetoric is in some ways "authentic," justified precisely because it treats these operas according to the critical discourse from which they originally emerged. What is more, as I have said above, this rhetoric can be called "authentic" not only in a historical perspective, but also in a contemporary one. Since the forces of repertory and canon still powerfully shape present-day production and consumption of opera, the discursive codification of the resistance to genre, which accompanied the formation of an operatic repertory and canon, lives on with them. The situation is rather different, however, when it comes to works from the first two centuries of opera. In historically aware critical discourse, their relationship to their putative genre is less frequently discussed than it was the case up to a couple of decades ago, since, on one hand, it would be historically inaccurate to frame it in terms of resistance, at least explicitly, but, on the other, no alternative widely shared critical model is available. Promoting works because they fulfill generic expectations, because they remain within the boundaries of their genres, or criticizing others because they go against such expectations and break such boundaries sounds preposterous, or at the very least provocative. And yet, there is no denying that, given its particularly strong genericity, opera suffers the most from a rhetoric of generic resistance, as proven by its aesthetic misfortunes over the last two centuries vis-à-vis other genres of music and theater. At the beginning of the twenty-first century, the issues raised by looking at opera from the point of view of genre seem as complex and problematic as ever.

See also: What Is Opera? Operatorio? The Concept of Opera

Bibliography

Adamson, John. 1999. "The Making of the Ancien-Régime Court." In *The Princely Courts of Europe, 1500–1750*, edited by John Adamson. 7–41. London: Weidenfeld & Nicholson.

Altman, Rick. 1999. *Film/Genre*. London: British Film Institute.

Betzwieser, Thomas. 2007. "Spielarten der deutschen Opernästhetik um 1800: Denkfiguren im Spannungsfeld von Gattungsreflexion und Bühnenkonvention." In Lippe 2007, 27–43.

Bianconi, Lorenzo. 1987. *Music in the Seventeenth Century*. Cambridge: Cambridge University Press.

Borghetti, Vincenzo. 2008. "Music and the Representation of Princely Power in the Fifteenth and Sixteenth Century." *Acta Musicologica* 80/2: 179–214.

Castelvecchi, Stefano. 2013. *Sentimental Opera: Questions of Genre in the Age of Bourgeois Drama*. Cambridge Studies in Opera. Cambridge: Cambridge University Press.

Charlton, David. 1992. "On Redefinitions of 'Rescue Opera.'" In *Music and the French Revolution*, edited by Malcolm Boyd, 169–188. Cambridge: Cambridge University Press.

De Van, Gilles. 1996. "Le grand opéra entre tragédie lyrique et drame romantique." *Il saggiatore musicale* 3: 325–360.

Di Giuseppe, Rosanna. 1996. "Opera: tradizione di una parola." *Drammaturgia* 3: 131–155.

Döhring, Sieghart. 1989. "Die Rettungsoper: Musiktheater im Wechselspiel politischer und ästhetischer Prozesse." In *Beethoven zwischen Revolution und Restauration*, edited by Helga Lühning and Sieghard Brandenburg, 109–136. Bonn: Beethoven-Haus.

Ellis, William Ashton, ed. and trans. 1892–1899. *Richard Wagner's Prose Works*. 8 vols. London: Kegan Paul.

Frow, John. 2006. *Genre*. London and New York: Routledge.

Genette, Gérard. 1997. *Paratexts: Thresholds of Interpretation*. Cambridge: Cambridge University Press.

Gerbino, Giuseppe, and Iain Fenlon. 2006. "Early Opera: The Initial Phase." In *European Music, 1520–1640*, edited by James Haar, 472–486. Woodbridge: The Boydell Press.

Groos, Arthur. 1995–1996. "Back to the Future: Hermeneutic Fantasies in *Der fliegende Holländer*." *19th-Century Music* 19/2: 191–211.

Habermas, Jürgen. [1962] 1989. *The Structural Transformation of the Public Sphere: An Inquiry into a Category of Bourgeois Society*, translated by Thomas Burger. Cambridge, MA: Massachusetts Institute of Technology Press.

Heller, Wendy. 2003. *Emblems of Eloquence: Opera and Women's Voices in Seventeenth-Century Venice*. Berkeley and Los Angeles: University of California Press.

Henze-Döhring, Sabine. 1986. *Opera seria, Opera buffa und Mozarts 'Don Giovanni': Zur Gattungskonvergenz in der italienischen Oper des 18. Jahrhunderts*. Laaber: Laaber.

Hugo, Victor. [1828] 1980. *Odes et Ballades*, edited by Pierre Albouy. Paris: Gallimard.

——. [1827] 1971. *Préface de Cromwell*, edited by Michel Cambien. Paris: Larousse.

Jacobshagen, Arnold. 2005. *Opera semiseria: Gattungskonvergenz und Kulturtransfer im Musiktheater*. Stuttgart: Steiner.

Klob, Karl Maria. 1913. *Die Oper von Gluck bis Wagner*. Ulm: Kerler.

Lacombe, Hervé. 2001. *The Keys to French Opera in the Nineteenth Century*, translated by Edward Schneider. Berkeley and Los Angeles: University of California Press.

Leopold, Silke. 2003. "Die Anfänge von Oper und die Probleme der Gattung." *Journal of Seventeenth-Century Music* 9. Online. Available: http://www.sscm-jscm.org/v9/no1/leopold.html1 (accessed August 2012).

LESMU. 2007. *Lessico della letteratura musicale italiana, 1490–1950*, edited by Fiamma Nicolodi and Paolo Trovato with Renato di Benedetto. Florence: Cesati. CD-ROM.

Lippe, Marcus Chr., ed. 2007. *Oper im Aufbruch: Gattungskonzepte des deutschsprachigen Musiktheaters um 1800*. Kassel: Bosse.

Longyear, Rey Morgan. 1959. "Notes on the Rescue Opera." *Musical Quarterly* 45/1: 49–66.

Manifesti. 1968. *I manifesti romantici del 1816 e gli scritti principali del 'Conciliatore' sul Romanticismo*, edited by Carlo Calcaterra. Turin: UTET.

Manzoni, Alessandro. [1823] 2008. *Lettre à Mr. C[hauvet] sur l'unité de temps et de lieu dans la tragédie*, edited by Carla Riccardi. Rome: Salerno.

McClary, Susan. 1992. *Georges Bizet: 'Carmen.'* Cambridge Opera Handbooks. Cambridge: Cambridge University Press.

Muir, Edward. 2007. *The Culture Wars of the Late Renaissance: Skeptics, Libertines, and Opera*. Cambridge, MA: Harvard University Press.

Naremore, James. 2008. *More Than Night: Film Noir in Its Contexts*. 2nd ed. Berkeley and Los Angeles: University of California Press.

Neale, Steve. 2000. *Genre and Hollywood*. London and New York: Routledge.

Rice, John A. 2007. "German Opera in Vienna around 1800: Joseph Weigl and *Die Schweizerfamilie*." In Lippe 2007, 313–322.

Romano, Dennis. 2006. "Commentary: Why Opera? The Politics of an Emerging Genre." *Journal of Interdisciplinary History* 36/3: 401–409.

Rosand, Ellen. 1991. *Opera in Seventeenth-Century Venice: The Creation of a Genre*. Berkeley and Los Angeles: University of California Press.

Rosmarin, Adena. 1985. *The Power of Genre*. Minneapolis: University of Minnesota Press.

Salzman, Eric, and Thomas Desi. 2008. *The New Music Theater: Seeing the Voice, Hearing the Body*. New York: Oxford University Press.

Schiller, Friedrich. [1800] 1966. *Naïve and Sentimental Poetry; and, On the Sublime: Two Essays*, translated by Julius A. Elias. New York: Ungar.

Schlegel, August Wilhelm. [1809–1811] 1879. *Lectures on Dramatic Art and Literature*, translated by John Black. London: Bell.

Schlegel, Friedrich. 1957. *Literary Notebooks 1797–1801*, edited by Hans Eichner. Toronto: University of Toronto Press.

Senici, Emanuele. 2004. "Tipologia dei generi nel teatro musicale." In *Storia della musica europea, Enciclopedia della musica*, vol. 4, edited by Jean-Jacques Nattiez, 624–640. Turin: Einaudi.

Sheppard, W. Anthony. 2001. *Revealing Masks: Exotic Influences and Ritualized Performance in Modernist Music Theater*. Berkeley and Los Angeles: University of California Press.

Stendhal. [1823] 2006. *Racine et Shakespeare (1818–1825) et autres textes de théorie romantique*, edited by Michel Crouzet. Paris: Champion.

Threadgold, Terry. 1989. "Talking about Genre: Ideologies and Incompatible Discourses." *Cultural Studies* 3/1: 101–127.

Trovato, Paolo. 1994. "Parole nuove nella letteratura musicale (con qualche considerazione di metodo)." In *Le parole della musica I: Studi sulla lingua della letteratura musicale in onore di Gianfranco Folena*, edited by Fiamma Nicolodi and Paolo Trovato, 3–29. Florence: Olschki.

Wagner, Richard. [1872] 1896. "On the Term 'Music Drama.'" In Ellis 1892–1899, V: 299–304.

——. [1851] 1893. *Opera and Drama*. In Ellis 1892–1899, II.

Weiss, Piero. 2002. *Opera: A History in Documents*. New York: Oxford University Press.

——. 1982. "Verdi and the Fusion of Genres." *Journal of the American Musicological Society* 35/1: 138–156.

CHAPTER 3

MUSICAL THEATER(S)

DEREK B. SCOTT

What Makes an Opera an Opera?

Tempting as it is to look for defining structural features, my contention is that what marks out a musical stage work as an opera is more a question of musical style and, in particular, the presence or absence of musical styles associated with commerce or entertainment. I am classifying such music in this chapter as the "Third Type" in order to help clarify a category, distinct from classical or folk music, that in other countries is known by such labels as *Unterhaltungsmusik*, *variétés*, *musica leggiera*, and λαϊκή μουσική. In the eighteenth century, popular styles could be incorporated into opera, as in *Die Zauberflöte*, without creating the same definitional problems that occur following the development of a music industry. The use or adaptation of later popular styles, as in *Die Dreigroschenoper*, becomes problematic. Significantly, this stage work ran very successfully on Broadway as *The Threepenny Opera*, but it is not in the regular repertory of any major opera company.

Strong contenders among musicals for the label "opera" in the first half of the twentieth century were Jerome Kern's *Show Boat* (1927), George Gershwin's *Porgy and Bess* (1935), Kurt Weill's *Street Scene* (1947), and Leonard Bernstein's *Candide* and *West Side Story* (both 1956). Then came a gap of some years, which may be put down to the impact of the rock revolution. After 1960, the musical faced a new situation: its musical style related less and less to the current mainstream popular style. Some critics make much of this. Joseph Swain calls it a "significant disjunction between the principal expressive tools of the theater and the most popular musical style of the surrounding culture" (Swain 1990: 360). Yet, although the rock style of the 1960s may have caused the musical to sound outmoded, this could scarcely have had much impact on the desire to emulate an already outmoded genre like opera. Besides, had not a similar situation arisen previously in the 1920s with jazz? An anti-opera turn could have been taken in the 1920s, when revues were challenging operettas in the popularity stakes, but in the next decade musical comedies won out (Block 2002: 85). All the same, there have surely been no more successful jazz musicals than there have been rock musicals.

Opera, being part of the classical tradition, took on the ideological values of that tradition as they were formulated in the nineteenth century, and embraced the ideas of moving forward, progressing, and "pushing the boundaries." Thus, a twentieth-century opera was expected to position itself in some way that related to the legacy of Wagner and late Verdi. One of the major problems faced by twentieth-century opera composers was the lack of any clear path forward after *Parsifal*. Yet still the idea prevailed that no return to the old "number opera" (made up of compartmentalized arias, duets, ensembles, and choruses) was possible. This problem did not exist for the musical, but it remains a reason that an important factor in the estimation of a musical as opera-like is that it does not contain too many obviously self-contained numbers. The features that will make a musical seem like an opera may be grouped into two categories. First, there are those associated with a high-status "serious" musical style: dissonant harmony, angular melody, and irregular rhythm or meter. Special care in avoiding dance patterns, except in a parodic, ironic, sour, or bitter context, will enhance the sense of high style. Second, there are historic conventions, especially those of the nineteenth century, that are widely seen as typifying opera: love duets, revenge arias, prayer arias, mad scenes, concerted ensembles, and dramatic recitatives.

In addition, the less spoken dialogue there is, the more the piece is likely to be found operatic. Opera is not defined by its being through-composed, but it is typified by being so. Some of the most dramatic effects in opera are achieved by having a character unexpectedly speak (for instance, Violetta on her death bed in *La traviata*). John Snelson holds that the less integrated a number is in a musical, the more it weakens an operatic comparison (2004: 101). Ironically, a typical way in which the musical differs from opera came about as a consequence of moves to integrate dance (a development often associated with *Oklahoma!* and *West Side Story*). Although many operas, especially French operas, have a ballet sequence, it is often self-contained and of little dramatic import (unlike the dream sequence in *Oklahoma!*). It may well be, however, that the musical's operatic aspirations were nurtured by the critical acclaim given to musicals that followed the integrated song and dance model. Generally, musicals make fewer demands on singers, and require more in the way of acting skill—and sometimes other performance skills, such as dance, acrobatics (Coleman's *Barnum*), or roller skating (Lloyd Webber's *Starlight Express*). Critics often trace the delight in spectacle back to French *grand opéra*, but it was also a feature of nineteenth-century popular theater, especially melodrama, which often employed startling stage effects and lots of traps. Even Gilbert and Sullivan went in for such things at times—the lighted wings of the fairies in *Iolanthe* and the living portraits scene in *Ruddigore*—and the American spectacle revues of the early twentieth century should not be forgotten. Harold Prince's spectacular production was a significant factor in the success of *Phantom of the Opera*: Few forgot the falling chandelier, or the boat crossing the underground lake among rising candelabras.

Form, Style, and Status: Sondheim's *Sweeney Todd*

What, in the end, defines an opera is not its form. *Die Zauberflöte* and *Carmen* cannot be distinguished as operas and *Show Boat* and *West Side Story* as musicals with reference to form alone. The crucial question is: Are they characterized predominantly by music of the Third Type? I have argued elsewhere that what happened in nineteenth-century London, Paris, New York, and Vienna changed perceptions completely about the nature of popular music and its perceived value (Scott 2008). After the revolution in popular music production in the nineteenth century, new styles developed in commercial urban environments that could not be accommodated satisfactorily within the categories of either "serious music" or "folk music." When composers wrote in popular commercial styles, they often opposed and offended the values of those who defended high art, whereas when Mozart wrote in a popular or folk-like style, it did not contradict the aesthetic values of his other music (Scott 2008: 6). However, in response to the work of Jacques Offenbach, Johann Strauss Jr., and Arthur Sullivan, the diminutive term "operetta" became the accepted label for opera that incorporated music of the Third Type. The Broadway musical differs from nineteenth-century operetta in that it mixes European music of the Third Type with American music of the Third Type, especially by assimilating African-American elements (as in the bluesy "Fish gotta swim" from Act II, scene 4, of *Show Boat*); the more it does so, the more it distinguishes itself from operetta. The first music heard as distinctly American, rather than European, had been found in blackface minstrelsy. This was an entertainment that did not call for an operatic voice, and in minstrel shows opera was frequently the subject of parody. Black musicals on Broadway in the 1890s, ragtime songs, syncopated dance music, and, a little later, blues and jazz all fed into the musical and revue, but were resisted by operetta composers. The sole example of an African-American influence in Lehár's *Die lustige Witwe* (1904) is a cakewalk, but it avoids the syncopation normally associated with that dance. Thus, to return to the inadequacy of distinctions made by reference to formal structure, Friml's *Rose-Marie* and Romberg's *The Desert Song* are more readily distinguished from *Show Boat* because of their European popular style rather than their form. Hence, it is no surprise that Sondheim's *A Little Night Music* has attracted the description "operetta," because of its European setting and extensive use of waltzes.

Stephen Citron also rejects arguments based on structure, but insists that the difference between a musical and an opera "lies in the expectations of the audience" (2001: 361). If a musical is performed by an opera company, he believes that the audience is led to think of it as opera. This is underlined by seeing singer-actors rather than actor-singers, and also by the style of singing: "Whether Lloyd Webber writes in through-sung fashion or Sondheim writes a fifteen-minute concerted number followed by dialogue is immaterial" (Citron 2001: 361). There is, indeed, a difference between operatic singers and musical theater singers, and a big problem for many lovers of opera who turn their ears to the musical is the kind of voice and vocal technique they encounter there. It can seem exaggerated and crude in its characterization of roles. It can also be perceived as unpleasant in timbre. These reactions stem from familiarity with the operatic voice and a consequent rejection of what would be inappropriate or ugly in a traditional operatic context. For that reason, the notion that vocal skill is neglected or unimportant to the musical needs to be countered by stressing that the musical brings its own vocal demands, which are various. For example, in Jo [Josephine] Estill's method of vocal training for musical theater (developed in the late 1980s), six voice qualities are specified, determined by the position of the larynx: speech (in which air pressure on the vocal folds is high), falsetto (vocal folds raised), cry (lifted larynx—as if about to moan), twang (nasal sound), opera, and belt (lifted larynx—as if about to scream) (see Estill 1997; Klimek 2005; and Kayes 2004: 154).

The issue of vulgarity of style, of course, remains. It has been suggested that, by employing the pseudonym Vernon Duke for his Broadway songs ("April in Paris" was his big hit of 1932, lyrics by E. Y. Harburg), composer Vladimir Dukelsky was able to "write songs uncomplicated by the highbrow modernism of the classical composer, while Dukelsky's music could remain undefiled by lowbrow show tunes" (Ziegel 2008: 106). The word "undefiled" here is instructive: the Third Type leaves a stain. This has been true since the days of the Strauss family in nineteenth-century Vienna (Riethmüller 1995: 1–17; Scott 2008: 88–89). Somewhat unexpectedly, however, the terms "highbrow" and "lowbrow" became subject to increasing erosion shortly after a last sustained attempt was made to pin down their social meanings in Pierre Bourdieu's aesthetic critique *Distinction* (1979), and this was bound to affect artistic production. Thus, Sondheim's *Sweeney Todd* appeared at an interesting moment when cultural categories were beginning to shift. It is not easy to classify the show tune elements in *Sweeney* as "lowbrow"—and that is only partly because of their often ironic function in the drama. For this reason alone, the debate about whether it is an opera or a musical is sure to continue. Swain suggests that Sondheim's domination of the Broadway stage in the 1970s and 1980s is "best described, perhaps, as a triumph of integrity over commercial interest, marked by an unflagging seriousness of purpose and an astounding dramatic range" (Swain 1990: 319). The key features of high-status artistic endorsement are here: integrity versus commerce, seriousness versus entertainment, and wide range versus narrowness (or repetitiveness). Few of Sondheim's works have made profits on Broadway, and that helps in terms of status.

With its almost through-composed structure, *Sweeney Todd* (1979) is regularly found by critics to approach opera more closely than his other stage works. After seeing Christopher Bond's play about the murderous barber, Sondheim had thoughts about turning it into an opera, and consulted John Dexter, a director of the Metropolitan Opera, who assured him it was suited to operatic treatment (Sondheim 1980: 3–14). Hugh Wheeler adapted Bond's play (itself based on a mid-nineteenth-century drama by George Dibdin Pitt) into a book for Sondheim to work from and create lyrics and music. There is a complicated plot and a lot of narrative, but the overriding theme of the work, for Sondheim, was obsession: "I was using the story as a metaphor for any kind of obsession" (see Zadan 1986: 245). Todd's obsession is revenge, and Sondheim succeeds in sustaining a particular mood or atmosphere throughout. This is obtained more by the use of leitmotifs than reprises. The ostinato pattern from the opening ballad returns, for example, in Todd's song "There Was a Barber and His Wife." Swain claims that Sondheim's leitmotifs are used in a Wagnerian way, but that is open to dispute. There is no sign of Wagner's ability to develop a leitmotif: consider the transformation of the "Rheingold" motif to depict the gloominess of the opening scene in *Die Götterdämmerung*, while maintaining a connection with the cause of the gloom. The timbre of a Sondheim score is the work of his regular orchestrator Jonathan Tunick. Tunick has commented that Sondheim is thorough in detailing harmony, melody, and rhythm in his piano scores, but neglectful of instrumentation (Rockwell 1983: 218). Sondheim's musical skill is not untutored; at one point he enrolled for lessons in composition with the arch-modernist Milton Babbitt at Princeton University. The prologue of *Sweeney Todd* is reminiscent of the style of Stravinsky's *Oedipus Rex*, with its use of ostinato and the oratorio-like intervention of the "company" as choral commentators. Pedal points and ostinati take the place of functional harmony in propelling the music forward. Diatonic dissonances are important (here, the ninth especially), and so, too, is quartal harmony, which works well with modal melodies because they do not demand functional harmony.

There are set pieces in *Sweeney*, such as the love duet and revenge aria so familiar from the operatic tradition. There are also references to popular genres, as in "By the Sea" for Todd and Mrs. Lovett, which takes up the unlikely rhythm (for nineteenth-century London) of the mambo. The opening ballad makes reference to the ancient melody of the *Dies irae*, a stock feature of the horror film. Likewise, the prologue's dissonant "Gothic organ" as signifier of the demonic is so familiar that it functions in the manner of a quotation. It is not so much the demonic it signifies, but the *use* of this device to signify the demonic—in other words, there is an expectation that it will be heard as a well-worn device, just as happens in the opening credits of a Wallace and Gromit animated film of 2005 when the title *The Curse of the Were-Rabbit* flashes onto the screen. The shock effect of the screaming factory whistle at the beginning of *Sweeney* is also a melodramatic gesture. Like the "Gothic organ," it comes with ready-made associations, and those associations are readily accepted rather than thwarted. The factory whistle serves no other purpose than to shock and, later on, its screaming sound accompanies the slashing of throats. This may be contrasted with Bartók's use of the piercing interval of the semitone to indicate the presence of blood behind each door in his opera *Bluebeard's Castle*. It is a sound that leads the drama, rather than merely accompanying Bluebeard's new wife's reactions. Nevertheless, the shock devices suit the melodramatic content of Sondheim's musical: Todd's recognition of having killed his wife is another shock—though since the music has never given any emotional depth to his relationship with his wife, a shock is all it is. At the close, the company starts pointing around the theater looking for Todd, when suddenly Todd and Mrs. Lovett rise from the grave. Again, it is horror film stuff—one thinks of Carrie's hand rising from the grave at the end of Brian de Palma's 1976 film *Carrie*.

It seems that we are not supposed to become emotionally engaged with any of the two-dimensional characters who populate this piece; instead, we witness a Brechtian rejection of illusionistic theater. Brecht wanted to make an audience critically aware of the social and political consequences of the actions of characters. The chorus interjections, the self-conscious melodrama, the moment when Todd breaks frame during his "epiphany" and turns on the audience, even the caricatures of Todd and Lovett used as the logo for the show—all may be taken as Brechtian devices for preventing an audience from slipping into passive reception. But what exactly is Sondheim trying to make us critically aware of in *Sweeney*? Is it anything beyond a warning not to be vengeful, otherwise we will hurt those we love? The *Sweeney* film of 2007 introduces more dialogue and tries to achieve more "realism." Thus, the choral commentary presents a problem, and the opening ballad is omitted. But *verismo* is not what *Sweeney* needs; it only puts it more firmly into the Vincent Price "camp horror" league. We already recognize a mixture of melodrama and camp horror when Todd holds his open razor up to the light and declares, "At last my arm is complete again."

Two of those who have made a case for regarding *Sweeney Todd* as an opera are John Rockwell (1983: 209–220) and Carey Blyton (1984). For Rockwell, the score is "Sondheim's most organically far-reaching to date," and the key features that make it deserving of being called an opera are: "its mosaic construction, rapidly shifting moods, recurrent leitmotifs and complex ensembles" (1983: 217). An example of a complex ensemble in *Sweeney* occurs in Act II, scene 2, when Todd, Anthony, and Johanna express simultaneously their differing feelings. Note that Rockwell's argument rests almost entirely on formal considerations. Blyton also puts forward the argument from design: "If anything gives full weight to the description of the work as an opera, it is the way in which the music is unified and given dramatic cohesion from song to song, and from act to act, by a host of technical means" (1984: 24). Rockwell maintains that it "belongs on the operatic stage far more deservedly than most of the new operas that jostle for position there" (Rockwell 1983: 217). It has, of course, been performed by opera companies in Chicago, Cologne, Helsinki, Leeds, New York, and elsewhere. Stephen Banfield remarks that it is not just in this case that the distinctions between musicals and operas "are becoming, or being, blurred," but he suggests that this may actually signal the need for "careful redefinition" (Banfield 1993: 287). Sondheim, himself, has suggested that *Sweeney* "is really an operetta, it requires operetta voices," voices he regards as capable of technical demands that fall somewhere above those required of Broadway singers, but below those required in opera (see Herbert 1989: 210, cited in Banfield 1993: 290). Tell that to the soprano who has to sing the Csárdás from *Die Fledermaus*!

Sondheim has compared his score to movie underscores, which could indicate that this may have been more of a reason for its musical continuity than any desire to emulate through-composed operas: it offered a solution to the need to maintain tension (Banfield 1993: 290). Banfield lights on another factor in the equation: *Sweeney Todd* is melodrama, and that genre relied in the past on the heightening of emotions via a musical underscore. He notes that *Sweeney* has the pace of melodrama, a pace more akin to spoken drama than to opera (Banfield 1993: 291). Banfield singles out "Green Finch and Linnet Bird" as "really operatic," but argues that this is an exception in a score that is still firmly rooted in musical theater in both the verbal style of the lyrics and the musical genres underpinning many of its numbers—patter songs, ballads, waltzes, and such (291). The role of Mrs. Lovett certainly calls for a non-operatic voice.

Blyton remarks: "From a purely musical point of view, the most interesting thing about *Sweeney Todd* is that Sondheim reveals in it that he is very much aware of what has been going on in 'serious' music since the turn of the century" (Blyton 1984: 20). Why is this the *most interesting thing* about the music? This is not a "purely musical" point; it is an ideologically loaded point, informed by notions of serious and trivial musical styles. It merely indicates that the writer approves of Sondheim's use of features associated with musical modernism. Because Blyton finds devices reminiscent of Britten and Stravinsky, it is all the more deserving of the label "opera"—Rodgers and Hammerstein have already been dismissed, by comparison, as "cosy family entertainment" (1984: 20). Blyton explains that the work's run of only a few months at the Theatre Royal, Drury Lane, was because it was "heard by the wrong audience," commenting that "[o]pera audiences are clearly prepared to accept much 'tougher' stories for musical treatments than those which support musicals" (1984: 26).

A few examples will present a flavor of its musical style, which is best described as eclectic. The Beadle's "Ladies in Their Sensitivities" is Britten-like, but the sequential treatment is too obvious for Britten. The Judge, in Todd's barber's chair, sings a ballad-opera-like tune ("You See, Sir, a Man Infatuate with Love"). Tobias's "Nothing's Gonna Harm You" is a typical Tin Pan Alley thirty-two-measure ABAB structure (it is actually thirty-four bars because of a two-measure transition added after the first AB). Anthony's love song to Johanna, "I Feel You Johanna," has lots of added ninths in the harmonic accompaniment; but adding a ninth to lend extra pungency to a chord has been around in musicals for some time: you can hear it in the first chord of "The Hills Are Alive" from *The Sound of Music*. There is an ironic use of waltz rhythm for Todd's and Mrs. Lovett's "little priest" duet that closes Act I, as Sweeney and Mrs. Lovett sing about the taste of various individuals once they have been turned into pies. The demonic waltz goes back to Liszt, but late-nineteenth-century Parisian cabaret knew *grotesquerie* such as this: for example, Maurice Mac-Nab's waltz song "Les Fœtus" (Scott 2008: 205–206). Sondheim's lyrics are at his most witty and inventive here. Sondheim has enjoyed much acclaim as a lyricist, from the time when he wrote lyrics for others (for example, *West Side Story*), to the period when he began writing both music and lyrics. Jim Lovensheimer describes Todd's "Epiphany" as "some of the angriest and most disturbing music ever written for the musical theatre" (Lovensheimer 2002: 188). Perhaps, but it remains within the category of the Third Type. A decade before *Sweeney*, there was a stage work concerning a character not unlike Todd, which contained some of the angriest and most disturbing music composed for the opera house; I am thinking of Harrison Birtwistle's *Punch and Judy* (1968).

The Megamusical and the Meganovel: *Les Misérables*

I now turn to two musicals that have claims to be considered operatic, but that are also characterized by the label "megamusical." Sternfeld describes the megamusical as epic and romantic, set in the past but dealing with broad human issues, sung throughout, and spectacular (2006: 1–3). Paul Prece and William Everett argue that "the concept of the megamusical constitutes a reinvigoration of nineteenth-century French grand opera" (2002: 246), and describe megamusicals as romantic sung-through musicals on themes of human suffering (often involving a sociopolitical message), whose impact is enhanced by dazzling stage effects. They compare the spectacle of the barricade in *Les Misérables* with the St. Bartholomew's Day massacre in Meyerbeer's *Les Huguenots* (Prece and Everett 2002: 246). It may be an oversimplification, but it is true that the set designs by John Napier are important to the effect of *Les Misérables*, especially the revolving floor (allowing the audience to see both sides of the barricade). Ironically, such things contributed to making initial reviewers wary and negative, with the critic of the London *Times*, Irving Wardle, suggesting that it was seduction by spectacle (cited in Sternfeld 2006: 186).

Les Misérables, music by Claude-Michel Schönberg, libretto Alain Boublil (1980/1989), was originally a concept album released in 1980 (orchestrated by John Cameron). Record sales enabled it to be performed in a version arranged for the arena of the Palais des Sports, Paris, in September 1980. Cameron Mackintosh, who heard the album in 1982, collaborated with the Royal Shakespeare Company and director Trevor Nunn to produce an English version at the Barbican Theatre, London, in October 1985. Herbert Kretzmer provided loose translations of Boublil's lyrics, as well as adding some of his own, such those in the song "Stars," which give depth to Javert's character (see Hugo [1862] 1995: I: 388 for a description of Javert's mindset: "infinite depth, authority, reason, *res judicata*, legal conscience, public prosecution, all the stars").[1] Valjean's role was changed from baritone to tenor to suit the performer Colm Wilkinson (Sternfeld 2006: 183). Courageously showing faith in the audience's reaction rather than that of the critics, Mackintosh moved it to the Palace Theatre in December. The first New York production premiered on March 12, 1987. At the tenth-anniversary concert in the Albert Hall in 1995, seventeen singers who had played the role of Jean Valjean in productions around the world made an appearance, each singing in the language of his own country. As I write, this musical has run continuously in London for twenty-six years (in 2004 it moved to the Queen's Theatre; see Figure 3.1). This may seem astonishing, since *Les Misérables* is a tragedy; but it is one that holds out hope, rather than engendering despair.

A difficulty for *Les Misérables* is that it is based on a canonic work of literature. On the one hand, this encourages awe, but, on the other, there are problems a reader now experiences with the tone of the original Victor Hugo novel. High on the list is the sometimes

FIGURE 3.1 *Les Misérables*, "the world's longest running musical," at the Queen's Theatre, London, January 2009. Photo Derek B. Scott.

unabashed sentimentality of the work, for instance, the description of Fantine on her deathbed: "Her whole body trembled with a kind of spreading of wings that were ready to carry her away, which you felt to be quivering but did not see"[2] (Hugo [1862] 1995: I: 380). Hugo's novel was, even in its day, accused by some critical voices of containing excessive sentimentality (Behr 1989: 21). Is the supposed sentimentalizing in the musical so much worse? It is neither my intention nor my wish to put the novel and the musical on an equal footing artistically; the cumulative effect of Hugo's panoramic vision is certainly not one of sentimentality, and at times he employs understatement to powerful emotional effect, as in Eponine's dying confession to Marius, "I think I was in love with you a little"[3] (II: 511). I do want to point out that, elsewhere, we make some allowances for the novel (we historicize it aesthetically), and we also need to make some allowances for the musical, which is as firmly situated in the context of the late-twentieth-century megamusical as Hugo's novel is in the conventions of the mid-nineteenth-century meganovel, such as Alexandre Dumas's *Le comte de Monte-Cristo* (1846).

The transformation of the French working class into Cockneys might strike some people as corny, but Hugo himself makes such a connection: "Jean Valjean had stolen a loaf of bread. An English statistic notes that in London four out of five thefts have hunger as their immediate cause"[4] (Hugo [1862] 1995: I: 140). Hugo also claims that Paris had its own Cockneys: its Cockney is called *le gandin*[5] (I:749). However, the English version of the musical does subject Hugo's work to a more substantial revision that aligns it with Dickensian Cockneys. Thénardier, in his "Master of the House" song, is closer to one of Dickens's villainous rogues than to Hugo's mean and vicious creation (to observe how revisions have been made, compare the character in Hugo ([1862] 1995: I: 497–499). Some scenes in the novel do offer themselves up readily as subjects suited to musical treatment. The following words, for example, almost act as a cue for what becomes Fantine's "I Dreamed a Dream" in the musical: "[I]n the workshop...she often turned away to wipe a tear. It was during the moments when she thought [the French word *songer*, here, also means to dream] of her child; perhaps also of the man whom she had loved"[6] (I: 250).

In an influential text, *Opera as Drama*, Kerman articulated his "central creed" that "in opera the dramatist is the *composer*" ([1956] 1988: xiii). What is crucial, for Kerman, is the way the composer interprets the action, narration, and drama in *music*. If the music does not function in this way, he suggests avoiding the term "opera." Kerman is not alone in emphasizing the primary role of music and, indeed, he cites Edward T. Cone's contention that a crucial principle of music drama is that "every important motivation must at some point be translated into musical terms" (Cone 1954: 119, cited in Kerman 1988: xv). There is a lot to be said in criticism of Kerman's theoretical framework, which rests on a rejection of matters relating to historical and cultural context, and accepts unproblematically the notion of a single, correct aesthetic truth (asserted by means of *ex cathedra* pronouncements about values). Yet if we go along with Kerman's idea of composer as dramatist, we should ask what the music tells us about character, about psychological states, and whether or not it reveals unspoken thoughts or makes unspoken (or unsung) dramatic connections.

While the plot links together the various ramifications of the drama, the solution to the problem of musical coherence over the time span of an opera or musical has to be sought elsewhere. The leitmotif has been a successful means of achieving this, but the musical has generally looked, instead, to the use of the reprise. There is, for instance, an effective use of reprise to convey dramatic irony of situation when the music of Valjean's reaction to the Bishop's forgiveness ("Yet why did I allow that man / To touch my soul and teach me love") reappears and adds psychological depth to Javert's soliloquy (which directly leads to his suicide): "How can I now allow this man / To hold dominion over me?" This is music carrying the drama, not just enhancing it. "I Dreamed a Dream" is effectively reprised when Valjean promises Fantine he will look after her little daughter Cosette. A more tenuous link is made with earlier music in Marius's song about his lost comrades, "Empty Chairs at Empty Tables"; it is part of a poignant scene not taken from the novel and was, indeed, added for the UK production. It is based on music from the scene between Valjean and the Bishop, at the latter's words "And remember this, my brother." So, the idea of remembering provides a rather thin justification for a reprise. Sternfeld suggests that when Fantine's death scene music returns as Eponine's song "On My Own," it links the two characters (Sternfeld 2006: 201). The music for Fantine's death, however, was actually a reprise of her own song "L'air de la misère," which featured only on the original French concept album. This song was given new lyrics and became Eponine's song of loneliness in the English production. A reprise can have the disadvantage of eating away at character building, especially if the music is associated with more than one character; it is also less likely to be developed or transformed. Fantine and Eponine are not the only characters to share music, and the excuse that dramatic connections are being made wears thin.

Swain argues: "The most signal link of the Broadway tradition with European Romantic opera is its dependence on the reprise for incisive dramatic effect. The reprise, of course, is Broadway's answer to the leitmotif" (Swain 1990: 358). Two things are conflated here: reprise and leitmotif. But they are different devices. Many operas show an interest in the psychological and dramatic possibilities of leitmotifs, and some operas certainly make use of reprise: Dido toward the end of Berlioz's *Les Troyens* and Otello at the end of Verdi's opera of that name are both given scenes in which the poignancy of their changed circumstances is enhanced by the effective use of reprise ("Adieu, fière cité," *Les Troyens*, Act V, scene 2, and "Un bacio . . . un bacio ancora," *Otello*, Act IV). The musical, on the other hand, inherits more of the operetta's penchant for reprising a good tune for the simple pleasure of hearing it repeated. This is a feature that occurs in the earliest examples: for instance, the catchy tune of the *fable* is reprised at the end of Offenbach's *Le financier et le savatier* (1856) for no compelling dramatic reason. It is not common to find redundant reprises in opera, although the various reprises of "In the Gipsy's Life" in Balfe's *Bohemian Girl* certainly seem to fit that description.

Commenting on the musical style of Schönberg-Boublil musicals, Prece and Everett claim that they "have their musical basis in folk-like melodies that are given a lavish treatment, largely through orchestration" (2002: 247). This is only half true of *Les Misérables*, and the orchestration is often unsubtle. Cosette's song "Castle on a Cloud" has a French character, but is unusual in its alternating measures of 3/4 and 2/4. The gamin Gavroche is given a folk-like air with cheeky, Artful Dodger–type lyrics that replace the former words based on his song in Hugo's novel, "C'est la faute à Voltaire" (II: 597–599). At other times, it is not the folk tradition that is referenced but, rather, older forms of commercial popular song. The revolutionary chorus "Do You Hear the People Sing?" is reminiscent of the verse section of George Root's American Civil War ballad "Tramp! Tramp! Tramp!" (see Music Example 3.1).

Other popular styles used have a feel of British and American pop of the 1960s, but also French chanson of that time. Insincerity is effectively represented in the "Waltz of Treachery" for the Thénardiers (another example of the use of waltz rhythm for ironic effect). Thénardier, the landlord, is well characterized musically, and the snaking chromaticisms found in the waltz are also used to represent his sleaziness and hypocrisy in "Master of the House," a song that treads the line between cabaret and vaudeville. There is evidence that Lloyd Webber is not alone in being influenced by Puccini, since Schönberg's music for the song "Bring Him Home," which was added to the English version, bears a striking similarity to the humming chorus from *Madama Butterfly*. Some elements of modernism are present in the score—for instance, the opening of the "Red and Black" ensemble—but they are few and far between. Although much of the music was composed by Schönberg before Boublil added words, the composer's work did

MUSIC EXAMPLE 3.1 Melody of "Tramp! Tramp! Tramp!" (George Root, 1864) and that of "Do You Hear the People Sing?" (*Les Misérables*, Act II). The latter has been put in the same key as the former in order to aid comparison.

Tramp! Tramp! Tramp!

Do you hear the people sing?

not end there. The Act I Finale, "One Day More," involving solo, ensemble, and chorus, reaches a peak of complexity with its allusions to previous themes intertwined in a contrapuntal mesh (see the lengthy excerpt given in Sternfeld 2006: 207–213; Javert's tune is new). There is subtle musical characterization within the ensemble, a technique indebted to the operatic legacy of Mozart, Donizetti, and Verdi. The music, in general, moves on constantly throughout *Les Misérables*, mixing recitative-like sections, songs, and ensembles, with barely a pause for applause. In the love scene between Cosette and Marius, one number moves into another, rather than there being a sustained love duet; it is entitled a "love montage" and includes interjections from Eponine (also in love with Marius).

Operatic Phantoms: Lloyd Weber and Hart's *The Phantom of the Opera*

The Phantom of the Opera, music by Andrew Lloyd Webber, lyrics by Charles Hart (with additional lyrics by Richard Stilgoe), is also based on a French novel—though one on a considerably smaller scale than *Les Misérables*. It opened in London at Her Majesty's Theatre in 1986 and in New York two years later. The location of the action is the Paris Opéra in 1881. The musical is intentionally more ghostly and mysterious than Gaston Leroux's novel: it concerns "a mystery never fully explained," according to the auctioneer in the prologue, whereas Leroux ensures that everything is amenable to rational explanation. The musical increases the melodrama and avoids moments of bathos, such as the Phantom's confession, "I'm neither an angel, nor genius, nor phantom . . . I'm Erik!"[7] (Leroux [1910] 1926: 161). The Phantom is more of a romantic figure, more of an "angel of music" than he is in the novel, where it is clear that it is the fault of Christine's father for putting such ideas into his daughter's head: "Her father claimed that all great musicians, all great artists receive, at least once in their lifetime, a visit from the Angel of Music"[8] (Leroux [1910]1926: 65).

Although Lloyd Webber has worked with political themes—*Evita* (1978), *The Beautiful Game* (2000)—he has often focused on the sufferings of individuals and their search for release. Whatever may be the operatic aspirations of *Phantom*, they should not be taken as evidence of a general desire to emulate opera on Lloyd Webber's part, since many of his best-known works (*Cats*, for example) are a long way from opera, and deliberately so. However, his output has rarely been governed by the normal expectations of musical theater. Snelson has argued that his work "has challenged the identity of the musical and forced reappraisal of the genre" (2004: 190). He claims that *Phantom* "questions the boundaries of musical and opera," and asks: "Is this a popular opera or an operatic musical?" He concludes that it is neither, and that "the cross-fertilization between the various forms of lyric theatre and between classical and pop music have given the work its own identity" (Snelson 2004: 122). But what does this actually mean? Is it unique? Is it a hybrid? It cannot be categorized? Sternfeld is more specific: for her, what makes *Phantom* operatic is the paucity of spoken dialogue, the presence of operatic voices (Carlotta the diva, and Piangi the tenor), the running together of scenes, the use of motifs and recurring themes (such as the "angel of music" theme), the building of ensembles with increasing numbers of characters singing different texts, and the perception by critics of Lloyd Webber's gain in sophistication and seriousness in this work (Sternfeld 2006: 234–235).

Phantom opens with a prologue (set in the present), and then has a flashback in time, as does *Sweeney Todd*. The signifiers of evil are as familiar as those in *Sweeney*: the "Gothic organ," low minor chords, dissonance, and chromaticism prominent among them (consider the music that the Phantom plays on the organ during the opening of Act I, scene 6). In Act II, scene 8, the Phantom's words "Hounded out by everyone" are accompanied by snatches of the *Dies irae*. There are also allusions to operatic styles throughout, although the predominant style of *Phantom* is still very much linked to musical theater. Sometimes a style associated with opera and another associated with musical theater are juxtaposed: for example, the vocal introduction to "Music of the Night" recollects in slightly varied form the harmonies of Tosca's "Vissi d'arte" (see Music Example 3.2), but when the song proper begins, it resembles "Come to Me, Bend to Me" from *Brigadoon* (lyrics by Alan Jay Lerner, music by Frederick Loewe, 1947) (see Music Example 3.3). Interestingly, Lloyd Webber had originally hoped to work with Lerner on *Phantom*. My intention here, I should emphasize, is to locate stylistic legacies rather than to suggest musical plagiarism.

The mixture of styles goes further, since Lloyd Webber, like Sullivan, has a wide range of stylistic references at his fingertips. Puccini often hovers in the background whenever Lloyd Webber is composing lyrical melody (from Evita's "Don't Cry for Me, Argentina" onward). Snelson offers some examples of motivic connections between Puccini and that of *Phantom* (2004: 178–180). In Act I, scene 8, the managers' duet "What a Way to Run a Business" is a number reminiscent of Gilbert and Sullivan. In contrast, the love duet for Raoul and Christine, "All I Ask of You," demonstrates, for those who doubt, that Lloyd Webber possesses a characterful melodic style of his own when he wishes. The

MUSIC EXAMPLE 3.2 Harmonies in "Vissi d'arte," *Tosca*, Act II, and "The Point of No Return," *Phantom*, Act II. The latter has been raised a tone to aid comparison.

"Vissi d'arte, vissi d'amore"

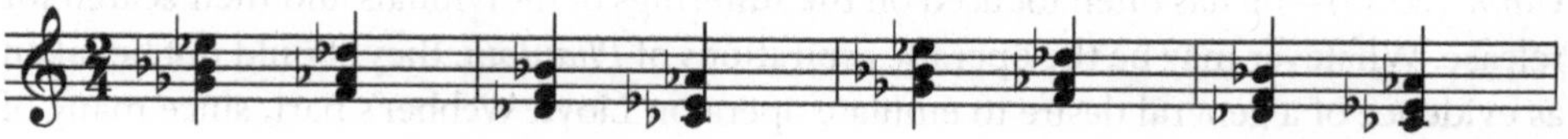

"I have brought you to the seat of sweet music's throne"

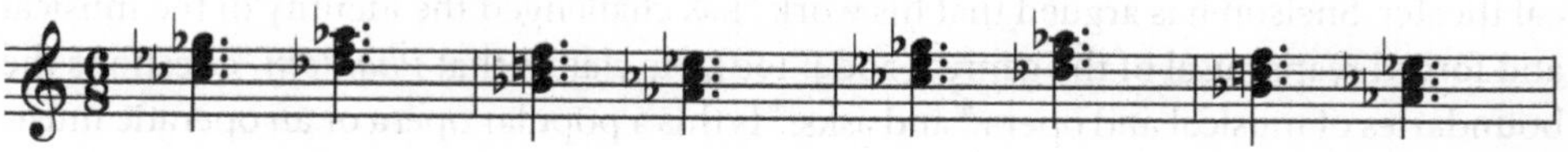

MUSIC EXAMPLE 3.3 Melody of "Come to Me, Bend to Me," *Brigadoon*, Act I, and "Music of the Night," *Phantom*, Act I.

Brigadoon

Phantom

falling ninths in the refrain are an effective and distinctive feature. Such melodic dissonance does present problems for harmonization; unsurprisingly, "All I Ask of You" has more in the way of octave doubling than the harmonizing one would expect of an operatic love duet. However, the duet for Christine and the Phantom, "In Sleep He Sang to Me," also lacks harmonizing of voices, and here the excuse cannot be the quantity of dissonant melodic notes. The reason for so much unison and octave doubling is a mystery. After all, in Act I, scene 8, there is an ensemble for Carlotta, Raoul, and the managers in which they all express themselves simultaneously in diverse ways. The ensemble "Prima Donna" also reveals a variety of characterization.

The duet for Christine and the Phantom, "In Sleep He Sang to Me," also illustrates Lloyd Webber's insensitivity to vocal register. The low *tessitura* of the first part of the duet calls for the ominous (and sonorous) tones of the chest register of the contralto. But, the effect is weak, since the voice required to cope with the punishingly high *tessitura* of the closing section of the duet is not one that possesses any power among these low As and Gs. The problem can, to some extent, be remedied by amplification, but that will merely make a voice louder without making its timbre richer. Compare Jerome Kern's music to "Old Man River" for an idiomatic treatment of vocal register across a wide compass. In the duet under discussion, the Phantom enters a fourth higher for his verse, the music having modulated from D minor to G minor; then there is a modulation down to E minor for Christine's next verse, and a modulation up to F minor for the last verse. The shifting tonality may increase the tension, but it is not enhanced by ever-rising pitch: the highest verse comes second. It concludes with what is meant to signify "operatic display" on the part of Christine, ending on E *in alt*. High *tessitura* and *melisma*, rather than rapid *coloratura*, are Lloyd Webber's signifiers for opera in this work. It is not just Christine who suffers: Why is the *tessitura* so high that it necessitates *falsetto* for the Phantom's "I Gave You My Music" at the end of Act I?

Lloyd Webber distinguishes stylistically the three fictional operas quoted within *Phantom*. *Hannibal* by Chalumeau represents French grand opera, *Il muto* by Albrizzio is Italian *opera buffa*, and the Phantom's own *Don Juan Triumphant* makes gestures toward modernism in its use of dissonance and whole-tone scales. It is not good use of time to debate the extent of parody in *Hannibal* or *Il muto*, because they are characterized only loosely. Characterization of *Hannibal* is so vague that a pop-inflected ballad "Think of Me" is presented as an unlikely aria from Act III. Ironically, the audience will no doubt prefer Christine's less operatic voice to that of the diva Carlotta, whom she is supposedly replacing. The song is lowered in pitch to reduce the operatic association of the high voice, but ends with a vocal cadenza on "ah," a gesture that is pointless as word painting but important as a signifier of opera. Snelson remarks that the onstage opera *Hannibal* is there to play to the "musical theatre audience's prejudice of opera, playing upon stereotypes," making the rest of *Phantom* appear more natural, despite its dialogue being sung rather than spoken (Snelson 2004: 108). Here is evidence, then, of a musical theater audience subject position, rather than that of an operatic audience. The awkward modernism of the music of *Don Juan Triumphant* in Act II can either be seen as inadequacy of technique on Lloyd Webber's part, or as a deliberate attempt to suggest such inadequacy on the Phantom's part. Once the Phantom makes his appearance in his own opera, the music loses its parodic elements; yet the duet "Past the Point of No Return" (the verse section of which uses the same music as that which introduced "Music of the Night") is supposed to be part of his opera.

Are Lloyd Webber's motifs and reprises ever developed? It is debatable. The Phantom's motif of descending chords may not develop, but Sternfeld holds that there are some less immediately memorable motifs that do mutate imaginatively, one such being what she labels the "story motif" (Sternfeld 2006: 245–247, and 381–385, which includes a list of recurring musical material in *Phantom*). But is that not because this is really more of a flexible melodic figure rather than a motif? Would one call a typical cadential formula in a recitative a motif? And what do the "story motif" transformations have to offer beyond lending cohesion to the work? Elsewhere, similar questions arise: What is the dramatic purpose of the reprise of the music-box "Masquerade" theme at "I must go—they'll wonder where I am" in Act I, scene 10? Why is Raoul singing the Phantom's music in this same scene? Why has Lloyd Webber decided to reprise the "Phantom of the Opera" tune here, as well as the introduction to "Music of the Night" (here sung by Christine)? It is difficult to find any more specific reason than that Raoul and Christine are talking about the Phantom.

The opening music of Act II makes use of reprises merely to remind people of the tunes they have heard—it has nothing to do with preparing for the first scene. In Act II, scene 3, the reprises from "She's the One" onward are of no significance except that this musical material previously served for a scene of disputation (in Act I, scene 8). However, when Raoul sings "Christine, Christine, don't think that I don't care" to the tune of "Prima donna," it could be a recognition of Christine's having just been given the opportunity of being the prima donna in the Phantom's opera *Don Juan Triumphant*. Many of the reprises add to the general cohesion of the score, but do not serve any particular dramatic or psychological purpose. That is why one is led to ask so often, "What's the point?"

Conclusion: Idiomatic Distinctions

I want to explore, in conclusion, some of the arguments set forth by Verdino-Süllwold (1990), since they relate closely to my concerns in this chapter and therefore allow me to revisit some of my arguments. She lists the "boundaries traditionally considered to separate opera from operetta and the musical" (1990: 32). The first is the supposed seriousness of the libretto, which she notes scarcely bears scrutiny in the case of some operas—she calls *Il trovatore* a "hodgepodge" (1990: 32). Moreover, this ignores the seriousness of subject matter in a number of musicals, beginning with *Show Boat* (1927). She asks: "Who can name a text in better control of such complex source material than that of *Les Misérables*?" (1990: 33). And, as another example, she adds, "if opera must explore epic passions and mythic legends, what of *Phantom*, which is truly a timeless re-telling of the beauty and the beast fable?" (1990: 33).

The second distinction she takes issue with is that operas are completely sung. This is not so, she remarks, while noting that *Les Misérables* fits this definition, as do, for the most part, *Sweeney Todd* and *Phantom of the Opera*. The third distinction is dance, although ballet was a feature of French opera. Nevertheless, in a musical it is common for the chorus and soloists to dance, too. Here, again, opera has its exceptions: Verdino-Süllwold cites Salome's dance in Richard Strauss's opera *Salome*, and the dance of the chorus in Arnold Schoenberg's *Moses und Aron* (1990: 34). The fourth distinction is the difference in vocal writing. Once more, there are exceptions: some operatic arias are direct and undecorated, while some operettas have vocally taxing roles—she mentions Cunégonde in Bernstein's *Candide* (1990: 34). But here there is confusion, because she has not taken account of distinctions between operetta and the musical; nor has she considered the full range of vocal techniques employed in musicals. This is where the concept of a Third Type helps to clarify matters; however, there is no recognition in this essay of popular styles of music that possess their own individual features and techniques. The "Broadway Belt" is not, for Verdino-Süllwold, a technique to be evaluated on its own terms, but merely a way in which performers with untrained voices have learned to cope with "scores made more complex than their natural equipment can deliver" (1990: 36). An example she offers to demonstrate that vocal demands in the musical can equal that of opera is Christine's almost three-octave span in *Phantom*, which she asserts "should silence complaints that Lloyd Webber's music is shallow and uncomplicated." Unfortunately, it does not succeed in doing so, because, as I have argued earlier, there is little evidence of any idiomatic feeling for the different registers of the voice and their tonal possibilities—it is, rather, as if the voice is being treated in the manner of a piano keyboard. Lloyd Webber has a tendency to wander into an uncomfortable vocal register without apparent regard for dramatic characterization or the singer's comfort. "Memory" from *Cats* provides another example: What is the reason for the low-pitched middle section? If you know the effect that different vocal registers can have on sung words, then you can use registers to great expressive effect. That is what Mozart, Verdi, Wagner, and Puccini understood, and their operas provide many examples of such knowledge being put into practice.

The fifth distinction is orchestration: the thinking being that a large orchestra and a complex arrangement will strengthen links between the musical and opera. However, noting that David Cullen helped Lloyd Webber with the orchestration of *Phantom*, and that Jonathan Tunick has provided similar services to Sondheim, Verdino-Süllwold asks: "Does the use of an orchestrator separate the musical composer from the operatic genius?" (1990: 36). She sidesteps the issue by insisting that an artistic work should stand "on its own artistic merits" (1990: 36). Agreed, but using an orchestrator surely means that the original music is composed with a much less precise attention to timbre and the idiomatic capabilities of instruments. Composing for violin, for instance, is not the same as composing for piano: It is not just a matter of staying within the instrument's range; it is knowing what is characteristic of the instrument and the technique needed to play it (you cannot, for example, make a distinction between *pizzicato*, *spiccato*, and *staccato* on piano). Furthermore, orchestrating it is not solely about timbre, but also figuration and counterpoint: For example, did the composer or the orchestrator add the instrumental countermelody to the first appearance of the words "Softly, deftly" in "Music of the Night"?

Toward the end of her article, Verdino-Süllwold (1990: 40) comes to what she calls the "trump card," the argument about the quality that "separated high art from low art." Indeed, this is not just a trump card, it is what ensures that the game is lost before it has even begun. She recognizes that Lloyd Webber's and Sondheim's stage works fail to achieve the accolade of "great art" because they are "show business" (1990: 41). Exactly so. However, her counterargument relies on dubious comparisons with the "glitzy" character of many operas and their productions. That misses the point. The music of the composers she mentions—Meyerbeer, Verdi, Puccini—related far more directly to the high art tradition than to the new popular forms of music for the nineteenth-century stage, such as music hall, minstrelsy, and vaudeville. It is not "largely an issue of contemporary taste," an idea she supports by saying "Verdi and Puccini were popular in their day" (1990: 41). The music of these composers was popular in the sense of "liked by many people" but not popular, or rarely so, in terms of possessing the same features that were to be found in music for the popular stage (including operetta). The musical is born of the Third Type, and this is difficult to recognize only because the Anglo-American term "popular" is so vague. I must emphasize, however, that I am not using this argument in an attempt to prove that none of the works I have discussed is an opera. Instead, I am trying to explain what the problems are in categorizing them as operas.

Swain points out that there is now a musical theater repertoire, and that this has undergone a "process of classification" (1990: 8). Yet though we might speak of a canon, even a "golden age," status problems remain, such as those that surface in the "is it an opera?" debate. Rockwell puts forward an analogy that has appealing simplicity as well as an apparent logic, but remains misguided: "There was a clear precedent for making opera out of popular musical theater: Mozart himself had done something similar with the German vaudeville *Singspiel* in *The Abduction from the Seraglio* and *The Magic Flute*" (1983: 210). Neither Mozart's style, nor that of the popular airs of his day, was music of the Third Type. In contrast, Sondheim's music is immersed in styles associated with the entertainment business: Rockwell remarks that his musical idiom involves "styles and procedures from every corner of the American popular song repertory" as well as opera (Rockwell 1983: 216). The composers of my other case studies are also steeped in the idioms of popular entertainment music. This, I stress, is the crucial point. What is more, contempt for consumers of the Third Type of music was scarcely any different in late 1980s New York to that felt in 1830s Vienna: "The semi-educated middle-class world loves Andrew Lloyd Webber," wrote Michael Feingold after the premiere of *Phantom*, with the same obvious distaste as the Viennese critic who announced in 1833, "A just indignation must seize everyone who, when Strauss plays, hears the names 'art and artist' desecrated by such frivolous stuff"[9] (Feingold 1988, quoted in Schönherr and Rienhöhl 1954: 100).

See also: What Is Opera? Operatorio? Genre, The Concept of Opera

Notes

1. "une profondeur infinie, l'autorité, la raison, la chose jugée, la conscience légale, la vindicte publique, toutes les étoiles."
2. "Toute sa personne tremblait de je ne sait quel déploiement d'ailes prêtes à s'entr'ouvrir et à l'emporter, qu'on sentait frémir, mais qu'on ne voyait pas."
3. "je crois que j'étais un peu amoureuse de vous."
4. "Jean Valjean avait volé un pain. Une statistique anglaise constate qu'à Londres quatre vols sur cinq ont pour cause immédiate la faim."
5. The term carried suggestions of a swank, dandy, or nut, which may not be thought to sum up the Cockney, but are part of the stereotype.
6. "dans l'atelier . . . elle se détournait souvent pour essuyer une larme. C'étaient les moments où elle songeait à son enfant; peut-être aussi à l'homme qu'elle avait aimé."
7. "Je ne suis ni ange, ni génie, ni fantôme. . . . Je suis Erik !"
8. "Le père Daaé prétendait que tous les grands musiciens, tous les grands artistes reçoivent, au moins une fois dans leur vie, la visite de l'Ange de la musique."
9. "Ein gerechter Unwille muß jeden ergreifen, der, wenn Strauß spielt, die Namen 'Kunst und Künstler' solcherart frivol entweihen hört."

Bibliography

Banfield, Stephen. 1993. *Sondheim's Broadway Musicals*. Ann Arbor: University of Michigan Press.

Behr, Edward. 1996. *Les Misérables: History in the Making*. New York: Arcade Publishing.

Block, Geoffrey. 2002. "American Musical Comedies of the 1920s and 1930s." In Everett and Laird 2002, 77–97.

Blyton, Carey. 1984. "Sondheim's *Sweeney Todd*—The Case for the Defence." *Tempo* 149 (June): 19–26.

Bourdieu, Pierre. [1979] 1989. *Distinction: A Social Critique of the Judgement of Taste*, translated by Richard Nice. London: Routledge.

Citron, Stephen. 2001. *Stephen Sondheim and Andrew Lloyd Webber: The New Musical*. New York: Oxford University Press.

Cone, Edward T. 1954. "The Old Man's Toys: Verdi's Last Operas." *Perspectives USA* 6: 114–133.

Estill, Jo. 1997. *Compulsory Figures of Voice: A User's Guide to Voice Quality*. Santa Rosa, CA: Estill Voice Training Systems.

Everett, William A., and Paul R. Laird, eds. 2002. *The Cambridge Companion to the Musical*. Cambridge: Cambridge University Press.

Feingold, Michael. 1988. "The Ghosts of Music Past." *The Village Voice* 33/5 (2 February).

Herbert, Trevor, ed., 1989. "Sondheim's Technique: Stephen Sondheim Interviewed by Trevor Herbert." In *Music and Text*, edited by Paul Driver and Rupert Christiansen. *Contemporary Music Review* 5/1: 199–214.

Hugo, Victor. [1862] 1995. *Les Misérables*, edited by Yves Gobain. Paris: Editions Gallimard.

Kerman, Joseph. [1956] 1988. *Opera as Drama*. Rev. ed. Berkeley and Los Angeles: University of California Press.

Kayes, Gillyanne. 2004. *Singing and the Actor*. 2nd ed. London: Black.

Klimek, Mary McDonald. 2005. *Estill Voice Training System Level Two: Figure Combinations for Six Voice Qualities*. Pittsburgh, PA: Estill Voice Training Systems International.

Leroux, Gaston. [1910] 1926. *Le Fantôme de l'Opéra*. Paris: Tallandier. (Orig. serialized in *Le Gaulois*, Sep. 23, 1909, to Jan. 8, 1910, then pub. Paris: Lafitte.)

Lovensheimer, Jim. 2002. "Stephen Sondheim and the Musical of the Outsider." In Everett and Laird 2002, 181–196.

Prece, Paul, and William A. Everett. 2002. "The Megamusical and Beyond: The Creation, Internationalisation and Impact of a Genre." In Everett and Laird 2002, 246–265.

Riethmüller, Albrecht. 1995. "Johann Strauss und der Makel der Popularität." In *Johann Strauss: Zwischen Kunstanspruch und Volksvergnüngen*, edited by Ludwig Finscher and Albrecht Riethmüller, 1–17. Darmstadt: Wissenschaftliche Buchgesellschaft.

Rockwell, John. 1983. *All-American Music: Composition in the Late Twentieth Century*. New York: Alfred A. Knopf.

Schönherr, Max, and Karl Rienhöhl. 1954. *Johann Strauss Vater: Ein Werkverzeichnis*. Vienna: Universal.

Scott, Derek B. 2008. *Sounds of the Metropolis: The 19th-Century Popular Music Revolution in London, New York, Paris, and Vienna*. New York: Oxford University Press.

Snelson, John. 2004. *Andrew Lloyd Webber*. New Haven: Yale University Press.

Sondheim, Stephen. 1980. "Larger Than Life: Reflections on Melodrama and Sweeney Todd." In *Melodrama*, edited by Daniel Gerould, 3–14. New York: Literary Forum.

Sternfeld, Jessica. 2006. *The Megamusical*. Bloomington: Indiana University Press.

Swain, Joseph P. 1990. *The Broadway Musical: A Critical and Musical Survey*. New York: Oxford University Press.

Swayne, Steve. 2005. *How Sondheim Got His Sound*. Ann Arbor: University of Michigan Press.

Verdino-Süllwold, Carla Maria. 1990. "Opera, Operetta, or Musical? Vanishing Distinctions in 20th Century Music Drama." *Opera Journal* 23/4: 31–43.

Warfield, Scott. 2002. "From *Hair* to *Rent*: Is 'Rock' a Four-Letter Word on Broadway." In Everett and Laird 2002, 231–245.

Zadan, Craig. 1986. *Sondheim & Co.* 2nd ed. New York: Harper and Row.

Ziegel, Aaron. 2008. "One Person, One Music: A Reassessment of the Duke-Dukelsky Musical Style." 105–106. *AMS/SMT Program and Abstracts*, Nashville.

Recordings

Les Misérables: Tragédie musicale de Alain Boublil et Claude-Michel Schönberg d'après l'œuvre de Victor Hugo, recorded Jan.–Apr. 1980. London: First Night Records, 1989.

Film

Sweeney Todd: The Demon Barber of Fleet Street. Directed by Tim Burton. DreamWorks Pictures, 2007. Released on DVD by DreamWorks Video in the United States and Warner Home Video in Europe, 2008.

CHAPTER 4

OPERATORIO?

MONIKA HENNEMANN

Visualizing Drama

Standard genre distinctions between opera and oratorio insist that the former is staged and the latter is not; opera is secular, oratorio is sacred. Yet there are numerous works, from secular oratorios to oratorio-like operas, that challenge these facile formulas—as does the remarkably prevalent practice of putting oratorios directly onto the stage. This chapter addresses "crossover" works and "crossover" productions: pieces and practices that might expand or even call into question our ideas of what operas and oratorios actually are, or ought to be.

The supposedly increasing desire for visual stimulus is a well-worn cliché of the modern age. Theater directors seem to regard Handel operas as unperformable without a plethora of fussy stage business to distract the audience from the unheavenly lengths of the *da capo* arias, and vast expenditure on visual effects has long since constituted the largest part of the price tag of many a Hollywood film. As early as 1929, the competition with film was the driving force behind C. T. Fairbairn's London stagings of choral works. As Harvey Grace has noted, "It is not that people are less fond of music, but that the taste of today, influenced by the cinema and by profusely illustrated daily journals, demands something with movement, drama, and colour" (Grace 1929: 689). These developments have naturally been deplored by those who regard them as a harmful distraction from the supposedly core expressive media of the art forms concerned—music in the case of opera, characterization and narrative in the case of film. Yet a fascination with the visual has been at the heart of dramatic theory since the time of the ancient Greeks, in a manner that affected musical performance long before Wagner coined his famously self-serving definition of music drama as "deeds of music made visible"[1] (Wagner [1872] 2004: 306). A few decades later, an even more crucial importance was attributed to these visual elements by another multidisciplinary artist, the Austrian expressionist Oskar Kokoschka. He claimed that "the act of seeing forms the basis of human awareness in certain cultural circles"[2] (Kokoschka [1947] 1956: 362).

In Aristotle's *Poetics*, drama was the *mimesis* (imitation) of an action, a direct re-enactment that was usefully contrasted to *diegesis*, the narrative retelling of an event (2008: 1–6). Although the two categories are to some extent related in that diegesis could be considered a subcategory of mimesis, an epic poem such as Homer's *Iliad* might confine itself to the latter, while Greek tragic drama had its fair share of both modes of presentation—the chorus would routinely narrate the historical background to the dramatic actions that the audience was presently to witness, or would comment upon those that had already been seen. Some actions—for example, the bloody murders that seemed to be such a tiresome part of life for Agamemnon, Electra, and other members of the house of Atreus—were regarded as altogether too horrific for mimesis, or even potentially blasphemous, given the religious nature of Greek dramatic festivals. They were accordingly never directly staged, but rather recounted by a messenger, accompanied by the sight of the victim's mangled corpse wheeled out on a trolley—less to provide proof that the gory deed had really taken place than to offer an arresting visual image on which the messenger's speech could elaborate.

But the comfortable theoretical contrast between mimesis and diegesis can also be somewhat misleading, at least as it might affect our assumptions about the actual performance of Greek epic and dramatic poetry. The Homeric poems were not primarily written texts to be meditated upon in private, but oral works intended for presentation before an audience. It seems highly unlikely that effective performers would have completely eschewed mimetic techniques in their delivery, especially in the long reported speeches that are such a prominent feature of the narrative. In a similar fashion, the tragic chorus did not simply recite its lines—it sang and danced as well, presumably in a manner that supported the verbal imagery. Visual stimulus linked to music was, therefore, rarely absent (a point not lost on Wagner when he forged his theory of the *Gesamtkunstwerk*), even if its extent was inevitably limited by the technical means available—no atmospheric lighting, elaborate scene changes, or revolving stages here.

In the same way that we might lose sight of the historical realities of classical Greek drama production by focusing too exclusively on abstract theories concerning its nature, we may also misunderstand certain trends in the history of musical performance by a too rigid attitude toward distinctions of genre. All music making before the age of recording involved a visual aspect unavoidable when performance was necessarily live. Disembodied sound, so routine to us, was largely confined to the enchanting Aeolian harp, or the haunting strains captured from afar so beloved of the Romantics—witness Berlioz's shepherds' piping "offstage" in the *Symphonie fantastique*, or Schumann's fondness for effects "wie aus der Ferne" ("as if from a distance"). Only with the advent of recorded sound did it suddenly become possible to detach completely the aural aspects of music production from the visual. Before this, an audience inevitably saw as well as heard music being performed. As a result, many treatises, from C. P. E. Bach's celebrated *Versuch über die wahre Art das Clavier zu spielen* onward, emphasized the need for players and singers to look the part, to underline the expression of the music with certain mimetic gestures and a suitable demeanor—or at the very least not to undermine the effect they were seeking to create by inappropriate appearance and actions. From the point of view of this aesthetic, a musician is himself an actor who, to quote C. P. E. Bach's adaptation of the Roman poet Horace, "cannot move others unless he himself is moved"[3] ([1753] 2008: I: 122).

Opera was only the most prominent of the musical genres that sought to provide a coherent dramatic framework to unite the unavoidably visual elements of music making with the aural. Just as its birth was directly linked to theories of Girolamo Mei and the members of the Florentine *Camerata* concerning the "re-creation" of Greek tragedy, the subsequent course of its life was also characterized by extensive aesthetic discussions, most notably in reams of prolix prose by Wagner (influenced, among others, by Adolf Bernhard Marx [1826], who in his later years insisted on the importance of extra-musical representation and drama for opera, and the pictorial powers of music in general). Yet theoretical disquisitions on what opera is, or should be, have also often had the effect of artificially isolating it from other genres—extolling it as the ultimate expression of visualized drama set to music—and of sidelining works that don't quite seem to be "proper" operas, although they may undeniably be dramas with music (see Robinson 1986; Kivy 1999; Scruton 1999).

Much-maligned crossover genres include the masque, the dramatic cantata, and the dramatic oratorio. The latter two—"sexless operatic embryos" ("geschlechtslose Opernembryonen"), to cite Wagner's scathing comment—are traditionally distinguished from opera mainly by the fact that they are not staged (1850: 102). Their only visual aspects should supposedly be the act of music making itself. They therefore confine themselves to Aristotle's *diegesis*, to the narration rather than the direct presentation of events, and thus avoid straying into the *mimesis* that is characteristic of genuine opera. It is the purpose of the central part of this chapter to argue that such a distinction is impossible to sustain historically. (Relevant recent treatments of genre distinctions include Lippe 2007; Mungen 2006; and Redepenning and Steinheuer, 2011. From the side of the oratorio, the foundational works in English are Smither 2000 and 1979–1980.)

Oratorio as Opera

The tendency to abominate rather than applaud stage settings of oratorios and cantatas is solidly entrenched in the literature. Nineteenth-century Handel pioneer Friedrich Chrysander castigated them as a "musical mishmash" (Chrysander 1870: 131) and for the musicologist Alfred Einstein they were, ludicrously, the "source of all evil" (1950: 206). The discomfort was understandable, even if the foaming phraseology was not. The staging of oratorios cuts extensively across convenient historical categories, especially after the genre had been pigeonholed as a "fit compromise between church and opera" ("treffliche Mittelgattung zwischen Kirche und Oper") by influential musical writers such as Friedrich Rochlitz (1832: IV: 77). The standard genre distinctions left no room for undesired experimentations, for if oratorios can be regularly presented on the stage like operas, what was the actual difference between an opera and an oratorio to be? A sacred subject—at least "sacred" in the sense of being based on a biblical source? Barely, as there are obviously operas on sacred subjects (such as Rossini's *Mosè in Egitto*, deemed in the libretto *Azione tragico-sacra*), just as there are secular oratorios, not the least Schumann's *Das Paradies und die Peri* and Elgar's *The Dream of Gerontius*. Works hovering inconveniently between genres include Anton Rubinstein's *Der Thurm zu Babel* (1869) and *Die Maccabäer* (1882), or Camille Saint-Saëns's *Samson et Dalila* (1877) (see also further discussion below). Even Handel's own favorite among his oratorios—*Theodora*—is a setting of a story for which one would search the Bible in vain. Perhaps the extensive use of the chorus might surely differentiate an oratorio from an opera? Here the specter of the long-neglected French *grand opéra* of Meyerbeer once more raises its inconvenient head. The chorus is certainly one of the principal players in many French *grand opéras*, and in those sister works influenced by the French fashion for elaborate choral numbers—so much so, in fact, that it was relatively straightforward for Wieland Wagner in 1950s Bayreuth to create a production of *Lohengrin* "in the oratorio style" simply by placing the chorus in static blocks on either side of the stage (see Carnegy 2006: 300–301).

But we do not have to wait for Wieland Wagner's consciously revisionist "new Bayreuth" to come across such a style of operatic staging. Aside from such imaginative pioneers, a static treatment of the chorus, and indeed the solo singers, has also been the default for stage directors with little idea what else to do. This was, to take just one example, a criticism leveled at Pierre Audi's staging at the Metropolitan Opera of Verdi's *Attila* in 2010 (see Audi 2010). A similar mindset can be clearly seen in current reviews of the English National Opera's production of John Adams's opera *The Death of Klinghoffer*, where several critics complained that the piece was "closer to oratorio than opera," which allegedly "robs the work of a real dramatic spine" (Clements 2012).

Almost a century before Wieland Wagner, Anton Rubinstein had conceived his now largely forgotten "spiritual operas" for a stage divided into two halves—one representing heaven, the other hell. Both halves were supplied with the requisite chorus (Rubinstein 1882: 46–54). Rubinstein even advocated the idea of constructing "churches of art," in other words, a Bayreuth-style dedicated theater for the performance of "sacred opera" (see Taylor 2007: 182–183; Täuschel 2001: 139–140; Schering [1911] 1988: 470). Another much better-known example of an attempt to make opera more static by conception is Stravinsky's *Oedipus Rex*, a so-called opera-oratorio, which premiered in 1928. But from the oratorio side of what might soon seem like an imaginary Berlin Wall separating genres, attempts to breathe dramatic life into oratorios through staged performances have taken place far more frequently than is usually acknowledged. So, does the opera/oratorio opposition, as so often presented in historiography, actually matter? We might simply consider naïve the expectation—so common in music history textbooks—that genre divisions should be black and white instead of gray. Nevertheless, this is to underestimate the ghetto-effect of our historical categories on works and performance practices that uncomfortably straddle familiar boundaries. Rubinstein's "spiritual operas" may well be forgotten today for better reasons than just that of ambiguous genre, but the fact remains that musicology has tended to ignore even once-popular works such as Félicien David's "Ode-Symphonie" *Le désert* (1844), Coleridge-Taylor's formerly famous *Hiawatha's Wedding Feast* (1899), or even at one point Berlioz's uncomfortably heterogeneous *Romeo and Juliet* and *Damnation of Faust* (on David's work, see Locke 1986 and Greenwald 2009 [especially 269–271], who alerts us to possible influences of not only David's *Le désert*, but also Haydn's *Creation*, on Verdi's *Attila*). Without the name of a major composer like Berlioz to back them up, even once-celebrated crossover pieces tended to fall into more than usually deep oblivion, occasionally to resurface in historical discussion as an example of the weird or exotic.

My contention in this chapter is that crossover works and performance practices, however despised or neglected by purists, were so common as to effectively constitute a part of the theatrical mainstream for the last three hundred years or so, throwing into question clear distinctions between opera and oratorio. Both genres were kindred ways of "visualizing drama." Staged performances of supposedly "undramatic" oratorios and cantatas appeared very frequently, especially in the nineteenth and early twentieth centuries. They were not, in other words, especially unusual, no more in fact than the opposite approach of "un-staging" operas for concert performances.

But this should, perhaps, not be a surprise. The practice of staging oratorios and related works was bound up with the very birth of the genre, and continues to the present day in major venues throughout the world. In 1985, for instance, the Royal Opera House in London, in conjunction with the Lyric Opera of Chicago and the Metropolitan Opera in New York, chose to celebrate the three hundredth anniversary of Handel's birth not with one of the composer's many operas, but with a staging of the oratorio *Samson*. Even Handel's *Messiah*, surely one of the least "dramatic" of all his oratorios, was produced by the English National Opera in 2009. (Other staged performances include those in West Berlin [1985] and Utrecht [2000], as well as by the American Opera Theater [2007], the Theater an der Wien [2009], and the Pittsburgh Symphony Orchestra [2011].)

Staging oratorios and cantatas seems to have been a particular specialty of the Metropolitan Opera throughout much of its history. It has carried on the practice in recent years with an operatic version of Berlioz's *Damnation of Faust* in the 2008–2009 season, notably advertised under the heading "opera." There seem to be no limits to what falls under that category: even Mozart's *Requiem*—in combination with the specially commissioned play "In der Schlangengrube" by Armin Petras and Jan Kauenhowe, based on interviews with dying patients at a Berlin hospice—found itself on the stage at the city's *Komische Oper* production by Sebastian Baumgarten in the very same season.

Ironically, the genre of Handelian oratorio initially took its familiar unstaged form for lack of anything better. As is well known, *Esther*, normally considered his first oratorio, was probably a reworking of an earlier masque of the same name. Handel's attempt to stage this revised *Esther* in 1732 came to nothing, owing to a ban on theatrical performances on sacred subjects by Edmund Gibson, the bishop of London (for a discussion, see Lang 1966: 278–280 and Burrows 2012: 214–215). Nevertheless, *Esther* was still performed in the King's Theatre, even if in rather restricted circumstances. The original advertisement in the *London Daily Journal* of April 19, 1732, for the forthcoming performance announced, "The Sacred Story of Esther, an Oratorio in English, formerly composed by Mr Handel, and now revised by him, with several additions, and to be performed with a great number of the best voices and instruments." A "nota bene" below this gives details of the typically British performance compromise that had been thrashed out following the bishop's ban: "there will be no action on the stage, but the theatre will be fitted out in a decent manner for the audience. The music to be disposed after the manner of the coronation service" (*LDJ* 1732: 288–289). The slightly embarrassed "but" after the admission of no action on stage would tell us, even if other aspects of the historical background were not known, that this manner of static staging without costumes, scenery, and action was hardly the first choice. It was, however, a surprising success, which Handel wasted no time in following up.

The lack of stage action in the first Handel oratorio was, therefore, a possible concession to circumstances rather than an active choice. The subsequent performance-practice history of the oratorio genre as a whole shows a similar vacillation over exactly how theatrical an oratorio could or should be. But it was later in the nineteenth century that examples of the "dramatic" performance of oratorios increased equally dramatically in number. Attempts to inject some extra interest into a potentially static genre ranged from the addition of a few pieces of stage business in concert performances to full-scale operatic presentations. In the 1880s the *Musical Times* commented with some disdain on partially dramatized performances of Haydn's *Creation* that had taken place in Cleveland, Ohio, in 1883, and in Paris in 1888, calling them a "violation of the sacred character" of the work. Quoting a local US journal, the *Musical Times* gave some details of the antics in the former that had excited its disapproval:

> In the beginning the audience-room was in literal chaos and darkness, and at the words "Let there be light," the electric lights flashed forth with such effective brilliancy that the audience were near breaking forth into wild demonstrations and deafening applause. (*MT* 1883: 439)

Of course, dispelling the darkness in such a dazzling fashion relied on Edison's recently invented electric technology, and would have been more difficult to achieve in former times, but it was just one of the many ways that an oratorio or cantata could be made more exciting. Haydn himself had taken great care for the premiere of the *Creation* that the selfsame passage should produce an exceptional effect, permitting not even his patron and translator of the text, Baron von Swieten, to see a copy of the score beforehand in order not to spoil the surprise (Temperley 1991: 35–36). Yet the producers of the Ohio *Creation* performance had an additional surprise in store. Again according to the *Musical Times*, "the climax was reached at the conclusion of the Oratorio, when *Eve* came forth and sang 'Home, sweet home,' accompanying herself on the piano" (*MT* 1883: 439).

Other notable attempts at dramatizing oratorios and cantatas included a fully staged production in 1860 of Mendelssohn's *Die erste Walpurgisnacht* in Karlsruhe, undertaken by the composer's close friend Eduard Devrient. According to Devrient's memoirs, even Mendelssohn himself—normally regarded as a "purist" in many other aspects

FIGURE 4.1 Joseph Urban. Costume drawings for a staged performance of Mendelssohn's *Die erste Walpurgisnacht* at the Boston Opera, 1910. Joseph Urban Archive, Rare Book and Manuscript Library, Columbia University.

of performance practice—was not against the idea of staging this work (Devrient 1872: 156), and the Devrient production proved to be one of several that subsequently took place in musical centers throughout Europe, including Vienna and Paris (see Cooper 2010: 190). A detailed account of a performance in Leipzig in 1862 was given by Wagner- and Liszt-advocate Richard Pohl, who fundamentally objected to staged productions of concerted works in principal (see Pohl 1862: 165–167). The trend reached American shores around 1910, when no less a figure than Joseph Urban—the renowned Viennese architect, children's book illustrator, and stage designer for the Vienna Opera House, the Boston Opera Company (between 1912 and 1914), the New York *Ziegfield Follies*, and the Metropolitan Opera (between 1917 and 1933)—took it upon himself to design the handsome stage sets for the American stage premiere. Figure 4.1 (from a portfolio of Urban's sketches in the library of Columbia University) gives a vivid idea of the lavish attention devoted to the costumes and sets.

But Mendelssohn was himself actively involved in other dramatic musical visualizations. He had played the piano for an 1833 private performance at the Academy of the Arts in Düsseldorf of Handel's *Israel in Egypt* with four *tableaux vivants* (Todd 2003: 286). His own oratorio *St. Paul* became the subject of such treatment in the same

FIGURE 4.2 Oskar Achenbach, "Ananias." Painting for a dramatized performance of Mendelssohn's *Paulus* in Düsseldorf, 1870, using *tableaux vivants*. Theaterwissenschaftliche Sammlung Universität zu Köln.

city in 1870. To celebrate the twenty-fifth anniversary of the town's *Künstlerliedertafel*, the oratorio was accompanied by dramatized *tableaux vivants* to assist the audience's attempts to follow the story. (The employment of *tableaux vivants* was by no means restricted to oratorios. Mendelssohn himself attended a performance of ten of his Lieder together with *tableaux vivants* in Frankfurt in 1839. See Seaton 2001: 693 and also Mendelssohn's letter of July 3, 1839, in Mendelssohn and Mendelssohn 1863: 161–162.)

For the *St. Paul* performance, the painter Oskar Achenbach was commissioned to provide the stage settings (see Figure 4.2); the choir and orchestra were placed in the stalls before the stage. After the overture, the curtain went up to reveal an Oriental landscape to illustrate the first scene.

The fact that this exotic picture was bizarrely accompanied by a distinctly non-exotic Lutheran chorale excited the particular disapproval of the well-known German musicologist Friedrich Chrysander. He made his relentlessly negative views known that same year in a long article entitled "Das Oratorium auf der Bühne" in the *Allgemeine musikalische Zeitung* (Chrysander 1870). Yet the production that Chrysander so abominated was judged a success by many critics of a less Puritanical bent. Wolfgang Müller of the *Augsburger Allgemeine Zeitung* waxed especially enthusiastic:

> If I were asked to describe my impression of the whole performance, I could say nothing but that I found it new and original, and that all expectations I had about this

> audacious attempt were wildly exceeded. [...] I believe that a performance on larger stages, such as the opera houses in Vienna, Berlin, and Munich would lead to incomparably better results.[4] (Müller in Chrysander 1870: 130–132)

In fact, pictorial assistance seems to have been especially prized in Düsseldorf. Even Beethoven's *Pastoral* Symphony was performed with such an accompaniment, turning it almost into the forerunner of a film score (see Smither 2000: 58; a similar performance of the *Pastoral* Symphony took place in mid-nineteenth-century London; see *MT* 1883: 439). One is reminded that a similar presentation, with diorama pictures to be commissioned from Buonaventura Genelli, was initially considered by Liszt for his *Dante* Symphony, before he decided that the torments of hell were better left to the imagination (Walker 1993: 50).

Chrysander, however, had no doubts about whom to blame for this unwelcome trend towards intrusion of opera into oratorio:

> Deep down, this whole enterprise to make an oratorio interesting through a staged performance, is owing to a taste over-stimulated by the modern operas [i.e., of Meyerbeer and Wagner], which can only be excited by unnaturally sharp spices that can be damaging for the organism.[5] (Chrysander 1870: 132)

He also turned his attack to other crossover genres, especially Anton Rubinstein's first "spiritual opera," which for Chrysander was a bastard child of opera and oratorio just as ridiculous as a staged *St. Paul*:

> In the meantime, [Rubinstein] has composed a "sacred opera" and has recently performed it in Königsberg and Vienna, to make the madness complete—in concert! A "sacred opera, consisting of solos and choirs," as the announcement claims. This musical gobbledygook, in which all concepts stumble against each other, suits the title of the chosen sacred opera like no other—"the tower of Babel"! May the undertaking end like that story. And certainly, that's how it will end.[6] (Chrysander 1870: 132)

Chrysander's contempt might have been all the greater had he known the genesis of Rubinstein's offending genre transgression. The Russian virtuoso's first successful oratorio, *Das verlorene Paradies* (1855), had in fact been conceived as an oratorio plain and simple. It was even premiered as such under Liszt in Weimar. Only in 1872 was it transformed into a "spiritual opera" as part of an attempted *Gattungsreform*, which was designed as a blow against what its composer saw as the unhealthy (even corrupt) dominance of Wagner over the operatic scene. Rubinstein did not advertise widely that the alterations needed to transform an oratorio into a "spiritual opera" were hardly extensive. In fact, they demonstrate once more the porous nature of genre divisions in the nineteenth century. The words "And God spake" were simply omitted from three of the chorus openings, thus turning the narrator's reported speech into a supposedly more thrillingly direct dramatic form (see Schering 1988: 469). From such tiny changes—from *diegesis* to *mimesis* in sixty seconds—was the entirely new genre of "spiritual opera" created. *Der Thurm zu Babel* underwent a similar transformation. However, Rubinstein's attempts to create a "Bayreuth for 'sacred operas'" through these compositions, his theoretical writings on the topic (Rubinstein 1882), and naturally by special theaters to be created for their performance did not ultimately fail owing to the insufficient excitement of direct speech; they failed because the music offered little of interest. More sustained success was achieved by another work that straddled the genre boundaries—Saint-Saëns's *Samson et Dalila* (1877), first conceived as an oratorio, but produced alternately as an opera (for a detailed account of the opera's origins, see Ratner 1985 and Locke 1991: especially 274). Saint-Saëns had composed an opening chorus in 1857 and had begun work on an oratorio on the subject in 1867, but was convinced by his librettist, Ferdinand Lemaire, that the story would be better suited to an opera). Here the music was simply stronger, rendering less important nagging questions about exactly what sort of piece *Samson et Dalila* actually should be.

Such questions, too, became less relevant as the practice of staging oratorios and cantatas gradually became a part of the theater mainstream, albeit a part often ignored in musicological scholarship. Though the custom was not without its critics—Chrysander was hardly a lone voice—the popularity of such productions proved to be a more than sufficient counterweight to aesthetic objections.

MENDELSSOHN'S "NEW *ELIJAH*"

Although the nineteenth and twentieth centuries saw notable stagings of a considerable number of oratorios, including Handel's *Jephtha* and even the little-known *Alexander Balus*, two works in particular have especially rich production histories: Mendelssohn's *Elijah* and Liszt's *St. Elizabeth* (for a somewhat dated list of stage revivals of Handel's oratorios, see Dean 1959: 662–664, who notes that the most popular work for staging was *Acis and Galatea*). Staged versions of these pieces seem to have been especially enticing because they could constitute an acceptable substitute for the mature operas that their respective composers had failed to complete. Mendelssohn's long-awaited *Lorelei* had remained a torso on his death in 1847, while Liszt's much-heralded *Sardanapale*, an opera based on Byron's play *Sardanapalus*, had eventually been abandoned only a few years later in 1851. While it is likely that Mendelssohn would have gone on to complete his work (he rarely failed to complete pieces that had reached such an advanced stage), Liszt was evidently unhappy with both the libretto of *Sardanapale* and his own sketches for the music. He never seriously considered writing another opera, turning instead to dramatic oratorio (see Hennemann 2004 and Hamilton 1996).

Dramatizations of *Elijah* included productions of (possibly) 1860, 1912, and 1920 in London, 1912 in New York, 1912 in Liverpool, 1932 in Southampton, and 1935 in Sheffield. (Unfortunately, the only source that mentions the 1860 performance, without providing any specifics, is Kurzhals-Reuter 1978: 226; for more on Sheffield, see Mackerness 1974.) For the latter, "modern stagecraft" was designed to provide not only

"Mendelssohn's vivid music, but wonderful scenes of oriental splendour" in a performance that employed around eight hundred participants (Mackerness 1974: 140). A few years before, the *Musical Times* of November 1920 had referred to the "extraordinary effect of Mendelssohn's Elijah as transferred to the stage" by the Moody-Manners opera company, a staging that was not only a staple of the company's repertoire, but also served as a model for the New York performances a little later (*MT* 1920: 761). Their highly successful financial model (unfortunately not transferred to the United States) was based on a calculated loss in London, balanced by a respectable profit in the "provinces"—Southampton and Liverpool, in this case. One of the performances' goals was to "attract singers, especially young singers, who have little desire to join the usual Choral Societies, but who will gladly take part in spectacular productions, to study standard choral works" (Mackerness 1974: 140). A separately printed libretto booklet was provided for the Moody-Manners production (see Figure 4.3), of which possibly only one copy survives today, in the British Library (Shelfmark Northcott M). The press lauded the "magic of the stage," which apparently made for "excellent entertainment" by giving "vividness and reality to the story, which cannot be made impressive [...] with soloists and chorus in evening dress and with book in hand." One critic of *The Musical Herald*

FIGURE 4.3 Front page of libretto booklet for a dramatized production of Mendelssohn's *Elijah* by the Moody-Manners Opera Company in London, 1920. The British Library, Northcott 155.

even admitted that he went "prepared to blame, and remained to praise!" (Dunstan 1912: 216).

In 1932, amateurs got in on the act, with the Southampton Musical Society giving a week's performance of *Elijah* "dramatized" with "Chorus, Orchestra, and Ballet numbering over 300 Performers." It was arranged and produced by T. C. Fairbairn and conducted by Arnold Williams. Six volunteer makeup artists transformed the good citizens of Southampton into temporary ancient Israelites so successfully that it was "doubtful if their own mothers would know them," the *Southern Daily Echo* claimed (*SDO* 1932: 2). This "much-anticipated... spectacle drama" was referred to as "New Elijah," and included additional dialogue intended to clarify the action to those members of the audience less familiar with the Old Testament. Although by present-day aesthetic standards an undertaking teetering on the verge of the ridiculous, the production was hailed by the press as "a great achievement" and attracted extensive coverage in local newspapers for several weeks.

Two years later the same producer put on a similar spectacle professionally in London's Albert Hall, this time with Albert Coates as the conductor. Here the vast arena was used to deploy the numerous Priests of Baal (W.R.A. 1934: 267). For some time, amazingly, this production was revived annually.

Perhaps even more remarkable from a modern, less flexible standpoint is the fact that such productions did not always confine themselves to the score of the work supposedly being performed. They could range much more widely, with the omission of some numbers and their replacement by favorite pieces from elsewhere in the composer's oeuvre. Musical directors used their power to cut, replace, and supplement with gusto. Of course, this practice is also found much more frequently than has sometimes been acknowledged in the performance of theater incidental music, and naturally recalls the fondness for routine insertion of certain "alien" hit numbers into opera productions in the first half of the nineteenth century (see Poriss 2009). The flourishing of theatrical oratorio well into the early decades of the twentieth century, complete with cuts and substitute numbers, once more calls into question routine ideas of the firm establishment of the "work concept" by the end of the nineteenth century (see Goehr 2009, especially chapter 4, where she suggests that the "work concept" emerged around 1800 as the domineering principle of composition). It is witness to the powerful desire not just to hear music, but to see it enacted in dramatic form. Not even the most "sacred" piece was necessarily treated as such. A typical approach, involving the usual extensive cutting, was suggested by Ferruccio Busoni for a staged production of Bach's *St. Matthew Passion* in an essay of 1921 titled "Zum Entwurfe einer szenischen Aufführung von J. S. Bach's Matthäuspassion" ("A Sketch of a Staged Production of J. S. Bach's *St. Matthew Passion*"; Busoni [1921] 1956: 140–142). Not wanting to do anything by halves, Busoni proposed cutting all of the arias, which supposedly unduly impeded the dramatic flow (141)—in his letter of May 31, 1919, to Hans Huber, he called them "the passing bigot's casual comment" (quoted and trans. in Beaumont 1987: 286). The action would take place on a stage intriguingly divided into two horizontal halves (see Rubinstein's vertical "heaven and hell" division), while the two choruses would stand in blocks to the left and right of the stage. The narrator was to be positioned in the middle of all this. Interestingly, a similar horizontal division of the stage featured in Keith Warner's 1999 production of—once again—*Lohengrin* at Bayreuth. Busoni's principal idea came to fruition most famously in Jonathan Miller's staging of Bach's work, first produced in 1993 and repeated in various places around the globe until the present day (its most recent reincarnation was a co-production between London's National Theatre and Southbank Sinfonia in 2011).

Although much of what actually happened musically in staged oratorio performances is naturally difficult to reconstruct in the absence of video recordings (or often even performance scores), we know in detail from newspaper reviews and other sources what was found necessary to "dramatize" the music of *Elijah* for the New York production of 1912. Alterations consisted of the addition of a number from Mendelssohn's opera fragment *Die Lorelei* (with an adapted text—the blond seductress Lorelei was effortlessly transformed into the Oriental beauty Jezebel) plus two intermezzi—the Andante from the *Italian Symphony* and an unspecified "Song without Words." For this large-scale series of performances, an opera company with more than one hundred members had been specially founded. An extensive tour of the United States was planned, but financial problems forced the drastic downsizing of these ambitions. The performances announced for Washington were canceled altogether, with the New York performances accordingly rescheduled from the spring of 1913 to December 1912. They seemed to mark the end of *Elijah* on stage in the United States, although the practice continued to thrive in England for many years to come.

Liszt's "Unholy" *Elizabeth*

Liszt's *Legend of Saint Elizabeth* had a similarly extensive theatrical production history. The same Joseph Urban who devised the stagings for the New York *Die erste Walpurgisnacht* and *Elijah* was involved in a dramatization of Liszt's oratorio, which was triumphantly announced in *The New York Times* as the Met's "next opera novelty" (*NYT* 1917) and premiered at the Met on January 3, 1918 (See Figure 4.4 and Figure 4.5).

The meticulous designs were not dissimilar from his sets for Wagner's operas. Other aspects of the production had been planned with a similar care. In view of wartime conditions, an English translation of the original German text was used, and in the publicity a strong emphasis was put on the fact that half the ensemble was now American (*NYT* 1918). Reviews made it clear that the production was partly intended as an attack on Wagner's dangerous dominance of the operatic repertoire—similar to Rubinstein's intentions with his "sacred operas." In the anti-German atmosphere of the times, the notably nationalistic Wagner was less than welcome on the stage of the Met. While this might be understandable in itself, to substitute a Wagner opera with a dramatized "New German School" oratorio by one of his most staunch supporters, originally set to a German text, and partially located in the Wartburg in Thuringia, seems like an especially inept response to patriotic concerns. As if to make up for the truly peculiar choice

FIGURE 4.4 Photograph of Urban's set drawing for the prologue of Liszt's *Saint Elizabeth* at the Metropolitan Opera, 1918. Joseph Urban Archive, Rare Book and Manuscript Library, Columbia University.

of work, the thoroughly American "Star-Spangled Banner"—not the national anthem quite yet, but already the "president's anthem"—was played by the orchestra during the interval (*NYT* 1918).[7]

The premiere of *St. Elizabeth* was a striking success, although it has to be admitted that Liszt would likely have disapproved of the production, despite his very vocal ambitions to unite the theater and church in music early on his life:

> This deeply religious, strong and effective music, which for the lack of another term we would like to call Music of Humanity, will unite THEATER and CHURCH on a massive scale. It will simultaneously be dramatic and sacred, magnificent and simple, pathetic and serious, fiery and wild, stormy and calm, high-spirited and tender.[8] (Liszt [1835] 2000: 59)

He had refused to attend the theatrical productions of *St. Elizabeth* that took place in Weimar—to some popular acclaim—in 1881 and 1884, evidently believing that the oratorio should not be used to give him an ersatz opera. Perhaps the failure of his tortuous attempts to complete a mature opera still rankled? Nevertheless, the public evidently did not share his distaste for blending the genres of opera and oratorio. In addition to stagings in Budapest and Vienna, an astonishing seventy-six performances of a dramatized *St. Elizabeth* took place in Prague in the decade after Liszt's death.

One could continue to describe in detail many other staged oratorio productions in the nineteenth and twentieth centuries, but the general point would remain the same. These productions were not all rare aberrations by the odd eccentric theater director,

FIGURE 4.5 Program for the production of Liszt's *Saint Elizabeth* at the Metropolitan Opera, 1918. Joseph Urban Archive, Rare Book and Manuscript Library, Columbia University.

or megalomaniac producer, or by well-meaning amateurs gone wild, but a mainstream part of theater history, however much some have tried to deplore or ignore the practice. They have taken place fairly often in many of the most important of the world's theaters, and continue to do so. And of course, when an oratorio gets staged, the performances tend to be repeated frequently, as with an operatic run. A concert might be rehearsed and then given once or twice, but a staged production like that of *St. Elizabeth* in Prague can end up with a run of seventy-six performances—quite a difference. Dramatizing oratorios may have been condemned aesthetically as a sideline in musical history, as a tastelessly inept practice that can only result in leaden choral operas, or embarrassingly active oratorios. But it would seem that the performers, and indeed their audiences, simply did not agree. The urge to visualize an initially only imagined drama was strong enough to break down genre boundaries that were palpably flimsy in the first place. In practice, it proved to be a very small step indeed from *diegesis* to *mimesis*.

See also: What Is Opera? Genre, Musical Theater(s), The Concept of Opera

Notes

1. "ersichtlich gewordene Thaten der Musik."
2. "Sehen ist eine Tätigkeit, welcher der Mensch bestimmter Kulturkreise sein Bewußtsein verdankt."
3. "In dem ein Musickus nicht anders rühren kann, er sey dann selbst gerührt; so muß er nothwendig sich selbst in alle Affeckten setzen können, welche er bey seinen Zuhörern erregen will; er giebt ihnen seine Empfindungen zu verstehen und bewegt sie solchergestallt am besten zur Mit-Empfindung."
4. "Soll ich nun den Eindruck der ganzen Aufführung schildern, so kann ich nichts anderes sagen, dass derselbe durchaus neu, originell war, und alle Erwartungen, die ich von diesem kühnen Versuch hegte, bei weitem übertraf. [. . .] Ich glaube, dass die Aufführung auf einer grossen Bühne, etwa in den Opernhäusern zu Wien, Berlin und München, ungleich grössere Erfolge erzielen dürfte."
5. "Hierüber bemerken wir einfach nur dass das ganze Unternehmen, ein Oratorium sich durch bühnenmässige Aufführung interessant zu machen, im letzten Grunde auf nichts anderes zurückzuführen ist, als auf eben den durch die moderne Oper [von Meyerbeer und Wagner] überreizten Geschmack, der nur noch durch unnatürlich scharfe, dem Organismus schädliche Gewürze erregt werden kann."
6. "Einstweilen aber hat er [Rubinstein] eine 'geistliche Oper' componirt und neulich in Königsberg und Wien, um die Tollheit voll zu machen, im—Concert aufgeführt! eine 'geistliche Oper, bestehend aus Soli und Chören,' wie die Anzeige besagt. Zu diesem musikalischen Kauderwelsch, in welchem alle Begriffe über einander stürzen, passt der Titel der gewählten geistlichen Oper unübertrefflich—'Der Thurmbau zu Babel'! Möge das Unterfangen enden wie dieser! und gewiss, es wird so enden."
7. Although the text of the "Star Spangled Banner" had already been written and set to the music of a popular British drinking song as early as 1814, it was officially adopted as the national anthem in 1931. It had been made the official tune for Navy events in 1889, and President Woodrow Wilson proclaimed it the national anthem of all armed forces in 1916.

In 1918, it was famously not only played at the Met, but also during the first game of the baseball World Series, where players and spectators joined in, cementing its use for nearly all sports events from that time onward.

8. "Diese zutiefst religiöse, starke und wirksame Musik, die wir in Ermangelung eines anderen <Namens> *Menschheitsmusik* nennen wollen, wird THEATER und KIRCHE in gewaltigen Ausmaßen vereinigen. Sie wird zugleich dramatisch und weihevoll sein, prachtvoll und einfach, pathetisch und ernst, feurig und wild, stürmisch und ruhig, heiter und zart."

Bibliography

Aristotle. 2008. *Poetics*, translated by S. H. Butcher. New York: Cosimo Classics.

Audi. 2010. Review of 2010 Metropolitan Opera Production of Verdi's *Attila*. Online. Available: http://diepresse.com/home/kultur/klassik/542560/Muti-und-Netrebko-in-New-York?_vl_backlink=/home/kultur/klassik/index.do (accessed August 8, 2012).

Bach, Carl Philipp Emanuel. [1753] 2008. *Versuch über die wahre Art das Clavier zu spielen*. Part I. Facsimile reprint. Kassel: Bärenreiter.

Barrett, Francis E. 1920. "Opera in London." *Musical Times* 61/933 (1 November): 752–761.

Beaumont, Antony, ed. 1987. *Ferruccio Busoni: Selected Letters*. New York: Columbia University Press.

Burrows, Donald. 2012. *Handel*. 2nd ed. New York: Oxford University Press.

Busoni, Ferruccio. [1921] 1956. "Zum Entwurf einer szenischen Aufführung von J. S. Bachs Matthäuspassion." In *Wesen und Einheit der Musik*, edited by Joachim Herrmann, 140–142. Berlin-Halensee: Max Hesses Verlag.

Carnegy, Patrick. 2006. *Wagner and the Art of the Theatre*. New Haven: Yale University Press.

Chrysander, Friedrich. 1870. "Das Oratorium auf der Bühne 1. Das Oratorium 'Paulus' von Mendelssohn in dramatischer Aufführung." *Leipziger allgemeine musikalische Zeitung* 5/17 (27 April): 130–132; 137–138; 145–146; 153–154; 160–163; 169–170; 177–179; 187–189; 195–196; 202–204; 210–211; 220–221.

Clements, Andrew. 2012. Review of Adams, *The Death of Klinghoffer*. *The Guardian* (26 February 012). Online. Available: http://www.guardian.co.uk/music/2012/feb/26/death-of-klinghoffer-review (accessed August 8, 2012).

Cooper, John Michael. 2010. *Mendelssohn, Goethe, and the Walpurgis Night: The Heathen Muse in European Culture, 1700–1850*. Rochester, NY: University of Rochester Press.

Dean, Winton. 1959. *Handel's Dramatic Oratorios and Masques*. New York: Oxford University Press.

Devrient, Eduard. 1872. *Meine Erinnerungen an Felix Mendelssohn-Bartholdy und seine Briefe an mich*. Leipzig: J. J. Weber.

Dunstan, R. 1912. "The Operatized 'Elijah.'" *The Musical Herald* (July): 216.

Einstein, Alfred. 1950. *Die Romantik in der Musik*. Vaduz: Liechtenstein-Verlag.

Frewin, Harrison. 1912. *Mendelssohn's Elijah: Complete Book of Lyrics and Words, With Biography of Felix Mendelssohn, Also Containing Four Gems from the Opera*. London: The Moody-Manners Opera Company.

Goehr, Lydia. 2009. *The Imaginary Museum of Musical Works: An Essay in the Philosophy of Music*. Rev. ed. New York: Oxford University Press.

Grace, Harvey. 1929. "The Dramatisation of Choral Works: A Talk with the Producer of 'Hiawatha.'" *Musical Times* 70/1038 (August 1): 689–693.

Greenwald, Helen. 2009. "*Son et lumière*: Verdi, *Attila*, and the Sunrise Over the Lagoon." *Cambridge Opera Journal* 21/3: 267–277.

Hamilton, Kenneth. 1996. "Not with a Bang but a Whimper: The Death of Liszt's *Sardanapale*." *Cambridge Opera Journal* 8/1: 45–58.

Hennemann, Monika. 2004. "Mendelssohn's Works for the Stage: From Liederspiel to *Lorelei*." In *Cambridge Companion to Mendelssohn*, edited by Peter Mercer-Taylor, 206–229. Cambridge: Cambridge University Press.

Kivy, Peter. 1999. *Osmin's Rage: Philosophical Reflections on Opera, Drama, and Text*. Rev. ed. Ithaca, NY: Cornell University Press.

Kokoschka, Oskar. [1947] 1956. "Bild, Sprache und Schrift." In *Schriften 1905–1955*, edited by Hans Maria Wingler, 362. Munich: Albert Langen/Georg Müller.

Kurzhals-Reuter, Arntrud. 1978. *Die Oratorien Felix Mendelssohn-Bartholdys: Untersuchungen zur Quellenlage, Entstehung, Gestaltung und Überlieferung*. Tutzing: Hans Schneider.

Lang, Paul Henry. 1966. *George Frideric Handel*. London: W. W. Norton.

LDJ. 1732. Advertisement for performances of Handel's *Esther*. *London Daily Journal* (April 19): 288–289.

Lippe, Marcus, ed. 2007. *Oper im Aufbruch: Gattungskonzepte des deutschsprachigen Musiktheaters um 1800*. Kassel: Bosse.

Liszt, Franz. [1835] 2000. "De la situation des artistes, et de leur condition dans le société" / "Zur Situation der Künstler und zu ihrer Stellung in der Gesellschaft." In *Sämtliche Schriften*, edited by Rainer Kleinertz, I: 2–65. Wiesbaden: Breitkopf & Härtel. First published (in six installments in French) in *Gazette musicale de Paris* 1835 18: 154–155; 19: 157–159, 20: 165–166; 30: 245–249; 35: 285–292; and 41: 332–333.

Locke, Ralph. 1991. "Constructing the Oriental 'Other': Saint-Saëns's *Samson et Dalila*." *Cambridge Opera Journal* 3/3 (1991): 261–302.

——. 1986. *Music, Musicians, and the Saint-Simonians*. Chicago: University of Chicago Press.

Mackerness, E[ric] D[avid]. 1974. *Somewhere Further North: A History of Music in Sheffield*. Sheffield, UK: Northend.

Marx, Adolf Bernhard. 1826. *Über Malerei in der Tonkunst: Ein Maigruss an die Kunstphilosophien*. Berlin: Finkesche Buchhandlung.

Mendelssohn Bartholdy, Paul, and Dr. Carl Mendelssohn Bartholdy, eds. 1863. *Letters of Felix Mendelssohn Bartholdy from 1833 to 1847*. Boston: Oliver Ditson.

MT. 1883. "Occasional Notes." [Review of Cleveland, OH, performances of Haydn's Creation]. *Musical Times* 24/486 (August 1): 439.

Müller, Wolfgang. 1870. "Rezension einer szenischen Aufführung von Mendelssohns Paulus am 2. April 1870." *Beilage* of the *Augsburger Allgemeine Zeitung* (April 9). Partially reprinted in Chrysander 1870.

Mungen, Anno Mungen. 2006. *'BilderMusik': Panoramen, Tableaux vivants und Lichtbilder als multimediale Darstellungsformen in Theater- und Musikaufführungen vom 19. Bis zum frühen 20. Jahrhundert*. 2 vols. Remscheid: Gardez!

NYT. 1917. "'St. Elizabeth' on Jan. 3." *New York Times* (December 19).

——. 1918. "St. Elizabeth Sung." *New York Times* (February 24).

Pohl, Richard. 1862. "Goethe-Mendelssohn's 'Erste Walpurgisnacht' auf der Bühne." *Neue Zeitschrift für Musik* 26/20 (May 16): 165–167.

Poriss, Hilary. 2009. *Changing the Score: Arias, Prima Donnas, and the Authority of Performance*. New York: Oxford University Press.

Ratner, Sabine. 1985. "La Genèse et la fortune de 'Samson et Dalila.'" *Cahiers Ivan Tourguéniev, Pauline Viardot, Maria Malibran* 9: 108–121.
Redepenning, Dorothea, and Joachim Steinheuer. 2011. *Inszenierung durch Musik: Der Komponist als Regisseur*. Kassel: Bärenreiter.
Robinson, Paul. 1986. *Opera and Ideas from Mozart to Strauss*. Ithaca, NY: Cornell University Press.
Rochlitz, Friedrich. [1824–1832] 1868. *Für Freunde der Tonkunst*. 4 vols. Leipzig: Carl Cnobloch.
Rubinstein, Anton. 1882. "Die geistliche Oper." In *Vor den Coulissen: Original-Blätter von Celebritäten des Theaters und der Musik*, edited by Josef Lewinsky, 46–54. Berlin: Hofmann.
Schering, Arnold. [1911] 1988. *Geschichte des Oratoriums*. Wiesbaden: Breitkopf & Härtel. Reprint.
Scruton, Roger. 1999. *The Aesthetics of Music*. New York: Oxford University Press.
Seaton, Douglass. 2001. "With Words: Mendelssohn's Vocal Songs." In *The Mendelssohn Companion*, 661–698. Westport, CT: Greenwood.
SDO. 1932. Review of staged performance of Mendelssohn's *Elijah* in Southampton, UK. *Southern Daily Echo* (May 2): 2.
Smither, Howard E. 2000. *A History of the Oratorio*. 4 vols. Chapel Hill: University of North Carolina Press.
——. 1979–1980. "Oratorio and Sacred Opera, 1700–1825: Terminology and Genre Distinction." *Proceedings of the Royal Musical Association* 106: 88–104.
Taylor, Philip. 2007. *Anton Rubinstein, A Life in Music*. Bloomington: Indiana University Press.
Täuschel, Annkatrin. 2001. *Rubinstein als Opernkomponist*. Berlin: Ernst Kuhn.
Temperley, Nicholas. 1991. *Haydn: The Creation*. Cambridge Music Handbooks. Cambridge: Cambridge University Press.
Todd, R. Larry. 2003. *Mendelssohn: A Life in Music*. New York: Oxford University Press.
Wagner, Richard. [1872] 2004. "Über die Benennung Musikdrama." In *Werke, Schriften und Briefe*, edited by Sven Friedrich, IX: 302–308. Berlin: Directmedia. Originally published in *Musikalisches Wochenblatt* 8 (November).
——. 1850. *Das Kunstwerk der Zukunft*. Leipzig: Otto Wigand.
Walker, Alan. 1993. *Franz Liszt: The Weimar Years*. Ithaca, NY: Cornell University Press.
W. R. A. 1934. "'Elijah' as Pageant." *Musical Times* 75/1093 (March 1): 267.

CHAPTER 5

THE CONCEPT OF OPERA

LYDIA GOEHR

Writing Opera's History

The concept of opera is inseparable from the writing of opera's history. Such a history may be written from different disciplinary and interdisciplinary standpoints. One may focus on the idea of genre, on opera's relation to the individual arts, on its constituent media, means, and technologies—once called its "machinery"—or on opera's contribution to ideas such as work, genius, or virtuosity; singing, diction, or acting; performativity, dramaturgy, or theatricality. One may track opera as a public, urban, or national institution according to ideas of carnival, festival, education, patronage, or consumption, or as a development out of theater and as a precursor to film. One may write opera's history along the lines of myth, religion, humanism, or secularization, or in materially contingent terms that reveal the changing statuses of composers, performers, singers, critics, and audiences. One may examine opera as a Baroque spectacle of marvel, charisma, and intoxication, or as an occasion for concentrated aesthetic experience. One may investigate opera as a representational or expressive art, as a mimetic or cathartic art, as an elite or popular art, or as an art for interpretation, performance, reproduction, or direction. One may connect opera allegorically or analogically to the rise or fall of nations and cultures, to different modes of government, authority, repression, subversion, or liberty, or by reference to divisions pertaining to race, gender, class, or colonial power. In the extensive literature spanning at least three centuries, these histories have been written to influence opera's conception, production, and reception. How one writes opera's history has always mattered to how one thinks about opera's past, present, and future.

Contest and Contestation

This chapter investigates opera as what philosophers have called an *essentially contested concept* (Gallie 1956). Notably in and after the 1950s, value-laden concepts belonging to science, politics, religion, and art were described this way, in part to put age-old theses about essentialism to rest. Moving away from analyzing concepts according to unchanging sets of essential and contingent properties, many philosophers argued in favor of treating concepts pragmatically and materially: as having revisable lives in dynamic and complex practices. True to the spirit of the argument, treating concepts as essentially contested became a highly contested affair. Some questioned the very language of concepts. Those interested in aesthetics tended to focus on the quarrel between essentialists and anti-essentialists. Others, interested in political and democratic theory, tended to look at the constant contestation of a particular concept's use. Here, I share with the latter in setting aside the matter of *essentialism* to concentrate on *contestation*. I prefer to speak of concepts as constantly contested, rather than as essentially contested. I take "contestation" as doubled up: to suggest a tense distinction between a more general idea of *antagonism*, *opposition*, and *challenge* and a more concrete idea of *contest*. Despite the closeness of the ideas, not all conceptual contestation is expressed through actual contests, and not all contests have conceptual contestation as their aim or result.

I investigate opera's concept historically, given a context in which the terms of the individual arts—music, painting, poetry, sculpture, architecture, dance, or ballet—have been *contested* often by *contests* being staged within the artworks themselves. This context is well described as *agonistic* and *paragonal*. Connecting opera's concept to the ancient Greek notion of *agôn*, or contest/debate (Lungstrum and Sauer 1997), and to the Renaissance idea of the *paragone*, or comparison/contest (Farago 1991), opens up a twofold path. It leads the concept, via a "fatherly" hand, to its claimed origins in Classical Athens and, via a "maternal" hand, to its claimed birth in Italy. The ancestral discourse of origin and birth begs for serious deconstruction. Yet its impact on opera's history is pervasive and undeniable. This chapter investigates the discourse critically, to reveal the concept's use and abuse in the many histories written—pro and contra opera as an art.

Perhaps because opera was "born" in Italy only in 1600 and not in 1500, surprisingly few scholars have addressed its beginnings against the agonistic context of the *paragone* that so affected the arts when, as it is said, the Renaissance was at its height. It is, however, revealing to do so (cf. Jahn 2005; Miersch 2008). The term *paragone* was used in 1817 to give title to the enormously influential preliminary book-passages written by Leonardo da Vinci; after this, the term became generic for a certain treatment of and attitude toward the arts. From the Latin *paragonizare*, the term means "comparison," but its use has always also been associated with "contest"—the *agôn* in par*agon*e and the creation of a paragon *qua* exemplar; hence, with assertions regarding one art or artwork as being more or less excellent or worthy than another (Farago 1991: 8–14). In general, investigating issues pertaining both to the contest of the arts and the influence of the agonistic arguments of Antiquity throws light on a history in which opera has never ceased contesting the terms of its media, means, aims, and values.

Aligned to music's history, opera's history has witnessed many famed quarrels or controversies, between Gioseffo Zarlino and Vincenzo Galilei, Claudio Monteverdi and Giovanni Maria Artusi, Jean-Philippe Rameau and Jean-Jacques Rousseau, Christoph Willibald Ritter von Gluck and Niccolò Piccinni, Richard Wagner and Friedrich Nietzsche. Such quarrels have set the ancient against the modern, the old against the new, theorists against practitioners, critics against producers, one national opera against another, melody against harmony, word against tone, eye against ear, and, finally, both reason and moral sense against any sense too closely aligned to corporeal pleasure. Opera's history has been written by reference to all these quarrels. Here, I focus on the issues raised by these quarrels more as they have been staged by and within the operas themselves.

Examples

Richard Strauss's *Capriccio* of 1942 is a late example of an *agonistic* and *paragonal* opera. Throughout and explicitly, its libretto reminds us of opera's history of contest and contestation. Doubly subtitled *Ein Konversationsstück für Musik*, it takes no side when pitting word against tone: *Prima le parole—dopo la musica! / Prima la musica—dopo le parole!* In one sense, it cannot take sides unless its aim is to bring the art of opera to its end. In another sense, it is prevented from taking sides. Although the contest takes place between a poet and a composer, it is staged with a supporting cast whose power is sufficient to displace the artistic contest between the tonal and verbal media by a personal and social contest between patrons and artists. Although artists desire the love of patrons and patrons that of artists, the love translates into a victory for art only on the condition that artists maintain their proper place in the social hierarchy. This is a typical displacement reflecting strategies of social discipline, found as often in opera as in the more general contest of the arts.

A second example is the 1670 *comédie-ballet* of Lully/Molière, *Le bourgeois gentilhomme*. It served as a model for *Capriccio*. In 1912, Strauss, Hofmannsthal, and Max Reinhardt staged its performance in German as *Der Bürger als Edelmann*. It gives an ironic role to philosophy. The philosopher enters the play to make peace in a contest between performing artists, each of whom seeks the favor of an aspiring bourgeois gentleman whose favor is not so obviously worth seeking. However, that the philosopher more enflames the contest than brings it to a rational solution demonstrates another aspect of competitive displacement: that the contest between the arts is nearly always made to submit to a contest between philosophy and the arts. Molière (2008: 266) condenses the original *platonic* quarrel by pitting the Music Master against the Dancing Master and then both against the Philosopher: "Philosophy is well enough," proclaims the Music Master, but there "is nothing so useful to a State as music," to which the Dancing Master responds: but there "is nothing so indispensable to mankind as dancing."

In the general contest of the arts, the arts are written about as though they were themselves seeking their own independence, autonomy, and agency. As a part of this search, the anthropomorphized arts like to ask whether, instead of waging sibling war among themselves, they would not benefit more by entering into friendly alliance, so that, together, they could take on philosophy or any other agent—political or religious—that aims to dictate their terms. In what ways specifically opera has resisted or encouraged just such a "sisterly" alliance for its own benefit is as persistent a question throughout opera's history as are related questions of discipline, censorship, and iconoclasm.

Another revealing example is Antonio Salieri's *Prima la musica e poi le parole* set against Mozart's *Der Schauspieldirektor*. Performed on the same evening in 1786 at opposite ends of the Royal Orangery in Vienna, Italian opera is pitted against German opera, *opera seria* against *opera buffa*, and one participant in the artistic process against another. Both works make competing parties and elements within the works sing together, to demonstrate the benefits of working together, of equality and cooperation, or to show in more inflated terms the benefits of aesthetic and moral harmony. The libretto of Mozart's piece thus concludes that great artists are such when they aspire to be the best in their arts, but become small when they promote their own greatness, or, as later reiterated in Peter Shaffer's play *Amadeus* (1979), great artists become small when they spend too much time comparing themselves with each other. This example illuminates another feature of competitive displacement: that a composer or librettist may well try to displace or at least to alleviate the wit or satire that characterizes an opera during its course by encouraging a moral sincerity at its end. To end on a resolved note of high-mindedness has long been one way for artists to placate their patrons.

Another example, reminiscent of Mozart's *Don Giovanni* (1787), is Rossini's 1812 *La pietra del paragone*, in which a nobleman, blessed with more money than charm, is the prize over which three women (Muses) comedically compete. So successful was this opera in its time, the record tells (Senici 2004: 13), that its composer was exempted from military service. Two more examples are Wagner's *Tannhäuser und der Sängerkrieg auf Wartburg* (1845) and his *Die Meistersinger von Nürnberg* (1868). In both, the contest over song and art is inextricably interwoven with the contestation of love, life, nature, community, spirituality, and sensuality. In both, a woman holding the proverbial laurel wreath is offered as the human prize to accompany the artistic one.

There are many more examples of agonistic and paragonal operas: serious, urgent, ironic, and satirical. Numerous operas show scenes of contest: archery, dueling, gambling, and card playing. Others pursue mythic contests between gods and humans in ways that bring attention to Olympian or triumphal themes. Pietro Metastasio's early eighteenth-century libretto *L'Olimpiade* was set no less than fifty times over the course of a single century (Segrave 2005). Countless operas treat personal and public heroism, victory, and defeat. Many of these works share a reference to Apollo or to his laurel wreath, which remains the case (as in Verdi's operas) even when myths or mythic contents are replaced or surpassed by stories of human history with naturalistic or realistic (*verismo*) themes. The Apollonian reference, which eventually becomes the blood-red thread of this chapter, appears also in works that aim to reinstate "the harmony of the world" in moments of war, crisis, or conscience. Set in the age of Johannes Kepler and thus coincident with opera's beginnings, Hindemith's opera *Die Harmonie der Welt* (1956–1957) repeats what many other operas and many other kinds of artworks do, when it returns through thoughts of celestial music to a significant *birth* moment in the past to inspire a cultural, intellectual, or social *rebirth* in the present.

Often when contests are staged between the arts, in significant part to increase the autonomous agency of the arts, the arts themselves are figured as Muses. This has encouraged an anthropomorphized discourse that has gendered the competitive "sister" arts as feminine. (For the first mention of "sistering," see Bundrick 2005: 52–54.) Yet when contests in operas are staged over the *arts* or between *artists*, they tend to focus on men, male gods, and male satyrs as their protagonists. When, in addition, these male figures happen to be artists as well, they tend more often to be poets, sculptors, and painters than either composers or musician-instrumentalists. Pfitzner's *Palestrina* (1917) and Lehár's *Paganini* (1925), contrasted with Donizetti's *Torquato Tasso* (1833) and Hindemith's *Mathis der Maler* (1934), are exceptions. Puccini's *Tosca* (1900) pays attention to a painter named Cavaradossi, and his *La bohème* (1896) to the painter and poet more than to either the philosopher or composer. This is different from Pfitzner's opera, which honors the noble composer, and thereby likely also the composer of the opera. Lehár's operetta punishes Paganini for his devilish musical powers. Opera as operetta already suggests a diminution of value, despite the envy that so many "serious" composers apparently had of Lehár's talent and success.

Musician-instrumentalists—whether they play strings or wind instruments—tend to be given small, albeit significant, roles on opera's stage. In Mozart's *Zauberflöte*, the instrument itself has more significance for the plot than the fact that Tamino is a flautist. In Kierkegaard's classic text (1988: 82), Tamino is denied the status of being a "musical" character, given a metaphysical commitment to assigning a universal significance to anyone who or anything that truly qualifies—hence, the decision to treat Don Giovanni or Don Juan not as a *character* but as a *role* driven and literally orchestrated by an "absolutely musical" *force* of an aesthetic world (see also Bloch 1985: 140–145). Before Hindemith's opera on Kepler, or Wagner's *Die Meistersinger*, Mozart's *Don Giovanni*, it was said, demonstrates, according to an age-old doctrine, how social or world harmony can be restored by showing, first, music's destructive, dissonant, and seductive power and then its unifying and pacifying potential. When music is expressed as the absolutely musical drive that *is* Don Giovanni, the bourgeois order is destroyed; when music is sung in final chorus or unison, the order is restored.

In many operas, a displacement is effected when figures like Orpheus, Pan, and even Tristan, known for their striking and cunning abilities as instrumentalists in original or earlier versions of their stories, are turned in later versions into instrument-less, singing lover-poets. This displacement is often accompanied by another: when the contest between singing lover-poets becomes a more urgent contest between critics. Here, the Midas theme enters opera's history: in J. S. Bach's secular cantata (BWV201) *Der Streit zwischen Phoebus und Pan. Geschwinde, ihr wirbelnden Winde* (1729); in Grétry's burlesque farce *Le jugement de Midas* (1778); as a play-within-a-play in Berlioz's *Benvenuto Cellini* (1838); and implicitly in Wagner's *Die Meistersinger* (Goehr 2011). Known for his ability to turn anything he touches into gold, Midas figures in these works mostly as the critic who is given the ears of an ass after judging the musical performance of Pan (or, in other versions, Marsyas) to be better than that of Phoebus/Apollo. In *Meistersinger*, Beckmesser receives a box on the ears—the townsfolk call him an ass—for rendering a similarly uninformed judgment. In this scene, Beckmesser is damned also for his not being able to tune his lute. His instrument, out of tune, serves less to accompany his song than to evidence a lack of *musicality* that is used to explain why a man such as he will always fail to win a woman (with a serenade), why his character is essentially capricious, and, finally, why a world or town that is determined by his sort of actions will fall from one moment to the next into total disorder. In the history of painting, the many musical instruments that are shown as out of tune or broken, hence, as tuneless, evidence the same metaphysical idea. The fact that an immoral music can bring the world to disarray and a moral music back to order connects the *Meistersinger* scene to the equally duplicitous scene of serenading in *Don Giovanni*. Given confusions of identity between the men in Mozart's case and the women in Wagner's, the many dangers of false *appearance* and *deception* are juxtaposed with the human, all-too-human, need for *illusion*—"Wahn, Wahn, überall Wahn."

In opera's history on and off stage, the roles of music and musicians, their voices and their instruments, have been strikingly antagonistic. The fact that the antagonism has often been expressed explicitly in the form of a contest is what has brought opera into contact with the general contest of the arts. The central claim of this chapter maintains that music, "her" musicians, their voices and their instruments, have always been opera's chief problem in ways that they have also been for music's "sister arts." To understand *opera* as a constantly contested concept is above all to understand the constant contestation of *music* as a concept.

The Birth Narrative

The discourse regarding opera's "origin" and "birth" reveals how persistently the contestation of opera's concept has pitted both aesthetic and social notions against each other, either to raise or to lower the status of opera regarded as an *art*. The same tension is found in the *paragone*, where much of what has been at stake for the various arts has been to prove their very status *as arts*. Here, "opera," "art," and "music" have all functioned as *evaluative terms*—honorifically and derogatorily—in ways that have affected their *classificatory* or *categorial* use. Whether opera or any one of the arts has been counted as primarily theoretical or practical, edificatory or entertaining, noble or low, liberal or mechanical, tragic or comic, dramatic or spectacular, representational or expressive has affected assessments regarding the ontological, moral, and social status of art's products, its producers and receivers.

Opera's history reveals a self-conscious struggle from the start over opera's parts, participants, conditions, and its name. It is not philosophically straightforward how one accounts for the fact that, although the term itself and the terms of the genre were established early on (Rosand 1991), "opera" as a generic, standardized, or umbrella term entered the history only about a century after, allegedly, the *first* exemplars were produced. Similarly, whether operas are better described by other designations, such as "music-theater," "musical tragedy," "comedy," or "melodrama"; *opera-ballo*, *favola*, or *attione in musica*; *dramma per musica* or *Musikdrama*; *Singspiel* or *Lehrstück*, depends on the significance, on the one hand, of aligning opera specifically to the concept of music, and, on the other, of naming or baptizing the products of "opera" in specific ways. The matter of naming proves most acute when it becomes an explicit issue for artists who want their products competitively to surpass those of others, or anxiously desire that their projects not be thought too similar to prior instances of the same art. Declarations regarding "opera" by many of its composers—from the earliest, through Verdi, Wagner, Debussy, Berg, Brecht and Weill, up to Cage, Adams, and Glass—are well understood in the competitive light of what Harold Bloom (1973), in his work on agonism and revisionism, called "the anxiety of influence." Further, whether one should include the *pre-opera* medieval processions or the Renaissance *intermedi*, or the *near-* or *almost-opera* oratorios, passion plays, and cantatas of earlier centuries, or the operettas, musicals, or multimedia installations of later centuries, and anything else going on outside the "West" depends on how open or closed opera historians determine opera's concept to be.

Decisions about the concept's scope are affected by whether "opera" is taken to designate *products* or *works*—and specifically musical products or works—prior to its referring to a complex *institution* or *practice*. Many early writings refer to the ancient Greek then Latin theatrical notion of *deus ex machina*: the practice of producing "a god from a machine." This reference suggests that the practice of staging divine, aesthetic, and political spectacles lay at the core of opera's concept long before the concept was used to refer to a *repertoire* of fully created *works* waiting to be performed and produced. Despite the closest translations of "opera" deriving from the Latin *opus*, "opera" referring to its *production* (*operatio*) captures more than "opera" referring to its *products*. The term "theater," linked to a universe or world, as in *theatrum mundi*, and the term *machina*, linked to something far greater than a piece of industrial equipment, suggests that priority should be given to finding in opera's core both the idea and art of *architecture*. When Wagner designed his total and future world of music drama, which he then baptized with the hallowed name "Bayreuth," he made explicit how important naming, titling, and terminology have always been for the practice of an art that has long been believed to have the institutional and architectonic potential as much to diminish as to ennoble humanity as a whole: the world taken as a stage (cf. Goehr 2009). Overall, the fact that "opera" has become the generic term for the entire art and institution, and for every product produced by and within the institution, is a persistent problem in itself.

What Comes First

From popular to expert accounts, opera historians have wanted to know which opera came first. Although it has rarely if ever been disputed that the "birth" happened in Italy, the reference to "Italy" has still meant contesting whether it happened in Florence,

Ferrara, Mantua, Siena, or Rome. "Few other genres have their beginnings as precisely determined as opera," Nino Pirrotta writes (1982: 237), after which he suggests that the first opera was not (as others believe) the Florentine *favola per musica, La Dafne* of 1598, with words by Ottavio Rinuccini and music by Jacopo Corsi and Jacopo Peri, but rather Peri's *Euridice* of 1600, again with words by Rinuccini. Pirrotta's grounds are evaluative: whereas the former was "immature" and "preliminary," the latter had a "full-fledged vitality." In his article "The First Printed Opera Libretto," F. W. Sternfeld (1978: 121) declares "without hesitation" that the first opera composer was Emilio de' Cavalieri, whose three-act *La rappresentazione di Anima e di Corpo* of 1600 qualified him to receive the "laurel of priority." Sternfeld then records how, in his preface to *Euridice*, Peri conceded that Cavalieri was the first to create the new kind of dramatic music ("la nostra musica su le scene"), to which, however, his most ardent competitor Giulio Caccini took exception, claiming the laurel for his own "nuove musiche." Given the contest over "firstness" under the guise of "newness," it was not uncommon for early composers and dramatists to stake their claim through written testimony or even duplicated publication, given a justified fear that a single publication might be lost or destroyed. When Piero Weiss (2002) much later produced a history of opera recording all these claims, he did so as a "history in documents," which means as a history of documents that survived.

Much of the birth discourse has identified the "first opera" by identifying the first composer or poet-dramatist-librettist. This has encouraged the idea that the birth was not that of a messy and complex *institution* or *practice* but that, rather, of already individuated *works*. Given, however, an extraordinary account from circa 1630, likely written by the Florentine Pierfrancesco Rinuccini—the son of the "first poet" of opera—maybe the laurel of priority should go to the *corago*, the general manager, director, and overseer of everything, including the carpentry, costume making, architecture, scene painting, singing and instrumental playing, dancing, acting, fencing, jousting, and tourneying (Savage and Sansone 1989). From the *corago*'s perspective—as from Wagner's later on—the invention of the total machinery not only made the production of the sublime poetry possible on the stage; it also prevented competitiveness. As Gerardo Guccini summarizes the "functional" rationale of the 1630 account: "by channeling these various specializations through a single functional hub, it would be possible to stop 'the ten or twelve arts or professions' from vying with each other for supremacy" (2002: 129).

This 1630 conception of what was not yet generically termed "opera" interestingly compares with John Dryden's conception fifty years later. In his preface to the Restoration piece *Albion and Albanius*, Dryden offered the description of a "poetical tale or fiction, represented by vocal and instrumental musick, adorned with scenes, machines, and dancing" (Dryden [1680] 1800: 152–153). Both conceptions award poetry first place in the total scheme, even if the point is also to define "opera" in relation to the *machinery* supporting the poetry from below. Whereas, however, the earlier conception functionally puts all supporting production elements on a par, Dryden's conception evaluates as soon as it distinguishes what *represents* by means of music from elements that *merely adorn*. This sort of distinction has long-term consequences. First, only when music is associated with expression, over and above its being a "mere" representation or accompaniment to poetry, is it put on a par with poetry, from which position music, as the medium now of pure or represent-less expression, then claims to rise above poetry. Second, Dryden's conception contributes to a history in which opera's "sublime" dimension is increasingly severed from the merely adorning machinery below. The severance opens up the possibility for opera to be regarded, first, in purely *aesthetic* terms, as sublime phantasmagoria or beautiful illusion and, second, in *ontological* terms, as though opera's total theatrical production were solely about its *works*. From both perspectives, what is demoted or concealed (under or behind the stage) is the supporting machinery and, with this, the human or mechanical labor. In general, in opera's history, as in that of the arts, the demotion of mechanical labor—the hostility toward machines or toward musicians who visibly play instruments—has been deemed not merely advantageous for sight, but actually essential to sustaining art's status as a *fine* or *pure art*.

The First/The Last

It takes little to curtail the almost obsessive preoccupation with opera's origin. From the earliest writings, historians have acknowledged that decisions regarding which "opera" came first depends on what one is looking for: the first suggestion or thought of opera, the first opera named as such, the first good or influential opera, the first surviving opera, opera's first private or public performance, the first fixed or semi-fixed libretto, the first printed score, the first opera identified in association with either a poet or a composer's name, or the first unified opera. Decisions have not only differed; they have also mattered. Consider Gluck's claim (noted by E. T. A. Hoffmann in 1814 [1989: 154]) that opera as a unified whole "in word, action, and music" is first demonstrated by his very own works, one teleological implication being that opera's birth or proper reform, or even the realization of opera's concept or essence, occurs two centuries later than is usually thought. Taken to its extreme, this sort of claim ends up supporting a teleological or historicist thesis, known under the Hegelian rubric of "the end of art," according to which opera's "final" or "true" birth signifies also the concept's end, conceived as either an achievement or a death. For what, it is asked, has opera to do once its concept or essence is realized, other than to reproduce itself without anywhere new or different to go? (Žižek and Dolar 2002: 1–19; Danto 1998; Goehr 2008: 79–107 and 257–305.)

Decisions about lastness have mattered as much as decisions about firstness, especially when the decisions have dialectically coincided. How does this happen? Consider the list of "first things" to be as agonistic as Leporello's list, so that it can also become a list of "last things," but where the latter list has only a single entry. This happens when a contender—a woman or a work—tries to attain a place not merely at the *top* but *beyond* the list: hence, as both first *and* last. Otherwise put, it is not enough for there to be a hierarchy of the arts if what is really wanted is for one contender to assume and achieve the final, supreme status of a *paragon* or, in Kierkegaard's terms, an incomparable classic.

In their shared history, both opera and music, and certain singular operatic women, have claimed exactly this sort of status. (Needless to say, being *beyond* the top is different from going *over* the top, which, often enough, is what opera is also accused of doing [Herwitz 2006].)

Let us extend our list now in the manner of the *Oxford English Dictionary*, to name the first opera house, opera singer, opera lover, opera audience, opera hat, opera ticket, or opera queen, so-called, who tends, as in Gluck's opera, to look back rather more to Orpheus than to Euridice. Recent studies suggest that implicit in Orpheus's melancholic song—a song that arguably marks opera's both beginning and end—is opera's violent suppression or concealment of homosexuality (Buller 1995; Robinson 1994; Berger 2008). When, according to some versions, the women (Maenads) killed Orpheus, both their shrieks and the brutal sounds of wind instruments and percussion were called upon to drown out his lyre and voice. After his death, his head, accompanied by the lyre, floated down a river that might well have been made from the blood of Marsyas, the poor, sibling wind-player whom Apollo flayed at the end of their contest over the morals of the musical art. What Orpheus's death suggests, and Marsyas's death makes explicit, is the inextricable relation between how both women and "musical men" have been treated by opera and how music and musicians have more generally been treated—the songs they have sung as well as the instruments they have played (Abbate 1991; McClary 1991).

If music or, as I will explain now, if *musica instrumentalis* has been one of opera's chief issues, this is because the concept of music has always been made to stand for the moral harmony of humanity—*musica humana*—and, by natural extension, the divine harmony of the world, *musica mundana* and *musica divina*.

Hybridity, Variability, Mobility

To treat opera's concept as covering the *production* over and above the individuated *products* suits the sort of flexibility evident in the more general history of the arts. Consider one of the oldest descriptions used against opera, that it was born as a merely "hybrid" genre or as a "dependent" or "bastard" art, constituted by the already developed, individual arts (Pirrotta 1982: 37–42; Rosand 1991: 34–65). In one, especially nineteenth-century, argument, opera's proponents looked back to an idealized origin in Antiquity to claim that before there were several arts, there was a single and unified conception or "ray" (*Lichtstrahl*) of art of which the several arts were "prismatic refractions" (*prismatische Brechungen*) (Ambros 1868: ix–x), or that before the arts went their separate ways, there was a total work of art. Although this view suited a myth recorded in Plato's *Timaeus*, it contradicted Aristotle's equally influential account in his *Poetics* of the more multiple genesis of tragic and comic drama. Otherwise put, the claim of original totality flew in the face of evolutionary "facts." According to the historian of Renaissance humanism Paul Oscar Kristeller (1951/1952), before the mid-eighteenth century, the so-called fine or beautiful arts were neither so clearly or purely individuated nor, indeed, packaged exclusively under a single, umbrella concept of art. Despite disputes regarding dating and details, Kristeller's thesis is persuasive in its suggestion that, throughout the combined and separate histories of the "arts," theorists and practitioners have always preoccupied themselves—as still they are preoccupied—with asking: What counts as art alongside or as opposed to craft? What separates or joins one medium from or to another? How are the separate arts related to an overarching concept of art? Under which circumstances should the arts be regarded as modes of invention or creation, or as productive and/or receptive disciplines or professions?

To speak of opera as "hybrid" in a non-accusatory way might be to celebrate the fact that opera is an art of mixed media, or, less statically, a dynamic art and example *par excellence* of multi-, trans-, or intermediality. Such a dynamic or fluid conception has recently motivated many multimedia productions, for example, Bill Viola's production from 2004–2005 drawn from Wagner's *Tristan*, with director Peter Sellars. Seemingly reacting to the closed commercial conditions associated with the modern work-concept, Viola titled his production *LOVE/DEATH: The Tristan Project* as though it would go on without end, as Tristan (but even more Isolde) desires to go on without end, so long as they have each other. The title *The Isolde Project* might have suited the project better. For all its newness, one of its points was an old one, reaching back to when the arts were all more mobile, fluid, or hybrid, when painting fused with sculpture or poetry with music in ways that confused any rigid or disciplinary scheme of classification. Indeed, without this sort of conceptual and medial mobility, would opera' "birth" in 1600 or, after that, its many intermedial revisions have been possible?

Some maintain that with the "systematization of the arts" came a certain sort of "fixity," according to which the borders of many artistic concepts were closed. However, it is also true that, despite the systematization, the arts have never really ceased moving in and out of each other's spaces. How systematization has prevented mobility or encouraged a resistance through mobility has always been an urgent question. Lessing ([1776] 1940) testified to the urgency in the mid-eighteenth century, as did Greenberg ([1940] 1986) and Adorno ([1965] 1978 and [1967] 1977) much later. Kristeller's history further reminds us that, even if one asserts that opera was born as a hybrid, bastard, or dependent art, one should not assume that its "parent" arts were thereby not hybrid, bastard, or dependent. They, too, have never ceased to claim different kinds of identity and difference from each other. From this perspective, one must also take care, when referring to *the* contest of the arts, to avoid suggesting that the many contests involved therein have always been fought on the same terms or with the same tools.

Many historians acknowledge that the atmosphere at opera's alleged "birth" was as self-conscious as it was competitive, given the many claims that opera was a "new musical" kind. Again, however, these claims should not be read as implying that, early on or at any time thereafter, opera's terms became so fixed as to merit no further negotiation. Modestly written, opera's history is revealed as a constantly contested affair. This truth is not belied but confirmed, rather, by the many histories that have more or less explicitly supported the long list of immodest claims about opera's first and only birth, rebirth, realization, renewal, or final reform.

Finally, on this methodological matter, to commit oneself to a more modest writing of opera's constant conceptual contestation is separate from either affirming or denying claims of naturalism or essentialism. Whether some arts are more natural than others or are essentially divided given distinctions of cognitive and emotional, bodily or mental sense is, at present, a most thorny topic. But it is not my topic here. I mention it only to reiterate that how opera's history has been written—in an essentialist or anti-essentialist mode—has profoundly shaped opera's conception, where "conception" concerns the matter of birth and origin, and, after this, of continuing life, in this case, the continuing production, reception, and evaluation of opera as institution and art.

A Master Narrative

For all the variability and complexity of the practice, one particular master narrative has persisted in the operas themselves and in the histories written. The conceptual logic of this narrative became fully explicit in the nineteenth century, although to acknowledge this complicates the claim that the first producers of opera were attempting *consciously* to create a new genre. Whereas recent histories suggest that there was very little naïve or unwitting about opera at its birth, earlier, more historicist histories tend to treat opera up to the point of Gluck and Mozart as a long and naïve pregnancy. What both approaches share is a view that the history has constantly negotiated opera's status as an *essentially* musical and musically myth-laden genre.

Recent histories tend to deconstruct or dismantle, or at least to complicate opera's birth narrative by compelling empirical arguments (Feldman 2007; Heller 2007). What is needed in addition is a rethinking of how the *historicism* that has dominated history and the *essentialism* that has dominated philosophy have encouraged or discouraged an operatic pursuit of sameness, timelessness, and universality to counter and surmount difference, ephemerality, and contingency. How opera and the arts have taken or refused to take the side of historicism and essentialism helps to explain their various entries into the agonistic arena.

As opera has been preoccupied with its status, so have the "individual" arts. In the *paragone*, artists have negotiated the terms of their arts, often to improve their own status, even while claiming arrogantly to have realized the concept of art to perfection. According to the agonistic teleology, more than *instantiating* the concept of art or of a particular art, the aim has been to *realize* it. Or, more than producing *examples*, the aim has been to produce the singular and supreme *paragon* or *exemplar*. In this arena, concepts are assumed to be of a contributor's own making, but a making endorsed by a classicizing and canonizing tradition, on the one hand, encouraged by Apollonian reward, on the other. Classicizing or antiquing art through philosophy, history, and myth has long been an effective way to legitimate both art's products and its producers. The rest of this chapter critically traces opera's master narrative by reference to Apollo, to show how music, musicians, and instrumentalists have always lain at the core of opera's agonistic concept—however opera's history has been written.

Apollo's Persistence

In the establishment of opera's "tradition," Apollo has dominated more than any other figure, more than Jove, Hercules, or Mercury, more than his antagonistic companions Dionysus and Bacchus, more even than Orpheus. Although Sternfeld (1993) opens *The Birth of Opera* thus: "In the beginning was the myth, and the myth was that of Orpheus," he, like many others, recognizes the pervasive presence of Apollo as both protagonist and disciplinary standard by which to judge the entire proceedings. While Orpheus tamed, Apollo harmonized. As father of the daughter Muses, as philosophical overseer or lawgiver of the sister arts, as musical contestant with lyre in hand, as a young god chasing a girl, as a young man shooting a python with an arrow from his bow, Apollo has played a manifold role that has been competitive and inspiring, but always also disciplinary. As Baroque figura, myth, totem, allegory, and metaphor, Apollo has served as the authoritative principle—a principle or standard *personified*—of the contest staged between the arts and between opera's constitutive media. The fact that Apollo appeared in what was arguably the very first opera—and in name, principle, or deed in so many operas thereafter—has served to legitimate not just *opera* but also *music* as an *art*.

Throughout his dialogues, Plato justified Apollo's appearance in matters particularly relevant to the education of a state's citizens. In his *Laws* (Book 2: 653c–654a), the Athenian (Socrates) observes that education, which consists in the correct disciplining of pleasures and pains, contradicts the nature of both the young and the old who, because they want to move either physically too much or mentally too little, are disinclined toward discipline. Pitying a human race "born to misery," Apollo—*Apollôn* the *mousêgetês* aided by the Muses and Dionysus—offered human beings thanksgiving feasts as periods of respite and as occasions to solidify discipline. To accommodate but also to control their desire for pleasure and joy, the gods taught humans how to experience rhythm and harmony. If, the Athenian concludes, this is the right account of human nature, then it is to Apollo and the Muses—and here Dionysus momentarily falls out of the picture—that we owe the *origin* of education and the arts.

Opera's First Subject

In an article subtitled "Poetic and Political Themes in the First Opera," Barbara Russano Hanning (1979) argues that Apollo deserves "primacy of place" because it is he who, in all his invincible glory, serves as the first opera's first subject. Apollo is chosen because this allows the opera to make a statement about the nature of the new art that it is declaring itself to be. Apollo's suffering in his dealings with Dafne/Daphne reflects the suffering that any artist must undergo for the sake of producing *new* art. When, at the opera's end, Dafne is transformed into a laurel tree, Apollo reflects upon the eternal existence Dafne has acquired, an endurance designed to serve the causes of politics and art. Apollo's reflection thus surpasses any feeling of loss, the loss of a living lover, turning a not completely happy ending (*lieto fine*) at least into a resolved one, as though it were he—Apollo—who intentionally effects her metamorphosis. Drawing on Ovid's *Metamorphoses* (I: lines 685–690), Apollo sings: "Since thou canst not be my bride, thou shalt at least be my tree. My hair, my lyre, my quiver shall always be entwined with thee, o laurel. With thee shall Roman generals wreathe their heads, when shouts of joy shall acclaim their triumph, and long processions climb the Capitol.... And as my head is ever young and my locks unshorn, so do thou keep the beauty of thy leaves perpetual" (Hanning 1979: 488).

Hanning argues that the denouement of the myth offered by this "first" opera sustains art's power. Even if Apollo cannot possess natural or female beauty, he triumphs over nature by immortalizing it through art. Here an analogy suggests itself to Bernini's famed sculpture, made from the rock specifically named for its ability to metamorphose. For opera or sculpture to effect the Apollonian metamorphosis required of art, it must do through art's *form* what marble does as nature's *matter*.

Hanning accentuates how much Apollo's laurel wreath or branch defines pictorial and verbal representations of political power. Cosimo I de' Medici represented and symbolized himself more than once as Apollo. Yet, the symbolism that serves the political cause is often tainted by the awareness that Apollo's victory has a pyrrhic aspect. Hanning mentions operas, which, though intended to demonstrate Apollo's certainty and strength, evidence a relinquishment of desire, or a bitterness, weakness, or "loss of nerve," as Karol Berger has more recently put it, for all Orphic opera under the general condition of modernity (2008: 42). Hanning quotes from the prologue for the 1611 version of *La Dafne*, which La Musica sings in Apollonian spirit. The lines express Rinuccini's resentment toward the Florentine court: "But when I thought, / because of my more beautiful song, / To adorn my locks with the most famous laurel, / A crowd whose name I do not deign to repeat, / Deprived me of all my esteem and reputation" (1979: 529). These words interestingly compare with the more ambitious and agonistic words, elsewhere recorded by Hanning (1973: 254–255), that Rinuccini gave to his Ovid to sing in the 1608 *La Dafne* (music by Marco da Gagliano): "I, who sang on the learned lyre about the flames of celestial lovers and their various transformations, so sweetly that the world still marvels at me....I appear to you tonight, o mortals."

In opera's history, librettists have often referred to Apollo when resisting patrons and critics. Georgia Cowart (2008: 163–167) describes a *livret* written for a ballet entitled *Aricie* for the Paris Opéra, in which Apollo is depicted, "as the perpetrator of injustice and cruelty for his refusal to allow Marsyas, a common mortal, to challenge the eulogies of his Muses." A Baroque piece of propaganda, the piece criticizes the censorial policies of an absolute king who presumes to take Apollo's identity for himself. That the piece can work in this way suggests something more general: the strategic and advantageous ability that any art has to swing a double sword against Apollo. While seeming to take Apollo's side for the "flattering" sake of courting the patron's favor, a work may simultaneously subvert this favor through expressions of sympathy for those—say, Marsyas—whom Apollo, in the name of eternal harmony, destroys.

Differently put, when an artwork shows Apollo rendering Dafne mute, or when it shows Apollo draining the "life and blood" of the python, as he drained the same of Marsyas (as we see in Titian's famed painting), the Apollonian or metamorphosing victory that the work dramatizes may deliberately fail to obliterate what this victory is meant to conceal: namely, all that is fragile, imperfect, temporal, mortal, and corporeal about humanity. Drawing on a motif associated with the work of Catherine Clément (1999): Although opera routinely "undoes" women, musical men, and musicians in the name of harmony and social discipline, it also demonstrates its ability—through women, musical men, and musicians—to sow *in the very same work* the subversive seeds of dissent.

Against this background, it is strikingly to opera's advantage to conceive of opera as an Ovidian art of metamorphosis. Ovid's poetic, witty, satirical, and subversive record of the ancient contests between gods and humans is everywhere evident in opera's history. Ovid records the many contests that result in the death, dismemberment, or restriction of musicians, singers, and women who by their human "craft"—doubly meant as both talent and hubris (hence, "craftiness")—challenge or threaten the gods, or, in more modern terms, the princes, kings, and sometimes tyrants of powerful states. When historians describe the cruelty hidden behind or made manifest by opera's spectacle (see also below), they show not only how Ovidian the art of opera has been, but also opera's ability, as just such an Ovidian art, to resist Apollo while simultaneously praising him, literally, to the heavens.

Educating the Citizens of a Nation

It is said that the standardization of the term "opera" was encouraged most when "opera" began to travel, when, for example, "Italian opera" arrived on the English stage. One might go even further to say that when "opera" was in Italy, no fixed or reflective top-down categorization of itself as "Italian opera" or even as "opera" was necessary, given the success of a practice to sustain itself through the mere fact that operatic productions were being produced. Or one might claim that one only needs a national categorization of opera when a nation feels threatened or dominated by a foreign art, as Germany or the United States sometimes felt dominated in the nineteenth century, or as France or England felt similarly a century or two earlier.

The last claim perhaps overstates the case. National opera, as national theater, also has positive aspirations associated with the building up of nation-states; hence, it is a product not only of fear. Nevertheless, fear is evident every time the contentious issues of language and comprehensibility are raised. The fact that the cultivated language of the *patrons* is not always the language of the *people* prompts questions regarding the constitution of the audience or the type of persons to whom the theater or opera is meant to be directed as a "national" institution. Further, given that national opera (and perhaps even national theater, too) is sometimes judged "foreign" in its own land brings the antagonistic relation between education and entertainment to the forefront of opera's concerns.

In 1711, Joseph Addison wrote that he was motivated most "to deliver" a record "down to posterity" of how Italian opera developed on the English stage, to explain to the "great grand-children" of his age "why their forefathers used to sit together like an audience of foreigners in their own country... to hear whole plays acted before them, in a tongue which they did not understand" ([1711] 1822: 22). What Addison meant by "Italian opera" wasn't completely obvious. Given his identification of *Arsinoe, Queen of Cyprus* as "the first opera that gave us a taste of Italian music," he selected a work composed by an Englishman, Thomas Clayton. Premiered in 1705, the opera was "after the Italian manner," although it was sung and spoken in English. Instead of declaring this opera Italian, Addison could have declared it the first English opera with Italian parents, which is how, effectively, Aaron Hill introduced Handel's *Rinaldo* in 1711 in his dedication to Queen Anne. As manager and actor, Hill declared that he was "no longer doubtful of succeeding in [his] Endeavor, to see the *English* OPERA more splendid than her MOTHER, the *Italian*." That Handel or Händel was German-born did nothing to deflate Hill's confidence, as Addison confirmed when he noted Hill's description of Handel as "the *Orpheus* of our Century"—the century of our England?—and of his opera as the "Son of Apollo, with a certain ray of Parnassus" (Addison [1711] 1822: 7; Weiss 2002: 66–67).

Addison wrote for a periodical that he helped found, *The Spectator*, as opposed to *The Listener*, which was founded only two centuries later, in 1929, by the British Broadcasting Corporation. Fearing the impact of opera sung in a foreign language, Addison posed the question most often asked of opera: whether it is an art primarily for the musical ear, such that turning one's eyes away from the spectacle or one's mind away from the drama is what *listeners* should do. What Addison feared most about Italian opera sung in Italian was the sort of "foreignness" that would encourage an English liking for an art that purportedly offered no educational value. If the eye was subordinated to the ear, word and image to tone, or thought to mere sensuousness, potentially mindful spectators would become, he feared, mindless listeners.

Addison opposed any tendency to believe that music and the listening ear were in fact the media that could most *save* opera from its allegedly barbaric tendency to serve as *mere* entertainments or spectacles. In pitting music against word and image, it was assumed that it was the *media* per se and not just a given *use* of it that was at fault. This assumption recalled Apollo's contest with Marsyas and Plato's arguments associated therewith. The primary reason for establishing the priority of words over tones, eyes over ears, reason over emotion, one city-state over another, or, nationalistically speaking, the Dorian over the Phrygian or Lydian mode, was that it mattered politically and morally which arts and which sorts of instruments one admitted into the *polis*. If this meant exaggerating the dangers of a medium per se—pipe-playing in principle as opposed to a particular playing of the pipe—this was justified by the urgency of the issue. "Music," Addison thus concluded to reinforce his complaint that "opera" was now *just* its music, "is certainly a very agreeable entertainment, but if it would take the entire possession of our ears, if it would make us incapable of hearing sense, if it would exclude arts that have a much greater tendency to the refinement of human nature; I must confess I would allow it no better quarter than Plato has done, who banishes it out of his Commonwealth" (Addison [1711] 1822: 22).

SETTING WORDS, SETTLING TERMS

Addison was neither the first nor the last to turn to Plato's (Apollonian) verdict on music when debating opera's constitution and values. In a letter written from Venice to Alessandro Striggio in Mantua, December 9, 1616, Monteverdi, caught up in the intrigues of a royal wedding, subtly challenged the instructions he had received to set a maritime fable, *Le nozze di Tetide*, to music (Stevens 1980: 115–118). As he suggested, the instructions for the poetry had obviously not been given by someone overly versed or trained in the musical art. For all the humbleness he showed his Lordship, and for all the respect he expressed (more or less) for the poet/librettist, the letter may be read between the lines as agonistic.

Though not initially won by "the composer," the contest with the poet was later so won—some say only in the nineteenth century—every time the poet or dramatist was relegated to the status of "the librettist," or every time the product was published (or recorded, as in this chapter, according to editorial decision) only under the composer's name. Early references to the designation "librettist" were typically without derogatory connotation. For a long time, conditions and conceptions were open enough to allow a text/libretto to be published under the name of the poet or dramatist, with or without a musical setting, or even variously published, in cases where there was more than one musical setting of the same text. This overall situation spurred two forms of competitiveness: one between composers and poet-dramatists and the other between composers who were aiming to produce the first or best musical setting of a text.

The early competitiveness was always driven by the need to raise both the abstract and concrete standing of the arts and their producers. For composers, to raise music's standing was often a matter of producing both a beautiful and a morally upstanding melody, *suitable* to the text. For music (*armonia*) properly to serve the delivered text (*orazione*), or for music to convey the correct sentiments and significance of the scene, one must, Monteverdi thus insisted in the aforementioned letter, employ the correct musical instruments. He quoted Plato in Latin: "cithara debet esse in civitate, et thibia in agris"—translated as "the cithara (or lyre) should be in the city, and the aulos/tibia (reed pipe/flute) in the country." This sentence drew on the enormously influential judgment from Plato's *Republic* (III: 399d), issued by Socrates to express his approval of Apollo's having banished Marsyas and his pipe to the countryside, leaving Apollo, with a straight bow and a simply strung lyre, to secure the values of the city. In other versions of the myth, it was Pan and not Marsyas who was banished, either with or without King Midas by his side. With Pan and Midas sent to a place where they no longer could do any harm, Marsyas was left in the town publicly to be flayed—for all to see. Interestingly, when Marsyas was associated with the town, he was not always flayed, as in Roman versions of the myth, when he was made to stand for the courage of his hubris in fighting for freedom against (Apollonian) tyranny. For reasons not unrelated, pertaining in this case to religious subversion, revolution, and discipline, spectacles of public punishment were later staged in the grand operas of Meyerbeer and Scribe.

In his letter to Striggio, Monteverdi did not directly refer to Apollo's contest with Marsyas or to Marsyas's punishment. He only mentioned the instruments that satyr figures like Marsyas played. Perhaps he was less concerned with the myth than with deciding the suitability of the sound to the situation and space; hence, his specification that if the scene of a text describes an event outside the city walls, in a rural or maritime space, wind instruments could and indeed should be used. Nevertheless, as evidenced in the oft-quoted foreword to the *Madrigali guerrieri et amorosi* of 1638, he well understood the moral and rhetorical stakes of misrepresenting or promoting the wrong sorts of situations and passions by the wrong musical or instrumental means (cf. Plett 2004: 373; Fabbri [1985] 1994: 240). Monteverdi's letter "to his Lordship" thus asks that the composer's decisions be taken seriously, for only someone fully knowledgeable about the art and craft of music should make decisions about which instruments and which melodies should be played. But behind the request lies his assumption that a composer could also understand an opera's moral and metaphysical stakes.

This request for authority must be understood in the light of the lesser or simply low position of earlier musicians, even "composers," compared with thinkers or theorists who occupied themselves with thoughts but not, professionally, with notations and instruments. To have compositional know-how was one thing; to have knowledge of matters moral and divine was another. Following Plato, it was long maintained that a merely practicing musician was little better than a servant who acted (to quote a twelfth-century writer) like a drunkard who always gets "home but does not in the least know by what path he returns" (Goehr [1992] 2007: 127); hence, the use of the term "know-how" instead of "knowledge" to distinguish persons who know by practice, inspiration, insobriety, madness, or touch, but not by reason, thought, or theory.

Following Pythagoras, Plato, and Aristotle, Boethius in the early sixth century (1989: 1–8) devoted a section in his *De institutione musica* to "what a musician is" (1989: 50–51) Those truly deserving the name *musicus* are those who produce correct judgments not by performance or "the servitude of work," but by engaging reason *entirely* in the contemplative mode, in the "sovereignty of speculation." Only the latter "make music" by "weighing reason," and reason is always superior to physical skill. Instrumentalists, accordingly, are named not after the "discipline" or "science" of music but from the instruments they play; hence, their functional and specific designations as "kitharists" and "auletes" (cf. Rouget 1985). For Boethius, correct judgment descends with all its disciplinary connotations from the high to the low, from theory to practice, from the master to "the slave," and, finally, in hierarchical terms, from *musica mundana* down through *musica humana* to *musica instrumentalis*. Even in his treatise *De institutione musica*, when he remarks that he *confines* his attention to the last, he never forgets the authority of the higher two. For this reason, he focuses far more on the principles of the harmony and construction of instrumental music and song than on their mere practice as such. In this way, his treatise accords with what he treats elsewhere, the moral and metaphysical consolations of the "musical muse" that *is* or *guides* philosophy. When, several centuries later, the Renaissance artists, including the early producers of opera, resume Boethius's thought, to put it to use in the *paragone*, they, too, negotiate the ramifications for the principle as well as for the production of music's concept.

Musica Mundana

To award Apollo first place in the writing of opera's history inflates the history, where inflation is the point. It does this by connecting opera's concept to a narrative not only of origin and birth but also of myth, and to a myth specifically associated with the concept of music. How has the narrative worked?

Music becomes opera's chief issue for the same reason that it becomes the same in the age-old contest of the arts. This is because what "music" is taken to mean always extends beyond either the instrumental art of tone or the vocal art of song. Given the inflation of music's concept, opera is drawn *backward* to its origin in Antiquity, to a mythic and ordered origin of art, and *upward* to the heavenly, celestial, or cosmic harmony of the spheres: *musica mundana* and *divina*. In this matter, Pythagorean science, Platonic and Boethian thought, and Apollonian myth all work together—typically in the Dorian mode.

Several early opera historians show that, above or alongside other musical figures, Apollo appears in so many of the early operas to lend to these productions the specific mythic content that justifies the necessary and not only incidental presence of music and song, captured in the idea of opera's being "sung throughout"; hence, without myth, no music or song, and, then, without music or song as a constant presence, no opera. This claim asks us, according to the narrative, to conceive of music empirically *and* metaphysically, as a *productive art* and as an Apollonian *principle* of moral order and harmony. Thus, it has never been enough apparently for opera to be sung throughout if opera was to move beyond *mere* sport, spectacle, or entertainment. Serving a divine and edificatory cause, opera was made from the start to *connect* the *production* to the *principle*.

In one of the first operas, the scene is set for what opera long after aims to secure in name and deed: Apollo's approval. In Monteverdi's *L'Orfeo* of 1607, the connection between production and principle is established through a vertical, platonic movement of descent and then ascent. The divine or celestial descends to aid humanity's ascent, thereby releasing humanity from all that is earthly, imperfect, or mundane.

The opera begins with La Musica singing, with golden lyre in hand, of her ability to inflame, charm, and soothe, but always so as to inspire humanity to seek the sonorous harmony of the heavens. At the end, when Orfeo believes all is lost, Apollo descends to console and counsel him. Rewriting the traditionally unhappy ending, Orfeo is allowed to ascend with Apollo in harmonious song, much as, later on, others ascend: in Gluck's *Alceste* (1767), in Bellini's *I Capuleti e i Montecchi* (1830), and in Verdi's *Aida* (1871). With Orfeo, all rise through song to a place where virtue and reward, or at least eternal love, are found in peace and delight. Having descended to a place of temptation, Orfeo ends *up* with the musical and Apollonian promise of eternal reward.

Rethinking the Birth Narrative through Music

Given the influence of the art and music historians Jacob Burckhardt ([1860] 1990) and A. W. Ambros ([1868] 1885), considerable attention has been paid to why (allegedly) the arts, of either singing or instrumental music, did not attain the sort of status that the other arts achieved in Italy around 1500, and why opera, as a decidedly musical art, was born only when the Renaissance, as Hugo Leichtentritt later put it, "had fully accomplished its mission" (1915: 622). This statement, the final of Leichtentritt's essay, might suggest different things: that opera's birth in 1600 was the birth of a "late" art and thus, fitting the times, the birth of a Baroque art; or that opera was born as the culmination of all that the Renaissance achieved; or, finally, that opera emerged as the art that it did as a result of the complex history of the musical art. The last best fits Leichtentritt's generally deflationary aim: to dispel the obsession with a mythically laden year, 1600. Already in 1915, he aimed to deconstruct opera's birth narrative by soberly situating opera's development in a long history in which music had generally fulfilled all sorts of social roles. "According to our present knowledge," he wrote, "instrumental music merely passed into a new phase of its development after 1600, after having been practised most extensively for centuries" (1915: 607).

Reinhard Strohm has also tempered the traditional narrative. Although "Italy was the cradle of the Renaissance, she did not give birth to what is often called 'Renaissance Music'" (2005: 540). Yet, he continues, this does not mean that there was no significant music in this period. There was; it is just that, first, it was not produced in Italy or, more accurately, was not produced in Italy by Italian composers. Composed elsewhere, it was often imported into Italy; thus the presence of notable northern European composers in the Italian courts. However, in my view, it is a tricky point whether the music that was produced ought still to be labeled "Renaissance music." Either the label remains too inflated or it becomes too deflated if it is used simply to capture anything that was going on anywhere during this period.

These and other music historians share a common strategy for deflating the judgment that opera was *born* in Italy *without precedent or predecessor.* It consists in re-describing music's condition in the period prior to opera's birth to subvert the traditional assertion that, of all the arts, the art of music thrived the least. Although this strategy is convincing and necessary, it risks aligning opera's birth too singularly with the empirical history of music. This alignment begs two questions at once, regarding what sort of *art* opera was at its birth and what concept of *music* most dominated its history thereafter.

These two questions are related. If the concept of music that has dominated opera extends beyond the empirical art of tone to point backward and upward to the Apollonian principle of harmony, then it follows that *whichever art opera has identified with over time, it has still been able to claim to embody the divine principle.* This is what the *paragone*, especially in the sixteenth century, urges us to consider. Despite the etymological intimacy, music as an *art* might not have a unique claim on *musica mundana* or on what in Antiquity more broadly went by the term *mousikê* (Murray and Wilson 2004). This claim turns on the relation assumed between the Greek and Latin terms *mousikê* and *musica.* When above, in summarizing Plato's argument from the *Laws,* I quoted the description of Apollo as *mousêgetês*, I left the description untranslated so that I could wait until now to describe the still common error of rendering it in English as "the master of music." Given the immediately preceding reference to the Muses, the phrase is better rendered as "their leader" or "the master of the Muses." The consequences of translating both the Greek and Latin terms simply as "music" have been *misleading* in matters of interpreting philosophical and theoretical texts, *reductionist* for the art of opera, and *acute* for the well-being of music's sister arts.

Paragone: Status and Contest

Many theorists and artists suggested early on that only if "musicians" could prove their subject theoretical, philosophical, or scientific—*ars liberalis* or *musica theoretica*—could they claim a unique relation to *musica mundana* or *divina.* Others claimed that if the other arts proved themselves liberal or theoretical, too, then nothing should prevent their also being described as musical. For the arts to be declared musical—as they were and still are—was to recognize their ability to embody all that Apollo and *mousikê* stood for: harmony, order, proportion, and unity, on the one hand, and inspiration and divinity, on the other. From this claim, another more agonistic one followed: that sometimes painting or poetry might show itself, without paradox, to be *more musical* or Muse-inspired (*mousikê*) than music. Recalling Horace's phrase "ut pictura poesis" (Lee 1967) or, by extension, "ut musica poesis" (Brown 1994)—as in one art so in the other—the ordering of the terms makes all the difference to the *agon*: hence, whether music, say, ought to follow or to lead painting or poetry in nature, ability, or form.

Under a Renaissance interpretation, Boethius's division of *musica* helps us to understand what was at stake for artists in the *paragone.* At this time, Boethius's view first reached prominence in the annals of the history of the arts. Given all that being inspired by the Muses (*mousikê*) meant, not just the art of music (*musica instrumentalis*) but also every mode or medium of art, as every task in human life (*musica humana*) was judged according to whether or not it approximated the silent harmony of the spheres (*musica mundana*). For the harmony to be silent meant, as Boethius noted, that it was inaudible to the imperfect human ear, indeed, to any corporeal sense, which is why one needed to employ one's reason to grasp it. The more reasonable, rational, or suitably proportioned the art or act, the more it approached the higher harmony. With these terms, the *paragone* may be read at its most agonistic as showing the resentment or envy of painters, poets, or sculptors that their arts were excluded from a schema that found *musica instrumentalis*—here read as the productive art of music—being placed alone on the third rung. Having listed all the reasons that painting is the superior art, Leonardo concluded: "since you have put music among the liberal arts, either you should put painting there or else take music away" (Farago 1991: 247; Winternitz 1970: 285).

But there was a tension in the argument: whether the status of *musica instrumentalis* as the "third rung" reflected an absolute or relative judgment. To declare *musica instrumentalis* absolutely low would likely have dissuaded painters and poets from wanting to join musicians on the rung. To declare it only as lower and thus as approximating something higher—*musica mundana*—would have encouraged their desire to be placed alongside. Leonardo put the point more or less this way: If painting and poetry are not to be placed on the ladder, then music does not belong there either. If they are to be put there, then this proves that they are proportioned and harmonious, too, and, as such, may then prove to be even more musical than music. And if they are more musical, then music as an art would benefit by their company. Music was not so sure. If music claimed opera as her art *alone*, then it would be, rather, painting and poetry that would benefit by *her* essential presence.

If this paragonal argument was tense, so was another. For it served neither artists nor their arts to aim to be *musical* only as a *liberal* matter of *theory*. Here, their agonism assumed a practical and mechanical dimension. Many claimed that, through its intervallic patterning of tones, music as a living instrumental or vocal art can mirror or express the Apollonian order of the world or harmony of the heavens with purity and immediacy. Others responded that, with their combined formal, emotional, and cognitive abilities to express, represent, and reflect upon their subject matter, painting and poetry can reach the same heights, if not with purity or immediacy, then more fully or completely. Indeed, with greater capacities for artistic *mediation*, that is, by being true precisely to their media as arts, were painting and poetry not thereby being true, and even truer, to Apollo's *principle*?

In his 1518 treatise *Instrumentorum opus*, Gaffurius noted (Miller 1977: 197) that according to the myth, although *all* the Muses were born from Apollo, Apollo gave his name to the art of music in particular. Many musicians, then and later, agreed. But the many Renaissance poets and painters did not, even if they otherwise embraced Gaffurius's treatise. In a contest or "divine colloquy" later staged in which Apollo sat as judge, Herder had Apollo chide music for claiming a special relationship to him and to the harmony and order for which he stood ([1785] 2006: 347–356). A contest that aimed to show the Apollonian harmony of the sister arts equally could not but help put music down when she claimed that the playing of her stringed instrument was alone in being an unmediated expression of what Apollo divinely played on his lyre. Apollo responded by reminding his daughter, first, that as father of all the Muses, he was just as closely related to the poet's pen and painter's brush, and, second, that whereas his heavenly music was necessarily perfect, his daughter's earthly music necessarily was not. With this claim, Apollo, helped by Herder, swung his own double-edged sword against both music and the other arts. Declaring earthly music to be necessarily or essentially imperfect allowed Herder to dismiss the allegedly degenerate instrumental music of his day, and elsewhere, in his piece "Tanz. Melodrama" (1802), to criticize the dominance of music in opera as causing the latter's deterioration. Second, declaring that earthly music is necessarily imperfect because it belongs to the world of imperfect appearance meant by extension that all arts are imperfect, which is a consequence with which every art had to deal. A similar *agon*, complicated by a political marriage that confused the Muses before Apollo sorted them out, was staged earlier than Herder's own "divine colloquy" in Gluck's *Il Parnaso confuso* of 1765.

Many of these arguments showed that although there were persistent attempts by artists to acquire Apollo's—and by association Plato's—approval, the artists sought this approval while yet aiming to be true to what their arts do as arts. When painters and poets represented, say, Apollo's contest with Marsyas, and there are countless examples, they often chose to follow Ovid in showing the punishment more than the contest, more the moral danger of music—the hubris of a human or satyr who dared to compete with a god—than music's joyful making in Marsyas's performance. To show disapproval of one sort of music or human action and approval of another was one way for painters and poets to raise their own standing as artists and, with this, the standing of their arts. And yet, even though, in self-censorship, they imposed upon themselves or accepted a moral discipline in the name of Platonic or Apollonian harmony, they often also subtly resisted the censorious verdicts passed on the arts by showing all that their arts could achieve as arts. How this double stand suited their art overall is as tense and interesting a question as whether the contest between the arts would have been so vigorous had the disciplining grip of philosophy, religion, and politics not been so strong.

Approximate Art and Endurance

For a long time, it was believed (à la Leonardo) that the nobility and beauty of an art rises the more that the exercise of manual or physical exertion diminishes: hence, painting's claim, with its delicate brushwork, to be nobler than heavily chiseled sculpture, and, by extension, poetry's verbal and textual claim to be more enduring than a merely temporal music produced instrumentally through performance. A contest that aimed to establish *ontological* differences between the arts given matters of time and space, endurance and transience, uniqueness and repeatability has always also been a contest aimed at proving the legitimacy of each art and artist, given upwardly mobile demands pertaining to morality, truth, and social status. To reach pure liberal status has meant reevaluating an art's necessarily impure mechanical means, turning the means into pure aesthetic *media*. The history of the arts, as opera's history, evidences a constant negotiation between aesthetic *media* and mechanical or technological *means*.

One way in which painters have dealt with the tension, and to serve their own cause, has been to occupy a suspended position between media and means. With the medieval exegetical principle of *invisibilia per visibilia* in hand, they have shown how, through the production *of appearance*, their art can access something *beyond* appearance. Consider the many "anagogical" *paintings* of "visual music," showing musicians—often Cecilia—gazing or pointing upward, in part agonistically to prove that the musical scene which leads *spectators* upward is present in the painting for all to *see*. That the instrumental music of the image is audibly silent renders visible the higher "silence" belonging to the music of the spheres.

Recall Hanning's description of Apollo's operatic triumph over Dafne as a metamorphosis achieved through the medium of art. One must now ask which artistic medium suited Apollo the most. When Apollo made art triumph over nature, and displaced transient with eternal beauty, did he achieve this by means of word, tone, or image? Music might embody the principle of harmony more *immediately* than any other art, but because of "her" material transience, she fails, so her sister arts long insisted, to preserve this principle in an adequate material form; hence, her necessary dependence upon them if opera was to be all that it could be. Given this argument, opera's history, like that of music, testifies to a constant pressure to prove, by whatever means, not only music's principled but also its material *endurance*. (To celebrate the contrary qualities—of passing temporality, sensuality, and so on—tells a quite other story, released from the pressure of metaphysics, morals, and discipline.)

Discipline and Descent

When the arts of instrumental performance and singing were attached to opera to make it the sort of art or genre it became, they were not so attached to demote opera to a transitory art of artificial or unnatural "affects," as it was sometimes accused of being, but rather (seriously or satirically) to attune or harmonize humanity through the rising and eternal movement of the soul. Otherwise put, much of opera's history has been dominated by the moving image of descent and ascent. This image highlights how far opera as an *art of presence and absence* has come to embody its "musicality" by means of what is seen *and* heard and of what is *not* seen and *not* heard.

In 1713, Nicolas Boileau produced a somewhat satirical sketch of an opera prologue, in which poetry and music argues over the excellence of their respective arts (1747: 442–445). It begins with La Musique claiming an immediate relationship to Apollo following

La Poésie's opening insult. "What! By vain harmonies and powerless sound can you claim to express all that I know how to say?" To which La Musique responds delicately: "But the soft transports that Apollo inspire in you I believe I can mingle with the sweet nature of my song." When, at the end, they are tempted to part ways—which naturally would not have suited the art of opera—harmony in the form of a "chorus" descends to reconcile them. "Let's forget our quarrels: we must work together for the good." Boileau remarks on the prologue's conclusion: "Thus did Apollo save us—SIC NOS SERVAVIT APOLLO" (Wygant 1995).

In 1915, Leichtentritt noted that "nearly thirty years before the first opera, a model of mise-en-scène... (demonstrated) the curious 'macchina,' the great machine which effect[ed] the opening of the clouds, the descent of gods or semigods from the sky: 'il ciel aperto'—the open sky—became an indispensable requisite of opera for 150 years and longer" (1915: 617). According to myth, the descent marked the beginning of time or history, when La Musica descended from the heavens to discipline or attune a discordant, irrational, and graceless humanity. But the descent was not without its complication. Following the stories recounted in Plato's *Timaeus*, La Musica not only *descended* to earth to lead humanity, its arts, and its earthly deeds away from imperfection; it also *fell* to earth, and presumably at a prior stage and in such a way that eternal wisdom gave way to earthly ignorance, envy, and scorn. The more La Musica assumed an earthly appearance the more *confused* it became with earthly forms of art: *musica instrumentalis*. The more confused it became—and "confusion" increasingly became a technical and judgmental term of the discourse—the more alienated humanity became from the wisdom and goodness to which La Musica in the celestial spheres was attached. Furthermore, when La Musica descended, it aligned itself to earthly manifestations *differently*, leaving critics thereafter with the task of determining which manifestations ought to be accepted into the city, and artists thereafter with the metaphysical-historical task of trying to retrieve something that humanity had lost. As one of the best-known choruses ("Va Pensiero" from *Nabucco*) sings to Verdi's melody of 1842: "Golden harp of the prophetic seers, / why do you hang mute upon the willow? / Rekindle our heart's memories and speak of times gone by!" Or as Shakespeare wrote on the verge of opera's birth in *The Merchant of Venice* (Act V, scene 1): "Such harmony is in immortal souls, / But whilst this muddy vesture of decay / Doth grossly close it in, / we cannot hear it."

In early opera, as in the prior *intermedi*, instrumental musicians descended by machines on clouds from the heavens: *musica ex machina*. Yet like angels in contemporary paintings (as in Raphael's *Cecilia*), though they played instruments or sang, they produced the sort of silent or celestial music that could not be heard in itself by ordinary mortals (Saslow 1996: 159–162). In the idea of descent, a tripartite division or "broken scene" (Strong 1996: 41) emerged, separating the *silent* music that corresponded to the harmonious movement of the heavens from a second music that was represented on the stage to *show* the descent of cosmic music to earth, which in turn was separated from a third music that was *heard but not always seen*. In this divided scene, the movement between music seen, heard, not seen, and not heard was strategically aimed to direct the audience's attention upward, while also aiding and rewarding it with a marvelous

Baroque spectacle. Instrumental musicians shown descending on clouds with their instruments were not necessarily or always the same instrumental musicians that produced the heard music. In opera, as much as in anagogical painting, poetry, or architecture, how one embodied music's descent in aesthetic form was how one demonstrated the power of the art to embody something "not of this world."

To produce a political image to correspond to the divine, aesthetic image, instrumental musicians were sometimes placed neither behind nor beneath the stage, as later became more common, but closer to where the most significant spectator of the event was placed—the prince or king in whose honor the event was organized. With "music" placed at the perspectival center of absolute power, its status was thereby raised. With its status raised, it helped legitimate the prince's authority as though he, through identification with Apollo, were pulling all the invisible strings. Increasingly, ideas were developed, regarding "broken scenes" and of how power was rendered visible through invisible means, to show how far opera as an art could be absolutist (for the king) and democratic (for the people) *simultaneously.* To have an audible music invisibly emanating from where the prince or king sat, yet corresponding to a visible music showing the descent of silent music onto the theater's stage, produced a total event that, by means of broken scenes of "music," finally unified the aesthetic spectacle with the political cause. It has been argued of opera in the eighteenth century that theatricality was understood no longer as an external instrument but as a constitutive trait of sovereign power (Strong 1996; Henaff 1996; Lichtenstein 1996). When, however, in the prior history was theatricality external? Maybe the power was not yet sovereign or absolute, but the power there was, of families and courts, had long embraced the theater and theatricality as part of its stage.

The theatrical movement between descent and ascent served the art of opera from the start, by showing that music could be as much a visual and verbal affair as an affair for tones, as much a matter of representation as for expression, and as much a matter for the eyes and mind as for the ears. That "music" increasingly became a matter only of audition and tonal form was what the history of opera has had to confront as long as it has aimed to retain its status as a total art of the theater. Such a total art reached a certain sort of culminating point in Wagner's Bayreuth, a half century after his death, when the crown that should have been placed on the head of Hans Sachs, in the name of Apollonian harmony and to bring *Die Meistersinger* to its end, was placed in one performance on the head of Adolf Hitler. This was only a repetition, however horrifying the image, of an age-old, aesthetic-political movement between that which exists in presence and absence both within and beyond the limits of opera's proscenium arch.

Discipline and Punish

Understanding the music's *double* role in the contest of the arts—as a mode or art of *production* and as a supreme, moral, and cosmic *principle*—helps to explain why so many dichotomizing decisions have been thought necessary: whether opera is primarily a representational or primarily an expressive art, an art for the eye or for the ear, for education or for entertainment, for understanding or for emotion, for interpretation or for performance—as though opera cannot, because it *should* not, be both or all these things at once. Another way to make the point is to show how "music" has been called upon as often to *demote* opera's status as art as to *raise* it. In the heavily loaded, binary oppositions just listed, music has either willingly taken or unwillingly been made to take the side of the latter: of expression, of the ear, of entertainment, and so on. This has caused problems for opera regarded as a branch of *music* so long as opera wanted to be taken seriously as an *art*, at least if expression, hearability, and entertainment were not to be trusted. Weighing up value—social, moral, and cognitive—with respect to these binary oppositions has always been how what has been considered true, good, and beautiful has been separated from what has been considered low, deceptive, and dangerous. Whereas harmony, rationality, and proportion have usually been identified with all that Apollo stood for, the contrary corporeal, virtuoso, devilish, or merely pleasurable dimensions of music or art have been identified with everything that Apollo put down. The added fact that these dimensions have often been termed "operatic" has only further challenged opera's bid—when in fact it has had this bid—to become an art worthy of its name (whatever its name).

In 1752, in the pamphlet *War*, or *Querelle des bouffons*, Rousseau responded to a performance of Giovanni Battista Pergolesi's two-act, comic intermezzo *La serva padrona* with a verse: "O inimitable Pergolesi, / When our unmerciful orchestra / Causes you to cry out under its clumsy violin, I believe contrary to fable, Marsyas flayed Apollo" (Rousseau 1825: 236; trans. Flint 1986: 174). Like many others, Rousseau drew upon the arguments of Antiquity that had shown Apollo more often in contest with musicians than anyone else, but not only for the obvious reason that Apollo himself was a musician (Winternitz 1979; Wyss 1996; Maniates 2000). Being the principal and principled overseer of the world's harmony, Apollo could have competed with anyone by any means and whatever art. When he did compete with musicians, Marsyas and Pan were most usually his opponents, though sometimes they were conflated with other figures and names. Interestingly, though Dionysus has always been Apollo's shadow figure, he has not generally been represented as competing with him in actual contest. What Marsyas and Pan shared was that they, like Orpheus, were extraordinarily talented or effective as musicians. Had they not been, Apollo would have had no reason to compete with them. Indeed, he entered into contest with them precisely to contest the means, ends, and modes of their talent. Talented in virtuoso skill or in their ability to move persons and animals through the charm of their melody, they were accused of having a *superficial* or merely *effective* musicality that was only and literally skin deep. When, at the contest's end, Apollo took Marsyas's skin, he demonstrated that musicality, like justice, has more to do with persons, their arts, and their acts, beyond what is merely *apparent*. In Plato's terms (and the end of his *Symposium*, when Socrates is compared to Marsyas, is particularly apt in this matter), to flatter with the musical art might have brought these persons worldly success or fame but, without the accompaniment of an inner morality, they were no better than the other sophistic or ambitious, well-dressed citizens populating and disrupting the city of Athens.

Further, that these musicians were often represented as half-human, as satyr- or animal-like, was meant to persuade those listening or looking not to be taken in by their merely external or outward appearances of musicality. In addition, they were almost always (though there are exceptions) associated with the playing of a wind or reed instrument—the instrument that the goddess Athena had so violently discarded in disgust. This was meant to remind an audience why (recalling Monteverdi), when such instruments are used in social or theatrical events, they ought to be used with extreme attention paid to their possible effects. Finally, that these musicians were represented in text and image as acting somehow indecently or violently was meant to reinforce the conclusion that they were less victims than willing, hubristic participants in this overall *agon*.

When Herder staged his contest of the arts, he was hardest on the art of music. He was not alone. The more the art or production of music claimed identity with music's divine principle, the more it was criticized for (hubristically) overstepping its limits. Music might have an immediate way of contacting the "invisible" or "silent" celestial music above, but it also, critics claimed, had the ability to bring shame and ruin to humanity the more it catered to the human, Bacchanalian or Dionysian desire for noisy pleasure and intoxication. Here was another motivation for hiding instrumental musicians from the stage or scene: wherever and whenever, the sight of them led persons downward to corporeal and lascivious sensations.

Rather surprisingly, contrary to the pervasive presence in sculpture, poetry, and painting of the contest between Apollo and Marsyas, there are few examples in opera, none of which is very well known. In 1628, Ottavio Tronsarelli wrote a "pastorale" of Marsyas (*Marsia*) for Cardinal Francesco Barberini's court. Apparently the contest was rewritten to produce a happy (suitably moral or Christian) ending (Olson 2004; Ford 1984; Hammond 1985 and 1994: 200–201). J. S. Bach's secular cantata *Der Streit zwischen Phoebus und Pan*, sometimes referred to as a *dramma per musica*, or as the closest Bach ever came to producing an opera, alludes to Apollo's contest with Marsyas, although it is focuses on Pan. In 1970, Einojuhani Rautavaara and Bengt V. Wall produced an ironic, comic opera *Apollo contra Marsyas* in which Apollo is made to stand for the high classics of Viennese music and Marsyas the jazzy or popular motifs, in this way reminding us of Ernst Krenek's 1927 opera *Jonny spielt auf*. Music's history, in contrast to opera's, especially after the Second World War, increasingly evidences examples of genuine sympathy toward Marsyas, as though Marsyas has finally come to stand for all the victims of oppression and war.

Unlike Orpheus and Bacchus, Dionysus also appears only in a few operas, for example, in Hans Werner Henze's *The Bassarids* (1966). Pan appears in Karol Szymanowski's *King Roger* (1926). In the latter, Dionysus is ultimately made to pay tribute to the sun-rising Apollo; in the former, Dionysian destruction finds no redemption. Pan also appears infrequently, and even less frequently as a distinctly "musical" figure, although he is given a leading role in Bach's Cantata mentioned above and in John Ernest

Galliard's *Pan and Syrinx.* He plays a minor role in Cavalli's *Gli amore d'Apollo e di Dafne* (1640) and in Purcell's *King Arthur, or the British Worthy* (1691). In general, that opera has not more often come to the defense of the musician, in contrast to music as a principle, is a signifi-cant theme on its own.

"Opera" before Opera: Toward the Total Work of Art

One way to deflate opera's traditional birth narrative is to look back at modes of near-opera production that preceded it. In this matter, the *intermedi* are exemplary. The fact that they overlapped with early operas in form, material, and personnel prompts one to ask why they constitute only opera's *proto*-history. Recent studies show that the *intermedi* and *La pellegrina*, in particular, introduced many of the Ovidian or agonistic themes that "opera proper" pursued.

First produced in the Teatro Mediceo degli Uffizi in 1589, *La pellegrina* celebrated the extravagant Florentine marriage of Ferdinando I de' Medici to Christine of Lorraine. The title originally referred to the main comedy by Girolamo Bargagli, between whose acts six separate *intermedi* were performed. To refer to the six in-between acts by the singular term *intermedio* begs the question of its unity—especially given that unity was in part what was being negotiated on the stage. It has long been argued that one way the *intermedi* gave birth to opera was by showing how a series of light, interval entertainments could assume a self-contained shape. At first, not necessarily connected to the others, each *intermedio* offered a spectacular diversion of myth, mime, dance, song, and machine of Baroque excess and irreality—a pantomime *sul gusto antico.* Gradually, however, the separate *intermedi* of a given evening or of a whole day—playing as it did with a day's actual passage of time—became more dramatically and musically unified. When the *intermedi* began to surpass the main theater piece, becoming itself the main event, this was the moment, according to the birth narrative, that gave "conceptual birth" to opera. Nevertheless, after the birth, it continued in production. With suitably adapted form, it became the agonistic pantomime or play-within-a-play staged, for example, as a *commedia dell'arte* in Strauss's 1912 *Ariadne auf Naxos* or as a Midas-play in 1838, in Berlioz's *Benvenuto Cellini.*

Nina Treadwell has rightly challenged this teleological birth narrative by questioning how far the *intermedi* were really aiming for a unified work of art (2009: 53). Still, the point of undermining the narrative is only to release the evidence from the narrative's top-down, overbearing force. After all, there is some evidence that the *intermedi* aided opera's bid for autonomy of attention and form. *La pellegrina* was noted immediately for the construction of its proscenium arch, elaborate machinery, costumes, and sets. What remained after the event were sketches drawn by the "architect" Bernardo Buontalenti (or drawings based thereon by Agostino Carracci and followers), some of the music, the poetic texts, detailed instructions for performance and instrumentation, and witness accounts. Giovanni Battista Strozzi the Younger (Sempé 2007) tells, in addition, of how the production was intended to impress its spectators for the challenge it offered to its own status as an accessory entertainment. What was once accessory was now the main event, a change that apparently justified thinking about the parts as forming somehow a unity. To each part Strozzi assigned a more or less Aristotelian characteristic: grandeur, astonishment, clarity, pleasure, proportion, and coherence.

Opera's history has largely depended upon its being separated sufficiently from the theater. One contentious way it has done this is by reference to its "musical" mode of division. Ellen Rosand notes that, in 1639, having produced a drama (for which Francesco Manelli composed music) titled *Delia*, Giulio Strozzi saw fit to preface his text with an argument establishing the naturalness of the three-act division as opposed to the theater's traditional five (1991: 53; also Solerti 1903: 7–8): "I have divided the work quite deliberately into three acts, a division common to all things: beginning, middle, and end," in contrast to the ancients who "made five in theirs, because they interspersed them with singing (i.e., choruses). This work, being wholly sung, has no need of so many pauses." Whether or not Strozzi was really marking a change or merely endorsing a practice already in place, his words testify to the development at opera's "birth" of a genre whose independence would be claimed in terms of the *constant presence* of music and song. The division of acts, as the issue of musical unification, never ceased preoccupying opera composers and librettists.

The subject of *La pellegrina* was chosen to prove and celebrate, through music and myth, the rightness or harmony of the union between royal personages from different political states. To every image of descent corresponded, if all went well, a final image of ascent. The six *intermedi* comprised Ovidian stories respectively regarding Apollo's slaying of the python at Delphi, the realm of the demons, Arion's encounter with a dolphin, and the gift, finally, of harmony and rhythm to humanity (Warburg 1999: 376–379). The second part staged a singing contest, itself in four parts, between the Muses and the Pierides, drawn from the fifth book of Ovid's *Metamorphoses*, with words by Rinuccini, set to music by Luca Marenzio. The contest tells of the "puffed up pride" of the nine daughters, otherwise called "foolish virgins," of a rich landowner named Pierus. Hubristically challenging the Muses to a song contest, the daughters insufficiently honor those who deserve honor. Transformed by the victorious Muses into magpies, the daughters are left endlessly to babble in words with ugly voices, denied forevermore the power of song.

Historicism and the Total Work of Art

In 1908, Romain Rolland prefaced a history of opera, from its "birth" to Mozart, with the claim that before its birth, opera had a history (1908: 19–20). Titling the preface "L'opéra avant l'opéra," he unwittingly threatened an infinite regress. For, once the *intermedi* are included in the history of opera *proper*, why not include the near-operas like Angelo Poliziano's 1480 Florentine tragedy *Orfeo*, or the medieval masquerades, spectacles, pageantries, and processions, or the music-festival-stagings and contests of Rome and Greece, on to where and when one can go back no further? Empirically speaking, there is nothing wrong with such a regress if what it tempers is the assumption that opera was born somehow without precedent. Nonetheless, it risks removing from opera's concept what for so long has been its distinctive *historicist* claim—which only from a contemporary perspective is a risk worth taking.

According to the historicist claim, opera was born, true to the spirit of the Renaissance, as a rebirth of what had allegedly been produced in Ancient Greece, though with conditions appropriate to the new age. The narrative endorsed three typical historicist strategies. First, it gave an honorific meaning to the idea of "firstness." Second, it meant that everything between the first opera and its origin in Antiquity had to be conceptually erased, as not a proper part of opera's history. Third, it meant that what empirically occurred in Antiquity had to be displaced by a mythic and metaphysical notion of ancient drama, such that it could serve, like the principle of *musica mundana*, as opera's true origin. If this historicist narrative gave to opera's concept its content at its birth in 1600, it continued to do so at nearly every other moment of reform, even at some moments in the twentieth century when one would have thought that the historicist narrative was most ripe for its dismantling.

When Wagner, for example, argued that opera should be reborn out of the spirit of Antiquity, he insisted that the birth be appropriate to the total social and aesthetic revolution he desired for his modern times. Looking back, he found an antique and idealized vision of the Greek tragic drama born out of the spirit of *mousikê* in which he included at least three bases in melody, poetry, and dance. In his evermore totalizing vision, he found the terms to *newly reunite* opera *qua* total *work* of art with opera *qua* entire social and aesthetic and even religious *institution*, especially when he identified an idealized portrait of Jesus with the same of Apollo (cf. Goehr 2011).

Metamorphosis comprised the subject matter of almost every poetic text produced at opera's birth, as also of an extraordinary number of libretti produced later. However, what metamorphosis made possible as well, according to the narrative, was an art of opera that could transform the relationship between the several arts, allegedly surpassing what each art could do by its means alone. The paragonal arguments of the sixteenth century urgently reappeared in the nineteenth, when the art of music—under the influence of the symphonic genre—claimed to have at last united music's production with music's principle. Given its new formal freedom, music ranked itself not merely at the top of the hierarchy of the arts but also beyond it, as the supreme synthesizing principle for the singular or total concept of art. At this moment, many claimed on music's behalf that, indeed, this daughter had always been correct in maintaining a special relationship to Apollo. Only with the supreme status of music so proved, the argument continued, could opera for the first time realize its concept as a truly musical art.

Yet, with the "symphonic" emancipation of the musical art, what constituted the musicality of opera became more problematic, not less. Empirically or artistically speaking, opera, as a hybrid art, was not reducible to music conceived of as a solely symphonic or purely instrumental genre. Without word, image, theatricality, and scene, opera would no longer be opera. To maintain opera as musical, it had to be admitted once again that musicality could extend beyond music as an art to show itself in all of opera's other dimensions. Thus, although by reference to music's emancipation as an art, opera was declared for the first time to have fully realized its concept, opera continued to do what in fact it had always done: explore ways of embodying the musical or harmonizing principle in *both* expressive *and* representational form. From these explorations emerged an opera regarded as a total work of art, which, though awarding priority to opera's immanently moving forms, refused to reduce opera to the instrumental art of music *alone*. *Tristan und Isolde* was an opera produced by Wagner in part to be exemplary of this argument.

Wagner sought the restorative power of *art*, *myth*, and *the aesthetic spirit* through both music's *principle* and its *production*. According to his view, which was shared by many, having finally won its autonomy or freedom from its mere dependence on representation (word and image), instrumental music, as the pure and immediate expression of the Schopenhauerian World-Will, could give back to opera not only its originary health but also, without paradox, a new and complete outer or representational form. Hence, again, to declare opera a *truly* or *purely* musical art was not incompatible with declaring opera more than an art for music *alone*. Through the power of music's expression, all the arts would be consummated or synthesized so as to render opera as much representational as expressive, as much for the eye as for the ear, as much for the total sensory experience of body and mind as for the total regeneration of art and society that had previously fallen into decadent division and alienation.

When Wagner described opera or music drama in terms of "deeds of music made visible" (*ersichtlich gewordene Thaten der Musik*), he aimed to turn opera away from the barbaric or artificial (*künstlich*) displays of empty spectacle and artificial unity into which it had allegedly fallen, and toward a total and serious theater in which tragic drama—the drama of a united *Volk*—was possible to actualize in modern times (Wagner [1872] 1983: IX: 276). Consistent with these terms, the *gesamt* of Wagner's *Gesamtkunstwerk* had a twofold, aesthetic and social, purpose: to effect a new union of the different media of the arts now regarded under a single umbrella concept of art (*Kunst*), and to restore *totality*—wholeness, health, and harmony—to a society that was typified by its modern, alienated institution of opera. Drawing explicitly on Feuerbach, Wagner described the conditions of alienation—and hence the modern condition of opera and the arts—in terms of caprice, artifice, luxury, egoism, fashion, and profit. Wagner made the Jewish connotations of these terms explicit when, following Feuerbach and others, he sought an explanation for how Jews had become the musicians and critics to oversee musical taste. Given the age-old contest and contestation of the arts, the final victor for Wagner was no single or total art at all, not even the art of music. Rather, the winner was or eventually would be the future *Volk* or community united, as we see at the end of *Meistersinger*, with the Apollonian principle grounded in "the natural tree of life." When Wagner argued for the concealment of the orchestra, part of what this implied was the "undoing" or "destruction (*Vernichtung*) of the "arbitrary" acts of art conceived as a means (*Mittel*). To avoid "the death of opera," art had to serve "the common aim of *all*": namely, the immediate and absolute portrayal of perfected human nature of —*der Menschen der Zukunft* (Wagner [1849] 1983: VI: 29).

To prove himself the first to do for opera what always, in his view, should have been done, Wagner denied the firstness of the first operas of Italy in 1600. In this claim, he was preempted. In 1814, when E. T. A. Hoffmann described opera under the condition of musical unity, he not only had painting or the "finished canvas" in mind (1989: 158); he aimed also to distinguish the new opera of his times from any that had gone before. "The Italians," he wrote (p. 152), "did not progress to the view that in opera word, action, and music should appear as a unified whole, and that this indivisible whole should create a total impression upon the listener. The music was to them more of an incidental accompaniment to the spectacle, and was only now and then allowed to emerge as an independent art creating its own effects [from *Effekt*]." Hoffmann's description was exaggerated, despite some disclaimers to the contrary (152 n. 262). Because he wanted to show that opera could only come of age when music was emancipated as an art, he was compelled to regard opera's birth in 1600 as having been only the first moment of potential in a long life of maturation.

Wagner pursued the same sort of argument. Although the Renaissance had witnessed the rebirth of the arts out of the decayed spirit that had followed Antiquity, it had not, given its liking for opulence and enchantment, fully developed opera as a serious, authentic, or free art. Only when the arts were united through the "expression of a free and beautiful public" would opera, born out of the spirit of ancient tragedy, be born not merely as a rebirth (*wiedergeboren*) but as a new, as though first, birth (*neuem geboren*) ([1849] 1983: III: 296–297).

Wagner acknowledged the value of much that preceded him and much that was Italian and French. Nevertheless, he spent inordinate amounts of time damning the operas of his own age for the agonistic sake of claiming the supreme promise of his own works. Rather more subtly, he elided the operas of 1600 in part by discussing them far less. Though Ambros described him in 1874 as "the modern Monteverdi," (Gregor-Dellin 1982: 726), Wagner hardly mentions Monteverdi by name, although this surely had partly to do with the state of knowledge regarding early opera in his time. Nevertheless, one way to read *Meistersinger* is in terms of Wagner's having wanted to produce an opera set in the period prior to opera's birth to show the terms of opera's true birth, the terms therefore by which his own opera would displace opera's first birth. To select the Maximilian and Lutheran age, in which Germany's painting and poetry had excelled, encouraged him to believe that he could realize opera as a musical-dramatic art as early Italian opera had not been able to do (Goehr 2011). Needless to say, proponents of Italian opera vehemently resisted Wagner's arguments, and so did proponents of the individual arts. There were many ways for opera and the arts to be musical without submitting to Wagner's demands for totality.

The Two Faces of Opera

Opera has always taken advantage of all sides of nearly every agonistic argument presented for or against it. In the nineteenth century, it was claimed increasingly to be the culmination or supreme synthesis of all arts and, hence, the only art, before film, that could bring the contest of the arts to an end, or at least change its terms once and for all. In the twentieth century, it was increasingly claimed to be the art, under Wagnerian influence, that helped bring art to its end, or opera to its last death. (As much as the birth narrative needs deconstructing, so, too, does the narrative of death.)

In 2006, in exploring "the nature of opera," Bernard Williams, inspired by W. H. Auden, described opera as the supreme anti-art of "manifest artifice." Whereas theater is an art *for interpretation*, Williams argued, opera is, or has finally become, an art *for performance* and for the staged performance of *singing* in particular. Instead of pitting German against French opera or Wagner against Bizet, as Nietzsche did before him, Williams drew on opera's manifest artifice—the staged performance of operatic singing—to account for why opera should be viewed not, as theater, in terms of its potential dramatic value as comedy or tragedy, but, as a sung spectacle, in terms of its success and popularity. With Puccini in mind, Williams contrasted opera's demand for excellent singers and song with theater's demand for deep interpretation. By means of song—constituting the musicality of opera—Puccini allegedly rendered more transparent than anyone before him opera's technique and conventions by explicitly staging its technique to secure or manipulate an effect. Opera's success, Williams continued, draws on its indestructible effectiveness, where effectiveness is what allows an audience to enjoy the spectacle of the singer's art for what it is: a spectacle. That the opera depends upon the audience's complicity in appreciating and desiring opera's *effectiveness* explains why (and again, this is a Nietzschean thought) an audience will return repeatedly to the opera house to enjoy what it already knows. Simply put, Williams concluded, the public goes to the opera to watch the wheels of its artifice turn.

The argument for opera as "manifest artifice" led Williams to *praise* Puccini's operas, even as he saw, in *Tosca* above all, the staging of profound cruelty. This observation did not lead Williams back into the domain of deep interpretation or to explore the long-standing accusations of artificiality or effect to which opera had long, if not always, been subjected. Rather, it explained to Williams—and here he was influenced by Joseph Kerman's classic text on opera *as* drama ([1956] 1988)—why some opera historians had shied away from Puccini in *disgust*. Although it is justified to think that opera historians never really shied away—so much, or that the distinction between interpretation and performance is indefensible for opera, in whole or part—it is less important than what Williams's argument reveals: namely, an ongoing willingness on the part of opera historians, as evidenced also in the operas themselves, to enter the agonistic arena for the moral and artistic sake of assessing opera's status as an *art*.

Williams's argument repeats what was long claimed about opera: that while punishing hubris has rendered opera edifying, its display has also rendered it entertaining. Although opera has long taught persons to leave the opera house encouraged less to act as though they were gods and more to strive as best they could to act in godlike ways, they have been taught this lesson by aesthetic *means* often at odds with the moral *end*, which is to say, by a manifestly artificial or extreme display of everything that they ought ultimately to reject. In this sense, opera has always staged what I would term the moral-aesthetic agonism or paradox of edificatory art. That it has been a cruel art, as ancient drama was cruel, has not contradicted but rather has partially accounted for its inherent spectacle and spectacular success. Singing on the stage is not opera's only draw.

Williams translated Wagner's phrase "ersichtlich gewordene Thaten der Musik" (usually translated as "deeds of music made visible") as "deeds of art made manifest." The difference is important: The former stresses the total aesthetic form; the latter emphasizes what is achieved by opera conceived as a self-conscious production of its own artifice. Nevertheless, Wagner, just as much as Puccini, understood opera's potential to manipulate its effect—for *performance*—while staging itself also as a drama of and for the theater, for *interpretation*. In this matter, it is useful to set Williams's comments on "effect" against Wagner's famed dismissal of Meyerbeer from his *Opera and Drama* (1851). "The secret of Meyerbeer's operatic music is—*Effect* [*Effekt*]," where by "effect," Wagner did not, he said, mean "the more familiar '*Wirkung*' [lit., a working]." Whereas, he explained, *Wirkung* assumes an antecedent *cause* and thus is grounded or motivated by something good—a "natural feeling"—*Effekt* does not. Meyerbeer's works are best described, accordingly, as effects or workings "without a cause (*ohne Ursache*) (Wagner [1851] 1983: VII: 98; [1893] 1983: II: 95). Wagner went on to show the alleged missed opportunities not only of Meyerbeer's obvious musical talent but also of much French or Italian opera, so that he could conclude that only a reborn German opera would express the grounded natural, and ancient Greek feeling of humanity, shed, as he saw it, of the Jewish or unmusical tendency to artifice.

Wagner was not the first, or the last, to associate opera's problem with superficial effect, or with a criticism of modernity that scapegoated or *satyr*ized the Jews. This means that, despite a common language, not all arguments against effect are to be read in Wagnerian terms. Williams's argument testifies more in fact to the impact of arguments from Antiquity—about drama, myth, and musicality—on opera, especially at its Italian moment of "culmination" in Puccini.

Conclusion

I have drawn on many paragonal arguments to explain why music and "her" musicians have together been *the chief issue* for opera's concept and production, as they have been in the broader contest of the arts. This is because music has been treated as both a "sister" art *and* a "fatherly" principle. Given that the daughter's constant claim to be the father's favorite has often led the other daughters to set her apart competitively as the most difficult daughter, music has been subject to the most inflating and to the most deflating of arguments.

By pulling at the threads of the "birth discourse" that has dominated so much of the writing of opera's history, I have shown how far this narrative has been drawn into another. The second narrative, equally pervasive, has stressed how far opera was "born" out of the spirit of a contest that was staged *between* the different arts in large order to sustain a certain moral, political, and social authority *over* the arts. Apollo *descended* from high onto opera's stage to control the *dissenting* elements of humanity.

Any writing of opera's history that turns its attention to Apollo quickly becomes a dichotomous and critical writing of its history, given the necessity to investigate—and thereby disclose—all that Apollo has conquered or destroyed for the sake of preserving or producing everything for which his name has been made to stand. Put differently, opera's complex alignment to, and identification with, "music" is what has brought the edificatory principle associated with Apollo to the agonistic core of its concept. The fact that Apollo's punishment of those with whom he entered into contest has so often been brutal has been seen not only in the quarrels regarding opera's form but also in its choice of subject matter. The laurel crown that has signified Apollo's victory over anyone who has entered into contest with him, threatened his authority, or defied his desires has served as a marker or icon in a history of opera that has always been concerned as much with sacred and secular political and religious victory as with moral and aesthetic discipline.

Whenever contemporary theorists write about what and whom opera has "undone," they have simultaneously performed the undoing of opera. Contemporary operas, like contemporary histories, treat of the voices "unsung" (Abbate 1991) or of persons seen "though other eyes" (Levin 1994). Yet, the contemporary writing of opera's history evidences one fragile hermeneutic question from which we have not escaped and perhaps cannot escape: How far is our writing about opera a writing on opera's behalf? What exactly would it mean to write for opera's demise? This question returns us to the very first point of this chapter: that although opera's concept may be written from more than one disciplinary or interdisciplinary standpoint, and although the tensions in writing the histories continue in subtle and complex ways to show themselves in the contemporary operas produced, writing opera's history continues to be an indispensable contribution to the determination of opera's concept: its ongoing, constantly contested conception, staging, production, and assessment.

See also: What Is Opera? Genre, Musical Theater(s), Operatorio? Opera between the Ancients and the Moderns

Bibliography

Abbate, Carolyn. 1991. *Unsung Voices: Opera and Musical Narrative in the Nineteenth Century*. Princeton, NJ: Princeton University Press.

Addison, Joseph, et al. [1711] 1822. *The Spectator with Notes and a General Index*. Philadelphia: Hickman and Hazzard.

Adorno, Theodor W. [1965] 1978. "Über einige Relationen zwischen Musik und Malerei." *Gesammelte Schriften* 16: 628–642. Frankfurt: Suhrkamp; translated by Susan Gillespie (1995) as "On Some Relationships between Music and Painting." *Musical Quarterly* 79/1: 66–79.

——. [1967] 1977. "Die Kunst und die Künste." *Gesammelte Schriften* 10.1: 432–453; translated by Rodney Livingstone (2003) as "Art and the Arts." In *Can One Live After Auschwitz? A Philosophical Reader*, edited by Rolf Tiedemann, 368–387. Stanford, CA: Stanford University Press.

——. [1937] 1971. "*Versuch über Wagner.*" *Gesammelte Schriften* 13. Frankfurt: Suhrkamp; translated by Rodney Livingston (2005) as *In Search of Wagner*. London: Verso.

Ambros, August Wilhelm. [1868] 1885. *Die Grenzen der Musik und Poesie: Eine Studie zur Aesthetik der Tonkunst*. 2nd ed. Leipzig: Heinrich Matthes; translated by J. H. Cornell (1893) as *The Boundaries of Music and Poetry: A Study in Musical Aesthetics*. New York: Schirmer.

Berger, Karol. 2008. *Bach's Cycle, Mozart's Arrow: An Essay on the Origins of Musical Modernity*. Berkeley and Los Angeles: University of California Press.

Bianconi, Lorenzo, and Giorgio Pestelli, eds. 2003. *Opera in Theory and Practice, Image and Myth*, translated by Kenneth Chalmers and Mary Whittall. *The History of Italian Opera* 6. Chicago: University of Chicago Press.

——. 2002. *Opera on Stage*, translated by Kate Singleton. *The History of Italian Opera* 5. Chicago: University of Chicago Press.

Blanning, Tim. 2008. *The Triumph of Music: The Rise of Composers, Musicians, and Their Art*. Cambridge, MA: Harvard University Press.

Bloch, Ernst. 1985. *Essays on the Philosophy of Music*, translated by Peter Palmer. Cambridge: Cambridge University Press.

Bloom, Harold. [1973] 1997. *The Anxiety of Influence: A Theory of Poetry*. New York: Oxford University Press.

Boethius, Anicius Manlius Severinus. 1989. *Fundamentals of Music*, edited by Claude V. Palisca and translated by Calvin M. Bower. New Haven: Yale University Press.

Boileau-Despréaux, Nicolas. 1747. *Œuvres*. Vol. 2, edited by M. de Saint-Marc. Paris: David & Durand.

Bokina, John. 2009. *Opera and Politics from Monteverdi to Henze*. New Haven: Yale University Press.

Brown, Howard M. 1994. "*Ut Musica Poesis*: Music and Poetry in France in the Late Sixteenth Century." *Early Music History* 13: 1–63.

Buller, Jeffrey L. 1995. "Looking Backwards: Baroque Opera and the Ending of the Orpheus Myth." *International Journal of the Classical Tradition* 1/3: 57–79.

Bundrick, Sheramy D. 2005. *Music and Image in Classical Athens*. Cambridge: Cambridge University Press.

Burckhardt, Jacob. [1860] 1990. *The Civilization of the Renaissance in Italy*, edited by Peter Murray and translated by S. G. C. Middlemore. London: Penguin.

Calcagno, Mauro. 2003. "Signifying Nothing: On the Aesthetics of Pure Voice in Early Venetian Opera." *Journal of Musicology* 20/4: 461–497.

Carter, Tim. 2000. *Monteverdi's Musical Theatre*. New Haven: Yale University Press.

Clément, Catherine. 1999. *Opera, or The Undoing of Women*, translated by Betsy Wing. Minneapolis: University of Minnesota Press.

Cowart, Georgia. 2008. *The Triumph of Pleasure: Louis XIV and the Politics of Spectacle*. Chicago: University of Chicago Press.

Danto, Arthur C. 1998. *After the End of Art: Contemporary Art and the Pale of History*. Princeton, NJ: Princeton University Press.

Dellamora, Richard, and Daniel Fischlin, eds. 1998. *The Work of Opera: Genre, Nationhood, and Sexual Difference*. New York: Columbia University Press.

Donington, Robert. 1991. *Opera and Its Symbols: The Unity of Words, Music, and Staging*. New Haven: Yale University Press.

Dryden, John. [1680] 1800. "Preface to Albion and Albanius." In *The Critical and Miscellaneous Prose Works of John Dryden*. Vol. 2, edited by Edmond Malone, 151–169. London: M. Baldwin and Son.

Ellis, William Ashton, ed. and trans. [1892–1899] 1995. *Richard Wagner's Prose Works*. 8 vols. London: Kegan Paul. Reprint. Lincoln: University of Nebraska Press.

Fabbri, Paolo. [1985] 1994. *Monteverdi*, translated by Tim Carter. Cambridge: Cambridge University Press.

Farago, Claire J. 1991. *Leonardo da Vinci's Paragone: A Critical Interpretation with a New Edition of the Text in the Codex Urbinas*. Boston: E. J. Brill.

Feldman, Martha. 2007. *Opera and Sovereignty: Transforming Myths in Eighteenth-Century Italy*. Chicago: University of Chicago Press.

Flint, Ellen R. 1986. "Jean-Jacques Rousseau's 'Lettre d'un symphoniste de l'académie royal de musique, à ses camarades dans l'orchestre'." *Musical Quarterly* 72/2: 170–179.

Ford, Terence. 1984. "Andrea Sacchi's 'Apollo Crowning the Singer Marc Antonio Pasqualini'." *Early Music* 12/1: 79–84.

Fulcher, Jane F. 1987. *The Nation's Image: French Grand Opera as Politics and Politicized Art*. Cambridge: Cambridge University Press.

Gaffurius, Franchinus. [1518] 1977. *De Harmonia musicorum instrumentorum opus*, edited by Clement A. Miller. Middleton, WI: A-R Editions.

Gallie, W. B. 1956. "Art as an Essentially Contested Concept." *Philosophical Quarterly* 6/23: 97–114.

Gerhard, Anselm. 1998. *The Urbanization of Opera: Music Theater in Paris in the Nineteenth Century*, translated by Mary Whittall. Chicago: University of Chicago Press.

Goehr, Lydia. 2011. "'—*wie ihn uns Meister Dürer gemalt*!' Contest, Myth, and Prophecy in Wagner's *Die Meistersinger von Nürnberg*." *Journal of the American Musicological Society* 64/1: 51–118.

——. 2009. "From Opera to Music Drama. Nominal Loss, Titular Gain." In *Richard Wagner and His World*, edited by Thomas S. Grey, 65–86. Princeton, NJ: Princeton University Press.

——. 2008. *Elective Affinities: Musical Essays on the History of Aesthetic Theory*. New York: Columbia University Press.

——. [1992] 2007. *The Imaginary Museum of Musical Works: An Essay in the Philosophy of Music*. New York: Oxford University Press.

Greenberg, Clement. [1940] 1986. "Towards a Newer Laocoön." In *Clement Greenberg: The Collected Essays and Criticism*, edited by John O'Brian, I: 23–37. Chicago: University of Chicago Press.

Gregor-Dellin, Martin. 1982. *Richard Wagner: Sein Leben—sein Werk—sein Jahrhundert. Dritter Teil: 1864–1882*. Munich: Piper.

Groos, Arthur, and Roger Parker, eds. 1988. *Reading Opera*. Princeton, NJ: Princeton University Press.

Guccini, Gerardo. 2002. "Directing Opera." In Bianconi and Pestelli, 125–176.

Hammond, Frederick. 1994. *Music and Spectacle in Baroque Rome: Barberini Patronage under Urban VIII*. New Haven: Yale University Press.

——. 1985. "More on Music in Casa Barberini." *Studi Musicali* 14: 235–261.

Hanning, Barbara Russano. 1979. "Glorious Apollo: Poetic and Political Themes in the First Opera." *Renaissance Quarterly* 32/4: 485–513.

———. 1973. "Apologia pro Ottavio Rinuccini." *Journal of the American Musicological Society* 26/2: 240–262.

Heartz, Daniel. 1967–1968. "From Garrick to Gluck: The Reform of Theatre and Opera in the Mid-Eighteenth Century." *Proceedings of the Royal Musical Association* 94: 111–127.

Heller, Wendy. 2007. "Venice's Mythic Empires: Truth and Verisimilitude in Venetian Opera." In Johnson et al. 2007, 35–52.

Hénaff, Marcel. 1996. "The Stage of Power." *SubStance* 25/2: 7–29.

Herder, Johann Gottfried von. [1802] 1809. "Tanz. Melodrama." In *Sämtliche Werke*, vol. 12: *Zur Schönen Literatur und Kunst*. 174–185. Tübingen: Cotta.

———. [1785] 2006. "Does Painting or Music Have a Greater Effect? A Divine Colloquy." In *Selected Writings on Aesthetics*, translated by Gregory Moore, 347–356. Princeton, NJ: Princeton University Press.

Herwitz, Daniel. 2006. "Kierkegaard Writes His Opera." In *The Don Giovanni Moment: Essays on the Legacy of an Opera*, edited by Lydia Goehr and Daniel Herwitz, 119–136. New York: Columbia University Press.

Hoffmann, E. T. A. 1989. *E. T. A. Hoffmann's Musical Writings: Kreisleriana, The Poet and the Composer, Music Criticism*, edited by David Charlton and translated by Martyn Clarke. Cambridge: Cambridge University Press.

Huebner, Steven. 1999. *French Opera at the Fin de Siècle: Wagnerism, Nationalism, and Style*. New York: Oxford University Press.

Hunter, Mary K., and James Webster, eds. 1997. *Opera Buffa in Mozart's Vienna*. Cambridge: Cambridge University Press.

Jahn, Bernhard. 2005. *Die Sinne und die Oper: Sinnlichkeit und das Problem ihrer Versprachlichung im Musiktheater des nord- und mitteldeutschen Raumes (1680–1740)*. Tübingen: Niemeyer.

Johnson, Victoria, Jane F. Fulcher, and Thomas Ertman, eds. 2007. *Opera and Society in Italy and France from Monteverdi to Bourdieu*. Cambridge: Cambridge University Press.

Katz, Ruth. 1986. *Divining the Powers of Music: Aesthetic Theory and the Origins of Opera*. New York: Pendragon.

Kerman, Joseph. [1956] 1988. *Opera as Drama*. Rev. ed. Berkeley and Los Angeles: University of California Press.

Kierkegaard, Søren. 1988. *Either/Or*. Part 1. In *Kierkegaard's Writings*. Vol. 3, edited and translated by Howard V. Hong and Edna H. Hong. Princeton, NJ: Princeton University Press.

Kirby, F. E. 1962. "Herder and Opera." *Journal of the American Musicological Society* 15/3: 316–329.

Kirkendale, Warren. 2003. "The Myth of the 'Birth of Opera' in the Florentine Camerata Debunked by Emilio de' Cavalieri: A Commemorative Lecture." *Opera Quarterly* 19/4: 631–643.

Kivy, Peter. 2009. *Antithetical Arts: On the Ancient Quarrel Between Literature and Music*. Oxford: Clarendon Press.

———. 1988. *Osmin's Rage: Philosophical Reflections on Opera, Drama, and Text*. Princeton, NJ: Princeton University Press.

Klein, Robert, and Henri Zerner, eds. 1966. *Italian Art 1500–1600: Sources and Documents*. Englewood Cliffs, NJ: Prentice-Hall.

Kristeller, Paul Oscar. 1951 and 1952. "The Modern System of the Arts: A Study in the History of Aesthetics." *Journal of the History of Ideas* 12/4: 496–527 and 13/1: 17–46.

Lee, Rensselaer W. 1967. *Ut Pictura Poesis: The Humanistic Theory of Painting*. New York: W. W. Norton.

Leichtentritt, Hugo. 1915. "The Renaissance Attitude Towards Music." *Musical Quarterly* 1/4: 604–622.

Leppert, Richard. 2011. "Music, Violence, and the Stakes of Listening." In *The Oxford Handbook of the New Cultural History of Music*, edited by Jane Fulcher, 39–67. New York: Oxford University Press.

Lessing, Gotthold Ephraim. [1776] 1984. *Laocoön: An Essay on the Limits of Painting and Poetry*, translated by Edward Allen McCormick. Baltimore: Johns Hopkins University Press.

Levin, David J., ed. 1994. *Opera through Other Eyes*. Stanford, CA: Stanford University Press.

Lichtenstein, Jacqueline. 1996. "The Representation of Power and the Power of Representation." *SubStance* 25/2: 81–92.

Liébert, Georges. 2004. *Nietzsche and Music*. Chicago: University of Chicago Press

Lindenberger, Herbert. 1998. *Opera in History from Monteverdi to Cage*. Stanford, CA: Stanford University Press.

Locke, Ralph P. 1993. "Reflections on Orientalism in Opera and Musical Theater." *Opera Quarterly* 10/1: 48–64.

Lungstrum, Janet, and Elizabeth Sauer, eds. 1997. *Agonistics: Arenas of Creative Contest*. Albany: State University of New York Press.

McClary, Susan. 1991. *Feminine Endings: Music, Gender, and Sexuality*. Minneapolis: University of Minnesota Press.

McGeary, Thomas. 1998. "Thomas Clayton and the Introduction of Italian Opera to England." *Philological Quarterly* 77/2: 171–186.

Miersch, Martin. 2008. "Zum Wettstreit der Künste in einer Barockoper." In *Gedächtnisparagone—Intermediale Konstellationen*, edited by Sabine Heiser and Christiane Holm, 169–190. Göttingen: Vandenhoeck & Ruprecht.

Maniates, Maria Rika. 2000. "Marsyas Agonistes." *Current Musicology* 69: 118–162.

Molière. 2008. *Don Juan: and Other Plays*, edited by Ian Maclean. New York: Oxford University Press.

Murray, Penelope, and Peter Wilson, eds. 2004. *Music and the Muses. The Culture of 'Mousikê' in the Classical Athenian City*. New York: Oxford University Press.

Olson, Todd P. 2004. "'Long Live the Knife': Andrea Sacchi's Portrait of Marc Antonio Pasqualini." *Art History* 27/5: 697–722.

Ossi, Massimo M. 2003. *Divining the Oracle: Monteverdi's Seconda Prattica*. Chicago: Chicago University Press.

Pirrotta, Nino. 1982. *Music and Theatre from Poliziano to Monteverdi*, translated by Elena Povoledo. Cambridge: Cambridge University Press.

——. 1966. "Music and Cultural Tendencies in 15th-Century Italy." *Journal of the American Musicological Society* 19/2: 127–161.

Plett, Heinrich F. 2004. *Rhetoric and Renaissance Culture*. Berlin: De Gruyter.

Radice, Mark A., ed. 1998. *Opera in Context: Essays on Historical Staging from the Late Renaissance to the Time of Puccini*. Portland, OR: Amadeus.

Robinson, Paul. 1994. "The Opera Queen: A Voice from the Closet." *Cambridge Opera Journal* 6/3: 283–291.

——. 1985. *Opera and Ideas: From Mozart to Strauss*. New York: Harper & Row.

Rolland, Romaine. 1908. *Musiciens d'autrefois*. Paris: Hachette.
Rosand, Ellen. 1991. *Opera in Seventeenth-Century Venice: The Creation of a Genre*. Berkeley and Los Angeles: University of California Press.
Rouget, Gilbert. 1985. *Music and Trance: A Theory of the Relations between Music and Possession*, translated by Brunhilde Biebuyck. Chicago: University of Chicago Press.
Rousseau, Jean-Jacques. 1825. *Œuvres completes. Écrits sur la musique*, edited by P. R. Argus. Paris: Dalibon.
Saslow, James M. 1996. *The Medici Wedding of 1589: Florentine Festival as Theatrum Mundi*. New Haven: Yale University Press.
Savage, Roger, and Matteo Sansone. 1989. "*Il Corago* and the Staging of Early Opera: Four Chapters from an Anonymous Treatise circa 1630." *Early Music* 17/4: 495–511.
Segrave, Jeffrey O. 2005. "Pietro Metastasio's L'Olimpiade and the Survival of the Olympic Idea in 18th Century Europe." *Olympika: The International Journal of Olympic Studies* 14: 1–28.
Sempé, Skip. 2007. *La Pellegrina. Intermedi 1589*. CD booklet, 23–25. Paradizo PA0004.
Senici, Emanuele, ed. 2004. *The Cambridge Companion to Rossini*. Cambridge: Cambridge University Press.
Solerti, Angelo. 1903. *Le origini del melodramma: Testimonianze dei contemporanei*. Turin: Fratelli Bocca.
Sollich, Robert, Clemens Risi, Sebastian Reus, and Stephan Jöris, eds. 2008. *Angst vor der Zerstörung: der Meister Künste zwischen Archiv und Erneuerung*. Berlin: Theater der Zeit.
Spitzer, John, and Neal Zaslaw. 2004. *The Birth of the Orchestra: History of an Institution: 1650–1815*. New York: Oxford University Press.
Stein, Louise K. 2006. "'*La música de dos orbes*': A Context for the First Opera of the Americas." *Opera Quarterly* 22/3–4: 433–458.
Sternfeld, Frederick W. 1993. *The Birth of Opera*. Oxford: Clarendon Press.
——. 1978. "The First Printed Opera Libretto." *Music & Letters* 59/2: 121–138.
Stevens, Denis, ed. and trans.1980. *The Letters of Claudio Monteverdi*. Oxford: Clarendon Press.
Strohm, Reinhard. 2005. *The Rise of European Music 1380–1500*. Cambridge: Cambridge University Press.
——. 1997. *Dramma per musica: Italian Opera Seria of the Eighteenth Century*. New Haven: Yale University Press.
Strong, Tracy B. 1996. "Theatricality, Public Space, and Music in Rousseau." *SubStance* 25/2: 110–127.
Strunk, W. Oliver. 1998. *Source Readings in Music History*. Rev. ed., edited by Leo Treitler. New York: W. W. Norton.
Tambling, Jeremy. 1996. *Opera and the Culture of Fascism*. Oxford: Clarendon Press.
Tomlinson, Gary. 2007. "Pastoral and Musical Magic in the Birth of Opera." In *Music and Historical Critique: Selected Essays*, 81–94. London: Ashgate Press.
——. 1999. *Metaphysical Song: An Essay on Opera*. Princeton, NJ: Princeton University Press.
——. 1987. *Monteverdi and the End of the Renaissance*. Berkeley and Los Angeles: University of California Press.
Treadwell, Nina. 2009. *Music and Wonder at the Medici Court: The 1589 Interludes for La Pellegrina*. Bloomington: Indiana University Press.
Treitler, Leo. 1990. *Music and the Historical Imagination*. Cambridge, MA: Harvard University Press.
Vergo, Peter. 2005. *That Divine Order: Music and the Visual Arts from Antiquity to the Eighteenth Century*. New York: Phaidon.

Wagner, Richard. 1983. *Dichtungen und Schriften*. 10 vols. Frankfurt: Insel.
Walker, D. P. 1976. "Joan Albert Ban and Mersenne's Musical Competition of 1640." *Music & Letters* 57/3: 233–255.
Warburg, Aby. 1999. *The Renewal of Pagan Antiquity: Contributions to the Cultural History of the European Renaissance*. Los Angeles: Getty Research Institute.
Weiss, Piero, ed. 2002. *Opera: A History in Documents*. New York: Oxford University Press.
Williams, Bernard. 2006. *On Opera*. New Haven: Yale University Press.
Winternitz, Emanuel. 1979. *Musical Instruments and Their Symbolism in Western Art*. New Haven: Yale University Press.
——. 1970. "The Role of Music in Leonardo's *Paragone*." In *Phenomenology and Social Reality: Essays in Memory of Alfred Schutz*, edited by Maurice Alexander Natanson, 270–296. The Hague: Nijhoff.
Wygant, Amy. 1995. "Boileau and the Sound of Satire." *Forum for Modern Language Studies* 31/2: 128–139.
Wyss, Edith. 1996. *The Myth of Apollo and Marsyas in the Art of the Italian Renaissance: An Inquiry into the Meaning of Images*. Newark, NJ: University of Delaware Press.
Žižek, Slavoj, and Mladen Dolar. 2002. *Opera's Second Death*. New York: Routledge.

PART II

WORDS, MUSIC, AND MEANING

The Libretto and the Score

CHAPTER 6

OFT-TOLD TALES

VINCENT GIROUD

Very few operas are set on an entirely original theme; as subjects go, to paraphrase Lorenzo Bianconi, opera "borrows for a living" (Bianconi 1987: 21). But within this general framework, a large part of the operatic tradition furthermore consists in resetting a theme treated in previous operas. This phenomenon can be observed throughout operatic history, from the origins to the present time, and affects all types of subjects: mythological, historical (or pseudo-historical), and those based on works of literature. It can take multiple configurations. At one extreme, the common reference is so tenuous that it is impossible to speak in terms of derivation: thus, save for the latent Masonic symbolism that *Zoroastre* and *Die Zauberflöte* have in common, Mozart's Sarastro and Rameau's Zoroaster are unrelated; nor is Massenet's Zarâstra (*Le mage*, 1891) indebted to either. In fact, the three libretti can virtually be described as original. At the opposite extreme, as in Lully's and Gluck's *Armide*, the text set to music is practically identical, or, as in the three operas based on Witold Gombrowicz's play *Yvonne, Princess of Burgundy* (respectively, by Boris Blacher [1973], Ulrich Wagner [1998], and Philippe Boesmans [2009]), it closely follows the same literary source. In between are all kinds of possibilities, depending on the relationship of the text (set to music) to its source (or sources), the various mediations that may intervene, and the musical and dramatic aesthetics involved.

Fabula versus Plot

When looking at operatic treatments of the same theme, it is useful to bear in mind the distinction made by Russian formalists between *fabula*, that is, the contents of the story reported in the source(s), and plot, the dramatic realization achieved in a specific libretto (Dahlhaus 2003: 77). This distinction, which goes back to Aristotelian poetics, is particularly pertinent in operas derived from ancient subjects, but it applies to more recent ones as well, for example, the many operas based on Ariosto and Tasso, or the eight or so versions of the Manon Lescaut "myth," each constituting a different "take" on the story invented by the Abbé Prévost. Modern sensibilities, trained, on the one hand, to privilege originality over imitation, on the other hand tend to rate adaptations according to their fidelity to their source. Our natural expectation is that the plot should respect and reflect the *fabula* as much as possible. One such ideal would be Carl Orff's *Antigonae* (1949), which is set directly on the Sophocles text, through the sole mediation of Hölderlin's German rendering. Previous ages tended to have the opposite attitude, prizing above all the original way in which the story was treated—the novel telling of an old tale. Whereas we admire Badoaro's libretto for Monteverdi's *Il ritorno d'Ulisse* (1640) for following faithfully the scheme of events narrated in the *Odyssey*, their contemporaries found it "lacking in invention" (Rosand 1991: 60). When he revisited the Ulysses story for Sacrati's *L'Ulisse errante* in 1644, Badoaro took, this time, considerable liberties with Homer. The earliest libretti based on Antigone—Pasqualigo for Orlandini (1718), Roccaforte for Galuppi (1751), and others—had nothing to do with Sophocles, instead loosely following other ancient sources, such as Euripides' lost play and Hyginus's *Fabulae* (see McClymonds 1992).

The *fabulae* that have inspired operatic treatments tend indeed to come from a great variety of sources and are seldom, if ever, unmediated. While the Florentine inventors of opera at the end of the sixteenth century, men of "humanist and classicist pretensions" (Bianconi 1987: 165), carefully presented and justified their invention, not as something radically new (which in truth it was) but as an imitation of Greek tragedy, none of the themes they selected—Adonis, Ariadne, Aurora and Cephalus, Daphne, Flora, Narcissus, Orpheus—was derived from the surviving corpus of Greek tragedies but came from non-theatrical Roman sources, especially Ovid (Ketterer 2003: 3ff.). When, in the last decades of the seventeenth century, Greek and Roman tragedy, in turn, began to attract opera librettists and composers, it was through the mediation of French classicism and its reinterpretation of Aristotle and Horace. Even when Shakespeare became a new source of inspiration at the end of the eighteenth century, it was through adaptations that often departed significantly from the early published sources. Steibelt's *Roméo et Juliette* (1793) is based on Ducis's edulcorated 1772 French version, in which Juliet wakes up before Romeo dies—a convention still in force when Gounod treated the subject in 1867. Felice Romani's libretto for Vaccai's *Romeo e Giulietta* (1825) and Bellini's *I Capuleti e i Montecchi* (1830) is derived, via Luigi Scevola's 1818 tragedy, not from Shakespeare but (like earlier theatrical operatic treatments of the story) from Renaissance sources, some of which, mediated through English adaptations, were used by Shakespeare. Shakespeare's play itself thus constitutes not so much a *fabula* as a plot derived from an earlier *fabula* preserved in a variety of sources, even though its subsequent preeminence gave it the status of a *fabula* from which a number of operatic plots were derived.

Intertextual Networks

The history of operatic settings of a similar theme is thus a dense intertextual network in which genetic reconstruction can be conjectural at best. This is especially the case in

Italian libretti of the pre-Metastasian and Metastasian tradition, in which, beginning in the 1690s, most operas were resettings of a preexisting libretto. The initial libretto—for example, Zeno's *Lucio Vero*, first set by Pollarolo in 1700 and reset around thirty times, or Metastasio's *Artaserse*, his most popular libretto, first set by Vinci in 1730 and reset more than eighty times—thus became an archetype, susceptible to revision by additions, insertions, cuts, retitling, or structural recasting (for example, from three to two acts, as in Mozart's *La clemenza di Tito*). Most of the resulting libretti—including some set by composers of the caliber of Handel, Vivaldi, and Gluck—thus present a complex pattern of "polygenetic filiation" (Strohm 2009: 93) that defies reconstitution, in which three different kinds of sources come into play: the "proximate source," which is the archetype by Zeno, Metastasio, or Pariati that is being reset; "intermediate sources," which can range from earlier operatic treatments of the same subject to other, unrelated sources, operatic or not; and "ultimate sources," in other words, the initial *fabula* or *fabulae* (usually mythological or pseudo-historical) from which the libretto and its archetype ultimately derive (Strohm 2009: 97). The archetype itself, rather than an adaptation of an earlier model, was usually an original work assembled from a variety of earlier sources transposed to fit the subject. Thus, as François Lévy has recently shown, Metastasio's *Demetrio*, first set by Caldara in 1731, ostensibly based on the life of the second-century B.C.E. Seleucid King Demetrios II as reported by various "ultimate" ancient sources, actually combines the plots of Corneille's *Don Sanche d'Aragon* and Quinault's *Astrate, roi de Tyr* (its "proximate sources"), enriching them with situations borrowed from Zeno and Pariati's *Astarto* and one from Racine's *Bérénice* ("intermediate sources"; see Lévy 2009: 218–238).

Even before the eighteenth century, the practice of libretto resetting played a part in the dissemination of opera beyond Italian borders: Cesti's highly popular *L'Orontea* (Innsbruck, 1656) has been shown to be a resetting of a libretto by Cicognini previously set by Lucio in 1649. At Hamburg in the 1680s, N. A. Strunck reused, in German translation, Quinault's *Alceste* and *Thésée* and, in 1693, set a German adaptation of Aureli's *L'Antigona delusa da Alceste*, originally set by Ziani in 1660. Equally remarkable is that the practice continued well into the nineteenth century, despite the higher premium placed by that time on originality. As late as 1828, Mercadante reset a version of Metastasio's *Adriano in Siria* (first set by Caldara in 1732); *Artaserse* and *Ipermestra* had an even longer afterlife—until 1840—and *Demetrio* the longest.

Instances of resetting a libretto are far fewer in French opera, and, with one important exception, were for export purposes, as in the case of Gluck resetting texts by Anseaume, Favart, Lemonnier, and Dancourt when in charge of the French opera theater in Vienna—or that of Boieldieu reusing Vial and Favières's libretto to Berton's *Aline, reine de Golconde* at St. Petersburg in 1804. The exception is Quinault, Lully's principal librettist, who, for all the criticism he suffered in his lifetime, eventually came to be considered an unsurpassable model. Resetting his libretti seemed therefore a logical outcome, even though Mondonville, when he first attempted to reset *Thésée* in 1765, was ridiculed for his presumption. It was certainly natural for Gluck, when he took his "reform" to France—first with a subject not hitherto treated

(*Iphigénie en Aulide*), then by returning to one of the earliest themes in opera (*Orphée et Eurydice*)—to measure himself successfully against Quinault and Lully's precedent by presenting his French version of *Alceste* in 1776. Gluck confronted Lully even more directly in 1777 by resetting Quinault's *Armide*, which was the Florentine composer's most admired work. Resetting Quinault had also become a tool in the rivalry set up by the Italianate camp between Gluck and Piccinni: Vismes, the Opéra director, initially tried to get them to reset Quinault's *Roland* (Piccinni's first contribution to the Opéra in early 1778). But whereas Gluck, save for the elimination of the prologue, had set Quinault's *Armide* text with few alterations, Piccinni's *Roland* libretto was adapted *au goût du jour* by Marmontel, who performed the same service for *Atys* in 1780. Vismes eventually succeeded in getting the two composers to compete by offering Piccinni an *Iphigénie en Tauride* to be set on a different libretto from the one Gluck was already working on.

While libretto resettings proper became less common in the nineteenth century, libretto transpositions, especially, remained a frequent form of theme resetting during the Romantic period. Donizetti's *Alina, regina di Golconda* (1828) is an adaptation of the 1766 Sedaine libretto for Monsigny (rather than the one set by Berton and Boieldieu); *Gianni di Parigi* (1830) is based on Saint-Just's libretto for Boieldieu's *Jean de Paris* (1812); *Betly* (1836) derives from Goethe's *Jery und Bätely*—itself a frequently reset *Singspiel*—by way of the libretto by Scribe and Mélesville for Adam's *Le châlet* (see Pendle 1974). *L'elisir d'amore* is a direct adaptation of Scribe's libretto for Auber's *Le philtre*, the main difference between the two versions being, as Mark Everist has shown, that Romani makes more room for duets and ensembles, whereas the Frenchman favors arias (see Everist 2009). The greatest of such transpositions is arguably Verdi's *Un ballo in maschera*, which, despite the change of locale eventually forced by the Roman censors on Verdi and his librettist Somma, is closely modeled on Scribe and Auber's *Gustave III*.

Endings

Whether reset, transposed, or originals derived from a common *fabula*, opera libretti on similar topics have had to deal with the long-established preference of audiences, well into the nineteenth century, for a happy ending. This was the case from the origin. As treated by Rinuccini for Peri's *Euridice* (1600), the story of Orpheus, the first oft-told tale of operatic history, departed from Ovid and other ancient sources in one significant aspect: instead of losing Eurydice a second time after bringing her back from the land of the dead, Orpheus was reunited with her and the couple supposedly lived happily ever after. This distortion of the ancient legend, to be sure, was in keeping with the circumstances of the opera's creation: since the work was intended to honor the wedding of Maria de' Medici to Henri IV of France, it made sense to present it as an allegory of marriage (rather than widowhood and death). A few years later, the first printing of

Striggio's libretto for Monteverdi's *L'Orfeo* (1607) had an implicitly tragic ending, with the Maenads invading the scene, singing and dancing—with the obvious implication that they were about to tear Orpheus to pieces; yet, on the evidence of the 1609 published score, Monteverdi reset the ending, cutting the Maenads' entrance and ending the opera with the apotheosis of the poet and his wife (Sternfeld 1993: 25–28). To be sure, Orpheus *does* get killed by the Maenads in the penultimate act of Landi's *La morte d'Orfeo*, published in 1619 (and possibly set to Landi's own libretto), but Act V ends with a similar apotheosis.

This overwhelming general preference for a *lieto* (rather than *funesto*) *fine*, even in plots based on a famously tragic *fabula*, continued into the end of the eighteenth century—as evidenced by the ending of Gluck's own treatment of the Orpheus legend. When he wrote *Didone* (1641) for Cavalli, Busenello did not hesitate to depart radically from Virgil, ending it not with the heroine's suicide, but with her marriage to Iarba, king of Getulia. The reluctance of operatic audiences, even when presented with a theme presumably familiar to most of their members, to accept a tragic denouement is further evidenced by the poor reception given in 1728 to Metastasio's first version (set by Vinci) of *Catone in Utica*: Romans (of all people) objected to the opera ending with Cato's suicide, and the poet, who had ended *Didone abbandonata* (1724) with the heroine's suicide, obliged: In the libretto reset by Leo in 1729, Cato's death was reported, rather than taking place on stage; when Vivaldi set *Catone* in 1737, the suicide had disappeared altogether (Ketterer 2009: 124–127). Operatic decorum thus frequently trumped fidelity to the source, even when the subject matter was drawn from a famous work of literature or, indeed, a historical source. A late evidence of the same trend is provided by Barbier and Carré fitting Ambroise Thomas's *Hamlet* (1868) with a happy denouement (though the original ending was retained in the alternative version prepared for the British premiere).

Tragic endings, however, gradually gained acceptance, especially in France, where it was understood that some degree of verisimilitude was to be expected, even when treating mythological subjects involving *merveilleux*: there was no question of making Juno "docile" or Medea "modest" (Kintzler 1991: 172–178). This stricter adherence to the spirit—if seldom to the letter—of the ancient myths may explain why Greek tragedy was adopted sooner in the French operatic tradition. In Cicognini's libretto to Cavalli's immensely popular *Giasone* (1649), Medea, save for her magic powers, has little to do with the character portrayed by Euripides and Seneca: she is thrown into the sea by Jason's attendant and the work ends with Jason's marriage to Hypsipile. As for Giovanni Faustini's *Medea placata*, it was rejected as "unpleasant" when his brother Marco tried to produce it posthumously in 1662 (Rosand 1991: 191). On the other hand, while taking liberties with the classical sources, both Charpentier's *Médée* (1693), on a libretto by Thomas Corneille, and Salomon's *Médée et Jason* (1713), on a libretto by the Abbé Pellegrin, respect its basic outline and do not extenuate the ending. By the time François-Benoît Hoffmann (for Cherubini, 1791), and Felice Romani (for Mayr, 1813) set the theme, there was no question of not following Euripides, Seneca, and Corneille (see Ewans 2007: 55–79).

Parody and Modern Transpositions

Two specific forms of intertextual relationship in operatic theme setting need specific attention: parody and modern transpositions.

Parody, in the sense of retelling a well-known theme in burlesque terms, is a long and distinguished tradition in operatic history, particularly in France, where the mock-heroic was an accepted, codified part of classical literary theory (see Genette 1997: 19–24). The earliest forms of *opéra comique* were satirical imitations of *tragédie en musique* presented at the fair theaters: thus Lesage and Gillier's *Arlequin Thétis* (1713) is a spoof on Collasse's *Thétis et Pélée* (1689), which had recently been revived at the Opéra, and their *Télémaque* (1715) a parody of Destouches's opera of the same title. That Pellegrin, the librettist of Destouche's *Télémaque* (1714), himself wrote the text of similar parodies for the fair theaters clearly indicates how the two worlds were interconnected. For a parody to be effective, it is, obviously, necessary that what is being parodied should be clearly recognizable, and this was evidently the case for fair theater audiences. By the same token, audiences attending performances of Hervé's *L'œil crevé* (1867) or *Le petit Faust* (1869) were supposed to be familiar with Rossini's *Guillaume Tell* and Gounod's *Faust* (which entered the Opéra repertory in that same year): the Rossini and Gounod operas, as it were, became the *fabulae* from which the burlesque plots were derived. The same observation applies to Offenbach's *Orphée aux enfers* which, ostensibly a parody of Gluck's *Orphée* (as made manifest by the short musical quotation heard in Act II), can be described, by extrapolation, as potentially parodying all Orpheus operas. That is even more the case with more recent examples, like Ibert's *Persée et Andromède* (1929) or Milhaud's mythological *opéras-minute* (1927–1928), which do not parody any specific work, but rather the respective *fabulae* from which the subjects parodied are issued.

Retelling an ancient or familiar theme by giving it a modern setting is a peculiar twentieth-century phenomenon. It may be related to the tendency, in philosophy and psychoanalysis, to reinterpret ancient and modern myths (including Shakespeare) in the light of modern scientific discoveries. It may also be tied to the rise of *Literaturoper*—in other words, the setting of the very text of a literary work, with practically no changes except for cuts—a phenomenon that tends to produce one-of-a-kind operas (who would reset *Pelléas*, *L'heure espagnole*, or *Dialogues des carmélites*?) but may also be found in oft-treated subjects, as with Orff's *Antigonae*. Modern transpositions are usually devoid of any satirical or playful intent and thus differ from parody or pastiche (see Genette 1997: 24–30), but like them they presuppose previous knowledge of the "hypotext" they derive from. To be sure, Milhaud's *Les malheurs d'Orphée* (1926) provides its own "keys," beginning with its title, because the Provençal peasant of Armand Lunel's libretto and his gypsy girlfriend are named Orphée and Eurydice. The same is true of Henze's *Boulevard Solitude* (1952), in which the characters, as in Walter Jockisch's scenario on which Grete Weil based her libretto, are called Manon Lescaut and Des Grieux, as in the Abbé Prévost novel, the story of which it retells in the context of post–World War

II Paris. The fact that Des Grieux, unnamed in Prévost's novella, is christened Armand opens a new intertextual vista by linking the story to that of *La dame aux camélias*, the source for Verdi's *La traviata* and itself a modern retelling of the Manon Lescaut story, in which Dumas brings up Prévost's novel at two crucial moments.

The Ariadne Myth

Most of the above observations can be verified if one looks at the various treatments of the Ariadne myth in operatic history: a Greek myth mediated by Roman sources, variously embellished according to French or Italian taste; later the subject of an archetype libretto frequently reset; revisited at the dawn of the Romantic age; rediscovered in novel ways in the twentieth century; modernized, parodied, transposed via modern mediations; and eventually the subject of a rare literal resetting.

Originally a goddess of nature in Minoan mythology—her name means "very holy"—Ariadne emerged early in Greek mythology, appearing in the context of three related episodes: her involvement with Theseus's slaying of the Minotaur; her subsequent abandonment; and her association with Dionysus and his cult. In operatic history, only Massenet has attempted to cover them all. Daughter of Minos, king of Crete, and Pasiphae, Ariadne is half-sister of the Minotaur, the monster born of her mother's affair with a bull (one of the earliest myths of bestiality). To avenge his son Androgeus, killed by the Athenians, Minos has been exacting from them, every ninth year, a tribute of seven young men and seven young women, to be devoured by the Minotaur (or, according to some authors, imprisoned). Theseus, son of Aegeus, king of Athens, volunteers to join the group. Ariadne falls in love with him and supplies the thread that allows him to escape from the Labyrinth after slaying the Minotaur. This episode is the most frequently treated in opera. Ariadne's subsequent abandonment was the moment favored by ancient authors: though no Greek or Roman tragedy on the subject has come to us, it was treated by Catullus and Ovid, among others. It is the basis of Monteverdi's lost opera (*L'Arianna*) and several seventeenth- and eighteenth-century treatments, before being revisited by Massenet, Strauss, and Milhaud.

Theseus's motivations in the abandonment were diversely interpreted by the ancients: some ascribed it to choice, others to accident, others to divine command—especially in accounts where Ariadne was *already* married to Dionysus, as suggested by the one reference to her in the *Odyssey*, which says that Artemis killed her in reprisal. In most versions, Theseus, notwithstanding his status as the national hero of Athens, is an unsympathetic, Jason-like figure, whereas Ariadne stands out as the woman betrayed, like Medea but without her magical powers and cruelty, and thus closer to Dido. One of the more human pictures of women passed to us from Antiquity, she might have been seen, by ancient standards, in a negative light, having betrayed her family to follow a stranger. But neither Catullus nor Ovid conveys such strictures, and their accounts strongly suggest a deeply sympathetic character.

While Theseus subsequently married Ariadne's sister, neither Euripides nor Seneca, in their tragedies on the Phaedra-Hippolytus episode, suggests that Phaedra caused her sister's abandonment. Only in modern times, beginning with Boccaccio's *Filocolo* (ca. 1336), was it assumed that Theseus had brought the two sisters with him from Crete and left one for the other. This love triangle recurs in several operatic treatments, from Conradi to Massenet. As for Ariadne's reaction to her lover's behavior, some authors, both ancient and modern, hint at a suicide, or at least suggest that she let herself die. In most accounts, however, Ariadne survives. Some early sources have her marry a priest of Dionysos, but in most sources it is Dionysos who rescues Ariadne from her grief and marries her, a union that produces several children. The apotheosis of the now semi-divine Ariadne is manifested, according to a legend reported in Ovid's *Metamorphoses*, when her wedding crown—a gift from Venus—becomes the nine-star constellation called Libera or, more commonly, Corona Borealis.

The Earliest Operatic Ariadnes

Like *L'Orfeo*, Monteverdi's *L'Arianna*, his second opera, was written for the Gonzaga court in Mantua. It was planned for the celebrations of the wedding of the Duke's eldest son and Margherita of Savoy in May 1608—a highly politicized alliance between two of northern Italy's powerful families. Referred to in the preparatory stages as a "pastoral" (but called *tragedia* in the published libretto), *L'Arianna* is in eight scenes. After a prologue in which Apollo greets the ducal bride, Venus introduces the story in the form of a dialogue with Cupid. The opera proper begins with Theseus and Ariadne being greeted by joyous Naxos fishermen. While Ariadne is asleep, Theseus's unnamed "counselor" persuades him—essentially for political reasons—to sail to Athens alone. After a chorus announcing dawn, a nervous Ariadne re-enters, accompanied by her confidante Dorilla. While the two of them go to the seashore, a messenger reports the departure of Theseus's ships and Ariadne's suicide attempt. Ariadne then sings her "Lamento," punctuated by choral interventions and Dorilla's comments. Ariadne leaves the stage again on hearing the hopeful announcement that ships (at first assumed to be the remorseful Theseus's) are approaching. She reappears in Bacchus's company—the chorus greets them as the "royal couple," an obvious reference to the Mantuan wedding—and sings of the happiness of love. Finally, Bacchus announces that Ariadne's golden hair will become a constellation.

While this happy ending suggests that *L'Arianna* was presented as an allegory of marriage, we know from the account of the 1608 festivities published in the same year that it was the "Lamento" that was found most affecting. This initial popularity explains why it has come to us in several versions, none of which includes the interventions from the chorus and Dorilla. *L'Arianna* was revived in the 1640 Carnival in Venice, but no copy of the entire score has surfaced.

The music of the first French *Ariadne* is not extant either. Its authors, the poet Pierre Perrin (ca. 1620–1675) and composer Robert Cambert (ca. 1628–1677), collaborated in what can be considered the first full-fledged French opera, *Pomone* (1669). Their *Ariane, ou Le mariage de Bacchus* was projected in 1659 and, like Monteverdi's work, was intended for a wedding—that of Louis XIV and the Spanish infanta, planned for the following year. *Ariane* was publicly rehearsed in Paris but never premiered there. It eventually reached the stage in London in 1674—the first opera performed in England and first French opera to be performed outside France (and in French). It was evidently presented at Nantes in 1687, after which the music disappeared.

A comparison between Rinuccini's libretto and Perrin's (in the revised form in which it has survived) illustrates the aesthetic contrast between the worlds of the late Italian Renaissance and the French Baroque. The allegorical prologue is a dialogue between four rivers—the Thames, the Seine, the Tiber, and the Po—with topical allusions to the marriage of James, Duke of York, to Mary of Modena. Act I, set in Bacchus's palace on Naxos, shows the god being celebrated for his victories in India. Venus begs him to turn his attention to love, Silenus to wine, and Mars and Bellone to military glory. In Act II, on the seashore, Bacchus witnesses Ariadne lamenting her abandonment, and Bacchants, Furies, dragons, and sea monsters dance an elaborate intermezzo. In Act III, set in a "desert," Bacchus tries to win Ariadne's heart, to Venus's delight and the consternation of Mars, Bellone, and Silenus. In Act IV, a magic sash presented by Venus and the Graces triggers Ariadne's change of heart. Act V is devoted to Ariadne's wedding and apotheosis. Anticipating *Ariadne auf Naxos*, Perrin's libretto unabashedly mixes comical and serious elements.

The third Ariadne opera—the earliest for which the entire music has survived—is Johann Georg Conradi's *Die schöne und getreue Ariadne* (*The beautiful and faithful Ariadne*). Set to a text by Christian Heinrich Postel (1658–1705), leading German librettist of the period, it was staged in 1691 at the Theater am Gänsemarkt at Hamburg, where Conradi was music director. Recently identified by George Buelow (1972) based on a manuscript in the Library of Congress, it is the only one of Conradi's nine operas to have been recovered. It combines French and Italian influences with more specific German features. Most of the action takes place on Crete and revolves on Ariadne's unrequited love for Theseus, who loves Phaedra and courts Ariadne solely to enlist her assistance in defeating the Minotaur. An unusual feature of Postel's libretto is the presence not just of Minos, who appears in several later versions, but also of Pasiphae, torn between her hatred toward Theseus and her desire to see the Minotaur, symbol of her shame, eliminated. Unaware of Ariadne's love for Theseus, she and Minos favor another suitor, Evanthes, who is actually Bacchus in disguise. Comical interventions are provided by Theseus's servant Pamphilius, including songs and choruses in praise of scissors-grinders. Set not on Naxos but on an unidentified island off the coast of Crete, the second part of Act III shows Theseus and Phaedra eloping while Ariadne is asleep. In a four-part scena, the heroine then expresses her grief and desire for vengeance. Evanthes, revealing himself, wins her hand, and Venus blesses their wedding. The work ends with songs and dances, while Ariadne's crown is seen in the sky.

Marin Marais's *Arianne et Bacchus*, the first opera he wrote entirely, was premiered in 1696. In the libretto by the otherwise unrecorded Saint-Jean, Naxos, a desert island in some settings, borders here on overcrowding. As in Donneau de Visé's *Le mariage de Bachus* (1672), its distant source, Ariadne is the victim of Juno's hostility toward Bacchus. In the first scene, she learns that Theseus (who never appears) has eloped with her sister. As in Thomas Corneille's *Ariane*, another source, Naxos is ruled by King Oenarus, whose sister Dircée is promised to Adraste, prince of Ithaca. Instead, Adraste falls in love with Ariadne. Meanwhile, Bacchus lands, greeted by Oenarus like visiting royalty, and he too begins to court Ariadne. Temporary hurdles include Juno taking Dircée's appearance and provoking Ariadne's jealousy by pretending that Bacchus has proposed to her—and Adraste calling on the Fury Alecto to drive Ariadne insane. Adraste is killed after rashly challenging Bacchus to a duel, and an apparition of Jupiter paves the way for the lovers' wedding and Ariadne's apotheosis. The work's musical highlight is Ariadne's sleep scene in Act III, in the tradition of similar passages in Lully's *Atys* and *Phaëton*.

Despite a cast headed by Marthe Le Rochois (Lully's first Armide), Marais's *Arianne* failed at the Opéra in 1696. Similarly, Jean-Joseph Mouret's *Ariane* only had one performance in 1717, though the music was praised. As in Pariati's contemporary version, Lagrance-Chancel and Roy's libretto takes place entirely in Crete—save for the independent prologue showing a Druidic mistletoe festival on the banks of the Seine. Theseus, incognito, has preceded the Athenian hostages and Ariadne has fallen in love with him. When Minos disembarks with the captives (here a yearly tribute), the group turns out to include Péribée, an Athenian princess once promised to Theseus. In Act II, set in Androgeus's tomb with the captives chained to its columns, Theseus reveals his identity, to Ariadne's dismay. To save him, Péribée agrees to marry Minos, but the ghost of Androgeus continues to demand vengeance. In the last act, set on the seashore before the entrance to the Labyrinth, Theseus and Ariane, reconciled, flee, leaving the betrayed Péribée to kill herself, while Minos swears revenge. The final tableau shows lightning striking down the Labyrinth and its ruins being swept away into the sea.

When Marais and Mouret wrote their *Arianes*, the popularity of the *tragédie en musique* as perfected by Lully and Quinault had declined, while *opéra-ballet* (then called simply "ballet") was on the rise. This new genre was launched in 1695 by Collasse's *Ballet des saisons*, on a libretto by the Abbé Pic, in which each season is represented by a short mythological scene associated with a particular kind of love. The Autumn act, subtitled "L'amour paisible," features Bacchus and Ariadne. After a monologue in which Ariadne wavers between *amour* and *gloire* in the manner of a Corneille heroine, she and Bacchus have a long dialogue, which results in her accepting his hand. The god of autumn joins them in a final trio while the chorus sings in praise of wine.

Mouret himself returned to the Ariadne theme in his *ballet héroïque*, *Les amours des dieux* (1727), on a libretto by Fuzelier in which her lament and Bacchus's wooing are essentially the pretext for a spectacular set change—the solitary shore becomes a pleasure grove—and celebratory songs and dances. The Ariadne story is also featured in Brassac's *L'empire de l'amour* (1733), in which it constitutes an *entrée* entitled "Les mortels." In Moncrif's libretto, which situates Ariadne's abandonment in Crete, Theseus cuts a particularly sorry figure: Courting Phaedra even in the middle of the preparations for his wedding to Ariadne, he manipulates her jealousy to convince her to elope with him. Unsuspecting until the end, Ariadne learns of his betrayal when her father bursts on stage in the middle of the prenuptial ceremony, and she faints in the arms of the priestesses of Venus.

Theseus, by contrast, projects a strongly positive image in Pariati's *Teseo in Creta*, the most frequently set operatic version of Ariadne's story. Pariati's plot is complicated by a twist found in none of the ancient sources. Ariadne, once captured by the Greeks, was brought up as the daughter of Archeus, King of Thebes, believing him to be her father, and comes to Crete with Theseus and the hostages. One of these, Carilda, is in love with Theseus, but he loves Ariadne and is loved by her. Carilda's name is drawn to be the first to be offered to the Minotaur, unless a champion fights for her. Although Theseus's friend Pirithous, who loves Carilda, offers to fight for her, Theseus insists on doing so, thereby provoking Ariadne's jealousy. More complications follow, some relating to Ariadne's secret identity (of which Theseus alone is aware), others to confusion over who loves whom, more still to Carilda's escape from the Labyrinth and to the involvement of an additional character, the Cretan general Tauride, son of Vulcan and possessor of a magic girdle without which the Athenians cannot be released and who himself has amorous designs on both Ariadne and Carilda. Twice victorious—over the Minotaur, then over Tauride—Theseus finally reveals Ariadne's identity and obtains from Minos her hand and the captives' release.

Pariati's libretto was first set in 1715 by the Florentine Francesco Conti, who held positions both as theorbist and composer at the Viennese court and whose wife Maria Landini starred as Ariadne—here a rather unsympathetic, jealous, petulant character (and therefore a natural recipient of arias in turn melancholy and furious). It was reused and adapted at least twenty-two times in the eighteenth century, beginning with Leonardo Leo's *pasticcio* (Naples, 1721) to music by Porpora, Bononcini, Leo himself, and Vivaldi, among others. In Leo's version, retitled *Arianna e Teseo*, the name of Theseus's rival and friend was changed, confusingly, from Piritoo to the more mellifluous Alceste, which it retained in all subsequent adaptations: Porpora (Venice, 1727), Feo (Turin, 1728), Leo (Rome, 1729, this time to his own music), and Riccardo Broschi, brother of the famous castrato Farinelli (Milan, 1731). Handel's *Arianna in Creta*, derived from Leo's Roman and Neapolitan versions, differs from Pariati's original by showing Theseus's fight with the Minotaur on stage. It also features, in Act II, a scene not found in any other Pariati-based libretto: The sleeping Theseus, at the command of a "venerable old Man on a cloud" personifying Sleep, is visited by dreams that foretell his forthcoming triumphs—a striking passage recalling similar moments in Lully and Rameau. *Arianna* was highly successful when it premiered in January 1734 at the Haymarket, with the castrato Carestini (who was to triumph as Ariodante a few months later) as Teseo.

The many composers who, after Handel, set their version of Pariati's text include the Maltese Girolamo Abos (Rome, 1748), Giuseppe Sarti (Copenhagen, 1756), Baldassare Galuppi (Padua, 1763), and Peter Winter (Venice, 1792). In some versions—for example,

Fischietti's (Naples, 1777)—Carilda was renamed Laodice. All these operas take *Arianna e Teseo* as their title, save for Winter's, called *Il sacrifizio di Creta, ossia Arianna e Teseo*.

While Pariati leaves out the Naxos episode, thus preserving Theseus's heroic stature, Benedetto Marcello's *Arianna*, subtitled "theatrical-musical piece [*intreccio scenico*] for five voices," is set entirely on the island. It is thought to have been premiered in 1726, not in a theater but at a "Casino dei Nobili" in Venice to mark a visit by Cardinal Ottoboni, and generically it belongs to the *serenata*. At the beginning of Vincenzo Cassini's libretto, Ariadne is asleep in a pavilion on the Naxos shore, while Theseus and Phaedra (a contralto role) are about to elope. Apprised of their flight by the distressed Ariadne, Bacchus, still incognito, unleashes a tempest that—as in Donneau de Visé's play a half-century before—brings back the fugitives. While feigning remorse, Theseus remains deaf to Ariadne's entreaties—her largo "Come mai puoi vedermi piangere," with two obbligato flutes, is the work's longest, most beautiful aria. Bacchus, realizing that he and Theseus are more likely to achieve their respective aims by being friends rather than enemies, makes his peace with him before revealing his identity. Theseus and Phaedra are forgiven and take part in the nuptial celebrations, where Silenus presents Ariadne with the famous wedding crown, the final chorus celebrating the "victor of the Indies."

Handel's choice of Ariadne as a subject is assumed to have been prompted by Porpora's *Arianna in Nasso*, the inaugural work staged by the company formed in 1733 under the name "Opera of the Nobility" to rival Handel's own Academy of Music. Behind this venture was a group of nobles, led by the Prince of Wales, and the castrato Senesino, who sang Porpora's Theseus. Rolli's libretto is modeled not on Pariati but on Stampa's libretto to Giovanni Porta's *dramma pastorale*, *Arianna nell'isola di Nasso* (Milan, 1723). The twist here is the unexpected presence on Naxos of Antiope, queen of the Amazons and wife of Theseus (and mother of Hippolytus). The work begins as Ariadne is waiting for Theseus on the Cretan shore in front of the gate of the Labyrinth. On Naxos, meanwhile, Pirithous is seeking Theseus (whom he has never met) to challenge him to a fight and turns for advice to Onaro, supposedly the high priest of Libero (one of Bacchus's alternate names) but in fact the god himself in disguise, who is already in love with Ariadne. When Ariadne and Theseus find themselves stranded on the island by a storm, Bacchus orders Theseus to leave Naxos with Antiope while Ariadne lies asleep in their tent. After Ariadne has discovered her lover's departure, Bacchus appears in all his glory on a chariot drawn by tigers, surrounded with Bacchants and Corybants. Ariadne is won over as if by magic and the opera concludes with her apotheosis. Theseus is presented more sympathetically than in other Naxos-based versions: He loves Ariadne until the end and abandons her only because Bacchus threatens to kill her unless he renounces her. Conversely, Bacchus—also a castrato part—comes out as an unscrupulous schemer. With twenty-three consecutive performances, Porpora's *Arianna* was the most successful of the operas he wrote during his five years in London.

One final Italian eighteenth-century setting of the Ariadne story, Pasquale Anfossi's *Il trionfo d'Arianna*, was premiered in Venice in 1781; it was heard in London three years later, with the castrato Pacchierotti, William Beckford's protégé, as Theseus. Lanfranchi Rossi's two-act libretto takes place entirely on Naxos (here "a wild uninhabited place"), where the trio of Ariadne, Theseus, and Phaedra is supplemented by a character of Rossi's invention, Narbale, who is in love with Phaedra. Theseus's hypocrisy—at some point, he assures Ariadne that "this place is void of treachery"—is partly extenuated by his heroism when a ship carrying Minos's troops, in pursuit of the fugitives, appears at the end of Act I. Act II culminates with the moonlit departure of the lovers, while the heroine is visited by premonitory dreams (represented as a pantomime). After her awakening and lament, Bacchus, returning from India, appears to a "sprightly symphony of drums, tymbals, and other oriental musical instruments" and the success of his courtship leads to more songs and dances.

One of the most important treatments of the Ariadne story in the eighteenth century, Benda's *Ariadne auf Naxos*, is strictly speaking not an opera but a melodrama, yet its influence was such that it belongs to operatic history. Its inspiration was Rousseau's 1772 *Pygmalion*, which combined for the first time a spoken text with an expressive musical background. Staged at Weimar in 1772, on Goethe's recommendation, *Pygmalion* made a deep impression on the German playwright Johann Christian Brandes (1735–1799), who wrote his *Ariadne* as a vehicle for his wife, adapting a poem on the same subject by Gerstenberg (which Johann Christoph Friedrich Bach had set as a cantata in 1774). Having unsuccessfully approached Anton Schweitzer, who had written the music for the Weimar *Pygmalion*, Brandes turned to the Bohemian composer Georg Anton Benda, Kappelldirector of Duke Friedrich III of Saxe Gotha. The premiere of their *Ariadne auf Naxos*, which took place at the Gotha court theater on January 27, 1775, was notable for another reason: the actors were, for the first time, dressed in costumes based on ancient models, in the spirit of the classical revival recently launched by Johann Joachim Winckelmann.

Labeled "duodrama," Brandes and Benda's *Ariadne* consists of two extended soliloquies (with brief interventions by an Oread nymph). First, an anguished Theseus, with Ariadne asleep at his feet, ponders his decision to flee Naxos and leave her behind. His motives are less selfish than in other versions: his Greek companions demand that they return to Greece and even threaten to kill Ariadne. After his departure, she wakes up and gradually realizes her predicament. Terrified by a storm that is breaking up, she throws herself into the sea. Benda skillfully rendered the mounting tension by gradually merging music and text, kept separate in the opening scene, to achieve, in the final moments, despite the absence of singing, a truly operatic effect. At the dawn of the Romantic age, Benda's was the most dramatic treatment the Ariadne story had received thus far. It is also the most human, with the intervention of Dionysos conspicuously missing. Audiences responded to its power and formal originality, with productions mounted in various German cities and internationally. In a famous letter he wrote to his father from Mannheim on November 12, 1778, Mozart expressed his enthusiasm for the score. Successfully staged in Paris in 1781, it was adapted by the librettist Moline and Alsatian composer Jean-Frédéric Edelmann (1749–1794) as a one-act *drame lyrique*, *Ariane dans l'île de Naxos*, staged at the Opéra in 1782, and subsequently mounted as far away as New York and St. Petersburg. Another imitation of Brandes and Benda, the melodrama *Ariadne Abandoned by Theseus in the Isle of Naxos*, was presented in New York in 1797, with music by Victor Pelissier, the first French-born composer active in the United States.

Ariadne versus Modernity

Owing to the century's distaste for mythological subjects, especially those involving gods and goddesses (except as objects of ridicule, as in Offenbach), only two Ariadne operas were recorded between 1800 and 1900: Anton Fischer's *Singspiel, Theseus und Ariadne*, on a text by Stegmayer, staged at the Theater an der Wien in 1809 (the year after the composer's death); and Nicola Benvenuti's *azione drammatica, Arianna e Teseo*, on a libretto by Nicolini, seen in Pisa in 1810.

Massenet's choice of Ariadne as a subject, in the early twentieth century, was an anti-Wagnerian statement: by turning to classical—as opposed to Nordic—mythology, he and his librettist Mendès, himself once a Wagnerite, promoted a Mediterranean, "Latin" form of lyric drama, with roots in French classical tragedy and in the eighteenth-century French and Italian operatic tradition. Act I, set in front of the gate to the Labyrinth, begins with Theseus fighting the Minotaur and ends with his triumphant departure for Greece with Ariadne and Phaedra. Act II takes place on the boat and features a storm in the tradition of eighteenth-century operatic tempests. Set in Naxos, Act III brings the situation to a crisis: Theseus has fallen in love with Phaedra, who is torn between love and guilt once Ariadne discovers the situation. At this point, Mendès introduces into the story a twist of his invention: After Phaedra, remorseful, curses a statue of Venus and is struck dead, Ariadne resolves, Orpheus-like, to bring her sister back from Hell, where she mollifies Persephone by presenting her with a bouquet of roses (a moment rendered by Massenet with one of his sensuous melodies). Overcome with gratitude, Theseus and Phaedra nevertheless flee together. The abandoned Ariadne walks into the sea, while the song of the Sirens, first introduced at the beginning of Act I, is heard again in the distance.

Unlike *Ariane*, which was well received at the Opéra in 1906, *Bacchus* was Massenet's single most disastrous failure, disappearing after five performances in 1909. Mendès's libretto came in for particularly harsh criticism. In the first act, set in Hell like Act IV of *Ariane*, Persephone learns about Ariadne being rescued by Bacchus and his taking her with him to India—a reversal of the tradition, which usually places their meeting *after* his return from India. A lifelong believer in the melodramatic form, Massenet set this prologue for three voices speaking on an orchestral background. Act II opens in Nepal, where the ascetic Buddhist community feels threatened by the arrival of the god of wine. With the help of giant monkeys, the army of Bacchus is defeated and he and Ariadne become the prisoners of Queen Amahelli, who falls in love with Bacchus and orders his release. After a danced celebration of the Dionysiac mysteries, the queen convinces Ariadne that Bacchus is doomed to perish at the stake unless someone sacrifices himself. Selflessly, Ariadne immediately offers to do so, stabbing herself on the pyre. Arrived too late on the scene, Bacchus implores Jupiter, who strikes the Indian queen dead, while Ariadne and her divine lover are transfigured.

The reasons for *Bacchus*'s failure seem to be due largely to its original form—closer to *opéra-ballet*, with its long symphonic interlude describing the battle, and dances occupying an entire tableau—and unusual subject. Critics were clearly put off by the philosophical underpinnings of Mendès's libretto, in which Bacchus stands for a kind of epicurianism in opposition to Eastern contemplative asceticism.

Strauss's *Ariadne auf Naxos* now occupies such a prominent place in the international operatic repertory that it is easy to forget that neither its original (1912) nor its revised version (1916) was an unqualified success at first. The work has a complex history. It was conceived within the project of an adaptation of *Le bourgeois gentilhomme* to be directed by Max Reinhardt, with the Ariadne opera, mixing serio and buffo elements, replacing the ceremony and dances that conclude Molière's comedy. It thus originated not so much as a modern version of the Greek myth but as a pastiche or even parody of earlier works. The choice of Ariadne as a subject, first mentioned in a March 1911 letter from Hofmannsthal to Strauss, was at first almost arbitrary, prompted by its universal, proverbial familiarity. Yet, as the project took shape, the poet came to see the myth as the illustration of a theme crucial to him: How can a constant heart be metamorphosed by the power of love?

In this version, by contrast with most previous settings, Theseus, often mentioned, never appears. Instead of focusing on the circumstances of the abandonment, Hofmannsthal confronted an issue that most previous settings had glossed over: Why should Ariadne, faithfulness personified, suddenly renounce her own self by responding to the love of an unknown god? At least one early treatment (Perrin) explained the metamorphosis by introducing a magical element. Others, when they did not end the Ariadne story with her suicide, left her change of heart unexplained, and thus dramatically unconvincing. Massenet and Mendès eschewed the difficulty by bypassing the meeting of Bacchus and Ariadne, which is retrospectively evoked in Act I of *Bacchus*. Hofmannsthal's heroine, until the end, remains unaware of the god's identity. Lost in her despair, having no hope except in the kingdom of death "where everything is pure," she nevertheless has not ignored the enthusiastic heralding of Bacchus by Najade, Dryade, and Echo. Her first impulse on hearing his voice is to identify him as Hermes, guide of souls to the netherworld. When he appears, she screams Theseus's name. Then she returns to her belief that she is facing the messenger of death. Her misapprehension is made more comprehensible by the way Bacchus is portrayed: not as the "victor of the Indies," surrounded with Bacchants and satyrs, but a beautiful young man, without ostensible divine attributes. He is recovering from an affair with the magician Circe, not normally associated with Bacchus in Antiquity but certainly well known (see Forsyth 1982) for changing men into beasts, and thus personifying love on its least spiritual level. His own confusion matches Ariadne's at first: he addresses her as an "enchantress" ready to recapture him with the help of a magic potion. As the scene progresses, Bacchus realizes his mistake but Ariadne doesn't and, forever faithful to Theseus, remains convinced that she is on her way to the Land of the Dead. This lack of communication makes for a highly unconventional love duet, which has divided critical opinion, and for which the 1912 and 1916 versions differ significantly: the earlier, where the uncomprehending Zerbinetta and Monsieur Jourdain have the last word, ironically highlighted the unattainable, spiritual quality of Ariadne's world; in the revised text, Zerbinetta's intervention is reduced to two lines, and the work ends with Bacchus's ecstatic declaration of love—a simpler, more conventional ending, more in line with the conclusions of previous Ariadne operas.

If Hofmannsthal's treatment can be called revisionist, that is even more the case in Milhaud's and Martinů's. *L'abandon d'Ariane* is the second work—and, lasting a mere twelve minutes, the longest—in Milhaud's set of *opéras-minute*, together with *L'enlèvement d'Europe* (1927) and *La délivrance de Thésée*, premiered as a trilogy at Wiesbaden in 1928. The three libretti are by Henri Hoppenot, a diplomat and former colleague in Brazil, where the composer had followed Claudel during the war. Hoppenot's take is a classic case of myth-debunking. In this version, Ariadne finds Theseus's attentions altogether unwelcome, nor is Theseus interested in Phaedra, though she loves him secretly. On Naxos, the sisters encounter a beggar, who is, in fact, the disguised Dionysos—for once given his Greek name—and is urged by his "gypsy Bacchants," as the libretto calls them, to solve the situation. Dionysos gets Theseus drunk, so that, seeing double, he believes he is leading away two women, whereas he is taking Phaedra alone, leaving behind a relieved Ariadne. Dionysos, who does not appear to be particularly in love with Ariadne, simply offers to fulfill her wish, which is to join Diana as a star in heaven. The briefest of choruses celebrates the happy event, ending on a comically out-of-place Racine quotation ("la fille de Minos et de Pasiphae") which takes the sopranos to a joyous high C. The parody is reflected in the music, which Milhaud wrote in two days: ostensibly retaining the operatic forms (arias, duets, ensembles, choruses), but compressed to such a extent that they are barely recognizable.

The source of Martinů's *Ariane* is *Le voyage de Thésée*, a 1943 play by Georges Neveux (1900–1982), the Ukrainian-born writer whose *Juliette, ou la clé des songes* had inspired Martinů's surrealist opera *Julietta* (1938). The composer prepared his own libretto by reducing Neveux's four acts to three scenes, lasting approximately forty-five minutes. As in Cocteau's and Anouilh's versions of Oedipus and Antigone, deliberate anachronisms make it impossible to tell whether we are in classical antiquity or not. The first scene shows a public square in Knossos, where seven young men from Athens have landed with a view to killing the Minotaur. Theseus, who is one of them, encounters a mysterious young woman. She herself has an appointment with the Minotaur—whom she has never met—and announces that she is about to marry a newly arrived stranger: Theseus. Disappointed by this course of events, one of the Athenian boys decides to look for the Minotaur himself and he gets killed. Resolving to avenge him, Theseus calls for the monster, only to confront, in the play's great *coup de théâtre*, his own image—the image, the Minotaur explains, of his happiness. By killing the Minotaur, Theseus renounces Ariadne's love. In the last scene, he and the boys sail away, while Ariadne, in a beautiful lyrical monologue—in Neveux's play part of her final dialogue with Theseus—bids farewell to her dream. Martinů's score responded to the oneiric quality of Neveux's text with nostalgic hints at the neoclassicism of the 1920s, a style conveyed from the opening *sinfonia*.

The persistent appeal of the Ariadne myth is evidenced by the three highly different operas that it has inspired in more recent times—two of them composed by women. Elzbieta Sikora's chamber opera *Ariadna*, after placing second at the 1978 Weber competition in Dresden, was premiered in Warsaw in 1979. The Polish composer (b. 1943) used a short dialogue by Cesare Pavese, "La vigna" (The vineyards), from his *Dialoghi con Leucò* (1947). Neither Theseus nor Bacchus appears in this version, which consists of a single scene: The grieving Ariadne is taunted by Leucothea, who introduces herself as the nymph of the island and announces the arrival of Dionysos, urging Ariadne to put her regrets behind her. Yet, despite Leucothea's final "Do not fear," Ariadne's forthcoming surrender to Bacchus, as translated by the composer in musical terms, sounds more like a threat than an apotheosis.

A different kind of ambiguity pervades Thea Musgrave's *The Voice of Ariadne*, also labeled "chamber opera," which was premiered at the Aldeburgh Festival in 1974. The libretto by the Peruvian-born Amalia Elguera is based on Henry James's short story *The Last of the Valerii*, in which an Italian count, married to an American heiress, becomes infatuated with a statue of Juno excavated on his estate, prompting the wife, in an act that resembles an exorcism, to have it reburied. In Musgrave's three-act opera, what is discovered is a pedestal bearing the name "Ariadne." The object of the count's infatuation is the voice of Ariadne calling for Theseus—its distant, otherworldly quality rendered through the use of a prerecorded tape. In the end, the countess succeeds in substituting her own voice for that of the mythological figure, and the opera ends with a meditative duet between husband and wife, emphasizing the symbolic scope of the myth.

Steeped in Monteverdi's music from his early years—his father, the German conductor Walter Goehr, was associated with its revival—the British composer Alexander Goehr (b. 1932) decided to reset to music Rinuccini's libretto to his lost opera. Premiered at Covent Garden in 1995, *Arianna*, "lost opera by Monteverdi, composed again by Alexander Goehr," omitted only the prologue for Apollo and a few occasional lines (especially in the choruses). The surviving "Lamento" is incorporated—and is indeed reinterpreted serially throughout the work—but is only faintly recognizable in its contemporary harmonization, while both the vocal declamation and the interventions of the chamber-size orchestra (notably the ritornellos and fanfares that accompany the more joyful moments) remain in the spirit of Monteverdi. With this postmodern version, the Ariadne theme may be said to have come to a full circle.

See also: Dramaturgy, What Is Opera? Opera between the Ancients and the Moderns

Bibliography

Bashford, Christina. 1991. "Perrin and Cambert's 'Ariane, ou Le Mariage de Bacchus' re-examined." *Music & Letters* 72/1: 1–26.

Bianconi, Lorenzo. 1987. *Music in the Seventeenth Century*, translated by David Bryant. Cambridge: Cambridge University Press.

Branger, Jean-Christophe. 2008. "*Ariane et Bacchus* de Massenet: un diptyque méditerranéen." In *Figures de l'Antiquité dans l'opéra français: Des 'Troyens' de Berlioz à 'Oedipe' d'Enesco*, edited by Jean-Christophe Branger and Vincent Giroud, 185–220. Saint-Étienne: Publications de l'Université de Saint-Étienne.

Buelow, George J. 1972. "*Die schöne und getreue Ariadne* (Hamburg 1691): A Lost Opera by J. G. Conradi Rediscovered." *Acta Musicologica* 44/1: 108–121.

Colas, Damien, and Alessandro Di Profio, eds. 2009. *D'une scène à l'autre. L'opéra italien en Europe*. 2 vols. II: *La musique à l'épreuve du théâtre*. Wavre: Mardaga.

Dahlhaus, Carl. 2003. "The Dramaturgy of Italian Opera." In *Opera in Theory and Practice, Image and Myth*, edited by Lorenzo Bianconi and Giorgio Pestelli, translated by Kenneth Chalmers and Mary Whittall. *The History of Italian Opera* 6, 73–150. Chicago: University of Chicago Press.

Daviau, Donald G., and George J. Buelow. 1975. *The 'Ariadne auf Naxos' of Hugo von Hofmannsthal and Richard Strauss*. Chapel Hill: University of North Carolina Press.

Everist, Mark. 2009. "A Transalpine Comedy: *L'elisir d'amore* and Cultural Transfer." In Colas and Di Profio 2009, 279–298.

Ewans, Michael. 2007. *Opera from the Greeks: Studies in the Poetics of Appropriation*. Aldershot: Ashgate.

Fabbri, Paolo. 1990. *Il Secolo cantante: Per una storia del libretto d'opera nel Seicento*. Bologna: Il Mulino.

Forsyth, Karen. 1982. *'Ariadne auf Naxos' by Hugo von Hofmannsthal and Richard Strauss: Its Genesis and Meaning*. New York: Oxford University Press.

Genette, Gérard. 1997. *Palimpsests: Literature in the Second Degree*, translated by Channa Newman and Claude Doubinsky. Lincoln: University of Nebraska Press.

Giroud, Vincent. 2010. *French Opera: A Short History*. New Haven: Yale University Press.

Granda, Giovanna. 1990. "Le peripezie di un libretto: Dal 'Teseo in Creta' all' 'Arianna e Teseo': Un testo per musica attraverso un secolo." In *La carriera di un librettista, Pietro Pariati da Reggio di Lombardia, con saggi di B. Dolley, H. Seifert, R. Strohm*, 291–488. Reggio Emilia: Società editrice Il Mulino.

Ieranò, Giorgio. 2007. *Il mito di Arianna: Da Omero a Borges*. Roma: Carocci.

Ketterer, Robert C. 2009. *Ancient Rome in Early Opera*. Urbana: University of Illinois Press.

——. 2003. "Why Early Opera Is Roman and Not Greek." *Cambridge Opera Journal* 15/1: 1–14.

Kimbell, David. 1991. *Italian Opera*. Cambridge: Cambridge University Press.

Kimberley, Nick. 1995. "Goehr, Monteverdi and 'Arianna.'" *Opera* 46/9: 1045–1047.

Kintzler, Catherine. 1991. *Poétique de l'opéra français de Corneille à Rousseau*. Paris: Minerve.

Lévy, François. 2009. "Métastase et le procédé de la contamination de sujets: le cas *Demetrio*." In Colas and Di Profio 2009, 215–238.

Malcomess, Hilde. 1993. *Die opéras minute von Darius Milhaud*. Orpheus-Schriftenreihe zu Grundfragen der Musik 71. Bonn: Verlag für systematische Musikwissenschaft GmbH.

McClymonds, Marita. 1992. "Antigone." *The New Grove Dictionary of Opera*. Online. Available: http://www.oxfordmusiconline.com/subscriber/article/grove/music/O005370 (accessed August 12, 2012).

Milliot, Sylvette, and Jérôme de La Gorce. 1991. *Marin Marais*. Paris: Fayard.

Pendle, Karin. 1974. "The Transformation of a Libretto: Goethe's 'Jery und Bätely.'" *Music & Letters* 5/1: 77–88.

Peyronie, André. 1988. "Ariane." In *Dictionnaire des mythes littéraires*. 2nd ed., 160–170. Monaco: Éditions du Rocher.

Picard, Timothée. 2005. "Mendès librettiste à la lumière de son wagnérisme." In *Catulle Mendès: L'énigme d'une disparition*, edited by Patrick Besnier, Sophie Lucet, and Nathalie Prince, 89–03. Rennes: Presses Universitaires de Rennes.

Rosand, Ellen. 1991. *Opera in Seventeenth-Century Venice: The Creation of a Genre*. Berkeley and Los Angeles: University of California Press.

Rose, Herbert Jennings, Charles Martin Robertson, and B.C. Dietrich. 1996. "Ariadne." *The Oxford Classical Dictionary*. 3rd ed., edited by Simon Hornblower and Anthony Spawforth, 156. New York: Oxford University Press.

Sternfeld, F. W. 1993. *The Birth of Opera*. Oxford: Clarendon Press.

Strohm, Reinhard. 2009. "La tragedia in maschera. French drama and Vivaldi's operas." In Colas and Di Profio 2009, 91–107.

——. 1997. *Dramma per musica: Italian Opera of the Eighteenth Century*. New Haven: Yale University Press.

Vatin, Claude. 2004. *Ariane et Dionysos: Un mythe de l'amour conjugal*. Paris: Éditions Rue d'Ulm, Presses de l'École normale supérieure.

Vyslouzil, Jiri. 1967. "The *Ariadne* of Bohuslav Martinů (Notes on the Genesis, Style and Ideas of the Work)." In *The Stage Works of Bohuslav Martinů*, edited by Rudolf Pecman, 195–203. Prague: [Czechoslovak Music Information Centre].

Waeber, Jacqueline. 2005. *En musique dans le texte: Le mélodrame, de Rousseau à Schoenberg*. Paris: Van Dieren.

Walsh, Stephen. 1974. "Musgrave's 'The Voice of Ariadne'." *Musical Times* 115/1576: 465–467.

CHAPTER 7

THE LANGUAGE OF NATIONAL STYLE

MARINA FROLOVA-WALKER

For Mozart, switching between *opera buffa* and *Singspiel* was quite unproblematic. Fifty years later, composers could not even countenance such a stylistic shift, although the practice of adapting scores to other national conventions persisted (hence the French versions of Tannhäuser and many other operas). As Carl Dahlhaus argued, "style" was endowed with an "existential" significance for the first time in the nineteenth century. No longer a mere assemblage of arbitrary conventions, style now had to carry the burden of authenticity. Thus,

> [a] national style, embodying the spirit of a people in musical sound, was conceived of as the expression of a form of existence, not merely as something which a composer could arbitrarily adopt and exchange [...]. (Dahlhaus 1980: 101)

Initially, as nationalism became a motor of cultural discourse, national style in opera was a problem only in countries that lay at the margins of operatic culture, such as Germany (where *Singspiel* prevailed) and Russia (where Italian opera had far greater prestige). But a reversal had taken place by the close of the nineteenth century, when the formerly confident operatic cultures of France and even Italy began to experience the anxiety of feeling invaded, contaminated, and even dominated by a foreign spirit—by Wagnerism (as Large and Weber point out, interest in Wagner grew into a cult, spurred imitations, and even engendered a kind of "social movement" [Large and Weber 1984: 1–27]).

In this chapter, following Dahlhaus, I will limit the discussion of opera and national style to the nineteenth and early twentieth centuries. I will focus initially on the two critical moments mentioned above: first, when the need for a national style came to the fore in the "marginal" operatic cultures of Germany and Russia, and second, drawing upon the research of other scholars, when Wagnerism brought the same need back to France and Italy. I will then concentrate on one particular way in which a national style can be evoked, namely through declamation faithful to the pitch and rhythms characteristic of a given language—and I will explore both the nationalist and universalist potential of such "dialogue operas" in Musorgsky, Debussy, and Janáček.

We shall take Germany, the cradle of nationalist thought, as our entry point: it was here that the discourse of national operatic style first emerged. Johann Gottfried Herder, who was the first to articulate the ideology of cultural nationalism, also hoped that opera would help to build the German nation. Unhappy with the chivalric content of most French opera and its superficial picturesqueness, he wrote:

> Oh for the creation of a new kind of German opera!—built on human foundations, with human music, declamation and decoration, but with feeling. Such a lofty goal, such a great task! (Herder 1878: 4: 484, trans. Meyer 2003: 4)

Although these words remained unpublished until 1846 (Meyer 2003: 4), many of Herder's compatriots—for example, Christoph Martin Wieland and Johann Georg Sulzer in the 1770s—nurtured similar hopes. While Britain and France enjoyed political and economic unity, Germany's defeats in the Napoleonic wars and its political fragmentation elicited compensatory efforts toward nation-building on the cultural front. According to Stephen Meyer (2003), the struggle for German opera consisted of three tasks: the creation of a new, through-composed German operatic form, the effort to create a new audience and win new prestige for operas in the German language, and the articulation of a new national ideology through music and drama (Meyer 2003: 8). These three tasks—aesthetic, social, and ideological—will remain points of reference throughout my discussion of opera and national style. Although only the aesthetic task would appear to have a direct bearing on stylistic issues, the social task was generally the most pressing: when there were no "national" works in the repertoire, or where audiences ignored such works, nationally conscious cultural elites strove to reverse the situation. Germany, during the 1810s and early 1820s, presents an early instance of this phenomenon: at the time, Italian troupes dominated the stages and received sponsorship from the German aristocracy; French opera was also prominent and popular across Germany, but Italian opera was considered the principal threat.

The New German Opera: *Der Freischütz* and *Euryanthe*

Weber's *Freischütz* opened the offensive against Italian domination, and it was perceived in precisely this way at the time, as "National-Oper" (Tusa 2006: 485). This perception only deepened later in the century, due to the writings of Wagner, and was expressed with particular eloquence around the time of Germany's unification by Friedrich Wilhelm Jähns (Wagner [1841] 1966; Tusa 2006: 484):

> Just as Germany on this very date (18 June 1815) liberated itself from the yoke of foreign domination, so too, exactly six years later, did German music liberate itself from the domination of foreign artistic elements.... Weber, the straightforward German,

> was directly confronted by the well-defended Spontini, but behind Spontini stood Rossini, perhaps still more dangerous, armed with those alluring sounds that so flatter the ear. In this victorious battle, Weber won the prize of [national] consciousness for the German people, and earned for them their own place in musico-dramatic art. (Jähns 1871: 311, trans. Meyer 2003: 111)

Der Freischütz drew from various established national symbols, such as the patriotic male chorus, and contributed, in its turn, to the construction of national identity: the combination of the folkloric, the natural (the forest), and the supernatural all came to be regarded as quintessentially German. As Susan Youens notes, at this fraught junction in European history, the German *Jäger* becomes a nationalistic emblem, a masculine heroic model of irresistible bravery and sexual appeal (Youens 1997: 43; Meyer 2003: 103).

Over the past century, dissenters such as Hermann Abert (1926), John Warrack (2001), and Carl Dahlhaus (1989) have argued that the opera was rather a deft combination of various French and even Italian models, with its main generic prototype to be found in *opéra comique* (Tusa 2006: 486–489). But cultural nationalism can embrace multitudes, and such arguments can strengthen rather than undermine the nationalist claims for *Der Freischütz*, since the notion that Germany should assimilate the best in European culture was also part of the rhetoric. Even Weber himself spoke (more than once) of the typical German, "eager for knowledge and demanding constant progress," absorbing "the exceptional of all others"; just when the reader might wonder whether this is all too attenuated to be considered nationalism, Weber reaches his point: The German demands a self-sufficient work of art, in which all the parts make up a beautiful and unified whole (Weber [1817] 1981: 207; Tusa 2003: 498).

For Weber himself, the ideal of the beautiful organic artwork was to be realized in his next opera, *Euryanthe*, a more self-consciously German creation. Organic unity demanded sung-through opera, rather than the fragmentation of *Singspiel*. Spohr and Weber raced to complete the first German opera proper, and both *Jessonda* and *Euryanthe* were premiered in 1823. As Spohr put it, "Another question is whether or not we Germans should finally elevate the opera into a thoroughly unified work of art by changing the dialogues of our opera into recitatives" (Spohr 1823: 463, trans. Meyer 2003: 11); his answer is obvious from the way he frames the question. And so it was *Euryanthe*, rather than *Der Freischütz*, which Weber now believed to be a proper model for future German opera, one that embodied the seriousness and depth of the German national character through its organic unity and harmonic richness (Tusa 2006: 502). Schumann followed *Euryanthe* painstakingly in *Genoveva* (1849), and Wagner also paid it close attention in *Lohengrin* (1848), although he also harbored reservations, complaining that Weber's model was often too pedantic and lacked sufficient popular appeal:

> What splitting of hairs in the declamation, what fussy use of this or that instrument to emphasize a single word! (Wagner 1834; Tusa 1991: 57)

The opera-going public, it would appear, agreed with Wagner in preferring a more broad-brush approach to the grand stage: Weber's deliberate cultivation of small-scale expression, his desire to render every moment of the score "characteristic," have pushed *Euryanthe* and *Genoveva* to the margins of the repertoire.

German opera was soon able to claim victory in the opera houses, with Italian opera companies rapidly losing ground to German-language troupes in the 1830s, but in the short term, the aesthetic goal of a growing body of great German operas was not attained, and the main beneficiary of the Italians' demise was French opera: German-language productions of Meyerbeer, Auber, and Halevy proved more appealing to German audiences than native fare (Meyer 2003: 158). It took several more decades and the titanic efforts of Wagner to reverse this situation (enlisting to the cause both his compositional skills and his anti-Semitic rhetoric).

Official and Cultural Nationalism in Russia: *A Life for the Tsar*

In the 1830s, Russian opera was still in its pre-*Freischütz* stage, unable to compete with the Italian and other foreign companies on Russian soil. Politically, Russia was in a very different position from Germany and seemed scarcely in need of nationalistic morale boosting, since it was already a unified state with an expanding imperial reach; in its encounter with Napoleon, it had emerged victorious, its armies chasing the French back to their homeland. In spite of this, cultural nationalism was on the rise as the cosmopolitan, Francophone habits of the aristocracy were eroding, and the dearth of indigenous art and literature (beyond Pushkin) left Russia lagging centuries behind its European competitors. Mikhail Glinka's opera *A Life for the Tsar* (*Zhizn' za tsarya*, 1836) deftly satisfied the needs of both the official court nationalism and also the more progressive, liberal variety (Taruskin 1997: 25–47). It served to glorify the establishment of the Romanov dynasty, becoming the permanent season-opener of the Imperial Theatres, but at the same time it was welcomed by Russia's Herderian cultural nationalists for elevating the Russian peasantry to high art on the operatic stage.

A decade after Germany's *Euryanthe* and *Jessonda*, Glinka provided Russians with their first sung-through opera in *A Life for the Tsar*. Achieving a high degree of formal unity in their operas was important to Weber and Glinka for two reasons: it allowed them to claim a higher artistic status for their operas, and it served as a patently anti-Italian gesture. Just as Weber had taken great pains over tonal planning (as in the use of keys delineating the devilish diminished seventh chord in the "Wolf's Glen" scene of *Der Freischütz*), Glinka attended carefully to his motivic connections and created thematic reminiscences; and again, like Weber, he prided himself on the art of transition from one number to another (see Frolova-Walker 2007: 102–104 and Taruskin 2005).

Glinka wanted to create an opera that captured a mood that was peculiarly Russian, distanced from the sunny character of Italian opera scores; he found the key in melancholy Russian popular and salon songs (romances). He applied these overlapping idioms quite consistently, although they are sometimes quite difficult to separate out, as the popular songs and romances drew much from various Western influences. To his Russian audience, however, the result was recognizably and pleasingly Russian, even if it stood alongside overtly Italian numbers, French-style ballet, and Germanic learned counterpoint. Russia, like Germany, took pride in its ability to assimilate and appropriate cultural goods, and considered it a national feature in itself. There was, however, another important aspect to Glinka's "Russian style": it was supposed to contrast with Polish local color (represented through the genres of the mazurka and the polonaise) for musico-dramatic reasons (the Poles were cast in the role of villains). A degree of ambiguity emerges between the idea of a Russian style as just one of the two local colors (Russian versus Polish) or as an overriding feature of the opera (Russian versus Italian). A confusion between these two conceptions seems to have persisted in the minds of Russian composers: Musorgsky compromised the thoroughgoing "existential" Russianness of *Boris Godunov* through the interpolation of Polish scenes (à la Glinka), while Rimsky-Korsakov, at the turn of the century, even composed whole operas in other "national styles" or local colors (*Servilia* was Italian, *Pan Voyevoda* [*The Governor*] Polish; see Frolova-Walker 2011).

Both Weber and Glinka vacillated between, on the one hand, that overriding national style that is intended as a profound reflection of national character, and, on the other, the much more easily achievable local color that satisfied itself with superficial characteristics. Neither imagined that the "national style" they created for a particular opera could establish itself outside that work, even in their own oeuvre, let alone the music of other composers. Weber took three diverse approaches to Germanness in *Freischütz*, *Euryanthe*, and *Oberon*, just as Glinka dropped the melancholy Russian idiom of *A Life* in order to take a new approach to Russianness in *Ruslan and Lyudmila* (1842). Even though this opera embodied Russian imperial ideology (Frolova-Walker 1997: 21–45), it did not attempt to create a homogeneous Russian style; rather, it presented an assemblage of distinct styles that sometimes corresponded to local color, but at other times did not, according to the composer's preferences (Lyudmila, the principal Russian heroine, was provided with both a Russian romance and a Rossinian aria, while the exotic character, Ratmir, was largely, but not exclusively, provided with characteristically exotic music). As with Weber, the second opera had less popular appeal than the first, but inspired imitations in like-minded followers, and *Ruslan* proved an even more potent inspiration for the composers of the "Five" (Mily Balakirev, Alexander Borodin, César Cui, Modest Musorgsky, Rimsky-Korsakov) than *Euryanthe* was for Wagner.

Manufacturing Italianness: Late Verdi and Puccini

As Thomas Grey has put it, "Italian opera never felt the need to mount a cultural offensive against the French. Unlike German opera in Weber's day, Italian opera suffered from no identity complex, at least not until the 'Wagner problem' starting in the 1870s" (Grey 2006: 562). As with most of the cases discussed in this chapter, it was a heightening of national self-consciousness that led to the sense of a foreign threat. The political unification of Italy in 1860 resulted in a movement to "create Italians" through patriotic education; in the oft-quoted phrase of one leading figure of the Risorgimento, Massimo d'Azeglio, "We have made Italy, now we must make Italians" ([1867] 1966). Opera thus became a national symbol that required protection. Until the 1870s, Italian operatic culture had remained remarkably closed, with only occasional performances of foreign operas such as Mozart and Meyerbeer (in Italian), but the next two decades saw not only the arrival of Wagner onto Italian stages (fraught with controversy and near-riots), but also the less startling, but steady progress of French grand opera. There was an effort by composers of the younger generation to make Italian operatic culture more cosmopolitan and progressive, as with Arrigo Boito's *Mefistofele* (1868), which was considered Wagnerian. The powerful publishing house of Ricordi became a partisan for conservatism, issuing a stream of anti-Wagnerian articles (Mallach 2007: 17). Verdi, too, became a cultural conservative in his pronouncements; the cosmopolitan works of Catalani, Franchetti, and the young Puccini made him painfully aware of the fragility of true Italian operatic culture (as he viewed it) (Mallach 2007: 119).

As Roger Parker (1997) has shown, Verdi's last opera, *Falstaff*, is in many ways a manifesto, a unique attempt to counteract Wagnerism while embracing some of its "progressive" features, such as through-composition and complex orchestral textures (1997: 100–125). Verdi's insistence that *Falstaff* was an old Italian story (supposedly predating Shakespeare) is indicative of his late-life cultural nationalism, as was his choice of the *buffa* genre. Interestingly, Verdi's abandonment in *Falstaff* of distinct numbers within the form does not lead to a continuous harmonic flow, as in Wagner: on the contrary, as Parker says, Verdi keeps cadencing almost obsessively (Parker 1997: 123; further research on the nature and meaning of *Falstaff*'s cadences can be found in Senici 2001 and Greenwald 2003a and 2003b). Verdi's appeal to Francesco Florimo in his letter of January 5, 1871, "Let us turn to the past: that will be progress,"[1] is embodied above all in the magisterial final fugue, as if illustrating his superior traditional training in counterpoint, the absence of which he so lamented in the young (Florimo 1883: 108, trans. Osborne 1971: 169).

While Verdi's status at the time was almost godlike, and his last opera immediately became iconic, its nationalism was too *recherché* to attract much popular support, and again we find the gap between nationalism in intention and reception that we have observed earlier in this chapter.

It was Puccini who became the new national symbol, "a constant sigh of pure, uncorrupted, unadulterated Italianness" (Wilson 2007: 2). His rise to national stardom was to a great extent engineered by the publisher Ricordi, using all the trappings of the emerging cult of the celebrity. The pro-Puccini rhetoric was in most cases anti-Wagnerian (even though Julian Budden had good reason to call him "Wagner's best Italian pupil" [1987: 332]). Puccini was deemed to be standing firm against a wave of decadence and degeneration to which Italy had succumbed; he was healthy while Wagner was diseased, he was spontaneously melodic where Wagner was sterile and systematic (Wilson

2007: 43). However, as Wilson (2007) has shown, the myth of Puccini as a national composer and successor to Verdi, created early in the composer's career (e.g., Shaw [1894] 1981: III: 217) and accompanying him throughout his life, was constantly challenged, reflecting Italy's social and cultural anxieties in the face of modernity. Fausto Torrefranca, for example, accused Puccini of writing music that was too strophic and symmetrical to reflect the contours of his texts, and also frowned upon his injections of mundane "realist" declamation—both fell afoul of Torrefranca's Wagnerian agenda (Torrefranca 1912: 74–75, 112–113; Groos and Parker 1987: 132–133). Wilson's assemblage of contemporaneous criticism shows how Puccini's style, which remained quite consistent over several decades, could be praised or castigated according to different agendas. It could be perceived as purely Italian or too internationalist, organically spontaneous or manufactured and episodic, perfectly melodic or too short-winded, virile or emasculated. Forever criticized for its un-heroic decadence and insufficient progressiveness, it was nevertheless happily appropriated by Fascism after Puccini's death (Wilson: 191–192). It seems that Puccini's style, which perhaps lacked the clear intentions typical of other nationalist composers, could be interpreted to fit almost any agenda. This case makes us realize all the more acutely that in settling the question "How national is this?" it is nationalist discourse itself that always has the last word.

A Naturalistic Response to Wagner: Charpentier's *Louise*

The French story runs in many respects parallel to the Italian: here is another confident operatic culture that comes to feel threatened by Wagner and Wagnerism. Although French operatic culture was much more cosmopolitan than Italian (it had generally been quite happy to embrace the Italian repertoire), Wagner nevertheless proved difficult to stomach. After *Tannhäuser*'s Paris run of 1861 ended in failure, Wagner retaliated with a series of anti-French essays, including the highly provocative farce *Eine Kapitulation* (translated into French in 1875) (Wagner [1873] 2005; Huebner 1999: 13; see also Grey 2009). This caused such a wave of resentment that further productions of Wagner in France were delayed, even though the composer was well established on the concert platform. The hostility to the staging of *Lohengrin* at the Opéra in 1891 culminated in demonstrations (there had been riots at the La Scala premiere twenty years earlier), but this failed to deter the arrival of heavyweights like *Die Walküre, Tristan*, and *Die Meistersinger* later in the 1890s (Huebner 1999: 16–17). As in Italy, Wagner represented much more than his music, and for the French, the German pill was especially bitter in the wake of their defeat in the Franco-Prussian War of 1870–1871. But if the mood had been one of universal rejection, these productions would never have taken place, and significant sections of the public were at least curious and often enthusiastic. The leaders of the younger generation of composers happily succumbed to the seductions of Wagner's music, and rushed to incorporate various Wagnerian features into their own works, for example Chabrier's *Gwendoline* (1886), d'Indy's *Fervaal* (1897), and Chausson's *Le roi Arthus* (1903). The French debates over Wagner and Wagnerism could be tortuous, with shifting allegiances: Saint-Saëns, for example, was at first a partisan for Wagner, but later became rather a French nationalist as a result of his association with the Societé Nationale, and by 1898, he was even defending the practice of spoken dialogue at the Opéra-Comique as a part of the national musical culture and therefore not something subject to changes in fashion (Saint-Saëns 1898; Huebner 1999: 197). The composer's turnaround is especially startling in the light of the struggles for national sung-through opera that had taken place in Russia and Germany three-quarters of a century earlier.

The alternative that commanded the most credibility in French culture of the time was Zola-esque naturalism. Human rather than mythical, modern rather than timeless, and concrete rather than abstract, Émile Zola's influence seemed to provide a healthy antidote to Wagner. Thus, Gustave Charpentier's *Louise* (1900) was deliberately designed to make a nationalist statement along naturalist lines, with the shabby urban realism of its Montmartre setting, the depiction of working-class life, and its attacks on conventional morality, together with a score containing the cries of street traders, references to popular musical genres in the bohemians' music, and even the use of a real sewing machine on stage. This "realism" was not much different from its slightly earlier counterpart, Italian *verismo*, but Bizet's *Carmen* (1875) provided an even earlier starting point. It must be conceded that by this date Wagner's legacy was too pervasive for Charpentier to repudiate it completely, and there are various Wagnerian reminiscences in the details of the score (not least the Tristanesque music for the lovers), in addition to the more general influence to be found in the opera's monumental scale (and the fact that it was intended as the first installment of a trilogy; in 1914 Charpentier completed *Julien, ou La vie du poète* charting the life of Louise's suitor). But for all this, Charpentier's opera could never be mistaken for the work of the avowed Wagnerians in French musical life, and Charpentier declared that he was deliberately trying to avoid the kind of Germanic complexity that compromised even the nature of French vocal writing (d'Indy being his primary target here):

> [W]e hear French works every day that sound like translations because of exasperating declamation which takes little account of strong beats and operates independently of modulations instead of motivating them. (Huret 1900; Huebner 1999: 437)

In opposition to such Wagnerian distortions in French text-setting, Charpentier pointed to Massenet's scores as a corrective. He decided on prose for his libretto (even Gounod had expressed a desire to set French prose) and claimed that he allowed the natural speed of declamation to govern musical events, with the "continuous symphony in the orchestra" being sufficiently flexible to keep apace. Charpentier was very close to Debussy in his polemics, even though the musical results are strikingly divergent: Charpentier's approach, for example, to syllabic declamation is much less radical than Debussy's and is interspersed with long cantabile melodies, judging correctly, it would seem, that purism would not be well received by the public. In the event, *Louise*, as a more "democratic" opera, had much greater box-office success than *Pelléas*, and a correspondingly greater impact on French nationalist discourse (initially, at least; more on this below). *Louise* also enjoyed a degree of good luck in its nationalist resonance: its naturalistic depiction of working-class life chimed with Zola at the moment of the writer's greatest national prestige, thanks to his famous article "J'accuse" (Zola 1898), exposing the lies and anti-Semitism of the French state over the Dreyfus affair. The critics were quick to mythologize *Louise*'s roots: the poet and critic Camille Mauclair, in his article "La fin du wagnérisme," compared it to sixteenth-century French chanson, both supposedly displaying the same native gift for realism (Mauclair 1904; Huebner 1999: 479).

Musorgsky, Debussy, Janáček: "Dialogue Opera" between the National and the Universal

Turning Russian Speech into Music

Glinka's "Russian style" in *A Life for the Tsar*, as we have seen, was created out of popular idioms of the day and was never intended for reuse outside that opera. For Musorgsky, however, this was not enough, and he devised an approach to musical declamation that was derived from the rhythmic and pitch patterning of Russian speech, thereby avoiding the arbitrariness of Glinka's Russian style. The music of the language as spoken in real life, together with the local and personal quirks a speaker will have absorbed, is converted into the vocal lines of song and opera, so that its Russianness is ingrained, sealed, and polished into the music. Musorgsky himself was well aware of the nationalist potential of his newfound principle: while reporting on the composition of his song cycle *Nursery*, for example, he claimed that he had portrayed children who were "Russians, with a strong local flavour" (Musorgsky [1873] 1981: 122). Ultimately, Musorgsky was able to stake a claim to Russianness thanks to the originality and progressive character of his operatic works, overcoming all the accrued Italian, German, and French clichés with one bold stroke. There were, of course, other markers of Russianness that Musorgsky shared with his contemporaries (folk-song quotations and imitations, church singing, and bell-ringing), but these were still filtered through Western conventions and were generally imposed from the outside on the preexisting Western operatic forms. Musorgskian declamation, as part of his overall realist aesthetic, is different, since it tends to erode these forms from within, imposing a much more radical change on the art form.

Unsurprisingly, Musorgsky's principles of musical declamation were soon established as a great nationalist achievement, and close reading of his recitatives was championed by Russian scholars, a practice that reached its peak in the work of Aleksey Ogolevets (1966), the compiler of a four-hundred-page volume that trawls through *Boris Godunov* phrase by phrase, with endlessly detailed and uniformly admiring commentary. According to Ogolevets:

> The words of the old man [Varlaam] convey a particularly carefree and joyful attitude. According to the normal rules which all [the rest] of Varlaam's part follows, the "upbeat" *kak u-te[kli]* should have been written in sixteenth notes, because in a normal dialogue, there is no stress to be heard on the word *kak*. But no! [Instead,] Musorgsky doubles the length of this would-be upbeat, and makes each note staccato. This devil-may-care delivery at the beginning of the phrase establishes a boastful intonation; here the "augmentation," in combination with the staccato, i.e. with the separation of each syllable, is very true to life. After a self-satisfied pause, the words *iz monastïrya* are uttered rapidly [...] The intonation of the phrase is utterly convincing. Its general expressiveness is strengthened by the non-syntactic caesura, which adds a touch of real "blasphemous" pleasure to Varlaam's boasting [...]. (Ogolevets 1966: 181)

Something, however, is amiss in the midst of all this scholarly activity: for Russian speakers, such commentary ought to be superfluous, since the connection between Musorgsky's vocal lines and real speech should be perfectly obvious without expert analysis. Non-Russians, on the other hand, simply have to take these commentators' judgments on trust: Who are they, after all, to doubt whether the "non-syntactic caesura" conveys "blasphemy" in a particular passage? Most Western commentators, accordingly, have accepted that Musorgskian declamation is the last word in authentic Russianness.

In spite of this general consensus, there are grounds for taking a universalist rather than a nationalist view of Musorgskian declamation. In his late autobiographical note of 1880, which was admittedly addressed to a Western readership, the composer avoided nationalist terms, famously declaring that his aim was to "converse with people" through his art and that he considered his principal achievement to be "the reproduction in musical sounds not only of emotional moods, but chiefly, of the moods conveyed through human speech"—"human," we should note, rather than "Russian" (Musorgsky 1971–1972: I: 270). Indeed, when he provided what he regarded as his own musical line of descent, he failed to name any Russian composers; the list ran as follows: Palestrina, Bach, Gluck, Beethoven, Berlioz, and Liszt (1971–1972: I: 270). As Taruskin so ably demonstrates, the roots of Musorgsky's speech-based musical realism lay in the Aristotelian aesthetic theories of Georg Gottfried Gervinus (1805–1871), from whose book (1868) comes the German counterpart, *Gefühlsstimmungen*, of Musorgsky's phrase "emotional moods" (Taruskin 1993: 71–95). These, according to Gervinus, can be conveyed through an *Empfindungsaccent*, a complex that includes various characteristics of speech, such as intonation, volume, intensity, and speed. The music of speech, he says, is the best resonator for emotions that outstrip the plain meaning of an utterance (Gervinus 1868: 19; Taruskin 1993: 78).

In his unfinished experimental opera, *The Marriage* (after Gogol's 1842 comedy), we find Musorgsky at his most scientific. We can imaginatively reconstruct the process of text setting: Attempting to fix Gogol's dialogue, together with the manner in which it would be delivered on stage, Musorgsky must have declaimed the lines to himself as an actor would, characterizing the part and perhaps exaggerating somewhat to make the result more suggestive for his musical purposes. He would then have notated the line, filtering the raw "data" through the limits of the available discrete pitches and the various rhythmic and metric conventions he was still prepared to recognize. Having completed this task, he would have fitted harmonies underneath; the unconventional melodic profiles, however, led him to some strikingly novel harmonic progressions. Working on his next opera, *Boris Godunov*, Musorgsky took a few steps back from the purist method he had employed in *The Marriage*, not least because even his most sympathetic colleagues had doubted the musicality of the results (Taruskin 1993: 94). Interestingly, he now restricted the more rigorous applications of the method to characters from the lower classes, and even then, the harmony was often allowed to shape the melody rather than the reverse. In the second version of *Boris* and in *Khovanshchina*, his third attempt at an opera, he retreated still further from his original declamatory ideal.

While it is undeniable that Musorgsky's songs and operatic dialogues have a universal appeal, how much is lost on non-Russian listeners? His vocal music suffers from two serious problems when presented to a non-Russian audience: When a translation is sung to convey the meaning of the text, the carefully honed correspondence between words and melody will be lost in all but a few lucky instances, making nonsense of the composer's choices; and whether or not the text is translated, the "emotional moods" carried by speech intonation vary significantly from one language to another (and so a friendly chat between Italians may sound like a blazing row to English passersby; a Venezuelan student once complained that my attempts at a clear and emphatic Russian delivery made him very tense as he imagined that I was scolding him). Perhaps then, after all, Musorgsky's musical declamation can only lead to an insular nationalist tradition that has little hope of communicating with a universal audience.

Debussy Reads Musorgsky

Setting this question aside for the moment, let us turn to Debussy, who adopted Musorgsky's methods in order to liberate himself from the overbearing influence of Wagner during the long gestation of *Pelléas et Mélisande* (Debussy already knew Wagner's scores intimately). In the autumn of 1893, he famously discarded the first draft of the crucial love scene, precisely because, as he wrote to Ernest Chausson on October 2, 1893, it was haunted by "the ghost of old Klingsor" (Lesure and Nichols 1987: 54–55), and began work on a "more personal" version that used "silence... as a means of expression" (Nichols and Langham Smith 1989: 33). This change of mind was preceded by an immersion into Musorgsky scores during the summer months, as recalled by his friend Raymond Bonheur (Bonheur 1926). Two of Debussy's letters to Chausson, dating from 1893, indicate an active interest in the Russian composer just as work on *Pelléas* was beginning. The first bears no specific date:

> As I have been very good, bring me some Mussorgsky.... (Dietschy 1990: 63)

The second is dated June 4:

> This information [Musorgsky's biographical details] comes from Jules de Brayer, from whose forehead shine, one might say, prophetic rays when he speaks of Mussorgsky, whom he ranks much above Wagner. He will be very useful to us for a particular project. (Dietschy 1990: 63)

A letter to Henri Lerolle of August 28, 1894, allows us to infer that Debussy began work on the *Nocturnes* simultaneously with the composition of the Yniold/Golaud scene (Act III, scene 4) for *Pelléas* (Lesure and Nichols 1987: 72–73). The first of the *Nocturnes* (*Nuages*) opens with an unmistakable quote from Musorgsky's *Sunless* (1874) song cycle, and this makes it much more likely that the hints of Musorgsky's *Nursery* cycle (1872) in the Yniold scene were the result of direct influence rather than chance resemblances (Debussy eventually published a rapturous review of the latter cycle, in 1901 [Lesure and Smith: 20–21]). Among other things, this would render his famous repetition of "petit père" in the Yniold scene a descendant of Musorgsky's repeated "nyanyushka ("Nanny dear") in the first song of *The Nursery*. Debussy matched Musorgsky's naturalistic representation of children's formulaic speech patterns, and was further inspired to delve into child psychology—that slippery continuum between disarming innocence and guileful manipulation.

Musorgsky led Debussy to make the declamatory style prevail in *Pelléas*, although in Debussy's case, the declamation is rather less actorly, and closer to the flatter profile of ordinary speech (in keeping with the character of Maeterlinck's symbolist drama). His revisions show that he was faced with the same decisions that Musorgsky had made before him: at times, it is the vocal line that leads, while the harmony complies; at other times, certain harmonic features are clearly of greatest importance to him, and these remain intact while the profile of the vocal line must adapt (Nichols and Langham Smith 1989: 49).

There is no evidence that Debussy was at this stage concerned with any nationalist potential in his new path, and indeed he initially resented nationalist and patriotic outpourings and ridiculed "national" artworks such as Charpentier's *Louise*. His interests lay in the human depths of his characters. As he wrote to Chausson on October 2, 1893: "I've been forcing myself to be Pelléas as well as Mélisande and I've gone looking for music behind all the veils she wraps around herself" (Lesure and Nichols 1987: 54–55). He commented further to Lerolle on August 28, 1894: "It's terrifying, the music's got to be profound and absolutely accurate! There's a 'petit père' that gives me nightmares" (Nichols and Langham Smith 1989: 35). His wish was to find a personal and progressive musical path, not to uphold the glory of the French nation. These two requirements—truth to himself, and progress—are interlinked in the warning he made in his letter to Godet (on December 18, 1911, before the Geneva premiere of *Pelléas*) that the representation of emotion in *Pelléas*, expressed without recourse to "stereotypes and leitmotifs," might be seen as almost "indecent" (Lesure and Nichols 1987: 251). But nationalist rhetoric caught up with *Pelléas* immediately after the premiere, and its anti-Wagnerian approach was celebrated as the new course for French music. As Steven Huebner has documented, the opera was seen to display various supposedly national qualities such as understatement, restraint, and French *génie de goût* very soon after its premiere, and Romain Rolland characteristically "positioned it in a direct line of filiation from the French works of Gluck (skipping over Wagner)" (Rolland 1908: 205; Huebner 1999: 478–479). And also, alas, skipping over Musorgsky—one form of cultural nationalism will rarely acknowledge the assistance it might have received from the artists of another nation. Still, when Debussy did eventually take up nationalism himself, he found a brother-in-arms in another Russian, this time Stravinsky, to whom he wrote (October 23, 1915) of the imperative to stop art from succumbing to "the Austro-German miasma" and to kill "this microbe of false grandeur, of organized ugliness" (Lesure and Nichols 1987: 308).

Janáček's "Obsession"

It would be very convenient if we could say that Leoš Janáček had taken up Musorgsky's methods, just as Debussy had done before him; Janáček was, after all, a Russophile Czech nationalist, famed above all for his dialogue operas. And yet it seems that he arrived at the same methods independently, in complete ignorance of Musorgsky (even if he continued to profess his ignorance rather longer than was plausible, after the similarities had already been pointed out). But given Janáček's musical interests, this independent rediscovery is entirely feasible: His exploration of folk song (which he conducted in a much more serious and scholarly manner than Musorgsky ever dreamed of) led him into such activities as notating street vendors' cries (there was a similar attempt by Russian ethnographers to notate these cries, and the results found their way into Stravinsky's *Petrushka*); from there, he broadened his inquiry into the musical aspects of the spoken word. Janáček even took recourse to stopwatches and other gadgetry in the hope of enhancing his researches, and he became obsessed with the latent music in the speech all around him, outstripping even Musorgsky here (for example, he captured the last words of his dying daughter in music notation, although in the context this can be seen as a touching rather than a perverse gesture). Like Debussy, he searched for a new approach to opera after his work in progress, *Jenůfa*, seemed to have reached a dead end; he set it aside for five years, and returned transformed by his investigations (had he been aware of Musorgsky's work, his journey could have been shortened). When he resumed work on *Jenůfa*, he went one step further than Musorgsky: not only did he present his dialogues naturalistically, but he also chose one signature speech-based motif for every scene or section within a scene, and he adopted this as the basis of his orchestral texture, often as an ostinato figure.

Once again, we find that Janáček's motivations are a mixture of nationalism and universalism. *Jenůfa*'s nationalist potential was fully exploited in the publicity surrounding the premiere, where it was presented as a "Moravian music drama," and one of the first reviewers publicized Janáček's own thoughts: "every translation of this specifically Moravian work is completely unthinkable without a complete rewriting of the music which has grown organically with people's speech" (Janáček 1911; Tyrrell 2006: I: 487). (Thus, the same question was raised that we set aside for later during our discussion of Musorgsky). On the other hand, Janáček often discussed his "speech melodies" in the universalist terms already familiar to us from Musorgsky and Debussy: "A speech melody is a faithful momentary musical expression of a human being; it is his soul and all his being like a photograph of the moment" (Janáček 1911; Tyrrell 2006: I: 478). He valued this approach not only for the access it offered to the psychological depth of his characters, but also for the exploration of the ever-varying contexts in which the words are uttered; like Musorgsky and Debussy, he believed that neither dimension had been present in opera previously:

> By stealth I listened to the speech of passers-by, I read the expression on their faces, my eyes tracked their every movement, I observed the area around the speakers, the company they kept, the time of day, lightness and darkness, coldness and warmth.
>
> I sensed a reflection of all this in the notated speech melody. How many variations of melody could be found for the same word! . . . But I suspected in the melody something deeper still, something that wasn't immediately apparent, that had been covered up; I sensed that in the melody there were traces of secret, inner events. In them I understood sadness as well as the outbreak of joy, determination and doubts, etc. (Janáček 1911; Tyrrell 2006: I: 480)

Any appreciation of *Jenůfa*'s nationalist potential was confined to Brno in the first years after the premiere, thanks at least in part to the complicated politics of nationalism/regionalism in the territories that were to form Czechoslovakia after the First World War. The Moravian character of the opera seemed too narrow for one of Janáček's most dogged critics, Zdeněk Nejedlý, who still extolled Smetana's brand of nationalism, but also argued that Janáček had chosen the wrong path in favoring folklorism over progressivism (Nejedlý 1916: 121–122; Tyrrell 2006: II: 94). Only when his operas found their way abroad were they fully appreciated for both their nationalism and their universal human appeal. Max Brod wrote admiringly of *Jenůfa*'s concluding scene, where "the music, until then stamped with an acutely national character . . . becomes general, merely musical music: the intermediate stage of ethnography has emptied into the great ocean of humanity" (Brod [1966] 2003: 39). Brod evidently finds much more in *Jenůfa* than Adorno, who condescendingly refers to it as a mere folkloristic piece (Botstein 2003: 34), but Brod still remains within the bounds of Herderian Romantic nationalism. In his arguments, Brod can arrive at a sober assessment of Janáček's personal craft as a composer, but at the same time, he adds his own Romantic belief that a primal, authentic *Volksgeist* was at work in the music. He realizes that in the hands of a lesser composer, the speech-melody approach could have been a dismal failure, and he points delightedly to one of the composer's most important inventions: namely, his naturalistic translation of the repetitions that characterize the speech of "people from rural areas" into repetitive musical structures that are stylized and "free-form"—in effect, this places them at a remove from their naturalistic origins, and instead they coalesce into a modernist device. Yet at the same time, Brod wants to see the root of the opera's stylistic unity in something "deeper than [Janáček's] personal genius." According to him, it lies, rather, in the fact that the speech melodies are, like folk songs, "genuine sounds of nature.... The genius of the people," he insists, "speaks from every measure" (Brod [1966] 2003: 37–43).

Brod's argument, if confused, perceptively hints at the path from universalism to nationalism and beyond that to universalism again, a path followed by Musorgsky, Debussy, and Janáček alike in their "dialogue operas." Each of the composers begins with the uncovering of a deep-seated human truth that has been hidden from art in the past. They research it almost scientifically, as the preoccupations of their age demanded, and just as Zola claimed to do: "my goal is scientific above all... I simply subjected two living bodies to the same analysis that surgeons perform on cadavers" (Zola [1868] 2008: 25; Mallach 2007: 12). The universal psychological truths thus uncovered are, however, wrapped in the rhythms and intonations of a particular language, in national clothing, threatening the potential universal appeal of the found truths with national insularity. But the enactment of the national aspect makes a profound impact on musical syntax that once again has a universal appeal to composers outside that nation. Naturalism, nationalism, and modernism truly go hand in hand here.

Translating the "Genius of a Nation"

Let us finally consider the issue that we set aside earlier, a practical matter that emerges from this tangle. The circulation of dialogue operas on the international stage summons translations into existence, but these are shot through with contradictions. The vocal lines of these operas stem from the pitch and rhythmic patterns of the original language within a dramatic context, and translation will therefore remove all motivation and sense from this compositional principle, leaving behind melodies that are merely wayward and arbitrary. But leaving these operas in their original languages (especially in the case of Moravian Czech and other lesser-known tongues) is no solution either, as the impact of the text is then lost; casting the music still further adrift from its original significance, surtitles offer only a partial remedy here. Serge Diaghilev was well aware of the problem when, in 1908, he presented *Boris Godunov* to his Parisian audience in the original Russian and cut the Gordian knot by removing the entire Inn Scene, where the declamatory manner was applied most consistently and radically. For its La Scala premiere (1909), *Boris* was translated into Italian, and this translation was also used by Toscanini at the Metropolitan Opera in 1913. A Met recording from 1939 demonstrates how the translation necessitated a partial recomposition of declamatory phrases, since Italian could not cope with Russian "mute endings," where words tail off into a string of unstressed syllables at the end (Musorgsky 1939).

With Debussy, similar problems arose, for example, in the English National Opera production of 1982, where the translator Hugh Macdonald also had to make minor modifications to Debussy's vocal lines in order to fit them to the consistently lower English syllable count (Howat 1982: 45–46). No one, however, dared suggest that any more radical recomposition should be undertaken in order to match the melodic contours of the vocal parts to the contours of the new English text as it would be spoken (and melodic changes might have necessitated harmonic changes, too). This was unthinkable, of course: It would have been deemed a gross intrusion into the fabric of the music. And yet, viewed dispassionately, such a move would have been the outcome if the logic of Debussy's compositional method had been followed.

Janáček, as it happens, was quite unperturbed by the translation of his operas into German, even though they were at first considered untranslatable (Tyrrell 2006: I: 488). If he had felt the need, he could have supervised the translations and adapted his music accordingly; instead, he allowed others to determine the translations, and to attach their German texts to his "Moravian" musical lines. Why did he not consider this a travesty? Do the speech patterns somehow cease to matter after they have been converted to music? Was the composer submitting to a necessary evil simply because this would enhance his finances and his international reputation? Or does his lack of concern tell us that we should not fetishize the authenticity of "speech melody," and that we should instead try to unravel the mythology that has accrued around it? This, indeed, has been the direction of many recent Janáček studies: Paul Wingfield has suggested that Janáček's method is not that distant from Wagner's (Wingfield 1992: 301), although this may be going too far, while Miloš Štědroň called his speech melody notations "artistically stylized objects" (Štědroň 1999: 80). Derek Katz noted that "Janacek's choices often seem motivated by musical rather than linguistic considerations" (Katz 2009: 23), an observation that can equally well be made of Musorgsky where *Boris Godunov* was concerned (but not *The Marriage*).

I would suggest that the "genius of the nation" (whatever that might be) is not easily conveyed through dialogue opera, even to native speakers of the composer's language. We find a series of obstacles impeding any direct communication from the composer to the listener, as I myself can judge in the case of Musorgsky. First, the speech patterns the composer has attempted to copy may be too far removed from the tendencies of present-day Russian speakers. The composer, in transferring the speech sounds to music, stretches, exaggerates, and molds them according to the promptings of his own imagination, using an array of discrete pitches (rather than allowing for the continuously changing pitch of normal speech); he then seeks out compromises between the resulting melody line and the need for some minimal degree of harmonic coherence. In addition to all these layers, the singers impose their own interpretive decisions on their performance (and a singer who is not a native speaker would be attempting this without any secure knowledge of the likely speech prototype!). Finally, we listeners must be lucky enough to catch the words, which in many performances are often difficult or impossible, owing to the singers' habits, the opera house's acoustic, and distractions from the listener's neighbors.

Even as a compatriot of Musorgsky's, I must confess that I often fail to grasp Musorgsky's speech prototypes while listening to a performance, even if I can extract them later while contemplating the score. During a performance, I am influenced much more by general parameters of speed and pitch (relaxed or urgent, subdued or excited) and therefore my perceptions are not so very different from those of non-Russian listeners (whether or not they know any Russian), and I might just as well listen to *Boris* in English translation. While a privileged native speaker's access to speech melody means better access to the comic nuances of the Inn Scene, or a more thrilling experience of the psychological battles in Prokofiev's *The Gambler* (*Igrok*), for example, we can still be struck and moved by Mélisande's "Je t'aime aussi" without being native French speakers. In any case, emotions and other psychological states are often so over-determined in opera that we can easily afford to miss one marker while noticing several others that give us the same information. It is quite normal for the words to elude opera-goers, even when the opera is sung in their own language. We may have a seat with a restricted view, or we may be viewing a production that deliberately distracts us or undermines the intentions of the composer and librettist. We may even be in the habit of reconstructing operas in our imagination from vocal scores. Listening to dialogue operas that were composed on the basis of speech patterns in another language is just one of a host of obstacles we successfully surmount in our regular experience of opera (if we generally failed, we would soon stop making the effort). If we broadly understand what the characters are talking about, then we know enough to make our operatic experiences worthwhile, and any further appreciation of subtleties in the construction of the melodic lines is merely an occasional bonus.

Debating Authenticity

Some clear recurring patterns emerge from all the examples above. The desire to create and maintain a self-consciously national style arises from a perceived threat of subordination to a foreign culture, and usually has deep social and political roots, such as immigration and war. The process is usually accompanied by public debate on what is required and what is to be avoided in any authentic national work. Composers will turn their backs on the offending foreign traditions and idioms (Rimsky-Korsakov described this *via negativa* method when talking about the formation of the "Russian style" [Frolova-Walker 2007: 207]), resulting in new national works that will be more (or less) melodic/declamatory/symphonic, small-scale/large-scale, or simple/complex than the negative model. Authentication is often sought in a folk tradition that is (rightly or wrongly) projected on the whole nation, or in a musical tradition from the nation's past (real or imagined). Further authentication is often drawn from close attention to the vernacular language, the pillar of every nationalist ideology, even though, as we have seen, this can lead to a paradoxical mélange of nationalist and universalist appeal. Composers of nationalist works still consistently hope for an international audience, and regard this as the standard for judging success, although the creation of such works is not a guarantee of enthusiastic reception even in the composer's home country. This means that a balance must be struck between insularity and openness—or, to re-describe the same dichotomy from an outsider's perspective, a balance between exoticism and familiarity.

And finally, nationalist quests are invariably entangled with the progressive/conservative dichotomy, and generally align themselves with what is regarded internationally as progressive. This is not merely coincidental, but arises from the consistent avoidance of an internationally dominant tradition, which pushes composers toward invention and innovation. For all the empty rhetoric and self-deception of many nationalist ideologies, they have served for this reason as a powerful catalyst to the artistic imagination.

On the reception side, however, the composer's intentions are not crucial on any of these counts. Whether this or that piece is received as a national artwork is above all dependent on the public discourse that develops around it. In the words of Michael Beckerman, when the nation "becomes a subtextual program for musical works [...] it is that which animates the musical style, allowing us to make connections between the narrow confines of a given piece and a larger, dynamic context" (Beckerman 1986: 73). A nationalist discourse is therefore the final arbiter on the national character of a given work or style, and nationalist composers can only strive for attention in this discourse, not only by incorporating plausibly national devices in their works, but also by writing music that is worth talking about by any standards.

See also: Versification, The German Libretto of the Early Nineteenth Century

Note

1. "torniamo all'antico, sarà un progresso."

Bibliography

Abert, Hermann. 1926. "Carl Maria von Weber und sein *Freischütz*." *Jahrbuch der Musikbibliothek Peters* 33: 9–29.

Beckerman, Michael, ed. 2003. *Janáček and His World*. Princeton, NJ: Princeton University Press.

——. 1986. "In Search of Czechness in Music." *19th-Century Music* 10/1: 61–73.

Bonheur, Raymond. 1926. "Souvenirs et impressions d'un compagnon de jeunesse." *La revue musicale* 7: 99–105 (3–9).

Botstein, Leon. 2003. "The Cultural Politics of Language and Music: Max Brod and Leoš Janáček." In Beckerman 2003, 13–54.

Brod, Max. [1966] 2003. "Max Brod on Leoš Janáček's *Jenůfa*," translated by Susan H. Gillespie. In Beckerman 2003, 37–43.

Budden, Julian. 1987. "Wagnerian Tendencies in Italian Opera." In *Music and Theatre: Essays in Honor of Winton Dean*, edited by Nigel Fortune, 299–332. New York: Cambridge University Press.

Csobádi, Peter, Gernot Gruber, et al., eds. 2003. *Politische Mythen und nationale Identitäten im (Musik-) Theater*. 2 Vols. Vorträge und Gespräche des Salzburger Symposions 2001. Wort und Musik: Salzburger Akademische Beiträge 54. Salzburg: Verlag Mueller-Speiser.

Dahlhaus, Carl. 1989. *Nineteenth-Century Music*, translated by J. Bradford Robinson. Berkeley and Los Angeles: University of California Press.

——. 1980. *Between Romanticism and Modernism: Four Studies in the Music of the Later Nineteenth Century*, translated by Mary Whittall. Berkeley and Los Angeles: University of California Press.

d'Azeglio, Massimo. [1867] 1966. *Things I Remember [I miei ricordi]*, translated by E. R. Vincent. New York: Oxford University Press.

Dietschy, Marcel. 1990. *A Portrait of Claude Debussy*, edited and translated by William Ashbrook and Margaret G. Cobb. Oxford: Clarendon Press.

Florimo, Francesco. 1883. *Riccardo Wagner ed i wagneristi*. Ancona: A. G. Morelli.

Frolova-Walker, Marina. 2011. "A Ukrainian Tune in Medieval France: Perceptions of Nationalism and Local Color in Russian Opera." *19th-Century Music* 35/2: 115–131.

——. 2007. *Russian Music and Nationalism from Glinka to Stalin*. New Haven: Yale University Press.

——. 1998. "'National in Form, Socialist in Content': Musical Nation-Building in the Soviet Republics." *Journal of the American Musicological Society* 51/2: 331–371.

——. 1997. "On *Ruslan* and Russianness." *Cambridge Opera Journal* 9/1: 21–45.

Fulcher, Jane. 1987. *The Nation's Image: French Grand Opera as Politics and Politicized Art*. Cambridge: Cambridge University Press.

Gervinus, Georg Gottfried. 1868. *Händel und Shakespeare*. Leipzig: W. Engelmann.

Giger, Andreas. 2008. *Verdi and the French Aesthetic: Verse, Stanza, and Melody in Nineteenth-Century Opera*. Cambridge: Cambridge University Press.

Greenwald, Helen. 2003a. "Decoding Verdi's Comic Vision: Towards a Theory of Comedy for the Late Nineteenth Century." *Verdi 2001. Atti del convegno internazionale di studi, Parma, New York, New Haven, 24 gennaio–1 febbraio 2001*. 2 vols., edited by Fabrizio Della Seta, Roberta Montemorra Marvin, and Marco Marica, I: 281–291. Florence: Olschki.

——. 2003b. "Opera and National Identity in the Late Nineteenth Century: Verdi, Wagner, and the 'Restoration of a Proper Society.'" In Csobádi et al. 2003, II: 545–554.

Grey, Thomas S. 2009. "*Eine Kapitulation*: Aristophanic Operetta as Cultural Warfare in 1870." In *Richard Wagner and His World*, edited by Thomas S. Grey, 87–122. Princeton, NJ: Princeton University Press.

——. 2006. "Commentary: Opera in the Age of Revolution." *Journal of Interdisciplinary History* 36/3: 555–567.

Groos, Arthur, and Roger Parker. 1987. *Giacomo Puccini: 'La bohème.'* Cambridge Opera Handbooks. Cambridge: Cambridge University Press.

Herder, Johann Gottfried von. 1878. "Einzelne Blätter zum 'Journal der Reise 1769.'" In *Herders sämtliche Werke*. 33 vols., edited by Bernhard Suphan, IV: 484. Berlin: Weidmann.

Howat, Roy. 1982. "English National Opera's *Pelléas and Mélisande* at the London Coliseum." *Cahiers Debussy* 6: 45–46.

Huebner, Steven. 1999. *French Opera at the Fin de Siècle: Wagnerism, Nationalism, and Style*. New York: Oxford University Press.

Huret, Jules. 1900. "Une idée d'artiste." *Le Figaro* (November 19).

Jähns, Friedrich Wilhelm. 1871. *Carl Maria von Weber in seinen Werken: Chronologisch-thematisches Verzeichniss einer sämtliche Compositionen nebst Angabe unvollständigen, verloren gegangene, zweifelhaften und untergeschobenen*. Berlin: Schlesinger'schen Buch- und Musikhandlung.

Janáček, Leoš. 1911. Interview in *Moravské noviny* (February 4).

Kaiser, Georg, ed. 1908. *Sämtliche Schriften von Carl Maria von Weber*. Berlin: Schuster & Loeffler.

Katz, Derek. 2009. *Janáček beyond the Borders*. Rochester, NY: University of Rochester Press.

Large, David Clay, and William Weber, eds. 1984. *Wagnerism in European Culture and Politics.* Ithaca, NY: Cornell University Press.

Lesure, François, and Roger Nichols, eds. 1987. *Debussy Letters*, translated by Roger Nichols. London: Faber and Faber.

——, and Richard Langham Smith, eds. 1977. *Debussy on Music.* London: Secker & Warburg; New York: Alfred A. Knopf.

Mallach, Allan. 2007. *The Autumn of Italian Opera from Verismo to Modernism, 1890–1915.* Boston: Northeastern University Press.

Mauclair, Camille. 1904. "La Fin du wagnérisme." *La Revue* (February 15).

Meyer, Stephen C. 2003. *Carl Maria von Weber and the Search for German Opera.* Bloomington: Indiana University Press.

Musorgsky, Modest. [1873] 1981. Musorgsky, Modest Petrovich. *Pis'ma.* Moscow: Muzïka.

——. 1971–1972. *Literaturnoye naslediye*, edited by A. A. Orlova and M. S. Pekelis. 2 vols. Moscow: Muzïka.

——. 1939. *Boris Godunov.* Metropolitan Opera Orchestra and Chorus, conducted by Ettore Panizza. Live performance, New York (December 9). Arkadia, 2000 2 CD GA2007.

Nejedlý, Zdeněk. 1916. "Leoša Janáčka 'Její pastorkyňa.'" *Smetana* 6: 117–124.

Nichols, Roger, and Richard Langham Smith, eds. and trans. 1989. *Claude Debussy: 'Pelléas et Mélisande.'* Cambridge Opera Handbooks. Cambridge: Cambridge University Press.

Ogolevets, Aleksey Stepanovich. 1966. *Vokal'naya dramaturgiya Musorgskogo.* Moscow: Muzïka.

Osborne, Charles, ed. and trans. 1971. *Letters of Giuseppe Verdi.* London: Gollancz.

Parker, Roger. 1997. *Leonora's Last Act: Essays in Verdian Discourse.* Princeton, NJ: Princeton University Press.

Rolland, Romain. 1908. *Musiciens d'aujourd'hui.* Paris: Hachette et cie.

Saint-Saëns, Camille. 1898. "Défense de l'Opéra-Comique." *Le Monde artiste* (May 8).

Senici, Emanuele. 2001. "Verdi's Falstaff at Italy's Fin de Siècle." *Musical Quarterly* 85/2: 274–310.

Shaw, George Bernard. [1894] 1981. "Born-Again Italian Opera." In *Shaw's Music.* 3 vols., edited by Dan Laurence, III: 214–221. London: Bodley Head.

Smaczny, Jan. 2003. "Grand Opera among the Czechs." *The Cambridge Companion to Grand Opera*, edited by David Charlton, 366–382. Cambridge: Cambridge University Press.

Spohr, Ludwig. 1823. "Aufruf and deutsche Komponisten." *Allgemeine musikalische Zeitung* 25: col. 457–464.

Štědroň, Miloš. 1999 "Direct Discourse and Speech Melody in Janáček's Operas." In *Janáček Studies*, edited by Paul Wingfield, 79–108. Cambridge: Cambridge University Press.

Taruskin, Richard. 2012. "Nationalism." In *Grove Music Online. Oxford Music Online.* Available: http://www.oxfordmusiconline.com/subscriber/article/grove/music/50846 (accessed July 21, 2012).

——. 2005. The Oxford History of Western Music. 5 vols. New York: Oxford University Press.

——. 1997. *Defining Russia Musically: Historical and Hermeneutical Essays.* Princeton, NJ: Princeton University Press.

——. 1993. *Musorgsky: Eight Essays and an Epilogue.* Princeton, NJ: Princeton University Press.

Torrefranca, Fausto. 1912. *Giacomo Puccini e l'opera internazionale.* Turin: Bocca.

Tusa, Michael C. 2006. "Cosmopolitanism and the National Opera: Weber's *Der Freischütz.*" *Journal of Interdisciplinary History* 36/3: 483–506.

——. 1991. *'Euryanthe' and Carl Maria von Weber's Dramaturgy of German Opera.* Oxford: Clarendon Press.

Tyrrell, John. 2006. *Janáček: Years of a Life.* 2 vols. London: Faber and Faber.

Wagner, Richard. [1834] “Die Deutsche Oper.” *Zeitung for die elegante Welt* 10 June. Online. Available: http://users.utu.fi/hansalmi/appen.html (accessed July 21, 2012).
——. [1841] 1966. “*Der Freischütz*: To the Paris Public.” In *Richard Wagner's Prose Works*, edited and translated by William Ashton Ellis, VII: 169–204. London: Kegan Paul..
——. [1873] 2005. “Eine Kapitulation.” In *Richard Wagner. Sämtliche Werke*. Vol. 31: *Dokumente und Texte zu unfollendeten Bühnenwerken*, edited by Isolde Vetter and Egon Voss, 307–339. Mainz: Schott.
Warrack, John. 2001. *German Opera: From the Beginnings to Wagner*. Cambridge: Cambridge University Press, 2001.
Weber, Carl Maria von. [1817] 1981. “To the Art-Loving Citizens of Dresden.” In *Carl Maria von Weber: Writings on Music*, edited by John Warrack and translated by Martin Cooper, 205–207. Cambridge: Cambridge University Press. [original in Dresden *Abend-Zeitung* 25 (January 29)].
Wilson, Alexandra. 2007. *The Puccini Problem: Opera, Nationalism, and Modernity*. Cambridge: Cambridge University Press.
Wingfield, Paul. 1992. “Janáček's Speech-Melody Theory in Concept and Practice.” *Cambridge Opera Journal* 4/3: 281–301.
Youens, Susan. 1997. *Schubert, Müller, and 'Die Schöne Müllerin.'* Cambridge: Cambridge University Press.
Zola, Émile. 1898. “J'accuse…! Lettre au président de la république.” *L'Aurore* (January 13): 1–2.
——. [1868, preface to the 2nd ed.] 2008. *Thérèse Raquin*, translated by Andrew Rothwell. New York: Oxford University Press.

CHAPTER 8

MUSICAL DRAMATURGY

DAMIEN COLAS

TRANSLATED BY EDWARD SCHNEIDER

It is perfectly obvious that opera is a particular form of theater: a particular form, that is, of stage action. Not so obvious is how to identify the elements that generate drama in an opera: to precisely describe operatic dramaturgy. This is evidenced by the inconclusive debate that has recurred throughout the history of music (Di Benedetto 1988). This chapter relates to an epistemological study of the ways in which operatic dramaturgy has been analyzed; more specifically, to a comparison of two schools of thought. According to one of these, the drama stems from the verbal text; according to the other, it originates in the musical elements. To avoid any ambiguity, the phrase "musical dramaturgy" will be understood here in its etymological sense of the "production (ἔργον) of theatrical action (δρᾶμα) through music." In that sense, musical dramaturgy is a sub-category of poetics. This definition is narrower than the generic "study of opera" seen in many university courses, but it covers more ground than theories of musical dramaturgy such as the one that Carl Dahlhaus strove to forge in the 1980s.

The Dramaturgy of the Libretto and Musical Dramaturgy: Seeking a New Paradigm

No matter what the approach, studying operatic dramaturgy eventually raises the question: What is the status of the libretto in the eyes of the student? For many, it goes without saying that an opera's dramaturgy corresponds precisely with that of its libretto; for them it is pointless to question this inherent equivalency. This applies, for example, to stage directors who base their work on the study of the verbal text—and sometimes of the verbal text alone. It applies also to students of comparative literature and of history, for whom the libretto is the prime object of analysis, and more generally to all who turn their attention to opera without being in a position to read the musical scores. To musicologists, on the other hand, it is by no means clear that the dramaturgy of an opera and that of its libretto are one and the same (Bianconi 1986: 7). The view that they are identical arises when a student intuitively, unknowingly peers at opera through a prism appropriate to spoken theater.

The approach by which all elements of an opera—music, staging, and performance—are explained on the basis of its libretto is not merely without foundation but also is easily shown to be false. So many characteristics of the genre demonstrate that this approach is neither applicable nor legitimate and thus that the theory of opera cannot be pondered in the same way as that of spoken theater. We need only think of the most obvious of these characteristics: the presence in every opera of passages where the sung text cannot be understood either because of the superposition of voices (for example, in a *largo concertato* in a nineteenth-century Italian opera or a contemplative ensemble in a German one) or because of the use of languages unknown to the audience. The popularity of Czech-school composers such as Smetana, Dvořák, and Janáček is out of all proportion to the number of music-lovers who speak the language. And works have been written in dead languages (Latin for Stravinsky's *Œdipus rex*, 1920, and Sanskrit for Philip Glass's *Satyagraha*, 1980) or invented ones (in the chorus of damned souls and demons in Berlioz's *La damnation de Faust*, 1846; the coded language for the Chief of the Gepopo in Ligeti's *Le grand macabre*, 1978, revised 1997; and the hypothetical reconstruction of the sound of ancient Egyptian in Glass's *Akhnaten*, 1983). Such passages do not prevent audiences from embracing and enjoying a work, and this cannot be explained by any theory of dramaturgical analysis of spoken theater.

Moreover, that viewpoint gives rise to spurious issues and notions of a kind that have cropped up throughout operatic history. One typical example is the accusation leveled against Italian opera by rationalist critics in the eighteenth century: "Too much music." In fact, that charge is illogical: one cannot complain that a genre is abusing the very medium on which it is founded. The confusion arises from a threefold premise whereby (a) the function of music is to illustrate the text; (b) the text antedates the music; and (c) in the dramatic genre, the music has no independent *raison d'être*. That premise may hold true from the narrow perspective of the dramaturgy of the libretto, but it entirely loses its validity when that perspective changes. The nineteenth-century accusation of "effect without cause" (*Wirkung ohne Ursache*) is likewise unfounded. The phrase, which Wagner used to denigrate Meyerbeer's dramaturgy (Wagner [1851] 1911: III: 301), had earlier been employed by Giuseppe Carpani with respect to Rossini ("effetti senza causa evidente"; Carpani 1824: 113). In both cases, the criticism, aimed at rather expansive musical forms that had a certain "effect" on the audience, was that they lacked *obvious* cause. This assumes that a musical structure must have an external justification—in the libretto—and does not even consider the possibility that cause can be found within the musical structure itself. The heteronomy of the musical discourse is seen as self-evident, and autonomy of any kind is rejected out of hand.

Hence, the limitations of dramaturgic analysis of the libretto call for a new paradigm. In the 1980s, Carl Dahlhaus proposed one to replace the premise that operatic dramaturgy equals the dramaturgy of the libretto: what he called the "fundamental proposition" of musical dramaturgy was that "the primary constituent of opera *as a drama* is the music" (Dahlhaus [1988] 2001: 467). While he was not the first writer to state this idea, his contribution was innovative in two respects, compared to the work of earlier theoreticians and musicologists from Pierjacopo Martello (1715) to Joseph Kerman (1956). First, by systematically questioning key ideas and concepts that had been accepted as given—often because of the intellectual authority of a respected writer—but that were in fact without foundation, he revealed internal contradictions in the dramaturgy of the libretto. Significantly, like his study of value judgments, "Sind musikalische Werturteile begründbar? ("Are Musical Value Judgments Justified?") (Dahlhaus [1985] 2001), his work on operatic dramaturgy reflects a foundationalist approach on the fringe of the traditional methodology of historical musicology. It is influenced by a school of thought linking it to the pioneering early twentieth-century work of Edmund Husserl on the theory of knowledge and David Hilbert on Euclidean geometry. Significantly, it was as he completed a deconstruction of arguments in Wagner's prose works (Dahlhaus [1971b] 2004) that Dahlhaus came to reassess number opera (Dahlhaus [1988] 2001) with a depth and rigor that ardent admirers of the genre had never previously mustered.

Second, Dahlhaus's intention was to forge an axiomatic theory on the basis of his fundamental proposition. For that reason, he did not lean on earlier critics and musicologists who had stated similar views; rather, he based his thinking on German literary criticism of the 1940s to 1960s, which tended toward axiomatism. From Emil Staiger (1946, 1953), Péter Szondi (1956), and Volker Klotz (1960) he borrowed the fundamental concepts of dramaturgy, which those writers had considered in the context of the written word. He then applied these to opera. It might seem surprising that Dahlhaus turned to the literary criticism of his day to deconstruct what had come about through the dramaturgy of the libretto. But in fact there is no contradiction: While the dramaturgy of the libretto in its narrowest sense explains musical elements as illustrations of a preexistent text—which is debatable, if only for the aforementioned reasons—the issues raised by Staiger, Szondi, and Klotz with respect to the theory of dramaturgy remain valid, irrespective of the media used to construct the drama. It is thus legitimate to apply these to opera.

Dahlhaus's theory, set out in a number of essays during the 1980s, remained unfinished. It focused on number opera—the foundation of Italian opera and various national schools derived from it—and thus could do no more than touch on issues specific to the mixing of song and spoken dialogue in comic genres such as *Singspiel*, *opéra comique*, *zarzuela*, and to *Literaturoper*, and it completely ignored the dramaturgy of the seventeenth- and eighteenth-century French *tragédie en musique*, which offered the only alternative to the Italian model. Nonetheless, his theory made it possible to bring out quite a few fundamental concepts that applied to a large part of the operatic literature.

The three case studies below were chosen to highlight the differences between the dramaturgy of the libretto and musical dramaturgy, to show how the latter gradually grew independent of the former, and to stress how a student's thinking will vary depending on the paradigm initially selected. The first two case studies relate to major dramaturgical problems—the portrayal of madness/folly and the portrayal of public uproar—faced by the creator of stage action, whether in a play, an opera, a ballet, or a puppet show. The third one describes how a well-known musical-dramaturgical tool was invented.

Madmen and Fools: The Depiction of Madness

Dramatists have always been drawn to the portrayal of madness and folly. There is nothing surprising about this: such behaviors invariably have an effect on those who witness them and can in that sense be described as theatrical. They take spectators by surprise, grab their attention, draw them out of their own thoughts. They arouse emotions ranging in intensity from mere surprise to compassion or fear. They meet two of the requirements that every playwright aims to fulfill: to draw the spectator in and to evoke emotions. The behavior of a madman or fool—even without the intermediary of the author's craft—inherently creates drama; in other words, it is "dramaturgic."

Yet the facets of madness and folly that are of interest to the playwright are not necessarily of interest to the musical dramatist. Shakespeare's fools (such as Feste in *Twelfth Night*) and Cervantes's Don Quixote have not to date provided rich material for musicians, and Parsifal—whom Wagner identifies as a "pure fool [pure of heart]"[1]—does not receive musical treatment specific to that status. Why is this? The folly of Feste, Don Quixote, and Parsifal relates to ignorance or rejection of the practical rules of dialogue that underlie social structures. Such behaviors fall squarely within the area of verbal expression and open up great creative possibilities for the writer of language. But they are of little benefit to the musician, at least within the resources of the seventeenth-to-nineteenth-century musical language.

On the other hand, the madness of Ophelia (*Hamlet*, 1868) and of Lucia (*Lucia di Lammermoor*, 1835) provided Ambroise Thomas and Gaetano Donizetti with rich subjects for musical treatment. Their madness is born not of a breakdown of reason but of unbearable suffering. For composers, the portrayal of madness is simply one category within the portrayal of suffering, for which they possess tried and true dramaturgic tools. In Lucia's mad scene, we see a blend of compositional strategies developed at various points in the history of opera, each appropriate to the musical portrayal of a particular symptom. To identify these it will be useful to return to two older examples.

When Egisto confronts his wife, Clori, who has betrayed him and who pretends not to recognize him, he sinks first into despair (Cavalli, *Egisto*, 1643, Act II, scene 1, "Lasso, io vivo"), then into madness. In the course of a lengthy recitative (Act III, scene 5, "Celesti fulmini") he swings between ferocious execration and desperate supplication, and his speech is marked by sudden, unpredictable shifts—a clear sign that he has lost his reason. Conventionally, "reason" is identified with mastery of one's reasoning (logic) and hence of the speech to which it gives rise (the *logos*). The madness of Ariosto's Orlando is like that of Egisto: both characters lose their reason when they come upon a tree carved with the names of their beloved and her new lover. To depict this in music, both Vivaldi (*Orlando furioso* 1727) and Handel (*Orlando* 1733) use recitative in the way Cavalli did (respectively in II: 13, "Ah sleale, ah spergiura" and II: 11 "Ah! stigie larve"), with the same emotional intensity and the same sudden shifts.

But Handel's duet for Angelica and Orlando ("Finché prendi ancor il sangue," III: 8) offers a completely different depiction of the character's madness. When Angelica attempts to calm him with her tears and contrition, Orlando is deaf to her words, locked into his determination to seek vengeance ("Sol ha sete di sangue il mio cor"). The obsessive nature of this madness—which cuts the character off from any contact with the world around him and condemns him to be his own prisoner—is conveyed through the repetitions that are part of the aria's construction.

A third symptom of madness appears in Donizetti's *Lucia*. After killing the man she was forced to marry, Lucia appears before the guests assembled in the castle, alienated from herself and unaware of the crime she has committed. Although, like Handel's Orlando, she is cut off from the world around her and is her own prisoner, this is because during her hallucinations her spirit and her mind have been possessed by an extrinsic power. The world she describes has no reality beyond her imagination, as emphasized by the strangeness of the sound of the glass harmonica that accompanies her.

Those three examples illustrate differing ways of musically depicting madness. They show that the creation of a dramaturgical tool in music is always the result of pairing a preexisting resource in the language of music with an *a posteriori* rationale for its use, within the theory of imitation. They also show the gradual movement from dramaturgy centered on the libretto to an ever deeper exploration of the dramaturgical powers of music itself.

Madness as Chaotic Discourse

The splintered discourse of Egisto, like that of Ottavia in her farewell in Monteverdi's *L'incoronazione di Poppea* (1642), reflects the distinction between recitative and aria, which is a foundation of the Venetian school. Those two compositional techniques were developed independently: Recitative was born at the start of the seventeenth century with the *stile rappresentativo* (Cavalieri, preface to *Rappresentazione di Anima e di Corpo*, 1600), while the easily identifiable self-contained and isometric nature and internal structure of aria already existed in Renaissance madrigals, songs, and instrumental dance music. They became two complementary elements for constructing an opera. The contrast between them in terms of compositional technique was used to reflect the contrast, in terms of the theory of imitation, between two concepts of *pathos*: the distinction between *lamento* in recitative and *lamento* in aria (Bianconi [1987] 1991: 219–235) corresponds to that between *perturbatio* and *morbus* (Dahlhaus [1988] 2001: 522).

In the third dialogue of his *Tusculan Disputations*, Cicero discusses those two Latin renderings of the Greek term *pathos*. When a person is stricken with *perturbatio* following a traumatic event, he or she loses the ability to reason since he is no longer able to organize his thoughts logically. The individual's discourse becomes chaotic, erratic, rambling, and unpredictable, and it is precisely its intensity and sudden shifts that, in terms of form, distinguish it from the flowing clarity of sane discourse. The hallucinations that are typical of what is today called schizophrenia fall into the category of *perturbatio*.

Recitative provides a clever solution for depicting this state of mind. Since its primary function is rhetorical, sung declamation can magnify the *cantus obscurior* of the verbal text (Cicero, *De Oratore*, 18.57). That is, it can use rhythm, intensity, and pitch to expand the contrasts already existing in the text. Moreover, recitative lacks its own musical structure: it is entirely linked to the words, and its musical organization is tethered to the organization of the text. The lack of coherence of the resulting musical form thus lends itself perfectly to translating verbal incoherence and unpredictability.

The association of recitative with *perturbatio*, developed in the seventeenth century, continued to be used by composers even when it had competition from other subsequent techniques for depicting madness. We still see it in the opening recitative of Lucia's mad scene, "Il dolce suono," where it is used to illustrate the intensity of the mental images that possess the character as she hallucinates.

Madness as Obsession

Recitative is marked by its dependence on the text. But the introduction of aria and the decision to make it the main structural element of opera from the second half of the seventeenth century until the first half of the nineteenth were two decisive steps toward the autonomy of musical discourse. With its pre-established structure based on repetition and on independence from the organization of the text, the form of an aria, unlike that of a recitative, cannot be described as merely setting the words to music. This liberation from the textual structure was criticized by those who viewed opera from a logocentric standpoint (Di Benedetto 1998: 19). Some contrasted the (vulgar and ephemeral) sensual pleasure of enjoying the music of an aria—and by extension an opera—with the (noble and enduring) intellectual pleasure derived from the text in recitative, which is akin to spoken drama (Di Benedetto 1988: 19). Others felt that repetition in an aria ran counter to the natural flow of discourse. Yet others condemned the juxtaposition of recitative and aria. All of these criticisms point to the tension between the dramaturgy of the libretto and that of the music, with the growing autonomy of the latter being seen as a betrayal of the former.

Audiences' acceptance of the aria and its enhanced role as the principal structural element of opera were a de facto refutation of criticism leveled against the use of this compositional practice. In matters of artistic creation, no theory that fails to encompass a technique that has gained public approval can be viewed as valid, even if the deductive reasoning behind it is correct. (Studying such reasoning is still useful because it helps to identify false premises through proof by contrapositive [*modus tollens*]. Dahlhaus regularly relied on such reasoning in his writing on musical dramaturgy.) By contrast, the justification of the aria as a dramaturgical tool was carried out retrospectively from both the poetic and the aesthetic angles.

In terms of poetics, aria lends itself to portraying the state of *morbus*, which Cicero described as a sickness deeply and tenaciously rooted in the spirit and from which the character (most often a woman) is incapable of freeing herself. Afflicted by *morbus*, she is imprisoned in her own suffering, and no one else can help her. Unlike recitative, whose sudden interruptions evoke the chaotic course of *perturbatio*, aria is first and foremost characterized by a "unity of mood" (Dahlhaus [1988] 2001: 522) that presents a clear musical image (*Abbild*) of the enduring nature of *morbus* (*Urbild*) (Serauky 1929). Hence, nothing prevents aria from continuing ad infinitum, which accounts for the great length of some seventeenth-century aria-*lamenti*, such as Monteverdi's *Lamento della ninfa* (*Eighth Book of Madrigals*, 1638), and eighteenth-century da capo arias of lamentation, such as "Ah! mio cor" from Handel's *Alcina* (1735).

Aria is characterized also by repetition, which can be viewed as a metaphor for mental obsession (Smith 1795: 154–155). The *immediate* repetition of a melodic fragment, in particular in an ostinato bass, obviously parallels the psychological state of withdrawal, in which the directionality needed for reasoning is absent. It is no coincidence that in the seventeenth century such repetition became a symbol of lament, and employed anew in the early twenty-first century in Amy Winehouse's "Back to Black" (2006) to express the grieving lover's perpetual return to misery (on the origins of the lament, see Rosand 1979). *Delayed* repetition does not weaken meaning: It strengthens it through contrast with the intervening passage. In the Orlando-Angelica duet in Handel's *Orlando*, the contrast between Orlando's unity of mood (*b*) and Angelica's (*a*)—which are stated nearly simultaneously and in the same meter—heightens the depiction of the obsessiveness of Orlando, who remains deaf to Angelica's pleas (see Music Example 8.1).

A similar use of repetition magnified by contrast is seen in the return to the A-section in the da capo lament "Ah! mio cor," when Alcina reverts to her original wretchedness after a momentary recovery in the B-section allegro ("Ma che fa gemendo Alcina?"). In such *Divergenzarien* (Kubik 1982), the juxtaposition of the two strophes (A and B) ingeniously combines the portrayal of *morbus*, through each strophe's own individual content, and the portrayal of *perturbatio*, through the striking contrasts in the transitions from A to B and from B back to A′.

Repetition can also serve aesthetically as a justification for the aria form, because it is what distinguishes listening to music from listening to speech. It had long been acknowledged that, in the depiction of passions, music makes a more powerful effect on the listener than other imitative arts (Smith 1795: 155)—thanks to the phenomenon of repetition, which played a central role according to seventeenth- and eighteenth-century theories of hearing (Gozza 2008). From Mersenne to Descartes, the pneumatic theory

MUSIC EXAMPLE 8.1 Handel, *Orlando* (1733). Angelica-Orlando duet. Without changing tempo, Handel sounds two opposite affects in succession, contrasting them through melody and orchestration.

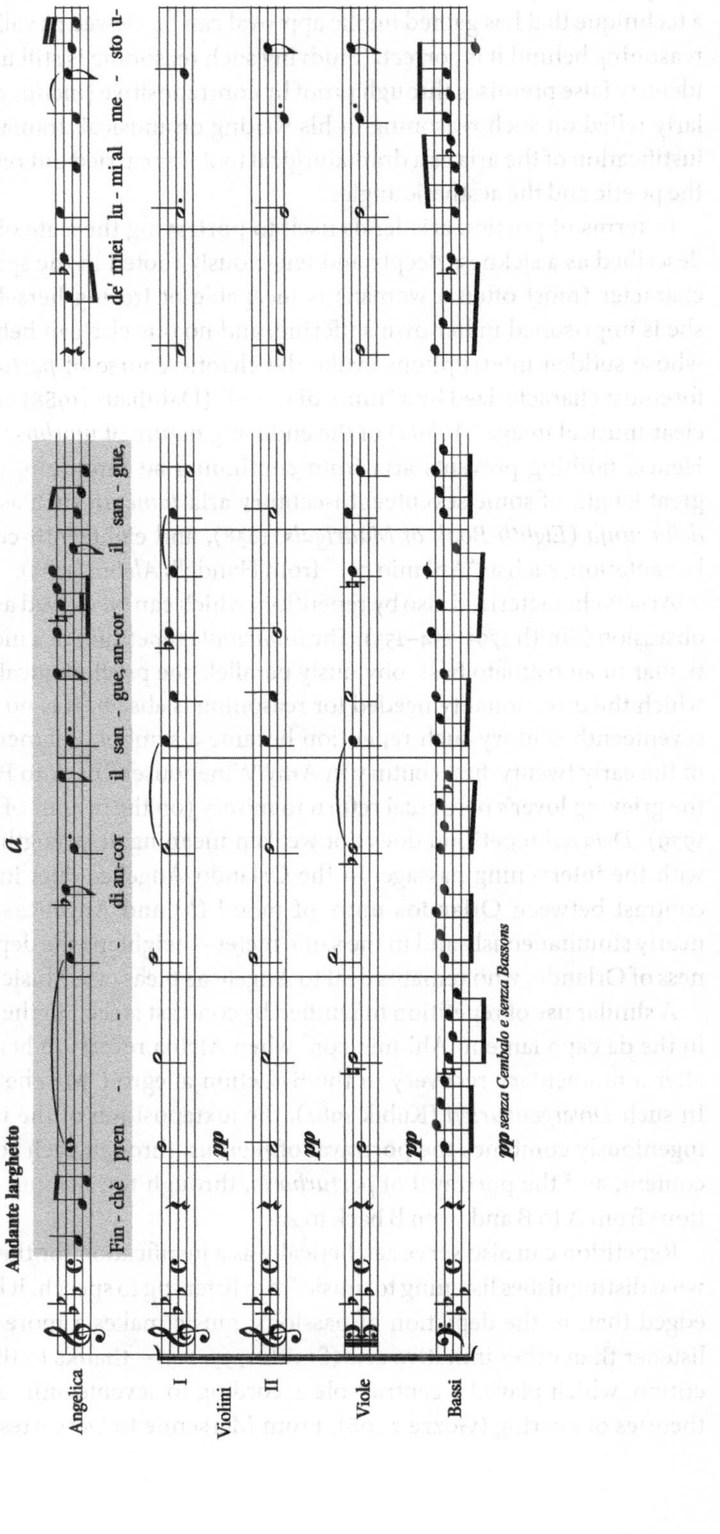

Ang
Orl
Vni I
II
Vle
B.
mor!
b
Sol ha se-te di san-gue il mio cor, sol ha se-te di san-gue, sol ha se-te di san-gue il mio cor,
con Cemb. e Bassons

of hearing viewed the air within the ear as a resonator whose job was to amplify and prolong sounds in order to transmit them to the "interior tribunal" of the mind (Aristotle, *De anima*, II, 8: 420a). Without repetition, the sonic signal would be too fleeting and would leave no mark on the brain. On the other hand, Descartes notes "all the evil that [the passions] can cause" when the ear's mechanism for repetition malfunctions and retains an impression "longer than necessary"[2] (Descartes 1649: §lxxiv). That describes the root of the kind of obsession that Cicero called *morbus*.

Madness as Going beyond the Self

Following the distinction between *perturbatio* and *morbus* set out in the seventeenth century, Diderot described another distinction during the eighteenth in his *Troisième entretien sur le Fils naturel* (1757). In his analysis of Clytemnestra's speech in Racine's *Iphigénie*, the philosopher writes of the link between the aposiopesis (the ellipsis following the words "dans son sang") and the line "J'entends gronder la foudre et sens trembler la terre":

Ô mère infortunée !
De festons odieux ma fille couronnée,
Tend la gorge aux couteaux par son père apprêtés.
Calchas va dans son sang… Barbares ! arrêtez ;
C'est le pur sang du dieu qui lance le tonnerre….
J'entends gronder la foudre et sens trembler la terre.

[O, wretched mother!
My daughter, crowned with hateful garlands,
Offers her throat to the blades readied by her father.
In her blood, Calchas shall… Barbarians, cease!
It is the pure blood of the thunder-god…
I hear the thunderbolt rumble and feel the Earth tremble.]

The speech is interrupted just as the scene that Clytemnestra is setting—that of the sacrifice of her daughter—would become unbearable if portrayed realistically. In his advice for setting the scene to music, Diderot proposes that this sudden silence in the speech be filled by a musical depiction of lightning and earthquake. Musical discourse would thus take over from verbal discourse as Clytemnestra is overcome by emotion, her mind frozen.

By suggesting this handover, Diderot delineates a key characteristic of musical dramaturgy: the use of the medium of music to express an emotion that, in its violence or intensity, goes not only beyond reason but, generally speaking, beyond all human limits—how much suffering can be borne or what can be expressed in speech. Music is employed to express something that is felt within, but that is infinitely greater than oneself—as paradoxical as it may seem—when the text summons up natural phenomena far beyond a human scale: thunderbolts and earthquakes. A fit of madness during which the character is "outside herself" is a specific case of this kind of upheaval caused by a sudden breach of human limits.

To depict these external forces of nature, Diderot gives two options. In the *style simple*, the thunder and lightning are evoked by the orchestra: a voice outside the human body. In the *style figuré*, they are evoked by the singer:

> The musician shall do with the voice what the other [style] assigns to the instrument[s]: He will make the thunderbolts rumble and make them fall in flashes. It is no longer Iphigenia's mother that I hear: it is the thunderbolt that roars; it is the Earth that trembles; it is the air that echoes with terrifying noises.[3] (Diderot 1674: V: 4)

Those two possibilities reflect the two contrasting traditions of the eighteenth century: the French *tragédie en musique*, with its preference for striking orchestral effects, and the Italian *opera seria*, with its inclination toward vocal virtuosity. In the latter, what makes it possible for the voice to express what is beyond the self—supra-human forces—is the series of variations expected in the repeat of the A-section in a da capo form (Colas 2008). For a character who is prey to madness and "outside himself," like Semele in "No, no, I'll take no less" (Handel, *Semele*, 1743, Act III, scene 4), the anticipated excesses in the ornamentation of the da capo and the striking contrast with the original vocal line are a metaphor for the character's possession by an overwhelmingly powerful force. In the cultural context of Stoic philosophy, the ornamentation reflects the hubris that has taken hold of the character: a human being's mad ambition to leave his allotted place in the cosmic order.

Transcending the self in anger, or possession by madness: these are two sides of the same coin and can be rendered musically in the same way. Lucia's mad scene shows how a nineteenth-century composer could exploit the abundant means of musical expression that had been developed over the previous two centuries. In that scene we find *perturbatio* in the abrupt shifts in the opening scena, with its aposiopeses ("un gelo mi serpeggia nel sen"; "Ohimè! Sorge il tremendo fantasma") and *morbus* in the melodic elongations of the cantabile ("ogni piacer più grato; mi fia con te diviso"). We find the *style simple* in the use of the glass harmonica and the *style figuré* in the ascent into the highest vocal register—both intended to depict the strangeness of Lucia's hallucinatory world.

A Scandal: The Depiction of Tumult

To depict a public uproar it is necessary to skirt the poetic principle of *mimesis*. In real life, such situations are avoided by using escape routes delineated in all cultures by the rules of verbal interaction. The need for public self-control means that everyone must offer an external face to others while also possessing a different, interior, face (Goffman 1956). Apart from some naturalist works of the turn of the nineteenth-to-twentieth centuries, serious theater tends not merely to omit the social niceties that are required for smooth verbal interaction and that ensure social equilibrium (Bühler 1933; Brown and Levinson 1987); more important, it gives prominence to episodes of conflict, rather than avoiding them. Professional actors reveal their interior face to the audience, like Cléopâtre in Corneille's *Rodogune* (1645, II: 2): "Connais-moi tout entière"; the "actors" that all members of society must be strive never to do so.

In a two-character confrontation—a template of the classic spoken theater in the seventeenth and eighteenth centuries—such conflict takes the form of oratorical fencing in which the verbal thrusts and parries can be extremely violent. In a public setting, it becomes a tumult: a socially forbidden situation in which the presence of witnesses alongside the protagonists exacerbates the situation and heightens the awkwardness. In theater, the exceptional is preferred to the usual in these cases; therein lies the break with strict conformity with the principle of *mimesis*. Another principle trumps it—that of interest: in the depiction of socially forbidden situations, the playwright is addressing the voyeur lurking in every audience member (Beaumarchais 1767: "If theater be a faithful depiction of what takes place in the world, the interest it holds for us is of necessity connected to the manner in which we see real objects"[4]). Here again, the dramatist's poetic approach is guided by aesthetic requirements.

There are many tumultuous scenes in nineteenth-century opera; two approaches can be distinguished. In the Act I finale of Rossini's *Il barbiere di Siviglia* (1816), the clamor in Dr. Bartolo's house, to which Count Almaviva has gained entry disguised as a drunken soldier in order to be with Rosina, is so great that the police arrive. As he is about to be arrested, Almaviva reveals his true identity (though only to the police). With this sudden change in the situation, the police are in a quandary. It is as though all who witness this scene are paralyzed and dumbstruck, which the music depicts in a *quadro di stupore* based on the progressive layering of the characters' asides. This polyphonic structure—the *largo concertato*—is the centerpiece of the finale, preceding the concluding *stretta*. In the Roman Carnival scene of Berlioz's *Benvenuto Cellini* (1837), the goldsmith Cellini kills Pompeo, a follower of his rival Fieramosca, who is disguised as a monk. After several measures of *rallentando* to indicate surprise, public anger is rendered by a sudden *accelerando* and the onset of the fugato "Assassiner un capucin !" (see Music Example 8.2).

In both cases, the tumult is illustrated for the audience with a sudden slowing of the musical discourse, corresponding to an expression of collective surprise, followed by an equally sudden acceleration. What is different is the moment to which the composer chooses to draw attention. In *Barbiere*, the emphasis is on the *concertato* "Fredda ed immobile," both because of the contrast with the preceding section, which is in a breathless tempo from start to finish, and because of the scale of the musical structure that portrays the freeze in the stage action. By comparison, the slowing of the action in *Benvenuto Cellini* after the murder of the Capuchin is no more than a simple transition to the following section. Rather than providing the keystone of the finale, it is merely a transitional structure on which the composer does not dwell. In neither case does the composer opt to linger on the very moment that triggers the uproar: both composers select events following that moment, though different ones. Rossini's tableau depicts the characters' speechlessness and perplexed silence, and Berlioz's the outrage and

MUSIC EXAMPLE 8.2 Berlioz, *Benvenuto Cellini* (1837). Act II Finale. This brief excerpt from a *concertato* shows the transition to the *allegro assai*. Here Berlioz depicts the tumult of the crowd following the assassination of the Capuchin, at the moment when time is slowed through a succession of three fermatas.

mounting anger of the crowd. Both approaches have equal validity within the theory of imitation.

Those examples illustrate two concurrent traditions. The first, established by Rossini and Donizetti in the 1810s to 1830s, places the *concertato* at the center of the finale and assigns a key structural function to the *quadro di stupore*. Until the end of the nineteenth century, a *fabula*'s potential for such a *concertato* was one of the determining factors—indeed, the primary one—for a composer in the choice of a subject. This is apparent in the Act I finale of Rossini's *Semiramide* (1823), which is built around the spectacular moment when King Ninus's ghost appears. It is also seen in Verdi's *Simon Boccanegra*, as revised with Arrigo Boito (1881): At the heart of this version, during the Council Chamber scene, they added the Doge's speech "Plebe! patrizi! popolo!" aimed at putting an end to fratricidal conflict. The Christ-like plea for peace and love—"E vo gridando pace, e vo gridando amor," derived from Petrarch's *Epistolae familiares*—is immediately followed and amplified by the polyphonic ensemble whose religious character provides the breadth required for the work's central political message (Budden 1973: II: 259). The *concertato* tradition spread beyond Italy and is found in French opera from Boieldieu to Offenbach (*La dame blanche*, 1825, Act II, auction scene, "Ô Ciel! quel est donc ce mystère ?"; *Les contes d'Hoffmann*, 1881, the Giulietta act, sextet with chorus, "Hélas ! mon cœur s'égare encore," composed by André Bloch), in Russian opera from Glinka to Tchaikovsky (*Ruslan and Ludmila*, 1842, Act I, no. 3 [abduction of Ludmila], "Какое чудное мгновенье—*Kakoe chudnoe mgnoven'e*"; *Eugene Onegin*, 1879, Act I, no. 16 [ball scene], "В вашем доме!—*V vashem dome!*") and even, in the guise of the contemplative ensemble, in German opera from Beethoven (*Fidelio*, 1814, Act I, scene 4, no. 3, "Mir ist so wunderbar") to Wagner (*Die Meistersinger von Nürnberg*, 1868, Act III, scene 4, "Selig, wie die Sonne meines Glückes lacht!") and Richard Strauss (*Capriccio*, 1942, scene 6, "Des Dichters Worte, wie leuchten sie klar!").

Compared with the success of the Italian-style *concertato*, the tradition that arose in France in the same period seems to amount to a counterculture. Like the *Benvenuto Cellini* carnival scene, the Act III finale of Auber's *Gustave III* (1833), following the public incident, makes use of an unresolved transition to a concluding ensemble in a rapid tempo. When Amélie's veil falls, the plotters recognize her as the wife of Ankarstrom, who is the only one to realize that she is the king's mistress: a secret scandal for him, and a farcical episode for the others. In the quartet with chorus, the section "La rencontre est jolie" overlays the *a parte* of Amélie (expressing shame) and Ankarstrom (the wish for vengeance) with the mockery of the plotters, who are all too eager to spread this latest morsel of gossip around the court. This French counter-model accentuates the originality of the Act II finale of Verdi's *Un ballo in maschera* (1859), specifically the passage "Ve' se di notte qui co' la sposa," which is inspired by it, and of the "ensembles of puzzlement" in German opera, which are dynamic and drive toward their conclusion. These are to be seen in Wagner (*Die Meistersinger von Nürnberg*, 1868, Act II, scene 6, finale, "Mit den Schuhen ward ich fertig schier!") and Richard Strauss (*Salome*, 1905, scene 4, quintet of Jews, "Seit dem Prophet Elias hat niemand Gott gesehen"; *Capriccio*, 1942, scene 9, octet, part 2 [*Streit-Ensemble*] "Aber so hört doch!"). For reasons to be considered below, the final fugue of Verdi's *Falstaff* (1893), "Tutto nel mondo è burla," can also be linked to this model.

Even more than recitatives and arias, ensembles raise various issues related to the dimension of time, such as the internal structure of closed numbers and their integration into an act. The question of the choice of the moment will be considered first, then that of the expansion and interruption of time, on which the Italian and French approaches differ.

The Choice of the Moment

Writing about the construction of the eighteenth-century *dramma per musica*, Hermann Abert (1926: 18) noted the lag between the climax of the chain of events being portrayed on stage—"external action"—and the musical climax, which often occurs "before or afterward."[5] This was even more marked in act finales in the nineteenth century, even becoming a signature of the genre. In all the aforementioned ensembles, the musical culmination takes place after the moment that triggers the uproar, which is the culmination of the external action. While it has been observed that this musical climax takes place immediately afterward in the Italian model and is postponed at the end of the ensemble in the French model, it is important to note that in both cases the composer places the exact moment triggering the uproar at the very end of the first section of the ensemble. These *tempi d'attacco* (Basevi 1859: 104, 191, 218) are built around the imminence of catastrophe, whether this comes about because of a sudden twist in the plot (as in the Act I finale of *Il barbiere di Siviglia*) or through an inexorable buildup of tension. In the latter case, sonic tools provide the composer with an ideal way, from the very outset of the section, to alert the listener to the approach of the breaking point. That was Verdi's approach in the *tempo d'attacco* of the Act II finale of *La traviata* (1853), where an unsettling rhythmic motif in the cellos and double basses shadows the actors' *parlante dialogico*.

The issue of "choice of the moment," as exemplified by the opposition between the French and the Italian schools, gives us a good standpoint from which to consider that of the musical tableau. Here, there is an inescapable parallel with the visual arts: Lacking the dimension of time, painters and sculptors are obliged at the outset to choose a moment in their treatment of any subject. This is not a major constraint in landscape painting or portraiture, but it is a key determining factor in history painting. We know from the diaries of his pupil Étienne-Jean Delécluze that Jacques-Louis David stressed that his students should avoid "the great crisis of the subject" (Pinelli 2000: 188). This is reflected in his *Leonidas at Thermopylae* (1814), where he depicts the oath of martyrdom before the battle, not the carnage the Persians wreaked upon the Spartan army. The "great crisis of the subject" to a painter and the apex of scenic action for the opera composer are two terms for a single reality. In both cases, direct portrayal is avoided: David chose the preceding moment; musicians choose the succeeding one.

The passage of time presents far more knotty problems when painting a picture in poetry, music, or drama. A painter is able to present the viewer with a tableau that the eye can immediately absorb in full—which by no means excludes the possibility of then contemplating it in detail for as long as you like. But a musician cannot present the listener with an entire picture in a fraction of a second. Attempts by composers to focus sharply on a single instant, reminiscent of the poetics of expressionism—although they are to be found, as in Mozart (*La clemenza di Tito*, 1791, Act I finale, the burning of Rome, cries of the offstage crowd in diminished sevenths)—reveal the relative poverty of music's means to express the instantaneous. The dimension of time is of course an asset, but it also imposes limitations. To create a tableau, the composer must give the illusion of halting the course of time, while of necessity working in the context of its duration.

Time Expanded

How does the composer create the illusion of expanding time? In the first movement of his *Pastoral* Symphony (1808), "Erwachen heiterer Empfindungen bey der Ankunft auf dem Lande" ("Arousal of Cheerful Feelings upon Arrival in the Country"), Beethoven does it with immediate repetition of melodic fragments, notably at the conclusion of the first theme, in which he avoids the procedure typical of classical form, which presses unremittingly forward. This respite creates an expansion of time that listeners of the day would have found unusual and that prompts a contemplative state. Such musical passages embody Lamartine's line, "Ô temps, suspends ton vol !" (*Le lac*, 1829). But while poetic lyricism is marked by recollection and evocation of the past (Staiger 1946), the expansion of time in music creates an "absolute present" that is self-contained and completely without reference to the past or the future (Dahlhaus, [1988] 2001: 470). This approach, embraced by the twentieth-century minimalist school (John Adams, *Nixon in China*, 1987; Richard Robbins, music for James Ivory's film *The Remains of the Day*, 1993), is perfect for creating an emotional environment in which time passes but that also projects a feeling of timelessness because there is no sense of development from a "before" to an "after."

An Italian-school *quadro di stupore* freezes time in a rather different way. When Ravenswood bursts in after the marriage contract has been signed in Walter Scott's novel *The Bride of Lammermoor* (1819, chapter 33), those present are described as "transfixed with surprise." The *concertato* of Donizetti's sextet (*Lucia di Lammermoor*, 1835) "Chi mi frena in tal momento?" fulfills the remit better than Scott's prose could ever have done. Under the tacit contract between author and reader in any work of fiction, Scott's events may be viewed as having actually taken place (a), and through the novel and the opera we know this story in two modes of artistic portrayal—(b) and (c)—each with its own conventions. In the reality of (a), the consternation of the guests lasts only seconds: etiquette requires that everyone recover as quickly as possible. In the novel (b), their collective astonishment is described in just a few words, which take about as long to read as the actual event would have taken to unfold. Drawing on the language of narratology (Müller 1948; Stepath 2006: 177–180), we note that the duration of the event being described ([a] *erzählte Zeit*) and the duration of the description ([b] *Erzählzeit*) correspond. But in Donizetti, the time devoted to the *quadro di stupore* (c) is out of all proportion to that of the actual event. In narratological terms, there is a disconnect between the time being represented ([a] *dargestellte Zeit*) and the time it takes to represent it ([c] *Darstellungszeit*). This discrepancy is one of the main characteristics of what Volker Klotz calls open-form drama (Klotz 1960). This category encompasses the non-Classicalist traditions of spoken theater (the theater of Golden-Age Spain and Elizabethan England) and number opera. (We must be careful about terminology here, because the latter—formed of *pezzi chiusi* ["closed" pieces]—falls within the category of *open*-form drama.) Dramas of this category give primacy to expression of the *hic et nunc* dissociated from any relationship that this moment might have with what comes before or after. By contrast, in closed-form drama—spoken theater in the Aristotelian tradition (classic French and German theater) and Wagnerian music-drama—every moment results from what comes before and prepares what follows, generating uninterrupted tension in the advance toward the denouement in such a way that no individual moment can stand on its own.

The musical construction of the *concertato* is not derived from that of the libretto's verse. It comes from the way in which the voices are combined, as in the contrapuntal madrigals of the *prima prattica*, a technique that had been barred from the nascent operatic form because of its unintelligibility: monody with accompaniment was the preferred vehicle for expressing emotion. How can we account for the restoration of polyphony? It may be explained precisely through the aforementioned "retrospective justification" under the theory of imitation. In the *quadro di stupore*, astonishment and speechlessness are made palpable in a polyphonic ensemble that seems to have arisen out of silence, which the audience accepts without question as believable.

The transition from intelligible speech to unintelligible but harmonious group speech indicates that the characters have been wrenched from the normal time-scale of the action and have moved into another, as into a parallel dimension. The *concertato*—as well as the contemplative ensemble to which it is related—is marked by a merging of emotions. Even if no single character's words can be understood, the shared emotions are clear. Here again, the self is transcended—not, this time, by the aforementioned concept of "beyond the self" but by a "self" that is dissolved into a group: individual voices are fused into a single expressive entity, and it becomes impossible to distinguish the individuals making up the group. This transcendence is made even more perceptible with the employment of the "groundswell," which almost literally lifts the listener, an ingenious technique honed by Italian composers beginning with Bellini and Donizetti (Kerman and Grey 1989). This merging differentiates the Italian-style *concertato* from the French or German ensemble of puzzlement, which gives priority to polyphonic multiplicity (however chaotic the result) and the intelligibility of fragments of text, recalling Renaissance street-cry songs. The final ensemble of Verdi's *Falstaff* (1893) falls into the same category.

Not surprisingly, when depicting this travel beyond the self to a collective self, composers drew on the resources of sacred music (Schmid 2009). Many Italian-type *concertati* are imbued with a sacred color; in portraying a collective self, they counterbalance the traditional portrayal of the individual self that reigns in the rest of the opera. A striking example is the ensemble "Qui me rendra ce mort ?" from Verdi's *Don Carlos* (1867): it was cut before the first performance, but Verdi recycled it in the "Lachrymosa" of the *Requiem* (1874). Hans von Bülow described Verdi's *Requiem* as "an opera in ecclesiastical vestments" (Voss 2004: 191), but in fact it seems that the opposite was the case: For decades opera had been drawing on the techniques of sacred music for numbers in which time was to be expanded.

It remains to justify the duration of these expansions of time. Here, Dahlhaus (2000–2007: II: 559) recalls the Aristotelian concept of "proper length," which conveys verisimilitude so long as it is commensurate with the intensity of the emotion being expressed (ἱκανὸς ὅρος τοῦ μεγέθους, Aristotle, *Poetics*, 1451a: 15). Aristotelian verisimilitude does not aim to reproduce reality; it seeks "truth in representation," where length is in keeping with the importance of the events or emotions being represented: The higher the emotion experienced by the characters, the longer the time that can legitimately be taken to express it.

Temporal Boundaries

The interruption of time and its expansion are two notions that cannot exist apart from one another. When an ensemble expands time—creating a disconnect between the time being represented and the time it takes to represent it—its opening and closing points correspond to the beginning and the end of the rupture between two time systems. This has been considered here in the context of large ensembles in act finales, but the issue of temporal boundaries and interruptions arises in all the forms of the number opera, from the aria and duet to the ensemble.

These interruptions can be an asset or a drawback. We have seen that the precise moment at which an uproar breaks out—as in the Act II finale of *La traviata* and in nineteenth-century Italian opera in general—coincides with the end of the *tempo d'attacco* and signals an imminent interruption of the boundaries of time. In the transition from one section to the next, the effect of a sudden contrast gives the composer a clever way to focus attention on an event on stage without needing to depict the moment or to halt the action. The moment is simply underscored in its temporal context. In the French model, the selected moment is marked, not through interruption using a slower tempo, as in the *concertato*, but by sudden acceleration. Zerlina's cry "Gente, aiuto; aiuto, gente!" in the Act II finale of Mozart's *Don Giovanni* (1787) coincides with an abrupt shift to a rapid tempo, accentuated by a change of key, which rouses the audience after the sleepy minuet. Rossini often uses these sudden, unexpected rhythmic twists.

Even more so than the expansion of time, interruption becomes a drawback viewed from the perspective of closed-form drama, as, for example, when we look at a duet on the basis of the spoken dialogue from which it is derived. For the Assur-Arsace duet "Bella immago degli dèi" in Act I of *Semiramide* (1823), Rossini used a common form for the duet, falling between bipartite aria and conventional (*solita forma*) ensemble and based on both of these (Balthazar 1989). The *cantabile* "D'un tenero amor" produces an abrupt drop in tension and interrupts the inexorable buildup that is the source of all the impact of the equivalent dialogue in Voltaire's tragedy (1748, Act I, scene 4). This drop is difficult to justify from the dramatic standpoint, however beautiful the *cantabile* may be. Bellini, who employed the same formal models as Rossini, appears to have been aware of the need to mitigate the interruption at the beginning of a *cantabile* by merging it with the preceding *primo tempo*, as he did so ingeniously in the Norma-Adalgisa duet in Act I of *Norma* (1831) (Colas 2004). In Wagner's view, the discontinuity of time was one of the main flaws of the number opera of his day. He was right to associate the succession of obvious seams with Italian opera; in *Die Meistersinger von Nürnberg* the members of the tailors' guild come onstage to a theme reminiscent of "Di tanti palpiti" from Rossini's *Tancredi* (1813). He also correctly associated it with the poetics of the *grand opéra* of Meyerbeer, who employed interruption and contrast, first of all, to resolve the problems inherent in the *grand opéra* form and, secondly, as a way to use music to create a poetics of mixed genres, similar to that of the romantic dramas of Victor Hugo (*Cromwell*, 1827, preface). Wagner sought to respond to this motley assortment with the flow of a through-composed music drama controlled by the teleology of closed-form drama, with which he began experimenting in *Tristan und Isolde* (1859). The sudden shifts typical of the open form are thus very rare in his works. One of the most striking—Ortrud's powerful challenge to Elsa during the Act II cathedral scene of *Lohengrin* (1850)—may be seen as a final borrowing from the French tradition, on which Wagner would then turn his back forever. Indeed, it has something in common with the papal bull scene in Donizetti's *La favorite* (1841).

Forging a Dramaturgic Tool: The Wagnerian Leitmotif

The above sections on the depiction of madness and public uproar describe two successive and complementary movements in the development of musical dramaturgy. First, we note the exploration of resources specific to the language of music, which inevitably led to liberation from the structure of the libretto. Second, these newly adopted musical techniques were granted dramatic justification *a posteriori* under the theory of imitation; this replaced direct justification through the verbal structure. Only when both these stages had been completed could it be said that a new musical-dramaturgic tool had been created. As a consequence, the development of musical dramaturgy was only possible through a shift from a theory of imitation limited to the textual material to an enlarged theory of imitation.

We can trace these stages in the creation of the Wagnerian leitmotif—which Wagner himself referred to as a "melodischer Moment" (*Oper und Drama*, 1851) or a

"Grundthema" (*Über die Anwendung der Musik auf das Drama*, 1879). This is a particularly interesting subject as it involves the orchestra: sounds that are inherently the most remote from the text. In Wagnerian drama, leitmotifs perform several functions with their origins in various eras and various contexts in the history of opera; these functions are nothing other than dramatic justifications that enable a process of composition to be used in the creation of a drama.

Signposting and Association

When Donner summons up the storm that produces the rainbow in the final scene of *Das Rheingold* (composed 1854; first performed 1869), we hear the storm-magic motif—the *Gewitterzaubermotif* (see Music Example 8.3).

MUSIC EXAMPLE 8.3 Wagner, *Das Rheingold* (1854). *Gewitterzaubermotif* (storm-magic motif), associated with Donner's call for the storm.

This theme is a signal that draws spectators' attention to the notable event that is taking place before them. That is signposting, a practice that Mahler (1896) mocked when he described the leitmotif system in precisely those road-sign terms. Musical signposting in the orchestra was related to stage effects and noises, such as thunder and lightning, which were common in many types of theater, including the most popular. This simple procedure helps to alert spectators to crucial moments in the action. In the nineteenth-century Parisian *mélodrame à grand spectacle*, there was a vocabulary of musical signposting for stock scenes, described here in the 1817 *Traité du mélodrame*:

> If the whole orchestra together produces muted and gloomy sounds, it means that the tyrant approaches, and the entire audience trembles; if the harmony is sweet and soft, the ill-fated lover will soon appear, and every heart will grow tender... In short, music is to each scene what approach avenues are to châteaux.[6] (A. Hugo et al. 1817: 55; Sala 1995: 78)

Once they had seen a few of these plays, audiences grew familiar with the language of the signposts and unfailingly discerned their meaning. *Mélodrame* also employed the related technique of association. According to Paul Ginisty, rather than being associated with a particular situation, association links a character with a musical color, as

> an apt use of resources corresponds to each character: a plaintive flute corresponds to the grief of the persecuted heroine; the double bass accompanies the tyrant; the comic is preceded by a brisk and lively melody.[7] (Ginisty 1910: 218)

Associative instrumentation emerged in the earliest days of operatic history, notably in Monteverdi's *L'Orfeo* (1607). In the scene in Hell, Charon "sings to the sound of a regal" and the chorus of spirits "to the sound of a regal, a wood-pipe organ, five trombones, two bass *viole da gamba* and a contrabass viol." In Rameau's *Hippolyte et Aricie* (1733), the timbre of four bassoons is heard throughout Act II, which is set in Hell. Unlike signposting, which is intended to draw attention to a pivotal moment, association is attached to a character, a situation, or a place and underscores its emotional mood. Whether its function is signposting or association, a musical theme is heard in conjunction with the representation on stage of the event, character, or place. It is a musical metaphor *in praesentia.*

Signposting and association are based on long-standing techniques of musical imitation; audiences immediately understand them for two reasons. First, the event (in the case of signposting), the character, or the place (in the case of association) serves as a caption for the musical image. The listener need not seek out meaning in the musical material, whether it be melody, rhythm, or instrumental timbre: The meaning is clearly provided through the simultaneous onstage action. Second, the musical image gallery benefits from codes that are clear to the audience, whether they be citations of music from beyond the opera (such as military or religious sounds) or physical imitation (a singing bird or a galloping horse) (Berlioz 1837). That explains the large role that signposting and association played in the introduction of new orchestral instruments which were initially used in this metaphoric way. The double bass was first used in the French opera orchestra by Marin Marais in his *Alcyone* (1701) to represent the rumble of thunder. When it became an established member of the orchestra, its timbre was no longer used metaphorically and, for the listener, it was stripped of its symbolic function (Kintzler 2011).

The technique of "mimographic music" (Smart 2004) that Auber used in *La muette de Portici* (1828) is in fact entirely based on signposting and association. Since the mute Fenella cannot make her voice heard, the orchestra substitutes for it, making use of the usual codes of both those functions. But here the musical metaphor is no longer limited to brief moments; rather, it is extended through entire scenes in which Fenella appears, using an internal thematic system. This demonstrates the rich potential of signposting and association, which had previously been used only in a limited manner.

Reminiscence, Contradiction, and Narration

In reminiscence, leitmotifs are used as metaphors *in absentia*: what they refer to is not present on stage. This function was first allocated to the orchestra in the eighteenth-century French repertoire and was then imported into German opera, notably Weber's *Euryanthe* (1823). In his *Poétique de la musique* (1785), Bernard de Lacépède wrote:

> The musician can recall these already-heard touching segments either by placing amidst the melodies of his characters the most notable melodies of the song he wishes to recall and whose effect he wishes to bring back, or by scattering these melodies in the accompaniments he causes to be heard, or by simply recalling the

> accompaniment of the segment whose aid he is seeking and by causing them to serve as accompaniment or as melody at a time when he has need of extrinsic beauty.[8] (Lacépède 1785: 124)

This laid the groundwork for a theory of reminiscence in music on the heels of the earliest examples of the technique in Grétry's *Richard Cœur de lion* (1784) and Lemoyne's *Électre* (1782).

As to assigning a narrative function to the orchestra, theory preceded practice. Oreste's line "Le calme rentre dans mon cœur" in Gluck's *Iphigénie en Tauride* (1779) is contradicted by murmuring in the strings, which clearly depicts tension and distress according to contemporary codes of musical imitation. Marmontel (*Supplément à l'Encyclopédie*, 1776) had already described the orchestra as a "second voice" independent from that of the character and even capable of contradicting it by revealing "his secret feelings" and displaying "the emotions that dominate and torment him." This ability would prove particularly useful to Wagner in rendering in music the many contradictory facets of Kundry in *Parsifal* (1882), who is the character furthest removed from opera designed to express emotions (Dahlhaus [1971a] 2004: 264–265).

In signposting and association, the link between orchestral sound and onstage event is obvious and direct. In reminiscence it becomes more distant, and it is at its most remote in contradiction, when the voice of the orchestra, in line with the principle of imitation, overlays the onstage action with an emotional element that is not to be seen there. At that point the orchestra can play the role of a narrator: the voice of the author, Wagner in this case, can overlay that of the character (Dahlhaus [1971b] 2004: 28).

The Structural Function

Much has been said (Dahlhaus [1971b] 2004: 82–95) about the historic divide—the theoretical groundwork for which had been laid in *Oper und Drama* (1851)—between the limited employment of leitmotifs in Wagner's romantic operas (*Der fliegende Holländer* [1843], *Tannhäuser* [1845], *Lohengrin* [1850]) and their structural use beginning with the *Ring* (1853). To make leitmotifs the fundamental unit for constructing a drama, Wagner had to alter their melodic profile, cease using them as "objects," make them more susceptible to transformation, and organize them into families (Cao 2010). In that way the network of leitmotifs could be a substitute for older formal principles such as metric structure and tonal plan: it formed an internal skeleton that would replace now-obsolete external scaffolding. While the leitmotif's structural function was decisive in the history of compositional systems, it was less so in terms of musical dramaturgy, for it was through its primary functions of signposting, reminiscence, and narration that the leitmotif had made its main contribution to the building of music-drama. Nonetheless, the gradual invention of this dramaturgical tool through the progressive concentration of numerous functions in a single orchestral motif was part of a broader trend that has been repeatedly described: liberation from the text, exploitation of musical resources, and justification in dramatic terms.

Extending the Sphere of Musical Dramaturgy

Were there no scenes of public uproar in eighteenth-century opera? When Ariodante believes he has seen Ginevra welcoming Polinesso into her apartments (Handel, *Ariodante*, 1735), the focus is on his solitary grief, expressed in the lament "Scherza infida." During the same period, the collective dimension of uproar is depicted in Bach's passions. Written in an instrumental style, the cries of the *turba* layer the crowd's emotion over the lamentations of the principal characters: fear ("Wohin?" no. 24 "Eilt, ihr angefochtnen Seelen," *St. John Passion*, 1724) or outrage ("Laßt ihn, haltet, bindet nicht!" no. 27a "So ist mein Jesus nun gefangen," *St. Matthew Passion*, 1727; see Music Example 8.4). This musical resource was not incorporated into opera because, owing to theatrical practices, choruses were not regularly used in opera houses until the second half of the eighteenth century. Composers had the technical ability to use this resource, but they had to wait several decades for it to become a common musical-dramaturgic tool.

Once we have abandoned the simplistic notion that the text of the libretto equals the drama, rich possibilities arise for the study of musical dramaturgy. Much work remains to be done, although there is no need to forge an axiomatic theory on the subject. In his pioneering work, Dahlhaus drew attention to many fundamental concepts, but others remain to be identified and studied. To give just one example, when viewed in terms of the distinction between *Darstellungszeit* (the time it takes to represent something) and *dargestellte Zeit* (the time being represented) the expansion of time is in fact but one option for disrupting the steady course of time. Its opposite—the contraction of time, in which a single musical piece brings together a number of moments drawn from a stretch of time that is longer than the time it takes to represent it—is often used in cinema. We see it in Miloš Forman's film adaptation of the musical comedy *Hair* (1979), in which the song "The Flesh Failures" encompasses Berger's departure from the training camp, his death in Vietnam, and, finally, the peace demonstrations on the Mall in Washington, D.C. What does this technique reveal to us about the characters and situations? What dramatic justification makes it acceptable to the audience? Those are questions for the student of musical dramaturgy.

Throughout the history of opera, the growth in the number of musical resources that were transformed into dramaturgical tools is paralleled by the increasing diversity of subjects on which operas could be based. In the eighteenth century, the lack of variety and the constant recourse to the same themes—love in particular—were frequently criticized. And it was observed that certain subjects, such as political controversy, were not

MUSIC EXAMPLE 8.4 Johann Sebastian Bach, *St. Matthew Passion* (1727). "Laßt ihn, haltet, bindet nicht!" from No. 27a "So ist mein Jesus nun gefangen." Here we see Bach's layering of two opposing affects between the two soloists (compassion) and the crowd (indignation).

S. solo
A. solo
S.
A.
T.
B.
fan
gen.
gen.
Laßt ihn, hal-tet, bin-det nicht!
Laßt ihn, hal-tet, bin-det nicht!
Laßt ihn, hal-tet, bin-det nicht!
Laßt ihn, hal-tet, bin-det nicht!
tutti
violini e viola all'unisono
flauti e oboi

suitable for opera. It was precisely the evolution of musical dramaturgy that ultimately widened those boundaries to embrace many new subjects as possibilities for operatic treatment. Political operas were born (Donizetti's *Dom Sébastien*, 1843, and Verdi's *Don Carlos*, 1867), followed by conversations set to music (Richard Strauss). This broadening of the range of musical dramaturgy is reflected in the emergence of *Literaturoper*. The very possibility of setting a text that had not originally been written for musical treatment, unlike librettos of the seventeenth through nineteenth centuries, shows that the scope of opera, initially narrower than that of spoken theater, ended up by being just as broad—indeed, broader.

Strauss's *Elektra* (1909) is in that category. Unlike the librettist, who wrote for a Rossini or a Verdi, Hofmannsthal had not been obliged to form his text within the constraints imposed by a composer's musical dramaturgy. Here, the alterations needed to transform stage play into opera were on a far smaller scale than the complete overhauls required for librettos from the seventeenth to the nineteenth century. The task consisted basically of making cuts, which was true also for Oscar Wilde's *Salomé* (1891), which Strauss set in 1905: the text is more concise in the operatic version because much of its expressive function is transferred to the music. On the other hand, Elektra's aria-like monologue "Orest! Orest!" was an addition; it is interesting to find that at the dawn of the twentieth century, opera still turned to a musical-dramaturgic resource that had been invented three hundred years earlier.

Still, that long-standing resource had become problematic over time. It bore the stamp of open-form drama characterized by frequent changes of timescale and by internal repetition. This became hard to justify in a post-Wagnerian world in which dramas are created in accordance with the closed-form system, with its single timescale and its teleology that frowns on melodic repetition. Yet in *Arabella* (1933) Strauss returned to aria structure, and did so with lyricism matching that of his orchestral songs. Four of the high points in the action are essentially arias: the Act I duet "Aber der richtige"; the monologue "Mein Elemer!"; the Act II duet "Und du wirst mein Gebieter sein"; and the final monologue "Das war sehr gut, Mandryka." When Arabella describes her Prince Charming and how she would recognize him at first sight, and when Mandryka tells of the Croatian custom of a woman offering a glass of water to her betrothed, each character escapes the time frame of ordinary life and flees to what Sigmund Freud called the waking dream (Freud 1908), which is normal for children but socially forbidden for adults. Something that is not permitted in real life becomes possible in aria. Here we find the characteristics mentioned above: suspension of time, a disparity between the time being represented and the time it takes to represent it, and a new form of transcending the self. We have discussed the "beyond the self" of possession by madness and the collective self of ensembles of bewilderment; here, it is a "dreamed self" that is expressed. For Strauss, aria was a possibility here because its dramatic justification had been updated and made to conform with the culture of his day. For, like any other form of dramaturgy, musical dramaturgy can succeed only when audiences both accept the verisimilitude of the musical discourse and are "enthralled and delighted" by it (Rousseau 1768). So, it is no accident that transcendence of the scale of the self is a constant theme in the compositional techniques discussed here. It appears that the travel beyond the self that is made possible by music is what causes the spectator to be so deeply moved—and is what audiences are looking for in opera.

See also: Versification, The Orchestra, Analysis

Notes

1. *Parsifal*, Act II, Kundry: "Dich nannt' ich, tör'ger Reiner / 'Fal parsi' / Dich, reinen Toren: 'Parsifal.'"
2. "tout le mal que [les passions] peuvent causer [...] plus qu'il n'est besoin."
3. "Le musicien fera exécuter, par la voix, ce que l'autre a réservé pour l'instrument : il fera gronder la foudre, il la fera tomber en éclats. Ce n'est plus la mère d'Iphigénie que j'entends : c'est la foudre qui gronde, c'est la terre qui tremble, c'est l'air qui retentit de bruits effrayants."
4. "Si le Théâtre est le tableau fidèle de ce qui se passe dans le monde, l'intérêt qu'il excite en nous a donc un rapport nécessaire à notre manière d'envisager les objets réels."
5. "Der musikalische Höhepunkt tritt meist entweder vor oder nach dem stofflich-dramatischen ein."
6. "Si tout l'orchestre, agissant à la fois, produit des sons sourds et lugubres, c'est que le tyran approche, et tout l'auditoire frémit ; si l'harmonie est douce et moelleuse, l'amante infortunée ne tardera pas à se montrer, et tous les cœurs s'attendrissent [...] En un mot, la musique est à chaque scène ce que les avenues sont aux châteaux."
7. "à chaque personnage correspond un judicieux emploi des ressources : la flûte plaintive correspond à la douleur de l'héroïne persécutée, la contre-basse accompagne le tyran, le comique est précédé d'une mélodie vive et animée."
8. "Le musicien peut rappeler ces morceaux touchans déja entendus, ou en plaçant au milieu des chants de ses personnages, les chants les plus marqués de l'air qu'il veut rappeler, & dont il veut faire revivre l'effet, ou en répandant ces chants dans les accompagnemens qu'il fait entendre, ou en rappelant simplement les accompagnemens du morceau dont il invoque le secours, & en les faisant servir d'accompagnemens ou de chant, dans le moment où il a besoin de beautés étrangères."

Bibliography

Abert, Hermann. 1926. *Grundprobleme der Operngeschichte*. Leipzig: Breitkopf & Härtel.

Basevi, Abramo. 1859. *Studio sulle opere di Giuseppe Verdi*. Florence: Tofani.

Beaumarchais, Pierre Caron de. 1767. "Essai sur le genre dramatique sérieux" [preface to *Eugénie* in the 2nd ed.]. Paris: Veuve Duchesne.

Berlioz, Hector. 1837. "De l'imitation musicale." *Revue et gazette musicale de Paris* (January 1 and 8).

Bianconi, Lorenzo. [1987] 1991. *Il seicento*. Turin: EDT.

——. 1986. "Introduzione." *La drammaturgia musicale*, 7–51. Bologna: Mulino.

——, and Giorgio Pestelli, eds. 1988. *Teorie e techniche, immagini e fantasmi. Storia dell'opera Italiana* 6. Turin: EDT.

Brown, Penelope, and Stephen C. Levinson. 1987. *Politeness: Some Universals in Language Usage*. Cambridge: Cambridge University Press.
Budden, Julian. 1978. *The Operas of Verdi*. 3 vols. New York: Oxford University Press.
Bühler, Karl. 1933. *Die Axiomatik der Sprachwissenschaft*. Frankfurt: Klostermann.
Cao, Hélène. 2010. "Leitmotif." *Dictionnaire encyclopédique Wagner*, edited by Timothée Picard. Arles: Actes Sud.
Carpani, Giuseppe. 1824. *Le rossiniane, ossia lettere musico-teatrali*. Padova: Minerva.
Colas, Damien. 2008. "Quale voce sentiamo nel da capo?" *Musica e storia* 16/3: 711–738.
——. 2004. "Duetto e *dialogue* a confronto: dal cantabile al 'dialogo musicale' nei duetti di Bellini." In *Vincenzo Bellini nel secondo centenario della morte*, edited by Graziella Seminara and Anna Tedesco, 149–184. Florence: Olschki.
Dahlhaus, Carl. 2000–2007. *Gesammelte Schriften*. 11 vols., edited by Hermann Danuser with Hans-Joachim Hinrichsen and Tobias Plebuch. Laaber: Laaber.
——. [1971a] 2004. "Richard Wagners Musikdramen." In Dahlhaus 2000–2007, VII: 141–273.
——. [1971b] 2004. "Wagners Konzeption des musikalischen Dramas." In Dahlhaus 2000–2007, VII: 11–140.
——. [1988] 2001. "Dramaturgie der italienischen Oper." In Dahlhaus 2000–2007, II: 467–545.
——. [1985] 2001. "Sind musikalische Werturteile begründbar?" In Dahlhaus 2000–2007, II: 110–117.
——. [1981] 2001. "Zeitstrukturen in der Oper." In Dahlhaus 2000–2007, II: 423–430.
Descartes, René. 1649. *Les passions de l'âme*. Paris: Legras.
Di Benedetto, Renato. 1988. "Poetiche e polemiche." In Bianconi and Pestelli 1988, 3–76.
Diderot, Denis. [1757] 1798. "Troisième entretien [sur *Le fils naturel*]." In *Œuvres de Denis Diderot*, edited by Jacques-André Naigeon, 183–238. Paris: Desray and Detervill.
Freud, Siegmund. 1908. "Der Dichter und das Phantasieren." *Neue Revue* 1: 716–724.
Ginisty, Paul. 1910. *Le mélodrame*. Paris: Louis-Michaud.
Goffman, Erving. 1956. *The Presentation of Self in Everyday Life*. Edinburgh: University of Edinburgh, Social Sciences Research Centre.
Gozza, Paolo. 2008. "Storia musicale dell'aria." *Musica e storia* 16/3: 519–531.
[Hugo, Abel, Armand Malitourne, and Jean Joseph Ader]. 1817. *Traité du mélodrame*. Paris: Delauney.
Kerman, Joseph. 1956. *Opera as Drama*. New York: Alfred A. Knopf.
——, and Thomas S. Grey. 1989. "Verdi's Groundswells: Surveying an Operatic Convention." In *Analyzing Opera: Verdi and Wagner*, edited by Roger Parker and Carolyn Abbate, 153–179. Berkeley and Los Angeles: University of California Press.
Kintzler, Catherine. 2011. "L'oreille, premier instrument de musique ?" *Methodos. Savoirs et textes*. Online. Available: http://methodos.revues.org/2542?lang=en (accessed February 6, 2014).
Klotz, Volker. 1960. *Geschlossene und offene Form im Drama*. München: C. Hanser.
Kubik, Reinhold. 1982. *Händels 'Rinaldo': Geschichte, Werk, Wirkung*. Neuhausen-Stuttgart: Hänssler.
Lacépède, Bernard de. 1785. *La poëtique de la musique*. Paris: Imprimerie de Monsieur.
Mahler, Gustav. 1996. Letter to Max Marschalk of 26 March 1896. In *Gustav Mahler. Briefe*, edited by Herta Blaukopf, 172. Wien: Paul Zsolnay.
Marmontel, Jean-François. 1776. "Accompagnement." *Supplément à l'Encyclopédie*, edited by Denis Diderot. Amsterdam: Rey.
Martello, Pierjacopo. 1715. *Della tragedia antica e moderna*. Roma: Francesco Gonzaga.

Müller, Günther. 1948. "Erzählzeit und erzählte Zeit." In *Festschrift für Paul Kluckhohn und Hermann Schneider*, edited by Tübinger Schülern, 195–212. Tübingen: Mohr-Siebeck.

Pinelli, Antonio. 2000. *Nel segno di Giano: Passato e futuro nell'arte europea tra Sette e Ottocento*. Roma: Carocci.

Rosand, Ellen. 1979. "The Descending Tetrachord: An Emblem of Lament." *Musical Quarterly* 65/3: 346–359.

Rousseau, Jean-Jacques. 1768. "Opéra." *Dictionnaire de musique*. Paris: Veuve Duchesne.

Sala, Emilio. 1995. *L'opera senza canto: Il melo romantico e l'invenzione della colonna sonora*. Venice: Marsilio.

Schmid, Manfred Hermann. 2009. "A French Connection: The Choral Settings in Mozart's *La clemenza di Tito*." *D'une scène à l'autre. L'opéra italien en Europe*. 2 vols. II: *La musique à l'épreuve du théâtre*, edited by Damien Colas and Alessandro Di Profio, 141–151. Wavre: Mardaga.

Serauky, Walter. 1929. *Die musikalische Nachahmungsästhetik im Zeitraum von 1700 bis 1850*. Münster: Helios.

Smart, Mary Ann. 2004. *Mimomania*. Berkeley and Los Angeles: University of California Press.

Smith, Adam. 1795. *Essays on Philosophical Subjects. Of the Nature of That Imitation Which Takes Place in What Are Called the Imitative Arts*. London: T. Cadell Junior and W. Davies.

Staiger, Emil. 1946. *Grundbegriffe der Poetik*. Zürich: Atlantis.

Stepath, Katrin. 2006. *Gegenwartskonzepte: Eine philosophisch-literaturwissenschaftliche Analyse temporaler Strukturen*. Würzburg: Königshausen & Neumann.

Szondi, Péter. 1956. *Theorie des modernen Dramas*. Frankfurt: Suhrkamp.

Voss, Egon. 2004. "'Oper im Kirchengewande'. Zur Rezeption von Verdis *Requiem* im deutschen Sprachraum." In *Das Bild der italienischen Oper in Deutschland*, edited by Sebastian Werr and Daniel Brandenburg, 191–199. Münster: LIT.

Wagner, Richard. [1851] 1911. *Sämtliche Schriften und Dichtungen*. 8 vols. III: *Oper und Drama*. Leipzig: Breitkopf & Härtel.

CHAPTER 9

VERSIFICATION

ANDREAS GIGER

Versification as a scholarly field investigates the structure of poetic verses, especially their meter (number of syllables), the position of accented and unaccented syllables, the position of the medial caesura (if appropriate), and the role of rhyme. Prosody, the aspect of versification primarily concerned with matters of accent and caesura, has a particularly strong influence on the structure of nineteenth-century operatic melody. This chapter shows that the composer often had a choice of approach and that this choice had musical consequences.

Approaches to Accentuation

Ever since the Second International Congress on Verdi Studies in 1969, musicologists have been considering the significance of prosody in explaining why the melodies of *Don Carlos* and, to a lesser extent, *Les vêpres siciliennes* are so different from those of Verdi's earlier operas (see especially Budden 1971 and Günther 1971). The findings have proven to be inconclusive because the research failed to take into account that by the nineteenth century, French versification encompassed more than one approach to accentuation and, as a consequence, reliance on only one approach inevitably distorted the picture. Having a choice does not mean, of course, that a composer would accentuate at random; it means that he had to accentuate based on his dramatic interpretation of the text. In other words, his choice would have rhetorical force.

It took so long to recognize the multiplicity of prosodic approaches because only one approach was predominant. It is described—among other places—in the popular treatise by Louis-Marie Quicherat (1850), which accounts for the setting of a great majority of verses in nineteenth-century French opera. According to this approach, each poetic meter (i.e., a verse with a specific number of syllables) includes a set number of accents falling on partly flexible positions of each verse (for a summary of Quicherat's rules, see Giger 2008: 12–13). For instance, an *octosyllabe* (verse of eight syllables) has, according

Table 9.1 Ambiguity of prosody in Brogni's "En mon âme." Halévy, *La Juive*, Act IV, scene 3

En mon âme une voix secrète	[3,6,8]	or	En mon âme une voix secrète	[3,8]
Parle pour elle et la défend?	[1,4,8]	or	Parle pour elle et la défend?	[4,8]
Et lorsque son bûcher s'apprête	[2,6,8]	or	Et lorsque son bûcher s'apprête	[6,8]
Je tremble du sort qui l'attend.	[2,5,8]	or	Je tremble du sort qui l'attend.	[2,8]

to Quicherat, an accent at the rhyme and on one or two additional, non-adjacent syllables (Quicherat 1850: 189). His phrase "un ou deux autres [accents] [one or two other accents]" implies a certain ambiguity (i.e., either two or three accents per verse) that scholarship has failed to acknowledge. The quatrain in Table 9.1 from Jacques Fromental Halévy's *La Juive* (Act IV, scene 3) illustrates this ambiguity. (The text is cited as Halévy set it; see Halévy n.d.: 329–330; for the libretto, see Scribe 1835: 14: 444; mute *e*s at the end of a word elide if the next word begins with a vowel; mute *e*s at the end of a verse are not counted when determining the poetic meter.)

A different, more fine-tuned approach concerns tonic accents, that is, all accents that mark the final syllable of even the smallest rhythmic group (not counting the *e muet*, of course) as in "je viens" or "père." This approach requires that all tonic accents be observed (to various degrees). Paul Pierson (1884), for instance, argues that

> Every segment has at its core a general accent of the period, which becomes the culminating accent of the segment . . . ; [hierarchically] below this culminating and unique accent, rule one or several comparatively weak accents, which, however, are individually endowed by a sufficient force to exert control over a system of weaker accents. (Pierson 1884: 158)

In the stanza from Halévy's *La Juive* cited above, Pierson's interpretation would correspond to Quicherat's with three accents; in other verses, however, Pierson would observe more accents. For example, an alexandrine (a verse of twelve syllables with a caesura on the sixth), according to Quicherat, has two accents in each hemistich, one at the caesura and one on any non-adjacent syllable; according to Pierson, however, the number of accents varies and would usually exceed those required by Quicherat, as in the following example from *Don Carlos* (Act II, tableau 2, scene 6; the caesura is marked by two vertical lines): "J'ai de ce prix sanglant ‖ payé la paix du monde" (Quicherat) and "J'**ai** de ce prix sanglant ‖ payé la paix du monde" (Pierson; *Don Carlos* Paris libretto 1867: 41).

While a sensitivity to secondary accents greater than Quicherat's leads us to Pierson, lesser sensitivity leads us to Otto Lubarsch (1879), who saw accents as points of arrival at the end of syntactic groups. As Lubarsch explains, syntactic groups tend to be relatively long and may encompass an entire verse:

> In French, the *Wortton* or the accentuation of an individual word is significantly reduced by the *Satzton*. . . . The French *Satzton* groups a series of conceptually related

Table 9.2 Prosodic interpretation of "En mon âme," according to Benloew

En mon âme une voix secrète	[2,4,6,8]
Parle pour elle et la défend?	[2,4,6,8]
Et lorsque son bûcher s'apprête	[2,4,6,8]
Je tremble du sort qui l'attend.	[2,4,6,8]

> words by assigning to the last limb of the chain a greater accent than to the other limbs. For example, the sentence "Cette maison est agré**able**," which forms a single conceptual chain, is pronounced in a way that the accent of its final word *agréable* stands out much more than all the other words of the sentence. (Lubarsch 1879: 5–6; see also Landry 1911: 191–192)

According to Lubarsch, the *octosyllabes* from *La Juive* might be accented, as in Quicherat's version, with only two accents, in the third verse perhaps with only one ("Et lorsque son bûcher s'apprête").

The prosodic interpretation could take yet another direction if one followed the practice of scanning (regularly alternating between accented and non-accented syllables), a practice still taught at schools and occasionally recommended in song. Pierson (1884: 227) criticized the practice but acknowledged its existence, while Louis Benloew (1862: 20–22, 24) accepted it in song and thus would have accepted the following extract from *La Juive* (see Table 9.2). Benloew (1862: 22) admits that such an interpretation creates a marked discrepancy between the tonic accent and the accent created by the scanning and warns that at the rhyme and (if the verse has one) the caesura, the two accents must coincide.

The Rhetoric of Accentuation

A composer's prosodic interpretation was determined by the emotion he intended to evoke. In most cases, Quicherat's approach works well but has only minimal rhetorical force, due to its broad application; in other cases, however, a less common approach enhances the desired emotion. Pierson's, for instance, even though it supposedly resembles "beautiful prose" (1884: 227), conveys a sense of agitation because it requires more accents than a speaker would normally observe. This sense of agitation recalls Richard Wagner's description in *Opera and Drama*:

> A faithful observance of the mode of expression we employ when our Feeling is highly wrought, even in ordinary life, will supply the poet with an unfailing measure for the number of accents in a natural Phrase.... [In] this... expression we emphasise far more strongly than usual—through the force of feeling—and also shift our

Table 9.3 Prosodic interpretation of Rodrigue's "O Roi, j'arrive de Flandre." Verdi, *Don Carlos*, Act II, tableau 2, scene 6

O Roi! || J'arrive de Flandre, ||	[2,4,7]
Ce pays jadis si beau! ||	[3,7]
Ce n'est [plus] qu'un désert de cendre, ||	[3,6,8]
Un lieu d'horreur, || un tombeau! ||	[2,4,7]
Là, || l'orphelin qui mendie ||	[1,4,7]
Et pleure par les chemins, ||	[2,7]
Tombe, || en fuyant l'incendie,	[1,4,7]
Sur des ossements humains! ||	[1,5,7]

accents closer together; while, to make these accents *im*press the hearer's Feeling as forcibly as we want to *ex*press in them our own feelings, we dwell on them in sharply lifted voice. These Accents round themselves instinctively into a phrase, or a main section of a phrase, during the outflow of the breath, and their number will always stand in direct ratio to the excitement; so that, for instance, an ireful, an *active* emotion will allow a greater number of Accents to be emitted in one breath, whereas a deep, a *suffering* one will consume the whole breath-force in fewer, more long-drawn tones. (Wagner [1852] 1966: 256–257)

In opera, Pierson's approach gained prevalence during the second half of the nineteenth century and is exemplified in "O Roi, j'arrive de Flandre" from Verdi's *Don Carlos* (Act II, tableau 2, scene 6), a political narrative in which Rodrigue confronts King Philip of Spain with the dismal situation of human rights in the Spanish-controlled region of Flanders (see Table 9.3). Even though the poetic meter remains constant (verses of seven syllables), the position of the accents changes from verse to verse (the strongest ones are followed by double-vertical lines). In his setting, Verdi observes the accents *and* their hierarchy, thus musically reflecting the high level of agitation conveyed by the text (see Günther and Petazzoni [1974] 1990: 236–238).

Scanning against tonic accents dates back to *opéra comique* and tends to occur in *romances* (such as "Une fièvre brûlante" from André-Ernest-Modeste Grétry's *Richard Coeur-de-lion* [Act II, scene 4; 1784]) and dance tunes (such as "Flamme vengeresse" from Daniel-François-Esprit Auber's *Le domino noir* [Act III, scene 4; 1837]). In grand opera, it acquires a rhetorical connotation with lightheartedness, often marked by an emphasis on memorable melody over correct accentuation; examples are numerous, including "Si j'ét**ai**s coquette! D**ieu**!" from Giacomo Meyerbeer's *Les Huguenots* (Act II, scene 5; 1836; scanned in trochees), "La brise s**ou**ffle au l**oi**n, plus légère et plus pure" from Verdi's *Les vêpres siciliennes* (Act V, scene 2; 1855; scanned in iambs), and "**Au** pal**ai**s des fées" from Verdi's *Don Carlos* (Act II, tableau 2, scene 1; 1867; scanned in trochees). In the examples by Meyerbeer and Verdi, tonic and rhythmic accents begin to conflict only in the second verse ("Pareille conquête, **oui**" and "Des rois Grenadins," respectively).

The prosodic approach of Lubarsch (1879) became more prominent in opera only toward the end of the nineteenth century, when periodic phrase structure gave way to freer, more speech-like melody. Its meaning, or range of meanings, still remains to be fully determined, but in Verdi's *Don Carlos* it is associated with a character's attempt to control his or her emotions. When King Philip accuses his wife, whom he suspects to be unfaithful, of talking to him too frankly, for instance, the king initially suppresses his emotions; two verses later, he loses his temper (i.e., he becomes agitated) and breaks into curses. Verdi reflects this change by first observing tonic accents only occasionally ("Vous me parlez avec hardiesse / Vous ne m'avez connu qu'en des jours de faiblesse") and eventually by observing every single one ("Alors, malh**eur** sur v**ous**... malh**eur**!").

Violated Accents and Caricature

Awareness of the prosodic variety and its significance also helps us interpret passages in which none of the theoretically sanctioned approaches applies, that is, in which accents are *truly* violated. In this case, too, a composer would have a dramatic purpose, usually caricature. In Adolphe Adam's *Le brasseur de Preston* (Act II, scene 18; 1838), for instance, the brewer Daniel Robinson stands in for his twin brother as an officer of the army without having the faintest idea of the responsibilities and code of behavior attached to the position. Despite many mishaps, he leads his troops to victory and recounts his adventure in the "Air du cheval" (see Werr 2002: 159–173, especially 168). Adam creates comedy by consistently subverting the rhythmic pattern established in the first verse. The result does not correspond, even remotely, with any of the standard prosodic approaches (see Table 9.4).

A similar situation appears in Richard Wagner's *Die Meistersinger von Nürnberg* (1868). Sixtus Beckmesser, the operatic version of the anti-Wagnerian critic Eduard Hanslick,

Table 9.4 Prosodic interpretations of Robinson's "Air du cheval." Adam, *Le brasseur de Preston*, Act II, scene 18

Accentuation according to Quicherat	Accentuation according to Pierson
Tout-à-l'heure tant bien que mal Le sergent me hisse à cheval Et, sans attendre mon signal, Je vois s'élancer l'animal;	Tout-à-l'heure tant bien que mal Le sergent me hisse à cheval Et, sans attendre mon signal, Je vois s'élancer l'animal;
Scanning according to Benloew	**Accentuation according to Adam**
Tout-à-l'heure tant bien que mal Le sergent me hisse à cheval Et, sans attendre mon signal, Je vois s'élancer l'animal;	Tout-à-l'heure tant bien que mal Le sergent me hisse à cheval Et, sans attendre mon signal, Je vois s'élancer l'animal;

appears under Eva's window for a trial run of the song with which he would like to win her as his bride at the upcoming song contest. The song (discussed in more detail below) is a caricature of a *Meisterlied* in every respect, not least in the garbled prosody. A proper interpretation of Wagner's prosodic approach requires some historical context, however, not only because nineteenth-century German operatic versification differs fundamentally from its French counterpart but also because, to the best of my knowledge, it has never been outlined in modern scholarly literature (the only study thoroughly covering German prosody in opera is Aikin 2002; it deals, however, with recitative, not aria, and is largely based on seventeenth-century operas for which the music has been lost).

Nineteenth-Century German Prosodic Standards

Prosodic standards for German librettos of the early nineteenth century date back to Opitz's reform in his *Buch von der deutschen Poeterey* (1624), in which the author notes only the iamb and trochee as acceptable meters and asserts that the German accent is one of stress and not duration:

> Furthermore, every verse is either iambic or trochaic, not by considering—as in Greek or Latin—a certain length of the syllables, but by recognizing, based on accents and intonation, which syllable is strong and which is weak.... Since, to the best of my knowledge, nobody, not even I, has carefully paid attention to [this rule], it seems just as important as it is in Latin to arrange the verses according to quantity or length.[1] (Opitz [1624] 1888: 182)

Despite Opitz's claim that any other rhythm is incompatible with German poetry, poets soon explored the dactyl and anapest as well (Breuer 1981: 170). They did not usually mix these poetic feet, however: structural variety in a poem remained limited to the arrangement of the rhyme, the number of verses per stanza, and the number of syllables per verse (Breuer 1981: 188). This aesthetic largely persisted until Friedrich Gottlieb Klopstock (1724–1803) revived rhythmic models of antiquity and Johann Gottfried Herder (1744–1803) praised rhythmically irregular verse rooted in the poetry of the people (Breuer 1981: 199–220). For both reformers, it was important that the rhythm match the poem's topic, imagery, lyricism, and melody (Herder [1773] 1892: 10; Klopstock called it "Mitausdruck der Gedanken [parallel expression of thoughts]"; see Breuer 1981: 192). But whereas Klopstock insisted on the connection with antiquity, Herder valued—similar to the concept of local color in opera—the connection with regional and socioeconomic segments of the population:

> In more than one province, I have come across folksongs, provincial songs, peasant songs that in terms of liveliness and rhythm, naiveté and strength of language are

Table 9.5 Poetic analysis of Agathe's aria. Weber, *Der Freischütz*, Act II, scene 2

Wie nahte mir der Schlummer,	recitative in iambs
Bevor ich ihn gesehn?–	
Ja, Liebe pflegt mit Kummer	
Stets Hand in Hand zu geh'n!	
Ob wohl der Mond auf seine Pfade lacht?	
Welch schöne Nacht!	
Leise, leise,	aria in trochees
Fromme Weise!	
Schwing' dich auf zum Sternenkreise.	
Lied, erschalle!	
Feiernd walle	
Mein Gebet zur Himmelshalle!–	

> equal to those of many of those [Scottish romances (and, by extension, songs of other peoples)]; but who collects them?... who pays attention to the songs of the people? in the streets, allies, fishmarkets? in the untrained rounds of the country folk? to songs that are often not scanned and badly rhymed?—who would want to collect them, print them for our critics, who are so good at counting syllables and at scanning?[2] (Herder [1773] 1892: 37)

The examples Herder cites—whether in the original German or in German translation—show that rhythmic consistency may be relaxed if justified by content. But despite Herder's efforts, true reform had to wait until Richard Wagner, who not only referred to the "unloveliness" of the iamb but also called for an

> *accent* which we place upon certain words or syllables [only] *for sake of intelligibleness.* This Accent, however, is by no means good for once and all..., but...varies in exact degree as this word or that syllable in the sentence is of stronger or weaker *import* for the meaning. (Wagner [1852] 1966: 241)

In German opera prior to Wagner's reform, verse intended for recitative was generally cast in iambs, verse for formal numbers in any of the principal four poetic feet (iambs, trochees, dactyls, or anapests). Verse for recitative tended to vary in length, verse for formal numbers tended to be consistent in length. An excerpt from Kind's libretto (Kind 1843: 30) for Carl Maria von Weber's *Der Freischütz* (Agathe's aria, Act II, scene 2) may serve as an example (see Table 9.5). The third and sixth verses of the aria portion are of distinct length only in theory; in practice, they combine two shorter verses into a longer one because neither "auf" in the middle of the third verse nor "Gebet" in the middle of the sixth would rhyme.

According to Herder, the poetic rhythm may change within a song—or, in our case, an aria—if justified by the drama. Ännchen's *Romanze* from *Der Freischütz* (Act III, scene 3; included in the 1823 libretto but not the 1843 libretto) provides a good example

Table 9.6 Poetic analysis of Ännchen's *Romanze* from Weber's *Der Freischütz*, Act III, scene 3

German text	Poetic feet	Translation
Einst träumte meiner seel'gen Base,	iambic tetrameters	Once my cousin—God rest her soul!—
Die Kammerthür' eröffne sich,		dreamt that her bedroom door was opened,
Und—kreideweiss ward ihre Nase;		and her nose went white as chalk,
Denn näher, furchtbar näher schlich		then nearer, terrifyingly nearer,
Ein Ungeheuer,	iambic dimeter	crept a monster
Mit Augen wie Feuer,	anapestic dimeters	with eyes like fire
Mit klirrender Kette[.]		and clanking chains.
Es nahte dem Bette,		It drew near the bed
In welchem sie schlief[—]		in which she was sleeping—
Ich meine die Base		I mean the cousin
Mit kreidiger Nase[—]		with the chalk-white nose—
Und stöhnte, ach! so hohl! und ächzte[,] [ach]! so tief!	iambic hexameter	and it moaned, oh so hollowly, and groaned, oh so deeply!
Sie kreuzte sich, rief,	anapestic dimeter	She crossed herself, and after
Nach manchem Angst- und Stossgebet[:]	iambic tetrameter	an anxious, urgent prayer, cried
Susanne! Marg[a]reth!	iambic trimeter	"Susanne! Margaret!"

(*Freischütz* 1823: 26). The *Romanze* begins in regular iambs as Ännchen introduces her cousin's nightmare. But exactly when the reason for the scare—the "Ungeheuer (Monster)"—is revealed, the poetic meter shifts, first to an iambic dimeter, then to anapestic dimeters, which are rarely pure but mixed with iambs, especially at the beginning of the verse (see Atkins 1923: 218). With this shift, the librettist presumably meant to attract attention, and Weber accordingly shifted to shorter phrases, adjusted the melodic rhythm to that of the text, and introduced the clarinets to create a supernatural effect (see Table 9.6).

In contrast to its French counterpart, German versification does not allow for multiple rhythmic interpretations of a verse. Whereas a German composer may downplay an accent, he must not violate prosody by stressing an unaccented syllable instead. Early nineteenth-century poetic theory, here in the words of Freese (1837), asserts this point with utmost clarity and in tandem with practice:

> In French—and most probably in many other languages as well and, admittedly to a far lesser extent, in the remaining romance ones—the tonic accent in versification is subordinate to the rhythm of the verse and inexorably absorbed by it; only on the ultimate and penultimate syllables does one remember the force of the [tonic accent]. In German, however, as in those languages that logically determine their intonation, the accentuation of single words and entire sentences already has taken shape so distinctly and firmly that a contrast between the two would be ugly and entirely contrary to the nature of our idiom.... The main rule imposes on the German poets a correspondence between the accent of the syllable and accent of the word on the one

> hand and accent of the verse on the other, so that in scanning and declamation, any accentually unnatural pronunciation of words is avoided, whether in their individual parts or their combination.[3] (Freese 1837: 89–90)

A composer encountering a change of poetic feet from one verse to another must therefore either adjust the text or respect the potential irregularities (as in Ännchen's *Romanze* discussed above); he must not, as a French composer might have done under the appropriate circumstances, scan against tonic accents. (For specific references to composition, see, for instance, von Zesen [1641] 1971: 26–27 and Rotth 1688: 3:146. See also Dove 1984: 620–621.)

The Marker Gets Marked by a Master: Beckmesser's "Serenade"

Prosody was part of Wagner's germinal idea for *Die Meistersinger von Nürnberg.* He envisioned a scene in which Hans Sachs critiques Beckmesser's serenade by answering every mistake with a hammer stroke on the shoes that the "marker" himself (Beckmesser) had left for repair. Sachs's hammer strokes are aimed at both the text and its musical treatment, but whereas the discrepancy between textual and musical accents has been mentioned frequently, the rhythmic qualities of the text itself have, to the best of my knowledge, never been addressed.

Wagner studied numerous texts on *Meistergesang* but left no evidence that he actually attempted to write an authentic *Meisterlied*, not with regard to the text and certainly not with regard to the music. Regardless of Wagner's intentions, the rhythm of Beckmesser's serenade may be evaluated according to the rules of a *Meisterlied* (the genre of the excerpt) or those of nineteenth-century opera (the genre of the overall work). The "historical" approach poses a problem because the primary sources on *Meistergesang* provide information only about rhyme, syllable count, and strophic schemes, not poetic feet (Breuer 1981: 131, 135–136). In any case, since the melodies of *Meistergesang* are most likely non-metrical and syllables are accented wherever necessary, changes in poetic feet would not cause a conflict between textual and musical accents (Warrack 1994a: 63).

Wagner's setting, however, *is* metrical, suggesting that an evaluation by nineteenth-century standards is more appropriate. The first *Bar* (stanza) of Beckmesser's serenade—which consists, as was common in *Meistergesang*, of twenty verses forming two *Stollen* and an *Abgesang*—shows that Wagner *mixed* poetic feet, not only from one verse to the next but also within verses (Wagner [1862] 1983: 48; see Table 9.7).

A comparison with either version of Walther's "Prize Song" (the version in the 1862 fair copy of the libretto, eventually discarded, and the version in the final libretto)—a song Wagner must have considered superior to Beckmesser's—shows that the

Table 9.7 Poetic analysis of Beckmesser's first *Bar*. Wagner, *Die Meistersinger von Nürnberg*, Act II, scene 6

Den Tag seh' ich erscheinen,	iambs	*Stollen* 1
der mir wohl gefall'n thut…	trochees	
Da fasst mein Herz sich einen	iambs	
guten und frischen Muth.	dactyl + trochees	
Da denk' ich nicht an Sterben,	iambs	
lieber an Werben	dactyls	
um jung Mägdeleins Hand.	anapests	
Warum wohl aller Tage	iambs	*Stollen* 2
schönster mag dieser sein?	dactyl + trochees	
Allen hier ich es sage:	trochee + dactyls	
weil ein schönes Fräulein	trochees	
von ihrem lieb'n Herrn Vater,	iambs	
wie gelobt hat er,	trochees	
ist bestimmt zum Ehstand.	trochees	
Wer sich getrau'	dactyls	*Abgesang*
der komm' un schau'	iambs	
dastehn die hold lieblich Jungfrau,	dactyls	
auf die ich all mein Hoffnung bau':	iambs	
darum ist der Tag so schön blau,	anapests	
als ich anfänglich fand.	trochee + dactyls	

Table 9.8 Beginning of Walther's "Prize Song" as it appears in the 1862 fair copy of the libretto. Wagner, *Die Meistersinger von Nürnberg*, Act III, scene 2

Fern	Pause
meiner Jugend gold'nen Toren	trochaic tetrameter
zog ich einst aus,	dactylic dimeter
in Betrachtung ganz verlogen:	trochaic tetrameter
väterlich Haus,	dactylic dimeter
kindliche Wiege,	dactylic dimeter
lebet wohl! ich eil', ich fliege	trochaic tetrameter
einer neuen Welt nun zu.	trochaic tetrameter

rhythmic shifts in Beckmesser's text by far outnumber those in Walther's (see McDonald 1977: 256–257); they suggest a lack of taste and portray Beckmesser as a poet with no sense of rhythm whatsoever. Table 9.8 shows the beginning of Walther's "Prize Song" as it appears in the 1862 fair copy of the libretto (as sung to Sachs early in Act III; Wagner [1862] 1983: 59); the most significant departure from an otherwise fairly regular metric treatment concerns the opening monosyllabic verse, a verse Adam Puschman (a student of Hans Sachs) calls a "Pause" (see Puschman [1571] 1888: 7).

Table 9.9 Beginning of Walther's "Prize Song" as it appears in the final version of the libretto. Wagner, *Die Meistersinger von Nürnberg*, Act III, scene 2

Morgenlich leuchtend in rosigem Schein,	dactylic tetrameter
von Blüt' und Duft	iambic dimeter
geschwellt die Luft,	iambic dimeter
voll aller Wonnen	iambic dimeter
nie ersonnen,	trochaic dimeter
ein Garten lud mich ein,	iambic trimeter
Gast ihm zu sein.	dactylic dimeter

Table 9.10 Beckmesser's scanning of the first *Bar*. Wagner, *Die Meistersinger von Nürnberg*, Act II, scene 6.

Den Tag seh' ich erscheinen,
der mir wohl gefall'n thut…
Da fasst mein Herz sich einen
guten und frischen Muth.
Da denk' ich nicht an Sterben,
lieber an Werben
um jung Mägdeleins Hand.
Warum wohl aller Tage
schönster mag dieser sein?
Allen hier ich es sage:
weil ein schönes Fräulein
von ihrem lieb'n Herrn Vater,
wie gelobt hat er,
ist bestimmt zum Ehstand.
Wer sich getrau'
der komm' und schau'
dastehn die hold lieblich Jungfrau,
auf die ich all mein Hoffnung bau':
darum ist der Tag so schön blau,
als ich anfänglich fand.

The final version of Walther's "Prize Song," too, is considerably more regular than Beckmesser's serenade, especially when we take into consideration that the verse "nie ersonnen" continues the iambic rhythm of the previous verses. The melody (the composition of which preceded the text) matches the continuous iambic rhythm of the poetry (see Warrack 1994b: 33 and Voss 1983: 16; see Table 9.9).

Beckmesser's setting compounds the problems of the poetic rhythm because he scans the entire text in iambs, regardless of the natural accents of the text (see Table 9.10). His treatment recalls French practice in which a composer may, for the sake of a more memorable melody and in the proper dramatic context, scan against tonic accents. Voss has more generally related this caricature of Beckmesser to "traditional opera [herkömmliche Oper]," especially Italian opera with its "indifference to accurate declamation [Gleichgültigkeit gegenüber sinngerechter Deklamation]," a type of opera in which "wrong accentuation and negligence do not matter [falsche Betonungen und Nachlässikgeit nicht ins Gewicht fallen]" (1981: 26–27; see also Vaget 2003: 197).

But Voss is not entirely accurate on two counts. First, Wagner seems to parody French, not Italian opera. While scanning against tonic accents does occur in Italian opera, it is normally restricted to the *quinario* (verse of five syllables) and its *doppio* form (coupled *quinari*) and involves the dactyl, not the iamb.[4] Similarly, Italian librettists in the middle of the nineteenth century avoided polymetric stanzas of the type found in Beckmesser's serenade, whereas their French counterparts employed them regularly.[5] The combination of scanning against tonic accents with polymetric stanzas is a particularly French characteristic, occurring in such numbers as Angèle's "Flamme vengeresse" from Auber's *Le domino noir* and Marguerite's "Si j'étais coquette! Dieu!" from *Les Huguenots*, both mentioned above.

Voss is also inaccurate when he claims that correct accentuation did not matter in French or Italian opera; the Italians had very specific prosodic rules (see below), and a French composer could scan against tonic accents only under the special circumstances described above. Therefore, when Wagner had Beckmesser scan his awkwardly lighthearted (or silly) polymetric text, he followed French practice in both text and music.

Our analysis contributes to the larger and ongoing controversy over the meaning of Beckmesser's serenade. The field of commentators is split between those who focus on Beckmesser as a representative of Jewishness as Wagner conceived it in "Das Judentum in der Musik" (for example, Millington 1991) and those who see him as a representative of non-German art, especially Italian and, occasionally, French opera (Vaget 2002: 202). As Grey (2002: 188) has shown, Wagner most probably did associate Beckmesser with the Jews but was satisfied for this association to remain "a kind of private subtext." Intimately familiar with French opera and bitter about his lack of success in Paris, especially with *Tannhäuser*, Wagner did not present the French approach to scanning as a subtext: he made it blatantly obvious.

Scanning in Italian Opera: Two Instances in *I due Foscari*

In Italian opera, scanning against tonic accents was not particularly common because librettists provided verse that either allowed for scanning without violating any accents or rendered scanning impossible. A *senario* (verse of six syllables) such as Aida's "L'insana parola," for instance, always includes an accent on the second and fifth syllables; since these must be observed and adjacent accents would always be treated as subordinate to the primary ones, the verse naturally invites scanning in anapests. The rules are somewhat more vague in the *settenario* (verse of seven syllables), requiring an accent on the second and sixth syllables, the fourth and sixth, or all three. While the *settenario* may invite scanning as well, it allows, if only two accents are observed, for one misaccentuation (Balthazar 1992: 7). In Zaccaria's verse "D'Egitto là sui lidi" from *Nabucco* (Act I, scene 2), for instance, the sixth and either the second or fourth syllables must be accented. Verdi complied, accenting the fourth and sixth but stressing the first over the second, in line with at least some of the theorists. Verdi's reason for misaccentuating "Egitto" on the first syllable had nothing to do with a potential urge to scan—the tonic accents would have allowed it naturally—but with establishing a melodic pattern that conveyed the drama (or he had conceived the melody prior to having the final text in hand).

Scanning Italian verses against tonic accents was not only uncommon but could become an issue. In the duet cabaletta for Jacopo and Lucrezia from *I due Foscari* (Act II, scene 2), for instance, Verdi accented the *settenari* "Ogni perduto bene / Nell'amor tuo godrò" not only on the fourth and sixth syllables but also on the second syllable, in line with at least some of the theorists but against the natural accent of "ogni" (which falls on the first syllable). In other words, he scanned against a natural accent of the text. The reason lies in the rhythm of the preceding verses, all of which naturally allow for scanning in iambs; only in the last two (quoted above), where the opening melody returns, does the poetic rhythm shift and lead to an incompatibility with the musical rhythm (see Music Example 9.1, upper line of text). It is not immediately clear why, in the autograph, these two verses were replaced and why they were replaced in a hand other than Verdi's. Even though the accentuation "Ogn**i** perduto bene" (instead of "**O**gni perduto bene") may strike us as somewhat odd today, numerous such examples exist, not least in the subsequent terzetto, where Verdi misaccentuated the same word, "ogni," in the same poetic meter, the *settenario* (in this case, Verdi does not scan, because he ignores the elision of "scordo" and "ogni."): "Nel t**uo** pat**e**rno ampl**e**sso / io sc**o**rdo ogn**i** dol**o**re." In the autograph, the latter instance is not corrected, suggesting that prosody was not the reason for the revision of the former instance.

Another possibility is censorship. We already know that the Roman censors, the strictest in Italy with regard to religion and morality, changed several passages in *I due Foscari* despite Francesco Maria Piave's claim, in his letter of November 9, 1844, to Ricordi, that they had approved the libretto "without changing a comma" (Abbiati 1959: I: 521; for censorship, see Giger 2009). It is certainly possible that they found the

MUSIC EXAMPLE 9.1 Verdi's setting of the last two verses of cabaletta text in the Jacopo-Lucrezia duet. *I due Foscari*, Act II, scene 2.

phrase "ogni perduto bene / nell'amor tuo godrò (in your love, I shall enjoy every lost good)" inappropriate and thus required that it be changed, whereas the more lenient (at least in regard to religion and morality) colleagues in Naples allowed the publishers Del Monaco, Cali, and Girard to print the text as Verdi had originally set it. Nevertheless, it is difficult to determine what exactly might have bothered the censors in Rome, which makes the censorial explanation as unconvincing as the prosodic one given above.

The solution appears in one of the opera's early manuscript copies, now housed at the Naples conservatory (*I due Foscari* Naples Copy: Act II: 66r–v). This copy, prepared under Ricordi's auspices before Verdi had made final revisions, was eventually updated in Verdi's hand and includes a note in the hand of a Ricordi scribe that "the old score serves to take the words for the new score [spartito vecchio serve per prendere le parole allo Spartito nuovo]" (*I due Foscari* Naples Copy: Act I: 80v), presumably suggesting that the words of this copy be used in any future score. When updating the manuscript copy, Verdi not only changed the text in the duet (*I due Foscari* Naples Copy: Act II: 66v) from "Ogn**i** perd**u**to bene / nell'**a**mor t**uo** godr**ò**" to "Perd**u**to ogn'**a**ltro b**e**ne / dell'**a**mor t**uo** vivr**ò**," he also changed the text in the terzetto from "Nel t**uo** pat**e**rno ampl**e**sso / Io sc**o**rdo ogn**i** dol**o**re" to "Nel t**uo** pat**e**rno ampl**e**sso / M**u**to si f**à** il dol**o**re." It turns out that scanning against tonic accents bothered Verdi after all, despite its theoretical legitimacy. Once Verdi had made these changes in the manuscript copy, a Ricordi scribe transferred to the autograph the first one (which thus appears in a hand other than Verdi's) but either failed or decided not to transfer the second one. The second change is indeed less successful, not only because the wording is awkward but also because the last syllable of "amplesso" is stretched over two notes and the syntactic structure of "Muto si fa' il dolore" does not fit the articulation and gesture of the melodic line (the slur in the second half of the measure ties "il" (which syntactically belongs to "dolore") to "fa" (see Music Example 9.2).

The reasons for the change must have lain in the reluctance to scan, not only because the misaccentuation of "ogni" would have been in line with prosodic theory but also because Verdi continued to resort to this kind of misaccentuation when it served his dramatic needs. In Medora's *romanza* from *Il corsaro* (1849), for instance, Verdi could easily have scanned the text—without violating any tonic accents ("Non s**o** le t**e**tre imm**a**gin**i** / fug**a**r del m**io** pens**ie**ro")—but misaccentuated "fug**a**r" for a dramatically

MUSIC EXAMPLE 9.2 Verdi's setting of "Nel tuo paterno amplesso." *I due Foscari*, Act II, scene 3, in the autograph and his correction in the Naples copy.

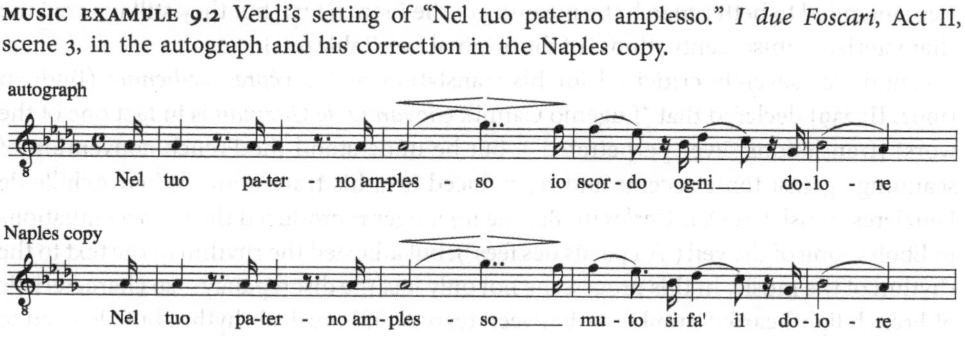

MUSIC EXAMPLE 9.3 Verdi's setting of "Non so le tetre immagini." *Il corsaro*, Act I, scene 4.

appropriate melodic quality (unlike *I due Foscari*, the autograph of *Il corsaro* shows no trace of revision here; see Hudson 1998: 31; see Music Example 9.3).

The reluctance of the Italians to scan against tonic accents is also evident in translations of Verdi's French operas into Italian. *Les vêpres siciliennes*, for instance, includes several arias in which Verdi scans against tonic accents. The first example of Table 9.11 shows Verdi's interpretation in iambs with accents on "jeun**e**s" instead of "j**eu**nes," "dont l**e**s fleurs" instead of "dont les fl**eu**rs," and "sont m**oi**ns fraîch**e**s" instead of "sont moins fr**aî**ches." An Italian translator had to decide whether he would reproduce the misaccentuations, which in French are integral to the overall effect, or avoid them in light of Italian sensibilities. Eugenio Caimi—an Italian exile working in Paris and presumably aware of the Italian reluctance to scan against tonic accents—allowed only one misaccentuation ("Dell**e**" instead of "D**e**lle"; for some sketchy biographical information on this obscure poet and translator active during the *Risorgimento*, see Giglio 1912: 279–280). Even this one instance seems to have raised objections and was "fixed"—in conjunction with a virtual retranslation—in the 1861 Turin libretto. (It is not yet clear who was responsible for the retranslation, but it may have been G. Sesto Giannini; see Toscani 2003: 505n.)

Caimi was bolder with Henri's "La brise souffle." Verdi's setting includes four misaccentuations ("l**é**gère **e**t" instead of "lég**è**re et," "p**a**raît" instead of "par**aî**t," "l'ond**e**" instead of "l'**o**nde," and "m**e** semble" instead of "me s**e**mble"), which Caimi nearly matched by including three ("Scend**o**no" instead of "Sc**e**ndono," "l'acque **i**n" instead of "l'**a**cque in," and "spos**a**no" instead of "sp**o**sano"), but as in the previous instance, the accentuation was corrected in later translations: both the 1856 and 1861 Turin librettos—the latter containing the version generally sung today—completely obliterate any irregularity, perfectly adjusting the textual rhythm to the music and thus sacrificing the special effect of carefree abandon to artificial smoothness. The revisions for the 1861 Turin performance were intended to better match the meaning of the French text, but they still ignored the characteristic "misaccentuations" of the original (see Table 9.11).

Caimi was severely criticized for his translation of *Les vêpres siciliennes* (Budden [1992: II: 239] declared that "Eugenio Caimi's *Giovanna de Guzman* is in fact one of the worst [translations] ever perpetrated"), but he understood the French convention of scanning against tonic accents and reproduced it in his translation. When Achille de Lauzières translated *Don Carlos* in 1867, he no longer reproduced the misaccentuations in Eboli's song of the veil ("Au palais des fées"), but adjusted the rhythm of the text to the rhythm of the music. In this process, he not only lost the discrepancy—so characteristic of French lighthearted numbers—between textual and musical rhythm but also had to

Table 9.11 Prosody of two ceremonial numbers from *Les vêpres siciliennes*, Act V, scene 2, in the original French and Italian translations

Paris, 1855: Merci, jeunes amies, De ces présens si doux! Dont les fleurs si jolies Sont moins fraîches que vous.	Parma, 1856; Turin, 1856: Il don m'è grato e pregio Di quei leggiadri fior; Delle vostr'alme ingenue Riflettono il candor! Turin, 1861: Mercè, dilette amiche, Di quei leggiadri fior; Il caro dono è immagine Del vostro bel candor!
Paris, 1855: La brise souffle au loin, || plus légère et plus pure Et de parfums plus doux || l'air paraît embaumé. L'onde plus mollement || et serpente et murmure, Et d'un rayon divin || tout me semble animé!	Parma, 1856: Scendono i zeffiretti—a carezzarmi il viso, E di profumi eletti—inondano il mio cor. L'acque in tenor gentile—il dolce mormorio Sposano al gaudio mio—col riso dell'amor. Turin, 1856: Il zeffiretto spira—a carezzarmi il viso, E di profumi eletti—ravviva questo cor. Del limpido ruscello—il dolce mormorio Unisce il gaudio mio—col riso dell'amor. Turin, 1861: La brezza aleggio intorno—a carezzarmi il viso, E di profumi eletti—imbalsamato è il cor. Più mollemente l'onda—con dolce mormorio S'unisce al canto mio—nel riso dell'amor.

Table 9.12 Prosody of Eboli's "Au palais des fées" in the original French and the Italian translation. *Don Carlos*, Act II, tableau 2, scene 1

Paris, 1867	Bologna, 1867
Au palais des fées, Des roi Grenadins, Devant les nymphées, Des ces beaux jardins,	Nei giardin—del bello Saracin—ostello, All'olezzo,—al rezzo Degli allôr,—dei fior.

resort to unusually poetic vocabulary ("olezzo" instead of "profumo" and "rezzo" instead of "ombra"; see Table 9.12).

In the past, scholars have drawn on versification to understand form, melodic style (Petrobelli 1989), and occasionally an opera's prevalent color (or *tinta*; Petrobelli 2000). This chapter has attempted to show that, with regard to its prosodic aspects, versification can do much more: It can underscore the rhetoric of an aria or phrase, contribute to the caricature of a character, play a role in determining what version of a particular text should be the principal one, and contribute to our understanding of the reasons why an opera is more effective in its original language than in translation; in other words, it can become an interpretive tool of importance similar to that of harmony, melody, or orchestration. These ramifications must be of concern not only to the composer, who must calculate the rhythmic effect of his melodies by taking into account both the rhythm of the music and its relationship to the rhythm of the text, but also the librettist, who must inspire the composer with a libretto not only of "palpable ambience, striking characters and… strong situations" (Powers 1990: 15) but also of potential for rhetorical effects.

See also: Musical Dramaturgy, The Language of National Style, The German Libretto of the Early Nineteenth Century

NOTES

1. "Nachmals ist auch ein jeder verß entweder ein iambicus oder trochaicus; nicht zwar das wir auff art der griechen vnnd lateiner eine gewisse grösse der sylben können inn acht nemen; sondern das wir aus den accenten vnnd dem thone erkennen, welche sylbe hoch vnnd welche niedrig gesetzt werden soll.... Wiewol nun meines wissens noch niemand, ich auch vor der zeit selber nicht, dieses genawe in acht genommen, scheinet es doch so hoch von nöthen zue sein, als hoch von nöthen ist, das die Lateiner nach den quantitatibus oder grössen der sylben ihre verse richten vnd reguliren."
2. "In mehr als einer Provinz sind mir Volkslieder, Provinziallieder, Bauernlieder bekannt, die an Lebhaftigkeit und Rhythmus, und Naivetät und Stärke der Sprache vielen derselben gewiß nichts nachgeben würden; nur wer ist der sie sammle?... der sich um Lieder des Volks bekümmre? auf Strassen, und Gassen und Fischmärkten? im ungelehrten Rundgesange des Landvolks? um Lieder, die oft nicht skandirt, und oft schlecht gereimt sind? wer wollte sie sammeln—wer für unsre Kritiker, die ja so gut Sylben zählen, und skandiren können, drucken lassen?"
3. "Im Französischen, sowie höchst wahrscheinlich auch in manchen anderen Sprachen und freilich in weit geringerem Maße in den übrigen Romanischen, bleibt der Silbenaccent bei der Versification völlig untergeordnet und wird von dem Versrhythmus unaufhaltsam fortgerissen; nur in der letzten und vorletzten Silbe erinnert man sich wiederum der Kraft des ersteren. Im Deutschen hingegen, wie überhaupt wohl in den logisch ihre Vertonung feststellenden Sprachen, hat sich der Sprachton in einzelnen Worten und ganzen Sätzen schon so bestimmt und fest ausgeprägt, daß ein Contrast beider durchaus übellautend und der Natur unseres Idioms gänzlich widerstreitend sein würde.... Die Hauptregel gebietet den Deutschen Dichtern Uebereinstimmung der Silben- und Wortaccente mit den Versaccenten, so dass durch Scansion und Declamation jede rücksichtlich der Betonung unnatürliche Aussprache der Wörter in ihren einzelnen Theilen, wie in ihrer Verbindung vermieden werde."
4. One of the most famous examples is the Duke's "La donna è mobile—qual piuma al vento" from *Rigoletto* and Manrico's "Di quella pira—L'orrendo foco" from *Il trovatore* (in both cases *quinari doppi* scanned in dactyls). See also Giger 2008: 47. Ritorni ([1841]: 106) suggests that the *endecasillabo* (verse of eleven syllables) "Canto l'armi pietose e il Capitano"

may, in a musical context, be scanned as follows: "Canto l'armi pietose e il Capitano." I am not aware of any such example in practice.

5. An exception was Arrigo Boito in his *Mefistofele* (1868; rev. 1875 and 1876); see Nikitopoulos 1994: 104–116. For a highly polymetric stanza in Meyerbeer, see Sélika's "Air du Sommeil" (*L'Africaine*, Act II, scene 1), which combines meters of five, six, and eight syllables.

Bibliography

Abbiati, Franco. 1959. *Giuseppe Verdi*. 4 vols. Milan: Ricordi.

Aiken, Judith. 2002. *A Language for German Opera: The Development of Forms and Formulas for Recitative and Aria in Seventeenth-Century German Libretti*. Wolfenbütteler Arbeiten zur Barockforschung 37. Wiesbaden: Harrassowitz.

Atkins, Henry Gibson. 1923. *A History of German Versification: Ten Centuries of Metrical Evolution*. London: Methuen.

Balthazar, Scott L. 1992. "The Rhythm of Text and Music in *Ottocento* Melody: An Empirical Reassessment in Light of Contemporary Treatises." *Current Musicology* 49: 5–28.

Benloew, Louis. 1862. *Précis d'une théorie des rhythmes. I: Rhythmes français et rhythmes latins*. Paris: Franck.

Bittong, Franz. 1869. *'Die Meistersinger,' oder: 'Das Judentum in der Musik': Parodistischer Scherz in 1 Akt*. Berlin: Krühn. Reprint in Fischer 2000, 329–352.

Breuer, Dieter. 1981. *Deutsche Metrik und Versgeschichte*. Munich: Fink.

Budden, Julian. 1971. "L'influenza della tradizione del grand opéra francese sulla struttura ritmica di *Don Carlo*." In Pavarani 1971, 311–318.

Csampai, Attila, and Dietmar Holland, eds. 1981. *Richard Wagner. 'Die Meistersinger von Nürnberg': Texte, Materialien, Kommentare*. Reinbek bei Hamburg: Rowohlt.

Dove, Richard. 1984. "Sound and Sense in the Classical Poetry of Platen." *The Modern Language Review* 79: 620–637.

Ellis, William Ashton, ed. and trans. [1892–1899] 1966. *Richard Wagner's Prose Works*. 8 vols. London: Kegan Paul. Reprint. New York: Broude Brothers.

Fischer, Jens Malte. 2000. *Richard Wagners 'Das Judentum in der Musik': Eine kritische Dokumentation als Beitrag zur Geschichte des Antisemitismus*. Frankfurt: Insel.

Freese, Carl Friedrich. 1837. *Deutsche Prosodie*. Stralsund: Löfflersche Buchhandlung.

Giger, Andreas. 2009. "La censura verdiana a Roma a metà dell'Ottocento," translated by Simonetta Ricciardi. In *I due Foscari*, edited by Marisa di Gregorio Casati. Quaderni del Festival Verdi, 92–111. Parma: Fondazione Teatro Regio di Parma and Istituto nazionale di studi verdiani.

——. 2008. *Verdi and the French Aesthetic: Verse, Stanza, and Melody in Nineteenth-Century Opera*. Cambridge: Cambridge University Press.

——. 2007. "Verismo: Origin, Corruption, and Redemption of an Operatic Term." *Journal of the American Musicological Society* 60/2: 271–316.

Giglio, Vittorio. 1912. *I fasti del cinquantanove: Ricordi civili e militari*. 2nd ed. Milan: Francesco Vallardi.

Grey, Thomas S. 2002. "Masters and Their Critics: Wagner, Hanslick, Beckmesser, and *Die Meistersinger*." In Vazsonyi 2002, 165–189.

Günther, Ursula, and Luciano Petazzoni, eds. [1974] 1990. *Giuseppe Verdi, Don Carlos: Edizione integrale delle varie versioni in cinque e in quattro atti (comprendente gli inediti verdiani a cura di Ursula Günther)*. 2 vols. Milan: Ricordi.

Günther, Ursula. 1971. "Le livret français de *Don Carlos*: Le premier acte et sa révision par Verdi." In Pavarani 1971, 90–140.

Halévy, Jacques Fromental. n.d. *La Juive*. Paris: Lemoine.

Herder, Johann Gottfried, et al. [1773] 1892. *Von deutscher Art und Kunst: Einige fliegende Blätter*. Hamburg: Bode. Reprint. Deutsche Litteraturdenkmale des 18. und 19. Jahrhunderts. Vols. 40–41. Stuttgart: Göschen'sche Verlagsanstalt.

Hudson, Elizabeth. 1998. "Critical Commentary" to Giuseppe Verdi, *Il corsaro*, edited by Elizabeth Hudson. *The Works of Giuseppe Verdi* [WGV]. Ser. I/13. Chicago: Chicago University Press; Milan: Ricordi.

Kind, Friedrich. 1843. *Freischütz-Buch*. Leipzig: Göschen.

Landry, Eugène. 1911. *La théorie du rythme et le rythme du français déclamé avec une étude expérimentale de la déclamation de plusieurs poètes et comédiens célèbres, du rythme des vers italiens, et des nuances de la durée dans la musique*. Paris: Champion.

Lubarsch, Otto. 1879. *Abriss der französischen Verslehre: Zum Gebrauch an höheren Lehranstalten*. Berlin: Weidmannsche Buchhandlung.

Mcdonald, William E. 1977. "Words, Music, and Dramatic Development in *Die Meistersinger*." *19th Century Music* 1/3: 246–260.

Millington, Barry. 1991. "Nuremberg Trial: Is There Anti-Semitism in *Die Meistersinger*?" *Cambridge Opera Journal* 3/3: 247–260.

Moreen, Robert Anthony. 1975. "Integration of Text Forms and Musical Forms in Verdi's Early Opera." PhD diss., Princeton University.

Nikitopoulos, Alison Terbell. 1994. "Arrigo Boito's *Mefistofele*: Poetry, Music, and Revisions." PhD diss., Princeton University.

Opitz, Martin. [1624] 1888. *Martin Opitzens Aristarchus sive de contemptu linguae Teutonicae und Buch von der Deutschen Poeterey*, edited by Georg Witkowski. Leipzig: Veit.

Pavarani, Marcello, ed. 1971. *Atti del II° congresso internazionale di studi verdiani, 30 luglio–5 agosto 1969*. Parma: Istituto di studi verdiani.

Petrobelli, Pierluigi. 2000. "De l'alexandrin à l'anapeste chez Verdi: Structure poétique et composition musicale dans *Un ballo in maschera*." In *L'Opéra en France et en Italie (1791–1925): Une scène privilégiée d'échanges littéraires et musicaux. Actes du colloque franco-italien tenu à l'Académie musicale de Villecroze (16–18 octobre 1997)*, edited by Hervé Lacombe, 215–222. Paris: Société française de musicologie.

——. 1989. "The Fusion of Styles." In *Giuseppe Verdi: 'A Masked Ball/Un ballo in maschera,'* edited by Nicholas John. English National Opera Guides 40, 9–14. London: John Calder; New York: Riverrun.

Pierson, Paul. 1884. *Métrique naturelle du langage*. Paris: Vieweg.

Powers, Harold. 1990. "Making Macbeth Musicable." In *Macbeth*, edited by Nicholas John. English National Opera Guide 41, 13–36. London: John Calder; New York: Riverrun.

Puschman, Adam. [1571] 1888. *Gründlicher Bericht des deutschen Meistergesangs, Erste Auflage (1571)*, edited by Richard Jonas. Neudrucke deutscher Literaturwerke des XVI. und XVII. Jahrhunderts 73. Halle a. S.: Niemeyer.

Quicherat, Louis-Marie. 1850. *Traité de versification française*. 2nd ed. Paris: Hachette.

Ritorni, Carlo Ritorni. 1841. *Ammaestramenti alla composizione d'ogni poema e d'ogni opera appartenente alla musica*. Milan: Pirola.

Rotth, Albrecht Christian. 1688. *Vollständige Deutsche Poesie in drey Teilen*. 2 vols. Leipzig: Friedrich Lanckischen Erben.

Scribe, Eugène. 1835. *Théâtre complet de M. Eugène Scribe, membre de l'Académie française*. 2nd ed. 24 vols. Paris: Aimé André.

Toscani, Claudio. 2003. "Verso francese e prosodia italiana: Osservazioni sulla traduzione delle *Vêpres siciliennes.*" In *Verdi 2001: Atti del convegno internazionale/Proceedings of the International Conference Parma—New York—New Haven, 24 gennaio–10 febbraio 2001/24 January–1 February 2001.* 2 vols., edited by Fabrizio Della Seta, Roberta Montemorra Marvin, and Marco Marica, II: 499–517. Florence: Olschki.

Vaget, Hans Rudolf. 2003. "'Du warst mein Feind von je': The Beckmesser Controversy Revisited." In Vazsonyi 2002, 190–208.

Vazsonyi, Nicholas, ed. 2002. *Wagner's 'Die Meistersinger': Performance, History, Representation.* Rochester, NY: University of Rochester Press.

Verdi, Giuseppe. Forthcoming. *I due Foscari,* edited by Andreas Giger. *The Works of Giuseppe Verdi* [WGV]. Ser. I/6. Chicago: University of Chicago Press; Milan: Ricordi.

Voss, Egon. 1983. "Die Entstehung der *Meistersinger von Nürnberg.*" In *Wagner, 'Die Meistersinger von Nürnberg': Faksimile der Reinschrift des Textbuchs von 1862, mit einem Aufsatz zur Entstehung des Werkes von Egon Voss.* 7–19. Mainz: Schott.

——. 1981. "Wagners *Meistersinger* als Oper des deutschen Bürgertums." In Csampai and Holland 1981, 9–31.

Wagner, Richard. [1862] 1983. *Wagner, 'Die Meistersinger von Nürnberg': Faksimile der Reinschrift des Textbuchs von 1862, mit einem Aufsatz zur Entstehung des Werkes von Egon Voss.* Mainz: Schott.

——. [1852] 1966. *Opera and Drama.* In Ellis [1892–1899] 1966, vol. 2.

——. 1869. *Das Judentum in der Musik* [revised version]. Leipzig: Weber.

——. [pseudonym K. Freigedank]. 1850. "Das Judentum in der Musik." *Neue Zeitschrift für Musik* 17/19 (September 3): 101–117; 20 (September 6): 109–112.

Warrack, John. 1994a. "Sachs, Beckmesser and Mastersong." In *Richard Wagner: 'Die Meistersinger von Nürnberg,'* edited by John Warrack, 49–65. Cambridge Opera Handbooks. Cambridge: Cambridge University Press.

——. 1994b. "The Sources and Genesis of the Text." In Warrack 1994a, 1–37.

Werr, Sebastian. 2002. *Musikalisches Drama und Boulevard: Französische Einflüsse auf die italienische Oper im 19. Jahrhundert.* Stuttgart: Metzler.

Zesen, Philipp von. [1641] 1971. *Deutscher Helicon.* In *Sämtliche Werke,* vol. 9, edited by Ulrich Maché. Berlin: De Gruyter.

Manuscripts

I due Foscari Naples Copy. Naples, Conservatorio San Pietro a Majella, OA-8-28/245.

Early Printed Librettos

Der Freischütz libretto. 1823. *DER/FREISCHÜTZ,*/OPER in Vier Abtheilungen./*in Musick Gesetzt*/von/*CARL MARIA VON WEBER./AMSTERDAM,*/Gedruckt bey SCHMIDTS & Co.

Don Carlos Paris libretto. 1867. DON/CARLOS/OPÉRA EN CINQ ACTES/PAROLES DE/MÉRY ET CAMILLE DU LOCLE/MUSIQUE DE/G. VERDI/Représenté, pour la première fois, à Paris, sur le théâtre Impérial de l'Opéra/le 11 Mars 1867/PARIS/MICHEL LÉVI | LÉON ESCUDIER.

Don Carlo Italian libretto. 1867. DON/CARLO/OPERA IN CINQUE ATTI/PAROLE DI/MÉRY e CAMILLO DU LOCLE/MUSICA DI/G. VERDI/TRADUZIONE ITALIANA DI ACHILLE DE LAUZIÈRES/DA RAPPRESENTARSI/AL GRAN TEATRO COMUNALE DI BOLOGNA/l'Autunno 1867/R. STABILIMENTO RICORDI.

Giovanna de Guzman Parma libretto. 1855–1856. GIOVANNA DE GUZMAN/OPERA IN CINQUE ATTI/MUSICA DEL MAESTRO/GIUSEPPE VERDI/Ufficiale della Legion d'Onore/*DA RAPPRESENTARSI*/AL TEATRO REGIO DI PARMA/*il Carnevale-Quaresima* 1855–56/MILANO/DALL'I. R. STABILIMENTO NAZIONALE PRIVILEGIATO DI/TITO DI GIO. RICORDI.

Giovanna de Guzman Turin libretto. 1855–1856. GIOVANNA DE GUZMAN/(MUSICA DE' VESPRI SICILIANI)/OPERA-BALLO IN 5 ATTI/DI/E. SCRIBE/POSTA IN MUSICA DAL M. CAVALIERE/GIUSEPPE VERDI/*da rappresentarsi*/AL TEATRO REGIO/NEL CARNEVAL-QUARESIMA 1855–56/TORINO/DALLA TIPOGRAFIA E LITOGRAFIA DI GIUSEPPE FODRATTI.

I vespri siciliani Turin libretto. 1861. I VESPRI SICILIANI/DRAMMA IN CINQUE ATTI/di E. Scribe e C. Duveyrier/MUSICA DEL MAESTRO CAV./GIUSEPPE VERDI/Ufficiale della Legion d'Onore/DA RAPPRESENTARSI/AL TEATRO CARIGNANO IN TORINO/l'Autunno 1861/MILANO/REGIO STABILIMENTO NAZIONALE/TITO DI GIO. RICORDI.

Les vêpres siciliennes Paris libretto. 1855. LES VÊPRES/SICILIENNES/OPÉRA EN CINQ ACTES/PAROLES DE/MM. E. SCRIBE ET CH. DUVEYRIER/MUSIQUE DE M. VERDI/DIVERTISSEMENTS DE M. L. PETIPA/Représenté pour la première fois à Paris, sur le théâtre de l'Académie impériale/de Musique, le 3 juin 1855/PARIS/MICHEL LÉVY FRÈRES, LIBRAIRES-ÉDITEURS/RUE VIVIENNE, 2 *bis* 1855.

CHAPTER 10

THE GERMAN LIBRETTO OF THE EARLY NINETEENTH CENTURY

JOHN WARRACK

SCARCELY had opera made its first appearance in German lands, with performances by visiting Italians in Salzburg in 1614, when German writers and musicians fell to arguing about how this beguiling new art form might be not merely imported but successfully transplanted. Whether or not Siegmund Staden's *Seelewig* of 1644 really deserves to be called the first German opera, as it so often is, depends on how opera is defined; but it is the first *Singspiel* of which the music is extant, and the score was accompanied by a running commentary on the artistic issues involved and how to perform the piece by the author of the text, Georg Philipp Harsdörffer. *Seelewig* was embedded in the fourth part of Harsdörffer's eight volumes of so-called *Frawenzimmer Gesprächspiele* (1641–1657), an *omnium gatherum* of prose, poetry, music, and especially dialogues, whose participants decide that opera reigns supreme among the arts, because it combines music, poetry, and painting. Accompanying this conclusion is the lament that no one will ever be found who unites these three talents in one person (Harsdörffer 1641–1657: IV: 76–209 and 533–666).

A precedent was thereby set for arguments that continued to occupy German writers and musicians for centuries. In his voluminous writings on opera, Johann Mattheson continually called for unity of the theatrical arts, in particular between the "sister" arts of poetry and music: "One should give much more consideration to their constant unity, preferably with each yielding a little to the other"[1] (Mattheson 1744: 32). Yet this multitalented and prolific (not to say prolix) author and composer seems never to have contemplated writing librettos for himself. However, the eighteenth century saw eminent writers happy to aid the art of opera by providing librettos, among them Christoph Martin Wieland, with four for Anton Schweitzer, notably *Alceste*, and Goethe, with his early *Singspiels* for Johann André and then for Johann Friedrich Reichardt and others during his Weimar years. Though, as with his lyric poetry, Goethe expected music to keep in its place as the enhancement of his words, Wieland sought a true unification, which he expounded principally in an essay of 1775. In this, he discusses the condition of

German opera, takes note of Algarotti's influential *Saggio sopra l'opera* (1755), and hopes for a Gluck who could bring about a "beautiful unison of all parts for the greater unity of the whole on the operatic stage"[2] (Wieland [1775] 1928). Only seven eighteenth-century German composers seem to have written librettos for themselves (Baumann 1985: III: 416–427). They include Carl August von Lichtenstein (who also wrote librettos for others), Johann Christoph Kaffka (who, on the other hand, was apt to pass off other men's work as his own), Carl Siegmund von Seckendorff (who worked in Weimar, where he attracted Goethe's disdain), and Christian Gotthilf Weisflog (essentially a church composer). Better known were Johann André and particularly Karl Dittersdorf. Despite Dittersdorf's interest in extended finales with continuous music, evident at its most effective in *Doktor und Apotheker* (1786), there is no indication, any more than with the others, that he was unifying words and music, rather than setting words deftly and often expressively in familiar *Singspiel* conventions. No discussion of these issues occurs in the autobiography he dictated to his son, *Lebensbeschreibung* (Leipzig, 1801). The repeated hopes of seventeenth- and eighteenth-century theorists for what they liked to describe as a *Zusammenfluss*—not merely an encounter, but a confluence into a single stream—continued to go unrealized.

Rochlitz, Weber, and Hoffmann

Perhaps this is not surprising, since no opera composer, not even the intelligent and gifted Mattheson, claimed creative literary gifts, even if some of them could cobble together a workmanlike libretto. But by the beginning of the nineteenth century, the situation was changing. Friedrich Rochlitz had challengingly opened what was to be his enormously influential journal, the Leipzig *Allgemeine musikalische Zeitung* (*AMZ*), with an essay, "Gedanken über die Oper [Thoughts on Opera]" (Rochlitz 1798), and followed it up with a variety of attempts to encourage German opera. Among those whom Rochlitz championed, and who wrote for the *AMZ*, were two of the most significant figures of Romanticism, with contrasting gifts: Carl Maria von Weber, a composer of genius with a vivid literary talent, and E. T. A. Hoffmann, a writer of genius with a vivid musical talent, by which at first he set greater store. Not surprisingly, both wrote critical and imaginative articles and stories in which they addressed the particularly German problem of the unification of words and music in opera. Hoffmann's view of Weber was equivocal, perhaps tinged with jealousy, though it still needs to be emphasized that he was not the author of the five articles in the *Vossische Zeitung*, hostile to *Der Freischütz* after its 1821 premiere, which have often been attributed to him (Benedict 1861; M. M. von Weber 1864: 324–325; Kron 1957). The misattribution was caused by an allegation in a letter of August 8, 1861, from Julius Benedict to Max Maria von Weber (Benedict 1861). Max Maria repeated the allegation, without mention of Benedict, in his biography of his father (M. M. von Weber 1864: II: 324–325). Thereafter it was repeated in books on both composers, and the articles were even republished under Hoffmann's name, until Wolfgang Kron demolished the case for his authorship (Kron 1957).[3] Weber, on the other hand, wholeheartedly saluted Hoffmann's *Undine* (1816) in words that echoed the earlier theorists but became famous in their own right, defining the ideal for German opera: "I am speaking of the kind of opera Germans want: a self-sufficient work of art in which every feature and every contribution by the related arts are molded together in a certain way and dissolve—to form a new world" (C. M. von Weber 1817). He then repeated the idea in his novel, with the difference that French opera was then included with German opera in this ideal (C. M. von Weber [1809–1820] 1981: 312–364).[4]

For his part, Hoffmann was much interested in the idea of words and music in Romantic opera springing unified from the same mind. He had tried writing his own texts in three of his first five attempts at opera. Too few of them have survived for any secure opinion to be formed, but the first, *Die Maske* (comp. 1799), suggests something closer to Viennese *Singspiel* than anything melding words and music into a new condition. In any case, he later abandoned the attempt. *Der Trank der Unsterblichkeit* (comp. 1808), though the first work styled *romantische Oper*, has as librettist not Hoffmann himself (despite the plot's "Hoffmannesque" interlocking of illusion and reality) but Count Julius von Soden, director of the theater in Bamberg where the anxious composer hoped, successfully, that this hastily composed piece would win him an appointment. Hoffmann's two most impressive operatic achievements also use other librettists: a later Bamberg director, Franz von Holbein, for a *grosse romantische Oper*, *Aurora* (comp. 1811–1812); and Friedrich de la Motte Fouqué, adapting his own popular tale for a *Zauberoper*, *Undine* (1816). In July 1812, when Hoffmann conceived the idea of an opera on Fouqué, he wrote to his publisher friend Julius Hitzig (one of his band of five friends fictionalized as his "Serapionsbrüder"), complaining that he was no good at versifying and asking for help; Hitzig duly got a libretto out of Fouqué for him by November 14. Yet the following September and October saw the writing of his tale *Der Dichter und der Komponist*, which later formed part of the *Serapionsbrüder* collection. Here, the composer Ludwig doubts his ability to write texts for himself, in the teeth of arguments from his friend Ferdinand; while in the framing dialogue, which Hoffmann added in 1819, Theodor (the musician aspect of Hoffmann's personality, and now made the "author" of the tale) also doubts the possibility of any single person writing an opera of equal worth in text and music. Nevertheless, the generally more practical Lothar prefaces the discussion by insisting, "I... believe that music and words flow from the inspired poet and composer in a *single* moment," and concludes it by rejecting Theodor's arguments, declaring, "I believe he will soon surprise us with an excellent opera whose libretto and music will be entirely his own. Everything that he has so sophistically argued concerning the impossibility of writing and composing an opera oneself may sound plausible enough, but it has not convinced me"[5] (Hoffmann 1813; Segebrecht 2001: 94,119). The implication is that in 1819 Hoffmann had not abandoned his faith in the ideal of a single, unified inspiration in a poet-composer, even though, especially having found himself deficient in the ability to write words for his own music, he was well aware of the practical difficulties. At the time of his death in 1822, he was at work on an opera based on Calderón, *Der Liebhaber nach dem Tode*, but again he employed a librettist, his friend Carl Wilhelm Salice-Contessa (who features as "Sylvester" among the Serapionsbrüder).

Weber, Kind, and *Der Freischütz*

From a different standpoint, Weber also fought shy of writing his own librettos, though he was willing to take a hand in them, a practice that was showing signs of growing increasingly active when he became mortally weakened by tuberculosis. His sense of dramatic proportion led him to make several important interventions in Friedrich Kind's text for his *romantische Oper, Der Freischütz.* Two of these included abandoning a planned Romanze for Cuno describing the origins of the shooting trial, "Herr Ottokar jagte durch Haid und durch Wald," instead of a spoken narration, and the deletion of a third stanza for Agathe's "Und ob die Wolke," both in the interests of dramatic momentum. In the "Wolf's Glen" finale of Act II, he rewrote Kind's prose in scene 5, providing Caspar with sung verse set against Samiel's spoken prose for the sake of the variety of means that marks its originality, but also underlining the dramatic point that while even the villainous Caspar has life in poetry and music, the diabolical Samiel is barren of humanizing art. Weber also wrote a second stanza for the "Huntsmen's Chorus," one in no way inferior to Kind's first stanza. The most substantial change was pressed on him by his wife Caroline, who as a singer perhaps had more conventional theatrical expectations than her husband: the removal of the opening scene in which the Hermit, fearful of the danger he believes is threatening Agathe, gives her a holy garland of roses for her protection. Cutting this brings the curtain up instead on the more familiar operatic opening of a scene-setting chorus, and relegates the Hermit to a last-minute *ex machina* appearance, something regretted by Kind and others, including Fouqué, with whom Kind attended a performance. Weber also cut from the finale ten of the Hermit's sermonizing lines, including the demand (echoing Jesus concerning the woman taken in adultery) as to which of those present would cast the first stone at Max (Schreiter 2007: 80). But these were improvements designed to tighten up the effectiveness of what remained essentially a *Singspiel*. Kind seems to have accepted Weber's amendments, if with some reluctance to judge by the variants in the republished texts which he supervised, and indeed to have been initially uncertain as to the nature of the work in hand—if, that is, we are to give credence to the account in his *Freischütz-Buch* of 1843 (see Figure 10.1), in the *Schöpfungsgeschichte* section whose nature is perhaps unwittingly well described by his subtitle "Biographische Novelle." In accepting collaboration with Weber, he initially made a distinction between two forms: "I must write a *Singspiel* or an opera for him [ich müsse ihm ein Singspiel oder eine Oper dichten]," but later had uncertainties about the respective rights of composer and librettist in an opera, as he described it:

> I recalled that I had read somewhere that even tragedy could attain its highest condition through being conjoined with opera. I considered what, in visits to the opera,

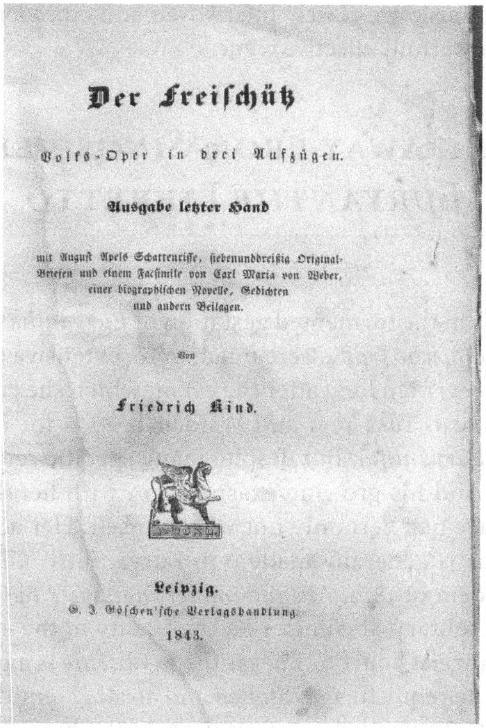

Der Freischütz

Volks-Oper in drei Aufzügen.

Ausgabe letzter Hand

mit August Apels Schattenrisse, siebenunddreißig Original-Briefen und einem Facsimile von Carl Maria von Weber, einer biographischen Novelle, Gedichten und andern Beilagen.

Von

Friedrich Kind.

Leipzig.

G. J. Göschen'sche Verlagshandlung.

1843.

FIGURE 10.1 Friedrich Kind, *Freischütz-Buch* (1843), title page. Collection of John Warrack.

> had struck me as advantageous or displeasing and unsuitable (for without internal criticism such things cannot be discarded), but I convinced myself that through a union of all the arts—poetry, music, action, painting, and dance—something of greatness would be achieved, and in respect of opera everything would be at the discretion of the poet.[6] (Kind 1843: 116–118)

Kind was probably unaware of the French influence on Weber: there can be no doubt that in filling his Prague and Dresden repertories with works by Méhul, Dalayrac, Grétry, Isouard, and other successful Parisian composers, Weber was preparing audiences but also himself for a new direction in German opera. There was in Méhul, especially, the kind of melodic grace that was to mark, for instance, Max's music in *Der Freischütz*. More important for the implications of libretto and hence musical form, there was also the characteristically French use of reminiscence motive, such as the recall of Caspar's diabolical piccolo trills in the "Wolf's Glen." Above all, there are the pervasive diminished sevenths of evil. These corrode the fundamentally diatonic harmony but also provide the key sequence to underpin the whole of that scene, an extraordinarily advanced use of subliminal tonality to match, in its disturbing effect, the dislocation of conventional means in the breaking up of the scene into disparate sections, with unexpected proportions of voice, speech, and orchestra. In a way that his librettist certainly did not anticipate, words and music are closely interwoven and cross-fertilize one another in this famous and still powerfully effective scene.

MOVING AWAY FROM *SINGSPIEL*: THE *EURYANTHE* LIBRETTO

Weber's interventions in the tormented gestation of *Euryanthe* (1823), described as a *grosse romantische-heroische Oper*, were much more extensive (Chezy 1840; Chezy's account was of course written long after the event, which she certainly remembered with advantages; see also Tusa 1991 and Waidelich 2008 for further discussion of words and music in *Euryanthe*). But despite many specific requests to his librettist Helmina von Chezy and his growing exasperation with her, he does not seem to have wanted to replace her, certainly not with himself. Her actual verses were not as consistently bad as is generally made out. Euryanthe's "Glöcklein im Thale," a previously written poem of 1812, *Abenddämmerung*, has a naïve charm well suited to Weber's music as, solitary, she muses on the beauty of the evening; and Adolar's troubadourish Romanze at court to Euryanthe *in absente* is a quite capably devised *Meistergesang*, with the requisite two *Stollen* and an *Abgesang*. It is the creakiness of the drama and the stereotyped characterization of the hero and heroine that have contributed most to the problems of *Euryanthe*, and in this Weber himself is not free from blame. With *Euryanthe* he was determined, in his aspirations for German opera, to move away from the *Singspiel* nature of *Der Freischütz* and to seek new forms generated by a new kind of libretto. Part of his intention was to build the use of motive into the dramatic and musical framework. Max Maria von Weber quotes him describing *Euryanthe* as "a pure dramatic attempt at making its effect entirely through the *unified collaboration of all the sister arts*"[7] (M. M. von Weber 1864: 600). He further quotes Weber as instructing Chezy, "When it comes to preparing the text, in God's name make my life really bitter with difficult metres, unexpected rhythms etc, that will lure ideas out of their lairs and force them along new paths"[8] (M. M. von Weber 1864: 363).

Chezy did her best. Act II opens with Lysiart's solo scene, a bold idea turning what might have been a straightforward Vengeance Aria depicting plain evil, as with Cherubini's Dourlinski or Beethoven's Pizarro, into an aria of uncertainty and self-reproach, one that introduced conscience-racked villainy as a feature of Romantic opera. Weber responds brilliantly, at first portraying Lysiart and his torment orchestrally before the entry of the voice, when Chezy provides him with just the "difficult metres" and "unexpected rhythms" for which he had asked:

> Wo berg' ich mich? Wo fänd' ich Fassung wieder?
> Ha! toller Frevlerwahn, du wahrst es ja.
> Der sie als leichte Beute sah!

Ihr Felsen, stürzt auf mich hernieder!
Du Widerhall, ruf' nicht das Ach
Des hoffnungslosen Strebens nach!
Nie wird sie mein, o ew'ger Qualen Hyder!

[Where can I hide myself? Where shall I recover myself?
Ha! A mad delusion, you were indeed,
To see her as easy prey!
Crash down upon me, you crags!
Echo, answer not the cry
Of a struggle without hope!
She will never be mine, you hydra of unending agonies.]

The stanza is of seven lines, not the expected eight; the rhyme scheme is, unusually, ABBACCA; and disturbing these patterns are lines whose irregular main stresses are 5544445. The calmer middle stanza is, contrastingly, more conventional and balanced, before Lysiart's anger rises again with a seven-line stanza of different irregularity from the first, and a rhyme scheme of AABABAB and main stresses of 43434(2)44 (the 2 is an inserted cry of "Doch, Hölle!"). There can be no doubt that this answered Weber's demands, and stimulated him to deliver the greatest scene in the opera, with words, wide-ranging vocal declamation, and orchestral depiction of a turbulent inner state, all bound together organically. While this is an original integration of words and music, it does not constitute of itself a new condition in opera. Weber further sought to pursue his cause with his use of motive; the motivic technique of *Euryanthe* does branch out into something new, and played a fundamental part in his evolving conception of the work.

Johann Nepomuk von Poissl

Though indebted to the example of French *opéra comique*, Weber's new musical strategy in *Euryanthe* also owes much to the example of one of the neglected figures of opera, Johann Nepomuk von Poissl. He was a composer greatly admired by Weber and also by Weber's mentors Georg Joseph Vogler and Franz Danzi, especially for his ambitions for the formation of German grand opera (the loss of Danzi's own *Iphigenia in Aulis*, of 1807, is the more regrettable as the *AMZ* praised it for the unity of words and music and took it as a text for urging German composers to greater efforts toward tragic opera [see *AMZ* 1807: 365–372]). Poissl's *Athalia* was hailed on its appearance in Munich in 1814 for its superiority to his previous operas:

> In composing *Athalia* he has progressed to another purpose, to a higher artistic goal; he has striven to give us, in the way that the Italians and the French have their own national opera, an emphatically *German* grand opera of a distinctive character. He has tried to solve this problem by uniting great power with charm. In this way his work is of a new kind: it is in more intimate accord with the drama and the

motive of the subject; it emphatically seizes hold of the character of the action in the individual scenes, and it remains true to them.[9] (*MTJ* 1814: 187–188; Waidelich 1996: 328)

Weber, usually quick to pounce on intrusive Italianisms in German opera, readily praised *Athalia* for its melodic quality, anticipating, with his approval of "italienische Gesanglieblichkeit," Wagner's commendation of Bellini. Weber also noted the manner in which "[t]he emotional crises in the action are judiciously characterized and contained by highly charged melodies which recur at crucial points. What were at first no more than hints are sure to appear later in undisguised form and with satisfying conviction"[10] (C. M. von Weber 1816a: 185). He was clearly singling out Poissl's imaginative use of a motive to characterize the violent Athalia and her driving forward of the plot until, finally, a livelier, fresher version of the motive is taken up by Joas as the throne passes to him. The action of this motive is kin to Weber's own serpentine theme for the deceitful Eglantine in *Euryanthe*, which it may well have suggested. It should also be noted that Johann Gottfried Wohlbrück's text, ingeniously adapting Racine's alexandrines into iambic pentameters, is handled by Poissl in freely flowing sequences of recitative, arioso, and more formal passages, with keen sensitivity to German prosody, again something new to German libretto, which would have impressed Weber and which left its mark on *Euryanthe*.

Perhaps the experience encouraged Poissl to return more systematically to the writing of his own librettos. He had made two earlier attempts with *Antigonus* (after Metastasio, 1808) and a *dramma eroico*, *Ottaviano in Sicilia* (1812); he now went on to write three more operas adapting Metastasio texts, *Der Wettkampf zu Olympia* (1815, after *L'Olimpiade*), its Metastasian companion piece *Nittetis* (1817), and *Issipile* (comp. 1818, unperformed), and he also wrote his own librettos for *La rappressaglia* (1820, after Cesare Sterbini), *Die Prinzessin von Provence* (1825, after Felice Romani), and *Zaide* (1843). With eight substantial operas, most of them in three acts, Poissl is a significant figure in the history of German opera for his efforts to unite composer and librettist in himself. As the review in the *Berliner AMZ* of a Munich performance of *Die Prinzessin von Provence* began, "It is a phenomenon as rare as it is pleasant when the poet and the composer of an opera unite in a *single* person.... The phenomenon is pleasant since the vital, finest adornment of a work of art, unity and diversity, can obviously only flourish in full bloom when blossoming from the power of an abundant *single* spirit"[11] (Stöpel 1827: 282–284). Introducing *Der Wettkampf zu Olimpia* to Dresden as part of his continuing championship of Poissl, Weber praised him for approaching this task "with scholarly erudition, indeed also with poetic talent." Though cautious in his definition of grand opera, Weber further insisted that it must be through-composed, "an opera in which the musical numbers are connected by a continuous *recitativo accompagnato*, fully orchestrated—in fact a scene where music holds court, surrounded by her courtiers who are in perpetual activity"[12] (C. M. von Weber 1820: 290). But while deserving Weber's encouragement, Poissl did not consistently manage to bring text and music together into a new condition. He was a capable writer, with a dramatic gift and the ability to choose plot and situation that suited him; but his work is still really a matter of Poissl the librettist providing Poissl the composer with a well-judged text, rather than finding the means whereby music and words blend to form "a new world."

Spohr's *Faust*

Just over three months after introducing and conducting Poissl's *Athalia* in Prague on May 21, 1816, Weber also introduced and conducted the first performance of Spohr's *Faust* there on September 1. The idea of motive was still in his mind: "A few melodies, felicitously and aptly devised, weave like delicate threads through the whole, and hold it together artistically"[13] (C. M. von Weber 1816b: 193; for a fuller discussion of Spohr and motive, see Brown 1984a: 75–85 and Brown 1984b: 25–27). If the metaphors are differently chosen, this reflects a difference in Spohr's motivic method. Joseph Bernard's libretto, which owes almost nothing to Goethe, is an undistinguished piece of work, but Spohr was seized by its basic theme, that of Faust, divided between his pure devotion to Röschen and his destructive lust for Kunigunde, believing vainly that by the exercise of his will and without God's help he can contend successfully with Mephistopheles. To this end, Spohr makes use not only of fairly straightforward reminiscence motives, but, more important to the fabric of the opera, motives identified with hell, with love, and to a slightly lesser extent with the turmoil of Faust's passionate nature, as shown in the opening measures of the overture (see Music Example 10.1).

These develop through the drama in a manner that can fairly be described as symphonic: leitmotive rather than reminiscence motive. He uses the hell motive, in particular, to underline the action of evil, to identify the source of destructive events, to add a musical dimension of ironic comment, and, in a particularly effective transformation, to insinuate itself into the orchestral line accompanying the wedding celebrations as the appalled Hugo becomes aware of Faust's seduction of his bride Kunigunde. *Faust* is an uneven work, but with such strokes it can suggest an opera in search of a better libretto. One was not found when Spohr took the opportunity of collaboration with his wife on the libretto of his last opera, *Die Kreuzfahrer*, to join words and music in what remains essentially a German version of French *grand opéra*.

MUSIC EXAMPLE 10.1 Louis Spohr, *Faust*, Overture, mm. 1–4.

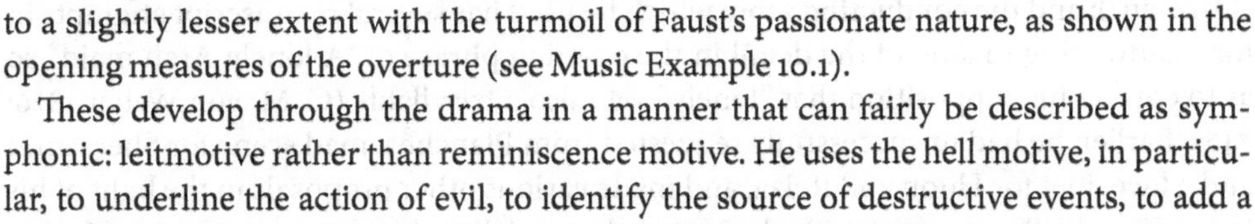

Weber's *Oberon*

As for his own *Oberon*, Weber embarked upon it with high hopes and did not realize until too late the unoperatic nature, by his own standards, of James Robinson Planché's entertainment, or the stilted manner of Planché's style. Arrived in London, a dying man, he wearily agreed to accommodate the popular tenor John Braham with an extra aria and to replace another that Braham seems to have found too taxing. But, his son Max Maria reported, he did not regard what was performed in London as the work's final form: "Verbal and written comments reveal that, for the subtler musical and dramatic sense of the German public, he intended to give it a different form in many of the numbers, and that he had even, as Caroline certainly wished, formed an inclination to turn the dialogue into recitative"[14] (M. M. von Weber 1864: 600).

What did he mean by this? Had he been granted health and energy in the forties of his life, which he did not live to see, how would he have rewritten *Oberon* as "der Oper die der Deutsche will [the opera that the Germans want]"? Certainly there would have been minor adjustments, since, understandably enough, the English that Weber had valiantly set himself to learn in Dresden remained uncertain. He would have found solutions to the few examples of mis-accentuation that mark the score, such as setting the first word of Reiza's "Ocean! Thou mighty monster" as a trisyllable (like the German "O-ze-an"); and the conducting score which he used has several manuscript attempts in his handwriting to amend the detail in the opening phrase of "A lonely Arab maid" so as to correct his supposition that "lonely" was also a trisyllable (C. M. von Weber 1826: 746). Earlier, he had unsuccessfully requested from Planché a mad scene for Sherasmin and a love duet for Huon and Reiza, and made various other proposals in the light of his increasing disillusionment with the text and especially with the entire nature of what Planché insisted was the kind of opera the English expected. Driven by the need to confer some kind of cohesion on the often widely separated numbers, he sought a unifying musical idea, and perhaps in this there are hints of what might have characterized a reworked *Oberon*.

They can only be hints, but they are there. The motives in *Oberon* derive from the simple rising three notes of the unaccompanied horn with which, when Weber came to write the overture, he opened the opera (for more, see Warrack 1976: 331–338). His method is quite different from the motivic techniques deriving from French opera that mark *Der Freischütz*, and from those, possibly also influenced by Poissl, which in turn mark *Euryanthe*. Infiltrating the vocal lines as well as providing the orchestra with developmental material, they are an adumbration of Wagner—and might have been more, had Weber lived to rewrite the opera as a through-composed work. The permeation of the score with the three-note theme, representing Oberon's horn and the action of rescuing magic, in constant transformations throughout the opera, anticipates, more closely than anything he had yet written, the growth of the opening Rhine arpeggios that suffuse *The Ring*, or the descending scale that starts as representation of Wotan's spear and becomes a deepening manifestation of his tragedy. What Weber does in *Oberon* also anticipates far more than could ever have been achieved within the scope of this magic opera of adventure. Wagner of course used reminiscence motive as part of the rich variety of his compositional techniques (as with, for instance, the Giants' lumbering fourths). But it is the element of symphonic development woven into the score of *Oberon* that points toward Wagner's subtlest achievements. The through-composition of the work would have necessitated a complete rewriting of the text as a new kind of libretto, and even if Weber had taken on the task himself, one can hardly imagine him achieving anything on the scale of Wagner.

Conclusion: *Singspiel*, Symphony, and Musical Motive

Weber, Hoffmann, Spohr, and Poissl were the four most striking composers of the early nineteenth century to explore the perennial German concern for the unification of words and music, something that had come to a head with the characteristically Romantic drawing closer of the different arts. At times they seemed to be on the brink of a breakthrough into what Wagner, after much pondering, trial and error, and many changes of mind, evolved with his many-faceted use of motive. It still needs emphasizing that there is no such single thing as "Wagnerian leitmotif," that almost every motive in *The Ring* has an individual nature, expressive function, and consequently manner of operating musically, from the straightforwardly referential to the subtly symphonic development of the drama in the music. Wagner himself was notoriously given to modifying facts to suit his convenience, and to changing his argument in the light of creative experience, but there is a ring of truth in his denial to Cosima of suggestions that he had developed "die Beethoven'sche Melodie," to which he added, "I could not have composed as I have done if Beethoven had never existed, but what I have used and developed are individual strokes of genius in my dramatic predecessors such as Auber himself, in whom I was led by something other than opera"[15] (Gregor-Dellin and Mack 1976–1977: II, 635). What must be meant with reference to Beethoven (the composer about whom Wagner wrote by far the most) is his genius for variation, something that developed from the conventional eighteenth-century decoration of a melody in his earliest works to the exploration of the essence of a theme that marks the late quartets, the late piano sonatas, and the "Diabelli" variations. The latter was a work that Wagner particularly admired since first hearing it, probably in Dresden in 1843, and he declared in 1881 that "with only three of these variations he could have written a symphony"[16] (Gregor-Dellin and Mack 1976–1977: II: 689). He was characteristically evasive about identifying his "dramatic predecessors," though he always admired Weber and went so far as to devote an entire essay to Auber (Wagner 1871).

That neither Weber nor Hoffmann nor Spohr made the move into fully symphonic dramatic motive seems on the face of it surprising. All composed symphonies, Spohr most prolifically and with the most notable success, as Hoffmann generously acknowledged when he hailed the First Symphony in a long analysis as a significant and promising work (Hoffmann 1811). It should also be asked why the German composers who gave symphonic form its genius in the eighteenth century and in some cases sustained it in the nineteenth century did not take their talent into the field of opera. Haydn shows no sign in his operas of his mastery of thematic development in symphony and string quartet, which so vitally influenced his contemporaries and successors. The operatic symphonic finales developed by Mozart come closest to a symphonic interpenetration of text and music, perhaps above all in the wit and wonder of the great Act II finale to *Le nozze di Figaro*, though without any working of reminiscence motive (his quotation of the catchphrase that gives *Così fan tutte* its title is no more than that—catchphrase not motive). As for Beethoven, *Fidelio* remains *Singspiel* raised to its highest level, and in his revisions he never sought to abandon it. His well-known model was Cherubini, whom he openly admired more than any other opera composer of the day, and whose use of Bouilly's libretto for *Les deux journées*, which he thought one of the best he knew, certainly affected his own choice of a Bouilly subject for *Fidelio*. There is no suggestion in what survives of his early attempt at Schikaneder's text *Vestas Feuer* that it would have transcended French *grand opéra* conventions; and though he continued to hunt for librettos, he never became seriously engaged with any of them (for a summary of these abortive operas, see Dean 1971: 381–386). In the case of Schubert, when he abandons lighter *Singspiel* pleasures for *Alfonso und Estrella* (comp. 1822) and the ambitious *heroisch-romantisch* opera *Fierrabras* (comp. 1823), though he makes perfunctory use of motive, he tends, despite his gift for developing long symphonic movements out of a few musical ideas, not to engage with dramatic development; indeed, sometimes he halts development and keeps the characters waiting until he has finished and they can get on with the plot. Something of the same problem afflicted Mendelssohn after his early *Singspiels* with *Die Hochzeit des Camacho* (1827), though he made original use of a reminiscence motive for Don Quixote first proposed in the overture. He spent the rest of his life seeking operatic subjects, having told Eduard Devrient in his letter of July 13, 1831 (from Milan), after the disappointing failure of *Camacho*, "Put a real opera [text] in my hand and in a couple of months it'll be composed, for every day I long afresh to write an opera.... And a text that doesn't really kindle me I won't set. If you know a man who's in a position to write an opera, for God's sake tell me about him: I look for nothing else"[17] (Devrient 1869: 91). Yet he rejected over fifty, chiefly when they seemed too French or Italian and did not fit his idea of what German opera might be (Hennemann 2002). After *Camacho*, he reverted to the *Singspiel* form of his earlier works with a *Liederspiel*, *Die Heimkehr aus der Fremde*, in 1829; too little survives of his only other opera attempt, *Die Loreley*, as late as 1847, for us to be certain of his intentions. Schumann, who declared in 1842 that his daily prayer was for German opera, contemplated numerous subjects before settling on his own not very satisfactory conflation of texts by

Ludwig Tieck and Friedrich Hebbel for *Genoveva* (1850), and considered two more subjects by Goethe and Schiller that never got beyond concert overtures (Jansen 1904: 220; see also Schumann's letter to Karl Koßmaly, September 1, 1842: "Do you know my morning and evening Artist's Prayer? It's called German Opera [Wissen Sie mein Morgen-und-abendliches Künstlergebet? Deutsche Oper heißt es]"). The hunt for librettos extended even to Brahms, perhaps of all the great German symphonic composers the one who seems the least likely to be drawn to opera but who also contemplated a wide range of subjects (Brody 1985–1986).

The situation was, in fact, one of confusion and frustration. A number of composers believed that the answer to the problem of German grand opera lay in the transplantation of French *grand opéra*, with its combination of the arts of poetry, music, scenery, and drama, after the fashion of Cherubini, Spontini, Auber, and later Meyerbeer. Perhaps this conjunction of the arts was the closest they would come to unification. But Spontini himself failed to provide a convincing example with any of the versions he made of his last opera, *Agnes von Hohenstaufen* in the late 1820s, and *grand opéra* remained essentially a conjunction or simultaneity of the arts rather than the *Zusammenfluss*, the confluence hoped for by the old theorists. An essential part of Wagner's genius was, as he himself believed, his absorption of the symphonic genius of Beethoven (whose Ninth Symphony he held to be music seeking the redemptive art of poetry) into music dramas to which he no longer wished to give the name "opera." But it was soon to prove that this was not the new dawn of "the music of the future," as the work of Wagner's epigones showed, for all the success of, for instance, Peter Cornelius in the realm of comedy with *Der Barbier von Bagdad* and to an extent in tragedy with *Der Cid*. The brief rise and total fall of August Bungert with his Homeric cycles was ample demonstration that Wagner, with his particular combination of talents, ambitions, and prodigious self-confidence, had not, for all his vast influence, provided a model. In one sense the dawn was really a twilight, as the arguments about composer and poet being the same man simmered down and cooled. What Wagner achieved proved to be unique, and individual, not the solution to an age-old problem.

Indeed, the ancient and worthy tradition of *Singspiel* had continued to serve well. While *Die Zauberflöte* and *Fidelio* are often taken as exceptions—masterpieces by two of the greatest geniuses in the history of music and therefore *hors concours*, transcending argument—their nature actually depends wholly upon the conjunction of spoken dialogue and music. The effectiveness of this balance is more obvious in comedy, when the narrative can speed ahead, comic exchanges cut with razor sharpness, and characterization can be made by means different from musical ones. Lortzing, a comparatively minor figure if an immensely popular one, was staunch in his upholding of opera with spoken dialogue. But speech also has its place in serious opera. The somewhat eerie effect that melodrama can produce was well known to Weber and ingeniously exploited by him in the "Wolf's Glen" scene, as it was again by Marschner in *Hans Heiling*. Its use in the dungeon scene of *Fidelio* anticipates these in intensifying Leonore's apprehension that all may not go well with her heroic enterprise. Yet aside from melodrama, though the spoken exchanges between the reunited Leonore and Florestan are often abbreviated or even cut in performance, there is something especially moving in the speaking of their words culminating at his question, "Treues Weib! Frau ohne Gleichen! Was hast du meinetwegen erduldet? [Faithful wife! Woman without equal! What have you suffered on my account?]," and her simple answer, "Nichts, mein Florestan," before they soar into the rapture of the duet. The full dialogue of *Fidelio* is nowadays almost always heavily cut, as is that of Mozart's *Singspiels* in both the North German and Viennese traditions (*Die Entführung* and *Die Zauberflöte*), that of *Der Freischütz*, and indeed of most *Singspiels* by other composers. Modern claims for "authenticity" seem not to extend to full performance of the text, which it is believed would weary a modern audience anxious to get on to the next piece of music. Probably it would, so distanced have we become from *Singspiel* as a common theatrical experience, an extension of our theater-going. This is the position it long held, and Goethe was speaking for it when he agreed with Beethoven in selecting *Les deux journées* as an ideal "because here the subject is so perfect that if given as a mere drama without music it could be seen with pleasure," and declared that "if *Der Freischütz* had not been so good a subject, the mere music would hardly have drawn such crowds; so Herr Kind should have some share in the credit"[18] (Biedermann 1890: V: October 9, 1828). Goethe is of course speaking as the author of a number of *Singspiels* in his Weimar years, in which the music is incidental to his drama. The point was satirically expressed in the cartoon displayed in Vienna bookshops showing the Virgin Mary (with the face of Carl Maria von Weber) holding the baby Jesus, the *Christkind* (with the face of Friedrich Kind), captioned, "Was wäre Maria ohne das Kind?"

The strength of the tradition has thereby been set out of perspective, and if it is unlikely to be recaptured, at least we should remember that in the early nineteenth century it was not universally seen as something to be grown beyond, and that even in one and the same composer a fruitful tension could exist between *Singspiel* and newer forms. To this tension we owe the individual character of major works by Weber, Spohr, Hoffmann, Schubert, Mendelssohn, and many more.

See also: Versification, Analyzing Opera, The Language of National Style, Opera Composition and Cultural Environment

Notes

1. "Man sollte vielmehr auf ihre beständige Einigkeit bedacht sein, und lieber von beyden Seiten etwas nachgeben."
2. "[...] schöne Zusammenstimmung aller Theile zur großen Einheit des Ganzen, auf dem lyrischen Schauplatze."
3. "Daß er [Hoffmann] *Weber's* oft bewährte Freundschaft seinem neuen Idol *Spontini* auf eine unwürdige Weise aufopferte, war am besten durch einen in der Vossischen Zeitung erschienen ausführlichen Bericht erwiesen, in welchem man seinen Styl nicht verkennen konnte und der, sehr schmeichelhaft für die ersten **Sänger**, den **Dichter** u. **Componisten** des Freischützen fürchterlich mitnahm. [That he (Hoffmann) sacrificed *Weber's* often

proved friendship to his new idol *Spontini* is best demonstrated by a detailed report that appeared in the *Vossische Zeitung*, in which one could not fail to recognise his style, and which treated the principal *singers* flatteringly, the *librettist* and *composer* of the *Freischütz* appallingly.]" I am grateful to Frau Eveline Bartlitz for drawing my attention to Benedict's letter.

4. "Ich von der Oper spreche, die der Deutsche will: ein in sich abgeschlosssenes Kunstwerk, wo alle Teile und Beiträge der verwandten und benutzten Künste ineinanderschmelzend verschwinden und auf gewisse Weise untergehend—eine neue Welt bilden."
5. "Ich ... glaube daß dem begeisterten Dichter und Komponisten Ton und Wort in *einem* Moment zuströmt ... ich glaube, daß er uns nächstens mit einer trefflichen Oper, die ihm, was Gedicht und Musik, betrifft, ganz allein angehört, überraschen wird. Alles, was er sophistischer Weise über die Unmöglichkeit selbst eine Oper zu dichten und zu komponieren vorgebracht, mag recht plausibel klingen, es hat mich aber nicht überzeugt."
6. "Ich entsann mich, irgenwo gelesen zu haben, daß sogar die Tragödie durch Verbindung mit der Oper ihre höchste Stufe erreichen werde. Ich bedachte, was mir beim Besuch der Opern—denn ohne innere Kritik war es dabei doch auch nicht abgegangen—vortheilhaft oder mißbilligend und unpassend vorgekommen war, aber ich überzeugte mich auch, daß durch Verbindung aller Künste, als der Poesie, der Musik, der Aktion, der Malerei und des Tanzes, ein Großes zu erreichen sey, und hierüber bei der Oper der Willkür des Dichters ja Alles anheim gestellt sey." Kind's book is at least in part an attempted justification of his importance in the success of the opera.
7. "[...] ein rein dramatischer Versuch, seine Wirkung nur von dem vereinigten Zusammenwirken aller Schwesterkünst."
8. "Wenn es an das Ausarbeiten des Textes geht, machen Sie mir in Gottes Namen das Leben mit schwierigen Versmaßen, unerwarteten Rhythmen u.s.w. recht sauer, das zwingt die Gedanken auf neue Wege und lockt sie aus ihren Schlupfwinkeln heraus."
9. "Bei der Composition der Athalia hat er sich noch einen andern Zweck, ein höheres Kunstziel vorgesetzt, er hat gestrebt, uns—wie Italiener und Franzosen ihre nationale Oper haben, auch eine in bestimmten Charakter hervorgehobene deutsche große Opernmusik zu geben. Er hat dieß Problem durch die Verbindung hoher Kraft mit Lieblichkeit zu lösen gesucht. Dadurch ist sein Komposition in einer neuen Art, sie ist in innigerem Einklange mit der Handlung und den Motiven des behandelten Stücks, sie nimmt bestimmt den Charakter der Handlung in den einzelnen Scenen an, und schmiegt sich treu an diesselbe." This is the only important modern study of Poissl's *Athalia*. (I have touched on Poissl and his use of motive in Warrack 2001: 288–295, but he still awaits the fuller critical study his work deserves.)
10. "Sinnig sind die Hauptmomente der Handlung und des Gefühles durch gewisse eindringende und herrlich wiederkehrende Melodien zusammengehalten und bezeichnet. Was früher Ahnung war, kehrt bestimmt später in voller erfreulicher Gewißheit wieder."
11. "Es ist eine so seltene als erfreuliche Erscheinung, wenn Dichter und Komponist einer Oper sich in e i n e r Person vereinigen ... Erfreulich aber ist die Erscheinung, denn der Kunstwerke nothwendigste schönste Zierde: Einheit und Mannigfaltigkeit kann offenbar nur aus e i n e s reichen Seelenlebens schönstem Walten im vollsten Glanz erblühen."
12. "mit wissenschaftlichen Kenntnisen, ja, selbst mit dichterischem Talente ... eine Oper, in der die Musikstücke durch fortlaufend instrumentierte Rezitative verbunden sind, und wo

demnach die Musik als Herrscherin, von allen ihren ununterbrochen in Tätigkeit gesetzten Krondienern umgeben, Hof hält."

13. "Glücklich und richtig berechnet gehen einige Melodien wie leise Faden durch das Ganze und halten es geistig zusammen."
14. "Mündliche und schriftliche Aeußerungen weisen darauf hin, daß er die Absicht hatte, ihr für den subtilern musikalischen und dramatischen Sinn des deutchen Publikums eine in vielen Stücken andere Gestalt zu geben, ja er hat sogar, wie Caroline bestimmt wußte, Neigung gehegt, den Dialog in Recitative umzuwandeln."
15. "Ich hätte nicht komponieren können, wie ich es getan habe, wenn Beethoven nicht gewesen wäre, aber was ich verwendet und erweitert habe, sind vereinzelte geniale Züge bei dramatischen Vorgängern wie selbst Auber, indem ich an etwas andrem mich hielt als die Oper."
16. "[. . .] mit je drei von diesen Variationen hätte er eine Symphonie schreiben können."
17. "[. . .] gieb mir eine rechte Oper in die Hand und in ein paar Monaten ist sie componirt, denn ich sehne mich jeden Tag von Neuen danach, eine Oper zu schreiben [. . .]. Und einen Text, der mich nicht ganz in Feuer setzt, componire ich nun einmal nicht. Wenn du einen Mann kennst, den im Stande ist, eine Oper zu dichten, so nenne ihn mir um Gotteswillen, ich suche nicht anderes."
18. "[. . .] denn hier ist das Sujet so vollkommen, daß man es ohne Musik als ein bloßes Stück geben könnte und man es mit Freuden sehen würde . . . Wäre der "Freischütz" kein so gutes Sujet, der Oper den Zulauf der Menge zu verschaffen, wie es nun der Fall ist, und man sollte daher dem Herrn Kind auch einige Ehre erzeigen."

BIBLIOGRAPHY

AMZ. 1807. Review of Danzi's *Iphigenia in Aulis*. *Allgemeine musikalische Zeitung* 9: 365–372.

Baumann, Thomas. 1985. *North German Opera in the Age of Goethe*. Cambridge: Cambridge University Press.

Benedict, Julius. 1861. Letter to Max Maria von Weber of 8 August. Copy by F. W. Jähns. Deutsche Staatsbibliothek, Berlin: Weberiana Mappe XIX. Cl. V.5. Nachtrag 8. Nr. 5.a.

Biedermann, Woldemar Fr. von, ed. 1890. *Goethes Gespräche*. Leipzig: F. W. von Biedermann.

Brody, Elaine. 1985–1986. "Operas in search of Brahms." *Opera Quarterly* 3/4: 24–37.

Brown, Clive. 1984a. *Louis Spohr*. Cambridge: Cambridge University Press.

——. 1984b. "Spohr, Faust and Leitmotif." *Musical Times* 125/1691: 25–27.

Chezy, Helmina von. 1840. "Carl Maria von Webers *Euryanthe*. Ein Beitrag zur Geschichte der deutschen Oper." *Neue Zeitschrift für Musik* 13/1–6: 9–11.

Dean, Winton. 1971. "Beethoven and Opera." In *The Beethoven Companion*, edited by Denis Arnold and Nigel Fortune, 331–386. London: Faber.

Devrient, Eduard. 1869. *Meine Erinnerungen an Felix Mendelssohn-Barthody und seine Briefe an mich*. Leipzig: J. J. Weber.

Dittersdorf, Karl Ditters von. 1801. *Lebensbeschreibung. Seinem Sohn in die Feder diktiert*. Leipzig: Breitkopf und Härtel.

Gregor-Dellin, Martin, and Dietrich Mack, eds. 1976–1977. *Cosima Wagner: Die Tagebücher 1869–1883*. 2 vols. Munich: Piper.

Harsdörffer, Georg Philipp. 1641–1657. *Seelewig*. In *Frawenzimmer Gesprächspiele*. 8 vols. Nuremberg.

Hennemann, Monika. 2002. "Mendelssohn, Opera, and the Libretto Problem." In *The Mendelssohns: Their Music in History*, edited by John Michael Cooper and Julie D. Prandl, 181–202. Oxford: Oxford University Press.

Hoffmann, Ernst Theodor. 1813. "Dichter und Komponist." *AMZ* 9: 793–806, 809–817. Republished with framing commentary as part of *Serapions=Brüder* (Berlin, 1819). Reprint. Segebrecht, Wulf, ed. 2001. *E. T. A. Hoffmann Sämtliche Werke*. Bd. 4. *Die Serapionsbrüder*. Frankfurt am Main: Deutscher Klassiker Verlag.

——. 1811. Review of Spohr's Symphony N. 1. *AMZ* 13: 797–806 and 813–809.

Jansen, F. Gustav, ed. 1904. *Robert Schumanns Briefe*. Neue Folge 2. Leipzig.

Kind, Friedrich. 1843. *Freischütz-Buch*. Leipzig: G. J. Göschen.

Kron, Wolfgang. 1957. *Die angeblichen Freischütz-Kritiken E.T. A. Hoffmanns*. Munich: Hueber.

Mattheson, Johann. 1744. *Die neueste Untersuchung der Singspiele*. Hamburg: C. Herold.

Morgan, Joseph E. 2009. "*Oberon*: A Reevaluation of Carl Maria von Weber." PhD diss., Brandeis University.

MTJ. 1814. Review of Poissl's *Athalia*. *Münchener Theater-Journal* 1/7:187–188.

Poissl, Johann Nepomuk. 1814. *Athalia*. D: Mbs St. th. 6.

Rochlitz, Friedrich. 1798. "Gedanken über die Oper." *AMZ* 1: 1–9.

Schreiter, Solveig. 2007. *Der Freischütz: Kritische Textbuch-Edition*. Munich: Allitera Verlag.

Segebrecht, Wulf, ed. 2001. *E. T. A. Hoffmann Sämtliche Werke*. Bd. 4. *Die Serapionsbrüder*. Frankfurt am Main: Deutscher Klassiker Verlag.

Spohr, Ludwig. [1816] 1853. *Faust*. Leipzig.

Staden, Siegmund. 1644. *Seelewig*. In Harsdörffer 1641–1657.

Stöpel, Franz. 1827. Review of Poissl's *Die Prinzessin von Provence*. *Berliner AMZ* 35: 282–284.

Tusa, Michael. 1991. *'Euryanthe' and Carl Maria von Weber's Dramaturgy of German Opera*. Oxford: Oxford University Press.

Waidelich, Till Gerrit. 2008. "'Durch Webers Betrügerey die Hände so gebunden': Helmina von Chezys Kampf um die Urheberrechte an ihrem *Euryanthe*-Libretto in ihrer Korrespondenz und Brief-Entwürfen." *Weberiana: Mitteilungen der Carl-Maria-von-Weber-Gesellschaft* 18, edited by Frank Ziegler, 33–69. Tutzing: Schneider.

——. 1996. "'Weder *Italienisch* noch *Französisch*, sondern rein Deutsch.' Johann Nepomuk Poißls *Athalia* als Oper 'ohngefehr im Genre der Gluck'schen.'" *Weber-Studien* 3, edited by Joachim Veit and Frank Ziegler, 318–346. Mainz.

Wagner, Richard. 1871. "Erinnerungen an Auber." *Musikalisches Wochenblatt*. Also in *Sämtliche Schriften und Dichtungen*. 16 vols. IX: 42–60. Leipzig.

Warrack, John. 2001. *German Opera: From the Beginnings to Wagner*. Cambridge: Cambridge University Press.

——. 1976. *Carl Maria von Weber*. 2nd ed. Cambridge: Cambridge University Press.

Weber, Carl Maria von. 1981. *Carl Maria von Weber: Writings on Music*, edited by John Warrack, translated by Martin Cooper. Cambridge: Cambridge University Press.

——. 1826. Oberon. GB-Lbl Add MS 27,746.

——. 1820. Introduction to Poissl's *Der Wettkampf zu Olympia*. [Dresden] *Abend-Zeitung* 64 (13 March). In C. M. von Weber 1981, 289–291.

——. 1809–1820. *Tonkünstlers Leben*. In C. M. von Weber 1981, 312–364.

——. 1817. Review of E. T. A. Hoffmann, *Undine*. *AMZ* 9: 201–208. In C. M. von Weber 1981, 200–205.

——. 1816a. Introduction to Poissl's *Athalia*. *Königliche kaiserliche privilegierte Prager Zeitung* 142 (May 21). In C. M. von Weber 1981, 184–187.

——. 1816b. Review of Spohr's *Faust. Königliche kaiserliche privilegierte Prager Zeitung* 245/1 (1 September). In C. M. von Weber 1981, 191–193.
Weber, Max Maria von. 1864–1866. *Carl Maria von Weber. Ein Lebensbild.* 3 vols. Leipzig: E. Keil.
Wieland, Christoph Martin. [1775] 1928. *Versuch über das deutsche Singspiel. Teutsche Merkur:* 3-4. Reprinted in *Wielands Gesammelte Schriften.* 23 vols., edited by Wilhelm Kurrelmeyer, XIV: 74–99. Berlin: Weidmann.

CHAPTER 11

ANALYSIS

WILLIAM DRABKIN

The Problem

If music analysis is concerned with breaking down a work into its constituent parts and examining how they fit together, how they function to produce something that is artistically meaningful to the listener, then the analysis of opera can, at best, be considered an extremely complex discipline in which music analysis—itself a complicated act—forms only part of the process.

There are many reasons for this. First, the music that goes into making an opera exists in a large number of formats and embraces a variety of genres. Assuming, for the moment, that we are concerned with a "number opera" made up of largely discrete units, an analysis would have to understand not only the workings of individual pieces but also the ways in which their succession is coherent and satisfying—not only as music but also in some sort of narrative way, as an unfolding drama. Such a task would be concerned with elements as varied as overtures, arias, duets, and larger ensembles. It would also have to account for finales, which themselves comprise a number of sections, each in its own tempo, each with its own internal structure. It might also have to consider stretches of recitative, music which, taken at face value, lacks sufficient melodic profile and variety of texture to be a useful subject for detailed scrutiny. To analyze an opera—to analyze its constituent parts and then to see how these fit together, musically and dramatically—is a multifaceted process that requires a considerable amount of intellectual gear-changing.

Second, opera is an unstable medium when set beside that bedrock of analysis, instrumental music. Most of the symphonies, concertos (disregarding cadenzas), and string quartets that have been laid out in the analyst's operating theater enjoy relatively fixed texts, with usually just a handful of discrepant notes, dynamics, slurs, and tempo markings distinguishing one authentic source from another; Beethoven's late quartet in B flat major, with its two finales, is the exception that almost proves the rule. The text of an opera—even an opera by a proverbial "German master"—can change in a number of ways. An aria may be replaced by another to lend novelty to a revival, or to better match the voice of a singer new to the cast. And the alterations do not have to be made in the same place; in replacing Don Ottavio's "Il mio tesoro" with "Dalla sua pace" for the Viennese revival of *Don Giovanni*, a mere seven months after the Prague premiere, Mozart changed the shape of both acts of the opera. The existence of alternative arias for Don Ottavio, and also for Donna Elvira, has led to a "hybrid" version of the opera, in which both alternatives are commonly included in performance. Though Mozart cannot be blamed for this, any analysis of his opera would consider the differences not only between the two authentic versions (including material for Vienna that is hardly ever performed today), but also a hybrid version that raises the profile of two characters. In the case of *Fidelio*, Beethoven took it upon himself to write a new overture for each revival, the last of which resulted—nearly a decade after the premiere—in his opera beginning and ending in different keys (see Tyson 1975, 1977).

Many operas in the canon have undergone revision more substantial than the replacement of individual numbers, whether to suit a different range of singers (e.g. a tenor Idamante instead of a castrato, for the concert revival of *Idomeneo* in 1786) or to reflect audience expectations in a particular country, for example the obligatory inclusion of ballet music in nineteenth-century performances at the Paris Opéra. There are also many operas that suffered change as the result of censorship, notably *Un ballo in maschera*, which Verdi revised extensively, altering along the way the opera's time, place, and title (see Gossett 2006: 489–532). In an extreme case, where artistry collided with practicality, the Paris suburban train timetable played a role in determining the musical text of the premiere of *Don Carlos*; it is hard to imagine the same fate befalling a late nineteenth-century symphony, even one by Bruckner, which was susceptible to the composer's own surgical knife. Even something as apparently modest as the transposition of an aria to accommodate a voice incapable of singing it well in its "original" key raises major issues for the many who are concerned with the role of tonality in the unfolding of a musical drama (see Puffett 1992 and Greenwald 1998).

A related phenomenon is the changes to the text of an opera that result from the practice of theater directors and, not least, of singers (see Poriss 2009). Some of these alterations have, over the course of time, attained canonic status; scholars have had to make a special plea for the "restoration" of numbers traditionally cut in performance, e.g. the two minor-character Act IV arias from *Le nozze di Figaro*. Thus, for instance, Wye Jamison Allanbrook (1983) correctly asserts that Marcellina's "Il capro ed la capretta" and Basilio's "In quegl'anni" are an integral part of the drama, "an important preface to Figaro's angry soliloquy," though she has greater difficulty eliciting any special musical worth in either of these posturing numbers (Allanbrook 1983: 159–167). Julian Rushton (1981) is more ruthlessly dismissive of them when he sets them beside the action-impeding arias in Act II of *Don Giovanni*, describing the latter as "great dramatic music, a term hardly applicable to the arias usually cut in Act IV of *Figaro*" (Rushton 1981: 54). Tim Carter offers a lukewarm defense of them, mainly on grounds of character portrayal and development (1987: 65); one could question, however, the timeliness of such qualities midway through the final act of a long stage work.

Sometimes the canonic status of a tradition has insinuated itself into the score, even into one prepared by a trained musicologist. Georg Schünemann, the director of the music division of the Prussian State Library in Berlin, indicated in his critical edition of *Così fan tutte* (prepared with conductor Kurt Soldan) that three numbers are "often omitted," including two of the tenor Ferrando's three arias. In marking items in the score with the note "bleibt oft fort [is often omitted]," the editors were probably observing a tradition of German productions of *Così*, rather than making value judgments about their musical worth (Mozart [1790] 1941). By contrast, the omission of a movement from a standard-repertory instrumental work, or its treatment as a performance option, is, to modern musicians, almost unthinkable.

What complicates the analysis of opera most of all is, of course, the status of the artwork as multimedia (and of analysis, advantageously, being "multivalent"; see Webster 1990, 1991; Atlas 1993). That does not, of course, make opera unique: There is much non-operatic music that is sung to a text, and there is much instrumental music that tells a story; and in both a human drama may unfold. The greater the need to coordinate a range of artistic parameters—for example poetic, tonal, and dramatic—the more likely it is for each of these to give up something of itself in order to work effectively for the form as a whole.

This means that even though composers of opera, in animating poetry and action through music, may be concerned with such things as developing themes, bringing a tonal argument to a successful conclusion, and creating a satisfying overall form, it is with the understanding that their audience may not react—or react consciously—to these specific musical achievements per se (about such audibility in Mozart, see Platoff 1996); rather, they will be enveloped by the combination of music, poetry, and drama together. Theorists like Heinrich Schenker will argue that musical works themselves reveal the laws of music to attentive listeners, and that the greatest composers have, while seeming to challenge these laws, revealed to us the ways in which they may be interpreted in new, hitherto unimagined, and thus "higher," ways. The theater may not, however, be the ideal forum for such challenges.

Is it possible, then, to imagine that opera composers, being aware of the need to take into account the multiple levels on which theater operates, must in some sense hold back on what they contribute at the musical level? Could operas be perceived as "under-composed" when set beside comparable works in other genres? Should we expect a string quartet or quintet by a great composer from the Classical period to be—musically—more challenging than one of his operas? Hard proof of the differences in intensity between two works of art is impossible to furnish, but the reader might wish to compare, for instance, the ways in which Mozart deploys his gifts for chromatic writing in the slow introductions to the overture to *Don Giovanni* and the first movement of the "Dissonance" Quartet. There is no denying the intensity of the former, and the power of those violin scales to instill a sense of terror in the listener—and to intensify that sense when the music is recapitulated in the penultimate scene of the opera, where the Commendatore-turned-statue confronts his assassin. But the false relations in the opening phrases of the "Dissonance" Quartet represent an altogether different class of compositional technique, one that would be too subtle to work its magic in the theater, where more immediate means of expression are required.

Nowhere are these issues considered more eloquently than in a work by the Austrian music theorist and doyen of modern tonal analysis, Heinrich Schenker. His early essay *The Decline of the Art of Composition* ([ca. 1907] 2005) remained virtually unknown for nearly a century and so has played no role in the debates about operatic analysis in the past forty years. Yet its unique status—both in the Schenker canon and as an early twentieth-century composition manifesto—lies in its attention to the issues of opera aesthetics and composition, ranging from Gluck to Wagner and taking in Mozart, Beethoven, Weber, Rossini, and Meyerbeer along the way. It was Schenker who first pointed out that Mozart's famous dictum, in a letter of October 3, 1781, to his father, about poetry being the "obedient daughter of music," was written as he was working on *Die Entführung aus dem Serail*, that is, some years before his collaboration with Lorenzo Da Ponte, and that it therefore does not necessarily apply to his later, more celebrated operatic output. Schenker then goes on to argue that, in Mozart's later operatic work—the *Decline* includes analytical remarks on three numbers from *Don Giovanni*—there is a "quantitative" musical deficit: that is, in the operas for which he is best known (and which are the most often written about) he recognized the need to sacrifice some of the musical richness with which his instrumental music is imbued—without the listener-spectator feeling in any way emotionally disappointed or intellectually shortchanged.

If, however, Mozart's operatic music, being in the service of the theater, has to make a certain amount of sacrifice, why should analysts become preoccupied with it? Put more positively, should not the analysis of Mozart strive to understand his greatest achievements and, in so doing, achieve greater insight into what Schenker called the "aristocratic" qualities of his art? If so, should this not be undertaken through such works as the quartets, quintets, and symphonies of the Viennese decade? One response to this question, which sparked heated rebuttal, was made by Joseph Kerman (1980) who, without of course knowing anything of Schenker's work on *Don Giovanni*, devotes much of his discussion to parsing differences between analysis and criticism, taking the work of Schenkerians as a distinctly problematic example of the elevation of German models of instrumental music in the name of scientific inquiry (Kerman 1980: 313).

There are several arguments against prioritizing Mozart's instrumental music over his operas. First, the end of analysis is not always an understanding of compositional technique. In this respect we must take "the art of composition" in Schenker's title at its face value, since his principal concern in this essay was the pernicious influence of nineteenth-century opera and other "associative" music on would-be composers of the early 1900s. Berlioz, Liszt, and, above all, Wagner, are the villains of Schenker's piece, for having diverted a later generation (Bruckner, Wolf, and Strauss) from the path carved for them by Beethoven—a path successfully taken only by Mendelssohn and Brahms. Thus, in the *Decline*, Schenker laments the fact that it was Wagner, not Beethoven, who took possession of Hugo Wolf's soul, corrupting the talented youth; elsewhere he attributes Bruckner's failings as a symphonist to the influence of Wagner, eradicating all trace of the good example of Mendelssohn in his formative years. (With Strauss, on the other hand, Schenker believed that the Wagnerian model merely compounded an innately impoverished talent.)

Second, it is impossible to divorce Wagner's style, which was held to be fundamental to the future course of music in the late nineteenth and early twentieth centuries, from its dramatic context. That the theatrically naïve Bruckner, as one anecdote has it, could have sat through a performance of his idol's *Tristan und Isolde* without once looking at the stage does not alter the fact that Wagner developed his musical language in and for the theater, and that the best of the Wagnerian critical canon—voice-leading graphs of the *Tristan* Prelude notwithstanding—acknowledges the inseparability of the words and the drama, and the philosophical sentiments they underpin, from the musical score.

Third and most obviously, there is more to music than what the great German masters are capable of teaching us; to mention just one field, recent analyses of Verdian opera—whatever their origins as a response to writings about Wagner—have contributed significantly to the breadth of our critical appreciation of opera. Schenker himself seems to have been more aware of this than he is usually credited with: his reviews of early Viennese productions of *Falstaff* suggest some of the elusive qualities in Verdi that, he believed, merited the careful critical attention that it has only lately received (Schenker [1891–1901] 1990: 44–48, 85–89).

One of the features that give opera a special status in the performing arts is the tension between, on the one hand, the complicated interrelationships between score (music), libretto (poetry), and stage action (drama) and, on the other, the ultimate conviction that we are concerned with a genre that is, after all, primarily musical. That is, I believe, what we mean when we refer to Wagner, Verdi, and Puccini as opera *composers*. That much seems to have been confirmed by Verdi himself, who on March 6, 1868, wrote to his friend and compatriot Count Opprandino Arrivabene that "in order to make an opera you must have primarily music in your blood" (cited in Sanguinetti 2006: 83). It is what we mean when we say that *Così fan tutte* is by Mozart, even when we are well aware that it was the product of an intimate collaboration between Mozart and Lorenzo Da Ponte. In this respect, operas differ from musicals, in which either the credits for the music, lyrics, and spoken dialogue (the "book") are shared equally, or the collaboration of composer and librettist is acknowledged in the general attribution of authorship, as in "Rodgers and Hammerstein," "Lerner and Loewe," "Gilbert and Sullivan"; their operatic equivalents, for example "Mozart and Da Ponte" or "Verdi and Piave," are never used. Moreover, we do not listen to operatic music all that differently from instrumental music, apart from the appeal of words as well as notes on our aural senses, and the fact that there is much to be seen as well. Music's effect, as music, is made through the laws of music; it is only when it is one of many elements affecting an audience that those effects are diffused and thus more difficult to pin down, that is, to explain as a harmonic progression, to put into graphic notation, to understand as an example of a certain form.

Ways of Analyzing Operatic Music

If successful accounts of music in general embrace a wide range of analytical parameters—harmony, theme and motive, counterpoint, style, rhetoric—then a successful account of operatic music must not only consider these features but also be capable of relating them to that which makes opera special, including text, drama, and spectacle (see Kerman 1988; Burton 1995 has devised a system for separating these functions in Puccini's operas). The sources of operatic music's power to move us, as viewing listeners, are nowhere more cogently set out than in Webster's 1991 theoretical essay on Mozart's arias; and if his table of "analytical parameters in an eighteenth-century aria" is restricted to the factors of production of a specific kind of operatic number written at a particular time (Webster 1991: 131), the breadth of his outline is sufficient reminder that the principles and techniques traditionally acquired in the advanced study of music theory represent only part of what is available for the close reading of opera.

Historically Based Explanations

One should not lose sight of the fact that much of what we have learned about opera, and indeed about music in general, has been told in non-technical terms. As Carolyn Abbate and Roger Parker explain at the outset of a volume of essays whose very concern is the analysis of opera, to "interpret" or "explain" an opera can simply mean "to contribute to a richer understanding of the work" (Abbate and Parker 1989b: 1). The overwhelming task facing the opera analyst may help to explain why some of the most enduring accounts of canonic works are by writers who wear their analytical accomplishments lightly and are able to "tell the story in familiar and friendly words." Few would dispute Abbate and Parker's assignment of such books as Edward Dent's *Mozart's Operas* (1913) and Ernest Newman's *Wagner Nights* (1949) as models of operatic storytelling. The writing of such books is often driven by the wealth of knowledge acquired over a lifetime's historical scholarship and practical experience in the theater. And while such experience intersects only rarely with the kind of skills that formal training in music analysis normally provides, there is no reason that the activities of historians and theorists cannot meet on common ground. Thus, for theorists for whom tonal coherence may be an important concern, and who, for instance, would see the key of D minor (yielding to major) as an important feature of the composition of *Don Giovanni*, Dent's research on the origins of the opera as a four-act structure, with Donna Anna's D major "Or sai che l'onore" concluding the first act (Dent [1913] 1947: 138), could be used in support of a position that tonality is a unifying factor on a number of different levels of composition.

Text Analysis as Determinant of Music Analysis

Most of an opera consists of sung music. And while the purely instrumental pieces (overtures, preludes, entr'actes) may be viewed as products of the composer working alone, whatever traditions and models may have influenced their design, the sung parts usually demand the fashioning of the musical materials around a previously written text, and this will have important consequences not only for musical meter and rhythm but also for tonality and character.

If, for instance, a stanza of Italian poetry—to begin with, often a quatrain—is roughly equivalent to a musical statement, then a pair of stanzas is an invitation to a composer to compose two connected but contrasting statements, for example a theme and a modulation to the dominant, or a first theme and a second theme. In other words, what would appear on the surface to invite strophic design—mere musical repetition, based on a repeating verse structure—can be used in a tonally more sophisticated form to propel the music into new territory, much as the change of words helps to advance a storyline or amplify the sentiments being expressed.

Further stanzas built in the same way could then be used for transitional material; where there is a shift in poetic construction, say, from a change either of meter, or of number of lines, or rhyme scheme, the music can—and should—reflect this by a corresponding change in design. The platform for studying the relationship between versification and music in early-nineteenth-century Italian opera (with a focus on Verdi) was set by Robert Moreen (1975), who includes detailed discussion of Italian prosody as well as its relationship to both small and large musical structures. Harold Powers (1987) takes a closer look at selected works of Verdi to determine the composer's actual practice against the posited norms, while Philip Gossett (2006: 364–406) takes the problem a step further by discussing composers' self-borrowing of music as well as the problem of translation (on contrafacta in Bellini, see Smart 2000, and for more on the relationship between text forms and scene structure in Rossini, Bellini, Donizetti, and Verdi, see Balthazar 1985). More recently, Andreas Giger (2008) has analyzed Verdi's settings of French texts, noting specifically the relationship between aesthetics, melody, rhythm, and compositional practice. Andrew Davis (2010) treats the deformation of poetic convention in Puccini's late works, while Nicholas Baragwanath (2011) takes a more holistic view of the ways that composers of Italian opera in the nineteenth century were schooled in the "rules" of melodic and poetic construction. In quite a different direction, Thomas Grey (1995) shows how Wagner took the opposite approach by theorizing about the origin of melody in speech (see also Dahlhaus 1965).

Tim Carter (1987) provides several classic examples of the ways in which poetic structure influenced musical structural in *Le nozze di Figaro*, though without belaboring his discussion with close readings of the music (Carter 1987: 74–87). Of particular interest is the way he sets out the verse structure of Figaro's first-act "Se vuol ballare" to show how the *versi sciolti* of the recitative give way to the lyrical five-syllable lines for the cavatina. We can take his discussion of the text a little further to see how the first two stanzas,

MUSIC EXAMPLE 11.1 Mozart, *Le nozze di Figaro*, Act I, no. 3 ("Se vuol ballare"), mm. 23–42.

being symmetrically constructed (both even begin with the same words, "Se vuol"), lend themselves well to "tonic" and "dominant" tonal areas in the cavatina.

Note, however, that the second stanza must serve two roles: as the bearer of the modulation to the dominant and the text of the dominant area itself (see Music Example 11.1). There follows a third quatrain, whose structure is subtly varied in two ways: It begins with a rhymed couplet (. . . piano / . . . arcano), which promotes greater forward musical development than the abbc pattern of stanzas 1 and 2. More crucially, the midline break allows Mozart to develop "Saprò" and "piano" separately, and independently, and so create the tension required for the return to the starting point to be a satisfying outcome.

This return occurs in two phases. The first, which sees a reprise only of the home key of F major, sets the fourth and final stanza, in which the quatrain structure has been expanded to six lines and two new poetic elements, near-rhyme (-endo / -ando) and *verso sdrucciolo* (a line ending with two unaccented syllables), are introduced. Both of these contribute to the forward thrust of this section of music, and thus promote a change of meter from 3/4 (minuet) to 2/4 (contredanse).

Two questions arise from this approach to Figaro's cavatina. First, is Mozart responding to Da Ponte's libretto, or is the libretto a response to the composer's demands for a particular structure that would fit his conception of Figaro's anger, and how it could be expressed in musical form? This question may be unanswerable, since we can only guess at how closely these two resident Viennese artists collaborated in shaping the opera. The second question concerns the final part of the aria, in which the opening of the minuet is recapitulated—Figaro repeats the first quatrain and its music exactly—and the orchestra rounds things off with a recall of the contredanse. An analysis of the poetic text itself cannot help us here. We can ask ourselves only what musical, or dramatic, factors were responsible for this: Did Mozart want to give added value to his principal character's first solo number? Or were a thematic reprise and a postlude needed to give sufficient weight to the cavatina, so that audiences would be able to hear the first three sung numbers of the opera as a subsection of Act I, sufficiently closed to allow the next part of the drama (featuring Marcellina and Bartolo) to make a new beginning?

Topical Analysis

The analysis of eighteenth-century music by topics (*topoi*)—the identification of the rhythmic and harmonic gestures or poses, and the understanding of musical discourse in terms of the opposition or interaction of these features—is a relatively recent phenomenon. While isolated examples of topical identification have featured in close readings of music for some time (see, for example, Noske [1977] 1990), especially the use of "ancient" styles with which to end forward-looking works (for example, the Minuet at the end of Beethoven's "Diabelli" Variations, and Mozart's *antichissima canzon*—fugue—as the final ensemble in *Don Giovanni*), the systematic presentation of topics and their application to the analysis of Classical music began with Leonard Ratner (1980) and was followed closely by Allanbrook (1983) a comprehensive and rigorous application of these theories to two canonic Mozart operas.

The basic premise here is that the character of the music is consistent with the character of the participants in the drama and that, in particular, rhythm and meter are of fundamental importance for that character portrayal. In this method of analysis, time signatures play an important role, with *alla breve* signatures ranged at one end of a two-dimensional spectrum, and "lighter" meters based on the eighth note at the other. The discipline, dignity, and poise that are associated with long-note pulses, for example the quintessentially sacred-music meters of 4/2 (and, later, ¢,) are thus set in opposition to such peasant dances as the 6/8 gigue or the 3/8 *deutscher Tanz* ("alla tedesca"). Occupying a middle ground are, on one side, the more refined sarabande (3/2 or 3/4) and the slow minuet (3/4), on the other side the march (4/4 or 2/4), the contredanse (2/4), and the Sicilian dance (12/8 or 6/8) (see Allanbrook 1983: Part I, especially 22 and 67). A classic exemplification of this theory is the dance scene from the Act I finale of *Don Giovanni*, in which Mozart contrives to have three pairs of characters dancing at the same time, accompanied by three on-stage orchestras, harmonically coordinated but each playing a different type of dance in a different meter (Allanbrook 1983: 275–287).

In this way, operatic music—above all, late-eighteenth-century opera—could be understood as a progression of *topoi* (topics, styles), which not only enhances the drama by bringing an extra dimension to the poetry of the libretto, but by creating its own world of musical diversity. The excitement generated by finales, featuring a wide-ranging array of characters, owes a great deal to this diversity and may account for the privileging of ensembles in close readings of Mozart in the analytical literature. Webster (1991: 102) noted this trend, attributing it to the (mis-)application of a "Wagnerian aesthetic" to Mozart's operas (see also Platoff 1989).

Compositional Process

If composition, as synthesis, may be viewed as the opposite procedure to analysis, then the interpretation of an operatic composer's decisions, whether by conscious planning (e.g., through sketches and other evidence of creative process) or in relationship to convention and norm, can be of paramount importance in arriving at an understanding of the finished product. Sketch studies have, of course, a long and distinguished pedigree, dating back to the work of Gustav Nottebohm on Beethoven in the 1860s and 1870s. The before-and-after comparisons that we get in such studies as Curt von Westernhagen's on Wagner's *Ring* (1976), Gossett's detailed analysis of the autograph of Verdi's *Ernani* (1987), and Linda Fairtile's study of Puccini's revisions (1995) are reminders of the potential for composers themselves to tell us what to look for—that is, to listen for—in their finished works. Of course, such "evidence" as may be found in a sketchbook, or an autograph score, can at best give us some idea of a composer's intent, which cannot be equated with meaning.

A related type of analysis is the study of an opera against the background of operatic convention, as a corrective to what Powers (1987) has called a "Germanic" or "North of the Alps" approach to instrumental music as the basis on which to find unifying features in an opera, or a unitary approach to composition (Powers 1987: 82). More may be learned, it is argued, by examining the design of a musical scene against what one might expect to find in a typical situation, what the early Verdi critic Abramo Basevi called "la solita forma" (Basevi 1859: 191). In a long and elaborate essay, drawing on many examples and citing the work of a wide range of modern commentators, Powers demonstrates that, throughout his career, Verdi neither slavishly followed the conventions of nineteenth-century operatic design nor disposed of them altogether when the dramatic situation called for something else, but rather shaped them according to the particular needs of that situation. This study may be thought of as a counterpart to Schenker's celebrated essay on "organicism" in sonatas of Haydn and Beethoven (Schenker [1926] 1996); for Verdi, as for the Viennese classical masters (whom he, too, greatly admired), musical forms were not empty shells that he filled but concepts with—and against—which he worked.

Tonal and Voice-Leading Approaches

The time of greatest interest in the analysis of opera, the last three decades of the twentieth century, coincides with the period in which Schenkerian theory gained a foothold—some would say stranglehold—in the analysis of tonal music more generally. It is hardly surprising, then, to find that Schenkerians have applied the principles of voice-leading analysis to the operatic repertory, even in spite of Schenker's early warning that the masters (by which he meant Mozart) did not write their most refined, "aristocratic" music for the theater and that, conversely, the most celebrated composers for the theater (by which he meant Gluck, Wagner, and the young Richard Strauss) wrote music that, from a technical point of view, fell short—in the case of Gluck and Strauss, far short—of what the masters had achieved. Wagner's principal failing, for the Schenker of 1907, is the absence of moment-to-moment connection in his scores. In *Das Rheingold*, scene 2, there is a passage in which the Valhalla leitmotif enters without any musically logical connection to what has gone before: it is stated simply because one of the giants is pointing to the castle that he and his brother have recently completed (Schenker [ca. 1907] 2005: 100–101). This Schenker contrasts with the opening scene of Act I of *Don Giovanni*, where even the simplest harmonic connection between two scenes, which results from the addition of a seventh to an F major chord so that it must resolve to B flat, is nonetheless a musical connection (Schenker [ca. 1907] 2005: 86).

Long after the *Decline*, Schenker continued to denounce Wagner for sacrificing musical coherence on the altar of music drama, though with different rhetoric. Instead of blaming him for the demise of the art in the nineteenth century, he simply maintained that Wagner was incapable of writing music with a solid underlying or "background" structure: his art was all surface and no depth (Schenker [1926] 1996: 29). A full-scale Schenkerian analysis of a Wagnerian music drama might, therefore, be seen as a contradiction in terms. But if we return to the tension between opera as drama, on the one hand, and opera as (operatic) music, on the other, the challenge of getting inside a piece of such considerable harmonic and contrapuntal complexity as a Wagner opera may be worth rising to, even if it requires new tools for the job, and the reforging of old ones. If Schenkerians apply Schenkerian theory to Wagner, that is because they regard Wagner's music as music. While Schenker denigrated even that classic of the analytical tradition, the *Tristan* Prelude, because the cello melody in measure 17 makes three return appearances, none of which advances the musical argument by exhibiting any variety of function (these sentiments appear in a paragraph on the *Tristan* Prelude that was cut at a late stage from his *Harmonielehre* of 1906; see Drabkin 2005: 22), his successors may view it as an honor, perhaps a duty, to make a voice-leading reduction of the most celebrated slow introduction in the music literature since Mozart's String Quartet in C (Mitchell 1967; appendix to Cube [ca. 1953] 1987). To see just how far Schenkerian theory, for want of a better word, moved over to Wagner's side in the course of the twentieth century, compare the following summary judgment:

> All musical movement and continuity are basically thought processes set to music [*vertonte Gedankenfolgen*]. His music follows the logic of thoughts and events incomparably more than the laws that reside in music itself.... He does not put together ideas from various elements, he builds no groups, he takes no care of the succession of keys, since he never has in mind a higher unity that is equivalent to any form. (Schenker [ca. 1907] 2005: 99)

with the following, taken from a full-length study of *Das Rheingold* and framed as a defense of Schenker against one of his severest critics:

> Each episode displays a clear formal/tonal design, which grows naturally out of the structure and content of the text. Thus [Carl] Dahlhaus's "logical/architectural" dialectic collapses: Wagner's forms are both logical *and* architectural. (Darcy 1993: 215)

The chromatic complexities of Wagner's mature operas notwithstanding—and there are few analyses of the music Wagner composed prior to the *Ring* operas—scholars have been eager to show that Schenkerian approaches are not only compatible with music drama but also have much to reveal in it. At one end of the spectrum, we have Warren Darcy's (1993) largely Schenkerian account of *Das Rheingold*, with dozens of voice-leading sketches embedded in a text that, though it has much to say about Wagner's dramaturgy, text setting, and compositional process, is primarily concerned with demonstrating tonal coherence in the large and small, and concludes with a synoptic view of the work (shown in three hierarchically related graphs) as a prolongation of D flat major by a $\hat{5}$–$\hat{6}$–$\hat{5}$ neighbor-note figure (Darcy 1993: 215–219, especially 217). To be sure, the graphic analyses acknowledge that the work begins in a different key, but its integration into the whole is somewhat unconventional: Instead of viewing E flat as an upper neighbor to D flat, Darcy reads an unfolding between the scenes' initial and final tonics, E flat major and C minor, as a pair of *lower* neighbor notes, almost a V^6 to the basic tonality of the opera.

At the opposite end, theorists have been content to show how a single phrase may be construed as a chromatic elaboration of a fundamental structure: *Tristan und Isolde* has provided two such examples. For a neat and elegant Schenkerian account of Wagner's setting of the so-called *Todesmotiv* (the leitmotif of Death, first heard near the beginning of Act I, scene 2, at Isolde's "Todgeweihtes Haupt! Todgeweihtes Herz!"), which was offered as a corrective to an earlier analysis of the passage intended to demonstrate the dissolution of tonality in the mature Wagner, see Cube (1984: 123–127, trans.

Drabkin 1985). A far more elaborate graphic reduction of another phrase from *Tristan*, the much-discussed "War Morold dir so wert" in Act I, middle of scene 5, appears in Darcy's survey of analytical approaches to Wagner (Darcy 1993: 45–58), as a corrective to Carl Dahlhaus's anti-Schenkerian reading of the passage (Dahlhaus 1980: 65–75) and as hard evidence for the position that, "[a]t the very least, a judicious use of Schenkerian techniques might help prevent the Dahlhaus syndrome of drawing grand conclusions from bungled analyses" (Darcy 1993: 55).

A midway position is taken by Patrick McCreless (1989), in a close reading of the music assigned to the three Norns in the Prologue to *Götterdämmerung*. His four-page middleground graph of this scene is one of the notational highlights of *Analyzing Opera* (Abbate and Parker 1989a), though it comes with a number of qualifications, heralded by section headings toward the end of the accompanying essay: After reading about "The Third Norn and a Certain Chord" and "The Third Norn, Who Is Different," it is time for us to learn why "Schenker Would Not Have Liked the Third Norn" (McCreless 1989: 288, 290). The music assigned to the Third Norn is built almost entirely around half-diminished seventh chords, and is thus more chromatic, more elusive, more modern than that of her sisters. Just as she is unable to catch hold of the golden rope of time, which eventually breaks, so Wagner's harmonies finally break loose from their moorings in the tonal system: The *Klang in der Natur*, like the World Ash Tree to which the rope was once tied, has been destroyed. If the analogy is overworked, it may be because McCreless has underestimated the modernity of the Norns' earlier music, and that what makes the Third Norn different from her sisters is that her music is new, whereas theirs recapitulates the themes associated with Wotan, Loge, Alberich, and other characters. McCreless's graph (292–295) shows a modulation from E flat minor to B minor across the scene predicated on the priority of E flat minor at the outset of the opera. He claims that this key "echoes the E flat major of the *Rheingold* 'Vorspiel' and the undisturbed state of the world [...]" (McCreless 1989: 282). Yet, as Music Example 11.2 shows, the explicit motivic connection to the *Rheingold* prelude—the Rhinemaidens' aquatic arpeggios—is given in measure 2, where the harmony changes to C flat major. We are confronted here with a Riemannian conundrum: Should the opening harmony be understood as i–VI in E flat minor, as McCreless's graphic analysis implies? Or is it the other way around, iii–I in C flat major, which would be more consistent with the conventional reading of Brünnhilde's awakening in the third act of *Siegfried*, of which the opening chords of this Prologue are a transposed repetition? The difficulties of Wagner's chromaticism aside, one cannot ignore the possibility that the style of other mid-nineteenth-century opera composers, particularly those for whom melodic continuity resides more in the voice than in the orchestra, is somewhat better suited to voice-leading analysis.

Verdi often creates continuity between keys by the harmonic reinterpretation of melodic scale-steps. This procedure, by which the key-note of a previous section has an important role to play in the next—often as the Schenkerian "primary tone" in a new key—is what links together the diverse sections of a scene as tonally disparate as, for instance, the love duet between Riccardo and Amelia in Act II of *Un ballo in maschera*, which is played out in no fewer than five keys.

MUSIC EXAMPLE 11.2 Wagner, *Die Götterdämmerung*, Prelude, mm. 1–8.

The continuity of pitch across sections of music has led some scholars—not only in Verdi, but elsewhere in the operatic repertory—to view operatic acts, even whole operas, as being in a single key, the ultimate claim of the "North of the Alps" analytical doctrine. For Verdi, a debate was initiated by Levarie (1978–1979) and continued by Kerman (1978–1979) and Marco (1979–1980) (see also Lawton 1982; Cone 1982; Parker and Brown 1983; Chusid 1989 and 1997; Greenwald 1998 summarizes the problem of tonal analysis in operatic repertoires and scholarly responses to it [see especially 521–524]). Claims about large-scale tonal unity in Mozart and Wagner have an older tradition (see Lorenz 1924–1933 and 1926–1927; Levarie 1952; for opposing views as they concern Mozart, see Webster 1987–1988 and 1990). Schenkerians now defend themselves against the charge that such key-orientated analyses are in any meaningful way Schenkerian; to be fair to their critics, however, there was always for Schenker a structural layer preceding even that of the *Ursatz*, namely, the "chord of nature," that is, the tonic triad resonating behind the background, and the entire foundations of Schenkerian theory are built on this fundamental concept that music is in a key. That Verdi's operas may be, in any sense, monotonal is something about which some Verdians (and scholars of other Italian repertoires) are now arguing for caution. (Arguments abound; see, for example, the exchange about Puccini's *Madama Butterfly* initiated by Atlas [1990–1991] and continued by Parker and Atlas [1992].)

According to a letter dating from 1868 (noted earlier), Verdi seems to have been adamant that the principal requisite in composing an opera was "to have music in your blood." As self-evident as this statement may seem, it has been used to support the case for prioritizing musical meanings in Verdi. To the claim that, in the mature Verdi, "the drama . . . is conveyed *primarily* through the music" (Sanguinetti 2006: 83), a corollary is tacitly appended, namely, that the course of the music is conveyed primarily through its graphic reductions. Giorgio Sanguinetti's example, in the second duet for Carlos and Elisabeth in *Don Carlos*, is difficult to follow, not least because the changes in tempo and musical character between musical sections are not matched to the phases in which the voice leading unfolds. The *scena*, which starts in E flat minor and ends in E flat major, comes close to being through-composed, with several major changes of tempo and internal lyrical sections beginning in D minor, G minor, B flat major, D flat major, E flat major, and C minor. While there is nothing mystical, or remote, about Schenkerian voice-leading graphs, they are useful only insofar as readers are willing to undertake a patient comparison with the musical score on which they are based. That, unsurprisingly, is not something most readers of opera criticism are disposed to doing: as we are reminded, or rather warned, by Abbate and Parker's opening lines, hard-core theorists are challenged by the plea "tell the story in familiar and friendly words" (see also Huebner 1992 and Rothstein 2008 for more on melody and voice leading in Verdi and Baragwanath 2008 on Puccini).

Analyzing Wagnerian Music Drama

In spite of Schenker's spiteful pronouncements about Wagner throughout his writings, there has been no shortage of attempts by theorists and analysts to come to terms with the major music dramas, from *Rheingold* to *Parsifal* (see, for example, Brinkmann 1972; Dahlhaus 1983; Lewin 1983–1984; McCreless 1982 and 1989; Bailey 1997; Darcy 1993; Grey 2008a; Whittall 2008; see Newcomb 1981 for a perspective on twentieth-century attempts at Wagnerian analysis). Indeed, it would be difficult to ignore the music of a successful opera composer whose music is so tightly harnessed to the text. And in spite of Schenker's harsh words about his musical syntax—evidenced above all by his inability to write a convincingly structured overture, and made all the more difficult to achieve by the banishment of word-repetition (Schenker [ca. 1907] 2005: 99–100)—Wagner's harmony is not only rich, but rich in ambiguity, and his thematic materials carry more weight than mere intervallic and rhythmic information.

Some motifs, moreover, openly defy the accusation of structural incohesiveness. The curse-motif in *Rheingold* (Music Example 11.3), for instance, is initially deployed in the form of a musical period, with the antecedent built upon arpeggiated half-diminished ninth chord F♯–A–C–E–G, the consequent resolving both its dissonances and its dominant harmony into the B minor, by which the earlier C–E–G triad is understood as a Neapolitan chord.

MUSIC EXAMPLE 11.3 Wagner, *Das Rheingold*, scene 4, Alberich's curse on the ring.

Similarly, the *Tarnhelm* motif, which Schenker readily admitted to be "a musical association of visionary beauty" (Schenker [ca. 1907] 2005: 100), is based on three chords for which no common tonality can be found; but Wagner embeds it in an antecedent-consequent pair (Music Example 11.4), in which it is not difficult to make out a near-textbook arpeggiation of a G sharp minor triad in the bass.

These suggestions prompt us to consider whether Wagner's music is more tonal—less un-Beethovenian—than Schenker would have had us believe, whether one can speak about a specifically harmonic design in his music dramas. Alfred Lorenz, writing around the same time that Schenker abandoned all hope of stemming the tide of serious discourse on nineteenth-century opera, had no difficulty developing Wagner's concept of "poetic-musical period" in such a way that each of Wagner's mature music dramas could be fit into a neat tonal-formal package; his own tetralogy (Lorenz 1924–1933) took barely a decade to complete. It is perhaps ironic, then, that in his seminal study of convention in Verdian opera, Powers (1987: 66) should lump the two together in the following way: "We [by which Powers does not mean himself] are unwittingly conditioned by the metaphor of ultimate organic unity that stems from Goethe and Wilhelm von Humboldt, whose music-theoretical heirs include both Lorenz and Schenker[,]" implying that the latter two named men were guilty of the same sort of

MUSIC EXAMPLE 11.4 Wagner, *Das Rheingold*, scene 4, "Tarnhelm" leitmotif.

crime. Schenker, for his part, kept his nose out of opera criticism after writing the *Niedergang* essay.

An exemplary expression of a more modern approach to Wagner is provided by Grey (2008a), whose explanation of leitmotif as the bearer of information, and as basis for thematic development, is complemented by a circumspect approach to using leitmotivic design as the key to unity in Wagnerian composition (Grey 2008b: 97). In his concise analysis of fifty-three measures from scene 4 of *Das Rheingold*, Grey describes Erda's appearance as "unusually self-contained" (for Wagner), even one that "suggests an operatic aria" (98). Without explicitly saying so, he characterizes its overall shape in terms that resonate with eighteenth-century form: an opening in C sharp minor, in which the earth-goddess introduces herself; a move to the relative major, in which she describes the work of her three daughters, the Norns; a period of harmonic instability, with a clear reference to the music of Alberich; and finally a return to C sharp minor, in which she repeats her admonition to Wotan about retaining possession of the ring. (It is hard not to think of the "Moonlight" Sonata here, even if Grey characterizes the return to C sharp as "no *da capo* but a peroration, or at any rate a culmination" [99].)

Crucial to the business of Wagnerian analysis, however, is the admission that the key of C sharp minor "appear[s]—like Erda herself—suddenly, without preparation"

(Grey 2008b: 99). This is the nub of Schenker's original objection—things that happen in the story are translated into musical material, without consideration for the specifically musical laws that govern their composition—and it sits uneasily beside his later explanation that Wagner has here "transform[ed] the free-standing aria into a 'poetic-musical period,' *integrated* within the larger, continuous *musical*-dramatic fabric" (Grey 2008a: 103; my emphasis). Where, in Mozart, the least sophisticated of all harmonic progressions might be used to effect a change of scene, for instance, the addition of a seventh to Leporello's F major "Notte giorno faticar" to set up Donna Anna's confrontation with Don Giovanni in the key of B flat (Schenker [ca. 1907] 2005: 86), no amount of theoretical wizardry can conjure a meaningful relationship between the C minor subdominant harmonies (iv, ii^6_5, and Neapolitan) supporting Wotan's furious expression of greed, on the one hand, and the C sharp minor tonality of Erda's warning. On the other hand, Schenker's summary dismissal of *Rheingold* on the basis of a page's worth of Fasolt's recitation in scene 2, is an equally selective case of analysis, whereby a whole work (and, for Schenker, an entire system of musical composition) stands or falls on a single example of a leitmotif—a transposition of the Valhalla theme—seeming to arise from nowhere (Schenker [1907] 2005: 100–101).

After Erda

For a detailed example of the analysis of music drama, I shall consider the passage in *Das Rheingold*, scene 4, in which Wotan agrees to pay the Giants in full to regain the goddess of youth, Freia. I have chosen this example because, on the one hand, it follows immediately from Erda's quasi-soliloquy and thus can be related to it, and, on the other, because it is so utterly different from it. Whereas Erda's solo stays in or close to the key of C sharp minor and is based mainly on a single idea and its "Neapolitan" inversion, the episode that follows is tonally unstable and makes use of an array of *Ring* motifs; it is also confrontational, with no fewer than five characters involved in the dialogue. Wotan, having been restrained by Fricka and Froh from following the earth goddess into the chasm into which she has disappeared, is caught in a moment of indecision, and Donner takes advantage of this by assuring the giants himself that they will get the ring. Freia's intercession on her own behalf slows down the tempo, giving Wotan further time for reflection; in the end he summons her to rejoin the gods, then throws the ring on the pile of gold in final payment for Valhalla. In an orchestral postlude, the gods take turns embracing Freia with joy.

Between Erda's disappearance and Donner's moment of resolution, a mere eight measures of transitional music elapse. The new section, which is marked at both ends by a substantial change in tempo and thematic material, is fifty-five measures long.

If Erda's entry was signaled by the most abrupt of harmonic progressions—the Neapolitan chord of C minor willfully reinvented as the tonic major of C sharp—her exit is followed by a progression that has at least some measure of tonal direction: as Wotan broods over her words of warning, and Fricka and Froh bar the way to her, the bass line pulls the harmony by chromatic steps, from G sharp (A flat) toward a dominant seventh chord built on E flat (see Music Example 11.5). In modern parlance, Erda's C sharp minor has morphed into the subdominant of A flat.

MUSIC EXAMPLE 11.5 Wagner, *Das Rheingold*, scene 4, seven measures before Donner's "Hört, ihr Riesen!"

WOTAN: "If I must [otherwise] worry and fear, then I must get hold of you and learn everything!"
FRICKA: "What do you intend, raging man?"
FROH: "Hold back, Wotan! Avoid the noble woman, [but] heed her word!"

Of course, a chromatic bass line is a conventional figure, even if its predictable course is mitigated by the angular melodic lines of Fricka's and Froh's intercessions. At the point of harmonic resolution, however, Wagner completely abandons the functional role of his dominant seventh, and instead makes it contrapuntal: $E\flat^{7}_{5}$–$^{6}_{4}$–$^{5}_{\natural 3}$–$\flat 3$. By lowering the third, he renounces all previous claims of E flat as a dominant; and while the status of that harmony is unclear, it underpins a statement of Erda's leitmotif.

By contrast, the chord progression that follows is as tonally purposeful as Donner's message is forthright (see Music Example 11.6). His offer of the gold to the giants is supported by a full cadential cycle in C flat major, I–vi–IV–ii–V$^{6}_{4}$ $^{5}_{3}$–I in measures 1–6, which is as clear an example of functional harmony as can be found anywhere in this opera. Freia's concerns about her companions' sincerity cast a cloud over the chord, adding an augmented sixth to C flat major (measures 7–8). Its temporary resolution to B♭ (as V$^{6}_{4}$ of E flat minor) is in turn reinterpreted as an inverted iv: this is clear enough from the V$^{(9)}_{7}$ chords of B flat minor in measures 10 and 13–14, which are themselves joined by a new augmented sixth. As nimble as Wagner's modulations may be, there is room for one more *non sequitur*: and it is again Erda's motif that articulates the harmonic rift, as attention shifts once more toward the brooding Wotan.

MUSIC EXAMPLE 11.6 Wagner, *Das Rheingold*, scene 4, "Hört, ihr Riesen!" mm. 1–18.

DONNER: "Giants: Return and listen! The gold will be given to you."
FREIA: "Dare I hope so? Do you [gods] think that Holda [= Freia] is really worth the ransom?

To resolve this harmonic impasse, Wagner simply returns to the beginning of the section, this time allowing Wotan himself to repeat the offer that had just been made by Donner (Music Example 11.7). A fanfare in C flat major introduces the Spear ("treaty") motif and a second cadential cycle, beginning in C flat major (I–V^{7}/IV–IV in measures

19–24) but modulating to E flat by the reinterpretation of IV as Neapolitan chord, is expanded internally by one deceptive cadence (vi in measure 29) and diverted from its expected resolution by another across measures 34–35: V–V^4_3/V, a favorite progression of the composer's.

MUSIC EXAMPLE 11.7 Wagner, *Das Rheingold*, scene 4, "Hört, ihr Riesen!" mm. 19–35.

WOTAN: "Come to me, Freia! You are freed. Now that you have been ransomed, bring us back our youth. Giants, take your ring!"

Motivically, Wotan's "Kehr' uns die Jugend zurück" brings together a number of crucial points in the opera, and may be seen as the key to the way in which *Das Rheingold* is held together. In scene 1, we heard Woglinde's "renunciation of love" motif (Music Example 11.8a), soon followed by Alberich's forswearing of love (Music Example 11.8b), with a recapitulation of the "renunciation" motif in the subsequent scene change. Scene 2 gives us the "golden apples" motif, first sung by Fafner, and Loge's paean to women ("Weibes Wonnne und Werth"), later followed by the "renunciation" motif in its original form (and key) and his harsh proclamation of the unwelcome news that Alberich had forsworn love and forged the ring (Music Example 11.8c).

MUSIC EXAMPLE 11.8a-d Wagner, *Das Rheingold*, Variants of the "Renunciation of Love" leitmotif.

This last motif, the minor-mode counterpart to "Weibes Wonne und Werth," becomes an important figure in the next two scene changes and is sung by Alberich after Wotan has torn the ring from his finger near the start of scene 4. When Wotan sings it himself as he pulls the ring from his own finger (Music Example 11.8d), the motif is effectively "neutralized," grounded in E flat major, the relative of the key in which it was first and most frequently heard. As can be seen from a comparison of first and last lines in Music Example 11.8, Wotan's gesture of submission not only recapitulates the "renunciation" theme in its original pitch structure but also pushes closer toward a perfect cadence; and by being set in the major, it suggests a happy ending. The twenty-one-measure instrumental postlude, in which the gods congratulate Freia on her safe return, gives Wagner further opportunity to confirm E flat as the intended goal, with a tonic pedal propping up the $V^7_{6\text{-}5}$ chord with which the episode concludes. The plot has, after all, come—nearly—full circle, with the gold stolen from the Rhinemaidens being paid to the Giants. And Wagner's music, appropriately, offers thematic recapitulation and temporary harmonic resolution.

What makes closure impossible is, of course, the further unfolding of the plot: the killing of Fasolt and, with it, the first effect of Alberich's curse upon the ring. Not only is E flat major abandoned, the "Renunciation" motif and all leitmotifs derived from stepwise motion are banished. The remaining music is dominated by motifs based on broken chords: those associated with Ring, the Curse, Donner's hammer, the rainbow leading to Valhalla, and Wotan's unsung flash of insight, which will become the Sword in the next evening's drama. In his magisterial study of the *Ring*, left incomplete at his death, Cooke (1979: 232–233) noted that the ransoming of Freia marks the point in the drama at which Wagner changed the sources of his plot. Viewed in terms of myth-setting, then, the ransoming of Freia is a concluding event; that Wagner has returned to the opening key of E flat major may not, after all, have been coincidental. The last part of the opera is thus tonally and thematically divorced from what has come just before it.

It would be wrong to extrapolate from this brief example that *Das Rheingold* is a work in E flat major, or even that it is a work that—like the *Ring* cycle as a whole, as some have argued—is marked by a progressive tonal shift from E flat to D flat. Nonetheless, the commonality of tone (or, in theoretical terminology, "pitch invariance") may be used as evidence underscoring the musical connection between the theft of the gold in the first scene of the opera and its last change of ownership in the last, and may be taken as evidence that tonality is a potent force in Wagnerian music drama. Ultimately, it cannot be denied that Wagner was fully aware of, or that he made full use of, the tonal system and its powers to move an audience. Indeed, his entire system of leitmotif construction and development is predicated upon the huge and almost limitlessly varied emotional forces residing in major and minor diatonicism and the chromaticism that binds them.

See also: Musical Dramaturgy, Versification, The Language of National Style, The German Libretto of the Early Nineteenth Century

Bibliography

Abbate, Carolyn, and Roger Parker. 1990. "Dismembering Mozart." *Cambridge Opera Journal* 2/2: 187–195.

——, eds. 1989a. *Analyzing Opera: Verdi and Wagner*. Berkeley and Los Angeles: University of California Press.

Abbate, Carolyn, and Roger Parker. 1989b. "Introduction: On Analyzing Opera." In Abbate and Parker 1989a, 1–24.

Allanbrook, Wye J. 1983. *Rhythmic Gesture in Mozart: 'Le nozze di Figaro' and 'Don Giovanni.'* Chicago: Chicago University Press.

Atlas, Allan. 1993. "Multivalence, Ambiguity and Non-Ambiguity: Puccini and the Polemicists." *Journal of the Royal Musical Association* 118/1: 73–93.

——. 1990–1991. "Crossed Stars and Crossed Tonal Areas in Puccini's *Madama Butterfly*." *19th-Century Music* 14/2: 186–196.

Bailey, Robert. 1977–1978. "The Structure of the *Ring* and its Evolution." *19th-Century Music* 1/1: 48–61.

Balthazar, Scott L. 1985 "Evolving Conventions in Italian Serious Opera: Scene Structure in the Works of Rossini, Bellini, Donizetti, and Verdi, 1810–1850." PhD diss., University of Pennsylvania.

Baragwanath, Nicholas. 2011. *The Italian Traditions and Puccini: Compositional Theory and Practice in Nineteenth-Century Opera*. Bloomington: Indiana University Press.

——. 2008. "Analytical Approaches to Selected Arias by Puccini." *Music Theory Online: A Journal of Criticism, Commentary, Research, and Scholarship*. 14/2. Online. Available: http://mtosmt.org/ (accessed August 13, 2012).

Basevi, Abramo. 1859. *Studio sulle opere di Giuseppe Verdi*. Florence: Tofani.

Brinkmann, Reinhold. 1972. "Drei der Fragen stell' ich mir frei'—Zur Wanderer-Szene im 1. Akt von Wagners Siegfried." *Jahrbuch des Staatlichen Institut für Musikforschung* 5: 120–162.

Brown, Matthew. 1989. "Isolde's Narrative: From *Hauptmotiv* to Tonal Model." In Abbate and Parker 1989a, 180–201.

Budden, Julian. 1992. *The Operas of Verdi*. 2nd ed., 3 vols. New York: Oxford University Press.

Burton, Deborah. 1995. "An Analysis of Puccini's *Tosca*: A Heuristic Approach to the Unifying Elements of the Opera." PhD diss., University of Michigan.

Carter, Tim. 1987. *W. A. Mozart: 'Le nozze di Figaro.'* Cambridge Opera Handbooks. Cambridge: Cambridge University Press.

Chusid, Martin. 1989. "The Tonality of *Rigoletto*." In Abbate and Parker 1989a, 241–261.

Cone, Edward T. 1982. "On the Road to *Otello*: Tonality and Structure in *Simon Boccanegra*." *Studi verdiani* 1: 72–98.

Cooke, Deryck. 1979. *I Saw the World End: A Study of Wagner's 'Ring.'* London: Oxford University Press.

Dahlhaus, Carl. 1983. "Tonalität und Form in Wagners *Ring des Nibelungen*." *Archiv für Musikwissenschaft* 40/3: 165–173.

——. 1980. *Between Romanticism and Modernism: Four Studies in the Music of the Later Nineteenth Century*, translated by Mary Whittall. Berkeley and Los Angeles: University of California Press.

——. 1979. *Richard Wagner's Music Dramas*. Cambridge: Cambridge University Press.

——. 1965. "Wagners Begriff der 'dichterisch-musikalischen Periode.'" In *Beiträge zur Geschichte der Musikanschauung im neunzehnten Jahrhundert*, edited by Walter Salmen, 169–187. Regensburg: Bosse.

Darcy, Warren. 1993. *Wagner's Das Rheingold*. Oxford: Clarendon Press.

Davis, Andrew. 2010. *Il trittico, Turandot, and Puccini's Late Style*. Bloomington: Indiana University Press.

Deathridge, John. 2008. *Wagner Beyond Good and Evil*. Berkeley and Los Angeles: University of California Press.

Dent, Edward J. [1913] 1947. *Mozart's Operas: A Critical Study*. 2nd ed. London: Oxford University Press.

Donington, Robert. 1963. *Wagner's "Ring" and Its Symbols: The Music and the Myth*. London: Faber and Faber.

Drabkin, William. 2005. "Schenker's 'Decline': an Introduction." *Music Analysis* 24/1–2: 3–31.

——. 1986. "The Musical Language of *La bohème*." In *Giacomo Puccini: La bohème*, edited by Arthur Groos and Roger Parker, 80–101. Cambridge Opera Handbooks. Cambridge: Cambridge University Press.

——. 1985. "Felix-Eberhard von Cube and the North-German Tradition of Schenkerism." *Proceedings of the Royal Musical Association* 111: 180–207.

Fairtile, Linda. 1995. "Giacomo Puccini's Operatic Revisions as Manifestations of His Compositional Priorities." PhD diss., New York University.

Giger, Andreas. 2008. *Verdi and the French Aesthetic: Verse, Stanza, and Melody in Nineteenth-Century Opera.* Cambridge: Cambridge University Press.

Gossett, Philip. 2006. *Divas and Scholars: Performing Italian Opera.* Chicago: University of Chicago Press.

——. 1989. "The Composition of *Ernani.*" In Abbate and Parker 1989a, 27–55.

——. 1970. "Gioachino Rossini and the Conventions of Composition." *Acta Musicologica* 42/1–2: 48–58.

Greenwald, Helen M. 1998. "Puccini, *Il tabarro*, and the Dilemma of Operatic Transposition." *Journal of the American Musicological Society* 51/3: 521–558.

——. 1991. "Dramatic Exposition and Musical Structure in Puccini's Operas." PhD diss., Graduate Center of the City University of New York.

Grey, Thomas S., ed. 2008a. *The Cambridge Companion to Wagner.* Cambridge: Cambridge University Press.

——. 2008b. "Leitmotif, Temporality, and Musical Design in the *Ring.*" In Grey 2008a, 85–114.

——. 1995. *Wagner's Musical Prose: Texts and Contexts.* Cambridge: Cambridge University Press.

Heartz, Daniel. 1980. "The Great Quartet in Mozart's *Idomeneo.*" *The Music Forum* 5: 233–256.

Hepokoski, James. 1989. "Verdi's Composition of *Otello*: The Act II Quartet." In Abbate and Parker 1989a, 125–149.

Huebner, Steven. 1992. "Lyric Form in *Ottocento* Opera." *Journal of the Royal Musical Association* 117/1: 123–147.

Kerman, Joseph. [1956] 1988. *Opera as Drama.* Rev. 2nd ed. Berkeley and Los Angeles: University of California Press.

——. 1980. "How We Got into Analysis, and How to Get Out." *Critical Inquiry* 7/2: 311–331.

——. 1978–1979. "Viewpoint." *19th-Century Music* 2/2: 186–191.

Lawton, David. 1989. "Tonal Systems in *Aida*, Act III." In Abbate and Parker 1989a, 262–275.

——. 1982. "Tonal Structure and Dramatic Action in *Rigoletto.*" *Verdi: Bollettino dell'istituto di studi verdiani* 3/9: 1559–1581.

Levarie, Siegmund. 1978–1979. "Key Relations in Verdi's *Un ballo in maschera.*" *19th-Century Music* 2/2: 143–147.

——. 1952. *Mozart's 'Le nozze di Figaro': A Critical Analysis.* Chicago: University of Chicago Press.

Lewin, David. 1983–1984. "Amfortas's Prayer to Titurel and the Role of D in *Parsifal*: The Tonal Spaces and the Drama of the Enharmonic C♭/B." *19th-Century Music* 7/3: 336–349.

Lorenz, Alfred. 1924–1933. *Das Geheimnis der Form bei Richard Wagner.* 4 vols. Berlin: Max Hesse.

McCreless, Patrick. 1989. "Schenker and the Norns." In Abbate and Parker 1989a, 276–297.

Marco, Guy. 1979–1980. "On Key Relations in Opera." *19th-Century Music* 3: 83–87.

Marvin, William M. 2003. "The Function of 'Rules' in *Die Meistersinger von Nürnberg.*" *Journal of Musicology* 20/3: 414–460.

Moreen, Robert A. 1975. "Integration of Text Forms and Musical Forms in Verdi's Early Operas." PhD diss., Princeton University.

Mozart, Wolfgang Amadeus. [1790] 1941. *Così fan tutte.* Score and piano arrangement, edited by Georg Schünemann and Kurt Soldan. Leipzig: Edition Peters.

Noske, Frits. [1977] 1990. *The Signifier and the Signified: Studies in the Operas of Mozart and Verdi.* Oxford: Clarendon Press.

Parker, Roger. 1989. "Motives and Recurring Themes in *Aida.*" In Abbate and Parker 1989a, 222–238.
——. 1981–1982. "Levels of Motivic Definition in Verdi's *Ernani.*" *19th-Century Music* 6/2: 141–150.
——, and Allan Atlas. 1992. "A Key for *Chi*? Tonal Areas in Puccini." *19th-Century Music* 15/3: 229–234.
——, and Matthew Brown. 1983. "Motivic and Tonal Interaction in Verdi's *Un ballo in maschera.*" *Journal of the American Musicological Society* 36/2: 243–265.
Petrobelli, Pierluigi. 1994. *Music in the Theater: Essays on Verdi and Other Composers*, with translations by Roger Parker. Princeton, NJ: Princeton University Press.
——. [1974] 1982. "Towards an Explanation of the Dramatic Structure of *Il trovatore.*" [Translated by William Drabkin.] *Music Analysis* 1/2: 129–141. Reprint. Petrobelli 1994, 100–112.
——. 1981. "Music in the Theatre—à propos of 'Aida'." In *Drama, Dance and Music*, edited by James Redmond, 9–42. Cambridge: Cambridge University Press. Reprint. Petrobelli 1994, 113–126.
Platoff, John. 1996. "Myths and Realities about Tonal Planning in Mozart's Operas." *Cambridge Opera Journal* 8/1: 3–15.
——. 1989. "Musical and Dramatic Structure in the Opera Buffa Finale." *The Journal of Musicology* 7/2: 191–230.
Poriss, Hilary. 2009. *Changing the Score: Arias, Prima Donnas, and the Authority of Performance.* New York: Oxford University Press.
Powers, Harold S. 1995. "One Halfstep at a Time: Tonal Transposition and 'Split Association' in Italian Opera." *Cambridge Opera Journal* 7/2: 135–164.
——. 1987. "'La solita forma' and 'the Uses of Convention.'" *Acta Musicologica* 59/1: 65–90.
Puffett, Derrick. 1992. "'Lass Er die Musi, wo sie ist': Pitch Specificity in Strauss." In *Richard Strauss and His World*, edited by Bryan Gilliam, 138–163. Princeton, NJ: Princeton University Press.
Ratner, Leonard. 1980. *Classic Music: Expression, Form, and Style.* New York: Schirmer.
Rothstein, William. 2008. "Common-tone Tonality in Italian Romantic Opera: An Introduction." *Music Theory Online: A Journal of Criticism, Commentary, Research, and Scholarship.* 14/1. Online. Available: http://mtosmt.org/ (accessed August 13, 2012).
Rushton, Julian. 1981. *W. A. Mozart: 'Don Giovanni.'* Cambridge Opera Handbooks. Cambridge: Cambridge University Press.
Sanguinetti, Giorgio. 2006. "Dramatic Functions of 'Tonal Field': The Second Duet 'Carlo–Élisabeth' in Verdi's *Don Carlos.*" In *Essays from the Third International Schenker Symposium*, edited by Allen Cadwallader and Jan Miyake, 81–102. Hildesheim: Georg Olms.
Schachter, Carl. 1987. "Analysis by Key: Another Look at Modulation." *Music Analysis* 6/3: 289–318.
Schenker, Heinrich. [ca. 1907] 2005. "The Decline of the Art of Composition: A Technical-Critical Study," edited and translated by William Drabkin. *Music Analysis* 24/1–2: 33–129.
——. [1926] 1996. "On Organicism in Sonata Form." *The Masterwork in Music*, vol. 2, edited by William Drabkin, 23–30. Cambridge: Cambridge University Press.
——. 1906. *Harmonielehre.* Stuttgart: J. G. Cott'asche Buchhandling Nachfolger.
Smart, Mary Ann. 2000. "In Praise of Convention: Formula and Experiment in Bellini's Self-Borrowings." *Journal of the American Musicological Society* 53/1: 25–68.
Tyson, Alan. 1977. "Yet Another 'Leonore' Overture?" *Music & Letters* 58/2: 192–203.

——. 1975. "The Problem of Beethoven's 'First' Leonore Overture." *Journal of the American Musicological Society* 28/2: 292–334.
Webster, James. 1991. "The Analysis of Mozart's Arias." In *Mozart Studies*, edited by Cliff Eisen, 101–199. Oxford: Clarendon Press.
——. 1990. "Mozart's Operas and the Myth of Musical Unity." *Cambridge Opera Journal* 2/2: 197–218.
——. 1987–1988. "To Understand Verdi and Wagner We Must Understand Mozart." *19th-Century Music* 11/2: 175–193.
Westernhagen, Curt von. 1976. *The Forging of the 'Ring': Richard Wagner's Composition Sketches for 'Der Ring Des Nibelungen,'* translated by Mary Whittall. Cambridge: Cambridge University Press.
Whittall, Arnold. 2008. "Criticism and Analysis: Current Perspectives." In Grey 2008a, 267–289.
——. 1983. "Wagner's Great Transition? From *Lohengrin* to *Das Rheingold*." *Music Analysis* 2/3: 269–280.
——. 1981. "The Music." In *Richard Wagner: 'Parsifal,'* edited by Lucy Beckett, 61–86. Cambridge Opera Handbooks. Cambridge: Cambridge University Press.

Humanism, Verisimilitude, and Voice

CHAPTER 12

OPERA BETWEEN THE ANCIENTS AND THE MODERNS

WENDY HELLER

> It has been the opinion of many, most Christian Queen, that the ancient Greeks and Romans, in representing their tragedies upon the stage, sang them throughout. But until now this noble manner of recitation has been neither revived nor (to my knowledge) even attempted by anyone, and I used to believe that this was due to the imperfection of the modern music, by far inferior to the ancient.[1]
>
> (Rinuccini, Preface to *L'Euridice*, 1600)

> The stingy narrow minds have corrupted the world, because, while they endeavor to wear ancient clothing, they render garments absurd with modern usage.[2]
>
> (Busenello, Preface to *Gli amori d'Apollo e di Dafne*, 1640)

From the moment in which Apollo used song to mourn Dafne's metamorphosis into a laurel tree, and Orfeo lamented the loss of Euridice, opera's links to the ancient world were forged in ways that—arguably—would never entirely be undone. Whether exploring the heroic deeds or misdeeds of the pagan gods, the adventures of epic heroes and the women they abandoned, or the vices and virtues of ancient monarchs, opera in the courts and public theaters of early modern Europe derived much of its inspiration from the expressive goals of ancient theater and the scope for imagination provided by the Greek and Roman world. Indeed, the comments of Rinuccini and Busenello cited above underscore the complex relationship between ancient and modern that was a factor in the creation of opera in the humanist epicenter of Florence and during its subsequent flowering, first in Venice, and then throughout early modern Europe.

On the surface, Rinuccini and Busenello have much in common. After all, they both collaborated with Claudio Monteverdi for two of his great masterpieces—Rinuccini for

Arianna and Busenello for *L'incoronazione di Poppea*. Yet, the prefaces to these works also remind us of their different perspectives, and reveal the great distance that opera traversed in only four decades. Rinuccini, who addresses his comments to Maria de' Medici, writes with an irrepressible optimism and pride on the innovative enterprise of opera. Believing that modern music is inferior to that of the ancients, Rinuccini is supremely confident that the method that had been undertaken by himself and Jacopo Peri in *La Dafne* as a simple test (*semplice prova*) succeeds not only in pleasing the nobility in all lands, but such esteemed listeners as the Grand Duchess and the Cardinals Dal Monte and Montalto. It scarcely matters that his opera ends happily, unlike the treatments of the story by Ovid and Virgil, in which Orpheus is ripped to shreds. Monteverdi, of course, takes a different approach to the problem by leaving two endings: the one of 1607, in which the Bacchantes are poised to dismember Orfeo, and the second one preserved in the 1609 score, in which Apollo, in a distinctly Christian, anti-pagan gesture, descends to escort his son to the heavens.

Busenello directs his comments not to a specific dedicatee, but rather to the reader of the Venetian libretto. As part of the *argomento*, the Preface serves not only to provide an introduction to the plot and its sources, but also to negotiate the distance between those sources and the drama about to unfold (Heller 2007). To be sure, some of those readers were noble—it would be incorrect to imagine that "public" opera in Venice was not designed at least in part for the upper classes—but the audience in the Venetian theaters was not exclusively so, and the success or failure of a work depended more upon its general popularity rather than its reception by a select group of elite listeners (on audiences in Venetian opera, see Rosand 1991 and Glixon and Glixon 2006). Busenello's tone in some ways reflects the changing relationship between librettist and audience, as well as the current status of sung drama. No longer do we sense the confidence that marked Rinuccini's enthusiastic endorsement of the new style. By the 1640s, when sung drama was no longer a novelty, Busenello dwells not on the superiority of ancient to modern music or the novelty of his own invention, but instead expresses disdain for those who slavishly adhere to ancient models. In so doing, he is not merely attempting to justify his distance from the ancients and the liberties that he takes in his librettos. He places himself squarely, along with his contemporaries, in the midst of the battle between the ancient and moderns.

The battle between ancients and moderns may have seemed particularly timely in the mid-seventeenth century, while the genre was still relatively new. But it would, in fact, remain relevant for librettists, composers, audiences, and critics over the next several hundred years. Even as opera takes its inspiration from antiquity to create dynamic accounts of an imagined past, by its very nature, it often falls short of the idealistic goals that we ascribe to its creators, even as reformers sought to recapture those ideals. Operatic retellings of ancient history, from Monteverdi's *Arianna* to Strauss's *Ariadne auf Naxos*, inevitably suffer from an artificiality and inauthenticity that has long discomfited critics.

In this essay, I reconsider operatic humanism and the conflicting strategies that composers, librettists, and producers used as they sought both to emulate the expressive goals of the ancients and to reinvent the past in their own image on the operatic stage. I propose that we go beyond the assumption that the genre's engagement with the philosophy, literature, and aesthetic values of the ancient world should be understood primarily in the context of the earliest operas or in the various bouts of classicizing and purifying reforms that often rendered works more distant from their classical models. Instead, I suggest that the problem is not that opera so often fails to conform to the humanistic ideals of its creators, but rather that critics have held the genre to a standard that actually never existed. Or to put it another way: opera came into its own in the seventeenth century as notions of humanism were in flux, when the pure reverence for the legacy of the ancients was not so much eroded as enriched with skepticism, humor, and irony—an appreciation of the darker side of Antiquity, even as the art and science of the modern world beckoned. Indeed, as this chapter will argue, it is this tension between the ancients and the moderns—so integral to opera from its inception—that has been one source of the genre's expressive power.

I begin my study with what I term irreverent "fantasies" about perceptions of the ancient world that shaped the thinking of early librettists, composers, and humanists. I then examine the battle between the ancients and moderns, as expressed by leading thinkers in late-sixteenth- and early-seventeenth-century Italy, that waged even as opera was in its infancy. Thereafter, I consider opera's habit of staging anachronism, where I show both the dramatic and musical consequences of integrating classical myth with modern writings (such as the Renaissance epics), a move deemed necessary to create a pleasurable drama, even as the rules of Aristotle were playfully transgressed. The chapter concludes with a commentary on several twentieth-century works that follow the paths of opera's originators by exploring modernity through the adaptation of ancient texts, similarly enriched with pleasurable anachronisms.

Fantasizing about the Ancients

> When the ancient musician sang any poem whatever, he first considered very diligently the character of the person speaking: his age, his sex, with whom he was speaking, and the effect he sought to produce by this means; and these conceptions, previously clothed by the poet in chosen words suited to such a need, the musician then expressed in the tone, and with the accents and gestures, the quantity and quality of sound, and the rhythm appropriate to the action and to such a person.
>
> (Galilei [1581] 1998: 466)

It is not surprising that scholars today, like their counterparts in the late sixteenth century, would be intrigued by Vincenzo Galilei's view of the ancient musician, who collaborated with the poet to create the perfect union between word and tone that "diligently" embodied the essence of the character represented. It may well be the power of this particular fantasy that has discouraged scholars from fully appreciating the ambivalence of opera's debt to the ancient world. Opera history, for better or worse, is in many respects a victim of its own mythology: a genre born of noble parents in a noble setting, arising from the desire of elite Florentine intellectuals, themselves inspired by humanistic fervor, to create a form of music that emulated the expressive power of Greek tragedy (standard writings on the birth of opera in Florence include Palisca 1989 and Pirrotta 1968). The story, too, is one of disappointment—as the genre, more often than not, due to literary abuses, the demands of singers, the desire for spectacle, profit, or generic impurity, fell short of expectations (see, for example, Freeman 1981 and Kerman 1988, both of whom echo the criticism of eighteenth-century opera reformers; see also Heller 1998b). This sense of disenchantment has left its mark on the historiography of early opera. For Gary Tomlinson (1999), the special nature of the word-tone relationship forged by Monteverdi and Rinuccini in Arianna's lament is the "climax of Renaissance humanism in music" (Tomlinson 1999: 24). The "natural alliance" between word and tone embodied in the mythic beings who sang in so many early operas celebrated the "higher orders of expression that are a supersensible part of the natural order itself." This is a feature of the genre that Tomlinson claims disappears in early modern opera, when the link to the supersensible was broken, and representation—through the musical expansion of the aria and the establishment of conventions—became the name of the game (Tomlinson 1999: 27). The order, harmony, and balance of the mythological cosmos conceived by such mythographers as Conti (1568) and Cartari (1556) provide Tomlinson with the perfect model of how the ancient myth might be relevant to late-Renaissance readers and viewers (Tomlinson 1999: 29–33). The fact that the gods might represent "the forces of nature and God" implies that the use of ancient myth in opera and musical theater during this fragile moment of humanist triumph has a pure and noble purpose (Tomlinson 1999: 30). "Such thinking," Tomlinson observes, "refutes the modern tendency to view the late Renaissance revival of ancient myth as little more than the pastime of idle metaphor-mongers and disengaged antiquarians" (1999: 30).

But perhaps there is a middle ground between the perfectly ordered cosmos and the pejorative view of "idle metaphor-mongers and disengaged antiquarians." The mythographers may have, as Tomlinson observes, "revealed what they considered to be truth in myths (30)," but they also had fun. The syntheses of ancient and Renaissance writings by Conti and Cartari are pleasurable reads, full of humor, irony, and contradictory allegories, and they became cherished reference sources for many subsequent artists and patrons with antiquarian interests (see Cartari 1556, which was republished numerous times throughout the remainder of the sixteenth and well into the seventeenth century; Conti 1568; Boccaccio [1360; 1472] 2011, a source for Cartari that provided iconographical and programmatic inspiration for poetry and art, as well as opera, well into the eighteenth century; see also Palma 1977). As Monteverdi and his colleagues explored the implications of the *seconda prattica*, both vocal and instrumental virtuosity became a tool of musical expression, and stagecraft became an increasingly valued component in musical theater, it is not surprising that some of the reverence toward the ancients began to erode. Truths, it turns out, aren't as entertaining as fictions.

Giuseppe Gerbino's (2009) cogent analysis of early opera's complex rapport with both pastoral and ancient tragedy demonstrates the extent to which the ancient genres—and particularly Aristotelian notions about tragedy—were contested even as opera was suffering its birth pangs. By the late sixteenth century, during the heyday of the pastoral, even while Rinuccini was formulating his first librettos, commentators were increasingly aware that tragedy had "outlived its utility" (Gerbino 2009: 396). "We are dealing," Gerbino observes, "with a vision of theater in which the Aristotelian theory of catharsis had been replaced by the Petrarchist belief in the healing power of poetry against the afflictions of love" (380). Thus, the earliest operas are necessarily mired in a theoretical-practical contradiction, inspired by the "declared humanistic intent to resurrect the spirit of Greek tragedy," as Gerbino puts it; yet the producers of opera chose for their primary model a genre for which there was no model in antiquity—the pastoral (381). The result is what he refers to as an irresolvable generic "dimorphism" in early opera: a tension between pastoral and tragedy in which the use of ancient myth as content—thus providing a genuine link to antiquity—is used to inspire "tragic pleasure," which is itself part of the Petrarchan legacy. Opera, as we will know, would find many new ways to inspire this "tragic pleasure," most notably with dying heroines (Gerbino 2009: 389–399).

Robert C. Ketterer provides yet another twist on the conventional views about opera's origins, first by reminding us that early opera was in fact "Roman and not Greek," and noting that we should not necessarily "take the generic and cultural claims for opera at face value" (Ketterer 2009: 3). A broader approach," Ketterer notes, "might suggest that early opera was "Hellenistic, not Classical [...] Imperial, not Democratic." Aristotle, he reminds us, did not in fact live in the era of the democratic *polis* that produced the tragedies that he so revered, and so for him, these dramas, too, were "classics" (Ketterer 2009: 3). Like Gerbino, Ketterer also calls our attention to the gap between theory and content in the formation of early opera. The stated aesthetic premise may be Greek, but the chosen subject matter, as he noted, was often indebted to Romans, or at least inflected by their influence: Greek myths were transmitted through Ovid, the pastoral poetry of Theocritus reshaped by Virgil, while the Greek-born Plutarch, a Roman citizen, proved to be one of the most important authorities on diverse aspects of the classical tradition (Ketterer 2009: 5).

Antichi e Moderni

If Gerbino and Ketterer are right, we might then more fruitfully regard opera in the early decades of the seventeenth century less as a purely humanistic enterprise than as a contested genre, mired from the outset in the Italian version of the battle between ancient and moderns that anticipated the better known "Querelle" involving Charles Perrault, Joachim Du Bellay, and Nicolas Boileau that would influence French opera during its crucial formative period (Fumaroli 2001: 12–18; Baron 1959: 3–22; and also

Guaragnella 2003. Rosand [2007: 329] invokes the battle of the ancient and moderns in relation to opera; for a discussion of issues raised by this, see Heller 2010b: 373–375). The debates about the ancients and moderns, as Hans Baron (1959) demonstrates, were an integral part of the Italian Renaissance; even the early Quattrocento writers such as Leon Bautista Alberti, who dedicated an Italian (Tuscan) manuscript of his treatise *De Pictura* (1435–1436) to the architect Brunelleschi, acknowledged that such skills "may not have been understood at all or known by the Ancients" (Baron 1959: 19). It is precisely this kind of thinking that led many at Northern Italian universities to champion the use of the vernacular rather than Latin as an appropriate language for high culture. Indeed, in his introduction to his edition of *De Pictura*, Rocco Sinisgalli hypothesizes that Alberti might have written it first in Tuscan before translating it into Latin (see Alberti [1435] 2011).

The Italian version of the quarrel was not a wholesale rejection of the principles of the ancients, but rather a reconstitution of their uses in the context of an increased awareness of the present—of "modern times"—as a period that is sufficiently glorious (after the period of so-called darkness from the fall of the Roman Empire to the Renaissance) to merit comparison with that of the ancients (Burke 1976 and Fumaroli 2001). For some, the championing of modernity was a reaction against a widespread tendency to view the world in decline—cosmically, morally, politically, culturally, and economically (Burke 1976)—an antidote to a prevailing pessimism. In so doing, the modernists advocated (against pagan culture) and in favor of the ennobling effect of Christianity on poetry and the arts.

Thus it is not uncommon to find early seventeenth-century writers Paolo Beni and Alessandro Tassoni championing Ariosto and Tasso over Homer and Virgil. In Beni's view, Venice is the "new and famous Athens," with worthy poets of her own, and he views Tasso as "a noble and graceful poet" who goes beyond all the ornaments and beauty of Homer and Virgil, "with a magnitude and majesty of ideas, a grandness and nobility of style, and a joy and sweetness of thinking that surmounts every human belief and genius"[3] (Beni [1607] 1612: 2; see also Diffley 1988; Tassoni ([1620] 1986: 841–934). Beni was among the first to use the word "modern" in this context, and he deemed Tasso and Ariosto worthy of comparison with their ancient models, Virgil and Homer, having "an original synthesis, entirely unknown in antiquity, but between grandeur and sweetness, force and grace, generosity and elegance"[4] (Fumaroli 2001: 73).

Tassoni takes the modernist position in his encyclopedic comparison of virtually all aspects of ancient and modern life, including not only poetry and music, but also clothing, architecture, art, jewelry, and warfare, while nonetheless retaining respect for ancient practices. Thus, for instance, he acknowledges the purity of ancient tragedy (chapter 14), unequaled by the moderns, and also applauds the "third species neither tragic nor comic, that is the pastorale," invented by the moderns, which he then divides into comic, tragic, and sylvan (*boscareccia*), exemplified by Guarini's *Il pastor fido* and Dante's *Divina Commedia*, termed a heroic satire (*eroisatirico*) (Tassoni [1620] 1986: 869). Tassoni situates his defense of modern music in the context of criticisms proffered by Plutarch, who—not unlike Galilei—compared the music of his own time unfavorably with that enjoyed by his predecessors. For Tassoni, both ancients and moderns are justified in complaining about music that "wounds the ear with an abstract, incomprehensible sweetness, as if many birds were singing together"[5] ([1620] 1986: 919). The ancients have no advantage, since there are modern musicians who do not confuse or break words but "seek to express themselves sweetly in such a way that their sense and harmony together goes to wound the hearts of the listeners"[6] ([1620] 1986: 919). He also proposes that "our Tuscan language," with its abundance of vowels at the beginning and at the end, is sweeter and smoother to pronounce than Greek or Latin and is thus better suited to music. He makes the case for the superiority of modern instrumental music by citing new instruments, such as the cornetto and the harpsichord ([1620] 1986: 919–920).

The comparisons between ancients and moderns are even more pointed in two volumes penned by Secondo Lancellotti (1623), an Olivetan monk, on the theme of "HOGGIdì" ("Today"). Lancellotti, who writes with a decidedly satirical tone, is not so much interested in glorifying the present as answering pedants—the "HOGGIdiani," who in their pessimism decry the present and bemoan the absence of Virgils, Homers, and Aristotles. Like Tassoni, who softened criticisms of modern music by reminding readers that the ancients complained of abuses in their own times, Lancellotti observes that the calamities and disasters of today were equally common in the past, and he argues persuasively in favor of modern innovations in both literature and music, even dedicating one of his two volumes to Urban VIII, the Barberini pope who would take the modernist stance in his patronage of the arts and sciences.

In a chapter entitled "That it is not now a new thing today that good literary men are often little recognized, neglected, and stepped upon," Lancellotti praises *tragicommedia* and the mixing of genres, citing dozens of examples of modern poetry[7] ([1623] 1637: XXVII: 309–339). His enthusiastic defense of modern music in the second volume (1636) echoes Tassoni, but while Tassoni praises only Gesualdo, Lancellotti singles out a host of musicians and singers associated with the *seconda prattica:* Monteverdi, Grandi, and Agazzari, and the exquisite singing of [Francesco] Rasi and Giulio Romano [Caccini][8] (Lancellotti 1636: XIV: 267–270). Intriguingly, Lancellotti recounts having had a discussion with Monteverdi in Venice some ten years ago about the "HOGGIdì." He recalls only that Monteverdi said something to him against the "HOGGIdiani" but since he didn't write it down at the time, it has all since vanished[9] (Lancellotti 1636: XIV: 276–277). (For further discussion on the ancients and moderns, see Holzer 1992, 1993; see also Carter 2006.)

For many writers during this period, including opera librettists, the fascination seems to have been with the juxtaposition of the ancient and modern eras. That is not to say that authors were no longer interested in emulating ancient practices; but those who advocated the modernist position often used satire—like Lancellotti—to underscore the difference between contemporary and classical authors. Thus, Tassoni's *La secchia rapita* (1622), a sort of farcical epic poem in which the "stolen bucket" plays the role of Helen of Troy in a fictional war between Modena and Bologna, reprinted numerous times in Italian, English, and French well into the nineteenth century, may have cast doubt on the singular authority of Homer and Virgil; yet his fantasy would have been meaningless without the ancient epic as an object of parody (Tassoni [1622] 1962). Giambattista Marino's controversial poem *L'Adone* showed how ancient myths could simultaneously be valued and exploited for their sensual properties, a point that would be critical not only in opera, but in all the arts (Marino [1623] 2007). Traiano Boccalini's *Ragguagli di Parnaso* (1612–1614, and 1669 [English translation]), a series of satirical news reports from Parnassus, demonstrated the consequences of enlisting ancient authorities to comment on the present (see Hendrix 1995; Fumaroli 2001: 29–32). The world of Apollo and his muses represented by Boccalini is not an idyllic intellectual or artistic paradise; rather, it was the setting for dialogues between ancient and modern writers and artists in a satirical vein. This is the realm, as Fumaroli notes, in which Seneca and Tacitus are "witnesses for the liberty of spirit under the terror of the Roman empire" (Fumaroli 2001: 44); where Petrarch can do battle with Martial over a presumed insult (Boccalini 1669: Century I/Advertisement 82: 139); and even the famous courtesan Thais could be admitted into Parnassus after she explained to Apollo the good that she might do for his court (Boccalini 1669: Century II/Advertisement 36: 239).

Wrinkles in Time: Anachronistic Encounters

It is not a coincidence that questions concerning the relative value of ancient literature and its attendant rules came to the fore on the Italian peninsula during the early decades of the seventeenth century, the period between the first operatic experiments in Florence and Mantua and the composition and performance of larger scale music dramas in Florence, Rome, and especially Venice. Indeed, in the theater, the battle between the ancients and the moderns was also played out through the juxtaposition of ancient precepts with modern fantasy. It is particularly revealing, for example, that Giulio Strozzi, who began his career by collaborating with Monteverdi long before the opening of the public opera theaters in Venice, named his 1620 play *Il natal d'amore* an "anacronismo," which he explains as follows:

> An anachronism means an error made in time. This error is more frequent among painters, because very often in a single painting they put together a variety of characters that flourish in many diverse times. I did the same in *The Birth of Love*, but I added there unity of action with its knot, and formed a tragedy of mankind from many stories according to my fancy. Thus, in all that I am distant from the rules and common laws, I erred in proper study in order to create a spectacle [*stravaganza*]. Plato in his dialogues created anachronisms and Virgil with his celebrated Aeneas and Dido showed us that it was not a sin to do this. If novelty will be pleasing, I will enjoy having satisfied the tastes of today, which is no small thing.[10] (Strozzi 1621: dedication)

Strozzi thus distances himself from the rules, specifically using anachronisms to provide his audience with novelty. Strozzi accomplishes this by bringing together in a single story a host of mythological characters defeated by love, all of whom would have been known to audiences through their individual narratives, including Hercules, Deineira, Ulysses, Penelope, Diana, and Orpheus.

Although this was a spoken play—only the last scene was set to music by Giovanni Rovetta—Strozzi's description of the work's relationship to ancient literature is echoed by numerous librettists writing for the Venetian stage, such as Busenello, who followed Strozzi's example and justifies his own flights of fancy in contriving for Dido and Aeneas to meet in his *La Didone* (1641) by noting Virgil's own anachronism in the *Aeneid*. In the libretto to Cavalli's lost opera *La Torilda* (1648), Pietro Paolo Bissari defends current theatrical practices (choruses, machines, dance, etc.) by citing a host of ancient precedents (on Bissari's use of ancient practices, see Heller 2003 and 2010a). Even a somewhat conservative Giacomo Badoaro rehearsed the ancient-modern controversy in the famous letter that prefaces the libretto to *Ulisse Errante*:

> The ancients have prescribed rules for many things, because they held themselves to the glory that the world should halt with their precepts, and [that] perhaps the ability to invent would be taken away from men of subsequent centuries [...]. Unhappy century, if the footprints of those from the past should force our feet to an unalterable path; one could indeed call this the century of the blind who don't know [anything] unless they are being guided [...].[11] (Badoaro 1644: 4–5)

Some writers, in fact, seem to be unsure as to where to position themselves in the battle. With the libretto for another lost opera of Cavalli's, *Amore innamorato* (1642), which we will consider in more detail below, the problem is exacerbated by the fact that it was a collaborative effort involving several members of the Venetian Accademia degli Incogniti: The poetry was written by Pietro Michiele, revised by Giovanni Fusconi, and the plot was suggested by Incogniti leader Giovanni Francesco Busenello (Michiele, 1642: prefatory note). Librettist Fusconi deals with the problem by assuring his readers that the "fable follows all the good rules taught by the masters": That is, it finishes in a single day, has only one plot, no extraneous incidents, and follows established customs[12] (Fusconi 1642: 7). As Ellen Rosand (1991: 47) has pointed out, this confident assertion is then immediately undermined by the claim that it is pointless to defend something that the ancient authors were also careless about. The present age, Fusconi notes, "is made up of private opinions and interests and thus does not believe in any rules except those of whim and passion"[13] (Fusconi 1642: 7).

All of these remarks are a manifestation of an urge to view the present as progress through comparison with the past. In order to define itself, this new style of entertainment not only needed to invoke ancient texts, rules, and procedure, but also the special kind of dissonance that arose from juxtaposing the ancient and the modern. Like Tassoni with the stolen bucket, librettists and composers continued to look to the *content* of Antiquity as a point of departure, while exploring discontinuities and disjunctions that ultimately provided much of the musical and dramatic expressivity. Once the topics for opera expanded beyond what Gerbino describes as the pastoral-tragedy dyad established by Rinuccini in the early years of the genre to include epic and history as well as mythology, opportunities for playing with temporal and generic discrepancies increased.

In some librettos, the play with anachronism occurs primarily on the level of myth, where the librettists, not unlike Strozzi in *Il natal d'amore*, altered well-known narratives by commingling characters who would normally never meet. Thus, for instance, although Cavalli's *Gli amori di Apollo e di Dafne* (1640) relies upon the same sources as Rinuccini's *La Dafne*, Busenello's libretto not only contradicts Aristotelian unities by bringing in multiple plots (a point that he justifies by citing *Il pastor fido* as an example), but also contrives for the conclusion of the opera to turn on an anachronism: As the thwarted romance between Apollo and Daphne comes to its inevitable conclusion with the nymph's transformation into a laurel tree, Busenello interjects into the story the goat-god Pan, who—though belonging to an earlier episode in Ovid's *Metamorphoses*—commiserated with Apollo about the women they loved, both of whom had been transformed into plants. Here the friction is not so much between ancient and modern as between two remarkably similar narratives; the fact that Pan, mourning the loss of Syrinx, wanders mistakenly from his own narrative into Apollo's story calls attention to the fragility of the genre itself. The tragic poignancy of Apollo's lament over Daphne's metamorphosis is thus transformed into a moment of homosocial bonding, albeit with a touch of humor—and a bit of social commentary on female sexuality that was undoubtedly indebted to contemporary Venetian sensibilities (Heller 2013a).

The librettist Giacinto Cicognini uses a similar strategy in one of the most popular operas of the period, *Giasone* (1649), also set by Francesco Cavalli. Although the Argonaut Jason was to meet Hypsipyle and abandon her long before encountering the sorceress Medea, Cicognini's libretto distorts the chronology and contrives for the two women competing for Jason's love to confront one another, thereby exploiting the coincidence implicit in Ovid's *Heroides*, where Jason is the only hero to receive letters from two abandoned women. When Hypsipyle's (Isifile's) final lament actually does the seemingly impossible—that is, persuade Jason to return to her—opera truly turns the classical world on its head (Heller 2013b).

In many instances, the clash between ancient and modern in terms of musical style is most notable in the treatment of invented characters that were added to the classical framework. This can be seen in three operas dealing with the Trojan War: Cavalli's *La Didone* (libretto by Busenello), Francesco Sacrati's *La finta pazza* (libretto by Giulio Strozzi), and Monteverdi's *Il ritorno d'Ulisse in patria* (libretto by Giacomo Badoaro), in which ostensibly minor characters are given expansive musical and dramatic roles that transform ancient courts into "modern" performance space, with appropriately up-to-date musical styles. In Cavalli's and Busenello's *La Didone*, the three Carthaginian ladies sing an imitative madrigal to criticize Dido's lack of chastity (Heller 1998). Thus, in both style and substance their utterances are distinct from those of the true Virgilian characters, while providing a modern perspective on them. The madrigals sung by the suitors in Monteverdi's *Il ritorno d'Ulisse in patria* are part of the entertainment in Ulisse's palace; Penelope's challenge is not only to resist their pleas for love, but also to withstand the pressure of their seductive musical style.

The play with anachronism is decidedly self-reflexive, exemplified by the appearance of a singing Eunuch in Sacrati's *La finta pazza* (Heller 2006; see also Rosand 1991: 110–120). Borrowing from Statius's *Achilleid*, the plot focuses on Achilles, who spent his youth, disguised as a woman, among the daughters of Lycomedes, where he fell in love with and impregnated Deidamia. Once Ulysses tricks him into revealing his true identity, Achilles' newfound enthusiasm for war causes him to abandon Deidamia, who then spends much of the opera feigning madness in an attempt to regain his love. Strozzi brilliantly integrates the Eunuch into the narrative by having him perform a canzonetta as part of the entertainment for Ulysses and his companions, providing a wry commentary on his castration and—by extension—Achilles' own somewhat fragile masculinity.

Another startling incongruity occurs in the aforementioned *Amore innamorato*, based on the tale of Cupid and Psyche from Apuleius's second-century novel *Metamorphoses*, or the *Golden Ass*, known, most notably, in Raphael's magnificent frescoes for the Palazzo Farnesina in Rome and his frescoes in the Palazzo Tè in Mantua (on the reception of Apuleius, see Accardo 2002; Ussia 2001; Carver 2007; see also Cavicchioli 2002). The novel, with its numerous episodes and changes of locale, is indeed an unruly narrative for a drama, scarcely following the Aristotelian unities, despite the use of the classic five-act structure. In this instance, the triumvirate of librettists from the Venetian Accademia degli Incogniti disrupt the familiar mythological narrative of the union between Cupid and Psyche (and the latter's eventual triumph over the jealousy of Venus) with the appearance of another familiar character from seventeenth-century life: the prostitute past her prime, referred to simply as "La Ruffiana," who attempts to convert others to the profession. Her Act II, scene 6, aria, in which she boasts of her power, would certainly have reminded viewers of a host of pseudo-pornographic literature on prostitution, such as Aretino's *Raggionamenti* and Ferrante Pallavicino's *La retorica della puttane* (Pallavicino [1642] 1992 and Heller 2004: 15–16, 994). I quote the text here:

LA RUFFIANA:	RUFFIAN WOMAN
Chi hà di me vanto maggiore ne la terra! Io trionfo d'ogni core, l'honestà per me s'attera. e mi glorio sol con l'arte, di rapir Venere a Marte.	Who has the advantage of me on earth? I triumph over every heart, the honest are drawn to me. I boast only with the art of stealing Venus for Mars.
Benché vecchia con l'occhiale veggo il bello, Per me solo Amor ha l'ale campidoglio m'è il bordello. E potrei far che Diana, divenisse cortegiana.	Although an old woman with eyeglasses I spot the handsome man, For me alone love has wings The brothel is my capital, And I could even turn Diana Into a courtesan
In me piovono i tesori degli avari, son ministri degli amori, Per me rubbam gli usurari. Le mie voci sono incanti, che consolano gli amanti.	The treasures of the greedy Are showered on me, They are ministers of love, Robbing moneylenders for my sake. My utterances are the spells that console lovers.

In Act IV, she will even try to lure Psyche out of the Underworld with the promise of more lovers. The improbable and anachronistic introduction of a Venetian-style courtesan thus allowed viewers to interpret the well-known tale in the context of contemporary courtesan culture.

The story of Psiche (Psyche) and Cupid, while central to *Amore innamorato*, is the interloper in another opera that is arguably even more indebted to the modern side of the debate: Francesco Cavalli's *La virtù de' strali d'amore* (1642), with a libretto by Giovanni Faustini (1642). Faustini may well be the most "modern" of all the librettists under discussion here, as he was best known for newly invented plots, although his most famous work, *La Calisto*, reveals a sophisticated knowledge of ancient sources (Heller 2004: 178–194; on Faustini, see Rosand 1991: 169–175). Closely bound to the practical side of opera production through his impresario brother, Faustini left no clues about his aesthetic concerns in his libretto prefaces. Yet, some of the librettist's approach to his craft can be gleaned both from the fact that he named his work a *tragicomica*—thus invoking genre hybridity best known from Guarini—and from the opera's prologue. Whereas Monteverdi gave prominence to Music in the prologue to *L'Orfeo* and Rinuccini gave voice to Ovid and Tragedy in *La Dafne* and *Euridice*, respectively, the protagonist of this prologue is Caprice: "I am he who, more lofty than anyone else, presumes to fly above every trite custom with unfamiliar ways and thought"[14] (Faustini 1642: 6). Caprice goes on to note that his *tragicomica* depends upon contrast: "I am Caprice, and from me you will see a work on this stage full of accidents at first tragic and later happy. Melpomene and Thalia were my muses, there were will be happenings with mortals, gods, and infernal creatures, mixed, yes, but not confused"[15] (Faustini 1642: 6).

Caprice does not underestimate his role, for the complex plot of *La virtù de' strali d'Amore* draws from both early modern and ancient sources and combines them in novel ways. The central narrative is indebted to the Italian Renaissance epics, in particular Ariosto's *Orlando furioso* and Tasso's *Gerusalemme liberata*, two "modern" works that figured prominently in the late-sixteenth-century debates between the ancients and moderns. The plot has numerous correspondences with the Renaissance chivalric tradition: there are two princes in pursuit of Cleria, a maiden who, like Ariosto's Angelica, is at first impervious to love; there is an evil sorceress, like Armida and Alcina, who bewitches a knight in an enchanted forest; there is also a good sorceress who heals a wounded knight and a jilted lover, Erabea, who spends much of the opera in male disguise. Faustini even goes so far as to name one of his characters Dalinda, a clear nod to the Ariodante episode in *Orlando furioso* (on the relatively few explicit uses of Ariosto in seventeenth-century opera, see Rosand 1984).

Yet, once again, the work is articulated by an intrusion from another time, in this case the realm of the gods. Act II opens, unexpectedly, with a celebration of the marriage of Cupid and Psiche, interrupted by Mars, who demands that Cupid use his power to resolve the human drama that had taken place in Act I—that is, to make Cleria desire the prince Pallante, who pursues her. Cupid, who resents Mars's interference, descends to earth determined to punish the unhappy Pallante still further. Angrily cursing womankind, Cupid falls asleep in the forest, only to be spied upon by the abandoned Erabea

MUSIC EXAMPLE 12.1 Francesco Cavalli, *La virtù de' strali d'amore*, Act III, scene 26, trio for Amore, Venere, and Psiche, I-Vnm, It. IV, 373 [=9897], f, 119 r-v.

(still in male disguise) lamenting her own sad fate. The result of this clash between the world of the gods and humans—and the ancient and modern sources—is remarkably violent. In an elegant reversal of conventional power structures, Erabea, in a symbolic act of sexual violence, penetrates Cupid with one of his own arrows.

Everything resolves happily for the various lovers in the penultimate scene, and Cupid and Psiche once again celebrate their immortal union; yet the contested relationship between the earthly and mythological realms is made explicit in the *lieto fine*. Rather than ending the opera with the usual love duet, Faustini and Cavalli provide us with a trio sung by three intertwined treble voices—Cupid, Psiche, and Venus—who (remarkable in a Cavalli opera) sing without continuo support, thus transporting listeners from the mortal world of conventional couplings to the undeniably sensual realm of the goddess of love (Music Example 12.1).

In so doing, Faustini and Cavalli strike a victory for the moderns: The gods may have the final word in this instance, but it is the juxtaposition of these two worlds—the capricious melding of classic myth with Renaissance epic—that provided the requisite dramatic and affective contrasts in *La virtù* that were so integral to seventeenth-century opera.

The Legacy of the Debate

We are thus left with a different view of opera's relationship to the ancient world. This is not a genre that tried to emulate the ancients, only to fail repeatedly in the attempt to maintain high standards. Rather, during its formative years, opera rode the bumpy waves of *seicento* humanism, a time in which the classics inspired neither reverence nor fidelity but playful irreverence. In so doing, opera played an active role in the lively contemporary discourse on modernity.

The question became particularly vexing in seventeenth-century France, where it was not only classical tragedy that was held up as a model but also an entirely modern creation—the tragedies of Racine, prompting critics both then and now to justify *tragédie en musique* in relation to ancient practices. Buford Norman notes that the Quinault-Lully operas "share the Aristotelian goals of Racinian tragedy (imitation of the passions and catharsis through rather formal and stylized means) and many of its principles (order, restraint, verisimilitude, necessity, propriety, and the dominance of the written word) but take a rather different approach" (Norman 2001: 4). This different approach, however, required the kind of modifications that were necessarily part of the modern side of the equation: a relaxing of the unities of time and place, the staging of supernatural or tragic events, the insertion of musical celebrations including airs and choruses, dances, and the prologues with their invocations of Louis XIV or seventeenth-century France—in other words, the same kinds of anachronisms that were also so vital to the Italian tradition. Thus, for instance, in Lully's *Alceste* (1674), which precipitated the first round of the French battle, Quinault added characters, plot lines, and *divertissements* to Euripides' *Alcestis*. While the alterations may have been less drastic than in the first Italian opera based on the *Alcestis* (Heller 2005), the inevitable anachronisms—such as the celebration in the Tuileries Garden during the Prologue—were no less disconcerting to adherents of a pure notion of classicism. Norman suggests that the tension between ancients and moderns apparent in the debates between Boileau and Perrault might be managed best by expanding our definitions of the classical rules:

> [...] it makes less sense to follow Boileau and view opera as an exception to classical rules and restraint than it does to see classicism as a temporary narrowing and focusing that occurs within a broader, more varied esthetic framework that privileges heroism, pleasure, spectacle, and the accommodation to the taste of the literate public. (Norman 2001: 4)

An essential part of that modernity, as Catherine Kintzler has shown, is the embrace of the *merveilleux*, a requirement for verisimilitude in the mythological realm (Kintzler 1991). Thus, if opera is going to represent the ancient world, it must by its very nature contradict the rules of verisimilitude established by ancient commentators.

Over the next few centuries, opera would frequently find itself on this contested ground, championed by members of both camps, often failing to satisfy either. Indeed, when seen through the lens of the debates between the ancients and moderns, the perennial bouts of operatic reform seem less to be about purifying the genre than smoothing over the tensions that were there at its very beginnings. In Metastasio's first opera libretto, *Didone abbandonata* (1724), for instance, the poet does not hesitate to add characters to the story of Dido and Aeneas, such as Araspe, the confidant of Iarba who loves Didone's sister Silene; but they are integrated into a narrative that—with the exception of the final scene—arguably owes far less to Virgil than any of its seventeenth-century predecessors. Even the famous dedication to *Alceste* (1769), in which Gluck (speaking for Calzabigi) expresses the desire to "restrict music to its true office of serving the poetry," results in a work that is closer to the ideals of Racine than Euripides (Gluck [1769] 1998).

Finally, we might note that it is not until the twentieth century that composers and librettists seem particularly eager to exploit and even celebrate the anachronisms and generic impurity that were integral to the Baroque. Indeed, it is paradoxical that the one opera that perhaps most celebrates anachronism—Richard Strauss and Hugo von Hofmannsthal's *Ariadne auf Naxos* (1912; rev. 1916)—should have been originally conceived as an entertainment within Molière's *Le bourgeois gentilhomme*, thus bringing ancient myth to life through a decidedly Baroque lens. Although the Molière was soon dropped—the opera was too long and unworkable in that form—composer and librettist would nonetheless retain the notion of Ariadne as an opera within the opera, replete with what Hofmannsthal regarded as a kind of ironic tension between Ariadne's mythic realm and that of the *commedia* characters (Frisch 2005: 220). Hofmannsthal describes this succinctly:

> What to divine souls is a real miracle is to the earth-bound nature of Zerbinetta just a love-affair. She sees in Ariadne's experience the only things she can see: the exchange of an old lover for a new one. And so these spiritual worlds are in the end ironically brought together in the only way in which they can be brought together: in non-comprehension. (Hofmannsthal and Strauss 1961: 94)

Notably, Hofmannsthal began crafting the libretto even as the Ariadne myth was used by several authors for yet another round of neo-classicizing reforms (Frisch 2005: 221–222). Zerbinetta's attempts to influence the lamenting Ariadne are not unlike the efforts of the Ruffiana woman in *Amore innamorato* to persuade Psyche to take up prostitution. In both instances, the mixing of genres and styles that openly defies the Aristotelian unities is staged as characters from the mythic and human worlds encounter one another in improbable, awkward ways that call attention to the artificiality of the whole undertaking.

Hans Werner Henze's *The Bassarids* (1966), with libretto by W. H. Auden and Chester Kallman, is yet another opera in which notions about modernity are explored through the adaption of an ancient text. The opera is based on *The Bacchae*, Euripides' grim final tragedy, in which Pentheus, having offended Dionysius by refusing to worship him, is torn apart by the wild Bacchantes, the women in his thrall. In the tragic ending of the play, Pentheus' mother Agave learns that the head she proudly displays to her father-in-law Cadmus is that of her son Pentheus.

The Bassarids premiered in 1966, at a time in which the counterculture's endorsement of a host of freedoms inspired a renewed interested in *The Bacchae*. Part of the complexity of the dialogue between the ancients and moderns embedded in *The Bassarids* has to do with the rather differing attitudes of the composer and librettists toward the material, in particular the moral question at the core of Euripides' play: To what extent is Dionysus a god to be revered or rejected? Like the modernists of the seventeenth century, who celebrated the triumph of Christianity over pagan culture, Auden and Kallman sought to redeem Euripides by redeeming Pentheus:

> We, as authors in the 20th century, writing for a public of the 20th century, felt it necessary that our Pentheus—while showing the same foolishness of method as in Euripides [...] should have a nobler motive than mere arrogance for his attempt. We have therefore made him into a platonic idealist, who has rejected the ancient polytheism in favor of a philosophical monism, involving the worship of a single, transcendental Good, which men can know only by controlling their passions [...]. (Auden and Kallman 1974: 834)

Pentheus's failure was self-repression—his inability to recognize or control the Dionysian elements in his own makeup (Morra 2007: 38–39).

Henze, on the other hand, saw the conflict in arguably simpler terms that resonated with his own increasingly Marxist orientation:

> The basic conflict in *The Bassarids* is between social repression and sexual liberation of the individual. It shows people as individuals breaking out of social context, as a road to freedom, as the intoxicating liberation of people who suddenly discover themselves, who release the Dionysus within themselves. (Henze 1982: 156)

That is not to say the Christian message isn't present; Dionysus takes on the role of Christ, while Mary is represented by the transfigured Semele (Thyone), the mother of Dionysus—both of whom are celebrated in the opera's ecstatic conclusion.

What is perhaps most interesting for the purposes of this chapter is the extent to which these differing interpretations of Euripides resulted in two quite different encounters between the ancients and moderns, albeit within a single opera. For Kallman and Auden, the history of opera and the use of anachronism provided a means to control Dionysus. As with *Ariadne auf Naxos*, the librettists initially placed Euripides in a distancing, Baroque frame that juxtaposed comic and serious elements. At their insistence, the first editions of the opera and libretto were subtitled "Opera Seria with Intermezzo in One Act," whereby Auden and Kallman "sought to combine the spirit of the ancient Greek satyr-drama with that of the seventeenth and eighteenth centuries, following the Baroque custom of inserting the two parts of a comic intermezzo after the first and second acts of a serious opera" (Ewans 2007: 166). Later replaced with an orchestral interlude, the Intermezzo—which depicted the dream of the sexually repressed Pentheus—was even set in the eighteenth century in a Rococo theater with neoclassical statuary (Ewans 2007: 166). Instead of trying to be neoclassical (they in fact condemned what they called "Gluck-y Greekiness"), they used a carefully constructed series of costumes. The chorus, for instance, begins in pseudo-Greek dress but by the end of the opera is attired entirely in modern dress, with more than a touch of the 1960s counterculture, thus presenting a "historical survey of religion and society" (Ewans 2007: 169), whereby the moderns had become appropriately enlightened.

For Henze, writing in a post-Bergian idiom, the invocation of music's past operated somewhat differently. Despite Auden and Kallman's invocation of *opera seria*, Henze chose a different historical model—the four-movement symphonies of Mozart and Beethoven, which "surrounded, subsumed, and ultimately transcended the historical dimensions that Auden and Kallman inserted into their libretto" (Ewans 2007: 172).

Nonetheless, we might hear an echo of opera's past in *The Bassarids*: the treatment of the chorus in the beginning reminds one of Gluck's *Alceste*, not to mention the initial fanfare that recalls the toccata that opens Monteverdi's *L'Orfeo*. This may be no coincidence; for with the triumph of Dionysus and the dismemberment of Pentheus, Auden, Kallman, and Henze—despite opposing approaches and differing political stances—bring us back to the origins of opera, and the conflict that Monteverdi and Striggio surely faced when deciding whether or not to let Orpheus face the violent anger of the Bacchantes or ascend to the heavens with his father Apollo. In the perennial battle between the ancients and the moderns, opera always stands on precarious ground.

See also: Verisimilitude, Voice, The Concept of Opera

Notes

1. "È stata opinione di molti, Cristanissima Regina, che gli Greci and Romani cantassero sulle scene le tragedie intere; ma sì nobil maniera di recitare nonché rinnovata, ma ne pur, che io sappia, fin qui era stata tentata da alcuna, e ciò mi credev'io per difetto della musica moderna di gran lunga all'antica inferiore."
2. "Gli'ingegni Stitici hanno corotto il Mondo, perché mentre si studia di portar l'abito antico, si rendono le vesti ridicole all'usanza moderna."
3. "Che a dirne il vero non può leggersi questo leggiadro e nobil poeta, che non sì riconosca in lui, oltre a tutti gli ornamenti e bellezze di Homero e Virgilio, un'ampiezza e maestà di concetti, una grandezza e nobiltà di stile, una felicità e soavità di ragionare, laqual sormonta ogni credenza & ingegno humano."
4. "Les deux grandes épopées italiannes ont opéré une synthèse très originale, entièrement inconnue de l'Antiquité, entre grandeur et doucer, force et grâce, génerosité et élégance."
5. "…che con suono in distinto ferisce l'orecchie d'una cotal dolcezza in astratto, che non s'intende, come sarebbe quella di multi uccelli, che cantassero unitamente."
6. "…ma cercano d'esprimerle dolcemente in guisa, che'l senso, e l'armonia loro vadano giustamente a ferire i cuori degli ascoltanti."
7. "Che non è cosa punto nuova d'HOGGIdì che Buoni e Letterari Huomoni siano bene spesso poco riconosciuti, anzi negletti, e calpestati."
8. "Che nelle Discipline Matematiche, cioè Geometria, Musica, Aritmetica, e Astrologia non sono mancati HOGGIdì gl'Ingegni."
9. "Fui dieci anni sono, cominciano a passarmi per la mente questo pensiero dell'HOGGIdì in Venetia da Claudio Monteverdi per discorrere seco come con Musico celebre de' nostri

tempi, e Maestro della Capella di San Marco e dissemi non sò che contra gli Hoggidiani, ma perché non lo posi in iscritto, suanì via il tutto."

10. Al delicato Lettore: "Significa Anacronismo uno error preso nel tempo. Questo error è molto frequente apresso i pittori, perché ben spesso in un sol quadro mettono insieme varii personaggi, che in tempi molto diversi fiorirono. Io fò il medesimo nel Natal d'Amore, ma vi hò aggiunta l'unità dell'azzione col suo nodo, e hò formata da molte favole a mio capriccio la tragedia del genere humano. Anzi in tutto quello, che mi sono allontanato dalle regole, e leggi communi, ho errato a bello studio per formare una stravaganze. Platone ne' suoi dialogi fece de gli Anacronismi, e Virgilio con quel celebre di Enea, e di Didone ci mostrò, che non era peccato il saperne fare. Se la novità piacerà, goderò di haver sodisfatto a gli humori di hoggidì, che non è poco."
11. "Hanno gli antichi prescritte in molte cose le regole, perché si tenevano a gloria, che il mondo si fermasse ne' loro precetti, e forse agli uomini del venturo secolo restasse levata la facoltà dell'inventare [. . .] . Infelice secolo, se l'orme dei passati obligassero il nostro piede al un'inalterabil camino; ben potrebbe chiamarsi questa l'età de' ciechi, che non sanno se non essere guidati."
12. A chi legge: "[. . . .] questa favola ha tutte le buone regole insegnate da' Maestri; che termina co'l giro d'un giorno, ò poco più; che è un'attione sola; che non ha accidente, che sia incompatibile; e che non travia punto dal costume [. . .]."
13. "[. . .] Il presente secolo composto d'opinioni, e d'interessi non crede ad altre regole, che a quelle del capriccio, e della passione."
14. "Io son colui, che più' d'ogn'altro altero / Di sorvolar presume / Ogni trito costume / Con modi insusitati, e co'l pensiero."
15. "Il Capriccio son' io, di me vedrete / Opra sù questa Scena / D'accidenti ripiena/E d'attioni pria meste, e poscia liete. / Melpemone, e Thalia furo mie Muse, / Saran con le mortali, / Le Divine, e l'Infernali / Cose in lei miste sì, ma non confuse."

Bibliography

Accardo, Pasquale J. 2002. *The Metamorphosis of Apuleius: Cupid and Psyche, Beauty and the Beast, King Kong.* Madison, NJ: Fairleigh Dickinson University Press.

Alberti, Leon Battista. [1435] 2011. *On Painting: A New Translation and Critical Edition*, edited and translated by Rocco Sinisgalli. Cambridge: Cambridge University Press.

Auden, W. H., and Chester Kallman. 1974. "Euripides for Today." *Musical Times* 115: 833–834.

Badoaro, Giacomo. 1644. *Ulisse errante.* Venice: Pinelli.

Baron, Hans. 1959. "The *Querelle* of the Ancients and Moderns." *Journal of the History of Ideas* 20/1: 3–22.

Beni, Paolo. [1607] 1612. *Comparatione di Torquato Tasso con Omero e Virgilio, insieme con la difesa dell'Ariosto paragonato ad Omero.* Padua: Martini.

Bissari, Pietro Paolo. 1662a. *Antiopa giustificata, drama guerriero. Attione seconda de gli applausi fatti all nascita dell'altezza Ser.ma Di Massimiliano Emanuele* [. . .]. Munich: Giovanni Jekelino.

——. 1662b. *Fedra incoronata, Drama Regio Musicale. Attione prima de gli applausi fatti alla nascita dell'altezza Ser.ma Di Massimiliano Emanuele* [. . .]. Munich: Giovanni Jekelino.

——. 1662c. *Medea Vendicativa, drama di foco. Attione terza de gli applausi fatti per la nascita dell'altezza Ser.ma Di Massimiliano Emanuele* [. . .]. Munich: Giovanni Jekelino.

Boccaccio, Giovanni. [ca. 1360; 1472] 2011. *Genealogia deorum gentillum*, edited and translated by Jon Solomon. *The I Tatti Renaissance Library*. Vol. 46. Cambridge, MA: Harvard University Press.

Boccalini, Traiano. 1669. *I ragguagli di Parnasso or, Advertisements from Parnassus in Two Centuries, with the Politick Touchstone. Written Originally in Italian by That Famous Traiano Boccalini and Now Put into English by the Right Honourable Henry Earl of Monmouth*. 2nd ed. London: Dring, Starkey, and Bassett.

——. 1612–1614. *De' ragguagli di Parnaso*. Venice: Farri.

Burke, Peter. 1976. "Tradition and Experience: The Idea of Decline from Bruni to Gibbon." *Daedalus* 105/3: 137–152.

Busenello, Giovanni Francesco. [1641] 1656. *La Didone*. Venice: Giuliani.

——. [1640] 1656. *Gli amori d'Apollo e di Dafne*. Venice: Giuliani.

Cartari, Vincenzo. 1556. *Le imagini con la spositione de i dei de gli antichi*. Venice: Marcolini.

Carter, Tim. 2006. "Italy, *iii*: 1600–1640." In *European Music, 1520–1540*, edited by James Haar, 91–100. Woodbridge, UK, and Rochester, NY: The Boydell Press.

Carver, Robert H. F. 2007. *The Protean Ass: The Metamorphoses of Apuleius from Antiquity to the Renaissance*. New York: Oxford University Press.

Cavicchioli, Sonio. 2002. *The Tale of Cupid and Psyche: An Illustrated History*. New York: Braziller.

Cecconi, Annamaria. 1999. "Medea vs Orfeo. Alla ricerca di un metà della potenza della musici al feminili." In *Orfeo, il mito, la musica. Percorsi tra musicologica e antropologia musicale*, edited by Stefano A. E. Leoni, 127–144. Turin: Trauben.

Conti, Natale. 1568. *Mythologiae sive explicationeum fabularum libri decem*. Venice: Comin Da Trino.

Diffley, Paul. 1988. *Paolo Beni: A Biographical and Critical Study*. New York: Oxford University Press.

Ewans, Michael. 2007. *Opera from the Greek: Studies in the Poetics of Appropriation*. Aldershot, UK: Ashgate, 2007.

Faustini, Giovanni. 1642. *La virtù de' strali d'amore*. Venice: Miloto.

Freeman, Robert. 1981. *Opera without Drama: Currents of Change in Italian Opera, 1675–1725*. Ann Arbor, MI: UMI Research Press.

Frisch, Walter. 2005. *German Modernism: Music and the Arts*. Berkeley and Los Angeles: University of California Press, 2005.

Fumaroli, Marc. 2001. "Les abeilles et les araignées." In *La Querelle des Anciens et des Modernes (XVIIe–XVIIIe siècles)*, edited and annotated by Anne-Marie Lecoq, 52–91. Paris: Gallimard.

Fusconi, Giovanni Battista. 1642. *Amore innamorato*. Venice: Surian.

Galilei, Vincenzo. [1581] 1998. *Discorso della musica antica, e della moderna*. Florence: Marescotti. "Dialogue on Ancient and Modern Music." [Edited by Gary Tomlinson.] In *Strunk's Source Readings in Music History*, edited by Leo Treitler, rev. ed., 462–467. New York: W. W. Norton.

Gerbino, Giuseppe. 2009. *Music and the Myth of Arcadia in Renaissance Italy*. Cambridge: Cambridge University Press.

Glixon, Beth L., and Jonathan E. 2006. *Inventing the Business of Opera: The Impresario and His World in Seventeenth-Century Venice*. AMS Studies in Music. New York: Oxford University Press.

Gluck, Christoph Willibald. 1769. *Alceste*. Vienna: Nella Stamparia Aulica di Giovanni Tomaso de Trattnern.

——. [1769] 1998. "Dedication for *Alceste*." [Edited by Wye J. Allanbrook.] In *Strunk's Source Readings in Music History*, edited by Leo Treitler, rev. ed., 932–934. New York: W. W. Norton.

Guaragnella, Pasquale. 2003. *Tra antichi e moderni: Morale e retorica nel Seicento Italiano*. Lecce: Argo.

Heller, Wendy. 2013a. "Daphne's Dilemma: Desire as Metamorphosis in Early Modern Opera." In *Structures of Feeling in Seventeenth-Century Expressive Culture*, edited by Susan McClary, 175–208. Toronto: University of Toronto Press.

——. 2013b. "Hypsipyle, Medea, and the Ovidian Imagination: Taming the Epic Hero in Cavalli's *Giasone*." In *Cavalli's Operas on the Modern Stage: Manuscript, Edition, Production*, edited by Ellen Rosand, 167–187. Aldershot, UK: Ashgate.

——. 2010a. "Phaedra's Handmaiden: Tragedy as Comedy and Spectacle in Seventeenth-Century Opera." In *Ancient Drama in Music for the Modern Stage*, edited by Peter Brown and Suzana Ograjensek, 67–84. Cambridge: Cambridge University Press.

——. 2010b. Review of Rosand 2007. *Journal of the American Musicological Society* 63/2: 367–377.

——. 2009. "Loving Theseus: The Spectacle of Feminine Passions on the Munich Stage (1662)." *Basler Jahrbuch für Historische Musikpraxis* 33: 197–201.

——. 2007. "Venice's Mythic Empires: Truth and Verisimilitude in Venetian Opera." In *Opera and Society in Italy and France from Monteverdi to Bourdieu*, edited by Victoria Johnson, Jane F. Fulcher, and Thomas Ertmann, 34–52. Cambridge: Cambridge University Press.

——. 2006. "The Castrato as Man: Trajectories from the Seventeenth Century." *British Journal for Eighteenth-Century Studies* 28/3: 307–321.

——. 2004. *Emblems of Eloquence: Opera and Women's Voices in Seventeenth-Century Venice*. Berkeley and Los Angeles: University of California Press.

——. 2003. "Dancing Desire on the Venetian Stage." *Cambridge Opera Journal* 15/3: 281–295.

——. 1998a. "*O castità bugiarda*: Dido, Opera, and the Convention of Abandonment." In *A Woman Scorn'd: The Myth of Dido—Queen of Carthage*, edited by Michael Burden, 169–225. London: Faber and Faber.

——. 1998b. "Reforming Achilles: Gender, Opera Seria, and the Rhetoric of the Enlightened Hero." *Early Music* 26/4: 526–581.

Hendrix, Harold. 1995. *Traiano Boccalini fra erudizione e polemica: ricerche sulla fortuna e bibliografia critica*. Florence: Olschki.

Henze, Hans Werner. 1982. *Music and Politics: Collected Writings 1953–81*, translated by Peter Labanyi. New York: Cornell University Press.

Holzer, Robert. 1993. "Monteverdi the Modernist: The Composer in Conversation with Secondo Lancellotti." Paper presented at the Annual Meeting of the Society of Seventeenth-Century Music, St. Louis, Missouri.

——. 1992. "'Sono d'altro garbo... le canzonette che si cantono oggi': Pietro della Valle on Music and Modernity in the Seventeenth Century." *Studi musicali* 22: 253–306.

Kerman, Joseph. [1956] 1988. *Opera and Drama*. Rev. ed. Berkeley and Los Angeles: University of California Press.

Ketterer, Robert C. 2009. *Ancient Rome in Early Opera*. Urbana and Chicago: University of Illinois Press.

——. 2003. "Why Early Opera Is Roman and Not Greek." *Cambridge Opera Journal* 15/1: 1–14.

Kintzler, Catherine. 1991. *Poétique de l'opéra français, de Corneille à Rousseau*. Paris: Minerve.

Lancellotti, Secondo. [1636] 1656. *L'Hoggidì overo gl'ingegni non inferioria' passati... Parte Seconda*. Venice: Guerigli.

——. [1623]. 1637. *L'Hoggidì overo Il Mondo non peggior ne più calamitoso del passato.* Venice: Guerigli.

Marino, Giambattista. [1623] 2007. *L'Adone*. In *Opere di Giambattista Marino*, edited by Marzio Piero and Luana Salvarani. Lavis: La Finestra.

Michiele, Pietro. 1642. *Rime... parte prime*. Venice: Guerigli.

Palisca, Claude. 1989. *The Florentine Camerata: Documentary Studies and Translations*. New Haven: Yale University Press.

Morra, Irene. 2007. *Twentieth-Century British Authors and the Rise of Opera in Britain.* Aldershot, UK: Ashgate.

Norman, Buford. 2001. *Touched by the Graces: The Libretti of Philippe Quinault in the Context of French Classicism*. Birmingham, AL: Summa Publications, 2001.

Pallavacino, Ferrante [1642] 1992. *La retorica delle puttane*, edited by Laura Coci. Parma: Fondazione Pietro Bembo.

Palma, Marco. 1977. "Cartari Vincenzo." *Dizionario Bibliografico degli Italiani*, edited by Alberti Ghisalberti. Vol. 20. Online. Available: http://www.treccani.it/Portale/elements/categoriesItems.jsp?pathFile=/sites/default/BancaDati/Dizionario_Biografico_degli_Italiani/VOL20/DIZIONARIO_BIOGRAFICO_DEGLI_ITALIANI_vol20_010585.xml (accessed February 6, 2014).

Pirrotta, Nino. 1968. "Early Opera and Aria." In *New Looks in Italian Opera: Essays in Honor of Donald J. Grout*, edited by William W. Austin, 237–280. Ithaca, NY: Cornell University Press.

Rinuccini, Ottavio. 1600. *L'Euridice d'Ottavio Rinuccini rappresentata nello sponsalitio della christianiss. Regina di Francia, e di Navarra*. Florence: Giunti.

Rosand, Ellen. 2007. *Monteverdi's Last Operas: A Venetian Trilogy*. Berkeley and Los Angeles: University of California Press.

——. 1991. *Opera in Seventeenth-Century Venice: The Creation of a Genre*. Berkeley and Los Angeles: University of California Press.

——. 1984. "Orlando in Seicento Venice: The Road Not Taken." In *Opera & Vivaldi*, edited by Michael Collins and Elise Kirk, 87–104. Austin: University of Texas Press.

Strozzi, Giulio. 1621. *Natal d'amore. Anacronismo. Seconda impressione*. Venice: Alberti.

Tassoni, Alessandro. [1620] 1986. *Pensieri e scritti preparatori*, edited by Pietro Puliatti. Book 10: 841–934. Modena: Panini.

——. [1622] 1962. *La secchia rapita*, edited by Pietro Papini. Florence: Sansoni.

Tomlinson, Gary. 1999. *Metaphysical Song: An Essay on Opera*. Princeton, NJ: Princeton University Press.

Ussia, Salvatore. 2001. *Amore innamorato: riscritture poetiche delle novelle di Amore e Psiche: secoli XV–XVII*. Vercelli: Mercurio.

CHAPTER 13

VERISIMILITUDE

THOMAS BETZWIESER

TRANSLATED BY JEFF TAPIA

Paradoxes of Medial Interplay

In Alain Resnais's 1997 film *On connaît la chanson*, a "comédie humaine" set in Paris, the dramatis personae suddenly and without warning begin to sing in the middle of their conversation. Their singing is not motivated in any way, nor is what they sing—French chansons—at all coherent. Song fragments pop up in the dialogue, only to disappear just as suddenly. However, the characters do not "really" sing—that is, with their own voices. Instead, they lip-synch (more or less in time) to preexisting, voiced-over music. The characters' body language remains largely unaffected by their singing; their gestures and movements are hardly any different than when speaking. And yet their singing and the music radically alter the cinematic fiction and, thereby, the reality of the plot. But they alter the audience's perception to an even greater degree, since viewers are left to wonder how long the characters in the film will continue speaking. In other words, the spectators can no longer assume that spoken dialogue will be the film's sole medium of communication. They are similarly jarred by the fact that the music is rendered only in fragments, instead of in complete set pieces as in other film musicals. Nonetheless, the musical numbers increasingly become extraterritorial realms for the audience during the course of the film, islands within a "sea" of everyday dialogue. By repeated viewings, the perception of the audience changes in that it begins regarding these musical islands selectively, similar to waiting for specific music in an opera. The chansons become fixed points within the diegesis, even though they are nothing more than a mere continuation of the dialogue.

With this in mind, one could interpret *On connaît la chanson* as a discourse on the functionality of music within the medium of film. It is, however, more than that. The film also touches upon central theoretical issues regarding opera, especially the aspect of the verisimilitude of singing. This question was *the* subject of aesthetic debates on the opera from the birth of the genre in the seventeenth century to well into the twentieth century. Ernst Krenek would even ask, though tongue-in-cheek, at the outset of the 1930s: "Why do people sing in opera on occasions where in real life they would only speak?" (Krenek [1932] 1958: 132–133). For Resnais's film the question initially seems easy to answer. The "people" change the medium just like in a *Singspiel*, especially when the spoken word is no longer deemed sufficient to express their emotions. This change in medium of the characters' speech could thus be justified as the dramaturgic foil to a music genre, in this case the dialogue opera. Even though such an explanation is based upon a (historically existent) theory, it still falls short. With the abrupt change in the forms of expression, Resnais questions not merely the verisimilitude of singing, but rather the interplay of the individual medium—speaking, singing, music—specifically with regard to their verisimilitude within the diegesis of film. The fact, however, that the chansons in Resnais's film never appear as genuinely diegetic music turns the singing into a second form of expression that is on par with the dialogue itself. In this way, the French director addresses the functionality of music as a whole—not just for the cinema, but for all forms of theater that incorporate music. For just as in opera, the aspect of plausibility (and implausibility) within *On connaît la chanson* becomes, one could say, its guiding principle. The questions which thereby arise are ultimately almost more relevant for opera than for cinema. Does a dialogue become a monologue once music comes into play? Do the interlocutors hear the music of their counterparts, or do they "react" only to the text? Does communication take place through, or rather within, the music? Is the music's expression unified (emotionally), or does it vary?

Significantly, it is precisely the oscillation between speaking and singing that is so unsettling about Resnais's film, thus perpetuating the problem of verisimilitude. Jacques Demy's *Les parapluies de Cherbourg* (1964) is a different matter altogether. In Demy's film, the characters sing continuously, even during realistic scenes. What makes this constellation so strange is the fact that the musical texture is presented in a completely different fashion than in traditional film musicals. Here, the composer (Michel Legrand) maintains his music largely in a recitative tone that could not be further from the spirit of standard Hollywood set pieces. Viewers are both bewildered and irritated when characters speak in recitative, regardless of whether they are in an auto repair shop or a clothing store. (One could rightly call *Les parapluies de Cherbourg* a veritable film opera.) After getting over this initial shock, the audience then has the same expectations as in an opera. Accepting that the characters' dialogue will be entirely sung, viewers will no longer question the fact—as opposed to viewers of the Resnais film. By no longer calling the verisimilitude of the communication into question, the audience signs a "contract" with the director regarding the form of communication. This new reality is thereby perceived to be completely coherent—in spite of the singing. In addition, the viewers very quickly learn that they have to give their undivided attention to the singing, otherwise they will not be able to follow the story. In other words, they are forced to accept the unusual mode of communication, unless they want to leave the theater dissatisfied. By accepting this artificial musical art form, the audience comes to the "reasonable" conclusion that it should regard the singing as speaking. In this way, the viewers transform the cinematic fiction into a "world of opera," complete with operatic "inhabitants" (Cone 1989), even though it is a fundamentally different art form.

Cinema provides an ideal example to shape our discussion of verisimilitude, especially since film is capable of representing all possible varieties of reality: historical and social, objective and subjective, public and private. Furthermore, song and music are not—except for in their diegetic function in the so-called film musical—automatically part of a re-created reality. As a medium of communication, song is both as implausible for today's moviegoers as recitative was in Italy in 1600 and as unusual as a sung tragedy *en musique* was in France in 1670. In some respects, the deliberate use of music in contemporary cinema is able to produce an aesthetic constellation similar to the new medium of sung theater that once opposed the traditional model of spoken drama. It can thus hardly be a coincidence that discussions of this problem have been taking place in the "home" of drama and film theory, namely, in French aesthetics. It was above all the models of French drama theory that were concerned with the issue of verisimilitude and illusion, and they have also become the focal point for considerations of opera. That being said, the following discussion will also be oriented along these theories, not simply to trace the persistence of this discussion in the sense of a *longue durée*, but rather to outline the strategies associated with the problem of verisimilitude that have been developed over time.

Examining the problem of verisimilitude in opera at the outset of the twenty-first century seems anachronistic, considering that this aesthetic category, so important for so long, has largely lost its validity in contemporary opera. If anything, it may still possess a certain degree of legitimacy for operas based on literature or historical events, such as Adams's *Nixon in China* (1987). Otherwise, it is obsolete. No one any longer will seriously question an opera such as *Das Mädchen mit den Schwefelhölzern* (1997) by Helmut Lachenmann—without a doubt one of the most important works of contemporary opera—in terms of verisimilitude. But this question hardly seems virulent anymore, even for the core repertoire of European opera. It is well known that modern *Regietheater*, with its postmodern-deconstructionist approach, has since marginalized the issue, and in some cases has even consciously attempted to do away with it altogether, whereas for works of post-dramatic theater, which frequently incorporate music or even become outright operatic, the category has literally vanished (Lehmann 1999).

On the face of it, then, the problem of verisimilitude in opera seems relevant today primarily as a historical phenomenon. And yet even for Lachenmann's opera, the category has apparently not lost all of its impact. *Das Mädchen mit den Schwefelhölzern* contains a rather long passage of a spoken text by Gudrun Enslin, a key figure of West German terrorism in the 1970s. This political text, which in some performances was recited by the composer himself, could imaginably be rendered in song, but would doubtlessly jar the audience. A sociopolitical text that is sung—offstage and without the physical presence of a character—really would lack verisimilitude since it obtains its particular effect precisely through the medium of spoken language. Lachenmann's Enslin monologue is representative of many contemporary operas in which the melodramatic configuration of texts takes on an important role within the musical work, frequently creating coherent narrative aggregates within a dramatic plot.

In spite of these rudiments of theatrical verisimilitude, the category nonetheless seems to be a historical one. As opposed to other categories, it has clearly lost its impact, something that, I believe, has also had historiographical consequences. Parameters such as vocal style, scoring, orchestral treatment, and so on can still be viewed under the umbrella of development, even for twentieth- and twenty-first-century opera. Following Adorno (1949), the criterion of compositional progress, or "historical state of the material" ("*Materialstand*"), can be applied to many works, be they by Schoenberg, Nono, Lachenmann, or—at the other end of the spectrum—Cage. And this criterion can certainly also be brought to bear on the technological side of the genre. The construction of theaters, stagecraft, and new instrument designs has gone through enormous developments that have also been invaluable to the *Gesamtkunstwerk* of the opera, while developments in scenography have given rise to increasingly intricate and complex means of depiction since the middle of the nineteenth century in cities like Naples, Paris, and Bayreuth. But it would ultimately be stagecraft that decisively conveyed the problem of verisimilitude. With this in mind, it seems almost paradoxical that the perfection of stage presentations in the twentieth century coincides with verisimilitude's dwindling relevance.

Most discussions of verisimilitude in opera basically assume the tacit premise that legitimate theater (where singing is absent) represents a form of art that can better depict events of a (familiar) world. Every discussion of verisimilitude is based on this premise, and it is empowered by the idea that theater is somehow subject to a kind of logicality of communication (mode of speaking, speech act). In light of the current culture of post-dramatic theater, such an equation could hardly be less appropriate. After all, drama theory is heading in a completely different direction (Fischer-Lichte 2004). In any case, contemporary spoken-word theater—if such a distinction to music-based theater is even valid anymore—is certainly just as far from a "concept of comprehension" as opera once was.

One of the paradoxes of opera history is that the question of theatrical verisimilitude is posed repeatedly, even though in principle the genre seems to be removed from any concept of illusionist theater. Without a doubt, the fundamental problem characterizing opera productions lies in the discontinuity between the "real time" of the dialogue and the way the musical numbers counteract it. On the other hand, opera is able to create its own time frames that structure the course of events independently of one another (Dahlhaus 1990). This core principle of opera is fundamentally opposed to an illusionist imitation of non-dramatic reality. The artistic division between outer and inner plot and the resulting leaps in time seem always to be opposed to the mimetic representation of reality. It is precisely the dramaturgy of the musical acts that contributes decisively to the artificial character of opera. In its various manifestations, "[i]t exhibits forms of interaction and plot that clearly distance themselves from non-dramatic reality" (Kämmerer 1990: 204).

Furthermore, we need to realize that the problem of verisimilitude primarily referred to the serious genres, such as *opéra seria*/*melodramma* and *tragédie lyrique*/*grand opéra*—in other words, to those genres that operated with material appropriate for speech-based theater. Other genres, such as *opera buffa*, the early *opéra comique* at the Théâtre de la foire, and operettas, remained nearly unaffected by questions of verisimilitude. Interestingly enough, regarding the use of contemporary material, this tradition can be traced up until the twentieth century, although from a different perspective: "[...] the factuality of the present is too strong to imagine as other than it is, too strong, at least, if the present situation involves strong emotions and suffering; it may be possible to write an *opera buffa* with a contemporary setting but not an *opera seria*" (Auden [1968] 1984: 83). The segment of opera history that the problem of verisimilitude refers to is thus limited indeed—and yet it still covers a substantial portion of opera.

Strategies of "As Ifs" and "Could Bes": A Historical View

The fact that the problem of verisimilitude in opera history comes across as a chimera has to do with its utterly theoretical quality; the underlying parameters of verisimilitude can hardly be "objectified." Presumably, this is because it is predominantly an issue of the eighteenth century, a time when taste reigned as the supreme authority of aesthetic judgment. It was primarily up to taste to decide whether nature had been rendered "correctly" or not. Taste (*le goût*) thus established itself as the paradigmatic category of art criticism. This certainly had tremendous consequences for music, since it was the establishment of this category that ultimately liberated the musical arts from the spell cast by the natural sciences and their fixation on objective data.

In the seventeenth century, and especially at the outset of opera history, every approach to the problem of verisimilitude was intensely rationalistic. The fundamental problem described above—namely, the question of how plausible it is for a dramatic plot to be either completely sung or accompanied by music—was already laid bare by this time. Even more than the question of whether a *lieto fine* should rightly have its place in this new art form, it was the problem of verisimilitude that writers, poets, philosophers, and, most of all, composers wrestled with. And ultimately it would remain the central theme in opera theory for a long time to come. Renato Di Benedetto (2003) has traced all the theoretical debates on Italian opera from 1600 through the nineteenth century. His approach, which takes into account the continuities and discontinuities of this present discussion, has remained the starting point for any work on the aesthetics of the opera of the *seicento* and *settecento*. Jacopo Peri was the first to examine this question regarding *recitar cantando*, that is, sung speech. The category of verisimilitude goes hand in hand with the birth of the operatic genre insofar as the "invention" of recitative was a direct consequence of deliberations on how the ancients would have solved the problem of song as speech. That, by contrast, such dramaturgic considerations regarding theatricality left Giulio Caccini cold sheds light on what one could call an early divergent position within opera aesthetics. Caccini turns his attention to the question of how the new singing style affects the composer's awareness in depicting emotions, whereby he also focuses on the singer's role. Simply put, whereas for Peri the verisimilitude of singing is given prominence, Caccini tends to concentrate more on the poetics of singing. This, then, also implies two completely different aesthetic perspectives on opera. Peri seeks to base his singing on a (fictive) verisimilitude of song in ancient drama, whereas Caccini's thought is heavily characterized by practical questions concerning the performances themselves.

With Giovanni Battista Doni's *Trattato della musica scenica* (1630)—which had limited "influence" before appearing in print in 1763—dramaturgic strategies are described for the first time that would become beneficial for the aspect of verisimilitude. Instead of having a drama that is continuously accompanied by music, Doni recommended devising an opera with three modes of presentation for the characters' discourse: sections for song, speech, and chorus should alternate. According to Doni, that would also ward off any threat of boredom. The anonymous treatise *Il corago* from the 1630s takes a similar stance by focusing on the antagonism and incompatibilities between the miraculous and the historically plausible. The text argues that whereas the miraculous and the magical allow for the use of stage effects, which work to counter boredom, it is nonetheless problematic to hear historical figures sing, especially when they are taking care of "state affairs." (The term "state affairs" also becomes a leitmotif in this context, despite the fact that the statesmen in the *dramma per musica* usually devoted themselves to "private business.")

It was essentially the use of history in Italian opera that made verisimilitude an ongoing subject of debate. Wendy Heller (2007) has shown how views on verisimilitude were so strongly influenced by their context by examining the libretto prefaces of Venetian libretti. Not only do these prefaces differentiate between two types of verisimilitude ("false verisimilitude" and "true verisimilitude"), but historical factuality was also made to conform to political factors in order "to create a verisimilar version of Roman history that accorded with the norms and political concerns of Venetian opera" (Heller 2007: 44). Thus, regarding Venetian opera, verisimilitude is specifically linked to the political. In other words, verisimilitude cannot be viewed solely as an absolute category within theater, but must (also) be understood as a contextual parameter.

The polymorphism of seventeenth-century Italian opera produced various strategies regarding verisimilitude, a few of which—such as Doni's proposal (1630) for the division of the characters' discourse—were virtually steamrolled by the history of composition. The establishment of Venetian opera at the close of the seventeenth century led to debates centering on a specific type of opera—debates that would eventually come to "reform" it. Thus, for Apostolo Zeno the problem of verisimilitude was fundamental to the extent that in his libretti he attempted to uphold the unity of time and action and the uniformity of his arsenal of characters. (As is known, comic and serious figures no longer coexist in Zeno.) Zeno was thoroughly literary. He was primarily interested in making the opera genre literary; the musical aspect—that is, the transformation of the text into music—was secondary for him.

The configuration of the category of verisimilitude within the discourse of opera aesthetics has many facets. One indispensable constituent is polemics, and, at the close of the seventeenth century, it had a name: Saint-Évremond. His essay *Sur les opéra* (1684), though it did not become influential until the eighteenth century, assembled almost all points of criticism then leveled at opera. Since Saint-Évremond was completely indebted to the aesthetics of classical French tragedy, his principal charge was that opera lacked a "closed form," which he felt was endangered by the "intrusion" of music. As a result, he viewed singing as something utterly preposterous and implausible per se. Music, according to him, ruptured the perfect unity of tragedy and destroyed verisimilitude, the "esprit de la représentation." As Doni had done before him, Saint-Évremond thus seeks a plausible, that is, logical dramaturgic basis to legitimize the existence of music. He finds what he is looking for in prayers and sacrificial and other religious rituals, in which he believed it was conceivable that one would sing. Yet since neither the French *tragédie en musique* nor the Italian *dramma per musica* corresponded in any way to his concepts, Saint-Évremond heaped opera with scathing attributes: fortuitous, monstrous, disproportioned, arbitrary, offensive. This fusion of aesthetic and moral categories would run like a red thread through opera theory from then on, frequently focusing on two categories: (im-)plausibility and (ir-)rationality. They come across as the *raison d'être* of opera. (Ironically, Saint-Évremond formulated an idea that—in spite of its blatant polemics—was absolutely prescient, namely, the subliminal presence of the author in musical drama. According to Saint-Évremond, since the composer allows his characters to sing, the musician lends them his own voice. As a result, the audience pays more attention to the omniscient presence of the composer than to the dramatis personae.)

Francesco Algarotti took the exact opposite position around the middle of the eighteenth century. He found opera to be, at least theoretically, "the quintessential and most ingenious" of artistic creations—something that betokens a shift within opera aesthetics. He does not call opera into question *a priori* because it is a composite work of art that unites different kinds of verisimilitude. He realizes, however, that opera still runs the fundamental risk of not having its individual parts proportionally related to each other. In fact, Algarotti felt that this condition was the norm. His judgment of Italian opera, together with its *convenienze ed inconvenienze teatrali*, is therefore equally sober and critical. A large part of his *Saggio sopra l'opera in musica* ([1763] 1989) centers on the idea that opera—precisely because its heterogeneous components create no aesthetic unity, and its mechanisms lack "order"—is a "composizione languida, sconnessa, inverisimile, mostruosa, grottesca ("a spiritless, disconnected, improbable, monstrous, grotesque composition") (Algarotti [1763] 1989: 9). Algarotti is thus primarily interested in the particular interaction of different art forms in this "composizione." As in the parallel work by Daniel Villeneuve, *Lettre sur le méchanisme de l'opéra italien* (1756; see Haas 1924), Algarotti considers, above all, the creation of theatrical illusions through the perfect collaboration (mechanism) of the constituents, text, music, and staging. Should this formation ever lose its equilibrium—for example, through the virtuosity of the castrati—the individual components, comparable to a nation, would have to be subjected to control and discipline. The question concerning the selection of material is of central importance for the problem of verisimilitude. Algarotti recommends selecting plots that take place long ago and far away, for only then is it plausible to hear the dramatis personae sing (Algarotti [1763] 1989: 19–20).

Algarotti's treatise acted as a spark for the reform of Italian opera beginning to take place around 1750 in cities like Vienna, Stuttgart, Parma, and Berlin. The accusations that initiated the reform are well known: unrealistic plots with complicated and stereotypical intrigues (including *lieto fine*), illogical divergence of musical and dramatic time (aria), "unrealistic" predominance of the monologue, and so on. Calzabigi, Verazi, and Coltellini tried to reform the libretto in attempts to counter these inherent "faults" of *opera seria*. How the problem of verisimilitude was treated—something that theorists had been grappling with for ages—thus represented an important impetus for reform. "In the name of verisimilitude and the dramatic principle, the reformers of opera could banish whatever excesses prevailed at the time" (Lindenberger 1984: 207).

Singing and Speaking: A Case Study for Medial Hybridity

A considerable portion of opera theory has been devoted to works that contain spoken dialogue (referred to hereafter as dialogue opera). The problem of verisimilitude is especially apparent in the genres *opéra comique* and *Singspiel* because of the ways completely different dramatic modes of expression—speaking and singing—converge. A large part of the debate centers on how these two modes of expression relate to each other, but extends far beyond that, since it also raises the issue of music's functionality. The question really comes down to what function music generally has in (dialogue) opera. That, in turn, implies the question of the dramaturgic legitimation of music—in other words, when and why music should "happen" and how it justifies its existence. These questions are obsolete for stage productions entirely set to music, such as *opera seria* and *melodramma*. Here again, the (old) problem of the verisimilitude of singing is raised, though from a different perspective—namely, in light of dramaturgic legitimacy on the one hand and theatrical communication on the other. Over the course of this debate, the motivation for music became the central aspect; its necessity resulted mainly from the coexistence of two completely different dramatic forms of expression for the dramatis personae.

The question surrounding the general function of music was first posed with regard to post-1750 *opéra comique*, which represented a new form of musical theater. Even though spoken text still largely comprised the dramatic essence of these works, one now considered the mix of *parlé* and *chanté* to be a unit. The fact that the *opéras comiques* were designated *nouveaux drames* (Nougaret 1769) reveals not only that the aesthetic judgment had changed with the loss of vaudeville's parodies, but that the texture of the genre now stood in a new light. Nonetheless, opera aesthetics still struggled with the coexistence of speech and song, which had consequences for both the manifestations of the genre (see Charlton 2000: essay II) and, to an even greater degree, the theoretical debates themselves (see Couvreur and Vendrix 1992).

To consider speech and song from the perspective of dramaturgical coherence implies posing the question of music's functionality. The question regarding the function and verisimilitude of opera song arose precisely where music was not clearly motivated by the dramatic text, where, in other words, it appeared just as naturally as in the through-composed genre. Without a doubt, the most striking aspect within the debate on the transformation of the *opéra comique* after 1750 is the acknowledgment of a change in theatrical communication. Since the (inter-)textual content associated with vaudeville parody was lost, theatrical communication also changed accordingly, seeing that the music now literally spoke for itself and no longer required any reference whatsoever to preexisting music or text. Thus, in his *Essai sur l'opéra-comique*, François-Antoine Quétant observes how ridiculous it is when a person, who would like to express something, "stops to listen to music"[1] (1764: 30). Quétant clearly sees in the alternation between speech and music a breach within theatrical illusion—not only for the audience, but for the dramatis personae as well. The statement that a character stops speaking in order to "listen to" the music (that is, to the ritornelle of an aria) demonstrates that the new music of the *opéra comique* has also changed the traditional system of communication.

Sébastien-Roch-Nicolas Chamfort, too, found it problematic when a character, overcome by emotion, pauses to "listen to" the music. In order to counter this "drawback"—namely, the hiatus at the intersection of song and speech—he recommends that the composer concentrate not merely on the character who is singing, but, to an even greater degree, on the attending dramatis personae[2] (Chamfort 1776: 344). Chamfort's demand would seem to tie into the desire for greater rigor in the characters' discourse; ultimately, however, it aims at something else. The music should (also) communicate something to the listener that cannot be captured by the characters' speech. More than ever before, the composer now finds himself in the role of a "commentator."

In light of such reflections, it was only a matter of time before the question was posed whether the music itself in *opéra comique* possessed different qualities and thus also obeyed different kinds of verisimilitude. None less than André-Ernest-Modeste Grétry, the predominant French composer between 1770 and 1800, developed an idea that has pervaded opera theory in various forms ever since. "Just because one often sings in *opéra comique* does not mean that one always sings. There is singing for speaking and singing for singing"[3] (Grétry [1789/1796] 1924: 267). Grétry's differentiation of operatic singing into "singing for speaking" and "singing for singing" may justly be deemed as a paradigm shift in the vision of opera music because he recognizes the different (dramaturgic) functions of music in singing. On the one hand, there is the category *chanter pour parler*, which represents a continuation of dialogue with other (musical) means. In this sense, singing is comparable to the characters' dialogue, even though the medium is completely different. On the other hand, there is music as a component of dramatic fiction—"realistic" or diegetic music, as it were, that can be viewed from the perspective of the dramatis personae as actual singing. (I proposed the term *drameninhärente Musik* [drama-inherent music] for any form of diegetic music in opera, embracing all sorts of music "inherent" to the drama/libretto, such as incidental music, stage song, stage music, etc. For the terminological discussion, see Betzwieser 2002: 24–30.)

Although the problem of verisimilitude is not mentioned *expressis verbis*, Grétry's differentiation actually goes to making opera song plausible, especially song that was no longer compatible with the categories of French aesthetics, such as, for example, the Italian virtuoso arietta. Grétry now calls such music—that can no longer be "explained" by dramatic verisimilitude—diegetic music: singing for the sake of singing. The French composer thereby acknowledges a fundamental disposition of music theater that is to become the *raison d'être* of opera in the nineteenth century: namely, the poetics of singing. Grétry recognizes that the poetic potential of an aria, in the sense of its expansion of autonomous musical elements, can no longer be measured with the yardstick of "stricte vraisemblance." He thus reacts to an apparent vacuum within aesthetics, since not a few critics censure the more technically demanding arias in French opera for their implausibility.

Under the label "chanter pour chanter" Grétry was also able to include all those types of musical numbers that were, so to speak, automatically diegetic in nature (romance, ballade, chanson, etc.). In this way, they were declared to be music "of greatest verisimilitude" since they represented, one could say, music to the first degree, that is, music on the same fictional level as the dialogue. It was not by chance that this type of diegetic music formed a mainstay within *opéra comique*. No other genre of music theater was so "shot-through" with drama-inherent music as the French dialogue opera.

Just as in French drama theory, opera debates in eighteenth-century German aesthetics also revolved around verisimilitude. And here as well there was a benchmark critic like Saint-Évremond who quickly became the "bad guy" of the opera world: Johann Christoph Gottsched (1700–1766). For Gottsched, opera was a "unification of a thousand improbabilities" that went against the grain of his elaborate, normative poetics. Yet as opposed to Saint-Évremond, Gottsched's word carried weight within theater aesthetics; his *Versuch einer critischen Dichtkunst* (Essay on a Critical Poetic Theory, [1730] 1751) proceeded to become one of the most highly recognized German theoretical works prior to Weimar classicism (see Bittmann 1992). Gottsched's critique was largely based on the performances given at the Hamburg Opera, the only German-language opera house up until that time. The absence of a genuinely German opera form—comparable to the *opera seria* or the *tragédie lyrique*—caused (after the Hamburg Opera closed in the 1740s) theory to focus largely on the new genre of the *Singspiel*.

It was Johann Friedrich Reichardt ([1774] 1782) above all who, with regard to verisimilitude, drew on the argument of "plausible" stage action. Reichardt saw German more as a "language of reason," incapable of expressing emotions. He thus considered the German language to be incompatible with a drama entirely set to music: "We are all quite aware that it is highly contrary to the nature of our language to sing in recitative throughout an entire play"[4] (161). The form of the *Singspiel* thus represented the logical conclusion of such a premise. But since singing is not exactly the natural form of communication in a *Singspiel*, it was necessary to provide a motive for the singing of the "mere human creatures" ("bloß menschlichen Geschöpfe"). A large part of German opera aesthetics between 1770 and 1800 (Reichardt, Goethe, E. T. A. Hoffmann, Tieck) thus centers on the problem of the dramaturgic motivation for music—a problem that had (meanwhile) become obsolete for *opera seria* and *tragédie lyrique*. Reichardt believes that in a *Singspiel* one should sing only at those times "where emotions have risen to such heights that words can no longer express them; where viewers have been so entirely transfixed by passion that their reason has been completely silenced, that sighs oppress their chests and tears befog their eyes, until, finally, they weep to the song of the suffering character on stage"[5] (Reichardt [1774] 1782: 162). Reichardt thus makes the use of music dependent upon the degree of portrayed emotion. In other words, singing is legitimized by a heightened emotional disposition with regard to the spoken texts preceding it. This idea was to become a leitmotif within German debates. Verisimilitude and dramatic logic were their central theories.

Debates on dialogue opera can be reduced to two schools of thought. The first, to which E. T. A. Hoffmann belonged, fundamentally declared the *Singspiel* to be an "absurdity." The second, as represented by Reichardt, Goethe, and Kotzebue, attempted to make "inconsistencies" in the dramaturgic motivations for music more plausible. Opera theory overall was thus furnished with new arguments, and Reichardt was a case in point. He does not speak (any longer) of the stage characters or singers and their emotions; instead, he wholly channels his interest onto the audience. The viewers should be gripped by emotion—to the same degree as the actors. And not only that, the emotions of the audience should be projected back onto the stage, resulting in the actors becoming the medium of the audience's emotions. This transforms the Baroque idea of the representation of emotion on the part of the actor into the idea of identification between stage character/composer and audience. This has consequences for the music since the concept of mimesis is thereby rendered obsolete. Nowhere is this made any clearer than in the debates on the concrete imitation of nature. As Reichardt observed, "But when Hiller creates wild, resounding music for a storm in *Die Jagd*, he does so not to express the roaring and blustering of the wind, but rather to awaken the same sentiment in the audience that a thunderstorm awakens in him"[6] (Reichardt [1774] 1782: 115).

Here, Reichardt even circumvents the mediating factor of the stage character by conflating the emotion of the recipient and the producer (composer). Even though this specific example of Johann Adam Hiller's *Die Jagd* (1770) has mainly to do with the problem of "musical painting," the theoretical approach still clearly tends toward verisimilitude via identification.

In Search of Verisimilitude: "Realistic" and "Operatic" Singing

It is not just dialogue opera that takes dramaturgic plausibility into account regarding the presence of music in drama. The question as to what extent music can represent different dramaturgic qualities also applies to through-composed genres. But since French opera aesthetics ultimately developed categories for the *tragédie lyrique* in step with contemporaneous (French) drama theory—though, as Kintzler (1991) has pointed out, under the modified concept of a "vraisemblance de merveilleux"—there were two aspects that harmonized less well with it: virtuoso singing and collective song. The former had appeared since the 1740s, especially in Rameau, under the term *ariette* (arietta). Within the context of the *tragédie lyrique*, arietta denotes—musically—not the diminutive of "air," but rather its exact opposite, namely, an even larger dimensioned solo vocal piece. Diderot and d'Alembert's *Encyclopédie* explicitly refers to the lexeme's change in meaning, according to which an arietta is now understood as a single-movement work usually cheerful in quality and sung with orchestral accompaniment[7] ("Ariette" in Diderot and d'Alembert [1751–1772]: I: 651). The place for such "virtuosic pieces" was frequently at the end of an act or toward the end of an entire opera, where they assumed their own extraterritorial space, as it were. In most cases, such ariettas were, as the *airs italiens* before them, irrelevant for the drama, disconnected from any dramaturgic plotting. Their importance lay primarily in vocal display and not in the story itself. "Italian" elements were thus subtly banished to a sort of holding pen that, consequently, was declared as the place of implausibility.

Collective song—that is, the choir—conflicted with verisimilitude to an even greater extent than the arietta did. The way in which the chorus was naturally considered a constitutive component of French opera stood at odds with its theoretical legitimation (Betzwieser 2000). Theater aesthetics was fundamentally skeptical of the participation of the choir in the *tragédie lyrique*. As to be expected, the cardinal question concerned the principal compatibility of the collective choir with "vraisemblance." Friedrich Melchior Grimm pointedly asked in the *Encyclopédie*: "How plausible is it actually for a multitude of individuals to articulate their feelings at the same time, and to do so with the same words and in one and the same musical movement? One would have to assume that they discussed everything beforehand and agreed on the air and words they would use to lend expression to their feelings in the respective scene"[8] ("Poème lyrique" in Diderot and d'Alembert [1751–1772]: XII: 832).

In light of a rationalistic opera theory, the question of a choir's verisimilitude was basically long overdue. Even though the fundamental paradox of opera—namely, that individuals express themselves while singing—had come to be accepted, attempts were still made to account for "realistic" forms (those present in theater) of verisimilitude. Grimm's comment above is more than just a rhetorical question; he is actually attempting to find a rational explanation for collective singing. In other words, a way out of the aporia of aesthetically legitimatizing the choir consisted, above all, in characterizing collective song as a partially pre-dramatic reality—that is, in declaring certain choral compositions to be preexistent music. That was especially important because the choir had now assumed much greater drama-relevant functions, thereby relinquishing its role as mere ceremonial (diegetic) music. With his proposal that choral song was music that the choir members had agreed upon in advance (in a type of pre-dramatic context), Grimm not only directed his attention to what was for "vraisemblance" the extremely delicate problem of simultaneous opera singing, but he also provided a theoretical solution. This idea was picked up by Jean-François Marmontel—also in the *Encyclopédie* (supplement)—and expanded in one crucial point. Marmontel proposed a distinction between choral movements that are to be viewed as musically preexistent to the drama (*chœur appris*/learned chorus), and those that are to be considered as collective, spontaneous expressions of emotions (*chœur impromptu*/spontaneous chorus) ("Chœur d'Opéra" in 1776b: II: 405–406). Unlike Grimm's notion, this distinction also implied the musical texture of the movement. Accordingly, the first type of choir, the "learned chorus," can "be artistically composed without ruining verisimilitude." Marmontel thus had invented a concept with which more complex, polyphonic structures of choral songs could be justified. On the other hand, with the "spontaneous chorus," the ad hoc interjections of Gluck's choruses could be classified under the theoretical model.

The idea that music does not originate directly from events on stage, but is also conceivable as a pre-dramatic element (from the viewpoint of the plot) called upon during the course of the drama had consequences for theoretical thought on the function of music. Grimm's concept that certain choruses were to be considered "learned" (and therefore as well known) threw the door wide open for differentiating various qualities of music, even in through-composed genres. It is no coincidence that it was Grimm himself who proposed (in a review of Monsigny's *Aline, reine de Golconde* in 1766) a term for such preexistent, mostly strophic, diegetic music, calling it a "pre-dramatic use"[9] (Grimm [1766/1879] 1877–1882: VII: 40). In other words, as long as songs—from the viewpoint of the plot—are identified as realistic, they automatically submit to a greater verisimilitude as music. They effectively represent music to the first degree, as opposed to music of a "discours dramatique" (Castil-Blaze 1820: 97), which is located on a different fictional level. Thus, by the year 1766, Grimm had, in some respects, already anticipated Grétry's concept of "chanter pour chanter" by linking song (chanson, romance couplet) to a clear dramaturgic disposition. In this way, Grimm and Grétry define the existence of two different "types" of opera music: diegetic and non-diegetic music.

Concepts often have a *longue durée* within a theoretical debate, and sometimes they reverberate through other discourses. The question of whether one can differentiate between various qualities or kinds of music in operatic works has been posed on numerous occasions since the end of the 1980s, especially from a post-structuralist perspective regarding the problem of authorship. The discourse, sparked by Edward T. Cone, could be captured under the heading "Rethinking Grétry," even though the French composer and his concepts are not specifically mentioned. Cone's essay "The World of Opera and Its Inhabitants" (Cone 1989), in which he returns to an idea he developed earlier (Cone 1974) of the composer as omniscient narrator within a work, zeroes in on the problem of the various functionalities of dramatic music. Cone identifies two different modalities of opera singing: "really singing" and "operatically singing," or "realistic music" and "operatic music" (Cone 1989: 126). "Realistic music" exists whenever the particular scene could be imagined as being sung in a play, in which case it would be considered "incidental music." If this is not the case, it is "operatic music": "Unlike incidental song, which occurs in situations calling for realistic singing, true operatic song replaces what in a more naturalistic medium would be ordinary speech" (Cone 1989: 126). However, Cone is unable to maintain this strict categorization since one and the same musical motif can potentially appear in both spheres (Cone 1989: 132). In order to counter the impossibility of such a clear differentiation, Cone develops the idea that one should view music as being written/composed by the personae. Thus, the characters know they are living in a completely musicalized world—that is, the opera. As a result, "they express themselves and communicate with one another in song" (Cone 1989: 132). Consequently, one is to consider the dramatis personae as the "creators" of their own music: "If the characters are composers, like all other composers, they are constantly 'thinking' music" (Cone 1989: 136). This model does help Cone to circumnavigate the blurry lines between "realistic" and "operatic" music, but the fact that we are supposed to imagine the dramatis personae as composers does not, in the end, answer the question of what "belongs to" this music and how we are to distinguish the characters' stage compositions from the music of "actual" composers, who, according to Cone, express themselves only through the orchestra. Cone was naturally aware that the idea of characters as composers led to a theoretical dead end. Nonetheless, the gist of his astute observations on the classification of opera music is still of great interest. And yet, one cannot help feeling that Cone, as well as Peter Kivy (1991), who followed up on Cone's work, both made the "wrong" genre the subject of their compelling theories. The question of to what extent opera music is "realistic music" or "operatic music" is actually much more apt for dialogue opera than for the through-composed genre. Nonetheless, Kivy and Cone place Mozart and Verdi at the center of their work, as if the paradigm for this issue could be established there and only there. In light of this, it is hardly surprising that their theories ended in controversy, even if the debate "only" applied to the above-named composers and, therefore, to the genre of opera that is fully set to music (for further discussion see Rosen 1992: 61–74 and Kivy 1992: 179–186). What is striking about this debate is that Cone's basic idea scarcely differs from the categorizations that Grétry, Grimm, and, later, Jouy and Castil-Blaze had formulated for dialogue opera. Cone, however, stringently developed them in terms of who the "creator" of such operatic music could be. Cone's model was further adapted by Carolyn Abbate, who introduced new terminology. She refers to the diegetic, drama-inherent portions of the opera as "phenomenal music," which she distinguishes from "noumenal music" (Abbate 1991: 5–7). Abbate convincingly argues that "phenomenal music" ultimately possesses genuinely narrative qualities that were fundamental for—or can be directly traced back to—musical narratives of nineteenth-century opera. Abbate was thereby able to newly inform the narrative strategies of Wagner's operas, especially the contexts of their musical references. One could say that she created a new "phenomenology" of the Wagnerian orchestral movement.

Where Does the Music Come From? Verisimilitude and the Orchestra

The fact that singing was accepted as an original form of expression for opera in the sense of a higher verisimilitude allowed song to become a kind of "reality" of fable and stage illusion. On the other hand, the instrumental portion of an opera, although no less intrinsic to the genre than the vocals, could hardly be viewed as part of the dramatic fiction. It is no coincidence, for example, that Pietro Metastasio wanted overall expression to be focused on the voice, and the arguments between the Lullistes and the Ramistes in the 1730s also reveal how emphasizing the orchestra represented an aesthetic problem. And so, the function of the orchestra increasingly became a problem for drama theory. However, the orchestra did not become the focus of interest until it began to shed its virtually affirmative role—until, in other words, it created its own individual expression above and beyond that of the characters' discourse.

Nonetheless, the orchestra played a subordinate role for a long time regarding the problem of verisimilitude. René Leibowitz rightly called the orchestra "un protagoniste invisible," in the chapter dedicated to it in his study *Les fantômes de l'opéra* (Leibowitz 1972: 109–144). For Leibowitz, the orchestra presents itself to listeners along various levels of perception. As opposed to the characters' singing, which is immediately accessible to the audience, the orchestra comes across "less consciously" (*moins consciente*). Leibowitz thereby also underscores different "levels" at which the orchestra makes itself known to the audience, that is, stands out from the musical movement. Hovering above the entire discourse is Meyerhold's dictum stating that in an opera the audience should completely forget that the characters are singing (instead of speaking)[10] (Meyerhold [1909] 1973: 126). The same also applies *mutatis mutandis* to the orchestra, which can clearly be seen in Leibowitz's paradigm of an orchestral approach, namely, Schoenberg's *Erwartung*. Here, the perfect merging of voice and orchestra to create a coherent illusion represents a higher operatic verisimilitude.

The question of the orchestra's functionality is essentially related to the problem of musico-theatrical communication because how the three media (text, music, stage) are conveyed also largely affects the question of theatrical verisimilitude. The communication between author, interpreter, and recipient is not insignificant regarding the creation of a coherent illusion. And it is precisely on this point that the problem of the orchestra turns virulent once one wishes to know what level the orchestra actually belongs to within the theatrical system of communication. Manfred Pfister distinguished between two systems of communication in drama: an inner system based on the speech of the dramatis personae, and an outer system composed of the relationship between author and recipient (Pfister [1977] 1997: 21). Whereas the inner communication system can be viewed as closed and corresponding to what Diderot calls everything that belongs within the "four walls" (in other words, the actual stage; see Diderot, *Discours sur la poésie dramatique* 1758 [2005]: 210–211),[11] the outer system is characterized by a direct relationship between author and recipient that, one could say, circumvents the inner system. (A paradigm for the presence of an outer system in opera is clearly Wagner's work, in which the author directly addresses the recipient by means of reminiscence motifs and leitmotifs.) In light of this model of communication, the relevant question for opera turns on the function of the orchestra: Should one view the orchestra/orchestral accompaniment as part of the inner or outer system? Does the orchestral music belong to the discourse of the dramatis personae, or does it primarily represent a medium that mediates between author and recipient? These questions were implicit with both Leibowitz and Cone.

It appears as though the communication systems in opera differ in degrees, based not primarily on the performance, but rather on the texture of the specific orchestral movement. In view of this, eighteenth-century opera is confronted with a different problem from the one Weber, Wagner, and Berg faced. If one considers (orchestral) music as a component of the characters' singing (which only represents a different mode of speaking, anyway), then *opera seria* and *tragédie lyrique* could be classified as "absolute drama" in Peter Szondi's sense, which is essentially characterized by the absence of the author (Szondi 1956: 13). In reference to Diderot, the orchestra would then lie within the four walls, as part of the inner system. In Wagner, however, the constellation is completely different. Music is no longer merely linked to the inner system; instead, it simultaneously establishes a strong outer bond between composer and audience. (Ironically, the orchestra is not visible in Wagner.) These two examples clearly demonstrate that although music can in principle serve as a "mediating narrative voice," as in the novel (Pfister [1977] 1997), it does not categorically possess codes directed "outward."

The question of whether (orchestral) music represents only the medium of communication, or if, instead, it already possesses concrete "narrative" qualities was posed in a theoretical context as early as the eighteenth century. The question primarily centered on the functionality of the orchestra within the opera and was therefore part of the "vraisemblance" debate. Once again, it was Marmontel who discussed the various qualities of orchestral accompaniment within opera ("Accompagnement" in 1776a: I: 115–116). In terms of the issue of verisimilitude, harmonic ("imiter le retentissement harmonieux de la voix"), imitative-descriptive (sea storm, thunder, wind etc.), and supportive accompaniment (accompanied-recitative) are all entirely unproblematic (Charlton 1997). Here, the orchestral accompaniment adopts the same musical perspective as the characters' discourse. All three types of accompaniment could be understood—according to Pfister—as a mediating vehicle for the inner communication system. However, Marmontel has a much more difficult time coming to terms with musical structures in which individual moments of the orchestral accompaniment run contrary to the characters' discourse. What plagues Marmontel is precisely the question of whether the orchestral accompaniment alone acts as the medium of communication, or whether a further "commenting" element is tied in with it. He has problems with this because in his definition of the term ("accompaniment") he postulated that all components of an operatic work must be beholden to the illusion on stage: "In vocal music, everything must have its own analogy to fiction and its plausibility. The verses, the song, the orchestra that accompany it together form a hypothesis whose principle is in nature"[12] (1776a: I: 115).

The central problem for Marmontel was whether orchestral music really does behave "analogously" to the stage fiction when a commenting or complementary quality is joined with the orchestra because the orchestral music transcends the vocals through its expressive power and thereby becomes a "seconde voix" (1776: I: 115–116). The clash of the "voix réelle" (singing voice) with a second voice, the "voix fictive" (orchestra), seems hardly to be resolvable in terms of verisimilitude. Although Marmontel, at the close of the eighteenth century, thereby specifies an original element of opera, he still has to explain this "collision" of two voices. He therefore argues to the effect that the varied sentiments the orchestral accompaniment is able to express are already inherent in the vocals. For Marmontel, the voice is a "miroir uni" ("one-dimensional mirror"), whereas the orchestra represents "un miroir à plusieurs faces" ("a mirror of many faces"): the accompaniment is "le supplément de la voix" ("the addition to the voice"). The orchestral accompaniment thus has "son motif dans la nature" and is thereby compatible with mimesis and verisimilitude.

The idea of considering the orchestra to be a "second voice" also implies—paradoxically—the possibility of a potentially contrasting function of the instrumental lines. With his theory, Marmontel anticipated the paradigmatic example of just such a contrasting usage: Orestes' "Le calme rentre dans mon cœur" in Gluck's *Iphigénie en Tauride* (1779), in which Orestes speaks of his newly found peace while the accompaniment expresses his true sentiment, anxiety. As Gary Tomlinson puts it, such "new orchestral powers are one of the early intimations in opera of the advent of a new subjectivity" (Tomlinson 1998: 59). Regardless of whether we agree with Marmontel's idea of viewing such an accompaniment as a "supplément de la voix," the decisive factor is that the orchestra is clearly aiming at the outer communication system, thus establishing a direct bond between author and recipient. In this way, an entirely new communicative strategy opens up within the theatrical system that causes the previous genre of "absolute drama" (*opera seria* and *tragédie lyrique*) to stumble over the aesthetic problem of verisimilitude.

So it is not surprising that, thereafter, the category of verisimilitude only plays a subordinate role within debates on the emancipation of orchestral accompaniment—for example, in the writings of Lacépède (Saloman 1974)—seeing that the discussion focused primarily on the audience, that is, on the aspect of effect. (The question of the orchestra's function within opera could not be answered entirely independent of its position within the theater since the visual presence of the orchestra inevitably poses the question of its role in creating illusion. As is commonly known, in his vision of a new kind of opera, Grétry opted for an "invisible" orchestra.) Grétry ultimately formulated a radical change in perspective by declaring the orchestra to be no longer compatible with the model of mimesis (Grétry [1789/1796] 1925: III: 151). It is interesting to note that Grétry used the physical non-presence of the orchestra (on the stage) as an argument against the mimetic model. Grétry considers the function of the orchestra to be geared toward the audience: the music "speaks" for the audience and represents its reaction to the events on stage. It is significant that Grétry explicitly includes within his theory the potentially contrastive quality of the accompaniment. In terms of Orestes' "Le calme rentre dans mon cœur," this means that the audience feels the actual emotional sentiments of the dramatis persona, which, for their part, are now manifested in the orchestra.

The "Irresistible" Power of Music

The entire debate on the functionality of the orchestra reveals how strongly opera theory centers on the problem of verisimilitude and that illusion, mimesis, and verisimilitude comprise the central categories of the discourse of opera aesthetics. The artificiality of opera with singing characters may have been an accepted configuration within aesthetic thought by the end of the eighteenth century, but most theorists still sought to base verisimilitude in the opera on "plausible" dramaturgy and communication. It would seem there is such a great degree of implausibility inherent in opera that each of its components has to be examined for its rational basis. The discussion of the orchestra, however, is new to the extent that it accounts for the historical developments of music following 1770, especially in terms of instrumental music's growth toward autonomy. For aesthetics, this development was, by all means, a point of no return since it would have been absurd to consider an elaborate orchestral movement by Weber, Meyerbeer, or Verdi as an "accessoire" to the characters' discourse. In that respect, the problem of verisimilitude regarding (opera) music had reached the end of the line.

The poetics of opera thereby adopted an idea already formulated by Rousseau (1768), namely, that the power of music should make the audience forget that the actors are singing. Rousseau had thus given the problem of verisimilitude a completely new twist; in fact, he turned it upside-down (Di Benedetto 2003: 40). Music was not to distance itself from the audience in order to (theoretically) legitimize the implausibility of theatrical singing; instead, music should get as close to the viewers as possible so that they are enthralled by it. Although Meyerhold had developed his position regarding opera in terms of performance and interpretation, whereas Rousseau did so against the foil of musical composition itself, their two paradigms are actually rather similar. For both of them the ultimate purpose is the same: in light of music's power, the audience is able to forget all the inconsistencies of opera—and so should all of opera's critics.

See also: The Concept of Opera, Opera between the Ancients and the Moderns, Musical Dramaturgy, Voice, The Orchestra, The Chorus

Notes

1. "[. . .] il est ridicule qu'un Personnage qui doit avoir des intérêts à démêler ou des sentimens à exprimer, s'arrête uniquement pour écouter de la Musique."
2. "Mais pour affaiblir autant que possible cet inconvénient, il faut que le musicien ait encore plus d'égard à l'acteur qui écoute qu'à celui qui chante."
3. "Quoique l'on chante souvent dans l'opéra comique, l'on ne chante pas toujours. Il y a chanter pour parler, et chanter pour chanter."
4. "Das ist unter uns allgemein erkannt, daß es der Natur unsrer Sprache höchst zuwider ist, das ganze Stück in Rezitativen abzusingen."

5. "[...] wo die Leidenschaft so hoch gestiegen, daß Worte sie nicht mehr ausdrücken: wo der Zuschauer schon so ganz in die Leidenschaft versetzt ist, daß alles Raisonnement in ihm schweigt, daß auch ihm schon Seufzer die Brust beklemmen, Thränen das Auge umnebeln, die er nun gleichsam in dem Gesange des Leidenden aushaucht, ausweint."
6. "Wenn aber Hiller in der *Jagd*, während des Sturms eine wilde, rauschende Symphonie spielen läßt, so geschieht dieses nicht, um das Sausen und Brausen des Windes auszudrücken, sondern um bey dem Zuschauer dieselbe Empfindung zu erregen, die ein Ungewittersturm bey ihm erregt."
7. " [...] grand morceau de musique d'un mouvement par l'ordinaire assez gai & marqué, qui se chante avec des accompagnements de symphonie."
8. "[...] avec quelle vraisemblance une assemblée entière ou tout un peuple pourra-t-il manifester son sentiment en chantant ensemble et en chœur le même couplet, les mêmes paroles, le même air? Il faudra donc supposer qu'ils se sont concertés d'avance, et qu'ils sont convenus entre eux de l'air et des paroles par lesquels ils exprimeraient leur sentiment sur ce qui fait le sujet de la scène, et qu'ils ne pouvaient savoir auparavant."
9. "[...] ils peuvent y être placés historiquement."
10. "Le drame musical doit être interprété de telle sorte que l'auditeur-spectateur ne se demande pas une seconde pourquoi les acteurs chantent dans ce drame au lieu de parler."
11. "Imaginez sur le bord du théâtre un grand mur qui vous sépare du parterre; jouez comme si la toile ne se levait pas."
12. "Dans la musique vocale, tout doit avoir son analogie avec la fiction, & sa vraisemblance comme elle. Les vers, le chant, la symphonie qui l'accompagne, forment ensemble une hypothèse, dont le principe est dans la nature."

Bibliography

Abbate, Carolyn. 2001. *In Search of Opera*. Princeton, NJ: Princeton University Press.

——. 1991. *Unsung Voices: Opera and Musical Narrative in the Nineteenth Century*. Princeton, NJ: Princeton University Press.

Adorno, Theodor W. 1949. *Philosophie der neuen Musik*. Tübingen: Mohr.

Algarotti, Francesco. [1763] 1989. *Saggio sopra l'opera in musica*. Venice: G. Pasquali. Reprint of the 1763 edition, edited by Annalisa Bini. Lucca: Libreria musicale italiana.

Arteaga, Esteban de. 1783–1785. *Le rivoluzioni del teatro musicale italiano della sua origine fine al presente*. Bologna: Forni.

Auden, W[ystan] H[ugh]. [1968] 1984. "The World of Opera." In *Secondary Worlds*, 76–102. London: Faber and Faber.

Bayerdörfer, Hans-Peter, ed. 1999. *Musiktheater als Herausforderung: Interdisziplinäre Facetten von Theater-und Musikwissenschaft*. Tübingen: Max Niemeyer Verlag.

Betzwieser, Thomas. 2008. "Bekannte Gesichter, gemischte Stimmen: Die mediale Transformation der Vaudeville-Praxis in Alain Resnais' *On connaît la chanson* (1997)." *Musiktheorie* 23: 179–188.

——. 2007. "Spielarten der deutschen Opernästhetik um 1800—Denkfiguren im Spannungsfeld von Gattungsreflexion und Bühnenkonvention." In *Oper im Aufbruch—Gattungskonzepte des deutschsprachigen Musiktheaters um 1800*, edited by Marcus Chr. Lippe, 27–43. Kassel: Gustav Bosse Verlag.

——. 2002. *Sprechen und Singen: Ästhetik und Erscheinungsformen der Dialogoper*. Stuttgart and Weimar: J. B. Metzler.

——. 2000. "Musical Setting and Scenic Movement: Chorus and *chœur dansé* in Eighteenth-Century Parisian Opéra." *Cambridge Opera Journal* 12/1: 1–28.
Bittmann, Anne-Rose. 1992. *Die Kategorie der Unwahrscheinlichkeit im opernästhetischen Schrifttum des 18. Jahrhunderts*. Frankfurt: Peter Lang.
Castil-Blaze, François Henri Joseph. 1820. *De L'Opéra en France*. Paris: Janet et Cotelle.
Chabanon, Michel. [1785] 1969. *De la Musique considérée en elle-même et dans ses rapports avec la parole, les langues, la poésie et le théâtre*. Paris: Pissot. Reprint. Geneva: Slatkine.
Chamfort, Sébastien-Roch-Nicolas. [1776] 1967. *Dictionnaire dramatique*. Paris: Lacombe. Reprint. Geneva: Slatkine.
Charlton, David. 2000. *French Opera 1730–1830: Meaning and Media*. Aldershot, UK: Ashgate.
——. 1997. "L'Orchestre et la métaphore du vivant de Mozart." In *Mozart: Les chemins de l'Europe. Actes du Congrès de Strasbourg 15–16 octobre 1991*, edited by Brigitte Massin, 105–112. Strasbourg: Éditions du Conseil de l'Europe.
——. 1987. "'L'art dramatico-musical': An Essay." In *Music and Theatre: Essays in Honour of Winton Dean*, edited by Nigel Fortune, 229–262. Cambridge: Cambridge University Press.
Cone, Edward T. 1989. "The World of Opera and its Inhabitants." In *Music: A View from Delft. Selected Essays*, edited by Robert P. Morgan, 125–138. Chicago: University of Chicago Press.
——. 1974. *The Composer's Voice*. Berkeley and Los Angeles: University of California Press.
Cook, Nicholas. 1998. *Analysing Musical Multimedia*. Oxford: Clarendon Press.
Couvreur, Manuel, and Philippe Vendrix. 1992. "Les Enjeux théoriques de l'Opéra-Comique." In *L'Opéra-Comique en France au XVIIIe siècle*, edited by Philippe Vendrix, 213–282. Liège: Mardaga.
Cowart, Georgia. 1981: *The Origins of Modern Criticism: French and Italian Music 1600–1750*. Ann Arbor: UMI Research Press.
Dahlhaus, Carl. 1990. "What Is a Musical Drama?" *Cambridge Opera Journal* 2/1: 95–111.
Di Benedetto, Renato. 2003. "Poetics and Polemics." [Translated by Kenneth Chalmers.] In *Opera in Theory and Practice, Image, and Myth*, edited by Lorenzo Bianconi and Giorgio Pestelli. *History of Italian Opera* 6, 1–71. Chicago: University of Chicago Press.
Diderot, Denis. [1758] 2005. *De la Poésie dramatique*, edited by Jean Goldzink. Paris: Flammarion.
——. [1773–1777/publ. posth. 1830] 1994. *Le paradoxe sur le comédien. Texte intégral*, edited by Joël Dupas. Paris: Seuil.
——, ed. 1776. *Supplément à l'Encyclopédie ou Dictionnaire raisonné des sciences, des arts et des métiers*. 5 vols. Amsterdam: Rey.
Diderot, Denis, and Jean le Rond d'Alembert, eds. 1751–1772. *Encyclopédie ou Dictionnaire raisonné des sciences, des arts et des métiers*. 28 vols. Paris: Briasson.
Didier, Beatrice. 1986. "Merveilleux et vérité. Les philosophes à la recherche d'une poétique de l'opéra." In *Les Écrivains français et l'opéra*, edited by Jean-Paul Capdevielle and Peter-Eckhard Knabe, 61–77. Cologne: dme-Verlag.
Doni, Giovanni Battista. 1763. "Trattato della musica scenica." *Lyra Barberina amphichordos*. Vol. 2. Florence.
Ferrero, Mercedes Viale. 1995. "Le indicibili variazioni del verosimile." In *Le parole della musica. Studi sul lessico della letteratura critica del teatro musicale in onore di Gianfranco Folena*, edited by Maria Teresa Muraro, 85–93. Florence: Olschki.
Fischer-Lichte, Erika. 2004. *Die Ästhetik des Performativen*. Frankfurt: Suhrkamp.
Girdlestone, Cuthbert. 1972. *La tragédie en musique (1673–1750) considérée comme genre littéraire*. Geneva: Droz.

Grétry, André-Ernest-Modeste. [1789/1796] 1924–1925. *Mémoires ou Essais sur la musique.* 3 vols. Bruxelles: Librairie Nationale d'Art et d'Histoire.

Grimm, Friedrich Melchior. [1766/1879] 1877–1882. Review of Monsigny's *Aline, reine de Golconde.* In *Correspondance littéraire, philosophique et critique par Grimm, Raynal et Meister.* 16 vols., edited by Maurice Tourneux, VII : 40–44. Paris: Garnier.

——. [1751–1772]. "Poème lyrique." In Diderot and d'Alembert 1751–1772, XII: 832.

Haas, Robert. 1924. "Josse de Villeneuves Brief über den Mechanismus der italienischen Oper von 1756." *Zeitschrift für Musikwissenschaft* 7: 129–163.

Heller, Wendy. 2007. "Venice's Mythic Empires: Truth and Verisimilitude in Venetian Opera." In *Opera and Society in Italy and France from Monteverdi to Bourdieu*, edited by Victoria Johnson, Jane E. Fulcher, and Thomas Ertman, 34–52. Cambridge: Cambridge University Press.

Kämmerer, Sebastian. 1990. *Illusionismus und Anti-Illusionismus im Musiktheater*. Anif/ Salzburg: Verlag Ursula Müller-Speiser.

Kerman, Joseph. [1956] 1988. *Opera as Drama*. Rev. ed. Berkeley and Los Angeles: University of California Press.

Kivy, Peter. 1999. *Osmin's Rage: Philosophical Reflections on Opera, Drama, and Text*. Ithaca, NY, and London: Cornell University Press.

——. 1992. "'Composers and 'Composers': A Response to David Rosen." *Cambridge Opera Journal* 4/2: 179–186.

——. 1991. "Opera Talk: A Philosophical 'phantasie'." *Cambridge Opera Journal* 3/1: 63–77.

Kintzler, Catherine. 2004. *Théâtre et opéra à l'âge classique*. Paris: Fayard.

——. 1991. *Poétique de l'opéra français de Corneille à Rousseau*. Paris: Minerve.

Krenek, Ernst. [1932] 1958. "Zur Situation der Opera." In *Zur Sprache gebracht: Essays über Musik*, edited by Friedrich Saathen, 130–138. Munich: Albert Langen-Georg Müller.

Le Cerf de la Viéville, Jean-Laurent. [1705] 1972. *Comparaison de la musique italienne et de la musique françoise*. 2nd ed. Brussels: François Foppens. Reprint. Geneva: Minkoff.

Lehmann, Hans-Thies. 1999. *Postdramatisches Theater*. Frankfurt: Verlag der Autoren. In English as *Postdramatic Theatre*, translated by Karen Jürs-Munby. London: Routledge [2006].

Leibowitz, René. 1972. *Les fantômes de l'opéra. Essais sur le théâtre lyrique*. Paris: Editions Gallimard.

Lindenberger, Herbert. 1984. *Opera, the Extravagant Art*. Ithaca, NY, and London: Cornell University Press.

Malipiero, Gian Francesco. 1924. *I profeti di Babilonia*. Milano: Bottega di Poesia.

Marmontel, Jean-François. 1776a. "Accompagnement." In Diderot 1776, I: 115–117.

——. 1776b. "Chœur d'Opéra." In Diderot 1776, II: 405–406.

Meyerhold, Vsevolod. [1909] 1973. "La Mise en scène de *Tristan et Isolde* au Théâtre Mariinsky." In Vsevolod Meyerhold, *Écrits sur le théâtre*, edited by Béatrice Picon-Vallin, I : 125–142. Lausanne: La Cité—L'Age d'Homme.

Nougaret, Jean-Baptiste. [1769] 1971. *De l'Art du théâtre où il est parlé des différents genres de spectacles et de la musique adaptée au théâtre*. Paris: Cailleau. Reprint. Geneva: Slatkine.

Pavis. Patrice. 1982. *Voix et images de la scène. Essais de sémiologie théâtrale*. Lille: Presses Universitaires de Lille.

Pfister, Manfred. 1997. *Das Drama. Theorie und Analyse*. 9th ed. München: Fink. In English as *The Theory and Analysis of Drama*, translated by John Halliday. Cambridge: Cambridge University Press [1991].

Quétant, François-Antoine. 1764. "Essai sur l'opéra-comique." In *Le Serrurier*, 29–31. Paris: Duchesne.

Raguenet, François. [1702–1705] 1987. *Parallèle des Italiens et des François, en ce qui regarde la musique et les opéras*. Paris: Moreau/Barbin. Reprint. Geneva: Minkoff.

Reichardt, Johann Friedrich. [1774] 1974. *Über die Deutsche comische Oper nebst einem Anhange eines freundschaftlichen Briefes über die musikalische Poesie*, edited by Walter Salmen. Hamburg: Bohn. Reprint. Munich: Katzbichler.

——. [1782] 1969. "Über das deutsche Singeschauspiel." *Musikalisches Kunstmagazin* 1: 4. Reprint. Hildesheim: Georg Olms.

Rosen, David. 1992. "Cone's and Kivy's 'World of Opera'." *Cambridge Opera Journal* 4/1: 61–74.

Rousseau, Jean-Jacques. 1979. *Ecrits sur la musique*, edited by Catherine Kintzler. Paris: Editions Stock.

——. 1768. "Opéra." *Dictionnaire de la musique*. Paris: Duchesne.

Saint-Évremond, Charles de Marguetel de Saint-Denis. [1684] 1966. "Sur les opéra." In *Œuvres en prose*, edited by René Ternois, III: 129–164. Paris: M. Didier.

Sajous D'Oria, Michèle. 2007. *Bleu et or. La scène et la salle en France au temps des Lumières*. Paris: CNRS Editions.

Saloman, Ora Frishberg. 1974. "The Orchestra in Le Sueur's Musical Aesthetics." *Musical Quarterly* 60/4: 616–624.

Strohm, Reinhard. 1997. *Dramma per musica: Italian opera seria of the Eighteenth Century*. New Haven: Yale University Press.

Szondi, Peter. [1956] 2007. *Die Theorie des modernen Dramas*. 26th ed. Frankfurt: Suhrkamp.

Tomlinson, Gary. 1998. *Metaphysical Song. An Essay in Opera*. Princeton, NJ: Princeton University Press.

CHAPTER 14

VOICE

MICHAL GROVER-FRIEDLANDER

The Art of the Voice

Several approaches to opera locate its aesthetic foundation in the singing voice, in that the media conceives of itself through the voice and the idea of the operatic voice. These approaches view the voice and the aesthetics of voice as embodying the single crucial condition, core, or essence that defines, constitutes, and determines the media. Opera is thus conceived as a phenomenon in which meaning is engendered in singing; singing reveals the nature and significance of that very capacity. The singing voice is positioned above all other constituents as that which is essential to opera; the attraction it exerts is the essence of the operatic as such. Accordingly, the goal in and of opera is to emphasize singing above everything else. What, in the deepest sense, accounts for the specificity of the world of opera is singing that is unlike any other. Whether the operatic voice is unique invokes the question of whether and in what ways an operatic voice differs from voices in other musical genres and modes of vocal performance, such as the lied and the oratorio, the musical and the operetta. There is also the related question of how the aesthetic, stylistic, and technical innovations that took place in music and opera and saw the expansion of music theater around the middle of the twentieth century have undermined this conception of the operatic voice. Other approaches emphasize opera's nature as a hybrid form of art, a total artwork, a multimedia or synaesthetic art (approaches not considered in this chapter), and position the voice alongside other signifying systems (text, scenery, etc.). These approaches stress the interrelationships among the different elements constructing opera, at the expense of the privilege of the voice.

The Unique Voice

The operatic voice is artificial, stylized, eccentric, extreme, extravagant, exaggerated, excessive, grotesque, bizarre, irrational, and absurd. It is a voice at the limit of human capacity, bordering on the unnatural. It is "superhuman" in its pyrotechnic acrobatic display. Calling for special production techniques, aspiring to powers of projection that can be heard over a huge orchestra and fill the vastest auditorium, it prides itself in the feats it achieves without technological intervention. The operatic voice is an exercise in concentrated intensity, all the while imparting an impression of ease in its technically flawless, emotionally charged execution. It is a voice that in unique ways bears on our conception of who is doing the singing and what that singing conveys. The operatic voice is heard within a strange world, where according to convention nearly everything is sung and enveloped in music.

The operatic voice fascinates. It is hyper-real and irrational. The listener is submerged within its affect. It is seductive and irresistible, and engenders states of ecstatic listening, passionate identification, introjection, the play of fantasy, and secret yearnings. It elicits physical, bodily, erotic responses; it is a desired voice, worshipped and fetishized; and it has its special forms of obsession, cult, fandom, and camp (Koestenbaum 1993; Abel 1996; Dame 1994; Leonardi and Pope 1996).

Such singing is transcendent and transformative, on the one hand, and repeatedly under the threat (and pleasure) of appearing shamefully ridiculous on the other. It is prey to parody and criticism and is under constant pressure to reform itself. Theodor W. Adorno claims that when parodying itself, opera is most true to itself (Adorno [1955] 1994: 26). Criticism of opera, ranging from early writers such as Dryden and Voltaire to the more recent Cage and Fluxus composers, is often directed toward the voice being over-stylized, preposterous, burdened by convention, constructed, emotionally over-the-top, extravagant, excessive, and decadent. Indeed, these are the very traits governing its modes of beauty. Consider, for example, the paradigmatic case of the castrato, whose beautiful voice evokes wonder and a state of rapture that stupefies the listener. The castrato's voice epitomizes the operatic voice because of its unusual, unnatural quality of timbre. It can deliver delicate lyricism, smooth sustained legato, even execution, unobtrusive register transfer, clear text, and nuanced dynamics. It is built on excellent breath control. It is a voice that resonates, exhibits infinite flexibility, variety, subtlety, agility, and virtuosity (Celletti 1991).

The Meaning of the Singing Voice

Concerning the nature of the operatic voice—its strange sounds, poetics of wonder, and outrageous impositions, as outlined above—there are no major aesthetic-theoretical disputes. Arguments arise instead about the sense of these voices, that is, about their mode of signification and the ways they construct meaning. Scholars disagree whether characters hear what they are doing as singing, whether they "know" they are singing or whether they inhabit a "cinematic" world in which, most of the time and for most of the characters, there is no soundtrack. Put differently, is the orchestral accompaniment part of what the character "says," "thinks," and "feels," or does it make up a general ambience, conveying the "composer's voice"? Are characters' utterances and their accompaniment, and those of others, perceived as song? Is it music for the inhabitants of opera? Are characters understood to be "composers" of the music? Do they also "write" the text? Does the music thus "originate" in them? Do they "hear" the other characters? Whose music is it in ensembles, who "composes" it, who "hears" it? Finally, whose "voice" is it when the orchestra sounds alone? This set of questions is contingent on another set about "realistic" singing (the plot indicates that a character really sings within the world of opera, for example, Desdemona's Willow song in Verdi's *Otello*) and "operatic" singing (what characters in opera do). These questions pertain to the metaphysics of the operatic utterance, and deal with the level of analogy between the world of opera and the world outside. Scholars argue for the understanding of operatic singing as a substitute for speech, or alternatively they argue that the character knows he is singing, means to be singing, and hears other characters, in their songs and accompaniment, to be singing.

Edward T. Cone (1988) claims that one cannot sustain the distinction between "realistic" and "operatic" singing. Cone proposes to think of the character as the creator of her singing, as the one who composes her own music, a composer-singer Orphic figure, who (usually) can be said to hear the accompaniment. Peter Kivy (1994) maintains the distinction between realistic and operatic singing but narrows the gap between the operatic realm and our ordinary ways of relating to the world. He argues that all instances of ordinary discourse are to some degree creative, improvisatory responses to novel situations; we are all authors of our words. Thus, a continuum exists among speakers, improvisatory poets, improvisatory singers, composers, and figures in the strange world of opera. In Kivy's matrix, the orchestral accompaniment expresses characters' gestures and bodily movements. For both Kivy and Cone, characters are composers expressing themselves in music.

David Rosen (1992) takes issue with Kivy's analogy to the real world and with the view that opera's inhabitants are singer-composers. In Rosen's account, opera does not maintain a consistent distinction between operatic and realistic singing. And here we can mention Adorno's claim that, in fact, the very meaning of opera is to be sought in contradiction (though not specifically the one alluded to here by Rosen) between real, live people who speak and the media of singing (Adorno [1955] 1994: 37). Rosen argues that an operatic character (usually) not only does not compose the accompanying music, but we must also assume that he does not hear it; neither can the orchestral music stand for the character's gestures, but rather might indicate inner emotional states. Stanley Cavell (1994) approaches the question as an issue about what singing does to speech. Singing does not represent speech; the two states, in fact, possess almost the opposite relation. Singing in opera brings out a problem about speaking and its conventionality, namely that in speaking something has been forgotten or repressed: a transformed world and a further self. The deadening or the loss of the world in speech and its recovery through song speak directly to the components of the myth of Orpheus. It is thus that singing in opera takes place between worlds. The raising of the voice in song opens up a passage between these worlds.

Another way of formulating the question about what the singing voice means in opera is through a duality different from that of "singing and speaking": phenomenal music (stage songs, when characters really sing) and noumenal music (what lies beyond the characters' sensibilities). Carolyn Abbate (1991) finds irruptions clustering around the borders of the phenomenal and the noumenal. These are uncanny sounds of what cannot normally be heard. In other words, the noumenal is not all of the opera's music, an ever-present sonorous envelope differentiated from phenomenal music, but within it there are irruptions of vocal gestures that reveal characters' awareness and knowledge of their inhabitants. They express the limit of phenomenal knowledge; it is here that characters become characters that hear, for example, Elektra in Strauss's opera of that name. Gary Tomlinson (1999), building on Abbate's differentiation between the two terms, postulates that the voice is impelled toward the borderline separating the phenomenal and the noumenal. The voice tends toward the noumenal limit.

Vicissitudes of Voice

The questions and codes about what it means to sing in opera are revealed to be far more complex when considered together with the conventions correlating voice types with character types and determining their function in the plot, their social role, gender, and so on. Catherine Clément (2000: 19) calls this the opera's vocal backdrop or society of voices. Vocal traits, including the mere range of the voice, stand for operatic subjectivity, as they convey a crucial determinant: the drama is acted out in the voices. For example, heroines who die are sopranos, like Violetta in Verdi's *La traviata*; lovers, usually rebels, are tenors, like Pelléas in Debussy's *Pelléas et Mélisande*; and basses often act in the sacred and religious fields, like Oroveso in Bellini's *Norma*.

That drama in opera resides in music rather than in narrative, situation, plot, and so forth as set in the libretto is a view advocated by Joseph Kerman ([1956] 1988), among others (Kerman does not privilege the singing voice but considers music as a whole). This is another way of formulating the claim that realism is not the context for understanding opera, nor indeed is the simple dichotomy between words and music. Opera as drama means, argues Kerman, that opera is a particular form of drama ([1956] 1988: 1). Ruth Katz (1994) opens up the question and considers different aesthetic approaches to music and drama, for instance that drama in opera aspires to the condition of music.

Other scholars, mostly those with a psychoanalytic orientation, go even further in draining language and words of meaning. They locate opera's essence in its construction of voices. The singing voice is not a character's utterance but the other way around: characters underscore opera's exclusive vicissitudes of voice. For example, Michel Poizat's (1992) underlying Lacanian supposition is that opera is the endless and painful quest for the original lost object. The pleasure in opera is the result of an illusory structure that brings one into proximity with original *jouissance* as the voice turns into a cry without signification. In forgetting the fundamental attachment of desire to language, this pleasure is ecstatic. Operatic singing derives its force not from the extravagance of the singing voice but from its pointing to the limits of vocal expression and to meaninglessness.

At its peak, opera touches on the edge or extremity of song and points to something beyond song, be it a cry or silence—for example Lulu's death cry in Berg's *Lulu* and Kundry's in Wagner's *Parsifal*. We are in the midst of the ever-old dichotomy between the singing voice, with its penchant for transcendence and intoxication (the singing voice is unbound, ambiguous, and disruptive; it is seductive and dangerous; and it renders the text unintelligible and thus forms a threat), and the abstract, rational, and logical spoken voice, which signifies and forms the law (Dolar 1996). For Poizat, opera is about the wish for the autonomization of voice, it is an attempt to approach pure voice, a detached voice-object, and an existence of voice alone. In this matrix, plot, text, and so on, serve the vicissitudes of voice; voice is not an intensified delivery of a text, its expressive or symbolic rendering. Rather, the plot and character delineation function to highlight the supreme value of voice (Poizat 1992).

Carolyn Abbate (1993) also develops an understanding of voice in opera that stands in contrast to obvious character delineation, narrative, and plot. Voice may manifest itself as a gesture in the orchestral, voiceless music that may be perceived as an act of enunciation creating its own narrative. These gestures in the music have no source in a particular character, nor are they anchored in a leitmotif, but are instead an expression of music as "personae." Abbate finds such an example in Strauss's *Salome*. These are "voices," argues Abbate, that control events and plots, subverting the "composer's voice" and enfolding a realm beyond narrative (Abbate 1991, 1993). Lawrence Kramer (2004) uses the term "wandering voice" to refer to the voice as a detached object. The term serves as a trope for opera as such. Wandering voice has three modalities through which it performs the operatic self and acts out the plot: a conditional mode (operatic voice proper, a heightened form), an unconditional mode (voice in extremis), and an absolute mode (the "beyond" of voice).

Body and Voice

A further empowering of voice is found in the notion that voice as such has "body" and possesses a materiality or physicality. The "grain of the voice" is the body in the singing voice (Barthes 1977). Voice is not only invisible and ephemeral but is partially matter; there is something in a voice or belonging to it that intimates mass, a presence beyond itself. This "body" is conceived either as a ghostly materiality arising and disappearing with the sound of the voice, or it is taken as something that leaves traces, remainders, and echoes of an event as though there were a lingering presence (Abbate 2001).

More common is the employment of body in the sense of embodiment and disembodiment. Here the determining pair is not "singing and speaking," "real and operatic singing," or "phenomenal and noumenal" but "voice and body": voice with regard to the body producing it (the body of the singer), to character (the construction of role, the visuality of the role enacted), and to listener (the voice resounding in the listening body, the visceral response).

The question of body and voice in opera obviously pertains not only to the status of what is seen compared to what is heard. Conventions governing the signification of the singer's body in relation to the voice are such that the voice range and the role are not biologically determined: castrato is here the paradigmatic case, but travesty, cross-dressing, and the overall preference for high voices all attest to this phenomenon. Voice categories are not determined by gender; indeed, the operatic voice is an example of the gendered-ness of the voice (Wood 1994; Dame 1994). The operatic voice challenges polarities and refuses categories of gender and sexuality that have been socially and culturally constructed (Wood 1994; Leonardi and Pope 1996; Abel 1996). Indeed, the operatic voice has loomed large in musicological queer theory because it allows us to reimagine, transgress, and sever the links among body, sex, voice, pitch, and timbre and thus to express conflict, paradox, and excess. In the writing of Koestenbaum (1993), the analogies between the operatic singing voice and sexuality, self-fashioning, and identity construction elicit a performative response whereby writing about opera becomes an attempt to recapture the ecstasies of the media and its voices.

Some scholars see the character embodied in the music and downplay the signification born of the body producing the singing; music overcomes, even cancels, the meaning born of the sight of the singer's body. No teenager can sing the part of Cio-Cio San (Madama Butterfly in Puccini's opera). Even though the role calls for a fifteen-year-old Japanese girl, only a highly trained older singer can be cast, thus inevitably not matching the physical qualifications called for by the role. The body is viewed as participating in the creation of the drama, but when it is absent, as in the case of studio recordings, the voice invents a presence. In other words, it is as if the body's signification changes once music sounds and voices sing. Similar to the paradoxical way in which words function in opera—they are indispensable but in fundamental ways disregarded—the body is indispensable but overlooked. Although there is a myth (though there is some truth to it) that opera singers require large bodies to produce their wondrous voices (Hutcheon and Hutcheon 2000)—voices are taken to reside "in" the very flesh, in the singer's physical dimensions—we "see" these bodies through what we "hear" of them. One outcome of privileging the singing voice in a predominantly acoustic domain—in which reflections and refractions are induced by the translation of the vocal into the visual, the body being a sign of the voice—is that singers require "no body" at all. In other words, an operatic performance demands a measure of "invisibility" (Koestenbaum 1993: 74). In the matrix of singer-role-voice-body, operatic "beings"—invisible-singers-in-visible-roles—cannot be reduced to the singer's presence, the formative effects of the singer's dramatic role, or any straightforward combination of the two (Grover-Friedlander 2011: 71). Other scholars do not adhere to the body's disappearance in the voice and emphasize instead singing's performativity, its presence as event (Duncan 2004).

The high measure of verisimilitude has periodically been questioned, historically by verismo composers such as Leoncavallo and Massenet and more recently by opera directors (Zeffirelli, for example) who take the singers' appearance to be the determining factor in casting them to match the role they perform. Indeed, opera is flexible enough to allow that the body and voice be synchronized and the visual and the vocal be matched.

Embodiment takes a turn in Cavell's account of opera's peculiar affinity of its voices and bodies. An operatic voice as such is disembodied within the body carrying it. To be sure, the body determines the voice in technical terms, what it can and cannot produce, but character in opera is not an outcome of the body and voice of the singer. Only a loose link connects the two. The voice does not determine the character, nor does the character determine the voice. A singer for Cavell has a unique body that cannot be detached from her voice; the link is irreproducible, but the voice is experienced as disembodied (Cavell 1994: 137). For Abbate, disembodiment is fundamental to opera, even as it is something that opera defends itself against. It is not an essential condition of opera's voices as such but a trick that increases or diminishes the power of the voice (Abbate 2001).

An Idea Behind the Voice

One way to explore the bizarre nature of the voice in opera, outlined thus far, is to consider the idea behind it, since one of its exceptional features is precisely the presence of such an idea. The idea is that of an invention of a phenomenon, of opera, that endows voices with power. Power takes on various forms: the recreation of a lost power (resurrection of the power that music once had in Greek tragedy); the revival of the dead (opera is ideationally founded on the myth of Orpheus); enchantment (the creation of such an illusion in a disenchanted world); a simulation of a symptom and its cure (in the psychoanalytic sense).

It is commonly held that opera originated in an act of invention achieved by a circle of theorists aiming to create a musical form that would revive the power of music in Greek tragedy. Opera is a media to explore the hidden powers behind the interaction of words and music. It has been marked with a peculiar sense of expectation about the power of such music, and has retained a certain nostalgia for lost, unheard, and absent voices. Indeed, it is the story of Orpheus, a tale about the power of the singing voice that serves as the media's founding myth and provides its recurring thematics. Many claim that all opera is Orphic. The Sirens are not a model for the origination of operatic song, since their song kills the listener. Neither can Ulysses be opera's ideal mythic listener, since if anything he allegorizes the capacity to resist song. Opera is about neither singing that kills the listener nor the capacity to withstand the power of song and refuse to listen. On the contrary, from the listener's point of view, opera involves abandoning oneself to song, anticipating beautiful singing, longing for intimations of a miraculous passage inherent in that singing, at the same time knowing that the singing will come to an end. The Orphic myth provides an understanding of the power of the operatic song as singing that tries to overturn death. Song manifests itself as the capacity to revive or to infuse a world of death with life, to musicalize the world. But the myth is as much about the success of song as the inability to sustain this success. Ultimately Orpheus fails, and Eurydice is resurrected for but a fleeting moment—thus showing that the ecstatic power of song cannot be sustained. Singing is shown to be essentially ephemeral; it reveals a world colored by transience. The origin of song in the myth is related to the impossibility of sustaining the world through song. The myth establishes a distinction between a song that revives but is transient and a gaze that kills and is permanent. Song revives the dead, but that revival is overturned by a gesture that is not acoustic. The visual is able to bring about the total collapse of whatever has been achieved by the vocal and the acoustic (Grover-Friedlander 2005: 7).

In Adorno's writing, opera is Orphic in the sense that it creates an illusion of enchantment or endeavors to preserve a magical dimension, an essentially auratic character, in the midst of a disenchanted world. Opera attempts to preserve the magical in a disillusioned world (Adorno [1955] 1994). In a similar vein, opera for Jean Starobinski has the singular power to transform bygone enchantments into present enchantment, since opera's "now," its "bodily presences," transcends "then." This is the only enchantment we have access to (Starobinski 2008). Peter Brooks finds that the operatic voice can act out emotion, in the psychoanalytic sense of reproducing it before our very eyes rather than merely imitating an affect. Moreover, the power of the operatic voice is unique in simultaneously being a performance of the symptom (the impasse) and its cure (the working through of the impasse). Opera's peculiar power of song is in resolution and cure (Brooks 2000).

The Power of the Operatic Voice as the Doubling of Worlds

We can formulate the power of the operatic voice as a doubling of worlds: past and present, the living and the dead, the enchanted and disenchanted, the deadlocked and cured. Let us linger briefly on one of these pairings: the power of the operatic voice to hover between worlds, one of which is either yearned for (Cavell 1994), not directly present to us (Abbate 1993, 2001), present at all costs (Žižek 2002), or turned perceptible (Tomlinson 1999). In all these accounts, the singing voice figures in some form as the passage, the in-between, the gate to something beyond itself. It is a figure for ephemerality and presence.

Cavell's account of opera's foundation is based on singing's power to cross over to the other world in an attempt to bring back the dead. Its origin should indeed be sought in the Orpheus myth. The power of singing to cross between worlds is also understood as the power to revive *this* world, to show it as transfigured, as though this world figured as the other. The revival of the world is coupled with an opposite notion of the world as lost and deadened. This is the realm of haunting, of an existence that takes place in neither world, in a limbo neither dead nor alive. Cavell puts forth the notion of singing as a figure for abandonment. Singing is not an expression of a character's inner life. Instead, it is a figure for the exposure of what lies beyond the confines of the work: singing opens up unbound reverberations of meaning. For Cavell, the excesses of opera are linked to deep intimations of ephemerality, the constant threat that singing will be terminated. What is nevertheless essential for Cavell is how even such excesses, transgressions, and failures reflect something quintessentially human—as though the human were essentially beyond itself, bringing out the contours of the human voice (Cavell 1994). Abbate expresses a related thought when stressing the presence of unheard song or music that sings itself, thus bringing out the unattainable nature of song or its inherent "beyond-ness." Its absent sounds make them resonate so powerfully (Abbate 2001). For Adorno, one is transfigured and exalted beyond ordinary existence through song. Opera's voices are costumes, disguises of heroes and gods that pertain to this transfiguration. Singing voices turn the meaningless into the meaningful as the singers' voices capture reflections of a meaning of life and its affirmation (Adorno [1955] 1994).

In Abbate's account, the origin of opera in the myth of Orpheus's singing excludes a crucial moment, namely Orpheus's postmortem dismemberment. Orpheus is decapitated, yet his singing resonates after death. This very aspect of the origin-myth of opera has repeatedly been left out of the media's history. Not wishing to acknowledge song's independence from the body or life of the singer, opera absents the singing head. But disembodiment finds its way back into opera in other forms. It serves, writes Abbate, instances of impossible singing, songs that can never exist. In Abbate's implied (rather than present) moments of music, there is a glimpse of another world (Abbate 2001). Abbate writes that opera always gives rise to two terms, whether they are speech versus music or operatic music versus phenomenal performance (Abbate 1991). The doubling of the world is reflected in the world above and the world below, or the transcendental and the material. Opera is a paradoxical amalgam of the two worlds. Abbate locates within the works themselves, in their different modes of singing, precisely the distinction between the material and the transcendental. Stage songs, phenomenal music, are special instances in opera where we glimpse the other world. In phenomenal music we get hints of the split between realms: between what characters inhabiting an opera customarily hear and what they hear when they sing. Another such glimpse is offered by the numinous intruder: a mysterious character, Faust for example, who breaches the opera and brings within its orbit the realm of the beyond. Or, finally, we glimpse another realm when opera imprints its nature as performance within the operatic work itself (Abbate 2001). Hans Gumbrecht (2004) describes something present in the performance that is beyond meaning: presence effects that are vocal remnants, remains of the voice—a vocal force, as it were, in the act of singing. This presence contains a notion of the performativity of the voice, otherwise beyond its meaning.

Slavoj Žižek relies on Lacan's notion of the two deaths. The first death is the biological and the second is the symbolic death in which there are no longer any haunting debts. It is in this zone, between the two deaths, that Žižek locates the Wagnerian singing voices. This "between-ness" is again a form of doubleness of the world that brings about the occasion for singing. It encompasses a sense of endlessness (for the Wagnerian hero, this undead existence, the prevention of the second death, is an eternity of suffering). In Žižek's matrix, the Wagnerian exemplary song emerges from the condition of existing as an undead monster, from the horror of immortality and an interminable existence of singing (Žižek and Dolar 2002).

Two worlds is the critical determinant of opera for Tomlinson as well, one accessible to the senses, the other not. Operatic singing is an experience of a metaphysics and physics, of the supersensible and sensible realms. This acquires different manifestations throughout history in accordance with changing models of subjectivity as opera for Tomlinson mirrors constructions of subjectivity in the subject it embodies. Tomlinson traces opera's voices approaching the noumenon as the limit case of the phenomenon. The subject is drawn toward the realm of the beyond, transcendent, noumenon. Opera has the power to envoice the imperceptible inaccessible realm and put its listeners in touch with invisible, supersensory realms (Tomlinson 1999).

Voice and Words: Death

Obviously, the most fundamental doubleness or division in opera is that of music and words. It takes on various forms, for example in relation to the limit of their interaction, the ways borders between words and music are transgressed, and fantasies about their possible union. The relationship between music and words is dealt with in terms of subservience, supremacy, and equality (Do words serve singing? Or vice versa? How do the rules of composition of two systems, music and poetry, work together?); in terms of form (text-oriented versus music-oriented scenes; intelligibility of the text where action and plot are advanced versus moments of vocal display where the voice frees itself from the constraints of textual intelligibility, the text is dismantled, and the voice is allowed full reign, and indeed is expected to be excessive and display virtuosity); in terms of expression (what is expressed, how the music reflects, contradicts, disregards, and goes beyond that which is conveyed by the text); in terms of conventions, and so on. The issue resurfaces under various headings in this volume. Here an exemplary mode of music-word doubleness will be mentioned—opera's death plots—as it is specifically theorized with respect to voice.

The abundance of death in opera has been accounted for in terms of the listener's investment, anxiety, and enjoyment, and in terms of the ways these reactions and the enacted plots mirror historical and cultural concepts and social structures. Some scholars conceive of the centrality of singing as that which explains opera's attraction to liminal situations, as these serve the expression of extreme singing. The quest for such singing brings about the excess of deaths in opera. Opera replays, ever again, the scene of death, releasing its central characters, one after the other, to that inner compulsion. In opera an intimate association is established between singing and death. The climax of singing is the most extreme form of being toward death. The relation of opera to death is found most importantly in the placement of the apotheosis of singing, and thus of what is termed "operatic," precisely in relation to and dependent on death: opera fashions death songs. I have argued that the death song is the height of singing expressed in the face of death. In such a death scene, the relation of music and meaning is reconfigured. It is the place where music overtakes narrative, the place where the plot lets go of its narrative logic in favor of singing. This operatic moment contains what its listeners have been waiting for all along: singing carries to the utmost the burden of the work. And yet there is also a sense of immortality that is consistent with death's obsessive presence. The repetition of song in the face of death from one opera to the other can be seen as a manifestation of the fantasy of song's power to revive the world, even if momentarily. It is as though the operatic voice wills precisely what is beyond human capacities—the reversal of death—but does so indirectly, subversively. The gesture of endless dying signifies the failure of death to hold sway. The repetition of song questions the finality of death, introducing a dimension of immortality. Endless dying is what opens to the dimension of immortality. It forms a kinship among works that subvert the recurring absoluteness of their individual deaths. Each opera kills anew, thereby also exposing the failure of death to master song. Put differently, death as a phenomenon in opera is not only to be understood from the obvious perspective of the libretto and the plot: death is immanent in the operatic singing voice (Grover-Friedlander 2005: 1–8). Clément (1988) claims that singing itself seems to kill the heroines in opera. We are deceived by opera's beautiful music, for it not only gives voice to and even causes these deaths but also encourages us to overlook or become amorally complicit in the murderous plot. For Poizat, the operatic voice is always impelled toward the extreme in an unattainable quest for a transcendent point that does not exist. Death plots allegorize the tendency of voice to reach beyond melodiousness, to achieve moments when listener and singer alike lose themselves in the singer's voice, dissolve in what becomes sheer voice, a vocal object (Poizat 1992). Žižek's formulation is that immersion in song kills; identification with the voice is the media of death (Žižek 2002). For Abbate, death functions as a utopian moment in which the opera seems to displace the authorial ("composer's") voice with a voice that has no source within the plot. She claims that death in the fictional space of an opera (what would end a character's life and imply the end of singing) is overshadowed by the concern with the fading away of the work itself. Abbate reconceives the place of life and death in relation to the work to reveal the work's livelihood. Simultaneous with the fading of every performance are its further resonances (Abbate 2001).

Afterlife of Voice

Can opera figure singing after death? Can it play out the scenario intimated by its foundation in Orphic singing? There are peculiar cases of singing being granted power in the face of death, cases which I identify as exemplifying an afterlife of singing (Grover-Friedlander 2011). These cases reformulate what operatic singing involves: death, the limit zone, is revisited or renegotiated, and a new extremity, a beyond of death, emerges around which singing is reconfigured. These cases exemplify a fantasy of opera, namely, its power to overturn mortality. Revitalization of the dead becomes part and parcel of the power granted singing, showing singing to be a presence beyond death. Put differently, a passage between the worlds of the living and the dead is what opera has always wished for. I have argued that the notion of an afterlife of singing serves to characterize a condition internal to singing (Grover-Friedlander 2011). It points to those cases where a breach occurs and there is a dissociation between the character's life trajectory and his or her singing, where singing itself takes on an afterlife in the face of the death of its carrier. Afterlives of singing are exceptional cases of the space of opera being invaded by singing after death, cases in which the entire space of the opera is affected by the presence of singing after death. Redrawing the boundaries of mortality through the notion of the afterlife of singing makes manifest a sphere of singing that has its own qualities and conjoined meanings. When singing is driven by the event of the protagonist's death but is not itself brought to an end by that death, we find ourselves in an alternate operatic world.

In the alternate space of opera, singing may overtake character. Singing, as it were, has its own being, and is not the emanation of the character's subjectivity. Such independence from character may manifest itself in various forms. It can result in the multiplication of singing voices inhabiting the same body, or in disembodied singing, or the merging of singing voices. Singing can be a locus of unity of more than one voice, or it can manifest itself through the failure of the attempt to put together voice and person after their intimate unity has been severed.

I consider two case studies of an afterlife of singing: Puccini's *Gianni Schicchi* and Hindemith's *Hin und zurück*. In the first, voice, singing, and song become independent of one another. Obviously, this is quite paradoxical: What could possibly distinguish one's voice (as one sings) from one's singing? There are operatic configurations that erect precisely such distinctions. Consider impersonation. In Puccini's *Gianni Schicchi* (1918), the title character attempts to impersonate the voice of (the dead) Buoso Donati in order to change the latter's will. The act constitutes, on an obvious level, the revival of the voice of the dead. What is more interesting and important, however, is that the opera's final moments are an apologia recited by Gianni Schicchi, supposedly many years after the events depicted, from hell. But, in fact, the voice given at the end to the dead permeates the opera as a whole. *Gianni Schicchi* undermines the presupposition that hell is kept separate from the world of the living and is to be confined to the opera's epilogue. Gianni Schicchi's afterlife in hell reflects back from the epilogue to the whole opera and refashions the character's operatic self as one that is simultaneously living and dead. If *Gianni Schicchi* is explicitly about a dead man being overtaken by a voice of the living man who dubs him—about how the dead are threatened by the living—then its implicit argument reveals the world of the living as itself permeated by death. In *Gianni Schicchi*, the main character sings by impersonating another's voice. But for those who stand to gain from this hoax and are threatened by its revelation, something more lies in the impersonation. Schicchi uses an earlier "song" and his usual voice in the midst of the impersonation. These serve as haunting reminders of falsehood thus becoming the voice of Schicchi himself making his presence known. The foreign voice (the impersonator's "real" voice) remains constantly present, even in the midst of the impersonated voice. Where then is the life and death of a character to be located? In an imitation of the dead? In a song? In a voice? Opera's expansion of the space of death, so that singing takes place beyond the boundaries of life, is then at the same time a re-articulation, even a transgression of the boundaries of singing itself. Singing as such becomes more present, becomes a being with its own identity and soul.

The notion of afterlife opens up hidden possibilities in the space of opera. It allows us to make intelligible a register of the voice that we intuitively sense to be essential to it and to reflect back on the meanings of the operatic voice as such and the sense of its haunting, resonating, unending presence (Grover-Friedlander 2011: 77–108).

Afterlives of singing have their own expanse of temporal possibilities. Traditional operatic singing creates self-enclosed moments that stop time. Operatic time manifests itself in moments of stillness, moments when time is suspended. Time does not flow forward in any customary sense; the unfolding narrative does not dominate the experience of time's progression. With operatic afterlives there is a rethinking of this temporal template and a further distortion of its temporal idiosyncrasy. Typically, the end is not foreshadowed but has already *occurred*. Take, for instance, a second case study: Paul Hindemith's twelve-minute opera *Hin und zurück* (*There and Back*, 1927, with a text by Marcellus Schiffer). The opera proceeds to a midpoint where the wife is killed by the jealous husband, followed by his suicide. At this caesura, a sage appears with peculiar words of wisdom:

> Looking down from above, no great difference exists
> If a man begins his life in the cradle,
> then proceeds 'til he meets death,
> or if he dies first, and follows from death to birth.
> Let us reverse this fate and make things turn back,
> Then I will show you, the logic changes not a jot,
> and all will be well as it was before.[1] (Hindemith 1927)

In the opera's second half, time is rewound. The opera goes backward textually and musically, retracing its steps and ending exactly at the point in time it began. The same text that led up to the double deaths now serves to "revive" the dead couple. A way to problematize a work's temporal boundary in examples of the afterlife of singing is to toy with beginnings and endings, with the edges of the work, questioning whether time has passed, whether anything has happened. *Hin und zurück* acts this out by changing the direction of the text line by line and by reversing the sequence of musical sections. The plot is now quite absurd, ending as it began with a deaf aunt knitting in her chair, oblivious to everything that has taken place, to the deaths and their miraculous undoing.

Utterances are comic and senseless, as though indeed singing was not the emanation of the character's subjectivity. *Hin und zurück* shows singing unfolding in a realm where life and death are interchangeable, where death and non-death are undifferentiated. Singing not only plays out the fantasy of reviving the dead, as in the myth of Orpheus, but also is itself what has been revived after death. Death no longer functions as a limit, climax, and end point. There is, then, no longer a unique climactic utterance with a perfect match to character. Hindemith's opera pokes fun at the abundance of deaths in opera, at operatic time, and at the notion of a unique climax in a sung death. *Hin und zurück* reformulates its relation to death by introducing a midpoint *deus ex machina* in which a higher power emerges from a trapdoor, disclaiming mortality. The sage declares that beginning at birth and ending in death is interchangeable with dying first then following a trajectory from death to life. It is a unique vocal expression set apart musically, textually, and dramaturgically, but its function is to parody mortality and opera; rather than serving the vicissitudes of death, it justifies its undoing.

One of the possibilities opened up by the notion of afterlife is fashioned as multiple occurrences in which singing is dispersed, split, multiplied, and echoed. Hearing similarly is keyed to recurrence rather than absorbed in a single, self-enclosed scene. The power of singing is in its resounding. Indeed, the entire second act—half of *Hin und zurück*—lasting the comic length of six minutes, echoes the first half of the opera in its totality. The same material often condensed is reversed in blocks. One of the rare textual changes is an incomplete "I'm dy. . ." of the murdered wife. One of the single moments where the music is treated in detail rather than in sections in which rewinding occurs on a minute level is in reversing the melodic direction in the opera's brief coloratura. There the melody descends rather than ascends, drawing attention to the voice. It is the opera's expression of singing. It is in a flash of melodic flourish that singing after death is reconfigured.

See also: Verisimilitude, Character, Meaning, Opera between the Ancients and the Moderns

Note

1. "Von ganz droben gesehn ist es ohne Belang, ob des Menschen Lebensgang von der Wiege vorwärts irrt, bis er verdirbt, oder ob er erst stirbt und nachher geboren wird. Laßt uns darum das Schicksal rückwärts drehen. Ihr werdet sehen, die Logik weicht nicht um ein Haar, und alles wird gut, wie es vorher war."

Bibliography

Abbate, Carolyn. 2001. *In Search of Opera*. Princeton, NJ: Princeton University Press.

——. 1993. "Opera; or, the Envoicing of Women." In *Musicology and Difference: Gender and Sexuality in Music Scholarship*, edited by Ruth Solie, 225–258. Berkeley and Los Angeles: University of California Press.

——. 1991. *Unsung Voices: Opera and Musical Narrative in the Nineteenth Century*. Princeton, NJ: Princeton University Press.

Abel, Sam. 1996. *Opera in the Flesh*. Boulder, CO: Westview Press.

Adorno, Theodor. [1955] 1994. "Bourgeois Opera." In *Opera Through Other Eyes*, edited and translated by David Levin, 25–44. Stanford, CA: Stanford University Press.

Barthes, Roland. 1977. "The Grain of the Voice." In *Image Music Text*, translated by Stephen Heath, 179–189. New York: The Noonday Press.
Brett, Philip, Elizabeth Wood, and Gary Thomas, eds. 1994. *Queering the Pitch: The New Gay and Lesbian Musicology*. New York: Routledge.
Brooks, Peter. 2000. "Body and Voice in Melodrama and Opera." In Smart 2000, 118–134.
Cavell, Stanley. 1994. "Opera and the Lease of Voice." In *A Pitch of Philosophy: Autobiographical Exercises*, 129–169. Cambridge: Harvard University Press.
Celletti, Rodolfo. 1991. *A History of Bel Canto*. Oxford: Clarendon Press.
Clément, Catherine. 2000. "Through Voices, History." In Smart 2000, 17–28.
——. 1988. *Opera, or the Undoing of Women*, translated by Betsy Wing. Minneapolis: University of Minnesota Press.
Cone, Edward T. 1988. "Opera and Its Inhabitants." In *A View from Delft*, edited by Robert Morgan, 125–138. Chicago: University of Chicago Press.
Dame, Joke. 1994. "Unveiled Voices: Sexual Difference and the Castrato." In Brett et al. 1994, 139–153.
Dolar, Mladen. 1996. "The Object Voice." In *Gaze and Voice as Love Objects*, edited by Renata Salecl and Slavoj Žižek, 7–31. Durham, NC: Duke University Press.
Duncan, Michelle. 2004. "The Operatic Scandal of the Singing Body." *Cambridge Opera Journal* 16/3: 283–306.
Grover-Friedlander, Michal. 2011. *Operatic Afterlives*. New York: Zone Books.
——. 2005. *Vocal Apparitions: The Attraction of Cinema to Opera*. Princeton, NJ: Princeton University Press.
Gumbrecht, Hans Ulrich. 2004. *Production of Presence: What Meaning Cannot Convey*. Stanford, CA: Stanford University Press.
Hindemith, Paul. 1927. *Hin und züruck*. Piano-vocal score. Text by Marcellus Schiffer, translated by Marion Farquhar. Mainz: B. Schott's Söhne.
Hutcheon, Linda, and Michael Hutcheon. 2000. *Bodily Charm: Living Opera*. Lincoln: University of Nebraska Press.
Katz, Ruth. 1994. *The Powers of Music: Aesthetic Theory and the Invention of Opera*. New Brunswick, NJ: Transaction Publishers.
Kerman, Joseph. [1956] 1988. *Opera as Drama*. Rev. ed. Berkeley and Los Angeles: University of California Press.
Kivy, Peter. 1994. "Speech, Song, and the Transparency of Media: A Note on Operatic Metaphysics." *The Journal of Aesthetics and Art Criticism* 52/1: 63–68.
Koestenbaum, Wayne. 1993. *The Queen's Throat: Opera, Homosexuality and the Mystery of Desire*. New York: Poseidon Press.
Kramer, Lawrence. 2004. "Voice and Its Beyonds." In *Opera and Modern Culture: Wagner and Strauss*, 221–228. Berkeley and Los Angeles: University of California Press.
Leonardi, Susan, and Rebecca Pope. 1996. *The Diva's Mouth: Body, Voice, Prima Donna Politics*. New Brunswick, NJ: Routledge.
Poizat, Michel. 1992. *The Angel's Cry: Beyond the Pleasure Principle in Opera*, translated by Arthur Denner. Ithaca, NY: Cornell University Press.
Rosen, David. 1992. "Cone's and Kivy's 'World of Opera.'" *Cambridge Opera Journal* 4/1: 61–74.
Smart, Mary Ann, ed. 2000. *Siren Songs: Representations of Gender and Sexuality in Opera*. Princeton, NJ: Princeton University Press.

Starobinski, Jean. 2008. *Enchantment: The Seductress in Opera*. New York: Columbia University Press.
Tomlinson, Gary. 1999. *Metaphysical Song: An Essay on Opera*. Princeton, NJ: Princeton University Press.
Wood, Elizabeth. 1994. "Sapphonic." In Brett et al. 1994, 27–66.
Žižek, Slavoj, and Mladen Dolar. 2002. *Opera's Second Death*. New York: Routledge.

CHAPTER 15

CHARACTERIZATION

JULIAN RUSHTON

Acts of Performance

Characterization is a disputed area in opera criticism. Its existence is usually admitted, but it is questioned whether the characterization of individuals as more than generalized human types derives entirely from the "play"—by which I mean the libretto and stage action—or derives in some essential way from the music.

Such discussions usually take place in the study, but opera is best experienced in the theater, where characterization may be received as the product of multiple creative voices—composer, librettist, singer—that emanate from an act of performance. Without music, opera would not be itself. The music should not be conceived as no more than decoration, designed to attract audiences either to a play that happens to be sung (or partly sung), or to a musical entertainment that justifies its length and lavishness by being presented in the guise of a drama (a "concert in costume"). These are the extremes of the operatic spectrum. At one end is the sung play; Debussy in *Pelléas et Mélisande* and Berg in *Wozzeck* delivered large parts of an existing spoken drama in types of speech-song, rather than adapting the original as a libretto (as is more usual). At the other end, a common misunderstanding of Baroque opera is to regard it as a "concert in costume," consisting largely of arias written to display the singers to best advantage. The core of the historically based modern repertory lies between these extremes: nobody could mistake *Le nozze di Figaro*, or *Otello*, for sung plays or concerts in costume, although both are based upon spoken dramas.

Neither of the extremes on the operatic spectrum needs to accommodate the idea of *musical* characterization. In a sung play, characterization can be attributed to the original—to Maeterlinck, to Büchner. In the concert in costume, attention is directed more to music than to dramatic characters as such. Crucial, therefore, to ideas of *musical* characterization are operas with a distinctive literary original, such as *Le mariage de Figaro* or *Othello*, and those that seem to turn on the vagaries of character and in which the sense of personality is a vital part of the experience: operas such as *Don Giovanni*, with its complex literary and popular antecedents, or—to take an example with no such antecedents—*Die Meistersinger*. But is that sense of personality the product merely of the words, or can it be attributed to the music?

The primacy of words in characterization is implicit in Gluck's comparison of poetry with draftsmanship; the musician brings the drawing to life by color and "by the well-chosen contrast of light and shade" (Howard 1995: 84; translated from the dedicatory Preface to *Alceste* [Vienna, 1769]. The words may have been written by the librettist, Ranieri de' Calzabigi, but Gluck authorized them). Wagner similarly appeared to question music's singularity when he urged that music should be a means to a dramatic end, rather than an end in itself (1887: 351). But neither of these great musical dramatists was referring to characterization. In persuasive discussions of this question, Peter Kivy concludes that music has only a limited role in characterizing the persons in the drama, even though he concedes Mozart's ability to persuade us that his music is "animating" a personality (Kivy 1993: 162). (It should be noted that Kivy employs "characterization" for the creation of types, and "animation" in the sense that I employ "characterization"; on this basis, he is right to say that "the means of *characterizing* the personages of an opera were available to any of Mozart's less talented contemporaries [his emphasis]" [1993: 163].) For Kivy, our perception that operatic characters possess psychological depth is an "illusion," an "aesthetic" or "artistic" effect (1988: 268–269, cited 1993: 167); characterization that is not illusory comes from the words.

Joseph Kerman lists three principal ways in which music can contribute to drama: characterization, action, and atmosphere. The first of these—not, as one might expect, the last—he calls "the most obvious":

> If feeling can be presented directly in music, as opera composers seem always to have believed (though philosophers have not always agreed with them), one agency of music in opera is to round out information about a character's thought and action with insight into his or her inner life of feeling. (Kerman [1956] 1988: 215)

Two demonstrations are required in support of this view: that music is indeed the agent that provides insight into a character's inner life of feeling, and that insight into a character's inner life of feeling constitutes characterization. Of Kerman's three musical contributions to drama, "action"—even if the product of inner feeling—is not considered here. But "atmosphere" intersects with Kivy's view of the limitation of music in matters of characterization.

Music produces atmosphere in a manner, and with a potency, not available to dramatic forms that eschew it. To evoke atmosphere—local color, weather, incipient dread—or to mark a cross-reference (through "leitmotif"), theaters used to employ orchestras to perform "incidental" music to spoken dramas, a tradition owing much to opera that fed into, and found a more permanent place in, film. Music achieves atmosphere through well understood styles, references, or topics. Where essentially atmospheric music, such as a slice of local color, seems to define an individual, it achieves the first, generic, stage of "characterization" through differentiation from other individuals. But from Kivy's point of view, this is no more than the sophisticated application of atmosphere, and thus of generic characterization, rather than "animation" or individualization. Pastoral music, for example, is a well-identified topic throughout the history of opera (see Ratner 1980; Allanbrook 1983; Monelle 2006). The application of a pastoral topic sets a scene, evokes an atmosphere. When a character sings in a pastoral manner, that person is typecast, perhaps as a peasant. The words may suggest a stupid peasant, a cunning peasant, a virtuous peasant, or a person of high rank disguised as a peasant; but such details emerge from the libretto more than the music. Music is thus relegated to a responsive role.

Rather than refute this view, which despite Kerman's advocacy is probably impossible, I would like to modify it. I suggest that musical characterization (Kivy's "animation") does exist, in the work of the best dramatic composers, although it works only in close association with literary characterization, in the libretto. It goes against the grain to relegate to a secondary position the one element that defines opera as a dramatic species—different from spoken drama, with or without "incidental" music, or film with non-diegetic or "expressive" music. In these other genres, individual characters do not *sing*. Thus it is only in musical drama that characters are experienced directly through music produced by individuals who are singers, and thus musicians.

Voices

Carolyn Abbate argues that music itself, never mind opera, is not solely the product of "the composer's voice"; she refers to "potentially multiple musical voices that inhabit a work" (1991: x)—even an instrumental work. Voices are further multiplied in opera; the incorporation of words into musical performance by singers adds the voice of the librettist. The composer's voice is only one—albeit an indispensable one—of those that reach us through performed music; we experience, indeed welcome, diversified performances based on the same musical score. In opera the individual singer's voice, emanating from an acting body, participates in the characterization suggested by the libretto and the musical score. The orchestra, too, has a voice, itself potentially multiple. Thus, for example, Gluck's oboe (*Iphigénie en Aulide*, Act I, scene 3) is the voice of Agamemnon's conscience; his agitated violas contradict the support given by the other strings to Orestes's deluded monologue, "Le calme rentre dans mon coeur" (*Iphigénie en Tauride*, Act II, scene 3). In the theater we, the audience, receive the voices of the singer, the orchestra, and (ideally) the poem, directly and together as the outcome of the creative energies of performer, composer, and librettist. But as everyone who attends an opera is aware, the work of the poet is often subdued by music. Even when opera is in the language of the audience, words are often rendered incomprehensible by repetition and melismatic setting, or simply made indistinguishable because of the difficulty in projecting them in the composed tessitura (in general, the higher the voice type and the higher the vocal line, the less distinguishable are the words). Yet it is surely the case that, in receiving signals from voice and orchestra, we receive something essential, even if we do not hear or understand all the words.

I make no apology for choosing familiar examples to explain my position. First, we should not underrate characterizations that may fairly be considered generic, or predominantly so, but where individuality of a kind stands out, at least in the music. Take Mozart, surely an exemplary operatic composer; Kivy's comments were provoked by the common perception that his characters seem almost to walk the earth, so familiar are their "speeches" (arias) and the dramas in which they are embedded, but he relegates the composer's work to the status of a beautiful illusion. Wye J. Allanbrook (1983) expounds modes of musical signification through rhythm, meter, and their exogenous associations. The gestures of march, minuet, or contredanse derive from material that existed before, and outside, the operas in which they appear. In *Le nozze di Figaro*, Lorenzo Da Ponte's libretto transformed French prose into Italian verse; but the words did not determine all of Mozart's choices of rhythmic gesture (explanations of Italian versification may be found in Gossett, 2006: 41–48, and Carter, 1987: 76–81). The march is an obvious topic when Figaro pretends to encourage Cherubino's (nonexistent) military ambition ("Non più andrai farfallone amoroso"). Less predictably, Figaro's "Si vuol ballare, signor contino" employs a kind of agitated minuet before breaking into a still faster contredanse. By finding "some aspects of Mozart's musical setting that do not seem attributable to Da Ponte" Tim Carter implies (without quite saying so) that other musical choices *were* dependent on the libretto, including Mozart's choice of meter (1987: 78). But the first words could fit a contredanse as well as a minuet; the poetic meter is the same in Giovanni's "projection of anger" in "Fin ch'an dal vino" (Kerman 1990: 119). When Figaro adopts the contredanse, the lines remain the same length (five syllables), but four-line stanzas (quatrains) are abandoned. That, however, did not determine Mozart's change from the parody of an aristocratic minuet to a contredanse, a meter suited to Figaro's own class. Certainly Mozart's characterization is generic in part, because he chose plausible rhythmic gestures from a repertoire that would be known to Figaro and his audience; but it is also individualizing, in that Figaro is perceived not merely as a servant, but as an angry servant in danger of losing control of himself—which would mean ruin to himself and his marriage. That loss of control communicates most directly, not by the words, but by the change of meter, which was Mozart's creative decision; and the characterization remains intact for an audience two centuries later. The concinnity of elements rounds out a characterization that is more than generic.

In *Don Giovanni*, the characters again range across social classes, without the bourgeois element in *Figaro*, but with a more central role for the pastoral. When peasants appear virtuous or likable, they sing in a higher style than when they appear unpleasant or doltish. When Zerlina and Masetto enter, they sing the same generic pastoral music, differing only in tessitura. Their diversity as persons appears in their arias. Masetto's impotent fury when Giovanni seems about to steal his girl ("Ho capito, signor, si") is in a single tempo, straightforwardly orchestrated; Zerlina's seductive charm as she wins Masetto back ("Batti, batti") is a two-tempo aria, colored by the only instrumental obbligato in the opera (violoncello, hardly a peasant instrument).

This differentiation could be considered no more than a beautiful musical reaction to what is intrinsic in the libretto, but in opera we experience characters primarily through the music they sing. Thus it is natural for opera critics to imply that the composer is the principal, if not the sole, creator of individualized operatic persons. Composer and librettist form a single author, as when Lior Barshack glosses "the radiant individuality of Mozart's characters" as "the extraordinary subtlety of individuation, of principal and peripheral characters, in the operas of Mozart and Da Ponte" (Barshack 2008: 47, 63). Mozart's finest operas are generically comedies; another opera based on an important play (Rossini's *Ermione*) provides an example rooted in tragedy. Philip Gossett writes: "In Ermione herself [...] Rossini created one of the most complex characters in the *bel canto* repertory" (2006: 6). Such a comment seems entirely natural, and only a philosopher, probably, would question it. A few lines earlier, however, Gossett remarks that the librettist Tottola "treats the opera's literary source, Racine's *Andromaque*, with both respect and appropriate freedom." While it is true that the change of eponymous heroine amounts to little, if any, shift of emphasis, there is no doubt that Racine (and his forebear Euripides) made Hermione an exceptionally complex character. So did Rossini "create" this characterization, or did he reflect and illustrate it with appropriate music? Gossett's wider objectives may have prevented him from explaining what is surely the case: that Rossini's Ermione, compared to her French model, is *differently* complex.

Humans versus Rhyming Aliens

It is hardly fair to restrict music's abilities in opera because music criticism has generally not chosen to identify and explain the musical elements that contribute to characterization. Edward T. Cone has identified the "inhabitants of the world of opera" as possessing "natural musicality": they "go around singing songs all the time" (Cone 1989: passim, cited 131, 138). From this starting point, albeit in a "philosophical 'phantasie,'" Kivy goes so far as to suggest that operatic folk are an alien race of "improvisational singer-composers" (Kivy 1993: 153). This would turn the inhabitants of French neoclassical dramas into a peculiar species, outwardly resembling humans, who speak only in rhymed Alexandrines (leaving aside that their mythical, legendary, or historical prototypes would have spoken Latin or Greek). Opera is never as consistent as Racine, even in its most carefully rationalized (Metastasian) form. It covers a spectrum from inarticulate sounds through speech to melismatic song, and so is nearer to Shakespearean drama, mainly in blank verse with the occasional rhyme and passages of prose. The "philosophical fantasy" compels us to understand that Shakespeare's historical and invented characters—Romans, kings and queens, Falstaff, Prospero—are skilled improvisers in the English language. The mythical, legendary, historical, or fictional characters in opera are still more talented, because they improvise both words and music (these points are rehearsed by Cone and Kivy, and received a detailed response from Rosen 1992).

I prefer an explanation that treats opera characters as human, rather than alien. Operatic dramas employ presentational modes that are musical: from its inception, the beauty and humanity of vocal music, and increasingly, through four centuries of operatic productivity, the evocative and expressive powers of instrumental music. The orchestra may seem to respond to a character's moods and actions, but it plays other roles, including the diegetic (off-stage hunting horns, for example). The individual singers are not producing these sounds, and we can only be sure they hear the diegetic ones, for the orchestra primarily speaks to the audience. Cone's argument compelled him to deny the existence of a separate category of diegetic ("realistic") song, something that would be sung in real life, or if the libretto were turned into, or back into, a spoken drama (Cherubino's song "Voi che sapete" is an obvious example). Yet although the distinction between diegetic and expressive singing is certainly not hard and fast, it inescapably exists. It is most apparent when the diegetic music is a deliberate stylistic anachronism, or is popular or sacred in idiom. In *Pikovaya dama* (Act II, scene 2), Tchaikovsky ventured outside his own idiom to use music by Grétry, which the character (the Countess) has certainly not invented for herself. In introducing popular or sacred idioms, composers usually retain a semblance of artistic unity by adapting their own style appropriately. In *Rigoletto*, the Duke's "La donna è mobile" masquerades as a "popular song" (Gossett 2006: 13). Cone's rejection of Jonathan Miller's karaoke solution (the accompaniment to "La donna è mobile" selected from a jukebox) seems misplaced (Cone 1989: 129). Recognition that some music is diegetic enhances individuation of a character. The Duke, fickleness personified, sings a popular song about the fickleness of women. Carmen's Habanera and Seguidilla are understood as drawn by the character from popular sources (McClary identifies these as "Cuban-style cabaret tune" and "pop tune"; 1992: 75, 87). Her second-act song and dance with castanets (and inescapably diegetic trumpets from the barracks) may be understood as made up on the spot, but that only makes sense if her normal "operatic" singing is not improvised. Kudrjáš in *Káťa Kabanova* (Act II) sings what must be heard as a diegetic song, folkloric despite its octatonicism. In *Wozzeck*, Marie (Act I, scene 3) uses the rhythm and contour of a functional genre, the lullaby, while remaining within the ambience of Berg's eclectic, near-atonal sound world. In *Peter Grimes*, the drinkers in the inn do not improvise "Old Joe has gone fishing" in septuple meter; it masquerades as an old catch, and is thus diegetic. The numerous sacred choruses of opera must also be understood as performed music: the chorales in *Die Meistersinger*, which could never be mistaken for Bach, or the Te Deum in *Tosca*, which sets Scarpia's lustful thoughts in such harsh relief. That such music is understood as diegetic increases operatic resources, and in many cases adds a dimension to characterization; otherwise, surely, composers would not have recourse to it so often, and not only in operas about singers—Orpheus operas, or *Die Meistersinger* and *Tosca*, where the principals (Walther, Tosca) function within the "play" as singers.

Prima la Musica

I propose that we should understand operatic characters in the light of certain truisms: that opera is, like all art, artificial, and is acted on a stage. Singing humans *represent* characters; they are not in any sense actual persons, or how could different singers perform the same roles? Opera *interprets* characters from myth, legend, history, or earlier fiction; more rarely, it tells of people invented purely for the purposes of a particular opera (an example is *Die Zauberflöte*). But what we witness in the theater is not any kind of reality, but the telling of a tale by artistic means.

The simplest objection to Kivy's negation of musical characterization is that it belongs in the philosopher's study rather than in experienced theater. The philosopher attempts to rationalize the phenomenon of opera by suggesting that its world is inhabited by a peculiar type of unreal people. It is clear from many of Kivy's remarks that he does not as a result feel alienated from them, nor does he want to diminish the composer's achievement; but any attempt to rationalize what was never meant to be rational seems misguided. In opera, we hear people singing rather than speaking. We attribute traits of character to them through direct absorption of what we hear, which is mostly music, even from the voices. Because sung words are difficult to distinguish, librettos used to be (and sometimes still are) on sale in the theater; now we have surtitles and not only for translations, but sometimes when the opera is in the presumed language of the audience. Such helpful practices, however, only enhance the sense that words, or detailed understanding of the words, lie half outside the performance of opera. Surtitles do not cover every word-repetition and extension; if they did, the singers might just as well select an effective syllable, and vocalize. For some of music's most individualized acts of performance, such as the Queen of Night's arias and Lucia's mad scene, the words will never be distinct enough to contribute to characterization.

So while admitting that the words are usually written before the music, and can have a great impact on what music is actually composed, opera criticism can still argue for the primacy of music: *Prima la musica e poi le parole*. Half a century ago, this view was eloquently expressed by Joseph Kerman: "opera is an art-form with its own integrity and its own particular limiting and liberating conventions" (1988: 4; these words appear in the first edition of *Opera as Drama* [New York: Vintage, 1956: 6–7]). And the primary element in the impact of opera in the theater is the music. Even with full comprehension of the words, through simultaneous reading, prior study, or even hearing them, the audience mainly comes to listen to the singers and the orchestra.

Of course, one hopes the singers can act. But what *is* acting in opera? This question is answered with some venom by the playwright David Hare: If operatic acting "by definition, must be different from anything we know as 'acting' in the theatre" that is "surely, another way of saying it's awful" (1996: 33). Indeed it *can* be awful, as it can in the spoken theater. But when it simply matches music whose requirements control the action to a degree Hare admits he cannot bear, it is not awful, but operatic. Hare's chief preoccupation is what he sees as the aesthetic, rather than ethical, political, or moral, reception of opera in late-twentieth-century Britain: "I do not believe it is enough for art to be beautiful. For me, it needs to be urgent as well" (1996: 34). With that I have no quarrel. Documentary sources make clear that operatic acting until well into the twentieth century tended toward a degree of stylization that any succeeding generation is likely to find curious at best, and—more likely—to mock; but the same is true of spoken theater, for who today acts like Garrick, Bernhardt, or Irving?

Acting styles date no less than spoken language or any other form of verbal communication. There can be no question of resorting to historic acting styles for all of the repertoire all of the time, but experiments in restoring the stylized acting of (for example) Baroque opera show not only its integrity and connectedness to the music, but also its effectiveness in conveying a specifically operatic type of human being. In any production, a degree of stylization recognizes that operatic characters come over as larger than life, and, with few exceptions, as egotistical. Even within the continuous textures of post-Wagnerian (or post-*verismo*) operas, the demands of the music rule out entirely fluid acting, and directors who share Hare's impatience with musically controlled tempi inevitably flounder, and fill the stage with unnecessary and distracting detail. Hare says that nothing has really improved since "the old days when opera singers just stood rooted to the spot and belted it out" (1996: 33), but this misses the essence of how opera works as a dramatic form. If instead we say "the old days when opera singers just stood still and sang" we can acknowledge that even in modern works, in the best interests of drama and characterization, singers should be allowed from time to time to do exactly that.

That music determines its speed of action is a quality of opera, not a defect: a quality that distinguishes it from other dramatic forms—though less markedly from poetic than from realistic drama. The eloquence of music creates operatic persons who dominate, or try to dominate, by delivering powerful emotions, and who control, or try to control, the action in their own interests. Some characters (mainly in Baroque or neoclassical opera) are prone to heroic self-sacrifice, but even this may be the ultimate gesture of egoism. Gluck's operas provide splendid examples: Alceste, Iphigenia, Orestes, Pylades. This mythological type is extended, in a radically different manner, by Wagner's development of Goethe's *ewig-weibliche* (Senta, Elizabeth, and Brünnhilde). But such magnificent operatic personae are not dependent on myth or ancient history; they spill over into nineteenth-century operas set in an identifiable social milieu. The deaths, in a halo of forgiveness, of Luisa Miller, murdered by her lover, or Violetta, dying of natural causes, are larger than life, entirely without the grim realism of the death by poison of their near-contemporary Emma Bovary. The demands of opera permit a singing ego almost to survive death: both Gilda in her sack and Werther after shooting himself die singing, like the mythic swan. Thus opera was lampooned before it was even invented in *A Midsummer Night's Dream*, when Theseus observes of Pyramus: "with the help of surgeon he might yet recover" (Act V, scene 1).

Even with the advent of *verismo* it is a mistake to expect realism in opera. However it is defined, *verismo* was nevertheless a vital stage in opera's evolution. *Verismo* arises from a *congeries* of elements, both within the "play" (natural, ordinary persons, including "low life," which for audiences could constitute a satisfactorily remote "other") and within the music. Musical characteristics include certain harmonic gestures, directness of melody, and post-Wagnerian continuity of orchestral texture (Giger 2007). Unless they retrench consciously, like *The Rake's Progress*, most operas since about 1900 owe some allegiance to *verismo*, which appears even in a post-Wagnerian tradition (Schreker, Korngold,

Strauss's *Intermezzo*). Ostensibly realistic operas still depend on a prevalence of inflated egos, for only such characters can justify the elaborate musical structures within which they operate. Objections might be raised to this assertion. What of *Wozzeck*, where the oversized egos (Captain, Doctor) are not the main characters, and are arguably mad? In *Peter Grimes* (unlike *Wozzeck*), the central character is the most solipsistic, and the most fully realized in music, but is also, in the end, mad. In Janáček's last operas we meet the intense solipsism of Emilia Marty (*Věc Makropulos*) and the prisoners in *Z mrtvého domu*—realist works, but no less concerned with self-centered characters than their near contemporary, Puccini's *Turandot*. Realism has somewhat retreated, in Tippett, Ligeti, Birtwistle, Glass, Adams, or Messiaen's monumentally hieratic *St François d'Assise*. But surely a Minotaur, a Richard Nixon, and a St. Francis, if we accept them on the operatic stage at all, can legitimately stand still and "belt it out."

Subtle Distinctions: Bizet, Verdi, and Wagner

If it is agreed that opera can put across dramatic personalities at all, it must be primarily by means of the music. The generic characterization Kivy does allow is an ubiquitous and valuable element in the armory of the opera composer; it can be achieved by topical allusion, differentiating in Mozart between the aristocratic and bucolic, and by music of identifiable ethnic character, as in *Carmen*. But individuals in these operas stand out against these background features. We not only distinguish Don Giovanni from Leporello by voice-type (baritone against bass) and musical style, but by individual traits which include imitating one another's style. We learn specifically about Giovanni's narcissism from the way he nearly derails his own imitation of Leporello in "Metà di voi qua vadano" (Rushton 1997: 421–423). Working with the license of near-realism and a rich eclecticism, Bizet found it easy to distinguish Carmen from Micaëla, but even with the significant difference in tessitura between these roles, a simple binary opposition achieved by generic music could have left both women, in E. M. Forster's terms, "flat" (1962: 75): Carmen, the gypsy "other"—unreliable, seductive, singing "Spanish" music; Micaëla, European, identifiable with a bourgeois audience, singing music no less identifiably French. If Micaëla is more than merely a dramatic foil to Carmen, it is her behavior in Act III, finding José in the brigands' encampment, that attributes to her a heroic if improbable determination, expressed in her self-examination by means of aria ("Je dis que rien ne m'épouvante"). In fully realistic drama, so gentle a character would not display her emotions at such length, even if nobody on stage is listening. We may swallow (just) the glittering waltz sung by Juliette in Gounod's opera because she is deceiving herself into believing she is not yet ready for love. Carmen herself has no such self-revealing aria, but she appears as a rounded individual less through "couleur locale" than through the fortune-telling scene in Act

III and her superb defiance in Act IV. She dwarfs those around her, including José, whose music, more than mere words, so strikingly differentiates him from the character in Mérimée's novella. One does not condone murder, but if we read José through his first sung utterance ("Parle-moi de ma mère") and his sentimental flower song, we cannot be surprised that someone like Carmen would abandon him, nor by the intensity of the loss that leads him to such an extremity, implicit in his most striking music: in Act I, the eloquent "instrumental outburst" when "he has yet to sing a note" (McClary 1992: 77–79), and throughout Act IV.

It might be argued that these different types of music constitute only congeries of generic characterizations, but one might equally ask how *else* a musical dramatist could create a rounded individual. No doubt Bizet was assisted by the quasi-realistic social and national environs, the local color that provides a background against which characters can be understood and stand out as individuals. But excellent characterization is not dependent on such obvious aids. Consider Verdi's Leonora, in *Il trovatore*, an opera that has received critical brickbats in the past for its conventionality, at least in the libretto (Budden calls it "the most conventional of libretto structures" [1978: 67]).

In the near-contemporary *Rigoletto* and *La traviata*, Verdi is admired for bending conventions, but in *Il trovatore* he chose a plot filled with coincidences, and provided three of the main characters with full double arias; only the fourth, Azucena, does not have one, a sign of her madness (a clear account of the conventional form of the double aria is in Budden 1973: 12–17).

The heroine's entrance aria (the cantabile "Tacea la notte" and cabaletta "Di tale amor") is conventional in form, but this does not make the characterization either flat or cautious. We know nothing about Leonora from the narration in the previous scene. By the end of her aria—when she leaves the stage—we know a great deal. Trivial things, such as that she is a maid of honor to the queen, we learn only from the words, and her relatively elevated social status is indicated by the presence of a confidant, Ines, who asks questions, exhorts Leonora to behave with decorum, and adds her voice to the climax of the cabaletta. The words also inform us that Leonora loves a troubadour, something that becomes apparent later when the tenor voice of Manrico is heard with plucked (diegetic) accompaniment. In the recitative, Leonora steers the modulations, each of which Ines accepts, and builds through tremolo, a cadence in E of some grandeur, and two enharmonic changes, toward an efflorescence of lyricism, even before the end of the recitative (see Music Example 15.1).

In "Tacea la notte" itself, her lyricism takes her soaring above the staff when the minor mode changes to major. The words refer to her lover, but as yet we learn nothing of him; rather, we learn about Leonora, who would be a different person if the same words were given a different, less extravagant, musical setting. In the *tempo di mezzo*, Ines upbraids Leonora, taking over a remote tonality (A minor) for herself. Again Leonora steers the decisive modulation through E flat to the A flat major of the cabaletta, a movement of energy and brilliance that bespeaks irresponsibility, perhaps, but also a constancy in love that will endure to the very bitter end (a cabaletta is not necessarily, or even usually, in the same key as a cantabile; a case can be made for Leonora showing exceptional determination to pursue her passion to the limit by her adherence to one key).

A contrasting example, also from Verdi, is the newly minted creation of a historical character. The unexpected rapport between Philip II in *Don Carlos* and Rodrigue (Posa: Act II, scene 2, of the five-act version) is one of this marvelous opera's numerous departures from history, but derives from its literary source, Schiller's tragedy. But the king's monologue that opens Act IV departs from Schiller, as Budden notes: "the immense

MUSIC EXAMPLE 15.1 Verdi, *Il trovatore*, Part I, scene 2, mm. 7–33.

MUSIC EXAMPLE 15.1 Continued

personal grief of Philip... is an invention of Verdi and his librettists" (1981: 120n). That could have been "of the librettists and Verdi"; but it is Verdi's music that lifts it above self-pity. Philip is endangered by his family and an unrealistically all-powerful church; worse, he is the victim of the impulse that led him to displace his heir, Carlos, by marrying his own son's betrothed ("Elle ne m'aime pas! Non, son coeur m'est fermé"). As with Berlioz's equally insomniac Herod in *L'enfance du Christ*, we come dangerously near to sympathizing with one who for much of the opera, as in history, appears in a grim light. Words alone would hardly take us so far. In the aria (Music Example 15.2), Verdi's oboe reminds us of Agamemnon's conscience, the "plaintive voice of nature" (*Iphigénie en Aulide*), and of the inner cry of Cassandra in Act I of Berlioz's *Les Troyens* (it hardly matters that Verdi is most unlikely to have known *Les Troyens*; a vocal score was published in 1863, but the first two acts were not included in the 1863 performances).

Budden remarks that the use of two horns in the minor key was "new in Verdi" (1981: III: 120). The distinctive feature of the horn passage is that it *looks* like music for natural horns, which could only have played it in the major mode. With valved instruments, the second horn could simply have doubled the first in thirds; instead it arpeggiates, as a natural horn necessarily would, but, also necessarily, in the major mode. Thus the minor mode contradicts the natural instruments' long association with the kingly

MUSIC EXAMPLE 15.2 Verdi, *Don Carlos* (original five-act version) Act IV, scene 1; Act III, scene 1 (four-act version), mm. 58–68.

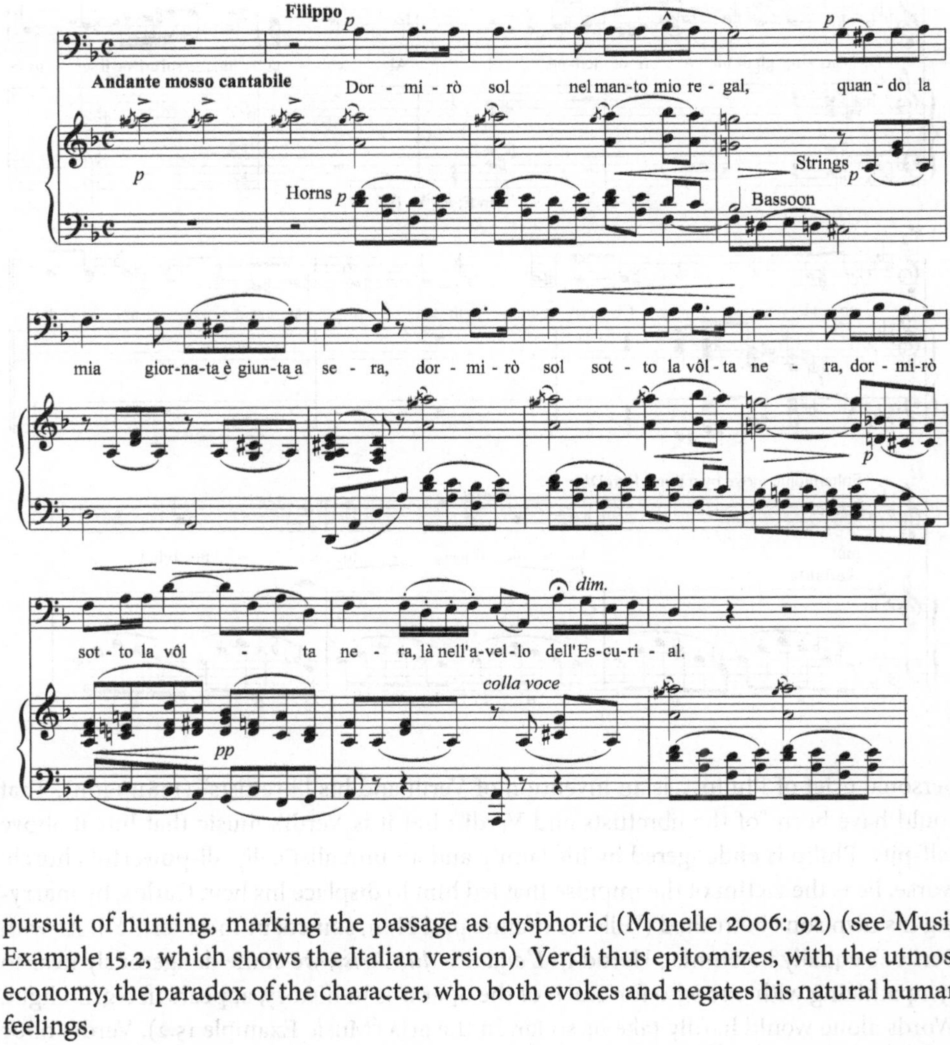

pursuit of hunting, marking the passage as dysphoric (Monelle 2006: 92) (see Music Example 15.2, which shows the Italian version). Verdi thus epitomizes, with the utmost economy, the paradox of the character, who both evokes and negates his natural human feelings.

I have argued elsewhere that musical signs tell us more than words about a character in Verdi's last opera: only the music fleetingly makes clear Ford's love for his wife, while with his conscious mind he is plotting to deceive Falstaff (Rushton 2004: 191–193). Another example concerns *Die Meistersinger*: despite Wagner's probable intention that we should despise Beckmesser, we are given an opportunity to find him endearing, if ridiculous (Rushton 2004: 193–197). This impression Wagner savagely overturns in the final scene, when Beckmesser fails to turn Walther's poem ("Morgenlich leuchtend im rosigen Schein") into a competent prize song, even muddling the words ("Morgen ich leuchte…"). This is cruel; but in the earlier scene (Act III, scene 3) Wagner also complicates Hans Sachs, who is less than frank in allowing Beckmesser to believe that he, not

Walther, is the author of the poem. Sachs says nothing literally dishonest, only promising that he will tell no one that the song is by him. Since he is not its author anyway, his promise is itself deceitful. But this piece of characterization is essentially verbal; Sachs's music does nothing to mark his serpentine mendacity, and in performance it is likely to pass unnoticed. Beckmesser's infectious delight, on the other hand, is entirely musical. At his "Was will ich mehr? Ich bin geborgen," the meter changes to a waltzing 3/8, plucked strings evoke the lute, and the orchestra, with many changes of meter (the waltz alternating freely with 2/4), performs a lively fantasia on the open-string motive of Beckmesser's instrument (elsewhere heard diegetically). He may be in pain from the beating he received the previous night, but his mind is dancing ("Beckmesser! Keiner besser!").

Die Meistersinger has many admirers (I am one), although some devotees of Wagner's other works have reservations (for instance, Deathridge 2008: x). Here, as elsewhere in Wagner, the complexity and effulgence of the music tend to overshadow occasional verbal inconsistencies (some can be attributed to the long gestation of *Der Ring des Nibelungen*). Arbitrary behavior is perhaps normal for mythical beings, gods, demigods, heroes, giants, and dragons; it does not compromise their characterization. Many such personages, in any case, will be perceived as "flat," however large they bulk on stage, in power of voice, and in the orchestra's motivic web. It is with no intention to diminish the magnificence of *Der Ring* that I suggest that Siegfried, if not quite flat, is somewhat artificially rounded by scenes of tenderness and nostalgia motivated by forest murmurs and a stab in the back. He gains more from the scene when he learns of the curse (*Götterdämmerung*, Act III, scene 1), where the tremendous music of his defiant speech is mainly based on motives familiar from *Das Rheingold* and *Die Walküre* (Music Example 15.3). His personal motive appears just once, dourly, on the bass trumpet. Otherwise the "Ring" motive is prominent, even in the voice. Siegfried lists his deeds to motives long associated with the spear, the sword, the dragon, and the disaster that will befall Valhalla, in music of restless tonality, with a predominance of half-diminished sevenths; then the major form of the "Rheingold" is accompanied by a rhythmic muttering associated with Alberich. The Rhinemaidens' music reemerges, but the climactic chords a few measures after the end of Music Example 15.3 evoke the corruption of the gold (I use conventional motive labels, aware that their signification may be over-simplified, and they tend to merge, as with the trumpet flourish that begins as the "Sword" morphing into Siegfried's horn call; that, however, does not affect my argument).

Brünnhilde is a rounded character long before achieving a motive all her own in the third opera in which she appears (*Götterdämmerung*, Prologue, scene 2). In *Die Walküre* she assimilates equine Valkyrie music, as Siegfried later assimilates his father's sword, but becomes fully herself in her plea to Wotan (*Die Walküre*, Act III), and still more by her sudden realization of her mortal, vulnerable femininity (*Siegfried*, Act III). Just as we expect increasingly rapturous love music, she falls silent (the bars preceding "Dort seh' ich Grane"), with harmonic darkening, a doom-laden string figure, the melancholy cor anglais, and low clarinets, all saying what words about a horse could never convey alone. From there her descent, in Act II of *Götterdämmerung*, to the human emotions of jealous rage and vengeance seems as convincing as it is moving.

A Simple Test

To take examples from Wagner rather than, say, Handel may seem to make my case more easily. But what Wagner did supremely well was not unprecedented. The motivic

MUSIC EXAMPLE 15.3 Wagner, *Götterdämmerung*, Act III, scene 1, mm. 363–387.

MUSIC EXAMPLE 15.3 Continued

allusions in Weber's "Wolf's Glen" scene (*Der Freischütz*, Act II) elevate the concept of "atmosphere" to the point where Max experiences psychological terror induced by his perception of supernatural phenomena, whether or not they are real. And Wagner was, of course, an inescapable influence, even in works of such contrary character as *Pelléas* and *Lulu*. The originality and insidious persuasiveness of the music in these and many other operas should allow us to say that character, as well as action and atmosphere, is conveyed to us by the composer. What I have argued may not be conclusive, and a philosopher would no doubt find ways to drive a wedge between my intellect and my conviction; whether philosophy could persuade me that I am actually wrong, however, is another question.

I end by proposing a simple test of whether music can characterize a rounded individual. Confine yourself to the libretto: Do the characters emerge vividly from it? Or do they emerge vividly only when they sing and the orchestra plays? Or put it this way: take the libretto and try to imagine entirely different music that is no less appropriate to the words. Is the resultant characterization the same?

To this question I would expect most musicians' answers to be "no." If animation of characters is an illusion, it is one as satisfying, and as legitimate, as any other artistic illusion, such as perspective in painting. Thus—even with Wagner, who also wrote the words—we can happily exclude the librettist and speak of Handel's Caesar and Cleopatra; Mozart's Figaro and Susanna; Verdi's Otello, Desdemona, and Falstaff; Debussy's Pelléas and Mélisande; and Berg's Wozzeck and Marie as humans that live by their music.

See also: What Is Opera? Verisimilitude, Voice, Meaning, Opera between the Ancients and the Moderns

Bibliography

Abbate, Carolyn. 1993. "Opera; or the Envoicing of Women." In *Musicology and Difference*, edited by Ruth Solie, 225–258. Berkeley and Los Angeles: University of California Press.

——. 1991. *Unsung Voices: Opera and Musical Narrative in the Nineteenth Century*. Princeton, NJ: Princeton University Press.

Allanbrook, Wye J. 1983. *Rhythmic Gesture in Mozart: 'Le nozze di Figaro' and 'Don Giovanni.'* Chicago: University of Chicago Press.

Barshack, Lior. 2008. "The Sovereignty of Pleasure: Sexual and Political Freedom in the Operas of Mozart and Da Ponte." *Law and Literature* 20/1: 47–67.

Budden, Julian. 1973–1981. *The Operas of Verdi*. 3 vols. London: Cassell.

Carter, Tim. 1987. *W. A. Mozart: 'Le nozze di Figaro.'* Cambridge Opera Handbooks. Cambridge: Cambridge University Press.

Cone, Edward T. 1989. "The World of Opera and Its Inhabitants." In *Music: A View from Delft. Selected Essays*, edited by Robert P. Morgan, 125–138. Chicago: University of Chicago Press.

Deathridge, John. 2008. *Wagner beyond Good and Evil*. Berkeley and Los Angeles: University of California Press.

Forster, Edward Morgan. 1962. *Aspects of the Novel*. Harmondsworth: Penguin Books.

Giger, Andreas. 2007. "Verismo: Origin, Corruption, and Redemption of an Operatic Term." *Journal of the American Musicological Society* 60/2: 271–315.

Gossett, Philip. 2006. *Divas and Scholars: Performing Italian Opera*. Chicago: University of Chicago Press.

Hare, David. 1996. "Why Opera Is Not for me." *BBC Music Magazine* 5/3 (November): 33–34.

Howard, Patricia. 1995. *Gluck: An Eighteenth-Century Portrait in Letters and Documents*. Oxford: Clarendon Press.

Hunter, Mary. 1999. *The Culture of Opera Buffa in Mozart's Vienna: A Poetics of Entertainment*. Princeton, NJ: Princeton University Press.

Kerman, Joseph. 1990. "Reading *Don Giovanni*." In *The Don Giovanni Book*, edited by Jonathan Miller, 108–125. London: Faber and Faber.

——. [1956] 1988. *Opera as Drama*. Rev. ed. Berkeley and Los Angeles: University of California Press.

Kivy, Peter. 1993. "Opera Talk: A Philosophical 'Phantasie'" and "How Did Mozart Do It? Living Conditions in the World of Opera." In *The Fine Art of Repetition*, 137–159 and 160–177. Cambridge: Cambridge University Press.

——. 1988. *Osmin's Rage: Philosophical Reflections on Opera, Drama, and Text.* Princeton, NJ: Princeton University Press.
McClary, Susan. 1992. *Georges Bizet: 'Carmen.'* Cambridge Opera Handbooks. Cambridge: Cambridge University Press.
Monelle, Raymond. 2006. *The Musical Topic: Hunt, Military and Pastoral.* Bloomington: Indiana University Press.
Ratner, Leonard G. 1980. *Classic Music: Expression, Form and Style.* New York: Schirmer.
Rosen, David. 1992. "Cone's and Kivy's 'World of Opera'." *Cambridge Opera Journal* 4/1: 61–74.
Rushton, Julian. 2004. "Speech, Song, and Deceiving Your Neighbour: Aspects of Dramaturgy in Wagner and Verdi." In *Theatre, Opera, and Performance in Italy from the Fifteenth Century to the Present. Essays in Honour of Richard Andrews*, edited by Brian Richardson, 107–122. Egham: The Society for Italian Studies.
——. 1997. "Buffo Roles in Mozart's Vienna: Tessitura and Tonality as Signs of Characterization." In *Opera Buffa in Mozart's Vienna*, edited by James Webster and Mary Hunter, 406–425. Cambridge: Cambridge University Press.
Wagner, Richard. 1887. *Oper und Drama. Gesammelte Schriften und Dichtungen*, III. Leipzig: Fritzsch.

CHAPTER 16

MEANING

LAWRENCE KRAMER

The glass chose to reflect only what he saw
Which was enough for his purpose: his image
Glazed, embalmed, projected at a 180-degree angle.
John Ashbery (1975)

The Reflective Moment

A convex mirror is like a stage on which you see yourself in distorted form and, just for that reason, see yourself truly: a glass, as John Ashbery's poem says, that somehow chooses what to reflect and yet always chooses what you already see. The convex mirror makes a handy allegory for the opera stage and its distinctive way with meaning. The distortion in the mirror is a disproportion of scale, which in opera typically takes the form of the gap between the largeness of the voices and the smallness of the distant, or at least distanced, bodies on stage. (Opera on screen obviously changes the equation, but not straightforwardly; the gap between voice and body is still there, only displaced between image stream and soundtrack. Opera on audio simply eliminates the bodies, widening the gap indefinitely.) In many operas, moreover, in a repertoire running, conservatively speaking, from Handel and Mozart through Puccini, there is a recurrent though uncertain moment in which audience self-reflection takes the place of voice and envelops the singers' bodies. That moment, as it happens, is also one in which opera, in the person(s) of the audience, reflects on itself and in so doing partly defines itself as a medium and a genre. The gesture is distinctive, although not unique. It is the fulcrum of the subject of this chapter, opera's relationship to meaning, and it therefore makes a good place to begin.

This reflective moment occurs in operas with distinct arias and duets, or numbers close enough to them to have definite boundaries. It is a familiar moment usually not worth a second thought: after an especially moving or virtuosic performance of a number, the audience interrupts the action by breaking into applause. On rare occasions—formerly not so rare—the applause prompts an encore, deferring even further the resumption of the action. But it doesn't matter; the performance then resumes as if nothing had happened. And indeed nothing has, except that the opera has been marked as just that, as opera, and doubly so: by the applause and by the voice. The reflective moment *inter*rupts the action without *dis*rupting it. But if one were to imagine a parallel moment in the performance of, say, a string quartet in which the cellist was given a round of applause after turning an eloquent phrase—well, that's the point: it's pretty hard to imagine. The operatic interruption is normal, the quartet interruption absurd, at least according to the traditional canons of listening to classical music. A more modest version of the same difference appears in the contrast between the curtain calls that follow each act of most operas and the strange rule that we are not supposed to applaud between the movements of a quartet or a symphony. Why is opera so happily interruptible?

The answer, as I have already suggested, is that the operatic interruption is of a piece with the foundational relationship of opera and meaning. The interruption is a moment of reflection that rewards the opera for becoming meaningful as measured by the expressive and technical accomplishments of its performance. But the constructive interruption is far from the only moment of its kind; it only applies to an opera, as if from without, the same principle that many operas apply to themselves from within. Part of the generic imperative of opera is to stage its own generic meaning, to stage its genre *as* its meaning, and to do so recurrently. When the audience gets involved, it is simply helping. Some operas, on Wagner's model, prefer to do without the help, but few choose to do without their own convex-mirror moments—Wagner's least of all. This moment of self-staging is both self-referential and self-celebratory, and it is each because it is the other. The cluster of relationships involved forms a primary feature, or more exactly a primary *figure*, of opera's identity. We will need to be increasingly specific about the details of that figure. Reflexivity is a mark of genre in general; particular genres assume their profile by the distinctive ways in which they observe what Derrida (1980) calls "the law of genre" and "re-mark" (remark on, mark again) their generic identity.

The particularities of this reflexive marking are especially important because, from a certain point of view, the question of meaning in opera is not much of a question at all. Opera means, as far as both its content and the content of its form go, in the same ways and for the same reasons as anything else. It means by and because of its provision for and/or its prompting of occasions of interpretation. In opera as elsewhere, meaning is the product of a surplus or a deficit of signification that can occur in any pertinent arena—of which opera has, obviously, a good many. Nonetheless, the exact devices by which opera engenders meaning may differ from those of other musical and mixed genres, and it is certainly possible to investigate opera from the point of view of media-specific devices, a point of view that is potentially both formal and historical.

Gender, Sexuality, Intermediality

Much recent work has done just that. From the late 1980s through the mid-1990s there was a veritable explosion of primarily feminist studies of the impact of gender and sexuality on the production of operatic meaning. Some of this work, such as Susan McClary's groundbreaking book on Bizet's *Carmen* (1992), Suzanne Cusick's work on Francesca Caccini (1993), Ralph Locke's essay on Saint-Saëns's *Samson et Dalila* (1991), and the first of my treatments of Strauss's *Salome* (1990, 2004), focused on the interplay of musical forms and cultural formations. Some, such as Terry Castle's essay on Brigitte Fassbaender (1995) and the tripartite "Staging Mozart's Women" by Wye Jamison Allanbrook, Mary Hunter, and Gretchen Wheelock (2000), focused on the meanings produced by particular performers and performances. Philip Brett's work on Britten (1993, 1994), Elizabeth Wood's on Ethel Smythe (1995), and Mitchell Morris's on Berg (1995), among many others, broadened the field to encompass gay and lesbian issues.

Subsequently, the interrelations of opera and cinema, or more broadly the technology and rhetoric of the moving image, came to the fore. Interest has gone not only to cinematic adaptation—the topic of two books by Marcia Citron (2000, 2010)—but also to the emergence of meaning from the affinities between the media themselves, the topic of many of the essays in two collections, Rose Theresa and Jeongwon Joe's *Between Opera and Cinema* (2002) and Jeremy Tambling's *A Night in at the Opera* (1994). Peter Franklin's seminal "Movies as Opera" (1994) traced the overlapping developments of proto-cinematic leanings in opera and the persistent entanglement of movies with opera, especially in the first half century of film history. An amusing measure of the interest in the mutual attraction of opera and cinema is that within a relatively short span no less than three serious readings of the Marx Brothers' *A Night at the Opera* were published by Stanley Cavell (1994), Michal Grover-Friedlander (2005), and myself (1994), all of them finding far more meaning than mere travesty in the movie's operatic mayhem.

Interdisciplinary or, more exactly, intermedial interests also flourished throughout this period, from Carolyn Abbate's investigation of the operatic uses of narrative (1991) to Mary Ann Smart's study of operatic gesture (2004) to Michael Halliwell's account of operas based on the work of Henry James (2005). Meanwhile, the traditional dismissal of operatic libretti as sources of meaning disappeared almost completely from the scholarly scene, though it has persisted in conventional public talk about opera. At the same time, there has been an exponential increase in the serious attention paid to specific productions as source of meaning (see, for example, Dellamora 1995; Locke 1995; Allanbrook, Hunter, and Wheelock 2000; and Levin 2006). By now, the devices acknowledged to produce meaning in opera amount to a surplus, not to say a surfeit. Or do they?

The Operatic Difference

With one obvious exception, to be noted soon, the device-oriented approach to the question of opera and meaning does not point to fundamental differences in the ways that opera and other musical or theatrical genres become meaningful. Music by itself may work with its traditional array of expressive resources joined, in performance, with accents, attitudes, and gestures; movies will surely work with image composition, mise-en-scène, shot types, editing rhythms, montage, pacing, gesture, script, actor personae, and much else, including (of course) music; opera may call on music, gesture, spectacle, libretti, production values, media, titles, casting, and so on. The resources of meaning are as different as they are abundant. Nonetheless, for the most part those differences are local and particular. They are not differences in the fundamental conditions of hermeneutic intelligibility.

In other words, the differences are contingent in a way that meaning itself—unless it is purposefully effaced—is not. A film can inflect its story by lighting direction and choice of film stock, an opera by changing its setting from one era and culture to another, but the semantic operations involved in interpreting the results are mutually consistent, if not quite identical. Northrop Frye observed the same nexus of difference and groundedness in his classic account of how narrative patterns and systems of images recur in different literary modes based on different "radicals of presentation"—the fundamental conditions by which words are addressed to an audience (Frye 1957). The originating conditions of acting, singing, and recounting correspond to the literary modes of drama, lyric, and narrative. Each mode can tell the same stories as the others and each can assimilate or appropriate the others to itself, but each does so in its own distinctive ways. Opera from this perspective is that strange hybrid in which all three radicals of presentation are equally necessary, although one of them—singing (not music, but singing)—is first among equals.

The Song Act

With singing we come to the operatic exception, which cuts across the continuities that otherwise structure the field of meaning. The exception is not singing itself but a certain vehicle of it, and one that really is unique to opera: operatic voice. To a large extent this voice defines itself as a force of rupture, something nearly impossible for other modalities to assimilate or appropriate. Opera as a genre depends on the difference between its own mode of vocalization and any other. For that reason the self-reflexive staging of opera is very often a staging of the assumption of voice.

The consequences for the production of operatic meaning will emerge as we go along. But one point to be noted immediately is that this self-staging is not, as such, a meta-theatrical *mise-en-abime*, although that is one form it may take, as it does most famously throughout Strauss's *Ariadne auf Naxos*, much of which is an opera (or rather a mismatched pair of operas) within an opera (on the *mise-en-abime* in *Ariadne*, see Frisch 1995: 227–244). Instead, the moment of self-staging is a moment of purely potential figuration, the acoustic-dramatic equivalent of a look in the convex mirror, be it a gaze or a glance, which permits but need not require the recognition of a revealingly distorted image. The moment is a proffer: a constellation of voice, action, and person that may be read, or not, as an allegory of the condition of both opera in general and of the particular opera in progress.

This moment typically involves what I call a "song act," on the analogy of the performative speech act (for the classic account of the performative speech act, see Austin 1962). Song acts occur as part of an opera's action—in film-theory language its diegesis, although there are many instances that hover ambiguously between diegetic and extradiegetic positions. Like speech acts, song acts either accomplish something specific in being uttered or distinctly "misfire." Operatic characters hear them as music, as opposed to the singing they hear as speech. Such acts have drawn commentary from Edward T. Cone (1974: 33) and Abbate (1991: 199–123), among others. Abbate speaks of "phenomenal song" in this context, but I prefer the more neutral "song acts" to avoid a Kantian framework that is not always appropriate even within the immediate post-Kantian era. Like its verbal analogue, the song act does what it does, or not, by channeling a certain force through its utterance—in opera through the sensory weight of the song act's performance as song. A regular effect of that force is to broach the possibility that the song act may be taken as an instance of generic self-staging.

It may, not must: the reflective moment becomes what it is by inviting or demanding interpretation, with all the uncertainties that this entails. But even when it remains opaque, the self-celebratory and self-reflective moment still stands out. Its doing so positions opera between and against two entirely incompatible conceptual positions, which represent the extreme poles of thought about the genre's meaning.

On the one hand, the moment declares that opera cannot be what Joseph Kerman memorably called it, a type of drama in which the dramatist is the composer (1956: 267), or, more fully, "a type of drama whose integral existence is determined from point to point and in the whole by musical articulation" (1956: 13). (Kerman also cites Edward T. Cone's statement that "the composer's conception of the text... is authoritative in defining the ultimate meaning of the work" [1956: 22]). The performative intervention in the song act disrupts the roles of the composer and the drama alike. Opera's vulnerability to refashioning by performance, something akin to what Judith Butler has called "linguistic vulnerability" in theorizing the effects of hurtful speech (1997: 1–6), almost literally takes center stage, where it proves as much an opportunity as a liability.

On the other hand, the same reflective moment declares that opera cannot be a form grounded in purely "drastic" occasions of pleasure and presence, as suggested by Abbate on the basis of a reading of the philosopher Vladimir Jankélévitch (Abbate 2004; Jankélévitch 2003). Those supposedly drastic episodes—which may or may not have reflective potential—are typically treated as if they interrupted nothing, as if the mimesis of the drama had not even been suspended but simply touched by a kind of syncope, a vertigo that the drama immediately reabsorbs. Meaning scatters like ripples in a pool and then, like the pool's reflecting surface, smoothly reassembles itself—hence the scenario of applause and participation with which this chapter began.

It is precisely this intermediacy between composition and loss of composure that defines the meaning of opera as a genre, that is, as the genre that stages itself as its own meaning over and above the meaning of the particular opera one is viewing. Opera can neither be confined to its presentation of concrete meaning nor can it transcend that presentation, and so—one might say, paraphrasing Friedrich Schlegel on the choice to have or to forgo an intellectual system—it must decide to do both (Schlegel [1798] 1982: 123). To cite a classic text by Roland Barthes, the divisions of which suggestively parallel the operatic *querelle*, opera can be neither a work nor Text, neither a definite and consumable form nor a constantly changing series of signifying-and-citing events (Barthes 1986).

In this respect, one might say that opera is like everything else, except that from this predicament it evolves the trait of identifying itself by staging its own intermediacy between mimetic or allegorical sense and enraptured nonsense. Opera seeks to perpetuate the "impossibility" of its own intermediate position. It does not necessarily seek simply to incarnate some transcendental presence or power, as conceived along Kantian lines by Gary Tomlinson (1999), nor to enunciate the pure "blue note" of what Michel Poizat calls the angel's cry (1992), a version of Jacques Lacan's *objet petit a*, which represents—always elusively—the obscure and unattainable object of desire. Even less, *pace* Slavoj Žižek (1997: 192), is opera as such a driven plea for mercy addressed to a personified form of Lacan's symbolic order, the big Other. Like the *mise-en-abime*, these are all possible realizations of a more primary condition. But one might say, drawing on other work by Žižek (1992: 3–6), that opera exemplifies the circularity of drive that seeks to envelop rather than to obtain its nominal goal. Opera, a form notoriously grounded in artifice and (even in its verismo moment) incapable of realistic illusion, recurrently seeks to embed in itself a dramatization of its own emergence into a meaning, and a space of meaning, that is too seductive or overpowering or absorbing to resist.

Voice in Action

How does it do that? To begin answering, we need to return, as one always does in opera, to the question of voice. Operatic voice is distinctive for the way it marks itself, designates itself, as voice, but a voice like no other. In contrast to the default or normative voice of communication, even of poetry and drama, operatic voice is not primarily a means of expression or transmission. Rather the reverse: operatic voice is the substance of something expressed or transmitted. It is an excess that escapes communication. We are supposed to apprehend this voice as emanating not from a person (nor, for the Lacanians in the neighborhood, from the big Other) but from the oracular cleft of its own possibility. The voice does not so much belong to the singer as the singer belongs to the voice.

Voice in this dispensation refers to itself, folds over on itself, not as a pure immediacy above or beyond reference, and not as the acoustic sublimation of a stage image, but as the effect of a vocal act that simultaneously opens and closes its distance or difference from itself. The voice absorbs the energy of its external reference back into the substance of its sound production but without obscuring the process of looping out and back. This quality has a poetic counterpart in styles of lyric verse that are receptive to oral lushness, poetry that enfolds itself acoustically, materially, marking itself as the trace of a voice that, even written, is still audible: Tennyson's "The moan of doves in immemorial elms, / And murmuring of innumerable bees" ("Come Down, O Maid," Tennyson 1958: 173), or Stevens's "The web is woven and you have to wear it, // The winter is made and you have to bear it, / The winter web, the winter woven, wind and wind" ("The Dwarf," Stevens 1954: 208).

Operatic voice can even achieve this thickened reflexivity by receding into a resonant absence, as in the limpid but mysterious series of "interview chords"—thirty-four floating triads in different orchestrations—that accompany the unseen and above all unheard dialogue in Britten's *Billy Budd* when Captain Vere explains to Billy why Billy must die. A more literal resonance attends the fleeting offstage voices that intervene in the action of numerous operas including Mozart's *Idomeneo*, Verdi's *Don Carlos* and *Rigoletto*, and Wagner's *Parsifal*—voices that wander from their bodily source and in so doing constitute what I have elsewhere suggested is the fundamental trope for opera itself (Kramer 2004: 221–228).

Symbolic versions of such wandering voice inform a series of key moments in an opera nearly contemporary with this writing, John Adams's *Doctor Atomic* (2005). The opera recounts the climatic days of the Manhattan Project, culminating in the detonation of the first atomic bomb in 1945. The libretto, compiled by Peter Sellars, is a "found" text; everything in it is drawn from archival sources, including statements by the participants, poetry by Donne, Baudelaire, and Muriel Rukeyser, and in one case what sounds like an extract from a scientific paper describing how to assemble the plutonium core of an atomic bomb. (Adams actually found it on the Internet.)

The assembly instructions receive a surprising setting: a sweetly lyrical, carefree, naïve air for women's chorus. The setting is immediately recognizable as a Siren song. It conveys the seductive allure of sweet science and the romance of the nuclear "Gadget," which the protagonist, J. Robert Oppenheimer, the scientific head of the project, must wrestle with as he weighs the moral consequences of devising and testing the bomb.

The assembly chorus wanders in from afar, sounding like nothing else in the opera. It bears a startling resemblance to the more literal Siren song that frames the Venusberg Bacchanal of Wagner's *Tannhäuser*; whether this is a direct allusion I can't say, but the family resemblance is unmistakable. Adams's scientific Sirens usurp the technological ideal attributed to Odysseus in Horkheimer and Adorno's famous account of the Homeric Sirens (Horkheimer and Adorno 1944: 32–36). Like their mythological sisters in Wagner, they beckon the listener, on stage and off, away from the world of history and its dangers and into a realm—here literally a sphere, the shape of the bomb—of dream and delusion. They sing whoever hears them out of place with the ravishment of operatic voice.

The consequences for Oppenheimer, as for Tannhäuser, are dire. Like Tannhäuser in the "Rome narrative" that recounts his moral abjection, Oppenheimer subsequently sings a long, tortured aria seeking a grace that, unlike Tannhäuser, he never receives, even pro forma. The text is Donne's Holy Sonnet beginning "Batter my heart, three-person'd God"; the line alludes not only to the Holy Trinity but to the name, Trinity, of the first atomic bomb test, the event that concludes the opera. (The historical

Oppenheimer named the test for the poem.) The aria, like the Siren song, wanders in from afar. Its preexisting torment does not so much anticipate or model Oppenheimer's as possess it, overtaking Oppenheimer's "own" voice with the voice of a merciless lucidity that Oppenheimer disavows even as he ventriloquizes it. The aria's incongruity and anachronism—it even suggests Baroque styles of text-setting—begin to chip away at the opera's documentary impulse and draw it into the mode of allegory. The birth of the atomic age no longer appears as the outcome of confused and conflicting values from everyone involved, even though the opera does dramatize these; instead, the historical events mirror the error of a heroic soul, a great man with a tragic flaw.

This process culminates with the Trinity test. Like *Tannhäuser*, *Dr. Atomic* ends with an event that is no event at all: for Tannhäuser a hypothetical redemption that appears as a cruel death, for Oppenheimer and his associates, including the opera audience, an apocalyptic explosion. Both works conclude by obliterating the memory of the Siren song. In Adams's case, this is the way the world ends: not with a whimper but a bang.

It is a bang we have to wait for, in dread, for longer than we think. The final moments of the opera stage the Trinity test in a distended version of real time. As we watch, we hear the countdown announced: twenty minutes to detonation, then five, then two, then one. But the actual time that elapses within this fictional five minutes is much greater, a compressed eternity—time enough not only to contemplate last things but also to ponder yet another allegory carried onto the scene by song acts from Oppenheimer's wife Kitty and her Indian maid Pasqualita.

The women are not present to witness the test; they sing from the distance of a split stage. In the Metropolitan Opera's 2008 production, they sing from the margins while the audience's eyes and ears are riveted to the center occupied by the test site. But their voices carry. Their singing wanders from afar onto the epoch-making scene like the cries of a traditional chorus of mourning women. Their song acts reflect not only on the looming event but also on its operatic mirroring. Pasqualita sings from a position of pastoral innocence that is about to be destroyed forever (another parallel to *Tannhäuser*, as we will see shortly); Kitty sings from the position of a wife whose love cannot keep her husband from yielding calamitously to the Siren song of the Gadget (Oppenheimer's Los Alamos is a technological Venusberg; his misplaced passion is a kind of nuclear adultery). The women's plaints resonate almost to the end. Kitty's equivocal line, "Dreamers wake in the night and sing their songs," describes exactly what happens on stage as the moment of detonation nears. Pasqualita's earlier refrain, sung to a traditional Tewa Indian melody, describes ironically what happens when the count reaches zero: "The cloud-flower blossoms."

A Case of Identity Crisis

To examine further the issues of meaning and reflexivity epitomized by moments like these, I will first delve into a paradigmatic example from a number opera and then turn to an opera meant to mark an epochal break with the number genre. The first part of this double case study does not need to be the first example its kind, or even the most representative; it needs only to stand out from an opera the persistence and prestige of which endows the reflective moment with the capacity to stand as an ideal type, regardless of changes in genre. The example comes from Mozart's *Don Giovanni*. It will be followed by a series of examples from *Tannhäuser*—another opera in which the licentiousness of voice plays a key role (although the drama involved is anything but *giocoso*) and the standard work that, *Ariadne* aside, is perhaps more invested in the issue of song acts and self-staging than any other.[1]

Don Giovanni is famously full of reflective song acts, including the catalogue aria in which Giovanni's servant Leporello narrates his master's erotic history; onstage extracts from three popular operas of the day, among them Mozart's own *Le nozze di Figaro*, on which the Don and Leporello comment critically during the climactic banquet scene; and the sepulchral admonitions of the Commendatore as his living-dead statue interrupts the banquet while the dark, stentorian music that opens the overture makes, as the statue does, an uncanny return. Kierkegaard (1848: 81–83, 93–94) may or may not have been right to suggest that the character Don Giovanni is the incarnation of unreflective immediacy, but the opera *Don Giovanni* preemptively dissents from Kierkegaard's identification of that immediacy with music, and with its own music in particular. *Don Giovanni* reflects on itself constantly. Even the elusive Don pauses amid his constant mobility to project his musical image in the convex mirror of the hectic "champagne" aria.

The scene with perhaps the greatest figurative potential occurs early in the second act, where the opera conspicuously suspends the prevailing narrative action and reflects itself in the mirror of a subplot, or not even that, in an episode of byplay. For no particular reason at this point, except that it is the sort of thing he does, Don Giovanni switches identities with Leporello. The servant, miming the master, persuades the susceptible Donna Elvira to come down from her balcony to join him in the street, after which the master, mimicking the servant, serenades Elvira's maid in an attempt at seduction that seems headed for success until it is interrupted by the flow of events as the chase for the fugitive Giovanni by his assorted antagonists resumes.

The double-sidedness of this identity exchange is essential to it. At a social level, as Michel Noiray observes, "Da Ponte and Mozart deny Leporello the ability to mime aristocracy in formal song, so that he can only address Elvira in recitative.... Don Giovanni, on the other hand, brilliantly deploys the popular idiom in his serenade" (Noiray 2006: 144). But the social positions here are less significant in themselves (they are obvious enough) than as a means for invoking, identifying, and destabilizing voice positions. Both halves of the scene disengage a voice from its proper body in terms that expose voice itself as an artifice, and more, an instrument of seduction half-created by its listener. Leporello's imitation is bad (the libretto says so) but it is quite successful because his recitative reflects what Elvira already hears and has always heard: the voice of the Giovanni whom she herself creates as a fiction and then desires against her better judgment. The audience hears not only what Elvira hears but also what she doesn't hear, and either way what it hears is a fabrication. More exactly, it is (or may be) opera, which is precisely what Elvira cannot resist.

As to Giovanni, his serenade not only forms the complement to Elvira's fiction but also compounds it, and compounds it doubly: first by producing formal song of remarkable charm and beauty, irresistible despite its transparent falsity, and second by visibly disengaging sound from its supposed source, as Giovanni "plays" his serenade on a mandolin, the "sound" of which actually comes from the orchestra, cushioned in pizzicato strings. The outcome is parallel in every respect to that of Leporello's deception of Elvira, which is this song act's convex mirror. The audience hears what the maid hears but also what she doesn't hear. And what she hears is (or may be) opera, which neither she nor, we surmise, anyone else can resist: surmise, because the maid is not a character like Elvira or Giovanni but a mere figure for susceptibility to operatic voice.

That voice, moreover, suggestively links the two parts of the scene when Giovanni's faux-Leporello serenade opens with an echo of a phrase that he, Giovanni, has sung in the trio for himself, Leporello, and Elvira that precedes the costume exchange (Noiray 2006: 144 observes this echo). The implication is, or may be, that Giovanni is just another victim of his own artifice, that he is really still singing "to" Elvira, whom he can now desire only in the socially inferior form of her maid. His own voice is not his own, even when it, and we, are well aware of that voice as the supposed reality, the natural presence, behind the disguise. As noted earlier, the swapping of voices and identities that culminates in this serenade is purely digressive within the opera's narrative; it is an extended interruption that has sometimes been pooh-poohed by critics (for example by Steptoe [1988: 185, 199]: "Don Giovanni has a less satisfying dramatic structure than Le nozze di Figaro. ... Dissatisfaction with Act II as a whole derives from the breakdown of [the] equilibrium [of serious and comic elements], and the artificial engineering of a series of comic incidents from the disguise of Don Giovanni as Leporello and vice versa"). But the interruption is the point. The exchanges offer the paired recitative and serenade as a twinned potential figure for the artifice of operatic voice that is elsewhere asked to sustain absorption in the drama. The success of the exchanges demonstrates that this artifice has the wherewithal to overcome reason and better judgment with surprising ease. Voice in opera, so the suggestion runs, is perfectly unnatural and perfect in its unnaturalness; it can draw the listener in better than anything put forward as natural or authentic.

This figure of voice can embody, or more exactly disembody, opera because the vocal power it invokes (not a casual term) is grounded in a rule and a technology of separation to which opera as a cultural institution distinctively binds itself. Reflecting on the condition of what she calls lyric possession, the state of being the will-less vehicle for the poetic or oracular power of a voice from elsewhere, the poet-critic Susan Stewart makes a striking *Giovanni*-like comparison:

> One might [...] recall the children's game in which one person stands behind another with the person in front keeping his hands behind his back, elbows protruding; the person behind puts her arms through the crooks of the partner's arms and moves her

> limbs in coordination with the facing partner's speech. A dissociation of voice from gesture, and gesture from the body result. Such forms of play, and expressions such as being [...] "beside one's self" provide a sample of ways in which we make possession manifest through qualities of dissociation. (Stewart 1995: 36)

The game described by Stewart resembles a common way of staging the first exchange, Leporello for Giovanni: Elvira hears Giovanni's voice in Leporello's bad imitation while Giovanni silently hovers (and sometimes even gestures) behind his other self. But whereas Stewart is addressing a state of exception, of possession by the other as dispossession of the self, opera takes the exception as a normal circumstance. For the singer or the audience to be overtaken and inhabited by a wandering voice, and more particularly by a voice that is not divine or oracular but human and artful, and just in those respects a surrogate for the divine or oracular, is the aim of operatic desire, or, if you will, of operatic drive.

The force of this desire is particularly telling in the second exchange, when the serving maid hears a strangely eloquent "Leporello" possessed of and by Don Giovanni's voice. Conjoined with the sensuous music, this is one of two paradigmatic seduction scenes in the opera, the other being Giovanni's smooth-talking of Zerlina to the aria "Là ci darem la mano." In both cases the Don's vaunted sexual magic fulfills itself only in musical artifice and only with a social inferior, a woman whose subordinate position is as much a figure for the subordination of the subject by operatic voice as it is a comment on the erotics and semiotics of class. Operatic voice as seduction is the voice Elvira only thinks she hears in the image of Giovanni assumed by Leporello, and this image, too, is a figure for opera. If Giovanni alone has the class privilege of throwing his voice, the opera singer alone has the laboriously acquired skill to do likewise (the voice thus won turns labor into aristocratic privilege). Unlike the figures of lyric possession, opera assumes that voice is not by nature detachable from its source but that it can become so by art. The art of operatic song is the art of detaching it.

Tannhäuser's Song Acts

The demonstration of that art resonates with particular irony in *Tannhäuser*. The minstrel-hero, whose own voice always gets the better of him, longs for immersion in a nature that he can never find no matter how close by it is. His best approximation comes early, when he encounters a naïve voice in the heart of pastoral nature itself, or so it seems. But the voice position that results is both fleeting and equivocal. Besides, it is only the first of many, each one more equivocal than the last.

Tannhäuser is organized around a series of song acts, one for each act of the opera: the just-noted pastoral air in Act I, Tannhäuser's entry in the song contest in Act II, and Wolfram's hymn to the evening star in Act III. Each of these songs acts marks Tannhäuser as a figure of lost voice, equally alienated from the sensory and the ideal, from mythology and history, from anarchy and custom. Tannhäuser comes to rest, and only briefly, in a place of transition between a false paradise and a failed community. That place, not surprisingly, is the German countryside, where the *Volk* live and speak in harmony with nature.

At the end of Act I, the spring song of a shepherd boy draws Tannhäuser back into this privileged locale. The scene, which also includes offstage bells and the approach of the pilgrims who chant the main theme of the overture, has been taken as an attempt to create an onstage refuge for innocent, anti-theatrical, anti-operatic presence (Abbate 1988; Levin 2006). The stage itself becomes the scene of an idyll when it hosts the acoustic reality of a simple folk-like song that is not heard but overheard, a song that simply arises as an emanation of its place. Perhaps ironically, though, the pastoral scene is not unique in its musical charm. The Venusberg also has a version of such music: the offstage song of the Sirens that frames the Bacchanal. (In the original, "Dresden" version of the opera [1845, revised 1847], Wagner's stage directions call only for the Siren song to be heard "from the far distance" as it departs; in the second, "Paris," version [1861, revised 1870], the song is marked as "invisible" from the outset.) The Sirens' song arrives as the first vocal music in the opera and departs as the prelude to the dialogue in which Tannhäuser tells Venus why he is leaving her. In its dissonant lyricism, this treble chorus, an uncanny counterpart to the shepherd's song, may be the most pristine and seductive music in the work (as well it should be!).

But the likeness goes only so far. The shepherd's tune is limpidly diatonic, which separates it not only from the Sirens' song but also from the entirety of the Venusberg music. Nature, ideally conceived, is not only the song's setting or ground but also its content. The song is the vehicle of a voice that has not yet learned the equivocal secret of operatic difference: a voice that is not fully "in" the opera at hand, voice on a threshold.

But this, too, goes only so far. Although the pastoral scene gives the immediate impression of presence exceeding representation and spontaneous music-making exceeding performance, the scene also, and with no delay, loops back on itself reflectively. It does so to expose the impression of acoustic innocence as an illusion and at the same time to allow both Tannhäuser and the audience to be impressed by a dream world they can observe but cannot enter. The scene depends on a series of discontinuities masquerading as unities: between the artifice of the shepherd's song and its expression of naturalness, between the singer taking the part of the shepherd boy and the boy "himself," and between the shepherd's pipe and its pastoral sound.

These discontinuities provide, even impose, reflective distance. They are precisely what this scene of unstaginess stages. Tannhäuser hears a boy and the boy's song but not the boy's performance; the song is sung, uttered, but it is not interpreted, not addressed to an audience; the song is all numinous. We, though, the audience, do not hear a shepherd's song but an operatic simulacrum of one, not folk music at all but its distanced idealization. And that means that what we hear is an operatic soprano voice giving a performance. We hear opera over Tannhäuser's shoulder.

In most performances, we also hear and see a mature woman imitating an adolescent boy. (Wagner's score simply calls for a soprano.) If we do, we are supposed to regard this traditionally most obvious of artifices, the trouser role, as an emanation of unspoiled nature. Even if the part is actually taken by a boy, his onstage presence is haunted by the woman who might have taken the part in his place—and vice versa for the woman. Even the boy "performs" in a sense that the shepherd does not. This equivocation places the dream of pastoral purity outside the erotic allegory—Venus versus Elisabeth—that otherwise structures the opera. That structure is momentarily excluded, though not precluded, by the sexually ambiguous figure of the shepherd.

Finally, we also see the equivocal shepherd "play" on a pipe he does not play while we hear an instrument we do not see. The pastoral pipe is supposed to be a shawm, but what we hear is its more refined descendant, the English horn. As with the mandolin in *Don Giovanni*, the instrument is separated from its sound—but with an added wrinkle. The separation of the instrument and its sound is not unusual in itself (it is a genre in its own right) but it becomes arresting here because of a second separation. The English horn actually *is* played onstage, but it remains unseen, so that its sound belongs audibly but not visibly to the space of the acoustic idyll. This refraction invites us to reflect on whose mode of hearing is right, "ours" or "Tannhäuser's," and to ask further if the question even makes sense—and further still to inhabit imaginatively the space between natural and operatic voice.

In the song contest, Tannhäuser affirms that operatic voice, the voice that performs, is inexorably drawn to sing about sexuality and to sexualize song, which is exactly what he does in the Venusberg. (Don Giovanni could have told him as much.) Indeed, Tannhäuser famously sings the same song in both the Venusberg and the Wartburg, in the first place with interjections from Venus, in the second without them—or rather with their absence constituting the unconscious of what he does sing and prompting a disavowal conveyed by his addition of an extra strophe (for more on this topic, see Hyer 2006). Tannhäuser the minstrel is a male Siren. He tries to be something else, but the gift of voice betrays him. It is not so much Tannhäuser as it is Tannhäuser's voice that refuses to be dishonest about sexuality and provokes an outburst of the hypocrisy and violence lurking just beneath the surface of the community that purports to welcome him. Song is not chaste; it is erotic by genre, which here means: performative and seductive in essence.

Song cannot escape this essence, even in prayer; we can hear it in the undertone of *Sehnsucht* that runs through the hymn to the evening star. In mourning Elisabeth even before she has died, Wolfram fuses her with her opposite as the object of an impossible desire. Like Tannhäuser, Wolfram is an involuntary Siren. As more than one commentator has observed, the evening star is—Venus (Müller and Wapnewski 1992: 29; Hyer 2006: 195). By the time Venus in person returns in Act III, Tannhäuser has exhausted the possibilities of the art of song, prayer included—hence the Pope's rejection of him. He has also exhausted the possibility of narrative; the Rome narrative has collapsed from within to become a lamentation. His voice has (been) broken.

All these failures are failures of vocal genre. They seem to run the gamut: the Rome narrative fails as ballad as the contest song and Wolfram's hymn have failed as minstrelsy. And then there is chorale, in which Tannhäuser does not, perhaps cannot, join.

He certainly cannot hear the Pilgrims' choral singing as pertaining in any way to him; he hears the communal song only as a force that excludes him (on the balladic element in the Rome narrative, see Abbate 1988; on the Pilgrims' chorus, see Kramer 2009). Even though this hearing proves mistaken, it is all that he ever knows; he dies before the truth reaches him. All he has left in the end is a plea (an expostulation—not a genre of song) and a name more blurted out than sung. His death is virtually the performative effect of his song act: "Blessed Elisabeth, pray for me!"

Meanwhile, Wolfram's *Abendstern* hymn both is and is not diegetic music, is not and yet still is a reflection in opera's convex mirror. It is diegetic for the obvious reason that the minstrel Wolfram delivers it as a hymn—he sings in character, the character sings. But it is reflective because the hymn is also a soliloquy or apostrophe, an address addressed to no one who can receive it. In this capacity it is not a hymn at all but a species of aria, an operatic type: the *preghiera*. The hymn's situation is similar to that of the shepherd's song: The *Abendstern* hymn is no more a hymn than the shepherd's song is a folk tune or the English horn is a shawm. Like Tannhäuser, Wolfram follows the law of operatic voice: what he sings he must perform, must take out of nature to be true to the nature of the voice as art. Wolfram's song is virtually a refugee from an Italian number opera, and its nineteenth-century reception—it was a favorite recital piece[2]—gives clear testimony to its status as an icon of Wagner's continuing embeddedness in the very operatic mode he was trying to escape.

The resulting entanglement is compounded later in Act III with the return of Venus, added by Wagner in the first revision (1847) of this much-revised opera. The returning goddess's address to her strayed lover, like Wolfram's to Elisabeth as the evening star, is strangely equivocal: As a figure in the narrative, does Venus speak or sing? We cannot really answer, which, like the interruption in the narrative of *Don Giovanni*, is precisely the point. And the point is again self-reflective. Venus's double framing by a "roseate light" (thus Wagner's stage directions) and a texture of shimmering strings and pulsating winds suggests a momentary indetermination of speech and song. The same duality plays about the reappearance itself: bearing forgiveness, Venus returns sincerely, but she also stages her return with exquisite theatricality.

We are thus invited to understand her return as a personified return of Opera itself, something that *this* opera would like both to spurn as debased and embrace as regenerate. The context for this ambivalence is Wagner's overt repulsion and covert attraction to French grand opera, the model to which he eventually sought to assimilate *Tannhäuser* for its Paris production in 1861. In 1852–1853 he wrote an essay, "On the Performance of *Tannhäuser*," that touches explicitly on this topic. Admonishing the performer of Elisabeth to avoid theatricality and operatic "juggling tricks," he makes plain the link (hardly a new one) between opera and a tawdry falseness of feeling. Both Elisabeth and Tannhäuser he identifies as characters with whom the performers should empathize. Venus is excluded from the category—more so by the essay than by the opera. Venus's return thus seems to incorporate a representation of the seductive trickery of the operatic genres that Wagner wishes to surmount but only, like Tannhäuser, by means of an extended passage through their domain.

Wagner seems to avoid discussing Venus, as if she made him uncomfortable. He notes that her part is "difficult" but requires only that the singer combine good looks with a firm conviction that Venus is "justified" (Wagner 1852–1853: 158). David Levin (2006) finds the locus of operatic falseness in the performativity of the Venusberg, to which Brian Hyer (2006) adds the suggestion that the Wartburg is no less performative—hence, one might surmise, Wagner's admonitions to his principal singers. Tannhäuser's problem is that he has no place in either of these equally performative fictive worlds, nor in any opera conceived to date—including *Tannhäuser*. (The possible exception is Meyerbeer's *Robert le diable*, from which Wagner is at telltale pains to distance himself; see Wagner 1852–1853: 157.)

The close of *Tannhäuser*, with its scenario of sacrifice and redemption and the triumphant return of the Pilgrims' chorus from the overture and pastoral scene—a *Don Giovanni*-like return, only inverted, and touched by the irony that the dead hero can no longer hear it—would thus represent an epochal change in the cultural status of opera generally. It is really opera, not Tannhäuser, that is redeemed by this close. The swarm of ecstatic pilgrims, an onstage audience to its own performance, celebrates the surmounting and/or transformation of theater by ritual, of modern illusion by inherited truth, or, in Walter Benjamin's terms, of art's exhibition value by its cult value (Benjamin 2003), or, in Theodor Adorno's terms, of mere art by the profound riddle that precedes it at the origins of culture (Adorno 1997; for further discussion, see Tiffany 2008). This destination matches the ending of *Doctor Atomic* in its aspiration to apocalyptic gravity. The massed orchestra and chorus boom out a meaning that consumes everything it touches.

More generally: although *Tannhäuser* is structured by the distribution of individual song acts, its dramatic resolution depends on the collective song act of the pilgrims' chorus. The chorus is theatrically transformative. But it is not *diegetically* transformative; it remains external to the narrative even in representing the narrative's concluding miracle, the sign of forgiveness, the flowering staff that Tannhäuser does not live to receive (for further discussion, see Kramer 2009). Forgiveness is withheld not only by the Pope but also by the composer. Only the two women, one vanished, the other a corpse, dispense it unconditionally.

The result is a decisive exposure of the gap between reflective song act and absorptive narrative. Opera recurrently stakes its fortunes on that gap, though not always with this degree of frankness. (The *Ring* cycle is the great exception, but that is a tale for another day.) It is only on the outside of song, where singing no longer hears itself, that the passions and actions of opera come into full flower, no matter whether their mode is tragic, comic, or ironic. But the meaning of those things remains inchoate unless and until some intervention, of which the song act is exemplary, draws out their links to the vicissitudes of vocal wandering, lyric possession, and the loop between reference and self-reference. Through operatic song the image of life is glazed, embalmed, projected at a 180-degree angle. But it is just in those respects that the image claims to be true to life, which is only ever lived through its fictions. The relationship between opera and meaning is an unending investigation of that dilemma.

See also: What Is Opera? Opera between the Ancients and the Moderns, Verisimilitude, Voice, Characterization

Notes

1. Quick reminders: in *Don Giovanni* the hero, a notorious rake, is pursued by three parties: Donna Anna, whose father, the Commandant of Seville, Giovanni has killed in a duel after attempting to "seduce" (she says rape) the daughter; Donna Elvira, a woman Giovanni has seduced and abandoned earlier; and Masetto, the fiancé of a peasant girl, Zerlina, whom Giovanni has all but seduced on stage. Giovanni is eventually accosted at a banquet (at his own invitation) by the living statue of the Commandant. He refuses to repent and the statue casts him into hell. In *Tannhäuser* the eponymous hero, a minstrel, begins in dalliance with Venus in her mythical home, the Venusberg. But he has already decided to return to the natural and social world and to his first love, Elisabeth. Once home again, in the Wartburg, he commits a brutal indiscretion during a song contest. After traveling to Rome as a penitent pilgrim only to be spurned by the Pope, he returns in despair to Germany, where Venus invites him to rejoin her. He is "redeemed" at the last minute—the last of his life—by the sacrificial death of Elisabeth, earlier the object of a famous onstage hymn by the minstrel Wolfram von Eschenbach. On the scare quotes around *redeemed*, see Kramer 2009. A far more complex self-staging occurs during the redemptive final scene of *Parsifal*; for an account, see Kramer 2006. The second act of Franz Schreker's *Der ferne Klang* (1912) travesties the song contest and places it in the modern equivalent of the Venusberg: a high-class brothel.
2. The hymn was popularized in an accessible piano transcription by Liszt as well as by vocal performances in the concert hall and parlor. Francis Hueffer, the music critic of the London *Times*, observed that the "melodious strains" in *Tannhäuser*, exemplified by the March of Act II and "Wolfram's Address to the Evening Star . . . [have] perhaps contributed more to the spreading of the author's name than any of his other works" (Hueffer 1881: 23). John Philip Sousa wrote that "I rarely play a programme without a Wagner number" and adds that the public is eager to hear complex scores as well as "the beautiful melodies like the 'Evening Star' " (Elson 1912: 644).

Bibliography

Abbate, Carolyn. 2004. "Music: Drastic or Gnostic?" *Critical Inquiry* 30/3: 505–536.

——. 1991. *Unsung Voices*. Princeton, NJ: Princeton University Press.

——. 1988. "Erik's Dream and Tannhäuser's Journey." In *Reading Opera*, edited by Arthur Groos and Roger Parker, 129–167. Princeton, NJ: Princeton University Press.

Adorno, Theodor W. 1997. *Aesthetic Theory*, edited by Gretel Adorno and Rolf Tiedemann, translated by Robert Hullot-Kantor. Minneapolis: University of Minnesota Press.

Allanbrook, Wye Jamison, Mary Hunter, and Gretchen Wheelock. 2000. "Staging Mozart's Women." In *Siren Songs: Representations of Gender and Sexuality in Opera*, edited by Mary Ann Smart, 47–66. Princeton, NJ: Princeton University Press.

Ashbery, John. 1975. *Self-Portrait in a Convex Mirror*. New York: Viking.

Austin, J. L. 1962. *How to Do Things with Words*, edited by J. O. Urmson and Marina Sbisa. Cambridge, MA: Harvard University Press.
Barthes, Roland. 1986. "From Work to Text." In *The Rustle of Language*, translated by Richard Howard, 56–64. Berkeley and Los Angeles: University of California Press.
Benjamin, Walter. 2003. "The Work of Art in the Age of its Technological Reproducibility" (third version). In *Selected Writings: Volume 4, 1938–1940*. 4 vols., edited by Howard Eiland and Michael W. Jennings, 251–283. Cambridge, MA: Harvard University Press.
Blackmer, Corinne E., and Patricia Juliana Smith, eds. 1995. *En Travesti: Women, Gender Subversion, Opera*. New York: Columbia University Press.
Brett, Philip. 1994. "Eros and Orientalism in Britten's Operas." In *Queering the Pitch: The New Gay and Lesbian Musicology*, edited by Philip Brett, Elizabeth Wood, and Gary Thomas, 235–256. New York: Routledge.
——. 1993. "Britten's Dream." In Solie 1993, 239–280.
Butler, Judith. 1997. *Excitable Speech: A Politics of the Performative*. New York: Routledge.
Castle, Terry. 1995. "In Praise of Brigitte Fassbaender: Reflections on Diva Worship." In Blackmer and Smith 1995, 20–58.
Cavell, Stanley. 1994. "Nothing Goes Without Saying." *London Review of Books* 16/1 (January 6): 3–5.
Citron, Marcia. 2010. *When Opera Meets Film*. Cambridge: Cambridge University Press.
——. 2000. *Opera on Screen*. New Haven: Yale University Press.
Cone, Edward T. 1974. *The Composer's Voice*. Berkeley and Los Angeles: University of California Press.
Cusick, Suzanne. 1993. "Of Women, Music, and Power: A Model from Seicento Florence." In Solie 1993, 281–304.
Deathridge, John. 2008. *Wagner beyond Good and Evil*. Berkeley and Los Angeles: University of California Press.
Dellamora, Richard. 1997. "Mozart and the Politics of Intimacy": *The Marriage of Figaro* in Toronto, Paris, and New York." In *The Work of Opera: Genre, Nationhood, and Sexual Difference*, edited by Richard Dellamora and Daniel Fischlin, 255–276. New York: Columbia University Press.
Derrida, Jacques. 1980. "The Law of Genre." [Translated by Avital Ronell.] *Critical Inquiry* 7/1: 55–82.
Eisen, Cliff, and Simon Keefe, eds. 2006. *The Cambridge Mozart Encyclopedia*. Cambridge: Cambridge University Press.
Elson, Louis Charles. 1912. *Modern Music and Musicians: Encyclopedia. V. I: A History of Music; Special Articles; Great Composers*. Princeton, NJ: The University Society.
Franklin, Peter. 1994. "Movies as Opera (Behind the Great Divide)." In Tambling 1994, 71–112.
Frisch, Walter. 2005. *German Modernism*. Berkeley and Los Angeles: University of California Press.
Frye, Northrop.1957. *Anatomy of Criticism*. Princeton: Princeton University Press
Grover-Friedlander, Michal. 2005. *Vocal Apparitions: The Attraction of Cinema to Opera*. Princeton, NJ: Princeton University Press.
Halliwell, Michael. 2005. *Opera and the Novel: The Case of Henry James*. Word and Music Studies 4. Amsterdam: Rodopi.
Heffer, Francis. 1881. *Richard Wagner*. New York: Scribner.
Horkheimer, Max, and Theodor W. Adorno. [1944] 2002. *Dialectic of Enlightenment*. New York: Continuum.

Hyer, Brian. 2006. "Response to David J. Levin. [Interstitial Redemption: Wagner's Tannhäuser and the Dramaturgical Vicissitudes of Music Drama]." *Monatshefte* 98/2: 192–197.

Jankélévitch, Vladimir. 2003. *Music and the Ineffable*, translated by Carolyn Abbate. Princeton, NJ: Princeton University Press.

Joe, Jeongwon, and Rose Theresa, eds. 2002. *Between Opera and Cinema*. New York: Routledge.

Kerman, Joseph. [1956] 1988. Opera as Drama. New York: Alfred A. Knopf. Reprint. Westport, CT: Greenwood Press.

Kierkegaard, Søren. [1843] 1992. *Either/Or: A Fragment of Life* (1843), translated by Alastair Hannay. London: Penguin.

Kramer, Lawrence. 2009. "Wagner's Gold Standard: *Tannhäuser* and the General Equivalent." *Cambridge Opera Journal* 21/2: 139–158.

——. 2006. "The Talking Wound and the Foolish Question: Symbolization in *Parsifal*." *Opera Quarterly* 22/2: 208–229.

——. [1990] 2004. "The Salome Complex." *Cambridge Opera Journal* 2/3: 269–295. Revised and expanded in *Opera and Modern Culture: Wagner and Strauss* by Lawrence Kramer, 128–166. Berkeley and Los Angeles: University of California Press.

——. 2001. *Musical Meaning: Toward a Critical History*. Berkeley and Los Angeles: University of California Press.

Levin, David. 2006. "Interstitial Redemption: Wagner's *Tannhäuser* and the Dramaturgical Vicissitudes of Music Drama." *Monatshefte* 98/2: 180–191.

——, ed., 1994. *Opera Through Other Eyes*. Stanford, CA: Stanford University Press.

Locke, Ralph. 1995. "What Are These Women Doing in Opera?" In Blackmer and Smith 1995, 59–98.

——. 1991. "Constructing the Oriental 'Other': Saint-Saens's Samson *et Dalila*." *Cambridge Opera Journal* 3/3: 261–302.

McClary, Susan. 1992. *Georges Bizet: 'Carmen.'* Cambridge Opera Handbooks. Cambridge: Cambridge University Press.

Morris, Mitchell. 1995. "Admiring the Countess Geschwitz." In Blackmer and Smith 1995, 348–370.

Müller, Ulrich, and Peter Wapnewski, eds. 1992. *Wagner Handbook*, translated by John Deathridge. Cambridge, MA: Harvard University Press.

Noiray, Michel. 2006. "*Don Giovanni*." In Eisen and Keefe 2006, 138–151.

Poizat, Michel. 1992. *The Angel's Cry: Beyond the Pleasure Principle in Opera*, translated by Arthur Denner. Ithaca, NY: Cornell University Press.

Schlegel, Friedrich. [1798] 1982. *Athenaeum* Fragments (1798), no. 53. In *German Romantic Criticism: Novalis, Schlegel, Schleiermacher, and Others*, edited by A. Leslie Willson, 120–124. New York: Continuum.

Smart, Mary Ann. 2004. *Mimomania: Music and Gesture in Nineteenth-Century Opera*. Berkeley and Los Angeles: University of California Press.

Solie, Ruth, ed. 1993. *Musicology and Difference*. Berkeley and Los Angeles: University of California Press.

Stevens, Wallace. 1954. *Collected Poems*. New York: Alfred A. Knopf.

Steptoe, Andrew. 1988. *The Mozart-Da Ponte Operas: The Cultural and Musical Background to 'Le nozze del Figaro,' 'Don Giovanni,' and 'Così fan tutte.'* Oxford: Clarendon Press.

Stewart, Susan. 1995. "Lyric Possession." *Critical Inquiry* 22/1: 34–63.

Tambling, Jeremy, ed. 1994. *A Night in at the Opera: Media Representations of Opera*. London: John Libbey.

Tennyson, Alfred. 1958. *Poems of Tennyson*, edited by Jerome F. Buckley. Boston: Houghton Mifflin.

Tiffany, Daniel. 2008. "Rhapsodic Measures." *Critical Inquiry* 34/5 (special issue): S146–S169.

Tomlinson, Gary. 1999. *Metaphysical Song: An Essay on Opera*. Princeton, NJ: Princeton University Press.

Wagner, Richard. [1853] 1898. "Ouvertüre zu *Tannhäuser*" [Overture to *Tannhäuser*]. In *Gesammelte Schriften und Dichtungen*, V. Leipzig: G. W. Fritzsch.

——. [1852–1853] 1898. "Über der Aufführung des *Tannhäuser*" (On the Performance of *Tannhäuser*). In *Gesammelte Schriften und Dichtungen*, V.

Wood, Elizabeth. 1995. "The Lesbian in the Opera: Desire Unmasked in Smyth's *Fantasio* and *Fête Galante*." In Blackmer and Smith 1995, 285–305.

Žižek, Slavoj. 1997. *The Plague of Fantasies*. London: Verso.

——. 1992. *Looking Awry: An Introduction to Jacques Lacan through Popular Culture*. Cambridge, MA: MIT Press.

——, and Mladen Dolar. 2001. *Opera's Second Death*. New York. Routledge.

PART III

PERFORMANCE AND PRODUCTION

CHAPTER 17

DIVAS AND DIVOS

HILARY PORISS

Introduction

Without adversity, a diva is just a singer.

(Pareles 2009)

On December 10, 2006, a remarkable event took place at the Teatro alla Scala in Milan, Italy. The opera that evening was Verdi's *Aida*, and Roberto Alagna sang the tenor role of Radames. Only minutes into the work, when Radames performs his famed aria "Celeste Aida," disaster struck, for Alagna failed to hit the final note of the piece, a high B flat, overreaching and landing unceremoniously on a grating and graceless B natural instead. The reaction from the Milanese spectators was merciless, boos and jeers reverberating throughout the house. Infuriated, Alagna did the unthinkable: he turned toward the audience, shook his fist furiously, and marched off the stage. On its own, this bold act would have been enough to set tongues throughout the operatic world wagging for weeks, but what happened next made the story even better. Alagna's understudy, Antonello Palombi—woefully unprepared for this unexpected turn of events—had only a matter of minutes to make his entrance. Without enough time to get into costume, Palombi walked on stage in his street clothes: black jeans and a blazer. It was in these "civvies" that he performed the rest of the first act, earning him a nine-minute ovation at the conclusion of the opera and allowing him to claim one of the most spectacular, or at least unusual, debuts in recent history.

Unsurprisingly, the press exploded with the news, most critics attacking Alagna for a lack of professionalism. Daniel J. Wakin, of the *New York Times*, for example, opened his review with this memorable invective: "In the history of operatic hissy fits, what happened at Teatro alla Scala in Milan during 'Aida' on Sunday night was a bravura performance" (Wakin 2006a); and Richard Owen, writing for *The Times* (London) included a damning quote from the production's director, Franco Zeffirelli: "A professional should never behave in this way. Alagna is too sensitive, it is too easy to hurt his feelings. He does not know how to act like a true star" (Owen 2006). Thanks to the newly influential blogosphere, moreover, opera fans around the world began hearing about and poring over the details of Alagna's tantrum only minutes after it occurred: Opera Chic's post (Opera Chic 2006), titled "Alagna Out of Aida: He's all like: C U L8R LAM3RZ [See You Later Lamers]!!" epitomized the excitement, fun, and fury generated by the singer. Blogging about it from the comfort of his apartment in New York City, moreover, Alex Ross commented: "I may be stuck home with a cold, but thanks to the miracle of the Internet I can still soak in the glamour, passion, and scandal of classical music" (Ross 2006).

But the "glamour, passion, and scandal" to which Ross refers is not endemic to the entire classical music world. A violinist storming off stage in the middle of a concerto or a pianist refusing to return to the keyboard following her first selection would undoubtedly stir up interest, but the widespread fascination that Alagna generated is unique to opera, and specifically, to its stars. More than any other musical genre, opera is utterly dependent on these performers—its "divas" and "divos"—for its successes, failures, for its very identity. The excitement surrounding this evening at La Scala had little to do with Verdi's music or Zeffirelli's vision; instead, it had everything to do with the singer and his actions. Indeed, according to one commentator, "[singers] are the lifeblood of the art, and without their competing talents opera would lose half its interest" (Sargeant 1973: 13); other fans would contend that without its prima donnas and leading men, opera would lose *all* of its interest.

It was not always thus. At the genre's inception, the profession of "singer" did not exist. As historian John Rosselli has carefully investigated, operas were too few and far between to occupy an artist's attention exclusively, and those who performed in the earliest courtly and public works tended to be either instrumentalists or actors who could also sing (Rosselli 1989). This situation began to shift toward the end of the seventeenth century, and by the middle of the eighteenth century—when opera seasons became an established component of social life in and outside Italy, and when demand for performers proliferated—musicians were able to devote themselves full-time to the art of singing. These years mark the precipitous rise of divas and divos to the top of operatic ranks, where they were worshipped by spectators, treated as royalty, and commanded salaries far higher than anyone else involved in productions. As the dean of Italian opera studies, Philip Gossett, has observed, "Manuel García, the first Almaviva in *Il barbiere di Siviglia*, was paid three times as much for singing the work as Rossini got for composing it, and the latter's contract obliged him 'to make where needed all those alterations necessary either to ensure the good reception of the music or to meet the circumstances and convenience of those same singers, at the simple request of the Impresario, because so it must be and no other way'" (Gossett 2006: xv). The primacy of singers remained unchallenged through the middle of the nineteenth century, and even today their influence remains strong.

The deep fascination that opera singers have garnered and the power they have exerted is reflected in the staggering volume of writing devoted to them over the past four centuries. Accounts of their lives, careers, and voices appear in a vast array of literature that includes (but is not limited to) newspapers, magazines, encyclopedias, biographies, autobiographies, letters, collections of anecdotes, cartoons, gossip columns, encyclopedias, novels, poetry, and more recently, blogs, websites, Facebook posts, and tweets. In their digests of this literature, both Rosselli and Sergio Durante have commented on its unwieldy nature—in Durante's words: "the material is vast and heterogeneous in its bibliographic forms, its target audience, its ends, and its language" (Durante 1998: 410). Andrew Farkas's annotated bibliography of "all the known writings *by* and *about* vocalists who pursued a stage or concert career as a singer" contains 1,850 items, and yet it is incomplete, as he admits (Farkas 1985: xii). Despite the abundance of this literature, a strikingly small proportion can be categorized as "serious" scholarship, for even though singers have always been central to the reception of opera, they—like most performers—have long taken a back seat to composers and their works. The *New Grove Dictionary of Opera* exemplifies this situation perfectly. While composers such as Verdi and Wagner receive multisection entries that sprawl across dozens of pages, their most famous contemporary interpreters are seldom allotted more than one perfunctory paragraph; the entries for Maria Callas (1923–1977) and Enrico Caruso (1873–1921), arguably two of the most influential musicians of the twentieth century, are only three and four paragraphs long, respectively. The rationale behind this general disparity is clear: the perceived "ephemeral" nature of the singer's art merits significantly less attention than the "permanent" contributions of opera's composers.

This outlook has begun to shift significantly over the past few decades. Once stranded on the periphery of musicological research, performers have gradually inched toward the center, and some of the most exciting work in the field of opera has, of late, occurred within the growing sub-discipline of diva and divo studies. In this chapter, I will explore this research, teasing out some of the most important themes and questions that are currently occupying the energies of scholars working in these fields. At the same time, I attempt to contextualize these newer studies in the centuries-old forums where discussions of singers have long occurred and where perceptions of these figures have been both constructed and reflected. To this end, I begin by exploring the stereotype of the diva/divo as divine monster, investigating the sway it has held over the reception of the world's most famous opera singers. This stereotype, however, is by no means the only lens through which singers have been viewed. Its binary opposition, that of the normal, down-to-earth, hard-working musician (exemplified beautifully by Palombi in Milan), represents an important alternative energizing many accounts of these figures. I then turn toward one of the most important concepts currently enlivening scholarship on singers: the idea that as a collaborative art form, the responsibility for the creation of operatic works falls, in part, on the shoulders of its practitioners, that they too possess artistic authority. By way of drawing both of these sections together, I conclude with a case study of Angelica Catalani, a prima donna whose life and career embody both the stereotype of the diva and the authority of the creative artist.

What Is a Diva?

> I didn't go to Venice of my own accord. I was sent there, forced to go, by that... that woman, she who has worshippers throughout the world, she who, despite a corrupt and failing body, limitless greed, and the personality of a broom, has—still, after all these years—the voice of an angel. It isn't surprising that she has power over me. Why shouldn't she? Even after a big meal, and I mean a big meal, she can walk onto a floodlit stage, stare into darkness and blinding glare, and then, with inimitable self-possession, make thousands weep. That all her gifts have been so concentrated is a miracle, and though she has no talent or virtue but this, it's more than enough. (Helprin 2004: 1)

So begins "Il Colore Ritrovato," a moving short story about an aging opera singer's agent. The narrator, Signor Cassati, has hundreds of clients, but his most valuable one, the soprano whose voice he discovered and on whom his entire thirty-year career has depended, is Rosanna Cardona, a divine monster. As this opening paragraph implies, Cardona is a difficult personality, to put it mildly, and over the course of the story we learn that she is temperamental, demanding, self-centered, irrational, unintelligent, greedy, financially extravagant, obnoxious, over-sexualized, and (unsurprisingly) fat. She is, in other words, a stereotypical diva, thoroughly unpleasant in "real life." But when she sings, she is transformed into a goddess, able to move her spectators to tears, and she is thereby forgiven, even adored, for her negative qualities.

This stereotype is almost as old as the genre itself, and although sopranos are most frequently accused of embodying these tendencies, mezzo-sopranos, tenors, baritones, basses, and (especially) castrati have also been exposed to its glory and its sting. ("Prima donna" carries similar meanings, but its origin as a term derived initially from contractual realities renders it somewhat less fraught. For a detailed discussion of the distinction between "diva" and "prima donna," see Cowgill and Poriss 2012: Introduction.) The term is gendered, but "diva" can be applied equally effectively to men (depending, of course, on the man), and the masculine form "divo" also carries a mixture of pejorative and magnificent connotations (a summary of scholarship concerning divo worship can be found in Henson 2007). The diva stereotype is not entirely distorted—it is, after all, a simple matter to compile an extensive list of misbehaviors on the part of the world's most glorious singers. Adelina Patti (1843–1919) sets an excellent example.

Patti was the premiere coloratura soprano during the second half of the nineteenth century, in constant demand at the world's greatest opera houses and incomparable in roles from the nineteenth-century Italian and French repertories. Knowing exactly what she was worth, she insisted on exorbitant sums for her appearances, earning so much money throughout her long career that she was able to purchase a castle in Wales (called Craig-y-nos), an edifice that contained a large indoor conservatory, a clock tower, and a private theater, among other amenities (Cone 1993; Klein 1920). According to legend, moreover, she terrorized impresarios, declining to set foot on stage without first receiving payment in full and forcing some managers to frantically assemble the necessary funds only minutes before the curtain was scheduled to rise. When an impresario complained that she earned more than the president of the United States, Patti supposedly responded, "Well then, let *him* sing." She was a notoriously weak actress who callously ignored the dramatic aspects of an opera; she ornamented her musical lines beyond recognition, exhibiting a complete disregard for composers' "intentions"; and she insisted that rehearsals were unnecessary for her, frequently showing up only for performances. At bottom, one could argue that Patti attended first and foremost to her own central place in the scheme of things, and only secondarily to all else concerning the opera productions in which she was involved.

Once on stage, however, Patti was glorious, and her biographers are vigilant in recording her vocal triumphs, describing the unique and spectacular nature of her voice in detail. She, like many other prima donnas and leading men, is remembered equally for her outrageous actions and for the power of her voice. The reputations of some divas are constructed almost entirely on unflattering anecdotes, an obvious example being Kathleen Battle (b. 1948). The stories involving this diva are as familiar as they are shocking: She complained to the Boston Symphony Orchestra when the Ritz-Carlton added peas to her pasta! She phoned her management in New York from a limousine in California to tell the driver to turn down the heat rather than asking him to do it herself! She requested a makeup artist prior to a radio interview! There can be little doubt that Battle is a difficult personality; nevertheless, it is dispiriting that these sensational anecdotes circulate more widely than do descriptions of her extraordinary artistry. As a stereotypical diva, she confirms all of the worst prejudices surrounding opera in general, and as such, there is little need or desire to inquire further into her career. Martin Kettle's comments in relation to Alagna's misdeeds at La Scala are relevant here: "many of the world's greatest opera singers, past and present, are remarkably normal, nice people [...]. But the world prefers its opera stars to be divine monsters" (Kettle 2006).

This construction of the divine monster has significant implications, for as is true of stereotypes in general, it distorts reality, casting poor light on those who do not deserve to be ridiculed, and in some cases, cutting off thoughtful discussion. Throughout her career, for example, Cecilia Bartoli (b. 1966) has been subject to accusations of diva-like behavior, but no more so than in 1998, when she performed the role of Susanna in the Metropolitan Opera's production of *Le nozze di Figaro*. The main point of contention concerned the character's two arias, "Venite, inginocchiatevi" and "Deh vieni, non tardar." Rather than sing this original pair, Bartoli performed two substitute arias that Mozart composed for a revival of the opera in 1789. Whether Bartoli was justified in making this alteration was a matter of intense (and unsettled) debate among critics and spectators, and the fallout has been discussed expertly elsewhere (see Parker 2006). Of interest here is the rhetoric that critics employed when they disagreed, often violently, with her decision to sing the substitution arias.

Writing for the *New York Times*, for instance, Anthony Tommasini (1998) took to the front lines against Bartoli, drawing on a number of characteristics that make up the negative stereotype of the divine monster for his weaponry. He opened his review in a fury: "There is a long tradition of conductors and opera houses catering to the whims of prima donnas. The tradition continues at the Metropolitan Opera, where Cecilia Bartoli, a singer of sensational popularity and, consequently, clout, is performing Susanna [...]." In the same article, he recycled a false rumor, claiming that Bartoli "showed up late" to rehearsals, he argued that she "insisted that her contract stipulate that she had the right to sing [the substitute arias]," and he declared that "both substitutes are frivolous works." The message is clear: Bartoli is a divine monster in the most pejorative sense of the term, someone who embraces power and uses it to set her own interests above those of Mozart. Stating this point outright was unnecessary—the allusion to "typical" attributes was sufficient.

Another sign of the ambivalence surrounding the divine monster can be located in the proliferation of anecdotes published in collections sporting evocative titles such as *Prima Donnas and Other Wild Beasts* (Wagner 1963) and *Demented: The World of the Opera Diva* (Mordden 1990), to name only a few. These books are packed with tales that reflect and reinforce the divine monster stereotype. In *Prima Donnas and Other Wild Beasts*, for example, Alan Wagner introduces the tenor Giuseppe Fancelli (1833–1887) as someone who was "particularly sure of his own importance," and who "was not the most astute of men" (Wagner 1961: 134). The punch line involves him signing his autograph with this inscription: "Faneli [*sic*] Primo Tenore Ass [*sic*]"; too dumb, in other words, to spell either his name or "assoluto" correctly. This story (like countless others) amuses by placing singers at the butt of a cruel joke: conceit and foolishness are a ridiculous and easily ridiculed combination.

The Lunch-Pail Musician

This mode of reception, highlighting foibles and flaws, winds its way through a wealth of writing, but it is by no means the only impulse that lies behind the copious literature on opera singers. There are many performers, both past and present, who have been shielded from this type of scorn—"normal" men and women. The nineteenth-century diva Giuditta Pasta (1797–1865), for example, was praised throughout her career for her superb acting and artistry; at the turn of the twentieth century, Ernestine Schumann-Heink went out of her way to emphasize her "normalness," portraying herself in the press as a mother of eight who cooked for her family between rehearsals and performances (Calico 2012); and today, Renée Fleming's reputation is grounded in her "all-American-girl" style, something she emphasizes throughout her autobiography (Fleming 2004). The unfettered adulation that many of these men and women have garnered for centuries has translated directly into articles and books concerning their lives, careers, and the effects they have had on spectators. As alluded to in the introduction of this chapter, it is impossible to generalize across the countless publications about these figures, but if pressed to identify a common denominator, one might maintain that this writing often conveys a widespread attempt to fend off, and even to reverse, the stigma of the divine monster.

Biographies and autobiographies are obvious, if not entirely reliable, places to look for an alternative to the construction of the divine monster. One of literally hundreds of examples appears in Luisa Tetrazzini's *My Life of Song* ([1922] 1977). Tetrazzini (1871–1940), whose career spanned from 1890 to 1934, was a leading coloratura soprano of her time, in possession of a dazzlingly agile voice that led her to excel in roles by Rossini, Donizetti, Verdi, Bizet, and many others. Her talent has never been questioned, and yet, as is true of most opera stars (indeed, of most famous people in general), her reputation was constructed on far more than artistic endeavors alone. Throughout her career, various facets of her private life were subject to intense scrutiny. She was widely rumored, for instance, to have had a voracious sexual appetite, and she was involved in relationships, occasionally scandalous ones, with a variety of men. She negotiated hard for the highest fees possible, and she often clashed fiercely with fellow singers and conductors. As Anne Shreffler (2001: 367) has remarked, "today's stereotype of the famous prima donna seems to be based largely on [Tetrazzini's] image (her stoutness, her financial extravagance, her tendency to cancel appearances, her affection for lap dogs and boy toys—traits by no means shared by all divas—have all become cemented into popular mythology)."

As if aware of this mythology and determined to counteract it, Tetrazzini reveals only a trace of these "diva"-like characteristics in her autobiography. In those pages, readers encounter a consummate artist who is thoroughly dedicated to music and willing to risk everything in service to her art. Although she does not depict herself as a saint, and is forthcoming about her fondness for luxurious surroundings and high fees, she neglects facets of her life that would blemish the image of a "respectable" woman (see Gattey 1995). What emerges is a description of a woman who is wholesome, generous, down-to-earth, and above all, extremely hard-working. She emphasizes her hearty work ethic throughout the autobiography, dedicating several pages to the time she devoted to learning new roles and recounting her experiences as a savvy impresario who single-handedly rescued several traveling opera troupes from ruin. One emerges from a reading of this memoir with an image of an artist who had quite a bit of dirt lodged deeply under her fingernails.

This image of a hard-working musician is by no means unusual; it is a construction that helps to counteract the myth of the divine monster. In some contexts, authors emphasize it unselfconsciously, a natural offshoot of the seemingly endless desire to recount the lives of men and women who did, in fact, work extremely hard. Clayton (1863) deserves special mention in this context. This volume is one of the earliest and finest examples of a common type of historical writing about prima donnas and leading men—collections of short biographical sketches of individual singers. (Other good early examples of this genre include Curzon 1898; Edwards 1888; Escudier 1840; Thurner 1883; more up-to-date examples include Christiansen 1985 and Pleasants 1966.) Clayton's discussions of forty-one prima donnas from the seventeenth through the nineteenth centuries contain a wealth of detail concerning the day-to-day activities of these women, their early training, and the paths they traveled on their way to the top of the profession. Although she occasionally engages in the type of hagiographic writing that is common in many biographies of opera stars, the bulk of this lengthy volume has the overall effect of pulling these "celestial" beings down to earth.

This urge to humanize plays a central role in contemporary conceptions of opera singers as well. Examples appear in a variety of trade publications, including Rasponi (1982), a collection of short descriptive sketches of fifty-two prima donnas whose careers spanned the first half of the twentieth century. This volume, which mirrors Clayton's in structure and goals, is saturated with references to the "normal" dispositions and hard work of the women it features. In the introduction to his interview with Lucrezia Bori (1887–1960), for example, Rasponi mentions her "gigantic efforts on behalf of her beloved Metropolitan Opera" (1982: 433), and prefaces the section on Amelita Galli-Curci (1882–1963) with this remark: "I had been so strongly warned of her arrogance that I was surprised at the cordiality with which she greeted me" (1982: 153). This fascination with peering behind the curtain extends to a desire to catch a glimpse of singers in their natural habitats. Matz (1995) contains dozens of brief vignettes that describe the mundane details of singers' lives. The chapter on Marian Anderson (1897–1993), for example, includes a sketch of the singer's home in Connecticut ("an 'L'-shaped eight-room, one-story house" that "hugs the ground on the knoll where it is built, deceiving the visitor as to its size" [1995: 53]); and from the chapter devoted to Robert Merrill (1917–2004), the reader learns that when seeking a new home, he and his wife looked for someplace that "would accommodate the singer, relaxer, party-giver, family man, informal host, sportsman, gardener, good neighbor and a new baby" (1995: 74). The message contrasts notably with the stereotype of the divine monster: at the end of the day, these men and women of the stage are no different from everyone else, pulling their pants off one leg at a time.

Once cognizant of the binary between the divine monster and the normal, hard-working musician, one notices manifestations that crop up in countless locations. The plot of the short story cited at the opening of this section, "Il Colore Ritrovato," for instance, pivots on Signor Cassati's chance encounter with a young, undiscovered singer. This woman is poor, humble, lovely, and thoroughly dedicated to the study of music. When Cassati first hears her, she has been performing on the street for hours, slaving away for enough coins to purchase her next meal. She is, in other words, everything that Rosanna Cardona is not, the opposite of a divine monster. And to return one final time to the evening of December 10, 2006, at Milan's La Scala, the episode with Alagna was exciting not only because the divo's actions were so outrageous, but also because his replacement was so thoroughly *normal*, right down to his street clothes. Verbal responses by each of the singers are illustrative. Alagna was unrepentant, convinced that his singing was flawless: "I sang beautifully, I was *bravissimo.* Too bad for those who didn't understand. [...] I sing with heart, with my blood" (Ross 2006). In contrast, Palombi's response to a reporter interested in getting at the singer's feelings and motivations is strikingly simple and modest: "I did my duty" (Wakin 2006b).

This binary opposition stands front and center in some of the most important research on opera singers that has emerged over the past few decades. The pioneering scholar in this area, Rosselli, has already received attention above, but his work merits more extended discussion. His exhaustive archival research on the Italian "opera industry" (1984) has uncovered details both small and large concerning to the day-to-day procedures of staging an opera from 1600 to the present, and in a later volume he turns his attention to the genre's practitioners (Rosselli 1992). This book is groundbreaking in the field for its approach. Rather than focusing exclusively on the stars of the operatic world, compiling biographical sketches in the style of Clayton, Rasponi, and others, Rosselli's interest falls on the broader issue of "the development and behaviour of the profession as a whole" (Rosselli 1992: 2). He devotes his attention to the day-to-day, addressing issues that pertain to training, payment, and a variety of other seemingly mundane details that together draw a fascinating picture of operatic production. This volume leaves readers with few illusions about the profession—this is a career that has historically been brutal for all but the very lucky few who have achieved fame, and even for those at the top, it can be grueling (Durante 1998 is also noteworthy in this context).

An important descendant of Rosselli's work is that of Susan Rutherford, who further investigates the theme of the working musician in *The Prima Donna and Opera, 1815–1930* (2006). As its title suggests, this book explores the challenges that have long confronted women in this profession, focusing not only on fame and fortune, but also on the quotidian aspects of a life dedicated to the stage. Rutherford's study resembles Rosselli's in its sweeping scope, seeking to "locate these singers within a broader history: one which includes not only the specificities of operatic stage practice, but the life beyond the opera house—the social, cultural and political framing that shaped individual experience, artistic endeavour and audience reception" (Rutherford 2006: 2). To this end, she provides a rich account of hundreds of singers—not only prima donnas, but also those members of the "supporting cast" whose careers lacked the glory and glamour of their more illustrious contemporaries.

Rutherford's book is particularly illuminating when her attention falls on case studies of individual performers such as Mary Garden (1874–1967) and Pauline Viardot (1821–1910). Among the most noteworthy is her discussion of Virginia Boccabadati (1828–1922), a "middle ranking singer who never quite achieved the success of a diva" (Rutherford 2006: 197). In her archival work, Rutherford uncovered nine letters sent by Boccabadati to her friend, the violinist and conductor Giulio Cesare Ferrarini. These missives, written between 1854 and 1861, provide a spotty, yet strikingly intimate account of the challenges inherent in balancing professional and personal demands (she was the unwed mother of a son who traveled with her on tours to various opera houses throughout Italy).

Although Boccabadati occasionally expresses satisfaction with her performances, the overall impression her letters leave, as Rutherford describes, is of a woman under immense pressure, plagued by anxiety and nerves. Following a performance of *La traviata* in Rovigo, Italy, where she sang the role of Violetta, for instance, she was in despair and complained to Ferrarini: "I have done all that I could, being very poorly in voice and extremely weak. The Public showed itself to be very content... but I was not pleased with myself and returned home profoundly saddened" (Rutherford 2006: 198); and in another, also sent from Rovigo, her mood did not improve even though her vocal health had been restored: "I am less sad since my voice is better, but I assure you that here one dies of boredom" (Rutherford 2006: 199). By 1861, Boccabadati had retired, and in a final note to Ferrarini she revealed that she was content at long last: "I am very happy as I had always *dreamed* of being [. . .]." Gone were the attacks of nerves that had long followed her, something she attributes to having left the stage: "I almost *never* sing any more," she writes with a touch of what seems to be delight. Having provided a powerful glimpse of the normalcy of this individual singer's experiences, Rutherford concludes with a description of Boccabadati that might easily apply to any number of performers: "hard-working and conscientious" as well as "relentlessly self-critical and never satisfied with her own efforts" (2006: 202).

Most recently, Kimberly White, in her dissertation, "The Cantatrice and the Profession of Singing at the Paris Opéra and Opéra Comique, 1830–1848" (2012), has made an enormous contribution to the study of women singers in France. Similar to Rutherford and Rosselli, White's concern lies not only with the rich and famous, but more broadly with the entire profession of singing and with those performers who never made it into the upper echelons. Through exhaustive archival research White reconstructs the major "life events" for women singers during this time period, exploring their training, debuts, contractual agreements, benefit concerts, retirements, and marriages. While she finds that life on stage was simple for some, most women engaged in this profession were forced to work very hard, continually pushing against cultural norms and actively constructing their images and celebrity. As accounts by White, Rutherford, Rosselli, and others illustrate, most opera singers are best understood not exclusively as divine monsters or as hard workers, but rather as inhabiting a realm somewhere in between. It goes without saying, moreover, that the fascination singers have held for scholars and opera lovers extends beyond these issues of image and stereotype. The question concerning who these performers "really are" has an important corollary that has received significant attention in the literature on prima donnas and leading men: What do these singers "do" and to what extent are they responsible for what audiences see and hear on stage? Another way of phrasing the question is this: Should singers be classified as "interpreters," artists who communicate the intentions of composers to spectators (whatever those intentions are thought to be), or are they "co-creators," artists who serve as collaborators, helping to generate musical texts?

To Interpret or to Create, That Is the Question

One approach to this question concerning the singer as collaborator has been to distinguish between those who publish their own compositions and those who do not. There are, after all, many gifted singer-composers active from the seventeenth century to the present, musicians who can unquestionably be labeled "creators." Ellen Rosand (1978), for instance, investigates the life and career of Barbara Strozzi (1619–1677), a court singer who, uniquely for a woman, published eight volumes of vocal music that included cantatas, madrigals, and ariettas. Many of Strozzi's contemporaries such as Francesco Rasi (1574–1621), Sigismondo d'India (ca. 1582–1629), Francesca Caccini (1587–1641), Giulio Caccini (1551–1618), and Jacopo Peri (1561–1633), to name only a few, also excelled as composers in addition to receiving attention for their accomplishments as singers (on Francesca Caccini, see Cusick 2009). In his comprehensive and absorbing monograph on the castrato Atto Melani (1626–1714), moreover, Freitas (2009) dedicates a chapter to Melani's compositional output, which consisted of fifteen cantatas. Although this *oeuvre* was small and lacked influence, as Freitas acknowledges, it is important for what it reveals about castratos in general: many of these singers were also highly trained composers, expected to be as adept at writing music as they were at performing it. The singer-songwriter phenomenon persisted well into the eighteenth century and extended to singers of all voice types, not only castratos. Throughout the nineteenth century, many stars of the opera stage produced music in a variety of genres. Isabella Colbran (1785–1845), Maria Malibran (1808–1836), and Pauline Viardot (1821–1910), to name but a few, all wrote songs and arias that they performed in public and private; and Manuel Garcia (1775–1832)—the father of Malibran and Viardot, and as mentioned above, Rossini's first Almaviva—was a prolific composer in addition to having led a highly successful career as a tenor. His operas *L'amante astuto* and *La figlia dell'aria* were among those produced by his troupe on their trip to New York City in 1825, and were thus among the first Italian operas sung in the original language in the United States.

This line of investigation has brought many vital insights to light, but it goes only a fraction of the way toward addressing the issue of whether singers might be considered co-creators of operatic works. What of the virtuosi who did not compose? Are they to be categorized as interpreters alone? A traditionalist might argue that a performer's primary responsibility is to act as a conduit through which a composer's vision is delivered to the audience. In the words of Ellen Harris: "A commonly held but infrequently spoken set of assumptions about music is that the composer as 'artist' achieves god-like status by creating a 'work of art' out of nothing" (Harris 1990: 301). This assumption has undergone gradual decay, however, and helping to erode it is the by now commonplace recognition among opera scholars that composers and librettists were not necessarily the only creative voices; on the contrary, opera production represents a collaborative enterprise in which singers, stage designers, spectators, and critics have helped to "create" the musical text (for discussion of this position, see Abbate and Parker 1989; Gossett 2006).

The question of what constitutes "creation" is by no means straightforward, however, and the work that scholars have produced in this area has unveiled a broad spectrum along which singers' contributions might be understood. On one end of this continuum are studies that attempt to grasp the sway that individual singers have held over composers. In her meticulous and engaging biographical study of the seventeenth-century virtuosa Silvia Gailarti Manni (dates unknown), for instance, Beth Glixon (1996) speculates briefly on this singer's role in the composition of Monteverdi's *Le nozze d'Enea con Lavinia* (1641; the music, however, is lost [see Rosand 2007]). Manni might have played the part of Silvia, a possibility suggested by the fact that the character's name is identical to the singer's. This is a minor character who appears in only two scenes, and yet even though the role is quite small, librettist and composer gave Silvia "a poignant lament of twenty-four verses." Glixon conjectures that this aria, which is quite substantial for a secondary role, may have been included as a way to "pay homage" to Manni. The shape of Monteverdi's operatic work, in other words, might have been affected directly by the unique talents of this singer—quite possibly, she was instrumental in the creation of this work.

Glixon's speculations ring true in large part because they conform to a well-known fact of opera production: Up through the nineteenth century and beyond, most composers tailored their works to the unique vocal talents of the singers who participated in their premieres. As Julian Budden (1973) has noted in reference to this circumstance, "when Mozart was a youth, no one would dream of composing an aria until he first heard the artist who was to perform it" (Budden 1973: I: 3; in this context, see also Gidwitz 1991). Indeed, opera history is crammed with evidence that composers worked very hard to please their performers and to write music they could sing well, fully aware that an opera's fate depended on how it sounded. Meyerbeer, for instance, rewrote substantial portions of his grand opera *Le Prophète* when the singers contracted to create the lead roles were not the ones he originally envisioned for the parts (Armstrong 1996). Verdi, furthermore, supplied star performers participating in revivals of his works with newly composed music when the need arose: For the tenor Mario, for instance, he fashioned a new cabaletta to introduce into a revival of *I due Foscari*, and for Sofia Loewe, he wrote a cavatina that she sang during performances of *Giovanna d'Arco*. "Non-definitive revisions" of this sort were commonplace throughout the early part of Verdi's career, when he was working to establish himself in the theatrical world and needed his singers' help to succeed (Lawton and Rosen 1974).

Mary Ann Smart (1994, 1997) has addressed the issue of singers' influence in a pair of articles that trace the lives of two prominent nineteenth-century prima donnas, Erminia Frezzolini (1818–1884) and Rosine Stoltz (1815–1903). In both cases, Smart references music written with these women's voices in mind (for Frezzolini, Verdi's *Giovanna d'Arco* and for Stoltz, Donizetti's *La favorite*), noting that the operas were composed in circumstances that encouraged collaboration. With regard to *La favorite*, commissioned by the Paris Opéra, Smart comments, for instance, that "[s]ince rehearsals for the beginning of a work usually began long before the last acts were composed, the specific abilities of the singers engaged for the premiere—and of course the demands they made on the composer for numbers that would highlight their strengths—could be highly influential in shaping vocal style and characterization" (1994: 183). She follows this observation with a comparison of solo music for the character Léonor with written descriptions of Stoltz's voice, noting significant similarities. Of the mezzo showpiece "O mon Fernand," for instance, Smart remarks that it "bears all the features [of Stoltz's voice] hinted at in the reviews: sharp shifts between extremes of range, extended passages in the low register, and an emphasis on declamation through short, intense phrases" (1994: 184).

Ann Shreffler's article on Strauss's *Ariadne auf Naxos* (2001) follows a similar line of thought. The question she pursues pertains to Zerbinetta's showpiece aria, "Großmächtige Prinzessin" from Richard Strauss's opera *Ariadne auf Naxos*: Specifically, why did Strauss saturate this number with fiery coloratura, a style that evoked nineteenth-century Italian and French opera, rather than twentieth-century German opera? Her response is multilayered. Part of Strauss's motivation, she argues, was to evoke the talents of not just one, but of a handful of coloratura singers active at the time he wrote the opera: "Margarethe Siems (who created the roles of Zerbinetta, Chrysothemis and the Marschallin), Selma Kurz (the 1916 Zerbinetta), Frieda Hempel (who was asked to sing Zerbinetta at the premiere), Luisa Tetrazzini, and others [...]" (Shreffler 2001: 361). Just as Donizetti, Verdi, and countless others followed the lead of their singers, in other words, so too did Strauss, at a time and within a musical tradition (early-twentieth-century Germanic) when composers were expected to wield the absolute final word over their works: "Zerbinetta's music [...] speaks with the voices of the coloratura sopranos whose vocal technique and improvisations inspired the aria" (Shreffler 2001: 369). As Shreffler illustrates, furthermore, Strauss aimed for more than a direct association with any one of these singers. Rather, by infusing this aria with coloratura, he sought to evoke a *type* of performer—the divine monster—in direct contrast to the other characters in the opera. In her words, "Strauss's use of coloratura can be seen as a signifying gesture, denoting characteristics associated with divas themselves (such as vivaciousness and temperament), but above all an essential *Italianità*, which contrasts with the Germanic style of the serious pair [Ariadne and Bacchus]" (Shreffler 2001: 361–362).

Whether their influence was direct (as in the cases that Smart investigates) or indirect (as Shreffler's example illustrates), prima donnas and leading men have continued to play powerful roles in helping to shape operatic works through the twentieth century to the present day. Benjamin Britten, for instance, tailored all of his important tenor roles—Peter Grimes, Albert Herring, Captain Vere (*Billy Budd*), and nearly a dozen others—to the unique vocal talents of tenor Peter Pears (1910–1986), and without their lifelong association, Britten's output undoubtedly would have sounded quite different. The "new" breed of contemporary singers, such as Dawn Upshaw (b. 1960) and Lorraine Hunt Lieberson (1954–2006), moreover, has also exerted significant influence. Upshaw is a recipient (2007) of a MacArthur Foundation ("genius") grant for championing new works and for working closely with composers on operas such as *L'amour de loin* (Kaija Saariaho), *Ainadamar* (Osvoldo Golijov), *The Great Gatsby* (John Harbison), and *Doctor Atomic* (John Adams). And Lieberson collaborated with her husband, the composer Peter Lieberson, on two sets of songs (*Rilke Songs* and *Neruda Songs*) and on his opera, *Ashoka's Dream*.

All of these singers, active from the seventeenth to the twenty-first centuries, as well as hundreds of others not mentioned here, have played integral roles in the process of generating operatic texts, but even so, a question remains open: To what extent does their influence constitute "creativity"? They are not literally responsible for the notes that were written, after all. This question can be fruitfully addressed by shifting one's gaze from text to performance. Through investigations of performance practices from the seventeenth through the nineteenth centuries, scholars have gained an intimate understanding of the relationship between score and singer, and of the degree to which performers were permitted, even required, to deviate from written texts. This understanding has particular bearing on the Italian repertory, for as Gossett (2006: 293) has explained, "[...] long after most European composers assumed that performers would try to respect their notation, composers of Italian opera continued to treat singers as collaborators." One lens through which to observe such collaboration is the art of ornamentation (see, for example, Caswell 1975; Celletti 1991; Crutchfield 1983, 1989, 1990; and Gossett 2006).

Among the earliest musicologists to explore this issue is Austin Caswell (1975),who provides an overview of nearly 150 embellishments that the prima donna Laure Cinti-Damoreau (1801–1863) made to a host of nineteenth-century operas (these ornaments are preserved in a set of seven notebooks that are housed at the Lilly Library of Indiana University). Caswell's concern lies primarily with nineteenth-century practices, but he opens his study with a pithy summary of what was at stake when singers from the seventeenth and eighteenth centuries embellished their arias: "From Monteverdi's *Orfeo* (1607) through the operas of Handel, the singer (especially the castrato) was assumed not so much to be portraying a character as he was presenting himself and displaying his virtuosic skill before an enthusiastic public. This was accomplished by the improvisation of *passaggi* to vary the repeat in a da capo aria and even by the more striking device of the cadenza" (Caswell 1975: 459). Indeed, Pierfrancesco Tosi (1654–1732), a castrato and voice instructor, engaged directly with this practice in his *Opinioni de'cantori antichi, e moderni* of 1723. This treatise, among the first of its kind, provides detailed instructions concerning the manner in which singers can and should differentiate their vocal lines from composers' directives at cadenzas, cadences, and other moments. Summarizing contemporary practice and its implications for performers, Tosi demonstrated that opera scores served only as starting points from which performers were expected to embellish. Just how creative eighteenth-century singers could get in their improvisatory freedom is the stuff of legend, particularly in the case of castratos. Traces of their inventiveness, as well as an understanding of how their creative efforts were received by spectators, can be located in archival materials and contemporary accounts of these figures (on the castrato Farinelli, in particular, see Feldman 2007: 69–83; other studies of castrati include Heriot 1956; Bergeron 1996; and Freitas 2009).

Known throughout the world for his stunning pyrotechnics and improvisations, Farinelli notated his embellishments in a handful of arias, one of which, "Son qual nave che agitata," by his brother, the composer Riccardo Broschi, is preserved in a presentation manuscript that Farinelli dedicated to Empress Maria Teresia on March 30, 1753. Feldman's detailed analysis of the castrato's ornaments illustrates not only that this performer was capable of extraordinary invention, but also that it was his *passaggi* and cadenzas, not Broschi's music, that enthralled and swayed spectators. In Feldman's words, "[Farinelli's] control over audience response through the wizardry of vocal gymnastics and his touching manipulation of affect marked him as a kind of Orphic magician who not only amazed and delighted, but 'subdued every hearer'" (Feldman 2007: 80). Such displays of a singer's own invention, rather than of a composer's, were not without critics throughout the eighteenth century and beyond: Agricola, who translated Tosi's treatise and appended his own commentary, for instance, took the position that composers held the right to limit performers' freedom of improvisation (Tosi and Agricola 1995); and displays of excessive ornamentation became the stuff of parody and ridicule among eighteenth-century writers (Marcello [1733] 1948, 1949; Martello [1715] 1980). Nevertheless, composers of the seventeenth and eighteenth centuries did not intend their works to be performed without input from their singers, and true artists were able to elegantly blend their own visions with that of composers.

Gossett (2006) has gone further than any other scholar in exploring the creative efforts of singers and their influence—both positive and negative—over operatic production throughout the nineteenth century. Not only does he demonstrate that, like their predecessors, the leading men and women of the nineteenth-century operatic stage were expected to ornament their vocal lines, he explores a variety of other means—such as cuts, transpositions, alternative versions, and substitution arias—through which they exerted their authority, and through which many singers continue to do so today. In my own work on the subject of substitution arias, moreover, I have attempted to demonstrate how a handful of famous prima donnas from the nineteenth century effectively "authored" versions of operas by Rossini, Donizetti, and Bellini by inserting arias into their scores that did not originally belong (Poriss 2009). When the mezzo-soprano Carolina Ungher (1803–1877) introduced an aria from Donizetti's *Ugo, conte di Parigi* into the same composer's *Marino Faliero*, for instance, not only had she undertaken a careful selection process in order to find the aria that functioned best in this new context, she also led the way for other prima donnas who later mimicked her choice. Throughout the history of opera, then, prima donnas and leading men have never failed to excite and thrill—a result of their larger-than-life actions as well as their abilities to influence and create individual operatic works. By no means simple conduits, divas and divos enliven the operatic world, setting it apart from other types of musical performance.

Portrait of a Diva

By way of summing up the issues raised throughout this chapter, I turn now to one individual prima donna, Angelica Catalani. Catalani (1780–1849) was one of the most famous and contentious figures of the nineteenth-century operatic stage; throughout her twenty-five-year career, she was beloved for her glorious voice and reviled for diva-like behavior. Catalani has survived in biographical and historical records as the epitome of a divine monster, obsessed with money and with showcasing her own talents rather than with respecting the integrity of operatic works (see, for instance, Mount

Edgcumbe 1973 and Hogarth 1838). The words uttered by her husband and manager, Paul Valabregue, have long characterized her supposedly inartistic approach toward performances and her utter conceit where her own talents were concerned: "My wife and four or five puppets... that's all that's necessary!" (Mount Edgcumbe 1973: 107). As long as she is on stage, in other words, nothing and no one else is required—all that matters is her voice.

Recent research on Catalani has demonstrated, however, that this image of a self-centered divine monster has been exaggerated. Cowgill (2012) offers the most thorough critical study, providing a much needed rehabilitation of this singer's biographical record, as well as a broader discussion of the manner in which many prima donnas have been all too easily pigeonholed as divine monsters. Walsh (1993), moreover, offers a vivid account of Catalani's artistry and the often rugged conditions under which she labored—to understand something of the environment in which she traveled and the volume of appearances she made in concert and on the opera stage is to know that this soprano worked harder than most throughout her career. As I have attempted to show in my own research, moreover, Catalani was also a creative artist whose influence spread throughout the operatic world. In particular, it was she who initiated the practice of singing theme-and-variation arias on themes by Rode, Mozart, Cimarosa, and others, music that she performed in concert and used as substitute arias. These numbers were subsequently taken up and performed by countless other prima donnas eager to capture a hint of her glory (Poriss 2009).

As an icon of diva behavior, on one hand, and a metaphor for the authority of the singer, on the other, Catalani emerges as a complicated figure. This intricate complex of characteristics is illustrated in a cartoon composed for the *Morning Post* of July 7, 1824, titled "The Cambridge Musical Squeeze!! -or- Double-Bass Entré to the Ochestra [*sic*]" (see Figure 17.1).

The cartoon was drawn by Isaac Robert Cruikshank (1789–1856), one of the most popular and successful graphic satirists of his day. It depicts a set of tumultuous events that occurred before and during a grand concert at the Senate House, Cambridge, on July 6, 1824. According to the *Morning Post* article that Cruikshank references in the lower right-hand corner, the concert featured a group of the most popular musicians working in Europe at the time, including the well-respected Giuditta Pasta and the reputedly monstrous Angelica Catalani (once again, this familiar binary takes center stage). This collection of accomplished performers attracted such a crush of spectators that the doors to the theater had to be closed thirty minutes prior to curtain time, forcing the singers and other artists to make their entrance through a window at the back of the building. Once inside, more disorder ensued when it was discovered that several of the orchestra's double basses, including that of Domenico Dragonetti, had been severely damaged.

The cartoon reimagines the space of these events, setting them all outside the Senate House, which stands in the background of the image. The middle ground features Catalani and the Bishop of Limerick ascending a ladder together toward the concert hall's makeshift window-entrance. To the left of the Bishop, squashed into the lower,

FIGURE 17.1 Isaac Robert Cruikshank, hand-colored etching, "The Cambridge Musical Squeeze!! -or- Double-Bass Entré to the Ochestra [*sic*]." © Victoria and Albert Museum, London.

left-hand corner of the window is Dragonetti, visibly exasperated and expressing his frustration over his damaged instrument. The man to the right of Catalani, holding a bass by its neck and speaking in a "French" accent, is most likely a caricature of her husband, Valabregue. A chaotic throng divided into two groups occupies the foreground: on the left side, a gaggle of learned Cambridge men, and to the right, a group of distinguished guests waiting their turn to climb the ladder into the concert hall.

This sketch, brimming with action and allusion, conveys more than a simple representation of events. Nearly every gesture, pose, and comment serves to deliver the message of Catalani as divine monster. The most obvious place where this is communicated is in Cruikshank's sketch of the singer—her rosy cheeks suggesting recent engagement in sexual activity, and her exposed leg, ankle, and arm implying openness to the male gaze. The Cambridge men below her take advantage of their position and stare lecherously up her dress, one exclaiming, "Fine legs by G-d," another uttering a string of obscenities loosely disguised as learned "Latin" prose ("horum," to take just the first term, clearly evokes "whore"). The impression of Catalani's wantonness is further enhanced by the fact that she is sandwiched between two men, neither of whom behaves properly: The Bishop grabs her waist, while his right leg inches up between hers; Valabregue on her other side offers to "push behind" and rests his nose delicately near that portion of her body, the tail of his speech balloon doubling as a wafting scent. What are we to make of the exaggerations in this image?

The cartoonist was alluding to the long-standing stereotype of the "loose" female opera singer, typecasting Catalani in a generic role. That Cruikshank selected Catalani as his central figure, moreover, indicates that this image referred to an allegory of a particular type of abuse: selling out, "prostituting" oneself for the sake of money and stardom. Cruikshank's cartoon, in other words, represents a familiar critique of the manner in which Catalani and many other singers handled their careers. Reinforcing this interpretation is the identity of the musical work that the chorister holds in the foreground of the cartoon, "Glorious Appollo [*sic*] from on High," the most famous glee composed by one of the best-known composers of the genre, Samuel Webbe. By placing this music in the chorister's hands, Cruikshank implies a performer willing to efface her own identity for the sake of a larger group, the normal, hard-working musician versus the divine monster.

But even if this message were the one Cruikshank intended, something more must be said, for despite all the slander directed at Catalani in this cartoon, she is the only person whose face is not caricatured, whose features are drawn in elegant proportion. Cruikshank took care to depict her favorably, compelling the viewer to peer beyond the surface and to imagine what might lie beyond the facade. Clearly, this singer is beloved, despite the implications that she embraces all of the bad behaviors for which many divas and divos have become known over the past four centuries. As such, Cruikshank's cartoon might be read more broadly as an allegory for the ambivalence and adulation that opera stars in general have long sparked. Simultaneously reviled and worshipped, the negative assumptions that might be thrown in their direction are easily forgotten when their talents are taken into consideration, when they *sing*. Catalani, Callas, Alagna, and so many others have enchanted and will continue to enchant long into the future. On the wings of their artistry and their voices, they float delicately above the fray, drowning out all other bustle and noise, and with them they carry their spectators far off into a divine realm.

See also: Castrato Acts, What Is Opera? Acting, Costumes, Gender

Bibliography

Abbate, Carolyn, and Roger Parker, eds. 1989. *Analyzing Opera: Verdi and Wagner*. Berkeley and Los Angeles: University of California Press.

Armstrong, Alan. 1996. "Gilbert-Louis Duprez and Gustave Roger in the Composition of Meyerbeer's *Le Prophète*." *Cambridge Opera Journal* 8/2: 147–165.

Bergeron, Katherine. 1996. "The Castrato as History." *Cambridge Opera Journal* 8/2: 164–184.

Blackmer, Corinne E., and Patricia Julianna Smith, eds. 1995. *En travesti: Women, Gender Subversion, Opera*. New York: Columbia University Press.

Budden, Julian. 1973–1981. *The Operas of Verdi*. 3 vols. New York: Oxford University Press.

Calico, Joy. 2012. "Staging Scandal with *Salome* and *Elektra*." In Cowgill and Poriss 2012, 61–82.

Castle, Terry. 1995. "In Praise of Brigitte Fassbaender: Reflections on Diva Worship." In Blackmer and Smith 1995, 20–58.

Caswell, Austin. 1975. "Mme Cinti-Damoreau and the Embellishment of Italian Opera in Paris, 1820–1845." *Journal of the American Musicological Society* 28/3: 459–492.

Celletti, Rodolfo. 1991. *A History of Bel Canto*. Oxford: Clarendon Press.

Christiansen, Rupert. 1985. *Prima Donna: A History*. New York: Viking.

Clayton, Ellen Creathorne. 1863. *Queens of Song: Being Memoirs of Some of the Most Celebrated Female Vocalists Who Have Appeared on the Lyric Stage, from the Earliest Days of Opera to the Present Time. To Which Is Added a Chronological List of All the Operas That Have Been Performed in Europe*. London: Smith, Elder, and Co.

Clément, Catherine. 1988. *Opera, or The Undoing of Women*, translated by Betsy Wing. Minneapolis: University of Minnesota Press.

Cone, John Frederick. 1993. *Adelina Patti: Queen of Hearts*. Portland, OR: Amadeus Press.

Cowgill, Rachel. 2012. "'Attitudes with a Shawl': Performance, Femininity, and Spectatorship at the Italian Opera in Early Nineteenth-Century London." In Cowgill and Poriss 2012, 217–251.

——, and Hilary Poriss, eds. 2012. *The Arts of the Prima Donna in the Long Nineteenth Century*. New York: Oxford University Press.

Crutchfield, Will. 1990. "Voices." In *Performance Practice: Music after 1600*, edited by Howard Mayer Brown and Stanley Sadie, 304–310. New York: W. W. Norton.

——. 1989. "The Prosodic Appoggiatura in the Music of Mozart and His Contemporaries." *Journal of the American Musicological Society* 42/2: 229–271.

——. 1983. "Vocal Ornamentation in Verdi: The Phonographic Evidence." *19th-Century Music* 7/1: 3–54.

Curzon, Henri de. 1898. *Croquis d'artistes*. Paris: Librairie Fischbacher.

Cusick, Suzanne. 2009. *Francesca Caccini at the Medici Court: Music and the Circulation of Power*. Chicago: University of Chicago Press.

Durante, Sergio. 1998. "The Opera Singer." In *Opera Production and Its Resources*, edited by Lorenzo Bianconi and Giorgio Pestelli, translated by Lydia G. Cochrane. *The History of Italian Opera* 4, 345–417. Chicago: University of Chicago Press.

Edwards, H. Sutherland. 1888. *The Prima Donna, Her History and Surroundings from the Seventeenth to the Nineteenth Century*. 2 vols. London: Remington and Co.

Escudier, Marie Pierre Yves, and Léon Escudier. 1840. *Études biographiques sur les chanteurs contemporains, précédées d'une Esquisse sur l'art du chant, par mm. Escudier frères*. Paris: J. Tessier.

Farkas, Andrew. 1985. *Opera and Concert Singers: An Annotated International Bibliography of Books and Pamphlets*. New York and London: Garland.

Feldman, Martha. 2007. *Opera and Sovereignty: Transforming Myths in Eighteenth-Century Italy*. Chicago: University of Chicago Press.

Fleming, Renée. 2004. *The Inner Voice: The Making of a Singer*. New York: Penguin Books.

Freitas, Roger. 2009. *Portrait of a Castrato: Politics, Patronage, and Music in the Life of Atto Melani*. Cambridge: Cambridge University Press.

Gattey, Charles Nelson. 1995. *Luisa Tetrazzini: The Florentine Nightingale*. Portland, OR: Amadeus Press.

Gidwitz, Patricia Lewy. 1991. " 'Ich bin die erste Sängerin': Vocal Profiles of Two Mozart Sopranos." *Early Music* 19/4: 565–579.

Glixon, Beth. 1996. "Scenes from the Life of Silvia Gailarti Manni, a Seventeenth-Century 'Virtuosa.' " *Early Music History* 15: 97–146.

Gossett, Philip. 2006. *Divas and Scholars: Performing Italian Opera*. Chicago: University of Chicago Press.

Harris, Ellen T. 1990. "Integrity and Improvisation in the Music of Handel." *Journal of Musicology* 8/3: 301–315.

Helprin, Mark. 2004. "Il Colore Ritrovato." In *The Pacific and Other Stories*, 1–34. New York: Penguin Press.

Henson, Karen. 2007. "Introduction: Divo Worship." *Cambridge Opera Journal* 19/1: 1–9.

Heriot, Angus. 1956. *The Castrati in Opera*. London: Secker & Warburg.

Hogarth, George. 1838. *Memoirs of the Musical Drama*. 2 vols. London: Richard Bentley.

Kettle, Martin. 2006. "A tantrum too far." *Guardian* (November 13).

Klein, Herman. [1920] 1978. *The Reign of Patti*. Reprint. New York: Da Capo Press.

Koestenbaum, Wayne. 1994. *The Queen's Throat: Opera, Homosexuality, and the Mystery of Desire*. New York: Vintage Books.

Lawton, David, and David Rosen. 1974. "Verdi's Non-Definitive Revisions: The Early Operas." *Atti del III° congresso internazionale di studi verdiani (Milano, Piccola Scala, 12–17 giugno 1972)*, 189–237. Parma: Istituto di studi verdiani.

Leonardi, Susan J., and Rebecca A. Pope, eds. 1996. *The Diva's Mouth: Body, Voice, Prima Donna Politics*. New Brunswick, NJ: Rutgers University Press.

Marcello, Benedetto. [1720] 1948/1949. *Il teatro alla moda*, translated by Reinhard Pauly. *Musical Quarterly* 34/3: 371–403 and 35/1: 85–105.

Martello, Pier Jacopo. [1715] 1980. *Della tragedia antica e moderna*. Rome: F. Gonzaga. Translated in Piero Weiss, "Pier Jacopo Martello on Opera (1715): Annotated Translation." *Musical Quarterly* 66/3: 378–403.

Matz, Mary Jane. 1955. *Opera Stars in the Sun: Intimate Glimpses of Metropolitan Opera Personalities*. New York: Farrar, Straus & Cudahy.

Mount Edgcumbe, Richard, Earl of. [1834] 1973. *Musical Reminiscences, Containing an Account of Italian Opera in England, from 1773*. Reprint. New York: Da Capo Press.

Opera Chic. 2006. "Alagna Out of Aida: He's all like: C U L8R LAM3RZ." (December 10). Online. Available: http://operachic.typepad.com (accessed August 14, 2012).

Owen, Richard. 2006. "Tenor Who Stormed off La Scala Stage Vows He Will Return." *The Times* (London) (December 13).
Pareles, Jon. 2009. "New CDs: Earning Diva Cred with Storm and Stress." *New York Times* (August 31).
Parker, Roger. 2006. *Remaking the Song: Operatic Visions and Revisions from Handel to Berio*. Berkeley and Los Angeles: University of California Press.
Pleasants, Henry. 1996. *The Great Singers: From the Dawn of Opera to Our Own Time*. New York: Simon and Schuster.
Poriss, Hilary. 2009. *Changing the Score: Arias, Prima Donnas, and the Authority of Performance*. AMS Studies in Music. New York: Oxford University Press.
Rasponi, Lanfranco. 1982. *The Last of the Prima Donnas*. New York: Alfred A. Knopf.
Rosand, Ellen. 2007. *Monteverdi's Last Operas: A Venetian Trilogy*. Berkeley and Los Angeles: University of California Press.
——. 1978. "Barbara Strozzi, *virtuosissima cantatrice*: The Composer's Voice." *Journal of the American Musicological Society* 31/2: 241–281.
Ross, Alex. 2006. "La Scala Scandal." (December 10). Online. Available: http://www.therestis-noise.com/2006/12/la_scala_scanda.html (accessed February 6, 2014).
Rosselli, John. 1992. *Singers of Italian Opera*. Cambridge: Cambridge University Press.
——. 1989. "From Princely Service to the Open Market: Singers of Italian Opera and Their Patrons, 1600–1850." *Cambridge Opera Journal* 1/1: 1–32.
——. 1984. *The Opera Industry in Italy from Cimarosa to Verdi: The Role of the Impresario*. Cambridge: Cambridge University Press.
Rutherford, Susan. 2007. "'La cantante delle passion': Giuditta Pasta and the Idea of Operatic Performance." *Cambridge Opera Journal* 19/2: 107–138.
——. 2006. *The Prima Donna and Opera, 1815–1930*. Cambridge: Cambridge University Press.
——. 1992. "The Voice of Freedom: Images of the Prima Donna." In *The New Woman and Her Sisters: Feminism and Theatre, 1850–1914*, edited by Vivian Gardner and Susan Rutherford, 95–113. Ann Arbor: University of Michigan Press.
Sargeant, Winthrop. 1973. *Divas: Impressions of Six Opera Superstars*. New York: Coward, McCann & Geoghegan.
Shreffler, Anne C. 2001. "The Coloratura's Voice: Another Look at Zerbinetta's Aria from *Ariadne auf Naxos*." In *Richard Strauss und die Moderne: Bericht über das Internationale Symposium München, 21. bis 23. Juli 1999*, edited by Birgit Bernd Edelmann, 360–390. Berlin: Henschel.
Smart, Mary Ann. 1997. "Verdi Sings Erminia Frezzolini." *Women and Music* 1: 33–45.
——. 1994. "The Lost Voice of Rosine Stoltz." *Cambridge Opera Journal* 6/1: 31–50.
Tetrazzini, Luisa. [1922] 1977. *My Life of Song*. Reprint. New York: Arno Press.
Thurner, Auguste. 1883. *Les reines du chant*. Paris: A. Hennuyer.
Tommasini, Anthony. 1998. "An Imbroglio for *Figaro*, Its Director and Bartoli." *New York Times* (November 9).
Tosi, Pierfrancesco. [1723] 1968. *Opinioni de' cantori antichi, e moderni*. Reprint. Monuments of Music and Music Literature in Facsimile, ser. 2. Music Literature 133. New York: Broude Brothers.
——, and Johann Friedrich Agricola. 1995. *Introduction to the Art of Singing*, translated by Julianne Baird. Cambridge: Cambridge University Press.
Wagner, Alan. 1961. *Prima Donnas and Other Wild Beasts*. Larchmont, NY: Argonaut.

Wakin, Daniel J. 2006a. "After La Scala Boos, a Tenor Boos Back." *New York Times* (December 13).
——. 2006b. "Stepping in for a Star, but Not Feeling Like One." *New York Times* (December 16).
Walsh, T. J. 1993. *Opera in Dublin, 1798–1820: Frederick Jones and the Crow Street Theatre.* New York: Oxford University Press.
White, Kimberly. 2012. "The Cantatrice and the Profession of Singing at the Paris Opéra and Opéra Comique, 1830-1848." PhD diss., McGill University.
Wierzbicki, James. 2001. "Dethroning the Divas: Satire Directed at Cuzzoni and Faustina." *Opera Quarterly* 17/2: 175–196.
Wood, Elizabeth. 1995. "The Lesbian in the Opera: Desire Unmasked in Smyth's Fantasio and Fête Galante." In Blackmer and Smith 1995, 285–305.

CHAPTER 18

CASTRATO ACTS

MARTHA FELDMAN

Tracking the Castrato

Picture yourself a young British aristocrat in 1733–1734, polishing off your education with a Grand Tour through Italy. A key strip of your itinerary takes you from Venice to Vicenza to Florence. It reverses the direction of a typical Grand Tour, which goes from Turin to Florence to Bologna to the Veneto and Venice, because you've set out to track the appearances of the stupendous castrato Carlo Broschi, known as Farinelli. If you were on this jaunt nowadays, people would call you an opera queen.[1]

Now imagine you're a young composer from across the Alps, commissioned to write for several opera seasons in Habsburg Milan. For the 1771 season you fashion some custom-made arias for the "powerful and voluminous" voice of soprano Giovanni Manzuoli, familiar from your mutual acquaintance with J. C. Bach in London six years earlier (Burney 1789: IV: 484–485). For 1772 you write for Venanzio Rauzzini (unknown to you), the leading male soprano in your new opera, for whom you also create a show-stopping motet *Exultate, jubilate* (K. 165 [158a]), done at the Theatine Church in Milan, January 17, 1773). Between engagements, you've headed east and south on the peninsula, finding singers in theaters, churches, and salons. In Cremona's 1770 production of *Demetrio*, the alto Giuseppe Cicognani strikes you with his "delightful voice" and "beautiful cantabile," unlike the young eunuchs playing secondary parts, who are merely "passable" (Anderson 1985: 110; he was Farnace in Mozart's *Mitridate, re di Ponto* [Milan, 1770]). Later that year, at the opera house in Naples, Giuseppe Aprile, whose "beautiful, even voice" you'd heard in a Milanese church in January 1770, "sings amazingly well" (Anderson 1985: 111, 143; Aprile played Cecilio in Mozart's *Lucio Silla* [Milan, 1772]). Cicognani and Aprile both hold forth in a salon concert given in Bologna by Count Pallavicino in spring that year—fortuitously, because you're also planning to visit the legendary Farinelli (now retired) in his nearby villa where, word has it, he may even sing for you (Anderson 1985: 123, 123 n2; on Farinelli's villa, see Boris 1998 and Boris and Cammarota 1990).

The protagonist of the first scenario is no nameless sybarite but the fourth Duke of Leeds, Thomas Osborne (1713–1781; McGeary 2002). By the time he reached Italy from London, he had pursued castrati in other performances, notably a number of Handel's works done by the renowned alto Senesino, who sang in London's luxurious opera scene.[2] While in Venice, the Duke managed to hear Farinelli in no less than three of his big roles—Arbace in Broschi's *Artaserse*, Demetrio in Porpora's *Berenice*, and Epitide in Giacomelli's *Merope*. The protagonist of the second scenario is of course Mozart, who while still a teenager traveled to Milan with his father to write two "serious operas" and a *festa teatrale*, all with prominent castrato parts.

Like Osborne and Mozart, countless nobles, poets, impresarios, composers, dignitaries, politicians, and other worldly men and women mapped their peregrinations onto those of castrati. When there was no vocational necessity to do so, there was generally a social impetus, for hearing the great castrati was de rigueur in the public agendas of middle- to upper-class Europeans, who were fascinated by them, often dazzled, astounded, and touched, and not infrequently (they claimed) disappointed or left cold. Expectations for castrato performances ran high, and going to hear them—like getting to see, hear, and be seen at the theaters where they played—was a must. Those who did not know how to get in or how to comport themselves once there were typically marked as outsiders or philistines, like the Branghton sisters of Frances Burney's epistolary novel *Evelina* (1778), who "torment" the heroine by jabbering through the performance of the wonderful Giuseppe Millico for whose "sweet voice" the refined protagonist feels "nothing but delight" (Burney 2002: 93).

Keynotes

In all these phenomena, castrati were part of a boom in two related industries that marked the early eighteenth century: the travel industry and a new celebrity media industry. By that era, castrati had long since become major players on the European stage. They had emerged in Italy's north Italian courts in the 1550s and first appeared in the Papal chapel in the next decade. By January 1607, the future Duke of Mantua Francesco Gonzaga could write his brother, "I have decided to have a play in music performed at Carnival this year, but as we have very few sopranos here, and those few not good, I should be grateful if Your Excellency would be kind enough to tell me if those castrati I heard when I was in Tuscany are still there" (Fenlon 1986: 167). The "play" was Monteverdi's court opera *L'Orfeo*, and the soprano the Duke ended up getting, Giovanni Gualberto Magli, took the roles of La Musica, Proserpina, and possibly La Speranza, most probably in an all-male cast, meaning that both Orfeo and the female Euridice would have been male trebles, too. During these early decades, castrati most often played gods, women, or saints. In Stefano Landi's *Sant'Alessio*, a Barberini opera from Rome 1632, the title character was played by a castrato—though that was rather exceptional during the first decades of the seventeenth century, when castrati were just beginning to proliferate in courts and chapels across Italy, Germany, and eventually the Iberian peninsula and beyond.

Critical to establishing castrati as leading men and to their proliferation in opera, usually as male lovers, was the advent in Venice of the commercial opera house in 1637. Most famous among castrato roles from the time is Emperor Nero in Monteverdi's *L'incoronazione di Poppea* (Venice, 1643), probably played by Stefano Costa. Male treble leads had appeared before *Poppea*—for example, the noble lover Egisto in Mazzocchi and Marazzoli's *Chi soffre speri* (Rome, Barbarini palace, 1637) and King Iarba in Cavalli's *Didone* (Venice, Teatro San Cassiano, 1641)—and shortly afterward there was Orfeo in Luigi Rossi's *Orfeo* (Paris, Palais Royal, 1647). A slew of operas ensued at midcentury, by which time the phenomenon had become widespread, thanks especially to its promotion by Cavalli. Examples include the roles of Giasone in *Giasone* (Venice, Teatro San Cassiano, 1649), Endimion in *Calisto* (Venice, Teatro San Apollinare, 1651), and (with two castrati each) the roles of Xerse and Arsemene in *Xerse* (Venice, Teatro SS. Giovanni e Paolo, 1655), Scipio and Luceio in *Scipione affricano* (Venice, Teatro SS. Giovanni e Paolo, 1664), and Farnace and Servilio in *Pompeo magno* (Teatro San Salvador, 1666). In the 1671 Roman revival of *Scipione affricano*, one of the most famous castrati of the latter half of the century, Siface (born Giovanni Francesco Grossi), gained such enormous fame playing Syphax that he took his moniker from the role. We will see below that in many such roles, castrati play men who have "forsaken true virility in favor of love" (Freitas 2003: 238 and passim, who argues that because loving women threatened loss of "vital heat," according to contemporary humoral theory, it was aligned with an emasculated castrato; 235–238).

As the numbers of large commercial opera houses increased steadily up to 1800, castrati appeared on stages in London (starting with Handel's *Rinaldo* of 1711), St. Petersburg (from the 1730s), and numerous other parts of Europe, excepting only France, which had its own tradition of opera based on indigenous drama and voice types. The best castrati followed extensive international travel itineraries for their work. Over a two-century span of industry growth, operatic competition stiffened for (and among) the best castrati, who by the late seventeenth century had come to be universally recognized as the most vocally elite group of singers. François Raguenet's comment following his travels in Italy are characteristic in hearing in castrato voices an affinity with the transhuman and a capacity to induce self-loss in listeners: "They sing like nightingales, they make you lose your balance and take your breath away"[3] (1702: 78–79). By Raguenet's time, castrati had come to represent the very physiognomy of the performer as star.

Accounts often suggest that castrato performance was above all about voice and secondarily about acting. A more native view might understand the castrato's voice as the principal medium of acting. Acting was, of course, also understood as physical gesture, following stylized conventions that prescribed imitating the passions in idealized forms, at least until the 1760s or so, coincident with a time when castrated singers were on the wane.

The way to learn acting was to look to sculptures and paintings as models of the passions, conceived in taxonomic terms. Taxonomies followed the general categories first codified by Descartes in his 1749 *Passions of the Soul* and extended by Le Brun's 1702 *Method for Learning to Draw the Passions* and Mattheson's 1739 *Complete Music Master* (Feldman 2003; Mattheson, *Der vollkomene Capellmeister*, Part 1, chap. 3 on passions, translated in Lenneberg 1958: 47–84 and 193–236). By the eighteenth century, when operatic castrati regularly performed in so-called *drammi per musica* (*opera seria*), the genre pressed out these codified passions as corresponding musical affects. Its dramaturgy consisted largely of short, distinct scenes that started with recitative and often culminated in an aria whose ending precipitated the singer's exit, nailing the emotional point after the reprise of the aria's main section. Arias were traditionally dominated by a single affect, normally with only a brief contrasting inner section shading the emotion of the main part. (Castrati did occasionally play in eighteenth-century comic opera, for example, Rinaldo in Galuppi's *Il filosofo di campagna* of 1754, but this was by far the exception.)

In delivering arias, castrati would typically strike a pose downstage center within the space of the proscenium arch, which formed a liminal borderland across which viewers and singers met. The positioning of singers within the proscenium did not preclude audience address and exchange but enabled it, to the advantage of singers attempting to attract the attention of viewers in the face of numerous ambient distractions (Feldman 2007: chapters 1 and 2). Some castrati abused their celebrity by willfully breaking the theatrical frame, dropping character to wave to friends, mug at the audience, or jest with fellow singers. The egregious Caffarelli (1710–1783) found out that there could be consequences for wholesale abandonment of decorum when the Bourbon government put him under house arrest, more than once (Heartz 2004).

All such practices, conventional and abusive, were predicated on the understanding that singing arias in the opera house was an agonistic activity in which singers struggled to outdo others or simply be heard. The oft-repeated story told by Charles Burney of Farinelli's battle with a trumpeter when he was a mere seventeen condenses such presumptions, framed in the scopophilic terms of an audience mesmerized by two gladiatorial performers, each intent on exhausting the other:

> He was seventeen years old when he left [. .. Naples] to go to Rome, where, during a run of an opera, there was a struggle every night between him and a famous player on the trumpet, in a song accompanied by that instrument: this, at first, seemed amicable and merely sportive, till the audience began to interest themselves in the contest, and to take different sides: After severally swelling out a note, in which each manifested the power of his lungs, and tried to rival the other in brilliancy and force, they had both a swell and a shake together, by thirds, which was continued so long, while the audience eagerly waited the event, that both seemed to be exhausted; and, in fact, the trumpeter, wholly spent, gave it up, thinking however his antagonist as much tired as himself, and that it would be a drawn battle; when Farinelli, with a smile on his countenance, shewing that he had only been sporting with him all this time, broke out all at once in the same breath, with fresh vigour, and not only swelled and shook the note, but ran the most rapid and difficult divisions, and was at last silenced only by the acclamations of the audience. From this period may be dated

> that superiority which he ever maintained over all his contemporaries. (Burney 1789: IV: 205–206)

Once some of the castrati had become operatic superstars, by the early eighteenth century, they were often divided into camps. In England the Duchess of Leeds couldn't stomach the few lingering supporters of Carestini, the castrato singing in Handel's Academy in rivalry with Farinelli, who had just begun his stint with Porpora's Opera of the Nobility. "I quarrel with those folks eternally, and tell them I wonder they are not ashamed to say so" (quoted in McGeary 2002: 205; spelling modernized). Even though Farinelli dominated the opera world before and after his arrival in London in 1734, he showed distrust and pride concerning other castrati. In a letter from Milan of September 26, 1731, he begged his patron Sicinio Pepoli to intervene with a certain Bolognese count in order that he not have to sing publicly an aria identified with Carestini, declaring that he would not sully his reputation thus, even if others sang his:

> For as long as I've been in this business there has never been a single occasion on which I've sung others' arias on the stage, especially those of that conceited [Carestini]. I myself enjoy the fact that others sing my arias in the theater and thus give me the pleasure of hearing them, as has often happened to me; so I don't want some vainglorious person able to boast that Farinelli sings his arias. (Vitali 2000: 89–90)

Farinelli's pride and exclusivity were the mark of a superstar, one who specialized in impersonating young nobles, heroes, and princes destined to rise in the social order. It's fair to say that the very top eighteenth-century castrati attained a status as virtual royal substitutes, and that their operatic displays of bravura in fiery allegros and emotion in pathetic ones were complicit in allowing them to compete and conquer as they negotiated the road to professional and social superiority—hence their constant efforts to raise the stakes on past performances (their own and others'), to exchange the most preeminent graces at court, and to display their lavish lifestyles with sovereign nonchalance. Vocal excess, like excessive wealth, resonated with the ability to make displays of squandering as a sign of sovereignty. Farinelli boasted that when he sang for the emperor and empress in Vienna he pulled off three great *messe di voce* in a row, adding that he was the only person "in his profession" ever to have been graced with singing privately for the imperial couple. Years later, he sent the imperial household a hubristic presentation manuscript (A-Wn 19111) as a keepsake of the extraordinary *passaggi*, cadenzas, and *messe di voce* for which he was renowned, rubricating all his own excesses (see Figure 18.1).

No sooner had some castrati become huge media stars, with composers writing down and even publishing their impossibly difficult music, than there were backlashes. Antonio Bernacchi (1685–1756) was renowned for singing *passaggi* of dazzling length and difficulty, but his teacher Pistocchi (1659–1726), possibly the best improviser of ornaments from the previous generation, was already said to have complained, "I taught you to sing, and you want to play." After his heyday Bernacchi was accused by the likes of Martinelli and Algarotti of sacrificing expression to virtuosic execution. Even the

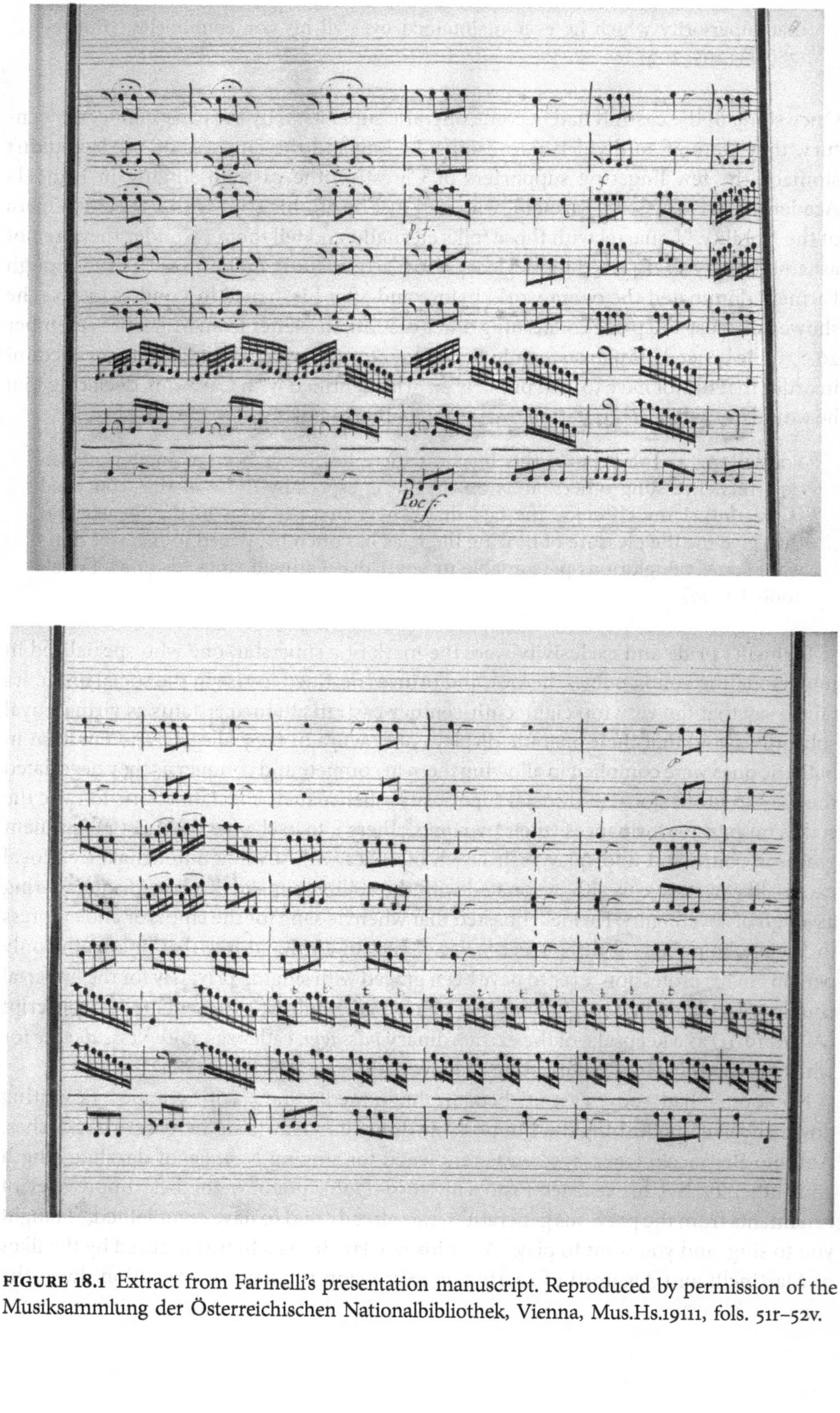

FIGURE 18.1 Extract from Farinelli's presentation manuscript. Reproduced by permission of the Musiksammlung der Österreichischen Nationalbibliothek, Vienna, Mus.Hs.19111, fols. 51r–52v.

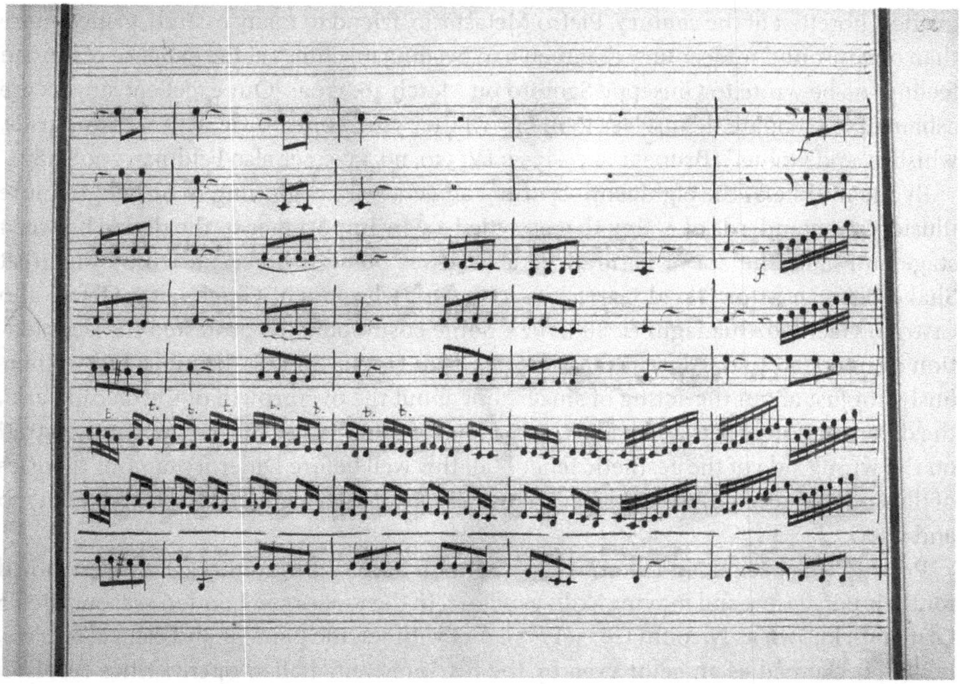

FIGURE 18.1 *Continued*

greatest librettist of the century, Pietro Metastasio, friend to many castrati, griped more than once around midcentury that men had become machines at the expense of human feeling. As he wrote to Giuseppe Santoro on March 26, 1764: "Our excellent singers are ashamed to compare themselves to men [...] they yearn only to vie with radiator grills, whistles, and violins" (Brunelli 1943–1954: IV: 350, no. 1375; see also Feldman 2008: 187).

By the middle of the eighteenth century, singers were beginning to be held to more illusionistic standards of acting that assigned a new importance to the divide between stage and hall. The era of naturalistic acting was being ushered in, led by the great Shakespearean actor David Garrick (1717–1779), who taught Gluck's first Orfeo, alto castrato Gaetano Guadagni (1728–1792). Some cosmopolitans protested the degradation of opera all told. Algarotti's *Essay on Opera* (1755; rev. 1763) complained vociferously not just about the acting of singers but about the overgrowth of the da capo aria, the deterioration of sets and ballets, and a host of other issues that de facto put castrati on the wrong side of the aesthetic fence—all this well before Diderot's famous theories of illusionistic acting were inscribed in his *Paradox of the Actor* (redacted between 1770 and 1784).

Prior to this period, and contrary to common accusation, some castrati were noted for their persuasive and moving skills as actors. In the 1708–1709 London season, Nicola Grimaldi, known as Nicolini (1673–1732), met with terrific popular and critical success, being proclaimed as an actor even by the fearsome anti-Italian opera critics Addison and Steele. Addison went so far as to suggest that Nicolini was better than some of England's own speaking actors—"I have often wished that our tragedians would copy after this great master in action. Could they make the same use of their arms and legs, and inform their faces with as significant looks and passions [...]!" ([1711] 1965: N. 13, March 15, quoted in Roach 1993: 69)—while Steele marveled at his ability to imitate perfectly the limbs of classical sculpture: "Every limb and every finger contributes to the part he acts, insomuch that a deaf man may go along with him in the sense of it. There is scarce a beautiful posture in an old statue which he does not plant himself in, as the different circumstances of the story give occasion for it" (Steele [1709–1710] 1899: N. 13, January 3, quoted in Roach 1993: 69, with further on Nicolini 68–69; also fundamental on acting is Barnett 1987).

What did such veneration and attacks have to do with castrati as figments of culture writ large? In Italy there was always a sense that castrati were both extraordinary and marginal (see Rosselli 1998 and Feldman 2009). They were marginal once castrated, since from that moment they were to dedicate themselves totally to their profession, which was essentially of the church. It also deprived them of their intended place in a patrilineal line (Feldman 2014: chap. 2). They were extraordinary because they received more rigorous training even than other boys, from whom they were largely isolated, and because they were inherently capable of that which other humans were not. Furthermore, since the large majority sang exclusively in church—with occasional release for some to do opera on the side and a good deal of church singing even for operatic castrati—Italians regarded them as essentially sacrificial beings, not least because they had shed blood to become, formally speaking, sacred celibates. Outside Italy, they received a less Catholic gloss, but their exceptional capabilities, combined with their gelded physical makeup, nevertheless marked them within society as a whole.

Accordingly, the late-seventeenth-century music historian Bontempi explained the exceptional capacities of the castrato as an exchange of potencies. In the venerated Baldassare Ferri he saw the procreative power of semen replaced by the magical power of song, expressed through utter purity of voice, perfect breath control, beauty and ease of passagework, and astonishing trills, variously combined with agility work, divisions, cadences, swelling, diminishing, and sweetness of nuance, with all of which Ferri could enchant every listener (*Historia musica* [1695] 1971). Ferri's nineteenth-century encomiast, fellow Perugian Count Giancarlo Conestabile, added that without the singer's "enormous chest" and lungs—a hormonal consequence of castration—these incredible feats would have been impossible (see Figure 18.2, a caricature of Senesino, seen alongside soprano Faustina Bordoni). Conestabile went on to vaunt Ferri's ability "to arrive sweetly on any note after the continuation of a very long and beautiful passaggio." The length of such a *passaggio* would not have allowed others to maintain breath control, but he, without taking a breath, could "burst forth" from it "into a very long and gorgeous trill and then pass into another *passaggio* even longer and more vigorous than the first," ascending and descending "from semitone to semitone without any break." By

FIGURE 18.2 Senesino, depicted with soprano Faustina Bordoni, in a caricature drawn by Venetian artist and librarian Anton Maria Zanetti il Vecchio (entitled *Francesco Bernardio detto il Senesino e Faustina Bordoni*). Reproduced from Zanetti's album by permission of the Istituto di storia dell'arte della Fondazione Giorgio Cini, Venice.

performing these "miracles of art," Ferri made himself "greater than a marvel and almost exceeded what is possible for humans" (Conestabili 1846: 9).

Surviving anecdotes about such feats can only occasionally be substantiated from seventeenth-century textual evidence, since it was generally expected that singers would add decorations, ideally *ex tempore*. Scores provide greater evidence during the active years of Farinelli, in the 1720s and 1730s, as composers began dictating passagework in at least some arias and for selected singers. Among numbers for which Farinelli was particularly famous is Giacomelli's bird-song aria "Quell'usignolo," with its endlessly mechanistic, instrumental divisions, and numerous cadenzas. More nuanced and equally hubristic are the runs and cadenzas composed by Farinelli's brother Riccardo Broschi in "Son qual nave che agitata," where the singer imagines himself as a ship buffeted in the waves. Farinelli began it with his famed *messa di voce*, followed by stupefying *passaggi* and plunging registral shifts, which are even more pronounced in another aria Riccardo wrote for him, "Qual guerriero in campo armato" (Feldman 2007: 71–80).

In their various skills, castrati counted as first among equals in attaining ideals of singing that were broadly shared until about 1840. Rounding out Bontempi's list of Ferri's virtues, they included beautiful unobstructed vocal sound, pure vowels, excellent diction, perfect intonation, light and rapid passagework, legato singing ("on the breath"), smoothly joined registers, evenness of timbre, and improvisational skill (cf. Wistreich 2002; Foreman 2006). Nevertheless, scores, treatises, and anecdotes make clear that castrato singing, while it differed vastly from individual to individual (like all singing), was marked by abilities rarely shared by contemporaneous females or tenors.

One was exceptional breath control, as displayed in long cadenzas, trills (often combined with complex passagework), and *messe di voce*. The last were all about supporting, sustaining, and controlling the flow of air, and became an emblem of castrato singing (Malkiewicz 1991). John Evelyn wrote in the late seventeenth century about Siface: "I heard the famous Singer the Eunuch Cifacca, esteemed the best in Europe & indeede his holding out & delicatenesse in extending & loosing a note with that incomparable softnesse, & sweetenesse was admirable" (De Beer 1959: 864). Farinelli boasted about executing three consecutive *messe di voce* when he sang for Emperor Karl VI at the Viennese court in 1732 (letter of March 31, 1732, in Vitali 2000: 99). The aria he must be referring to, "Son qual nave" (facsimile reproduction in Schmitz 1955: 76–93), appears in Farinelli's presentation manuscript (A-Wn 19111), which includes six of his arias in all of which his own ornaments and cadenzas are rubricated in red (see again Figure 18.1).

Farinelli's story about singing it for Karl VI was confirmed years later, when music historian Charles Burney recalled the singer's 1734 London debut in the pastiche *Artaserse*:

> In the famous air *Son qual Nave*..., the first note he sung was taken with such delicacy, swelled by minute degrees to such an amazing volume, and afterwards diminished in the same manner to a mere point, that it was applauded for a full five minutes.... After this he set off with such brilliancy and rapidity of execution, that it was difficult for the violins of those days to keep pace with him. (Scholes 1959: 154)

Arguably castrati also possessed easier-than-usual access to a chest-dominant sound in the fifth or even octave above F4—hence the many reports of the powerful, piercing resonance ("ring" or "formant") that many produced in high registers, for which the large lungs many of them had would have put considerable subglottal pressure against the vocal cords, producing the same rich overtones of a modern-day tenor singing at the top of his range, but with considerably more ease and continuity with lower registers (cf. Potter, 2009: chapter 2). Quantz's observation that Senesino "sang Allegros with great fire, and marked rapid divisions, from the chest, in an articulate and pleasing manner," points to easy access to "chest" even in agility work, a claim borne out by Handel's arias for him ("Herrn Johann Joachim Quantzens Lebenslauf von ihm selbst entworfen," in Marpurg [1754] 1970: 197–250; repr. in Kahl 1948; Eng. trans. Nettl 1951: 280–319; on Handel's arias, see LaRue 1995: chap. 5).

Finally, castrati were also identified with the ability to make large, rapid registral shifts, whether by sudden wide leaps or by moving swiftly through *passaggi* of wide ambitus, presumably with a light tone (for an example from Rauzzini's very difficult *Solfeggi* [1808], see Potter 2009: 41). Such shifts were commonly exploited for virtuosic effect, and to bring out different timbral and expressive possibilities of head and chest (*voce di petto* and *voce di testa*, sometimes called "falsetto"). Musical evidence suggests that only a handful of non-castrated sopranos, much less tenors, shared that ability—Lucrezia Agujari (1743–1783), Regina Mingotti (1722–1808; Pollerus 2009), and Nancy Storace (1766–1817) were exceptions (indeed, Frey 2007 shows that Storace, Mozart's Susanna, was competing vocally with castrati in the late 1770s and 1780s)—whereas it was common among castrati (Feldman 2014: chap. 3). Salieri's *Prima la musica e poi le parole* (Vienna, 1786), a send-up of late eighteenth-century *opera seria*, had Storace parody castrato Luigi Marchesi (1755–1829) by incorporating excerpts with exaggerated registral shifts and arpeggiated coloratura (*bombe*) from his acclaimed performance in Sarti's *Giulio Sabino*, done in Vienna the previous year (Rice 1998: 378–381, 383–384).

What Gender Is This Voice?

Before and after the great wars, castrati were studied with intensity by only a few figures, all working in a relatively objectivist mode. The first major ground was broken by the German doctor Franz Haböck, whose five-hundred-page study drew primary sources together with basic medical understandings and interviews with the last living castrati in Rome to create what remains the central scholarly monograph on the subject (Haböck 1927). In the late 1980s and early 1990s, the British-Italian historian John Rosselli added much to the social and institutional dimensions of knowledge about castrati, in writings that are unparalleled for reliability and wide-ranging archival sleuthing (see especially Rosselli 1988a, 1988b, and 1992). Between these periods came the monograph by Futurist cineaste, photographer, and literato Anton Giulio Bragaglia (1959, with gems culled from obscure Italian literary manuscripts).

But all in all, before the 1980s castrati drew little attention from musicologists, intent on studying works, artifacts, biography, and philology and not performers, gender, or the body, much less the "performative" as a kind of intersubjective communication (exceptions include Freeman 1974; Benoit 1971; Weaver and Weaver 1977; and later the brilliant essays about friendship and iconography by Heartz [1984, 1990, and 1994]). For most scholars before the late 1980s, the fact of a high voice issuing from a man's body was aesthetically incongruous and psychologically inimical. Once castrati began to be studied more abundantly, they were often turned into the stuff of dreams, fantasies, and repressed desires. The trend was adumbrated by novelist Anne Rice's Freudian-tinged dip into castrato erotica *Cry to Heaven* (1982), which tracks a young eighteenth-century nobleman who has been castrated by his father and driven out of Venice, where he—rather than the father—had stood to inherit the family wealth, and who thus exemplifies the classic Freudian boy's fear of castration by his father (Keller and Morgan 2000: chap. 3). Unlike the sexual identity of castrati conjured up by some contemporaneous musicologists, the sex of Rice's protagonist is crystal clear, but his sexual desires are suggestively complex and mysterious.

But musicology by then was being mediated by other idols. The late 1980s unleashed a bumper crop of gender-bending, gender-blending studies inspired by the projects of two fountainheads of later twentieth-century cultural studies: Mikhail Bakhtin's history of the carnivalesque body and Michel Foucault's histories of sexuality, institutions, and epistemes. Though each was utterly unlike the other, the central texts of both figures were monumentally influential across the disciplines from the 1970s onward and equally forcible in heaving off an avalanche of imitations and variations, repackaged with the new (quasi-)Foucauldian watchwords of desire, power, discourse, control, and discipline and the (quasi-)Bakhtinian ones of cross-dressing, masquerade, impersonation, androgyny, inversion, reversal, passing, performativity, ventriloquism, embodiment, tricksterism, transgendering, and transvestism (see Stallybrass and White 1986; Epstein and Straub 1991; Garber 1992). Prima facie, all these added up to a motley congeries of studies, yet in the so-called new musicology they jostled together in celebration of boundary crossings and institutional critiques, new canons of knowledge and the body, and new ways of distinguishing the imaginary from the "real." Reductively speaking, somewhere between Foucault's dystopia and Bakhtin's utopia musicologists came upon a knowledge factory where the two met and connected over their one dark, shared obsession, namely the rule of institutions, especially over the human body.

When the improbable Foucault/Bakhtin comet hit planet Musicology, there was hardly a better place for it to land than on the castrati. Not only did their sex strike modern-day onlookers as indeterminate, but not infrequently they had played female parts (as females did male ones). While some downplayed the castrato's cross-dressing and sexual status as incidental (e.g., Keyser 1988; Moindrot 1993: 102 and passim), others, like Birthe Schwarz, argued that castrato cross-dressing, with its elements of disguise and confusion of sexes, had erotic fascination for viewers (Schwarz 1998). Castrati thus gave cause to celebrate the early modern opera house as a space of freedom from wider social repression.

Yet only a few castrato studies had sufficient evidence to give real footings to their claims. As Freitas (2003) has shown, most begged the question of what cultural meanings the castrato's sexual status actually held on or offstage, even recent studies indebted to the ideas of Roland Barthes (1915–1980). Barthes in our calculus should count as the third giant cultural critic who powerfully influenced writings on castrati and castrato performance, indeed pointedly so. (The poststructural philosopher Jacques Derrida affected musicology decisively, but not so greatly castrato studies.) Especially influential have been Barthes's essays "The Grain of the Voice" (1977: chap. 12) and *S/Z* (1974), an ambitious semiotic analysis of Balzac's novella *Sarrasine* (1830). In the torso of the novella, the young sculptor Sarrasine is obsessed with a young singer named La Zambinella whom he perceives to be a woman but who later drives him mad when he discovers that "she" is a castrated man. Temperament relates to gender here, along the lines of what Barthes called an "axis of castration," connecting the castrated man with a castrating androgyne—hence S slash Z. The castrato's Lacanian phallus—the socio-psychological instrument, not the physical one—is critical to this axis because his alleged androgyny makes him ambiguous to observers. Semantically, therefore, the castrato of *S/Z* is a void, given physical form in the ghostly, eerily manicured old castrato who forms the backstory of *Sarrasine* and the rich family he provisions.

"The Grain of the Voice" claims that that ambiguous void is fundamental to the very status of voice as a hollow signifier. For Barthes, castrati were erotic yet "without sex" or sexual "density," for their sexuality had left the overall body to "lodge" exclusively "in the throat," a phallus with no other station (Barthes 1974: 110; see also Kowaleski-Wallace 1992; Reynolds 1995 resonates with the Bakhtinian strain, but also the Lacanian/Barthesian, in saying that the castrato "pointed away from ordinary meanings of the voice . . . and directed the listening ear to the particularities of the voice itself" [37]).

It's fair to say that Barthes produced the modern psychoanalytic road map of the castrato. Under his sway and (less directly) that of Lacan, swarms of castrato savants have seen sex as absenting the castrato's body and settling in the voice (however "hollow"), by which means listeners are thought to have been (and still be) imbued with a kind of erotic ecstasy (*jouissance* in Lacanian jargon). The first major instantiation of this theory was produced by the Lacanian psychoanalyst Michel Poizat in *The Angel's Cry: Beyond the Pleasure Principle in Opera*, a 1992 translation from the more pointedly titled French original *L'opéra, ou le cri de l'ange: Essai sur le jouissance de l'amateur d'opéra* (Poizat 1986). Though the book concerns the effects on listeners of opera singers generally, the key to their effects lies with the castrato, that singing angel whose "virility" is "displaced into his voice" in a song that is beyond sex, beyond words, and beyond sense (all Lacanian terms: *hors-sexe, hors-parole, hors-sens*). The "alchemy of voice" purges it of sexual demarcation (Poizat [1986] 1992: 119). (Cf. Joke Dame 1994, who draws on *Sarrasine* to assert a Freudian sublimated homoerotics as explanation for certain historical descriptions of castrati as feminine in body but masculine in voice—piercing, sustained, powerful.)

Wayne Koestenbaum (1993) extended the Lacanian/Barthesian sense of voice to the diva, specifically to diva worship by gay men. His *The Queen's Throat: Opera,*

Homosexuality, and the Mystery of Desire is a delightful, maddening, and insightful autobiographical book that did much to launch the field of diva studies, understanding the castrato as the byway to appreciating diva desire. Specifically, the key to the castrato's lost vocal art is embedded nostalgically in the mid-nineteenth-century term "bel canto," codified about 1860 at the same time as "homosexual." For Koestenbaum the coincidence is no coincidence. Rather, it speaks to contemporaneous efforts to lure an Other, with Foucauldian inexorability, into "cure" and "recovery" (surely a dialectical one in this instance). Moreover, "opera culture," as it "fantasizes about a lost age," also relates—almost serendipitously, it seems—to psychoanalysis:

> Observe voice culture's affinity with psychoanalysis. Both systems believe in expressing hidden material, confessing secrets. And both discourses take castration seriously: voice culture wants to recapture the castrato's scandalous vocal plentitude, while psychoanalysis imagines castration as identity's foundation—star player in the psyche's interminable opera. (Koestenbaum 1993: 159)

If Koestenbaum's most important move for castrato performance studies lies in his spot-on analysis of cults of (female) diva worship, it nonetheless allows us to extrapolate on issues that castrati raise only implicitly. "We love" Callas, for example,

> because she incarnated vocal multiplicity and heterogeneity. She had three voices: chest tones like a contralto, an inconsistent, cloudy, yet beautiful middle register [a singer would say the voice was "covered" in the *passaggio* between registers], and a piercing top that was fleet in coloratura but often metallic. One colleague said that Callas had three hundred voices. Callas, a chameleon, stepped in and out of registers like quick costume changes. (Koestenbaum 1993: 145)

Not only was Callas a master of registral shifts, she was also adored for being brilliantly perfect yet not *always* brilliantly perfect but always being brave and compelling. She was fey and vulnerable when she wasn't imperious, or was both at once. For all her flaws, she was a true star and truly exceeded the best. Thanks to Koestenbaum, we begin to see that Callas was not unlike a superb castrato—a Caffarelli, or Siface, or even a (better-behaved) Farinelli.

Critically speaking, Koestenbaum takes us some distance back to the body that various strains of literary criticism had removed. Freitas has since done much to put back the historical body. His work on Atto Melani (1626–1714) and the larger contexts of his life shows that castrati were real sexual beings who often had sex lives and whose sex lives help us understand their sex appeal (among other things), both off- and onstage (Freitas 2009, especially chap. 4). In the seventeenth century, where most of Freitas's evidence lies, he discerns an Apollonian castrato, often found desirable by both men and women—not despite but because of his effeminate voice and looks, including plump soft neck, cheeks, and hands and a lack of an Adam's apple or beard (evident in Bartolomeo Nazari's famous portrait of Farinelli done when the singer was twenty-nine; see Figure 18.3). In this gloss, castrati were grown-up boys, nicknamed with diminutives such as Matteuccio, or later Senesino, Farinelli, Cusanino, and the like (recalling

FIGURE 18.3 For physiological and hormonal reasons, castrati also often had long limbs, which are evident in this depiction of Farinelli in a painting by Bartolomeo Nazari in the first year of Farinelli's London sojourn, 1734, when the singer was twenty-nine years old. Image courtesy of the Royal College of Music, London.

the feminine Cherubino, meaning "little cherub," in *Figaro*). Heartz (1990) might be read to support Freitas. About the inclusion of the little song "Son pastorello amante" in Giaquinto's majestic portrait of Farinelli, Heartz asks, "This regal figure wishes to be identified as an amorous little shepherd?" (1990: 48).

Much of Freitas's theory is grounded in Laqueur's influential study (1990) of cultural constructions of sex "from the Greeks to Freud," according to which early moderns still conceived sex in Galenic terms. The model is essentially "one-sexed" in presupposing a single continuous sexual form that graduates vertically from the imperfect female upward to the perfect male—indeed, the female is an outside-in male (or vice versa). Laqueur's analysis says that over many centuries of historical time, one great paradigmatic shift took place in cultural and scientific understandings of sex and gender, and that it happened around 1750, when sex was reconceived in the now familiar binary terms of male-versus-female—terms newly embedded in scientific language as an already-given in which "almost everything one wants to say about sex... already has in it a claim about gender" (Laqueur 1990: 10 and 151ff.). Importantly, the theory sees this shift as coinciding with the acme of Enlightenment thought, when Galenic views were weakening.

Not all historians of medicine and science have agreed with Laqueur's analysis, and some think the divide is cut too cleanly. Park and Nye (1991), for example, challenged Laqueur on grounds that no single early modern model of sex held sway, but rather two main threads, Aristotelian and Hippocratic/Galenic, and that, additionally, a two-sex model dates back to the Greeks (see response in Laqueur 2007: 85–89). But musicologists have been quite receptive, having already become intrigued by the possibility of a rupture between early modern and modern times following Foucault's posited epistemic break and Bakhtin's early modern body as an open, porous site in which such liquids as blood, semen, and milk are fungible. For Balme (1999), the emergent two-sex model explained the reaction against castrati in the later eighteenth century, while for Liebscher (2000: 47–51) the one-sex model showed that *travesti* practices, when castrati played women (especially in Rome where women were forbidden from the stage), were possible because castrati thrived in a time when there was no fixed notion of sexual status or identity. Freitas's work explains the castrato's stage appeal more specifically by positing him as a "frozen boy," halted in a primordial Galenic middle ground between a fully evolved male and a female, genitally speaking, and thus deprived of the "vital heat" that made evolution from one to the other possible.

Voice Machines

Over the last hundred years, the quest to locate the castrato's voice has coincided with various attempts to reproduce it. In 1902 and 1904 the Gramophone and Typewriter Company undertook to record the "last castrato," papal singer Alessandro Moreschi, a local celebrity who was sought out for his historical significance. Attempts to revive castrato vocal parts followed. The 1920 Göttingen staging of Handel's *Rodelinda*, put on by art historian Oskar Hagen, used tenors and basses for high male roles. Paul Henry Lang (1966: 169–173) likewise advocated transposing castrato parts downwards to avert the intolerable consequences of a male part being played by a female (cf. Feldman 2014: chap. 3; Lang's view is echoed by DeMarco 2002: especially 174–175). Nikolaus Harnoncourt settled on women's voices (cf. Rosand 1979; Burrows 1988), but by about 1980 that became unpalatable for many aficionados of the early music movement. The solution, ironically, was to make recourse to countertenors, whose mode of vocal production and output could hardly be further from those of castrati, which are better approximated by the power, substance, and ring of strong-voiced females.

Lately, reproductions of the castrato voice have taken a different turn, most famously in Gérard Corbiau's 1995 feature film *Farinelli*. Corbiau's film—at once majestic and inane—portrayed Farinelli and his brother (doubling as manager) in tawdry sex scenes collaborating to compensate for the castrato's lack: the virile brother slides atop the female conquests of the emasculated one at the moment before climax, thus reworking the Oedipal complex with a novel gloss on "castrato performance" as Farinelli gazes sadly at the moment of orgasm he misses out on. But if the film depicts his sexual ability in undersupply, his voice is oversupplied, thanks to a painstaking recreation by the Paris studios of IRCAM, which morphed the female coloratura Ewa Mallas Godlewska with the countertenor Derek Lee Ragin to create a single voice of presumably greater power, resonance, and range than either alone could muster. The result, though meticulously wrought, was neither fish nor fowl, which may account for the fact that it's not well lip-synched. It is a synthetically otherworldly voice, more likely to produce curiosity than rapture (see Bergeron 1996; Miller 1997; and Harris 1997).

A decade later, the BBC produced a one-hour docu-research program called "Handel and the Castrati" that featured electronic manipulations of various voices to simulate the powerful, presumably chesty sound of the lost castrato. Produced by Francesca Kemp with hosting by countertenor Nicolas Clapton, the program placed vocal manipulations in the hands of David Howard, Professor and Head of the Audio Laboratory in the Department of Electronics at the University of York. Howard's reconstruction stands front and center in the show, though its real hero might be seen as the young Darren Abrahams, a tenor who consents to screech in full-out chest voice throughout the neighborhood of C5 above middle C in a sacrificial performance truly worthy of a castrato (imagine that on the third phrase of Handel's "Ombra mai fu" with text "cara ed amabile"—"Singing in the pain," indeed, as Sean Coughlan titled his BBC essay on the show; Coughlan 2006). In the end, Howard combined the acoustic material of the tenor's high chest with the voice of hormonally "natural" male soprano Michael Maniaci and leavened the two with a child's voice. (Maniaci rose to fame playing a last-minute Armando in Meyerbeer's *Il crociato in Egitto* in a production at Venice's La Fenice, originally sung in Paris by nineteenth-century castrato Giambattista Velluti.) The result is another synthetically re-engineered cyber-voice, which once again highlights, however inadvertently, the irreducible difference between an electro-human amalgam and a single sentient, living organism. At the end of the BBC program, a continuo player repines that it's difficult to accompany a voice that isn't produced by a single person (Coughlan 2006; Scott 2007).

Exactly so. The problem points up a difficulty in all research on castrato performance that tries to reimagine even a single castrato, much less the castrati. For not just every voice, but every pair of lungs, every actor, and every mind and soul of every castrato was distinct from every other, just as surely as all horses' teeth and hens' toes. We confront this irreducible difference when we consider that until well into the nineteenth century, every score was written to outfit a particular singer (as Mozart outfitted scores for Cicognani, Manzuoli, and Rauzzini). And even once that was no longer necessarily the case, every score was still differently realized in every performance.

It's ironic, then, that recent work and debates on castrati have centered on a product of vocal engineering, rather than on historical variations in physical development as they might relate to variations in vocal character. Promising in current trends, by contrast, is research into the broad flows of meaning and material exchange that underpin the phenomenon of castrati as ways to peer into an imagined historical castrato. Bonnie Gordon, for example, has been exploring how castrati constituted one category among many of animate and inanimate phenomena that impinged on received categories of the organic and the material, human and machine, in an age preoccupied with virtuoso performances otherwise manifested in extravagant stage machines, elaborate garden topiary, and complex displays of fireworks. Through this optic, she asks how castrati enhanced possibilities of the virtuosic, or allowed urges toward it to be expressed and experienced at a time when passions for collecting curiosities, including wondrous machines, were running high (see Gordon 2011 and note her book-in-progress *Voice Machines: The Castrato, the Cat Piano, and Other Strange Sounds*). Similarly, for the period of decline, literary critic Gillen D'Arcy Wood effectively extends such questions forward to the 1770s and beyond, understanding castrati in the context of "virtuosophobia," the new dread of what today we might call "extreme singing" and the physical manipulations effected to enable it (Wood 2010).

Demise

As a breed, castrati were always outsiders, but they were relatively unmarked until the eighteenth century, since castrations were carried out not only—perhaps not even mainly—to produce singers, but to cure boys and men of humoral imbalances caused by gout, kidney stones, hernias, and other ills for which removal of the testicles was an age-old Galenic therapy (Gerbino 2004; Gentilcore 2006). At some point, probably in the earlier seventeenth century, as castrato voices came to be increasingly wanted, the numbers castrated for therapeutic reasons undoubtedly dropped relative to the numbers castrated for music (at least among prepubescent boys). Almost simultaneously, the elite medical and scientific establishments were growing ever more suspicious of Galenic medicine. This development merged with enlightened views of human integrity and of the inviolability of the child of innocence, which French philosophes, Italian illuminati, and other cosmopolitan intellectuals were promoting, following the lead of Rousseau (see the classic Ariès 1962: especially 411–415). The combination spelled eventual death for castrati onstage. By the mid-eighteenth century, many adamant critiques of castrating boys had emerged from the educated elite (Feldman 2009). No longer just the butt of conventional, good-natured satire, the castrato became a real subjective and social danger. The Marquis de Sade ([1967] 1995: 68) watched the castrato Giuseppe Millico—a Gluckian famed for his command of the pathetic style—in the leading male role in Gazzaniga's *Perseus ed Andromaca* (Florence, 1775) and was horror-struck by his "high, clear voice" coming from a "large, fatty, somewhat ill-formed body." In 1781 John Moore was even less sympathetic to "these wretched castratos" with their "artificial trills" (1797: II: 89–90).

Castrati were also morally problematic because they symbolized mechanical virtuosity, which was anathema to the naturalistic ideals of Romantics. In a recent essay on the final return to the London stage in 1824–1825 of Giambattista Velluti (1780–1861), the last major castrato to sing in a large public theater, James Q. Davies (2005) explains this development with an armory of documentary and contextual evidence, which shows how hostile Velluti's critical reception was when he went to London to perform in the revival of Meyerbeer's *Il crociato in Egitto*. As one critic wrote, Velluti "came upon" his ear "like the spectral moan of an unearthly being." He had become an unthinkable being in the face of new conceptions of what Davies calls "embodied vocality" and naturalness in expression—and this just as castration "descended into a psychological, culturally vexed or repressed sphere," with castration anxiety emerging as an originary theme in human development (Davies 2005: 273). Eventually, castrated men became intolerable on the stage, and the parts they had played were taken by female mezzos and contraltos in male dress (Ratliff 1997; Hadlock 2004; André 2006).

Rossini's reaction to Velluti's singing of his aria "Perché mai le luci aprimmo" in *Aureliano in Palmira* (1814) has become the symbolic death knell of the castrato. In Stendhal's account, Velluti, in full bloom during the performances, "made shameless abuse of his prodigious gifts" by adding to each rehearsal more and more extravagant ornamentation, until finally at the performance he obscured the aria beyond recognition. Thereafter the composer, we read, learned to dominate singers. Rossini resolved that in the future "every scrap of ornamentation, every vestige of a *fioritura*" would "constitute an integral part of the song itself, and the whole lot, without exception, will be noted down in the score" (Stendhal [1824] 1985: 340–342, quote 342). In the historical imaginary, the beauty of the castrato's singing, founded on the improvisation and nuance that Rossini was only later to call bel canto, faded from that moment on like a daylily in the dusk.

See also: Divas and Divos, Acting, Gender

Notes

1. My thanks to Will Crutchfield and Drew Minter for much help in thinking about matters of the castrato's voice, as well as to Winifred Faix Brown, Felicity Laurence, John Potter, and Richard Wistreich.
2. The Duke left London on May 22, 1733, and was in Venice in December and January 1733–1734, Vicenza in May 1734, and Florence that July. Thomas McGeary has kindly apprised me of unpublished letters by the Dowager Duchess of Leeds written from London in 1731–1734 that suggest the Duke was seeing Handel's opera company there before and after his stay in Oxford; one letter from the Duke's friend Lord Romney refers to a performance with Senesino of Handel's oratorio *Esther* in 1733, which the two had seen (McGeary 1998). Between 1731 and 1733, Senesino also sang in Handel's *Scipione* (revival, November 3, 1730), *Poro* (February 2, 1731), *Ezio* (January 15, 1732), *Sosarme, re di Media* (February 15, 1732), and *Orlando* (January 27, 1733) and in some revivals and revisions of Handel's oratorio *Esther* (premiere, Crown and Anchor Tavern in the Strand, February 23, 1732), including the expanded English-language version at the King's Theatre, May 2, 1732 (probably referred to in Romney's letter), and his oratorio *Deborah* (March 17, 1733). On Senesino, with emphasis on the *Radamisto* revisions of December 1720, see LaRue 1995: chap. 5.
3. "[...] des sons de voix de Rossignol ; ce sont des haleines à faire perdre terre, et à vous ôter presque la Respiration [...]."

Bibliography

Addison, Joseph. [1711] 1965. *The Spectator*. 5 vols. Oxford: Clarendon Press.

Algarotti, Francesco. 1767. *An Essay on the Opera*. London: L. David and C. Reymers.

Anderson, Emily, ed. and trans. 1985. *The Letters of Mozart and His Family*. 3rd ed. New York: W. W. Norton.

André, Naomi. 2006. *Voicing Gender: Castrati, Travesti, and the Second Woman in Early-Nineteenth-Century Italian Opera*. Bloomington: Indiana University Press.

Ariès, Philippe. 1962. *Centuries of Childhood: A Social History of Family Life*, translated by Robert Baldick. New York: Vintage Books.

Balme, Christopher B. 1999. "'Of Pipes and Parts': Die Kastraten im Diskurs der Darstellungstheorie des frühen 18. Jahrhunderts." In *Musiktheater als Herausforderung: Interdisziplinäre Facetten von Theater- und Musikwissenschaft*, edited by Hans-Peter Bayerdörfer, 127–138. Tübingen: Max Niemeyer.

Barnett, Dene, with the assistance of Jeannette Massy-Westropp. 1987. *The Art of Gesture: The Practices and Principles of 18th-Century Acting*. Heidelberg: Carl Winter Universitätsverlag.

Barthes, Roland. 1977. "The Grain of the Voice." In *Image—Music—Text*, translated by Stephen Heath, 179–189. New York: Hill & Wang.

——. 1974. *S/Z*, translated by Richard Miller. New York: Hill & Wang.

Beghelli, Marco, and Raffaele Talmelli. 2011. *Ermafrodite armoniche: il contralto nell'Ottocento*. Varese: Zecchini.

Belcastro, Maria Giovanna, et al. 2011. "*Hyperostosis frontalis interna* (HFI) and Castration: The Case of the Famous Singer Farinelli (1705–1782)." *Journal of Anatomy* 219/5: 632–637.

Benoit, Marcelle. 1971. *Versailles et les musiciens du roi, 1661–1733*. Paris: A. & J. Picard.

Bergeron, Katherine. 1996. "The Castrato as History." *Cambridge Opera Journal* 8/2: 167–184.

Berry, Helen. 2011. *The Castrato and His Wife*. New York: Oxford University Press.

Bontempi, Giovanni Angelini. [1695] 1971. *Historia musica*. [Perugia]. Reprint. Biblioteca Musica Bononiensis 2/48. Bologna: Forni.

Boris, Francesca. 1998. "Il Farinello: La villa perduta." *Il carrobbio: Tradizioni, problemi, immagini dell'Emilia Romagna* 24: 157–172.

——, and Giampietro Cammarota. 1990. "La collezione di Carlo Broschi detto Farinelli." *Accademia Clementina: atti e memorie* 27, nuova serie: 183–237.

Bragaglia, Anton Giulio. 1959. *Degli "evirati cantori": Contributo alla storia del teatro*. Florence: Sansoni Antiquiriato.

Brunelli, Bruno, ed. 1943–1954. *Pietro Metastasio: Tutte le opere*. 5 vols. Milan: Mondadori.

Burney, Charles. 1789. *A General History of Music*. 2nd ed. 4 vols. London: G. G. J. and J. Robinson.

Burney, Frances. [1778] 2002. *Evelina; or, The History of a Young Lady's Entrance into the World*, edited by Edward A. Bloom with an Introduction and Notes by Vivien Jones. New York: Oxford University Press.

Burrows, Donald. 1988. "Die Kastratenrollen in Händels Londoner Opern: Probleme und Lösungsvorschläge." In *Händel auf dem Theater*, edited by Hans Joachim Marx, 85–93. Laaber: Laaber.

Conestabili, Giancarlo. 1846. *Notizie biografiche di Baldassarre Ferri: Musico celebratissimo*. Perugia: Bartelli.

Coughlan, Sean. 2006. "Singing in the Pain." *BBC News Magazine.* Rev. March 29, 2006. Online. Available: http://news.bbc.co.uk/2/hi/uk_news/magazine/4853432.stm (accessed February 6, 2014).

Dame, Joke. 1994. "Unveiled Voices: Sexual Difference and the Castrato." In *Queering the Pitch*, edited by Philip Brett, Elizabeth Wood, and Gary C. Thomas, 139–154. New York: Routledge.

Davies, James Q. 2005. "'Velluti in speculum': The Twilight of the Castrato." *Cambridge Opera Journal* 17/3: 271–301.

De Beer, E. S. 1959. *The Diary of John Evelyn*. London: Oxford University Press.

DeMarco, Laura. 2002. "The Fact of the Castrato and the Myth of the Countertenor." *Musical Quarterly* 86/1: 174–185.

Diderot, Denis. 1994. "The Paradox of Acting." In *Selected Writings on Arts and Literature*, translated by Geoffrey Bremner. London: Penguin Books.

Dolan, Emily I., and John Tresch. 2011. "A Sublime Invasion: Meyerbeer, Balzac, and the Opera Machine." *Opera Quarterly* 27/1: 4–31.

Epstein, Julia, and Kristina Straub, eds. 1991. *Body Guards: The Cultural Politics of Gender Ambiguity*. New York: Routledge.

Farinelli (Carlo Broschi). 2007. *Arie per Carlo Broschi Farinelli*, edited by Luigi Verdi and Maria Pia Jacoboni, preface by Carlo Vitali. Roma: Bardi.

Feldman, Martha. 2014. *The Castrato: Reflections on Natures and Kinds*. Berkeley and Los Angeles: University of California Press.

——. 2009. "Strange Births and Surprising Kin: The Castrato's Tale." In *Italy's Eighteenth-Century: Gender and Culture in the Age of the Grand Tour*, edited by Paula Findlen, Wendy Ryworth, and Catherine Sama, 175–202, 400–414. Stanford, CA: Stanford University Press.

——. 2008. "Denaturing the Castrato." *Opera Quarterly* 24/3–4:178–199.

——. 2007. *Opera and Sovereignty: Transforming Myths in Eighteenth-Century Opera*. Chicago: University of Chicago Press.

——. 2003. "Music and the Order of the Passions." In *Representing the Passions: Bodies, Visions, Texts*, edited by Richard Meyer, 37–67. Los Angeles: Getty Trust Publications.

Fenlon, Ian. 1986. "Correspondence Relating to the Early Mantuan Performances." In *Claudio Monteverdi, 'Orfeo,'* edited by John Whenham, 167–172. Cambridge Opera Handbooks. Cambridge: Cambridge University Press.

Finucci, Valeria. 2003. *The Manly Masquerade: Masculinity, Paternity, and Castration in the Italian Renaissance*. Durham: Duke University Press.

Foreman, Edward. 2006. *The Art of Bel Canto in the Italian Baroque: A Study of the Original Sources*. Minneapolis: Pro Musica Press.

Freeman, Robert. 1974. "Farinello and His Repertory." In *Studies in Renaissance and Baroque Music in Honor of Arthur Mendel*, edited by Robert L. Marshall, 301–330. Kassel: Bärenreiter.

Freitas, Roger. 2009. *Portrait of a Castrato: Politics, Patronage, and Music in the Life of Atto Melani*. Cambridge: Cambridge University Press.

——. 2003. "The Eroticism of Emasculation: Confronting the Baroque Body of the Castrato." *Journal of Musicology* 20/2: 196–249.

Frey, Emily. 2007. "Negotiating Gender and Genre: Soprano Voices in Late Eighteenth-Century Opera." Paper read at conference on "The Castrato." Music Department, University of California at Berkeley, December 8, 2007.

Garber, Marjorie. 1992. *Vested Interests: Cross-Dressing and Cultural Anxiety*. London: Routledge.
Gentilcore, David. 2006. *Medical Charlatanism in Early Modern Italy*. New York: Oxford University Press.
Gerbino, Giuseppe. 2004. "The Quest for the Soprano Voice: Castrati in Renaissance Italy." *Studi musicali* 33: 303–357.
Gordon, Bonnie. 2011. "The Castrato Meets the Cyborg." *Opera Quarterly* 27/1: 94–122.
——. 2008. "Orfeo's Machines." *Opera Quarterly* 24/3–4: 200–222.
Haböck, Franz. 1927. *Die Kastraten und ihre Gesangskunst: Eine Gesangsphysiologische, kultur- und musikhistorische Studien*. Stuttgart: Deutsche Verlags-Anstalt.
Hadlock, Heather. 2004. "Women Playing Men in Italian Opera, 1810–1835." In *Women's Voices across Musical Worlds*, edited by Jane A. Bernstein, 285–307. Boston: Northeastern University Press.
Harris, Ellen T. 1997. "Twentieth-Century Farinelli." *Musical Quarterly* 81/2: 180–189.
Heartz, Daniel. 2004. "Caffarelli's Caprices." In *Music Observed: Studies in Memory of William C. Holmes*, edited by Colleen Reardon and Susan Parisi, 195–207. Warren, MI: Harmonie Park Press.
——. 1994. "Portrait of a Primo Uomo: Carlo Scalzi in Venice, ca. 1740." In *Musikalische Ikonographie*, edited by Harald Heckmann, Monika Holl, and Hans Joachim Marx, 133–146. Laaber: Laaber.
——. 1990. "Farinelli Revisited." *Early Music* 18/3: 430–433, 435, 437–441, 443.
——. 1984. "Farinelli and Metastasio: Rival Twins of Public Favour." *Early Music* 12/3: 358–366.
Historia musica. [Perugia, 1695] 1971. Reprint. Biblioteca Musica Bononiensis 2/48. Bologna: Forni.
Kahl, Willi. 1948. *Selbstbiographien deutscher Musiker des XVIII. Jahrhunderts*. Cologne: Staufen.
Keller, James R., and Gwendolyn A. Morgan. 2000. *Anne Rice and Sexual Politics*. London: McFarland.
Keyser, Dorothy. 1988. "Cross-Sexual Casting in Baroque Opera: Musical and Theatrical Conventions." *Opera Quarterly* 5/4: 46–57.
Koestenbaum, Wayne. 1993. *The Queen's Throat: Opera, Homosexuality, and the Mystery of Desire*. New York: Da Capo Press.
Kowaleski-Wallace, Beth. 1992. "Shunning the Bearded Kiss: Castrati and the Definition of Female Sexuality." *Prose Studies* 15/2: 153–170.
Lang, Paul Henry. 1966. *George Frideric Handel*. New York: W. W. Norton.
Laqueur, Thomas. 2007. "Response: Men with a Past." *Cambridge Opera Journal* 19/1: 85–89.
——. 1990. *Making Sex: Body and Gender from the Greeks to Freud*. Cambridge, MA: Harvard University Press.
LaRue, C. Steven. 1995. *Handel and His Singers: The Creation of the Royal Academy Operas, 1720–1728*. Oxford: Clarendon Press.
Lenneberg, Hans. 1958. "Johann Mattheson on Affect and Rhetoric in Music." *Journal of Music Theory* 2/1: 47–84 and 2/2: 193–236.
Liebscher, Julia. 2000. "Das Kastratentum im Diskurs von Thomas Laqueurs 'One-Sex-Model.'" In *Frauen- und Männerbilder in der Musik: Festschrift für Eva Rieger zum 60. Geburtstag*, edited by Freia Hoffmann, Jane Bowers, and Ruth Heckmann, 47–51. Oldenburg: Bibliotheks- und Informationssystem der Universität Oldenberg.

Malkiewicz, Michael. 1991. "Zur Verkörperung des Kastraten im Musiknotat: Die 'Stimme des Kastraten' in den Opern von Wolfgang Amadeus Mozart." In *Verkörperung*, edited by Erika Fischer-Lichte, Christian Horn, and Matthias Warstat, 309–323. Tübingen: Francke.

Marpurg, Friedrich Wilhelm. [1754] 1970. *Historisch-kritische Beyträge zur Aufnahme der Musik*. Vol. 1. Reprint. Hildesheim: G. Olms.

Marquis de Sade [Donatien Alphonse François]. [1772–1776?] 1995. *Voyage d'Italie*, edited by Maurice Lever. Paris: Fayard.

McGeary, Thomas. 2002. "Farinelli and the Duke of Leeds: 'Tanto mio amico e patrone particolare.'" *Early Music* 30/2: 202–213.

——. 2000a. "Repressing Female Desire on the London Opera Stage, 1724–1727." *Women & Music: A Journal of Gender and Culture* 4: 40–58.

——. 2000b. "Verse Epistles on Italian Opera Singers, 1724–1736." *RMA Research Chronicle* 33: 29–88.

——. 1998. "Handel, Prince Frederick, and the Opera of the Nobility Reconsidered." *Göttinger Händel-Beiträge* 7: 156–178.

——. 1994. "Gendering Opera: Italian Opera as the Feminine Other in Britain, 1700–42." *Journal of Musicological Research* 14: 17–34.

Miller, Felicia. 1997. "Farinelli's Electronic Hermaphrodite and the Contralto Tradition." In *The Work of Opera: Genre, Nationhood, and Sexual Difference*, edited by Richard Dellamora and Daniel Fischlin, 73–92. New York: Columbia University Press.

Moindrot, Isabelle. 1993. *L'opéra seria, ou le regne des castrats*. Paris: Fayard.

Moore, John. [1779] 1787. *A View of Society and Manners in Italy*. 4th ed. 2 vols. London: Printed for A. Strahan and T. Cadell.

Nettl, Paul. [1951] 1969. *Forgotten Musicians*. New York: Greenwood Press.

Park, Katharine, and Robert Nye. 1991. "Destiny Is Anatomy." Review of Thomas Laqueur, *Making Sex: Body and Gender from the Greeks to Freud* [Harvard University Press]. *New Republic* 204/7: 53–57.

Poizat, Michel. [1986] 1992. *The Angel's Cry: Beyond the Pleasure Principle in Opera*, translated by Arthur Denner. Ithaca, NY: Cornell University Press.

Pollerus, Christine 2009. "Singing Coloratura in the 1750s." Paper read at the National Early Musical Association International Conference on "Singing Music from 1500–1900: Style, Technique, Knowledge, Assertion, Experiment." University of York, July 7–10, 2009.

Potter, John. 2009. *Tenor: History of a Voice*. New Haven: Yale University Press.

Raguenet, François. 1702. *Paralèle des Italiens et des François, en ce Qui regarde La Musique et l'Opéra*. Paris: Moreau.

Ratliff, Joy. 1997. "Women in Pants: Male Roles for the Mezzo-Soprano or Contralto Voice." D.M.A. diss., University of Maryland at College Park.

Reynolds, Margaret. 1995. "Ruggiero's Deceptions, Cherubino's Distractions." In *En travesti: Women, Gender Subversion, Opera*, edited by Corinne E. Blackmer and Julianna Smith, 132–151. New York: Columbia University Press.

Rice, John A. 1998. *Antonio Salieri and Viennese Opera*. Chicago: University of Chicago Press.

Roach, Joseph R. 1993. *The Player's Passion: Studies in the Science of Acting*. Ann Arbor: University of Michigan Press.

Rosand, Ellen. 1979. "Francesco Cavalli in Modern Edition." *Current Musicology* 27: 77–78.

Rosselli, John. 1992. *Singers of Italian Opera: The History of a Profession*. Cambridge: Cambridge University Press.

———. 1988a. "L'apprendistato del cantante italiano: rapporti contrattuali fra allievi e insegnanti dal Cinquecento al Novecento." *Rivista italiana di musicologia* 23: 157–181.

———. 1988b. "The Castrati as a Professional Group and as a Social Phenomenon, 1550–1850." *Acta Musicologica* 60/2: 143–179.

Schmitz, Hans-Peter. 1955. *Die Kunst der Verzierung im 18. Jahrhundert: Instrumentale und vokale Musizierpraxis in Beispielen*. Kassel: Bärenreiter.

Scholes, Percy A., ed. 1959. Charles Burney, *An Eighteenth-Century Musical Tour in France and Italy*. London: Oxford University Press.

Schwarz, Birthe. 1998. "Das Spiel mit den Geschlechterrollen: Kastraten und Primadonnen im Musiktheater des 18. Jahrhunderts." In *Gender Studies und Musik: Geschlechterrollen und ihre Bedeutung für die Musikwissenschaft*, edited by Stefan Fragner, Jan Hemming, and Beate Kutschke, 75–84. Regensburg: Con Brio.

Scott, Robert Dawson. 2007. "The Man with the 300-Year-Old Voice: Michael Maniaci's Unique Soprano Voice Gives Him the Air of an Antique Castrato." *Times Online*. Available: http://www.thetimes.co.uk/tto/arts/music/classical/article1870312.ece (accessed February 6, 2014).

Stallybrass, Peter, and Allon White. 1986. *The Politics and Poetics of Transgression*. Ithaca, NY: Cornell University Press.

Steele, Richard. [1709–1710] 1899. *The Tatler*. London: Duckworth.

Stendhal [Marie-Henri Beyle]. [1824] 1985. *Life of Rossini*, translated by Richard N. Coe. London: Calder and Boyars.

Vitali, Carlo, with Francesca Boris, eds. 2000. Carlo Broschi detto il Farinelli, *La solitudine amica: lettere al conte Sicinio Pepoli*. Palermo: Sellerio.

Weaver, Robert Lamar, and Norma Wright Weaver. 1977. "Materiale per le biografie dei fratelli Melani." *Rivista italiana di musicologia* 12: 252–295.

Wistreich, Richard. 2002. "Reconstructing Pre-Romantic Singing Technique." In *Cambridge Companion to Singing*, edited by John Potter, 178–191, 258–261. Cambridge: Cambridge University Press.

Wood, Gillen D'Arcy. 2010. *Romanticism and Music Culture in Britain, 1770–1840: Virtue and Virtuosity*. Cambridge: Cambridge University Press.

CHAPTER 19

REHEARSAL PRACTICES

MARK EVERIST

In his novel *The Lyre of Orpheus*, Robertson Davies (1988) has one of the characters surrounding the first performance in modern times of E. T. A. Hoffmann's fictitious opera *The Magnanimous Cuckold* assemble a *Regiebuch*, a record of the rehearsals, production, and compositional changes made during the preparations. The strongly antiquarian interest is played out in a comic mode, attempting to juxtapose creative and documentary impulses in favor of the former. But documenting a production is a modern obsession, triggered at least in part by Max Reinhardt's development of the *Regiebuch* in the early years of the twentieth century, as evidenced by the publication of the *Regiebuch* (more along the lines of Davies than Reinhardt) for Harrison Birtwistle's 2008 *The Minotaur*, premiered at Covent Garden, which "chronicles the development of the production, with its diversions from, and clarifications of, the text as well as the composer's reaction to these" (Samuel 2008: 215; Samuel 1992; Styan 1982).

Such a modern preoccupation is something of an irony, given the difficulty of recovering details of rehearsals from the past, and this dilemma may well underpin the rare and scattered nature of writing on the subject, which sits ill with the plethora of studies of contemporary, observable, rehearsal practices and techniques. Much of what can be read is based on the survival of individual documents, such as the diaries of the Bayreuth choreographer and *régisseur* Richard Fricke, from 1875 to 1876, which tell us so much about Wagner's rehearsals (Deaville and Baker 1998; see also Porges [1876] 1983), or Carl Ludwig Junker's *Einige der vornehmsten Pflichten eines Kapellmeisters oder Musikdirektors* a century earlier (Junker 1782). And recent work on Ravel's *L'heure espagnole* has been based on the discovery of a single document, the marked-up score of the Opéra-Comique's *régisseur*, Ernest Carbonne (Kilpatrick 2009). Accounts of rehearsal that go beyond single documents are rare, but Miehling's (2000) explanation of rehearsal in Baroque opera and Ziegler's (2007) examination of Weber in Dresden are important broader studies that underpin the concerns of this chapter.

It is no surprise that Ziegler (2007) focuses on almost exactly the midpoint in the history of opera, beginning in 1817 when Weber moved to Dresden; at this juncture, widespread documentary survival of the sorts of ephemeral material that can be brought to bear on such questions as rehearsal begin to be preserved in sufficient numbers to make the historical examination of rehearsal possible (see, for example Rosselli et al. 1992). And nowhere is the survival of ephemera more pronounced than in nineteenth-century Paris. But even here, details of the rehearsal process from the protagonists themselves are rare for the simple reason that, on the spot, most of their communications tend to be verbal, with little written record. Circumstances such as those surrounding the preparations for Mozart's *Die Entführung aus dem Serail* in 1782, however well-known, are somewhat rare: if Mozart's father had been in Vienna rather than Salzburg, we would know nothing of Ludwig Fischer's low notes or Caterina Cavalieri's flexible throat (Baumann 1987: 12–26). The focus in this chapter on Paris in the first half of the nineteenth century, then, is a result of the survival of material both administrative and personal (such circumstances make the section on France in Rosselli et al. 1992, taken merely from Véron's memoirs and Berlioz's account of the failure of *Benvenuto Cellini* even more inexplicable; see Véron 1853–1856 and Cairns 1977).

Meyerbeer, *Robert le diable*, *Les Huguenots*, and the Académie Royale de Musique

The planning, organization, and execution of the rehearsal schedules at the Académie Royale de Musique (otherwise known as the Paris Opéra) in the 1830s had a curiously modern feel to them, as befitted the world's premier opera institution. Even half a century later, composers outside the capital of the nineteenth century would have envied the luxury of the number, extent, and duration of the rehearsals for their work. But luxury came at a cost. By the 1830s, there was a clear tradition of over-composition on the part of the composer, which meant that it would be expected that material would be cut both during rehearsal and even immediately after the premiere (more on this later). This resulted in significant complexity since any sort of cutting in such a work as Meyerbeer's *Robert le diable* or *Les Huguenots* entailed tidying up around the edges, which in turn required the recomposition of transitions and related passages—which could be done quite quickly—and then recopying, which took longer. So, for example, Meyerbeer, in his diary entry for December 23, 1835 noted both the cutting of the *morceau d'ensemble* in Act III of *Les Huguenots* and the rehearsal of the surrounding context the day after (Letellier 1999: 467). Two days later, he was with Aimé-Ambroise-Simon Leborne, the head of the copyists bureau, discussing the link between scenes 1 and 2 of the same work (Letellier 1999: 467). Furthermore, there was the very real expectation that the work would continue to be modified after its premiere on February 29, 1836. Perhaps the most striking example of this practice is Halévy's *La Juive*, in which three consecutive numbers were excised from the beginning of Act III after the premiere, reducing the dimensions of the role of Eudoxie by about half (Hallman 2002: 228–230). And for *Robert le diable*, Meyerbeer insisted on rehearsals on two consecutive days between the first and second performances; a series of undated notes in his diary indicates that rehearsals during December 1831—although small scale and precisely targeted—continued unabated throughout what was an intense period of performances: of the last eighteen performances in 1831 at the Académie Royale de Musique, fourteen were of *Robert le diable* (Letellier 1999: I: 421–422). As will be seen, one mitigating factor in the otherwise intense rehearsal schedule was that arrangements for each of the principal artistic domains—music, dance, and staging—were controlled separately, at least in the early stages of the work. Although nothing is known of the rehearsals for the ballet in *Les Huguenots*, the survival of dancer and choreographer Marie Taglioni's diary gives the same details for the rehearsals of the dance elements of *Robert le diable* as Meyerbeer's diary does for the music and the *mise en scène* (*F-Po*, Fonds Taglioni R 25).

The number of soloists' rehearsals for both *Robert le diable* and *Les Huguenots* is almost impossible to establish. It is, however, certain that they were among the first to start: in the case of *Robert le diable* they began on July 16, 1831, four months before the premiere, and in the case of *Les Huguenots*, eight months before the premiere (Letellier 1999: 416, 462). These took place either in Meyerbeer's hotel or in apartments hired specifically for the purpose; such arrangements must be viewed as atypical since composers domiciled in Paris (Halévy, Niedermeyer, or Auber, for example) would have had their own apartments and probably access to other rehearsal spaces. In Meyerbeer's case, rehearsals for *Robert le diable* were much ameliorated by his move from Auteuil (where he had been since June 9) to the Hotel Wagram (now the Hotel Meurice, 228 rue de Rivoli) on September 28, 1831 (Letellier 1999: 416, 418). By August 1835, two months after beginning production, Meyerbeer still rehearsed separately (for an hour's duration) with Cornélie Falcon and Adolphe Nourrit, and as late as January he continued rehearsals with Maria-Dolorès-Bénédicta-Joséphine Nau and Serda, mainly because the role of St. Bris had been enlarged late in the day to take account of the excision of the role of Catherine de' Médicis by the Censor (Letellier 1999: 463).

But even before the rehearsals for the soloists had begun, those for the chorus had started, and for multiple works at once. Thus, for *Robert le diable* they were under way by June 25, 1831 (six months before the premiere), even though there were no fewer than twelve choral rehearsals between June 2 and 27, 1835, for *Les Huguenots*, on average one every two days (Letellier 1999: 416, 462). Given that the chorus was involved in performances of the complete repertoire (*Robert le diable, Guillaume Tell, Gustave III, Don Juan*, and *La Juive*) during this period, this must have taxed the chorus' stamina—not to say patience—to the limit. The situation must have caused Meyerbeer concern as well, since in July 1835 he approached Halévy, the *chef du chant*, about using students from the Conservatoire for the chorus (Letellier 1999: 416). Whether his intent was to increase the size of the Opéra chorus or to offer them relief is not clear, but it is certainly the case that for *Les Huguenots* six new tenors and basses were recruited to the chorus in September 1835, surely an attempt to boost volume or quality or both (Letellier 1999: 464). Much less well-known than the *Foyer de la danse*, so often captured in images of all media, the

Opéra's *foyer du chœur* was adjacent and just behind the stage, and it was presumably here that such rehearsals took place.

Assembling an exact chronology of rehearsals is hampered by documents that are occasionally inexact. Thus it is not entirely certain if sectional rehearsals preceded full orchestral rehearsals or overlapped with them. Meyerbeer certainly held rehearsals for the woodwinds in *Les Huguenots* on October 28, 1835, and for the strings on November 3 and 18, but it is not clear if the rehearsal of Act III on September 14, for example, included the full orchestra (Letellier 1999: 464). Meyerbeer could, nevertheless, report that the tenth orchestral rehearsal had taken place on January 9, 1836 (Letellier 1999: 471). In the case of *Robert le diable*, it seems fairly clear that string rehearsals began on September 27 and the first orchestral rehearsal (of thirteen) took place on October 8, 1831 (Letellier 1999: 417–418). It has to be assumed that these rehearsals were directed by the conductor of the Opéra, François-Antoine Habeneck, since, for example, we know that on October 19, 1831, Meyerbeer met with Habeneck, specifically to go through the Act III finale. Still, on February 11, 1836, shortly before the premiere of *Les Huguenots*, Meyerbeer himself rehearsed the entire ensemble (singers and orchestra)—in the style of an Italian *maestro*—from a piano in the orchestra (Letellier 1999: 418, 473). There is no indication that any orchestral rehearsals—full or sectional—took place anywhere else than in the auditorium itself.

What distinguishes the Académie Royale de Musique from so many other opera houses of the period was its staging, so it is no surprise to find that rehearsals for the *mise en scène* were as important as those for the soloists, chorus, orchestra, or *corps de ballet*. Isolating rehearsals just for the *mise en scène* alone is unproblematic: these took place on October 17, 1831, for *Robert le diable* and on October 6, 1835, for *Les Huguenots* (Letellier 1999: 418, 464). Further detail for *Robert* is not forthcoming, but all the rehearsals for *Les Huguenots* that took place in November 1835 (with the exception of a single string sectional rehearsal on November 18; see Table 19.1) were both in the auditorium and with the *mise en scène*.

Lighting was left until the dress rehearsals, and given the technological limitations of this part of the operation, it is hardly surprising, although the arrangements for *Les Huguenots* left both Meyerbeer and librettist Eugène Scribe unsatisfied until just before the premiere (Letellier 1999: 473). Also left until late were the rehearsals for the onstage band, and various other technical details: the shooting machine in Act V of *Les Huguenots* occupied a good deal of energy, and inexplicably the horses and litter for Marguerite de Valois's Act III entry seem to have been left until the last minute (Letellier 1999: 473). In addition to one-on-one meetings with Habeneck and Halévy, Meyerbeer also rehearsed alone with the principal cellist Norblin at a point at which the plan was to accompany Raoul's Act I aria "Plus blanche que la blanche ermine" with a solo cello rather than—as it turned out—Chrétien Urhan's viola d'amore (Letellier 1999: 464).

Given that the Académie Royale de Musique was committed to around fifteen performances a month (Monday, Wednesday, and Friday, with the occasional Sunday in the 1830s), and that the same artists who were involved in rehearsals for *Les Huguenots* in 1835 were those who were performing *Robert le diable*, *La Juive*, *Don Juan*, and other standard repertory of the period, rehearsals could only take place on days when there were no public performances. Add in additional rehearsals for revivals, and the schedule could begin to look congested, as the account for November 1835 in Table 19.1 shows.[1] A single complaint by Meyerbeer in his diary entry of November 26, 1835, to the effect that nine rehearsals had been missed because of the revival of Rossini's *Le siège de Corinthe*, permits a reconstruction of the entire month's activity. Rehearsals began on November 5 for the scheduled premiere on November 27, which did not, in fact, take place until December 4. Moreover, the empty space on the schedule for Saturday,

Table 19.1 Performance and Rehearsal Schedule at the Paris Opéra, November 1835

Day	*Date*	*Public Performance*	*Other*
Sunday	Nov. 1		
Monday	Nov. 2	*Robert le diable*	
Tuesday	Nov. 3		*Les Huguenots*, 1st string rehearsal
Wednesday	Nov. 4	*La Juive*	
Thursday	Nov. 5		*Le siège de Corinthe*, rehearsal 1
Friday	Nov. 6	*Robert le diable*	
Saturday	Nov. 7		*Les Huguenots*, rehearsal
Sunday	Nov. 8		*Le siège de Corinthe*, rehearsal 2
Monday	Nov. 9	*Moïse; L'Ile des pirates*	
Tuesday	Nov. 10		*Le siège de Corinthe*, rehearsal 3
Wednesday	Nov. 11	*La tentation; Le comte Ory; La somnambule*	
Thursday	Nov. 12		*Les Huguenots*, first rehearsal of Act I; ditto Act II
Friday	Nov. 13	*Don Juan*	
Saturday	Nov. 14		*Le siège de Corinthe*, rehearsal 4
Sunday	Nov. 15	*La Juive*	
Monday	Nov. 16	*Le philtre; La révolte au sérail*	
Tuesday	Nov. 17		*Les Huguenots*, rehearsal at 12.00
Wednesday	Nov. 18	*Gustave III*	
Thursday	Nov. 19		*Le siège de Corinthe*, rehearsal 5
Friday	Nov. 20	*Robert le diable*	
Saturday	Nov. 21		*Le siège de Corinthe*, rehearsal 6
Sunday	Nov. 22		*Le siège de Corinthe*, rehearsal 7
Monday	Nov. 23	*Le comte Ory; L'Ile des pirates*	*Les Huguenots*, choral rehearsal, Acts IV and V
Tuesday	Nov. 24		*Le siège de Corinthe*, rehearsal 8
Wednesday	Nov. 25	*Guillaume Tell; Gustave III*	
Thursday	Nov. 26		*Le siège de Corinthe*, rehearsal 9
Friday	Nov. 27	Projected premiere of revival of *Le siège de Corinthe*	
Saturday	Nov. 28		
Sunday	Nov. 29	*Robert le diable*	
Monday	Nov. 30	*La muette de Portici*	

November 28 (also empty in Meyerbeer's diary) suggests that the day was used for a further rehearsal of the work.

Performances during November reflect the normal pattern for the mid-1830s: nine evenings given over exclusively to a single *grand opéra*, and five to a combination of opera and ballet; two of these feature separate acts of operas (*morcellé*), and three feature the new genre of *petit opéra* through its two principal representatives, Rossini's *Le comte Ory* and Auber's *Le philtre* (for a full account of the relationship between ballet, *petit opéra*, and the process of *morcellement*, see Everist 2010: 195–231). The five rehearsals for *Les Huguenots* as opposed to the nine or more for *Le siège de Corinthe* would be replicated, but in *Les Huguenots*' favor in early February as its premiere drew near.

Premieres at the Paris Opéra throughout the nineteenth century were in general well resourced, often to the point of luxury. When such luxury was very occasionally denied, it was a moment of public outrage and institutional scandal. Much the same could be said for such revivals as those of *Le siège de Corinthe* in 1835, discussed in the previous paragraphs. Such productions—premieres and revivals—profited from an institution that functioned like a well-oiled machine, and that permitted the complex rehearsal pattern already outlined. Central to this machine was the mechanism for copying, preserving, and gaining access to performance material. The current collections of performance material, housed in the library at the Palais Garnier, give only a shadowy view of their past use, now that they are merely archival documents and are no longer used for performance (see *Archives* 1988: 32). But the names of successive generations of artists crossed out on the copies of, say, Eudoxie's *rôle* in *La Juive*, are eloquent testimony to the quality of the performance material at the Opéra, used over and over again from 1835 into the twentieth century (*F-Po* Mat. 19. 315: [6–8]). And however valuable the material is to the current understanding of *grand opéra* (and its value is immense), its centrality to the continuing presence of such works as *La Juive*, *Robert le diable*, *Guillaume Tell*, and so on, in the repertory of Europe's most important opera house is beyond question.

Grand Opéra outside Paris

The surviving performance material could not be said to be central for performances and rehearsal outside Paris, even outside the Opéra—although the licensing system made it impossible for any of the works performed there to appear on any other Parisian stage. Provincial stages were dependent on the material—musical, textual, and scenic—published in Paris, and performance material and rehearsals were thus based on printed material or copies thereof. Coupled with the greater instability of provincial opera houses, such dependence threw much of the responsibility for assembling performance materials onto the performers themselves.

Most artists were excluded from the luxurious arrangements that reigned at the Paris Opéra. Most striking were those who tried to gain access either to the Opéra or to any of the state-supported opera houses and theaters in the capital (such as the Opéra-Comique, the Théâtre Italien, and so on). The serried ranks of Conservatoire-trained singers ready to audition and then to début at one of Paris's opera houses, as well as the singers arriving in the capital from the provinces to try their luck, all needed material for rehearsal and performance (White 2012). Similarly, any sort of concert performance, in Paris or elsewhere, even by stars of the Opéra, would require a different sort of performance material. As much as in the provinces, in such cases artists had to rely on material that they could buy in the shops owned by the major publishers of the day: Troupenas, Schlesinger, Escudier, Pacini, and so on.

Publishers were central to the delivery of opera outside such organizations as the Paris Opéra, and by the mid-1830s could control almost all the material for a given work. Thus for *La Juive*, the publisher Maurice Schlesinger had negotiated a position with Halévy, Scribe, and the management of the Opéra for the exclusive publication of the full score (Halévy *La Juive* FS), the piano-vocal score (Halévy *La Juive* PV), the orchestral parts, and score arranged for piano alone without voices but with obbligato flute or violin; he also published extracts (*morceaux détachés*) from the opera, which were available either with piano accompaniment, guitar accompaniment, or with full orchestra; such extracts would often appear in multiple transpositions and could involve complete numbers, parts of numbers, or—in some cases—both (a complete set of the *morceaux détachés* is preserved as part of the *dépôt légal* in the Bibliothèque nationale de France *F-Pn:* Vm².766). So far, this was fairly routine, if ambitious, but Schlesinger expanded his activities from the mid-1830s onward to include the publication of the libretto (Scribe *La Juive*), and also—although this does not relate to questions of rehearsal—the publication and sale of a large slice of the myriad arrangements, variation-sets, fantasias, *Souvenirs, Mosaïques*, and so on, based on one or more themes from the opera; in 1835 alone, he published sixteen works for piano solo, four for two violins, six for flute(s), three for guitar, two for *cornet à pistons*, and one each for cello and clarinet (the advertisement for *Morceaux et arrangements pour divers instruments sur les motifs de la Juive* appeared on the first page of every *morceau détaché* underneath the thematic catalogue).

Costs of published material were carefully controlled. Full scores and parts that were likely to be purchased by institutions rather than individuals were, for *La Juive*, priced at 300 and 350 francs, respectively, whereas the piano-vocal score was sold for 40 francs. Hardly any instrumental work cost more than 10 francs, and *morceaux détachés* with piano (rather than orchestral) accompaniment ranged from 2 francs for a very short number to 12 francs for the *grand trio* from Act II. Such cost-structures were developed to maximize profit from sales, but only indirectly for the convenience of those who might use them. Among this latter group were those who used published extracts in the theater for professional purposes. Central to the publishers' campaigns of distribution were the collections of *morceaux détachés*; unlike other types of material (with the possible exception of keyboard arrangements), the fates of these documents were subject to the pressures and pleasures of the collector, who could range from those whose professional leanings lay elsewhere to those for whom such a collection of *morceaux détachés* was essential to their livelihood. Of interest in this latter context is Pierre-Luc Ciceri, leading set designer in Paris 1824–1847, who owned albums that were unlikely to have been of firsthand importance to his career, but are of interest in reconstructing what his musical horizons might have been. One volume is a collection exclusively of *romances*, whereas the other contains the first three years of Blangini's *La lyre des dames* (also collections of romances) to which Ciceri presumably subscribed in the early 1820s (*F-Pn* 4° Y.326). Another volume, however, also includes *airs, duos*, and *trios* from French and Italian opera, the latest of which is Charles-Simon Catel's *Wallace* of 1817 (*F-Pn* 4° Y.327). Similarly, an album that might well have belonged to Jean-François Gail, son of Sophie Gail, author of *Réflexions sur le goût musical en France* and of texts for Berlioz and the *morceaux de concours* for the *Prix de Rome*, contains not only a large number of *romances* but also *morceaux détachés* from *opéras comiques* by Auber, Boieldieu, and Catel. Important here is that more than one number appears from each opera, suggesting that the work as a whole had an importance for the owner that transcended that of a single aria. There are two numbers from Auber's *Le maçon* and three each from Auber's *La fiancée* and Boieldieu's *Les deux nuits* (*F-Pn* 4° Y.319), suggesting that the original operatic context of these arias was as important as the content of the arias themselves.

Approaching the business of operatic rehearsal yet again, an anonymous collection of *morceaux détachés* and *romances* puts the latter into an appendix at the end of the volume, clearly differentiated from the opera excerpts collected toward the beginning, which include multiple numbers from the pastiche based on Mozart's *Die Zauberflöte*, *Les mystères d'Isis*, Winter's *Tamerlan*, and Boieldieu's *La fête du village voisin* as well as single numbers by Catel, Méhul, Grétry, Niccolo, and Berton. Much of the music (the Mozart pastiche and the Winter) was originally written for the singer Marie-Thérèse Davoux-Maillard, and it may well be that this collection could have been associated with a soprano of the next generation (*F-Pn* 4° Y.332).

More clearly and perhaps purposefully organized is a collection belonging to Mr. Chomel (*F-Pn* 4° Y.301), possibly a younger relation of the Conservatoire-trained soprano, Amélie-Adèle Chomel/Chaumel, known in Italy as *La Comelli*, who married Rubini in 1819, and who sang at the Opéra-Comique from 1816 to 1818 (see Fétis 1860–1865: VII: 344). This is a collection of *morceaux détachés*, all from operas by Boieldieu, and all preserved in chronological order: *Le nouveau seigneur de village* (1813), *La fête du village voisin* (1816), *Le petit chaperon rouge* (1818), and *Les voitures versées* (1820). To look at the first of these, it might be thought that this was an attempt to collect together all the music for the role of Frontin, sung originally by Nicolas-Jean Blaise Martin, the legendary *basse-taille* from the Opéra-Comique: the three numbers that survive are the Act I duo for Blaise and Frontin (the celebrated "duo de la bouteille"), the *air* for Frontin "Paix, paix, taisez-vous," and the duo for Frontin and Babet (the latter role created by Louise-Thérèse-Antoinette Regnault). But the last number in the opera, the ensemble number that also features two solos by Frontin, is missing. Thus, while the volume includes 90 percent or more of the music written for Martin in the role of Frontin, it could not have served as a comprehensive rehearsal tool for any of Martin's successors. Furthermore, the selections from the other Boieldieu operas in the volume are significantly more heterogeneous: of the five extracts from *La fête du village voisin*, all are for different characters, and the only logic behind the selection of the extracts from *Le petit chaperon rouge* initially seems to be an attempt to capture all the music in the opera except for the choruses (numbers 1 and 6, and the trio, number 8); this, however, fails to account for the omission of the *rêve, cavatine et duo* (number 9), and the *airs* (numbers 11, 13, and 14).

Significantly more complex but no less ambiguous is the surviving compilation of vocal music belonging to Anne-Cécile Saint-Aubin, known better as Cécile Duret during her career at the Opéra-Comique from 1805 to 1820. She and her sister, Alexandrine, were the daughters of Jeanne-Charlotte Saint-Aubin, a star of the Comédie Italienne (then the Opéra-Comique) from 1786 to 1808, who had previously sung in the provinces and briefly in 1786 at the Académie Royale de Musique (Forbes 1992 and also Fétis 1860–1865: III: 90). Given the date and range of the contents, and the fact that the volume is attributed to "Mlle Saint-Aubin," it seems reasonable to conclude that the compilation was assembled during Cécile Saint-Aubin's teenage years (she was born in 1785) but before she married and began her career at the Opéra-Comique in 1805 at the age of twenty (*F-Pn* L. 2146). The volume must have been assembled between 1804 and 1814 since the binder, Terzuolo, described himself as "Papetier de l'Empereur"; most of Terzuolo's work appears to date from before the Revolution, which supports a dating earlier in that period. Moreover, the latest work in the compilation, Gaveaux's *Le diable en vacances*, dates from 1805.

Saint-Aubin's volume consists of six types of material, largely collected discretely, as follows: printed freestanding *romances*, printed *romances* from published collections and periodicals, printed opera excerpts, manuscript opera excerpts, manuscript *romances*, and a manuscript collection of keyboard items.

The two opera collections are relevant here. The manuscript collection consists of excerpts from the following operas:

- *Le diable en vacances* (Gaveaux; 1805 Opéra-Comique [OC])
- *Oedipe à Colone* (Sacchini; 1787 Académie Royale de Musique [ARM]) x 2
- *Phèdre* (Lemoyne; 1786 ARM) x 2
- *Renaud* (Sacchini; 1783 ARM)
- *Le calife de Bagdad* (Boieldieu; 1800 OC)
- *Richard cœur de lion* (Grétry; 1784 OC) x 2
- *Stratonice* (Méhul; 1792 [OC, later reworked for ARM]).

This is an eclectic collection of material, perhaps reflecting to a degree the artistic priorities of Saint-Aubin's mother, including classics of the *opéra comique* repertory as well as works she may well have studied during or shortly after her brief sojourn at the Académie Royale de Musique.

The printed collection, which itself includes three embedded manuscript items, is more coherent:

- *Le calife de Bagdad* (Boieldieu; 1800 OC)
- *Une folie* (Méhul; 1802 OC) x 2

- *La belle Arsène* (Monsigny; 1773 OC)
- *Alexis, ou L'erreur d'un père* (Dalayrac; 1798 OC) MS
- *Le prisonnier, ou La ressemblance* (Della-Maria; 1798 OC) MS
- *Palma, ou Le voyage en Grèce* (Plantade; 1798 OC) MS
- *Le prisonnier, ou La ressemblance* (Della-Maria; 1798 OC)
- *Toberne, ou Le pêcheur suédois* (Bruni; 1795 OC)
- *L'épicure* (Cherubini; 1800 OC)
- *Bion* (Méhul; 1801 OC).

All the inclusions here are from *opéra comique*, and with a single exception fall into the period 1795–1802. The exception, the excerpt from Monsigny's *La belle Arsène*, dated originally from 1773 but survives in Saint-Aubin's book in an arrangement published by Thomassin in 1784; its position in this otherwise closely controlled group remains anomalous. The presence of both printed and manuscript material in this section argues that media was not the criterion for distinguishing it from the exclusively manuscript section, and that Cécile assembled her compilation either from printed copies or hand-written copies of prints as they became available.

The repertory is exactly what Saint-Aubin's mother would have known well, and indeed, were it not for the unequivocal attribution of the volume to *Mlle* Saint-Aubin, it would be tempting to associate it with her mother (who, born Jeanne-Charlotte Schroeder, would never have been called Mlle Saint-Aubin). Saint-Aubin's compilation then, seems to have been a study volume assembled by a promising student with a successful career at the Opéra-Comique ahead of her. It is tempting to see the two collections, if they are not separated by media, as representative of her two spells at the Conservatoire: the first from *15 germinal an xi* (April 5, 1803) to 1805 with significant input from her mother, and the second, after a false start in public in 1805, from that year to 1808.

Two contrasting modes of rehearsal—on the one hand, the institutionally supported premiere at the opera house and, on the other, the ad hoc assimilation of printed extracts and manuscript copy—throw into relief a document akin to the latter that attempts to imitate the former. Assembling a *rôle*—a document that contains all the music for a given artist in a single work—was relatively straightforward for *opéra comique*, where the kinetic parts of the work were in spoken dialogue, did not involve music at all, and could be learned and rehearsed from the printed libretto or—where it was included—in the piano-vocal score. The first part of M. Chomel's compilation already discussed comes very close to a *rôle* for Frontin in Boieldieu's *Le nouveau seigneur de village*, for example. Through-composed *grand opéra*, however, posed a different sort of problem. Not only was all the kinetic material in the opera in accompanied recitative, but—certainly by the 1830s—the boundaries between recitative and composed number were so blurred that extracting material for *morceaux détachés* became more and more subject to variation, and more ambitious ensembles meant that that a *rôle* would not just include the solo and ensemble numbers in which an artist was formally involved, but also an ensemble or recitative in which they might have a part that ran only a few measures. Any artist trying to assemble all the material they would need would have the choice of either spending money on an unwieldy piano-vocal score or of constructing their own *rôle*.

Grand Opéra: Rehearsing *ad hoc*

A hitherto unknown document presents an attempt to construct a *rôle* out of preexisting printed *morceaux détachés* by supplementing them with manuscript copies of those parts of the piano-vocal score that were relevant, and systematically preserves the complete *rôles* of Eudoxie in Halévy's *La Juive* (1835), of Isabelle de Bavière from the same composer's *Charles VI* (1843), and of Paola from Flotow's *L'âme en peine* (1846; the document is currently in the possession of the author; hereafter *GB-SO*). The first two of these roles had been taken by Julie-Aimée Vansteenkiste (known as Julie Dorus until her marriage in 1833, and thereafter as Julie Dorus-Gras), and the third by Maria Nau (for both artists, see Kutsch and Riemens 2003: II: 1215–1216 and V: 3299–3300). Although the role of Paola is that of a *prima donna*, it is in what was known as a *petit opéra*, one designed to support *ballet-pantomime*; the roles in *La Juive* and *Charles VI*—both *grands opéras* central to the repertory of the Académie Royale de Musique during the July Monarchy—were secondary to those of Rachel and Odette (the female leads in the two respective operas). The document thus falls into three sections (orthography and capitalization follows original source): (1) La Juive/Musique d'Halevy/Paroles d'E. Scribe/Role d'Eudoxie—fols. 1r–22v; (2) Charles VI/Musique d'halévy, paroles de M[s] Delavigne/Rôle d'Isabelle de Bavière—fols. 23r–46v; (3) L'Ame en Peine/Musique de Flotow, paroles de St Georges/Role de Paola—fols. 47r–76v. Each comprises the printed *morceaux détachés* required to make up the main parts of the *rôle* and manuscript copies of the rest made from Schlesinger's piano-vocal score.

The *rôle* for Isabelle de Bavière in *Charles VI*, for example, contains nothing for the first two numbers in the work; her first music consists of those interpolations in the *chœur de chasse* "La fanfare" that she sings and are copied on fol. 23v; they correspond to pages 40–42 of the piano-vocal score (Halévy *Charles VI* PV), and pages 104–107 of the full score (Halévy *Charles VI* FS). This is followed by the printed *morceau détaché* that includes the *duo* "Respect à ce Roi" for Odette (sung by Rosine Stolz at the premiere) and Isabelle de Bavière (*GB-SO*, fols. 24–30v) and this corresponds to pages 45–55 of the piano-vocal score and pages 118–147 of the full score. Figure 19.1 gives the opening in the *morceau détaché*.

But in the complete work, the duo is prefaced by a twelve-bar recitative for Isabelle and Raymond, which is omitted in the *morceau détaché*, since it is not required for concert or domestic use, but is critical for the rehearsal of the work for the theater (Figure 19.2); accordingly, these twelve bars are written out in skeleton in *GB-SO* (fol. 23v) (Figure 19.3, lowest three staves).

In *GB-SO* may be observed the cues—that are underscored—to separate them out from the material that Isabelle sings. As may be also seen from Figure 19.3, the stage indications

FIGURE 19.1 Halévy, *Charles VI*, duo for Isabelle de Bavière and Odette, "Respect à ce Roi," *morceau détaché* in *GB-SO*, fol. 24v. Collection of Mark Everist.

FIGURE 19.2 *Charles VI*, Opéra en 5 actes, *Paroles de Mrs Germain et Casimir Delavigne.* Musique de F. Halévy. Partition avec Acc^t^ de Piano, *arrangée par Ch. Schwenke. Prix 40^f^ net / a Paris, chez* M^CE^ Schlesinger, *Rue Richelieu, 97*, 45.

FIGURE 19.3 Halévy, *Charles VI*, duo for Isabelle de Bavière and Odette, "Respect à ce Roi," manuscript vocal line of recitative in *GB-SO*, fol. 23v. Collection of Mark Everist.

and other orientation are carefully included on the bottom two staves ("à Raymond," "à Odette," etc.). At the bottom right of the page is the cue to proceed to the printed version of the duo "de suite le Duo gravé," and the careful indications—"C'est votre fille" marked "à Raymond," "Approchez-vous" marked "à Odette" and "Sortez" marked "à Raymond"—give some clue as to which version of the printed score these manuscript notes might have been copied. The piano-vocal score gives merely the last of these (Figure 19.2), while the full score the last two. Only the libretto gives all three indications that appear in *GB-SO*; it must therefore be assumed that the compiler of *GB-SO* had access not only either to the piano-vocal or full score but also to the printed libretto (Delavigne *Charles VI*). In short, the copy in *GB-SO* pulls from the printed score, the libretto, and the *morceaux détachés* everything that is needed for the *rôle* of Isabelle de Bavière in this number.

As in the case of the *chœur de chasse*, Isabelle's brief contribution to the *entr'acte et air* "Gloire au maître" is copied out by hand (*GB-SO* fol. 38r; piano-vocal score, 78). The *morceau détaché* of the following *Villanelle et air* "Quant le soleil" omits all the music for the chorus that accompanies this number. While for most of the time this makes no difference to the *rôle* of Isabelle (since she sings at the same time), there is a moment between the andante "L'amant loin de son doux" and the allegro moderato "Au concert succède le bal," which in *GB-SO* are noted in pencil on the printed extract ("13 mesures de plus, pour le chœur"; fol. 35r) as is the cue for the ballet at the end of the number (fol. 37r). The music for Isabelle's contribution to the following recitative and to the Act II finale are added in manuscript on folio 38r. Isabelle takes no part in Act III of *Charles VI* until the finale, and here her music is written out in *GB-SO* folios 44r–44v; the same is the case for her contributions in Act IV to the scène "Au roi je demands raison" (*GB-SO* fol. 44v) and the Act IV finale (*GB-SO* fols. 45r–46r). Although Isabelle appears in the fifth act of the opera, the lines that she has in the libretto were never set; she has no music to sing and nothing appears in *GB-SO*.

The extent to which the *rôles* in *GB-SO* resemble those generated officially by the Académie Royale de Musique may be gauged by a comparison of some of the material from *L'âme en peine*. Pacini-Bonoldi's *morceau détaché* edition of the duet for Paolo and Léopold from Act I of the opera excludes a lengthy passage for the two soloists, just before Paolo's *romance* "Prends cet anneau" and replaces it with a modulatory passage that moves from E flat major to G major (Figure 19.4).

To produce something that would permit the use of the document for rehearsal of the work in the theater, the original passage had to be reinstated from the piano vocal score, and the eight measures that replaced them in the *morceau détaché* suppressed (deleted in pencil in the *morceau détaché* in *GB-SO* and visible in Figure 19.4); the passage from the piano-vocal score is given as Figure 19.5, showing the original ending and the beginning of its continuation "Heureuse et calme," and may be compared to the manuscript copy in *GB-SO* (Figure 19.6, staves 7–9), and in turn to the relevant pages in Maria Nau's original MS *rôle* for the Opéra (Figure 19.7). What the comparisons show is the near-equivalence of the reading in the piano-vocal score with that of Maria Nau's *rôle*, the suppression of a significant part of the duet in the Pacini-Bonoldi *morceau détaché*, and its reinstatement from the piano-vocal score in the composite *rôle GB-SO*.

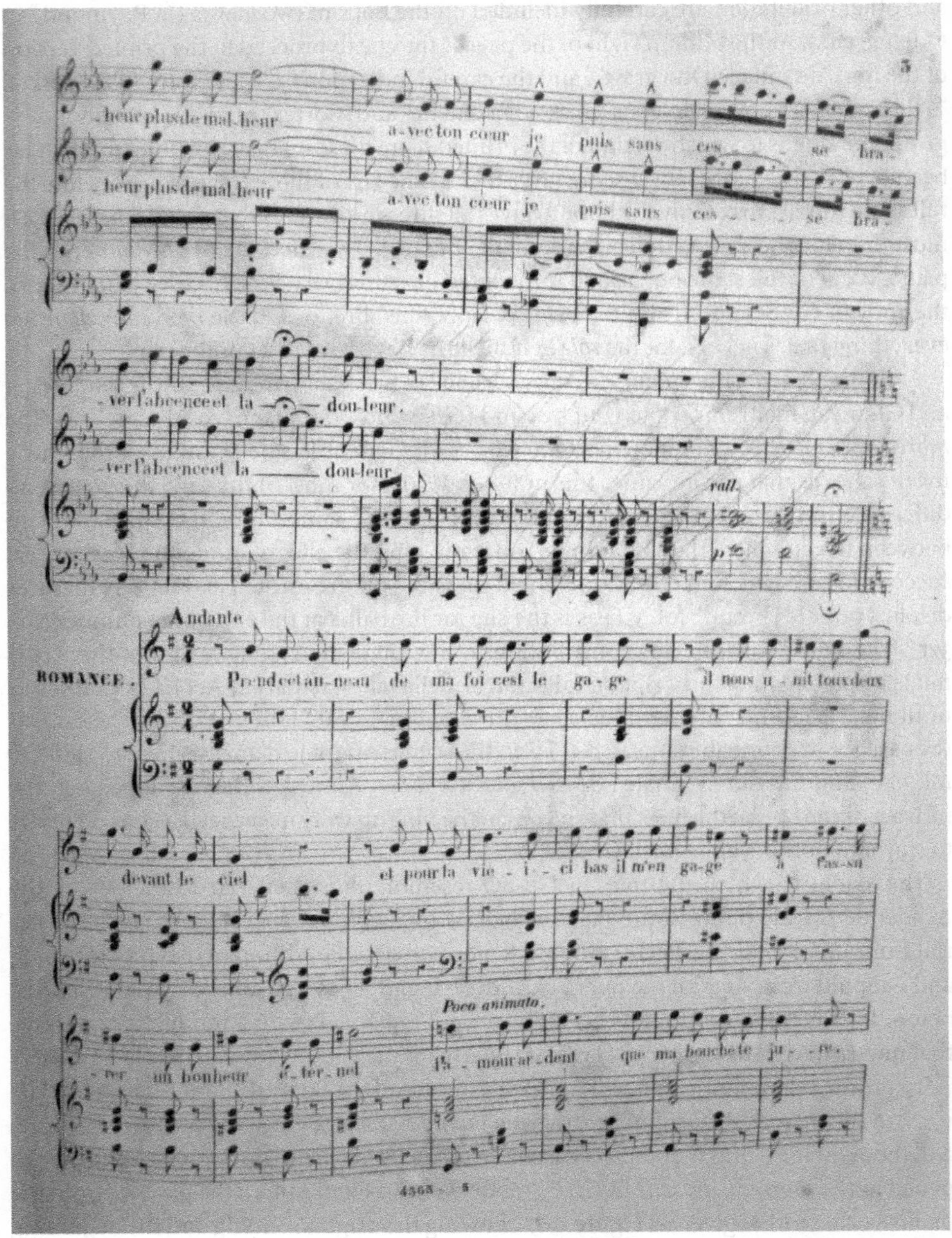

FIGURE 19.4 Flotow, *L'âme en peine*, duo for Léopold and Paola, "Ô doux transport," *morceau détaché* in *GB-SO*, fol. 55r. Collection of Mark Everist.

FIGURE 19.5 L'AME en PEINE / Opéra / En Deux Actes / Paroles de M^{r} de St Georges / Musique / DE / F. DE FLOTOW. / Prix net 12^{f} / PARIS, chez F. BONOLDI, 13 Rue Taitbout, 29.

FIGURE 19.6 Flotow, *L'âme en peine*, duo for Léopold and Paola, "Ô doux transport," MS addition in *GB-SO*, fol. 47v. Collection of Mark Everist.

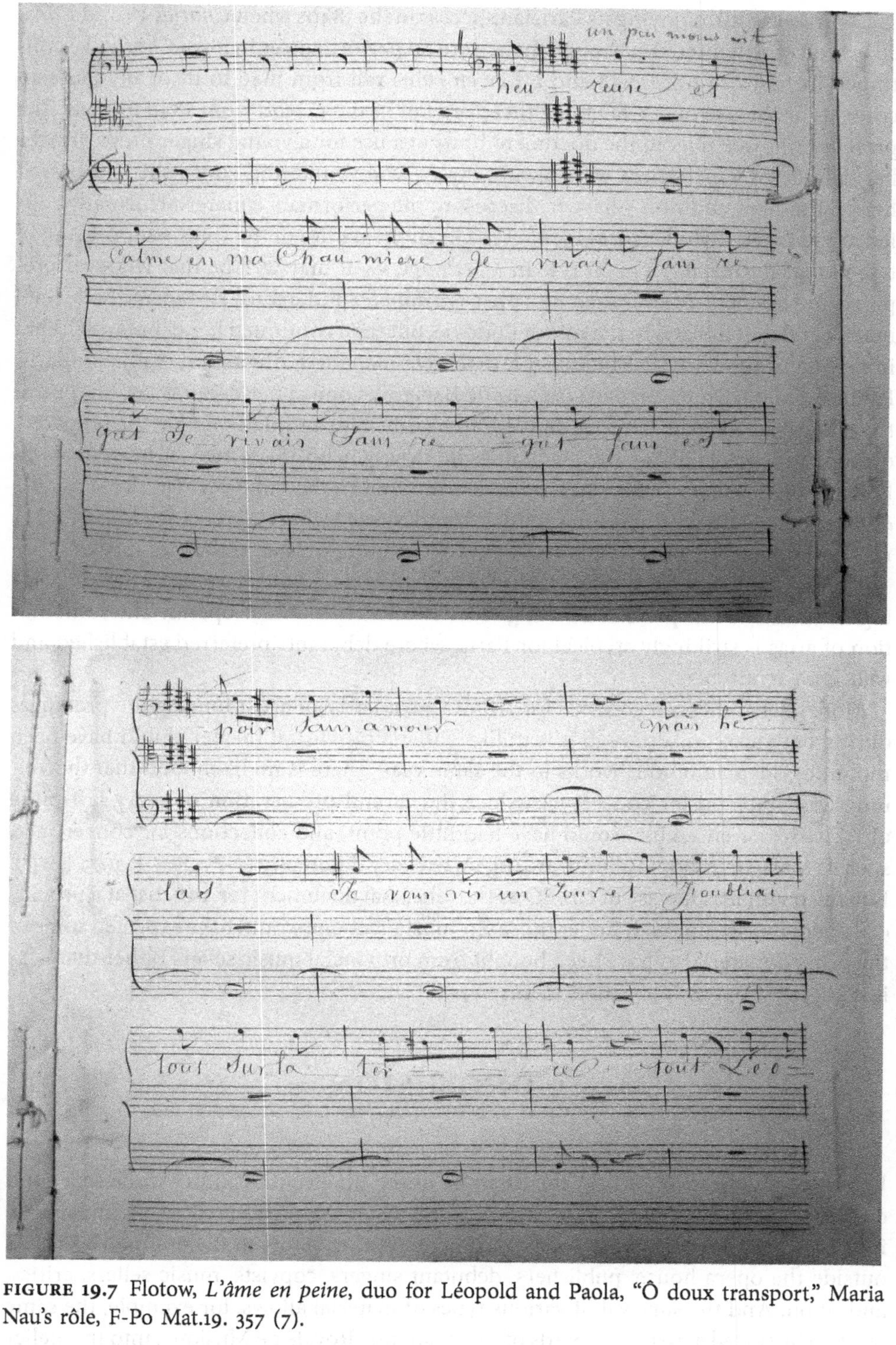

FIGURE 19.7 Flotow, *L'âme en peine*, duo for Léopold and Paola, "Ô doux transport," Maria Nau's rôle, F-Po Mat.19. 357 (7).

La Juive was still enjoying its Parisian success in the 1840s when *Charles VI* and *L'âme en peine* were premiered, although there were no performances in 1850. *Charles VI* continued its first run until 1848 and *L'âme en peine* ran from 1846 to 1850; any Parisian context for the use of *GB-SO* must therefore fall in the period from 1846 to 1848. The presence of three *rôles* in the document hints at a use for a young singer preparing for her débuts (of which there were always three) who would not—until she had passed her preliminary audition—have had access to the performance material formally copied at the Opéra (Muller 1974–1976: 173). Given the nature of the roles—supporting in two *grands opéras* and a main role in a *petit opéra*—it may well be that whoever prepared and used *GB-SO* was seeking a post as a *double* (understudy). Mademoiselle Rabi made her debut in Paris in the role of Eudoxie, but then continued her débuts as Urbain in *Les Huguenots* and Alice in *Robert le diable* (*Le ménestrel*, August 30, 1846). Similarly, Pauline-Eulalie Dameron used Isabelle de Bavière as one of her début roles, but one of the others was Alice in *Robert le diable*. Other plausible candidates for having prepared, owned, and used *GB-SO* are Mademoiselle Roissy, who made two of her débuts as Eudoxie on February 7, 1847, and as Isabelle on June 20 the same year (*Revue et gazette des théâtres*, Feburary 7 and June 20, 1847), and Marie Hébert-Massy (née Massy, 1813–1875), who sang for some time at the Opéra-Comique and later in the provinces.

Making a debut with these three roles at the Opéra would have been out of keeping with the normal practice of using older extracts from older operas. The combination of arias is strikingly atypical for Paris, where debutants preferred established and well-known numbers.

More likely rehearsal contexts for *GB-SO* are a Parisian artist touring the provinces during her vacation, although it is unlikely that a provincial theater would have been mounting such ambitious works in the same year. There is no likelihood that the volume was prepared for concert use, since the careful preservation of every last piece of recitative or ensemble would have had little point, and collections for concert use, such as Mariette Alboni's album, are organized very differently (*F-Pn* Rés. F. 1074 [1–3]). Equally possible is the use of *GB-SO* as the rehearsal document for an artist at a provincial opera house, although under those circumstances one would have expected some of the printed material to have been bought from provincial music sellers rather than—as is the case—from the publishers themselves.

Conclusion

Rehearsal practices in Paris in the first half of the nineteenth century disclose a good deal about the ways in which the various elements in a new production might play one into another. They also reveal the engagement of other actors in the drama who reside outside the opera house: publishers, debutant singers, copyists, music sellers, critics, and so on. And the survival of various types of material allows, for example, the same work to be traced across the boards of the Académie Royale de Musique, into the atelier of the music publisher, and into the salon of the artist in a way that permits individual surviving documents to be clearly associated with otherwise very public events: to be able to examine the document that Cornélie Falcon used to rehearse the role of Rachel, or that Julie Dorus-Gras used for the part of Eudoxie—and then to be able to do this for any work of that type—is a real rarity. Similarly, the near-obsessive record of his life kept by Giacomo Meyerbeer makes possible a synthesis of a large amount of disparate material, as the accounts of *Robert le diable* and *Les Huguenots* show.

Comparisons with modern rehearsal practices are easily made. True, the sudden illness of a Siegfried at Covent Garden in the 1990s could be covered with some ease, even if the understudy also fell sick and a third Siegfried had to fly from Stuttgart just in time for the performance, and in 1835 such a sequence of events would probably have resulted in cancellation. And cancellation at short notice was a much more common feature of the early nineteenth century than today. But if Robertson Davies's character were to go back 160 years, armed with pencil and notebook, the *Regiebuch* might not seem quite so different from the fictional one he wrote for *The Magnanimous Cuckold*.

See also: Production Aesthetics and Materials, Acting

Notes

1. Table 19.1 is constructed from a close reading of Meyerbeer's diaries (both the entries themselves and their implication) calibrated against the *Journal de l'Opéra*. Chronopera 2012 purports to duplicate this material, but fails, for example, to include any information for November 27, 1835 (the date is completely absent), which as Table 19.1 shows, was the aborted premiere of the revival of *Le siège de Corinthe*, replaced by a three-act version of Rossini's *Guillaume Tell*, Act V of Auber's *Gustave III*, and the ballet *Flore et Zéphire*. See *Le journal des débats*, November 28, 1835.

Bibliography

Archives. 1988. *Archives de l'Opéra de Paris: Inventaire Sommaire*. Paris: Bibliothèque Nationale.

Bauman, Thomas. 1987. *W. A. Mozart: 'Die Entführung aus dem Serail.'* Cambridge Opera Handbooks. Cambridge: Cambridge University Press.

Cairns, David, ed. and trans. 1977. *The Memoirs of Hector Berlioz, Member of the French Institute, Including His Travels to Italy, Germany, Russia and England*. London: Victor Gollanz.

Chronopera. 2012. Online. Available: http://chronopera.free.fr (accessed February 6, 2014).

Davies, Robertson. 1998. *The Lyre of Orpheus*. Toronto: Macmillan.

Deaville James A., and Evan Baker, eds. 1998. *Wagner in Rehearsal, 1875–1876: The Diaries of Richard Fricke*. Stuyvesant, NY: Pendragon.

Devriès, Anik, and Lesure, François. 1978–1988. *Dictionnaire des éditeurs de musique français*. 2 vols. Archives de l'édition musicale française 4. Geneva: Minkoff.

Everist, Mark. 2010. *"Grand opéra—petit opéra: Parisian Opera and Ballet from the Restoration to the Second Empire." 19th-Century Music* 33/3: 195–231.

Fétis, François-Joseph. 1860–1865a. "Duret, Anne-Cécile." *Biographie universelle des musiciens et bibliographie générale de la musique*. 8 vols. 2nd ed. [with supplement in 2 vols]. III: 90. Paris: Firmin Didot.

——. 1860–1865b. "Rubini, Jean-Baptiste." *Biographie universelle des musiciens* VII: 344.

Forbes, Elizabeth. 1992. "Saint-Aubin, Jeanne Charlotte." *The New Grove Dictionary of Opera*. Online. Available: http://www.oxfordmusiconline.com/subscriber/article/grove/music/O904517 (accessed February 6, 2014).

Hallman, Diana. 2002. *Opera, Liberalism and Antisemitism in Nineteenth-Century France: The Politics of Halévy's 'La Juive.'* Cambridge Studies in Opera. Cambridge: Cambridge University Press.

Junker, Carl Ludwig. 1782. *Einige der vornehmsten Pflichten eines Kapellmeisters oder Musikdirektors*. Winterthur: Steiner.

Kilpatrick, Emily. 2009. "The Carbonne Copy: Tracing the Première of *L'heure espagnole*." *Revue de musicologie* 95/1: 97–135.

Kutsch, Karl-Josef, and Leo Riemens. 2003. *Großes Sängerlexeikon*. 4 vols. Bern and Stuttgart: Francke [1987–1994]; 4th ed. 7 vols. Munich: Saur.

Letellier, Robert, trans. 1999. *The Diaries of Giacomo Meyerbeer: vol. 1, 1791–1839*. Madison, WI, and Teaneck, NJ: Fairleigh Dickinson University Press; London: Associated University Press.

Miehling, Klaus. 2000. "Direktion und Dirigieren in der Barockoper." *Basler Jahrbuch für historische Musikpraxis* 24: 25–47.

Muller, Jean-Pierre. 1974–1976. "L'usage des 'trois débuts' dans l'art lyrique au 19e siècle." *Revue belge de Musicologie* 28: 172–186.

Porges, Heinrich. [1876] 1983. *Wagner Rehearsing the 'Ring': An Eyewitness Account of the Stage Rehearsal of the First Bayreuth Festival*, translated by Robert L. Jacobs. Cambridge: Cambridge University Press.

Rosselli, John, et al. 1992. "Rehearsal." *The New Grove Dictionary of Opera*. Online. Available: http://www.oxfordmusiconline.com/subscriber/article/grove/music/O904517 (accessed January 21, 2014).

Samuel, Rhian. 2008. "Birtwistle's *The Minotaur*: The Opera and a Diary of its First Production." *Cambridge Opera Journal* 20/2: 215–236.

——. 1992. "Birtwistle's *Gawain*: An Essay and a Diary." *Cambridge Opera Journal* 4/2: 193–178.

Styan, John Louis. 1982. *Max Reinhardt*. Directors in Perspective. Cambridge: Cambridge University Press.

Véron, Louis. 1853–1856. *Mémoires d'un bourgeois de Paris*. 6 vols. Paris: Gouet.

White, Kimberly. 2012. "The Cantatrice and the Profession of Singing at the Paris Opéra and Opéra Comique, 1830–1848." PhD diss., McGill University.

Ziegler, Frank. 2007. "Webers Probenarbeit an der Dresdner Oper." In *Tagungsbericht Dresden 2006 sowie weitere Aufsätze und Quellenstudien: Bericht über das Symposion 'Carl Maria von Weber—der Dresdner Kapellmeister und der Orchesterstil seiner Zeit' in der Hochschule für Musik 'Carl Maria von Weber' in Dresden am 13. und 14. Oktober 2006 sowie freie Aufsätze und Quellenstudien*, edited by Manuel Gervink, Frank Heidelberger, and Franz Ziegler. Weber-Studien 8, 91–115. Mainz: Schott.

PRIMARY SOURCES 1: MANUSCRIPT

F-Po Mat.19. 315 (6-8).
F-Po RE 234 and 235.
F-Po, Fonds Taglioni R 25
Journal de l'Opéra (*F-Po* MS without shelfmark)

PRIMARY SOURCES 2: PRINTED

Delavigne *Charles VI*. CHARLES VI, OPÉRA EN CINQ ACTES, / Paroles de MM. CASIMIR DELAVIGNE / et GERMAIN DELAVIGNE,/MUSIQUE DE/F. HALÉVY, / Membre de l'Institut, REPRÉSENTÉ POUR LA PREMIÈRE FOIS / *Sur le Théâtre de l'Académie Royale de Musique*, Le 15 mars 1843 / Prix: 1 franc / PARIS, / MAURICE SCHLESINGER, ÉDITEUR DE MUSIQUE, / 97 RUE RICHELIEU. / JONAS, LIBRAIRE DE L'OPÉRA. / 1843.
F-Pn 4° Y.301.
F-Pn 4° Y.319.
F-Pn 4° Y.326.
F-Pn 4° Y.327.
F-Pn 4° Y.332
Halévy *Charles VI* PV. CHARLES VI / Opéra en 5 actes, / *Paroles de Mrs Germain et Casimir Delavigne* / Musique de / F. HALÉVY. / Partition avec Acc[t] de Piano / *arrangée par / Ch. Schwenke / Prix 40f net / A PARIS, chez* M[CE] SCHLESINGER, *Rue Richelieu, 97.*
Halévy *La juive* FS. LA JUIVE / Opéra en cinq actes / paroles / *de Mr E. Scribe* / Musique de / F. HALEVY. / *à son illustre Maitre et Ami* / L. CHERUBINI / Membre de l'Institut / Directeur du Conservatoire royal de Musique de Paris & C / Parties d'Orch. 350[f] / Partition 300[r] / Représenté pour la première fois à Paris, sur le théâtre de l'académie Royale de Musique / le 23 Février 1835 / *PARIS, chez* MAURICE SCHLESINGER *Rue Richelieu.*
Halévy *La juive* PV. LA JUIVE / Opera en 5 Actes/Paroles de M. E. Scribe / *Musique de* F. Halevy / Partition de Piano arrangée par F. Hiller / PRIX 40 F[CS] NET. / *Paris Chez Maurice Schlesinger, 97 rue Richelieu.*
L'AME en PEINE / Opéra / En Deux Actes / Paroles de M[r] de St Georges / Musique / DE / F. DE FLOTOW. / Prix net 12f / PARIS, chez F. BONOLDI, 13 Rue Taitbout.
Le journal des débats, 28 November 1835.
Le ménestrel, 30 August 1846.
Revue et gazette des théâtres, 7 February and 20 June 1847.
SCRIBE *La juive*. LA JUIVE / OPÉRA EN CINQ ACTES / PAROLES DE M. E. SCRIBE, MUSIQUE DE M. F. HALEVY, / *Divertissemens de M. Taglioni*; / REPRÉSENTÉ POUR LA PREMIÈRE FOIS / *Sur le Théâtre de l'Académie Royale de Musique* / LE 23 FÉVRIER 1835 /—/ Prix: 1 franc. / PARIS, / MAURICE SCHLESINGER, ÉDITEUR, / J.-N. BARBA, LIBRAIRE, AU PALAIS-ROYAL, / Derrière le Théâtre-Français /—/ 1835. / IMP. D'ÉVERTAT, RUE DU CADRAN, 16 <*F-Pn* Th[B] 1932 A>.

CHAPTER 20

ACTING

SIMON WILLIAMS

Opera and the Absence of Acting

Theater, as Peter Brook has memorably defined it, exists simply when there is a space for one person to walk across and another person to observe this (Brook 1998: 9). Most theatrical performances are more complex than this, but the actor's presence is theater's most elemental component and the main conduit through which the audience's attention is drawn to the stage and fastened there for the duration of the performance. Acting is foundational for all theater. In representational theater, which accounts for the majority of operatic performance seen today, acting entails the embodiment of a character that has an identity different from the actor's own. In the words of Clive Barker, it incorporates the "transformation of one human being into another ... conditioned by circumstances of time, space, and character which are not those of the person undergoing the transformation" (Barker 1989: 110). Acting also involves the conveyance of the emotions of the fictional character to audience members, who respond either by finding those emotions recreated in themselves or by feeling other emotions that may or may not be sympathetic toward the character. The successful actor must possess highly developed mimetic, or imitative, abilities, the power to imagine and externalize the inner life of the character, complete control of physical and vocal skills, and a presence that excites or otherwise moves an audience.

Singing and acting are not practices that have always coexisted happily. Most theorists of operatic performance will agree that highly developed powers of characterization are essential to the successful realization of a role. Emilio de' Cavalieri, one of the earliest composers of opera, insisted that the singer "should express the words well, so that they may be understood, and accompany them with gestures and movements, not only of the hands but other gestures that are an efficacious aid in moving the affections" (Cavalieri [1600] 1967: n.p.; MacClintock 1979: 183). Giovanni Battista Mancini, a leading singing teacher of the eighteenth century, claimed that "in order to be a perfect actor merely singing is not enough, but the knowledge of reciting and acting well is required too"

(Mancini 1774: 165; Barnett 1987: 17); Wagner insisted that his singers' acting talents be as versatile as their singing, and Verdi urged singers to pay close attention to characterization. Today, many teachers consider that operatic performance can only be effective when the acting capacities of the performer are as fully developed as the singing (Balk 1985: 9). Nevertheless, acting and singing are often felt to be in conflict, as if one can only be practiced at the expense of the other, and when that happens, acting may have to go to the wall. "I do not know if a perfect Singer can at the same time be a perfect actor," wrote the eighteenth-century singer and teacher Pietro Francesco Tosi. "[...] It being, however, much more difficult to sing well than to act well, the Merit of the first is beyond the second" (Tosi [1723] 1968: 152). Two hundred years later, Konstantin Stanislavski complained that an indifference, even hostility, to acting well had become a fixed attitude in the operatic profession. Most singers, he argued, ignore acting entirely: "not only do they not study it, they treat it with disdain, taking pride in the fact that they are *singers* and not just actors" (Stanislavski 1961: 330). While Stanislavski's dictum cannot be taken as applying to all opera singers, many of whom successfully combine acting and singing, it is not at all unusual to feel the absence of such fusion on the operatic stage today. Even the most accomplished singing-actors sense a fundamental incompatibility between acting and singing. "It is almost impossible to sing and really act at the same time," Natalie Dessay has gone on record as saying. "For me, acting is receiving and singing is giving, and that is why [acting in opera] is so difficult" (Mead 2009: 54).

The specific demands that opera makes on the actor are still relatively unexplored. Extended theoretical and historical discussions of operatic acting as distinct from acting in spoken theater are hard to come by. Evidence of singers' acting abilities is available anecdotally from histories and biographies and from comments scattered through memoirs and reviews. Recent research includes only one volume that explores the technical relationship between music and gesture in nineteenth-century opera (Smart 2004), another that concentrates systematically on the theatrical aspects of singers' careers and on their capacity as actors (Rutherford 2006, see especially chapter 7), and an engaging survey of the corporeal aspects of operatic composition and performance, but which only touches on issues of acting tangentially (Hutcheon and Hutcheon 2000). Among contemporary singers, it is Renée Fleming's autobiography, *The Inner Voice*, that provides the most insights into the nature of acting in opera (Fleming 2004). Meanwhile, *The New Grove Dictionary of Opera*, which is a font of information on opera as a theatrical practice, devotes a dozen pages to stage lighting, twenty-eight to stage design, twenty-seven to production, and fifteen to singing, but does not even include an entry on acting.

Despite the uneasy relationship between acting and singing, for at least the last one hundred years, discussions of operatic performance have been continuously informed by a sense that each generation considers that acting values have become increasingly important in contrast to the previous generation. With the advent of *verismo* in the late nineteenth century, a vivid and often sensational realism came to be practiced by some singers. In the 1940s, a growing attention to realistic performance on the operatic stage was attributed to the influence of the movies (Mitchell 1970: 53); and twenty years later, an important teacher and practitioner claimed that in opera "the importance of acting has been overlooked by too many" but now the situation appears to be improving (Volbach 1967: 48). Today, we also pay tribute to the increased attention to acting and the theatrical dimensions of opera, so much so that Peter Gelb, General Manager of the Metropolitan Opera, can claim that "the raising of theatrical standards will be 'the salvation of opera'" (Isherwood 2007).

There are many reasons for an increased attention to acting in opera over the last one hundred years. This is the period in which the operatic repertoire has been stubbornly narrowed down to a few dozen works, and as the same pieces come to be repeated time and time again, for the sheer sake of variety we wish to see them performed in different interpretations. Stage directors have also become a major presence in operatic production, and they often require singers to be effective actors. More recently, opera has become easily available on DVD and on HD screen transmissions, so that singers are expected physically to complement their roles and to display histrionic powers that are equal to their vocal abilities; and quite simply, opera is much more interesting when it is acted with energy, precision, and imagination than when it is not. Acting classes have recently begun to find their way into the curricula of music academies. Fleming recalls that when she began her training as a singer (in the late 1970s), in major conservatoires such as Eastman and Juilliard, there was no crossover between the drama and music divisions (Fleming 2004: 27), but now it is common for singers to take acting classes, and there are several manuals and textbooks that outline the training of the singer in which singing and acting are fused (Balk 1985). Although one can still see the bad old "park and bark" style of acting being practiced in opera houses, perhaps the days are largely gone when operatic acting, in the ironic words of Ernest Newman (paraphrased by director Frank Corsaro) consisted of a singer raising her arms as "an indication that something's afoot. If she raises both arms, it is a sign of disaster" (Corsaro 1978: 5).

Acting in Opera and the Spoken Theater

But is the representation of character and communication between actor and audience the same in opera as in spoken drama? Probably not. Actors in spoken drama speak out of silence; the dialogue they engage in more often than not seems to resemble the speech and pace of everyday conversation. Actors can, either individually or collectively, determine the pace of the work in which they are performing; and usually they act against a set or sets that are scaled to the dimensions of the human body and within a theater space where there is a good chance that they can establish fairly intimate contact with most, if not all, members of the audience. Actors in the spoken theater are, by and large, in control of the space in which they perform and the action that they are representing. In contrast, singing actors have to perform under circumstances that most speaking actors would find intolerably restrictive. For a start, they are very rarely surrounded by silence; between them and the audience is the orchestra, an insistent, often clamorous entity, whose very presence requires the singers to produce great volume and resonance in order to be heard above it. The immense physical effort demanded by such singing does not provide an ideal foundation for subtle characterization, as it tends to encourage gestures that are sweeping and generalized rather than highly nuanced. The orchestra and the conductor also control one of the actor's key resources, the freedom to set the rhythm of the performance. Accuracy in rhythm is critical to the success of any stage production, so a corresponding sense of rhythm is an essential attribute for the actor; in contrast, the opera singer must submit to rhythms generated by the conductor and, in doing so, abandon one of the defining characteristics of artistic freedom for the actor.

Despite the vagaries of historical nomenclature, song and speech are both "legitimate" dramatic languages, but they are perhaps best suited to exploring different aspects of human behavior and may therefore require different modes of acting. As a general rule, speech is most suited to explore the median ranges of human experience, and it can begin to lose efficacy as it moves toward the extremes of experience. Only complex and forceful dramatic verse such as Shakespeare's, or, in modern drama, a concentrated playing of the subtext can articulate these extremes to any degree of satisfaction. Opera, however, occupies extremes with greater ease than spoken drama does. Its music *is* the poetry and it tends to have no subtext, as that too is taken up by the music. Music provides access to characters' emotions in ways that are more direct and overt than in spoken drama, and the size with which these emotions are articulated tends to be enlarged by musical treatment. If such emotional passages are ineptly performed, they can appear to be inflated in contrast to spoken drama. Music provides a highly effective means of exploring and making explicit the secret corners of characters' psychic lives, so from *bel canto* works such as *La sonnambula* or *Lucia di Lammermoor* through *Tristan und Isolde* to *Pelléas et Mélisande* and expressionist operas such as Korngold's *Die tote Stadt*, much opera has centered on the expression of romantic and erotic longings, recondite emotions, and passions of extraordinary intensity. However, opera is not only at home in exploring the intimate strata of our emotional lives, it also excels in representing great public events, such as military parades, religious rituals, affairs of state, wars, trials, and riots, and in painting landscapes that can endow characters with heroic stature, as can be demonstrated by the progression of opera from the grand court spectacles of the seventeenth century through nineteenth-century grand opera and beyond. Although the ground that lies between the extremes of intimacy and grandeur—the discursive drama of ideas, the comedy of manners and wit, the domestic drama of everyday life—is not absent from the operatic repertoire (as can be seen, for example, from works such as *Le nozze di Figaro* or *La bohème*), this range of human discourse is perhaps more appropriately conveyed through spoken dialogue and through gestures employed in the performance of realistic drama. In fact, realism is not of much utility in conveying either the private or the grand dimensions of operatic action, so something more is required of the singing actor, a manner that is either grander and more elevated than realism, or more remote from it. To make operatic action credible on stage, a formal, sometimes even arcane repertoire of gestures, movements, and postures might be utilized.

The space of the opera stage is quite often larger than that utilized in the spoken theater, and the auditorium of the opera house is so vast that speaking actors would have great difficulty in commanding it. While the speaking actor performs to audiences ranging from a few dozen individuals to at the most a little over a thousand, opera, for economic and institutional reasons, is usually performed in theaters with auditoria that can hold up to four thousand and, if in the open air, several thousand more. The sheer magnitude of operatic performance space only strengthens the need to develop an approach to gesture different from that employed by speaking actors. In opera, as in spoken theater, gestures may reveal the inner life of the characters, but as they are also governed by the music, they tend, on the whole, to unfold more slowly than in spoken drama, their artificiality is more apparent and their duration more attenuated, often to the point of mannerism. In fact, the musical basis of opera encourages the singing actor to develop a style that draws heavily on a gestural mode of acting that is outdated in the spoken theater, associated as it is primarily with the melodrama of the nineteenth century and a style of tragic acting from earlier periods.

The very existence of music in opera can lead to claims that "the quality of acting is usually below the standard acceptable in the spoken theater" (Osnes 2001: 159), a statement that, if true, might be backed up by the argument that, as people do not sing in everyday life, there is no need for them to create a character whose bearing on stage resembles the way humans behave in everyday life. But such an objection betrays a misunderstanding of the nature of dramatic language. All language on stage is artificial, even speech; none of us, for example, in our everyday lives speak in Shakespearean verse, or are as witty as the characters of Wilde and Shaw, or make poetry from a limited vocabulary as Pinter's or Mamet's characters do. Music is yet one more overlay of poetry or heightened expression, and the singing actor must find a way to incorporate it into mimetic performance, just as the speaking actor does with the intensified language of poetic drama.

A corollary of the assumption that singing is not a credible dramatic language is that the words that are sung do not matter. Such thinking seems to lie behind Jerry Fodor's recent claim in the *Times Literary Supplement* that "most libretti cannot be taken seriously [and] but for the music they couldn't hope to hold the stage" (Fodor 2007). True enough; no libretti, not even the literary ones by Wagner and Hofmannsthal, can stand as plays in their own right and they were never intended to, but this does not mean that the drama they articulate "cannot be taken seriously." Most libretti, especially in the modern period, have been adapted from preexisting dramatic or literary material, which has already found audiences or readers for whom it was credible, and there is no reason to assume that an effective adaptation into opera should not be taken seriously as well. Some libretti, such as Myfanwy Piper's for Benjamin Britten's *The Turn of the Screw*, or, more recently, Meredith Oakes's for Thomas Ades's *The Tempest*, contain stunning poetry, but they have been designed specifically as a basis upon which music can develop its own capacities as a dramatic language, not as dramatic works in themselves.

In fact, music, whether or not it carries specific meaning in its non-vocal genres, does carry meaning in opera by its function as the prime medium of dramatic action. As such it can realize with unnerving accuracy intimate states of mind, represent with clarity the emotional flux of the character's lives, and explicitly shape the dramatic action. The opera singer must employ voice and body to interpret, with an equivalent exactitude, the character in a way that makes the action credible and coherent.

All of this indicates that the implied dichotomy between singing and acting, which has been at the basis of much of the suspicion of acting in opera, is a false one, because singing in opera is not separate from acting—it is part of it. The singing voice is as devoted to the representation of character as are facial expressions, bodily gestures and stances, movements, patterns of intonation and stress, and byplay. Not all opera singers might agree with Renée Fleming when she claims that "my primary goal is to make the audience forget that I am singing" (Fleming 2004: 156), or with Natalie Dessay, who is reported as saying that "her highest artistic ambition [is] to embody a character so persuasively, and tell a story so convincingly, that the audience forgets she is singing" (Mead 2009: 54). Indeed, the very conditions of operatic performance make it extremely difficult for us to forget the artistic means, particularly the singing, that the performers use (Lindenberger 1984: 130), but the voice alone, unaided by any mimetic skills in the singer, is challenged to convey the complexity of dramatic character that is germane to the operas that compose the repertoire today.

Acting: From Presentation to Representation

How, historically, has the singing actor risen to the histrionic challenge offered by operatic roles and are the solutions discovered by previous generations of singers viable in the theater today? Since the institution of opera at the turn of the sixteenth into the seventeenth century, theater has changed substantially; the spatial dynamic between actors and audiences, the understanding of dramatic character, and the means of realizing it have gone through several transformations. Until well into the nineteenth century, the auditorium was fully lit and the stage shared conceptual space with the audience. In the course of that century, however, the progressive darkening of the auditorium and the increased proficiency in creating scenic illusion through the construction of realistically detailed or evocative and atmospheric sets, aided by improvements in lighting, meant that by the start of the twentieth century the stage appeared to represent a world separate from that of the audience, one into which spectators peered as if privileged onlookers.

These changes radically influenced the singing actor. From the earliest years, acting in serious or tragic opera was tied closely to the music; in every movement and gesture the actor was expected to complement and never violate the music. Marco da Gagliano, in a preface to his *La Dafne* (Mantua, 1608), instructs the actor that "his singing and gestures should be full of majesty, more or less in accordance with the loftiness of the music. He must take care that every gesture and step follow the beat of the music and singing" (Gagliano [1608] 1979: 190). The illusion of nobility arising from harmonious unity of the body with the music suited well the elevated milieu of *opera seria*, and it was sustained until the end of the eighteenth century. Throughout this period, spoken tragedy and *opera seria* were performed through a complex language of gestures, stances, and poses that had its origins in the rhetorical practices of ancient Rome. It was a refined system in which character was represented in ideal form, and decorum, harmony, and beauty were prime markers of the performer's excellence, while "nature," as it was manifested through the emotions, was never felt in any rawness but was always under the controlling influence of "art." Although the realistic depiction of character was not even contemplated, the system of gesture and movement, available to us today in Barnett's exhaustively detailed catalogue of gestures drawn from major acting treatises of the seventeenth, eighteenth, and early nineteenth centuries (Barnett 1987), served as a precise code that covered an extensive range of human emotions and motivations and would have been easily understood by audiences. As performers in *opera seria* were customarily arrayed in heavy drapes, with *tonnelets* (skirts similar to the tutus of ballet) worn by men and voluminous floor-length skirts by women, and, for the most elevated characters, large waving plumes on their helmets, gestures had to be executed with the utmost care. In opera, the balletic slowness of such acting would have been more pronounced than in spoken tragedy, because, even though recitatives were delivered quite fast, it takes longer to express emotions in music than in words, so poses were sustained to the point of mannerism and transitions were slower. Indeed, François-Joseph Talma, the most accomplished classical actor in Revolutionary France, when he once acted in opera found it exceptionally difficult to fill out the long gaps necessitated by the music (Rutherford 2006: 233–234). The performance of *opera buffa*, *Singspiel*, *opéra comique*, and other mixed forms was more informal and, in contrast to *seria*, required a greater sense of ensemble; Mozart's comic operas, for example, with their extended and complex finales, could not be performed without a seemingly spontaneous communication between the actors.

Even though the formal, gestural language of *opera seria* might be used as a basis for the performance of some opera today, audiences are likely to find it artificial and even preposterous, as it articulates a code whose meaning has been largely lost today. Furthermore, it has about it the aura of rhetoric and therefore works most effectively in a theatrical configuration where direct communication between the actor and the audience is possible. But the architectural and scenic changes that occurred in the course of the nineteenth century gave rise to a theater where that was no longer possible as action, in both opera and spoken drama, tended increasingly, as the century progressed, toward either the graphically realistic or the vague and suggestive. In neither instance would the declarative, unambiguous gestures of *seria* serve any function. Smart, in her minutely observed study of the relationship between gesture and music in nineteenth-century opera, points out that the few treatises of gesture that did appear at this time, such as Aristippe's *Théorie de l'art du comédien* (1826), Carlo Blasis's *The Code of Terpsichore*

([1828] 1830), and Edward P. Thwing's *Drill Book on Vocal Culture and Gesture* (1876), tended to replicate their eighteenth-century sources (Smart 2004: 16). On stage, however, something different was happening; "the notion of gesture as a language in itself, worthy of dictionary-like exegesis, was gradually replaced by research that signaled the awakening of more modern concerns, conceiving gesture as involuntary physiological response or as unconscious manifestation of psychic depth" (Smart 2004: 17), a process that culminated in naturalism or its operatic equivalent, *verismo*. This different understanding of the nature of gesture implied a different relationship between the body and the music it expressed, which resulted in an increasing freedom of the singer's body from the music and the gradual abandonment of any attempt to have gesture move in total harmony with the music.

This new mode of theatricality was already apparent in the performance of Italian opera in the early nineteenth century. The romantic concern with subjectivity found a fertile field in the emotional lives of the desolate heroes and heroines of *bel canto* opera, and singers, if they were to explore these shadowy areas fully, needed to develop a mimesis that brought psychological turmoil and distress to the surface, in contrast to the *seria* of previous generations, which had been concerned with projecting ideal and morally admirable images of human experience. In the great *bel canto* roles, the noble heroes of *seria* were replaced by lovers whose aberrant desires tore apart the social fabric, and who were driven, either by external coercion or inner turmoil, to catastrophic pathological extremes—in Bellini's *La sonnambula* and *I puritani* to the brink of madness, or in Donizetti's *Lucia di Lammermoor* beyond madness into murder and suicide. The *bel canto* period produced the first great prima donnas of the operatic stage, who charted the emotional life of their characters not only through delivery of the vocal line—many of the major female singers sang mezzo-soprano rather than pure soprano and some could cover up to three octaves—but through intonation, accentuation, gesture, facial expression, posture, and byplay, all of which struck audiences as original and unprecedented. As a general rule, until the Romantic period, performers, in opera and spoken theater, had been admired to the degree that they mastered formulas and tropes that had been practiced for generations, so performance had been a repetition of past patterns and the assertion of a generalized and unchanging truth. But with the advent of Romanticism, the individuality of the singer and the originality of the performance caught the attention of audiences, so acting that invested individuality in a role began to earn applause. Some singers, such as Giuditta Pasta (1797–1865), who created three of Bellini's major roles (Amina in *La sonnambula*, Norma, and Beatrice di Tenda, as well as Donizetti's Anna Bolena), and Pauline Viardot (1821–1910) seemed to stay within a framework they had created for the character and sustained an aura of dignity reminiscent of *seria*, while suggesting emotional turbulence beneath a marmoreal surface; in so doing they served as bridges between older rhetorical and newer mimetic styles of acting. Others, such as Maria Malibran (1808–1836) and Wilhelmine Schröder-Devrient (1804–1860), who inspired the youthful Wagner, created characters, both from *bel canto* and earlier operas, that seemed to be in excess of what was written and frequently aroused ferment as to the appropriateness of their histrionic contributions.

An unsigned review of Malibran (referred to as Madame de Beriot) as "Fidelio" in *The Musical World* (May 13, 1836: 140) takes issue with her "tendency to bring every point into [...] equally high relief. The unwearied activity of her mind leads her to make even the minutiae of her part over-important [...] having made a point, she is determined you shall feel she has made it" (Rutherford 2006: 240).

While a greater attention to psychological detail in operatic acting complemented an increasing realism in stage settings, any tendency toward realism in acting was resisted by increases in the size of the average auditorium and stage, which accommodated the larger audiences produced by the rapidly growing cities of the nineteenth century. In order for singers' characters to be read, even from the middle of the stalls, broad gestures had to be adopted that were reminiscent less of *opera seria*, more of the melodrama that prevailed in the popular theater. Smart concludes her study of gesture in nineteenth-century opera with the telling observation that even in the latter part of the century, in Wagner's music dramas and Verdi's mature grand operas, in which the conventions of melodrama were challenged and the gestural patterns associated with it were disappearing, a use of gesture that reveals the inner state of the character constantly rubs shoulders with passages in which the composer requires of the singers "a gestural model of music and movement" (Smart 2004: 203). The height of realism in opera composition was reached with Italian *verismo* and corresponding works in other countries at the turn of the nineteenth into the twentieth century, which gave rise to a generation of singers who intensified the focus on realistic detail. The most notable of these were the French soprano Emma Calvé (1858–1942), whose intense renderings of roles such as Santuzza, Carmen, and Ophelia in Thomas's *Hamlet* owed much to Eleonora Duse, as did the acting of the more restrained Italian soprano Claudia Muzio (1889–1936). Indeed, memories of Duse's sparing, minimalistic approach to acting may well have been in Puccini's mind as he crafted the characterization of Mimì in *La bohème* (Greenwald 2012: 290). In contrast, the flamboyant Scottish soprano Mary Garden (1874–1967) brought a notably vivid and often sexually provocative interpretation to a wide range of roles from the classic and modern repertoire.

Despite the movement toward realism that marked the production of theater over the long nineteenth century, acting practices developed during the eighteenth century hung on with remarkable persistency in the performance of opera, and vestiges can still be traced today. George Bernard Shaw, who entertained the lowest opinion of singers' histrionic skills, claimed that "operatic actors [...] wholly substitute mannerisms of the feeblest sort for acting" and complained that "even the few singers [...] who are specially celebrated for their acting, would be celebrated for their deficiency if they were placed in an equally prominent position in drama" (Shaw [1886] 1981: I: 435). In 1915, a manual, *Acting in Opera* by George Edward Shea, was published that claimed to be based upon current operatic performance practices in Europe; it prescribed specific gestures and movements for specific emotions and situations and evoked the idea of operatic performance as a slowly executed ballet, in which all movement occurs in exact harmony with the music. Movement synchronized to music can still be seen in the opera house, practiced by soloists and choruses alike, but it can so easily appear as overemphatic and mannered that it can serve as the cause of unintentional laughter, the most deadly enemy of tragic pathos the theater has to offer.

Acting and Ensemble

Evidence of the turn toward realism in the performance of opera can be found in the production books—*livrets scèniques* in France or *disposizioni sceniche* in Italian—that recorded productions in major opera houses from the late 1820s in France and the 1850s in Italy. Initially, these books gave relatively little indication as to how individual singers should interpret their roles, though the production book for *Otello*, based on the La Scala production of 1887, indicates three solos where singers should use their imagination in developing their characters (Busch 1988: II: 528, 565–566, 600). Comparing the *Otello* book to production books from earlier decades, there is abundant evidence that blocking had grown more complex as the nineteenth century progressed, a development that made clear the realistic ambitions of the operatic theater; in particular, precise instructions as to how soloists should move in relation to each other suggest that those responsible for staging the productions were aware of how the play of mind between the principal characters can be expressed through movement on stage. While the prime interest of these books remains scenic, they offer evidence that the concept of operatic performance as an ensemble, in which the impact of the production on the audience is achieved through the combined efforts of principals and chorus rather than through spectacular solo performances, was taking hold in the course of the nineteenth century. It was in the theatrical work of Richard Wagner that this idea was most thoroughly explored and developed.

Wagner's antipathy toward the way opera was produced in his own time was based in large part on his view that the stage was treated as a platform for a display of the singers' virtuosity and that audiences were encouraged to pay attention solely to their skills as singers, not as interpreters of dramatic character. From his earliest, quasi-satirical articles on the Parisian opera (see Wagner [1840] 1896: 207) to his extended stage rehearsals with the singers for the first complete production of *The Ring* at Bayreuth in 1876, Wagner campaigned against mere vocal virtuosity on the stage. In its place he sought an approach to acting that allowed the singer to realize from moment to moment the changing volitional life of the character as expressed in the vocal line and the orchestra. He envisaged a unity of physical gesture, movement, and singing, through which the singers subordinated their talents to the larger purpose of creating a seamless work of art, seamlessness being a defining quality of the *Gesamtkunstwerk*. This entailed the abandonment of self-conscious theatricality and the creation of an illusion that the production absorbs the audience through its similarity to actual life. On the grounds that "art…ceases to be art from the moment it presents itself as Art to our reflecting consciousness," Wagner argued that the actor's "whole essence is reproductiveness whose root we find as the bent to copy with all possible deception the individuality of other persons and their demeanour in the incidents of everyday life" (Wagner [1872] 1896: 214). But Wagner, who proved in rehearsal to be a strikingly resourceful actor himself, could never entirely wean his singers from declarative gestures, so that much of the acting in the first *Ring* cycle at Bayreuth in 1876 and at the *Festspielhaus* for several decades after his death was often wooden and overemphatic. The gesture reinforced what had already been stated in the music, and this practice of "double-marking" had the effect of impeding rather than facilitating the flow of the action, thereby creating a self-conscious theatricality rather than avoiding it.

The mode of ensemble acting that would have brought Wagner's ideal opera performance closer to fulfillment was developed by Stanislavski, the Russian director and actor, best known as the first director of Chekhov's plays and one of the founders of the Moscow Art Theatre. Opera was, however, of equal if not more interest to Stanislavski than spoken drama was, and during the early revolutionary years he ran a studio in which he attempted to apply principles of naturalistic acting to the performance of opera. He, like Wagner, conceived of performance as a process of sacrifice, in which performers subordinated their individual needs to the interests of the entire performance. Stanislavski considered this surrender to be easier for the opera singer than for the speaking actor, precisely because music usurps the actor's prerogative to control the rhythm of the action. "Opera," he claimed, "is much easier than drama. For in opera the rhythm is already there" (Stanislavski 1961: 169). Once the singer has discovered this, in a process identical to that followed by the speaking actor, she creates a "circle of attention" that provides parameters for the role and using the "affective memory" brings the unconscious strata of the character, articulated in the music, to physical realization, ultimately to create a "through-line of action" for the character, which is devoid of any trace of theatrical convention. Stanislavski's attempts to create productions in which the singer's role unfolds, as it were, spontaneously with the music were confined primarily to the studio, as the structure of the operatic profession did not allow for the prolonged rehearsals that were necessary for him to develop a seamless ensemble. He drew many of his insights into opera from the acting of Fyodor Chaliapin (1873–1938), whose capacity to sing over both the baritone and bass registers and to transform himself physically into whichever role he played allowed him to craft performances in which characterization was governed entirely by the inner life of the character; therefore at each performance his presentation seemed fresh and urgent.

Stanislavski never fulfilled his ambitions for a permanent ensemble of operatic actors; this was accomplished by the Austrian stage director Walter Felsenstein (1901–1975), who, as director of the Komische Oper in East Berlin from 1947, produced a series of model productions in which all aspects of performance were subordinated to articulating the dramatic action. As with Stanislavski, singers were expected to construct detailed pasts for their characters and to develop them with total disregard for theatrical convention; they should become "unreservedly believable." But Felsenstein's most important demand was that his singers should act as if singing were the only way in which they could express themselves. When this happens, the energies of the singer begin to challenge and even incorporate those of the conductor, the orchestra, or the stage director, so the singer becomes the "creative fashioner" of the opera (Fuchs 1991: 15). With Felsenstein, the singing-actor becomes the dominant presence in operatic performance, but only if the singing is subsumed within the acting. Once this happens successfully, and the motivation of the actors emerges clearly, they become the unifying powers within the performance, even to the extent of instilling motivation into the orchestra.

Modern Modes of Operatic Acting

Felsenstein insisted that his own brand of music theater should not be regarded as a template for all opera production. "Advocates of the consistent music theater," he wrote, "should [...] not try to insert themselves where they are neither wanted nor needed" (cited in Fuchs 1991: 14). His comment is a reminder that operatic performance today takes place in several contexts and in several different styles; furthermore, the ideal of the seamlessly staged work of art is not the only one available to us. To take the most obvious example, opera is still performed, often to the great satisfaction of audiences, in the setting of the concert hall. In such an environment, acting even of the sketchiest nature tends to be out of place or even a touch embarrassing. Not all productions attempt to provide as vivid a sense of life within the characters as did Stanislavski's and Felsenstein's. The static mode of staging, in the symbolist tradition, implicated in the theories of Adolphe Appia and introduced on the stage by Wieland Wagner, has continued into our own time with directors such as Robert Wilson. They may ask the singers to disclose the character within the role, but they do so in a manner that is slow, hieratic, and rarely disrupted by any upswell of volatility. As the appeal of such productions is usually pictorial, actors are components in a visual composition, rather than interpreters of character. Although few modern directors encourage the adoption of the rhetorical gestures of earlier operatic acting—Wilson is greatly indebted to acting styles of the East Asian theater—symbolist performance has a ritualistic aura that recalls the formality with which *opera seria* was produced prior to the nineteenth century. The formal nature of operatic gesture also works to the advantage of operas staged in the style of Bertolt Brecht's Epic theater, which has had a major influence on operatic production since the 1970s. In Brecht the inner life of the character is also a secondary concern; instead, audience attention is directed toward the social polemic, and the aim of the actors will be to demonstrate how their characters' behavior is prompted mainly by those social forces that are driving the action.

Acting in Opera: Callas

A striking appearance, a vivid acting technique, and the capacity to use the voice to explore the emotional intricacies of character are assets that are becoming essential in opera today, because while audiences may be drawn to operatic performance by the music, they often find themselves held in the opera house by the theater. Whether the last one hundred years have been prodigal of great singing actors is not an easy matter to judge as, until recently, one has had to rely primarily upon written sources that either focus solely on the voice or provide information about the acting that is primarily anecdotal. For example, the performances of Maria Callas may have been documented more copiously than those of any other singer, because in the minds of many opera-goers, she stands as the most consummate actor of opera in the second half of the twentieth century. But exactly why she should have this reputation is uncertain. In David Lowe's anthology of reviews, essays, and memoirs of Callas—perhaps the most useful source book on the singer—tribute after tribute is made to the quality of her acting. From the start of her career she was praised for her "dramatic instinct [and] the intensity of her acting" (Herzog 1944; Lowe 1986: 17), and in mid-career there cannot have been many who would have disagreed that "as an actress [...] [she] must be reckoned among the greats" (Smith 1957; Lowe 1986: 69), but detailed concrete descriptions of her acting are difficult to come by.

In part, her reputation as an actor may have arisen from the drama within her voice, which is apparent from her many recordings. The imperfections of her singing have been exhaustively documented—the flawed vocal technique, the three registers that were never integrated, her frequent inability to stay on pitch, and her shrillness on top—as have its extraordinary beauties—her "mezza voce of opulence and warmth" (Lowe, 36), her astounding legato, the hollow tones of her lower register, and the compassion that her voice could both express and attract. More than one voice can be heard in her singing, as if it itself is the site of drama. Whether an unbroken stream of silvery sound delivered with a flawless vocal technique is inappropriate for a singing-actor depends primarily upon the way in which it is put to use, but Callas's voice was dramatic through its very composition and the disparity with which its parts were related to each other.

A similar disparity may have been apparent in her acting on stage. In Act II of *Tosca*, in her celebrated comeback at Covent Garden in 1964, she covered a wide emotional range, the extremes of which led her to adopt strikingly different modes of acting. The visual record of this performance (Callas 2002) indicates that she was a vivid, naturalistic actor. Passages in which she expresses vulnerability and inner distress or in which she struggles with the agents who are manhandling Cavaradossi are executed with moment-to-moment exactitude, and her body and face express the turmoil within Tosca to the minutest detail. There were moments, however, where naturalism was transformed into a mode of acting reminiscent of the ancient gestural tradition. As Callas's Tosca pleads with Scarpia, she does so with arms and hands outstretched and shoulders flung back in the manner prescribed by handbooks dating back to the earliest eighteenth century. Similarly, moments of fury and pathos are presented grandly in a manner that even has a touch of the archaic about it and arouses associations with the acting of classical tragedy. Whether a consistent characterization lies beneath these different modes is a question for each observer to decide, but each moment is executed with a calculated knowledge of its theatrical impact.

As John Steane has commented, it is absurd to claim that Callas introduced the phenomenon of acting onto the operatic stage (Steane 1996: II: 254). In fact, her popularity as a performer may have resided not in any originality in her acting, but in the opposite; she consummated, with more completeness and flair than previous singers, a mode of acting that was specific to opera, one that could be defined neither by naturalistic attention to detail and motivation, nor by formal gestures, but by the tension between them. Indeed, Callas could move from one to the other without any sense of disruption, as each moment was justified by a level of intensity that was determined by the orchestra and the vocal line. It was not only through the depth of her characterization that she made her impact, but through the deliberation and sparseness of her acting, as with just a single movement of her arm she could make "the audience sit forward, gripped by the stimulus of a dynamic personality in action" (Lowe 1986: 42). Callas was a master of sparse suggestive acting, a minimalism that had been first observed by Wagner almost a century earlier (see also Ardoin [1987] 1998; Seletsky 2004; Cazaux 2010; and Grover-Friedlander 2011).

Acting in Opera: *Parsifal*

Much expressive acting in opera may reside in the tension between the realistic representation of characters' emotions and a stylized mode of gesture and movement, which would often be considered excessive in spoken drama. But toward the end of his life, when he was directing the first production of *Parsifal* at Bayreuth, Wagner clearly modified his ideas of what constituted successful mimesis on the operatic stage. While directing the *Ring* he had expected full characterization and unmodified realism from his actors, but in directing *Parsifal* six years later, he found that both realism and declarative rhetorical gestures lacked power; rather, he wrote, "a half-uplifting of one arm, a characteristic movement of the hand, the head, was quite enough to emphasize a somewhat heightened feeling" (Wagner [1882] 1897: 307). At the time this suggestive approach to characterization might have seemed particular to *Parsifal*, a drama in which realistic aspects of action are reduced and characters address a level of consciousness that lies outside the immediate ambit of everyday experience. Most of the action is unequivocally symbolic, and the extreme slowness with which the score unfolds does not seem to invite the actors to employ the rhythms of physical life. Consequently, for most of its performance history *Parsifal* has been performed with singers maintaining static poses in stagings that tend, in the two outer acts especially, to rely heavily on a ritual that parallels religious ceremony with reduced attention to representing individual character.

While passivity and stillness may open the minds of audiences to associative aspects of *Parsifal*'s music, they can mask the multiple strata of the action. A judicious use of realistic acting combined with the sparer mode of acting Wagner had encouraged, however, can both endow that action with greater specificity and give weight and precision to the symbolism. One of the most widely seen productions of *Parsifal* over the last decade has been the one directed by Nicholas Lehnhoff, first staged at the ENO in 1999, later in San Francisco, Chicago, and Baden-Baden, where it was filmed in 2005 (Wagner/Lehnhoff 2005). This *Parsifal*, set in a barren, post-apocalyptic world, without a scintilla of nature in Raimund Bauer's designs, refers more to military than religious ritual in this severe staging. The prime interest of the production, therefore, resides not in the possibility of a divine presence that will save humanity, but in the capacity of human beings to find salvation in themselves. It is therefore through the actuality of the singers' presence and the specificity of their acting that the conception of the production is realized.

Despite his secular perspective, Lehnhoff's understanding of the action is neither radical nor idiosyncratic. He probes psychological realms that were soon to be explored by such near contemporaries of Wagner as Ibsen, Freud, and Stanislavski, whose actors were devoted to uncovering the unconscious fears, desires, and impulses that govern human behavior. The key to Lehnhoff's reading is the anxiety that is introduced in the Prelude at the point where the evocative opening theme returns and loses its haunting aura of boundless distance through worrying repetitions of a single phrase, which lends the Prelude an air of hysteria that confounds any sense of comfort the theme might have initially conveyed. It centers the action on psychic distress within and dysfunction between the characters.

While Lehnhoff's production incorporates the minimalist approach to acting advocated by Wagner, it is not the only method employed. The Ibsenesque angle on the action requires actors to move precisely from moment to moment. This banishes any sense of the mystical in their relationships and conveys a reductive view of the human condition. In Act I, Gurnemanz (Matti Salminen) is irascible and uncertain of himself, constantly on the verge, it would seem, of despair; Amfortas (Thomas Hampson) lives in self-pity and terror, partly as a result of his wound, but even more out of fear of Titurel, his father; the knights are filled with childish contempt for Kundry (Waltraud Meier), which arises from the unease she causes them by arousing their sexuality; and Parsifal (Christopher Ventris) is nothing more than a figure of thoughtless violence. It is a circumscribed world in which characters are marked not so much by their difference from others as by their common trait—an urge to violence sparked by fear arising from unresolved divisions and inner tensions. This is not a world in which the individual is isolated. Although Wagner's poem unfolds in a series of soliloquies, Lehnhoff's staging resists this by insisting on an illusion of constant dialogue. The knights, for example, actively respond to Gurnemanz's soliloquies as if engaged in an exchange with him. All characters in the opening act are tied to each other by bonds, which are established through an acting that is concrete and psychologically specific and which intensifies the claustrophobia of a society determined by brutality, fear, and ignorance. The cold, resentful suppression, which dominates the action, is broken by startling moments of violence. In the absence of the divine, what little development there is in this act consists primarily in Gurnemanz learning compassion.

Operatic action tends to occupy the extremes rather than the median of human experience and so realistic acting can have limited efficacy. It works best when providing insights into the emotional life described by the music. Once those emotions intensify and drive the action more overtly, realism has reached its limits. The acting in Lehnhoff's

Parsifal moves in two potentially contrary directions. Passages of extreme torment, such as Kundry's unsuccessful seduction of Parsifal in Act II and Amfortas's agony during the final scene, are realized through expressionistic acting in which movement is jagged and impulsive, facial expressions reach grotesque contortions, and screams and explosive shouts punctuate the music. At the same time, though the divine is never present, the action consistently works toward a realization of a sublime state, in this instance, through the growth of love between Parsifal and Kundry, who by initially choosing denial, resolve the conflicts that have been impeding them. Upon this they will build, it is implied, a freer society. Such a utopian vision would be betrayed if it were literally depicted on stage. Ultimately it must reside in the audience's imagination and memory. It is at this point that Wagner's acting of "half-indication" proves most effective. As Kundry leads Parsifal and a few other knights offstage to this new fertile world, the slow, measured control of their formal progress indicates that they now possess themselves and points the attention of the audience toward the world they are going to create.

The success of Lehnhoff's *Parsifal* is dependent upon the actor and on finely observed variations in acting style. The humanization of the action and the avoidance of any trappings of the Romantic theater place intense and unyielding focus on the actor, but in so doing, a multivalent and complex understanding of Wagner's final opera as a process of human growth is established that resists, quite effectively, the vaguer modes of representation that can often attend this work when it is treated as a drama of religious salvation.

See also: Divas and Divos, Rehearsal Practices, Production Aesthetics and Materials, *Regietheater*/Director's Theater

Bibliography

Ardoin, John. [1987] 1998. *Callas at Juilliard: The Master Classes.* New York: Alfred A. Knopf. Reprint. Portland, OR: Amadeus Press.

Aristippe, [Felix]. 1826. *Théorie de l'art du comédien*. Paris: A. Leroux.

Balk, H. Wesley. 1985. *The Complete Singer-Actor: Training for Music Theater.* 2nd ed. Minneapolis: University of Minnesota Press.

Barker, Clive. 1989. *Theatre Games: A New Approach to Drama Training.* London: Methuen.

Barnett, Dene, with the assistance of Jeanette Massy-Westropp. 1987. *The Art of Gesture: The Practices and Principles of 18th Century Acting.* Heidelberg: Carl Winter Universitätsverlag.

Blasis, Carlo. [1828] 1830. *The Code of Terpsichore*, translated by R. Barton. London: Edward Bull.

Bogart, Anne, and Tina Landau. 2005. *The Viewpoints Book.* New York: Theatre Communications Group.

Borovsky, Victor. 1988. *Chaliapin: A Critical Biography.* London: Hamish Hamilton.

Brook, Peter. 1998. *The Empty Space: A Book about the Theatre: Deadly, Holy, Rough, Immediate.* New York: Touchstone.

Busch, Hans, ed. and trans. 1988. *Verdi's 'Otello' and 'Simon Boccanegra'* [Revised version] *in Letters and Documents.* 2 vols. Oxford: Clarendon Press.

Callas, Maria. 2002. *The Eternal Maria Callas*. DVD EMI Classic 5 00720 9.
Cavalieri, Emilio De'. [1600] 1967. *Rappresentazione di Anima, et di Corpo, Nuovamente posta in Musica dal Sig. Emilio del Cavalliere per recitar cantando.* Facsimile edition (n.p.). Bologna: Forni. In MacClintock 1979, 182–184.
Cazaux, Chantal. 2010. "'Son Tosca!': Tosca et ses interprètes." In *Victorien Sardou: Le théâtre et les arts*, edited by Isabelle Moindrot, 157–166. Rennes: Universitaires de Rennes.
Corsaro, Frank. 1978. *Maverick: A Director's Personal Experience in Opera and Theater.* New York: Vanguard.
Ellis, William Ashton, ed. and trans. 1892–1899. *Richard Wagner's Prose Works.* 8 vols. London: Kegan Paul.
Fleming, Renée. 2004. *The Inner Voice: The Making of a Singer*. New York: Penguin.
Fodor, Jerry. 2007. "Life in Tune." Review of Bernard Williams, *On Opera* (New Haven: Yale University Press, 2006). *Times Literary Supplement* (January 17). Online. Available: https://login.the-tls.co.uk/?gotoUrl=http%3A%2F%2Fwww.the-tls.co.uk%2Ftls%2Freviews%2Farts_and_commentary%2Farticle728232.ece (accessed February 6, 2014).
Fuchs, Peter Paul, ed. and trans. 1991. *The Music Theatre of Walter Felsenstein.* London: Quartet Books.
Gagliano, Marco da. [1608] 1979. "Preface to *Dafne*." In MacClintock 1979, 186–193.
Greenwald, Helen. 2012. "*Ars moriendi:* Reflections on the Death of Mimì." In *The Arts of the Prima Donna in the Long Nineteenth Century*, edited by Rachel Cowgill and Hilary Poriss, 271–304. New York: Oxford University Press.
Grover-Friedlander, Michal. 2011. *Operatic Afterlives*. New York: Zone Books.
Herzog, Friedrich W. 1944. Review of *Tiefland. Deutsche Nachrichten in Griechenland*, translated by Henry Wisneski. In Lowe 1986, 17.
Hutcheon, Linda, and Michael Hutcheon. 2000. *Bodily Charm, Living Opera*. Lincoln: University of Nebraska Press.
Isherwood, Charles. 2007. "Operatic Acting? Oxymoron No More." *New York Times* (September 9). Online. Available: http://www.nytimes.com/2007/09/09/arts/music/09char.html (accessed February 6, 2014).
Lindenberger, Herbert. 1984. *Opera: The Extravagant Art*. Ithaca, NY: Cornell University Press.
Lowe, David A., ed. 1986. *Callas As They Saw Her*. New York: Ungar.
MacClintock, Carol. 1979. *Readings in the History of Music in Performance*. Bloomington: Indiana University Press.
Mancini, Giovanni Battista. 1774. *Pensieri e riflessioni pratiche sopra il canto figurato.* Vienna: Ghelen.
Mitchell, Ronald E. 1970. *Opera: Dead or Alive*. Madison, Milwaukee: University of Wisconsin Press.
Mead, Rebecca. 2009. "The Actress: A Soprano's Ambivalent Relationship with her Voice." *The New Yorker* (March 2). Online. Available: http://www.newyorker.com/reporting/2009/03/02/090302fa_fact_mead (accessed February 6, 2014).
Osnes, Beth. 2001. *Acting: An Encyclopedia of Traditional Culture*. Santa Barbara, CA: ABC-CLIO.
Rutherford, Susan. 2006. *The Prima Donna and Opera*, 1815–1930. Cambridge: Cambridge University Press.
Seletsky, Robert. 2004. "The Performance Practice of Maria Callas: Interpretation and Instinct." *Opera Quarterly* 20/4: 587–602.

Shaw, George Bernard. [1886] 1981. "Palmy Days at the Opera." *Shaw's Music*. 3 vols., edited by Dan H. Laurence. I: 432–437. New York: Dodd Mead.

Shea, George E. [1915] 1980. *Acting in Opera*. Reprint. New York: Da Capo.

Smart, Mary Ann. 2004. *Mimomania: Music and Gesture in Nineteenth-Century Opera*. Berkeley and Los Angeles: University of California Press.

Smith, Brittain, trans. 1957. Unsigned review of 1957 concert in Zurich, *Lucia di Lammermoor* (Rome), and *La sonnambula* (Cologne). *Kölnische Rundschau*.

Steane, John. 1996. *Singers of the Century*. 3 vols. Portland: Amadeus Press.

Stanislavski, Konstantin. 2008. *My Life in Art*, edited and translated by Jean Benedetti. London: Routledge.

——. 1961. *Stanislavsky on the Art of the Stage*, translated by David Magarshack. New York: Hill & Wang.

Tosi, Piero Francesco. [1723] 1968. *Opinioni de' cantori antichi e moderni*, translated [1743] by John Ernest Galliard as *Observations on the Florid Song; or Sentiments on the Ancient and Modern Singers*. London: J. Wilcox. Reprint. New York and London: Johnson.

Thwing, Edward P. 1876. *Drill Book on Vocal Culture and Gesture*. New York: Funk & Wagnalls.

Volbach, Walther R. 1967. *Problems of Opera Production*. 2nd rev. ed. [n.p.]: Archon Books.

Wagner, Richard. [1912–1914]. *Sämtliche Schriften und Dichtungen* [*SSD*], edited by Hans von Wolzogen and Richard Sternfeld. 16 vols. Leipzig: Breitkopf & Härtel.

——. [1882] 1897. "Das Bühneneweihfestspiel in Bayreuth" ["*Parsifal* at Bayreuth"]. In *SSD*, X: 297–308; Ellis, VI: 301–312.

——. [1872] 1896. "Über Schauspieler und Sänger" ["Actors and Singers"]. In *SSD*, IX: 61–126; Ellis, V: 157–228.

——. [1840] 1896. "Der Virtuos und der Künstler" ["The Virtuoso and the Artist"]. In *SSD*, I: 167–179. Ellis, VII: 108–122.

Wagner [Richard]/Lehnhoff, Nicholas. 2005. *Parsifal*. DVD. Cond. Kent Nagano BBC/Opus Arte. OA 0915 D.

CHAPTER 21

THE CHORUS

RYAN MINOR

Singing Celebrities

In the spring of 2007, the Metropolitan Opera in New York held a contest. The occasion was a new production of Gluck's *Orfeo ed Euridice*, directed and choreographed by Mark Morris, in which each member of the chorus was costumed as a famous historical figure (see Figure 21.1). Perhaps sensing some free publicity, the Met invited the public to identify as many of the figures as possible. After the contest was over, the opera house's website featured a complete guide to this elaborate chorus, which was now revealed to include an eclectic collection of over one hundred personalities ranging from Golda Meir to Montezuma to Marlene Dietrich (detailed pictures of the chorus are available at Metropolitan Opera 2012). The figures were difficult to recognize from most seats in the house, but viewed in its entirety Morris's chorus, and the amphitheater that housed it, dominated the staging. And as the central—indeed, only—dramaturgical idea Morris brought to the production, his chorus also came to dominate the staging's critical reception as well. Reactions were mixed, although one commentator held out hope that the curiously overwrought treatment of the chorus did have a point to make: "The concept risks cuteness but achieves pathos: celebrities are apparently doomed to spend eternity in a V.I.P. area designed by Richard Serra" (Ross 2007). So conceived, Morris's chorus of famous names from the past amounted to more than mere costumed spectacle, or at least more than spectacle alone; it illustrated a leveling effect meted out by death itself.

Be that as it may, one might well ask what any of the celebrities in Morris's chorus had to do with Gluck's opera, or why it was necessary to place so much attention on particular individuals to begin with, given that Morris's stated intent was simply to provide a chorus that functioned as "witnesses from history" (Sheek 2009). The implication, of course, was that the chorus's pronouncements on Orfeo's travails carried more weight if they were issued by "witnesses" that had themselves made history—rather like the retired sports icons who now serve as TV commentators. Moreover, in the context of a production already overflowing with marquee names (in addition to Morris, James

FIGURE 21.1 Mark Morris's production of *Orfeo ed Euridice*. Photo: Ken Howard/Metropolitan Opera.

Levine conducted, Isaac Mizrahi designed the costumes, and, initially, the late and irreplaceable Lorraine Hunt Lieberson was slated to sing Orfeo), this chorus, comprising solely famous people, seemed at times not so much a dramaturgical statement as it was an extension of the star-studded roster behind the rest of the production. This was not simply a chorus made up of distinct individuals, but of distinctly famous individuals. Perhaps inevitably, luxury casting had now managed to infiltrate an entirely make-believe realm, as if to assure the audience that even the otherwise anonymous chorus was actually an exclusive collection of historical A-listers.

The Dramaturgical Problem

Wittingly or not, Morris's staging underlined a central issue in thinking about the chorus's role in opera. In assigning distinct personages to individual chorus members, and thus highlighting the question of who or what constitutes a chorus—which in turn raises the question of whether the group represents one or multiple subjectivities (or maybe something in between)—Morris implicitly engaged a long-standing discussion concerning the identity, source, and accountability of the opera chorus. After all, the chorus's often lavish, even nonsensical, onstage appearances have not always been grounded in a concrete identity, much less one that is clearly necessitated by the drama;

the opera chorus has had a marked tendency to metastasize into something larger, less focused, and significantly more extravagant than a simple character alone. Thus the desire to assign a provenance to choral utterance—to pin down, and even slim down, the chorus—has also formed an important part of operatic reforms (not the least of which, ironically, was Gluck's own). Morris's production is instructive on this count as well, perched as it is on the perilously thin line that separates dramaturgical concept from empty spectacle, and a chorus that serves a dramatic function from a chorus that serves a decorative one. Richard Wagner's famous accusation that the opera chorus often functioned merely as musical scenery is perhaps the best-known formulation of this complaint, and it is a charge that hits uncomfortably close to home for Morris's staging, in which the choral amphitheatre and its residents almost always *are* the set (Wagner 1888a). But as we will see below, Wagner and countless other reformers of the opera chorus were generally only successful in identifying the problem, not solving it. For as much as the opera chorus has been difficult to stage, difficult to theorize, and difficult to keep under control, for virtually all of operatic history—from the Baroque, through the cycles of reform, and to the present—it has also been difficult to do without.

Modeling the Greeks: Collective Sentiments

Probably the most basic function of the opera chorus, ranging from its early years to the present, is also its most traditional, and familiar, task: providing reflection and commentary on the drama. This was, of course, the chorus's role in ancient Greek tragedy, and it is no accident that early opera—which self-consciously attempted to model itself after contemporary understanding of classical tragedy in so many ways—would also look to its ancient forebear in this respect as well (a brief overview of the chorus in the earliest opera, starting in the 1580s, can be found in Grout 1963). But whereas early opera in general sought to cultivate the new musical language and textures of monody as a means of reanimating the expressive ideals of Greek tragedy, for the most part the specifically choral music made little break with the past.[1] In Monteverdi's *L'Orfeo*, for instance, the chorus's "Ahi, caso acerbo" following the announcement of Euridice's death is essentially a madrigal. One reason for the difference in musical language is obvious: monody's expressive flexibility, its quicksilver harmonic and rhythmic shifts, is much harder to achieve in an ensemble of multiple singers than it is for soloist and basso continuo alone. It is also frequently asserted that the continued use of madrigal textures for the chorus helped to provide a textural contrast to the soloists' monody. Either way, however, the result is hardly one of expediency alone; "Ahi, caso acerbo" functions equally well as a *seconda prattica* madrigal and as a touching dramatic reflection on Euridice's death. (Much the same can be said about "With Drooping Wings" at the end of Purcell's *Dido and Aeneas*, a choral reflection on death and sacrifice that—to this listener at least—is just as moving as the much more famous solo lament that immediately precedes it.)

Italian Baroque opera after *L'Orfeo* rarely included choruses—they were essentially absent from Venetian opera, later became a target of the Arcadian reforms, and are exceptionally rare in Metastasian libretti as well as Handel's operas—and as a result, it arguably never developed a uniquely operatic musical language to express collective sentiment. Exactly the opposite was the case in France. In the works of Lully and Rameau the chorus forms a crucial part of the music, drama, and spectacle, primarily in (but not limited to) the *divertissements*. Thus, not surprisingly, given the centrality of the chorus to *ancien régime* opera, this is also the repertory in which the chorus's role has attracted the most attention from both contemporary theorists and present-day musicologists (Harris-Warrick 1994; Kintzler 2007). Much of this attention has focused on the relations between the chorus and other entities, and in this sense the significance of the chorus in opera of the *ancien régime* is not its particularity but rather its integration into a larger system of political and aesthetic representation. Certainly a stage filled with flying chariots or an Incan sun festival, elaborately costumed and often masked dancers, and the king's own instrumentalists—not to mention the king's proxy himself, embodied in the central mythological character—can hardly be considered a forum for choral expression alone (Harris-Warrick 1994). (Nor would the concept of a chorus unto itself, unhinged from the broader artistic and political systems in which it participated, have made much sense to contemporary writers or audiences.) At the very least, one should probably think more in terms of "society" or even *le peuple*, given that the term *chœur* generally referred not simply to a group of singers but also to the dancers who shared the stage with them (for a broader consideration of what might count as *le peuple*, see Kintzler 2007). Indeed, so mutually imbricated were choral singing and dancing in this repertory that figuring out when the chorus sang and when the dancers danced in any one number marked *chœur* has formed a virtual cottage industry of musicological analysis (on this question, see, among many, Harris-Warrick and Marsh 1994).

All the same, the importance of the chorus (broadly conceived) to this repertory is hard to overstate, both in comparison to contemporary Italian opera as well as to the music accorded the soloists. Put bluntly: "Societies in French opera...get the richest music" (Harris-Warrick 2007: 53). Not only was the chorus unbound by the strict rhythmic patterns that dictated the soloists' declamations, but its music was also accompanied by the rhythms and literal presence of dance, as well as the full orchestra, often in elaborate and lengthy numbers that formed the pillars of the opera's formal structures (Jacobshagen 1997). It is precisely these elements, particularly heard in contrast to the relative austerity of the soloists' music, that most obviously separate *tragédie lyrique* from mere *tragédie*. And since French spoken theater was itself focused on the same classical and mythological subjects as contemporary operas, one of the main tasks of constructing an opera libretto was the regular and sustained inclusion of these choral/dance *divertissements* that provided scenic and musical richness. In Catherine Kintzler's wonderful metaphor: "The librettists of musical tragedy use the same keyboard, so to speak, as do stage dramatists, but they push a kind of 'shift' key which introduces another world, a world of marvels" (Kintzler 2007: 74).

It was a "shift key" that librettists pushed with some frequency, resulting in scenes such as the elaborate celebrations for "the different peoples of Greece" in the last act of Lully's *Alceste*, the panic scene (replete with an earthquake and tidal wave) in Rameau's *Les Boréades*, or the peace-pipe ceremony in his *Les Indes galantes*. The list is long and impressive. But to focus on spectacle alone as the chorus's sole operatic function in *ancien régime* opera, or—more pointedly—to situate spectacle in a zero-sum game in opposition to dramatic function, is to import a grossly anachronistic aesthetic. Such a focus also perpetuates the reductive claim that this repertory consists only of a "universe of total mastery" in which the entire operatic arsenal (allegorical plot, scenery, danced and sung spectacle) served no function other than dishing out lavish helpings of royalist propaganda (the phrase is Downing Thomas's, although his frustration is shared by many; see Thomas 2002: 127).

Hence many recent writers have begun to emphasize that the chorus's contribution was not simply its physical and vocal presence per se, but also its ability, through that presence, to introduce contrasting registers of human society into the otherwise narrowly elite roster of mythological heroes and heroines. Kintzler, for instance, has pointed out that the "enchanted pastoral" provided an entrée for the "middle ranks of humanity" such as shepherds to find a place on the stage, just as the chorus served a "suspensive function" by embodying the codes of propriety and social order to which the hero must ultimately prove his loyalty by the end of the drama. By contrast, a chorus of narrow-minded confidants can provide a useful foil for the superhuman values of the principles: "committed to a vulgar point of view that contrasts with that of their masters, they do not understand heroism and thereby call attention to it" (Kintzler 2007: 78). As the embodiment of an established order (good or bad), the onstage society does not decorate the *tragédie lyrique* so much as it provides one of its central forces.

Nor should we forget that the chorus in Lully and Rameau can also serve that most basic function of simple commentary and reflection. Consider, for instance, the moment in Act II of *Armide* when the chorus of "bergers et bergères heroïques" laments Renaud's dogged resistance to Armide's charms: "Ah! What error! What folly! / Not to enjoy life! / It is for games and love / that we were given beautiful days."[2] Following a brief orchestral introduction, Lully's setting of this text is in many ways a textbook moment of choral commentary, taken straight from an Attic playbook. The first half of the text is reaction, set to short, almost breathless phrases, as the shepherds take in the sad sight of Renaud's stubbornness. The second half then steps back to reflect on the situation. The chorus sings almost entirely in root-position chords, as if to underscore the solidity of its reflections, and near homophony, to demonstrate its unanimity. This emphatically rooted quality of the chorus's music is nicely offset by scoring for treble voices alone; along with the soothing prelude that surrounds the chorus, as Renaud falls asleep and is subsequently enchanted by the nymphs in Armide's employ, it is a beguiling moment (for a sense of who would have sung what in this scene, see Rosow 1987).

As well it should be, though, for as Rebecca Harris-Warrick has pointed out, the opera relies on "mechanisms of displacement" whereby "Armide's seductiveness gets activated more through the singing and dancing bodies of her followers than it does through her own utterances" (Harris-Warrick 2007: 66). This displacement has roots both in the generic traditions of choral spectacle and pastoral enchantment and in the political requirements of theatrical representation. After all, Armide's seductive allure is hardly the basis for an allegory of heroic rule, not only because she herself is no model of noble self-control, but also because Renaud is not particularly well-suited for the role either. Seen in the context of a heroine who cannot control her passions and a hero who is dangerously subject to them (if only through trickery), *Armide*'s displacement of reflective sentiment onto the chorus provides some degree of calm and measured repose, in addition to the scenic and musical splendor that was always its métier. In stark contrast to the wavering desires and loyalties of the opera's two ostensible sovereigns, the chorus's equipoise and unanimity of sentiment are a variant on Kintzler's "suspensive" function, grounding the drama in established forms of reflection and spectacle until Renaud can finally come to his senses at the end of the opera. So conceived, it matters little whose side the chorus is actually on at any given moment; although the beautiful chorus for "bergères" is actually sung by demons that Armide has momentarily transformed into creatures more befitting a scene of pastoral beauty, the function of the chorus—which frames Armide's seduction in terms of an unobjectionable truism about love—remains the same. The fact that the chorus of disguised demons functions, looks, and sounds much like any other chorus in Lully's operas is precisely the point, particularly in its implicit parallel between Renaud and the audience: both are susceptible to sway of the *divertissement*.

Verisimilitude and the Aesthetics of Passion

A century later, by contrast, it did matter whose side the chorus was on, and it did matter whether a chorus was singing as "itself" or, in the case of our *Armide* example, had assumed another identity for the sake of effect. At issue, in fact, was effect itself, the growing gap between the official aims of *ancien régime* opera and what audiences actually seemed to take away from it. To return briefly to the *Armide* example, for instance, we might momentarily take leave of the chorus to note that it was Armide's passionate "Enfin il est en ma puissance," and not an example of Renaud's heroism, that quickly became the opera's iconic moment. Part of this discrepancy lies with Renaud, who as Downing Thomas has noted is particularly illustrative of the disparity in Lully between the "peerless hero of the prologue and the problematic and threadbare figures of male glory" that subsequently appear in the operas (Thomas 2002: 99). But if Renaud lacks the requisite heroism to sustain the drama, Armide is easily able to carry the entire weight of the opera's emotional trajectory. She is, as Thomas suggests, an agent of the operatic sublime, and as such she is at the vanguard of an aesthetics of passion that would guide operatic composition not only in later *ancien régime* France but well beyond it in the High Baroque and *empfindsam* aesthetics that dominated Europe for much of the eighteenth century.

This much is canonical operatic history; what is less well known is how these aesthetics of passion would affect the chorus. And yet what happened next—initially in France, the only repertory at this point historically that either composed for, or thought critically about, the opera chorus—is probably the most crucial moment in the opera chorus's evolution (one might also call it a devolution) from a crucial participant in the genre to one of the genre's most frequent, even embarrassing, lightning rods for reform. The core of the matter was verisimilitude. At its heart a plea for dramaturgical transparency and simplicity, the doctrine of *vraisemblance* called for a one-to-one correlation between the performer singing a dramatic text and the character that performer is portraying. More broadly, verisimilitude also sought to dismiss the superfluous and the rehearsed in favor of the essential and the spontaneous. This was not an easy test for the chorus to pass. Not only did it seem unlikely that a group of people would naturally utter the same sentiment at the same time, but the only way of explaining this unanimity and simultaneity of sentiment was to presume that the chorus had already rehearsed its utterances. Hence the chorus not only ran afoul of verisimilitude's demand that a single expression stem from a single character, but it also introduced a gaping temporal seam into the drama. As one writer complained in Diderot's *Encyclopédie*, "One would have to assume that [the members of the chorus] had been consulted in advance, that they had agreed on the tune and the words with which they would express their feelings about the topic of the scene, and that they could have known about it in advance" (the entry is Friedrich Melchior Grimm's, on the *poème lyrique*, translated and quoted in Betzwieser 2000: 2). By contrast, a character like Armide was ideal: during her throes of passion, it was easy to believe that Armide the performer is both experiencing and presenting the story of Armide the character in unmediated, unrehearsed "real time." No advance arrangements are necessary to coordinate Armide's story with her reactions to it; the doctrine of verisimilitude and an aesthetics of (individual) passion are virtually coterminous. But a group response was another matter, and the chorus of Lully or Rameau was not particularly well equipped to handle the challenge.

By the mid-eighteenth century, then, the use of the chorus was "out of proportion with its tenuous legitimacy in dramatic theory" (Betzwieser 2000: 2). It also turns out that the chorus was less than compelling in its onstage comportment. One often-quoted complaint from the *Encyclopédie* makes a persuasive, and humorous, case for reform: "Choruses fill the theater, and are a very agreeable spectacle; but they are left immobile in their place; one hears them say occasionally that 'the earth gives way under my foot,' that they 'perish,' etc., during which they remain calmly in place, without moving an inch" (the entry is Louis de Cahusac's, on the *chœur*, translated and quoted in Betzwieser 2000: 4). Calls for reform of the opera chorus therefore became increasingly insistent by the 1760s, fueled by both a focus on verisimilitude within works and the related insistence that, if nothing else, chorus members begin to move onstage and visually inhabit the reflective characters they were ostensibly portraying. In theory, the latter reform was the simpler of the two to enact, and it seems to have centered on Gluck; whereas Lully's Act II chorus from *Armide* would have split the duties of singing and dancing between the chorus and the dancers, Gluck's setting of the same text calls for a pantomimic *chœur dansé* in which the chorus would almost certainly have moved, if not to the same choreography as the dancers (Betzwieser 2000; Jacobshagen 1997). Indeed, Gluck's animated demonstrations during rehearsal of how a chorus might move and act onstage serve as an amusing counterweight to the equally amusing (and frequent) descriptions of the lifeless chorus that had become entrenched by midcentury (Betzwieser 2000: 28).

Verisimilitude within works, on the other hand, was harder to reform—particularly as long as the only standard for its adjudication was the ideal of one character uttering one expression as an unmediated response to the unfolding drama. But as much as the French operatic establishment was committed to dramatic verisimilitude, it was also committed to the chorus; after all, even complaints such as the one above admit that choruses are ultimately "a very agreeable spectacle." One solution, promoted by Jean-François Marmontel, provided a provisional way out of the quandary by drawing a distinction between the *chœur appris* and the *chœur impromptu*: between a chorus that would naturally be pre-rehearsed (a song of praise, or a ceremonial number) and a chorus that seemed to be uttered on the spur of the moment. In the nineteenth century the *chœur impromptu* would become the gold standard, as an unmediated expression of the people, but for the encyclopedists the idea of a spontaneous, collective utterance was simply too far-fetched; only choral scenes that essentially announced their own lack of spontaneity, and whose music was literally performed as "music" onstage, could be squared with the dramatic realism of contemporary theory. It thus fell to the *chœur appris* to fulfill the dictates of verisimilitude, and it is probably for this reason as much as it is political fealty that we have the eighteenth century to thank for so many scenes of choral ceremony (Betzwieser 2000; Jacobshagen 1997: 107–113).

The anguished discussions among Marmontel and other French critics midcentury were followed by the reforms of Gluck, whose prescriptions for a chorus that moved and acted onstage were reinforced by his works themselves, and their reintegration of the chorus into the drama (Schneider 2000). Yet as much as Gluck's reform operas were to have a palpable effect on the art form's broader contours, it is harder to say that they had as revolutionary or as lasting an impact on the chorus. For one thing, it was works such as *Iphigénie en Aulide* (most prominently) that tended to accord the chorus a greater role as a dramatic character, whereas the reform operas such as *Alceste* and *Orfeo ed Euridice* assigned the chorus its traditional task of reflective commentary—hence Mark Morris's staging of celebrity commentators for the latter work. But more important than whether choral reflection should count as a step forward or backward was the realization that it simply falls on the wrong side of Marmontel's schema: by definition, reflection can hardly aspire to the condition of the *chœur appris*. Reflection happens after an event, not in preparation for it. And while it undoubtedly provides a measure of spontaneity, it is that very spontaneity that causes collective reflection to fail the test of verisimilitude; particularly with a chorus like Morris's, made up so emphatically of individuals, the notion that this group could make the same utterance at the same time is impossible to support without a more developed concept of group identity. Such a concept would in fact come soon, with nineteenth-century nationalism. But for the time being, eighteenth-century aesthetics were hamstrung when it came to the chorus, stuck between the theoretically unimpeachable but dramatically stillborn spectacle of the *chœur appris* on the one hand and the emotionally compelling but theoretically problematic *chœur impromptu* on the other. And in this sense it is no surprise that eighteenth-century opera after Rameau failed to develop a fundamentally new conception of the chorus—and that Gluck's "reforms" essentially reinstated the chorus of Lully.

Utopian Moments

Mozart's operas mainly reflect this impasse, although they obliquely hint at some alternatives. For the most part, his choruses are familiar standbys: the polis (*Idomeneo*, *Die Zauberflöte*), cheerful peasants (*Le nozze di Figaro*, *Don Giovanni*), or conveyors of local color (*Die Entführung aus dem Serail*). Virtually all of these examples are songs of praise or thanksgiving, and they easily fit the bill of the *chœur appris*. Yet to that last category of "local color" we might also append the related but somewhat more mysterious subcategory of "sounds from elsewhere," which would encompass the men's chorus summoning Don Giovanni to hell, as well as the chipper march for offstage voices in *Così fan tutte* that announces the alleged departure and arrival of Guglielmo and Ferrando. These latter two examples are neither reflective nor dramatic (in the sense of being issued from a participating character in the drama); nor do they provide much beyond an atmospheric representation of a different locale. But it is in the very difference of that locale—somewhere else, yet close enough to be heard—that we can see in these choruses not only an extension of the scope of operatic presentation beyond the space onstage, but also the representation of that expanded space through choral voices. Both of these aspirations will recur with some intensity in nineteenth-century opera, particularly with its otherworldly (either angelic or demonic) choruses of offstage spirits and scenes of approaching armies, processions, or mobs.

The most recognizable and most important form of collective expression in Mozart is not, however, the chorus per se, but rather the ensemble. And although there are dangers in viewing the ensemble as an ersatz chorus—starting with the obvious fact that Mozart wrote choruses, too—it is also true that there are undeniable similarities between Mozart's *opera buffa* ensembles and some of the politically charged choruses of nineteenth-century opera. The most obvious example here is *Figaro*, and particularly the final scene, in which the Count is granted forgiveness not only by his beleaguered wife but in fact the entire cast of principals—which in its inclusion of all possible classes, ages, and genders comes as close as anything else in late eighteenth-century opera to presenting a social collectivity. As Mladen Dolar has suggested, this scene presents not just an interaction among individuals but also a "community growing from particular interests and inclinations and combining them to form a common harmony, without having to sacrifice them [. . .]" (Dolar 2002: 31). When the entire cast joins the Countess to sing that "tutti contenti saremo così," set to some of Mozart's most famously sublime music—an andante hymn binding all the voices in simple homophony—it is hard not to hear some sort of gesture toward collectivity that extends well beyond the generic requirements of a concluding tutti. (It should be noted, however, that this andante is probably performed too slowly in modern performances, and that a faster tempo does shake some, though certainly not all, of the hymnic feel. See Will 2007.) Dolar has even described the moment as "the emphatically condensed utopian moment of the bourgeois community, the moment of *liberté égalité fraternité*" (Dolar 2002: 40). Although its gesture is one of repetition and not generation—the "chorus" borrows the Countess's material rather than coming up with its own—one could also argue that it is precisely in assuming the subject position of the Countess, in granting itself the same musical space and the same moral authority, that Mozart's assemblage of characters makes the boldest move yet toward a kind of collective agency. This is a community that has effectively turned the tables on its ostensible ruler (the Count); to invoke Ivan Nagel's trenchant analysis of the politics behind eighteenth-century opera, we might say that this community has begun to possess its own autonomy, and as a result is in the position to grant, rather than simply receive, mercy (Nagel 1991).

Similar moments for a reflective ensemble close other Mozart operas, albeit with generally fewer characters, and in many ways these ensembles are a clear anticipation of the kind of collective moral authority that nineteenth-century opera will assign to the chorus. On the other hand, the very fact that Mozart could convincingly locate communal sentiment in an ensemble of soloists suggests that these sentiments can effectively be conveyed without a chorus—and perhaps even more convincingly, since they come from characters who have each taken a unique and traceable part in the action. The end of *Figaro* may well mark the "utopian moment of the bourgeois community," and it may do so in ways that draw heavily on both choral idioms (the hymn texture) and emerging notions of collective autonomy, but it ultimately does so without the chorus, which made its last, short appearance in the previous act. And in this sense, it is hard to avoid the suspicion that the verisimilitude debates midcentury introduced some formidable seeds of doubt about the viability of the opera chorus that have never been fully dispelled. As I have suggested, nationalism will certainly offer one solution to the question of a chorus's identity, and thereby secure the source and authority of choral sentiment. Yet it is precisely the terms of that solution, the assumption that a chorus cannot serve its traditional role of reflective contemplation without a strenuously advertised grounding in a concrete identity, that reveal the underlying quandary: a chorus could no longer be "simply" a chorus. It had become, perhaps permanently, an object of reform and suspicion.

A Collective Individuality?

Such was the sorry state of the chorus of the late eighteenth century—a beset and decaying remnant of its seventeenth-century predecessor—that one recent critic could even claim that in the nineteenth century "a new character emerged on to the operatic stage: the chorus" (Rutherford 2006: 1). Across a wide spectrum of repertory, ranging from *Les Huguenots* to *Boris Godunov*, and *Die Meistersinger von Nürnberg* to *Macbeth*, the nineteenth-century chorus is indeed a new character insofar as its explicitly political (national, regional, or confessional) credentials as the voice of "the people," together with its expanded proportions, provided the opera chorus with a moral and sonic authority it had never before possessed. And not only did the chorus benefit from this new infusion of a nameable personality, but the politics of identity also benefited from the newly enlivened chorus as well. Yet as mutually beneficial as this new choral ideal may have been, its "birth" was largely one of happenstance. Regardless of whether the nineteenth-century chorus should be considered something entirely new or simply a reworked version of an older model (Opera Chorus 2.0, as it were), one could hardly make the claim that the various political forces providing this new identity were themselves products of, or answers to, the verisimilitude debates in mid-eighteenth-century France; dramatic realism did not bring about the French Revolution. Rather, the nineteenth-century opera chorus was, for the most part, the offspring of an accidental if fortunate convergence between political movements in need of a public face (and voice) and an artistic institution in need of a dramaturgical upgrade.

In the utter transparency of its provenance—representing Huguenots, gypsies, Scottish exiles, and so forth—the standard opera chorus of the nineteenth century is undoubtedly the easiest of any period to understand dramatically, and it is perhaps not coincidental that it is also the easiest to understand musically as well, with its steady diet of unison melodies, folk tunes (both real and imagined), and an almost overbearing aura of homespun goodness. All the same, however, this insistent grounding of the chorus in a monolithic communal identity prompted an almost immediate theoretical backlash. Giuseppe Mazzini, the Italian politician, famously demanded in 1836 a "collective individuality" of the opera chorus in place of its overweening homogeneity; instead of all those unison choruses, he sought more variety and spontaneity to reflect the vitality of the people themselves (Mazzini 2004). Across the Alps, Richard Wagner soon made a similar claim in his 1851 *Oper und Drama*, charging not only that the opera chorus amounted to little more than musical scenery, but more importantly that no amount of reform could ever change the situation; the opera chorus "is only vital and convincing in drama when it is completely dispossessed of its trivial pronouncements *en masse*. A mass can never interest, only merely astound, us: only exactly differentiated individuals can captivate our sympathies" (Wagner 1888a: 162). Appropriating Shakespeare's one-person choruses as a predecessor in his fight against the overcrowded stage, Wagner promised not only to pare down the opera chorus but in fact to banish it entirely (Wagner 1888b). Of course, Wagner was not successful in his crusade to rid the stage of the chorus, as a quick glance through his own oeuvre reveals. This failure is hardly surprising, however, since an equally quick glance through his own essays makes clear how crucial the notion of *das Volk* was to his program of artistic and political renewal. Although Wagner insisted that *das Volk* should take its rightful place as spectators of the music drama, and not participants in it, he was also rarely capable of forgoing the satisfaction of staging a chorus that fulfilled his political needs (Minor 2005).

Three Cases of *Chœur Impromptu*: The Good Citizens of Nuremberg, Valladolid, and Moscow

Consider *Die Meistersinger*, whose enormous assemblage of Nuremberg citizens singing the praises of Hans Sachs at the work's close serves as a not particularly subtle metaphor for the kind of reception Wagner hoped his own works and political program might engender. In theory, this monumental scene should enjoy at least partial immunity against the charge of empty spectacle, since it so strenuously provides the chorus with an identity (*das Volk*, though more specifically the citizens of Nuremberg serving as a proxy for Germans in general), and Wagner even goes to great lengths to highlight individual reactions to the song contest. And yet the cumulative effect, particularly at the end of the opera, is nothing other than monumental homogeneity. Of course, that is exactly the point of nineteenth-century nationalist rhetoric—an organic and indivisible populace, preferably large and formidable—but as *Die Meistersinger* shows, the aim of staging a national community does not go very far in guarding against choral spectacle; in fact, it would seem to encourage it. Named spectacle is still spectacle all the same.

If the chorus that ends *Die Meistersinger* reinstates the very sort of overwhelming choral mass that Wagner had promised to dissolve, the scene for the Nuremberg guilds on the festival meadow might seem to work in the opposite direction, by providing some internal differentiation among the chorus—in Mazzini's words, a "collective individuality." Yet the scene, in which the guilds' incessant bickering over their own importance is set to some of the most embarrassingly banal music in Wagner's entire oeuvre, is not only difficult to stage convincingly. (Most recently, Wagner's great-granddaughter Katharina—together with dramaturge Robert Sollich—simply replaced the scene with a naughty burlesque; the guilds are mercifully absent, although the music and text remain unchanged, as is house policy. See Wagner 2009 DVD.) It also seems to go nowhere, since the laborious distinctions that Wagner attempts to introduce within his chorus are immediately forgotten the moment Hans Sachs steps onstage and the monumental crowd is once more reinstated. *Das Volk*, after all, is singular (as, notably, are *le peuple* and *il popolo*), and it is difficult to subdivide a rhetorical category whose homogeneity was its chief attraction to begin with. Indeed, in both cases—the painfully condescending "quarrel" among the Nuremberg guilds, and the huge crowd scene ending the opera—we can see the price that the chorus paid for its admission back onto the operatic stage. It now has an identity, an official badge conferring sufficient credentials to pass verisimilar muster, but it is precisely this transparency that also advertises the chorus's own tethers. And in no way is this kind of chorus limited to Wagner; the famous line from *H.M.S. Pinafore*—"I know the value of a kindly chorus"—could refer to any number of opera choruses from the nineteenth century, most of which primarily offer up their own, highly overdetermined, voices in praise of someone else, with little regard to the fact that the puppet strings are so visibly on display (Gossett 1996: 43–45).

And yet if we view some opera choruses diachronically rather than synchronically—that is, through their experiences and proclamations over the course of the drama, as opposed to their strictly homogeneous identity at one given moment—it is also evident that the nineteenth century was capable of providing some measure of heterogeneity to its chorus, by allowing it to change its mind. To be sure, this linear heterogeneity is not quite the vertical "collective individuality" Mazzini had requested, but it does at least give some sense that the chorus could be a sentient and alert communal presence—if also a capricious one. Hagen's minions in *Götterdämmerung* are one example, as they react to his killing of Siegfried, but far stronger cases can be made for *Don Carlos* (to varying degrees in both versions) and *Boris Godunov* (in its later version). In the Verdi, the turning point is the auto-da-fé scene, in which the Spanish people initially sing in support of the gruesome display of state power, but later join the Flemish deputies to oppose the king. As James Parakilas has noted, the crowd's subsequent return to the opening music, "recrossing the lines of power and turning their backs on the sympathies they have just evoked," illustrates not only the coercive powers of the state but also the people's germinal resistance to it (Parakilas 1992: 184). The effect is even stronger in the original, Parisian version of the opera, in which the people subsequently form a mob in order to release Carlos from prison, but are then rebuffed, and thus perform yet another volte-face by pledging allegiance to the church and the king once again. *Boris Godunov* goes a step further in its vertiginous swings of public opinion: The chorus, which initially pledges its utmost, and abject, devotion to Boris at the beginning of the opera, returns at the end in the 1872 revision as a mob that cruelly harasses one of Boris's boyars before pledging its new devotion to the Pretender. Moreover, the opening scene is a vast expansion of the original Pushkin, whereas the latter scene is entirely absent from it; clearly the depiction of a people veering from servitude to cockiness, and questions about the crowd's ability to function as a rational and autonomous actor, took on a signal importance in the opera's revisions (Kowal-Wolk 1992: 86–110).

All three of these cases are witness to the nineteenth-century triumph of the *chœur impromptu*—and particularly *Don Carlos* and *Boris Godunov*, which thematize a progression from the prepackaged *chœur appris* (the songs of praise with which the auto-da-fé and coronation scenes begin) to the spontaneous *chœur impromptu*. The valence of this progression is not always positive—Mussorgsky's opera is certainly not an optimistic portrayal of communal wisdom—but in both cases the chorus provides a space for the operas to explore the potential and the danger of a collective that is learning to supplement servitude with agency. This transition has an obvious nationalist appeal, regardless of whether communal autonomy or simply better autocracy is the intended message, and thus it is hardly a surprise that the nineteenth-century opera chorus has figured prominently in nationalist and political movements, as well as the historiography surrounding them. "Va, pensiero" from *Nabucco* is the most famous example, although scholars continue to disagree on whether this chorus's nearly mythic status—written for Hebrew slaves, but apparently understood by Risorgimento patriots as a stand-in for Italian nationalists—accrued immediately or only later in the century (Parker 1997; Smart 2004). *Guillaume Tell*, which functions much the same way for the lore of the 1830 revolution in Paris as *Nabucco* does for that of the Risorgimento, has similarly generated both irresistible anecdotes as well as scholarly skepticism; in the case of the Rossini, Benjamin Walton has suggested that for much of the opera the chorus is hardly a revolutionary agent yearning to control its own destiny, but in fact a relatively passive community that is content to rely on God or Tell to solve its problems (Walton 2007).

The Politics of Verisimilitude

Yet if the importance of the opera chorus as either progenitor or reflection of nineteenth-century political movements may at times have been overstated, it is nonetheless clear that chorus *members* were themselves highly suspect politically. Susan Rutherford has uncovered *rapporti serali* from the Teatro Regio in Parma indicating that the political affiliations of the house's chorus members were continually monitored, with help of the police, and in fact the chorus had to swear an oath of allegiance—to God, the Spanish Infanta, and his heirs—after the failed 1848 revolutions. To be sure, not all the concerns recorded in the *rapporti* were political; one especially enjoyable entry involves a chorus member who, having neglected to leave the stage in time, "provided an unexpected third member for the entombing of Radames and Aida and was later fined for making 'useless jokes' during their final touching duet." But as Rutherford suggests, scrutinizing the political persuasions of chorus members was one of the more serious concerns for the state as far as the opera house was concerned, particularly since it was the chorus who was given those very numbers ("Va, pensiero," or "O Signore dal tetto natio" in *I Lombardi*) that could so easily be understood as thinly veiled political allegories (Rutherford 2006: 4–6). And this underlying unease with the chorus's own political sympathies would seem to point to a fear that its task of representing the people could easily tip over into simply *being* the people if its members themselves shared revolutionary sentiments—something we might call verisimilitude with a vengeance. Along these lines, Philip Gossett has recently shown that the patriotic choruses composed after the *cinque giornate* in March 1848, when Milan was freed from Austrian censorship, make explicit the sentiments that had earlier been cloaked in metaphor. In other words, stripping away the veneer of operatic representation made clear that that veneer had not been particularly thick to start with. The non-operatic, uncensored choruses seem retroactively to confirm the revolutionary undercurrent of their operatic predecessors—so much so that, following the reinstatement of Austrian rule, censorship of earlier opera choruses became stricter than it was before 1848 (Gossett 2007).

There is, however, an underlying similarity between the choruses with veiled revolutionary sentiments (regardless of when, or how often, they were actually mobilized for political or historiographical aims) and the choruses that simply proclaim allegiance to their ruler: Both are "kindly" in their own way. Both are ultimately what Nietzsche would call the "serving chorus," providing a mouthpiece for someone, or something, else (Nietzsche 1967: 65). In fact, it would be difficult to find a nineteenth-century chorus whose chief task was *not* a kind of political or dramaturgical servitude. The unnamed chorus in *Fidelio* that suddenly appears out of nowhere at the opera's end to celebrate the happy turn of events; the chorus at the beginning of *La traviata* that, "flushed" from its nonstop partying, is employed to represent the symptoms of Violetta's dissolute ways (Groos 1995: 242); the *bel canto* choruses that can be trusted to provide arpeggios or other forms of chordal support beneath a soloist's cabaletta; even the spectacular French operatic chorus of the nineteenth century that, to quote Parakilas's apt formulation, "puts the 'grand' in grand opera" (2003: 76)—in all of these cases it is hard to avoid the suspicion that the chorus has been defined solely through its function, its potential to supply scenic, sonic, or political backup. As much as it may complicate certain narratives about the chorus's importance—including those cited approvingly in the preceding paragraph—it is also not unsurprising that Luigi Torchi could write of Verdi's operas, on the occasion of the composer's death, that "[t]he chorus is a vulgar instrument of sonority, an apparatus of effect and, as such, intervenes in opera merely to provide alternate effects" (Torchi 1901: 312, quoted in Engelhardt 1988: 26).[3] After all, it is only as an "instrument" or "apparatus," even a highly sympathetic one, that the chorus could be called upon to serve so many functions in the first place. If the very same chorus at the Paris Opéra that populated *ancien régime* opera could, just months later, be used to populate revolutionary works—and what is more, to serve as the very embodiment of their revolutionary principles—the question is not whether the opera chorus of the long nineteenth century served a political purpose, but rather whether it ever served its *own* purpose (Parakilas 2003: 77; Bartlet 1992). Yet what would that purpose be? It is not an easy question to answer, and the difficulty in formulating a response goes a long way toward explaining the attraction that the chorus held for so many composers, politicians, and national publics.

Unruly Mobs

The preceding argument—that by the nineteenth century the opera chorus was "kindly" *by definition*, and did not so much come into its own, but rather someone else's own—holds for most twentieth-century opera as well. Whatever privations the new century may have inflicted on its actual populations, the opera stage seems to have maintained an unending supply of virtuous simple folk, stolid burghers, eager revolutionaries, and angry mobs to help make political or dramaturgical points. Prokofiev's *War and Peace* is a good example of this essentially nineteenth-century use of the chorus, with its large number of soldiers and patriots ready at any turn—and there are many—to sing another hymn to Mother Russia. (Indeed, the story of Prokofiev's revisions to the opera is largely the story of his adding more choral numbers.) Glass's *Satyagraha* broadens the scope a bit more, with the chorus portraying both a white mob as well as the nonviolent participants of the "March of Five Thousand," but here, too, the use of the chorus to embody certain elements or potentials of modern society—one very bad, and one very good—is entirely in keeping with the mobs and the virtuous downtrodden of nineteenth-century opera.

Yet if we pursue the comparison of mobs in particular, we can see some important differences in the twentieth century. In *Simon Boccanegra*, to take a classical example from the nineteenth century, the rioting plebians are calmed by Boccanegra, even to the point of joining him in a plea for peace; good leaders, it is shown, can create good citizens (see, e.g., Gossett 1996). But looking at many later examples, even just in the first decade of the new century, we can see that the mob is no longer an entity whose primary goal onstage is to illustrate the baleful but reversible effects of bad leadership. Rather, the mob has become a violent and primitive life force, the manifestation of an unconscious and irrational herd instinct. In Zemlinsky's *Der Traumgörge*, for instance, the mob is not simply an unchecked force that just needs checking; the whole point is that it cannot be checked, at least for long (Minor 2009). Moreover, the mob cannot be easily separated from the principals: Görge, the main character, does defend himself and his love interest from the mob, but he had himself *joined* the mob just one scene earlier. In fact, much of early-twentieth-century opera seems deeply concerned not only with the eruptions of mob violence, but the very attraction of that violence. The lynch mob in *La fanciulla del West*, the bloodthirsty crowd in *Turandot*, the aggressively nasty chorus of townspeople in d'Albert's *Tiefland*, and the peasant mob in *Mathis der Maler* are all undoubtedly portrayed in a negative light, but it is a light that also illuminates the appeal of that crowd to the main characters who are tempted (often with success) to join its ranks or support its demands. In a sense, we might say that a nineteenth-century investment in the value and appeal of collective sentiment has joined forces with a twentieth-century insistence on the violent irrationality of that sentiment. And not surprisingly, corralling these forces becomes one of the goals of operatic leadership. *Turandot*, for instance, would seem to be a textbook case of the investment in, and manipulation of, the chorus's desire for violent spectacle—leading some recent commentators to claim that Puccini's work "delivers opera to fascism" (Steinberg and Stewart-Steinberg 2007: 268).

This operatic exploration of crowd psychology has obvious and legible roots in contemporary politics, in particular the simultaneous fear of, and desire for, mass revolution in the first few decades of the century. In this sense the opera chorus was an insistently contemporary figure. But especially in the twentieth century, the chorus was also a useful emblem of the past, above all the religious past. In both Messiaen's *Saint François d'Assise* and Pfitzner's *Palestrina*, for instance, the chorus can provide a sonic and visual representation of divine inspiration or imprimatur—in the Messiaen, the hummed major triad accompanying Francis's foretaste of heaven, and in Pfitzner's opera the chorus of angels that helps provide material for Palestrina's triumphant mass setting. Alternately, and perhaps more reflective of the twentieth century's intensely ambivalent relationship to both religious doctrine as well as the past more generally, are operas in which the chorus embodies both a religious and aesthetic conservatism and a more modern, and frequently secular, alternative. Szymanowski's *King Roger*, for instance, regularly employs the chorus to depict Byzantine religious rituals as well as danced Dionysian ecstasy. By contrast, *Moses und Aron* reverses the terms: it juxtaposes rigorously modern counterpoint with an elaborate danced chorus of the golden calf—complete with rape, sacrifice, and suicide—that depicts not only of a kind of ancient religious ceremony but also quite transparently the inclination toward mass violence that would soon grip Schoenberg's Germany, and that had been so frequently anticipated by the early-twentieth-century operatic mob.

The Complications of Spectatorship

Moses und Aron is not, however, merely concerned with Dionysian revelry, and if we look elsewhere in the opera we can also see a use of the chorus that is not only more experimental in general, but also begins to move outside the kind of representational and verisimilar stranglehold that has defined the chorus for much of its operatic career. The chorus that sings as the burning bush, for instance, is of interest both for its stylistic innovation—a speaking chorus—as well as its utter disregard for verisimilitude. And this resolutely non-verisimilar use of the chorus is all the more notable because it is juxtaposed, in the same work, with the much more traditional choruses of the dance of the golden calf and the lamenting Israelites—a juxtaposition that Schoenberg also explored in *Die glückliche Hand*, with its chorus that alternately expresses communal reflection and the protagonist's own consciousness. Milhaud's *Christophe Colomb* is probably the most thoroughgoing in its exploration of a chorus that is both part of the action and part reflective outsider. Moreover, especially in an opera that is both allegorical and non-chronological, the work's combination of representational and reflective choruses, choral support for the narrator, and spoken and wordless choruses makes it difficult to draw any clear distinction between actor and spectator, contemporary and descendent, and verisimilar or abstract utterance. *Intolleranza 1960* goes a step further, dissolving many of the chorus's texts into isolated syllables, but its most notable and notorious innovation is Nono's use of loudspeakers, which broadcast the chorus into the auditorium in a way that seems to erase an easy distinction between chorus and audience—a distinction that, given the work's scathing critique of postwar Europe, many would have preferred to leave intact. (At one point, the chorus steps back to ask the audience: "Are you accomplices with the herd"?)

Strictly speaking, such a connection between chorus and audience does not reinstate verisimilitude. But it does, once again, attempt to give a name to the chorus, to assign it an identity of sorts, and in that sense it is not so far removed from the nineteenth-century choruses that were employed to promote a particular point of view. The difference, rather, is the extent and the bite of the politics involved. Nono's opera was followed by some infamous Verdi stagings in Germany that took a similar tack in employing the chorus to deliver their political critiques; Hans Neuenfels's 1981 production of *Aida* in Frankfurt, for instance, was a notable *succès de scandale* in its use of an onstage chorus that was explicitly intended to mirror the audience, and even respond to it, during some of the opera's most notorious Orientalist fantasies (Weber 1994; for an account of this staging, together with others by Neuenfels and Peter Konwitschny, see Risi 2002). Nono's and Neuenfels's pointed analogy—that spectatorship *of* opera bears an uncomfortable likeness to spectatorship *within* opera, to all those choruses who cheer on or simply tolerate acts of violence—quickly became a cliché, albeit a generally effective one, in critically ambitious opera stagings in the last several decades. But perhaps we can see its rapid spread as a renewed attempt to reinstate the idea of the chorus, and its cousin in the audience, as both reflection and arbitrator of communal morality. Certainly the end of Zimmermann's *Die Soldaten*, with its extended choral cry accompanying images of the atom bomb, would seem to make a similar point in expanding the chorus's representational role beyond verisimilar rigidity (Poizat 1992: 91). And in this sense we might see the last few decades as a return of sorts: not, *pace* Mark Morris, to the chorus as bloated, costumed spectacle, but to that most ancient of choruses, one that represents nothing less than humanity itself.

See also: Politics, Verisimilitude, Musical Dramaturgy

Notes

1. For a detailed look at the breaks and continuities between madrigal and opera, and between the late Renaissance and the early Baroque, see Calcagno 2012.
2. "Ah ! Quelle erreur ! Quelle folie ! /De ne pas jouir de la vie ! /C'est aux jeux, c'est aux amours, /Qu'il faut donner les beaux jours."
3. "Il coro è un volgare strumento di sonorità, un apparato di effetto è, come tale, interviene nell'opera per il bisogno di alternare effetti."

Bibliography

Bartlet, M. Elizabeth C. 1992. "The New Repertory at the Opéra during the Reign of Terror: Revolutionary Rhetoric and Operatic Consequences." In *Music and the French Revolution*, edited by Malcom Boyd, 107–156. Cambridge: Cambridge University Press.

Betzwieser, Thomas. 2000. "Musical Setting and Scenic Movement: Chorus and chœur dansé in Eighteenth-Century Parisian Opéra." *Cambridge Opera Journal* 12/1: 1–28.

Calcagno, Mauro. 2012. *From Madrigal to Opera: Performing the Self in Early Modern Italy*. Berkeley and Los Angeles: University of California Press.

Dolar, Mladen. 2002. "If Music Be the Food of Love." In Slavoj Žižek and Mladen Dolar, *Opera's Second Death*, 1–102. New York: Routledge.

Engelhardt, Markus. 1988. *Die Chöre in den Frühen Opern Giuseppe Verdis*. Tutzing: Hans Schneider.

Gossett, Philip. 2007. "'Edizioni distrutte' and the Significance of Operatic Choruses during the Risorgimento." In Johnson et al. 2007, 181–243.

——. 1990. "Becoming a Citizen: The Chorus in *Risorgimento* Opera." *Cambridge Opera Journal* 2/1: 41–64.

Groos, Arthur. 1995. "'TB Sheets': Love and Disease in *La traviata*." *Cambridge Opera Journal* 7/3: 233–260.

Grout, Donald Jay. 1963. "The Chorus in Early Opera." In *Festschrift Friedrich Blume. Zum 70. Geburtstag*, edited by Anna Amalie Abert and Wilhelm Pfannkuch, 151–161. Kassel: Bärenreiter.

Harris-Warrick, Rebecca. 2007. "Lully's On-Stage Societies." In Johnson et al. 2007, 53–71.

——. 1994. "Magnificence in Motion: Stage Musicians in Lully's Ballets and Operas." *Cambridge Opera Journal* 6/3: 189–203.

——, and Carol G. Marsh, 1994. *Musical Theatre at the Court of Louis XIV: 'Le Mariage de la Grosse Cathos.'* Cambridge: Cambridge University Press.

Jacobshagen, Arnold. 1997. *Der Chor in der französischen Oper des späten Ancien régime*. Frankfurt: Peter Lang.

Johnson, Victoria, Jane F. Fulcher, and Thomas Ertman, eds. 2007. *Opera and Society in Italy and France from Monteverdi to Bourdieu*. Cambridge: Cambridge University Press.

Kintzler, Catherine. 2007. "Representations of le *peuple* in French Opera, 1673–1764." In Johnson et al. 2007, 72–86.

Kowal-Wolk, Larissa. 1992. *Die Huldigungschöre in russischen Opern des 19. Jahrhunderts*. Frankfurt: Peter Lang.

Mazzini, Giuseppe. 2004. *Giuseppe Mazzini's 'Philosophy of Music' (1836): Envisioning a Social Opera*, translated by Emilie Ashurst Venturi, edited and annotated by Franco Sciannameo. Lewiston, NY: Edwin Mellon.

Metropolitan Opera. 2012. Online. Available: http://metoperafamily.org/metopera/_img/news/contest.main.jpg (accessed January 6, 2009).

Minor, Ryan. 2009. "Zemlinsky und das Kollektiv." In *Alexander von Zemlinsky und die Moderne*, edited by Katharina John, 54–59. Berlin: Nicolaische Verlagsbuchhandlung.

——. 2005. "Wagner's Last Chorus: Consecrating Space and Spectatorship in *Parsifal*." *Cambridge Opera Journal* 17/1: 1–36.

Nagel, Ivan. 1991. *Autonomy and Mercy: Reflections on Mozart's Operas*, translated by Marion Faber and Ivan Nagel. Cambridge, MA: Harvard University Press.

Nietzsche, Friedrich. 1967. *The Birth of Tragedy*, translated by Walter Kaufmann. New York: Vintage.

Parakilas, James. 2003. "The Chorus." In *The Cambridge Companion to Grand Opera*, edited by David Charlton, 76–92. Cambridge: Cambridge University Press.

——. 1992. "Political Representation and the Chorus in Nineteenth-Century Opera." *19th-Century Music* 16/2: 181–202.

Parker, Roger. 1997. "'Va pensiero' and the Insidious Mastery of Song." In *Leonora's Last Act: Essays in Verdian Discourse*, 20–41. Princeton, NJ: Princeton University Press.

Poizat, Michel. 1992. *The Angel's Cry: Beyond the Pleasure Principle in Opera*, translated by Arthur Denner. Ithaca, NY: Cornell University Press.

Risi, Clemens. 2002. "Shedding Light on the Audience: Hans Neuenfels and Peter Konwitschny Stage Verdi (and Verdians)." *Cambridge Opera Journal* 14/1–2: 201–210.

Rosow, Lois. "Performing a Choral Dialogue by Lully." *Early Music* 15/3: 325–335.

Ross, Alex. 2007. "Underworld," *The New Yorker* (May 21). Online. Available: http://www.newyorker.com/arts/critics/musical/2007/05/21/070521crmu_music_ross (accessed February 6, 2014).

Rutherford, Susan. 2006. "'Crime and Punishment': Tales of the Opera Chorus in Nineteenth-Century Parma." *Nineteenth Century Theatre & Film* 33/2: 1–11.

Schneider, Herbert. 2000. "Gluck and Lully." In *Lully Studies*, edited by John Hajdu Heyer, 243–271. Cambridge: Cambridge University Press.

Sheek, Charles. 2009. "Dance in *Orfeo*." In *Playbill*. The Metropolitan Opera. Program book for the opera (January 9): 40–41.

Smart, Mary Ann. 2004. "Verdi, Italian Romanticism, and the Risorgimento." In *The Cambridge Companion to Verdi*, edited by Scott L. Balthazar, 29–45. Cambridge: Cambridge University Press.

Steinberg, Michael P., and Suzanne Stewart-Steinberg. 2007. "Fascism and the Operatic Unconscious." In Johnson et al. 2007, 267–288.

Thomas, Downing. 2002. *Aesthetics of Opera in the Ancien Régime, 1647–1785*. Cambridge: Cambridge University Press.

Torchi, Luigi. 1901. "Arte contemporanea: L'opera di Giuseppe Verdi e i suoi caratteri principali." *Rivista musicale italiana* 8: 279–325.

Wagner, Richard. 2009. *Die Meistersinger von Nürnberg*. Bayreuther Festspiele, directed by Katharina Wagner with dramaturgy by Robert Sollich. United Motion, BF Medien DVD BF1231978.

——. 1888a. *Oper und Drama*. In *Gesammelte Schriften und Dichtungen* [*GSD*]. IV. Leipzig: Fritzsch.

——. 1888b. "Über Schauspieler und Sänger." In *GSD* IX: 189–274.

Walton, Benjamin. 2007. *Rossini in Restoration Paris: The Sound of Modern Life*. Cambridge: Cambridge University Press.

Weber, Samuel. 1994. "Taking Place: Toward a Theater of Dislocation." In *Opera Through Other Eyes*, edited by David Levin, 107–146. Stanford, CA: Stanford University Press.

Will, Richard. 2007. "The Ambivalence of Mozart's Countess." In *Music, Libraries, Scholarship: Essays in Honor of Lenore Coral*, edited by James Cassaro, 31–53. Madison, WI: A-R Editions.

CHAPTER 22

THE ORCHESTRA

ALESSANDRO DI PROFIO

TRANSLATED BY JULIA GRELLA O'CONNELL

INSTITUTIONS AND TRADITIONS

THE historiography of music has long overlooked, if not completely ignored, the opera orchestra, neglecting such basic matters as the placement of musicians in physical space, the division of musicians' roles into core members of the orchestra and players hired on an as-needed basis, the acoustic properties of the concert hall, and the position of the conductor (on the orchestra in general, see Mahling and Rösing 1997: 835–852). Recently, however, scholarly teams such as John Spitzer and Neil Zaslaw (2004) and Niels Martin Jensen and Franco Piperno (2008) have begun to adopt this more global approach to the study of the opera orchestra.

The post–World War II orchestra, internationalized and founded on an order established in the 1870s, is in fact the product of a long process of transformation that has brought many disparities into conformity but also fails to explain many other differences among orchestras, including those that concern performance spaces—church, theater, or concert hall—sometimes in the same city and even within the same institution. For this reason, it is inaccurate to speak of *the* "Mozart orchestra" (no less of *the* "Verdi orchestra"). There were distinct differences not only between the orchestra of the Regio Ducale of Milan (which presented the premieres of Mozart's *Mitridate, re di Ponto* in 1770 and *Ascanio in Alba* in 1771), and that of Munich (which presented *Idomeneo* in 1781), but even between the orchestras of the two theaters that hosted the 1787 premiere (National Theatre, Prague) and the 1788 revival (Burgtheater, Vienna) of *Don Giovanni*, despite their geographic proximity and the short time elapsed between the two productions. As Dexter Edge has shown, for example, the Act II trombone parts in Mozart's autograph score were suppressed in Vienna (1992: 77–78). Mozart also composed to suit the assets of his available performers. While he tailored vocal lines to individual singers, "to fit [...] as perfectly as a well-made suit of clothes," as he wrote to his father on February 28, 1778 (Anderson 1938: II: 736; Bauer and Deutsch 1962–1975: II: 304), he also extended this compositional principle to the instrumental components of his operas (Zaslaw 1992: 200). There were variables, however. Singers were, essentially, the movable parts of a specific production and traveled from one season to the next, but orchestral players in a given city were unchanging, hired permanently within their cities. Change on that front, moreover, could generate unrest, even as late as 1870–1871, when the recruitment of Bolognese musicians to the orchestra of La Scala caused a commotion (see Rostagno 2002b: 186). Orchestras were not entirely dependent upon the skills of any individual musician (though the case of the Viennese clarinetist Anton Stadler, for whom Mozart composed his clarinet concerto and quintet, is an exception), but rather upon local traditions, which proved themselves capable of steering both the compositional gesture and its execution.

While these traditions persisted, their conservative effects were also counterbalanced by several diverse factors: (a) Opera, and in particular Italian opera, was an export in most cities, and as such demanded international standards, including those for orchestral playing. (b) In the nineteenth century, conductors began to travel from city to city: Gasparo Spontini, for instance, divided his activities between Paris and Berlin, after an earlier, Italian phase; Hans von Bülow's early career was in Italy; and Emanuele Muzio went to the United States. Eventually conductors, like vocal soloists, went on tour, as was the case with Arturo Toscanini. (c) Even orchestras themselves began to go on tour: the orchestra of La Scala, for example, participated in the 1878 World's Fair at the Trocadero in Paris. (d) Finally, sound reproduction, first with the advent of radio and then with the popularity of recordings, accelerated and consolidated this move toward homogenization on an international scale, though still in progress by the first half of the twentieth century. Modern conductors' preferences regarding placement of instruments, for example, attest to the persistence of old local traditions. Thus, Stokowski favored an antiphonal division for the violins, while Toscanini preferred proximal unity between first and second violins (Koury: 319–320). The inherent paradox is that, even in the postwar period, when the opera orchestra had become substantially homogeneous, it was possible to find, in one institution or another, yet another trend that pushed for further reorganization of the orchestra: that is, historically informed performance. Fidelity to the repertoire and the context of its creation, along with a new executive practice, exalted rather than leveled location-specific orchestral traditions (for instance, in the 1950s the Hamburg Orchestra, under Eugen Jochum, began to play Mozart with a reduced string section; see Corneloup 1955: 224).

This chapter seeks to clear the overgrowth from these old paths and illuminate the ways in which they have stayed the same. I take account of these variations in four chronologically ordered case studies that focus on the particularities of different locales, the types of instruments used and their placement, rehearsal practice, and the emergence of the conductor. Even though the names of Verdi and Wagner have been associated from the nineteenth century through World War I by way of the historiography of music with a strong national identity—Italianness and Germanness—the truth is that both composers used foreign models, in particular the Paris Opéra.

The "Orchestra" before the Orchestra: From Monteverdi to (Monteverdi and) Cavalli

Did the evolution of Monteverdi's operatic *oeuvre*, as Richard Taruskin puts it, from Monteverdi to Monteverdi—that is, from the Monteverdi of *L'Orfeo* to the Monteverdi of *L'incoronazione di Poppea*—really have much to do with the orchestra (2005: II: 1)? In the first engraving of *L'Orfeo*, Monteverdi indicated his orchestration with particular care, noting different instrument types and their numbers:

> two harpsichords, two double-basses, ten *viole da braccio*, one double-harp, two piccolo violins *alla francese*, two *chitaroni* [*sic:* in fact, the score called for three], two organs *di legno*, three bass viols, four trombones [*sic*: five], one *regale* [in fact there were more than one], two cornets, one *flautino alla vigesima seconda* [*sic:* two], one *clarino* trumpet with three muted trumpets. (Monteverdi [1609] 1998)

Monteverdi's instrumentation corresponds to various expressive and symbolic criteria, and his highly detailed stage directions also project his interest in evoking distinct atmospheres. Thus, the wood organ (*organo di legno*) and the chitarrone signify an atmosphere of funereal sorrow, while the instruments with dark and ponderous timbres, trombones in particular, evoke the underworld. And for the change of scene at the end of Act II, Monteverdi instructs the louder instruments (cornets, trombones, and *regali*) to "fall silent," and the softer ones (i.e., viols *da braccio*, organs, harpsichords, etc.) to begin the *ritornello* (Monteverdi [1609] 1998: 88). At the beginning of the last act, however, Monteverdi positioned the wood organs and the chitarroni in opposite corners to produce the stereophonic effect of Orfeo's lament answered by an echo (Monteverdi [1609] 1998: 89).

Monteverdi's contemporaries soon became aware of his prodigious orchestra. Important evidence includes Giovanni Battista Doni's comments on the lush sound and variety of instruments used in performances of *L'Orfeo* (and Cavalieri's *Rappresentazione d'Anima et di Corpo*) in Rome and Florence:

> In the performances of sung drama at which I found myself here in Rome and in Florence, I saw a great variety of instruments employed, so many, in fact, that they were treated almost with indifference, including those most noble: harpsichords, viols, theorbos, lutes, lyres and more which I cannot name, but in particular, harpsichords exceedingly grand in form [...]. (Doni [1633–1635] 1763: 221)

Moreover, we can presume from the surviving fragment (the "Lament"), as well as the testimony of contemporary sources, that Monteverdi's *Arianna* offered the same sort of instrumental richness. *L'Orfeo* was also one of the most celebrated examples of the sixteenth-century phenomenon of festival opera in which elaborate orchestration fulfilled the twofold purpose of underscoring the event's importance and honoring its patrons (Tarr and Walker 1978: 148; Rosand 1991: 10; see also Spitzer and Zaslaw 2004 and Schmidt 1976: 391, 407–408 regarding another festival opera, Cesti's *Il pomo d'oro*).

In reality, Monteverdi's *L'Orfeo*, along with subsequent festival operas, carried on the instrumental conventions of the mid-Renaissance. But, when operatic activity shifted to Venice, the polychromatic sonorities of this tradition faded and were replaced by a pronounced monochromaticism, an orchestra composed essentially of violins, lutes, harpsichords, and occasionally organs or chromatic harps (trombones and cornets, while still important to sacred music, rarely heard in opera, were used mainly to support specialized moments, such as underworld scenes). Sources attest that the orchestra of San Cassiano was relatively small, including several harpsichords, one theorbo, and a single trumpet (see Prunières 1931: 17), and that the orchestra of San Cassiano employed sixteen musicians; in reality, however, a reconstruction of the ensemble based on archival documents leads us to believe that the number was much smaller. The Venetian impresario Marco Faustini (see Glixon and Glixon 2006: 350–352) attests to the constant presence, in the years 1650–1660, of two or three harpsichords (most likely the first harpsichordist was the composer, who alternated with the second harpsichordist for arias and recitatives, while the third played only in purely instrumental or ballet sections), one theorbo, two violins, and one *violone*. In the account books kept by impresarios, there is evidence of only one booking of a trumpet player: in general, the strings were called upon to imitate the sound of trumpets (Rosand 1991: 328–332). Only with Carlo Pallavicino's *Il Nerone* (1679) do we begin to see a new, quantitative progression of instruments in opera orchestras; according to the *Mercure galant*, there could be as many as forty musicians (Beat 1968: 285).

Two explanations for the reduction in the size of the orchestra in the Venetian period were that (a) the opening of public theaters and the expenditure for singers required that other resources be cut, and (b) a new aesthetic that advocated for the representation of the passions in ways beyond the symbolic employment of instruments in a score (see Weaver 1964: 85–88, especially regarding the emergence of this new idiom with the example of Monteverdi's 1624 dramatic madrigal *Il combattimento di Tancredi e Clorinda*).

But the first question is whether, regarding *L'Orfeo*, one can accurately speak of an orchestra at all. The case has been made by Broder (1960), Zaslaw (1988), and Staehelin (1972) that the "orchestra" of *L'Orfeo* is only an orchestra in an ethnomusicological sense, meaning an ensemble of instruments that by definition would also include Renaissance consorts (see also Brown 1973: 77–82). The accepted modern understanding of the orchestra, however, views it as a progressively defined entity: its "birth" does not correspond to any identifiable moment either in time or in geographical space. It is, rather, an aggregate of music-historical evolutionary processes (see Zaslaw 1988).

With the rise of public opera in Venice, three directions in the formation and management of the orchestra that would have lasting repercussions began to take shape: (a) The orchestra favored a fixed ensemble (although many of the players in the Venetian opera orchestras were not necessarily Venetian, but foreigners who became residents or freelancers from other regions). (b) The composer had rights as the leader of the production, as evidenced, for example, by the contract struck between Cavalli and the Teatro San Cassiano on July 24, 1658. (c) The new operatic system centered on singers to the disadvantage of instrumentalists (for details about budget distribution see Glixon and Glixon 2006: 223; Bianconi and Walker 1984: 235–237). What is most important is to understand from this is that the evolution of the opera orchestra followed the same course as the other components of opera, forging their identities in the same place (Venice) and at the same time (after 1637).

Evolution, Not Revolution: The Paris Opéra

As in Italy, sixteenth-century France saw the growth of a new operatic genre from the musical roots of the previous century. The entire history of opera in France is characterized by the weight of tradition counterbalanced by a constant search for novelty, and the opera orchestra, from Lully to the experiments of Messiaen, illustrates this ambivalence.

If the central role of Lully in the organization of French musical life under Louis XIV (1638–1715) and, later, in the construction of a new genre, the *tragédie en musique*, was ever in doubt, it must be remembered that Lully inherited a musical structure that was already crumbling, and which he himself ably buried. The *Chambre* and the *Grande Écurie*, the two musical pillars of court and chapel, had been founded by François I (1494–1547). Under the control of the *Chambre* were the *Vingt-quatre violons du roi* (also known as the *Grande bande*) and the *Petits violons du roi* (the *Petite bande*, later called the *Violons du cabinet*). The musical framework of the *Écurie* (twelve trumpets, eight *fifres* and drums, fifteen sackbuts, oboes, cornets, and one *musette*) hardly varied from 1571 until the reign of Louis XIV (Anthony 2003). None of these ensembles, however, was a true "orchestra" in the modern sense, but rather, a consort organized by instrument type (see Zaslaw 1988).

Lully made use of both the *Petite bande* and the *Grande bande* in his quest to create a single orchestra with greater instrumental variety and a more opulent sound (La Gorce 2002: 132–135). This model had already been foreshadowed in Luigi Rossi's *Orfeo* (1647), which added harpsichords, theorbos, lutes, and guitars to the forces of the *Vingt-quatre violins du roi* (Hammond 1996: 124). Even before the foundation of the Académie in 1669, the expansion of Lully's orchestra, sometimes to as many as eighty-four musicians (as in the ballets *Alcidiane* [1658] and *La raillerie* [1659]), was noted by his contemporaries (for example, Jean Loret, in his journal, *La muse historique* [see La Gorce 2002: 132]). Similar instrumental richness was heard again—and astonishingly so—on the occasion of the reprise of Cavalli's opera *Xerse* (1660), with ballet music composed by Lully. The numbers and sound diverged significantly from the trajectory of Italian opera-orchestral practice. Cavalli's orchestra in Venice had recently undergone a simplification, at least in the context of the newly complex orchestral arrangements in that city (see above). Though this may seem a contradiction in terms, it is not, because the operas of Cavalli, even with their sparer orchestration, functioned almost as "festival operas" in the sociological and musical context of the court of Louis XIV, and adopted that genre's musical means. Indeed, while, as previously noted, the Renaissance model of the musical consort served as common ground for sixteenth-century orchestras, the Italian opera orchestra evolved in the context of economic incentives that resulted from opera's move from court into the public sphere.

In France, on the other hand, it was only in 1761 that a fundamental reorganization of the musical system was ordered: The *Chapelle* and the *Chambre* were united into a single organization, while the *Vingt-quatre violons du roi* ceased their activity. But even the organization of ensembles by instrument family had a lasting effect on music composition through the specifically French innovation of writing for strings in five parts: *dessus, haute-contre, taille, quinte,* and *basse.* This practice had already been much in evidence in music written for ballets—the *Ballet comique de la Royne* (1581) is a well-known example—and was later taken up by Lully. The orchestra of the Opéra preserved the practice of five-part writing until the 1720s, when a four-part structure was adopted (La Gorce 1990: 29–30; traces of the old practice can be found as late as 1803 in Cherubini's opera *Anacréon*). Nonetheless, it was only around the end of the 1740s that scores in four parts became commonplace: in that decade, the *hautes-contres* and *tailles* were consolidated into a single viola part. When the *quintes* were eliminated, the works of Lully were readjusted to the new four-part system (Rosow 1981: 219). In the post-Lully period, the orchestra suffered a polarization between the *dessus* (the highest violin part) and the *basses* (the lowest) that led to both the weakening of the middle voices and to the standard division of the violins into first and second parts, which would henceforth be strictly enforced. Indeed, this separation of the upper strings was the premise for the French orchestra's adoption of the string quartet structure (first and second violins, viola, and cello). This structure was already in use in Italy and in other European orchestras, but its application in France had to wait for the fusion of the *hautes-contres* and *tailles de violon,* still employed separately by Lully's successor Rameau, as evidenced by his opera *Les Boréades* (ca. 1763).

If five-part orchestral writing was a French anomaly, the organization of the orchestra into two groups (*petit chœur* and *grand chœur,* already traceable in Robert Cambert's 1671 pastorale *Pomone* and evident in full force at least until 1790) probably had a connection with the Italian practice of the *tutti* and the *concertino.* As in the Italian system, the two groups did not share the same function: the *petit chœur* accompanied the vocal soloists in the recitatives and airs, whereas the *grand chœur* accompanied the choral numbers, performed the *ouvertures, ritournelles,* and *symphonies,* and later the dances introduced by Lully into every act of his operas. As Rousseau observed, the *petit chœur* unified a group of soloists (paid better than those of the rest of the orchestra) that comprised the *basso continuo* (1768: 97); in the time of Lully, at least according to representations from court, they numbered about ten: two harpsichords, four lutes and theorbos, two violins, and one or two *basses de violon.* At the start of the eighteenth century, the *petit chœur* did not play in the pieces that demanded the greatest volume (the *ouvertures*, choral numbers, and the majority of the dances).

Conservatism and Experimentation: Instrumental Color

In the transition from the orchestra of Lully to that of his successor Rameau, instrumental color changed markedly; some instruments, including the theorbo, disappeared (see Sadler 1980). New instruments, however, were introduced, for example, the double-bass used for the storm scene in Marin Marais's 1706 *Alcyone* and the clarinet, beginning with Rameau's 1749 *Zoroastre* (see La Laurencie 1913). Other instruments were structurally or functionally modified. Some parts were versatile enough to be performed on more than one instrument, while other score indications (for instance, that for *fluttes*) referred not to specific instruments, but rather, to a group. Rameau's orchestra was composed primarily of strings—sixteen or seventeen violins, six violas (including three *haute-contres* and three *tailles*), four *basses du petit chœur*, eight or nine *basses du grand chœur*—rounded out by two oboes, flutes and *petite flute*, trumpets, bassoons, and timpani. The majority of the registries of the Opéra specify six flutes and oboes (played by the same musicians, and therefore rarely written together in the score) and four or five bassoons (an instrument that evolved considerably under Rameau's tenure).

In the Rameau era, other instruments were used sporadically, though not consistently enough to justify the establishment of stable "chairs" for them, since they could be relied upon to be played by other instrumentalists: the *corno di caccia*, or natural horn, was, for instance, played by a violist; the *musette* and *tambourin* by one of the bassists of the *petit chœur*, and the timpani by a violinist; the *flageolets* that appear in Act II of *Platée* were most likely played by the oboists. The trombone—introduced by Gluck—was at first played by the horn players, with a trombone position only established in 1790, when parts for *serpentone* (a relative of the tuba) were added to the orchestra. The harp traveled over a similar course: It was tried out in the French version of Gluck's *Orfeo* in 1774, and was institutionalized beginning in 1781. The practice of double appointments was encouraged in the cases of instruments like trumpets, *tamburi*, timpani, and *tamburini* (see Sadler 1981: 61). The percussion section, whose members were long considered stage rather than orchestra personnel (and were only brought under the rubric of the orchestra in 1827), was enlarged toward the end of the eighteenth and the beginning of the nineteenth centuries by Lemoyne, Catel, Cherubini, and Spontini.

The Opéra was placed under the protection of the public, that is, under the aegis of the city of Paris or of the nation, according to the changing times (see Wild 1989: 299–321). This external intervention led to a much earlier institutionalization of the profession of orchestra musician than occurred elsewhere and provided an unprecedented level of security and stability. Nevertheless, the actual number of musicians in the orchestra of the Opéra grew rather slowly. Between 1704, the year for which the first official list of musicians employed by the Opéra has been identified, and 1768 (La Gorce 1979), the ensemble vacillated between forty-three and fifty musicians, while over the next few years between seventy-four and seventy-seven musicians worked at the Opéra and the number increased to one hundred by 1907 (Spitzer and Zaslaw 2004: 188–189). Still, these numbers do not give an accurate account of the actual ranks of musicians who played in the orchestra each night: not all the chair-holding musicians were present at each performance (much less at every rehearsal). Moreover, the theater made frequent use of "ringers" hired on a per-rehearsal or per-performance basis, especially when unusual instruments were called for. As noted by Pierre (1888) and elaborated upon by Colas (2008: 146–148), the orchestra of the Opéra operated at two levels, one stable and the other variable. The stable ensemble consisted of "fixed" instruments (strings, woodwinds, brass) and remained essentially unchanged throughout the century. The variables changed from opera to opera, as "exotic" instruments were added for "local color" or to play in only a very few specific instances (overtures, ballets, choruses, marches, and ritual scenes). When one of these "new" instruments made its entrance in the course of an aria, it never accompanied the singer. The nineteenth-century French opera orchestra thus consisted of a stable complement of musicians, enhanced by others added as needed, a situation that emerged from the structure originally conceived by Lully and fulfilled the two conjoined functions of the Opéra as an institution: preserver of tradition and leader of innovation.

In the first half of the nineteenth century, Meyerbeer and especially Halévy vied with one another in their quest for new instruments. In *Guido et Ginevra* (1838), Halévy introduced the *mélophone*, invented only the year before by Pierre-Charles Leclerc, and the valved trombone; in his 1852 *Le Juif errant*, he wrote a part for *jeu de timbres* (glockenspiel). Instruments like the tam-tam and the organ, introduced by Meyerbeer in his *Robert le diable* (1831), were not left to "sediment" (to use Colas's term [2008]), but rather expanded the rank of "fixed" instruments in the orchestra. This incessant instrumental innovation was encouraged not only by the musical compositions themselves, but also by musicological and organological research, for which the *expositions universelles* were important means of diffusion. The vitality of this experimentation was exemplified by Adolphe Sax, whose activities contributed to making Paris the *locus classicus* for the musical avant-garde in the nineteenth century. Sax's career at the Opéra began in 1847, when he became the superintendent of "external" musicians, that is, those hired to play unusual instruments or members of military bands engaged to play either onstage or from the wings in certain martial scenes. Sax thus garnered expertise both in furnishing instruments and in finding the musicians who could play them. His collaboration with the Opéra ultimately had a three-part function: to supplant "old" instruments with new ones, to expand the fundamental structure of the orchestra by adding new "fixed" instruments, and to conduct onstage instrumental ensembles when necessary (for more on Sax, see De Keyser 2006 and Haine 1980).

Military orchestras had been longtime collaborators with traditional orchestras in certain sections of operatic works, a practice that was also widespread outside France. In the mid-nineteenth century, there were two opposing views of military music. One, represented by Neapolitan composer Michele Carafa, was essentially traditionalist; the other, represented by Sax, was more innovative. These two differing conceptions reached a musical confrontation, as it were, in a public concert in 1845, and it was Sax's that dominated. Among other things, the development of wind instruments initiated a discussion in France about what constituted instrument families. As Fétis, who lamented the lost "variety" of the Monteverdi orchestra, observed (1827: 278–279), while the strings had a certain homogeneity because they all were members of the same species of violin, the flute and the clarinet, in spite of the fact that both were woodwinds, were unique and separate entities. Kreutzer (1845) and Lavoix (1878: 467–468) noted that military music in the second half of the nineteenth century had in fact returned to a method of organization into instrument families typical of the Renaissance consort. Indeed, Sax based his work on the four-part division of voices (into bass, tenor, contralto, and soprano) used by the strings: the saxophone family, which comprises five instruments ranging from low to high, follows the same principle (Colas 2008: 166–168).

Nevertheless, the weight of tradition proved to be heavy, reining in innovations that came about too quickly: Natural horns, for example, would hold fast to their position in the orchestra until the second half of the nineteenth century, in spite of the fact that the first valved horns had been introduced in Paris as early as 1827 and were used for the first time in an opera, alongside natural horns, in Halévy's *La Juive* (1835). The ophicleide, introduced into the orchestra in 1822, remained there until the Salle Le Peletier (the home of the Opéra for more than a half-century before the new Palais Garnier took its place in 1875) was destroyed by fire in 1873, by which time it had already been supplanted by the tuba (Pierre 1888; Audéon, Colas, and Di Profio 2008: 229–230).

The Plan of the Orchestra: The Placement of Musicians

The idea of a place specific to operatic performance—first the Salle Le Peletier and then the Palais Garnier—reflects both a new preoccupation with acoustics and a growing awareness of the power of dramatic spectacle. François Devret, the architect of Le Peletier, was also the author of a treatise on the orchestra (ca. 1820). Devret placed the violins at the center of the orchestra with the violas on its flanks. The brass were at stage left (*côté cour*) and the winds at stage right (*côté jardin*), while a broad external semicircle was made up of violins, contrabasses, and percussion. The orchestra used three trombones, three flutes (one of them for solos), and four bassoons. As Elizabeth Bartlet has observed, this perfectly symmetrical arrangement reflects the historical development of the theatrical orchestra itself: the first woodwinds in the orchestra—the oboes—were placed near the violins, which made up the original nucleus; flutes, and later clarinets, were added to this pattern in the order of their introduction into the ensemble (1996: 33–35).

Emmanuel Hervé (2012: 131–134) has recently drawn attention to the orchestral plan published in Alexandre Choron and Adrien de Lafage's manual of vocal and instrumental music (1836–1838: VI [1837]). The image shown in Figure 22.1 has six points of interest: (1) "*Table de Renvoi*" ("reference table"), which provides a list of numbered instruments that correspond to the plans in the other figures; (2) Fig. A, plan of the Dresden Opera orchestra in 1754; (3) Fig. B, Plan of the Paris Opéra in the 1830s; (4) Choron's proposal for the placement of the orchestra in relation to the stage and the audience; (5) Fig. F, the concert orchestra of the Paris Conservatoire as arranged by Habeneck; and (6) Fig. H, large amateur concert orchestra in Vienna 1812. Of particular interest for the purposes of this chapter are the two plans proposed by Choron for the orchestra of the Paris Opéra. The primary feature of this particular plan is the fact that it groups all the woodwinds not specially designated for solos in the center, opposite the brass section; the violins are placed to the left and right of this center, and the cellos and basses are lined up in a row behind the conductor but in front of the audience (see Figure 22.1).

This placement, with slight variations, is confirmed in an orchestral plan from the eighteenth and nineteenth centuries given by conductor Ernest Altès to his successor Henri Kling (Koury 1986: 267–268). According to French tradition, the basses formed a sort of protective wall around the other instruments of the orchestra, as evidenced by contemporary iconographical documents (see Figures 22.2 and 22.3).

Choron also published the orchestral seating plan of the Théâtre-Italien, an opera house that hybridized French and Italian musical conventions that underscored the uniqueness of the Opéra. Thus, first and second violins were seated together (although the modern practice of dividing the violins was already in use at the Berlin Opera as early as 1776, when it was directed by Johann Friedrich Reichardt; see Koury 1986: 33–34). Cellos and basses were positioned along the two sides of the orchestra, and the harpsichord—an instrument that had been absent from the orchestra pit of the Opéra since 1776—was still used together with a cello and a bass, following the seventeenth- and eighteenth-century practice of assembling the *continuo* instruments near one another. In the nineteenth century, a single harpsichord or piano began to replace the two keyboard instruments of the typical Italian orchestra (Meuci 1994: 444), and the Théâtre-Italien followed suit.

The Position of the Conductor

A comparison of the two published plans by Choron reveals another difference in the instrument arrangements at the Opéra and the Théâtre-Italien: the conductor of the former was directly in front of the stage, while the conductor of the latter was positioned more toward the center. At the Opéra, this position of the director remained unchanged until 1906: the conductor stood close to the stage and behind the musicians, watching the singers. Contemporary iconography confirms this practice for the Opéra, but also for other Parisian theatres, including the Opéra-Comique, the Opéra-National, and the Théâtre-Italien (see Figures 22.2, 22.3, and 22.4). In the case of the latter, the journal *L'illustration* (April 1, 1843) published an engraving of Donizetti on the occasion of the premiere of *Don Pasquale* that appears to contradict the seating plans given by Choron; this divergence from the norm nonetheless suggests that, true to its hybrid character, the Théâtre-Italien was more changeable, or at least more open to experimentation

It was thus for the Opéra as well. Much later, Verdi conducted the French premiere of *Aida* in 1880 from a similar position, in front of the stage, as illustrated in a well-known

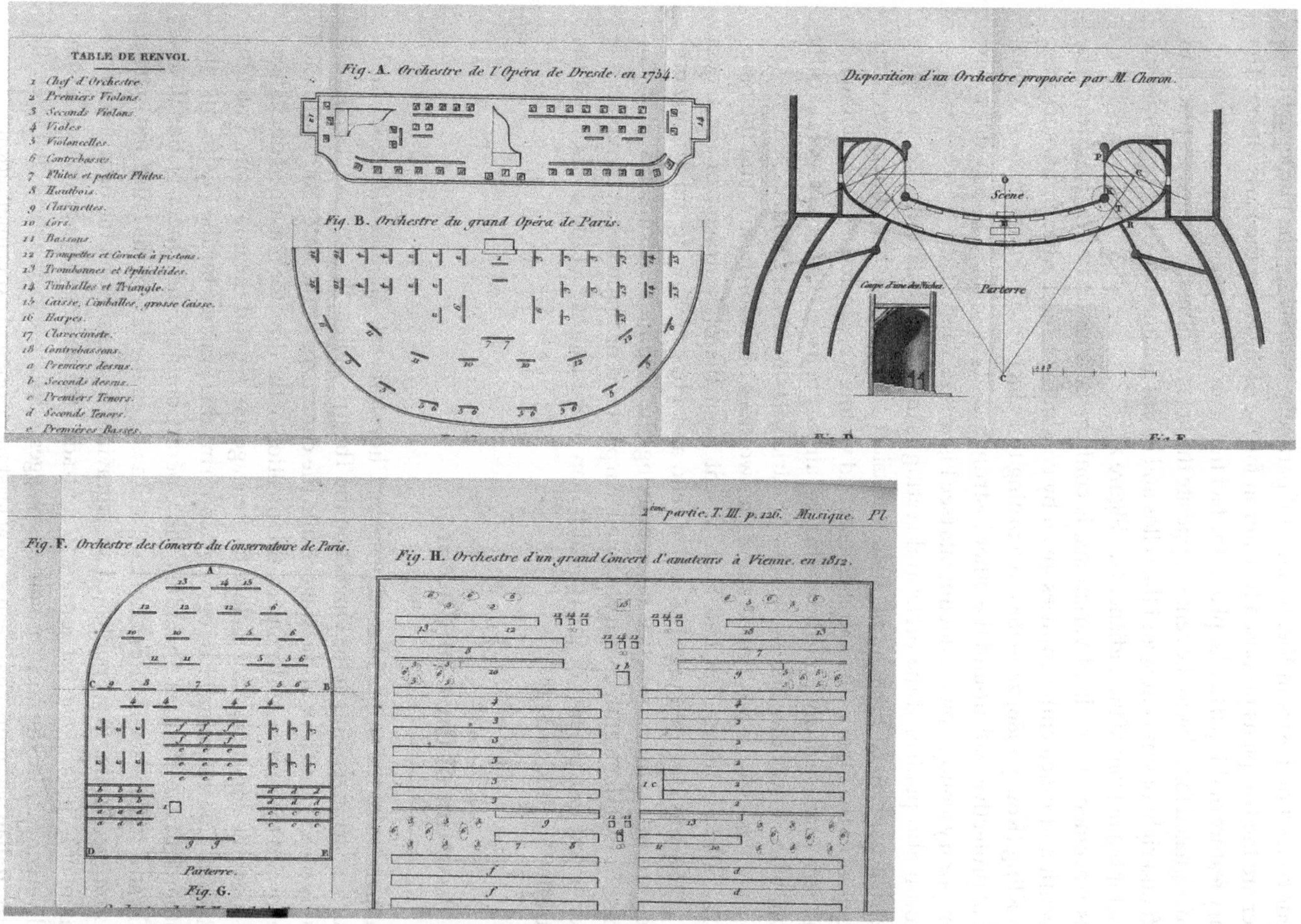

FIGURE 22.1 Orchestra seating plans in Dresden, Paris, and Vienna with a proposed arrangement by Alexandre Choron. Alexandre Choron and Adrien de Lafage, *Manuel complet de musique vocale et instrumentale*, libro VI, Paris: Roret, 1836–1838. With appreciation for the assistance of the Institut de recherche sur le patrimoine musical en France (IRPMF, Paris).

FIGURE 22.2 "Théâtre de l'Opéra. Opéra de *Charles VI*, paroles de MM. Casimir et Germain Delavigne, musique de M. F. Halévy. Cinquième acte, dernière décoration." In *L'illustration*, March 18, 1843, 41. Collection of Alessandro Di Profio.

print that appeared in *Le monde illustré* (April 3, 1880; see Figure 22.5). The composer is shown seated before the stage, turned slightly to face the first violins at his left, with his back to the other musicians: this placement of the conductor was also observed on occasion in England and in the German-speaking lands (for eyewitness accounts, see Koury 1986: 33–34, 247). Nevertheless, it was in France that the practice took firm hold.

As illogical as it may seem to the modern opera audience, the placement of the conductor at the foot of the stage served an important purpose, since the conductor's traditional function had been to support both the vocal soloists and the opera chorus and to keep order by noisily beating time with a baton (Charlton 1993). The emphasis, therefore, was on the stage rather than the pit, as Schroeder confirms: "In small theatres, or where the company through a frequently changing ensemble is not very sure, the conductor will do better to take a position close to the stage, in order to render the utmost assistance in any failure of memory that may happen" (1889: 63). It cannot have been by accident that this positioning of the conductor evolved mainly in France, where the operatic genre (first as *tragédie en musique*, later as *grand opéra*), in contrast to its Italian counterpart, was conceived as a complex theatrical spectacle in which large choruses played a functional music-dramatic role.

FIGURE 22.3 "Théâtre de l'Opéra-Comique. Une scène d'*Angélique et Médor* (d'Ambroise Thomas)." In *L'illustration*, June 10, 1843, 237. Collection of Alessandro Di Profio.

FIGURE 22.4 "Théâtre-Italien. Une scène de *Don Pasquale*, deuxième acte." In *L'illustration*, April 1, 1843, 72. With appreciation for the assistance of the Institut de recherche sur le patrimoine musical en France (IRPMF, Paris).

FIGURE 22.5 Verdi conducting the orchestra in a performance of *Aida*. In *Le monde illustré*, April 3, 1880. Collection of Alessandro Di Profio.

This concept of opera as grand theatrical spectacle, as well as the role of Paris as the nineteenth-century European capital, explains the enormous pressure upon French musicians to endure extremely long rehearsal periods compared with the usual practice of Italian houses. Thus, for example, rehearsals for Verdi's *Les vêpres siciliennes* began at the Opéra on October 1, 1854, months before the opera's premiere on June 13, 1855, while Verdi was allotted only about three weeks of rehearsal time for the premiere of *Rigoletto* at La Fenice in Venice in 1851.

Toward Verdi's Conception of the La Scala Orchestra

In the first three quarters of the nineteenth century, the Italian opera orchestra underwent almost continual changes, leading up to its modern-day plan, which came into existence during the generation of Ponchielli, Leoncavallo, Mascagni, Puccini, and the mature Verdi. As Antonio Rostagno has emphasized, diverse musical factors were at the root of the Italian orchestral revolution of the 1870s: (a) a growing interest in symphonic concerts; (b) a new rivalry between orchestra societies and opera orchestras; (c) the practice of the most important cities' orchestras sharing the best players among them; (d) the need of theaters for new, young composers, such as Ponchielli and Boito, but also for those, like Verdi, whose greatness had been confirmed, in order to generate box-office revenue; and (e) the growing Italian appreciation for French-style *grand opéra* à la Meyerbeer. This new sensitivity to the quality and size of the orchestra, however, was preceded by a long, slow transformation marked by regional differences and resistance to the foreign model, attitudes that lingered in an Italy that was politically unified only in 1861 (Rostagno 1996: 130–131).

"Like the Grand Opéra of Paris": Structure and Design of the Italian Opera Orchestra

In the Italian orchestra of the eighteenth century, the numerical ratio of violins to the lower strings was two to one (Meucci 1994: 436), while in the rest of Europe it was generally three to two (Zaslaw 1976–1977: 171–177). During the course of the nineteenth century, the tendency was to equalize the number of strings with regard to the numbers of other instruments. La Scala, on the other hand, from its opening in 1778 until the 1845–1846 season, decreased its number of string players from fifty-one out of a total of seventy-two musicians to forty-six, a change that only slightly modified the internal balance of instruments (Meucci 1994: 439).

One of the dominant characteristics of the Italian opera orchestra was the modest presence of middle-register strings, with a preference for those in the extreme outer registers demonstrated by a large number of violins and basses. This seems a peculiarity when compared with other European orchestras described by Leopold Mozart, who noted in the orchestra for *Mitridate re di Ponto* twenty-eight violins, six violas, two cellos, and six basses (in addition to two oboes, two flutes, two bassoons, and two harpsichords; see Anderson 1938: I: 255–256; Bauer and Deutsch 1962–1975: I: 408). The basses were the foundation of the Italian opera orchestra, while the cellos (traditionally used for the continuo) began by the nineteenth century to double the basses an octave higher and also to play solo lines. The double-bass is one of the instruments that best illustrates Italian regional peculiarities: from one orchestra to another, we find appreciable differences in its number and placement as well as in its physical features. A bass with three strings tuned in ascending fourths (A1-D-G) was commonly used in Italy, while its German counterpart had four strings ascending to E1, and in France, the instrument was tuned by ascending fifths (G1-D-A). Nevertheless, there were exceptions to the Italian standard, even in the first decades of the century: the Florentine orchestra of the Pergola, for instance, following the German model, restricted its number of double-basses, and, as an article in the *Allgemeine musikalische Zeitung* noted in 1813, used a four-stringed bass (Staffieri 1996: 189). The orchestra of La Scala adopted a hybrid solution between the French and Italian practices, lowering the pitch of the lowest string by a full step to tune them G1-D-G (see Rostagno 2002a: 284). Italian orchestras, nonetheless, resisted adopting the four-stringed bass for many years; Luigi Negri, principal bassist at La Scala, encountered one at the Universal Exposition in Paris in 1878 and was not impressed by it:

> The four-stringed bass is much less convenient than the three-stringed bass [. . .]. I have heard of foreign orchestras in which the four-stringed bass is in use: I was at the Trocadero [touring orchestra of La Scala in Paris in 1878], yet, I confess that this instrument has no special effect.[1] (*GMM* 1881: 263, cited in Rostagno 2002a: 285)

Giovanni Bottesini (1869), who conducted the Cairo premiere of *Aida* (December 24, 1871), suggested that the four-stringed bass's fullness and clarity of sound were lacking compared to those of the three-stringed instrument (Bottesini 1869: 7–8), and in 1881, Giulio Ricordi defended the three-stringed model before the Congress of Italian Musicians (*GMM* 1881: 264, cited in Rostagno 2002a: 285). At this same Congress, the Istituto Musicale of Florence proposed that both three- and four-stringed basses be included in Italian orchestras, a pan-European practice that followed the example of the Paris Opéra, as evidenced in the orchestra plans of Pietro Lichtenthal ([1826] 1970: I: Table 1) and the observations of François-Auguste Gevaert (1863: 36).

The first director of the Milan Conservatory, Bonifazio Asioli, divided the orchestra into two "bodies," which he called the primary and the secondary. The first was made up of the string quartet, the second by the wind instruments. The essential method of apportioning instruments per part, in this case, was "to multiply in unison each instrument making up the Quartet, to the point at which a true balance is found between each of the two bodies"[2] of the orchestra (Asioli 1836: III: 35). Most likely following the structure of La Scala's orchestra from 1825, Asioli delineated the ideal proportions of three orchestras of varying sizes—small, medium, and large. In each case the number of strings increases, as does the type and number of brass. Thus, for example, there are no trumpets in the small orchestra, while the medium orchestra features one trumpet, and the large two trumpets and one trombone (Asioli 1836: III: 35).

Johann Joachim Quantz had already indicated another possibility for an orchestra of between four and twelve violins, with other instruments assigned proportionally ([1752] 1962: 214). This principle of proportion also goes far to explain Wagner's reaction to Spontini's request to have twelve double-basses—a number well in line with Italian tradition—in the orchestra for the Dresden premiere of *La vestale* in 1844. Wagner was not surprised so much by the number of basses Spontini desired as by the consequently much greater number of "balancing" instruments that would need to be obtained, which would swell the orchestra to an even greater size than that of Asioli's "orchestra grande" (Wagner [1865–1880] 1983: 278).

Asioli, moreover, warned against the excessive use of woodwinds, which he claimed could drown out the singers' voices. In the early years of the nineteenth century, the massive influx of woodwinds and percussion into the Italian orchestra was probably intended to balance it with the developing stage band, which had already been present in Italian opera before Rossini. Moreover, there were institutional relationships between the band and the orchestra, as at La Scala, including the siphoning off of musicians from one group to the other. These relationships supported the adoption of new instruments such as the horn and the valved trumpet, which had been used in the stage band before their introduction into the orchestra (Meucci 1994: 457–459).

Italian productions of foreign operas, such as that of Meyerbeer's *Robert le diable* in Naples, also spurred changes to the orchestra, both in increased numbers of already existing instruments and in the introduction of completely new ones. La Scala in the period from 1816 to 1830, under the direction of Alessandro Rolla and later Franco Faccio (1871–1889), increased the numbers of already existing instruments, introduced new ones, and modified the internal balance of the instruments and the placement of individual sections. These changes were to some degree inspired by practice in other European theaters. In 1834 the La Scala orchestra experimented with a new seating order, proposed by Donizetti and based on the model of the Imperial Theatre of Vienna, in which the string quartet was reunited in the center of the pit (see Gassner 1844, reproduced in Koury 1986: 255). But the order established under Rolla was soon restored, which prolonged the eighteenth-century Italian tradition, as evidenced in, among others, the 1752 plan of the Teatro Regio di Torino, shown in a painting by Giovanni Michele Graneri (1708–1762), *Sala del Teatro Regio di Torino* (ca. 1752). It was long believed that this painting, attributed to Pietro Domenico Olivero represented Francesco Feo's *Arsace* (1740), which opened the Regio. In fact, the painting is by Graneri and depicts Ignazio Balbi's *Lucio Papirio dittatore*, in the scenes of the Galiani brothers. (The painting is housed at the Palazzo Madama, Museo civico d'Arte antica, in Torino and may be viewed at Torino 2013.)

Between 1844 and 1846, the orchestra underwent a few changes, including moving players so that they could more easily see the conductor, consolidating the strings to the left of the conductor and the winds to his right, although keeping the brass separated with horns on one side and trumpets and trombones on the other (see the statement of Francesco Antonio Biscottini [1846], in Meucci 1987–1988). The Italian custom of keeping double basses separate was also maintained, but would become obsolete by the second half of the nineteenth century (Staffieri 2002: 226–227). Out of these experiments would emerge a quest for sonic homogeneity that would form the basis for all future orchestral modifications. One of the direct models for these transformations was in fact the orchestra of the Paris Opéra, to which the *Gazzetta musicale di Milano* would dedicate an article in January 1848 (*GMM* 1848: 1–3). One of the key players of Milanese musical life at midcentury was Alberto Mazzucato, a composer, teacher, conductor, and journalist, who had been to Paris, where he was suitably impressed by the orchestra (see the comments by Fétis ([1860–1865] 2001: III: 536).

Conductors who were aware of the organizational structure of Parisian orchestras—including Italians Angelo Mariani, Muzio, and Faccio, who visited Paris in 1862—would inevitably compare one institution with another, bringing into sharp focus the relative weaknesses of the Italian orchestra, whose function was before all else to support the singers and the drama onstage. Not surprisingly, the midcentury restructuring of La Scala's orchestra (noted earlier) directly preceded the premiere there of Meyerbeer's

Robert le diable in 1846, and the premiere of his *L'Africaine* twenty years later made further changes necessary. Mazzucato had insisted in numerous articles published in the *Gazzeta musicale di Milano* on the inadequacies of the Scala orchestra when it had to contend not only with the works of Meyerbeer but also the works of Italian composers, including Rossini (*Guillaume Tell*) and Donizetti (*Maria di Rohan* and *Linda di Chamounix*), who were writing for audiences on the other side of the Alps.

This last point brings to light another aspect of a complex debate: the integration into the new Italian operatic repertoire of orchestral writing that owed a great deal to the French and German traditions and the consequent need for an increasingly higher level of musicianship. In this sense, Mazzucato's activism can be seen as just one thread in a wide net of influences woven from many strands. One of the strongest of these strands was held by Verdi, who had kept away from La Scala for almost twenty-five years after the disappointing production of his *Giovanna d'Arco* in 1845. With the support of the music publisher Ricordi, Verdi pushed for reform, both quantitative and qualitative, in the orchestra of La Scala; because his own instrumental writing called for a high level of skill, these reforms, when enacted, would have an obvious impact upon the performance of his operas. If a new, and permanent, increase in the size of the organization took place between 1856 and 1858, coinciding with the arrival of Mazzucato as *maestro concertatore*, still more considerable structural changes occurred in the decade from 1863 to 1873, an evolution accompanied by the mounting of three operas by Verdi: *Don Carlos* in 1868, the premiere of the second version of *La forza del destino* (1869), and the Italian premiere of *Aida* (1872).

Indeed, in 1871, the commission for the reform of Italian conservatories, presided over by Verdi, presented a report on the structure of the two most important Italian orchestras, those at La Scala and the Teatro San Carlo in Naples. Verdi's principal recommendation was that the strings in the lower and middle registers be reinforced, resulting in a 1:2 ratio of violas, cellos, and basses to violins (Harwood 1986: 117). For the La Scala premiere of *Aida*, in particular, the woodwinds and horns were moved closer to the conductor, where they could see the violas and cello. The conductor no longer turned his back on the orchestra (more on this below), and the loudest instruments, including trombones and percussion, were placed at a greater distance from the audience (see Rostagno 2002a: 270).

These interventions also responded to two immediate necessities: the need for effective growth (the forces assembled for *Aida* swelled La Scala's orchestra from eighty-five parts to ninety-five) in order to achieve a sonority both "fat" and "round," as Verdi explained in his letter of January 13, 1872, to Bottesini (Cesari and Luzio 1913: 679; Busch 1978: 277), and in his letter of July 10, 1871, to Giulio Ricordi, he noted the corresponding need to reorganize the internal balance of the instruments to obtain a better blend (Cesari and Luzio 1913: 264; Busch 1978: 183). Not coincidentally, the critic Filippo Filippi immediately noticed the debt this new structure owed to the French model and wrote in *La perseveranza* of September 25, 1871, "The orchestra [of La Scala] will before long be ordered like that of the *Grand Opéra* of Paris, and like those of all the other great foreign theatres"[3] (Filippi 1871: 2, quoted in Rostagno 2002b: 190). More than twenty years later, around the time of the premiere of *Falstaff* in 1893, Verdi, in a letter to Edoardo

Mascheroni of December 8, admitted his responsibility for the new arrangement of the orchestra in 1871: "I believe [...] that the orchestra, such as it is, is well arranged and balanced; and I do not say this because I was responsible for ordering it thus when it premiered *Aida*, but rather because the instruments blend well this way, in particular the strings, which form a closed circle in the middle of the winds and especially the brasses"[4] (Cesari and Luzio 1913: 691). Indeed, in the reorganization of the Italian orchestra, Verdi's own debt to French *grand opéra* was evident, just as it was already apparent in his historiographical approach to the drama.

The Conductor

Another important transformation in the orchestra of La Scala, which had been restructured for the European premiere of *Aida*, concerned the position of the conductor. No longer would he stand at the center, surrounded by instruments, but at the back of the orchestra pit, in such a way that he was able to see the entire orchestra—in other words, he assumed the "modern" position. In this case, the French method was not taken as a model. The new position taken by the conductor of La Scala was in fact the end point of a long process of evolution concerning the physical location of the conductor, as much as his function: In fact, the two were inevitably conflated in the face of the new form of opera imposed in the second half of the nineteenth century. Following a seventeenth-century tradition, the composer conducted at least the first three performances of his own opera from the keyboard, seated at the first harpsichord, while the *maestro al cembalo* of the theater took the second harpsichord; after the first performances, the *maestro al cembalo* would once again assume his position, vacating the second harpsichord to his assistant. This was the system described by Leopold Mozart in a letter to his wife on the occasion of the premiere of *Mitridate, re di Ponto* in 1771 (Mozart 1938: I: 263). Conducting *al cembalo* remained a fairly common practice as late as the mid-nineteenth century; Rossini conducted the London premiere of his *Zelmira* in 1824 in this manner, as did Pacini in 1831 and Verdi in 1845 (Chusid 1990: 22); even Muzio and Mariani experimented with this method at the beginning of their careers. In fact, the musician seated at the harpsichord functioned as concertmaster; he prepared the singers without the orchestra and conducted most of the full rehearsals, which also focused almost exclusively on the singers, often to the detriment of the instrumental parts. Nonetheless, if the orchestra was not up to snuff, as was often the case, the production could still go on, even with great success, as long as the singers were good. As Bellini wrote on April 5, 1828, to Francesco Florimo before the premiere of *Bianca e Fernando*: "In general, the production is half-baked where the orchestra is concerned; but I am satisfied with it, because the singers know their parts so well that they pull the orchestra along with them [...] and since the singers set the tempi, all will go well"[5] (Florimo 1882: 319).

On the other hand, this practice of effective disequilibrium between the preparation of the singers and that of the orchestra was not well-adapted to new operatic musical forms in the second half of the nineteenth century. For this reason, Mariani began rehearsing the orchestra a week earlier than usual for the October 27, 1867, production of *Don Carlos* at Bologna. Moreover, Mariani repeatedly insisted to Verdi upon the necessity of rehearsing the orchestra separately for the reprise of *La forza del destino* at Vicenza in 1869 (Zoppi 1947: 129). The division of rehearsals into those for vocal soloists and those for the orchestra before bringing the two parts together was soon tied to another particularity of the Italian system, the practice of maintaining parallel conducting roles for the concertmaster at the keyboard, who would conduct the singers in performance, and the first-chair violinist, who would conduct the orchestra (Fairtile 1997). As Lauro Rossi (1850) emphasizes, this practice, unique in Europe, was regarded with greater skepticism from all sides as new musical forms and approaches to staging increasingly imposed the need for greater executive control over the production. Mariani, when reviewing his rehearsal schedules, made a point of centralizing these directorial duties and taking them upon himself (he declared in his *Autobiography* that he was the first conductor to do so; Mariani 1866). He was not quite right about that, however. The few precedents for this role included Giuseppe Scaramelli, who conducted *I masnadieri* in Fiume in 1848, and Muzio, who conducted the 1854 premiere of *Rigoletto* at the Carcano in Milan (see Chusid 1990: 23). At La Scala, the first "M[aestr]o. Concertatore e Dir[ettore]. per le Opere," Mazzucato, was appointed during the 1867–1868 season.

Not surprisingly, individual styles of conducting emerged as a result of this change in directorial responsibility. Early examples include Mariani's direction of *Don Carlos* at Bologna and Faccio's direction of *Aida*. Faccio epitomized a conducting style that Verdi referred to in his letter of September 1, 1871, to Draneth Bey as "devout" (Cesari and Luzio 1913: 269–270; Busch 1978: 210), as it sought to translate into action the very will of the composer by following closely every notation made in the rehearsal process. Mariani, on the other hand, was set free artistically by Verdi (as he was by Wagner when he conducted the 1871 premiere of *Lohengrin* in Bologna); Mariani was convinced not only of his ability to carry out the composer's intentions, but of even being able to convey them *better* than the composer might have done without him. In effect, Faccio's approach is inscribed in the history of conducting with the implication that the composer's direction of rehearsals constituted the ultimate creative act. The case of Mariani, on the other hand, opened the door to a new musical-executive praxis, one that would wrest the work of the conductor from the composer's control. The evolution of the operatic repertoire, with performances in the second half of the nineteenth century coming more and more to be dominated by reprises rather than premieres, only served to favor this second approach, of which Toscanini would become the emblem.

The Ideal Orchestra: The Rise of Wagner

Wagner was as much a driving force behind the changes in the organization of the nineteenth-century orchestra (discussed above) as for the transformation of contemporary practices of orchestration. Although historiography tends to view Wagner as *sui generis*, he absorbed and amalgamated the nineteenth-century European musical experience, beginning with the lessons of Beethoven (in particular, those of the Ninth Symphony) and the innovations of Weber, especially in *Der Freischütz.* He also borrowed from Bellini as much as he criticized him, and owed much to the French (Halévy and especially Meyerbeer). Wagner's mature works, and the concomitant physical materialization of his life's vision with the opening of the theater at Bayreuth, were the final result of a process that had been some forty years in the making.

In both his theoretical treatises and his letters, Wagner turned his attention again and again to the question of the orchestra, which was already part of a wide-ranging German theoretical debate that also engaged Joseph Fröhlich (1810–1811), Augustin Sundelin (1828), Ferdinand Simon Gassner (1842, 1844), and Carl Czerny ([1848] 1979), all of whom wrote numerous articles on the subject in periodicals such as the *Allgemeine musikalische Zeitung* and in dictionaries (Riemann 1882). They even cited Berlioz's *Traité d'instrumentation* (1843), which had greatly influenced several generations of German musicians, including Richard Strauss, who later brought out a revised translation in 1905. While mainly concerned with problems of orchestration, the debate also drew attention to the actual structure of the orchestra and especially the balance between instrumental groups.

The orchestras with which Wagner worked at the beginning of his career can only be construed as malnourished. For example, the orchestra of the theater at Magdeburg, as described by the composer in 1836 and verified by documents from several years prior, most likely employed only sixteen string players and thirteen woodwinds, augmented by players from the local military band (Carse 1948: 54; for detail on orchestras Wagner conducted at Königsberg and Riga, see Bebbington 1984: 103–104). The breaking point for Wagner came, however, with his sojourn in Paris from September 1839 to April 1842, when he heard the orchestras at both the Opéra and the Société du Conservatoire, conducted by François Habeneck. When Wagner returned to Germany, he began restructuring the orchestra, beginning with *Rienzi* at Dresden in 1842 (Koury 1986: 133). As Kapellmeister in Dresden, Wagner also submitted more than forty recommendations (in *Die Königliche Kapelle betreffend*) to the director of the theater Baron August von Lüttichau, as he attempted to form a national German theater (Wagner [1848] 1912: II: 233–273 and [1846] 1914: XII: 151–204). A few years later (1850–1854), he tried to merge the two orchestras at Zurich (Wagner 1953: 459–463), and for his national theater project in Saxony (1848–1849), he proposed a permanent orchestra consisting of sixty-two musicians, including, in addition to the strings, three flutes, three oboes (including an English horn), three clarinets (including a bass clarinet), three bassoons, three horns, three trumpets, three trombones, and one timpani (Koury 1986: 134).

The evolution of Wagner's orchestration consisted in the synthesis and enrichment of the tradition of Haydn and Mozart along with yet another model, the medium-sized orchestra (Bebbington 1984: 121), which came very close to the one proposed by Asioli (see above). The organization of the strings was at the heart of the recommendations

Wagner had originally formulated in Dresden in 1846, culminating in the *Ring* cycle, which featured the truly revolutionary number of sixty-four strings (sixteen first violins, sixteen second violins, twelve violas, twelve cellos, and eight basses), with proportions similar to those proposed by Berlioz (four violins per part, three violas, three cellos, and two basses). By the time of its official inauguration in 1876, the orchestra at Bayreuth boasted 116 players, essentially made up of permanent hires (although additions were made when necessary; see, for example, Lavignac 1951: 519). This ongoing accumulation of instruments nevertheless imparted a majestic quality to the orchestra and did not obscure another important tendency in Wagner: his use of divided instrumental parts and orchestral instruments as soloists, rather than as *tutti*. In a sense, Wagner's most innovative writing for the orchestra was the music he composed for the middle parts, especially the viola, an instrument that had since the 1830s been almost completely neglected in German orchestras (an exception is Weber's *Der Freischütz*).

Wagner's interest in organological innovation is well known: he requested Wilhelm Heckel to develop a new type of bassoon, introduced at Bayreuth in 1879. And, although he continued to write for the natural horn, Wagner also introduced the valved horn in *Rienzi* (Halévy had already used it in *La Juive* in 1835). The expansion of the horns, to eight in the *Ring* cycle, was characteristic of Wagner's mature works. Inspired by the innovative spirit of Adolphe Sax (whose work he became acquainted with in Paris in 1853), Wagner also invented his own instrument, the so-called Wagner tuba, which was probably first used at Bayreuth in 1875. In general, Wagner always showed a predilection for low notes in the woodwinds and brass, as evidenced in the Wagner tuba, the bass tuba, bass clarinet, and another instrument of his own invention, the bass trombone (for an analysis of the evolution of Wagner's orchestra by instrumental group, see Burton 1992).

The Bayreuth Festspielhaus

The reorganization of the Wagnerian orchestra went hand in hand with his entirely new conception of theatrical space. The acoustic characteristics of this space and the configuration of the orchestra pit, as well as rehearsal conditions and instrument maintenance, all had a direct impact on Wagner's ideas about the ideal orchestra. In his preface to the libretto for the *Ring* cycle, Wagner foresaw a hidden conductor directing an "invisible" orchestra, which would be capable of producing a "transfigured" sound (Barth 1975: 199–200). But even an idea so seemingly particular to Wagner was in fact tethered to a wider European trend: Grétry had already suggested it in his *Mémoires* (1797: III: 32), and the architects Claude Nicolas Ledoux (at Besançon in 1784) and Karl Friedrich Schinkel at (Berlin in 1821) had written of their plans for a hidden orchestra pit placed deep in the ground. Nonetheless, after various projects spurred by Wagner in Munich in 1865, the idea of a *mystischer Abgrund* (a "mystical pit") was fully realized at the Bayreuth Festspielhaus, based on a project originally conceived by architect Gottfried Semper. As Lavignac, who also reproduced the seating charts, described it:

> The instruments are grouped by family, just as in the great symphonic concerts, except in one regard that is exactly the opposite, which is that the conductor and the violins are placed on high, and the louder instruments lower down, all the way at the bottom; and also the first violins are at the right and the second violins at the left, which makes the Bayreuth orchestra simply an ordinary orchestra in reverse.[6] (Lavignac 1951: 54)

In fact, the disparities between the orchestra of the concert hall and that of the theater, both in terms of structure and of seating, were essentially abolished at Bayreuth. Wagner probably used Spontini's seating plans for the 1844 Dresden *La vestale* (noted earlier), as a starting point, bringing to them his own modifications in which, for example, he did not unite cellos and basses at the center of the pit, even though the arrangement was standard for German theaters (Bebbington 1984: 151–152, 172–173). He also positioned the conductor far from the stage, which required a greater number of rehearsals in order to reassure the singers. Altogether, Wagner's changes symbolized a new concept of musical spectacle: a *total* artwork (or *Gesamtkunstwerk*), placed entirely under the direction of the conductor, who, from this position, could assume control of the whole.

Epilogue: Challenging the "Idea" of an Opera Orchestra

The twentieth century conferred upon the orchestra an administrative stability that was unknown during the preceding centuries; the world's principal opera theaters had at last settled on the practice of hiring both orchestral players and conductors on a permanent basis. At the same time, in the wake of diverse artistic experimentation, the twentieth century called into question both the function and the very concept of the opera orchestra itself.

From the point of view of orchestral size and balance, two opposing tendencies came to the fore. On the one hand, Wagnerism continued to make itself felt not only in Germany, but also in Italy and France, where vast orchestras dominated. The orchestra for Hugo Wolf's *Der Corregidor* (1896), for example, was as sumptuous as that of *Die Meistersinger*, while that for Debussy's *Pelléas et Mélisande* (1902) essentially recast the orchestral model set forth by *Parsifal*. Even Olivier Messiaen, whose admiration for Wagner influenced his activities both as a composer and as a theorist, used for his 1983 opera *Saint François d'Assise* a chorus of 150 singers and an orchestra of 120 players, including three *ondes Martenot* and thirty-eight percussion instruments; twenty rehearsals were needed to put the show together for its premiere.

On the other hand, we find the opposing tendency toward chamber opera, which makes use of restricted instrumental forces. For example, in *Ariadne auf Naxos*, Strauss specified in the score just six violins, four violas, four cellos, two basses, woodwinds and horns in pairs, a trumpet, a piano, and two harps. Darius Milhaud, in *Les malheurs d'Orphée* (1926), called for only solo woodwinds and strings, and in *Hin und zurück* (1927), Hindemith wrote for an ensemble of nine wind instruments, two pianos, and a harmonium.

From a stylistic point of view, the directions taken by opera composers in the twentieth century were myriad and diverse and directly affected by consideration of the orchestra and its history. The revival of an eighteenth-century aesthetic sensibility explains, for example, why Benjamin Britten specified that the conductor accompany the recitatives in *The Rape of Lucretia* (1946) from the piano or Stravinsky's use in *The Rake's Progress* (1951) of eighteenth-century conventions, including basso continuo, orchestrated ritornelli, and obbligato winds. At the same time, composers continued to cultivate a taste for exoticism (see Sheppard 2001), for example, the gong in Britten's *Death in Venice* (1973), which evokes an atmosphere of hedonistic indulgence (Griffiths 1994: 331). Above all, novelty was drawn from jazz, which influenced many opera composers, including Kurt Weill and Darius Milhaud.

A radical reassessment of what makes an orchestra, and how an orchestra should function in opera, was initiated by the avant-garde in the 1960s. In 1962 Luigi Nono devised criteria that characterized traditional opera, among them the presence of a "unique focus as much on the visual as on the sonic planes"[7] (Nono 1985). The fixed rapport between the audience and the spectacle, as in a ritual, and the prospect of a unique and central source of sound became subjects of discussion in the new theater of the avant-garde. Radio added the possibility of further sonic integration, joining the realities of electronic or concrete music and instrumental music in a single medium, the amplified speaker. This evolution was sociological as well, since with radio the privileged place of production was no longer the opera house (Ferrari 2000: 20–21). Thus, the "premieres" of many operas took place via radio transmission, including Gian Carlo Menotti's *The Old Maid and the Thief* (1939), broadcast on NBC radio, and Luigi Dallapiccola's *Il prigioniero* (1949), broadcast by RAI in Turin. With their 1955 "radio play" *Ritratto di città* (Portrait of a City, subtitled *studio per una rappresentazione radiofonica* [study for radio performance]), Luciano Berio, Bruno Maderna, and Roberto Leydi sought to demonstrate the resources of the recording studios of RAI in Milan by uniting instrumental sounds with electronic ones. With this work, opera historiography witnessed the invention of a new genre: opera not *transmitted by* radio, but *composed for* radio. Further experimentation followed with Bruno Maderna's "radio opera" *Don Perlimplin*, a "Serenata for a satellite" (1961) and Stravinsky's *The Flood* (1962) for CBS television.

The introduction of electronic instruments also forced a restructuring of the orchestra, as the new instruments were integrated into the traditional company, as was the case with the *ondes Martenot*, used by Messiaen to create special effects (see Tchamkerten 2007: 72). John Adams used a synthesizer in his score for *Nixon in China* (1987), after Philip Glass's *Einstein on the Beach* (1976). Tod Machover's *Valis* (1987) is accompanied entirely by a computer, and Steve Reich produces melodies and images generated by computer in *The Cave* (1993), which calls for eighteen musicians, images projected on five video screens, prerecorded spoken interviews, and both live and sampled music.

The continuous mutation of the orchestra in the twentieth century also, paradoxically, involved a return to the performance practices of an earlier era, but not simply as such re-contextualized elements as basso continuo. Based on the pioneering research of instrument-maker Arnold Dolmetsch (1858–1940), period performance practice came into the mainstream in the second half of the century, along with a reawakening of interest in early repertoire (see Parrott and Peres Da Costa 2002). The effort to resurrect period practices and the growing comfort with use of critical editions of scores based upon primary sources and old treatises have had inevitable consequences for the orchestra with the introduction of period instruments and adjusted concert pitch to reflect the historical context for the first execution of the work; the organization of the orchestra; the proportions of instrumental groups; and the placement of the musicians according to information gleaned from contemporary documents and iconography. The paradox is that in the post–World War II period, at a time when the opera orchestra had finally become essentially homogeneous throughout Europe, the phenomenon of historically informed performance stimulated a rethinking of the orchestra based upon the repertoire being performed and the context of its creation. Furthermore, an even newer style of performance practice has worked against the impetus toward standardization of the orchestra to form hybrid ensembles that blend period-instrument specialists into more traditional fixed ensembles.

The experimentation of the avant-garde, on the one hand, and the phenomenon of historically informed performance, on the other, have not only succeeded in challenging the very idea of a "standardized" orchestra, but have shown that, even today, this venerable institution can be endlessly transformed according to the requirements of a single opera.

See also: Historically Informed Performance

NOTES

1. "Il contrabbasso a 4 corde presenta una comodità molto minore di quella del contrabbasso a tre corde [. . .]. Io ho sentito delle orchestre straniere in cui il contrabbasso a 4 corde è in uso: sono stato al Trocadero [tournée dell'orchestra della Scala a Parigi nel 1878], eppure, confesso che questo istrumento non mi ha fatto nessun effetto speciale."
2. "moltiplicare in unisono ciascun istromento formante il Quartetto, sino a quel punto in cui trovasi una giusta proporzione tra l'uno e l'altro corpo."
3. "L'orchestra sarà disposta, presso a poco, come al *Grand Opéra* di Parigi e come in tutti i grandi teatri all'estero."
4. "Credo [. . .] che l'orchestra, tal quale è, sia ben collocata e distribuita; e non dico questo perché io sia stato il colpevole che così la fissai quando diedi *Aida*, ma perché gli strumenti s'impastano bene, e gli archi accerchiano e chiudono nel mezzo gli istromenti da fiato, specialmente gli ottoni."
5. "In generale lo spettacolo è immaturo per l'orchestra; ma io sono contento perché gli stessi cantanti, sapendo bene la loro parte, se la trascineranno con loro, [. . .] e i tempi li staccheranno i cantanti, e così andrà bene."

6. " [...] les instruments sont groupés par familles exactement comme dans les grands concerts symphoniques, sauf que c'est juste le contraire, que le chef d'orchestre et les violons sont en haut, et les instruments bruyants en bas, tout au fond; sauf aussi que les premiers violons sont à droite, les seconds à gauche; c'est tout simplement un orchestre ordinaire renversé."
7. "centro focale unico tanto sul piano visivo che sul piano sonoro."

Bibliography

Anderson, Emily, ed. and trans. 1938. *The Letters of Mozart and His Family*. 2 vols. London: Macmillan.

Anthony, James R. [1974] 2003. *French Baroque Music (from Beaujoyeulx to Rameau)*. Portland: Amadeus Press.

Asioli, Bonifazio. [1836]. *Il maestro di composizione ossia Seguito del trattato d'armonia*. 4 vols. [Milan: Ricordi].

Audéon, Hervé, Damien Colas, and Alessandro Di Profio. 2008. "The Orchestras of the Paris Opera Houses in the Nineteenth Century." In Jensen and Piperno 2008, II: 217–258.

Barth, Herbert, Dietrich Mack, and Egon Voss, eds. 1975. *Wagner: A Documentary Biography*. New York: Oxford University Press.

Bartlet, M. Elizabeth C. 1996. *'Guillaume Tell' di Gioachino Rossini: Fonti iconografiche*. Pesaro: Fondazione Rossini.

Bauer, Wilhelm A., and Otto Erich Deutsch, eds. 1962–1975. *Mozarts Briefe und Aufzeichnungen*. 4 vols. Kassel: Bärenreiter.

Beat, Janet. 1968. "Monteverdi and the Opera Orchestra of His Time." In *The Monteverdi Companion*, edited by Denis Arnold and Nigel Fortune, 277–301. London: Faber and Faber.

Bebbington, Warren A. 1984. "The Orchestral Conducting Practice of Richard Wagner." PhD diss., City University of New York.

Berlioz, Hector. 1905. *Instrumentationslehre*, translated and edited by Richard Strauss. Leipzig: C. F. Peters.

——. 1864. *Instrumentationslehre*, translated by Alfred Dörffel. Leipzig: Gustav Heinze.

——. 1843. *Grand traité d'instrumentation et d'orchestration modernes*. Paris: Schonenberger.

Bianconi, Lorenzo, and Thomas Walker. 1984. "Production, Consumption and Political Function of Seventeenth-Century Opera." *Early Music History* 4: 209–296.

Biscottini, Francesco Antonio. [1846] "Relazione alla direzione generale dei teatri di Milano." Ms. [1846], I-Mt 85.

Bottesini, Giovanni. [ca. 1869]. *Metodo di contrabbasso*. Milan: Ricordi.

Broder, Nathan. 1960. "The Beginnings of the Orchestra." *Journal of the American Musicological Society* 13/1–3: 174–180.

Brown, Howard Mayer. 1973. *Sixteenth-Century Instrumentation: The Music for the Florentine Intermedii*. Musicological Studies and Documents 30. [Dallas?]: American Institute of Musicology.

Burton, Jonathan. 1992. "Orchestration." In *The Wagner Compendium*, edited by Barry Millington, 334–347. New York: Schirmer.

Busch, Hans. 1978. *Verdi's 'Aida': The History of an Opera in Letters and Documents*. Minneapolis: University of Minnesota Press.

Carse, Adam. 1948. *The Orchestra from Beethoven to Berlioz: A History of the Orchestra in the First Half of the 19th Century and of the Development of Orchestral Baton Conducting.* New York: Broude Brothers.

Cavallini, Ivano. 1998. *Il direttore d'orchestra: Genesi e storia di un'arte.* Venice: Marsilio.

Cesari, Gaetano, and Alessandro Luzio, eds. 1913. *I copialettere di Giuseppe Verdi.* Milan: Stucchi Ceretti.

Charlton, David. 1993. "'A *maître d'orchestre*... conducts': New and Old Evidence on French Practice." *Early Music* 21/3: 340–353.

Choron, Alexandre, and Adrien de Lafage. 1836–1838. *Manuel complet de musique vocale et instrumentale.* Paris: Roret.

Chusid, Martin. 1990. "A Letter by the Composer about *Giovanna d'Arco* and Some Remarks on the Division of Musical Direction in Verdi's Day." *Performance Practice Review* 3/1: 7–57.

Colas, Damien. 2008. "Halévy and His Contribution to the Evolution of the Orchestra in the Mid-Nineteenth Century." In Jensen and Piperno 2008, II: 143–184.

Corneloup, Marcel. 1955. *L'orchestre et ses instruments.* Paris: Presses de l'Ile de France.

Czerny, Carl. [1848] 1979. *School of Practical Composition.* London: R. Cocks & Co. Reprint. New York: Da Capo Press.

De Keyser, Ignace. 2006. "Adolphe Sax and the Paris Opéra." In *Brass Scholarship in Review: Proceedings of the Historic Society Conference. Cité de la musique, Paris 1999,* edited by Stewart Carter, 133–169. Hillsdale, NY: Pendragon.

Di Profio, Alessandro. 2010. "L'ours à la baguette: Verdi, chef d'orchestre à Paris." *Musiques, images et instruments* 12: 130–168.

Doni, Giovanni Battista. 1763. "Trattato della musica scenica." In *De' trattati di musica di Gio. Battista Doni,* edited by Anton Francesco Gori, II: 1–144. Florence: Stamperia imperiale.

Edge, Dexter. 1992. "Mozart's Viennese Orchestras." *Early Music* 20/1: 62–88.

Fairtile, Linda. 1997. "Musical Direction in Verdi's Middle-Period Operas." In *Verdi's Middle Period (1849–59): Source Studies, Analysis and Performance Practice,* edited by Martin Chusid, 413–426. Chicago: University of Chicago Press.

Ferrari, Giordano. 2000. *Les débuts du théâtre musical d'avant-garde en Italie: Berio, Evangelisti, Maderna.* Paris: L'Harmattan.

Fétis, François-Joseph. [1860–1865] 2001. *Biographie universelle des musiciens et bibliographie générale de la musique.* 5 vols. Paris: Tchou.

——. 1827. "Des révolutions de l'orchestre." *Revue de Paris* (April): 269–280.

Filippi, Filippo. 1871. "Appendice. Rassegna drammatico-musicale: Cose della Scala." *La perseveranza* 13 (September 25): 2.

Florimo, Francesco. 1882. *Memorie e lettere: Bellini.* Florence: G. Barbera.

Fröhlich, Joseph. 1810–1811. *Vollständige theoretische-praktische Musikschule für alle beym Orchester gebräuchliche wichtigere Instrumente.* Bonn: n. p.

Galeazzi, Francesco. 1791–1796. *Elementi teorico-pratici di musica, con un saggio sopra l'arte di suonare il violino.* 2 vols. Rome: Pilucchi Cracas.

Gassner, Ferdinand Simon. 1844. *Dirigent und Ripienist für angehende Musikdirigenten, Musiker und Musikfreunde.* Karlsruhe: Gross.

——. 1842. *Partiturkenntniss: ein Leitfaden zum Selbstunterricht für angehende Tonsetzer.* Karlsruhe: Gross.

Gevaert, François-Auguste. 1863. *Traité général d'instrumentation exposé méthodique des principes de cet art dans leur application à l'orchestre, à la musique d'harmonie et de fanfares, etc.* Gand: Gevaert.

Glixon, Beth, and Jonathan Glixon. 2006. *Inventing the Business of Opera: The Impresario and His World in Seventeenth-Century Venice*. AMS Studies in Music. New York: Oxford University Press.
GMM. 1881. "Seconda seduta. Congresso dei musicisti italiani." *Gazzetta musicale di Milano* 36/29 (July 17): 263.
——. 1848. "Nozioni storico-statistiche sull'orchestra dell'Opéra." *Gazzetta musicale di Milano* 7/1 (January 5): 1–3.
Grétry, André-Ernst-Modeste. 1797. *Mémoires ou Essais sur la musique*. Paris: Imprimerie de la République.
Griffiths, Paul. 1994. "The Twentieth Century." In *The Oxford Illustrated History of Opera*, edited by Roger Parker, 279–349. New York: Oxford University Press.
Haine, Malou. 1980. *Adolphe Sax (1814–1894). Sa vie, son œuvre et ses instruments de musique*. Brussels: Editions de l'Université de Bruxelles.
Hammond, Frederick. 1996. "Orpheus in a New Key: The Barberini and the Rossi-Buti *l'Orfeo*." *Studi musicali* 25: 103–125.
Harwood, Gregory W. 1986. "Verdi's Reform of the Italian Opera Orchestra." *19th-Century Music* 10/2: 108–134.
Hervé, Emmanuel. 2012. *L'orchestre de l'Opéra de Paris à travers le cas de 'Robert le diable' de Meyerbeer (1831–1864)*. Pesaro: Fondazione Rossini.
Jensen, Luke. 1991. "The Emergence of the Modern Conductor in 19th-Century Italian Opera." *Performance Practice Review* 4/1: 34–63.
Jensen, Niels Martin, and Franco Piperno, eds. 2008. *The Opera Orchestra in 18th- and 19th-Century Europe*. 2 vols. Berlin: Berliner Wissenschafts-Verlag.
Koury, Daniel J. 1986. *Orchestral Performance Practices in the Nineteenth Century. Size, Proportions, and Seating*. Ann Arbor, MI: UMI Press.
La Gorce, Jérôme de. 2002. *Jean-Baptiste Lully*. Paris: Fayard.
——. 1990. "L'orchestre de l'Opéra et son évolution de Campra a Rameau." *Revue de musicologie* 76/1: 23–43.
——. 1979. "L'Académie Royale de Musique en 1704, d'après les documents inédits conservés dans les archives notariales." *Revue de musicologie* 65/2: 160–191.
La Laurencie, Lionel de. 1913. "Rameau et les clarinettes." *Le Mercure musical* 9: 27–28.
Lavignac, Albert. [1897] 1951. *Le voyage artistique à Bayreuth*. Paris: Librairie Delagraven.
Lavoix, Henri, 1878. *Histoire de l'instrumentation depuis le XVIe siècle jusqu'à nos jours*. Paris: Firmin-Didot.
Lemaître, Edmond 1986. "L'orchestre dans le théâtre lyrique français chez les continuateurs de Lully, 1687–1715." *Recherches sur la musique française classique* 24: 107–127.
Lichtenthal, Pietro. [1826] 1970. *Dizionario e bibliografia della musica*. 4 vols. Bologna: Forni.
Mahling, Christoph-Hellmut, and Helmut Rösing. 1997. "Orchester." In *MGG2* (*Die Musik in Geschichte und Gegenwart*), *Sachteil*, edited by Ludwig Finscher and Friedrich Blume, VII: 812–852. Kassel: Bärenreiter.
Mariani, Angelo. 1866. *Autobiografia* [November 1866]. I-Bca: Ms. Landoni, Cartone IX, 1.
Meucci, Renato. 1994. "La trasformazione dell'orchestra in Italia al tempo di Rossini." In *Gioachino Rossini, 1792–1992. Il testo e la scena. Atti del convegno 1992*, edited by Paolo Fabbri, 431–464. Pesaro: Fondazione Rossini.
——. 1987–1988. "Osservazioni del m. Francesco Antonio Biscottini sull'orchestra scaligera del 1846." *Il flauto dolce* 17–18: 41–44.
Monteverdi, Claudio. [1609] 1998. *L'Orfeo*, edited by Elisabeth Schmierer. Laaber: Laaber. Facsimile. Venice: Amadino.

Nono, Luigi. 1985. "Possibilité et nécessité d'un nouveau théâtre musical." *Contrechamps* 4: 55–67.

Parrott, Andrew, and Neal Peres Da Costa. 2002. "Performance practice." In *The Oxford Companion to Music*. Online. Available: http://www.oxfordmusiconline.com/subscriber/article/opr/t114/e5090 (accessed May 25, 2011).

Pierre, Constant. 1888. *Histoire de la composition de l'orchestre de l'Opéra depuis Cambert jusqu'à nos jours*. F-Pn: Rés., Vmc. 53.

Piperno, Franco, ed. 1996. "Le orchestre dei teatri d'opera italiani nell'Ottocento. Bilancio provvisorio di una ricerca." *Studi verdiani* 11: 119–221.

Prunières, Henri. 1931. *Cavalli et l'opéra vénitien au* XVIIe *siècle*. Paris: Rieder.

Quantz, Johann Joachim. [1752] 1966. *On Playing the Flute*, translated by Edward R. Reilly. London: Faber & Faber.

Riemann, Hugo. 1882. *Musik-Lexikon: die Theorie und Geschichte der Musik*. Leipzig: Verlag des Bibliographischen Instituts.

Rosand, Ellen. 1991. *Opera in 17th-Century Venice: The Creation of a Genre*. Berkeley and Los Angeles: University of California Press.

Rosow, Lois. 1981. "Lully's *Armide* at the Paris Opéra: A Performance History: 1686–1766." PhD diss., Brandeis University.

Rossi, Lauro. 1850. "Le prime necessità di un'impresa teatrale in musica." *L'Italia musicale* 2: 146–150.

Rostagno, Antonio. 2002a. "*Aida* e l'orchestra. Le prime esecuzioni, le partiture, le prassi esecutive." *Studi verdiani* 16: 265–292.

——. 2002b. "La Scala verso la moderna orchestra. Gli eventi e i motivi delle riforme da Merelli ad 'Aida'." *Studi verdiani* 16: 157–216.

——. 2000. "Verdi e Mariani." In *Giuseppe Verdi, genovese*, edited by Roberto Iovino and Stefano Verdino, 33–60. Lucca: Libreria musicale italiana.

——. 1996. "Milano, Teatro alla Scala (1816–1861) (AR)." *Studi verdiani* 11: 163–181.

Rousseau, Jean-Jacques. 1768. *Dictionnaire de musique*. Paris: Duchesne.

Sadler, Graham. 1981–1982. "Rameau and the Orchestra." *Proceedings of the Royal Musical Association* 108: 47–68.

——. 1980. "The Role of the Keyboard Continuo in French Opera, 1673–1776." *Early Music* 8/2: 148–157.

Schmidt, Carl B. 1976. "Antonio Cesti's *Il pomo d'oro*: A Reexamination of a Famous Hapsburg Court Spectacle." *Journal of the American Musicological Society* 29/3: 381–412.

Schroeder, Carl. 1889. *Handbook of Conducting*, edited and translated by John Matthews. London: Augner.

Sheppard, W. Anthony. 2001. *Revealing Masks: Exotic Influences and Ritualized Performance in Modernist Music Theater*. Berkeley and Los Angeles: University of California Press.

Spitzer, John, and Neal Zaslaw. 2004. *The Birth of the Orchestra: History of an Institution, 1650–1815*. New York: Oxford University Press.

Staehelin, Martin. 1972. "Orchester." *Handwörterbuch der musicalischen Terminologie*, edited by Hans Heinrich Eggebrecht. Wiesbaden: F. Steiner.

Staffieri, Gloria. 2002. "'Un'altra esecuzione è possibile.' *Robert le Diable* e la riforma delle orchestre italiane negli anni Quaranta." *Studi verdiani* 16: 219–246.

——. 1996. "Firenze, Teatro della Pergola (1823–1848)." *Studi verdiani* 11: 181–204.

Sundelin, Augustin. 1828. *Die Instrumentierung für das Orchester*. Berlin: Wagenführ.

Tarr, Edward H., and Thomas Walker 1978. "'Bellici carmi, festivo fragor': Die Verwendung der Trompete in der italienischen Oper des 17. Jahrhunderts." *Hamburger Jahrbuch für Musikwissenschaft* 3: 143–203.

Taruskin, Richard. 2005. *Music in the Seventeenth and Eighteenth Centuries. The Oxford History of Western Music* 2. New York: Oxford University Press.

Tchamkerten, Jacques. 2007. "From *Fête des belles eaux* to *Saint François d'Assise*: The Evolution of the Writing for Ondes Martenot in the Music of Olivier Messiaen." In *Olivier Messiaen: Music, Art and Literature*, edited by Christopher Dingle and Nigel Simeone, 63–78. Aldershot, UK: Ashgate.

Torino. 2013. Giovanni Michele Graneri (1708–1762), *Sala del Teatro Regio di Torino* (ca 1752). Online. Available: http://it.wikipedia.org/wiki/File:Pietro_Domenico_Oliviero_-_The_Royal_Theater_in_Turin.jpg (accessed June 1, 2013).

Wagner, Richard. [1865–1880] 1983. *My Life*, translated by Andrew Gray. Cambridge: Cambridge University Press.

——. 1953. *Briefe. Die Sammlung Burrel*, edited by John N. Burk. Frankfurt: S. Fischer.

——. 1911–1916. *Sämtliche Schriften und Dichtungen* [*SSD*], edited by Hans von Wolzogen and Richard Sternfeld. 16 vols. Leipzig: Breitkopf & Härtel.

——. [1846] 1914. "Die Königliche Kapelle betreffend." In *SSD*, XII: 151–204.

——. [1848] 1912. "Entwurf zur Organisation eines deutschen National Theaters für das Königreich Sachsen." In *SSD*, II: 233–273.

Weaver, Robert L. 1986. "The Consolidation of the Main Elements of the Orchestra: 1470–1768." In *The Orchestra: Origins and Transformations*, edited by Joan Peyser, 1–36. New York: Charles Scribner's Sons.

——. 1964. "The Orchestra in Early Italian Opera." *Journal of the American Musicological Society* 17/1: 83–89.

Wild, Nicole. 1989. *Dictionnaire des théâtres parisiens au XIXe siècle*. Paris: Aux amateurs de livres.

Zaslaw, Neal. 1997. "Les orchestres mozartiens européens." In *Mozart: les chemins de l'Europe*, edited by Brigitte Massin, 113–122. Strasbourg: Editions du conseil de l'Europe.

——. 1992. "Mozart's Orchestras: Applying Historical Knowledge to Modern Performances." *Early Music* 20/2: 197–205.

——. 1988. "When is an Orchestra not an Orchestra?" *Early Music* 16/4: 483–495.

——. 1976–1977. "Toward the Revival of the Classical Orchestra." *Proceedings of the Royal Musical Association* 103: 158–187.

Zoppi, Umberto. 1947. *Angelo Mariani, Giuseppe Verdi e Teresa Stolz in un carteggio inedito*. Milan: Garzanti.

CHAPTER 23

DANCE

LINDA J. TOMKO

In the past twenty years, studies of dance and opera have issued chiefly from scholars working in the discipline of musicology, and in some instances also from dance history and dance studies. While the multiple-media and interdisciplinary status of opera itself might seem to beckon to scholars possessing different expertise to join forces in collaborative investigations, such a way of proceeding has been tapped only occasionally (Harris-Warrick and Marsh [1994] and Price, Milhous, and Hume [1995] offer immediate exception to this generalization. Still, the economies of academic institutions tend to organize research, and rewards to researchers, along disciplinary lines). Among the issues that have preoccupied a number of scholars situated in these fields, a primary concern has been the materiality of dance in opera, that is, conceptualizing or tracking the very "stuff" of dance in opera productions. Less widely pursued as a consistent node of inquiry has been study of ways in which dance in opera, and opera itself operated *in* societies: how it exerted impact, what kinds of impact, and to what effect. These two strands focus the scrutiny conducted by this chapter, with respect to research and debates about dance and opera, in Europe of the seventeenth to the mid-nineteenth centuries. A case study of Mark Morris's late-twentieth-century filmic *Dido and Aeneas* illuminates the debates through a performance optic.

Materializing Dance in and in Connection with Opera

The vitality of the "early music movement" from the mid-twentieth century has provided steady impetus for at least sixty years to scholars who grappled with dance's historical presence and participation in opera. One of the strengths of this "early music movement" has been its tendency to query period dance practices for the insights they can offer on the music performance practice of the period. For all the gaps and lacunae in surviving musical scores and records, the textual status of dance in opera is more challenging still; relatively few are the periods in which detailed choreographic records were made, and for which they are still extant. It is perhaps not surprising that dance in operas from the 1670s to 1730s has received some of the most sustained study, since dance scores from that period are extant, recorded in the Favier and the Beauchamps-Feuillet systems of notation (Harris-Warrick and Marsh 1994; Hilton 1997). While scores using the latter system survive in significant number, almost all were created as scores from 1700 or later. That means that some dance notation scores are available from early eighteenth-century revivals of *tragédies en musiques* by Quinault and Lully, but not from the period of their creation in the 1670s and 1680s. Further, a handful of choreographies at best are notated from any given production, and no large ensemble dance notations from the opera stage were recorded. Rebecca Harris-Warrick and Carol Marsh (1994) have brought to light a *mascarade* from 1688, thoroughly recorded in Favier notation that provides valuable information about staging as well as dancing. Its data derive from a single production; the question is how far it may be extrapolated.

The galvanizing impact of the "early music movement" is still to be felt in the continuing drive to produce period operas, as evidenced by the biennial Boston Early Music Festival in the United States and the fully staged operas that anchor it, as one example, and the New Chamber Opera series mounted at New College, in Oxford, England, as another. The producers of several-hour operas certainly benefit from some of the findings about the materiality of dance in opera. For example, Rebecca Harris-Warrick's systematic research on the conventions for dancing in French Baroque operas offers grounds for deciding when *not* to dance in a Lullian *divertissement*. Harris-Warrick has delineated an aesthetic of "continuity" and a principle of "single focus" at work in the interleaving of choreographies amidst vocal texts and instrumental texts in Lullian *divertissements*, which typically occurred within each of five acts in a *tragédie en musique* (Harris-Warrick 1999: 193–194; 1998: 65–67). Vocal music and dancing did not compete simultaneously for the viewers' attention, but rather occurred in some alternation, except at times in final choruses whose texts had been well established earlier and thus could sustain viewers' apprehension in concert with dancing. As well, Harris-Warrick has shown that dance in French Baroque opera is structured in group scenes and that a sense of community thereby receives visible in addition to aural expression (Harris-Warrick 1999: 199; 1998: 66). From both a present-day production and a historicizing perspective, research has endeavored to discover when and where dance occurred in operas (within acts, as was the case in French operas, or between acts, in Italian operas); when dancers entered the stage, how long they stayed, and when and how they exited in relation to others onstage, even from which zone of the stage. In addition to such crucial questions of logistics or navigation of the scenic landscape and temporal unfolding of an opera production, musicological research has asked how the dancing operated aesthetically: how it interacted with the instrumental and vocal musics; how it related to the texts of the *livrets*; and how it participated—if it did—in the drama unfolded by the produced work. Marian Smith's investigation of *musique parlante* in connection with dance in Parisian operas of the first third of the nineteenth century indicates that the connotative connections summoned up by *musique parlante*—the instrumental citation of popular or familiar songs or tunes in a ballet's music—brought particular words to mind that informed spectators' reception of the narrative and the dancing taking place onstage (Smith 2000: 101–110). This period strategy differs from that of a seventeenth-century Lullian *divertissement*; while both require recourse to text to seal a meaning, for the latter the texts sung onstage provide the particular context in and through which spectators took in the dancing presented in the same *divertissement* (Harris-Warrick 1998: 57, 64; 1999: 193). The garnering of such insights has required painstaking empirical research, of a kind that musicology has honed and burnished, and it has typically been applied to dance in operas of the seventeenth through mid-nineteenth centuries. From that point onward, the vocabularies of classical ballet that supplied a large part of opera choreography for the nineteenth and twentieth centuries receive very little parsing, perhaps because present-day opportunities to see classical ballet lexicons and syntax in action seem plentiful or accessible.

What musicological research has not foregrounded for the seventeenth and eighteenth centuries has been the corporeal means put into play by dance in opera, and ways in which different fashionings of dancing bodies entered into and circulated debates of their day. This arguably can be traced to lack of recorded choreography, but an example from analysis of fifteenth- and sixteenth-century dancing suggests that step-by-step recordings of choreography do not hold all the answers. In *The Dancing Body and Renaissance Choreography*, Mark Franko stresses that "known steps of the social dance repertory were improvised upon and transformed in ballets de cour" (Franko 1986: 3), but that the treatises which set out Renaissance dance vocabulary and choreographies left unstated the perspective on movement quality that informed those "choreographic descriptions" (1986: 5). That is, "[t]reatises tell us to some degree what to dance but not how to dance it" (1986: 10). Franko discerns a tension between movement and stasis within individual step units of the vocabulary, and in transitions from one step and posture to another. He reads this as an evidence of period concerns about dancing; he himself is concerned with showing dancing's connection to civility, and how it exerted effects on its viewers. Franko's finding and his focus on a theory of the body in Renaissance dancing differ greatly from the valorization of court dance as a way station on the (almost inevitable) progress toward autonomous dance that characterized a master narrative of Euro-American theatrical dancing in the early days of academic dance history study. (The synthesizing, editorial commentary that accompanies primary source readings in Cohen [1974] offers a widely circulated example of such a master narrative. For a critique of telic narratives that preceded critiques subsequently forwarded from critical theory bases, see Chapman [1979–1980].) It also prompts researchers to query connections made between moving bodies and period contestations, such as those about class or religion, for example, articulated in embodied practices.

For most periods within seventeenth- through early-nineteenth-century opera, especially when choreographic records are lacking, musicologists have grappled with materializing the dancing in operas by means of an emerging procedure of parsing the affects of musical numbers for scenes and *divertissements* in which dancing occurs. Wye Jamison Allanbrook (1983) offered an early example of this (in addition to other kinds of analysis) in *Rhythmic Gesture in Mozart: 'Le nozze di Figaro' and 'Don Giovanni.'*

Bruce Alan Brown (1991) provides eloquent readings in this vein of the movement plan for a number of pantomime ballets and dance in *opéra-comique* in *Gluck and the French Theatre in Vienna*. With many fewer scores extant than librettos surviving for seventeenth-century Venetian opera, Irene Alm (2003) unpacked the associations circulated by music types, in articles written before her too-early death, and in "Winged Feet and Mute Eloquence" in *Cambridge Opera Journal*, posthumously edited by Wendy Heller and Rebecca Harris-Warrick. In effect, these investigations piece together via the accompanying music the semiotic code, or codes, obtaining for dancing connected with opera productions in their respective periods, although the authors do not designate them formal codes. What the mapped sequences of affects or feeling states lay out are points in the operas' forward-moving trajectories. And while these sequences certainly do summon up acoustically sensuous dimensions of the feeling states, they are unable to unpack how the dancing bodies make corporeal contributions to the presentation of sensuous experience in tandem with the music. To be sure, demographic or ethnic data about the danced characters are certainly capable of conveyance through the movement plan of musical numbers. Such analysis does not necessarily make manifest the ordinating force of particular constructions of dancing bodies therein, be that the gendering, cultural othering, or racing of those constructions.

Running in parallel with the mapping of affective musical trajectories is a concern in musicological studies with the institutional structures that enabled presentation of opera and dance in and in connection with opera. Alm again offers an excellent example with her characterization of different theaters that staged opera in seventeenth-century Venice, including the stage size; obligations of the *maestro di balli* and identification of dance makers when possible; size and typical gendering of dance troupes; and aspects of dance style as these are deduced with respect to a repertoire that was not recorded (Alm 1996c). In a spate of articles, she points out the completely professional status of dancers connected with Venetian operas and the presence of female dancers alongside males from the 1630s. And she brings home the difference that the commercial nature of public theaters exerted on opera finances. The situation in seventeenth-century Venice was remarkably different from that in Paris. Kathleen Hansell (2002) addresses similar kinds of points about the constitution of dance troupes, circulation of dancers, dance makers, and works in her prodigious research on dance in connection with opera produced in Italian cities, from the earliest days of the new genre through the 1870s. She also searches out by whom music for entr'acte ballets was composed, what musical forces it employed, salaries and categories or *emploi* for dancers, and shifts in genres of ballet across the periods. She further maps the different tastes for types of opera in different Italian cities and the vital matter of shifts in finance. Because there was no unified Italy until the nineteenth century, the focus on cities offers salutary contrast with situations in France and England, for instance. What played to favor in one city did not in another; thus, in interesting ways, Hansell shows that the new genre of opera in Italian cities was articulated in interaction with those who saw it. And the focus on city/commercial orientation of dance in opera allows researchers and readers alike to ask the significance of opera when its production was not ruler-driven. Hansell's rigorous charting of change over time makes quite clear that for Italian practice, dance in connection with opera meant ballets staged *between* acts of opera, and that dance was no less important to the ontological status of opera by virtue of its entr'acte sequencing. (Alm treats the seventeenth-century onset of this pattern.) In this Hansell helps set on its heels the telic view in dance historiography, mentioned above, of dance's "progress" toward autonomous status, and the picture given of *ballet d'action* as signaling the onset of this independence. For, as Hansell shows, ballets with through-composed action conveyed solely by dance and music could very well constitute the danced material presented between acts of eighteenth-century Italian operas. Her analysis additionally broadens previous dance historical narratives by writing into eighteenth-century dance history the circumstances and practices in Italian cities, where previously only Marian Hannah Winter (1974) had given them much due. And it expands our understanding of dance as a crucial component in an array or even collation of experiences that viewers encountered as constitutive of opera.

Marian Smith's study of mime and pantomime ballet in connection with the Paris Opéra (2000) shows a similar intertwining of opera and ballet as constitutive of viewers' experience of opera as a spectatorial practice. Her study also suggests when the disaggregation of the two commenced. In his assessment of the conditions of possibility for reform opera's emergence in Gluck's Vienna, Brown (1991) likewise emphasizes the importance of material conditions (whence financial support for production, what configuration of genres and houses provided stages), acting together with available artistic talent and, crucially here also, management. In a notable collaborative study that assessed Italian opera in late eighteenth-century London, musicologist Curtis Price and theater historians Judith Milhous and Robert Hume (1995) demonstrate, in no uncertain terms, the impact of financial mismanagement on the downward spiral of the King's Theatre, Haymarket, in the 1780s and its subsequent struggle with the rival Pantheon Theatre. In their emphases on institutional matrices, financial instruments, and frameworks for funding, these studies feed and sustain a long-term musicological balancing of aesthetic queries with economic ones—a concern that, if not new, has been renewed in dance studies analyses of the millennium.[1]

Intense scrutiny, by different researchers, of dance and opera in Italy, France, Austria, and England during different eras of the seventeenth, eighteenth, and nineteenth centuries has followed in some respects the area studies or national tradition patterns within musicology that also have been organized along genre lines. In so doing, it also makes manifest the strands of difference among what in dance history master narratives had long been deemed the pan-European spread of, for example, a French noble style of dance in the late seventeenth and early eighteenth centuries, and a vogue for *ballet d'action* from the mid-eighteenth to nineteenth centuries, by which latter time it was considered to constitute a norm. The empirical digging and parsing of change over time by scholars mentioned above have enabled revision of any sense of homogeneity that previously obtained in previous dance accounts. While *la belle danse* spread widely across Europe, it was styled differently in different countries, even as it maintained some features in common. (Marsh [1985] made a detailed argument for a distinctive

English style. Russell [2006] and his translation [2012] of Gottfried Taubert's 1717 *Rechtschaffener Tantzmeister* offer valuable perspective on intersections of the French model with German particularity.) More important still, the advent of *ballet d'action* is shown to have proceeded not by utter paradigm shift, as Thomas Kuhn presented this model of change in *The Structure of Scientific Revolutions* ([1962] 1970), but rather as one mode of dance making that agitated among other modes still much in practice: it was part of a multiply configured choreographic scene.

Expression

In tandem with scholarly differentiation of this "Euro-scape" of dance in and in connection with opera, investigation of dance "expression" has continued apace, and here as well scholars have brought into view different practices at different sites, rather than a singular pan-European model. Fairly early in her distinguished research on dance in the *divertissements* of Lully's *tragédies en musique*, Harris-Warrick articulated the valuable distinction that codified movement was but one of several kinds of designed movement presented to audiences. That is, movement of the type recorded in early eighteenth-century dance notation scores was but one type of movement fashioned for the stage, and other types circulated that were both different and not notated. The movements of the *Trembleurs*, people from "*climats glacés*," in the Quinault/Lully opera *Isis*, for example, were described by the Abbé Dubos ([1719, 1748] 1978) as resembling none of the usual movements seen in operas (Harris-Warrick 2000: 47–48; 1999: 195). Further, dances of such characters as Furies are presumed to differ considerably from the danced vocabulary and syntax of noble and even pastoral types. Harris-Warrick has at times assigned to the categories of "pantomime" and "mimesis" the performance of occupational stances and gestures, and actions like the combat among soldiers sparked in Act IV of *Cadmus*. She contrasts this conveyance of meaning to the movement that is intended to be read by audiences as "actual dancing" (Harris-Warrick 1999: 189, 195; 1996: 62), what might also be called "representations of quotidian dancing by characters in the narrative" (this phrasing is my own). Continuing to work on the question, she has posited such categories as end points on a spectrum of representation (Harris-Warrick 2007a: 214). Alm's writing on seventeenth-century Venetian opera uses a similar categorization with regard to occupational procedures or activity representations. She also embraced as sorts of pantomime the stage use of props for smoking or drinking, for example, and the assumption of bodily stances (possibly by children, she wrote) to enact baboons (Alm 1996b: 94–98; 1996c: 106). This capacious designation of pantomime as a category of designed stage movement is so broad as almost to diminish its usefulness; neither does it acknowledge period differences in what constituted pantomime, such as the grammatical operation of a sign system in nineteenth-century ballet pantomime with which characters used gestures to make syntactical statements (e.g., "I love you"; "let us dance together"). Alm also intimates what Hansell argues fully with regard to a distinctive Italian approach to pantomime. Alm cites Giovanni Battista Doni's 1630s *Trattato della musica scenica* and his advocacy of "match[ing] the movements to the subject of the ballo," maintaining that "use of a large choreographic vocabulary of movements, steps, and gestures carefully tailored to each subject is an essential characteristic of Italian theatrical dance throughout the seventeenth century" (Alm 1996c: 89–90). Hansell argues that pantomime by seventeenth- and eighteenth-century Italian dancers was full-bodied, embracing all the person's corporeal resources, which could include acrobatic skills and aerial style (2002: 183, 189), and that this disposition of body parts and capacities differed from mime used in other countries. Bongiovanni (2005) treats pantomime and virtuoso dancing as two related but different aspects of the Italian grotesque dancer's skills. In unpacking some period critiques of grotesque dancing voiced by literati and Neapolitan partisans of Jean-Georges Noverre's choreographic approach, he emphasizes critics' distaste for virtuosic dancing. Hansell (2002) seems to place more emphasis on the two skill sets as conjoined. Alm, Hansell, and Bongiovanni catalyze deserved re-equilibration of dance historical accounts that privileged the French scene and French aesthetics.

Englishman John Weaver put his praise for Italian mimes into print in the 1710s, and his own efforts to develop a gestural system for performance in his innovative "theatrical entertainments of dancing" have been steadily visited by scholars exploring dance's route toward autonomous status and storying capacity (Ralph 1985). The credit long accrued to Weaver has more recently been extended to recognize the collaboration and skills of the performers who enacted this vision of danced meaning-making, as dance historian Moira Goff (2007) has shown with particular respect to dancer Hester Santlow on the London stage. Musicologist Sarah McCleave (1995, 1998, 2007, 2007–2008) and dance studies scholar Susan Foster (1996: 1–12) have turned attention to Marie Sallé's skills and impact on, respectively, Handel's 1734 London operas and several Rameau operas, and a century's shift in how French ballets positioned their female characters as agents, or not. The revising of an erstwhile male-gendered pattern of innovation in danced expression is an important gain from these researches. Equally vital is McCleave's recent querying and historicization of the very concept of expression in dance as it shifted for different theorists during the parts of the eighteenth century when Sallé both created and performed dances in operas, and when, McCleave argues, Noverre's *ballet d'action* responded in part to Sallé's impress (McCleave 2007–2008). McCleave's recent work begins to bridge the explanatory gap between the meaning-making accomplished by articulation of a single affective state via a given choreography in a Lullian *divertissement* (such as a sarabande or passepied) and the communication of a complete action through a sequencing of changing affective gestures in a Sallé choreography for the London stage or Paris Opéra.

In a related vein, research by Mary Cyr (1995a), Antonia Banducci (1993), and Thomas Betzwieser (2000) has deepened present-day understanding of how stage movement by members of the chorus forwarded a French opera's trajectory, at different points in the eighteenth century. All three built upon Lois Rosow's findings in "Performing a Choral Dialogue by Lully" (1987) and the picture presented there of the chorus's assignment to the sides of the stage, without further locomotion in the course of scenes. Cyr's early argument (1995a) from iconographic sources about the chorus's potential gesturing did not account for conventions of visual representation at work in costume designs, for example. Banducci's (1993) thorough parsing of a promptbook for a 1748 production of Campra's *Tancrède* by Madame de Pompadour's troupe at Versailles persuasively limned some of the emphases that conventional and also unusual timing and spatial locations of choruses' entrances and exits could lend to a production. In a 2004 article that gives substantive attention to prompt-notes for a 1778 revival of *Armide*, planned for the Opéra but not performed, Banducci explores the relationship between stage dance and dancers and the movement of the chorus. She creates the capacity for readers to imagine the hierarchical stage space of French opera as, at given points, a mutually constituted swath of bodies not limited in its impact to the activity of the soloists or the danced ensembles. Betzwieser (2000) focuses attention on Gluck's putting of the chorus into motion—granting them locomotion—together with dancers in his Paris reform operas. Reading commentaries from the mid- to late eighteenth century, together with libretti and scores, Betzwieser argues that the pivot for this change came with a shift in musical setting: polyphonic music was used as accompaniment for dancing, where previously it had served as surrogate for movement. The careful, data-based refigurings of the stage by these scholars do not, perhaps not yet, address whether (and if so, whether individually or in unison) the range of eighteenth-century dramatic gestures set out by Dene Barnett's research (1987) were those of which period chorus members availed themselves (and which present-day performers of Baroque opera frequently access).

Scholarly attention to bodily "expression," and to the chorus and its scenic movement, thus broadens the conceptualization of movement practice in play with respect to dance located within the acts of operas, as in the French model, and staged in entr'acte connection with operas, as in the Italian model. Research drives to materialize movement practices have resulted in heavy emphasis on establishing the ontological status of the practices—not interruption, not parenthetical, as Harris-Warrick put it (1998: 67; 1999: 193), and to trace their dramaturgical function, the latter generally conceived as ways that movement practices forward the trajectory of plot or story.

Conceptualizing How Dance and Opera Joined Debates in Societies

The "materializing" approach to exploring dance and movement in and in connection with opera tends to plumb the historical surround for grist with which to explain, substantiate, and even theorize the aesthetics, performance practices, and repertories of operas and their dancing. Another approach, running concurrently in the last twenty years, tends to scrutinize how dance and movement practice in and in connection with opera take action in and with respect to their historical, political, and social surround—what I will call here a culturalist approach. Empirical procedures of the materializing approach are fundamental to the culturalist approach, too, but in the latter, analysis turns outward from the genre to query the circulation of its productions, to inspect how dance and opera enter into period debates and represent—sometimes contesting, at other times consolidating—constructions of being, knowledge, and power in their societies. The public balls that grew up around the Paris Opéra in the eighteenth century and again in the nineteenth century have provided one kind of topos productive for culturalist analysis. Richard Semmens's study (2004) of the eighteenth-century *bals publics*, from inauguration through the 1780s, immediately pinpoints the economic connection between commercial balls and Opéra music. Revenues generated by the public balls supplied financial resources for debt-reduction, first in connection with a Magasin, a new services building that opened in 1715, and later with the Opéra's overall finances (Semmens 2004: 57–59). What Semmens also unpacks is the *bals*' currency as a kind of "vortex of behavior"—here I use Joseph Roach's (1996) term—that is, a locus where the force of past customs, etiquettes, and corporeal techniques eddied without complete erasure as new behaviors and traditions formulated. Semmens distinguished formal balls (often court balls) from the public balls. The conduct of formal balls projected dancers' status and emphasized the display of rank, or rank as achieved and embodied via a group dance event; whereas public balls subverted the projection of status through their requirement of masking and the evening-long agenda of participants' attempts to unmask others through conversational ploys and, implicitly, engage in sexual encounters. To derive the distinction, Semmens parsed the materiality of *bals* as events: entrances and exits; decision making about the repertoire to be danced; specifics of the orchestras' instrumentation, leadership, musicians, and their employment; the architecture of the *bal* space—and relations over time among the longways-formation contredanses and the cotillion and *contredanse à la française* choreographies for fixed numbers of persons. He argues that the public balls created a space for the articulation of individuals *qua* individuals. For all participants, the gauge of access or entry to the public ball was ability to pay, not social rank, and for women especially, the ability to take initiative in the ploys and pursuit of unmasking upended the gendered subordination that marked their daily life, at least through the 1760s and the onset of gendered changes to masking and conventionalized ball apparel. What Semmens discerns is the conceptual and ambient space that public balls afforded for emergence of individualized subjectivity, though he does not use that term. He notes the marginalization of dancing—contredanses were pushed to the two ends of the ball floor, together with their orchestras—and the allocation of space at the center of the floor to the subversive play of unmasking. Semmens thus connects the loss of dance's status-projection capacities in the public ball context with possibilities for resistance to still-dominant gender and class hierarchies in French society.

Maribeth Clark's (1998) culturalist analysis assesses nineteenth-century public balls and examines the balls as topoi for period operas. Her dissertation probes how commercially published quadrille dance music, and social dancing of quadrille choreographies, conditioned ways in which people heard opera music and also music arranged from operas. By speaking to what can be called the "re-purposing" of opera music and its channeling to a music-buying public, she underlines the instability of opera in the first half of the nineteenth century, suggesting that it was prone to unravel. That is, Clark argues, the supposed coherence of grand opera works proved to be tenuous or provisional, as tunes or topoi from grand opera were readily selected and arranged for commercial markets and social dance consumption. Clearly engaging with reception of opera music and its circulation in several types of channels, Clark links balls and dance music to issues of courtship, spectators' perceptions of women's dancing bodies, and even nation, as she forwards the idea that the meanings for music are not dictated by the music, but can be gleaned and constructed by its receivers—indeed, its users.

The capacity of dance and movement in opera to construct social meanings is eloquently voiced by Susan McClary's (1991) discussion of Bizet's *Carmen*. McClary calls attention to the lead character's sensuous moving body, specifically her hips, as referenced and indicated by the music, and argues for the music as a register of sexuality (1991: 57; 1992: 54, 56). In other writing she proposes the production of different cultural bodies in the music, such as French and Italian bodies, by means of the qualities of motion that the music suggests (McClary 1995; 1998).

Gender

Gender has in fact long supplied a prominent focus in culturalist analyses of dance and movement practice in connection with opera. Early momentum to consider constructions, and contestations, of gender allocations put into play by opera was generated by Catherine Clément's *Opera, or the Undoing of Women* ([1988] 1999). It exposed how opera's "beautiful music" obfuscated and belied the subordination of women spelled out by the "words" (the *livret*). Both Maribeth Clark (1998) and Marian Smith (2000) point to masculinist readings of dancers in Romantic ballet and opera that circulated in period news and literary accounts, and Smith additionally speaks to the way that plots provide instruction, even tutelage, for women on gender roles prevailing in French society. Semmens (2004) points to the temporary shifts in gender power, however short-lived, that eighteenth-century Opéra balls provided women masqueraders. Julia Prest's (2006) assessment of cross-casting and cross-dressing in seventeenth-century French court ballets addresses a format that included vocal and instrumental music but was predecessor to French opera. Prest (2006: 1) distinguishes cross-casting ("male actors playing female roles") from cross-dressing ("the female roles disguising themselves as men *within* the fiction of the film"), illustrating with an example drawn from the film *Monty Python's Life of Brian* (1979). Her analysis relies heavily on *livrets* for parsing the impact of the dancing that constituted an important element of the *entrées*, the structural components from which court ballets were made. Prest resists a single interpretation and insists that the impact of cross-casting and cross-dressing is particular to the situations and genres in which it appears (she addresses Shakespearean plays and castrati in French opera, in addition to dancers in court ballet.) Nonetheless, she connects cross-dressing and cross-casting to cultural anxieties about identities in the periods and genres she surveys, mapping ways that productions reached out to join debates about, comment on, and offer alternatives with respect to the social configurations that people navigated on daily and long-term bases.

Scholars have just begun to scratch the surface of dance's implication in the signaling of gender or sexuality in seventeenth- and eighteenth-century opera. Harris-Warrick has set out some preliminary earmarks of a gender code for dance assignments in Lullian *divertissements*, while calling for further work. Rapid, vigorous music is frequently given for male characters, gentler triple meter used for female characters or mixed male-female groups, she noted early in her research trajectory (Harris-Warrick 1998: 64) In recent writing on Lully's *Cadmus et Hermione* (2008), she notes a shift evident after 1681, when female dancers began to appear on the Opéra stage and when Quinault configured *divertissements* to include female personages to advantage. Lully's music changed in response, she says: "The dance airs that Lully composed for women or for mixed groups were clearly different from those destined for men alone"[2] (Harris-Warrick 2008: 231). She further observes a "particular structure to be found in certain dances by Lully for male characters' roles, the first part of which has the allure of an entrée grave and irregular structures (5+6 measures), whereas the second part, while keeping the same meter, accelerates via jerky rhythms and doubling of note values"[3] (2008: 241–242). How the dancing person bodies forth gender, if she or he does, in concert with other recognized music and dance types, is still to be theorized. So too are the seventeenth- and eighteenth-century implications of same-sex dances for two or three people, which are available for scrutiny among notated scores.

Ideological Critique

While culturalist analyses of dance and movement in opera have deftly pursued several ways in which dance and movement in opera have participated in and sometimes contested particular period debates about gender or identity, Cowart's *The Triumph of Pleasure* (2008) expands the scope of ideological critique that opera can be seen to have proffered via late-seventeenth and early-eighteenth-century *opéra-ballet*. Cowart paces through court ballet under Louis XIII and XIV, *comédie-ballets, tragédies lyriques*, and *opéra-ballet*, pulling apart the aesthetic messages offered by these production types to show the resistant strand bound together with the royally enjoined strand of meaning. She focuses on the deployment of spectacle (which she broadly defines as dance and music) in the production types, and on the topos of the Muses as recurring features of the double-coded message that productions delivered. Her analysis attributes to the producing artists considerable agency in selecting the Muses topos, and she delineates the *libertin* circles in which several of them moved, locating additional sources and philosophies that underpinned their resistive stances to the king's perceived excesses. And she illuminates patronage offered by political contenders, as the new genre of *opéra-ballet* emerged in the wake of Lully's demise, Louis XIV's decreasing interest in musical theater, and the growing importance of the Opéra venue, as opposed to the court, as locus and symbol of a counter-public sphere imbued with resistance to the monarch's aggrandizement and self-memorializing system of artistic production.

Cowart's argument highlights the intertextuality between earlier and later production types, and it places much emphasis on the power of spectacle to provide a vehicle for political engagement and cloaked resistance. Her analysis relies heavily on music and *livret* materials, which it reads with sophistication, and iconography, especially with regard to *opéra-ballets* and interpretation of the *fête galante* motif. A number of notated dance scores do exist for the period of the inauguration and flourishing of *opéra-ballet*. Cowart does not draw on these herself, but rather takes up Sarah Cohen's (2000) analysis of the minuet dance type, for example, as an optic for imaginatively parsing spatial trajectories in period images depicting Cytherean parties. For culturalist as for materializing approaches, multivariable analysis remains challenging to enact for appraising dance and movement in and connected with opera. Cowart's is one of the most broad-ranging endeavors to date, and it speaks both to the constitutive features of the production types it analyzes and to the period struggles that the productions entered into, however veiled that participation had to be.

Mark Morris's filmic *Dido and Aeneas* (1995)

To date, neither the materializing nor the culturalist approach has displaced the other in the academy, or with regard to scholarly explorations of dance in and in connection with opera. While the former approach seems to buttress a concern with genres and their distinctions that has been characteristic of modernist inquiry in the mid- and late twentieth century, and the latter strives to reconceptualize how artistic practices constitute even as they are constituted by the milieu in which they circulate, the two can play into each other. That this is possible, and can be productive, is vividly shown in Mark Morris's 1995 film conception and choreography of *Dido and Aeneas*, using music by Henry Purcell and *livret* materials from that work's 1680s English production(s).[4] Morris has enjoyed several collaborations in addition to *Dido and Aeneas* for which he provided choreography for contemporary productions of period operas, including Gluck's *Orfeo ed Euridice* (1996), Rameau's *Platée* (1997), and Purcell's *King Arthur* (2006). While the musical forces typically pursue period performance practices, no period choreographic scores specific to these works survive for dance directors to mobilize. Morris's choreographic approach has tended to a hybrid of present-day and period choreographic strategies, put to work with movement vocabularies that borrow eclectically from modern dance and ballet lexicons, but also invent movement as needed. The DVD publication of Morris's *Dido and Aeneas* renders it still more widely accessible than Morris's stage production of the work, which premiered in 1989, and thus the analysis that follows is keyed to the commercially recorded production (Morris 1995).

Morris's 1995 *Dido* is danced in its entirety, with choral and instrumental music provided by the noted period music ensemble Tafelmusik, conducted by Jeanne Lamon, and the Tafelmusik Chamber Choir. And while both chorus and solo singers are shown from time to time in the DVD frame, none of the singers tread the stage. Instead, the plot is enacted by solo dancers who emerge from and return to the dancing chorus, together with Morris in the dual dance role of Dido and Sorceress, and Guillermo Resto as the dancing Aeneas. This makes for steady change in the texture of the dancing forces, that is, alternation of danced duets, solos, and danced ensembles, and that very contrast enacts a widely held value in seventeenth- and eighteenth-century Baroque opera. Whereas dancers in French opera would seldom have danced while the chorus sang, Morris puts the dancing chorus in motion to choral as well as instrumental music. (The ensemble dances during the vocal section of "Come away, fellow sailors"[5] and also during the purely instrumental music that immediately follows, for example.)

In terms of "blocking" for performers and the spatial designs configured by dancing bodies, Morris shows exquisite sensitivity to the period value placed on symmetry. As the overture commences, the dancers mount steps to a raised rectangular platform that serves as the dancing space for the entire production. Aeneas climbs the steps stage left, Dido and the dance chorus stage right, and this early imbalance of forces pits Aeneas against Dido's group, raising questions from the outset about the outcome of their (d)alliance. Stepping up onto low balustrades that girdle the dancing space, Aeneas and the chorus turn sharply, in profile, gazing in opposite directions; then they switch those directions; then they step into the arena for action. Morris's choreography returns a number of times to profile facings, be that of Dido face to face with Aeneas, or Belinda and the Second Woman mimicking that mirror symmetry as the two royals woo, or segments of the dancing chorus symmetrically disposed across lateral and sagittal axes of the stage. Dido's air "Ah! Belinda" mobilizes the two in a danced phrase using first mirror image symmetry, and then coaxial symmetry, before Belinda steps aside for a new phrase that Dido pursues solo. Further echoing period staging practices, Morris frequently places members of the dancing chorus in lines at two sides of the stage, but he just as often riffs on convention and distributes them along a low balustrade at the upstage border, or aligns two lines of dancers at one side of the stage with none at the other. In bold disregard of stage wisdom that cautions dancers against turning their backs on the audience for any sustained period, Morris frequently plants Dido center stage, turned upstage to watch the chorus's dancing. In the "Fear no danger" danced chorus, this seated figure cheekily registers Dido as choreographer of her court, just as Morris is choreographer of his troupe. The trope is reinforced when the Sorceress and witches engage in danced call and response during "In our deep vaulted cell" and the Echo Dance of the Furies that follows. Here is explicit postmodern self-reflexivity, and wry comment.

Morris's hybrid approach continues with the movement he fashions for this production. Male and female chorus dancers share the same movement vocabulary and also a full-bodied approach to imitative and abstract action that likely would have gained approval from eighteenth-century Italian *grotteschi*. Morris devised a lexicon of gestures that noticeably recur and that cite body parts and linked concepts, such as a dancer's two flared hands pressed one above the other beneath the sternum, to signal heart and also "pain"; or the profile, vertical stance topped by arched back and backward-flung head, resounding visually as "death." Some bodily motions enact the movement quality mentioned in the associated sung text. This occurs in "Grief increases by concealing" when Dido stirs the air with her forearms to depict the turbulence of "storm," and when she circles an elongated arm with punctuated stops to picture the vigor of Anchises' valor that is attributed to Aeneas. And it happens there again in the succeeding pendular arm swing and reclining posture that register this hero's reputed "softness." Sometimes Morris has the dancers avail themselves of quotidian behavior, as when Aeneas lies atop Dido in the "Grove" scene, to consummate their union.

The 1680s *Dido* was performed at least once by female students at a boarding school in Chelsea; it is not known how Aeneas was portrayed. In addition to the culturalist question of gender assignments in dance, Morris's cross-casting of himself as both Dido and the Sorceress in the 1995 filmic production puts sexuality into play in a dual register of past and present. Morris capably dances a representation of femininity that, despite its character's indecision, is appropriately strong in relation to the softness of Aeneas's role; indeed, this Dido even slaps Aeneas. But cross-casting is not (yet) commonplace in mainstream Euro-American contemporary choreography; to present-day viewers, Morris and Resto's enactment of the heterosexual couple Dido and Aeneas simultaneously reads as a same-sex couple. This brings home the shift(s) in Western conceptions of sexuality since the seventeenth century, when it was deemed possible for elite English men to maintain "masculinity" while engaging in sexual relations with lower-class men, as well as with women (Bray 1995). The same-sex casting of the lead couple in Morris's *Dido* perhaps also illuminates, by means of contrast, the relations of power and submission expected of women, even of queens, in patriarchal marriage. Musicologist Ellen Harris reads the main subject of the seventeenth-century *Dido and Aeneas* in related vein as a cautionary tale for period young women—"the Dido legend was suitably adapted as a morality for the girls of Josias Priest's boarding school who acted the drama," and she points to the last line in Thomas D'Urfey's 1689 Epilogue to *Dido*, "... to save us from those grand deceivers, men" in corroboration (Harris 1987: 33). Reading against the heteronormative grain, Judith Peraino views *Dido* as situating the Sorceress and Dido in a sadomasochistic relationship: The Sorceress takes pleasure in tormenting Dido, and Dido takes pleasure in suffering (Peraino 1995: 114–115). Not only can Dido and the Sorceress be read as a " 'homosexual' dyad," but the 1689 performance at Priest's school for young gentlewomen "allows for the 'working out' of the underlying homosexual dynamics at play in the homosocial environment of the boarding schools" (Peraino 1995: 121, 127). Susan Foster extrapolates from the 1680s *Dido* to imagine a different ending in which Belinda and Dido go off together as a lesbian couple to the Canary Islands (Foster 2007: 129). Neither writer's argument nods to the same-sex casting in Morris's filmic *Dido*, and only the stage-performed *Dido* had been capable of viewing when Peraino's article was in press. Their circulation nonetheless echoes and extends the opportunity and imperative to scrutinize sexuality that Morris's casting foregrounds. And their circulation links textual argument with the embodied culturalist argument that Morris's casting proffers.

Morris's 1995 *Dido* brings to the fore a second set of culturalist concerns, those of empire, trade, and dominating cultural others. Empire is cited three times in the 1995 *Dido and Aeneas* vocal text: chorus members happily assimilate "empire growing" to "pleasures flowing" as they urge Dido to encourage Aeneas; Aeneas sues for Dido's acceptance, imploring, "If not for mine, for empire's sake"; and the injured Dido spurns Aeneas's repentance with "To your promis'd empire fly, and let forsaken Dido die." However readily the love story offers competition to this theme, empire cannot be gainsaid. If one takes Aeneas to stand for classical Troy and the (white) colonial power of seventeenth-century Europe, Dido, queen of Carthage (in today's Tunisia), could stand for classical-era Africa (even though, per *Bulfinch's Mythology*, she relocated from Tyre, in present-day Lebanon), the city's orientation to commerce, and, broadly, the continent's seventeenth-century trade in slaves (Bulfinch 1998: 241–242). Morris complicates this interpretation of Aeneas's role by casting a black performer, whom audiences might well read as the subordinated member of a mixed-race couple in today's still racist social power structure, and by casting himself, a white performer, in the role of an African Dido. What the casting highlights by the very reversal it introduces is the dependence of seventeenth-century English plantations on the slave labor that worked its crops in Jamaica, Barbados, and the Leeward Islands. Also, from the 1670s when the Royal African Company was chartered, England would contest and then overtake the Dutch in the slave trade (Norton et al. 1986: 51–52, 64–65). Analyzing Noverre's eighteenth-century *Dido and Aeneas*, Foster suggests the possible interpretations of Dido as either exotic/African or white/French, the latter in view of and anticipating France's nineteenth-century colonization of Algeria (2007: 128–129). The legacy of the African diaspora in which England participated is still agitating today; here, too, Morris's casting creates an intertext between past and present.

Coeval with issues of diaspora that the 1995 *Dido* raises is a second register of empire, this one linked to the consumer revolution of late-seventeenth- and early-eighteenth-century England that commerce and bluewater policy brought about. As David Porter (2002) persuasively argues, trade with China and the fashions of chinoiserie that cycled through English culture came to be attributed to females, their interests, and their gender allocation, while also linked to contest between emerging theories of aesthetic value. The "pleasures flowing" that, early in the production, the *Dido* chorus cites as a result of "empire growing" can be understood to signal the sensuous experiencing of the China wares that began to circulate in England in the late seventeenth century. Further, the simultaneous novelty and seeming timelessness of China goods within English culture could

> exercise such extraordinary and seemingly subversive appeal only in a context where the destiny assigned by family pedigree was increasingly subject to the flux of social mobility, and the traditional role of women in the reproduction of the social order was being undermined within the increasingly contested and anxiety-ridden field of

> gender identity. The consumers of chinoiserie were the bricoleurs of the new commercial society. (Porter 2002: 408)

To be sure, the boarding school performance of *Dido and Aeneas* occurred as England's China trade began to burgeon, but note that "in the 1690s, Queen Mary was renowned for her magnificent porcelain collection" (Porter 2002: 396). Both the 1680s production(s) and Morris's 1995 *Dido and Aeneas* offer viewers and readers, past and present, a frame in which to acknowledge connections between empire as commerce, sensuous pleasures, and configuration of gendered agency.

What Morris's 1995 *Dido and Aeneas* offers, I suggest, is a palimpsest. Its dance design acknowledges choreographic strategies past, but also some of twentieth-century currency. The work offers viewers access to concerns about sexuality, domination of cultural others by trading them as chattel, and shifting grounds of gender ordination, in dual registers of the past and the present. Without replicating a 1680s production, it brings together dimensions of materializing research on period performance with culturalist concerns about ways in which artistic production intervened, and sometimes was complicit, in structures of domination and in/equality of their day. Whether this was Morris's express intention, whether he deemed this a reworking of *Dido* or a re-purposing of it, is less central than the work's effects, and these effects are at least twofold. In terms of his own career trajectory, *Dido* offered Morris the challenge of working with a storied music and vocal score, and as a filmic composition, at a time in the late twentieth century when critical kudos for "experimental" choreography continued to valorize the distancing of concert dance choreography from musical structures that might dominate it. Certainly Morris's involvement with period opera projects has brought his work to the attention of new audiences who might otherwise not have encountered it. As well, *Dido* enabled him to continue and extend the querying of gender, sexuality, and race staged in contemporary theatrical dance, as he had done with, for example, *The Hard Nut*, a jaunty revision of the nineteenth-century classical ballet that had come to be a Christmas-time theatrical staple in the United States. The 1995 *Dido* offers up a palimpsest[6] of past and present concerns about how to articulate dance with vocal and instrumental music; how to tap past bodily and musical performance practices; and how to weigh dance in and in connection with opera, as a production kind that both constituted, and took steps to resist, structures of being, knowledge, and power in its times. For today's times, it also suggests that the materializing and the culturalist scholarly approaches might aspire to test each other's findings, to ask in what they sustain, or do not, each other's theorizing, tuning in, all the while, to the reciprocal interplay between pasts and presents.

See also: Politics, Historically Informed Performance

Notes

1. Foster (2002) offers a more thorough economic analysis than others since Garafola (1989) and her articulation of emphasis on "Enterprise" in addition to that of "Art" and "Audience." For attention to institutional issues, see Tomko 1999.

2. "Les airs de danse que Lully a composés pour des femmes ou pour des troupes mixtes sont nettement différents de ceux qu'il destinait aux homes seuls."
3. "Le 'Premier air pour les Statues'... a une carrure particulière qu'on retrouve dans certaines danses de Lully pour des rôles de caractère masculins : la première partie a l'allure d'une entrée grave et des carrures irrégulières (5+6 mesures), tandis que la seconde, tout en gardant le même signe de mesure, propose une accélération par des rythmes saccadés en doublant la valeur des notes."
4. Scholars agree that Purcell and Tate's *Dido and Aeneas* was performed in 1689, for which an Epilogue by Thomas D'Urfey exists. The date of the *first* production was thrown into vigorous question by Bruce Wood and Andrew Pinnock's 1992 article "'Unscarr'd by Turning Times'?" which sparked numerous rejoinders. For some of these, see Buttrey 1992; Goldie 1992; Adams 1993; Price 1994; Walkling 1994, 1995; Wood and Pinnock 1994, 1995. More than a decade later, new data stirred comment again; see White 2009; Price and Walkling 2011; Pinnock 2012. Dates for the first performance (whether that was at court or at Josias Priest's boarding school in Chelsea) discussed in the debates fell in the 1680s. Hence my use of the descriptor "1680s."
5. For consistency in referring to the 1995 DVD, I use text from the libretto posted on the Mark Morris Dance Group website (Morris 2012). See also Price 1986 for a critical edition and score.
6. After this chapter entered the editorial and production processes, Andrew Walkling (2010), too, described *Dido and Aeneas* as a palimpsest.

Bibliography

Adams, Martin. 1993. "More on Dating *Dido*." *Early Music* 21/3: 510.

Allanbrook, Wye Jamison. 1983. *Rhythmic Gesture in Mozart: 'Le nozze di Figaro' and 'Don Giovanni.'* Chicago: University of Chicago Press.

Alm, Irene. 2003. "Winged Feet and Mute Eloquence: Dance in Seventeenth-century Venetian Opera," edited by Wendy Heller and Rebecca Harris-Warrick. *Cambridge Opera Journal* 15/3: 216–280.

——. 1996a. "Operatic Ballroom Scenes and the Arrival of French Social Dance in Venice." *Studi musicali* 25: 345–371.

——. 1996b. "Pantomime in Seventeenth-Century Venetian Theatrical Dance." In *Creature di Prometeo. Il Ballo Teatrale. Dal Divertimento al Dramma. Studi offerti a Aurel M. Milloss*, edited by Giovanni Morelli, 87–102. Florence: Olschki.

——. 1996c. "Theatrical Dance in Venetian Opera 1637–1660." In *L'arte della danza ai tempi di Claudio Monteverdi. Atti del convegno internazionale Torino, 6–7 settembre 1993*, edited by Angelo Chiarle, 95–111. Turin: Istituto per i beni musicali in Piemonte.

——. 1995. "Humanism and Theatrical Dance in Early Opera." *Musica Disciplina* 49: 79–93.

Banducci, Antonia L. 2004. "Staging and Its Dramatic Effect in French Baroque Opera: Evidence from Prompt Notes." *Eighteenth-Century Music* 1/1: 5–28.

——. 1993. "Staging a *Tragédie en Musique*: A 1748 Promptbook of Campra's *Tancrède*." *Early Music* 21/2: 180–190.

Barnett, Dene, with the assistance of Jeanette Massy-Westropp. 1987. *The Art of Gesture: The Practices and Principles of 18th-Century Acting*. Heidelberg: Carl Winter Universitätsverlag.

Bauman, Thomas, and Marita P. McClymonds, eds. 1995. *Opera and the Enlightenment*. Cambridge: Cambridge University Press.

Betzwieser, Thomas. 2000. "Musical Setting and Scenic Movement: Chorus and *Chœur Dansé* in Eighteenth-Century Parisian Opéra." *Cambridge Opera Journal* 12/1: 1–28.

Bongiovanni, Salvatore. 2005. "Magri in Naples: Defending the Italian Dance Tradition," translated by Bruce Alan Brown. In *The Grotesque Dancer on the Eighteenth-Century Stage: Gennaro Magri and His World*, edited by Rebecca Harris-Warrick and Bruce Alan Brown, 91–108. Madison: University of Wisconsin Press.

Bray, Alan. 1995. *Homosexuality in Renaissance England*. New York: Columbia University Press.

Brown, Bruce Alan. 2009. "Le Ballet-Pantomime Reformé et son Nouveau Public: Paris, Vienne." In Waeber 2009, 197–213.

——. 1995. "*Zéphire et Flore*: A 'Galant' Early Ballet by Angiolini and Gluck." In Bauman and McClymonds 1995, 189–216.

——. 1991. *Gluck and the French Theatre in Vienna*. Oxford: Clarendon Press.

Bulfinch, Thomas. 1998. *Bulfinch's Mythology*. New York: Modern Library.

Burden, Michael. 2007. "To Repeat (or Not to Repeat?): Dance Cues in Restoration English Opera." *Early Music* 35/3: 397–417.

Buttrey, John. 1992. "The Dating of *Dido*." *Early Music* 20/4: 703.

Chapman, John. 1979–1980. "The Aesthetic Interpretation of Dance History." *Dance Chronicle* 3/3: 254–274.

Clark, Maribeth. 1998. "Understanding French Grand Opera through Dance." PhD diss., University of Pennsylvania.

Clément, Catherine. [1988] 1999. *Opera, or the Undoing of Women*, translated by Betsy Wing. Minneapolis: University of Minnesota Press.

Cohen, Sarah R. 2000. *Art, Dance, and the Body in French Culture of the Ancien Régime*. Cambridge: Cambridge University Press.

Cohen, Selma Jeanne, ed. 1974. *Dance as a Theatre Art: Source Readings in Dance History from 1581 to the Present*. New York: Dodd, Mead.

Cowart, Georgia. 2008. *The Triumph of Pleasure: Louis XIV and the Politics of Spectacle*. Chicago: University of Chicago Press.

Cyr, Mary. 1995a. "The Dramatic role of the Chorus in French Opera: Evidence for the Use of Gesture, 1670–1770." In Bauman and McClymonds 1995, 105–118.

——. 1995b. "The Paris Opéra Chorus during the Time of Rameau." *Music & Letters* 76/1: 32–51.

Dubos, Abbé [Jean-Baptiste]. [1719, 1748] 1978. *Critical Reflections on Poetry, Painting, and Music* [*Réflexions critiques sur la poésie et sur la peinture*]. 5th ed., translated by Thomas Nugent. London: Printed for J. Nourse. Reprint. New York: AMS Press.

Foster, Susan. 2007. "Dido's Otherness: Choreographing Race and Gender in the *Ballet d'Action*." In *Dance Discourses: Keywords in Dance Research*, edited by Susanne Franco and Marina Nordera, 121–130. London: Routledge.

——. 2002. *Dances That Describe Themselves: The Improvised Choreography of Richard Bull*. Middletown, CT: Wesleyan University Press.

——. 1996. *Choreography and Narrative: Ballet's Staging of Story and Desire*. Bloomington: Indiana University Press.

Franko, Mark. 1987. "The Notion of 'Fantasmata' in Fifteenth-Century Italian Dance Treatises." Congress on Research in Dance. *Dance Research Annual* 16: 68–86.

——. 1986. *The Dancing Body in Renaissance Choreography*. Birmingham, NY: Summa Publications.

Garafola, Lynn. 1989. *Diaghilev's Ballets Russes*. New York: Oxford University Press.

Goff, Moira. 2007. *The Incomparable Hester Santlow: A Dancer-Actress on the Georgian Stage*. Performance in the Long Eighteenth Century: Studies in Theatre, Music, Dance. Aldershot, UK: Ashgate.

Goldie, Mark. 1992. "The Earliest Notice of Purcell's *Dido and Aeneas*." *Early Music* 20/3: 393–400.

Hansell, Kathleen Kuzmick. 2002. "Theatrical Ballet and Italian Opera." [English original]. In *Opera on Stage*, edited by Lorenzo Bianconi and Giorgio Pestelli, translated by Kate Singleton. *The History of Italian Opera* 5: 177–301. Chicago: University of Chicago Press.

Harris, Ellen T. 1987. *Henry Purcell's 'Dido and Aeneas.'* Oxford: Clarendon Press.

Harris-Warrick, Rebecca. 2009. "Ballet, Pantomime, and the Sung Word in the Operas of Rameau." In *Coll'astuzia, col giudizio: Essays in Honor of Neal Zaslaw*, edited by Cliff Eisen, 31–61. Ann Arbor: Steglein.

——. 2008. "La Danse dans *Cadmus & Hermione*." In *Cadmus and Hermione (1673) de Jean-Baptiste Lully et Philippe Quinault*, edited by Jean Duron, 231–250. Wavre: Mardaga.

——. 2007a. "Dance and Representation in the Operas of Lully." In *'L'esprit français' und die Musik Europas: Entstehung, Einfluss und Grenzen einer ästhetischen Doktrin; Festschrift für Herbert Schneider*, edited by Michelle Biget-Manfroy and Rainer Schmusch. Hildesheim: Georg Olms Verlag.

——. 2007b. "Lully's On-stage Societies." In Johnson et al. 2007, 53–71.

——. 2003. "Staging Venice." *Cambridge Opera Journal* 15/3: 297–316.

——. 2000. "The Phrase Structure of Lully's Dance Music." In *Lully Studies*, edited by John Hajdu Heyer, 32–56. Cambridge: Cambridge University Press.

——. 1999. "'Toute Danse Doit Exprimer, Peindre…': Finding the Drama in the Operatic Divertissement." In *Basler Jahrbuch für historische Musikpraxis* 23, edited by Peter Reidemeister, 187–210. Winterthur, Switzerland: Amadeus.

——. 1998. "Recovering the Lullian Divertissement." In McCleave 1998, 55–80.

——. 1990. "Contexts for Choreographies: Notated Dances Set to the Music of Jean-Baptiste Lully." In *Jean-Baptiste Lully. Actes du colloque/Kongressbericht Saint-Germain-en-Laye—Heidelberg 1987*, edited by Jérôme de La Gorce and Herbert Schneider, 433–455. Laaber: Laaber-Verlag.

——, and Bruce Alan Brown, eds. 2005. *The Grotesque Dancer on the Eighteenth-Century Stage: Gennaro Magri and His World*. Studies in Dance History. Madison: University of Wisconsin Press.

——, and Carol G. Marsh. 1994. *Musical Theatre at the Court of Louis XIV: 'Le Mariage de la Grosse Cathos.'* Cambridge Musical Texts and Monographs. Cambridge: Cambridge University Press.

Heller, Wendy. 2003. "Dancing Desire on the Venetian Stage." *Cambridge Opera Journal* 15/3: 281–295.

Hilton, Wendy. 1997. *Dance and Music of Court and Theatre: Selected Writings of Wendy Hilton*. Stuyvesant, NY: Pendragon.

Jeschke, Claudia. 1991. "From Ballet de Cour to Ballet en Action: The Transformation of Dance Aesthetics and Performance at the End of the Seventeenth and Beginning of the Eighteenth Centuries." *Theatre History Studies* 11: 107–122.

Johnson, Victoria, Jane F. Fulcher, and Thomas Ertman, eds. 2007. *Opera and Society in Italy and France from Monteverdi to Bourdieu*. Cambridge: Cambridge University Press.

Kintzler, Catherine. 2007. "Representations of *le peuple* in French Opera, 1673–1764." In Johnson et al. 2007, 72–86.

Kuhn, Thomas. [1962] 1970. *The Structure of Scientific Revolutions*. Chicago: University of Chicago Press.

Lenman, Bruce P. 1990. "The English and Dutch East India Companies and the Birth of Consumerism in the Augustan World." *Eighteenth-Century Life* 14/1: 47–65.

Marsh, Carol. 1985. "French Court Dance in England, 1706–1740: A Study of the Sources." PhD diss., The Graduate Center of The City University of New York.
McClary, Susan. 1998. "Unruly Passions and Courtly Dances: Technologies of the Body in Baroque Music." In *From the Royal to the Republican Body: Incorporating the Political in Seventeenth-and Eighteenth-Century France*, edited by Sara E. Melzer and Kathryn Norberg, 85–112. Berkeley and Los Angeles: University of California Press.
——. 1995. "Music, the Pythagoreans, and the Body." In *Choreographing History*, edited by Susan Foster, 82–104. Bloomington: Indiana University Press.
——. 1992. *Georges Bizet, 'Carmen.'* Cambridge Opera Handbooks. Cambridge: Cambridge University Press.
——. 1991. *Feminine Endings: Music, Gender, and Sexuality*. Minneapolis: University of Minnesota Press.
McCleave, Sarah. 2007–2008. "Marie Sallé and the Development of the *Ballet en Action*." *Journal of the Society for Musicology in Ireland* 3: 1–23. Online. Available: http://www.music.ucc.ie/jsmi/index.php/jsmi/issue/view (accessed August 15, 2012).
——. 2007. "Sallé, Handel, Rameau and the Development of Narrative Dance Music." In *Die Beziehung von Musik und Choreographie im Ballett; Bericht vom Internationalen Symposium an der Hochschule für Musik und Theater, Leipzig 23–25 März 2006*, edited by Michael Malkiewicz and Jorg Rothkamm, 105–119. Berlin: Vorwerk 8.
——. 1998. "English and French Theatrical Sources: The Repertoire of Marie Sallé." In McCleave ed., 1998, 13–32.
——. 1995. "Marie Sallé as Muse: Handel's Music for Mime." *The Consort* 51/1: 13–23.
——, ed. 1998. *Dance and Music in French Baroque Theatre: Sources and Interpretations*. Study Texts 3. London: Institute of Advanced Musical Studies, King's College London.
Morris, Mark. 2012. Mark Morris Dance Group website. Online. Available: http://markmorrisdancegroup.org/resources/works (accessed August 15, 2012).
——. 1995. *Dido and Aeneas*. DVD. Mark Morris Dance Group, Tafelmusik Orchestra and Chamber Choir. Canada: Rhombus Media.
Norton, Mary Beth, David M. Katzman, et al. 1986. *A People and a Nation: A History of the United States*. 2nd ed. Boston: Houghton Mifflin.
Orr, Bridget. 2001. *Empire on the English Stage: 1660–1714*. Cambridge: Cambridge University Press.
Peraino, Judith A. 1995. "I Am an Opera: Identifying with Henry Purcell's *Dido and Aeneas*." In *En Travesti: Women, Gender Subversion, Opera*, edited by Corinne E. Blackmer and Patricia Juliana Smith, 99–131. New York: Columbia University Press.
Pinnock, Andrew. 2012. "*Deus ex machina*: A Royal Witness to the Court Origin of Purcell's *Dido and Aeneas*." *Early Music* 40/2: 265–278.
Porter, David L. 2002. "Monstrous Beauty: Eighteenth-Century Fashion and the Aesthetics of the Chinese Taste." *Eighteenth-Century Studies* 35/3: 395–411.
Powell, Jocelyn. 1988. "Dance and Drama in the Eighteenth Century: David Garrick and Jean Georges Noverre." *Word & Image* 4/3–4: 678–691.
Prest, Julia. 2006. *Theatre under Louis XIV: Cross-Casting and the Performance of Gender in Drama, Ballet, and Opera*. New York: Palgrave Macmillan.
Price, Curtis. 1994. "*Dido and Aeneas*: Questions of Style and Evidence." *Early Music* 22/1: 115–125.
——, ed. 1986. *Henry Purcell, 'Dido and Aeneas': An Opera*. Norton Critical Scores. New York: W. W. Norton.

Price, Curtis, and Andrew R. Walkling. 2011. "Communications." *Journal of the American Musicological Society* 64/1:266–274.
Price, Curtis, Judith Milhous, and Robert D. Hume. 1995. *Italian Opera in Late Eighteenth-Century London*, Vol. 1: *The King's Theatre, Haymarket 1778–1791*. Oxford: Clarendon Press.
Ralph, Richard. 1985. *The Life and Works of John Weaver*. New York: Dance Horizons.
Roach, Joseph. 1996. *Cities of the Dead: Circum-Atlantic Performance*. New York: Columbia University Press.
Rosow, Lois. 1987. "Performing a Choral Dialogue by Lully." *Early Music* 15/3: 325–335.
Russell, Tilden. 2012. *The Compleat Dancing Master: A Translation of Gottfried Taubert's 'Rechtschaffener Tantzmeister' (1717)*. 2 vols. New York: Peter Lang.
——. 2006. "The Minuet According to Taubert." *Dance Research* [UK] 24/2: 138–162.
Sawkins, Lionel. 1996. "*Trembleurs* and Cold People: How Should They Shiver?" In *Performing the Music of Henry Purcell*, edited by Michael Burden, 243–264. Oxford: Clarendon Press.
Schwartz, Judith L. 1998. "The Passacaille in Lully's *Armide*: Phrase Structure in the Choreography and the Music." *Early Music* 26/2: 300–320.
Semmens, Richard. 2004. *The* bals publics *at the Paris Opéra in the Eighteenth Century*. Dance & Music Series 13. Hillsdale, NY: Pendragon Press.
Smith, Marion. 2000. *Ballet and Opera in the Age of Giselle*. Princeton, NJ: Princeton University Press.
Thomas, Downing. 2002. *Aesthetics of Opera in the Ancien Régime, 1647–1785*. Cambridge: Cambridge University Press.
Tomko, Linda J. 2011. "Harlequin Choreographies: Repetition, Difference, and Representation." In *'The Stage's Glory': John Rich, 1692–1761*, edited by Berta Joncus and Jeremy Barlow, 99–137. Newark: University of Delaware Press.
——. 2008. "Mr. Isaac's *The Pastorall* and Issues of 'Party.'" In *Dance, Spectacle, and the Body Politick, 1250–1750*, edited by Jennifer Nevile, 241–263. Bloomington: Indiana University Press.
——. 2005. "Magri's Grotteschi." In Harris-Warrick and Brown 2005, 151–172.
——. 1999. *Dancing Class: Gender, Ethnicity, and Social Divides in American Dance, 1890–1920*. Bloomington: Indiana University Press.
——. 1997. "Issues of Nation in Isaac's *The Union*." *Dance Research* [UK] 15/2: 99–125.
Waeber, Jacqueline, ed. 2009. *Musique et geste en France de Lully à la Revolution: Études sur la musique, le théâtre et la danse*. Frankfurt: Peter Lang.
Walkling, Andrew R. 2010. "The Masque of Actaeon and the Antimasque of Mercury: Dance, Dramatic Structure, and Tragic Exposition in *Dido and Aeneas*." *Journal of the American Musicological Society* 63/2: 191–242.
——. 1995. "Political Allegory in Purcell's 'Dido and Aeneas'." *Music & Letters* 76/4: 540–571.
——. 1994. "'The Dating of Purcell's *Dido and Aeneas*'?: A Reply to Bruce Wood and Andrew Pinnock." *Early Music* 22/3: 469–481.
White, Bryan. 2009. "Letter from Aleppo: Dating the Chelsea School Performance of *Dido and Aeneas*." *Early Music* 38/3: 417–428.
Winter, Marian Hannah. 1974. *The Pre-Romantic Ballet*. London: Pitman.
Wood, Bruce, and Andrew Pinnock. 1995. "Not Known at This Address: More on the Dating of *Dido*." *Early Music* 23/1: 188–189.
——. 1994. "'Singin' in the Rain': Yet More on Dating *Dido*." *Early Music* 22/2: 365–367.
——. 1992. "'Unscarr'd by Turning Times'?: The Dating of Purcell's *Dido and Aeneas*." *Early Music* 20/3: 373–390.

CHAPTER 24

PRODUCTION AESTHETICS AND MATERIALS

KATHERINE SYER

EFFORTS to record the visual dimensions of opera—the motion and expression of singers/actors as well as scenographic elements—got under way in systematic fashion during the first half of the nineteenth century. Serving primarily as a means of coordinating all of the non-musical elements involved in an increasingly complex and specialized multimedia art form, these detailed staging manuals also aimed to ensure uniform practices in revivals, in the same theater or elsewhere. Scholarly attention to such materials and to opera production matters in general has increased steadily since the 1970s. Heated debates concerning strongly revisionist stagings of standard repertory works directed attention to the ways works were first staged. It is surely no coincidence that this growing interest in production history coincided with a period in which opera became commercially available in forms that support repeated viewing and close scrutiny. Amateur and professional audio-visual recordings of opera productions now abound on YouTube. Theaters regularly archive recordings of their productions, further enhancing the notion of production as a durable artistic element.

Indicative of a broadening lens in opera studies beyond musical terms, production history is a standard feature of the English National Opera Guides, which began to be published in 1980, and the Cambridge Opera Handbooks that started appearing in 1981. An interdisciplinary air breathes throughout two specialized journals, *Opera Quarterly* and *Cambridge Opera Journal*, launched in 1983 and 1989, respectively, and through the four volumes of *The New Grove Dictionary of Opera*, from 1992. Also noteworthy is the *Storia dell'opera italiana* series edited by Lorenzo Bianconi and Giorgio Pestelli. While only three of the intended six volumes have appeared (original Italian versions 1987–1988; English translations 1998–2003), two of these stand as a comprehensive treatment of the visual aspects of Italian opera, with each contributor displaying a nuanced sensitivity to the musical works being staged. Evan Baker (2013) maps a broader European context in *From the Score to the Stage: An Illustrated History of Continental Opera Production and Staging*.

Of course, not all opera producers have felt a need to document fully the visual aspects of performance. Still, creative scholars working with uneven evidence and a wide range of sources continue to shed light on what opera audiences have seen onstage across more than four hundred years. Even in the absence of staging manuals or some kind of illustrated promptbook, our picture of opera through the eras has become vastly richer at a time when opera staging and design—for better or worse—is now often accorded extraordinary status. This chapter examines some of the sources—pictorial renderings, annotated libretti, production books, and Internet-based materials—that document and preserve the "look" of opera from its earliest days. A chronological view of these sources reveals their evolving aesthetic underpinnings as well as the celebratory, commemorative, pragmatic and other reasons why our historical picture of opera is the way it is.

Early Italian Opera: A Spectacular Springboard

Opera's emergence as a distinctive genre characterized by pervasive music—primarily vocal—was intertwined with other evolving multimedia forms of theater. Lavish court-sponsored entertainments were most likely to be documented in ways that hinted at matters of production and design. Beyond impressing large live audiences—including some witnesses who wrote detailed descriptions of their experiences—these spectacular events were occasionally rendered in engravings that patrons would distribute to their peers. Such images might, however, have improved upon reality in order to encourage admiration and perhaps envy (Viale Ferrero 2002). Simpler vocal dramas with roots in the madrigal and pastoral tradition tended to stimulate less documentation. Contrasts in scope and attention to visual effects could be vast. Consider, for example, the performances of *Il rapimento di Cefalo* and *Euridice* in 1600 in Florence. Both were mounted during the wedding celebrations of Maria de' Medici and Henri IV of France and both can be categorized as operas, the former with continuous music by Caccini, who also contributed material to Peri's score for *Euridice*. Bernardo Buontalenti carried out the designs for *Il rapimento di Cefalo* along the lines of the most elaborate *intermedii*, for an audience of some 3,800 members of the court. The scenography for *Euridice* involved a curtained stage with sets, costumed performers, and a means of lighting, but the performance was an altogether more intimate event. No stage machinery was involved, and there were only two set changes of a very basic kind (Ossi 1998). With visual splendor de-emphasized, the subtle expressivity of the human voice came to the fore. While sophisticated stagecraft was to play an important role in the future of opera, the heritage of more modest (and less often recorded) late Renaissance theater traditions would also prove influential.

Commercial opera for a paying public involved a different set of concerns from those of court opera, with the figure of the impresario emerging to play a central organizational role (Rosselli 1984). In this environment, funds needed to be balanced more delicately so that audience expectations and tastes would be met without overspending resources. The commissioning of engravings was not a valued endeavor. The paper trail left by the nascent business of opera has nevertheless yielded an impression of changing staging practices and priorities during this time. In the period from 1637 through the 1680s, as public opera and hybrid models sprouted, informative financial documents survive for private Roman performances of Virgilio Mazzocchi and Marco Marazzoli's *Chi soffre speri* (1637/1639), involving court-employed artists, and Francesco Cavalli's *Antioco*, first performed in 1659 at the public Teatro San Cassiano in Venice. In the profit-driven environment, singers and the composer gained stature and financial reward, while support for the orchestra and stagecraft became less strong. A third case involving an impresario working in Reggio Emilia in 1683, with ducal support, was also relatively sparing in its use of spectacular visual effects (Bianconi and Walker 1984). By this later date, finances and aesthetics had clearly shifted toward a singer-dominated art form, with the solo aria as its primary component and a more predictable, streamlined approach to staging and design. Visual novelty and variety, which had initially helped attract audiences to the art form in Venice, gradually yielded to the standardization of some aspects of production (Rosand 1991).

Papers related to the Venetian impresario Marco Faustini have helped flesh out our understanding of staging and design practices in the 1650s and 1660s. We now understand that the number of different sets used per production gradually increased midcentury, with fewer sets used on average for pastoral works. Giacomo Torelli's mechanization of scene changes at the Teatro Novissimo (1641–1645) helps account for the change. With sliding painted flats already in use, a practice connected to the increasingly popular proscenium-framed stage, Torelli's system linked them together in a framework involving a central axle, ropes, and counterweights. This manner of synchronizing changes of scenery simplified the whole process, reducing the number of stagehands required. The system proved widely influential and enduring, as did the deep, symmetrically balanced central design perspective that it favored. Without detailed staging manuals, our understanding of how these sets were maneuvered often relies on informed guesswork. It was long thought, logically enough, that the most encompassing or framing set in a production—the *scena maestra*—remained in place throughout and was altered in varying degrees as the scenes changed. However, recently unearthed documents indicate that the *scena maestra* was actually removed when not in full use. Fresh evidence has also come to light that care was taken to vary re-used sets in order to make them distinctive. The practice of a theater operating mostly with a group of stock sets, a *dotazione*, only became typical of opera production toward the end of the seventeenth century (Glixon and Glixon 2006).

A comparison of surviving set designs for three operas produced in a public theater (1642), the theater of a private patron (1680), and a court theater (1690), respectively, has also contributed to a more nuanced understanding of seventeenth-century practices. Consistent in all three works is the alternation of natural exterior scenes with architecturally defined ones (interior settings for the most part), and each features a horrid scene—grotto, temple of revenge, mine—that involved a variety of flying machines and traps. Stage machinery was used more consistently throughout the acts of the court opera (Viale Ferrero 2002). Typical of works that might travel to other public venues, Francesco Sacrati's *Il Bellerofonte* (1642) featured elaborate celebratory material in its Prologue—a glorification of the city of Venice that Torelli designed for the public Teatro Novissimo. Such prefatory material could be modified easily or even removed, according to different facilities and local interests.

High-profile dynasties of theater designers and others dedicated to the execution of private and public opera emerged to satisfy growing interest in the genre. Although the amount of materials that survive for individual productions is uneven, the travels of such teams clearly disseminated their characteristic approaches and techniques. Torelli, together with the multitalented choreographer Giovan Battista Balbi, for example, took his designs and staging system to Paris in 1645. Successive generations of artisans with wide-ranging and overlapping skills are found in the Mauro family, who worked mostly for public theaters, as did the Galliari family in the eighteenth century. Exceptionally prolific and influential were the Galli Bibienas, who were predominantly affiliated with court opera, as was Ludovico Burnacini in Vienna and the Vigarani family in Paris. Of particular note are Ferdinando Galli Bibiena's (1656–1743) multi-perspective stage designs, which opened up alternatives to seventeenth-century traditions and offered greater visual fascination in lieu of mechanical marvels. By the early years of the eighteenth century, the technology of the operatic theater was in place for the next century, and some fresh stimulus in the area of design was on the horizon.

The expressive movement of singers and dancers in early opera remains challenging to envision, even with a reasonably good sense of the surroundings in which they performed. In commercial venues, rehearsal time devoted to the creative coordination of singers with the physical means of production (*mise en scène*) could be scant. The dramatic coaching of singers as an ensemble was also uncommon. Still, individuals with a particularly strong theatrical vision could play a strong overall shaping role. Giovan Battista Balbi was one such figure. Attention to the interpretation and acting of solo singers tended, however, to be handled individually in private coaching sessions with the house poet (Guccini 2002). The situation with ballet is exacerbated by the dearth of surviving musical scores and notated choreography. Libretti contain very little in the way of details concerning danced numbers. Approximately one-third of seventeenth-century operatic scores have survived, and in these scores the music that would have been choreographed is often missing. Of the surviving scores, markings for dances (*balli*) are sometimes simply absent where libretti, engravings, and written descriptions indicate they indeed were performed. The reasons for dance's seemingly tangential position are twofold: The choreographed music was frequently composed by someone other than the composer(s) of the rest of the work, and these segments would mostly be rehearsed independently by a professional dance troupe. The music for dances was thus separate from the rest of the score most of the time (Hansell 2002). In any case, the music is generally of limited value as the transmission of professional choreography was an oral and corporeal tradition (treatises were aimed at amateur dancers in courtly environments).

Close attention to this aspect of early Venetian opera suggests that the ballets were rather exotic and athletic when compared with the more familiar, socialized forms of theatrical dance that developed in France (Alm 2003). The dances in Italian opera initially embodied a surfeit of sensuality—extensions of expressivity that went beyond the capabilities of the singing voice (Heller 2003).

Opera in France: A Regal Affair

Louis XIV's enthusiasm for theatrical entertainments bore strong implications for the ways opera took root in French soil. Generously supported and usually carefully prepared, indigenous French opera was launched in an intimate relationship with a court whose members often performed the dual roles of performers and audience. The king's personal passion for dance influenced opera, even after he himself quit the stage in 1670; dance is central to the *tragédie en musique* (or *tragédie lyrique*) form of opera established by Jean-Baptiste Lully and the librettist Philippe Quinault soon thereafter. As a pedagogical tool and also an effort to memorialize dance, Louis XIV commissioned Pierre Beauchamp, director of the Académie Royale de Danse starting in 1681, and chief choreographer for opera until 1687, to develop a notational style. As a result, around 350 dances—47 of them specifically intended for the Opéra—were recorded and could be taught to court dancers. Also known by the name Beauchamp-Feuillet, the notation system was first self-published by Raoul-Auger Feuillet in 1700.

Performance venues in Paris and the various court residences occupied by Louis XIV were not especially well-suited to elaborate theatrical performances. The Théâtre du Palais-Royal, a cramped space in all respects, served as the home of the Académie Royale de Musique (later simply known as the Opéra), French opera's quasi-public arm. When, in 1674, Lully moved into the theater with his designer and machinist Carlo Vigarani, the stage still bore the traces of renovations undertaken by Torelli (1645–1647), as well as subsequent modifications made by Molière. Renovations overseen by Lully and Vigarani seem to have endured until the theater was beset by fire in 1763. Although the public could buy tickets to opera performances at the Palais Royal, the operas presented there generally premiered at court; production resources as well as audience members overlapped considerably at the revivals (Coeyman 2000). That Lully's operas continued to be performed at the Palais Royal decades after his death contributed to a long, stable period in terms of production aesthetics, with French audiences favoring magical visual effects and specific historical details. A singular pictorial rendering of the theater in use during an opera performance is of a revival of Lully's *Armide* in 1747 (Zaslaw 1983). This depiction, coupled with contemporary accounts, indicates that the theater's small stage limited its ability to embrace developments such as multi-perspective set designs.

A rare promptbook used for performances of André Campra's *Tancrède* in 1748 offers a revealing glimpse of the ways that contemporary court opera was executed (Banducci 1993). Although the production was mounted in a small, temporary theater at Versailles, connections via personnel who also worked at the Opéra suggest that it was not atypical. Sadly, stage designs for the Versailles production do not exist. Still, the basis of the promptbook is a score, not a libretto, and the directions are thus unusually specific. They clearly indicate at which measure entrances and exits were to be made. In a number of instances, soloists entered only a few measures before the end of their number's instrumental introduction, thereby allowing the music to assume importance in preparing the scene and building suspense. In contrast to what is otherwise known of theater blocking practices of the time (Barnett and Massy-Westropp 1987), this source seems to emphasize stage left (associated with the king) in rank and dramatic position over stage right (associated with the queen). Some exceptional moments in which singers were to be engaged in dramatic acting and movement about the stage are also indicated.

The *Tancrède* promptbook remains the only known such source for an opera prior to 1750, aside from a libretto with annotations (Figure 24.1) associated with performances of Handel's *Radamisto* in London in 1720. Less detailed than the *Tancrède* source, it nevertheless crucially illuminates how a number of supernumeraries (at least twenty-six) functioned to clarify the roles and ranks of the principal singers (Milhous and Hume 1986).

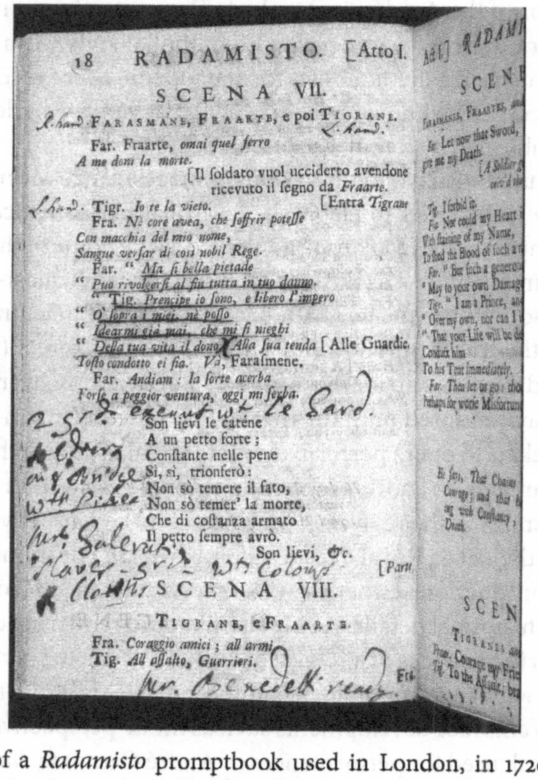

FIGURE 24.1 Pages of a *Radamisto* promptbook used in London, in 1720, featuring annotations that clarify details about entrances and exits, the placement of singers, and even sound effects. © Victoria and Albert Museum.

In Paris, supernumeraries would be drawn from the chorus and corps of dancers. That a promptbook would have been used for *Tancrède* is logical enough. French operas involved relatively large singing casts, including groups of people that needed to be well organized. The chorus had at this time become an insignificant presence in Italian opera, but the French remained accustomed to seeing and hearing many performers active on the operatic stage. Some of the richest music in a French opera accompanied groups of performers. Furthermore, while *divertissement* may be a useful term to reference the part of the act dominated by masses of characters and dancers, its suggestion of being a diversion from the main drama is unfortunate and misleading (Harris-Warwick 2007). The chorus came to play an even greater role in French opera in the nineteenth century as an active, politicized body. The gradual nature of this evolution, starting in the late eighteenth century, laid the groundwork for Parisian grand opera, with its elaborate production practices and tendency to record aspects of the stage action in greater and greater detail (Jacobshagen, 1997).

Italian Opera through the Romantic Era: The Quest for Originality

Eighteenth-century Italian opera reified, in the form of *opera seria*, into a predictable aria-based structure with equally regularized production practices. In widespread performance, however, it was the essential malleability of *opera seria* that proved to be one of its greatest assets (Feldman 1995). Libretti were heavily recycled and modified. With new musical settings of select numbers tailored to fit individual singers, they had hardly a chance of fitting, *in toto*, another cast. Comic opera, in the form of *intermezzi* and later *opera buffa*, was also voice driven but simpler in terms of staging requirements. Less costly to produce and more portable, productions of comic opera outnumbered those of *opera seria* by midcentury. Continuing to develop musically and dramatically, if not substantially in matters of production, comic opera remained in the shadows in terms of social and cultural prestige, as well as sponsorship (Piperno 2002).

The unstable nature of musical scores remained characteristic of Italian opera well into the nineteenth century. In some cases, the number and nature of modifications could stretch the sense of cohesion to the point of breaking. Even a librettist as influential as Pietro Metastasio, who had a keen theatrical sense and oversaw the production of his works in Vienna in the 1730s, had limited impact on the realization of his dramas elsewhere. The tendency to accommodate specific singers still prevailed a century later, when Felice Romani (1788–1865), another librettist of impressive dramatic vision, endeavored to promote intact, persuasive performances of his works. In Romani's time, contracts dictated how far the responsibilities of a librettist or composer might extend into the sphere of production (Roccatagliati and Henson 1996). A significant change in the way that composers were paid decisively enhanced their status and influence in this period: they began to earn streams of payments from revivals. In France, the Société des Auteurs et Compositeurs Dramatiques aimed to support performance rights for creators of artistic works. Giovanni Ricordi offered an alternative to Italian composers, who were accustomed to being paid only if they were personally involved in a production. Instead of forfeiting all performance rights to the theater or impresario that employed them, composers could now pass control of the rental and publication of scores to Ricordi, who in turn offered payments for all revivals (Gossett 2006). Scores were not entirely safeguarded from manipulation, but recognition of composers' efforts and the work's status as an artistic entity nevertheless grew. This configuration encouraged composers such as Verdi, whose dramatic vision included careful attention to staging matters, to exercise new levels of authority in this sphere.

A reliable basis of repeatable repertoire balanced new works in the programs of many Italian opera houses in the early nineteenth century. Starting with *Tancredi* (1813), Rossini's works proved durable and circulated widely. The designs for revival productions in this period tended to reflect the distinctive artistic personalities of institutional designers and their different approaches to historical elements, which were a focal point of interest in costuming as well. Soon after, engravings or lithographs began to circulate as normative set designs; Alessandro Sanquirico's designs for productions at Milan's Teatro alla Scala were especially favored until his retirement in 1832 (Viale Ferrero, 2002). The original designs for the premieres of Rossini's works in Venice in 1813 had not been circulated in any way. Rediscovered only in the 1960s, the sketches of Giuseppe Borsato, Francesco Bagnara, and Giuseppe Bertoja bear subtle signs of Romanticism (Povoledo 1969). The situation was completely different for the premiere of Rossini's final opera, *Guillaume Tell*, in Paris (1829). Two years earlier, the Comité de Mise en Scène had been established to review and coordinate all aspects of design and production at the Opéra. The set designs for *Guillaume Tell*—all freshly conceived and built especially for the premiere—highlighted the distinctiveness of the production. Documents elaborating on the designs and blocking of the premiere of *Guillaume Tell* included the *livret de mise en scène* prepared by Jacques Solomé, which was made specifically as a guide for revivals. Copies of *livrets* such as this one traveled with the repertoire well past French borders.

La Scala also had a production committee around this time, although it only involved two painters. Sanquirico served as its advisor from 1832 to 1849, charged with the mandate of controlling all design elements (Viale Ferrero 2002). Specialized set and costume designs could convey potent, multivalent types of meaning. Even mountainous landscapes and rustic settings gained fresh expressive associations in coordination with politically laced dramas (much as they had done in *Guillaume Tell*) about virginal heroines in Alpine settings (Senici, 2005): Bellini's *La sonnambula* (1831), Donizetti's *Linda di Chamounix* (1842), and Verdi's *Luisa Miller* (1849).

While it seems that more rigorous attention was paid to scenery and costumes than to stage action in Italian theaters, unpublished documents continue to shed light on actual working methods. The case of the composer Luigi Ricci (1805–1869), active at La Scala throughout the 1830s, is instructive (Izzo 2010). Ricci's autograph manuscripts bear numerous, detailed stage directions that were not published in the libretti and scores for his operas. The more skeletal versions in print served as the basis for productions in which a house poet would have been responsible for realizing the stage actions in detail. Ricci's annotations reflect his aims for those productions that he directed himself. Using his own score instead of a libretto-style promptbook, his indications for stage actions could be specific to a musical gesture; furthermore, they reflect a conceptualization of gesture that to some degree was intertwined with the very composition of the score. If we try to imagine the stage business from printed performance materials and libretti alone, we can only perceive the vague, static outlines of what actually took place on stage. Ricci's additional entries in his score come closer to revealing the dynamic and sophisticated level of choreography so natural to the comic genre that he favored.

The Operatic Stage Transformed through Light

Increasingly individual productions reflected the Romantic focus on originality, which fueled a concomitant exploration of new scenographic options. An opera such as Carl Maria von Weber's *Der Freischütz* (Berlin, 1821), for example, combined well-worn Baroque practices with unusual machinery and progressive techniques involving colored chemical reactions in the "Wolf's Glen" scene concluding Act II (Bomberger 1998). The scene's intensive use of special effects, novel in itself, also included a special light source that could suddenly render the diabolical character Samiel visible from behind his hiding place (a rock painted onto gauze).

Of all the technological developments that touched upon theater practices in the nineteenth century, those concerned with lighting had the most far-reaching impact (Bergman 1977). With the introduction of gas lighting in theaters in the early decades of the nineteenth century, and incandescent electric light toward the century's close, the quantity and quality of illumination changed. Such changes impacted on all visual aspects of the stage: Everything from the materials and colors used in sets and costumes to makeup, blocking, and gesture needed to work well with the newer light sources or combinations of light sources employed in a given theater. With the usable lit part of the stage much expanded, the upstage area proved more suitable for imagery painted on broad canvases and three-dimensional set pieces, or *practicables*. The resultant increased complexity in design and stage motion stimulated the documentation of these aspects of production in detail.

In the later 1820s, the situation that emerged in Paris (and that scarcely could be replicated elsewhere) reflected the extraordinary resources of the Opéra, then housed in the Salle Le Peletier. On account of the Opéra's institutional nature, generations of prominent and distinctive designers were provided with generous means for carrying out their work. A centralized archive of production materials for both ballet and opera was especially encouraged. Beginning in 1805, all costume-design sketches were collected;

regular conservation of set designs started in 1861 (Wild 1987/1994 and Join-Dieterle 1988).

The Comité de Mise en Scène's mission to attain high production standards emerged in the context of a sophisticated entertainment world in which the Opéra had proven itself to be wanting. Popular shows in Paris's boulevard theaters and the dioramas of Louis-Jacques-Mandé Daguerre, best known for his contributions to photography, paved the way for fresh emphasis on verisimilitude and masterful illusions onstage (Pendle 1987). A compressed transition from nighttime to daytime, for example, could be handled with adjustable gas lighting. Vast painted canvases with three-dimensional extensions might depict unusual and arresting scenes such as large battles or a volcanic eruption. Working as a scene painter at the Opéra, Daguerre's interest in realistic lighting effects and his use of a curved broad canvas backdrop, or cyclorama, helped to refine naturalism onstage. The logical extension of this kind of approach is found in Puccini's partnership with David Belasco in *Madama Butterfly* (1905) and *La fanciulla del West* (1910) (Greenwald 1998).

Until the last years of the nineteenth century, electric and other special forms of light were used selectively, while gas remained the primary means to light stages and auditoriums. With the waning tendency to keep auditoriums lit during performance, experimentation with different intensities of light and contrasting chiaroscuro effects gained in their effectiveness. The ballet of spectral nuns in the cloister scene of Meyerbeer and Scribe's *Robert le diable* (1831) proved to be a captivating expression of ambiguity—the result of closely coordinated production elements (Guest and Jürgensen 1998). Henri Duponchel, in a role close to that of a modern director, exercised his training as a designer on the setting, executed by Pierre-Luc Charles Cicéri. Meyerbeer's autograph score contains personal annotations concerning stage motion and pantomime. The warm yellowish glow of the gas lighting enhanced the mystery of the scene while the bright harshness of electric light focused on the character Bertram at the peak of his temptation. Atypically, the cost for Duponchel's costumes exceeded that for the sets. Given the concern with historical realism that prevailed during this period, it is noteworthy that the costuming was not stylistically unified. The principal female character Alice was dressed in the style of the Restoration, which may have prompted the opera's first audiences to sense the drama's pressing concerns as more topical than historical (Fulcher 1987).

Parisian *Livrets de Mise en Scène*

Recent scholarship concerning Parisian grand opera is an industry in itself, although the repertoire at its core is limited and quite famously exhausted itself. Attention to production matters has remained strong ever since H. Robert Cohen published two volumes of *livrets de mise en scène* for grand operas and *opéra comiques* produced in Paris (Cohen 1988, 1991). These staging manuals include floor plans, descriptions of sets, costumes, movements, and the like—tantalizing invitations for us to imagine how stage directions in scores and libretti were realized. A sophisticated production process evolved to suit the needs of grand opera whereby the efforts of many highly specialized professionals could be coordinated smoothly. Elements of design are treated extensively in the staging manuals, as the goal was often a specific historical image; these were further supported by documents associated with the pictorial sketching of the sets and costumes. Generally speaking, later nineteenth-century *livrets de mise en scène* are more detailed in all categories, reflecting both increased complexity and an increased desire to record as many details of the staging as possible (Langer 1997).

It is tempting to regard *livrets* associated with a Parisian premiere as capturing an idealized form of authorial intent extending directly from the score. However, practicality coexists with prescription, and some of the manuals are frankly difficult to pinpoint to a specific date. Multiple staging manuals exist for Auber's *Fra Diavolo* (first performed in 1830); each individual *livret* is perhaps best understood as reflecting a relatively discrete phase in production practices that evolved across decades (Jacobshagen 2001). The *livrets* for the four main Meyerbeer operas are especially rich sources for understanding stage technology in use between 1831 and 1836, although one dimension—lighting effects—is explained solely in descriptive rather than technical fashion (Baumann 1995). Documents pertaining to the luxurious premiere production of Halévy's *La Juive* (1835) reveal the subjective tone of the manual's scribe. Prepared as the production was developed and hence virtually complete by the final dress rehearsal, the *livret* captures the last-minute excision of two scenes from the score in the form of revisions (Newark 2001). The detailed insights that can be gleaned from such staging manuals reveal a theatrical world in lively flux.

Grand opera's links with other theatrical genres—melodrama and other forms of popular theater, *opéra comique* and ballet—are the focus of a growing body of literature (Hibberd 2009; Smart 2005; Wild 1997). Gesture and its relation to music is a special case with a mute character such as Fenella in Auber's *La muette de Portici*, for example, whose un-operatic mode of expression is limited to pantomime; she is better understood among her melodramatic relatives. The original *livret de mise en scène* of *La muette* expands upon stage directions in the score, but as is so often the case, there is a gap between such descriptions and a full enactment of the role. Filling in that gap to some extent is the system of oratory developed by François Delsarte, who sang for a time at the Opéra-Comique but rounded out his career as an influential teacher of singing and rhetoric (Delsarte [1882] 1892).

The connections between dance-based pantomime, with its musically grounded narrative, and opera represent an especially fresh and provocative avenue for research given ballet's then intimate connection to nineteenth-century opera. Operatic allusions to social dances had long sharpened the political contours of operatic dramas—Mozart's *Le nozze di Figaro* (1786) and *Don Giovanni* (1787) offer examples that are thoroughly integrated with the drama (Allanbrook **1983**). Operatically hybrid ballet-pantomimes flourished at the Opéra during the 1830s and 1840s (Smith, 2000). The Parisian mandate to include a ballet within an opera is best known from the adjustments that Verdi and Wagner made to preexisting scores for performances there. Verdi himself favored dramatically justified dance within his operas. We cannot imagine *Aida* without its choreographed displays; the separable *divertissements* that he composed are more easily forgotten. With the potential to spill beyond the borders of danced segments, dance-related rhythms imply motion and open up a choreographic dimension. In the case of Verdi's creative process, the rhythmic shape of dance forms and the stage action they imply seem to have helped him frame dramatic situations that would also contain arias and choruses (Jürgensen 2001).

Two Commanding Visionaries of the Nineteenth-Century Lyric Stage: Verdi and Wagner

Despite the different cultural traditions associated with Giuseppe Verdi and Richard Wagner, and the obvious differences in the sorts of dramas they shaped, both composers were "men of the theater," keenly interested in the entire process of shaping a musical drama and bringing it to the stage. They both gained experience with the incomparable production resources in Paris, expanding their awareness of what could be achieved and of the kind of approach to staging that supported such excellence. *Les vêpres siciliennes* (1855) was one of many Paris productions with which Verdi would be involved. Years after his efforts to reach a Parisian stage with either *Rienzi* or *Der fliegende Holländer* failed, Wagner experienced a partial success with his *Tannhäuser* at the Opéra in 1861, despite the early withdrawal of the work following scandalous disruptions. Following these pivotal experiences, both artists moved decisively in the direction of creating model productions of their operas. Their main ideas about staging and design were to be considered part of the work. Through astonishing good fortune and much audacity and determination, Wagner's desire to assume control over all aspects of the production of *Der Ring des Nibelungen* involved the construction of his own Festival Theater in Bayreuth (Syer 2009). Verdi, by contrast, honed his skills at dealing effectively with a collection of theaters that presented the premieres and revivals of his works.

Verdi's most important production experiences prior to working in Paris were his repeated interactions with the designer Giuseppe Bertoja and the technical team at Venice's La Fenice (Baker 1998a). This extended relationship shaped Verdi's awareness of dramatic and scenic possibilities at a time when the neoclassical legacies of designers such as Sanquirico (La Scala) and Antonio Niccolini (Teatro San Carlo) had faded. Gas lighting was installed at La Fenice in 1844 (see Greenwald 2009). Such technological changes had an obvious and immediate impact on the changing visual manifestation of Verdi's operas (Langer 2001). The premiere of *Rigoletto* (1851) featured a novel use of plastic decorations such as multilevel platforms and stairs, as well as the sophisticated atmospheric lighting and special sound effects for the storm in the third act (Baker 1998b). The dramaturgy of this concluding, experimental act is entirely bound up with technical and aesthetic options that became available to Verdi. It is hardly a surprise, given the sort of technical precision required in such a scene, that Verdi would adopt the method of documenting the visual aspects of his productions in a staging manual (*disposizione scenica*) soon after *Les vêpres siciliennes* was produced in Paris.

The *disposizione scenica* for *Otello* (1887) is Verdi's most elaborate (see Hepokoski and Viale Ferrero 1990 and Bush 1988). It dwells extensively on the Act I storm and contains the first explicit mention (in such a manual) of the use of electric light to depict lightning. In terms of acting, Verdi expected a consistently intense kind of character portrayal involving gestures that were then somewhat exaggerated and outmoded. Not particularly satisfied with the premiere production, Verdi involved himself with rehearsals of *Falstaff* with a mind to do things differently. He was intimately involved and by all accounts found the experience and the production more satisfying (Hepokoski 1985). Ricordi planned to issue a staging manual for *Falstaff* but none exists. The *disposizioni sceniche* that Ricordi did issue likely met with Verdi's approval, even if it is difficult to assess precisely which directions are his (Rosen 1981). The staging manual for *Otello* contains fascinating descriptions of pantomime action that enlivened scenes for which stage directions are otherwise completely lacking in printed scores (Coe 1978). How relevant are such sources for performances today? David Rosen and Andrew Porter have both emphasized how many of the directions in Verdi's *disposizioni sceniche* are not bound to the historical stage. On the contrary, they mostly clarify the drama in gestural terms related to precise moments in the score and sometimes demonstrate optimal stage layouts for matters of musical balance (Rosen 2001 and Porter 2001).

Wagner's ideas about the theater and the production history of his works began to command fresh attention in the period around the centenary of *Der Ring des Nibelungen* in 1976, in part due to the controversial, revisionist staging of the *Ring* in Bayreuth that year (Bauer 1982). For some, the Bayreuth theater that he opened in 1876 still serves as the ideal environment to hear his works, especially *Parsifal*, the only opera Wagner composed with experience of the structure's unusual acoustic properties. Even more than with the *Ring*, *Parsifal*'s first production is closely connected to the Bayreuth theater and its technical capabilities (Syer 2005). The design of the simple amphitheater-shaped auditorium suggests a reincarnation of the mythic legacy of antiquity, and Wagner was indeed deeply interested in Greek tragedy. A double proscenium sets the auditorium at a slight remove from the stage, which crowns its concealed orchestra pit. When it opened, the theater was equipped with cutting-edge technology—especially regarding the production of steam and special lighting effects—thanks to Wagner's enlistment of the support of outstanding technical personnel (Baumann 1980; Kreuzer 2011). Wagner's own scenic and stage directions, however, have not played a significant role in any Bayreuth production since the early 1990s. His non-realistic brand of illusionism, in particular, has encouraged directors and designers to seek other interpretive solutions (Ashman 2008).

Wagner's Path to Producing the *Ring* and *Parsifal* in Bayreuth

Although he had less experience staging his own operas as compared with Verdi, Wagner had become accustomed to excellent facilities and support already during his tenure at the Dresden Court Theater in the 1840s. While in exile, beginning in 1849, he had no direct involvement with the staging of his works. Still, he corresponded at length with Liszt at the time of the premiere of *Lohengrin* in Weimar (1850) and he wrote pamphlets on matters especially important to him regarding the production of *Der fliegende Holländer* and *Tannhäuser* (1852). His writings include technical details about special effects involving lighting, as well as details about gestures that he wanted to be paced so as to coordinate with specific moments in the music. A telling indication of the musical foundation of Wagner's dramatic conception is his ardent wish and explicit demand for the production team to reference the score instead of libretti. Accordingly, he included generous set descriptions and stage directions in the published versions of his scores.

Through the overwhelming financial support of King Ludwig II of Bavaria, a series of productions of Wagner's works conceived as models were presented in Munich starting in 1864. The spotlight switched from older works to premieres with *Tristan und Isolde* in 1865. The original designs for this work, long prized for its modernity, have received less critical attention than those for his other operas, likely as they involved few challenges in terms of stagecraft (Petzet and Petzet 1970). On account of the need for a larger orchestra pit, the production was relocated from the Rococo-styled Cuvilliés Theater to the larger, more restrained aesthetic milieu of the Court Theater. Resituating Angelo Quaglio II's sets for Act I within the Cuvilliés Theater helps to illuminate an aspect of Wagner's visual aesthetic that is often overlooked and misunderstood: he actively integrated older design and staging practices into his operas in order to set more progressive dimensions of his works into relief (Figure 24.2).

The opening of *Tristan und Isolde* illustrates this general strategy. The stage that we first see is foreshortened. Its full depth and a view of the sea are revealed only at the end of the first scene when Isolde, feeling suffocated, calls out for air and the tapestries that form the rear of her tent on the ship's deck are drawn open. The sailor's song first heard right after the prelude is then heard a second time, a retake that brackets the opening scene as if it were a prologue. The opening of the tapestries at the end of the first scene also articulates this dramatic structure and visually complements the front draperies of Isolde's tent, which in turn resemble a split theater curtain raised up by ropes, which also figure in the ship's rigging. In the Cuvilliés Theater (and in many similarly styled Rococo and Baroque theaters), this overtly self-conscious red curtain imagery would have also forged a visual connection to *trompe l'œil* swags "draped" over the railing of the balcony that rings the auditorium at the level of the royal box.

FIGURE 24.2 Model for Angelo Quaglio II's set designs for Act I of *Tristan und Isolde*. Photo by Rudolf Betz, reproduced courtesy of the Deutsches Theatermuseum. The model is housed at the Ludwig II Museum at Herrenchiemsee.

Closer study of backward-glancing, theatrically reflexive moments in Wagner's later works yields a more nuanced understanding of his visual aesthetic than has resulted from overemphasis on the metaphysical dimensions of his dramas. Wagner conceived the first visual manifestation of his god Wotan, for example, as dark thunderclouds that would produce lightning and thereby start a fire that would surround and protect Brünnhilde. Then, as he wrote the three dramas preceding *Siegfried's Tod* (*Siegfried's Death*)—the opera that would be revised and renamed as *Götterdämmerung*—he began to imagine Wotan onstage in human form. Wagner's earliest ideas for Wotan can be traced to his 1847 adaptation of Gluck's *Iphigénie en Aulide* on account of stage directions that are nearly identical for the stormy scene in *Siegfried's Tod*. For the scene in Gluck's opera in which the goddess Diane's change of heart was expressed by another character, Wagner opted for the more conventional solution of a *dea ex machina* (unaware of Gluck's like-minded revision). In Wagner's treatment, Artemis (Diana) arrives via dark storm clouds—quintessentially Baroque entrance vehicles for angered gods—undergirded by a thunder machine that loudly culminates in a strike of lightning. After this spectacularly old-fashioned mode of arrival, the atmosphere calms for Artemis to deliver her benevolent message (which contains textual and musical allusions to Wagner's then unfinished *Lohengrin*). Although the character Wotan evolved significantly as Wagner revised the *Ring* libretto over many years, traces of his initial inspiration percolated through to the completed composition. Wotan's tempestuous nature remained a distinctive part of his characterization as his role in the drama expanded, including the use of a specially constructed thunder machine for the god's angrier appearances. The stormy milieu was meanwhile preserved in the scene in *Götterdämmerung* that was heavily rewritten to feature Waltraute. Wagner's recourse to older staging practices in association with Wotan underscores the fundamental idea that his god would be an antiquated figure.

Gesture, for Wagner, was not simply indicative of emotional states but yet another expression of pervasive aspects of character that he instilled in the music and drama. Julius Hey, a vocal pedagogue who was much impressed by Wagner's coaching of Ludwig Schnorr von Carolsfeld for the role of Tristan, also observed rehearsals for Act I of *Siegfried* in Bayreuth. He described how Wagner could fully imagine the distinctive physical language of his characters; he enacted Mime (without caricature) as an awkward schoolmaster type opposite Georg Unger's Siegfried (Hey 1911). Heinrich Porges, another observer whom Wagner enlisted to keep a record of the staging rehearsals of the *Ring*, noted revealing details of Loge's characterization. With regard to scene 2 of *Das Rheingold*, Porges mentioned Loge's ironic carefree gaiety, likening his chromatic musical theme to flames delighting in their destructive power. He also documented Wagner's suggestion that Loge's gestures and movements should convey his restless nature as a fire-god (Porges 1983). Although Wagner did not leave anything along the lines of a concentrated staging manual, his requests that various members of the creative team make production notes during rehearsals yielded a wealth of recorded details, as do the models and design sketches for his productions.

Wagner's unusual scenographic expectations stem from the non-historical nature of his dramas and his preference for complicated depictions of enchanted spaces or forces. Recalling French theater entertainments popular earlier in the century, the series of large painted scrolls that were unwound to reveal changing scenery during the transformation to the mystical world of the Grail in *Parsifal* proved especially challenging to coordinate with music (Baker 1998a). Wagner struggled to find a suitable visual language for sets and costumes that was natural and allusive but not fussy; he found it difficult to find designers not hamstrung by the prevailing artistic trends toward historical detail. The costumes by Carl Doepler for the *Ring*, for example, frustrated him for this reason. In the first revival of the *Ring* in 1896, Cosima Wagner aimed at something simpler with classical robes. This was surely a move in the direction of Wagner's wishes, yet the costumes of 1876 were preferred by audiences who mistakenly thought they represented the intentions of the composer (Carnegy 2006). For a work that was so closely associated with Wagner's theater in Bayreuth and challenging to produce, the *Ring*'s early production history as a touring show is rather curious. With the whole production able to fit into five cargo rail cars, the *Ring* traveled to dozens of theaters of varying sizes and capabilities. Organized by Angelo Neumann, the staging was overseen by the young conductor Anton Seidl, whom Wagner had coached for years to be his virtual double.

In the year of Wagner's death, Houston Stewart Chamberlain (later to marry into the Wagner clan) met Adolphe Appia and subsequently guided his theatrical education. Through Chamberlain's influence, Appia worked in Dresden with Hugo Bähr, one of the most significant early experimenters with electric light in theaters. His carbon-arc lights and projections were used to animate the stage image in *Ring* performances in 1876. At that time, the contrast between the warm glow of gaslight and bright electric light was often hard to coordinate effectively; the result in 1876 was not ideal. In *Parsifal*, Wagner used electricity more selectively, for the illumination of the Grail as well as Kundry in Act II, when she first becomes visible to Parsifal. Full electrification of the Bayreuth theater only happened a few years after Wagner's death. When Appia embraced the subtler ways that electric light was being used by the end of the 1880s, he found a way to conceptually resolve what he saw as a lack of compatibility between the visual and musical-dramatic aspects of Wagner's works as they were produced in Bayreuth. His suggestions for new approaches to design were famously rebuffed by Cosima Wagner, who sustained an approach to stage design that was intended for gaslit stages well after the Bayreuth stage had been fully modernized. Through copyright law, she maintained nearly exclusive control over the staging of *Parsifal* for thirty years, with only subtle changes being introduced to the production toward the end of that period. No other opera has been bound so tightly to the theater of its creation and to its original production, which through time became a morbidly inflexible and hence ironic tribute to one of opera's most vibrantly creative theatrical figures.

Modernism: The Gateway to More Choices

Supported by developments in lighting technology, the expansion of design options that began to emerge around the turn of the twentieth century had a profound impact on opera production. A range of aesthetic alternatives to a naturalistic kind of realism began to color the look of both new works and revivals of older operas. In this context, the chance of experiencing an opera production whose designs, manner of acting, and stage action might be radically different from that initially envisioned by its creators naturally increased. The advent of commercial film as a competitive entertainment genre only encouraged the production trend in the direction of modernity, while offering designers and directors another medium for rendering sets and even layers of stage action. Digital and interactive technologies have further multiplied the options for design and gesture.

The means for tracking the flow of images and actions (if not the full technical explanation of every element) in production still often centers on a heavily annotated score, sometimes with interleaved pages to support the inclusion of graphics. As stage directors and designers have assumed a more central and autonomous role in the production of opera, promptbooks of various kinds have been created to suit the needs of the artists involved and the particularities of the production. The reliance on printed and written records is, however, rapidly yielding to digital media. Staging manuals will certainly not prove to be an exception given technological developments in iPad capabilities. The means of coordinating production elements during performance must adapt according to the medium in play. One creative solution emerged in the *Ring* conceived for Valencia and Florence (2007–2009) by the group known as La Fura dels Baus, headed by Carlus Padrissa. To streamline the execution of a number of simultaneous, complex cues, a computer program was designed that was triggered by a keyboard player performing a reduction of the orchestral score in real time.

In concluding our discussion of a subject continuously in flux, Wagner's *Ring* also offers us apt examples of the ways the unique appearance of an opera production can be documented in recent times. It goes without saying that the *Ring* is an exceptionally challenging work to design and stage, often involving extraordinary financial resources and thus perhaps inviting memorialization. The director Joachim Herz and designer Rudolf Heinrich were acutely aware that the production they developed in Leipzig (1973–1976) was radically novel and sure to stimulate controversy. They preserved countless records of conversations and communications which led to decisions that influenced the design and staging of their production. These materials then served as the basis of a two-volume "behind the scenes" documentary publication (Marion Reinisch 1975 and Röhlig 1980). Elaborate books, often handsomely illustrated with design sketches and photographs, have accompanied most new *Ring* productions since. Internet-based variants of this tendency to record the creative process as well as the final achievement include the blog maintained by Kasper Bech Holten and his production team during the development of their *Ring* in Copenhagen in 2003–2006 (Holten 2005–2006) and the array of interviews and trailers that are available on opera company websites. Susan Froemke's full feature-length film *Wagner's Dream* (2012) is an exceptional case that charts five years of the development of the *Ring* production directed by Robert Lepage for the New York Metropolitan Opera. Complementing the increased availability of commercial audio-visual recordings of opera productions in recent decades are such efforts that explore why and how a particular staging looks the ways it does.

See also: Operatorio? Historically Informed Performance, Operatic Images, Dance, Verisimilitude, The Chorus

Bibliography

Allanbrook, Wye J. 1983. *Rhythmic Gesture in Mozart: 'Le nozze di Figaro' and 'Don Giovanni.'* Chicago: University of Chicago Press.

Alm, Irene. 2003. "Winged Feet and Mute Eloquence: Dance in Seventeenth-Century Venetian Opera." *Cambridge Opera Journal* 15/3: 216–280.

Ashman, Mike. 2008. "Wagner on Stage: Aesthetic, Dramaturgical, and Social Considerations." In *The Cambridge Companion to Wagner*, edited by Thomas S. Grey, 246–275. Cambridge: Cambridge University Press.

Baker, Evan. 2013. *From the Score to the Stage: An Illustrated History of Continental Opera Production and Staging*. Chicago: University of Chicago Press.

——. 1998a. "Richard Wagner and His Search for the Ideal Theatrical Space." In Radice 1998, 241–278.

——. 1998b. "Verdi's Operas and Giuseppe Bertoja's Designs at the Gran Teatro la Fenice, Venice." In Radice 1998, 209–240.

Banducci, Antonia. 1993. "Staging a *tragédie en musique*: A 1748 Promptbook of Campra's *Tancrède*." *Early Music* 21/2: 181–190.

Barnett, Dene, with the assistance of Jeannette Massy-Westropp. 1987. *The Art of Gesture: The Practices and Principles of 18th-Century Acting*. Heidelberg: Carl Winter Universitätsverlag.

Bauer, Georg Oswald. 1983. *Richard Wagner: The Stage Designs and Productions from the Premieres to the Present*, translated by Stewart Spencer. New York: Rizzoli.

Baumann, Carl-Friedrich. 1995. "Livrets als bühnentechnische Quelle." In *Giacomo Meyerbeer, Musik als Welterfahrung: Festschrift für Heinz Becker zum 70. Gerburtstag*, edited by Sieghart Döhring und Jürgen Schläder, 9–29. Munich: Ricordi.

——. 1980. *Bühnentechnik im Festspielhaus Bayreuth*. Munich: Prestel.

Bergman, Gösta M. 1977. *Lighting in the Theatre*. Stockholm: Almquist & Wiksell.

Bianconi, Lorenzo, and Giorgio Pestelli, eds. 2002. *Opera on Stage*, translated by Kate Singleton. *The History of Italian Opera* 5. Chicago: University of Chicago Press.

——. 1998. *Opera Production and Its Resources*, translated by Lydia G. Cochrane. *The History of Italian Opera* 4. Chicago: University of Chicago Press.

Bianconi, Lorenzo, and Thomas Walker. 1984. "Production, Consumption and Political Function of Seventeenth-Century Opera." *Early Music History* 4: 209–296.

Bomberger, E. Douglas. 1998. "The Neues Schauspielhaus in Berlin and the Premiere of Carl Maria von Weber's *Der Freischütz*." In Radice 1998, 147–170.

Bush, Hans, ed. and trans. 1988. *Verdi's 'Otello' and 'Simon Boccanegra' in Letters and Documents*. 2 vols. Oxford: Clarendon Press.

Carnegy, Patrick. 2006. *Wagner and the Art of the Theatre*. New Haven: Yale University Press.

Carter, Tim. 2003. "Rediscovering II *rapimento di Cefalo*." *Journal of Seventeenth-Century Music* 9/1. Online. Available: http://sscm-jscm.press.illinois.edu/v9/no1/carter.html (accessed August 15, 2012).

Charlton, David, ed. 2003. *The Cambridge Companion to Grand Opera*. Cambridge: Cambridge University Press.

Coe, Doug. 1978. "The Original Production Book for *Otello*: An Introduction." *19-Century Music* 2/2: 148–158.

Coeyman, Barbara. 2000. "Walking through Lully's Opera Theatre in the Palais Royal." In *Lully Studies*, edited by John Hajdu Heyer, 216–242. Cambridge: Cambridge University Press.

Cohen, H. Robert. 1991. *The Original Staging Manuals for Twelve Parisian Operatic Premières*. Stuyvesant, NY: Pendragon.

——. 1988. *The Original Staging Manuals for Ten Parisian Operatic Premieres 1824–1843*. Stuyvesant, NY: Pendragon.

Delsarte, François. [1882] 1892. *Delsarte's System of Oratory, Including the Complete Works of M. l'abbe Delaumosne and Mme. Angelique Arnaud (Pupils of Delsarte) with the Literary Remains of Francois Delsarte*. 4th ed., translated by Frances A. Shaw. New York: E. S. Werner. Online. Available: http://www.gutenberg.org/files/12200/12200-h/12200-h.htm (accessed August 15, 2012).

Feldman, Martha. 1995. "Magic Mirrors and the Seria Stage: Thoughts toward a Ritual View." *Journal of the American Musicological Society* 48/3: 423–484.

Feuillet, Raoul-Auger. [1700] 1979. *Chorégraphie ou l'art de décrire la dance par caractères, figures et signes démonstratifs*. Hildesheim: Olms.

Fulcher, Jane. 1987. *The Nation's Image: French Grand Opera as Politics and Politicized Art*. Cambridge: Cambridge University Press.

Glixon, Jonathan E., and Beth L. Glixon. 2006. *Inventing the Business of Opera: The Impresario and His World in Seventeenth-Century Venice*. AMS Studies in Music. New York: Oxford University Press.

Gossett, Philip. 2006. *Divas and Scholars: Performing Italian Opera*. Chicago: University of Chicago Press.

Greenwald, Helen M. 2009. "*Son et lumière*: Verdi, *Attila*, and the Sunrise over the Lagoon." *Cambridge Opera Journal* 21/3: 267–277.

——. 1998. "Belasco, Puccini, and the California Sunset." In Radice 1998, 279–296.

Guccini, Gerardo. 2002. "Directing Opera." In Bianconi and Pestelli 2002, 125–176.

Guest, Ann Hutchinson, and Knud Arne Jürgensen. *'Robert le diable': The Ballet of the Nuns*. New York: Routledge, 1998.

Hansell, Kathleen. 2002. "Theatrical Ballet and Italian Opera." In Bianconi and Pestelli 2002, 177–308.

Harris-Warwick, Rebecca. 2007. "Lully's On-Stage Societies." In *Opera and Society in Italy and France from Monteverdi to Bourdieu*, edited by Victoria Johnson, Jane E. Fulcher, and Thomas Ertman, 53–71. Cambridge: Cambridge University Press.

Heller, Wendy. 2003. "Dancing Desire on the Venetian Stage." *Cambridge Opera Journal* 15/3: 281–295.

Hepokoski, James A. 1985. "Under the Eye of the Verdian Bear: Notes on the Rehearsals and Première of *Falstaff*." *Musical Quarterly* 71/2: 135–156.

——, and Mercedes Viale Ferrero. 1990. *'Otello' di Giuseppe Verdi*. Milan: Ricordi.

Hey, Julius. 1911. *Richard Wagner als Vortragsmeister*. Leipzig: Breitkopf and Härtel.

Hibberd, Sarah. 2009. *French Grand Opera and the Historical Imagination*. Cambridge: Cambridge University Press.

Holten, Kasper Bech. 2005–2006. "The Copenhagen Ring: Director's Blog." Online. Available: http://www.old.kglteater.dk/bloguk/default.htm (accessed August 15, 2012).

Izzo, Francesco. 2010. "Comic Sights: Stage Directions in Luigi Ricci's Autograph Scores." In *Fashions and Legacies of Nineteenth-Century Italian Opera*, edited by Roberta Montemorra Marvin and Hilary Poriss, 176–195. Cambridge: Cambridge University Press.

Jacobshagen, Arnold. 2001. "Staging at the Opéra-Comique in Nineteenth-Century Paris: Auber's '*Fra Diavolo*' and the *livrets de mise-en-scène*." *Cambridge Opera Journal* 13/3: 239–260.

——. 1997. *Der Chor in der französischen Oper des späten Ancien Régime*. Frankfurt: Peter Lang.

Join-Dieterle, Catherine. 1988. *Les décors de scène de l'Opéra de Paris à l'époque romantique*. Paris: Picard.

Jürgensen, Knud Arne. 2001. "An Avenue Unexplored: The Divertissement and the Opéra-Ballet." In Latham and Parker 2001, 91–102.

Kreuzer, Gundula. 2011. "Wagner-Dampf: Steam in *Der Ring des Nibelungen* and Operatic Production." *Opera Quarterly* 27/2: 179–218.

Langer, Arne. 2001. "Die Optische Dimensions: Szenentypen, Bühnenräume, Kostüme, Dekorationen, Bewegugung, Tanz." In *Verdi Handbuch*, edited by Anselm Gerhard and Uwe Schweikert, 249–276. Stuttgart: Metzler; Kassel: Bärenreiter.

——. 1997. *Der Regissuer und die Aufzeichnungspraxis der Opernregie im 19. Jahrhundert.* Frankfurt: Peter Lang.

Latham, Alison, and Roger Parker, eds. 2001. *Verdi in Performance.* New York: Oxford University Press.

Milhous, Judith, and Robert D. Hume. 1986. "A Prompt Copy of Handel's 'Radamisto'." *Musical Times* 127/1719: 316–321.

Newark, Cormac. 2001. "Ceremony, Celebration, and Spectacle in *La Juive*." In *Reading Critics Reading: Opera and Ballet Criticism in France from the Revolution to 1848*, edited by Roger Parker and Mary Ann Smart, 155–187. New York: Oxford University Press.

Olivier, Philippe. 2007. *Der Ring des Nibelungen in Bayreuth: Von den Anfängen bis heute.* Mainz: Schott.

Ossi, Massimo. 1998. "*Dalle macchine… la maraviglia:* Bernardo Buontalenti's *Il rapimento di Cefalo* at the Medici Theater in 1600." In Radice 1998, 15–35.

Pendle, Karin. 1987. "The Boulevard Theaters and Continuity in French Opera of the Nineteenth Century." In *Music in Paris in the Eighteen-Thirties*, edited by Peter Bloom, 509–535. Stuyvesant, NY: Pendragon Press.

Petzet, Detta, and Michael Petzet. 1970. *Die Richard Wagner Bühne König Ludwigs II.* Munich: Prestel Verlag.

Piperno, Franco. 1998. "Opera Production to 1780." In Bianconi and Pestelli 1998, 1–79.

Porges, Heinrich. 1983. *Wagner Rehearsing the 'Ring,'* translated by Robert L. Jacobs. Cambridge: Cambridge University Press.

Porter, Andrew. 2001. "In Praise of the Pragmatic." In Latham and Parker 2001, 23–27.

Povoledo, Elena. 1969. "Les premières représentations des opéras de Rossini et la tradition scénographique de l'époque." In *Anatomy of an Illusion: Studies in Nineteenth-Century Scene Design. Lectures of the Fourth International Congress on Theatre Research, Amsterdam 1965*, 31–34. Amsterdam: Scheltema & Holkema.

Radice, Mark, ed. 1998. *Opera in Context: Essays on Historical Staging from the Late Renaissance to the Time of Puccini.* Portland, OR: Amadeus Press.

Reinisch, Marion, ed. 1975. *Joachim Herz inszeniert Richard Wagners 'Ring des Nibelungen' am Opernhaus Leipzig: I. Teil 'Das Rheingold,' 'Die Walküre.'* Berlin: Akademie der Künste der Deutschen Demokratischen Republik.

Roccatagliati, Alessandro, and Karen Henson. 1996. "Felice Romani, Librettist by Trade." *Cambridge Opera Journal* 8/2: 113–145.

Röhlig, Eginhard, ed. 1980. *Joachim Herz inszeniert Richard Wagners 'Ring des Nibelungen' am Opernhaus Leipzig: II. Teil 'Siegfried,' 'Götterdämmerung.'* Berlin: Akademie der Künste der Deutschen Demokratischen Republik.

Rosand, Ellen. 1991. *Opera in Seventeenth-Century Venice: The Creation of a Genre.* Berkeley and Los Angeles: University of California Press.

Rosen, David. 2001. "On Staging That Matters." In Latham and Parker 2001, 28–33.

——. 1981. "The Staging of Verdi's Operas: An Introduction to the Ricordi *Disposizioni sceniche*." In *Interdisciplinary Horizons in the Study of Musical Traditions, East and West: The Twelfth Congress of the International Musicological Society, August 21–27, 1977, University of California, Berkeley, California; Final Report*, edited by Daniel Heartz and Bonnie Wade, 444–453. Kassel: Bärenreiter.

Rosselli, John. 1984. *The Opera Industry in Italy from Cimarosa to Verdi.* Cambridge: Cambridge University Press.

Senici, Emanuele. 2005. *Landscape and Gender in Italian Opera: The Alpine Virgin from Bellini to Puccini.* Cambridge: Cambridge University Press.

Smart, Mary Ann. 2005. *Mimomania: Music and Gesture in Nineteenth-Century Opera.* Berkeley and Los Angeles: University of California Press.
Smith, Marian. 2000. *Ballet and Opera in the Age of 'Giselle.'* Princeton, NJ: Princeton University Press.
Syer, Katherine. 2009. "From Page to Stage: Wagner as *Regisseur*." In *Wagner and his World*, edited by Thomas S. Grey, 3–26. Princeton, NJ: Princeton University Press.
——. 2005. "Parsifal on Stage." In *A Companion to Wagner's 'Parsifal,'* edited by William Kinderman and Katherine Syer, 277–338. Rochester NY: Camden House.
Viale Ferrero, Mercedes. 2002. "Stage and Set." In Bianconi and Pestelli 2002, 1–124.
Wild, Nicole. 1997. "La mise en scène a l'Opéra-Comique sous la Restauration." In *Die Opera Comique und ihr Einfluß auf das europäische Musiktheater im 19. Jahrhundert*, edited by Herbert Schneider und Nicole Wild, 183–210. Hildesheim: George Olms Verlag.
——. 1987/1994. *Décors et costumes du XIXe siècle a l'Opéra de Paris.* 2 vols. Paris: Bibliothèque Nationale.
Zaslaw, Neal 1983. "Observations: At the Paris Opéra in 1747." *Early Music* 11/ 4: 515–516.

CHAPTER 25

COSTUMES

VERONICA ISAAC

As dress historians have long been conscious, the clothes that we wear play a key role in constructing our social identity (Greenblatt 1984; Taylor 2002). The garments in which we choose to dress ourselves can be manipulated to advertise or disguise our professions, political leanings, taste, and age. Whether we reject, embrace, or create our own fashion, the clothing we adopt and how we adorn ourselves make an immediate visual statement, signifying our desire to conform to, or opt out of, society. The theater has often been described as a "mirror" of the public world, which though often deliberately skewed or imperfect, mimics our habitats, behavior, and clothing. The characters that inhabit this contrived universe wear garments that, even when endeavoring to recreate a past or imagined world, are inextricably connected with contemporary dress. Stage costumes thus offer an exciting opportunity to study the social significance of fashion, to examine how we recreate ourselves in our own images, while exploring a fascinating strand of both musical and theatrical history.

Theater historians have played a leading role in identifying the problems and issues connected with research in this area, and opera scholars are now beginning to build upon this work (see, for example, Bignami 2010, 2005; Breward 2004, 2011; De Marly 1962; Jowers 1992; Kaplan and Stowell 1994; Laver 1964; Majer 2012; Monks 2010). Further work on operatic costume has emerged within the field of scenography, where costumes are considered among other tools of production (see, for example, on Italian opera, Biggi 2010; Jesurum 2010; Viale Ferrero 2004, 2002, 2000, 1984). Costumes have also been considered in discussions of individual composers, works, and productions (for instance, Ashman 1992; Clark 2003; Crespi Morbio 2000). A primary concern among scholars has been to identify source material through which to carry out such research. Inventories provided by performance venues such as theaters and royal residences offer an invaluable record of a production, but contemporary exhibition and museum catalogues can also prove an excellent starting point. Of course, an important goal is to find the costumes themselves, but without additional evidence pertaining to actual use, confusion can arise as to origin and purpose, since garments often traveled, not only from place to place, but from one production to the next. Of great help in identifying and determining the initial use of a particular garment are sketches, engravings, and paintings, which provide iconographic evidence, not least for operatic characters drawn from history and mythology, but also clues to contemporary personal attire (see, for example, La Gorce 1997; Massip 1990; Wild 1987; an overview of opera costume may be found in Van Witsen 1981).

Many of the issues surrounding the role of costume in opera were discussed in March 2012 at a conference devoted to the subject held at the Fondazione Cini in Venice: *Fashioning Opera and Musical Theater: Stage Costumes from the Late Renaissance to 1900* (De Lucca 2014). Several papers were devoted to establishing methodologies (Busseti and Jesurum 2014) and identifying sources, specifically collections in theaters, including two Neapolitan venues, the Teatro San Carlo (Maione and Seller 2014) and the Conservatorio San Pietro a Majella (De Simone and Maccavino 2014), and the royal opera house in Stockholm (Tråvén 2014). Other papers addressed productions of works by Scarlatti, Verdi, and Wagner, as well as genres like the English masque. The many speakers included several pioneering scholars of fashion, textiles, costumes, and stage design in Italy, among them Doretta Davanzo Poli (2011, 2007, 2002), Bruna Niccoli (2005, 2004), and Paola Bignami, whose collaboration with Charlotte Ossicini, *Il quadrimensionale instabile: Manuale per lo studio del costume teatrale* (2010), is among the first texts to explore the challenges connected with documenting garments that frequently depart from the materials, silhouettes, and even scale by which historic dress can usually be dated and defined.

One of the main concerns for the scholar of costumes is to identify the precise ways in which fashion—that is, personal dress and its trends—is distinct from stage costumes, designed to symbolize or represent a particular style, concept, or era rather than conscientiously replicate the reality. It is essential to remain aware that these are garments constructed to project an illusion which, while dazzling under stage lights, was never intended to be subject to close and sustained inspection. When analyzing costume design, and surviving garments in particular, we must also consider the practical accommodations that costume designers are obliged to make to assist movement on stage, facilitate the athletic art of singing, flatter the wearer, and delight contemporary taste and imagination. The real people who inhabited these costumes frequently owned them, sometimes even developed a celebrated association with them, and thus also shaped their physical and historical identity. Garments may often outlive their original purpose and may be passed through generations, acquiring an altered appearance, a new meaning, and a different owner, thus accruing along the way their own "biographies." This chapter will address each of these issues and will conclude with a study of the costumes for Gilbert and Sullivan's 1881 *Patience*, which, as will be seen, was tailored by its creators to lampoon the ideological and sartorial vanities of late-nineteenth-century London audiences.

Defining Costume

What distinguishes "a costume" from any other historic garment, from ritual garb to personal wardrobe to uniforms? The fact that it is still common practice to refer to historic clothing as "costumes" rather than "dress" further complicates the problem. While surviving advertisements show that nineteenth-century shoppers were familiar with the use of the word "costume" to signify both garments for everyday and stage wear, its meaning has altered over time. As a result many dress historians now seem to prefer the term "dress" or "fashion" rather than "costume," a shift affirmed by the launch in 1997 of the journal *Fashion Theory* and the 2007 re-branding of the Museum of Costume in Bath, United Kingdom (first opened in 1963) as the Fashion Museum. Yet, despite the fact that some scholars have begun to call for a reassessment of terminology, the traditional use persists. Even if the term "costume" could be reclaimed, there remains the risk that further confusion may result from the fact that the rejection of "costume" as a technical designation has become inextricably linked to the continued struggle to establish dress history as a legitimate area for academic research (Taylor 2002: 1). This, albeit unintentional, association of "costume" with an outdated and undisciplined approach to the study of dress history threatens to further undermine efforts to encourage scholarship specifically on "costumes." Before the study of theatrical garments can be established as a distinct and valid area of dress and theater history, it is, therefore, vital to reclaim the word "costume" as a term specifically reserved for, and relating to, garments used for performance.

In order to achieve this aim, it is necessary to determine exactly what garments will be encompassed by the word "costume." The *Oxford English Dictionary* (*OED*) defines costume (the noun) as "[a] set of clothes in a style typical of a particular country or historical period: *authentic Elizabethan costumes*" (*OED* online). The *OED* traces the origin of the word to the early eighteenth century from the French and Italian *costume*, meaning "custom, fashion, habit," derived in turn from the Latin *consuetude*. For the purposes of this chapter, a clearer delineation of its meaning is required. From this point onward, I will therefore employ the term "costume" specifically to signify a garment, or associated accessory, specifically created to be used, or worn, in a live performance before an audience.

The type of performance in which the costume is worn is not restricted to, but will in most cases be connected with, a production in a theater or equivalent arena, be this spoken theater or opera. While the garment in question may have been designed to replicate the fashions associated with a particular country or historic period, in this instance "costume" will also be taken to encompass dress with no distinctive historic or regional features. It will exclude any garments that were not used for a live performance, but the term "live performance" could be expanded to include costumes created for twentieth- and twenty-first-century rock and pop performance and also the masques and private theatricals staged in courts and private houses from the late sixteenth century onward.

Given this emphasis on the correct use of terminology, it is important to address the fact that throughout this chapter I will alternate the terms "theatrical costume" and "opera costume" to demonstrate that similar methodology and source material can be employed for the study of costumes created for both spoken theater and opera productions. The importance of acknowledging the clear stylistic differences between the two forms of performance must not be overlooked, however, particularly with regard to the impact that these distinctions have on costume.

In both opera and spoken theater productions, one of the chief purposes of an actor's costume is to provide a visual signal of his or her dramatic significance within the production. In most instances, the more elaborate or distinctive the garment, the more important and substantial the role will be. There are, of course, exceptions to this rule, particularly in productions where the principal characters are of a low social status, a case in point being Verdi's 1871 opera, *Aida*, in which the title role is that of a captive Ethiopian princess, forced to serve as a slave. The character of Aida is a particularly interesting case, since the costume of "slave" is inauthentic for a person of high station, and not one intended by the wearer. To mitigate the effect and cue the audience in such cases where a character is wearing the "wrong" attire, designers frequently provide other clues to the true identity through hair, makeup, or accessories—in the case of Aida, almost never obliterating the expected beauty of the heroic captive princess. When responding to such narratives, the costume designer is faced with the task of ensuring that the dramatic significance of a character is made evident through a costume, which though visually arresting, is consistent with the social position he or she occupies within the narrative (Van Witsen 1981: 9). In addition to highlighting characters' dramatic significance, costumes are often required to express something of their wearers' inner nature. For example, the elaborate or overly fastidious garments of Baron Scarpia in Giacomo Puccini's *Tosca* (1900) can communicate arrogance or villainy, while Mozart and Da Ponte made clear their intention to humiliate Elvira in *Don Giovanni* (1787) by dressing her in traveling clothing for her first entrance.

The physical demands on performers must also be taken into account. Often the nature of the role will determine the degree to which creativity and the desire for dramatic effect can be allowed to overcome the practical considerations of whether a performer will actually be able to move in an unwieldy and heavy costume. This was clearly the artistic intention behind a costume that Cecil Beaton (1904–1980) designed for the 1963 production of *Turandot* at the Royal Opera House, now part of the *Royal Opera House Collection* (ROH 2012). The vivid red and pink silk costume is decorated with circles of appliqué and includes a striking gold and red jeweled headdress with upright spikes fanning out in a half circle above the wearer's head. The element of the costume that commands attention, however, is the immense red cloak, bordered in gold and with the wide hanging sleeves deliberately lined in a contrasting bright blue. This cloak flows out in a train several meters long and its weight was such that the singer (initially Amy Shuard) could only wear it in Act I, where she does not sing (ROH 2012).

The shifts that have occurred in the style and nature of operatic performances over time have also had a significant impact on costume design. The costume drawings by Silvio degli Alli for the 1658 production of Cavalli's *L'Ipermestra* offer an illustration of some of the earliest forms of costume associated with the genre. As Christine Jeanneret (2012) has discovered, not only do drawings survive, but also designs for scenery and accounts of those who witnessed the spectacle—most important, that of Orazio Ricasoli Rucellai (1604–1673), whose description of the production was decorated with Alli's engravings. By piecing together the evidence contained within these sources, one is able to identify some of the figures involved in the design and construction of the costumes and also to establish a clearer sense of the costumes themselves. Phrases gleaned from surviving descriptions, wardrobe inventories, and even financial accounts can expand the perception of a two-dimensional drawing, revealing that a cloak was made of silk or a tunic was bordered with glittering gold embroidery. Still, it is often the images of garments that provide the most vivid sense of how a production might have looked on the stage. Even so, an image must be treated with caution, particularly those such as Alli's engravings, which were created after a production to illustrate a published account. One cannot dismiss the strong temptation toward idealization, or the risk that the artist may have had to rely on a hurried sketch or even a secondhand description on which to base the final engraving. The often ambiguous nature of the source material is a major challenge for all those researching costume for the stage, and the further back in history one attempts to probe, the more significant a problem it becomes. That is not to say that all claims about the conventions identified in costume from the seventeenth or eighteenth centuries cannot be fully substantiated. It is simply that it is essential that researchers analyzing costumes from any era acknowledge the scope for diversity as well as the inescapable flaws in source material.

Elements of the stiff formality and classical influences evident in visual representations of late seventeenth-century costumes can still be seen in the depictions of the costumes that featured in eighteenth-century productions (Lecomte 1820). As surviving designs, playbills, engravings, and supporting archival material attest, by this period certain garments appear to have become specifically associated with opera and the balletic performances that often accompanied them. One such garment was the "tonnelet" worn by male performers. Engravings by artists such as Jean Bérain the Younger (1678–1726) show that the tonnelet, which generally took the form of a sleeveless, three-quarter length tunic with a stiff, wide skirt, originated in the late seventeenth century. The costumes that both Jean Bérain (1637–1711) and his son designed for both opera productions and court festivals may have helped to popularize the tonnelet as a dominant form of dress within productions during this period.

A costume in this style (Figure 25.1) survives within the collections of the Department of Theatre and Performance, Victoria and Albert Museum (V&A). The costume comes from a private theater at Meleto Castle, Tuscany, which was opened in 1741. Though not directly associated with an operatic production, it is among the earliest surviving examples of a garment made specifically for the stage, and is also likely to have been used for masques and other entertainments, which included dancing. The costume is made from heavy velvet, believed to have originally been crimson in color, now faded to a rust red. The bodice and layered skirt are decorated with a stylized design of flowers and scrolls in raised silver embroidery. Furnishing velvet was used to create the "ground" of the costume; both this rich fabric and the precious metal thread used for the embroidery would have glowed in the candlelit interior of the theater.

By the mid- to late eighteenth century, the number of extant costumes increases, and large collections of material from the 1770s survive in the wardrobe of the Royal Opera House, Sweden. Marianne Tråvén (2012) has been able to match many of these surviving costumes with a concurrent Inventory of the Costume Workshop, and also with sample

FIGURE 25.1 Red velvet tonnelet, 1741. © Victoria and Albert Museum, S.92-1978.

books that belonged to the merchants who may have supplied the fabrics (now held in the State Archive). Tråvén has shown that this range of source material can be examined alongside books and prints of costume designs originally within the library of King Gustav III (1747–1792), which are now part of Musik-och teaterbiblioteket (The Music and Theater Museum), Stockholm (see Stockholm 2012). This allows the researcher to piece together a vision, not only of the production itself, but also of the king's keen involvement in, and financial support of, the productions staged by the Royal Opera in Stockholm in the late eighteenth century.

There are some clearly definable periods during which both theatrical and operatic costumes were strongly influenced by offstage dress, and when new fashions in mainstream dress prompted a shift in the garments being worn on the stage. As paintings by artists such as Johann Zoffany (1733–1810) reveal, the connections between on- and offstage dress were especially close throughout the mid- to late eighteenth century. Around 1780, for instance, the new fashion for simpler, classically inspired garments for everyday female dress led to the adoption of lighter draped tunics for female performers. The costumes of male performers also underwent a dramatic change, and the heavy tonnelets were abandoned in favor of jackets and knee breeches. This shift in costume design facilitated major advances in dance technique. As can be seen from the engravings René Gaillard (ca. 1719–1790) produced from the costumes that Jean Baptiste Martin (fl. 1748–1757) designed for the Paris Opera (Gaillard 1733), the wide, stiff skirts of the costumes, often supported on panniers or hooped petticoats, previously worn by female dancers, had forced performers to adopt a formal, distant style of dance. The new softer style of costumes, however, allowed the performers much more freedom of movement and, as a hand-colored lithograph of André Deshayes as Achilles and James Harvey D'Egville as Ulysses in D'Egville's ballet *Achille et Déidamie* at the King's Theatre in 1804 reveals

FIGURE 25.2 Hand-colored lithograph of André Deshayes as Achilles and James Harvey D'Egville as Ulysses in D'Egville's ballet *Achille et Déidamie* at King's Theatre 1804. © Victoria and Albert Museum, E.4973-1968.

(Figure 25.2), dancers were now able to dance close beside, or behind, one another, and the man could lift and support his partner.

As Van Witsen's analysis of the costumes from the 1871 premiere of Verdi's *Aida* has shown, contemporary fashions can also exert an unintentional influence over the costume designer's work. On this occasion, despite the fact that costumes had been executed under the supervision of the French Egyptologist Auguste Mariette, both scenery and garments still "had an air of 1871 about them." Indeed, as the surviving photographs show, the women's costumes "had all but a bustle silhouette" (Van Witsen 1994: 1). The importance of photographs as a source for researchers investigating opera costume from the nineteenth century cannot be understated, yet even this pictorial record must be treated with circumspection.

The *cartes des visites* prints (2¼ by 3½ inches) produced from 1854 and the larger cabinet cards (6½ by 4½ inches) that replaced them circa 1866 provide a crucial visual record of stage costumes from the mid-nineteenth century. What must be remembered when analyzing these images, however, is that nearly all the photographs from this time would have been taken in a studio rather than on the stage. Therefore, while in some instances it is very clear that efforts may have been made to replicate elements of the set and to recreate, or at least evoke, scenes from the production, the photographs cannot be relied upon as a true record of how the costume would have looked on the stage. Furthermore, although color photography was first invented in the mid-nineteenth century, it was not until the 1950s that color photographs became widely available. As a result, while some images have been hand tinted or colored, most of them are black and white or sepia, and therefore reveal little or no information about the original colors of the costumes they depict. In order to discover more about the color and texture of a costume, a researcher is either forced to turn to surviving hand-colored designs or paintings, or, where they exist, to the garments themselves.

Extant Garments

Unfortunately, the costumes that do survive after live performances seldom conform to the researcher's vision of the original production. Not only are they likely to be damaged through use or faded and tarnished over time, they also rarely live up to the exotic and dramatic images outlined in the original designs or preserved in intricate engravings. To mitigate this disillusionment and to fully understand stage costumes, it is essential to maintain an awareness of the original purpose of these garments.

The stage costumes that do become part of a historic costume collection after a production are an exception to the norm. Indeed, the majority of costumes are either discarded or returned to the wardrobe to be recycled and adapted at a future date. For designers and makers, the key considerations are the short term visual impact of the garment together with its ability to withstand hard and repeated wear. Designers such as Oliver Messel (1904–1978), battling with the shortage of fabrics occasioned by the rationing after World War II, were, therefore, content to employ materials such as candy wrappers, dishcloths, and gilded pipe cleaners to achieve the desired effect for their stage costumes, and gave little thought to the eventual fate of garments that were never intended to be retained for a long period of time (Messel 2012). It is the curators and researchers, rather than the original creators and wearers, who are concerned about the long-term stability of the materials used and the fact that paste stones and synthetic fabrics that look stunning from a distance or under dramatic lighting are often something of a disappointment when inspected at close range. Such delicacy was something singers themselves were conscious of. In one notable example recounted by John Rosselli, soprano Rosa Ponselle refused to sing at the dress rehearsal of the 1929 production of *Norma* at Covent Garden because she worried that her fragile costume would suffer from the additional wear (Rosselli 1992: 184).

All historic dress and textiles are vulnerable to the damage that can result from long-term exposure to light, dust, and fluctuations in temperature and relative humidity. Perspiration also breaks down fibers and stains fabric and is a particular issue with garments that were worn under hot stage lights and, in the case of dance costumes, used in physically demanding performances. A production that proves particularly successful is likely to have a long run of performances and may possibly remain within a company's repertoire for an extended period. For this reason, costumes for both chorus members and leading performers will often need to be repaired, and frequently remade, especially if a role is recast or a costume is particularly fragile. Furthermore, as surviving costumes from the Bolshoi Ballet's 1901 production of *Swan Lake*, now held by the Victoria and Albert Museum (V&A), demonstrate, several almost identical versions of the same outfit might be made for members of the chorus; makers generally only create one, or perhaps two, versions of a costume intended for a leading role. As a result, the costumes associated with principal roles are generally worn much more heavily than those used by members of the chorus, and accumulate significant structural damage.

Another issue with which curators of stage costume have to contend is the damage that designers and makers inflict upon costumes for dramatic effect. For example, within the Victoria and Albert collections are surviving costumes from the 1892 production of William Shakespeare's *King Lear* at the Lyceum Theatre (in which Sir Henry Irving [1838–1905] played the title role) that exemplify the impact of this deliberate "distressing" of fabrics. Indeed, the garments that Irving wore in the storm scene (Act III, scene 2) are broken-down versions of the elaborate tunics and cloaks the actor wore in previous acts of the play, but made from much rougher and less expensive fabrics. As a 2012 production at Glyndebourne, Sussex, demonstrated, within opera one of the most obvious instances of intentional "distressing" can often be seen in the garments created for Cinderella in Gioachino Rossini's (1792–1868) *La Cenerentola*. The impact of the elaborate gown in which Angelina (Cenerentola) dazzles both guests and audiences in the ball scene would be greatly reduced if the rags she has worn for earlier scenes were not sufficiently tattered and stained with cinders.

It is also important to recall that the costumes now being examined at close hand were originally intended to be viewed from seats several meters away and only when illuminated by some form of softened artificial lighting. Re-imagining the effect of scale, distance, and lighting on a costume is a challenge that all those analyzing such garments must overcome. Yet, having outlined all the problems and disappointments that can result from direct contact with a stage costume, it is important to stress that not all costumes are roughly made or exaggerated, and many provide examples of extremely intricate embroidery and expert construction. As Barbara Hodgdon (2006) enthuses, "one of the pleasures of the archive is the thrill of touching a costume's fabric, feeling its weight and drape in one's hand" (2006: 140).

These are garments "indelibly imprinted with performance" (Hodgdon 2006: 140). Handling such garments therefore not only exposes evidence of wear but also makes apparent the manner in which elaborate decoration and costly materials were often reserved for the section of the costumes visible to the audience, with panels of plain cheap fabric often being used for areas that could be concealed under cloaks, skirts, and jackets. A direct encounter with a costume, such as that worn by Irving in the title role of W. G. Wills and Percy Fitzgerald's 1878 play *Vanderdecken* (again in the V&A collections), can also reveal evidence of the manner in which fabrics have been combined for theatrical effect. The faceted beads that were sewn across the surface of the cloak have been covered in a layer of black gauze. This muffling layer of gauze rendered the actor invisible when lurking at the rear of the stage, and meant that he could emerge suddenly from the shadows when the beads were illuminated by a beam of gaslight.

In seeking to recover the impact of a costume within the original production, one is always, as Hodgdon put it, carrying out "a recontextualization from surviving remains" (2006: 138). As she makes apparent, however, extant garments have a crucial part to play in these efforts, not least because being able to discover the true color, weight, and texture of garments depicted in still black and white or sepia photographs makes it possible to "re-animate" these frozen images (Hodgdon 2006: 143).

Multiple Identities

One of the key problems faced when researching and documenting extant costumes stems from the fact that not only were costumes seldom reserved for a single scene within a production, but also that they frequently reappeared in other works within a performer's or company's repertoire. Some singers—sopranos, in particular—were known to carry their own custom-made costumes from city to city and from production to production (Rosselli 1992: 161), while others even became identified with a particular piece of clothing or an accessory. One notable example is Angelica Catalani, who created something of a sensation by her so-called *leçons de grace*, a series of poses executed with the aid of a shawl (Cowgill 2012: 220–222 and passim). Among the oldest examples of personal accoutrements in the *Royal Opera House Company Collections* (ROH 2012) is a pair of delicate white satin shoes embellished with lace and diamante, worn by the famous Spanish soprano Adelina Patti (1843–1919). Patti wore the shoes both as Violetta in Verdi's *La traviata*, and as Lucia in Gaetano Donizetti's *Lucia di Lammermoor*. The debates and uncertainty that often surround the provenance of a costume can call into question its authenticity as a record of a performance, particularly as the perceived historical value of a surviving costume is often determined by the status of the performer for whom it was originally made.

For many scholars, such "things" have their own stories to tell. Igor Kopytoff argued that it is possible to create the "biography of an object," that by asking "the same range of cultural questions" of an object as one would of an individual, such as "What are the recognized 'ages' or periods in a thing's life?" and "Where does the thing come from and who made it?" it would be possible to construct its "biography" (Kopytoff 1986: 66). For Kopytoff the value of these "biographies of things" lies in their ability to "make salient what might otherwise remain obscure"; indeed, for anthropologists they make it possible to explore the manner in which "alien objects" are "culturally redefined and put to use" (Kopytoff 1986: 67). Although Kopytoff's research focuses upon the anthropological implications of "cultural redefinition," his biographical mode of analysis is equally applicable to theatrical costume. In the case of the costumes that now survive in museum stores, for instance, the formal acquisition of the costume by a museum curator transforms the garment from an ephemeral object into an item deemed worthy of long-term preservation and expert care. Furthermore, the construction of "biographies" for such garments provides a tool through which to explore the numerous "associations" and "identities" that a costume can accumulate during a life cycle that often includes not only damage, repair and alteration, but potentially the transfer to different performers and productions.

For similar reasons the semiotic approach, used by Susan Pearce to explore the "chain of meanings" that individual objects accumulate over time, provides a pertinent means of documenting and investigating the "multiple identities" that are an inherent part of a stage costume (Pearce 1994). Pearce argues that "meaning develops as an interactive process between thing and viewer." As a result, any interpretation is inevitably selective and is shaped by the experience of the interpreter, while the object itself remains "richer than any of its realizations" (Pearce 1994: 19). Her discussion highlights "the power" and "emotional potency" of the "actual object." Most important, it reminds those investigating theatrical costume to acknowledge and remain conscious of the degree to which their own preconceptions and experiences can influence their reaction to, and interpretation of, extant garments (Pearce 1994: 26).

A New "Aesthetic Opera": W. S. Gilbert and Arthur Sullivan's *Patience*

The first performance of the opera *Patience, or Bunthorne's Bride* took place at the Opera Comique (London) on April 24, 1881. The libretto had been written by W. S. Gilbert and the music for the production composed by Arthur Sullivan. This was not their first collaboration, having already worked together on a novelty piece called *Thespis* for the Gaiety Theatre in 1871; four years later, Richard D'Oyly Carte (1844–1901) persuaded them to collaborate again on *Trial by Jury* staged at the Royalty Theatre. *Patience* could, however, be taken to mark a key point in a partnership which, while often tense and argumentative, was nevertheless extraordinarily productive and successful and endured for over twenty years.

Though the continuing appeal of the operas created by Gilbert and Sullivan is testament to the timelessness of their work, it is clear that the popularity of Gilbert's librettos among nineteenth-century audiences also stemmed from their topicality. This is particularly evident in the case of *Patience.* Written when the craze for Aestheticism was at its height, many of the individuals who featured in the production were immediately recognizable as caricatures of famous promoters of the principles and attire associated with the movement.

Alison Adburgham, for instance, firmly identifies the poet Reginald Bunthorne, played by George Grossmith and "complete with his monocle," as a caricature of the painter James Abbott McNeill Whistler (1834–1903) (Adburgham, 1975). She also upholds the argument made by many critics that Archibald Grosvenor "was unmistakably Oscar Wilde." In support of her case, Adburgham draws attention to lyrics from Bunthorne's solo in Act I, "If you walk down Piccadilly with a poppy or a lily" (Gilbert & Sullivan 1881: 15). This was, as she goes on to state, exactly what Wilde had done, "attired in a loose shirt with Byron collar and large knotted green tie, velvet knee breeches, silk stockings and velvet beret" (Adburgham 1975: 30). Wilde was taking the lily to offer in homage to a society beauty hailed as the embodiment of all the classical grace to which the Aesthete should aspire, Lillie Langtry (1853–1929).

As the following discussion will make apparent, it was not only through the storyline and characters that Gilbert sought to satirize the more extreme elements of Aestheticism, but also through costumes in which the leading performers were dressed. Before an in-depth analysis of these aesthetically inspired costumes can be carried out, however, it is necessary to establish the principles at the heart of the Aesthetic movement, and precisely why the garments and behavior adopted by its enthusiasts attracted such extensive ridicule.

The Cult of Beauty

The full impact and extent of the Aesthetic movement has been widely discussed and explored elsewhere (Newton 1974; Prettejohn 2007; Gere 2008), most recently in the exhibition "The Cult of Beauty" (Victoria and Albert Museum, April–July 2011). As one of the exhibition's curators, Stephen Calloway, commented in the accompanying book, the Aesthetic movement

> [...] sought to redefine the artist primarily as a super sensitive seeker after ideal beauty. Artists engaged in the creation of this new kind of exquisite art had a need, it was held, to look constantly upon beauty, to surround themselves only with exquisite things [...]. (Calloway 2011: 90)

Paintings of studios and interiors inhabited by artists loyal to the ideals of the movement provide a sense of the kind of environment that its followers sought to create. These ranged from the stark, Japanese-inspired simplicity of Whistler's studio, seen in his 1865 painting *The Artist in His Studio* (image at Whistler 1865) to the extravagant Oriental style depicted in *The Drawing Room, Townsend House*, which was the décor adopted by the Alma Tadema family for their North London home (image at Alma Tadema 1883).

The influence of Aestheticism extended beyond the mode of decoration employed for one's home to encompass the manner in which one adorned one's physical person. Handbooks were published offering guidance on the most flattering styles and colors for those who wished to adopt Aesthetic dress (Haweis 1878; Higgin 1885) and, as Edwina Ehrman found,

> women wishing to dress artistically were recommended to look for inspiration in paintings, particularly those of the Pre-Raphaelite artists, and in books about period

FIGURE 25.3 William Richmond Blake, *Portrait of Mrs. Luke Ionides*, 1882. © Victoria and Albert Museum, E.1062:1, 2-2003.

> costume where they would find attractive sleeve details and decorative combinations of colours and fabrics. (Ehrman 2011: 207)

Contemporary photographs and paintings of women who supported the movement, such as Mary Frances (fl. 1886), wife of the artist Walter Crane (1845–1916) (image at Holleyer 1886), and Mrs. Luke Ionides (Figure 25.3), provide a sense of the styles that were adopted. The 1886 sepia photograph cannot record the colors of Frances's dress but it does display the loose cut of the garment, the smocking at the softly gathered neckline, and the delicate floral pattern with which the fabric is printed. In the case of Mrs. Ionides, the vivid rust red of her gown dominates the 1882 portrait. As with Frances, the bodice of Ionides's dress is softly pleated, and both women wear dresses where the waistline has been raised above the natural level to a point slightly below the bust. "The Empire Line," as it has been termed, was particularly associated with the Regency Period (ca. 1800–1815); many depictions of Aesthetic dress were influenced by the fashions of this period, as well as by the Greek and Roman garments depicted in classical statuary that originally inspired these Regency fashions.

One of the reasons that Aesthetic dress attracted such extensive criticism was the degree to which it departed from the silhouette and colors promoted as part of mainstream fashion. By the 1880s, most women relied upon the support of a rigid corset with channels of bone or steel at its core, and tight lacing at the rear to achieve the narrow waist, raised bustline, and curved hips that were the essential foundation for the fashions of the period (V&A/Pix 2012a). In addition to her corset, a woman also required a hooped bustle, decorously referred to as a dress improver, or at the very least a bustle pad to support the skirts that projected in a soft curve behind her (V&A/Pix 2012b). Although extant garments reveal that not all Aesthetic dress was free from the stiff boning associated with the constrictive fashions of the late nineteenth century, many women who favored Aesthetic garments, among them the actress Ellen Terry (1847–1928), did stop wearing corsets, and pleating and tucks were used to achieve a soft, draped effect. (A wide selection of images of Terry both in and out of role can be found on the Victoria and Albert Museum's website, "Search the Collections." See, in particular, V&A/Pix 2012c and V&A/Pix 2012d.) The vivid purples and blues that could be achieved with the chemical (aniline) dyes discovered in the 1850s were still extremely fashionable, as were dresses covered with contrasting and complex layers of trimming. The majority of Aesthetes rejected these chemical dyes, preferring the softer green, ochre, and indigo tones that could be achieved with natural dyes.

Poets, Lilies, and Potatoes

Patience is set in the mythical environs of Castle Bunthorne, where a group of young maidens have fallen hopelessly in love with the "morbid and mystic poet" Reginald Bunthorne. Much to the despair of the maidens, Bunthorne has himself fallen in love, but with the village milkmaid Patience, who is entirely indifferent to and somewhat dismayed by Bunthorne's urgent professions of his affection. Further disasters seem imminent when a group of Dragoons, previously engaged to these maidens, return to claim their brides; the situation is made worse by the arrival of the handsome poet Archibald Grosvenor, with whom all the women, Patience included, fall instantly in love. Determined to regain the affections of their betrothed, the Dragoons exchange their uniforms for Aesthetic dress and, though this transformation is more comic than heroic, their sacrifice earns the love of the maidens.

In response to the terrifying threats of a distraught Bunthorne, Archibald Grosvenor agrees to cut his hair and adopt the dress and manners of a commonplace young man. Seeing their hero abandon his Aesthetic attire, all the lovesick maidens follow suit, and by the conclusion of the opera everyone except Bunthorne and Lady Jane has discarded their Aesthetic dress. All these "everyday young men and women" and even the "pretty massive" Lady Jane find a soul mate, leaving only the Aesthete Bunthorne alone and forced to content himself "with a tulip or lily."

The programs and publicity connected with *Patience* highlighted its status as "A new Aesthetic Opera." This emphasis on the novelty of the piece did not pass unnoticed among the critics, who were quick to point out that this was not the first dramatic production to take up the new craze for Aestheticism as it subject matter. As a writer for the *Saturday Review* in June 1881 declared, "Already no chorus is complete in any new farce without a pale faced, long haired young man, with his hat on the back of his head and a flower as big as a frying pan in his hand" (V&A/Clips).

A production that many reviewers identified as a direct rival to *Patience* was Sir Francis Cowley Burnard's (1836–1917) play *The Colonel*, which had been produced at the Prince of Wales Theatre some two months before *Patience* opened at the Opera Comique (V&A/Clips). Many aspects of the plot of *The Colonel*, not least its focus on a group of naïve young maidens, easily seduced by the false lure of Aestheticism, resonate with the storyline followed in *Patience*, and both could be said to illustrate what a reviewer in *Punch*, who dubs himself "A. Philistine," described as "the discomfiture of the Aesthete and the triumph of common sense" (Philistine 1881: 81). There were, however, aspects of *Patience* that set the production apart, not least, as Jane W. Stedman has remarked, the fact that Gilbert devised stage pictures in the styles of contemporary Aesthetic painters, including Leighton's *Daphnephoria* (1878), and Burne-Jones's *Design from Romance of the Rose* (1881) (Stedman 1996: 183).

Whether or not *Patience* could be said to have been following or leading a trend, the success of the production was such that it transferred to the newly built Savoy Theatre in October 1881, and subsequently toured America.

Classical Draperies

It appears that Gilbert's contribution to the production extended far beyond writing the libretto, and descriptions of rehearsals suggest that he took on a role comparable to that of a "stage director" (Darlington 1951: 33–34). Furthermore, when George Du Maurier (1834–1896), famous for his popular caricatures of Aesthetes in the satirical periodical *Punch*, proved unavailable to design the costumes, Gilbert chose to take responsibility for the designs himself (Stedman 1996: 183).

In both *The Colonel* and *Patience*, fabrics from the House of Liberty, the newly established department store, were used for the costumes. Described by Wilde as "the chosen resort of the artistic shopper," Liberty's was already establishing a reputation as the place to go "for aesthetic furnishings, for peacock's feathers, and blue-and-white china, Japanese fans and screens, for Japanese 'leather' wallpapers to make modish dadoes" (Adburgham 1975: 31–32). The commercial and artistic success of this collaboration was such that Gilbert turned to the shop again when creating the 1885 production of *The Mikado*, and Arthur Liberty (1843–1917) is said to have sent special envoys to Japan to study the clothes worn there and bring back exactly the right materials to costume the cast and dress the stage sets (Adburgham 1975: 31–32).

Gilbert's appreciation of the subtleties and significance of costume becomes immediately evident upon a detailed examination of the costumes. For instance, even elements of the costume worn by the "blithe and gay" Patience, Leonora Braham (1853–1931), make direct reference to imagery associated with Aesthetic dress (image at Braham 1881). Some dramatic license has been taken, as Braham appeared in a costume that was more reminiscent of a fashionable 1880s walking dress, with a swathed skirt and tightly fitting bodice, than the plain, practical printed cottons or linens that were more likely to have been worn by a working-class woman, even a rustic milkmaid (though an equally idealized costume is worn by the haymakers in Thomas Armstrong's 1869 painting *The Hay Field* [Armstrong 1869]). The sunflowers massed under the brim of Braham's hat had been adopted by the movement, along with the lily, as one of its symbols. Moreover, the same motif featured repeatedly in fireplace surrounds and on decorative furnishings. Exaggerated versions of the flower also often appeared in the caricatures of Aesthetes, such as that featured on a music sheet cover for a humorous song ridiculing members of the movement, entitled "The High Art Maiden," written by Herbert Harraden circa 1885 (image at Harraden 1885).

It is, however, not Patience, but the lovesick maidens who are first revealed when the curtain rises. These "young Ladies," all "wearing aesthetic draperies," were grouped around the stage and in front of a backdrop showing the exterior of Castle Bunthorne. Each lady was equipped with a lute, mandolin, or other similar instrument, and the stage directions instructed them to appear "in the last stage of despair" (Gilbert and Sullivan 1881: 5).

In the absence of extant garments from the production, much of the analysis is dependent on the surviving black and white or sepia photographs of the performers. Indications of the original colors can be found, however, in the description by the critic in *The Sporting Times*, who complained about the Pre-Raphaelite red wig and "gaudy" blue dress worn by Jessie Bond as Lady Angela, as well as the "sickly" greens of other costumes (image at Bond 1881). Further information is provided by a reviewer in *The Pall Mall Gazette*, which declared Gilbert's aesthetic costumes exquisitely beautiful, "unlike the vulgar raw reds, yellows, and blues of the chorus's dresses when they become everyday young girls" (Stedman 1996: 183–184). As a comparison of sketches from the 1881 souvenir program with paintings such as *The Mill: Girls Dancing to Music by a River* by Edward Burne-Jones (1870–1872) shows (image at Burne-Jones 1870–1872), the influence of Aesthetic paintings on the style of the classical draperies, with probably deliberate reference to these works, is immediately apparent. Indeed, as subsequent analysis will show, Gilbert's eye for design clearly extended beyond the dresses themselves to encompass the accessories worn and carried by his leading ladies.

This parallel between the theatrical costumes and Aesthetic paintings is particularly apparent in the garments worn by May Fortescue (1862–1950) as Lady Ella. Photographs of the actress as she appeared in the 1881 production reveal the detail of lilies just visible on the bodice of her dress and the bracelets that twine about her arms (image at Fortescue 1881).

Like her fellow maidens, she is carrying an instrument, in this case a lyre. The design of the maiden's dresses bears a particularly strong resemblance to those depicted in paintings such as *The Midday Slumbers* (1881) and *A Greek Woman* (1869) by the artist Sir Lawrence Alma Tadema (1836–1912; see Alma Tadema 2012 for access to his complete works and Alma Tadema 1869 for *A Greek Woman*). The loose, hanging sleeves, gathered into knots at the shoulder, which feature in both paintings, were replicated in Gilbert's costume designs. The silhouette of the flowing, layered skirts also echoes those seen in the paintings. In the case of Lady Ella, there is an even stronger link with the artist, as her bracelets may owe their inspiration to a remarkably similar piece of jewelry, a serpent armlet, worn by Alma Tadema's second wife, Laura Theresa, who was also an artist in her own right (image at Alma Tadema 1870; see also Phillips 2011: 208–2011, figure 182 on p. 208).

Certain aspects of the costumes worn by Julia Gwynne (1856–1934) as Lady Saphir (Figure 25.4) and Jessie Bond (1853–1942) as Lady Angela (image at Bond 1881) are also

FIGURE 25.4 Black and white photograph showing Julia Gwynne as "Saphir," 1881. © Victoria and Albert Museum, S.146:144-2007.

worthy of comment, not least because of the connections that can be traced between these costumes and surviving examples of Aesthetic dress (see *Patience* 1882). The costumes of both actresses are bordered with bands of decoration at the hem and neckline, and the delicate open sleeves have been softly gathered into knots. The images chosen for these decorative borders make direct reference to similar motifs that appear in examples of extant Aesthetic dress and also feature in the décor of the period. The most obvious connection in this instance is between the Daisy Pattern from which William Morris's 1864 design takes its name (Figure 25.5) and the floral motif that appears on the dress of both Bond and Gwynne. Similarly, while the cut of their bodices is not directly comparable to this later silk, satin, and chiffon dress from the collection of Platt Hall, Manchester, the overall design is strikingly similar (image at Liberty 2012).

The costume worn by Alice Barnett (1846–1901) as Lady Jane is also of interest. Designed to support Lady Jane's description of herself as "not pretty. Massive," it was cut in the tunic style that was often used for Aesthetic dress (Figure 25.6). In this instance, however, it is not the cut of the costume but the bold design, which dominates the front of the tunic, that attracts attention (image at Barnett 1881).

The review in *The Referee* published on April 24, 1881, provides a wonderfully apt summary of the outfit, describing Miss Barnett as "a gigantic nocturne in black and

FIGURE 25.5 "Daisy Wallpaper," block printed in distemper colors, William Morris, 1864. © Victoria and Albert Museum, E.2222-1913.

FIGURE 25.6 Black and white photograph showing Alice Barnett as "Lady Jane," 1881. © Victoria and Albert Museum, S.146:143-2007.

peacock green" (V&A/Clips). This description creates an immediate and deliberate link with the work of another leading figure in the Aesthetic movement, the artist James Abbott McNeill Whistler. Whistler's series of "Nocturnes," which featured in the opening show at the Grosvenor Gallery, had become famous when they were severely condemned by the art critic John Ruskin (1819–1900; see the image at Whistler 1875). The peacock, which is at the center of this bold design, was an image favored by members of the Aesthetic movement and regularly appeared in artwork and furnishing designs. The most famous example of this is perhaps *The Peacock Room*, which Whistler designed at enormous expense for the London home of Frederick Richards Leyland (1832–1892) circa 1877–1888 (a panorama image may be seen at Whistler 1876).

An Aesthetic Sham

The Aesthetic dress worn by the male performers in *Patience* all follows a very similar cut and design and consists of a dark velvet jacket and fitted knee breeches, soft "pumps," and in most cases a soft, wide-brimmed hat, as shown in Figure 25.7. These outfits owed their inspiration in part to the knee breeches that characterized the male fashions of the

FIGURE 25.7 Photograph of George Grossmith as Reginald Bunthorne in *Patience* at the Opera Comique, 1881. © Victoria and Albert Museum, S.146:183-2007.

Regency era, but also to the values promoted by the Rational Dress movement, which advocated the healthiness of clothing that allowed freedom of movement and the beneficial effect of wearing wool next to the skin (Newton 1974: 89–115).

Described by one reviewer as "an idyllic poet in black velvet with long fair hair" (V&A/Clips), the outfit worn by Grosvenor reflects a fashion that was common among male Aesthetes (Figure 25.8). Yet there is also a strong case to suggest that Gilbert's design was an intentional reference to the mode of attire adopted by Oscar Wilde, who at this point was establishing himself as an arbiter of taste within the Aesthetic movement (Figure 25.9).

Though Gilbert was careful to make no direct reference to Wilde, the connection would have been immediately apparent to audiences, and indeed to Wilde himself. D'Oyly Carte was swift to recognize the value of cultivating the support of an individual who was becoming an increasingly influential figure within society, and offered to finance Wilde's 1882 tour of America. According to Josephine Lee, in return Wilde agreed to schedule his arrival in American cities so that it would coincide with the "opening of the opera, acting, as Max Beerbohm suggested, as a 'sandwich board for *Patience*'" (Lee 2010: 18–19).

FIGURE 25.8 Photograph of Rutland Barrington as Archibald Grosvenor in *Patience* at the Opera Comique. © Victoria and Albert Museum, S.146:181-2007.

FIGURE 25.9 Photograph of Oscar Wilde taken by the American photographer Napoleon Sarony. Wilde is dressed in knee breeches, quilted jacket, and loose neck tie, 1882. National Portrait Gallery, NPG P24.

As can be seen in the color illustration of the Dragoons that appears on a music sheet cover for "The Patience Polka" (sold to promote the production) and published by Chappell & Company, London, circa 1881 (image at Polka 1881), the bright tones and stiff fabrics of the heavy wool uniforms trimmed with gold braid that the Dragoons wear when they make their first appearance provided a deliberate, and visually effective, contrast with the attire favored by Bunthorne and Grosvenor. Unfortunately for the Dragoons, the maidens who once admired these uniforms have now developed "exalted perceptions" and "etherealized" tastes (Lee 2010: 18). They therefore advise the "fleshly" Dragoon Guards to exchange their bright primary colored uniforms for, as described by Lady Jane in Act I, a "cobwebby grey velvet, with a tender bloom like cold gravy, which, made Florentine fourteenth-century, trimmed with Venetian leather and Spanish altar lace, and surmounted with something Japanese—it matters not what—would at least be Early English!" (Gilbert & Sullivan 1881: 13).

As Figure 25.10 shows, this unflattering change in attire and the ridiculous postures adopted by the Dragoons offered the ideal opportunity to mock the exaggerated dress

FIGURE 25.10 Richard Temple as Colonel Calverley, Durward Lely as Lieutenant the Duke of Dunstable, and Frank Thornton as Major Murgatroyd in *Patience*, at the Opera Comique. © Victoria and Albert Museum, S.146:163-2007.

and behavior of those whose affection of Aestheticism is "born of a morbid love of admiration" (Gilbert and Sullivan 1881: 14).

Everyday Young Girls

> Enter Grosvenor, followed by all the "every-day young girls," who are followed by Chorus of Dragoons. He has had his hair cut, and is dressed in an ordinary suit of dittos and a pot hat. They all dance cheerfully round the stage (in marked contrast to their former languor). (Gilbert and Sullivan 1881: 38)

It is perhaps not surprising that, as stage directions from the final scene quoted above make evident, the happy conclusion of the production is dependent upon the return to everyday dress and sensibilities. Indeed, the only character who clings to his feigned Aestheticism is the unhappy "sham," Bunthorne.

The fate of Bunthorne, deprived of "his bride" and reduced to the companionship of a "tulip or lily," is just one illustration of the degree to which criticism and ridicule are directed toward those who are "an Aesthetic sham," rather than genuine followers of the movement. This careful management of the narrative may explain how the production was able to satirize the movement so effectively, and yet create an opera, which, according to *The Pall Mall Gazette* (April 25, 1881), "did not injure the true aesthetic tree" (*Pall Mall* 1881).

Many factors united to engineer the success of *Patience*, which ran for over 578 performances. The visual impact of dress and set and the sharp wit of Gilbert's libretto synergized perfectly with Sullivan's score, which was redolent with an "air of languor and yearning" that was perfectly designed for the satirical purpose of opera (*Pall Mall* 1881). As Gilbert declared in the libretto:

> If this is not exactly right, we hope you won't upbraid;
> You can't get high Aesthetic taste, like trousers, ready made
> True views on Mediaevalism, Time alone will bring
> But, as far as we can judge, it's something like this sort of thing.
>
> (Gilbert and Sullivan 1881: 32)

See also: Production Aesthetics and Materials, Historically Informed Performance, Operatic Images

Bibliography

Adburgham, Alison. 1975. *Liberty's: A Biography of a Shop*. London: George Allen & Unwin Ltd.

Ashman, Mike. 1992. "Producing Wagner." In *Wagner in Performance*, edited by Barry Millington and Stewart Spencer, 29–47. New Haven: Yale University Press.

Benedettini, Floridia, Bruna Niccoli, and Carla Tolomeo, eds. 2006. *I barocchi: costumi di scena della Fondazione Cerratelli e sculture di Carla Tolomeo*. Milan: IdeArte; Viareggio: Idea books.

Biggi, Maria Ida. 2010. "La presenza dei personaggi nelle incisioni di Alessandro Sanquirico." In Biggi and Gallarti 2010, 151–166.

——, and Paolo Gallarati, eds. 2010. *L'immaginario scenografico e la realizzazione musicale: Atti del Convegno in onore di Mercedes Viale Ferrero (2009)*. Turin: Edizioni Orso dell'Alessandria.

Bignami, Paola. 2005. *Storia del costume teatrale: Oggetti per esibirsi nello spettacolo e in società*. Rome: Carocci.

——, and Ossicini, Charlotte. 2010. *Il quadrimensionale instabile: Manuale per lo studio del costume teatrale*. Turin: UTET University.

Bradley, Ian. 1996. *Complete Annotated Gilbert and Sullivan*. New York: Oxford University Press.

Breward, Christopher. 2010. "'At Home at St James': Dress, Décor, and the Problem of Fashion in Edwardian Theatre." In *The Edwardian Sense: Art, Design and Performance in Britain, 1901–1910*, edited by Morna O'Neill and Michael Hart, 141–165. New Haven: Yale University Press.

Breward, Christopher. 2004. *Fashioning London: Clothing and the Modern Metropolis*. Oxford and New York: Berg.

Bryant, Barbara. 2011. "The Grosvenor Gallery, Patronage and the Aesthetic Portrait." In Calloway and Federle Orr 2011, 156-177.
Busseti, Vincenza, and Olga Jesurum. 2014. "Giubbino, farsetto, inquartata: La catalogazione dei costume teatrali e la questione del lemmario." In De Lucca 2014.
Calloway, Stephen. 2011. "The Palace of Art: Artists Collections and Their Houses." In Calloway and Federle Orr 2011, 88–109.
——, and Lynn Federle Orr, eds. 2011. *The Cult of Beauty: The Aesthetic Movement 1860–1900.* London: V&A.
Campagnol, Isabella. 2007. "Venice 1870–1930. The Rediscovery of the Arts and Crafts in Dress." *Dress: The Journal of the Costume Society of America* 34: 33–44.
Carr, Alice Vansittart. 1926. *Mrs. J. Comyns Carr's Reminiscences.* London: Hutchinson & Co.
Carter, Michael. 2003. *Fashion Classics: From Carlyle to Barthes.* Oxford: Berg.
Cavanagh, John, and Sidney Jackson Jowers, eds. 2000. *Theatrical Costume, Masks, Make-Up and Wigs: A Bibliography and Iconography.* London and New York: Routledge.
Clark, Caryl. 2003. "Fabricating Magic: Costuming Salieri's 'Armida'." *Early Music* 31/3: 451–461.
Cowgill, Rachel. 2012. "'Attitudes with a Shawl': Performance, Femininity, and Spectatorship at the Italian Opera in Early Nineteenth-Century London." In *The Arts of the Prima Donna in the Long Nineteenth Century*, edited by Rachel Cowgill and Hilary Poriss, 217–251. New York: Oxford University Press.
Craig, Edith, and Christopher St. John, eds. 1933. *Ellen Terry's Memoirs.* London: Victor Gollancz.
Crespi Morbio, Vittoria. 2000. "I Costumi." In *Giuseppe Verdi: l'uomo, l'opera, il mito*, edited by Francesco Degrada, 276–287. Milan: Skira.
Cumming, Valerie. 2004. *Understanding Fashion History.* London: B. T. Batsford.
——. 1987. "Ellen Terry: An Aesthetic Actress and Her Clothing." *Costume* 21: 67–74.
Darlington, William A. 1951. *The World of Gilbert and Sullivan.* London: Peter Nevill.
Davanzo Poli, Doretta. 2011. *Venice-Burano. The Lace Museum.* Venice: Marsilio.
——. 2007. *Twentieth-Century Fabrics: European and American Designers and Manufacturers.* Milan: Skira.
——. 2002. *Abiti antiche e moderni dei veneziani.* Venice: Neri Pozza.
Davis, Tracey C. 1991. *Actresses as Working Women: Their Social Identity in Victorian Culture.* London: Routledge.
De Lucca, Valeria, ed. 2014. *Fashioning Opera and Musical Theater: Stage Costumes from the Late Renaissance to 1900.* [Proceedings of conference held March 29–April 1 2012, Venice: Fondazione Cini, Isola San Giorgio Maggiore]. Venice: Fondazione Giorgio Cini.
De Marly, Diana. 1982. *Costume on the Stage: 1600–1940.* London: B. T. Batsford.
De Simone, Paola, and Nicolò Maccavino. 2014. "I figurini della Collezione Carlo Guillaume: Dalla Biblioteca del Conservatorio San Pietro a Majella una fonte d'archivio ancora inedita per l'Ottocento musicale e coreutico sulla scena dei Reali Teatri di Napoli." In De Lucca 2014.
Erhman, Edwina. 2011. "Women's Dress." In Calloway and Federle Orr 2011, 206–208.
Fauque, Claude. 2011. *Costumes de scène: A travers les collections du CNCS.* Paris: Editions de la Martinière.
Fowler, James. 1989. "Archives of the Dance: Early Dance Holdings of the Theatre Museum, London." *Dance Research* 7/2: 81–88.
Gere, Charlotte. 2010. *Artistic Circles: Design and Decoration in the Aesthetic Movement.* London: V&A Publishing.

Gilbert, W. S., and Arthur Sullivan. 1881. *An Entirely New and Original Aesthetic Opera in Two Acts Entitled Patience, or Bunthorne's Bride*. London: Chapell & Co. Online. Available: http://archive.org/stream/entirelyneworigioosulluoft#page/6/mode/2up (accessed August 8, 2012).

Greenblatt, Stephen. 1984. *Renaissance Self-Fashioning: From More to Shakespeare*. Chicago: University of Chicago Press.

Hall-Witt, Jennifer. 2007. *Fashionable Acts: Opera and Elite Culture in London, 1780–1880*. Lebanon: University of New Hampshire Press.

Haweis, Mary. [1878] 2005. *The Art of Beauty*. New York: Harper & Brother's. Reprint. Kessinger.

Higgin, Louis. [1885] 2008. *Art as Applied to Dress: With Special Reference to Harmonious Colouring*. Oxford: J. S.Virtue. Reprint. Pranava Books.

Hodgdon, Barbara. 2006. "Shopping in the Archives: Material Mnemonics." In *Remembering Shakespeare, Memory, Performance*, edited by Peter Holland, 135–168. Cambridge: Cambridge University Press.

Isaac, Veronica. 2008. "From Ellen Terry's Beetlewing Dress to David Tennant's Leather Trousers: An Investigation of the Preservation and Presentation of Theatrical Costume in British Theatres and Museums." M.A. thesis, University of Southampton, UK.

Jeanneret, Christine. 2012. "Emblems, Portraits, Characters and Affects: Costume Drawings for *Ipermestra* (1658)." Paper read at "Fashioning Opera and Musical Theatre: Stage Costumes from the Late Renaissance to 1900." Conference, March 29–April 1. Venice: Fondazione Cini. Isola di San Giorgio Maggiore.

Jesurum, Olga. 2010. "Discorso sul metodo': Per un metodologia dello studio sulla scenografia ottocentesca." In Biggi and Gallarati 2010, 193–202.

Jones, Alice Rosalind, and Peter Stallybrass. 2000. *Renaissance Clothing and the Materials of Memory*. Cambridge: Cambridge University Press.

Jowers, Sidney Jackson. 1992. "Costumes." In *The New Grove Dictionary of Opera*. Online. Available: http://www.oxfordmusiconline.com/subscriber/article/grove/music/O005329 (accessed July 14, 2012).

Kaplan, Joel H., and Sheila Stowell. 1994. *Theatre and Fashion: Oscar Wilde to the Suffragettes*. Cambridge: Cambridge University Press.

Kopytoff, Igor. 1986. "The Cultural Biography of Things: Commoditization as Process." In *The Social Life of Things: Commodities in Cultural Perspective*, edited by Arjun Appadurai, 64–91. Cambridge: Cambridge University Press.

La Gorce, Jérôme de. 1997. *Féeries d'opéra: Décors, machines, et costumes en France, 1645–1765*. Paris: Éditions de Patrimoine.

Laver, James. 1964. *Costume in the Theatre*. London: Harrap.

Lecomte, Hippolyte. 1820. *Costumes de Théatre de 1670 à 1820*. Paris. Delpech.

Lee, Josephine. 2010. *The Japan of Pure Invention: Gilbert and Sullivan's Mikado*. Minneapolis: University of Minnesota Press.

Lublin, Robert. 2011. *Costuming the Shakespearean Stage: Visual Codes of Representation in Early Modern Theatre and Culture*. Aldershot, UK: Ashgate.

Maione, Paologiovanni, and Francesca Seller. 2014. "Il magazzino delle meraviglie. Inventari e regolamenti per i costumi del Teatro di San Carlo nell'Ottocento." In De Lucca 2014.

Majer, Michele, ed. 2012. *Staging Fashion 1880–1920: Lily Elsie, Jane Harding and Billie Burke*. New Haven: Yale University Press.

Marshall, Gail. 1998. *Actresses of the Victorian Stage*. Cambridge: Cambridge University Press.

Massip, Catherine, ed. 1990. *Voyage en musique: Cent ans d'exotisme—Décors et costumes dans le spectacle lyriques en France.* Boulogne-Billancourt: Centre Boulogne-Billancourt.

Meisel, Martin. 1983. *Realizations: Narrative, Pictorial, and Theatrical Arts in Nineteenth-Century England.* Princeton, NJ: Princeton University Press.

Messel. 2012. *Biography of Oliver Messel.* Online. Available: http://www.vam.ac.uk/content/articles/b/biography-oliver-messel/ (accessed August 8, 2012).

Mikhail, E. H. 1979. *Oscar Wilde: Interviews and Recollections.* London: Macmillan.

Monks, Aoife. 2009. *The Actor in Costume.* London: Palgrave Macmillan.

Nathan, Archie. 1960. *Costumes by Nathan.* Newnes: London.

Newton, Stella Mary. 1974. *"Health Art and Reason": Dress Reformers of the 19th Century.* London: Murray.

Niccoli, Bruna. 2004. "Official Dress and Courtly Fashion in Genoese Entries." In *Europa Triumphans: Court and Civic Festivals in Early Modern Europe.* 2 vols., edited by J. R. Mulryne, Helen Watanabe-O'Kelly, and Margaret Shewring, I: 261–273. Aldershot, UK: Ashgate.

——, and Roberta Orsi Landini. 2005. *Moda a Firenze, 1540–1580: Lo stile di Eleonora di Toledo e la sua influenza.* Florence: Pagliai Polistampa.

Pall Mall. 1881. *The Pall Mall Gazette* (April 25). Online. Available: http://diamond.boisestate.edu/gas/patience/reviews/1881opcom/810425pmg.html (accessed August 8, 2012).

Pearce, Susan. 1994. "Objects as Meaning; or Narrating the Past." In *Interpreting Objects and Collections,* edited by Susan Pearce, 19–29. New York: Routledge.

Philistine, A. 1881. *Punch.* (February 19). Online. Available: http://www.xix-e.pierre-marteau.com/ed/colonel/criticism.html (accessed August 8, 2012).

Phillips, Clare. 2011. "Jewellery." In Calloway and Federle Orr 2011, 208–211.

Prettejohn, Elizabeth. 2007. *Art for Art's Sake: Aestheticism in Victorian Painting.* New Haven: Yale University Press.

Ravelhofer, Barbara. 2006. *The Early Stuart Masque: Dance, Costume, and Music.* New York: Oxford University Press.

Robertson, Walford Graham. 1931. *Time Was.* London: Hutchinson.

Rosselli, John. 1992. *Singers of Italian Opera: The History of a Profession.* Cambridge: Cambridge University Press.

Stedman, Jane W. 1996. *W. S. Gilbert: A Classic Victorian and His Theatre.* New York: Oxford University Press.

Stowell, Sheila. 2012. "Lucile and the Theatricalization of Fashion." In Majer 2012: 60–76.

Taylor, Lou. 2002. *The Study of Dress History.* Manchester: Manchester University Press.

Tonkovich, Jennifer. 2005. "Claude Gillot's Costume Designs for the Paris Opéra: Some New Sources." *The Burlington Magazine* 147/1225: 248–252.

Tråvén, Marianne. 2014. "The Inventory after Gustav III as a Source for the Work of the Costume Workshop of the Royal Opera in Stockholm between 1773 and 1792." In De Lucca 2014.

V&A/Clips.2012. Press clippings from the Production File for *Patience,* Opera Comique (1881), in the collection of the Department of Theatre and Performance (most absent page numbers and exact dates). Items referenced include: *Daily Telegraph* (April 25, 1881); *The Illustrated Sporting and Dramatic News* (1881); *Illustrated London News* (1881); *Saturday Review* (June 1881); *The Referee* (April 24, 1881).

Van Witsen, Leo. 1981. *Costuming in Opera: Who Wears What and Why.* 2 vols. Bloomington: Indiana University Press.

Viale Ferrero, Mercedes. 2004. "Staging Rossini." [Translated by Rosa Solinas.] In *The Cambridge Companion to Rossini,* edited by Emanuele Senici, 204–215. Cambridge: Cambridge University Press.

——. 2002. "Stage and Set." In *Opera on Stage*, edited by Lorenzo Bianconi and Giorgio Pestelli, translated by Kate Singleton. *The History of Italian Opera* 5: 1–123. Chicago: University of Chicago Press.

——. 2000. "'Con solo abito in bianco senza velo in testa': Una raccolta di figurini nell'archivio storico del Teatro Regio di Torino." In *'Una piacente estate di San Martino': Studi e ricerche per i settant'anni di Marcello Conati*, edited by Marco Capra, 357–379. Lucca: Libreria musicale italiana.

——. 1984. "Costume Designs by Alessandro Sanquirico and others for ballets performed at the Teatro alla Scala, Milan, 1820–24." *Dance Research* 2/2: 24–40.

Wild, Nicole. 1987. *Décors et costumes du XIXe siècle. I: Opéra de Paris*. Paris: Bibliothèque National de France.

Wren, Gayden. 2001. *A Most Ingenious Paradox: The Art of Gilbert and Sullivan*. New York: Oxford University Press.

Relevant Web-Based Sources

Comédie. 2012. *L'art du costume à la Comédie-Française*. http://www.cncs.fr/expositions/a-l-affiche/la-com%C9die-fran%C7aise/31 A website created to accompany the exhibition *L'art du costume à la Comédie-Française*, Centre national du costume de scène de Moulins, June 11–December 30, 2011 (accessed June 22, 2012).

London. 2012. Museum of London Collections Online. http://www.museumoflondon.org.uk/Collections-Research/Collections-online/ An online resource catalogues records and images for some of the pieces from the Museum's vast collection.

ROH. 212. Royal Opera House Company Collections. http://www.rohcollections.org.uk/ The online catalogue of the Royal Opera House Company Collections. (accessed June 22, 2012).

Stockholm. 2012. Musik/Teater Museet (Music/Theater Museum) Stockholm. http://www.musikmuseet.se/?l=en A comprehensive overview of the collections. (accessed August 8, 2012).

V&A. 2012. Search the Collections, Victoria and Albert Museum. http://collections.vam.ac.uk/ The online catalogue of the Victoria and Albert Museum.

V&A/Opera. 2012. http://www.vam.ac.uk/content/articles/o-9/19th-century-opera/ A brief but useful overview of key developments in opera in Britain during the nineteenth century. (accessed June 14, 2012).

Images on the Web

Alma Tadema. 2012. A comprehensive selection of the works of the artist Sir Lawrence Alma Tadema. NB: many of the images are not dated. Online. Available: http://www.alma-tadema.org/ (accessed August 8, 2012).

Alma Tadema. 1883. Anna Alma Tadema, *The Drawing Room, Townsend House*, 1883 [Royal Academy of Art]. Online. Available: http://www.racollection.org.uk/ixbin/indexplus?_IXACTION_=file&_IXFILE_=templates/search/works.html (accessed August 20, 2012).

Alma Tadema, Sir Lawrence. 1870. *Serpent Armlet*, inscribed in Greek letters and worn by Laura Theresa Alma Tadema when painted by her husband. Ca. 1870. [Private Collection]. In Calloway 2011 (Private Collection). Online. Available: http://www.historyextra.com/gallery/cult-beauty# (accessed August 31, 2012).

Alma Tadema, Sir Lawrence. 1869. *A Greek Woman* (oil on canvas). [Private Collection]. Online. Available: http://www.the-athenaeum.org/art/detail.php?ID=367 (accessed August 31, 2012).

Armstrong, Thomas. 1869. *The Hay Field*, 1869 [V&A Collections]. Online. Available: http://collections.vam.ac.uk/item/O16459/the-hay-field-oil-painting-armstrong-thomas/ (accessed August 8, 2012).

Bond. 1881. Black and white photograph of Jessie Bond as Lady Angela. Online. Available: http://math.boisestate.edu/gas/books/bond/006.html (accessed September 1, 2012).

Braham. 1881. Signed photograph of Leonora Braham in the title role of *Patience* at the Opera Comique, 1881 [National Portrait Gallery Collections, NPG x6415]. Online. Available: http://www.npg.org.uk/collections.php (accessed August 31, 2012).

Burne-Jones, Edward. 1870–1872. Oil painting, *The Mill: Girls Dancing to Music by a River*. [V&A Collections, CAI.8]. Online. Available: http://collections.vam.ac.uk/item/O14964/the-mill-girls-dancing-to-oil-painting-burne-jones-edward/ (accessed August 31, 2012).

Fortescue. 1881. Photograph of May Fortescue as Lady Ella in *Patience* at the Opera Comique, [V&A Collections, S.146:81-2007]. Online. Available: http://collections.vam.ac.uk/item/O231127/guy-little-theatrical-photograph-photograph-unknown/ (accessed August 8, 2012).

Gaillard, René. 1733. Engraving by René Gaillard (ca. 1719–1790) of the costume that Jean Baptiste Martin (fl. 1748–1757) designed for a Fury in *Hippolyte et Aricie* (1733) by Jean-Philippe Rameau (1683–1764). [Bibliothèque de l'arsenal, Paris, France] Online. Available: http://www.scholarsresource.com/browse/work/2144665100 (accessed August 31, 2012). [Small image only].

Harraden, Herbert. 1885. Sheet music cover: "High Art Maiden." Online. Available: http://www.lookandlearn.com/history-images/XJ845755/The-High-Art-Maiden?img=0&search=affectation&cat=&bool=phrase (accessed August 31, 2012).

Holleyer. Frederick. [ca.] 1886. Photograph of Mary Frances Crane. [V&A Collections, 7811-1938]. Online. Available: http://collections.vam.ac.uk/item/O88743/mary-frances-mrs-walter-crane-photograph-hollyer-frederick/ (accessed August 31, 2012).

Liberty. 2012. "*Hera*" *Dress*. Silk satin and silk crepe chiffon, trimmed with glass beads. House of Liberty, 1904–1905. [Platt Hall, Manchester]. Online. Available: http://www.manchestergalleries.org/the-collections/search-the-collection/display.php?EMUSESSID=4a30a17779353ea4586828115778ad81&irn=17163 (accessed August 8, 2012).

Patience. 1882. Color posters produced to promote American tour of the production circa 1882 and printed by A. S. Seers, New York. Online. Available: http://math.boisestate.edu/gas/patience/posters/index.html (accessed August 8, 2012).

Polka. 1881. Hand tinted cover of sheet music for the "Patience Polka." Online. Available: http://diamond.boisestate.edu/gas/patience/illus_mus/covers.html (accessed September 1, 2012).

V&A/Pix. 2012. Digitized images of all garments and photographs cited from the V&A Collections. Online. Available: http://collections.vam.ac.uk/ (accessed August 8, 2012).

V&A/Pix. 2012a. T.84&A-1980, Red sateen, beige leather and whalebone, with a steel spoon-shaped busk, circa 1883, V&A Collections. Online. Available: http://collections.vam.ac.uk/item/O58915/corset-unknown/ (accessed August 20, 2012).

V&A/Pix. 2012b. T.57-1980, Woven and padded horsehair bustle pad, England, ca. 1875, V&A Collections. Online. Available: http://collections.vam.ac.uk/item/O88753/bustle-pad-unknown/ (accessed August 20, 2012).

V&A/Pix. 2012c. Sepia photograph of Terry in a loose fitting dress. She is not wearing a corset beneath. Image taken by the photographer Herbert Rose Barraud circa 1880–1890. Online. Available: http://collections.vam.ac.uk/item/O141666/guy-little-theatrical-photograph-photograph-barraud-herbert-rose/ (accessed October 16, 2012).

V&A/Pix. 2012d. Sepia photograph of Terry in a loose fitting dress. She is not wearing a corset beneath. Image taken by the photographer Arthur Ellis circa 1880–1890. Online. Available: http://collections.vam.ac.uk/item/O141716/guy-little-theatrical-photograph-photograph-ellis-alfred/ (accessed October 16, 2012).

Whistler, J. M. 1876. The recreation of *The Peacock Room*. Purchased by Charles Lang Freer in 1904 and transported to his home in Detroit. Freer Art Gallery. Online. Available: http://www.asia.si.edu/exhibitions/current/peacockRoom/pano.asp (accessed August 8, 2012).

Whistler, J. M. 1875. *Nocturne in Black and Gold: The Falling Rocket*. The Detroit Institute of Arts. Online. Available: http://www.dia.org/object-info/7d1a59d3-6163-440a-925a-b0978f1f8811.aspx?position=4 (accessed August 8, 2012).

Whistler, J. M. 1865. *The Artist in His Studio*. Art Institute of Chicago. Online. Available: http://www.artic.edu/aic/collections/artwork/65709?search_no=3&index=0 (accessed August 20, 2012).

CHAPTER 26

REGIETHEATER/DIRECTOR'S THEATER

ULRICH MÜLLER

What Is *Regietheater*?

Regietheater is a German term, and also something that was "invented" in the German-speaking realm. Should one listen today to a discussion of theater experts following the opening night of a stage production, it is virtually impossible not to hear this word in various usages, from agreement to displeasure, and frequently in an aggressive debate about the merits or weaknesses of the piece in question. It has become the *Lieblingswort* (favorite term) of the German *feuilleton* (Döhring 2007: 31). There have been heated arguments between people who consider *Regietheater* innovative and interesting and those who condemn it as unfitting or even repelling.

Part of the difficulty in the usage of this term stems from the fact that there are two understood meanings of it, both of which refer to the staging of dramas and/or musical theater. The term is a compound German noun, the two roots of which both have classical origins, that is, Greek and Latin (such compound nouns are very common in the German language): *Regie* (directing a theater production) and *Theater*; the term *Regie* has been in use in German since the end of the eighteenth century (from Latin *regere* [to direct] via French *régie*); Greek *théatron* means a location, where you can "see" something, and *Theater* has been used in German since the seventeenth century (via French *théâtre*). On the one hand, *Regietheater* generally implies that *Regie* is as important as the text and the music; on the other, there is an understanding of the term reserved primarily for provocative or disparaging purposes: a type of *Regie* that seeks to dominate the drama, to deconstruct it, to question it, even to transform the story and/or interpret it in a new way. We do not know when or by whom the word *Regietheater* was composed. Richard Wagner was one of the first composers who tried to direct performances of his own operas, namely at his Bayreuth Festival in 1876 (*Der Ring des Nibelungen*) and his 1882 production of *Parsifal*; but he was only partially satisfied with the staging (Bauer 1992: 506).

It is a difficult task to discuss *Regietheater* and its context, and it can only be done in a highly subjective manner. One must know who is speaking, what expertise he or she has on the subject, and with which kind of theater he or she is familiar. New productions all over the world that can be considered in the context of *Regietheater* are regularly discussed in print. Recently, a number of books, including conference proceedings and monographs about certain directors and stage designers, have appeared (see, for example, Alonge 2006; Schläder 2006; Levin 2007 [on Wagner, Mozart, Verdi, and Zemlinsky]; Gutjahr 2008; Sollich et al. 2008; and Latham and Parker 2001 [on Verdi]; much about performances may also be found in Edward Said's 2008 collection of reviews). But such books do not necessarily mirror the full range of what is a mixed public reaction and are sometimes more or less apologetic in favor of *Regietheater*. Frequently, they are concerned with (often small) selections of operas, authors, or directors, because there is hardly a chance for individuals to know (and that means for modern productions to have seen on stage) all important performances; videos represent only a sample of theatrical reality (see videography).

German writers are mostly intense supporters of *Regietheater*, while others follow more cautiously. For example, David Levin comments, "Opera onstage remains a forum for surprise, dismay, and delight," but also notes, that "the fact [...] that *any* work can be made to signify almost anything does not mean that anything goes" (Levin 2007: 207). Said, however, simply observes, "Productions should emphasize, I believe, the connection between an operatic work and its immediate context to a late-twentieth century audience" (Said 2008: 117). Monographs and readers about Wagner are legion in German-speaking countries, and the newer ones support even extreme forms of *Regietheater*. Two publications should be specifically mentioned, the first of which is an exhaustive book about Wagner performances by a British author, Patrick Carnegy (2006). Carnegy, dramaturg at the Royal Opera House London and music critic, presents a very broad and well-balanced survey of how operas have been produced in the last decades, and not only regarding Wagner. The second is the publication of the proceedings of the 2005 symposium about *Regietheater* organized by the International Salzburg Association, the University of Salzburg, and the Salzburg Festival (Kühnel et al. 2007). The symposium focused on Mozart's operas, and its publication features not only case studies about Mozart reception from Goethe (Schanze) to Jean-Pierre Ponnelle (Kii-Ming Lo), Peter Sellars (Felten), and *Zauberflöte* (Greenwald, Scott, Rothschild, and Vysloužilová), but also basic essays about *Regietheater* (Kühnel, Döhring, Müller) as well as pro and contra arguments by Peter Csobádi, Joachim Herz, Raimund Jakob, Michael Rosenfeld, and Thomas Rothschild.

From Stage Director to *Regisseur*

It must be kept in mind that (at all times and in all places) theater requires an adequate location, either open-air or in a building like a temple, church, or a theater; there must be one or several actors, preferably some kind of costumes and scenery, and of course, an audience. At least one person must organize and control the entire event, and be responsible for ensuring that everything and everybody is at the right place at the right time. For the classical Greek theater, these duties had to be done by several individuals: the poet, the *didaskalos* (teacher, master) and the *choregos* (master of the chorus). The *regens ludi* (master of the play) fulfilled the same function for performances of medieval religious plays, or stage masters for such different types of theater as the Japanese Noh, the theater of Shakespeare's epoch, or Baroque court shows.

The French word *mis-en-scène* precisely describes the responsibilities of these individuals, namely to "put" the drama onto the stage, that is, "in scene" (in Italian: *mettere in scena*), with the collaboration of the impresario, the stage master, and the actors. We must also assume that at all times there was a contemporary living tradition of how to present a play—which, of course, was always changing, but also provided a standard aesthetic framework. Goethe, for example, was for many years director of the Weimar court theater and in 1803 taught two of his actors ninety-one rules for acting ("Didaskalien," later correctly titled "Regeln für Schauspieler" [Rules for Actors], translated in Woehl 1927, written down in 1824 by J. P. Eckermann and posthumously published in 1832 and numerous times thereafter; see Goethe [1803] 1833). Several years earlier, probably in 1794, Goethe had already delineated rules on how to perform an opera, specifically Mozart's *Zauberflöte* (Schanze 2007).

Regietheater, understood in neutral terms, began in the early twentieth century, when some stage directors (*Regisseure*) in the German-speaking countries began to disagree with the established bourgeois theater, which promoted a Romantic style of staging and acting. These stage directors then made a concerted effort to dominate theater productions, starting with dramas, and soon moving on to operas. Some designers and directors conceived productions that were no longer realistic, but used abstract and symbolic forms, the new technologies of electric lighting, the cyclorama (*Rundhorizont*, a semi-circular curtain or wall used as background to suggest limitless space, replacing the traditional side curtains), and revolving stages. In the realm of opera, Adolph Appia (1862–1928) of Switzerland and Edward Gordon Craig (1872–1966) of Britain should be mentioned, and later, several German directors and designers of the Weimar Republic (i.e., Germany in the 1920s), for example, the teams of Oskar Hagen, Hans Niedecken-Gebhard and Hein Heckroth (operas of Händel in Göttingen), and Erich Maria Rabenalt and Wilhelm Reinking (Darmstadt). Later, in Berlin at Otto Klemperer's *Kroll-Oper*, Rabenalt and Reinking, together with Jürgen Fehling and others, tried to establish a more abstract style, but without lasting success. (For discussion of some of these, see Peusch 1984; Carnegy 2006: 234–260; and Levin 2007: 37–39.) More successful were Gustav Mahler and Alfred Roller in Vienna, Hans Gregor (who founded the pre-war Komische Oper in Berlin) and—for dramas—Max Reinhardt, who was one of the founders of the Salzburg Festival. The Salzburg Festival was based on a concept devised by Hugo von Hofmannsthal to rediscover and preserve the Baroque-Catholic cultural heritage of Austria after the collapse of the Habsburg Empire (see, with many details, Gallup 1987; stressing the ideological context, see Steinberg 2000). It became more and more international, especially after World War II under the direction of Herbert von Karajan (1908–1989). Wagner's Bayreuth Festival (which he founded in

1876; see later discussion) also became a testing ground for directorial innovation, and even Richard's son Siegfried Wagner (1869–1930) tried to change, very cautiously, the traditional methods of staging. But this kind of *Regietheater* ended abruptly with the rise to power of National Socialism and the ensuing dictatorship that established itself in 1933 in Germany and in 1938 in Austria; only in neutral Switzerland (Zürich) could aspects of the free and progressive theater tradition survive.

Modern *Regietheater*: The Early Years

The work of two directors can be considered as defining the beginnings of modern *Regietheater*: Wieland Wagner (Bayreuth Festival, 1917–1966), and Walter Felsenstein (Komische Oper Berlin/ GDR, 1901–1975). When in 1951 Wieland and his brother Wolfgang re-opened their grandfather Richard's Bayreuth Festival, they announced a clear departure from former styles of performing Wagner by clearing the stage—and also trying to clear out the former dreadful affiliation with the ideology of National Socialism. There are several books and many articles about the "New Bayreuth" and Wieland Wagner (see, for example, Schäfer 1970; Mack 1978; Barth 1980; Müller and Wapnewski 1992; Eckert 2001; Carnegy 2006; and Kapsamer 2010). Carnegy notes:

> Wieland and his younger brother Wolfgang, aged thirty-four and thirty-one respectively, had been entrusted with the reopening of the festival after their mother Winifred [the English-born widow of Richard's son Siegfried, who died in 1930] had been effectively dispossessed by a denazification court. Over the festival lay the shameful shadow of the Führer's appropriation of it as a cultural flagship for the Reich. [...] When Wieland spoke of the necessity of "entrümpeln"—of clearing out the rubbish and making a clean start—he was speaking of more than tired old scenery, costumes and stage props. (Carnegy 2006: 263)

It was a provocation for the "Grail Temple" of Wagnerism, and reactions were exceedingly heated: Wieland's staging of the *Ring* and above all of *Parsifal* (1951) were more or less empty, using light, colors, and a huge cyclorama, which allowed all of the attention to be focused on the singers and their acting on a central disc (*Scheibe*). There are many photographs of Wieland Wagner's productions; he also designed both the stage and the costumes, but unfortunately there are only two full videos (*Tristan und Isolde* and *Die Walküre*), which were taped at a complete guest appearance at the Osaka Festival in Japan, in 1967, shortly after Wieland's death (but only in black and white and of modest technical quality; see Wieland Wagner 1967 DVD).

By the time of his death in 1966, Wieland Wagner had radically transformed the style of directing Wagner's operas, transposing the theories of Sigmund Freud, C. G. Jung, and Rudolf Steiner to the stage: he presented human relations through the lens of psychoanalysis, combined it with the archetypes and symbolism of *Tiefenpsychologie* (depth psychology), and applied concepts of *Anthroposophie* about the meaning of colors.

According to Carnegy, "Wieland's emphasis on the Greek rather than the German affinities on the universality of a psychological reading of myth had cut the operas from their historical anchorages. He had effectively de-historicized them," creating a stage of mythology (Carnegy 2006: 309). Articles by the philologist Wolfgang Schadewaldt (University of Tübingen; see Müller and Wapnewski 1992) and the dramaturg Lynn Snook about Wagner's mythology (Snook 2009) also influenced Wieland, but probably not the writings of Robert Donington (1963), "whose Jungian analysis [...], although quite independently conceived, reads almost like a screen play for Wieland's productions" (Carnegy 2006: 305). In his last years Wieland tried to inject modern sociology into some of his productions (*Meistersinger*, Bayreuth 1964; *Lulu*, Stuttgart 1966).

Walter Felsenstein, director of the Komische Oper Berlin from 1947 until his death in 1975, also substantially influenced the style of directing operas, not by using symbolic forms or shapes, but by strict concentration on dramatic veracity; for him the drama was as essential as the music, and his artists and even the chorus became singing actors and actresses (see Melchinger 1961; Fuchs 1991 [with an excellent foreword by the editor]; Braunmüller 2002; Homann 2005; see also the interview with Joachim Herz, *Der neue Merker* 2002 [Förster and Zöllner {2002} 2009]). Felsenstein presented all of his productions in the German language to make them intelligible to his audience; he re-examined the sources of the plays, and produced new and trustworthy translations of the non-German libretti. His productions not only seemed to be realistic or even naturalistic, but also presented tales of timeless meaning and significance. His successor at the Komische Oper, Joachim Herz, called this style *komödiantischen Realismus* ("comic realism"; see Herz 1984). Several productions of Felsenstein (among them Verdi's *Otello*, Offenbach's *Tales of Hoffmann* and Bartók's *Barbe-bleue* [*Bluebeard*], and Janáček's *The Cunning Little Vixen*) were filmed by Georg Mielke (2001) in the German Democratic Republic, in German, and were released in 2008. The evolution of *Regietheater* went considerably further and became a widespread method of staging operas, especially the relatively small number of pieces in the standard repertoire.

Modern *Regietheater*: An Invective

Modern use of the term *Regietheater*, as mentioned earlier, means something quite different: productions in which the director and his team present the drama or musical theater in what is often a surprisingly new and often provocative manner, specifically the director's personal interpretation of the drama to a modern audience. John Lahr, in a review of Gordon Edelstein's 2010 production of Tennessee Williams's *Glass Menagerie* (Laura Pels Theatre, New York), accused such a director of "trying to claim co-authorship of a play that he imperfectly understands" (Lahr 2010).

A well-known and much-discussed example of what is meant by this idea of "co-authorship" or *Regietheater* is the production of Mozart's *Entführung aus dem Serail* at the Komische Oper in Berlin (2004), directed by Calixto Bieito. This opera, with a libretto by Stephanie the Younger, adapted from the text of Friedrich Bretzner of Leipzig, debuted on July 16, 1782, at the Imperial Theater (the Old Burgtheater) in Vienna, and became Mozart's greatest success in his lifetime. It is a so-called *Türkenoper* (Turkish opera), telling the story of two European couples, Konstanze and Belmonte and Blonde and Pedrillo, three of whom were captured by Muslim pirates and sold as slaves to the rich and mighty pasha Bassa Selim, whose property is guarded by Osmin, a both cruel and comical figure. The two couples, led by Belmonte and Pedrillo, try to escape, are caught again, and await execution. But in the end Bassa pardons them and lets them sail back to their homelands. Such a finale characterizes this opera as an Enlightenment piece that exhibits tolerance and generosity (in German: *Humanitäts-Oper*).

Bieito's production in Berlin had nothing to do with an Eastern country or any contrast between Christians and Muslims, but rather takes place in a contemporary European brothel, the owners and guardians of which are Selim and Osmin (see Herz 2007; Benoit-Otis 2007; and Buschinger 2007). The two couples are depicted as modern sex slaves. Of course, there can be no merciful finale: Selim, Osmin, and several prostitutes are killed, Konstanze commits suicide, and Belmonte becomes the new "supervisor" of the brothel. Several journalists applauded, including Kai Luehrs-Kaiser on Kulturradio am Morgen, who remarked, "Generosity, Mozart's nice 'dizziness of tolerance,' is nowadays passé"[1] (quoted by Herz 2007: 83), and many more people came to the box office than usual (Herz 2007: 83). An intelligently made scandal sells, at least at the moment.

In 1997 in Salzburg, François Abu Salem (1951–2010) transferred the location of *Die Entführung* to a contemporary Palestinian military camp (Salem 2003 DVD), but the basic plot was kept intact. Six years later (2003), in Salzburg, Stefan Herheim "deconstructed" the opera (Herheim 2006 DVD). The online review in *mostly opera* (2008) commented ironically,

> The music is Mozart's. The recitatives are new. The story is completely new. *Die Entführung* is completely deconstructed. There is simply no real action. Bassa Selim is written out. In modern costumes we are presented with a line-up of scenes exploring the relations between men and women, accompanied by Stefan Herheim's newly written dialogue. (*mostly opera* 2008)

MODERN *REGIETHEATER*: SOCIAL AND ARTISTIC CONTEXT

Productions that can be considered representative of modern *Regietheater* currently dominate the cultural pages in newspapers and magazines internationally, and examples of sometimes very different styles can be seen in many theaters, from those in large cities to medium-sized and even small theaters. There are two reasons that account for this in the German-speaking realm, in particular: first, German theaters are for the most part highly subsidized by the state. Roughly only 15 percent of the expenses of opera houses are actually earned by box office sales; there is no real tradition of sponsorship, as the burden of financing is normally carried by the state, counties, or cities (i.e., the taxpayers). Second, the German-speaking realm still has the highest density of theaters in relation to population around the world. Not only are there opera houses, that is, theaters dedicated to musical productions, in many large cities, such as Berlin, Hamburg, Cologne, Dresden, Leipzig, Stuttgart, Munich, Vienna, Graz, or Zürich, but many smaller cities and towns have their own houses, including a so-called *Dreisparten-Theater*, meaning a multifunctional theater that presents dramas, operas/operettas, and ballets (and more recently, also musicals). Of course, there are partly subsidized opera houses in many a non-German metropolis, including Milan, Paris, Brussels, or Amsterdam, London, and New York, to name only a few. But there is a reason for the distinctive German opera scene: until the beginning of the nineteenth century, large parts of the German-speaking domain were fragmented into numerous independent states of various size, of ecclesiastical territories, and free cities (*Reichsstädte*), and all the large cities and many of the smaller ones held the ambition to have their own local theater(s). All of them were financed by the government, that is, kings, princes, bishops, and city councils. Many of them survived their tumultuous histories (which explains why a large number still exist) as well as the financial system, which has not changed fundamentally. As a result, the *Intendanten* (impresarios) of these theaters have been only partly dependent on immediate box office success, and have had to struggle increasingly for public attention; in general, it has been worse to be considered old-fashioned than to sell few tickets.

Audience response is always mixed. Often, there is some or even much booing and hissing at the end of a performance, and discussions between people are full of controversy and in many cases aggressive. The responses of the printed press or other media are generally more favorable, at least in the German-speaking areas: if journalists and members of the audience applaud conservative and/or traditional productions, they are scolded for not being "trendy" or "en vogue," and many of them are worried about such a reputation. Alex Ross describes the situation with convincing irony and remarkable candor in his review of Christoph Schlingensief's 2004 *Parsifal* at Bayreuth:

> We then saw a sped-up film of one rabbit decomposing [as a symbol of Wagner's grail], its body frothing as the maggots did their work [...]. Schlingensief's dead-rabbit climax was something new: for the first time, I left a theatre feeling, like, ready to hurl. The trouble with this sort of provocation is that if you criticize it, even with an involuntary emetic reflex, you end up playing a role that the instigator has written for you. You are cast as the reactionary, the sentimentalist, the sort of person who requires a kitschy white dove, as if white doves and rotting rabbits were the only option. You are suspected of harboring Fascist tendencies. [...] When the curtain fell, the audience responded with the loudest, lustiest boos I've heard outside of Yankee stadium. Less than a third of the audience applauded when Schlingensief took his bow. In other words: a triumph. A curious charade played out in the press afterward: everyone denied that anything untoward had happened. [...] When I read

> the reviews two days later, I was amazed to discover that there hadn't been any scandal at all—only a few boos perhaps. A new reality was agreed upon that had little to do with what had happened in the theatre. It's all politics, of course. Because German opera houses are heavily supported by state and local governments, the audience's opinion is relatively immaterial; productions are bought and sold in a marketplace of intellectual publicity. (Ross 2004)

Ross explains why adverse reactions are widespread, but only rarely printed. Birgit Meyer (2007), dramaturg at the Vienna Volksoper, catalogued a number of reactions by the audience of this opera house (between 1999 and 2004), which reveal a recurring tolerance, mostly a product of the principle "Just close your eyes and listen to the music." But there do exist dissenting reactions in some extreme cases, such as to the *Madama Butterfly* directed by Stefan Herheim in 2003–2004 (Volksoper Vienna). In this production, Cio-Cio San is killed by the composer Puccini (who is also present on the stage and is finally asked to do so by a fictive staged audience!) because she refuses to commit suicide, as is demanded by the plot of the opera. Skeptics prophesize that the audience will soon leave the box offices and cease to attend performances. But that is by far too pessimistic an expectation, and there are no such indications of such, at least not at this time.

There is a joke that one should be reimbursed for the price a ticket if the production of a drama or opera differs too much from the written text (in the United States, some theater box offices post a disclaimer that no refunds will be granted to dissatisfied viewers). And indeed, after a 2001 performance of Johann Strauss's *Die Fledermaus*, directed by Hans Neuenfels at the Salzburg Festival (DVD), a furious fan went to court, claiming that the Festival had substituted a work different from the one for which he had bought his ticket (see Jakob 2007: 97). It is true that the production no longer had anything to do with the Viennese bourgeoisie, and that, for example, Prinz Orlofsky, originally a rich Russian snob and/or sponsor, was presented as a drug-addicted Göring-like Nazi. Nevertheless, the courts (*Landesgericht* and *Bezirksgericht* Salzburg) decided against the plaintiff, in favor of the principle of artistic freedom.

If the copyright to a piece has expired, the directors are totally free to interpret an opera as they wish; for operas that are still copyrighted the authors and/or the modern owners of the copyright can stop a production, which—probably for financial reasons—rarely happens. Again an example from the Salzburg festival: the Hungarian composer György Ligeti angrily protested Peter Sellars's 1997 transformation of his opera *Le grand macabre* (1974–1978) from a lustful Bacchanalian story into a post-atomic apocalypse. In the end, Ligeti did not veto the production, perhaps submitting to the principle that a distorted performance at a prestigious festival is still better than no performance at all (see Umbach 1997). Rare are cases in which a singer disagrees and withdraws from a production; only a world-famous and nearly indispensable conductor like Riccardo Muti could afford to do so, as happened in Salzburg in 1992. Muti disagreed completely with Ursel and Karl-Ernst Hermann's production of *La clemenza di Tito* (transferred from the Théâtre Royale de la Monnaie, Brussels) and withdrew; it was finally conducted by Gustav Kuhn (Hermann 1992 DVD). *New York Times* critic Edward Rothstein (1992) commented, "Ancient Rome was nowhere to be seen. The main set is a sleek, glistening white stage shell, a pristine, almost antiseptic chamber." Several times, Muti was privileged to choose "his" director in Salzburg, as in 2011 when he selected Peter Stein for Verdi's *Macbeth*, which became a success with the audience, but less for the journalists. Muti's choice for the 2005 *Zauberflöte*, however, ended with a scandal: "The new production of *Die Zauberflöte* met with a storm of protest and loud choruses of booing because stage director Graham Vick had transferred the action to an old peoples' home. [...] This is the latest in a series of perverse productions of Mozart operas at this Mozartian haven" (Greenfield 2005). The production had to be replaced for 2006 (the year of the Mozart jubilee) with a new staging by Pierre Audi, again conducted by Muti (Audi 2006 DVD).

Modern *Regietheater*: Typologies and Contradictions

Jürgen Kühnel (2007) categorizes several interrelated types of modern *Regietheater*: (1) symbolic, even allegorical stagings (typical of Wieland Wagner); (2) the drama-based comic-realistic approach (for example, Felsenstein and Herz); (3) the transposition of the story into the time of the author(s) and/or the present time; and (4) the staging not of the story, but of the mental reflexes and reactions of the director (and the directing team). Kühnel calls transpositions of time period "diegetic transformations," which necessitate "pragmatic transformation," that is, the nearly stereotyped use of iconic objects, including sunglasses, suitcases, traveling coats, tennis matches, television monitors, machine guns, modern uniforms (above all, of the Nazi SS), bicycles, and cars (2007: 23). He deems the more interior approach "semantic transformation," and presents several variations of it: strict, even rigorous revision of the characters, for example, Don Giovanni as an impotent seducer; alteration of the end of a story (i.e., Don Giovanni murdered by his servant Leporello as in Martin Kusej's production, Salzburg 2002; DVD: 2006); or ironic, satiric, or cynical deconstruction of an opera (as noted throughout this chapter).

But there is a paradox in the contemporary staging of operas, namely a fundamental disparity between what is shown on stage by directors of *Regietheater* and what can be heard from the orchestra and the opera singers. The strongest antithesis to *Regietheater* is *Werktreue*, a term often used in discussions of contemporary staging. It means "fidelity" to the work to be staged—to its words, libretto, and author's intent (Müller 2004, 2007). It was Cosima Wagner, Richard Wagner's widow and for many years director of the Bayreuth Festival, who stressed that everything should be shown as the "master" had written and conceived it (Bauer 1992: 508–509). *Werktreue* became an important term in the early 1950s when the new style of Wieland Wagner was vigorously discussed. *Werktreue* is, however, essentially impossible; to stage an opera as the author(s) wanted it or, much more strictly, as they staged it (for example, Richard Strauss and Hugo von Hofmannsthal), is no longer possible: theater is constantly being influenced by developments, modes, and fashions, and, surprisingly, more so than other visual media such as painting or even film. We can never look upon a stage as Mozart or Wagner did, because there is a span of one or two intervening centuries, filled with experiences and transformations of the stage environment, which provide other references and associations that cannot be expunged from memory.

On the other hand, *Werktreue* performances of the music itself—by the orchestra and the singers—seem more possible. Over the last few decades, musical *Werktreue*, often called in German *Originalklang* (historically correct, original sound, or more currently, historically informed performance), has become an expectation, and it is now virtually unthinkable to perform, say, Bach's *St. Matthew Passion* or *Brandenburg Concertos* with a large symphonic orchestra, as was done a half-century ago, all of which makes for an interesting contradiction insofar as opera is concerned. Even though many conductors try to perform operatic music as near or even as true as possible to the written musical notes, with original instruments and with an original-sized orchestra, many at the same time accept stage productions that sometimes present something very different. Thus, for example, Nikolaus Harnoncourt, one of the Austrian founding fathers of the *Originalklang* movement, did not decline to conduct the 2002–2003 Salzburg production of *Don Giovanni* as it was conceived by Kusej (see the earlier discussion). But *Werktreue* in musical matters as well as staging is a mirage. Our competence and ability to listen has changed throughout the centuries with the advent of every new musical form, song, or style, and we cannot listen to a Baroque piece without later references impinging on our consciousness. Moreover, the advent of critical editions has revealed more definitively the fluidity of the opera score, especially in the nineteenth century, insofar as performance practice is concerned.

A Visualization of Subtext(s)?

The over-all concept of modern *Regietheater* can be explained by the principle of "subtext," that is, one or more parallel texts or messages that lie below the surface of the manifest text: when one speaks or writes, there are always connotations and allusions that lie "below the surface" of the spoken or written words (see Müller 2004, 2007). These subtexts are highly subjective and personal, and they differ from one individual to the next. One important aspect of *Regietheater* is the intention to visualize the perceived or suspected subtext or subtexts of an opera. The extremely subjective character of subtext(s) also explains why the reactions of the audience often differ so greatly; there is no right or wrong, only agreement or disagreement. For example, if a director, before 1989, staged Beethoven's *Fidelio* in front of the Berlin Wall with Pizarro's soldiers dressed in SS uniforms and carrying machine guns, the response can only be a subjective one. The same is true if a director mistrusts Beethoven's optimistic finale and its message, and demonstrates that by changing what the audience anticipates it will see on stage.

Such a theory can explain the principles behind modern *Regietheater*, but also stimulate some possibly unanswerable questions: How far from an "original" text may directors stray when interpreting a drama or an opera before it becomes unacceptable? May they, for example, change time and locality, one or some characters, the finale, or the whole story? May they deride and ridicule the play? May they delete or add new texts, change the libretto, and even the music?

It can be astonishing to consider the ways in which even authors and composers of the distant past—long before the advent of modern *Regietheater*—have re-interpreted their own works. Da Ponte and Mozart, for example, not only made additions and deletions for the production of *Don Giovanni* in Vienna (premiere: Prague 1787), but even changed the finale. Annals of performance practice, moreover, reveal how frequently singers added or substituted new arias to existing works (see Poriss 2009). Goethe, director of the Court Theater at Weimar, asked Christian August Vulpius to rework thoroughly the "immoral story" of *Così fan tutte* and also to adjust "illogical" parts of *Die Zauberflöte*, including the sung parts of the libretti (see Ueberschlag 2005 and Wunderlich et al. 2007). Da Ponte's story of *Così fan tutte* was generally thought to be dishonest and cynical, and its early performance history reveals that the text as well as the whole story were significantly changed several times (see Hunter 1999: 247–298); only starting around 1900 has the more-or-less "original" version been staged (see Vill 1978).

Composers have also been known to alter the work of their colleagues, past and present. Richard Wagner had no problems reworking Gluck's *Iphigénie en Aulide* (Dresden 1847) or adapting Mozart's *Don Giovanni* (Zürich 1850; see Deathridge et al 1986: WWV 77 and WWV 83), while Richard Strauss, who inaugurated the renaissance of the original *Così fan tutte* (but in German, in Munich, 1898), nevertheless later "overhauled" Mozart's *Idomeneo* for Vienna in 1931, the same year of Ermanno Wolf-Ferrari's production for Munich. It should be kept in mind that it is necessary to this day to "arrange" (in German: *einrichten*) the text of a drama and sometimes even an opera for a particular performance by deleting some words, parts, or scenes or sometimes also by shifting a scene. Once more, it was Wagner who authorized the extensive cutting of both the text and the music of the love duet in his *Tristan und Isolde*, a version that is sometimes still used, namely in favor of the singers (Voss 1971).

But those adaptations, which have been made mostly (but not always) for "technical" reasons, are not what is meant today when people discuss modern *Regietheater*; rather, they refer to re-interpretations, deconstructions, and stagings of subtexts by directors of the last few decades. One more example, discussed by Michael Bartsch (2005), seems appropriate in the context of twenty-first-century economics: in Dresden in 2004, Volker Lösch directed Gerhart Hauptmann's drama *Die Weber* (which depicts the social problems caused by industrialization in the nineteenth century) and brought onto the stage thirty-three unemployed workers, who recited their own texts about losing a job (see Balme 2008). Hauptmann's granddaughter Anna Hauptmann (who inherited the rights of the drama) and the publishing house (Felix Bloch Erben) went to court in Dresden and tried to prohibit that production, achieving only minor success (see McGowan 2008: 132–135).

Sometimes even the very possibility that a classic work will be misinterpreted could yield a harsh response. Thus, as happened in late summer 2011, Stephen Sondheim provoked a heated discussion about the limits of new theater productions. Patrick Healy (2011) reported that Diane Paulus, artistic director of the American Repertory Theatre, and playwright Suzan-Lori Parks were planning to rewrite sections of *Porgy and Bess* for a staging in Cambridge, Massachusetts (later to be transferred to Broadway). According to Healy, Paulus and Parks intended "making it both widely accessible and artistically fresh. [Therefore, they] created scenes, invented biographical details and, in their most radical move, added a more hopeful ending." Five days later (August 10), an indignant Sondheim wrote to the *New York Times*, arguing that "there is a difference between reinterpretation and wholesale rewriting," which would result in "distorting" this opera (Sondheim 2011). At that moment, however, nothing could be said about the quality of the production, because it was still in rehearsal. As it turned out, the production was far less disruptive than originally imagined by a concerned public.

The final decision about modern *Regietheater* must be made by the audience, because there is no theater without spectators. As long as people buy tickets for such productions at the box office, modern *Regietheater* will be alive and kicking; if the audience doesn't financially support any theatrical endeavor, even the German subsidized theater system won't be able to survive. Levin stresses, "Productions that look new are not necessarily strong; conversely, a traditional-looking production is not necessarily reactionary" (1997: 52).

Regietheater on "Record": Wagner's *Ring* and the "Complete Mozart" (*Mozart 22*)

Since the 1951 re-opening of the Bayreuth Festival (*Neu-Bayreuth*), the number of live productions and audio (at first on LP) and visual recordings of Wagner's *Ring* has increased exponentially. The history of the *Ring* productions has been documented in several monographs, including Eckert (2001), Carnegy (2006), and Schmidt-Reiter (2010), but none of these authors can know the full range of *Ring* productions. To gain as complete a picture as possible, it is necessary to consider numerous reviews of specific productions, among them nearly all Bayreuth *Rings* after World War II, and the increasing number of video and DVD releases. An exhaustive discography (until 2005) was published in the *wagnerspectrum* by Kurt Malisch (2006: I: 239–255; 2: 221–233), and Mike Ashman regularly discusses Wagner and *Ring* DVDs in the same periodical. Excellent information about Wagner on audio and video can be found in the publications of the British Wagner Society (*Wagner*/*Wagner News*).

The dialectic reaction to Wieland Wagner's style began in 1970–1974 with productions of the *Ring* in the medium-sized opera theater in Kassel (directed by Ulrich Melchinger, stage and costumes by Thomas Richter-Forgach), and continued in 1973–1976 in Leipzig (Joachim Herz and Rudolf Heinrich; discussed later). In Bayreuth in 1976 yet another veritable scandal was provoked by the "Centennial *Ring*" (Patrice Chéreau and Richard Peduzzi with costumes by Jacques Schmidt; DVD). All three productions (Kassel, Leipzig, Bayreuth) radically de-mythologized the *Ring* and put the story in its ideological and social context, transposing it to the time of Wagner (Herz) or to the modern era (Melchinger, Herz, Chéreau); these productions might not be directly influenced by, but may be seen in the context of, several factors: the 1968 protests at European universities, Marxism, and, regarding Wagner himself, George Bernard Shaw's book *The Perfect Wagnerite* (1898).

Whereas the productions in Kassel and Leipzig provoked a sensation among opera and Wagner specialists, Chéreau generated a widely known scandal: part of the audience in Bayreuth and many journalists applauded, but others, familiar with the timeless symbolic style of Wieland and his successors, were infuriated and even tried to disrupt the performances. But Chéreau, like Melchinger and Herz, did not deconstruct or even change the story of the tetralogy; rather, he simply emphasized its social and political message (which accords with Wagner's own concept and text). The production was highly controversial, and I remember quite well how, at the 1976 Bayreuth Festival, gentlemen in the audience wearing tuxedos used *Trillerpfeifen* (referee whistles) in order to disrupt the performance. Ironically, Chéreau's production is now considered a more or less acceptable example of modern opera staging (see Carnegy 2006: 356–364).

Many more *Ring* productions have been staged since that time at both large and middle-sized opera theaters, and some general developments can be identified in these productions. Romantic or conventional interpretations became extremely rare, as most of them combine some kind of political or social subtext with modernized versions of symbolism and abstract reduction. Outstanding among them is the extremely media-genic *Ring*—the so-called *Designer-Ring* of the German designer Gudrun Müller, who uses the name "Rosalie" (Bayreuth 1994–1998, director Alfred Kirchner; DVD: *Götterdämmerung*; see "Rosalie" ca. 1997; and the photos in Bauer 2000). Even middle-sized theaters succeeded in staging high-quality *Ring* productions, for example, an innovative co-production of the *Vereinigte Bühnen* Graz and the Landestheater Salzburg 1987–1990, directed by Christian Pöppelreiter/ Jörg Kossdorff (see Irmer and Pöppelreiter 1992; Fuchs 2004: 94–97).

Two large Mozart projects must also be noted when discussing *Regietheater*. From 1986 to 1988, the American director Peter Sellars presented highly controversial productions of the three Da Ponte operas of Mozart at the PepsiCo Summerfare festival in Purchase, New York; Sellars transposed the events of *Le nozze di Figaro* into the high society of New York's Trump Tower, *Don Giovanni* into a sub-proletarian street in the Bronx, and set *Così fan tutte* in a diner at a gas station, all modern social contexts where the original stories are hardly any longer functional. Sellars's Mozartian experiments came to a sudden end because Pepsi terminated its sponsorship of the 1989 summer festival (a dark omen for fully supported productions), though later in 1989 the performances were once more produced in Vienna by Austrian TV (DVDs). Writing about these productions, the British music critic Lucasta Miller (2006) borrowed Austrian pop star Falco's (Johann Hölzel, 1957–1998) refrain, "Rock me Amadeus," noting:

> [Sellars] is willing to risk absurdity, but to do so with such intense conviction that at his best he transforms what could have been silly into something sublime. [. . .] In his uncanny wide-eyed innocence, as in his phenomenal work ethic, there is something that seems, in its idiosyncratic way, essentially American. (Miller 2006)

The other project, a real Mozart "Marathon," was conceived in 2006 by Peter Ruzicka, then artistic director of the Salzburg Festival. Within five weeks he had staged and videotaped (DVD) all twenty-two operas of Mozart; each opera was directed by a different team, using different styles and methods, from Romantic (Pierre Audi: *Zauberflöte*) to provocative *Regietheater* (Kusej: *Don Giovanni;* Herheim: *Entführung*, discussed earlier), but with mostly convincing modern stagings. The series of productions (with the DVD box and excellent program books edited by Susanne Stähr) showcases different approaches to producing the operas of one eminent composer.

Joachim Herz (1924–2010)

When Joachim Herz died in 2010, most obituaries agreed with *Theaterkompass* (2010): "There can be no doubt that Joachim Herz is one of the most important opera directors of our time." Herz, a disciple of Heinz Arnold and Walter Felsenstein, became the latter's assistant in 1956, and was director of the opera at Leipzig (1959–1976), *Intendant* of the Komische Oper Berlin/GDR (1976–1981), and *Chefregisseur* of the Semper-Oper Dresden (1981–1991). He studied musicology, unlike nearly all other theater directors, and was also a fascinating author and teacher. He was guest professor at the University of Salzburg (teaching a seminar with Oswald Panagl and myself), published several books (see bibliography), became a sought-after speaker at academic conferences, and was honored by a *Festschrift* (Ursula Müller et al. 1989). While living in the German Democratic Republic (without ever becoming a member of the Communist Party), he also directed operas in West Germany (Wiesbaden, Essen, Hamburg, Munich), Austria (Vienna; Salzburg: with guest performances in Japan), Buenos Aires, Moscow, Helsinki, Copenhagen, Tallinn, Bern, Zürich, Vancouver, and Great Britain (English and Welsh National Opera)—altogether 126 productions of sixty operas. Much information about him can be found in Benz (1998), Carnegy (2006), and in an exhaustive interview in the leading Austrian opera magazine *Der Neue Merker* (Herz 2002); Herz's own books are, of course, the principal source for his thoughts about theater.

Herz can be called a protagonist of the second generation of modern *Musiktheater*, after Walter Felsenstein and Wieland Wagner. He had two leading principles: presenting the "truthfulness of the action" (see Fuchs 1991: 151), achieved by very "close reading" (Herz 1990: 27–28) and interpretation as a "social-political corrective to psychologizing and abstraction." He combined these ideas with those of Felsenstein and Bertolt Brecht

(Carnegy 2006: 340), and mostly used the language of his audience (Herz 1990: 24–28; for more on Herz in Salzburg during the "Ära Lutz Hochstraate," see Fuchs 2004).

What may be the most groundbreaking example of Herz's work is his *Madama Butterfly*, a success produced worldwide: Komische Oper Berlin (1978, German), Welsh National Opera Cardiff (1979, English), Zürich (1987, Italian with surtitles), Vancouver (1987, English), and Salzburg (1998, Italian with surtitles). In 1978 Herz was the first opera director who took the many different versions of Puccini's opera into account when staging it, an experiment he later discussed in some detail (see Herz 1989: 254–259; 1980: 239–261). After "excavating" the different versions, he presented his own reconstruction of what he called "Puccini's *Ur-Butterfly*," following the first version of Milan 1904, combined with some of the later changes, to focus on the story of Cio-Cio San and Pinkerton as the meeting of "two nations, two civilizations—painful clash: one side mercilessly possessive, the other prevailing in the final catastrophe"[2] (Herz 1989: 259). It was no academic reconstruction, rather one conceived for a stage production, which still presented a moving tragic love story within the detailed frame of the social and cultural differences between Japan and the Western world in the late nineteenth century; as such, it was akin to Sondheim's *Pacific Overtures* (1976), which Herz (as he told me in a private conversation) knew very well and esteemed highly. Herz's work on the opera actually predates much of the musicological research done since the 1990s (Groos 1994; Groos et al. 2005). The Berlin production was taped by GDR-TV (by Georg Mielke, see his article 2001), but, like other TV videos of Herz's opera productions, it is not yet available commercially.

Herz called his method of directing *realistisch-komödiantisch*, meaning not simply "realistic," but rather the more complex "veracity in presenting a story on stage" (Herz 1989:186–187). Further important examples of his productions include Weill and Brecht's *Aufstieg und Fall der Stadt Mahagonny* (Berlin 1977, Munich 1984), Shostakovitch's *The Nose* (Dresden 1986), Richard Strauss's *Die Frau ohne Schatten* (Leipzig 1965), *Salome* (London 1975, Dresden 1988), and *Die ägyptische Helena* (Dresden 1981, Munich 1989), *Don Giovanni* (Salzburg 1989; see Herz 1990), *Rosenkavalier* (Dresden 1985, Salzburg 1993) and Ligeti's *Grand macabre* (Leipzig 1991).

Most influential were Herz's Wagner productions, which became real trendsetters. Outstanding among these is his 1960 *Meistersinger* for Leipzig, which opened the rebuilt Leipzig Opernhaus, where it was performed in a Globe-style theater (disputing the abstraction of Wieland Wagner; see Herz 1989: 99), which, surprisingly, Wieland later copied in Bayreuth 1963 (Herz 2010: 330 n. 53). Following these successes were *Der fliegende Holländer* (Komische Oper Berlin 1962, and repeated in 1963 at the Bolshoi in Moscow, the first production there by a foreigner), and his film version (1964, correctly titled "a film *after* Richard Wagner"; see Podroschko 1989; Calico 2010), which transferred the action into the nineteenth century (with Daland as head of a "a prosperous 1840s ship owner's household"; see Carnegy 2006: 324 and Herz 2010: 247–249), all within the framework of Senta's "dream" (Herz 1989: 103–107; 2010: 253–256). Herz used two technical systems, including a wide screen for the dream sequences and a normal-sized one for "reality," and also conceived a surprising happy end, in which

Senta leaves her depressing bourgeoisie home. Both the dream frame (copied, for example, by Harry Kupfer, Bayreuth 1978; DVD) and the transfer of the action to the epoch of the composer became a worldwide trend that is so common that most theater-goers today don't know who "invented" these ideas.

The climax of Herz's Wagner productions was his *Ring* in Leipzig (1973–1976). Influenced by Bernard Shaw's *The Perfect Wagnerite* (1898), Herz and Rudolf Heinrich (stage design) combined, as mentioned, the principles of Felsenstein and Brecht, showing the protagonists of the tetralogy not as mythological entities but "primarily as humans [...] as recognizable people caught up in the social and political drama of the mid-nineteenth century" (Carnegy 2006: 332). There is no video of this *Ring*, but it is well documented by photos as well Herz's own detailed comments and notes (1989: 152–205; 2010: 278–339), and three important publications (Herz et al. 1975/1980; Benz 1998; Carnegy 2006: 331–343). Two scenes from Herz's *Ring* stand out: in *Götterdämmerung*, Act III, the added presence of Wotan, apparently half-mad, grieving and saluting in an avenue of eagle-crowned monuments during Siegfried's funeral march (Figure 26.1), and the gods' ascent into Valhalla in *Das Rheingold* (Figure 26.2), described by Carnegy (2006: 336) as a "composite of well known grandiose buildings from the 19th century."

On the occasion of Herz's eightieth birthday, *Welt Online* praised his achievements, noting he "has revolutionized Wagner interpretation [...]. Since that time there was

FIGURE 26.1 Joachim Herz, Leipzig 1976: *Götterdämmerung*, Act III, funeral march for Siegfried. From the Herz *Nachlass* with the kind permission of Dr. Kristel Pappel-Herz.

FIGURE 26.2 Joachim Herz, Leipzig 1973: *Rheingold*, finale. From the Herz *Nachlass* with the kind permission of Dr. Kristel Pappel-Herz.

hardly a Wagner production without *Gründerzeit-Look* [referring to the vogue of productions that evoked the time of the second industrial revolution]. Chéreau's Bayreuth *Ring* was completely based on the innovation of Herz. Today that alone would have made this native Dresdener into a superstar in the world of modern opera production"[3] (*Welt Online* 2004). While he was a trailblazer for modern *Regietheater*, he nevertheless fiercely polemicized against opera productions that "deconstructed" plot and action in the extreme—even late in life, when he wrote his lively philippic (Herz 2007), accusing ill-informed directors of staging their individual neuroses.

Postscriptum

> 'Music has a face: leave it alone. If you don't like it, don't play it; but don't change it.' So said Paul Hindemith, one of the 20th century's foremost classical composers. [...] If you believe that a stage work is *fundamentally* flawed, then why not leave it alone and do another piece instead?
>
> (Teachout 2011)

See also: What Is Opera? Production Aesthetics and Materials, Historically Informed Performance, Operatic Images

Notes

1. "Mozarts schöner Humanitätsdusel am Schluss, ist in heutiger Welt passé."
2. "Zwei Nationen, zwei Welten. Schmerzhafter Aufprall: die eine bedenkenlos okkupierend, die andere im Untergang sich behauptend."
3. "Er hat die Wagner-Interpretation revolutioniert [...] Fürderhin gab es kaum eine Wagner—Inszenierung ohne Gründerzeit-Look. Chéreaus Bayreuther [...] 'Ring' basierte gänzlich auf der Herzschen Innovation, die allein schon den geborenen Dresdener heutzutage zum Superstar des Opernregiebetriebes gemacht hätte."

Bibliography

Alonge, Roberto. 2006. *Il teatro dei registi: Scriptori di enigmi e poeti della scena*. Rome/Bari: Laterza.

Artioli, Umberto, ed. 2004. *Il teatro di regia: Genesi ed evoluzione (1870–1950)*. Rome: Carocci.

Balme, Christopher. 2008. "Werktreue: Aufstieg und Niedergang eines fundamentalistischen Begriffs." In Gutjahr 2008, 43–51.

Bartsch, Michael. 2005. "Die Weber in Dresden." *DJV-Kurier*. Online. Available: http://www.djv-sachsen.de/kurier52/Diagramme_Umfrage/diagramme_umfrage.htm (accessed February 6, 2014).

Bauer, Oswald G. 2000. *Rosalie: Bilder zum Ring. Bayreuther Festspiele 1994–1998*. Ostfildern-Ruit: Hatje Cantz.

——. 1992. "Performance History: A Brief Survey," translated by Stewart Spencer. In Müller and Wapnewski 1992, 502–523.

Benoit-Otis, Marie-Hélène. 2007. "Zwischen Werktreue und Regietheater: Fassungen des Dialogs in Inszenierungen von Mozarts *Die Entführung aus dem Serail*." In Kühnel et al. 2007, 216–228.

Benz, Marion. 1998: *Die Wagner-Inszenierungen von Joachim Herz: Studie zur theatralen Wagner-Rezeption in der DDR*. Diss. University of Erlangen-Nuremberg.

Brauneck, Manfred. 1995. *Theater im 20. Jahrhundert: Programmschriften, Stilperioden, Reformmodelle*. Reinbek: Rowohlt.

Braunmüller, Robert. 2002. *Oper als Drama. Das realistische Musiktheater Walter Felsensteins*. Tübingen: Niemeyer.

Buschinger, Danielle. 2007 "Die Berliner Inszenierungen von Mozarts *Così fan tutte* und *Die Entführung aus dem Serail*." In Kühnel et al. 2007, 229–238.

Calico, Joy H. 2010. "Wagner in East Germany: Joachim Herz' *Der fliegende Holländer* (1964)." In *Wagner and Cinema*, edited by Jeongwon Joe and Sander L. Gilman, 294–311. Bloomington: Indiana University Press.

Carnegy, Patrick. 2006. *Wagner and the Art of the Theatre*. New Haven: Yale University Press.

Csobádi, Peter. 2007. "'Wer ist der Herr? Was gibt dem Herrn Befugnis?' Reflexion über die Grenzen von Regie und Poesie." In Kühnel et al. 2007, 54–67.

——, et al., eds. 2001. *Das Musiktheater in den audiovisuellen Medien: '. . . ersichtlich gewordene Taten der Musik.' Vorträge und Gespräche des Salzburger Symposions 1999*. Anif/ Salzburg: Mueller-Speiser.

Deathridge, John et al., eds. 1986. *Wagner-Werk-Verzeichnis (WWV): Verzeichnis der musikalischen Werke Richard Wagners und ihrer Quellen*. Mainz: Schott.

Donington, Robert. 1963. *Wagner's 'Ring' and Its Symbols: The Music and the Myth*. London: Faber and Faber.

Döhring, Sieghart. 2007. "Gedanken zum Regietheater." In Kühnel et al. 2007, 31–34.

Eckert, Nora. 2001. *Der Ring des Nibelungen und seine Inszenierungen von 1876 bis 2001*. Hamburg: Europäische Verlagsanstalt/Rotbuch.

——. 1995. *Von der Oper zum Musiktheater. Wegbereiter und Regisseure*. Berlin: Henschel.

Felsenstein, Walter, and Joachim Herz. 1976. *Musiktheater. Beiträge zur Methodik und zu Inszenierungskonzepten*. Leipzig: Reclam.

Felten, Uta. 2007. "'Senza alcun ordine la danza sia.' Peter Sellars und Luc Bondys *Don Giovanni-Inszenierungen im intermedialen Streit*." In Kühnel et al. 2007, 259–266.

Förster, Rico, and Ivo Zöllner. [2002] 2009. "Interview mit Regisseur Joachim Herz." *Der Neue Merker* 22/155. Online. Available: http://www.der-neue-merker.at/druck.php?area=33&pgm_00013_id=60&pgm_00040_id=14 (accessed February 6, 2014).

Fuchs, Christian Martin, ed. 2004. *Theaterzauber. Salzburger Landestheater: Die Ära Hochstraate*. Salzburg: Landestheater.

Fuchs, Peter Paul, ed. [1975] 1991. *The Music Theatre of Walter Felsenstein: Collected Articles, Speeches and Interviews by Walter Felsenstein and Others*. London: Quartet Books.

Fuhrich, Edda, and Gisela Prossnitz. 1990. *Die Salzburger Festspiele. Ihre Geschichte in Daten, Zeitzeugnissen und Bildern. Band 1. 1920–1945*. Salzburg: Residenz.

Gallup, Stephen. 1987. *A History of the Salzburg Festival*. London: Weidenfeld and Nicholson.

Goethe, Johann Wolfgang. [1803] 1833. "Schauspielkunst: Regeln für Schauspieler." In Goethe, *Werke: Vollständige Ausgabe letzter Hand*, vol. 44: 286–315. Stuttgart and Tübingen: Cotta. Online. Available: http://books.google.com/books?id=KjFapjIhLTAC&q=regeln+fur+schauspieler#v=snippet&q=regeln%20fur%20schauspieler&f=false (accessed February 6, 2014).

Greenfield, Edward. 2005. "*Die Zauberflöte/Mitridate*/Salzburg." *The Guardian* (August 23). Online. Available: http://www.theguardian.com/music/2005/aug/24/classicalmusicandopera (accessed February 6, 2014).

Greenwald, Helen. 2007. "The Practice of Performance in *Die Zauberflöte*." In Kühnel et al. 2007, 321–330.

Groos, Arthur 1994. "Lieutenant F. B. Pinkerton: Problems in the Genesis and Performance of *Madama Butterfly*." In *The Puccini Companion*, edited by William Weaver and Simonetta Puccini, 169–201. New York: W. W. Norton.

——, et al., eds. 2005. *Madama Butterfly: Fonti e Documenti della Genesi*. Lucca: Centro studi Giacomo Puccini/Lucca: Maria Pacini Fazzi.

Gutjahr, Ortrud, ed. 2008. *Regietheater! Wie sich über Inszenierungen streiten lässt*. Würzburg: Königshausen & Neumann.

Healy, Patrick. 2011. "It Ain't Necessarily 'Porgy'." *New York Times* (August 5). Online. Available: http://www.nytimes.com/2011/08/07/theater/porgy-and-bess-with-audra-mcdonald.html?pagewanted=all (accessed February 6, 2014).

Herz, Joachim. 2010–2012. *Oper mit Herz. Das Musiktheater des Joachim Herz*. 3 vols., edited by Michael Heinemann and Kristel Pappel. Köln: Dohr [collected essays, notes, etc.].

——. 2007. "Diskussionsbeitrag zu *Idomeneo*." In Kühnel et al. 2007, 202–205.

——. 1990. *Joachim Herz inszeniert 'Don Giovanni' in Salzburg. Abbildungen, neue deutsche Übersetzung, Essays, Materialien*, edited by Ulrich Müller and Oswald Panagl. Anif-Salzburg: Mueller-Speiser.

——. 1989. *Theater—Kunst des erfüllten Augenblicks. Briefe, Vorträge, Notate, Gespräche, Essays*, edited by Ilse Kobán. Berlin: Henschel.

——. 1985. *'Und Figaro läßt sich scheiden': Oper als Idee und Interpretation*. Munich: Piper.

——. 1984. "Die realistisch-komödiantische Wagnerinterpretation 1960–1976." In *Richard Wagner 1883–1983*, 3–32 [with many photos].

——. 1980. "Zur Urfassung von Puccinis 'Madam Butterfly' [with discussion and 3 photos]." In Wiesmann 1980, 239–264.

——, Marion Reinisch, and Eginhard Röhlig. 1975/1980. *Joachim Herz inszeniert Richard Wagners 'Ring des Nibelungen' am Opernhaus Leipzig*. 2 vols. Arbeitshefte 21/ 29 der Akademie der Künste der DDR. Berlin: Akademie der Künste.

Hiss, Guido. 2005. "Die Geburt des Regietheaters aus dem Geist des Gesamtkunstwerks." In *Synthetische Visionen: Theater als Gesamtkunstwerk von 1800 bis 2000*, edited by Guido Hiss, 123–162. Munich: epodium.

Homann, Rainer. 2005. *Die Partitur als Regiebuch. Walter Felsensteins Musiktheater*. Osnabrück: epos.

Hunter, Mary. 1999. *The Culture of Opera Buffa in Mozart's Vienna: A Poetics of Entertainment*. Princeton, NJ: Princeton University Press.

Irmer, Hans-Joachim, and Christian Pöppelreiter, eds. 1992. *Richard Wagner, 'Der Ring des Nibelungen,' Graz und Salzburg 1987–1990*. Anif/Salzburg: Mueller-Speiser [with many photos].

Jakob, Raimund. 2007. "Regieoper und/oder Werktreue? Jurisprudenzielle und psychosoziologische Gedanken zum Bühnenwerk von W. A. Mozart." In Kühnel et al. 2007, 89–99.

Kapsamer, Ingrid. 2010. *Wieland Wagner. Wegbereiter und Weltwirkung*. Wien: Styria.

Kim, Yun Geol. 2006. *Der Stellenwert Max Reinhardts in der Entwicklung des modernen Regietheaters: Reinhardts Theater als suggestive Anstalt*. Trier: WTV.

Konold, Wulf. 1997. "Musiktheater. I: Inszenierungen." *Die Musik in Geschichte und Gegenwart. Sachteil VI*. 2nd ed., edited by Ludwig Finscher. Kassel: Bärenreiter/Metzler [with a comprehensive bibliography, especially of shorter articles].

Kriechbaumer, Robert. 2011. *Salzburger Festspiele 1990–2001: Die Ära Mortier/Landesmann*. Salzburg: Jung & Jung.

Kühnel, Jürgen. 2007. "Regietheater. Konzeption und Praxis am Beispiel Mozarts. Versuch einter Typologie." In Kühnel et al. 2007, 13–30.

——. 2001. "'...mit neuen Augen anschauen.' Anmerkungen zum Thema Oper und Regietheater." In *Zeit-'Wart Gegen'-Geist. Beiträge über Phänomene der Kultur unserer Zeit. Festschrift Sigrid Wiesmann*, edited by Hannes Grossek, 289–310. Vienna: Reischl & Grossek.

——. 1984. "Über Wieland Wagner." In *Richard Wagner 1883–1983: Die Rezeption im 19. und 20. Jahrhundert: Gesammelte Beiträge des Salzburger Symposions*, edited by Gerhard Croll et al., 491–514. Stuttgarter Arbeiten zur Germanistik 129. Stuttgart: H.D. Heinz.

——, Ulrich Müller, and Oswald Panagl, eds. 2007. *'Regietheater.' Konzeption und Praxis am Beispiel der Bühnenwerke Mozarts. Mit einem Anhang zu Franz Schrekers 'Die Gezeichneten.' Salzburger Symposion 2005*. Anif/Salzburg: Mueller-Speiser.

Lahr, John. 2010. "Telling It Like It Isn't: *The Glass Menagerie* Re-Staged." *The New Yorker* (April 5). Online. Available: http://www.newyorker.com/arts/critics/theatre/2010/04/05/100405crth_theatre_lahr?currentPage=all (accessed February 6,2014).

Latham, Alison, and Roger Parker, eds. 2001. *Verdi in Performance*. New York: Oxford University Press.

Levin, David J. 2007. *Unsettling Opera. Staging Mozart, Verdi, Wagner, and Zemlinsky*. Chicago: University of Chicago Press.

——. 1997. "Reading a Staging/Staging a Reading." *Cambridge Opera Journal* 9/1: 47–71.

Lo, Kii-Ming. 2007. "Die filmische Umsetzung der Ouvertüren von Mozarts Opern durch Jean-Pierre Ponnelle." In Kühnel et al. 2007, 364–375.

Malisch, Kurt. 2006. "Die Quadratur des *Rings*—oder: Der *Ring*, der nie gelungen? Richard Wagners *Ring*-Tetralogie im discographischen Vergleich." *wagnerspectrum* 1: 239–255; 2: 221–233.

McGowan, Moray. 2008. "What Was the *Wende* and What of the *Volk? Fidelio's* Questions and *The Weavers'* Answers." In *Theatre in the Berlin Republic: German Drama Since Reunification*, edited by Denise Varney, 115–140. Frankfurt: Peter Lang.

Melchinger, Siegfried. 1961. *Musiktheater: Walter Felsenstein*. Bremen: Schünemann.

Meyer, Birgit. 2007. "Regietheater im Spannungsfeld zwischen künstlerischem Anspruch, Kulturauftrag, ökonomischen Zwängen und Kulturpolitik am Beispiel der Volksoper Wien. Ein Statement aus dem Theateralltag." In Kühnel et al. 2007, 100–112.

Mielke, Georg. 2001. "Oper als Bildungsauftrag. Dreißig Jahre Musiktheater im Fernsehen der DDR." In Csobádi et al. 2001, 143–151.

Miller, Lucasta. 2006. "Rock Me Amadeus." *The Guardian* (June 2). Online. Available: http://www.guardian.co.uk/stage/2006/jun/03/theatre.mozart (accessed February 6, 2014).

mostly opera. 2008. "Stefan Herheim Abducts the Abduction." Online. Available: http://mostlyopera.blogspot.com/2008/08/stefan-herheim-abducts-abduction.html (accessed February 6, 2014).

Müller, Ulrich. 2007. "Problemfall Oper? Werktreue, Originalklang, Regietheater: Essay zu einem aktuellen Problem des Musiktheaters. Mit einer Übersicht: *Don Giovanni* in Salzburg." In Kühnel et al. 2007, 35–53.

——. 2004. "Werktreue, Originalklang, Regietheater—zu einem aktuellen Problemkreis des Musiktheaters." *Österreichische Musikzeitschrift* 59/7: 10–19.

——. 1992. "Wagner and Antiquity." In Müller and Wapnewski 1992, 227–235.

——, and Peter Wapnewski, eds. 1992. *Wagner Handbook*. Translation edited by John Deathridge. Cambridge, MA: Harvard University Press.

Müller, Ursula, et al., eds. 1989. *Opern und Opernfiguren: Festschrift für Joachim Herz*. Anif/Salzburg: Mueller-Speiser.

Peusch, Vibeke. 1984. *Opernregie—Regieoper: Avantgardistisches Musiktheater in der Weimarer Republik*. Frankfurt: Tende.

Podroschko, Sirikit. 1989. "Senta, oder: 'Der fliegende Holländer' von Joachim Herz, ein Film nach Richard Wagner (1964)." In Ursula Müller et al. 1989, 227–239.

Poriss, Hilary. 2009. *Changing the Score: Arias, Prima Donnas, and the Authority of Performance*. New York: Oxford University Press.

Prossnitz, Gisela, and Robert Kriechbaumer. 2007. *Die Salzburger Festspiele 1945–1960*. 2 vols. Salzburg: Jung & Jung.

Raphael, Aksinia, ed. 2005. *Werkstatt Musiktheater: Walter Felsenstein in Bildern von Clemens Kohl*. Berlin: Henschel.

Richard Wagner 1883–1983. Die Rezeption im 19. und 20. Jahrhundert. Gesammelte Beiträge des Salzburger Symposions. 1984. Stuttgart: Heinz.

"Rosalie." [ca. 2007]. "*Götterdämmerung* DVD." Photos of the *Ring* production and TV clip of *Götterdämmerung* finale. Online. Available: http://www.wagneropera.net/DVD/Gotterdammerung/DVD-Gotterdammerung-Kirchner.htm (accessed February 6, 2014).

Rosenfeld, Michael. 2007. "Regie zwischen Kunst und Geschmacklosigkeit. Ungehaltenes Referat eines ungehaltenen Zuschauers." In Kühnel et al. 2007, 113–125.

Ross, Alex. 2004. "Nausea: A New *Parsifal* at Bayreuth." *The New Yorker* (August 9). Online. Available: http://www.newyorker.com/archive/2004/08/09/040809crmu_music1?currentPage=all (accessed February 6, 2014).

Rothschild, Thomas. 2007. "'Das ist der Teufel sicherlich'. Papageno trifft Monostatos. Ein Vergleich." In Kühnel et al. 2007, 331–337.

Rothstein, Edward. 1992. "In Salzburg, an Original *Clemenza* That Takes Opera Seria Seriously." *New York Times* (July 29). Online. Available: http://www.nytimes.com/1992/07/29/arts/review-music-in-salzburg-an-original-clemenza-that-takes-opera-seria-seriously.html (accessed February 6, 2014).

Schäfer, Walter Erich. 1970. *Wieland Wagner. Persönlichkeit und Leistung.* Tübingen: Wunderlich.

Schanze, Helmut. 2007. "Goethe als '*Regisseur*' der *Zauberflöte*. Über den Beginn des 'Regietheaters.'" In Kühnel et al. 2007, 157–165.

Schläder, Jürgen, ed. 2006. *OperMachtTheaterBilder* [!]. *Neue Wirklichkeiten des Regietheaters.* Berlin: Henschel.

Schmid-Reiter, Isolde. 2010. *Richard Wagners 'Der Ring des Nibelungen.' Europäische Traditionen und Paradigmen.* Regensburg: ConBrio. *Schwerpunkt / focusing on Regietheater (= wagnerspectrum 2/ 2005)*, 2005. Würzburg: Königshausen & Neumann.

Scott, Derek. B. 2007. "A Problem of Race in Directing *Die Zauberflöte*." In Kühnel et al. 2007, 338–344.

Shaw, Bernard. 1898. *The Perfect Wagnerite: A Commentary on the 'Ring of the Nibelungs.'* London: Grant Richards.

Skelton, Geoffrey 1971. *Wieland Wagner: The Positive Sceptic.* London: Gollancz.

Snook, Lynn. 2009. *Wagners Mythische Modelle*, edited by Ulrike Feld and Wolfgang Behrens. Anif/Salzburg: Mueller-Speiser.

Sollich, Robert, Clemens Risi, Sebastian Reus, and Stephan Jöris, eds. 2008. *Angst vor der Zerstörung. Der Meister Künste zwischen Archiv und Erneuerung.* Recherchen 52. Berlin: Theater der Zeit.

Sondheim, Stephen. 2011: "Stephen Sondheim Takes Issue with Plan for Revamped 'Porgy and Bess'." *New York Times* (August 10). Online. Available: http://artsbeat.blogs.nytimes.com/2011/08/10/stephen-sondheim-takes-issue-with-plan-for-revamped-porgy-and-bess/ (accessed February 6, 2014).

Steinberg, Michael P. [1990] 2000. *The Meaning of the Salzburg Festival: Austria as Theater and Ideology, 1890–1930.* Ithaca, NY: Cornell University Press.

Teachout, Terry. 2011. "Rewriting 'Porgy and Bess'—Is the Text of a Classic Ever Sacred?" *New York Times* (September 2). Online. Available: http://online.wsj.com/article/SB1000142405311190478740457653075197101559 0 (accessed February 6, 2014).

Theaterkompass. 2010. "Zum Tod des Opernregisseurs und -Intendanten Joachim Herz." *Theaterkompass.* Online. Available: http://www.theaterkompass.at/news-einzelansicht+M583382d5497.html (accessed February 6, 2014).

Umbach, Klaus. 1997. "Kalaschnikow und Kuckucksuhr." *Der Spiegel* 32. Online. Available: http://www.spiegel.de/spiegel/print/d-8757047.html (accessed February 6, 2014).

Vill, Susanne, ed. 1978. *Così fan tutte. Beiträge zur Wirkungsgeschichte von Mozarts Oper.* Bayreuth: Mühlscher Universitätsverlag Fehr.

Voss, Egon. 1971. "Wagners Striche im Tristan." *Neue Zeitschrift für Musik* 132: 644–647.

Vysloužilová, Věra. 2007. "Mozarts *Zauberflöte* am Nationaltheater Prag 1956/57." In Kühnel et al. 2007, 345–351.

Wagner/Wagner News. (1953–). *Wagner Society.* Online. Available: http://www.wagnersociety.org/ (accessed February 6, 2014).

Wagnerspectrum. (2005–). Online. Available: http://www.wagnerspectrum.de/ (accessed February 6, 2014).

Welt Online. 2004. "Glückwunsch:Joachim Herz wird 80." *Welt Online* (June 15). Online. Available: http://www.welt.de/printwelt/article320405/Glueckwunsch_Joachim_Herz_wird_80.html (accessed February 6, 2014).

Wiesmann, Sigrid, ed. 1980. *Werk und Wiedergabe: Musiktheater exemplarisch interpretiert.* Bayreuth: Mühl.

Woehl, Arthur. 1927. "Goethe's 'Rules for Actors': A Translation with an Introduction." *Quarterly Journal of Speech* 13/3: 243–264.

Wunderlich, Werner, et al. 2007. *Mozarts 'Zauberflöte' und ihre Dichter. Schikaneder—Vulpius—Goethe—Zuccalmaglio. Faksimiles und Editionen von Textbuch, Bearbeitungen und Fortsetzungen der Mozart-Oper.* Anif/Salzburg: Mueller-Speiser.

Videography

Abu Salem. 2003. Mozart, *Die Entführung aus dem Serail,* Salzburg 1997. DVD. Image Entertainment.

Audi, Pierre. 2006. Mozart, *Die Zauberflöte.* DVD. Mozart 22/Decca.

Bieito, Calixto. 2004. Mozart, *Die Entführung aus dem Serail,* Komische Oper Berlin (Video clips). Online. Available: http://www.dailymotion.com/video/x6anze_mozart-s-die-entfuhrung-aus-dem-ser_music (accessed February 6, 2014).

Chéreau, Patrice. 1980. Wagner, *Der Ring des Nibelungen.* 5 DVDs: Deutsche Grammophon 1980.

Felsenstein, Walter. 2008. Felsenstein-Edition, 12 DVDs: Arthaus Musik.

Herheim, Stefan. 2006. Mozart, *Die Entführung aus dem Serail,* Salzburg 2003. DVD 2006: Mozart 22/Decca.

Hermann, Ursel and Karl-Ernst. 1992. Mozart, *La clemenza di Tito.* Video excerpt. Online. Available: http://www.youtube.com/watch?v=4kDkaDZRro4 (accessed February 6, 2014).

Herz, Joachim. 1964. Wagner, *Der fliegende Holländer:* Ein Film nach Richard Wagner. VHS/Disc Dreamife/ Niho Monitor. Information Online. Available: http://www.operadis-opera-discography.org.uk/CLWAFLIE.HTM#25 (accessed February 6, 2014).

——. (n.d.) TV Videos (*Così fan tutte, Freischütz, Land Bum-Bum* [Katzer], *Madam Butterfly, Mahagonny, Nose, Rosenkavalier, Salome, Xerxes, Zauberflöte/ Act II*: Not yet available on DVD (see Mielke 2001).

Kupfer, Harry. 1985. Wagner, *Der fliegende Holländer,* Bayreuth 1978. DVD Deutsche Grammophon (recorded 1985).

Kusej, Martin. 2006. Mozart, *Don Giovanni*. DVD. Mozart 22/ Decca. *Mozart 22*. 33 DVDs of live recordings of all Mozart operas. Salzburger Festspiele 2006. Decca.

Pöppelreiter, Christian, and Jörg Kossdorff. 1990. Richard Wagner, *Der Ring des Nibelungen:* DVD House of Opera.

"Rosalie." 2007. Wagner, *Götterdämmerung*. DVD. Deutsche Grammophon. Wagner, Wieland. 1963–1965. *Wagner* rehearsal excerpts. Online. Available: http://wn.com/Wieland_Wagner (accessed August 16, 2012).

"Rosalie." [ca. 2007]. http://www.wagneropera.net/DVD/Gotterdammerung/DVD-Gotterdammerung-Kirchner.htm (accessed February 6, 2014).

Wagner, Wieland. 1967. Wagner, *Tristan und Isolde*. Osaka. DVD. House of Opera-1967.

——. 1967 *Die Walküre*. Osaka. VHS video (no longer available).

CHAPTER 27

HISTORICALLY INFORMED PERFORMANCE

MARY HUNTER

What Is Historically Informed Performance?

"Historically informed" and "historically aware" are terms that, since the 1990s, have essentially replaced the earlier term "authentic" to indicate performance practices and attitudes that directly or indirectly rely on documentary sources from the time of the work to inform interpretative decisions about the acoustic, conceptual, and (in the case of opera) visual environment in which a work was originally created.

The word "authentic" has fallen out of favor not only because complete authenticity is unachievable, but also because it has been criticized as a stultifying ideal for performance. Richard Taruskin is the best-known and perhaps fiercest musicological critic of the culture of authenticity in Early Music performance—the term "Early Music" being used to indicate not only music written several hundred years ago, but also performed now with some attention to documentary evidence about performance practice. Taruskin points out, among other things, that the desire for a perfect simulacrum of an earlier performance is in fact a paradigmatic modernist stance (Taruskin 1995: 164–173). In a different essay he distinguishes between Early Music as the rediscovery of lesser-known works and Early Music as an ideology of performance that rethinks well-known ones (Taruskin 1992: 126). This distinction, however, does not allow for the ways in which newly unearthed repertory often stimulates new habits of performance—the stylized gestures necessary to French Baroque opera are a case in point. Other commentaries on the ideology of historically informed performance include those by John Butt (2002), Nicholas Kenyon (1988), Bruce Haynes (2007), and Laurence Dreyfus (1983). Harry Haskell's history of the Early Music movement is a valuable chronicle (Haskell 1988). Practitioners of historically informed performance have long asserted that their efforts—based on research but informed by their modern musical intuitions—were not simply "reconstructive," but as musically creative as those of "non-authentic" performance (Harnoncourt 1988: 49; Jacobs 2007).

Opera has always been integral to the Early Music movement, both in its aspect of unearthing and presenting lesser-known works (Westrup 1925; Haskell 1988) and in its corollary re-institution of historically informed habits of performance (Dreyfus, Kerman, et al. 1992: 126). The Handel operas, for example, first at the Halle Händel Festival from the 1920s, then at the Barber Institute of the University of Birmingham in the 1950s and 1960s, and eventually more widely, have been central to both performers' and scholars' thinking not only about Handel himself, but also about the stage-worthiness of da capo arias, the plausibility of *opera seria*, and the revivability of vocal techniques that stress agility and diction over volume. More recently, a renewed interest in performing French Baroque operas—particularly on the parts of Alan Curtis (director of Il Complesso Barocco), William Christie (director of Les Arts Florissants), Claude Malgloire (director of La Grande Écurie at la Chambre du Roy), Marc Minkowski (director of Les Musiciens du Louvre), and Vincent Dumestre (director of Le Poème Harmonique)—has drawn on and contributed to scholarship on rhetorical acting style, stage gesture, and dance; their evocations of Baroque stage deportment and vocal style have radiated out from this repertory both to other operas and to non-dramatic music. Finally, the biennial Boston Early Music Festival has, almost since its inception in 1980, oriented itself around a Baroque opera whose production prominently advertises its historical bona fides.

Occasional productions like those mentioned above, and at venues like the International Händel-Festspiele at Göttingen, the Slottsteater in Drottningholm, Sweden, the court theater at Versailles, and the Schlosstheater at Schwetzingen, are on the leading edge of the historical performance movement in opera. Such productions, while no longer completely novel, remain "niche" events, focused on works from 1600 to about 1750 (though Mozart is sometimes included) and aimed at an audience of period—rather than opera—enthusiasts. In tandem with these elaborately historicized and special productions of Baroque opera, however, mainstream opera productions have exponentially increased their inclusion of certain elements of historical performance. For example, in the last couple of decades many modern-instrument performers have also learned something about an older version of their instrument, often translating that back onto their performance on the modern one; Early Music conductors like Sir John Eliot Gardiner, Nicholas McGegan, Nicolaus Harnoncourt, and Sir Roger Norrington have found themselves in front of modern ensembles, asking those performers to try ancient practices ("software") on modern instruments ("hardware"); and the countertenor voice, once an exclusive attribute of the Early Music scene—often used as a (less than accurate) substitute for the mercifully unreconstructable castrato—has become normal in mainstream productions of opera. Thus, for example, within the last decade or so, productions of Handel operas at venues as traditionally inhospitable to Early Music as the Metropolitan Opera and the Houston Grand Opera have used countertenor voices and a highly articulated and nuanced style of instrumental playing on modern instruments that derives directly from more self-consciously revivalist performances.

This penetration of the historically informed into the mainstream raises the question of what now can or should count as a "historically informed" production of opera. However, drawing lines between "informed" and "uninformed," or "aware" and "unaware" performances is not a useful enterprise. There is, for one thing, no need for the morality contest that any arbitrarily drawn line would suggest. (Haynes [2007: 11] gives an amusing list of opposites to "authentic.") Moreover, "historical informedness" is a moving target. What may count today as "historically informed" may drop off the list as soon as new or better historical information becomes available, or as performance styles intended to startle listeners instead make them comfortable, or simply as tastes change.

A more useful and interesting question than which productions belong (or not) in the pantheon of the historically informed, is how any production of any opera places itself in relation to history, and what kinds of historical work have informed the production. This has the advantage not only of dealing open-mindedly with various degrees of "historical informedness," but also of allowing the student or scholar to think about post-Baroque operas, which have mostly not enjoyed the reconstructive attention given to earlier works. The question is admittedly very general, even vague, but I would argue that this generality is necessary as we ask about the relation between historically informed performance and opera—partly because opera as a full theatrical experience has so many dimensions in which historical research can be put to use, and partly because that same multidimensionality raises not only more, but different issues than is the case in non-dramatic music. In other words, it seems to me that the topic "historically informed performance and opera" is both more complex than, and quite distinct from, the topic "historically informed performance and [non-dramatic] music," and requires a broader approach.

Surprisingly, historical performance in opera has not yet been addressed in this way. The philosophical or meta-level discussions of historical performance in general tend to shy away from opera, even though opera was at the forefront of the rediscovery of seventeenth-century music (see Crutchfield 1988, for example), and, as mentioned above, some kinds of Early Music practices were integral to, or originated in, opera performances. In addition, although opera performance and production are becoming increasingly notable and respectable objects of scholarly study, self-described historically informed performance has not been much considered in that field. (Abbate 2000; Levin 2007; Latham and Parker 2001; *Opera Quarterly* 2005–present, especially its "Notes from the Stage" section; and *Cambridge Opera Journal* 2004 all attend to performance, for example, but do not pay attention to issues of historicity as they are normally understood in the performance-practice community.) There are, of course, vast numbers of essays and books on historical issues attached to the performance of opera, but these tend either to provide the historical information that might bring a modern performance of a particular opera or sub-repertory closer to its historical condition (e.g., Harris-Warrick and Marsh 1994; Rice 2009; Johnson 1995), or to comment on the historical quality of productions without subjecting the enterprise as a whole to methodological investigation (e.g., Banducci 2005; Burgess 2006 is an exception), or to describe what musicians and directors do to evoke the historicity of a given work or repertory (see Christie 1993, and some interviews in Sherman 1997). The purpose of this chapter, then, is to suggest the beginnings of a broader approach to the historicity of opera performance, starting from the obvious but crucial observation that operas are multidimensional theatrical events, not just musical works.

The usual criterion for categorizing a production of an opera as historically informed or aware has been the use of historical instruments. But as noted above, the absence of historical hardware no longer means that historical performance practices will be ignored. Nor does the use of gut-strung violins and one-key flutes guarantee that the staging will be "historical." Indeed, modern instruments and big vibrato-filled voices often accompany staged representations that reflect considerable historical research. One of the important differences between most opera and other kinds of music is that, with its narrative structure and specific settings and characters, it cannot avoid locating itself in history; in that sense, essentially *all* productions of opera are in one way or another "historically informed."

The Domains of Historicity in Opera Production

Opera productions evidence their relation to history in three main domains: the visual, the aural, and the ideological.

The Visual Domain

The visual domain—that is, the stage set, lighting, costumes, and blocking practices—is the first and most obvious indication of a production's sense of history. Opera sets and costumes demonstrate a range of historical awareness: reconstruction, evocation, and historical sampling are all used, and there is no predictable relation between historical visual style in general and historical awareness in the sonic dimension of a production. It has long been normal in mainstream productions to evoke the period (and place) of an opera's composition, particularly when the opera deals with subject matter more or less contemporary to it. Thus, *La traviata* in a plausible replica of mid-nineteenth-century Paris and its environs, *Così fan tutte* in something that viewers will recognize as eighteenth-century Italy (if not exactly Naples), and *Wozzeck* in early-twentieth-century Germany are all settings that recognize the historical location of the works; productions that use these settings often show no other evidence of historical awareness. It is also conventional to stage operas set in times earlier than the period of composition in the fictional epoch of the plot: *Orfeo* in classical antiquity, *Die Meistersinger* in the mid-sixteenth century, *Don Carlos* in the sixteenth century. As with productions set in the time of the opera's composition, recognition of the period of the action is not necessarily accompanied by other kinds of historical awareness.

Mainstream productions set in the time of, or depicted by, an opera typically *evoke* rather than *reconstruct* the period in question: for example, eighteenth-century costumes (especially female ones) have often eschewed the large powdered wigs of the time, especially for characters considered "natural," so that their faces seem more "human" to the audience. Twentieth-century productions of *Le nozze di Figaro* quite often put the Countess in some version of an eighteenth-century wig, for example, but productions of *Die Zauberflöte* essentially never put Pamina in a comparable headpiece, despite evidence from contemporary illustrations that she would have worn one. Moreover, designers do not restrict themselves to the kinds of fabrics available in the time represented, and the corseting is normally less rigorous than historical corseting. But when combined with stage sets that evoke the same period as the costumes, the overall visual effect is of a coherent and recognizable moment in the past. However, it is important to note that the particular form of that coherence relies on a given audience's conventional understanding of the period in question: the sets and costumes in mainstream opera productions are typically not a jarring experience for their audiences (Stieglitz 2012). That means that a late-twentieth-century version of a given period may look quite different from a late-nineteenth-century version of the same period. Sometimes, a highly eclectic mainstream production, like Graham Vick's version of Mozart's early opera seria, *Mitridate, re di Ponto*, which uses a modern orchestra and does not announce itself as an Early Music production, will make reference to the historical imagination of the opera's period. In this case, the costumes for Mitridate himself and his son Sifare borrow the outline of eighteenth-century representations of ancient military costumes, and Aspasia's ridiculously wide panniered skirt is a kind of commentary on aristocratic female dress of the time (Ford 2009; Turin 2012).

In contrast, the productions that advertise themselves as historically informed and that make a point of historicizing the visual dimension tend to reproduce the costumes of the opera's own period with more rigor than the more "evocative" modern productions (compare, for example, Martín y Soler 1993 with Mozart 2006). And if the opera is on a mythical or historical subject, some historically informed productions will construct sets and costumes that would have signified the location of the myth to the opera's first audiences rather than using the actual architecture and costumes of the classical period. Historically informed productions of French Baroque operas on mythical themes, for example, often (correctly) dress the singers in Baroque costumes rather than tunics and pepla. The Boston Early Music Festival productions of Lully's *Thesée* and *Psyché* were of this sort, for example; the sets were not mechanically "authentic," nor did they copy original stage designs. But they were historically correct in locating these myths firmly among French Baroque architecture and garden design.

For obvious logistical reasons, it is unusual for modern productions to reproduce, or even evoke, the stage mechanics of an opera's original period, even when the period itself is depicted on the stage. For example, the sliding wing-flats of the Baroque perspective stage, which allowed instant scene-changes in the view of the audience, have rarely been imitated in modern theaters—or even in retrofitted older ones. A few small court theaters preserved from the eighteenth century, like Drottningholm in Sweden, or Český Krumlov in the Czech Republic, can use the original stage mechanics because they are fitted so to do, and in very recent years the Centre de Musique Baroque de Versailles has been working on constructing eighteenth-century sets in the French court theaters. However, even when the scenery and other machinery is old, for reasons of safety the candles, oil-lamp footlights, and gaslights of the old theaters have normally disappeared from these preserved theaters, sometimes being replaced by low-wattage electric lights designed to flicker like candles. Even this degree of historical informedness, however, fails to reproduce the smoke and heat of actual candles and oil lamps. (The recent production by Vincent Dumestre and Benjamin Lazar of Lully's *Cadmus et Hermione* [Lully 2008] was in fact fully candle-lit [though electric light was needed to film it], but this is not a practice likely to spread.) Unlike the evocation of a period in the sets and costumes, the reconstruction of historical stage mechanics is normally (at least at the time of writing) accompanied by historically aware musical performance (for more on the history of stage machinery and set design, see Baker 2013).

Another important visual domain in operatic production is the use of historical gestures and blocking practices. Such practices are less rare than historically based lighting, but still not close to mainstream. Although modern operatic acting (even onscreen) is not exactly naturalistic, stage behavior in Baroque, Classical, and even Romantic opera was even less so. Singers relied on a stock of conventional gestures and postures to indicate particular emotional states—grief, pity, surprise, love, and so on (Barnett 1987: passim; Hepokoski 2001: 15). Even into the twentieth century, these gestures were used to communicate the particular words of the operatic texts as well as the general emotional situation of the singer. Such pantomime-like gestures made sense in a world of relatively dim lighting, noisy audiences, and no surtitles, providing a backup (or perhaps even a primary) system for comprehension. Moreover, if the well-lit portion of the stage was small (often the case with candles and oil lamps), the singers needed to face the audience, stand relatively close to the front of the stage, and not move out of the pool of light to be visible. In this situation, the rhetorical gestures also provided movement and visual interest that might otherwise be lacking. These rhetorical gestures also link to the postures and movements of Baroque dance, which has also undergone a striking revival on the modern historically aware stage (Hilton 1981; Little and Marsh 1992; Lancelot 1996; Alm 2003; Harris-Warrick and Brown 2005). Blocking practices until the nineteenth century also tended to arrange characters according to social hierarchy, something contemporary audiences would instinctively have understood (Savage 1998: 589–590). Nowadays, most audiences would find the rhetorical gestures excessively formulaic or "melodramatic" (or both), as they survive mostly in pantomime and cartoons, while the hierarchical placement of characters is incomprehensible to most moderns. Present-day productions that either obviously evoke or use these staging practices are thus clearly making a bid to count as thoroughly historically informed, and are always accompanied by historically aware music making.

The final visual domain to be considered here is the placement and appearance of the orchestra. Although most modern opera houses have pits, the orchestra for most opera before the late nineteenth century was placed on the floor in front of the stage, which meant it was more fully visible, especially from the upper levels of the theater, than are most pit orchestras today. The direction of the orchestra was also undertaken by either the continuo keyboard player or the concert master, or a combination of the two: conductors standing in front of the opera orchestra were not a regular feature of operatic life until the early to mid-nineteenth century (Spitzer and Zaslaw 1992). In modern productions of early opera, the orchestra naturally has to be placed where there is room. Even where the theater allows the orchestra to be placed on the floor in front of the stage, the players tend to be organized in the modern ways, rather than along a single long music stand, which is what many pictures from the early centuries show. Most modern performance of operas, regardless of the visual style of the production, and even in the most rigorously reconstructionist performances, leave the orchestra in the usual modern formal wear, or in Early Music black shirts and trousers (or dresses). At Drottningholm, however, the orchestra wears a kind of eighteenth-century livery to enhance the period feel of the whole experience. This attempt at historical authenticity, however, is complicated by the inclusion of women (wearing the same masculine livery), which was not eighteenth-century practice.

The Sonic Domain

As in any other kind of music, historical awareness in opera can be shown in both the hardware (instruments) and the software (playing and singing techniques and styles) of the musical performance. Generally speaking, in productions that use the full panoply of old instruments, the players use techniques and articulations that ultimately (if indirectly) rely on historical evidence, and, as noted above, the use of historical hard- and software inarguably locates such a performance within the fold of the historically informed. The relation of the voice to performances that count as historically aware is more complex than that of the instruments. The hardware/software distinction is blurred, to put it mildly, partly because there is no external physical object to reconstruct, but also partly because few operatic singers can make a living singing only Early Music, and there are limitations on the amount of historical sound and practice they can embed into their basic techniques if they have to switch styles regularly. However, one voice—the countertenor—is analogous to hardware, in that, as it is used today, it is essentially a different instrument from the "natural" voices of both men and women. For many years the use of a countertenor has been a sign of historical awareness: castrato roles that in earlier modern productions would have been sung by women or transposed down an octave by natural-voiced men are now often sung by countertenors (Young, 2007). However, in a fascinating countermovement, just as countertenors are beginning to be routine in mainstream productions of Baroque operas, performances advertising themselves as particularly historically aware increasingly use women in these roles because the *sound* may be closer in timbre to the castrato than is the countertenor. Thus one kind of production, which may now be viewed as more historically accurate, seems to value the *software* of a more "authentic" vocal timbre, and the other, which may now be viewed as less historically informed, uses the *hardware* of a closer-to-authentic biology and visual effect. An easily available and striking example of a female-sung castrato role is Monica Bacelli's performance of the title role in *Tamerlano* (Handel 2001). Of course, what counts as historically informed singing changes rapidly from one generation of singers to another. At the time of writing, despite overwhelming evidence of enormous variability in the seventeenth and eighteenth centuries, the default Early Music voice in modern times has a light timbre, great agility, a narrow vibrato, and clear diction. Perhaps not surprisingly if we take seriously Taruskin's observation that "authentic" performance is actually a modernist ideal, the singers who tend to appear in the most historically aware opera productions are also often those who sing a lot of modern music. Interestingly, the few singers who have made significant efforts to make their basic vocal production conform to what they have learned from the old treatises have not had the largest careers in staged productions of early operas, perhaps because they are relatively few and would stick out uncomfortably in a cast of merely light-voiced singers, and perhaps because the effect of this kind of singing can be de-familiarizing in ways that are found to be unappealing for opera (see the later discussion). Julianne Baird's comments about the importance of a singer's capacity to maintain his or her individuality are relevant here (Sherman 1997: 241).

The Ideological Domain

If we think of ideology as the basic attitudes of producers and performers to their work, we may discern two currently basic ideologies of historically informed performance, and these map quite neatly onto two repertories of opera. The first ideology is that it would be almost unthinkable to perform certain works—even in the great standard-repertory opera houses—without the sonic environment provided by Baroque instruments and "default" Baroque-style singing. For such productions it seems to be the norm now to import a period-instrument group into the house to replace the modern-instrument orchestra. For example, for a recent production of Monteverdi's *L'incoronazione di Poppea* at Glyndebourne, and even when it was transported to the cavernous Albert Hall, the instrumental parts were provided by the Orchestra of the Age of Enlightenment. The second ideology is that historical hardware and performance practices are an option rather than a necessity. The first attitude pertains particularly to early seventeenth-century works, especially those by Monteverdi, which have found their way into the standard repertory, and to French Baroque opera. The second is perhaps best exemplified in relation to the operas of Handel, though it can apply to any repertory of works in the standard repertory. In the case of Monteverdi and other seventeenth-century works, the sense of the necessity of a Baroque acoustic environment probably arises in part from the facts that the "orchestra" bears very little resemblance to the ensemble bearing that name for most of operatic history, and that the improvisatory skills and sensitivity to declamation required of the instrumental musicians are very different from the skills cultivated by most modern orchestral players (see, however, Curtis 1997: 136–137). Thus, unless the instrumental ensemble uses now-unfashionable arrangements by the likes of Denis Stevens and Raymond Leppard, the music can really only be realized by musicians trained in Early Music techniques, and those capacities normally go along with the use of historical instruments. (In other words, modern opera-house orchestras are mostly not capable of realizing this music.) With respect to French Baroque opera, whose productions also almost exclusively use historical instruments (an exception being the 2000 production of Rameau's *Platée* [1745] at New York's City Opera, which used the resident house orchestra plus harpsichord and recorders), the case is somewhat different. Here the instrumentation is closer to "orchestral" in the modern sense, the orchestral parts are more fully (if not always completely) written out, and they are closer to what a modern opera-house orchestra would be used to playing. However, the style—especially with respect to rhythm, timbre, and declamation—is quite different from the better- (or at least longer-) known German and Italian repertory, let alone more modern works. It took the pioneering late twentieth-century work of Curtis (1997) and then Christie (1997), who immersed himself in the relevant historical documentation and founded Les Arts Florissants, a period-instrument and vocal ensemble, to find a performance style that made modern sense of the music, especially of Lully and Rameau (Christie 1993: passim). Christie's performances and recordings have essentially created the current "default" style for this music, and although many different ensembles have taken up the repertory, the ideals of a lush but transparent sound, perfect intonation, rhythmic life and flexibility, and exquisite sensitivity to the sound of the voice and to the words—all of which are more fully or easily achievable with the old instruments—have become pervasive. In addition, the many historically informed recordings of both Monteverdi and French Baroque operas have disseminated this now-"default" sound far beyond the relatively small numbers of theaters able and willing to mount productions of these operas.

In the case of Handel, his music (if not his operas), unlike that of Monteverdi or Lully or Rameau, has long been part of broad public consciousness. Moreover, the longer and broader history of Handel opera performances makes a wonderful case study in the changes in historically informed performance (both the sound itself and the issues of primary concern) over time. The performances at the Halle Festival, which in the early days were quite self-consciously revivals, had the scores rewritten to suit the taste of the times: the orchestration was vastly inflated, the castrato parts were transposed to natural male voices, and very often the da capos were cut. Historical consciousness in these productions was focused on the point that these operas were by a great (German) composer and that they were fundamentally stageworthy (Haskell 1983: 137–139). The mid-twentieth-century English (Barber Institute) productions were more "historically informed" in the sense that they were more likely to perform the castrato roles at pitch and also more likely to take the da capos. But, apart from the harpsichord, they did not use historical instruments, and the tiny stage enforced minimal scenic display (Hunter 2009; Dean 2006: 488). And although countertenors made occasional appearances in these productions (Alfred Deller was a frequent participant), they more often used women in the heroic roles: Dame Janet Baker was a frequent singer in this milieu. Dame

Janet's voice would not now be considered a particularly "Baroque" voice, and the rhythmically and coloristically rather uniform sound of her passagework does not match early twenty-first century ideas about historically informed Baroque singing, but in her time (and indeed, beyond it), her Handel performances were considered both musically convincing and historically revelatory. Winton Dean, for example, wrote, "Dame Janet Baker's performance as Ariodante far outstrips the rest. With her flexibility, delicacy and unfailing sense of line, and total commitment to the drama, she does justice to a part she has long made her own [...]. In Act 3 in particular she is incomparable. She knows how to accommodate da capo ornaments: Those of the other singers, though seldom out of style, are apt to sound contrived or intrusive" (Dean 1981: 33–34). These midcentury productions certainly did not claim to recreate a historically "authentic" theatrical experience; rather, in a modernist vein, they concentrated on reproducing the contents of the scores as respectfully as possible, given modern means. This history, plus the greater familiarity of Handel's music in comparison to that of Monteverdi, Lully, or Rameau, has meant that audiences (and performers) have in mind a wide range of sonic possibilities for Handel operatic performance; and even now, Handel operas are more likely than Monteverdi or French Baroque works to be performed using modern instruments (with varying degrees of influence from Early Music practices). The use of modern instruments and, often, relatively well-known singers of mainstream operatic repertory locate the works in a "Baroque period" that feels entirely familiar to the majority of opera- and concert-goers rather than presenting a "field trip" to another musical era.

As mentioned above, the deployment of a historical sonic dimension—whether in Handel, Monteverdi, or the French repertory—by no means implies that the visual dimension will be comparably historical. Indeed, the ideology of "mixed" productions (modern or postmodern staging with old instruments) is quite explicitly that the opera being presented is an inherently appealing entertainment, in which the historically informed instrumental playing is both a pleasurable element and evidence of due respect to the composer (see the "making-of" portion of Monteverdi 2007). The combination of rigorously researched playing on historical instruments and strikingly modern and imaginative—and often highly physical—staging is, as of this writing, increasingly normal (e.g., Monteverdi 2007, where the entire cast dances). The arguments for this juxtaposition of historicities are a rich mixture of commercial realism, historical justification, and "timeless" performative contextualizing. For example, in the "making-of" segment of the DVD of the 2005 Glyndebourne production of Handel's *Giulio Cesare*, directed by David McVicar (Handel 2005), the performers and directors often refer to the connection they are making with the audience, which is clearly of great satisfaction to them, and which undoubtedly feeds into the stage life of the work. Throughout his interviews, David McVicar describes a variety of analogies between Handel's world and ours: For example, the question of imperialism is salient in both, which justifies the late nineteenth-century colonial setting. He also claims that Handel's musical rhythms are often from the "popular dance" of his own time, which justifies the Broadway/West End and Bollywood-style dancing throughout the production; and that Handel was a man of the theater (always wanting to put on a good show), which justifies the physicality of the production. McVicar's is a version of historical awareness, of course, but one more interested in historical knowledge about the *effects* of a show rather than its *means*, explicitly what the production most strenuously aims at recapturing. This is not a new ideology, nor one unique to opera. Arguments about playing Bach on the modern piano, for example, reflect it, as does, of course, the textual "violence" done to Mozart among many others in the nineteenth century in the name of making his operas palatable or appealing to a then-modern audience. What is new and different in this kind of opera production, particularly with those operas for which historical instruments are considered a choice rather than a necessity, is the postmodern layering of a research-based historical (even if not reconstructionist) musical idiom with a joyfully modern stage life, and a thoroughly modern approach to the expressive innards of the work. The *Giulio Cesare* performers interviewed in this segment had all learned something about Baroque performance practices, especially ornamentation and cadenza-making, but their chief concern in communicating the opera was the question "what kind of person is this character?" and the answer to that question for each of them seemed to come from a thoroughly modern and psychological, rather than a historicized and social-political, sense of human nature.

In some recent productions of early opera, then, there is a complex combination of ideologies. "Historically informed" instrumental (and to a lesser extent, vocal) music collaborates with what we might call a "historically rethought" visual dimension. A set of historically "uninformed" attitudes to characterization then operates within these sonic and visual frames. Obviously, any given production of an opera may manifest different ideologies of historicity, but separating out the visual, sonic, and ideological or attitudinal domains allows us to see how history plays into production.

The Unique Role of Historical Performance in Opera

Partly because historicity demonstrates itself in so many *domains* of opera, partly because it demonstrates itself in so many different *ways*, often simultaneously, and partly because of the nature of opera as a medium, historical awareness in opera means something quite different than it does in non-dramatic music. It is obvious that the multilayered or multi-domained nature of opera would make an "authentic" production even more elusive than it is in non-dramatic music (even supposing that it were desirable), and even a historically informed production is a more complex and cumbersome ideal than in non-dramatic music. But more important to opera's unique version of historical performance than its multidimensionality is its explicitly human content and its frank reliance for meaning and effect upon the manipulation of the audience's sympathies and capacities for identification. These inherent characteristics of many repertories of opera, when coupled with a widely held modern expectation of *all* opera that audience members should be able to "relate to" operatic characters, or at least place them in their own system of moral and social values, richly complicate the notion of historically informed performance, because the perceived need for a "human" connection between the audience and the operatic characters has had profound effects on production choices.

A production advertising itself as historically informed has essentially two choices about the basic ethos of its characters. One possibility is to make them transhistorically human (i.e., recognizably like "us") despite the unfamiliar setting; the other is to make them case studies of a particular historical type or examples of a cultural archetype. The first choice is vastly more common than the second. Techniques for "humanizing" a historical character—that is, for making him or her appear more familiar to a given audience—include having the makeup and hairstyle approximate the familiar styles of the audience's time and place, even when the costume is (more or less) historical. (Van Witsen 1981 is full of anecdotes about singers insisting that their costumes look good by the standards of their own day, but it also seems probable that there is often a directorial hand in the choice visually to "familiarize" a character by means of the hairstyle and makeup.) In addition, familiar gestures and body language, whether throughout or as comic relief from a less familiar demeanor, make the characters seem closer to "our" reality; and "unmarked" vocal production associates the work and characters with works and characters that may be more familiar in the repertory. The way the singers themselves conceptualize the characters also feeds in, more or less subtly, to the "universal," or at least transhistorical qualities of the characters; as noted above, it is striking that when singers are interviewed about their roles in opera, they tend to understand them in modern "pop-psych" terms, regardless of the period or historical apparatus of the production. This clearly allows them to make sense of what they have to do and to communicate something that is viscerally meaningful to them about the people they are pretending to be. Further, if the opera belongs in the canon or is otherwise familiar, even the most conspicuously historically informed productions will often adhere to oral-tradition conventions about the characters or their relationships in order (perhaps unconsciously) to retain what we perceive as their humanity. For example, most Giulio Cesares have not only lower but heavier voices than their Cleopatras, most Susannas are smaller than their Countesses, most Commendatores are large. Imagining the opposites (soubrette Cesare, statuesque Susanna, diminutive Commendatore) drives home the ways in which we "know" these characters. A fully "historical" performance might retain Cesare's relatively richer voice, if it could be demonstrated that that was the norm in the performances Handel supervised, but would probably ask him to engage in flowing dance-like or rhetorical postures and gestures, rather than striding in a macho way around the stage; and such a production would require Figaro to wring his hands while singing "Se vuol ballare," since that is in the stage directions. Many audience members would find these moves unpleasantly de-familiarizing.

Such de-familiarization was for a long time the stuff of the Early Music movement in general: in the 1970s and 1980s, at its most extreme distance from "regular," "bourgeois" symphony and opera performances, the "movement" looked and felt like a bunch of hippies not only finding unfamiliar ancient music to add to the canon, but also appropriating and reinventing the familiar canonic repertory with an almost messianic zeal for both "truth" and "freedom" defined against mainstream practices (Shelemay 2001: 6ff). But the zeal to re-imagine familiar music weakened precisely at the point where the re-imagining crossed from the acoustic world into the psychological. For example, the 1980s Drottningholm productions of the late Mozart operas were case studies in *not* historicizing or de-familiarizing the characters and action, despite the way they quite radically re-imagined the orchestral music. And more recent productions of these much-loved works with original instruments have not moved in the direction of historical staging practices. Indeed, Sir John Eliot Gardiner's 1995 production of *Die Zauberflöte* at the Concertgebouw (Mozart 1996) implicitly asserted that the dramatic illusion was secondary to the music, as the orchestra was visually front and center, the "scenery" was provided only intermittently by the acrobatic modern-dance group Pilobolus, and the characters (in marvelously fanciful costumes) moved around—and sometimes among—the orchestra. Gardiner's 1992 production of *Così fan tutte* at the Théâtre du Châtelet (Mozart 1993) was more conventionally staged (though the orchestra was still visible to the audience), and the costumes and scenery were gorgeously evocative of the late eighteenth century, but the physical presences, voices, and stage behavior of the singers were entirely modern.

To move into even more familiar repertory, there is more detailed information about the original productions of many Verdi operas than there is about any other pre-twentieth-century repertory except nineteenth-century French opera, whose *livrets scéniques* preserved the details of production as integral parts of "the work" (Hepokoski 2001: 12). Eight of Verdi's late operas have left *disposizioni sceniche*, based on the French *livrets scéniques*, which describe the blocking in exquisite detail. In addition, sound recordings of at least one of Verdi's original singers were made (Maurel 1993), and some of the theaters in which the operas were premiered still stand; the technical means exist to reproduce mid-nineteenth-century instruments, and there are players to play them in a historical manner. In addition, there is a much-heralded series of editions of Verdi operas that painstakingly reconstruct the stages of composition and production for these works, so that it is often possible to do exactly the version of a work that Verdi wrote for, say, the very first performance (Verdi 1983–). But with the exception of Gardiner's 1993 semi-staged performance of *Falstaff* on original instruments, which used the same setup as that described above for *Die Zauberflöte* (Verdi 2001), and a 1989 Sarasota opera performance of *Rigoletto*, which tried some melodramatic acting, gas-lighting effects, and vocal production that approximated what the conductor knew about earlier vocal techniques (and was deemed unpersuasive by John Rockwell [1989]), there have been almost no thoroughgoing attempts to stage Verdi in a historically informed manner. Hepokoski argues against the idea on the grounds that a production that followed the *disposizione scenica* could not help but be received as a "modern, historicized commentary" on production practices more familiar to a modern audience (Hepokoski 2001: 19). Further, Roger Parker writes more baldly, "few of us today would [...] be happy to see the chorus move all in step, with regimental discipline about the stage; or for the singers to make a series of elaborate and (to us) melodramatic gestures as they sing" (Parker 2007: viii–ix).

"Few of us would be happy" may be a true statement, and it may justify not applying the full panoply of historical devices and techniques to familiar operas. But it exposes the institutional and commercial underpinnings of most mainstream opera production that reinforce the conceptual distinctions between historically informed productions of opera and those of other kinds of music. Opera has always been "about" moving its public, about forging a visceral but specific connection between the situations and events on stage and the situations and events in and beyond the auditorium. Today, those situations and events seem to have to be rooted in the psychologically plausible, even when they spread out into the political or social realms. In other words, if there is no visceral sympathy with the characters or their plights, there is, as far as many people are concerned, no opera. De-familiarizing the characters is, then, a dangerous move, particularly when opera is such an expensive proposition: if "few of us are happy," there are no patrons. All of these things are less true with non-operatic music: institutionally, most non-operatic music is cheaper to mount, and thus depends for its existence on the "happiness" of fewer people. Aesthetically, there is less "danger" in de-familiarizing non-dramatic music because the very identities of the audience are (with certain exceptions) less at issue, and most non-dramatic music offers the audience a wider variety of ways of relating to it.

French Baroque opera is an interesting case in the "de-familiarization" stakes; as noted above, it is routinely produced in quite carefully historical garb and with very thoroughly researched musical practices. There are a number of reasons that this repertory is particularly adapted for pervasively historicizing productions. One is that because it was a court-monopolized entertainment, and because the operas of both Lully and Rameau (but especially the former) were performed repeatedly and for a long period of time in essentially the same way, there is an unusual fullness of documentation about the early productions (Thomas 1992). It was also theorized and discussed in its own time with a remarkable degree of self-consciousness, so the aesthetic framework is unusually clear. The reason for its modern suitability for highly historicized production is that it represents a remarkably coherent and self-contained political and social world from a much-valued period in French history. Thus the French government is willing to help fund the restoration and revival of the repertory as part of the national patrimony; popular success is a benefit but not a necessity for a project to be carried out, as is the case with the Centre de Musique Baroque de Versailles. The third and most profound reason is that its aesthetic, although intended to delight the audience, did not then, and cannot reasonably be construed now, to rely on complex or (often) even plausible psychological portraiture; rather it created a literally marvelous and delightful world, which, in the famous words of Jean La Bruyère, was supposed to enchant the spirit, the ears, and the eyes equally (La Bruyère [1694] 1951: 79). The mythical (rather than historical) basis and clear allegorical meanings of most of the stories in this repertory also contribute to this aesthetic. Compared to the inner life or motivation of a character who needs to be sympathetic to be dramatically effective, "Le merveilleux" is easier to re-create (given sufficient knowledge and money). Finally, and related to this third point, French Baroque opera is fertile terrain for historically informed performance because it is relatively unfamiliar; not only are the works themselves unfamiliar, but the style is not something much heard in mainstream modern-instrument musical culture, and thus there is much less dead weight of "classic" performances to dislodge.

In addition to William Christie's pioneering work and that of the Boston Early Music Festival, the Centre de Musique Baroque de Versailles, in conjunction with the ensemble Poème Harmonique with music director Vincent Dumestre and stage director Benjamin Lazar, has recently (2008) followed up on its exacting production of *Le bourgeois gentilhomme* with a reconstruction of Lully's first full opera, *Cadmus et Hermione* (Lully 2008). These latter productions are notable for using old French pronunciation, for a pervasive use of rhetorical gesture, and for extraordinarily detailed reconstructions of Baroque sets, costumes, lighting, and stage mechanics. Lazar and Dumestre claim that the more they study the historical record, the more their imaginations are stimulated; and indeed, the sets, choreography, and costumes are created anew within the conventions and constraints of the historical information, rather than being copied from particular originals (Lazar 2008). Nevertheless, for the audience (even watching the screen version) the experience is of relatively uncomplicated time-travel of a sort impossible for productions of better-known operas.

Examples of Historically Informed Production: "Collage" or "Timelessness"

Most historically informed opera productions are not, as we have seen, as thorough in every dimension as the Dumestre/Lazar *Cadmus et Hermione*. Most historically informed productions open more obvious hermeneutic windows onto the complex historical location they occupy. Take the recent Opera Atelier (Toronto) production of Lully's *Persée*, a thoroughly researched but "looser" reconstruction of a work by the French Baroque master (Lully 2005). The instruments are "original," the singing is cognizant of seventeenth-century French performance practice, the body language often evokes the rhetorical gestures of the stage of that period, and the choreography uses period vocabulary. In addition, the work is unfamiliar: it is an allegory about French royal power, and it needs some historical contextualization to make any sense at all in the modern world. Director Marshall Pinkoski and choreographer Jeanette Zingg predictably insist that this is not a revival or reconstruction, but rather a fully modern entertainment "within the stylistic constraints" of the French Baroque. And, not surprisingly, there are a variety of cracks in the armature of historicization. One example concerns the most psychologically immediate character, Mérope, who nurses a hopeless passion for Persée, and utters her misery several times in the course of the opera. Her laments are sung with the continuous rhetorical hand gestures common in this style (strikingly unlike modern stage behavior), but the singer Monica Whicher's distinctly modern voice, her barely historical coiffure, and even the slightly prom-dress quality of the top end of her costume all break down the historical distance between this character and the audience, turning Lully's study of a static (if also touching) *Affekt* into a character emotionally plausible in the world of the audience. A different example is Meduse (Medusa), the villain Persée must kill, who is played by a male singer, as Lully intended. The singer in this production (who doubles as the good king Céphée, which Lully did not intend) makes Meduse a wonderfully campy, drag-queen presence. No doubt the original production played up the ever-comic potential of a man playing an older or unappealing woman, and the original singer of the role specialized in comic roles, but this production inserts recognizably modern body language into this predominantly historicizing production for comic effect (for a slightly different reading see Bolduc 2005: sections 5.3 and 6).

In both these examples, the directors and performers have used modernity to move the audience—once to sympathy and once to ridicule. Significantly, the invocation of modernity to create sympathy is "silent" or at least muted—that is, most people will not even notice the signs of modernity that make Mérope a particularly appealing character. In contrast, the evocation of modernity to the ends of laughter and ridicule is entirely obvious: Meduse's campy posturing is very obviously out of step with most of the production. In both cases, however, the production engages in a kind of collage of historical layers, or a series of "bridges" from one historical location to another. It may be ironic that the sense of collage in this production emerges from the fact that sight and sound are largely coherent with each other (both being historicized), so that these, and other, moments of modernity seem "pasted on" to a historical basis.

A 1998 production of Monteverdi's *L'Orfeo* works somewhat differently with respect to its historical location. The music is directed by eminent Early Music specialist René Jacobs; it is a ravishing realization of the score, with a lush variety of continuo realizations. The choral singing is the "white" sound usual in many Early Music performances, and the solo singing is in the default Early Music, light, articulate, but highly rhetorical style. The set is almost completely bare, and the costumes are a mixture of vaguely Asian loose jackets and pants, comic hazmat suits for the demons of hell, and a singlet and green paint for Caronte. The overall concept, which includes pervasive dancing, was designed by modern-dance choreographer Trisha Brown. As with the 2005 Glyndebourne *Giulio Cesare* discussed above, the obvious intellectual response to this is that it is a collage of historical and modern elements. However, one does not experience the juxtapositions or "edges" of the different elements in the way that one would expect in a true collage. In the interview included with the DVD of this production, René Jacobs claims (just like Pinkoski and Zingg) that his style of music making, however thoroughly researched, is modern, but this of course is only partly true. It is, rather, a modern way of representing Monteverdi's acoustic world. Thus the *lack* of collage-effect, or better, the sense of continuity in this production, is not due to the inherent modernity of the aural dimension; rather it is partly due to *our* sense at the turn of the twenty-first century that early instruments are the norm for Monteverdi, and thus that an obviously modern (in some sense "normal") staging is perfectly in step with the music. Up until the late 1980s or 1990s, historically informed music making in the context of modern staging would have felt much more discontinuous, because at that point the ethos of original instrument performance was both much more self-consciously reconstructionist, and much more self-consciously dedicated to making (especially familiar) music "other" (Shelemay 2001: 9). Thus at that point in time an "original" sonic dimension joined to modern visuals felt as though the two were pulling in opposite directions. Another reason for the felt seamlessness of this *Orfeo* production may simply be the trickle-down effect of postmodernity—by the early twenty-first century the shocking effects of supposedly incongruous historical juxtapositions in art have worn off, and a variety of circumstances (not least the Internet) have contributed to a kind of "flattening out" of our historical sense. The past several decades' rise of *Regietheater* in the operatic world overall has vastly widened the possible aesthetic, historical, and social frames for all opera, such that the coexistence of a theorbo and Cirque du Soleil aerial dancing in the same production is certainly no more (indeed, probably less) jarring than the introduction of oral sex into *Die Entführung aus dem Serail* (Mozart 2004). Finally, the relative seamlessness and "timelessness" of the Brown/Jacobs production is also due to *Orfeo's* status as a myth, existing outside the frame of history; there is no impetus to try to place the events in any particular period, as there is in the politically salient *Persée*; and where there is no basis in a particular historical period, there is less possibility of historical collage.

Conclusion

One might ask whether a "historically informed" opera production like the Trisha Brown/Rene Jacobs *Orfeo*, with its early instruments, Early Music singing style, and modern staging, is the *opposite* of the currently mainstream "historically uninformed" (but not *Regietheater*) productions of most operas with their modern instruments, modern singing styles, but historical settings. Putting this *Orfeo* next to the Opera Atelier's *Persée*, let alone next to a "standard" Metropolitan Opera production of *La traviata*, confirms the notion, introduced above, that even an *implicit* binary opposition between historically "informed" and historically "uninformed" productions is a deeply unhelpful way to think about historicity in operatic performance. Opposition does not work as an analytical tool. More helpful is to consider the *placement* and *quality* of the interfaces between modernity and the historical. This kind of consideration is both more possible and more necessary in opera than in non-dramatic music—possible because the different domains of opera are distinct enough to allow this kind of analysis, and necessary because any opera's meanings (and the meanings of any production) are radically diminished without some sense of their historical location (or locations).

I suggested above that opera producers and performers typically make conscious and unconscious choices about the borders of "authenticity" in order to retain (or challenge) an audience's familiar frameworks of sympathy with and distance from the characters (or character types); but these decisions also keep the operas in their familiar institutional places as either "standard repertory" (e.g., Verdi), or "standard historical repertory" (e.g., Monteverdi and Handel), or "historical revival" (e.g., French Baroque opera). A decision, for example, to de-familiarize a Verdi opera by using the "authentic" blocking and gestures is also a decision to change its institutional and financial status in our culture. Similarly (but less radically), a decision to do a Rameau opera with modern instruments, voices, and mainstream musical habits, in an important opera house, is assertion that the work has joined the central canon of "universally" accessible works, and that as such, it can attract the same audience as Puccini. Choices about historicity in opera production are not only more complex than "informed" versus "uninformed"; they are about the meaning of this genre in modern life.

See also: Regietheater/Director's Theater, Costumes, Castrato Acts, Dance

Bibliography

Abbate, Carolyn. 2004. "Music—Drastic or Gnostic." *Critical Inquiry* 30: 505–536.

——. 2000. *In Search of Opera*. Princeton, NJ: Princeton University Press.

Alm, Irene. 2003. "Winged Feet and Mute Eloquence: Dance in Seventeenth-Century Venetian Opera," edited by Rebecca Harris-Warrick and Wendy Heller. *Cambridge Opera Journal* 15: 216–80.

Baker, Evan. 2013. *From the Score to the Stage: An Illustrated History of Continental Opera Production and Staging*. Chicago: University of Chicago Press.

Banducci, Antonia. 2005. "The Opera Atelier Performance (Toronto, 2000): The Spirit of Lully on the Modern Stage." *Journal of Seventeenth-Century Music* 10. Online. Available: http://www.sscm-jscm.org/v10/no1/banducci.html (accessed February 6, 2014).

Barnett, Dene, with the assistance of Jeanette Massy-Westropp. 1987. *The Art of Gesture: The Practices and Principles of 18th Century Acting*. Heidelberg: Carl Winter Universitätsverlag.

Bolduc, Benoit. 2005. "From Marvel to Camp, Medusa for the Twenty-First Century." *Journal of Seventeenth-Century Music* 10. Online. Available: http://www.sscm-jscm.org/v10/no1/bolduc.html (accessed February 6, 2014).

Burgess, Geoffrey. 2006. "Revisiting *Atys*: Reflections on Les Arts Florissants' Production." *Early Music* 34/3: 465–478.

Butt, John. 2002. *Playing with History: The Historical Approach to Musical Performance*. Cambridge: Cambridge University Press.

Conati, Marcello, and Natalia Grilli, eds. 1993. *'Simon Boccanegra' di Giuseppe Verdi*. Milan: Ricordi.

Cambridge Opera Journal. 2004. Vol. 16/3 (November 2004). Special issue on performance.

Christie, William. 1997. "At Home with the Idiom: William Christie on the French Baroque." In Sherman 1997, 257–272.

——. 1993. "The Elusive World of the French Baroque." *Early Music* 21/2: 262–266.

Crutchfield, Will. 1988. "Fashion, Conviction, and Performance Style." In Kenyon 1988, 19–26.

Curtis, Alan. 1997. "Every Detail of This Music Has Something to Do with Language." In Sherman 1997, 134–141.

Dean, Winton. 2006. *Handel's Operas 1728–1741*. Melton: Boydell and Brewer.

——. 1981. Review of Handel's *Ariodante* with Dame Janet Baker. *Musical Times* 122 (January): 33–34.

Dreyfus, Laurence. 1983. "Early Music Defended against Its Devotees: A Theory of Historical Performance in the Twentieth Century." *Musical Quarterly* 69/3: 297–322.

——, Joseph Kerman, Joshua Kosman, et al. 1992. "The Early Music Debate; Ancients, Moderns and Postmoderns." *Journal of Musicology* 10/1: 113–130.

Ford, Bruce. 2009. Picture of *Mitridate* costume. Online. Available: www.tenorbruceford.com/newandnoteworthy.html (accessed January 7, 2013).

Handel, Georg Friedrich. 2005. DVD: Georg Frideric Handel, *Giulio Cesare*. Dir. David McVicar. Cond. William Christie. Opus Arte 0950 D (2006), DVD 3.

——. 2001 DVD. *Tamerlano*. Dir. Jonathan Miller. Cond. Nicholas McGegan. Arthaus DVD 100 703.

Harnoncourt, Nikolaus. 1988. "Articulation." In *Baroque Music Today: Baroque Music as Speech: Ways to a New Understanding of Music*, translated by Mary O'Neill, 39–49. Portland, OR: Amadeus Press.

Harris-Warrick, Rebecca, and Carol Marsh. 1994. *Musical Theatre at the Court of Louis XIV: Le marriage de la Grosse Cathos*. Cambridge: Cambridge University Press.

Harris-Warrick, Rebecca, and Bruce Alan Brown, eds. 2005. *The Grotesque Dancer on the Eighteenth-Century Stage: Gennaro Magri and His World*. Madison: University of Wisconsin Press.

Haskell, Harry. 1988. *The Early Music Movement: A History*. London: Thames and Hudson.

Haynes, Bruce. 2007. *The End of Early Music: A Period Performer's History of Music for the Twenty-First Century*. New York: Oxford University Press.

Hepokoski, James. 2001. "Staging Verdi's Operas: The Single, 'Correct,' Performance." In Latham and Parker 2001, 11–22.

——, and Mercedes Viale Ferrero, eds. 1994. *'Otello' di Giuseppe Verdi*. Milan: Ricordi.

Hilton, Wendy. 1981. *Dance of Court and Theater: The French Noble Style*, edited by Caroline Gaynor, labanotation by Mireille Backer. Princeton, NJ: Princeton University Press.

Hunter, Shelagh. 2009. Personal conversation.

Johnson, James. 1995. *Listening in Paris: A Cultural History*. Berkeley and Los Angeles: University of California Press.

Kenyon, Nicholas, ed. 1988. *Authenticity and Early Music*. New York: Oxford University Press.

La Bruyère, Jean. [1694] 1951. *Les caractères ou les moeurs de ce siècle*. In *Oeuvres complètes*, edited by Julien Benda. Paris: Gallimard.

Lancelot, Francine. 1996. *La belle danse: Catalogue raisoné fait en l'an 1995*. Paris: Van Dieren.

Latham, Alison, and Roger Parker, eds. 2001. *Verdi in Performance*. New York: Oxford University Press.

Lazar, Benjamin. 2008. Interview with Lazar and Vincent Dumestre. Online. Available: http://www.royaumont.com/fondation_abbaye/interview_vincent_dumestre__benjamin_lazar.823.0.html (accessed February 6, 2014).

Levin, David. 2007. *Unsettling Opera*. Chicago: University of Chicago Press.

Little, Meredith, and Carol G. Marsh. 1992. *La Danse Noble: An Inventory of Dances and Sources*. New York: Broude Bros.
Lully, Jean-Baptiste. 2008. DVD: *Cadmus et Hermione*. Dir. Benjamin Lazar. Alpha 701.
——. 2005. DVD: *Le bourgeois gentilhomme*. Dir. Benjamin Lazar. Alpha 700.
Martín y Soler, Vicente. 1993. Costume illustration. Online. Available: http://www.canvasmanagement.com/cv.php?id=68&lang=e (accessed July 26, 2009). This website is no longer available.
Marvin, Roberta Montemorra. 2001. "Verdi Scholarship at the Beginning of the Twenty-first Century. *Nineteenth-Century Studies* 15: 89–97.
Maurel, Victor. 1993. *Victor Maurel, the Complete Recordings*. GEMM CD 9027.
Monteverdi, Claudio. 2007. DVD: *L'Orfeo*. Cond. René Jacobs. Dir. Trisha Brown. Harmonia Mundi 9909003.04.
Mozart, Wolfgang Amadeus. 2006. DVD: *Così fan tutte*, dir. Nicholas Hytner. (Costume illustration). Online. Available: http://www.opusarte.com/product?q=Cosi (accessed January 7, 2013).
——. 1996. VHS: *Die Zauberflöte*. Dir. John Eliot Gardiner. Archiv Production Video.
——. 1993. DVD: *Così fan tutte*. Dir. John Eliot Gardiner. Archiv Produktion 440 072 536-3.
Opera Quarterly. 2005. Vol. 21 (summer) until 2011. "Notes from the Stage."
Parker, Roger. 2007. *The New Grove Guide to Verdi and His Operas*. New York: Oxford University Press.
Petrobelli, Pierluigi, and Fabrizio della Seta, eds. 1996. *La realizzazione scenica dello spettacolo verdiano: Atti del congresso internazionale 28, 10 Settembre 1994*. Parma: Istituto nazionale di studi verdiani.
Rameau, Jean-Philippe. 1995. *Hippolyte et Aricie*. CD. *Les Indes Galantes* (Opus Arte 2005), *Les Paladins* (Opus Arte 2005), *Les Boréades* (Opus Arte 2004), *Zoroastre* (Opus Arte 2007), *La guirlande* (Erato 2001), *Zéphyr* (Erato, 2001), (Archiv 1995), *Les fêtes d'Hébé* (Erato 1997), *Castor et Pollux* (Opus Arte 2008), *Pigmalion* (Centaur 2010), *Nelée et Myrthis* (Harmonia Mundi 2008), and *Anacréon* (1757) (Deutsche Grammophon 1996).
Rice, John A. 2009. *Mozart on the Stage*. Cambridge: Cambridge University Press.
Rockwell, John. 1989. "A Try at Authenticity in Sarasota *'Rigoletto'*." *New York Times* (February 26). Online. Available: http://www.nytimes.com/1989/02/26/arts/review-opera-a-try-at-authenticity-in-sarasota-rigoletto.html (accessed February 6, 2014).
——. 1986. Review. "Home Video: New Cassettes: From Kilt to White Tie." *New York Times* (August 31): A 20.
Rosen, David, and Marinella Pigozzi, eds. 2002. *'Un ballo in maschera' di Giuseppe Verdi*. Milan: Ricordi.
Savage, Roger. 1998. "Staging an Opera: Letters from the Cesarian Poet." *Early Music* 26: 583–595.
Shelemay, Kay. 2001. "Toward an Ethnomusicology of the Early Music Movement: Thoughts on Bridging Disciplines and Musical Worlds." *Ethnomusicology* 45:1–29.
Sherman, Bernard. 1997. *Inside Early Music: Conversations with Performers*. New York: Oxford University Press.
Slavko, Pavel. 2002. Interview re: The Stage Machinery at Český Krumlov Castle Theater. Online. Available: http://www.radio.cz/en/article/11909 (accessed February 6, 2014).
Spitzer, John, and Neal Zaslaw. 1992. "Conductor." In *The New Grove Dictionary of Opera. Online*. Available: http://www.oxfordmusiconline.com/subscriber/article/grove/music/O901114 (accessed August 16, 2012).

Stieglitz, Sandy.2012. *Sandy's Opera Gallery*. Online. Available: www.cs.princeton.edu/~san (accessed February 6, 2014).

Taruskin, Richard. 1995. "The Modern Sound of Early Music." In *Text and Act: Essays on Music and Performance*, 164–172. New York: Oxford University Press.

——. 1992. "The Early Music Debate: Ancients, Moderns and Postmoderns." *Journal of Musicology* 10/1: 113–130.

Thomas, Downing. 1992. *Aesthetics of Opera in the Ancien Régime, 1647–1785*. Cambridge: Cambridge University Press.

Turin. 2012. Turin opera seria. (Opera seria Roman costumes). Online. Available: http://www.classiquenews.com/images/articles/opera_seria_baroque_acteurs_scene.jpg (accessed February 6, 2014).

Van Witsen, Leo. 1981. *Costuming in Opera: Who Wears What and Why*. Bloomington: Indiana University Press.

Verdi, Giuseppe. 1983–. *The Works of Giuseppe Verdi*. Series I: The Operas, edited by Philip Gossett. Chicago: University of Chicago Press; Milan: Ricordi.

——. 2001. *Falstaff*. Cond. John Eliot Gardiner. Philips CD 462-603.

Westrup, Jack. 1925. "Monteverde's [*sic*] Orfeo." *Musical Times* 66: 1096–1100.

Young, Marcia. 2007. "Boys and Girls Together." *Opera News* 72 (August): 26–29.

PART IV

OPERA AND SOCIETY

CHAPTER 28

OPERA COMPOSITION AND CULTURAL ENVIRONMENT

MARIANNE BETZ

> Did I never talk to you about my fine principles [...]? They comprise never again to try an opera or marriage.[1]
>
> (Brahms in a letter to Joseph Viktor Widmann, January 7, 1888; Kalbeck 1915: 72)

Successes, Failures, Opportunities, and Resistance

The history of opera is most often written as a history of successes on stage, with side notes for the failures. Nonetheless, the failures remain of interest, as does the question of why composers did *not* write an opera or gave up after a try. The purpose of this chapter is to explore some of the cultural factors that encouraged or hindered composers to engage with opera. Bach and Brahms come immediately to mind in this context as non-opera composers, Beethoven and Schumann as examples of those who gave up. *Fidelio* (1805/1814) continues to incite controversial discussions about Beethoven's lucky hand in dealing with the genre and the dramatic impact of the subject, mostly because of the work's astonishing final hybrid form, amalgamating heroic French rescue opera, German *Singspiel*, and melodrama. But Schumann's *Genoveva* (1850) was nearly immediately forgotten after a few performances (Warrack 2001). Decidedly written as a German opera, the latter could not catch up with the popularity of mainstream French grand opera and Italian opera (Hanslick 1880; Billington 1987). Much in contrast to these unfortunate operatic ambitions of composers with otherwise overall successfully received musical output is the resistance toward this popular genre exemplified by Bach and Brahms.

Bach was fond of what he called "die schönen Dresdener Liederchen"—the beautiful Dresden songs. According to his biographer Forkel, he attended performances at the Dresden opera several times after 1731, usually together with his eldest son Wilhelm Friedemann (Forkel [1802] 1982: 86); he may also have attended performances on trips to Hamburg or Weißenfels (Wolff 1988). A friend of Johann Adolf Hasse and his wife Faustina Bordoni, Bach must have been at the Dresden premiere of Johann Adolf Hasse's *Cleofide* on September 13, 1731 (Wolff 1988: 167), the only opera of the many Bach may have seen that is actually documented. In spite of his own enormous output of dramatic vocal works, such as the *Passions*, Bach himself did not write an opera. Some of his secular cantatas bear the subtitle "dramma per musica"; though this indicates their structure as dialogues to be performed in concert, it does not point to staging. Nonetheless, the elaborate handling and refining of the musical styles introduced by contemporary stage works in his very own music indicate the composer's familiarity with current examples of the genre (Wolff 1988: 168). One explanation for the absence of opera in Bach's work may be his workload, which throughout his life was dominated by mostly church-affiliated duties. Weimar was the first place in which Bach was stationed that had an opera house, founded in 1696. Yet Weimar's operatic life did not blossom in those days (Schrickel 1928; Huschke 1998: 1923). Apart from that, Bach's focus as court organist and "Cammermusicus" from 1708 had to be on organ, church, and other instrumental music. During the following years at the Cöthen court, Bach was much involved in secular music, focusing on chamber and orchestral works. At Leipzig, finally, his professional environment from 1723 for over two decades, Bach's obligations nearly all had to do with Protestant church music. An opera house had been founded in Leipzig in 1693, but economic problems forced it to close in 1720. Thus only traveling opera troupes performed in Leipzig in the next few years, among these, after 1744, some Italian companies (Warrack 2001: 30, 63). It was not until after the end of the Prussian-Austrian war in 1763 that regular stage productions were put on again.

Thus the grounds for Bach's "abstinence" from the genre, a paradox considering his general interest in the repertoire, trace back to a variety of causes. The strong musical family background did not include a close affiliation to opera; church and town musician were the predominant professions in Bach's family. Bach's cousin Johann Nicolaus (1669–1753) composed a student scene in operatic style ("Der Jenaische Wein—und Bierrufer"), which may have included acting, while Johann Ludwig (1677–1731), another cousin, is documented as conductor of an opera in Meiningen (Böhme 1969: 60, 125; Koch 1968: 300–301). Bach did not study with teachers who would have introduced him to the theater, nor did the places where he lived and worked have a flourishing operatic life during that time. Consequently, he missed the stimulus that might be expected through contact with the specific infrastructure of opera, including stage settings, scenery, machines, costumes, choreography, and so on. Beyond that, several influential people in Bach's Protestant surroundings cultivated a distance toward the genre: in his contract dated May 5, 1723, Bach had to confirm that his music would not be "*opernhafftig*" ("opera-like") (Neumann 1963: 177), but instead would aim to increase the devotion of listeners. Certainly this obligation, juxtaposing opera and devotion as two disparate values, did not stimulate experiments with the operatic style in ways other than those Bach adopted into his Leipzig vocal works.

Although Johannes Brahms (1833–1897) also came from a Protestant milieu, the explanations for his reserve toward the genre are different from those imagined for Bach. Brahms's career very soon tended toward that of a pianist and composer. His role play as a young man with the other "Johannes," the fictitious "Kreisler" figure from E. T. A. Hoffmann's stories (a musician oscillating between geniality and lunacy but consoling his enthusiastic and over-sensible soul with Bach, Beethoven, and Burgundy) already indicated Brahms's aesthetic and musical orientation. Much like his literary alter ego, Brahms emphasized instrumental music as a language without words, an understanding of music that made Hoffmann and many others rank instrumental music at the top of a hierarchy of musical genres. Robert Schumann's prophetic editorial "Neue Bahnen" in the *Neue Zeitschrift für Musik* in 1853 describes the author's vision of the musical future awaiting the emerging genius Brahms. There Schumann writes of sonata, symphony, piano and chamber music, choir, and orchestra in relation to the young composer, but omits any reference to the stage. Maybe this eclipse simply reacted to the fact that up until then Brahms had not written any stage work, maybe it reflected the aesthetic ranking of instrumental music over vocal music. This flashes up in Schumann's emphasis on sonata and symphony as "songs whose poetry one would understand without knowing the words,"[2] a phrase highlighting the author's aesthetics but, as a side effect, also unveiling his very own troubles with opera, which he would have preferred as "opera without text" (Schumann 1853: 185; Billington 1987: 11–12). Although the most influential persons in Brahms's younger years, Joseph Joachim and Robert and Clara Schumann, were not themselves closely affiliated with opera, there was no lack of role models. Had Brahms searched for mentors, he certainly would have found them, just as he could have received the necessary operatic inputs from a place with an operatic infrastructure and a vivid opera life. Yet, how much was Brahms really tempted by opera? A lot of assumptions have been made about Brahms's resistance to both marriage and opera. Carol Hess, for example, examined the possibility that Brahms's cantata *Rinaldo* is an autobiographical statement reflecting his own role in love affairs, leaving the seductress Armida without voice, yet highlighting the situation of Rinaldo who, torn between his longing and reason, finally succeeds in freeing himself from all fetters (Hess 1998: 63–89). Reiber (2001) scrutinized Brahms's various attempts at finding a suitable libretto, a problem that Schumann, Beethoven, and others had faced as well. As documented in the memoirs of Brahms's contemporary Richard Heuberger, Brahms was sometimes drawn to Mozart as his ideal of an opera composer, with *Le nozze di Figaro* being his favorite piece (Reiber 2001: 16). However, even if Brahms had found what he judged to be an acceptable opera book, one that suited his well-educated literary taste, he still would have had to find his place in the opera world. Schumann's enthusiastic inaugural address of Brahms in 1853 ("Neue Bahnen") had nourished the ongoing antagonism between the progressive *Neudeutsche Schule* and the conservatives.

The unfortunate public dispute starting around 1860 and focusing on Brahms, who was counted as representing conservatism, did not make stylistic choices easier, as the preference for musical genres became a marker for each of the groups. In their early texts both Wagner and Liszt, leading figures of the progressive movement, had elaborated on the idea of musical progress. Although Franz Liszt himself finished only one opera (*Don Sanche*, 1824/1825), which can even be regarded as a study work, he felt strongly drawn to the genre. In 1843 he wrote to Marie d'Agoult about his plans for composing an opera after the end of his virtuoso career (Szelényi 1977: 216–217). He wanted to highlight the genre, which he did in his opera transcriptions and paraphrases, but also as the writer of numerous texts dedicated to the dramaturgy and the aesthetics of musical drama (Redepenning 1989: viii–x). Wagner in particular emphasized musical drama as a natural conclusion of the aesthetic impact of Beethoven's Ninth Symphony, and thus dominated the discussion of contemporary opera. The conservatives, consequently, postulated that progress meant focusing on autonomous instrumental music; the legacy of the Vienna Classic era made symphony and string quartet the top ranked genres. As Hanslick wrote in 1854:

> What *instrumental music* is unable to achieve, lies also beyond the pale of *music proper*; for it alone is pure and self-subsistent music. No matter whether we regard vocal music as superior to, or more effective than instrumental music [...] we cannot help admitting that the term "music," in its true meaning, must exclude compositions in which words are set to music.[3] (Hanslick 1854: 20)

Hence, especially in the Germanic countries, many influential voices including, again, Hanslick, regarded opera as aesthetically inferior: "All musical poetry is human-made [...] pervaded by elements of quicker or slower mortality. Among the big forms in music again opera is the most compound, the most conventional and thus the most ephemeral"[4] (Hanslick 1875: vii). Since the late eighteenth century, authors like Tieck and Wackenroder had eulogized concert halls as churches or cathedrals, a parallel that focused on performance venues for symphonic music or oratorio, and certainly not on opera houses or theaters (Dahlhaus 1989: 77ff.).

The success of *Ein deutsches Requiem*, premiered in 1868, made Brahms famous. With the cantata *Rinaldo* op. 50 on Goethe's poem *Rinaldo* from 1811 (Torkewitz 1995: 709–719), performed in Vienna in 1869, Brahms came close to putting a dramatic text into music, probably the closest he ever came to a stage work. Yet reviewers, including Hanslick, remarked on the lack of dramatic suggestion and coloring in Brahms's music. Emphasizing the hybrid character of Goethe's poem, Hanslick critically demanded a corresponding musical style that should oscillate between opera, cantata, and Lied (Hanslick 1886: 386). In the same year, Wagner's *Rheingold* was premiered in Munich, preceded in 1868 by *Die Meistersinger von Nürnberg*. Would Brahms at this point have dared to bring out an opera, a genre in which he, at the height of his career, was actually a beginner? As in the case of Schumann, any opera of Brahms would have had to survive the inevitable comparison with the Italian and French repertoire and by then, of course, Wagner. Brahms evidently still tried to find a proper subject. However, his famous comment from 1888 (see above), linking his resistance to both marriage and opera, marks the deadline for his considerations and finally for his way to solve the opera dilemma for himself: He resisted the temptation (Reiber 2001: 13ff).

Operatic "Conditions"

It appears that certain factors affect the development of a composer as an opera or a non-opera composer. One possible point of entry is biography, where issues like the influence of role models, inputs through contact with infrastructure, and so on, come into play. The Bach family, of whom no one was closely affiliated to the theater world, contrasts immensely with, for example, the family background of a composer like Carl Maria von Weber (1786–1826), who grew up in a theatrical environment. The Webers, a musical family for generations, were theater people: the mother, Genovefa Brenner, had been a singer; the father, Franz Anton, was a former "Stadtmusicus" who became director of his own theater troupe (Veit 2001). Moreover, Carl Maria's cousins, the daughters of his uncle Fridolin Weber, singer and violinist of the Mannheim electoral chapel, were the sopranos Aloysia and Constanze Weber, the latter being Mozart's wife. The "kleine Carl Weber" had appeared on stage as a five-year-old (Veit 2001: 13–14) and at the age of twelve had finished his first opera *Die Macht der Liebe und des Weins*, dedicated to the power of love and wine, about which he probably did not know much at the time. On June 27, 1811, Weber wrote to his friend Johann Gänsbacher that he was "waiting painfully for a good opera book, not feeling at ease without an opera in hand"[5] (Weber [1811] 2003; Veit 2001: 17), revealing his enormous commitment to the genre. A similar enthusiasm for opera, much in contrast to Brahms's later reserve toward it, is evidenced by a posting in the Leipziger *Allgemeine musikalische Zeitung* in which Weber, in an outburst of theater-blood, urged German poets (*die Dichter Deutschlands*) to write and submit librettos: "The undersigned wishes to receive as quickly as possible a good opera text, which he intends to set in music and reward decently"[6] (Weber 1813: 24). Weber's duties in his major positions in Prague and Dresden, both operatic centers, corresponded to his enormous dramatic talent as composer and conductor. While, on the one hand, he contributed to the operatic ambitions nourished in these places, he, on the other hand, found inspiration for himself, for instance with the emerging focus on German opera as a new species of the genre.

While Weber's particular talent enabled the success of *Der Freischütz* (1821) as a splendid example of German opera, German opera on the whole did not advance to a blossoming new branch of the repertoire. The operas of German composers, like Schumann, who tried their hand, did not compete successfully with the contemporary repertoire, particularly Italian opera. The performance conditions, singers, and musicians were also not on par (Warrack 2001: 338–339). Although traveling to Italy for many musicians in the nineteenth century meant a journey to the homeland of music, Otto Nicolai's motivation for his sojourn to Italy had a unique background: he wanted to "Italianize" himself as much as possible to overcome the obstacle of being a German composer and become successful in opera, combining the German school and Italian *leggerezza*, like his role model Mozart (Schröder 1892: 78ff.). Much in contrast to Meyerbeer, who had similar reasons for traveling to Italy and managed to make a career as an opera composer, Nicolai's only real later success, ironically, was the German opera *Die lustigen Weiber von Windsor* (1849).

Individual case studies inevitably lead to a more general questioning of "operatic conditions," a phrase used in 1924 by American critic Carl Engel (referring to George Whitefield Chadwick's failed operatic venture, *The Padrone*, which is discussed in more detail below). With this in mind, we can parse out several different types of context that are necessary for operatic life both to flourish and to inspire artistic productivity:

1. An adequate social environment is necessary for the implementation of opera into the cultural life of a societal or regional setting. In history, first courts and then towns became the centers of opera. As artistic hubs they consequently began to develop dynamics of their own, attracting composers, singers, and other artists. Furthermore, opera as part of social life advanced to become a marker of sophisticated societal behavior.
2. Opera needs to be acknowledged as an elevated form of musical art, beyond any moral doubt. The reserve toward theater in general and opera in particular, based on religious and moral arguments, influenced the musical life of many places and hindered the blossoming of opera.
3. The aesthetic appreciation of opera relates to musical hierarchy in general, but also more specifically to the place of opera in the context of other species of vocal and dramatic music. During the nineteenth century, the idea emerged that the German-speaking countries were destined to be the homelands of pure instrumental music, leaving opera to Italy and France. This helped to establish categories of evaluation, and of nationalist thinking in music, which created ideological obstacles for composers of the post-Beethoven generations (Hanslick 1880: 268).
4. A common understanding of the possible languages, the subjects, and the texts is necessary. This is usually connected to the social, moral, and aesthetic acceptance of opera.

Importing Opera in Pre-War America

One of the most fertile contexts for considering "operatic conditions" is pre–World War I America, where an astonishing number of renowned composers did not engage with opera, in spite of their sympathy with the genre. European operatic "hits" reached North American stages very quickly. It was a crucial moment when Italian opera, sung in Italian, promoted by no less than Lorenzo Da Ponte and presented by the ensemble of Manuel García, reached New York City in 1825 with performances of Rossini's *Il barbiere di Siviglia*, and a few months later, Mozart's *Don Giovanni* (Müller 1991; Dizikes 1993: 3–88). These and other masterworks of the European operatic repertoire began to serve as models for "opera" in the United States. However, such aspirations for American opera, written and produced by Americans and sung in English, did not enable nineteenth-century American composers to find an easy way to Americanize opera as a "grass-roots" genre. Many works, though staged, did not become part of the repertoire; others were not staged at all. Even composers who were otherwise successful struggled with opera, tried their hand, gave up after a failure, or did not write an opera at all.

"Germanic" musical life and musical thinking had an enormous impact on American musicians (Graziano 2006). Until World War I, studying in Germany or Austria was regarded as a must for most American musicians (Bomberger 1991; Betz 2000: 531–536), making in effect a pilgrimage to the cradles of classical music. Composers like Bach and Brahms, who did not compose operas, were regarded as part of the musical canon in the United States, while other "Germanic" composers of the canon, like Beethoven or Mendelssohn, were mostly received as composers of other genres, and were not as affiliated with theater. Therefore, both the influence of musical aesthetics cultivated in the German-speaking world and promoted in the United States by authors like John Sullivan Dwight, and the existence of role models have to be considered important factors for musical preferences: key to an understanding of the artistic paths that American composers chose.

The development of operatic life in the United States before the twentieth century has several strands: the import of the European repertoire, the setup of a network for opera in the emerging cultural life of the country, and the struggling for American "grand opera," in the sense of the English use of the term, meaning serious opera (Kirk 2001). In contrast to non-scenic music, opera for a long time was confronted by a strong moral resistance to the stage in general, especially in parts of the country with strong Puritan influence. As the Reverend Thomas E. Thomas made clear in 1866: "The vitality of the stage is but one form of the vitality of sin. The theatre is old but human depravity is older. [...] Theatrical amusements are but one manifestation of man's debasement in his apostacy [*sic*] of his maker" (Thomas 1866: 5). Nonetheless, the history of musical theater reaches back into the colonial era and is characterized by an enormous diversity of styles. At first, the word "opera" was used in a rather broad sense compared with the European understanding of the term. The ballad farce *Flora; or, Hob in the Well* by John Hippisley, performed in Charleston, South Carolina, in 1735, is counted, according to Preston, as the first opera "mounted in English-speaking America" (Preston 2002: 4), while James Ralph's *The Fashionable Lady* is considered the first opera written by an American, though it had its first performance in London in 1729 (McKay 1979: 360–367). To a huge extent, operatic life was based on reception: stage productions, mostly from the English ballad opera repertory and performed in English, were presented by itinerant ensembles, similar to the way that theater life existed in the British Isles, where traveling companies distributed the repertory from London throughout the country (Preston 2002: 4). All forms of musical theater were presented to audiences "from all parts of society," which expected theater mainly to be entertaining (Ahlquist 1997: xi). The strength of the resistance against the stage, particularly in New England, is documented by the "Act preventing Stage-Plays and other Theatrical Entertainments." This Act, prohibiting any theatrical performance, was passed by the Massachusetts legislature in 1750 (Massachusetts Bay 1878: III/24: 500). In 1778, a Resolution of the Continental Congress banned all activities that might have disturbed the revolutionary spirit, and suspended thus the development of theatrical life in general until after the revolution:

> *Resolved*, That any person holding an office under the United States, who shall act, promote, encourage or attend such plays, shall be deemed unworthy to hold such office, and shall be accordingly dismissed. [...] *Resolved*. That it be, and it is hereby, earnestly recommended to the several States to take the most effectual measures for the encouragement thereof, *and for the suppressing theatrical entertainment*, horse-racing, gaming, and such other diversions as are *productive of idleness, dissipation, and a general depravity of principles and manners*. (Ford 1908: 1001, 1018; emphasis original)

Theatrical activity soon boomed anew. In many places, especially in the fast growing cities on the East Coast, permanent theaters were established (Dizikes 1993: 58–60). French opera had been made popular in French-speaking New Orleans after 1792, when French troupes presented the contemporary opera repertoire. In 1825 the García troupe introduced Italian opera to New York (Müller 1991: 30–31). Now this was a significant change: highlights of the European repertoire, sung in a language incomprehensible to most parts of the audience, reached America, where they advanced to become models for "opera." Da Ponte soon started a subscription for a theater intended exclusively for Italian opera, which opened with Rossini's *La gazza ladra* on November 18, 1833 (Dizikes 1993: 75). That economic reasons caused the closing of the house in 1835—it finally burned down in 1839—reveals the dilemma of the enterprise. Although the repertoire was accepted as top-class, beyond any moral objection, the unintelligible language made the performances unsuitable for American audiences. While New York counted as a future "Paris of the New World" (Ahlquist 1997: 45), the networks for cultural activity generally—and opera specifically—still had to be built up. In contrast to European conventions, opera in the United States was a commercial event, open to whoever could afford to buy a ticket, but thus also dependent on its financial success. Entertainment was an eminent factor for success. Beyond that, a New York audience differed completely in class and education from a European public. Karin Ahlquist's description of the interior of the New York Park Theatre analyzes the plan of the house according to class and gender of the various groups of the audience and their usual seating, including the boxes frequented by prostitutes and their male clientele (Ahlquist 1997: 5–8).

The history of opera in New York did not end with this episode. With its many immigrant communities, which maintained their own orchestras and ethnic theaters, the city was a culturally bustling place, on its way to becoming a hub for opera (Koegel 2006).

Yet the setback had brought up a question that would become crucial for the development of the genre and the particular approach of American composers to it.

Boston

> Opera has been an exotic save in two cities, New York and New Orleans, the former having been the musical centre of the country in operatic matters from the very beginning. Boston [...] is provincial in the matter of grand opera. (Elson 1904: 361)

In contrast to New York and, of course, New Orleans, Boston's audiences held out against opera performed on stage for longer, though collections of the most popular songs and arias, often arranged for instruments, had been sold successfully in local bookstores during the colonial era (McKay 1985: 137–138). Although the colonial prohibition was revoked in 1792, and as a consequence two theaters were erected (Dizikes 1993: 150), the programs opened the field only "occasionally [for] an Opera" (McKay 1985: 141), due to the enduring anti-theater sentiments. Boston appeared to be "wholly given over to Handel, Haydn, and psalms" (Elson 1904: 99). Singing, emphasized as a New England custom, was cultivated in singing schools dedicated to sacred music, whereas the oratorio was fostered by the famous Handel and Haydn Society, founded in 1815. Yet, "oratorio" covered more than just one genre, as Frederic Ritter pointed out in 1883: "In the United States [...] the meaning of the word 'oratorio' was rather an ambiguous one: any concert by different composers was called an oratorio" (Ritter 1883: 113). Discussion and writing about music gained more and more importance and contributed to Boston's general claim of intellectual leadership, especially in comparison with New York (Broyles 1992: 13), which, by contrast, had more variety in styles and programs presented, as described in an 1862 issue of *Dwight's Musical Journal*:

> New York unfolds of course a richer programme. Her large German population, and abundant supply of good musicians, make more and larger undertakings in the higher field of music a necessity. Yet always until very lately, in Symphony, Oratorio and classical Quartet performances Boston has borne the palm. But New York has a permanent Orchestral Society, on a much ampler scale than ours [...] In New York, too, as we have seen by the excellent letters of our correspondent(s), they have Opera—and *German* Opera too—which looks like a settled thing, an institution, where such things as Mozart's *Seraglio* and *Zauberflöte*, Weber's *Freyschütz*, and many a good thing we only hear *about* in these parts [...]. (*DJM* 1862: 247)

In Boston, musical aesthetics were most prominently promulgated by John Sullivan Dwight, who demanded pure music (Saloman 1995: 61–62). By this he meant music without words, such as symphonic and chamber music, which became more and more established in Boston as the superior forms of instrumental music. Boston's often-described musical development "from psalmody to symphony" (Broyles 1992: 8) followed a switch in musical thinking, imbibing more and more a metaphysical approach toward instrumental music. This was similar to the Romantic aesthetics of the Beethoven and post-Beethoven era in the German-speaking countries, and subsequently eclipsed opera. Meanwhile, music education, another emerging Boston domain, confirmed values that attributed moral purposes to music—in contrast, for instance, to dance (Ritter 1883: 244–247). Lowell Mason, the proponent of musical instruction at public schools and "one of the most important and powerful men in American music history," focused on singing and instrumental music as the main subjects of musical pedagogy (Broyles 1990: 4). His own experiences of European musical life made him appreciate opera, although he ranked it decidedly lower than church and instrumental music: "The principal objections to the Opera in America do not exist to it as it is here [...] Indeed the only objection to it is the impurity, or immoral tendency of the text" (Broyles 1990: 74–75). Mason's travel journals reveal that the captivating performances which he attended in famous places like London, Berlin, Dresden, and Paris changed his attitude. Yet he still objected to the immorality of the plots—something that for a long time remained an obstacle to the approval of opera by Americans and which consequently stimulated the wish for specifically American opera, addressing appropriate American subjects (Broyles 1992: 304).

The second Boston Theater was built in 1854 in order to make cultural life more attractive for business travelers (Dizikes 1993: 165–166). It was intended that both spoken drama and opera should be staged here, the latter offered by touring ensembles. Performances included famous works, such as *Fidelio* in 1854, *Carmen* (1879), *Fra Diavolo* (1830), and, of course, Italian opera, now no longer presented merely in anglicized versions (Broyles 1992: 300). However, one of the highlights was the first American performance of what was going to become a landmark of English musical theater: *H.M.S. Pinafore* by Gilbert and Sullivan, staged in Boston in November 1878, just a couple of months after the London premiere.

Second New England School

Still in 1904, Louis Elson remarked in the *History of American Music* that "in the domain of opera America has as yet done but little" (Elson 1904: 233). Nineteenth-century composers like William H. Fry (1813–1864) in Philadelphia and George Bristow (1825–1898) in New York had eagerly ventured to bring out their own operas: Fry's *Leonora* was premiered in 1845 in Philadelphia, Bristow's *Rip Van Winkle* in 1855 in New York.

However, New England composers from Paine to Ives remained more hesitant. The so-called Second New England School encompassed composers who were New Englanders (Broyles 2004: 236–237) and, having been Boston-based at some point in their lives, were influenced by the prevailing mental climate and musical preferences of their surroundings. Musically they were prolific in symphony, chamber music, song, and, of course, sacred music. Several also tried their hands at stage works. Yet none of them managed to fill the gap and become *the* American opera composer.

Among those who never tried their hands at opera are Arthur Foote (1853–1937) and Edward MacDowell (1860–1908); the latter, in spite of being born in New York and having spent a great deal of his life there, is occasionally counted as part of the group. Foote, an organist, was open to many types of music. He launched a chamber music series, composed several well-received orchestral works, and even attended the first Bayreuth Festival in 1876, but as a composer, he remained distant from opera. The same is true for MacDowell, who composed neither an opera nor a symphony as he focused on a virtuoso career as a pianist-composer. His own instrumental music shows an inclination for literary stimuli and programmatic ideas, possibly due to the influence of the Liszt circle (Bomberger 1991: 199, 261).

John Knowles Paine (1839–1906), the doyen of the Second New England School, wrote various stage works, and also worked on an opera. After studies in Germany he became an organist and a theory teacher, and was finally appointed to Harvard University, where he became the first professor of music in 1875. Renowned for his two symphonies, his *Mass*, and the oratorio *St. Peter*, he served as a role model for younger American composers. With the incidental music for the Greek dramas *Oedipus tyrannus* (1881) and *The Birds* (1902), Paine's reputation was enhanced. This was possibly partly due to the literary rank that Greek drama had for the intellectual audiences of Cambridge and Boston. Likewise, the choice of a text by Milton for the cantata *The Nativity* op. 39 was positively reviewed: "In 'The Nativity' he [Paine] shows once more that the fine artistic instinct which enables him to draw musical inspiration from fine poetry without allowing the fancy of a poet to lure him away from the true domain of music [. . .]" (In *Boston Evening Transcript*, May 3, 1883: 1). By contrast, Paine's only grand opera, *Azara* (Schmidt 1980), on which he continued to work from 1883 until 1898, was only partly performed and never fully staged. It is based on a story set in medieval Provence, which Paine, on the basis of a French *chante-fable* from the thirteenth century, worked out for a libretto and finally had translated into German. Vocal scores were published with German and English texts in 1901, and the full score, with the English text, printed by Breitkopf & Härtel appeared in 1908, paid for by Paine's widow (Schmidt 1980: 213–214). The critics lauded the music for its "strong Wagnerian characteristics" (Schmidt 1980: 562–563). While instrumental and vocal excerpts of *Azara* were performed separately, the work as a whole was given in a concert version in Boston in 1907, one year after Paine's death. Plans for a performance of the work with English text at the Metropolitan Opera House in 1907 could not be realized because of a lack of singers who could have sung the English texts (Kirk 2001: 130).

While there is not much information about Paine's motivation for opera composition, the reasons that drove George Whitefield Chadwick (1854–1931) and Amy Beach (1867–1944) are well documented. Both were eager to compose an American opera and therefore searched for an appropriate and truly American subject. Beach had considered a topic like "Rip Van Winkle" for a possible opera, but it was not until 1932 that she finally composed a one-act opera, *Cabildo*, based on a story about Pierre Lafitte, a pirate who supported Andrew Jackson during the siege of New Orleans (Block 1998: 274–281). The topic is reflected by the integration of Creole tunes into the music. Because of the depression and the war, *Cabildo* could only be staged posthumously on February 27, 1945; it remains unpublished.

George Whitefield Chadwick

Chadwick had repeatedly picked up Americanisms on the level of both musical idiom and musical topics in his instrumental works. In 1878, while still a student, he had written an overture called "Rip Van Winkle" on the story by Washington Irving. Later, several of his symphonic and chamber music works, such as the *Symphonic Sketches* (1904) and the fourth string quartet (1896), were praised for their American sound (Betz 2000). Highly motivated to compose grand opera after the success of a couple of other stage works, including two operettas and a burlesque, he yearned "But oh for a good opera book. A book that will *act*—[...] with a real atmosphere and with real emotions—if possible with some amusing comedy and with some opportunity for dramatic climaxes. Who, Oh who will make this for me? And soon!" (Chadwick: May 1, 1911). Trained in Leipzig and Munich, Chadwick started as an organist; however, he decided to become a symphony composer, a dream that did come true (Betz 2005). This ambition had been nourished through his studies with Salomon Jadassohn and Carl Reinecke, both of whom had prepared him mentally for a future career in symphony, and maybe a performance at the Gewandhaus—but not for opera. Yet Chadwick attended all kinds of theater performances at Leipzig and later, in 1883 and in 1887, even traveled to Bayreuth. Whether on those rare occasions in Boston or New York, or on his trips through the United States and Europe, Chadwick, with a growing fondness for the genre, hardly missed any chance of seeing opera: "On Wednesday we had Cavalleria + Pagliacci with the great Caruso [...] it is mighty good fun" (Chadwick: March 4, 1905). The success of his oratorio *Judith*, premiered at the Worcester Festival in 1901, made Chadwick for a moment consider developing a scenic version of the work he himself had labeled a "lyric drama," an idea he soon gave up because of the hybrid character of such an arrangement: "This performance of Judith was an excellent opportunity for me to find out what sort of a piece it really is and whether I was justified in considering the possibility of a stage performance. After hearing it I came to the conclusion that no amount of excision would make the first act seem like anything but an oratorio. A modern one to be sure, and more or less dramatic, but still not with the footlight smell that everything for the theatre *must* have, whether the music is good or bad. The same is true of the last act [...]" (Chadwick: November 26, 1911).

The wish for American opera as an American artifact was in the air. In 1908 the Metropolitan Opera House announced a competition in an attempt to encourage composers to produce American opera (Betz 2002, 2003). The rules stipulated that the composer had to be American-born, the composition a grand opera, and the libretto in English. The prize was finally awarded to Horatio Parker (1863–1919) for his opera *Mona*, on the story of a British princess revolting against the Romans around 100 A.D. Chadwick, one of the jury members, recorded his impression of the compositions, which he found disappointing: "Today I finished my batch of operas for the Metropolitan competition including Parkers [*sic*] which of course I could not help recognizing. His is decidedly the best of the lot but suffers as do most of them from too many *words*, and too little *action*.... *After all these other fellows get through showing us how not to write operas I would like to try my hand*" (Chadwick: March 4, 1911; my emphasis). On March 18, 1910, *The Pipe of Desire* by Frederick Converse (1871–1940), like Parker a friend and former student of Chadwick's, had been performed as the first American opera at the Metropolitan Opera. Parker's *Mona*, which premiered on March 14, 1912, at the Met had four performances; his following opera, *Fairyland*, which premiered in Los Angeles on July 1, 1915, had six. Slightly worse was the fate of Converse's operas. *The Pipe of Desire* had only two performances (see Metropolitan Opera 1883–1966). Converse's *The Sacrifice* was premiered on March 3, 1911, at the Boston Opera House, but two further operas (*Beauty and the Beast* 1913, *The Immigrants* 1914) remained unperformed.

However, Chadwick judged *Mona* an unsatisfactory experience: "His piece is hardly an opera at all. It is an idyll [...]" (Chadwick: January 5, 1911). His frustration became the stimulus for outlining the scenario for an opera called *The Padrone*, which ultimately became a two-act work with an interlude (the first page of Chadwick's autograph manuscript is shown in Figure 28.1). Chadwick's libretto, on a subject of his own devising and finished by the playwright David Kilburn Stevens (1860–1946), dealt with the influx of Italian immigrants arriving in the United States, a very relevant issue around 1910. The subject was especially relevant to Boston, where more and more Italians settled in the North End, a topic of controversial discussion. The main theme of the plot was the encounter of Italians and Americans, two ethnic groups that Chadwick at first wanted to emphasize by the use of both the English and Italian languages—especially as this seemed to facilitate a production at the Met. On December 5, 1912, the by now all-English piano-vocal score was submitted to the Met, with the names of composer and librettist hidden by a pasting on the cover. When, in 1913, the score was returned from the Metropolitan Opera with the cursory remark that the opera was found unsuitable for a production, it became clear that Chadwick's project had failed. Apparently the rejection had much to do with the realism of the story. Like other operas, including famous verismo works like *Cavalleria rusticana* and *Pagliacci*, premiered in the United States in 1891 and 1893, *The Padrone* deals with everyday life. It openly displays the economic situation and a lack of education of disadvantaged Italians who, after their arrival in the United States, became dependent on both their already Americanized compatriots and the American officials, who allowed those *padroni* to boss around and exploit the newly arrived. The opera thus emphasized a weak spot in the current US immigration policy, which at that time, incited by Jacob A. Riis's "How the Other Half Lives" (1890), provoked the socio-criticism of "muckraker" journalists and authors. Such a topic evidently did not suit an opera house financed by wealthy box-holders who would find a confrontation with contemporary problems of their own country on stage scandalous

FIGURE 28.1 George Whitefield Chadwick, *The Padrone*: Opening page of autograph score. From the archives at New England Conservatory, Boston.

and, literally, out of place (Betz 2012). Chadwick never received any detailed explanation of what exactly made his opera unsuitable for a Metropolitan Opera production, for example, whether the language should have been more colloquial, whether the bilingual scheme should have been kept, whether the musical characterization of the ethnic groups by a tarantella and an American ditty should have been extended, or whether certain parts of the work should have been shortened or extended for a better effect on stage. Thus he could only rely on what his friend, the music critic Henry Krehbiel, reported to him and which Chadwick recorded in his *Memoirs*. Krehbiel alluded to the contemporary subject being the offensive part of the work:

> Gatti-Casazza disliked the book because it was a drama of life among the humble Italians, and probably too true to life, and that it had been played through by Morgenstern one of the accompanists who reported unfavorably on it. So there is the consideration that American composers get from the leading American opera house! Another cat in the meal is the fact that Victor Herbert has a new one-act opera [i.e. *Madeleine*, New York 1914] which he is pushing through Kahn. *The Padrone* is now in the hands of Dippel who will, I think, at least read it through. (Chadwick: first entry 1913).

Chadwick still finished the full orchestra score, but hardly ever mentioned *The Padrone* again. The opera remained unstaged during the composer's lifetime, the setback marking a decisive caesura in his career. He had intended to fill the gap with an opera that fulfilled all requirements of an American artifact and that might have had a chance to stand for a new type of operatic repertoire, had it been judged favorably.

Operatic Conditions Once More

The discrepancy between the career of this highly talented, renowned composer of orchestral and vocal music and his non-success in opera made Carl Engel speculate late in 1924 about what might have become of American opera if Chadwick had had a proper chance, summarizing thus: "Operatic conditions in America did not encourage Mr. Chadwick to develop the dramatic side of his musical gifts" (Engel 1924: 447). Chadwick, who of all Second New England School composers struggled the most to become an opera composer, failed—and for several reasons. He lacked both opera-friendly teachers and role models, and the inspiration and experience of a vigorous local operatic life and a theater-friendly ambience. More important, though integrated well into Boston's famous symphonic and choral networks, he lacked integration into an operatic network. The insurmountable hurdles with which composers like Chadwick or Paine were confronted were scrutinized by Oscar Sonneck in 1905: "The struggle against the apathy of the public, [...] against the commercial cowardice and avarice of the managers, seems hopeless" (Sonneck [1921] 1968: 92).

New York had become the American marketplace of opera and was famous for its performances and even premieres of Wagner, Verdi, and Puccini in casts that included the star singers and top conductors of that time. American opera in general, and a work like *The Padrone* in particular, would have been an experiment outside this canon and consequently an entrepreneurial risk. By contrast, Boston did not provide satisfactory "operatic conditions" (and, as of this writing, apparently still does not; see Guerrieri 2012). All attempts to implement a permanent and vibrant opera culture failed. Until the opening of the Boston Opera House in 1909 on Huntington Avenue, the second Boston Theater had served as a venue for operatic performances presented by various companies. Unfortunately, the new Opera House, intended for the newly founded Boston Opera Company as a resident company that planned to cooperate with the Metropolitan Opera, the Chicago, and the Philadelphia ensembles, had to close again after only six seasons; it was finally demolished in 1958. Meanwhile, Symphony Hall, which since 1900 had been in its new building a few blocks away from the Opera House, gradually became a temple of high-class orchestral music. For too long moral, aesthetic, and musical objections to opera had existed, just as the idea of instrumental music being the more valuable had dominated the musical understanding.

New England composers of the generations of Paine and Chadwick, even including a number of their students, did not have many chances to become successful opera composers unless they moved to New York in order to merge into that city's networks. In 1905 Oscar Sonneck noted:

> [...] today we are as far from American opera of artistic importance as we have ever been. Not that our composers lack the power to write dramatic music, but our operatic life has been trimmed into a hot-house product. The one Metropolitan Opera House of New York supplies the whole country with opera [...] Under these circumstances there is neither place nor time for the production of American operas, and our composers have almost stopped trying their hands at this sadly neglected branch. (Sonneck [1921]1968: 91–92)

On New England, he dryly remarked in his overview of the history of opera in the United States in 1915: "The people of New England received a taste of opera" (Sonneck [1915] 1963: 161). What would have been essential, beyond a mere taste, would have been a nutrient medium, deriving from a climate that was predisposed for the American variety of a European genre and thus for a new component of American musical and cultural identity.

See also: How Opera Traveled, The Operatic Canon, Patronage, Audiences

Notes

1. "Habe ich Ihnen nie von meinen schönen Prinzipien gesprochen [...]? Dazu gehört: keine Oper und keine Heirat mehr zu versuchen."
2. "Lieder, deren Poesie man, ohne die Worte zu kennen, verstehen würde."
3. "Was die *Instrumentalmusik* nicht kann, von dem darf nie gesagt werden, die *Musik* könne es; denn nur sie ist reine, absolute *Tonkunst*. Ob man nun die Vocal = oder die Instrumentalmusik an Werth und Wirkung vorziehen wolle [...] man wird stets einräumen müssen, dass der Begriff 'Tonkunst' in einem auf Textworte componirten Musikstück nicht rein aufgehe."
4. "Alle Tondichtung ist Menschenwerk [...] durchzogen von Elementen schnellerer oder langsamerer Sterblichkeit. Unter den großen Musikformen ist wieder die Oper die zusammengesetzteste, conventionellste und daher vergänglichste."
5. "Ich warte mit Schmerzen auf einen guten neuen OpernText, denn wenn ich keine Oper unter den Fäusten habe ist mir nicht wohl."
6. "Der Unterzeichnete wünscht so bald als möglich in den Besitz eines guten Opern-Textes zu kommen, den er in Musik setzen und anständig honoriren will."

Bibliography

Ahlquist, Karin. 1997. *Democracy at the Opera: Music, Theater and Culture in New York City 1815–1860*. Urbana: University of Illinois Press.

Betz, Marianne. 2012. "'But oh for a good opera book!' George Whitefield Chadwicks (1854–1931) Oper 'The Padrone.'" In *Musik und kulturelle Identität*. 3 vols., edited by Detlef Altenburg and Rainer Bayreuther. Bericht über den XIII. Internationalen Kongress der Gesellschaft für Musikforschung Weimar 2004, II: 506–515. Kassel: Bärenreiter.

——. 2005. "Zwischen Sinfonie und Orgel. Der Komponist und Kirchenmusiker George Whitefield Chadwick." *Musik und Kirche* 75/1: 34–39.

——. 2003. "Verismo all'americana: Auf der Suche nach einer amerikanischen Oper." *Zibaldone. Zeitschrift für italienische Kultur der Gegenwart* 35: 32–49.

——. 2002. "American Women as Opera Figures: Puccini's 'Fanciulla del West' versus Chadwick's Marietta in 'The Padrone'." *Journal of the American Music Research Center, University of Colorado at Boulder* 12: 1–9.

——. 2000. "Amerikanische Studierende am Leipziger Konservatorium. Zum Beispiel George W. Chadwick." In *Musikkonzepte—Konzepte der Musikwissenschaft*. 2 vols., edited by Kathrin Eberl and Wolfgang Ruf. Kongressbericht der Gesellschaft für Musikforschung Halle 1998, II: 531–536. Kassel: Bärenreiter.

Billington, Steven M. 1987. "Robert Schumann's '*Genoveva*': A Source Study." PhD diss., New York University.

Block, Adrienne Fried. 1998. *Amy Beach: Passionate Victorian*. New York: Oxford University Press.

Böhme, Erdmann W. [1931] 1969. *Die frühdeutsche Oper in Thüringen*. Reprint. Giebing: Emil Katzbichler.

Bomberger, E. Douglas. 1991. "The German Musical Training of American Students 1850–1900." PhD diss., University of Maryland.

Borroff, Edith. 1992. *American Operas. A Checklist*. Warren, MI: Harmonie Park Press.

Broyles, Michael. 2004: "Art Music from 1860 to 1920." In *The Cambridge History of American Music*, edited by David Nicholls, 214–254. Cambridge: Cambridge University Press.

——. 1992. *Music of the Highest Class: Elitism and Populism in Antebellum Boston*. New Haven: Yale University Press.

——, ed. 1990. *A Yankee Musician in Europe: The 1837 Journals of Lowell Mason*. Ann Arbor: UMI Research Press.

Chadwick, George W. Memoirs [unpublished]. Archives of the New England Conservatory of Music, Boston.

Dahlhaus, Carl. 1989. "Metaphysik der Instrumentalmusik." In *Die Musik des 19. Jahrhunderts*. Neues Handbuch der Musikwissenschaft 6: 73–78. Laaber: Laaber.

Dizikes, John. 1993. *Opera in America: A Cultural History*. New Haven: Yale University Press.

DJM. 1862. "Boston, November 1, 1862: What's for the Winter?" *Dwight's Journal of Music* 22/5 (November 1): 246–247.

Elson, Louis. 1904. *The History of American Music*. London: Macmillan.

Engel, Carl. 1924. "George W. Chadwick." *Musical Quarterly* 10/3: 438–457.

Ford, Worthington Ch., ed. 1908. *A Century of Lawmaking for a New Nation: U.S. Congressional Documents and Debates, 1774–1875. Journals of the Continental Congress*, Volume 12, Sept. 2–Dec. 31, 1778. Washington, DC: Government Printing Office.

Forkel, Johann N. [1802] 1982. *Über Johann Sebastian Bachs Leben, Kunst und Kunstwerke*. Reprint. Berlin: Henschelverlag.

Freeman, Charles. 1999. "American Realism and Progressivism in Chadwick's *The Padrone* and Converse's *The Immigrants*." PhD diss., Florida State University.

Graziano, John, ed. 2006. *European Music and Musicians in New York City 1840–1900*. Rochester, NY: University of Rochester Press.

Guerrieri, Matthew. 2012. "Why Boston Is 'Not an Opera Town'." *The Boston Globe* (January 15). Online. Available: http://articles.boston.com/2012-01-15/ideas/30626744_1_opera-house-boston-lyric-opera-metropolitan-opera#.TyLoB45jd98 (accessed August 16, 2012).

Hanslick, Eduard. 1886. *Concerte, Componisten und Virtuosen der letzten fünfzehn Jahre. 1870–1885*. Berlin: Allgemeiner Verein für Deutsche Literatur.

——. 1880. "Robert Schumann als Operncomponist—*Genovefa*." In *Die moderne Oper: Kritiken und Studien*. Berlin: A. Hofmann.

——. 1875. *Die moderne Oper: Kritiken und Studien*. Berlin: A. Hofmann.

——. 1854. *Vom Musikalisch-Schönen*. Leipzig: R. Weigel.

Hess, Carol. 1998. "'Als wahres volles Menschenbild': Brahms's *Rinaldo* and Autobiographical Allusion." *Brahms Studies* 2, edited by David Brodbeck, 63–89. Lincoln: University of Nebraska Press.

Horowitz, Joseph. 2005. *Classical Music in America: A History of Its Rise and Fall*. New York: W. W. Norton.

Huschke, Wolfram. 1998. "Weimar." In *Die Musik in Geschichte und Gegenwart*, edited by Ludwig Finscher. Sachteil 9, 1912–1930. Kassel: Bärenreiter.

Johnson, Claudia D. 2008. *Church and Stage: The Theatre as Target of Religious Condemnation in Nineteenth Century America*. Jefferson, NC: McFarland.

Johnson, H. Earle. 1979. *First Performances in America. To 1900. Works with Orchestra*. Detroit: College Music Society.

——. 1943. *Musical Interludes in Boston. 1795–1830*. New York: Columbia University Press.

Kalbeck, Max. 1915. *Johannes Brahms: Briefe an Joseph Viktor Widmann, Ellen und Ferdinand Vetter, Adolf Schubring*. Briefwechsel VIII. Berlin: Verlag der deutschen Brahmsgesellschaft.

Kirk, Elise K. 2001. *American Opera*. Urbana: University of Illinois Press.

Koch, Herbert. 1968. "Johann Nikolaus, der 'Jenaer' Bach." *Die Musikforschung* 21: 290–304.

Koegel, John. 2006. "The Development of the German American Musical Stage in New York City, 1840–1890." In Graziano 2006, 149–181.

Marvin, Roberta Montemorra. 2006. "Burlesques, Barriers, Borders, and Boundaries." In *Operatic Migrations*, edited by Roberta Montemorra Marvin and Downing A. Thomas, 205–217. Aldershot, UK: Ashgate.

Massachusetts Bay. 1878. *The Acts and Resolves, Public and Private, of the Province of the Massachusetts Bay*. Vol 3. Boston: Albert and Wright 1878, Acts of 1750.

Mattfeld, Julius. [1927] 1976. *A Hundred Years of Grand Opera in New York*. Reprint, New York: AMS Press.

——. 1963. *A Handbook of American Operatic Premieres 1731–1962*. Detroit Studies in Music Bibliography 5. Detroit: Information Service.

McKay, David. 1985. "Opera in Colonial Boston." *American Music* 3/2: 133–142.

——. 1979. "The Fashionable Lady." *Musical Quarterly* 65/3: 360–367.

Metropolitan Opera. 1883–1966. Metropolitan Opera Company, 1883–1966: A Collection of Newspaper Clippings, New York Public Library, call n.* ZB 769.

Müller, Ulrich. 1991. "Don Giovanni in New York, oder: Lorenzo Da Pontes 'Musikalische Bienen'." In *Don Giovanni in New York*, edited by Ulrich Müller and Oswald Panagl, 27–41. Anif/Salzburg: Verlag Müller-Speiser.

Neumann, Werner, and Schulze Hans-Joachim, eds. 1963. *Schriftstücke von der Hand Johann Sebastian Bachs*. Bach-Dokumente I (supplement to the *Neue Bach-Ausgabe*). Kassel: Bärenreiter.

Preston, Katherine. 2002. "American Musical Theatre before the Twentieth Century." In *The Cambridge Companion to the Musical*, edited by William A. Everett and Paul R. Laird, 4–28. Cambridge: Cambridge University Press.

Redepenning, Dorothea, and Britta Schilling, eds. 1989. *Franz Liszt, Dramaturgische Blätter*. Sämtliche Schriften 5. Wiesbaden: Breitkopf & Härtel.

Reiber, Joachim. 2001. "Suche, Versuche, Versuchungen: Brahms und die Oper." In *Internationaler Brahms-Kongress Gmunden 1997. Kongressbericht*, edited by Ingrid Fuchs, 13–30. Tutzing: Schneider.

Ritter, Frederic L. 1883. *Music in America*. New York: Charles Scribner's Sons.

Saloman, Ora F. 1995. *Beethoven's Symphonies and J. S. Dwight: The Birth of American Music Criticism*. Boston: Northeastern University Press.

Schmidt, John C. 1980. *The Life and Works of John Knowles Paine*. Studies in Musicology 34. Ann Arbor: UMI Research Press.

Schrickel, Leonhard. 1928. *Geschichte des Weimarer Theaters von seinen Anfängen bis heute*. Weimar: Pauses-Verlag.

Schröder, Bernhard. 1892. *Otto Nicolais Tagebücher nebst Biographischen Ergänzungen*. Leipzig: Breitkopf und Härtel.

Sonneck, Oscar. [1921] 1968. *Miscellaneous Studies in the History of Music*. Reprint. New York: DaCapo Press.

——. [1915] 1963. *Early Opera in America*. Reprint. New York: Benjamin Blom.

Schumann, Robert. 1853. "Neue Bahnen." *Neue Zeitschrift für Musik* 39/18 (October 28): 185–186.

Szelényi, Lászlo. 1977. "Liszts Opernpläne. Ein wenig bekanntes Kapitel aus dem Schaffen des Komponisten." In *Liszt Studien* 1. Kongress-Bericht Eisenstadt 1975, edited by Wolfgang Suppan, 215–224. Graz: Akademische Verlagsanstalt.

Thomas, Thomas E. 1866. *The Theatre: A Sermon Delivered in the First Presbyterian Church, Dayton, Ohio, Dec. 24, 1865*. Dayton, OH: Payne and Holden.

Torkewitz, Dieter. 1995. "Brahms' *Rinaldo*." In *Torquato Tasso in Deutschland: Seine Wirkung in Literatur, Kunst und Musik seit der Mitte des 18. Jahrhunderts*, edited by Achim Aurnhammer, 709–719. Berlin/New York: Walter de Gruyter.

Veit, Joachim. 2001. *Carl Maria von Weber: ... wenn ich keine Oper unter den Fäusten habe ist mir nicht wohl. Eine Dokumentation zum Opernschaffen. Ausstellung der Staatsbibliothek zu Berlin—Preußischer Kulturbesitz*. Wiesbaden: Reichert.

Warrack, John. 2001. *German Opera: From the Beginnings to Wagner*. Cambridge: Cambridge University Press.

Weber, Carl Maria von. 1813. "Aufforderung." *Allgemeine musikalische Zeitung* 15 (March 12): 24.

——. [1811] 2003. Letter of June 27, 1811, to Johann Gänsbacher. *Digitale Gesamtausgabe (WeGA). Korrespondenz* Online. Available: http://www.weber-gesamtausgabe.de/de/A002068/Korrespondenz/A040408 (accessed August 16, 2012).

Wolff, Christoph. 1988. "Anmerkungen zu Bach und 'Cleofide' (Dresden 1731)." In *Johann Sebastian Bachs Spätwerk und dessen Umfeld. Bericht über das wissenschaftliche Symposion anläßlich des 61. Bachfestes der Neuen Bachgesellschaft Duisburg 1986*, edited by Christoph Wolff, 167–169. Kassel: Bärenreiter.

CHAPTER 29

PATRONAGE

VALERIA DE LUCCA

At the time of its origins in the courts of late Renaissance Italy, opera was the quintessential "princely entertainment," the highest expression of the cultural finesse and social status of the member of the aristocracy who sponsored its production—the patron (Annibaldi 2001: 31–32). Only the patron's high standing and wealth could explain the splendor of sets, machines, and costumes, the extraordinary talent of the singers, the beauty of music and poetry. The subject matter of the opera—heroic adventures, royal passions, and mythological loves and transformations—was most explicitly the embodiment of the patron's nobility, a manifestation of his or her cultural sensibility, and often a vehicle for key social and political messages. Offstage elements—the selected and educated audience, the theatrical space, the commemorative printed libretto—all contributed to glorify the image of the patron, whose wealth and social status made the performance possible.

Four centuries into the history of opera, traces of those opulent and elitist beginnings are still evident in opera houses across the world. Compared to ballet, spoken drama, and instrumental music, opera continues to be not only the most expensive of the performing arts to produce, but also the genre that has drawn the smallest audiences, a wealthy and educated elite that accounts for only a very small percentage of the population that attends concerts and other cultural events (Towse 2003: 342; Bereson 2002: 2–3). Opera's charms and its high costs are embedded in its complex combination of music, poetry, scenery, costumes, machines, special effects, large cast, orchestra, and often very costly principal singers. But most important, throughout the centuries opera has remained a symbol of the rulers and the wealthy, who have supported it since its inception. The history of opera is thus inextricably intertwined with the history of its patrons, who not only sustained it financially, but also shaped its form and content in profound and persistent ways.

Patrons, Entrepreneurs, or Philanthropists?

But who is an opera "patron," and how can we define opera "patronage"? The terms defy a univocal definition since their meaning changes not only with time and place, but also with disciplinary perspective. According to the *Oxford English Dictionary* (*OED* 1989), the term "patron" (from Latin *patronus* [protector of clients, defender], from *pater, patr* [father]) has a double meaning, "superior" but also "protector." The word "patronage" thus refers to "the action of a patron giving influential support, favor, encouragement, or countenance to a person, institution, work, art, etc. Originally implying the action of a superior" (*OED* 1989). In other languages, the corresponding terms have a different root and refer specifically to the arts. To mention a few examples, in Italian, French, Spanish, and German, the terms *mecenatismo, mécénat, mecenazgo*, and *Mäzen* all derive from the name of Gaius Cilnius Maecenas (ca. 70 B.C.–8 B.C.), who generously supported artists and intellectuals at the time of Emperor Augustus, most notably Virgil and Horace. In these languages the term loses the intrinsic connotation of "superiority" and is often used to indicate the generous and enlightened support of the arts for the pure benefit of the artists and of the community. The question is not insignificant, since, as we shall see, the social and economic superiority of the "patron" is in fact what has come to define "patronage" in most recent opera scholarship.

Indeed, a patron is first of all someone who offers support to artists and to the production of a work, from its composition to its performance, not only in the form of material goods and funding, but also of security and prestige. The past four decades have seen an increase in the number of studies devoted to the social and political implications of opera production and management, underlying a shift in scholars' attention from what Annibaldi has defined as an "idealistic and romantic vision of patronage [...] in which the financial support lavished on an artist is fundamentally a tribute to his genius" to an "anthropological perspective [...] according to which musical patronage is essentially the production and management of sound symbols of a group or a class"[1] (Annibaldi 1993: 14). The result of this shift in musicological studies is that "patronage" has become a broad field of inquiry concerned primarily with the role that opera played in diverse social, political, and cultural milieux (see, for example, *New Grove Opera*, which lacks an entry on "patronage" but discusses it within the entry "Sociology of Opera" [see Rosselli 1992b]). In other words, while patrons' financial support to artists remains a central concern for any investigation on patronage (and often serves as the primary and ultimate proof of a patronage relationship), the ways in which patrons' support shaped operatic production, influencing its contents, forms, performance, and reception histories, and the diverse kinds of financial and managerial support that opera has received throughout its history and across the Western world have taken center stage.

Even within these two more circumscribed areas, defining "patronage" is not always a straightforward endeavor. If we accept the definition of "patron" as the individual who offers financial and artistic support to the production of an opera (in the form of the individuals behind it), from composition to performance, thus influencing the genre to fit his or her tastes and sociopolitical needs, we must face the fact that in some contexts this "individual" might be difficult to identify. Much work has been done to read opera production under rulers such as Pope Urban VIII (Murata 1981; Hammond 1994), Louis XIV (Isherwood 1973; Downing 2002: 53–99; Cowart 2008), King Ludwig of Bavaria (Eger 1992), and the Austrian Empress Marie Therese (Rice 2003), to mention a few enthusiastic supporters of the genre, as a manifestation of their personal and political visions. As opera became a business, however, its production grew into a more complex web of social relationships, with theater owners who rented their space to an impresario to make a profit, and most important, aristocrats and wealthy individuals who funded opera production and supported impresarios, composers, poets, singers, and musicians. Thus, in the commercial theaters the role of the "patron" seems to be taken over by many agents, including the paying audiences that ultimately determined the success or failure of an opera season (Glixon and Glixon 2006: 305–313; Feldman 2011: 354; Cowart 2008: xxii, 112–113, and passim; Johnson 1995; Gerhard 1998). The question becomes even more complex if we consider that the term "patron" is still applied today to those wealthy individuals who offer financial and organizational support to a specific opera production or steady contributions and endowments to not-for-profit institutions, opera houses, and festivals. Often referred to as philanthropists and benefactors, modern-day patrons supported the production of opera during most of the last century (Locke 1993, 1997) and their contributions, both financial and managerial, are still essential to its production today (Schanke 2007), calling into question the possibility of opera's survival as an independent and sustainable business model.

In the remaining sections of this chapter I will explore the double nature of the patronage of opera—as a way to construct the public identity of a patron, but also as a form of support to the production of opera. I will use examples from seventeenth-century Italy to discuss how early patrons established fundamental practices at court and in the public theaters that survive to this day: how patrons engaged with composers, singers, librettists, and impresarios, managed their finances, and most of all used opera to further their personal ambitions and define themselves for posterity.

Opera and the Construction of the Patron

The ways in which opera represents the social status, cultural, political, and social interests of the patron can best be observed in the courts of early modern Europe (Annibaldi 1998: 173–174). In these sociopolitical microcosms, rulers and wealthy aristocrats surrounded themselves with scientists, scholars, poets, and artists whose scientific discoveries, literary achievements, and artistic production celebrated the family name and often acquired a profoundly political relevance. In this context, opera was an essential element of diplomacy, image-building, and public celebration, exemplifying the complexity and multiplicity of aims that patronage could attain. It is no coincidence that at court the performance of an opera often marked the climax of public ceremonies such as weddings, military victories, or diplomatic visits. Indeed, Jacopo Peri, Giulio Caccini, and Ottavio Rinuccini's *Euridice*, the first opera of which a score has survived to this day in its entirety, was performed in Florence in 1600 to celebrate the wedding of Maria de' Medici to Henri IV of France. As such, opera's musical and verbal contents had to be carefully constructed, often resulting in strict control or even censorship, and its performance painstakingly planned so as to achieve the intended goal, which was ultimately to legitimize the power of the ruler.

This was particularly crucial when the ruler was a woman, since in male-dominated societies, such as the Italian courts of the early modern period, women were rarely, if ever, allowed to govern. During its illustrious and long history, for example, the Medici court in Florence was only once ruled by women, between 1621 and 1628, when the death of Grand Duke Cosimo II de' Medici left his wife, Archduchess Maria Magdalena of Austria, and mother, Christine of Lorraine, in charge of governing Tuscany until his son came of age. The ways in which the two regents of Florence used patronage of the arts, particularly of opera and musical theater, is exemplary of the political, social, and diplomatic tensions that could be articulated in operas of the time, reminding us that the genre was far from being considered mere "court entertainment." As rulers of one of the most powerful and influential courts in Europe, Maria Magdalena and Christine had to construct an official image that would legitimize their regency not only in the eyes of their court and of the Florentines, but also in those of international allies and opponents. But most important, as Kelley Harness (2006) and Suzanne Cusick (2009) have amply demonstrated, this process of image-making through their patronage of the arts helped them legitimize their gender, something that male rulers were not required to do. Women in early modern Italy could become rulers only under extraordinary circumstances, as in this case the premature death of a male relative. Since patronage of the arts was one of the activities that noblewomen were allowed to cultivate, it often functioned as a powerful means of self-identification by allowing them to respond to the limitations imposed by a patriarchal society (Reiss and Wilkins 2001: 1–17, 37–50; De Lucca 2011b: 382). Artists were required to participate actively in the subtle art of constructing the image of their patron by the skillful use of their talents. As Harness points out, "rulers were active, although not sole authors of their self-fashioning" and the court itself enjoyed the reflected light emanating from the image of a powerful patron and of stable rule (Harness 2006: 3). This reminds us that in this respect, patronage can be better understood as an exchange between patrons and artists: patrons offered artists financial support and powerful protection, while artists contributed to the fabrication of the patrons' public image. Thus, "constructing the patron" in the tightly knit society of the early modern European courts was the result of the actions of multiple parties, a collective enterprise whose positive effects could benefit both patron and artist.

The two essential ingredients for the manufacture of the public *persona* of the patron were the commission of a new work and its production. While in some cases it is difficult to assess the extent to which patrons and artists collaborated and patrons directly influenced artistic production, there are instances in which documentary evidence can help us identify their respective contributions. Archduchess Maria Magdalena, who was the main agent behind the commission and production of operas and musical theatrical works staged during the regency, carefully chose the subjects of these spectacles, supervised the rehearsals, and in some cases even cast the performers. On many occasions she worked together with the musicians and poets in her service, whereas at other times she suggested the literary source herself. Joining a long tradition of women rulers who had to portray themselves as chaste, strong, emotionally stable, and capable of controlling political power, Maria Magdalena selected themes and images that would reinforce and validate her strength as a ruler. For example, the frescoes, paintings, and musico-dramatic entertainments she commissioned boasted a number of virgin martyrs and biblical women, including Saint Ursula (Andrea Salvadori and Marco da Gagliano's *La regina Sant'Orsola*) and Judith (Salvadori and Gagliano's *La Giuditta*), women chosen by God to save their people and defeat tyranny and oppression and who displayed the virtues and strengths of the regents' desired public image (Harness 2006: 79–99, 113–140). Epic-chivalric tales could also convey the required message: the Christian virgin sorceress Melissa saves Ruggiero from the evil enchantress Alcina in *La liberazione di Ruggiero dall'isola d'Alcina* (libretto by Saracinelli and music by Francesca Caccini) (Harness 2006: 152–162), whereas through the mythological tale of *La Flora* (libretto by Salvadori, music by Gagliano and Peri), in which Venus restores Cupid's powers to unite Flora and Zephyr, the regents celebrated the wedding of Maria Magdalena's daughter Margherita to Odoardo Farnese of Parma, while at the same time ratifying the transfer of power to the new Grand Duke Ferdinando II and marking the end of the regency (Harness 2006: 165–195).

The next step was the rendition of the subject matter in musical and literary forms that would convey the intended messages. Indeed, one could argue that the most important decision was the choice of composer and librettist, whose music and text had to embody the sense of control, power, strength, and female virtue that the regents required for their self-fashioning agenda (Harness 2006: 71, 83–88). The task, however, was more complicated, as musical theatrical entertainments could bear more than one message. So, for example, the well-known episode from Ariosto's *Orlando furioso*, in which the sorceress Melissa has to free Ruggiero from the enchantress Alcina, becomes both an opportunity to display the virtues of Archduchess Maria Magdalena while communicating the regents' desire to arrange a marriage between the guest for whom *La liberazione* was performed, Prince Wladyslaw of Poland, and Maria Magdalena's daughter. In order to achieve the desired results, the well-known literary source was manipulated by Saracinelli and Caccini to accommodate scenes that were considered essential to the regents' messages and borrowed from another very popular literary poem at the time, Tasso's *Gerusalemme liberata*, while the music was carefully crafted to sharpen the contrast between the irrational and overly expressive Alcina and the controlled Melissa (Harness 2006: 152–162). According to Cusick, Caccini's portrayal of Alcina's "proliferating speech and explosive heat" was meant to be a clear sign of excessive sexual behavior, a female attribute that the regents firmly refused in their self-fashioning strategy. Melissa's musical and poetic language, on the contrary, deftly articulated on stage the anxieties surrounding the figure of Archduchess Magdalena's "mannish, foreign ways." The sorceress seemed "to exercise princely control over the contradictions of gender and ethnicity within her own persona," a clear indication "that the virago archduchess whose power she so obviously represented could do the same" (Cusick 2009: 208–209).

Finally, the performance of the work was as important as the work itself in conveying the messages of power, grandeur, control, and ability to rule: the Archduchess personally supervised the recruiting of singers and musicians, examined the set designs before the performance, and had a say even on the number of horses to be employed in the ballet that concluded *La liberazione di Ruggiero* (Harness 2006: 71, 152). Despite their use of musico-dramatic works to convey a legitimized image of themselves to their visitors and guests, it is not surprising that the regents were indeed the principal audience of the performances: the theatrical space was built so as to offer the rulers the optimal perspective and ultimate enjoyment of the performance; at the same time, their central position in the theater made them one of the main features of the spectacle itself (Harness 2006: 13–14).

Negotiating Space

Maria Magdalena and Christine's effective strategies of patronage of the arts, and particularly of dramatic music, presuppose that they paid the exorbitant bills to produce and stage the operas and musico-dramatic spectacles performed during the regency. In so doing, they were dedicatees, principal audience, and sole financial supporters of the works they had helped to create. Not surprisingly, then, the operas produced at court during their regency embodied their tastes and sociopolitical agenda. However, as is well known, in 1637 the first public opera theater opened to a paying audience in Venice, and once opera became a profitable enterprise, priorities and aims changed rapidly and radically for its producers: Who was the intended audience of a performance now? Whose social and political vision had to be embedded into the work? What determined the success of an opera production? And most important, who paid the bills? To be sure, opera's move from the court to the open market required that the producers—financial investors and impresarios—also satisfied the needs of a new fundamental agent: a paying audience that consisted of a varied group of differently wealthy individuals; inevitably, in the context of commercial opera, the term "patronage" acquires a completely new meaning.

Bianconi and Walker's seminal study on the "production, consumption and political function of seventeenth-century opera" (Bianconi and Walker 1984 [paper first presented at the twelfth meeting of the International Musicological Society in 1977]) was among the first to address the question of the economic aspects of the management of both court and commercial opera theaters. Their thorough examination of three forms of support of opera in seventeenth-century Italy—the court system of Rome, the commercial theater of Venice, and the institutional support of the city in Reggio Emilia—paved the way for a number of studies on the economic and social mechanisms of opera production. This in turn raises the question of the "patronage" of opera in systems other than the court. Indeed, the coexistence of court and commercial systems, which characterized most of the history of opera during the *ancien régime*, meant that the aristocracy had to take over a new role to exert control over, and possibly gain a profit from, opera production.

Seventeenth-century Venice and its public theaters are emblematic of the new dynamics behind the production of commercial opera and of the complexity of webs of social relationships in a context in which theater owners, impresarios, and wealthy opera lovers all contributed to stage a spectacle that would appeal to a broader audience than that which attended operas at court (Glixon and Glixon 2006). The well-documented case of the Grimani family, Venetian aristocrats turned businessmen, who at different times over the centuries owned four theaters in Venice, offers an example of the most successful of Venetian aristocratic entrepreneurships related to opera. Most theaters in Venice, or at least the most successful enterprises, were built or owned by members of the aristocracy and, as at court, the splendor of the venue was identified with the nobility of the owner. In most cases, the theater was managed by an impresario, who paid rent to the owners of the theater and who invested capital in the enterprise. Beginning in 1639, the Grimani family built theaters *ad hoc* for the performance of opera. The rent the impresario paid to the owner was the reason that the noble owner of the theater was usually the only one to gain a profit from the operation. Once the impresario had paid his rent, he could enjoy a reasonable amount of freedom in matters that concerned the production of opera, including the recruiting and casting of singers and the choice of repertory. There were, of course, exceptions, and on several occasions the Grimani intervened on matters of recruiting and choices of repertory, even exerting some degree of control over the subject matter of the libretti produced in their theaters (Calcagno 2006). As at court, theater owners could also be the dedicatees of operas and had the power to influence the impresario's decisions.

The impresario was the real "risk-taker." Since the impresario's profit depended mostly on the sale of tickets, the rent of boxes and the sale of seats, the choice of the opera, and the recruiting of good singers were matters of preeminent importance: the success of the opera production was crucial for a return of the capital invested. For this reason, unlike at court, opera in Venice had to please not only the owners of the theater, or the principal financial investors, but also a large paying audience with diverse social and cultural backgrounds. Indeed, in Glixon and Glixon's view, the general audience and the impresario acquire a more central role than suggested by Bianconi and Walker (1984), both for their financial contribution to the operatic production and the social and artistic functions they fulfilled (Glixon and Glixon 2006: 17–33, 315–322). By reassessing the role that audience and impresarios played in the Venetian operatic world, they conclude that all the parties involved—"theater owner, the boxholder, the impresario, the investors and lenders, the dedicatee of the libretto, and the ticket-buying audience"—expand the definition of patronage *tout court* in the specific context of commercial opera in Venice. The city of Venice itself might be viewed, they argue, as the real patron of opera in the *Serenissima* (Glixon and Glixon 2006: 322).

The involvement of noble entrepreneurs in the activities of the Venetian theaters was not, however, limited to the wealthy residents of the lagoon who invested capital in the venture and expected a financial return. The success of commercial theaters attracted the attention of numerous aristocrats from courts and cities outside Venice who were eager to exert some control over the newly born system. Unlike most courts in Europe, Venetian theaters were not self-contained and self-sufficient worlds: they needed singers, stage designers, dancers, composers, and poets, the most renowned of whom were still, at this time, members of the households of rulers and nobles around Europe. Antonio Cesti, who composed some of the most successful operas of the seventeenth century, was first employed by the Archduke Ferdinand Karl in Innsbruck and later by the Emperor in Vienna, even while accepting commissions from the Venetian commercial theaters (Schmidt 1978); Francesco Cavalli, one of the most successful and prolific composers of Venetian operas, maintained his employment with the Cappella di San Marco until his death, first as organist and later as *maestro di cappella*. In quite the same way, some of the most sought-after singers of the time worked for the Medici family (Mamone 2003), the Duke of Savoy (Rosselli 1992a; Viale Ferrero 1976), the Bentivoglio family from Ferrara (Fabris 1999; Monaldini 2001), the Colonna of Rome (De Lucca 2009: chapter 2), and the Dukes of Mantua (Glixon and Glixon 2006). Competition and tensions between the two worlds of court and public theater were thus not unusual, especially when it came to controlling the movements of well-known and talented singers from the court (or in some cases the church) to the public stage. In 1667 the Duke of Savoy notoriously threatened one of his singers, castrato Giovanni Antonio Cavagna (at the time employed in Venice), with "the effects of our rightful indignation" if he should desert him to accept the employment of another patron (Viale Ferrero 1976: 271–294).

Other aristocrats were more collaborative. During the 1660s, for example, Lorenzo Onofrio Colonna and his wife Maria Mancini, who belonged to one of the most illustrious families in Rome, became very influential supporters of impresario Marco Faustini of the Venetian Teatro SS. Giovanni e Paolo. The Colonna were arguably some of the most important patrons of opera in Rome during the 1660s and 1670s. They supported composers of the caliber of Antonio Cesti, Alessandro Stradella, and Alessandro Scarlatti and poets including Nicolò Minato and Giovanni Filippo Apolloni; they commissioned new works and produced an astounding number of operas in their Roman palaces; they employed some of the most renowned singers, including sopranos Antonia Coresi and Giulia Masotti and castrato Giuseppe Fede; and they assembled one of the most extraordinary collections of opera scores and librettos of the time. Unlike other Roman aristocrats with a passion for opera, the Colonna's patronage reached beyond Rome, particularly during the early 1660s when, as Maria Mancini records in her autobiography, "Pope Alexander, because of an aversion he had towards all divertissements, had banned even the plays"[2] (Mancini [1677] 1998: 49). Thus, probably motivated by both the great fame of the Venetian operatic stages and the austere policy of the church toward theatrical entertainments in Rome, the couple began to spend long periods of time on the lagoon, where they became deeply involved with the production of opera during three carnival seasons between 1663 and 1667. The couple's interaction with impresario Marco Faustini of the Teatro SS. Giovanni e Paolo during these years exemplifies the diverse functions that aristocratic patrons could have in the context of commercial enterprises, revealing that the boundaries between the worlds of court and commercial opera were, and indeed remained for many years to come, extraordinarily fluid.

While some wealthy individuals invested financial capital in the theatrical enterprise, functioning as what Glixon and Glixon define as the "investors," the Colonna acted mostly as "protectors": with no legal or financial obligations to the theater, they used their name, prestige, social status, and knowledge of the operatic world to maximize the resources of the theater's owners and impresario (Glixon and Glixon 2006: 4). Indeed, the Colonna helped Marco Faustini with two crucial aspects of the production: recruiting the best singers available and choosing the repertory. In so doing, their contribution went arguably beyond a financial investment, since it guaranteed the success of three opera seasons.

Procuring good singers had become as crucial a factor for the success of the opera season as it was difficult a task. By the 1660s, singers were already the most expensive and indispensable commodities on the operatic stages, and their progressive "professionalization" gave them enough freedom to move between the court, the church, and the public theater. This, in turn, could spark competition not only between patrons and impresarios, but also among patrons themselves, eager to secure the most "valuable" singers available. On the public stage as well, singers were often known as belonging to one patron or another. Thus, for example, Maria Mancini, praising Cavagna's performance in 1667 of Cesti's *Il Tito* at the Teatro SS. Giovanni e Paolo, identifies him as "one of the musicians of His Highness [the Duke of Savoy]" (Mancini [1677] 1998: 53). And in quite the same way, composer Andrea Ziani in his letter of April 3, 1666, to Faustini refers to Antonia Coresi, who performed in the same production, as "the lady of the Most Excellent Prince [Colonna]"[3] (Ziani 1666; Schmidt 1978: 462, 464). Singers, well aware of their newly acquired power, tried to take full advantage of both the protection of their patrons and the fame and earnings that came with the new operatic open market.

For some singers, life could be easy. Soprano Antonia Coresi, one of the most highly paid prima donnas of the time, was Maria Mancini Colonna's lady-in-waiting. Together with her husband, tenor Nicola Coresi, they were employed by the Colonna family between 1661 and 1669 and lived in Rome in their palace. When Nicola and Antonia had commitments in Venice, they traveled with the Colonna and the rest of the *famiglia*. At a time in which impresarios often tried to economize on singers' contracts, it was a great advantage for the Coresi not to worry, like other singers, about travel expenses, which could be quite onerous. Furthermore, once in Venice, the Coresi enjoyed all the benefits of being employees of supportive patrons: they were guaranteed such luxuries as lodging at a comfortable aristocratic palace, new clothes, and gondolas to move around the city. Despite such lavish benefits, during their time in Venice Antonia and Nicola continued to receive their salary of five Roman scudi a month, a very low amount if compared to the extraordinary figures that impresarios were offering Antonia to sing in Venice, but a clear sign that the reputation and protection of the Colonna family were worth more than any monetary compensation. Moreover, the Coresi enjoyed unusual freedom to make their own decisions about singing commitments. In a letter of September 22, 1666, to impresario Faustini, for example, Nicola expresses his gratitude to his patron for allowing him to decide whether he and his wife wanted to sing in a production of Ziani's *Annibale in Capua* in Milan in 1665:

> Here [Milan] they are preparing *Annibale in Capua*, and they do not have any other good singer but Cavagnino, who is performing in it under [the threat] of violence by his padrone who thought the opera was organized by the Governor. They pushed very hard to have Sig.ra Antonia and me, but when I found out that this opera was not done by the Governor of Milan, and that the Contestabile [Colonna] my Signore would be so kind as to let us decide freely if we want to do it or not, I made such high requests that it was impossible to find an agreement, and thus I have stayed out of it, for my great satisfaction.[4] (Coresi 1666b)

And even when it came to determining salary, Lorenzo Onofrio allowed Nicola to conduct the negotiations directly with the impresario. As Nicola wrote to Faustini on September 2, 1666, "I heard from a letter that Sig. Girolimo Loredano wrote to the Sig. Contestabile [Colonna] that Your Excellency wants me to perform under the contract done for my wife, and I respond 'no'. . ."[5] (Coresi 1666a).

But for other singers, life could be much more complicated, especially if their patrons did not travel to Venice or, as for Cavagna, opposed the singers' travels. In these cases, while still maintaining their relationship of employment with their "principal patrons," singers could look for the "protection" of an individual who could assist them "in moving between the creative and the mercenary worlds, and as an advisor and intermediary, by helping to secure advantageous working conditions" (Glixon and Glixon 2006: 173). During the 1666–1667 season, the Colonna acted as protectors of two singers who were not part of their household, the above-mentioned castrato Giovanni Antonio Cavagna and soprano Giulia Masotti. Their relationship with the Colonna family is emblematic of a shift in the conception of patronage, which becomes a much more fluid phenomenon when singers became coveted and acquired the necessary power to move from one patron to another as they pleased. As we have seen, in 1666 the Duke of Savoy had reluctantly allowed Cavagna to go to Venice under the condition that he would return to Turin at his command. Concerned by his patron's hostility toward his Venetian plans, in his letter of November 1, 1666, Cavagna begged Faustini to find him a powerful and understanding protector in Venice:

> With this [letter] I inform you now of my arrival in Turin; I am waiting for nothing but the return of the court, which is in the mountains bear hunting, to leave once and for all, since it is impossible for me to live any longer among the malignity of these *musici* without feeling in danger. [. . .] Since I believe I will come to Venice without any protection, and for several reasons I desire to have a protector, I beg you to find me lodging with the *Contestabile* [Colonna] or [his brother in law] the Duke of Nivers, so that I could enjoy their protection and not be forced by the [other] nobles to sing for every venue they organize, which thing—as you know—I detest over any other; since for my better reputation I have always been in Venice under the protection of the Signori Princes of Parma or of the Duke of Savoy, I would not like, if I

> could [avoid it], to be diminished from my position of the past. I recommend this affair to your prudence with great secrecy.[6] (Cavagna 1666; Glixon and Glixon 2006: 206)

Colonna offered everything he needed: the prestige of his family name guaranteed the singer enough public exposure and publicity; furthermore, he was also less demanding than other noblemen of his rank when it came to asking the singer to perform in private contexts.

During the same 1666–1667 season, Giulia Masotti, a soprano under the patronage of the Chigi family in Rome and an old acquaintance of the Colonna's, also had to ask Lorenzo Onofrio and Maria Mancini for help: she was engaged to sing at the Teatro SS. Giovanni e Paolo, but refused to interact with the impresario directly. Instead, she preferred to use Lorenzo Onofrio and Maria Mancini Colonna (probably because of their higher social standing) as intermediaries to help her negotiate the best conditions of employment (Glixon and Glixon 2006: 213). Masotti's requests were numerous, and the well-documented negotiations went on for several weeks (Glixon and Glixon 2006: 209–214; Brunelli 1941: 330–333; Rosselli 1989: 11–12; Rosand 1991: chapter 8; Glixon 1995: 524–526; De Lucca forthcoming). The prima donna was concerned with not offending her previous "protector" in Venice, the Duchess of Parma, and on October 9, 1666, she asked the Colonna to confirm their protection of her for the year (Masotti 1666). Furthermore, she did not want to pay for her travel expenses up front, but demanded an advance from the impresario, which Colonna provided. Finally, she did not like the part Faustini sent her. Here again, the mediation of the Colonna was essential to guarantee the recruitment of the soprano. As we read from a letter that Colonna sent to Faustini on October 20, 1666:

> Also, looking for an opera in Rome is not [my] task, since it is you who have to pick one. I only dare to suggest that if you spend everything you have to get the best singers, you should then try to have an opera that in the libretto and in the music could properly accompany the excellence of the singers; and on this subject Sig.ra Giulia is right; because she was much more appreciated and well received in La Dori, an old opera, than in La Rosilena, a new opera, and perhaps she recognized the part you sent her to Rome as mediocre.[7] (Colonna 1666)

This missive reveals that Faustini had asked Colonna for help to select the opera for the season, since many singers had complained about the opera he had chosen, *Il tiranno umiliato d'Amore, overo Il Meraspe* (libretto by Marco Faustini's deceased brother Giovanni Faustini and music by Carlo Pallavicino). Colonna seems at first reluctant to help Faustini, even though in the end, and probably under the influence of Giulia Masotti, he suggests Cesti's *La Dori*, Masotti's warhorse and one of the Colonna's favorite operas. The fact that Marco Faustini had asked Colonna for help choosing a work to perform points to another crucial aspect of the collaboration between patrons and impresarios: impresarios could not only count on the patrons' tastes, but also on their often vast collections of scores at a time in which these precious artifacts circulated in restricted circles and in very limited exemplars.

Not surprisingly, in January 1667 *La Dori* opened at the Teatro SS. Giovanni e Paolo. The libretto printed for the production bears many traces of the Colonna's contribution to the season. First, it refers to the difficult process of finding the score. As we read in the protest to the reader:

> [...] we encountered many difficulties in finding the original score of the music, in adapting it, and in transposing the parts; we overcame all difficulties with just a short delay; but then in only eight days here it appears for your enjoyment.[8] (*La Dori* 1667, "Lettore")

It is very likely that the Colonna were able to provide their own score of *La Dori* so that Masotti and Faustini would be equally satisfied. Furthermore, the libretto acknowledges the family's contribution with the recruiting of the singers in the form of a dedication to Maria Mancini Colonna, here compared to the "column" that sustained the temple of Apollo:

> With [this Column] the royal palace of the Sun is built, because the protection it exerts over so many Muses, who are the *virtuosi* who sing in the opera, makes it become an Apollo in Parnassus.[9] (*La Dori* 1667, dedication)

In addition to Giulia Masotti in the title role, the stellar cast for that season at the Teatro Grimani featured the best singers available on the market, including Giovanni Antonio Cavagna as the *primo uomo* and Antonia Coresi as the *seconda donna*. The principal singers had enjoyed the advantages of the Colonna's "benigna protezione," and impresario Faustini could count on a production that promised to generate good revenue.

The case of the Teatro SS. Giovanni e Paolo during the 1660s serves as a perfect example of the complexity of the operation of commercial theaters, in Venice as well as in other cities in which the "Venetian system" became the model. As Glixon and Glixon have argued, "all of the possible sources of income—annual box rentals, tickets sales, and contributions of wealthy supporters—were required to meet the high costs of this elaborate art form" (2006: 322). But in addition to financial contributions, impresarios also needed help recruiting singers, finding performance materials, obtaining new works, and cultivating their web of social relationships. By offering the impresario this kind of support, individuals like the Colonna—patrons turned protectors of the public theaters—contributed in crucial ways to the success of an opera season and ultimately to the survival of the "business" of opera.

Opera remained indeed a risky—but apparently worthy—business. As the model of opera production of the Venetian theaters spread around Europe, patrons, impresarios, and artists collaborated to make it a profitable and durable enterprise. And despite the frequent setbacks, the commercial theater became a fertile environment for the production of most of the masterpieces in the history of the genre. The social, political, and economic conventions and machinations of this four-hundred-year-old system soon became such entrenched cultural phenomena that they lent themselves to satire very early along the continuum of opera's history. Notable among a long list of self-referential works is Mozart's *Der Schauspieldirektor* (1786), which not only pokes fun at impresarios, bankers, and singers, but also the genre itself. In the twentieth century, these same institutions were both mocked and celebrated in the 1935 Marx Brothers film comedy *A Night at the Opera*, which features a greedy and snobbish impresario, a socially ambitious female patron, a pair of young singers, and a sly huckster and his cohorts, who upend the proceedings and eventually ensure a happy ending marked by an operatic performance.

Conclusions

Four centuries after the Colonna's involvement with the Teatro SS. Giovanni e Paolo, patrons still play an essential role in the support of opera production in most theaters around the world. Entering the Metropolitan Opera, one cannot fail to notice the list of patrons and benefactors of the theater engraved in bold letters on an imposing gray marble wall. These wealthy individuals are the heirs of a long tradition of patrons who for centuries have supported opera in various ways, not only through financial investment but also through their commitment of time, energy, and knowledge. The thread that connects these "angels of our time" (Schanke 2007) to the patrons of the past is still visible: just as in centuries past, patrons of the Metropolitan Opera are rewarded by "prominent donor recognition in *Playbill*, the annual Season Book and other Met publications" for a generous financial contribution to the theater. For an even more generous gift, their names can be engraved "on the Golden Horseshoe plaque on the Mercedes T. Bass Grand Tier of the Opera House," or they can be entitled to receive the "Dedication of a performance in their honor every two years, including a prominent listing on the cast page of the program" (Metropolitan Opera 2012). In a way, their recognition is not unlike the kind of tribute given to the Colonna in Venice for their contribution to the 1666–1667 opera season. Indeed, as in seventeenth-century Venice, no opera house today can rely exclusively on box office revenue. No matter how expensive admission prices can be, the high costs of a successful opera production seem inevitably to call for diverse forms of external support, including different degrees of government funding (through taxpayers' money), corporate sponsorships, and private patronage.

The mission of opera patrons today is sometimes called into question, especially because most of the private donations made to nonprofit institutions, like opera companies, are tax exempt. The fact that governments around the world are willing to support opera as a cultural phenomenon that cannot sustain itself has deep ramifications. As Ruth Bereson has argued, "Plainly, opera is not merely the best supported of the arts, it is also a symbol of the continuity of governments and, most important of all, an integral part of state ceremonial" (2002: 3). But beyond opera's symbolic value, the discussion about the need to support opera houses through tax exemption is taking center stage at a time of global financial struggle (Holcombe 2000).

As opera enters its fifth century, can a new, sustainable business model be devised for its survival? Could larger audiences and smaller production costs mark the beginning of a new era for the genre? And ultimately, is opera still so intimately connected to the social status, wealth, and vision of its patrons, or could it survive without them?

See also: What Is Opera? Audiences, How Opera Traveled, The Operatic Canon, Opera Composition and Cultural Environment, Censorship, Gender

Notes

1. "visione idealistico-romantica del mecenatismo [...] in cui il sostegno economico profuso a un artista è fondamentalmente un tributo al genio di lui" to a "prospettiva antropologica [...] secondo la quale il mecenatismo musicale si risolve essenzialmente nella produzione e nella gestione di simboli sonori di gruppo e di classe."
2. "A notre retour à Rome, d'où le Pape Alexandre, par une aversion qu'il avait pour tous les divertissements, avait banni jusqu'aux comédies, Monsieur le Connétable continuant ses soins, et s'efforçant de réparer cette disette de plaisirs [...]."
3. "Ho inteso le meraviglie del Tito opera veramente decantata qui al segno maggiore non tanto per il drama, stimato più per la dicitura che per il soggetto, quanto per la musica e gli recitanti, inter quos, la donna dell'Ecc.mo Principe esaltata alle stelle, e poi il S. Cavagnino, e Donati, veramente d'essi degni applauso."
4. "Qui fanno l'Annibale in Capua, e non ci hanno altro recitante bono che Cavagnino, quale ci recita per forza violentato dal suo Padrone che ha creduto che la faccia il Governatore. Hanno fatto grandissime forze per aver la Sig.ra Antonia e me, ma io quando ho saputo che detta opera non la faceva il Governatore di Milano, e che il Contestabile mio Sig.re si è compiaciuto lasciarmi la libertà del fare o non fare, mi son messi in pretensioni così alte che non è stato possibile aggiustarsi, e così con mia sodisfazione ne sono restato fuori."
5. "Ho inteso da una lettera del Sig.r Girolimo Loredano scritta al Sig.r Contestabile che V.S. pretende che io sia obbligato a recitare con la scritta fatta per mia moglie, et io gli rispondo di no..."
6. "Per questa li aviso il mio arivo in Turino; non attendo che il ritorno della corte, quale è fra le montagne alla caccia del orso per sbrigarmi una volta per sempre essendomi impossibile il poter più vivere fra la malignità di questi musici senza pericolare [...] Come che credo di venir a Venezia senza alcuna prottezione così desidero per più capi averne qualche d'una che però in confidenza la suplico se potesse trovarmi l'aloggio in casa e del Sig. Duca di Nivers o del Sig. Contestabile il procurarmelo come da sè perch'io possi godere di quella prottezione et non esser forzato dalla nobiltà a cantare in ogni loro cosa che sa ch'io molto aborisco; si come per mia maggior riputazione essendo sempre stato in Venezia sotto la prottezione delli Sig.ri Prencipi di Parma o Duca di Savoia onde non vorrei potendo decadere dal passato. Raccomando con ogni secretezza il negozio alla sua prudenza mentre tutto affetto li bacio le mani." See also Glixon and Glixon (2006: 206). For more on Cavagna's relationship with the Duke of Savoy during the season of 1666–1667, see Viale Ferrero 1976: 159; Rosand 1991: 224; and Rosselli 1989: 7, 9–10.
7. "Mi fo lecito però di dire che spendendo tutto in musici si dovrebbe cercare a fare un'opera che nelle parole, e nella musica accompagnasse l'eccellenza de' recitanti, et in questo fa parlare con raggione la Sig.ra Giulia; mentre lei fu molto più stimata e accetta nella Dori opera vecchia, che nella Rosilena opera nuova, e forse la sua parte inviatagli in Roma sarrà stata riconosciuta per mediocre."

8. "Si è incontrato molte difficoltà, così nel ritrovare l'originale della musica, come nell'aggiustarlo, e nel trasportare le parti; si è superato il tutto con qualche dilazione; ma poi in soli otto giorni comparisce in scena per sodisfarti: si sono aggionte alcune ariette per maggiormente adornare il drama; godi intanto delle voci angeliche, che la rappresentano, e della musica celeste e ammirabile del Signor Cavalier Cesti."
9. "Con essa è fabricata la reggia del sole, poichè la Prottezione, che tiene di tante muse, che sono li virtuosi rappresentanti nel drama, la fa divenire un Apollo in Parnaso."

Bibliography

Annibaldi, Claudio. 2001. "Uno 'spettacolo veramente da principi': Committenza e recezione dell'opera aulica nel primo Seicento." In *"Lo stupor dell'invenzione": Firenze e la nascita dell'opera. Atti del convegno internazionale (Florence, October 5–6, 2000)*, edited by Piero Gargiulo, 31–60. Florence: Olschki.

——. 1998. "Towards a Theory of Musical Patronage in the Renaissance and Baroque: The Perspective from Anthropology and Semiotics." *Recercare* 10: 174–180.

——. 1996. "Tipologia della committenza musicale nella Venezia seicentesca." In *Musica, scienza e idee nella Serenissima durante il Seicento: Atti del convegno internazionale*, edited by Francesco Passadore and Franco Rossi. Venice: Fondazione Levi.

Apolloni, Giovanni Filippo. 1667. *La Dori, overo lo schiavo regio*. Venice: Francesco Nicolini and Stefano Curti.

Baumol, William, and William G. Bowen. 1966. *Performing Arts, the Economic Dilemma: A Study of Problems Common to Theater, Opera, Music, and Dance*. New York: Twentieth Century Fund.

Bereson, Ruth. 2002. *The Operatic State: Cultural Policy and the Opera House*. London and New York: Routledge.

Bianconi, Lorenzo, and Giorgio Morelli. 1982. *Antonio Vivaldi: teatro musicale, cultura e società*. Florence: Olschki.

Bianconi, Lorenzo, and Giorgio Pestelli, eds. 1998. *Opera Production and Its Resources*, translated by Lydia G. Cochrane. *The History of Italian Opera* 4. Chicago: University of Chicago Press.

Bianconi, Lorenzo, and Thomas Walker. 1984. "Production, Consumption and Political Function of Seventeenth-Century Opera." *Early Music History* 4: 209–296.

——. 1975. "Dalla *Finta pazza* alla *Veremonda*: Storie di Febiarmonici." *Rivista Italiana di Musicologia* 10: 379–454.

Brown, Bruce Alan. 1989. "Maria Theresa's Vienna." In *The Classical Era: From the 1740s to the End of the 18th Century*, edited by Neal Zaslaw, 99–125. Englewood Cliffs, NJ: Prentice Hall.

Brunelli, Bruno. 1941. "L'impresario in angustie." *Rivista italiana del dramma* 3: 311–341.

Burke, Peter. 1987. *The Historical Anthropology of Early Modern Italy: Essays on Perception and Communication*. Cambridge: Cambridge University Press.

Burrows, Donald, and Robert Hume. 1991. "George I, the Haymarket Opera Company and Handel's Water Music." *Early Music* 19/3: 323–341.

Calcagno, Mauro. 2006. "Censoring *Eliogabalo* in Seventeenth-Century Venice." *Journal of Interdisciplinary History* 36/3: 355–377.

Carter, Tim. 2012. "Monteverdi, Early Opera and a Question of Genre: The Case of *Andromeda* (1620)." *Journal of the Royal Musical Association* 137/1: 1–34.

Cavagna, Giovanni Antonio. 1666. I-Vas, SGSM, b. 188, ff. 47r and 48r–48v.
Clark, Caryl. 2005. "Haydn in the Theater: The Operas." In *The Cambridge Companion to Haydn*, edited by Caryl Clark, 176–199. Cambridge: Cambridge University Press.
Colonna, Lorenzo Onofrio. 1666. I-Vas, SGSM, b. 188, f.345.
Coresi, Nicola. 1666a. I-Vas, SGSM, b. 188, f. 271.
——. 1666b. I-Vas, SGSM, b. 188, f. 281.
Cowart, Georgia. 2008. *The Triumph of Pleasure: Louis XIV and the Politics of Spectacle*. Chicago: University of Chicago Press.
Cusick, Suzanne. 2009. *Francesca Caccini at the Medici Court: Music and the Circulation of Power*. Chicago: University of Chicago Press.
De Lucca, Valeria. 2014. "The Power of the Prima Donna: Giulia Masotti's Repertory of Choice." *Journal of Seventeenth-Century Music*.
——. 2011a. "*L'Alcasta* and the Emergence of Collective Patronage in Mid-Seventeenth-Century Rome." *The Journal of Musicology* 28/2: 195–230.
——. 2011b. "Strategies of Women Patrons of Music and Theatre in Rome: Maria Mancini Colonna, Queen Christina of Sweden, and Women of Their Circles." *Renaissance Studies* 25/3: 374–392.
Eger, Manfred. 1992. "The Patronage of King Ludwig II." In *The Wagner Handbook*, edited by Ulrich Müller and Peter Wapnewski; translation edited by John Deathridge, 317–326. Cambridge, MA: Harvard University Press.
Fabris, Dinko. 1999. *Mecenati e musici: documenti sul patronato artistico dei Bentivoglio di Ferrara nell'epoca di Monteverdi (1585–1645)*. Lucca: Libreria musicale italiana.
Feldman, Martha. 2007. *Opera and Sovereignty: Transforming Myths in Eighteenth-Century Italy*. Chicago: University of Chicago Press.
Glixon, Beth. 1995. "Private Lives of Public Women: Prima Donnas in Mid-Seventeenth-Century Venice." *Music & Letters* 76/4: 509–531.
Glixon, Jonathan E., and Beth L. Glixon. 2006. *Inventing the Business of Opera: The Impresario and His World in Seventeenth-Century Venice*. New York: Oxford University Press.
Gerhard, Anselm. 1998. *The Urbanization of Opera: Music Theater in Paris in the Nineteenth Century*, translated by Mary Whittall. Chicago: University of Chicago Press.
Hammond, Frederick. 1994. *Music and Spectacle in Baroque Rome: Barberini Patronage under Urban VIII*. New Haven: Yale University Press.
Hanning, Barbara Russano. 1979. "Glorious Apollo: Poetic and Political Themes in the First Opera." *Renaissance Quarterly* 32: 485–513.
Harness, Kelley. 2006. *Echoes of Women's Voices: Music, Art, and Female Patronage in Early Modern Florence*. Chicago: University of Chicago Press.
Harris-Warrick, Rebecca. 2007. "Lully's On-Stage Societies." In *Opera and Society in Italy and France from Monteverdi to Bourdieu*, edited by Victoria Johnson, Jane F. Fulcher, and Thomas Ertman, 53–71. Cambridge: Cambridge University Press.
Hill, John W. [1971] 1997. *Roman Monody, Cantata, and Opera from the Circles around Cardinal Montalto*. Oxford: Clarendon Press. Reprint. New York: Oxford University Press.
Holcombe, Randall G. 2000. *Writing Off Ideas: Taxation, Foundations, and Philanthropy in America*. Oakland, CA: Independent Institute.
Hunter, David. 2009. "Royal Patronage of Handel in Britain: The Rewards of Pensions and Office." In *Handel Studies: A Gedenkschrift for Howard Serwer*, edited by Richard G. King, 127–153. Hillsdale, NY: Pendragon Press.

——. 2000. "Patronizing Handel, Inventing Audiences: The Intersections of Class, Money, Music and History." *Early Music* 28/1: 32–49.

Isherwood, Robert M. 1973. *Music in the Service of the King: France in the Seventeenth Century*. Ithaca, NY: Cornell University Press.

Johnson, James H. 1995. *Listening in Paris: A Cultural History*. Berkeley and Los Angeles: University of California Press.

Levine, Lawrence W. 1988. *Highbrow/Lowbrow: The Emergence of Cultural Hierarchy in America*. Cambridge, MA: Harvard University Press.

Locke, Ralph. 1993. "Music Lovers, Patrons, and the 'Sacralization' of Culture in America." *19th-Century Music* 17/2: 149–173.

——, and Cyrilla Barr, eds. 1997. *Cultivating Music in America: Women Patrons and Activists since 1860*. Berkeley and Los Angeles: University of California Press.

Mamone, Sara. 2003. "Most Serene Brothers-Princes-Impresarios: Theater in Florence under the Management and Protection of Mattias, Giovan Carlo, and Leopoldo de' Medici." *Journal of Seventeenth-Century Music* 9/1. Online. Available: http://sscm-jscm.press.illinois.edu/v9/no1/mamone.html (accessed January 21, 2014).

Mancini, Maria. [1677] 1998. *La vérité dans son jour*, edited by Patricia Francis Cholakian and Elizabeth C. Goldsmith. Delmar, NY: Scholars' Facsimiles and Reprints.

Masotti, Giulia. 1666. I-Vas, SGSM, b. 188, f. 301–302.

Metropolitan Opera. 2012. Online. Available: http://www.metoperafamily.org/metopera/support/membership_patron/major_gifts.aspx (accessed August 25, 2012).

Milhous, Judith. 1984. "Opera Finances in London, 1674–1738." *Journal of the American Musicological Society* 37/3: 567–592.

——, and Robert D. Hume. 1999. "Heidegger and the Management of the Haymarket Opera, 1713–17." *Early Music* 27/1: 65–84.

——. 1983. "New Light on Handel and the Royal Academy of Music in 1720." *Theatre Journal* 35: 149–167.

Monaldini, Sergio. 2001. *L'orto dell'esperidi: musici, attori e artisti nel patrocinio della famiglia Bentivoglio (1646–1685)*. Lucca: Libreria musicale italiana.

Monod, Paul. 2006. "The Politics of Handel's Early London Operas, 1711–1718." *Journal of Interdisciplinary History* 36/3: 445–472.

Murata, Margaret. 1981. *Operas for the Papal Court, 1631–1668*. Ann Arbor, MI: UMI Research Press.

Piperno, Franco. 1998. "Opera Production to 1780." In Bianconi and Pestelli 1998, 1–79.

Reiss, Sheryl E., and David G. Wilkins, eds. 2001. *Beyond Isabella: Secular Women Patrons of Art in Renaissance Italy*. Kirksville: Truman State University Press.

Rice, John A. 2003. *Empress Marie Therese and Music at the Viennese Court, 1792–1807*. Cambridge: Cambridge University Press.

——. 1995. "Leopold II, Mozart, and the Return to a Golden Age." In *Opera and the Enlightenment*, edited by Thomas Bauman and Marita Petzoldt McClymonds, 271–298. Cambridge: Cambridge University Press.

——. 1989. "Vienna under Joseph II and Leopold II." In *The Classical Era: From the 1740s to the End of the 18th Century*, edited by Neal Zaslaw, 126–165. Englewood Cliffs, NJ: Prentice Hall.

Rosand, Ellen. 1991. *Opera in Seventeenth-Century Venice: The Creation of a Genre*. Berkeley and Los Angeles: University of California Press.

Rosselli, John. 1992a. *Singers of Italian Opera: The History of a Profession*. Cambridge: Cambridge University Press.

——. 1992b. "Sociology of Opera." *The New Grove Dictionary of Opera*. Online. Available: http://www.oxfordmusiconline.com/subscriber/article/grove/music/O005915 (accessed January 21, 2014).
——. 1991. *Music and Musicians in Nineteenth-Century Italy*. London: Batsford.
——. 1989. "From Princely Service to the Open Market: Singers of Italian Opera and Their Patrons, 1600–1850." *Cambridge Opera Journal* 1/1: 1–32.
——. 1984. *The Opera Industry in Italy from Cimarosa to Verdi: The Role of the Impresario*. Cambridge: Cambridge University Press.
Schanke, Robert A., ed. 2007. *Angels in the American Theater: Patrons, Patronage, and Philanthropy*. Carbondale: Southern Illinois University Press.
Schmidt, Carl B. 1978. "An Episode in the History of Venetian Opera: The "Tito" Commission (1665–66)." *Journal of the American Musicological Society* 31/3: 442–466.
Snowman, Daniel. *The Gilded Stage: A Social History of Opera*. London: Atlantic Books.
Stein, Louise K. 1993. *Songs of Mortals, Dialogues of the Gods: Music and Theatre in Seventeenth-Century Spain*. Oxford: Clarendon Press.
Thomas, Downing. 2002. *Aesthetics of Opera in the Ancien Régime, 1647–1785*. Cambridge: Cambridge University Press.
Towse, Ruth, ed. 2007. *Recent Developments in Cultural Economics*. Cheltenham: Edward Elgar.
Towse, Ruth. 2003. *A Handbook of Cultural Economics*. Cheltenham: Edward Elgar.
——. 1997. *Cultural Economics: The Arts, the Heritage and the Media Industries*. 2 vols. Cheltenham: Edward Elgar.
Useem, Michael. 1984. *The Inner Circle: Large Corporations and the Rise of Business Political Activity in the U.S. and U.K.* New York: Oxford University Press.
Viale Ferrero, Mercedes. 1976. "Repliche a Torino di melodrammi veneziani." In *Venezia e il melodramma nel Seicento*, edited by Maria Teresa Muraro, 159–164. Florence: Olschki.
Wolff, Christoph. 2012. *Mozart at the Gateway to His Fortune: Serving the Emperor, 1788–1791*. New York: W. W. Norton.
Ziani, Andrea. 1666. I-Vas, SGSM, b. 188, f. 255.

CHAPTER 30

AUDIENCES

GEORGIA COWART

THE subject of opera audiences as a field of study emerged in the 1990s, in the wake of the "cultural turn" of the previous two decades. More specifically, it arose from the growing displacement of attention from the work of art as formal object and result of authorial intention to the reader or audience as the source of more relative and pluralistic interpretations (Barthes 1968). The application of these ideas to the audiences of theater has encouraged an expanded interest in the cultural effects of performance, especially on the individual spectator and segments of the audience comprising, for example, women and gays. Concomitantly, a view of culture as the object of consumption has led to an emphasis on the role of the public as consumers, and on the role of cultural consumption in the construction of identity (Brewer and Bermingham 1995).

The literature to date, mostly the work of North American cultural historians, has focused largely on eighteenth- and nineteenth-century Paris, London, and New York, though musicologists have also begun to treat audiences as part of the broader social, cultural, and commercial context. These contributions have revealed important new dimensions of opera, including the function of the opera house as a social and cultural environment. Although most of the current literature focuses on the behaviors and demographics of opera audiences, the importance of the subject for future study extends beyond these parameters into the wider arenas of reception, taste, and aesthetics, all of which emanate from the interactions of audiences with operatic works, styles, and performances.

OPERA AUDIENCES AND THE MOVE FROM COURT TO URBAN SETTINGS

Little has been written on early opera and court entertainments from the point of view of their audiences. The literature to date has begun to address a few central problems: What exactly was the dividing line between private or court opera and public opera in terms of the audience, as patrons, attendees, and taste-setters? How did princes continue to control or influence opera after it moved to the public arena? How, when, and why did that influence wane?

Early Florentine opera was developed in the laboratory of the Camerata, a group of nobles and intellectuals seeking to recreate the effects of ancient Greek drama. The Camerata's emphasis on the emotional effects of opera, stimulated by the Aristotelian studies of Girolamo Mei, grew from the search for a cathartic, audience-focused art that would result not only in entertainment but also in personal and societal transformation (Palisca 1954a, 1954b). As opera developed at courts and in the public sphere, the genre quickly adapted to two primary exigencies: the need for princely glorification and for festive pleasure, aims overshadowing but never completely extinguishing the view of opera as a means, like ancient rhetoric, of moving and instructing a malleable audience.

When rulers sponsored opera as court entertainment, it was natural to use the genre as propaganda for their power, both through its heroic content and the lavish scale on which it was produced. Rulers offered opera to their court as a sign of their beneficence and as a way of glorifying the reign, especially during the carnival season, when business affairs and military operations slackened or ceased. The element of propaganda tended to frame the festive function of court opera, while an aura of pleasure marked the privilege and prestige of its courtly audience. Opera retained its association with carnival both in its hedonistic orientation and in the practice, frequent among audiences throughout the early modern period, of wearing masks. Appearing incognito allowed a certain liberation from social formalities and was accompanied by a seemingly endless fascination with games of identity and self-presentation (Johnson 2011; Knif 1995: 216; Glixon and Glixon 2006: 19, 314).

When opera moved into the public sphere, in 1637 in Venice, and in the later seventeenth century in France and England, it tended to reflect the tastes and propensities of an aristocratic class (in Venice, the ruling oligarchy). The function of noble families not only as the audience, but as the patrons of opera—often at a commercial loss in business terms—has created some confusion as to whether early Venetian opera might adhere more to the courtly than to the public model (Glixon and Glixon 2006: 295–296). One important difference was the participation of all social classes. Though the presence of the lower class may have been negligible in terms of economic contribution to the opera as a commercial venture, it undoubtedly influenced the aesthetic character of operatic works—for example, in the incorporation of crowd-pleasing burlesque scenes (Rosand 1991: 14).

In states with a strong ruler, the growth of opera as a public phenomenon occurred in stages that could be politically fraught. Feldman (2007) looks at the ways in which the absolutist principles on which *opera seria* was based could be altered, manipulated, and subverted as Italian audiences became increasingly more diverse. In France, with the establishment of a public opera house in 1669, a "dual audience" arose, as operas were typically performed first at court, during the carnival season, and later in Paris during the spring. Public audiences of the Old Regime overlapped to some extent with those for court entertainments, as courtiers and members of the royal family habitually frequented the Paris Opéra (the Académie Royale de Musique). Unlike in Venice, comic scenes were quickly expunged from the *tragédie en musique*, as being unfit to depict the royal virtues of heroism and self-sacrifice.

In the seventeenth and eighteenth centuries, an emerging public opera gradually took on the function of mirror to a privileged urban society. From its beginnings in Italy, early opera glorified its public audience and the experience of opera-going in much the same way as court entertainments glorified the court (Rosand 1991: 110–124). In France, especially in the *opéra-ballet* of the early eighteenth century, the praise of a public society replaced and at times subverted the traditional praise of the monarch (Cowart 2008). Moving away from the glorification of an upper-class audience, nineteenth-century opera related instead to a shared urban experience. Gerhard (1988) analyzes French *grand opéra*, with its depiction of violent historical events, its replacement of horrific for heroic endings, and its general sense of disillusionment, as a reflection of the rapid "urbanization" of Paris in the early nineteenth century.

Operas could serve not only as the reflection, but also the product of audience values and expectations. Both Gaetano Donizetti and Giuseppe Verdi, for example, were particularly sensitive to the tastes of the public. Donizetti's correspondence attests to a preoccupation with its judgment and a propensity to modify his operas in response (Sorba 2005: 597–614). Verdi's relationship to Italian revolutionary ideologies and to the censors, and the wider relationships among opera, its audiences, and nineteenth-century Italian politics have received scattered and widely divergent interpretations. (A useful review of the literature on this subject is provided by Davis 2005: 569–594.)

Opera Audiences and the Transition from "Event" to "Work" Aesthetic

Did early opera audiences really listen, and if not, when did they begin to do so? This question has served as the focus of much of the literature to date. From the early seventeenth century, the very concept of opera derived as much from a performative audience as from the performance onstage, and as much from the theater-going experience as from the operatic repertoire. From the beginnings of public opera across Europe and in Russia and North America, conversation, business dealings, political meetings, and amorous assignations constituted the normal activity of audience members, as did eating and drinking, circulating, gambling, and receiving acquaintances in one's box. Members of an upper-class elite occupied the most prestigious boxes, commonly those located on the lowest tiers. The royal box was typically the most central of these, though in the late eighteenth century it could also be located to the side of the proscenium arch. Beginning with the earliest public opera houses, boxes could be bought or rented for successive seasons, and for many the main focus of opera-going remained the opportunity to visit and entertain acquaintances in their salon-like atmosphere. In some theaters, box holders could also install decorations and hang wallpaper and curtains. Opera-goers arrived fashionably late and left as they pleased, the banging of doors mingling with conversation as part of the general ambience.

When audiences did interact with the performance on stage, it was not uncommon (especially in Italy, but also to an extent in other countries) to applaud frequently and frantically, or to halt the dramatic action by noisily demanding encores. Alternately, they showed disapproval by booing, exiting the theater *en masse*, violently hissing and whistling, stamping their feet, and on occasion rioting. Bouquets could be thrown, but so could all manner of food, including the proverbial rotten tomato as well as apple cores, orange peels, eggs, gingerbread, eggplants, pieces of sausage, and even whole wieners. Opera everywhere was subject to cabals and factions, but in Paris and London, professional claques, often paid by the management, noisily supported the performers, while rival claques were hired by their enemies. And especially in Paris, members of the audience sang lustily along with the performers onstage.

This exuberant world of opera-going was also a libertine one. Police records from eighteenth-century Paris indicate that influential noblemen often placed their mistresses in the opera chorus or *corps de ballet* for reasons having to do less with professionalism than with the immunity from prosecution granted to performers in official theaters. Gentlemen regularly left their boxes to visit singers and dancers (*filles de l'Opéra*, as they were known in Paris) backstage. Opera houses typically functioned as magnets for prostitutes, who solicited opera-goers in the corridors and vestibules (Cowart 1994: 205–220). In seventeenth-century Venice, special boxes were designated for that city's famous courtesans (Glixon and Glixon 2006: 301–302). Until the early 1850s, the disreputable third tier of many North American houses was given over to prostitution (Preston [1993] 2001: 17; Ahlquist 1997: 5). Critics and moralists commonly railed against the immorality of the opera house, and operatic artists, patrons, and managements often found themselves in conflict with church and political authorities. In eighteenth-century Boston, a moralistic opposition to opera among the upper class delayed the genre's establishment in that city until 1791—considerably later than in New York, Philadelphia, and Charleston (McKay 1985: 140).

In the first book-length study of audience behavior at the opera, James H. Johnson (1995) traces the transition from opera-going as "social duty" to a more intensely subjective experience between 1750 and 1850. The extent to which Johnson pushes his claims of audience rowdiness in the earlier period has been challenged by Wood and Sadler (2000: 30) and by Charlton (2012: 186–198), but the trend toward increasing audience attentiveness has been documented across a wide range of opera houses in Europe and America. Jennifer Hall-Witt (2007) describes a parallel but slightly later transition in England between 1780 and 1880. For the earlier, more "chatty" period, she uses the term "event aesthetic," a phrase that captures not only the pleasurable but also the performative aspect of opera-going. This aesthetic depended on a fluid boundary between the stage and the brightly lit auditorium, in which the boxes themselves constituted miniature proscenium stages. In addition, until the late eighteenth century, spectators were often seated onstage, along the sides of the performance area, where they could indulge in self-display while enjoying the dual spectacles unfolding simultaneously on the stage and in the hall.

Audience behavior at court, as well as public behavior in the presence of a visiting monarch, was probably characterized by a higher level of decorum than that associated with the public opera house. Dr. Burney, for example, noted that eighteenth-century audiences in the San Carlo theater in Naples were distinctly less noisy whenever the king was in attendance (Lindenberger 1984: 237). David R. B. Kimbell notes that in nineteenth-century Turin and Naples, where the opera houses were also court theaters, there was a ban on applause when the court was present, although exceptions could be made if the monarch gave a sign (Kimbell 1981: 43). William Weber documents more attentive and submissive court audiences at opera performances at Versailles in 1664 and in Vienna in 1668. In general, Weber believes that even public audiences may have listened more carefully, though in ways different from present-day audiences, than the evidence has been taken to indicate (1997: 678–691). Johnson attributes increased audience attentiveness to a growing bourgeois emphasis on respectability, the affective qualities of a new repertoire featuring works of Gluck and later Beethoven, and the new culture of *sensibilité* arising in the 1780s. To those causes may be added a weakening of the subscription system, causing patrons who had owned or occupied the same box year after year to be dispersed throughout the theater. With a broader swath of society attending the opera, and with the high nobility less concentrated in the lower boxes, socializing gave way to more focused listening. Whereas in France the move to polite attentiveness came about in part through the weakening of the influence of aristocratic values, in England it was the aristocrats themselves who embraced a more respectable demeanor from the early years of Queen Victoria's reign (1837–1901) (Hall-Witt 2007: 7–8).

Lawrence Levine argues that American opera audiences' embrace of quiet listening came about largely as a means of differentiating themselves, through "highbrow" behaviors and tastes, from the rowdy lower classes. Early nineteenth-century Italian opera, like Shakespearean drama, had drawn an audience as unified in its tastes as it was diverse in its social makeup. This aesthetic unity was sundered only in the last decades of the century by what Levine calls an emerging "sacralization of culture." The result was a new perception of opera as transcendental experience and opera houses as "temples," inspiring in the initiated an attitude of hushed awe and meditative inspiration (Levine 1988: 85–168).

By the late nineteenth century, the new etiquette of quiet listening had overtaken all the major operatic centers (Müller 2006: 167–187). However diverse its causes, a common thread may be found in the "work concept." This phenomenon took hold in the early nineteenth century, along with the more universal acceptance of a Western musical canon (Goehr [1994] 2007). The perception of operas as artworks deserving of careful attention, rather than as background to social events, supported the shift toward a more reverential attitude. In Germany, where the work concept was enthusiastically embraced, attentive listening reached unprecedented, quasi-religious extremes. It culminated in Wagner's Festspielhaus in Bayreuth, where the orchestra pit was hidden, the hall darkened, and boxes abolished altogether (Gay 1995: 11–35).

The trend toward increased decorum was universal though relative; such a reverential attitude never completely took hold in countries such as Italy, where audiences continued to exhibit more extroverted behaviors. Accounts of Louis Spohr and Giacomo Meyerbeer indicate that nineteenth-century Italian audiences' lack of inhibition far exceeded the norm for the rest of Europe. Audiences in the northern towns of Bologna, Modena, Reggio, and Parma were deemed the most unpredictable and dangerous, with a reputation for frequent rioting. Florentine audiences at the aristocratic theater of La Pergola were known for their restraint, but at La Pagliano, a more popular venue, a bench was once thrown at the impresario from the fifth tier, and a cod's head at a baritone whose performance failed to please. Such use of projectiles was part of a long Italian tradition that also included a live owl attached to a wreath, thrown at a singer in Palermo in 1844, and in the 1950s, a bunch of radishes and leeks thrown at Maria Callas by a supporter of Renata Tebaldi (Kimbell 1981: 61; Rosselli 1984: 153).

Arturo Toscanini, conductor at La Scala from 1898, initiated a massive program of audience reform. He had the house lights lowered, curbed spontaneous applause, and abolished sight-blocking ladies' hats. He was unable, however, to suppress the practice of encores, a frustration that caused him to walk out of a performance at the end of the 1902 season, not to return until 1906. In 1908, he left again for the Metropolitan Opera in New York, where, reigning until 1915, he continued to battle the trappings of the "event aesthetic." Returning once again to a reorganized La Scala from 1920 to 1929, he eventually did succeed in imposing a lasting ban on the encore (Cairns 1992). From 1933, when Feodor Chaliapin sang Gioachino Rossini's *Il barbiere di Siviglia*, no encores were heard in that house until February 2007, when in response to an explosive demonstration the Peruvian tenor Juan Diego Flórez was allowed to encore "Ah, mes amis" from Donizetti's *La fille du régiment* (Gurewitsch 2008). In April 2008, Flórez again made history by breaching a similar ban at the Met, where encores had also been outlawed for most of the century (an exception was Luciano Pavarotti's repeat of the third-act tenor aria from Puccini's *Tosca* in 1994). After Flórez's encore, the Met's general manager Peter Gelb declared the ban ended, as a way of making opera "as entertaining and exciting for the audience as it can be" (Wakin 2008).

Audience Demographics

The idea of a "public" has been compared to a mirage, eluding attempts at either statistical or philosophical definitions (Sorlin 1992). In many ways the audiences of the past are similarly difficult to describe, define, or quantify. For early opera, the only consistently reliable sources are subscriber lists. Though often preserving the names and professions of box holders, these can throw light only on the uppermost level of opera-going, reinforcing the impression given by newspaper reviews and reports that opera was a strictly upper-class affair. But despite the influence of the aristocracy in shaping the tone and atmosphere of early opera, this class constituted only a part of the opera-going public. Less prestigious boxes, procured on a nightly basis, were most commonly occupied by lower-ranking nobles or members of the upper bourgeoisie. The least affluent opera-goers were relegated to the uppermost galleries, or in some houses to the highest tier of boxes.

The area on the floor, known as the "pit" (later "stalls") in England, the *parterre* in France and Germany, and the *poltrone* in Italy, was typically filled with officers, government officials, travelers, students, and servants, but it could also attract "persons of quality." The English pit served as a showplace for dandies competing with the performers for attention; the wide aisles to either side were known as "fop-allies" or "Fop's Alley." In the mid-nineteenth century, ladies began to populate this area when its rough pit benches were converted to more comfortable stall seats (Hall-Witt 2007: 4–5). The unruly *parterre* of the Paris Opéra was long a standing-room male preserve, tightly packed with up to 890 single ticket holders and gentlemen taking a break from the boxes. Composers and librettists occupied this space until the late eighteenth century, when police, hoping to mitigate the jeers and whistles of jealous authors, banished them to the amphitheater at the back of the auditorium (Johnson 1995: 18; Charlton 2012: 187).

Across Europe into the nineteenth century, the numbers of laborers is thought to have been low, since according to general salary ranges even the most inexpensive ticket prices would have been more or less prohibitive. It was not uncommon, however, for lackeys and other servants to accompany their masters to the opera, and to take their place in the floor area. In Italy, they could then be summoned to anterooms, commonly situated across the corridor from the boxes, to prepare food and beverages. At La Scala between 1778 and 1796, preferential rates in the *poltrone* were given to "blackcoats," the majordomos, secretaries, and stewards of noble box holders. By 1820 most of these places had been taken over by middle-class opera patrons (Rosselli 1992).

The nineteenth century saw the increased participation of the bourgeoisie, but not in any steady or uniform manner. In London, the establishment of Covent Garden as an opera house in 1847 initiated a class rivalry with Her Majesty's Theatre, but it involved a split between upper and lower aristocracy rather than the middle classes the supporters of Covent Garden had hoped to attract (Hall-Witt 1997: 5). The audiences for *opera buffa* in Mozart's Vienna and for *opéra comique* in nineteenth-century Paris were also quite aristocratic (Hunter 1999: 13; Huebner 1989: 216). Although the management of the Opéra began to cater to the bourgeoisie in the 1830s, its efforts attracted mainly the upper stratum of that class. In time, an aristocracy of wealth began to replace the old aristocracy of birth (Johnson 1995: 241–246). In Berlin, although the court opera was opened to the public in the eighteenth century, the only non-aristocratic group admitted (by invitation) was army officers. Around 1800, the audience consisted of mostly the nobility, the military and administrative officials. Only well into the nineteenth century was it also opened to civil servants, merchants, bankers, homeowners, and affluent craftsmen, and, on Sundays, to members of the working class such as craftsmen, journeymen, household maids, and other servants (Walter 1997: 319).

In South America, as in New York or London, the producers of nineteenth-century opera were Italians and the consumers were the local elites. At the Teatro Colón in Buenos Aires, for example, the Hispo-Argentines imposed a "cold" tone of "Spanish dignity rather than Italian enthusiasm," although the gender-separate galleries were dominated by Italian immigrants (Rosselli 1990: 170). Waves of Italian immigration to Argentina, Uruguay, and Chile in the last third of the nineteenth century created a demand for lower-price, popular opera houses catering to middle- and lower-class audiences. Buenos Aires's Teatro Doria (later Marconi), an example of the more plebian end, was originally a wooden barn, located outside the city center near a market and railway station, and filled in the hot season with "butchers in shirtsleeves smoking tremendous Italian cigars and spitting to right and left" (Rosselli 1990: 175). This popular operatic tradition continued into the 1950s, but finally disappeared as a result of the assimilation of the Italian immigrant population and the loss of an Italian operatic hegemony (Rosselli 1990: 181).

Social segregation at the opera was created by ticket pricing, tacit agreement, and in some cases, written regulations (Ahlquist 2007: 6). In eighteenth-century Russia, official regulations governed who was permitted to sit, according to rank, in different places in the theater. The removal of these regulations in the nineteenth century did little to change the status quo (Buckler 2000: 26). In eighteenth- and nineteenth-century Paris and London, the *beau monde* or "World," a cosmopolitan mix of nobles, wealthy bourgeois, professionals, artists, and even courtesans, tended to resist the rigid divisions of Vienna, for example, where a wooden barrier separated nobles from commoners (Weber 2000: 171).

In the United States in the early nineteenth century, the theater was considered to be a democratizing institution, frequented by persons of all classes and races—though the use of separate entrances often prevented the occupants of boxes, pit, and gallery from rubbing shoulders. African-Americans were required to sit in the gallery, and in the South they had it to themselves. In the St. Charles Theater in New Orleans, an important destination for traveling opera companies, the gallery was divided into separate sections for free blacks and slaves (Preston [1993] 2001: 16, 280). According to Joseph Patrick Roppolo, the St. Charles's privileged elite formed a "thin circle of elegance," sandwiched between a more diverse gathering that included, in addition to the black audience mentioned above, "housewives, clerks, salesmen, shopkeepers, prostitutes, vagabonds, and drunks," as well as longshoremen and steamboat workers (1950: 125–126). Between 1860 and 1914, the number and size of opera audiences reached a peak as the number of works in the repertoire dwindled. Since then, competition by the phonograph, cinema, radio, television, and more recently, the Internet has led to a decrease in numbers at the opera house but, at the same time, to new audiences for opera in the home and the movie theater. It remains to be seen whether the recent collapse of the recording industry will lead to a renewed interest in opera productions, either in the opera house itself or by way of live broadcasts.

Thanks to increasingly sophisticated mechanisms of market research, more accurate information on the composition, participation, and taste of contemporary audiences is now being obtained by opera houses themselves. Rosanne Martorella has used this kind of information to gauge the relationship of audience to repertoire. She attributes the conservative repertoire of the Metropolitan Opera and the Chicago Lyric Opera to their reliance on subscription performances to fill the house and supply a minimal financial base. As an example she mentions White Paper published by the Metropolitan Opera House in 1971, blaming an unadventurous repertoire on the necessity of submitting to box office demands. Citing the lack of government support, the report points to opera houses in European countries, where the difference between box-office receipts and expenses (amounting to 90 percent in Sweden and 70 percent in Germany, for example) was made up by government subsidy (Martorella 1977: 354–366). While somewhat more adventurous programming has characterized institutions like the New York City Opera, before its recent demise, and the San Francisco Opera, with its younger, less subscriber-dominated audience, one must look to university-affiliated institutions for the regular production of the avant-garde and non-mainstream repertoire.

Since 1982, the National Endowment for the Arts, in conjunction with the Bureau of the Census, has published demographic data on public participation in the arts. The results of this process have yielded a wealth of information on opera-going in the United States. For example, the percentage of opera-goers, always low compared to attendees at other performing-arts events, held steady at around 3 percent of the population in the 1982, 1992, and 2002 surveys; in 2008, it dropped to 2.1 percent. The percentage of the population claiming to "like" opera dropped to 8.3 percent in 2008 from 10–12 percent in previous decades. Figures for 2008 indicate a pronounced relationship between opera-going, formal education, and income. About two-thirds of adults who attended at least one opera in that year had a college or graduate degree, and more than half earned $75,000 or more (25 percent earned at least $150,000). Attendance for most age categories of opera-goers has dropped somewhat or changed only slightly in number from 2002 to 2008; the only exception is for adults aged 35–44, whose presence increased by 6.2 percent since 2002. About 5 percent of adults watched or listened to a recorded or live broadcast of opera in 2008, down from 12 percent in 1982 and 1992. In 2008, 84.8 percent of the audience for live performances was white, and about 59 percent female (National Endowment for the Arts 2009; DiMaggio and Mukhtar 2004: 169–194).

The perception of opera audiences as a small, elite contingent of the population, concentrated in major urban centers, is currently being challenged by the continuing success of the Metropolitan Opera's "Live in HD" broadcasts and the emergence of high-definition broadcast series in other cities. It is further challenged by the success of various forms of "pop opera," or opera that exists outside the confines of the traditional opera house. While opera has always bridged the divide between classical and popular music (a divide only recognized since the nineteenth century), since the late twentieth century pop opera (sometimes known as "popera") has created a new audience and transformed the music industry. A concert by the Three Tenors (Plácido Domingo, Luciano Pavarotti, and José Carreras) in Dodger Stadium in 1994, for example, yielded around $13.5 million in ticket sales and reached an audience of around 1.3 billion via worldwide telecasts. Multi-platinum albums by the likes of Il Divo, Andrea Bocelli,

Sarah Brightman, and Josh Groban continue to dominate the new Billboard chart for "crossover," in addition to yielding a new Grammy category (Branstetter 2009: 1–3).

Gender and Identity

Several recent studies have treated gender and identity at the opera. Georgia Cowart (1994) has looked at commentary by critics and moralists condemning women's fascination for opera and their participation as opera-goers in early modern Paris. Hall-Witt (2007: 19–22) has documented ways in which London society women used their box as a base for tending family status and shaping social networks, while peripatetic males traversed the theater in the era of the "event aesthetic." For younger women, the opera box, one of the few sites available for the mingling of men and women at the upper reaches of society, served as the venue *par excellence* for meeting and interacting with potential marriage prospects. Particularly in the nineteenth century, a wealth of fictional literature appropriated the "opera-box trope" as a backdrop for the drama that took place there on a nightly basis between the sexes and among individuals representing the fine gradations of a social hierarchy (Solie 1997: 185–208). The institution of the afternoon matinee in late nineteenth-century New York has been seen as the catalyst for an increase in opera-going among women (Block 2008: 193–216). In general, women with some degree of social status in the eighteenth and nineteenth centuries were able to wield a certain social authority at the opera. Any such authority is absent in the theater of our own time, according to feminist commentator Jill Dolan (1988), who sees the female audience member as an outsider in the male-dominated world of spectatorship.

In 1993, Wayne Koestenbaum, a poet and cultural critic, interwove personal subjectivity and sociological observation to document the phenomenon of the "opera queen," the gay man obsessed with opera for reasons involving listening, desire, divas, and sexual identity (Koestenbaum 1993). Paul Robinson elaborated on this phenomenon in his essay, "The Opera Queen: A Voice from the Closet" ([1994] 2002). Mitchell Morris brought the opera queen to a musicological readership around the same time in his exploration of the opera queen's fascination with performance, with a critical language capable of articulating the erotic, and with various ways of "queening" the canon (1993: 184–200). The phenomenon of the opera queen is generally considered to have declined after its heyday in the closeted 1950s, largely because of the growing freedom of gay men to meet in other places and because of the disappearance of vinyl opera recordings, with which it was closely associated (Clum 1994).

Much remains to be done before a more comprehensive history of opera audiences can begin to be adumbrated. Interestingly, some of the widest gaps coincide with the areas in which the canon has retained the strongest hold, most notably, in Italy and the German-speaking countries. Opera archives, subscriber lists, newspaper reviews and reports, letters, diaries, and statistical data await study. Finally, methodologies involving literary representations of opera audiences, as well as the depiction of stage audiences within opera itself, promise to yield equally valuable though different kinds of cultural insights (Gossett 1990: 41–64; Parakilas 1992: 181–202; Minor 1995: 1–36; Solie 1997: 185–208; Buckler 2000.) The study of such representations can, when supported by other forms of evidence, contribute to an understanding of opera-going; they can also convey symbolic messages holding resonant cultural and political meanings. A case study will demonstrate how audiences were represented in productions at the Paris Opéra in the late years of Louis XIV's reign, and how the audience-centered aesthetic developed in these works influenced Antoine Watteau's well-known painting, *The Pilgrimage to Cythera* (1717).

The Staging of the Audience in the Era of the Sun King

The theater provided one of the few venues in Old-Regime France where different social classes could congregate, and as such it served as a potent political symbol. A series of depictions of stage audiences in late seventeenth- and early eighteenth-century operatic works demonstrates how the audience was used as the metonymic signifier of a Parisian public during the reign of Louis XIV (1643–1715). Through a sophisticated system of intertextual allusion, these works alternately characterized audiences as the collective victim of an absolutist, militaristic regime or the liberated beneficiaries of the pleasures and freedoms of the Parisian metropolis. The series begins with *Le bourgeois gentilhomme* (1670), the last comedy-ballet of Jean-Baptiste Lully and Molière, produced a few years before the introduction of French opera. Unlike the court ballet, which had glorified Louis and his court, the comedy-ballet was known for its satiric humor, sparing neither the king nor the nobility. The epilogue to *Le bourgeois gentilhomme*, entitled "Le ballet des nations" (Lully [1670] 2006: 216–268), was introduced and concluded by the comic staging of a public audience, in some regards a representation of Molière's own audience in Paris. In it, various factions, representing different levels of society as well as foreigners and provincials, collide and compete in the face of a shortage of seats and libretti. After this study in social diversity, the stage audience settles down to view a ballet, by means of which it collectively undergoes a profound transformation. In a brief closing chorus, its pseudo-contrapuntal quarreling is transformed into a harmonious, hymn-like declaration of pleasure and awe at the privilege of viewing entertainment fit for gods. This privilege, formerly available only to the king and his court, has now raised the public audience to the level of kings or "gods" themselves. In sum, the scene depicts a utopia of theater, itself an agent in the transformation of society from a chaotic diversity to a harmonious union.

Le bourgeois gentilhomme was the last collaboration between Lully and Molière, and one of the last works in a series of comedy-ballets embodying a comic, irreverent spirit that was virtually eradicated in the 1670s. Instead, that decade saw the introduction of opera, known as the *tragédie en musique* or musical tragedy, by Jean-Baptiste Lully and his librettist Philippe Quinault. This genre featured the heroic content and lofty tone appropriate to the image of a king approaching the apogee of his power. Its seriousness may be seen in the prologue of a transitional stage piece by Lully, *Les fêtes de l'Amour et de Bacchus* ([1672] 1971: I: 40), a reworking of the audience scene from the *Bourgeois gentilhomme*. Here, instead of depicting a utopia of theater, as in the original comedy-ballet, the scene is revised to conform to more conventional sovereign praise. The action takes place in a palatial room rather than an ordinary public theater. The initial chorus, with its burlesque confusion, is halted abruptly by the imperious recitative of an absolutist Muse, who insists that the audience cease its common squabbling and speak in a high style more appropriate to a glorious king. For the remainder of the prologue, three Muses command the rambunctious, lively, and diverse audience of *Le bourgeois gentilhomme* to sing a stilted, artificial tribute to the king, which they dictate line by line. This scene, written in the year of Molière's death, marks the decline of the comedy-ballet and the manifesto of the new opera, a royal entertainment emphasizing tragedy and heroism. Inaugurating the direct intervention of royal propaganda in the affairs of the Opéra, it hints at an intention to stamp the king's august identity on this urban venue and to silence the collective voice of a heteroglot audience.

These two depictions of a stage audience provide respective models for an audience-centered versus a sovereign-centered aesthetic and ideology. While the earlier work depicts a subjective audience, unruly in its demeanor but capable of being overcome and transformed by the beauty of spectacle, the later work depicts a subjugated audience, constrained to obediently praise a king with interests different from its own. This sovereign-centered aesthetic characterized the prologues of the *tragédie en musique*, which coincided with the height of a propaganda of glory in the 1670s. Stage audiences do not figure in these works, though the audience at the Opéra was surely expected to identify with the large choruses representing the populace paying tribute to the power of Louis XIV. Conflating the Paris audience with these massed voices, passages in many of the prologues of these works rhetorically enjoin those in attendance to add their voices to the monumental praise of the Sun King.

Just after Lully's death in 1687, in a period characterized by increasing financial deprivation and overweening militarism, the stage audience reappeared as a vehicle of political critique. In the prologue of *Orphée* (1688), an opera by Lully's son Louis Lully, an audience expecting to be entertained finds only an empty theater, through whose back portico may be seen the bleak signs of winter. Venus, coming to the aid of the disappointed audience, condemns superfluous pomp and the horrors of war. Her lament for her son Orpheus is joined by the Games and Pleasures, as well as Cupid and the Graces. It befits the subversive implications of the opera, which represents both the bereft audience and the artists of the theater as the victims of an absolute, intolerant, and militaristic ruler.

Though the *tragédie en musique* continued as an official genre well into the eighteenth century, the 1690s saw the emergence of a new genre, the *opéra-ballet*. An audience-pleasing mix of light operatic action, song, and dance, it offered entertainment based on colorful settings with elaborate costumes and stage designs. In fact, many of these works represented satiric reversals of the plots of the court ballets of an earlier era, in which Louis XIV had danced the roles of powerful gods and heroes. Also, just as the court ballet of Louis's youth had celebrated his court as the home of luxury and abundance, these Parisian works glorified the Opéra and its audience as a privileged social elite.

Between 1699 and 1710, a series of *opéra-ballets* set against the backdrop of Venetian carnival presented a libertine, public Paris under the mask of Venice. Their focus, rather than on the king, is on the entertainments and audiences of Paris-*qua*-Venice. Ballets, comedies, balls, gambling halls, and street charlatans all make an appearance. In two of these works, charlatans hustle the crowds, inviting them to "step right up" to urban spectacles that are joyous and inclusive. *Le carnaval de Venise* (1699), by André Campra, plays directly off the prologue, tragic plot, and ideological associations of Louis Lully's *Orphée*. For the intense tragedy and deprived audience of the earlier work, it substitutes a delighted audience witnessing a comic opera featuring Pluto (the villainous surrogate of Louis XIV in Louis Lully's *Orphée)* as a ridiculous buffoon. In an elaborate staging, boxes filled with satisfied spectators descend on either side of the stage and remain throughout the inserted opera (Cowart 2001a, 2008).

Another group of *opéra-ballets*, on the subject of Cythera, equates the utopia of Venus's sacred isle with the Parisian *opéra-ballet* and its audience. Venus and her son Cupid, the rulers of an inclusive, libertine society, represent the antithesis of the devout, absolutist monarch. In these works, pleasurable *fêtes galantes* feature lovers singing the praise of Venus. The final scene of Louis Bourgeois's *Les amours déguisés* (1713) depicts the audience of a *fête* in honor of Cupid. This diverse stage audience, including citizens of many nations who have come together to celebrate the triumph of the god of love, is subtly equated with the audience of the Opéra itself, known for its libertinism as the Temple of Cupid or the Temple of Venus.

Another Cytherean *opéra-ballet*, *Le triomphe des arts* (1700, music by Michel de la Barre), more pointedly alludes to the Paris Opéra as a self-reflexive Cythera, and its audience as the microcosm of a public society. Its entries celebrate architecture as stage design, music as the score of the *opéra-ballet*, living sculpture as dance, and poetry as the *livret* of this new art form. They also celebrate a new breed of artists working in these fields. The final scene of this work features a chorus representing Dance and a soloist representing Music, celebrating the victory of Pygmalion, love, and the arts. Various allusions hint that the coming to life of Pygmalion's statue represents the depiction of a new society coming to life through the arts of the *opéra-ballet*. A singer costumed as a sailor communicates directly to the audience, inviting its members to embark on the seas of desire. As a whole, the entries of *Le triomphe des arts* may be read as the successive awakening of the arts of the *opéra-ballet* itself, and the final scene as a direct appeal to its audience to join in its cult of peace and freedom. The *livret* of this work was written by Antoine Houdar de La Motte, the leader of the Moderns in the famous Quarrel between the Ancients and the Moderns. It may be considered a defense of an early eighteenth-century modernism and of the libertine theater, especially the Opéra, against the attacks of the antitheatrical lobby.

A series of musical comedies at the Comédie-Française and the Parisian fairground theaters further develop the myth of Cythera as an allusion to the theater and its audience. A musical comedy by Florent Carton Dancourt, entitled *Les trois cousines* (1700), transfers the myth to modern-day France. In its final *divertissement*, young village couples costumed as pilgrims prepare to make a "pilgrimage" to the shrine of Cupid, which may be interpreted as the libertine haunts of Paris and, more particularly, the theater. Dancourt makes specific reference to the inclusive nature of this shrine, where all social classes are welcome. A few years later, in a series of plays by Louis Fuzelier at the fairground theaters, audience members are invited to come as "pilgrims" to the theater itself.

The painter Jean-Antoine Watteau worked at the Paris Opéra, probably as a set painter, shortly after his arrival in Paris in 1702. Many of his later works were based on themes and characters of the Parisian stage (Cowart 2001b, 2009). His most famous painting, *The Pilgrimage to Cythera* (1717), summarizes the *opéra-ballet*'s imagery of a libertine, politically oppositional, audience-centered Cythera. Many elements of this painting, especially the later version (ca. 1718–1719) of the work now housed in the Charlottenburg Palace in Berlin (Figure 30.1), can be explained through reference to the *livrets* and the frontispieces of the *opéra-ballets Le triomphe des arts* and *Les amours*

FIGURE 30.1 Jean-Antoine Watteau, *The Pilgrimage to Cythera* (Berlin: Charlottenburg Palace), oil on canvas, ca. 1718–1719. Art Resource.

déguisés, Dancourt's play *Les trois cousines*, and the various plays of Fuselier at the fairground theaters. In the painting, a group of pilgrims, so designated by the characteristic staff and cape of pilgrims to religious shrines, pays homage to the statue of Venus and Cupid on her sacred isle. This imagery is directly derived from *Le triomphe des arts*, including its cult of Venus on a sacred island where couples pay homage to the goddess, and its invitation to its audience to embark on the seas of love and pleasure. It further alludes to Dancourt's play and Fuzelier's series of plays equating pilgrims with the audience of theater.

Like the *opéra-ballet Le triomphe des arts*, Watteau's *Pilgrimage* invites its own audience into the transformative experience of the arts and the birth of a new society. On the right, the statue of Venus and her cupids, coming to life out of the grey stone, echoes the awakening of the stone cupids on the Temple of Cupid in the *opéra-ballet*. The peaceful nature of this society is indicated by Venus, as she holds Cupid's arrows out of reach. This gesture may also refer to the victory of Venus over the militant Minerva, goddess of war, in the prologue to *Les amours déguisés*. Signifying this victory, a coat of arms has been placed as an offering at the foot of the statue, while a cupid pulls a laurel wreath, symbol of victory, from the armor to the feet of Venus. Entering on the lower right of the painting, the viewer is swept into a chain of lovers that progresses toward the embarkation to the left.

The point of embarkation may be seen to resemble a parting theater curtain, equating the voyage of love and pleasure with the experience of spectacle and the arts, and the lovers with the audience. The arch-like formation of cupids over the boat, playing on and reversing the phenomenon of the royal entry through an *arc de triomphe*, literally celebrates a triumphal "entry" of a public audience into an art of societal regeneration represented by the theater. As in Dancourt's play, this process embraces the upper class, literally the aristocratically dressed individuals placed high on the hill to the viewer's right, and the lower class (dressed in peasant weskits, straw hats, and unkempt suits), symbolically placed below. As they approach the ship, this stratification breaks down, as aristocrats and commoners alike have boarded or are preparing to do so. In fact, in the original version of the painting, now at the Louvre, Watteau clearly adorned the head of one of the peasants with a laurel wreath—the symbol of victory more commonly associated with the king (Cowart 2001b: 2009).

In summary, the operatic treatment of Cythera and Watteau's Cytherian vision have replaced the praise of the king with the praise of the new arts of the *opéra-ballet* and its audience. Certainly the audience of the Paris Opéra had always taken pleasure in staging themselves. This act of staging, moreover, had accrued added significance as the king withdrew from attendance at the opera. William Weber (2007) has traced a growing social and cultural cosmopolitanism occurring in capital cities, especially Paris and London, in the eighteenth century. In the new order, fundamentally different from the old courtly order, authority was founded upon the empowerment of the public. The opera was the central institution within this newly empowered public, since it was the primary meeting place for members of an international elite. In depicting stage audiences, then, creators of the *opéra- ballet* and related genres may be understood to have harnessed the power of a new kind of staging as a way of representing a new kind of power—the power of the theatrical audience, and particularly the audience of opera, which has now become the icon of a new cultural authority.

See also: Patronage, How Opera Traveled, Autographs, Memorabilia, and the Aesthetics of Collecting, The Operatic Canon, Operatic Images, Gender

Bibliography

Adorno, Theodor W. 1993. "Bourgeois Opera." In *Opera through Other Eyes*, edited and translated by David J. Levin, 14–41. Stanford CA: Stanford University Press.

Ahlquist, Karen. 1997. *Democracy at the Opera: Music, Theater, and Culture in New York City, 1815–1860*. Urbana: University of Illinois Press.

Barthes, Roland. 1999. "The Death of the Author." In *Image—Music—Text*, translated by Stephen Heath, 42–46. New York: Noonday Press.

Bereson, Ruth. 2002. *The Operatic State*. London: Routledge.

Block, Adrienne Fried. 2008. "Matinee Mania, or the Regendering of Nineteenth-Century Audiences in New York City." *19th-Century Music* 31/3: 193–216.

Botstein, Leon. 1999. "The Audience." *Musical Quarterly* 83/4: 479–486.

Branstetter, Leah. 2006. "Angels and Arctic Monkeys: A Study of Opera Crossover." Master's thesis, University of Cincinnati.

Brewer, John, and Ann Bermingham, eds. 1995. *The Consumption of Culture, 1600–1800: Image, Object, Text*. London: Routledge.

Buckler, Julie A. 2000. *The Literary Lorgnette: Attending Opera in Imperial Russia*. Stanford, CA: Stanford University Press.

Burden, Michael. 2008. "'Play It Again Sam': The 'Encore' in 18th-Century London Opera." Oxford University Research Archive. Online. Available: http://ora.ouls.ox.ac.uk/objects/uuid%3A6ec725fe-0ec1-4dbf-98e7-19d9170de22c (accessed August 17, 2012).

Butsch, Richard. 2000. *The Making of American Audiences: From Stage to Television, 1750–1990*. Cambridge: Cambridge University Press.

Cairns, David. "Arturo Toscanini." 1992. *The New Grove Dictionary of Opera*. Online. Available: http://www.oxfordmusiconline.com/subscriber/article/grove/music/28197 (accessed August 17, 2012).

Charlton, David. 2012. *Opera in the Age of Rousseau: Music, Confrontation, Realism*. Cambridge Studies in Opera. Cambridge: Cambridge University Press.

Clum, John M. 1994. "Opera without Queens/Queens without Opera." *Performing Arts Journal* 16/2: 107–115.

Conrad, Peter. 1987. *A Song of Love and Death: The Meaning of Opera*. New York: Poseidon Press.

Cowart, Georgia J. 2009. "The Musical Theater in Watteau's Paris." In *Watteau, Music, and Theater*, edited by Katharine Baetjer, 9–18. New York: Metropolitan Museum of Art and Yale University Press.

——. 2008. *The Triumph of Pleasure: Louis XIV and the Politics of Spectacle*. Chicago: University of Chicago Press.

——. 2001a. "Carnival in Venice or Protest in Paris? Louis XIV and the Politics of Subversion at the Paris Opéra." *Journal of the American Musicological Society* 54/2: 265–302.

——. 2001b. "Watteau's *Pilgrimage to Cythera* and the Subversive Ideology of the Opera-Ballet." *Art Bulletin* 83: 460–478.

——. 1994. "Of Women, Sex, and Folly: Opera under the Old Regime." *Cambridge Opera Journal* 6/3: 205–220.

Crosten, William L. 1972. *French Grand Opera: An Art and a Business*. New York: Da Capo Press.

Davis, John Anthony. 2005. "Opera and Absolutism in Restoration Italy, 1815–1860." *Journal of Interdisciplinary History* 36/4: 569–594.

Dill, Charles. 1998. *Monstrous Opera: Rameau and the Tragic Tradition*. Princeton, NJ: Princeton University Press.

DiMaggio, Paul, and Toqir Mukhtar. 2004. "Arts Participation as Cultural Capital in the United States, 1982–2002: Signs of Decline?" *Poetics* 32: 169–194.

Dolan, Jill. 1988. *The Feminist Spectator as Critic*. Ann Arbor, MI: UMI Research Press, 1988.

Feldman, Martha. 2007. *Opera and Sovereignty: Transforming Myth in Eighteenth-Century Italy*. Chicago: University of Chicago Press.

Fenner, Theodore. 1994. *Opera in London: Views of the Press, 1785–1830*. Carbondale: Southern Illinois University Press.

Fulcher, Jane. 1987. *The Nation's Image: French Grand Opera as Politics and Politicized Art*. Cambridge: Cambridge University Press.

Gay, Peter. 1995. *The Naked Heart*. Vol. 4 of *The Bourgeois Experience: Victoria to Freud*. New York: W. W. Norton.

Gerhard, Anselm. 1998. *The Urbanization of Opera: Music Theater in Paris in the Nineteenth Century*, translated by Mary Whittall. Chicago: University of Chicago Press.

Glixon, Beth L., and Jonathan E. 2006. *Inventing the Business of Opera: The Impresario and His World in Seventeenth-Century Venice*. AMS Studies in Music. New York: Oxford University Press.

Goehr, Lydia. [1992] 2007. *The Imaginary Museum of Musical Works: An Essay in the Philosophy of Music*. Reprint. New York: Oxford University Press.

Gossett, Philip. 1990. "Becoming a Citizen: The Chorus in 'Risorgimento' Opera." *Cambridge Opera Journal* 2/1: 41–64.

Gurewitsch, Matthew. "Frisky Young Tenors on Operatic War Horses." *New York Times* (April 20). Online. Available: http://www.nytimes.com/2008/04/20/arts/music/20gure.html (accessed August 17, 2012).

Hall-Witt, Jennifer. 2007. *Fashionable Acts: Opera and Elite Culture in London, 1780–1880*. Durham: University of New Hampshire Press.

Harris-Warrick, Rebecca. 2007. "Lully's On-Stage Societies." In Johnson et al. 2007, 53–71.

Huebner, Steven. 1989. "Opera Audiences in Paris 1830–1870." *Music & Letters* 70/2: 206–225.

Hunter, Mary. 1999. *The Culture of Opera Buffa in Mozart's Vienna: A Poetics of Entertainment*. Princeton, NJ: Princeton University Press.

Johnson, James H. 2011. *Venice Incognito: Masks in the Serene Republic*. Berkeley and Los Angeles: University of California Press.

——. 1995. *Listening in Paris: A Cultural History*. Studies on the History of Society and Culture 21, edited by Victoria E. Bonnell and Lynn Hunt. Berkeley and Los Angeles: University of California Press.

Johnson, Victoria, Jane F. Fulcher, and Thomas Ertman, eds. 2007. *Opera and Society in Italy and France from Monteverdi to Bourdieu*. Cambridge: Cambridge University Press.

Kimbell, David R. B. 1981. *Verdi in the Age of Italian Romanticism*. Cambridge: Cambridge University Press.

Knif, Henrik. 1995. *Gentlemen and Spectators: Studies in Journals, Opera, and the Social Scene in Late Stuart London*. Helsinki: Finnish Historical Society.

Koestenbaum, Wayne. 1993. *The Queen's Throat: Opera, Homosexuality, and the Mystery of Desire*. New York: Poseidon.

La Gorce, Jérôme de. 1992. *L'Opéra à Paris au temps de Louis XIV: Histoire d'un théâtre*. Paris: Desjonquères.

Langhans, Edward A. 1992. "Seating." In The New Grove Dictionary of Opera, edited by Stanley Sadie. Grove Music Online. Oxford Music Online. Available: http://www.oxfordmusiconline.com/subscriber/article/grove/music/O004893 (accessed August 18, 2012).

Levine, Lawrence. 1988. *Highbrow/Lowbrow: The Emergence of Cultural Hierarchy in America*. Cambridge, MA: Harvard University Press.

Lindenberger, Herbert. 1984. *Opera: The Extravagant Art*. Ithaca, NY: Cornell University Press.

Lully, Jean-Baptiste. [1670] 2006. *Le bourgeois gentilhomme*, edited by Herbert Schneider. In *Oeuvres complètes*, edited by Jérôme de La Gorce and Herbert Schneider. Series 2. Vol. 4. Hildesheim: Georg Olms.

——. [1672] 1971. *Les fêtes de l'Amour et de Bacchus*. In *Recueil général des opéras représentés par L'Académie Royale de Musique depuis son établissement*. 3 vols. Geneva: Slatkine Reprint. Originally published in Paris, 1703–1746.

Martorella, Rosanne. 1977. "The Relationship between Box Office and Repertoire: A Case Study of Opera." *The Sociological Quarterly* 18/3: 354–366.

McKay, David. 1985. "Opera in Colonial Boston." *American Music* 3/2: 133–142.

Minor, Ryan. 2005. "Wagner's Last Chorus: Consecrating Space and Spectatorship in *Parsifal*." *Cambridge Opera Journal* 17/1: 1–36.

Morris, Mitchell. 1993. "Reading as an Opera Queen." In *Musicology and Difference: Gender and Sexuality in Music Scholarship*, edited by Ruth A. Solie, 184–200. Berkeley and Los Angeles: University of California Press.

Muir, Edward. 2005. "Why Venice? Venetian Society and the Success of Early Opera." *Journal of Interdisciplinary History* 36/3: 331–353.

Müller, Sven Oliver. 2006. "Distinktion, Demonstration und Disziplinierung: Veränderungen in Publikumsverhalten in Londoner und Berliner Opernhäusern im 19. Jahrhundert." *International Review of the Aesthetics and Sociology of Music* 37/2: 167–187.

Nalbach, Daniel. 1972. *The King's Theatre, 1704–1867*. London: Society for Theatre Research.

National Endowment for the Arts, Office of Research and Analysis. 2009. Survey of Public Participation in the Arts. Research Division Report 49. Online. Available: www.nea.gov/research/index.html (accessed August 18, 2012).

Palisca, Claude V. 1954a. "The Beginnings of Baroque Music: Its Roots in Sixteenth-Century Theory and Polemics." PhD diss., Harvard University.

——. 1954b. "Girolamo Mei: Mentor to the Florentine Camerata." *Musical Quarterly* 40/1: 1–20.

Parakilas, James. 1992. "Political Representation and the Chorus in Nineteenth-Century Opera." *19th-Century Music* 16/2: 181–202.

Pasler, Jann. 2008. "Pelléas and Power: Forces behind the Reception of Debussy's Opera." In Pasler, *Writing Through Music: Essays on Music, Culture, and Politics*, 181–212. New York: Oxford University Press.

Preston, Katherine K. [1993] 2001. *Opera on the Road: Traveling Opera Troupes in the United States, 1825–60*. Urbana: University of Illinois Press.

Rao, Nancy Yunhwa. 2000. "Racial Essences and Historical Invisibility: Chinese Opera in New York, 1930." *Cambridge Opera Journal* 12/2: 135–162.

Ravel, Jeffrey S. 1999. *The Contested Parterre: Public Theater and French Political Culture, 1680–1791*. Ithaca, NY: Cornell University Press.

——. 1993. "Seating the Public: Spheres and Loathing in the Paris Theaters, 1777–1778." *French Historical Studies* 18: 173–210.
Raynor, Henry. 1978. *Music and Society since 1815*. New York: Taplinger.
Robinson, Paul. [1994] 2002. "The Opera Queen: A Voice from the Closet." In *Opera, Sex, and Other Vital Matters*, 157–169. Chicago: University of Chicago Press. Originally published in *Cambridge Opera Journal* 6/3: 283–291.
Roppolo, Joseph Patrick. 1950. "Audiences in New Orleans Theatre, 1845–1861." *Tulane Studies in English* 2: 121–135. New Orleans: Tulane University Press.
Rosand, Ellen. 1991. *Opera in Seventeenth-Century Venice: The Creation of a Genre*. Berkeley and Los Angeles: University of California Press.
Rosselli, John. 1992. "Sociology of Opera." In *The New Grove Dictionary of Opera*, edited by Stanley Sadie. *Grove Music Online. Oxford Music Online*. Available: http://www.oxfordmusiconline.com/subscriber/article/grove/music/O005915 (accessed August 18, 2012).
——. 1990. "The Opera Business and the Italian Immigrant Community in Latin America 1820–1930: The Example of Buenos Aires." *Past and Present* 127: 155–182.
——. 1984. *The Opera Industry in Italy from Cimarosa to Verdi: The Role of the Impresario*. Cambridge: Cambridge University Press.
Solie, Ruth. 1997. "Fictions of the Opera Box." In *Genre, Nationhood, and Sexual Difference*, edited by Richard Dellamora and Daniel Fischlin, 185–208. New York: Columbia University Press.
Sorba, Carlotta. 1995. "To Please the Public: Composers and Audiences in Nineteenth-Century Italy." *Journal of Interdisciplinary History* 36/4: 595–614.
Sorlin, Pierre. 1992. "Le mirage du public." *Revue d'histoire moderne et contemporaine* 39/1: 86–102.
Wakin, Daniel J. 2008. "Ban on Solo Encores at the Met? Ban, What Ban?" *New York Times* (April 23; rev. April 25). Online. Available: http://www.nytimes.com/2008/04/23/arts/music/23aria.html (accessed August 18, 2012).
Walsh, T. J. *Opera in Dublin, 1798–1820: Frederic Jones and the Crow Street Theatre*. New York: Oxford University Press, 1993.
Walter, Michael. 1997. *Die Oper ist ein Irrenhaus: Sozialgeschichte der Oper im 19. Jahrhundert*. Stuttgart: Metzler.
Weber, William. 2007. "Opera and the Cultural Authority of the Capital City." In Johnson et al. 2007, 160–180.
——. [1975] 2004. *Music and the Middle Class: The Social Structure of Concert Life in Paris and Vienna between 1830 and 1848*. 2nd ed. Aldershot, UK: Ashgate.
——. 1997. "Did People Listen in the Eighteenth Century?" *Early Music* 25/4: 678–691.
——. 1993. "L'institution et son public: L'Opéra à Paris et à Londres au XVIIIe siècle." *Annales E.S.C.* 48/6: 1519–1540.
Wood, Caroline, and Graham Sadler. 2000. *French Baroque Opera: A Reader*. Aldershot, UK: Ashgate.
Zaslaw, Neal. 1983. "At the Paris Opera in 1747." *Early Music* 11/4: 515–516.

CHAPTER 31

AUTOGRAPHS, MEMORABILIA, AND THE AESTHETICS OF COLLECTING

DANIELA MACCHIONE

TRANSLATED BY JULIA GRELLA O'CONNELL

> The artist produces in a kind of state of grace, of exaltation that fascinates the amateur—the name given to the client [...]—and that stands in opposition to modern production.[1]
>
> (Godbout 2008: 332)

Documenting the Art of Music Collecting

Opera autographs remain a small, but popular component in the larger market for rare books and manuscripts. The direction of this market is influenced by many factors, and to gather statistics from it is a frustrating undertaking, because, among other reasons, the autograph market exists through a network of private sales, trades, and agreements that elude every attempt at proper documentation. Statistics gathered from bibliographical tools like annual records of sales at auctions would, inevitably, be incomplete. For example, the *American Book Prices Current* (ABPC 1895–), an Anglo-American repository that annually gathers information about books and manuscripts sold at auction (only by those auction houses listed in the publication) does not include unsold items or those sold from book sellers and antiquarians; it does not even record all of the items since, for instance, multiple lots of miscellanea are actually excluded.

Sales catalogues from the major firms of the antiquarian market reveal much about market demand, taste, client motivation, and cultural management. Finding sales catalogues through institutional resources, however, is not at all a simple matter. For example, the *Répertoire International de Littérature Musicale* (RILM, a comprehensive bibliography of publications in music) registers only a few hundred catalogues, most of which are very recent and come from big auction houses. The libraries and archives of auction houses and antiquarian book sellers would seem to offer the most promising results, if it weren't for the fact that finding complete collections of sales catalogues in a single archive is also very difficult. Moreover, we cannot count on libraries to conserve sales catalogues, mainly because they are considered ephemera, articles made for circumscribed and temporary events like sales; in some countries, auction and sales catalogues are not even considered publications. The most useful instrument for diachronic tracking of antiquarian booksellers' activities is, perhaps, the *Sales Catalogues Index Project Input* (SCIPIO), now accessible through the *Online Computer Library Center* (OCLC, available in participating libraries), which provides information about auction sales catalogues from all major North American and European auction houses, as well as many private sales from the end of the sixteenth century to the present. Only a few musicological journals, mostly Anglo-American and dedicated to a particular composer, such as the *Beethoven Journal*, regularly include reports of sales of specific interest to the particular publication. Thematic catalogues provide information regarding autograph sources that circulate in the antiquarian market and belong to private collectors, but the research is not usually driven in any systematic way.

Music collecting is an activity that has always been closely associated with music-producing systems, but in the musicological arena, the phenomenon of "collecting" as a broader human phenomenon *tout-court*—a historical, socio-anthropological, economic manifestation of that same system—appears to be a field of only marginal interest, little explored and only rarely confronted as a topic for autonomous research, consigned, rather, to studies of a bibliographic nature, catalogues, and essays on single collections, collectors, or antiquarian firms. While economic aspects of the music market and publishing industry have long occupied scholars, expanded consideration of music collecting as another expression of that same market does not seem to have been attempted.

The following pages do not address all aspects of this interdisciplinary phenomenon, passing over, for example, the merits of the music collections for research, and for the variety of musicological literature and music enterprises like critical editions, which owe much to autographs and early editions and speak for themselves. The intention of this chapter, rather, is to share some reflections on the social dynamics of the production and transmission of collectible objects, specifically the privately owned autographs that circulate under the radar and inspire the work conducted in *OperaCat*.[2]

OperaCat is a database of descriptions drawn from sales catalogues of various types of manuscript materials—autograph letters, documents, musical manuscripts (scribal as well as autographs from working manuscripts, sketches, and drafts to pages from albums and smaller musical quotation), signed photographs—relating to the Italian opera composers Gioachino Rossini, Gaetano Donizetti, Vincenzo Bellini, Giuseppe Verdi, and Giacomo Puccini.[3] *OperaCat* offers a representative assortment of operatic collectibles that have circulated in the official antiquarian market, while revealing the tendencies of opera collecting over the last 150 years.

A peculiar separation from the creators, the original owners and collectors, seems to condemn these *fliegende* autographs to perpetual motion, sporadically disappearing from and re-emerging in the gold mines of the international antiquarian market and collections. Apprehended in transit from one collection to another, whether private or public, some of the objects recorded in *OperaCat* are now known, studied, published, or, at the very least, made accessible to libraries, while many others survive only as descriptions in sales catalogues.

Systematic Collecting: A Definition

My discussion focuses on the socio-historical peculiarities of private music collecting and follows psychiatrist Peter Subkowski's definition of systematic collecting, which in its narrowest sense

> (1) refers to seeking, selecting, gathering, and storing of objects that have a subjective value for the collector, and in most cases includes some attempt at completion. The collection of intangibles such as knowledge is not considered collecting, as the object or thing is not securely available;
> (2) is [...] systematic (in the sense of series formation) and, as a rule, limited to a definable and delineable area or topic [...], which can be outlined in, for instance, auction catalogues, or through other collections;
> (3) is comprehensive and has depth, including an interest in secondary literature and background information;
> (4) tends to have an affective, passionate grasp on the person engaged in it;
> (5) is furthermore a relatively constant behavior over time, and not just a short-term fad. (Subkowski 2006: 385)

Collecting is thus, above all else, a human behavior. Subkowski's definition, however, does not distinguish between different forms of collecting or the different kinds of objects being collected (for example, art as opposed to books or autographs, rather than albums or stamps). And, perhaps symptomatic of a certain fractiousness of some disciplines toward the economic sphere, Subkowski does not refer to the marketplace, where the seeking and selecting, selling and acquisition of the objects, and, as we will see, sometimes even the creation of the objects, is decided.

"Ce Qui Circule Entre Nous": Prices and Value

According to conventional wisdom, collectors who flaunt their acquisitions share more details about their transactions particularly when they believe they have bought—possibly below cost or, in other words, at a lesser price than the presumed "real" value (determined by whom?)— a *unicum*, an object whose value wasn't previously grasped either by the seller or other collectors and connoisseurs. Clearly, we have been dealing here with different meanings of the term "value."

In this context, the collector has at least two expectations: that the originality of an individual field of interest will be recognized, and that there will be an objective correspondence between the value of a collectible object and its price. When talking about collecting, price and value are the most controversial topics and the ones subject to the most unofficial chatter. Let us turn our attention now to some of the most frequently asked questions: are price and value of any object of art (and for our purposes, an autograph) reconcilable? And, apart from its objective details—its rarity, age, and condition—where does the value of an autograph reside? If its use-value is the reason a given item is on the market and its exchange-value is the worth ascribed to said item by the market, what carries and retains the autographs in the market? How is it that the association of an autograph with celebrity seems to suffice, perhaps even more than its content or its original function? In short, what type of "merchandise" is an autograph? And, finally, why collect autographs at all?

In a discussion of art, gifts, and the market in his book, sociologist Jacques Godbout of the MAUSS (*Mouvement anti-utilitariste dans les sciences sociales*) wonders at the fact that "merchandise" like a painting such as Van Gogh's *Irises* can pass from the artist to his brother and then reap $54 million on the market without ever having increased either its utility or its rarity (Godbout 2008: 329). Beethoven provides us with an even more familiar example. In 1827, immediately after his death, Beethoven's sketchbooks (containing his musical ideas) were estimated as being worth about 10 florins, around €155 ($200) according to modern calculation (for an approximate conversion rate from florins [1830 Convention Coins] to Euros, see BHM 2009). In May 2002, at Sotheby's in London, a folio of sketches for the Ninth Symphony was sold for about £1.3 million[4] (about $1.8 million), almost the same price, £1.12 million (about $1.95 million) paid three years later, on December 1, 2005, again at Sotheby's in London, for the autograph of the version for piano four-hands of the *Grosse Fuge*. After decades spent away from publicity and in private hands, and despite the commonly held view that collectors jealously protect their treasures from the public, both of the two Beethoven manuscripts were donated in 2006 by their last buyer, Bruce Kovner, to the Juilliard School, where they are now available to scholars.

As an analogous contrast, I turn to James Coover (1989), whose works are fundamental bibliographic tools for the scholar of music collecting. Coover cites the case of Mendelssohn's autograph of the *Fingal's Cave Overture*, sold at auction for only £52 in 1875, the same year in which the engraving plates and rights for one of the most popular works of music-hall composer Charles Coote fetched £990 (Coover 1989: 56). Coover dismisses the question by affirming that these kinds of disproportionately irreconcilable values are innate to the marketplace. The reason for such dynamic pricing contrasts, however, does not seem to reside *sic et simpliciter* in the uncertainty of the market, in the mechanisms of auctions, or in the costly performances by their facilitators in the spirit of capitalism. In May 2002, the same *Fingal's Cave* autograph was sold for £600, in the very same auction at which the symphonic sketch by Beethoven, mentioned above, was sold for a price almost four times greater. This raises the issue of how reception, at least insofar as the myth of the artist, and academic interest influence the market. Yet another Beethoven case is illuminating. As made clear by Douglas Johnson, Alan Tyson, and Robert Winter (1985), the dispersion of the Beethoven sketchbooks

> began almost at once, and by the 1860s, when scholarly interest in them was first aroused by Thayer and Nottebohm, most of the sketchbooks were in new hands. [...] And of course the value of the sketchbooks had been enhanced both by the publicity accorded them by scholars and by the more general glorification of Beethoven himself. (Johnson, Tyson, and Winter 1985: 18)

Value has components whose utility and exchange are shared by some individuals and not by others. These components are both subjective and social, and may be observed from a historical perspective, but their proportions are not really quantifiable, either objectively or in absolute monetary terms.

Music Collecting and Cultural Models

A discussion of value should not be separated from its sociocultural context. The same transformations wrought upon the production, circulation, and reception of music by cultural politics, social economics, taste, models of knowing, and relevant organization of knowledge (which has come to bear upon both music historiography and theories of musical consumption) seem also to have influenced musical collecting. While appreciation of autographs has grown since the first decades of the nineteenth century, music and opera collections have been an integral part of the largest private libraries for centuries, reflecting varied geographical, historical, cultural, and political circumstances. I follow here with a few examples.

In France during the late seventeenth and early eighteenth centuries, music collections flourished in a climate in which new trends in the organization of knowledge resulted in a new interest in creative expression, which also influenced the ideas and ideals behind the choices people made about their own libraries. Musical collections described in coeval auction catalogues include operas and contemporary ballets, with a rather remarkable preference—posthumous—for the works of Jean-Baptiste Lully. Another marketing revelation of the same era is that the *livrets* (or librettos) were more desirable than the music. Musical scores, however, would soon mount a serious challenge to this state of affairs, thanks to the demands of the growing market for amateur and drawing-room music-making, as well as the transformation of private libraries, rich in early operatic editions, into collectors' libraries. These dynamics do not seem so different from those of more than a hundred years later, as music publishing declined under the blows of other popular forms of musical entertainment, such as the gramophone, which laid the groundwork for the new fad of recordings collecting, a determining factor in contemporary musical consumption as well, thanks to new digital technologies.

As revealed in his 1771 *Catalogue des livres*, Pietro Leopoldo, grand duke of Tuscany (the future Holy Roman Emperor Leopoldo II), possessed a library of around 1,570 titles, of which 114 were musical scores, including instrumental music, anthologies of songs and arias, sacred music, and around 60 opera scores (Leopoldo 1771).[5] The opera scores, in particular, bear the clear imprint of the Hapsburg Court Opera and were all contemporary works. The tendency to turn to the past in opera collecting seems in fact to be a relatively recent trend, appearing with the rise of the notion of "operatic repertory" and encouraged by the important role played in the formation of public taste by the so-called canon.

The case of the Scalvini Collection of operatic editions preserved at the Istituto Nazionale di Studi Verdiani in Parma offers an illuminating look at musical collecting in nineteenth-century Italy (Pompilio 1991–1992). A conspicuous part of the collection was originally assembled by the aristocratic Milanese bibliophile and devoted opera lover Giovanni Battista Cagnola, who was also an amateur musician and composer, a stereotypical nineteenth-century collector of music. It was only in the 1850s that Cagnola began to look back at operatic works from preceding years and to fill the gaps in his collection of operas, which consisted mostly of works by Rossini, Mercadante, Donizetti, Bellini, and Verdi. This change in direction was influenced by the confluence of many contemporary factors: opera revivals; comprehensive publishing projects like the complete editions of the "great" composers, which began in those years; and last, though not least, a growing, widespread interest—if not a true "fever"—that developed for Italian opera composers, also abroad. This phenomenon of "composer-centeredness" has also helped to define the collecting phenomenon.

Overrating the Artist

Forcing his investigative gaze, Godbout asks: "To what universe can a product of this kind belong, a universe in which, according to all evidence, the artist is overestimated at the expense of the work?"[6] (Godbout 2008: 329). Although the separation between performer and spectator would manifest itself fairly early in Western music, "composer-centeredness" began to appear in the nineteenth century and grew in the wake of broader changes in the conception of artistic creativity and *auctoritas*. Among other things, the focus on the creative individual also led to a new consideration of the act of writing, of authorship, and of manuscripts.

In October 1843, just a few weeks before the premiere of his *Dom Sebastien, roi du Portugal* in Paris, Donizetti, needing written permission from the queen of Portugal in order to dedicate his new opera to her, pressured the Marquis Ricci, Chargé d'affaires for the king of Sardinia and Lisbon, for assistance. As Donizetti wrote in a letter to the singer Natale Costantini, "To further entice him, I wrote a romanza for him, and

I myself copied it as an autograph in the letter [...] not that I attach any worth to things of that kind, but one day someone might ask him to see my handwriting out of curiosity"[7] (Libreria Antiquaria Luigi Banzi s.d. *OperaCat* ID 2245). Well aware of the generosity of his gift, Donizetti clearly intended to titillate the personal satisfaction as well as the ambition for worldly prestige that possession of an autograph could ensure—in this case, an actual piece of vocal chamber music expressly composed and copied by one of the most noted composers of the time.

Pierre Jules Fontaine (one of the first biographers specifically interested in the collecting of autographs) defined an autograph manuscript in his *Des collections d'autographes, et de l'utilité qu'on en peut retirer* of 1834 as "the soul, the mind of the man of God"[8] (Fontaine 1834: 10). Above all, Fontaine saw an autograph collection as a copious source of documents useful to bibliography, history, and literature. But he also believed that an autograph could preserve "the mind of the person who wrote it, [...] show it in its true light"; in it one can "even [...] divine his character through the shape of his writing"[9] (Fontaine 1834: 6). It was in these years that modern graphology, as a method of personality analysis, first emerged in France. And while the discipline of "sketch studies" was just beginning, Fontaine reminded his readers that "[i]n a letter, a man somehow gives himself up to his correspondent, and is reflected as in a mirror; a manuscript presents the real talent of an author, as well as the corrections, the variants that are sown, and the different movements of his mind"[10] (Fontaine 1834: 6). In the arts, the process of production occupies a central role; antiquarians and clients inside the market, as well as the hosts of consumers (including scholars) outside the market, attribute great importance to context—to how and in what mental and spiritual state the result was obtained.

It is not surprising, then, that the letters, documents, and autograph musical manuscripts that shed so much light on creative circumstances are among the most desired pieces in the music collecting market.

Autograph Collecting: The Intellectual Benefits and Pleasures of a Liberal Curiosity

While preserving manuscripts is a very old practice, the modern systematic collection of handwritten documents by famous persons—gathered, ordered, and considered together as a unitary whole—began in the Enlightenment and paralleled the birth of such modern ideas as that of "museum" and "antiquariat." Requests forwarded directly to interested parties or entrusted via word of mouth, private agreements for the sale as well as the exchange of autographs, have always been common enough; but the first half of the nineteenth century saw the advent of public sales dedicated to autographs. According to Fontaine, the first sale of this kind took place in Paris in 1820; the oldest catalogue of autographs recorded in SCIPIO is from Sotheby's in London from 1819, while the earliest sales catalogue recorded in *OperaCat* (ID 4288–4290) that pertains exclusively to autographs (and includes Italian opera) was published in January 1853. This catalogue, prepared in London by the firm of Puttick & Simpson (1853), publicizes some letters of Donizetti, dead since 1848, and also of Rossini, still living at the time. The earliest document in *OperaCat* referring to a sale of autographs is a letter by Rossini to Giuseppe Mattei, apparently written on January 3, 1851, in which the composer expresses his surprise that in England his autograph sold for ten pounds sterling (Christie's 1994; *OperaCat* ID 1214).

Not surprisingly, the collection and sale of Italian opera autographs was much more widely practiced north of the Alps. England, France, and the German-speaking lands are traditionally indicated as the initiators of autograph commerce, which soon reached the United States, where letters of Rossini, Donizetti, and Bellini were already commonly available at auction in the 1850s. In the first half of the nineteenth century, however, the gold mine of musical autographs was Vienna, and the "canon" of Viennese classicism still vaunts the highest quotes on the market. Moreover, the same antiquarian interest that nourished autograph collecting in the Hapsburg capital simultaneously sowed the seeds for one of the first schools of modern musicology, as the most eminent music scholars moved in the same circles as the enlightened amateurs and collectors of the Empire. Among them was Aloys Fuchs, one of the first systematic acquirers of musical autographs, whose collection is often cited in the catalogues of composers' works (Schaal 1966).

In Italy, notwithstanding the wealth of archives, interest in music autograph collecting spread later. In a letter to the publisher Antonio Pacini in France, most probably written in the middle of the 1830s, Donizetti sketched a curious image of "a stream of French gentlemen" who had come to Naples in search of manuscripts and musical lessons from him, apparently with poor results, and were ready to move on (Kenneth W. Rendell Gallery s.d.; *OperaCat* ID 4744). In the same letter we learn that Donizetti himself was caught up in a search for manuscripts on behalf of Cherubini (a collector himself), although he despaired of finding anything.

Italian musical periodicals of the 1850s still considered the collecting of musical autographs to be an imported craze that was less expensive than collecting art. An article in *L'Italia musicale* (September 25, 1850) sounds particularly modern in its not-so-subtle criticism that autograph collecting would be conditioned by the often vacuous celebrity accorded by newspapers to individuals of dubious merit as well as the apparent difficulty of outsiders, unbelievers, or the uninitiated to comprehend the peculiar dynamic of value pricing in the antiquarian market:

> The mania for autograph collecting is coming into vogue even among ourselves. It is an inexpensive type of collecting compared to that of paintings, books, cameos, or medals. In this world, every man who even for only a single day in his village school scribbled four marks on a piece of paper can, one day or another, see his scribbles in a collection of autographs. Once upon a time, one venerated as precious relics the signatures of the greatest men—writers, poets, princes and so on. Now, instead,

> every person whose name has been published two or three times in the Gazette, or among the Arrivals and Departures or in the articles, deserves his characters conserved within a file of autographs. The price of these varies according to their rarity, and, therefore, in inverse proportion to the amount of words that the authors have written.[11] (*LIM* 1850)

With the acquisition of musical autographs, public institutions declared their intention to preserve the memory of the past for younger generations. Music publishers were instead interested in the most extensive collections of complete manuscripts, engraving plates, and copyrights. Private collectors directed their attention to smaller pieces, for the most part individual documents, letters, or manuscripts, as sources of knowledge as well as of a special, more intimate pleasure.

In 1852, an announcement appeared in the Italian music press, noting that the son of Domenico Cimarosa, "due to his exquisite sense of generosity and his love for the teaching of that art which garnered his father so many laurels,"[12] far from freely donating the collection of his father's autographs that he had inherited from Cardinal Consalvi, preferred instead to sell it to the archives of the *Collegio di Musica* of Naples for two thousand ducats and an annuity of sixty ducats, "rather than to the music publishers who had offered him more than double that amount"[13] (*LIM* 1852). In the same year, news that the pianist Sigismond Thalberg had acquired a collection of musical autographs made the rounds of the international music press. The anecdotes that always seem to arise around such announcements recount that a few days after the acquisition, the virtuoso confessed to a friend that although he knew the collection would not yield him any revenue, his excitement over its "godimenti intellettuali" ("intellectual pleasures") and "contenuto morale" ("moral content") was enough to disrupt his sleep (*LIM* 1853). It seems that Thalberg admitted to having paid an amount more than ten times greater than the sum the autographs could have fetched at auction, quite different from what the parsimonious "Cousin Pons" would have done—another type of collector and musician painted with a detailed, if perhaps clinical eye, a few years earlier by writer and collector himself Honoré de Balzac in his 1848 novel of the same name.

Already undermining the reputation of collecting, even in this era, were its perceived tendencies toward mania and obsession. Thalberg's historical rival Franz Liszt used to keep his distance from such activities, and declared himself absolutely *not* to be a collector of autographs. However, even he succumbed. In June 1852, the celebrated Liszt was most probably searching for a type of pleasure not entirely dissimilar to Thalberg's when he asked Clara Schumann—in vain—to give him Robert Schumann's signed score of *Manfred* (La Mara 1894: I: letter 86). In fact, it is fair to assume this was the sort of pleasure that by 1855 would drive Liszt to covet the signed letters of Wagner, which he considered "a perfectly inalienable benefit to me," as he wrote to the director of orchestra August Kiel, who also sought autographs (La Mara 1894: I: letter 143).

In that century of nationalist revolutions, other merits were also ascribed to autographs. In the introductory essay for the sales catalogue of a collection of autographs prepared for auction on March 4, 1867, by the New York firm of Leavitt, Strebeigh &

Company, the autographs are said to be "eminently conducive to patriotism" (Leavitt, Strebeigh & Co. 1867). As attested by various letters and "relics" in their possession, among which were locks of hair, the autograph collector Giuseppe Verdi and his wife Giuseppina were particularly proud of autographed notes sent to them by a man they considered to be an icon of the Italian nation—indeed, a "living saint"—the writer Alessandro Manzoni (see, for example, Luzio 1927: 555, 558). As for eminent musicians who represented the Italian spirit, Verdi, in a letter from 1870, consistent both with the assertion that the true essence of Italian music lies in its polyphonic vocal tradition and with the growing interest in Italian sacred music, asked his friend Cesare Vigna for an autograph of Benedetto Marcello, which would have been dearer to him than a letter by Rossini, although he said he possessed various examples of the latter (Libreria Musicale Gallini 2001; *OperaCat* ID 2556). In short, it is clear from collected testimonials that the value of an autograph is a reflection of the owner's personal experience, as the object becomes an extension of both its author and the collector himself.

A Bond-Value

Although they live in the marketplace and are valued and exchanged in monetary terms, autographs and objects of art tend to evade the logic of capitalist exchange. An autograph is not a common good of consumption, its use-value is not a conventional one, and its market is not that of common transactions. Collecting's issues of solipsism notwithstanding, an autograph possesses a third value, of linkage, or bond-value that renews itself in its circulation from the moment of its creation.

The value of the bond corresponds first and foremost to the value of the product itself in the construction or expansion of ties between the individuals, artist/producer and enjoyer/user. An autograph possesses the potential for greater socialization, having been produced in order to enhance (or not) the original connection (though in some cases the connection is established only after its creation) among artists, collectors, scholars, fans, or the merely curious, and between them and their field of interest and/or marketing.

In the game of association played in the music system, collecting represents one of the possible actions and strategies on an equal plane with the means of production and their drivers, the composers' public and private relationships, and the audience of users and potential collectors. We will now look at the rules and mechanisms of this game by examining certain types of autographs recorded in *OperaCat*.

Collectibles: Text and Paratext

Autographs of Rossini, Verdi, and Puccini began to circulate among collectors while the composers were still alive. Sometimes the composers themselves gave them away or their families or the original recipients sold them. But this traffic can be even more complex. Thus, for example, in his last years, Rossini saw some of the autographs no longer in his possession return to him through the hands of new owners looking for an authenticating signature. Moreover, the largesse of Rossini's widow in disposing of her dead husband's handwritten relics is well known.

In 1926, two years after the death of Puccini, musical manuscript collectors could regularly find for sale drafts and sketches that the composer had signed and occasionally given to friends and admirers. Much earlier, however, at the height of his international success and with innumerable autograph signatures on quotes of his most celebrated melodies, on the title pages of printed editions, or on photographs in circulation, Puccini must have been aware that collectors would eventually take an interest in his personal letters to friends and relatives (see the auction held by Karl Ernst Henrici on October 20, 1913, while the composer was still alive). Nonetheless, Puccini probably could not foresee at that time that even the intimate letters sent to his lovers would become hunted quarry in the antiquarian market. In December 2008 a sensation was caused by the reappearance of all the letters that Verdi wrote to a soprano over thirty years, from 1877 until 1900, hailed as a "confirmation" (although yet to be proven) of their love affair (Torno 2008).[14]

The ethical aspects of the phenomenon are consistent, sometimes particularly delicate, and not only in regard to the boundaries of the public dimension of the artist's personal life, but also in the treatment reserved for many autographs. It is not, in fact, rare to see entire manuscripts dismembered or private letters detached from their legitimate signatures, and last but not least, instances of forgery.

In the shadow of the great interest aroused by letters and more or less intact musical manuscripts, there is also within the antiquarian market a world of small collectible autographs whose size and function would seem to exclude them from the domain of "art," but which are clearly sought out in order to create interpersonal relationships with that domain, even if ephemeral ones. A significant number of these small specimens recorded in *OperaCat* were originally conceived as souvenirs: gifts requested by the recipients or spontaneously given by the composers themselves to friends, patrons, and admirers—all potential collectors. But the cache of these items also includes promotional gadgets, photographs, and postcards, products of commercial initiatives created to launch a production, to promote composers and performers, and to both create and gratify the expectations of the public. Throughout the nineteenth century, autograph albums filled with the signatures of famous people were all the rage, particularly it seems, among women, in a practice that dates back to the *album amicorum*, the paper ancestor of social networks like Facebook. Autograph albums usually contained dedications or simple signatures, drawings, and a bit later photographs, brief compositions, or excerpts from favorite arias, as in the case of Charlotte de Rothschild's "Livre d'Or," which includes an exceptional array of compositions from Rossini to Bernstein (see Gossett 2013). In 1824, Rossini contributed to the album of the Polish composer and piano virtuosa Maria Szymanowska a page of music drawn from the opera *Ermione* (Act II, scene 9, *gran scena* sung by Ermione, "Un'empia mel rapì"). Not unlike other composers of that era, Rossini would later reuse this same melody in many of his iterations of "Mi lagnerò tacendo," the numerous short vocal compositions he set to the arietta text from *Siroe* by Metastasio (1726). Even today, new versions of "Mi lagnerò tacendo" continue to emerge from private collections and on the antiquarian market, thus prolonging a game that had begun almost two hundred years ago by Rossini himself. He was clearly well aware from the very beginning of his career of his privileged status as "sovereign composer," no longer subordinate to aristocratic protectors even if, at least out of ceremony, he was still obliged to his more respectable public. In fact, in the same production system that allowed works to premiere even without an official benefactor, sponsors still required that the composers recognize and pay respect to social conventions. The many brief compositions Rossini based on "Mi lagnerò tacendo" are not in fact "silent" (*tacendo*) at all, forming a still open system of textual variants that involves both musical structure and morphology as well as every other paratextual aspect of the pages of an album. Thus, the absolute uniqueness that the fact of being an autograph should guarantee fades, as in the case of the "Mi lagnerò tacendo" spin-offs. But fading along with it is one of the other illusions implicitly established between the recipient/consumer and the artist/producer—that is, that one can become a participant in "Art" and in the artists' community by possessing a work of art. Both of these illusions present a potential challenge that Rossini seems to have intuited, if not knowingly taken up. Already in the nineteenth century, the industrialist Alfred Bolivet, driven by his obsession to complete collections, attempted to put together these similar album pages, which Rossini had dispensed with such generosity, only to give up, probably when faced with their proliferation. Rossini's original burst of creativity is here seen in the virtuosity of the entirety of the variations on the same, short, regular verses and in the general plan of their dissemination and dispersion, rather than in the creation of any one of these settings taken individually.[15]

A broader political shift is also observable through these small autographs, illuminated by paratextual elements such as dedications, sometimes to unknown people. The presence of a dedication demonstrates more than anything an interpersonal relationship. If the practice is observed over a long period of time, for example, in the first half of the nineteenth century, as the artistic and economic independence guaranteed by the burgeoning music market began to consolidate, it is possible to see that the function of autographed musical souvenirs seems to pass slowly from that of a musical tribute to individual patron, benefactor, or friend to a recognition—a due and increasingly standardized one—given to one's larger public. As autographed collectibles proliferated, they also lost their musical content, gaining instead advertising or promotional content. Moreover, with few exceptions, the dimension of music autographs reduced in direct proportion to their circulation and the separation between the actor (i.e., the composer or performer) and the spectator (the consumer), which resulted, conversely, in a growing interest in the person-artist.

While in the first half of the nineteenth century short but complete compositions found in album pages were particularly popular, beginning in the 1850s, the "musical quotations" from the openings of the most celebrated arias enjoyed considerable success. These quotations often consist of a few musical bars copied out and signed, all virtually identical, without any appreciable distinctive feature except for dates or dedications, when present.

In the mid-nineteenth century, the invention of photography created a new type of collectible that soon became very popular, and which remains useful today as a documentary source for productions, costuming, scenery, and performers: the autographed photograph. The very earliest literature on collecting recommends that collectors organize their autographs in an album, ordered in sections by subject, and prefaced with a portrait of the auteur. The early contribution by photography to the success of visiting cards in the early 1850s, a true "must have" of that era, and the subsequent great success of the souvenir photo and photo-postcards are documented in *OperaCat* by the portraits that Rossini commissioned during his last Parisian years from the famous firms of Nadar (pseudonym of writer and caricaturist Gaspard-Félix Tournachon [1820–1910]) and Numa Blanc. Rossini used these photographs as visiting cards to honor his guests, friends, and acquaintances. But one may cite as well the numerous postcards (mailed or given out in person) complete with a photographic portrait of Puccini, the fascinating composer particularly appreciated by the female public, and even more so for his fame as a *tombeur de femmes*. By the last quarter of the nineteenth century, photographs were widely used in promotional strategies by the opera industry, which was, and remains, particularly attentive to the images of its performers. The standard mass-produced photographic autograph consists of a portrait, like so many others in circulation, marked by a single autographic element: the signature, the basic-degree inscription. Their number in the market is still considerable, and their value/price does not reach the exorbitant amounts that musical manuscripts command.

Is this all perhaps a manifestation of the end of the aristocratic notion of "Art," denounced in the first decades of the last century, and does it signify the coming of art to the masses? It is a rather duplicitous phenomenon that, on the one hand, sees collecting keeping an aura of intellectual aristocracy, and on the other, assimilating itself to the standards of mass consumption typical, for example, of fanaticism. According to collectors, what makes a difference in the search for collectibles is as much one's artistic sensibility as one's knowledge, but above all else, the economic ability to make such an investment.

An autograph—just one of the cards played by collectors in the above-mentioned members-only associative game of the musical system—is, above all, a powerful entity to be sought out and collected, to create interpersonal relationships, to engage in competitions with or renew alliances between composers and the different "consumers," even across the distance of time. Thanks to the peculiar orbit to which an autograph belongs, it is, in the end, a symbolic universe.

The Art of Collecting and the Social System

As we have seen, collecting is a topic of multidisciplinary interest at the intersection of history, economics, and sociology. On the one side, sociohistorical literature dominates the non-economic aspects of the phenomenon, but on the other, the market, particularly the market of the auction house, has long been investigated from a purely economic perspective. The limits of the latter, as well as those of a rigorously anthropological and sociological view, have been examined as a subdiscipline of the sociology of art, which studies the art market and collecting as aspects of the complex relationship between art and society, alongside the figure of the artist, his or her works, and his or her public.

As early as the 1960s, art historian Francis Haskell ([1962] 1980) began to study the metamorphosis of taste through the prism of collectors and patrons. A similar endeavor in the field of historical musicology was also undertaken with the goal of understanding music patronage; although very little is known about the earliest music collectors and only very few catalogues documenting the music holdings of the most ancient libraries have survived, scholars have shown that the figures of the musical collector and the musical patron tend not only to coincide, but to often superimpose themselves on the figure of the "dilettante" (see, for example, Pompilio 1991–1992 and Florimo [1880–1882] 2002). In the nineteenth century, typical musical autograph collectors included aristocrats; amateur musicians with artistic ambitions that were never fully satisfied; *nouveaux-riches* who built libraries and autograph collections that would demonstrate the solidity of their acquired social status, in a field traditionally open only to the wealthiest and most aristocratic families; and, finally, people of culture and knowledge, very often librarians or musicians themselves.

Thus, while collecting is a practice sometimes dissimulated in a more exclusive activity, thanks to the particularity—sometimes eccentricity, rarity, and market value—of collectible objects, it is also possible to speak of a common attitude among collectors that manifests itself more democratically in the quotidian sphere. The urge to collect has in fact psychodynamic and sociological, in addition to anthropological, roots.

While a collection reflects the taste of an era, it also speaks for its gatherer, hence the ongoing fascination with when and how to build a collection, the philosophy underlying collecting, and the personal motives of the collector. Not so different, indeed, from fanaticism, collecting can also be seen as a form of narcissism, an extension of the individual ego into objects that in turn exercise their own autonomy upon, and in the end, actually appropriate, the collector. James J. Fuld, for example, called his living room full of musical first editions—his "non-argumentative friends"—his "psychiatric crutch" (Fuld 1976: 479). Moreover, according to Subkowski, "collecting represents a specific form of object relating and way of handling primary loss trauma [...] Under certain circumstances collecting can also result in a successful Gestalt or way of life" (Subkowski 2006: 383). In fact, as early as the nineteenth century, collecting was actually a subject of psychiatric research, which considered it a typical example of the kind of obsessive-compulsive behavior through which certain manic-depressive disorders manifested themselves.

In France in the mid-seventeenth century, Fontaine actually used the word "mania" when describing autograph collecting, distinguishing the amateurs, the "merely curious, whom one could call *autographomanes*, making an analogy to bibliomanes,"[16] from the "connoisseurs, whom one can call *autographophiles*, because they resemble bibliophiles"[17]

(Fontaine 1834: 5–6). He was clearly referring to the work of the English bibliographer Thomas Frognall Dibdin, who published a book in 1809, suggestively titled *Bibliomania*, which proved to be very popular in the nineteenth century, so much so that it went into several editions (Dibdin [1809] 2010). In the second half of the century, the word "maniac" was already commonly used when referring to collecting, and became common currency in the early twentieth century, used in 1913 by Puccini, who sent his nephew two visiting cards, presumably bearing his signature, accompanied by the following note: "Here are 2 cards for the autograph maniacs"[18] (Lion Heart 2006; *OperaCat* ID 902). What, exactly, is the nature of the power exerted by such a signature that it engenders a maniacal passion that raises its market value, even above that of its own content? Anthropology suggests that the signature, a guarantee of the autograph, is an "author-carrier."

"The fetish of the art market is the master's name," wrote Walter Benjamin in his essay on the collector and historian Eduard Fuchs (Benjamin 1974: II: 503). The term "fetish" implies the veneration of inanimate objects by virtue of the spirit, divinity, or magic power that one believes is alive within them. Autographs would enjoy the ascribed virtues of such powers, and the materialization of the author and of his creative spirit in his calligraphy and autographed name would thus make them objects of reverence. Signatures cut out from larger documents circulate in the antiquarian markets, sold singly as if they were relics, that category of objects that allegedly retain the supernatural graces of an extraordinary person, a hero, or a saint who may once have held them. The autographed corner torn away (who knows by whom) from Beethoven's Ninth Symphony and said to have been kept by the pianist and collector Alfred Cortot, conserved in a pendant of his watch chain, is such a relic (Traficante 1970; Hyatt King and Neighbour 1966: 8). Just as relics have played an important role in the consolidation of religions and the cults of certain saints, musical relics have also helped in the construction of the cult of the composer. We have already mentioned Beethoven's sketches, but a quasi-religious adoration has led fans and collectors to treasure as relics another type of "discarded" object. When in 2001 the Milanese antiquarian Gallini sold one of the many locks of Verdi's hair that had been circulating in the market, the anonymous catalogue editor asked if one should regard the hair with the same romantic-fetishistic spirit of our ancestors, or as a carrier of the composer's DNA (Libreria Musicale Gallini 2001). Not entirely different from the old approach, this last, more "scientific" vision makes a clear appeal to the anthropological metonymy of the "part-for-whole possession." Why would one collect DNA? The most acclaimed operatic locks were probably those of Bellini, in which Francesco Florimo, who founded the cult of the Sicilian composer, saw in this truncated part of his dear friend something that was "apparently inanimate, but throbs and lives"[19] (Florimo [1880–1882] 2002: II: 143). That hair should possess some secret power is already a potent biblical image; José Gil discusses the nature of this power in the context of the body's residues in which he traces a floating signifier between symbol and object:

> Amulets, talismans, gris-gris, elixirs, and relics hold tamed energies inside them. It is interesting to note that these traces of the floating signifier are insignificant in themselves: their lowly stature calls forth the potency of the energy put into play [...]

> These little bits of something contain an energy stored away that is intimately associated with them, and, because of their very nature, they are positioned as mere stages to the reserves of energy that circulate beneath the symbolic. (Gil 1998: 100–101)

The relic-autograph would then share power of the symbol. It is this energy of symbols that is capable of sparking a peculiar bond-value, that between the extraordinary and the ordinary. As Krzysztof Pomian summarizes it:

> [Collectible objects] are considered in the context of the exchange that unites gods and men, heroes and ordinary mortals, the afterlife and the earthly world, the beginning of time and the present, the far and the near. Hence their connection with religion, only to be replaced in modern times with aesthetic and scientific interests, or more recently, with the ideological affirmation of national entities.[20] (Pomian 1978: 364)

The Gift

Let us now attempt a rereading of the phenomenon of collecting and the impulse to collect autographs, in particular, from an unconventional (in our field) yet compelling sociological perspective, that of the phenomenon of "the gift" and its theory. Godbout writes: "The artist [...] has transformed the producer-user relationship in the community of 'art lovers'"[21] (Godbout 2008: 343). Not being able to escape a relationship with his clients, the artist sublimates this relationship by ensuring that the customer and all other agents in the system of artistic production are in communion with his creative experience. This is a concession, a gift that the artist gives to his public in various ways: through the performance, sale, and circulation of his work to the revelation of his artistic intent (and his private sphere), he seals those relationships that keep his Art alive by giving it larger, social meaning. For Godbout and the leaders of MAUSS, the French social scientific movement inspired by Marcel Mauss (see above), artistic creativity is an experience of the social fact that is the gift. Music collecting as a practice in which one manifests the receiving of Art is therefore locatable in the broader framework of the theory of the gift, the notion of receiving and reciprocating.

The disputes and controversies that surround it notwithstanding, the social theory of Mauss on *le don* (set forth for the first time in his *Essai sur le don*, published in 1924, a comparative study on the gift within traditional archaic cultures) continues to inspire scholars. According to this theory, social actions, and therefore institutions themselves, are not simply the result of purely individual self-interest, nor of purely social obligation, but derive, rather, from a union of the smallest intersections of giving and receiving that would connect all social phenomena. While I will not delve deeper into gift theory here, it is, nonetheless, crucial to mention that the power within a given object, similar in nature to the energy of symbols, would allow it to live on its own and circulate in order to return eventually to its donor (Mauss [1924] 1990).

What kind of gift, then, is art? At a more informed level, a musical work is often spoken of in terms of generosity: that shown by the composer in the music, that of the performers in their execution, and that recognized by the public in the reception reserved for a work of art.

It is, again, in terms of gift giving and receiving that Jean Starobinski in his book *Largesse* novelizes the struggles of the artist in the creative process:

> For every gift granted how many have remained incomplete or have been rejected. [...] The artist at work persists, worrying about what *that* will produce, ready to persevere, ready to abandon the game. And while he *gives himself* to his work, while he *gives form* to his work of art, he puts off the decision to accept or reject the result. The destination remains open. Will he finally consent to his work, will he *give* his assent? He may make it a gift to the public, or to a friend, who for the moment assumes the role of the beholder par excellence. The possibility of this final gift illuminates all of his earlier labour. (Starobinski 1997: 17)

Is this a romantic conception of art, already outdated, or a well-established way in which to consider the compositional process?

As already seen, the central role assumed by the artist and the creative process in the nineteenth century had a major impact on the collecting of musical autographs. After all, the majority of operatic autographs in circulation even today date from, or at least refer to, opera of the 1800s and early 1900s. Before beginning their independent lives as collectible objects, many autographs were in fact distributed voluntarily in order to consolidate the producer-user relationship, giving the illusion of a shared creative experience in a more confidential form. Once on the market, their value renews itself, despite material and temporal separation from the original players, and continues to grow in the community of art lovers. The original artistic energy, itself a gift with the potential for greater socialization, continues to reciprocate through passion, time, money, and creativity. Indeed, collecting itself is a form of creativity that touches on interest, knowledge, imagination, intuition, and business skills. Whether or not they choose to share their treasures, collectors usually possess a passionate curiosity about what they collect, and often have a profound knowledge of the subject. The vast number of collections that are ultimately bequeathed or donated to the larger public (a model of circulation that takes autographs from a public donor to private enjoyment and eventually to a larger fruition), and used frequently by scholars, confirms their universal cultural benefit and reflects positively on the original creator-donor, as they reveal certain aspects of their lives and creative processes.

Such objects can lose their symbolic power as their energy moves elsewhere. This occurs when the meaning of the original is no longer recognized and the object ceases to embody a challenge to its receivers. Technology and fashion can condition the social stability built around such objects. Some sellers claim, for example, to have noted a diminished interest in tactile collectibles, such as dedications, photographs, and autographs, on the part of the younger generations of small collectors, who are more interested in digital objects.

The context of artistic creativity in which we position our understanding of collecting can seem inadequate when considered with a more disenchanted gaze. One could, for example, turn to Marx, who states in the first chapter of *Das Kapital* that the power causing objects to circulate is fetishism of the merchandise and not the force of the object itself, a gift. The logic of capitalism, however, is not able to explain by itself all of the aspects of the "universe" within which the art market operates. The solution to the tension present in collecting and in the economic and non-economic aspects of the phenomenon, strongly rooted in the symbolic, are beyond the scope of this chapter, which has instead addressed the phenomenon in terms of relationships, rather than acts, or the isolated actors. Despite the many changes that have occurred throughout the history of collectible objects and the manner of their creation, circulation, and acquisition, the world of opera collectors, fans, scholars, consumers, lovers, composers, singers, sellers, libraries, museums, and foundations has exercised upon the operatic autograph those relationships that keep institutions, including opera, alive.

See also: Audiences, The Operatic Canon, How Opera Traveled, Sources

Notes

1. "L'artista produce in una specie di stato di grazia, di esaltazione che affascina l'amatore—nome dato al cliente [...]—e che sta all'opposto della produzione moderna."
2. *OperaCat is* funded by the Mellon Distinguished Achievement Award granted to Philip Gossett of the University of Chicago.
3. The autographs mentioned here and registered on *OperaCat* are noted in the text with a brief bibliographic citation of the related sale catalogues and identification number (*OperaCat* ID) that corresponds to the appropriate record in the database.
4. The following year a scribal full score of the same symphony marked throughout by the composer was bought for about £2.1 million at Sotheby's in London by a private collector.
5. Very few copies of this catalogue are known to have survived; the copy consulted for the purposes of this essay is currently preserved at the Grolier Club Library of New York.
6. "A quale universo può appartenere un prodotto del genere, un universo in cui, con tutta evidenza, c'è sopravvalutazione dell'artista a scapito dell'opera?"
7. "Per tentare di più il Marchese gli feci una romanza, e la copiai io stesso sulla lettera come autografo [...] non già che io a tal cose attacchi prezzo, ma può ben darsi che alcuno un giorno gli domandi i miei caratteri per semplice curiosità."
8. "l'âme, la pensée de l'homme de Dieu."
9. "La pensée de la personne qui a écrit, de la montrer dans son vrai jour, et soubvent même de faire deviner son caractère, par la forme de son écriture."
10. "Dans une lettre, l'homme s'abandonne en quelque sorte à son correspondant, et se reflète comme dans un miroir ; un manuscrit présente le talent réel d'un auteur, et les corrections, les variantes qu'il y a semées, et les divers mouvemens de sa pensée."
11. "La smania di raccogliere autografi prende ogni dì maggior voga anche da noi. È una collezione che si può fare a miglior mercato che quello di quadri, di libri, di cammei, di medaglie. Ogni uomo di questo mondo, che fu anche per un sol giorno alla scuola del villaggio a scarabocchiare quattro aste s'un pezzo di carta, può un dì o l'altro vedere i suoi scarabocchi

in una raccolta di autografi. Un tempo si veneravano come reliquie preziosissime gli autografi d'uomini sommi, letterati, poeti, principi ecc. adesso invece ogni cristiano, il cui nome sia stato due o tre volte stampato sulla Gazzetta, o fra gli Arrivi e Partenze o sotto gli articoli comunicati, è degno che i suoi caratteri si conservino in una cartella di autografi. Il prezzo d'essi varia secondo la rarità, è cioè in ragione inversa della somma delle parole che gli autori hanno scritto."

12. "Per isquisito senso di generosità e di amore all'insegnamento di quell'arte, in cui tanti allori raccolse il genitore."
13. "Anzi che agli editori di musica che gli avevano offerto più del doppio di tal somma."
14. Additional information provided in a private communication by Laura Nicora of Milan (author of the expert report on the correspondence to the buyer). The correspondence also includes other letters to the singer written by Giuseppina Strepponi (Verdi's wife), alone or together with her husband.
15. A critical edition of the versions of "Mi lagnerò tacendo" is being prepared by Philip Gossett and Patricia Brauner for the *Works of Gioachino Rossini* published by Bärenreiter.
16. "curieux, qu'on peut appeler autographomanes, par analogie à bibliomanes."
17. "connaisseurs, qu'on peut appeler autographophiles, parce qu'ils ressemblent aux bibliophiles."
18. "Eccole le 2 cartoline per i maniaci di autografi."
19. "che apparentement inanimate, pure palpita e vive."
20. "[Gli oggetti da collezione] sono considerati nel quadro dello scambio che unisce gli dei e gli uomini, gli eroi e comuni mortali, l'aldilà e il mondo terreno, il tempo delle origini e il presente, il lontano e il vicino. Di qui il loro legame con la religione, solo in età moderna sostituito da interessi estetici, scientifici o più recentemente ancora dall'affermazione ideologica di entità nazionali."
21. "L'artista [...] ha trasformato il rapporto produttore-utente in una comunità di "amatori d'arte." Non potendo sottrarsi al rapporto con la clientela, l'artista sublima tale rapporto facendo in modo che il cliente e tutti gli altri agenti del sistema di produzione artistica siano in comunione con la sua esperienza creativa."

Bibliography

ABPC. 1895–. *American Book Prices Current*. Washington, DC: Daniel J. Leab.

Albrecht, Otto E., and Stephen Roe, 2003. "Collections, private." In *Grove Music Online. Oxford Music Online*. Available: http://www.oxfordmusiconline.com/subscriber/article/grove/music/06108 (accessed August 23, 2012).

Benjamin, Walter. 1972. "Eduard Fuchs, der Sammler und der Historiker." *Gesammelte Schriften*, edited by Rolf Tiedemann and Hermann Schweppenhauser, II: 465–505. Frankfurt am Main: Suhrkamp. Translated in *The Essential Frankfurt School Reader*, edited by Andrew Arato and Eike Gebhardt, 225–253. New York: Continuum International, 1982.

BHM. 2009. *Beethoven's Capital: "All These Notes Don't Pay My Needs."* Beethoven-Haus Museum. Online. Available: http://www.beethoven-haus-bonn.de/sixcms/media.php/75/kurzf_hrer_geld_engl.pdf (accessed February 6, 2014).

Bianconi, Lorenzo, and Giorgio Pestelli, eds. 1998. *Opera Production and Its Resources*, translated by Lydia G. Cochrane. *The History of Italian Opera* 4. Chicago: University of Chicago Press.

Caillé, Alain, and Jacques Godbout, eds. 2001. *The World of the Gift*. London and Montreal: McGill-Queen's University Press.

Christie's. 1994. Auction catalogue n. 5207, June 29, 994, Lot 118. *OperaCat* ID 1214.

Cohen, Albert. 2000. "Musicians, Amateurs and Collectors: Early French Auction Catalogues as Musical Sources." *Music & Letters* 81/1: 1–12.

Connell, Philip. 2000. "Bibliomania: Book Collecting, Cultural Politics, and the Rise of Literary Heritage in Romantic Britain." *Representation* 71: 24–47.

Coover, James B. 2001. *Private Music Collections. Catalogs and Cognate Literature*. Warren, Michigan: Harmonie Park Press.

——. 1989. "Puttick's Auctions: Windows on the Retail Music Trade." *Journal of the Royal Musical Association* 114/1: 56–68.

——. 1988. *Antiquarian Catalogues of Music Interest*. London: Mansell.

Coral, Leonore. 2003. "Music Dealers and Antiquarians." In *Grove Music Online. Oxford Music Online*. Available: http://www.oxfordmusiconline.com/subscriber/article/grove/music/19435 (accessed February 6, 2014).

Dibdin, Thomas Frognall. [1809] 2010. *Bibliomania, or Book Madness: A Bibliographical Romance, in Six Parts*. London: Creery. Reprint. Cambridge: Cambridge University Press.

Fabbri, Paolo. 2001. *Rossini nelle raccolte Piancastelli di Forlì*. Lucca: Libreria musicale italiana.

Florimo, Francesco. [1880–1882] 2002. *Le scuola musicale di Napoli e i suoi Conservatori*. 4 vols. Naples: Morano. Reprint. Bologna: Forni.

Fontaine, Jules-Pierre. 1836. *Manuel de l'amateur d'autographes*. Paris: P. Morta.

——. 1834. *Des Collections d'autographes, et de l'utilité qu'on en peut retirer*. Paris: L'Auteur.

Fuld, James J. 1976. "Surrounded by One's Friends." *Notes* 32/3: 479–490.

Gil, José. 1998. *Metamorphoses of the Body*, translated by Stephen Muecke. Minneapolis: University of Minnesota Press.

Godbout, Jacques. [2007] 2008. *Quello che circola tra noi: Dare, ricevere, ricambiare*, translated by Paolo Gomarasca. Milan: Vita e Pensiero. Originally published as *Ce qui circule entre nous. Donner, recevoir, rendre*. Paris: Editions du Seuil.

Gombrich, Ernst. 1987. *Reflections on the History of Art: Views and Reviews*. Oxford: Phaidon.

——. 1979. *Ideals and Idols: Essays on Values in History and Art*. Oxford: Phaidon.

Gossett, Philip. 2013. "The Livre d'or of Charlotte de Rothschild." In *Word, Image, and Song: Essays on Musical Voices*. 2 vols., edited by Rebecca Cypess, Beth L. Glixon, and Nathan Link, II: 187–212. Rochester: University of Rochester Press.

Graber, David. 2005. "Fetishism as social creativity or, Fetishes are gods in the process of construction." *Anthropological Theory* 5: 407–438.

Haskell, Francis. [1962] 1980. *Patrons and Painters: Art and Society in Baroque Italy*. New Haven: Yale University Press. Originally published London: Chatto & Windus.

——. 1976. *Rediscoveries in Art: Some Aspects of Taste, Fashion, and Collecting in England and France*. London: Phaidon.

Hyatt King, Alexander, and Oliver W. Neighbour. 1966. "Printed Music from the Collection of Alfred Cortot." *The British Museum Quarterly* 31/1–2: 8–16.

Henrici, Karl Ernst. 1913. Auction catalogue n. XVII, October 20, 1913, Lot 215. *OperaCat* ID 5341.

JHC. 1989–. *The Journal of the History of Collections*.

Johnson, Douglas, Alan Tyson, and Robert Winter, eds. 1985. *The Beethoven Sketchbooks. History—Reconstruction—Inventory*. California Studies in 19th Century Music 4. Berkeley and Los Angeles: University of California Press.

Kunard, Andrea. 2006. "Traditions of Collecting and Remembering. Gender, Class, and the Nineteenth-Century Sentiment Album and Photographic Album." *Early Popular Visual Culture* 4/3: 227–243.

La Mara. 1894. *Letters of Franz Liszt. Collected and edited by La Mara.* Translated by Constance Bache. 2 vols. New York: Charles Scribner's Sons.

Leopoldo. 1771. *Catalogue des livres du cabinet particulier de LL.AA.RR.* Florence: Imprimerie granducale.

LIM. 1853. "Thalberg." *L'Italia musicale* 5/53 (2 July): 213.

——. 1852. *L'Italia musicale* 4/57 (17 July): 226.

——. 1850. "Gli autografi." *L'Italia musicale* 2/69 (September 25): 275–276.

Leavitt, Strebeigh & Co. 1867. Auction catalogue. March 4, 1867.

Libreria Antiquaria Luigi Banzi. Sales catalogue n. 2 [s.d.], Lot 57. *OperaCat* ID 2245.

Libreria Musicale Gallini. 2001. Sales catalogue "Giuseppe Verdi," Lot 595. *OperaCat* ID 2556.

Lion Heart Autographs. 2006. Electronic sales catalogue, Lot 13697. *OperaCat* ID 902. Online. Available: www.lionheartautographs.com (accessed February 6, 2014).

Luzio, Alessandro. 1927. *Profili biografici e bozzetti storici.* 2 vols. Milan: Casa editrice L. F. Cogliati.

Mauss, Marcel. 1990. *The Gift: The Form and Reason for Exchange in Archaic Societies*, translated by W. D. Halls. London: Routledge.

McCourt, Tom. 2005. "Collecting Music in the Digital Realm." *Popular Music and Society* 28/2: 249–252.

OperaCat. 2014. Online. Available: http://operacat.uchicago.edu/ (accessed June 17, 2014).

Pomian, Krzysztof. 1990. *Collectors and Curiosities: Paris and Venice, 1500–1800*, translated by Elizabeth Wiles-Portier. Cambridge, UK: Polity Press; Cambridge, MA: Basil Blackwell.

——. 1978. "Collezione." In *Enciclopedia Einaudi*, 330–364. Milan: Einaudi.

Pompilio, Angelo. 1991–1992. "La collezione Scalvini dell'Istituto Nazionale di Studi Verdiani. Il melodramma italiano dell'Ottocento tra collezionismo ed editoria musicale." *Studi verdiani* 7: 111–188 and 8: 118–143.

Puttick & Simpson. 1853. Auction catalogue, January 25, 1853, Lot 384, 391, 392. *OperaCat* ID 4288–4290.

Rendell, Kenneth W. Gallery. Sales catalogue n. 193, Lot 30. *OperaCat* ID 4744.

Sandvoss, Cornel. 2005. *Fans: The Mirror of Consumption.* Cambridge, UK: Polity Press.

Schaal, Richard. 1966. *Quellen und Forschungen zur Wiener Musiksammlung von Aloys Fuchs.* Österreichische Akademie der Wissenschaften. Philosophische-historische Klasse. Sitzungsbericht 251. Band I. Abhandlung. Veröffentlichungen der Kommission für Musikforschung 5. Vienna: Hermann Böhlaus.

Starobinski, Jean. 1997. *Largesse*, translated by Jane Marie Todd. Chicago: University of Chicago Press.

Stroh, Patricia. 2007. "Beethoven in the Auction Market: A Twenty-Year Review." *Notes* 63/3: 533–564.

Subkowski, Peter. 2006. "On the Psychodynamics of Collecting." *International Journal of Psychoanalysis* 87/2: 383–401.

Torno, Armando. 2008. "'Saremo soli!': i segreti di Verdi e Teresa Stolz." *Corriere della sera* (December 1). Online. Available: http://archiviostorico.corriere.it/2008/dicembre/01/Saremo_soli_segreti_Verdi_Teresa_co_9_081201042.shtml (accessed February 6, 2014).

Traficante, Frank. 1970. "Dispersal of the Cortot Collection: 290 Treatises in Lexington." *Notes* 26/4: 713–717.

Waterman, Sue. 2005. "Collecting the Nineteenth Century." *Representation* 90: 98–128.

CHAPTER 32

POLITICS

MARC A. WEINER

The Political in Opera

To speak of "opera and politics" is to be more evocative than precise, because the phrase may direct one's attention to any number of different objects of inquiry and modes of interpretation. Most often, it implies a given political system, specific historical personages associated with worldly power, or attendant issues conveyed, explicitly or by suggestion only, in the dramatic setting (Arblaster 1992; McClary 1985: 154–156). One thinks, in this sense, of Shuisky's ambitions for the czar's throne in Mussorgsky's *Boris Godunov*, of the subjugation of Flanders in Verdi's opera set in sixteenth-century Spain, *Don Carlos*, the *ancien régime*'s waning power in Mozart's *Le nozze de Figaro*, the depiction of the Saint Bartholomew's Day Massacre in Meyerbeer's *Les Huguenots*, or of Richard Nixon's encounter with Mao Tse-Tung in Adams's *Nixon in China*. Another understanding focuses on the specific historical setting in which a given operatic work was composed and/or received, such as the Egyptian commission and premiere of Verdi's *Aida* (Said 1994: 115), the performance of the first version of Beethoven's *Fidelio* before an audience of Napoleon's officers in 1805 Vienna (Riezler 1971: 38), the role of the monarchy of Louis Philippe in the development of Meyerbeer's *Robert le diable* (Fulcher 2002: 64–78), or Pfitzner's veiled rejection of parliamentary democracies in *Palestrina* (Bokina 1997: 129–140; Weiner 2009: 56–60, 153). Investigations into opera and politics have concerned the affiliations of given composers (Verdi's identification with the Risorgimento, Britten's pacifism, Schoenberg's Zionism), as well as the role that politics played in their professional careers (Mozart's dependence upon Joseph II, Prokofiev's and Shostakovich's interdictions under Stalin, Wagner's flight from Dresden for accusations of meddling in Saxon politics) (Carr 2008; Naegele 1995: 201–226, 322–354).

But a work might also convey the "political" only in a far more general sense, as in the xenophobic rejection of foreign, non-German culture in Wagner's *Die Meistersinger*, or of the French (in a parodistic manner, rather than emphatically as in Wagner) in Britten's *Billy Budd*. In this vein, the notion of the nationalistic and populist *Volksoper* is associated with a number of works, from Weber's *Der Freischütz* and Mussorgsky's *Khovanshchina* to Humperdink's *Hänsel und Gretel* and Mascagni's *Cavalleria rusticana.* Operas are often thought of as representative of a given national sensibility; Bartók's *Bluebeard's Castle* is deemed very East European, Wagner's *Ring* singularly Germanic, and Britten is said to have essentially reinvented the English opera (Brett 1983: 92, 95; Brett 2006: 23). Then there is the notion of the "politicization" of a work, which imprints upon an opera a signification initially unintended by, and for some critics even antithetical to, the wishes of the composer, as in the argument that Hitler's celebration of the Wagnerian music drama as a glorification of all things Aryan—with all of its biological, racist meaning in the 1930s and 1940s—was an unfortunate distortion of the works as Wagner conceived them in the nineteenth century (Borchmeyer 1992: 183–185; Hanisch 1992: 200; Krohn 1992: 186, 201; Weiner 1995: 2, 14–21, 27–30; Rüsen 2000: 16–17; Potter 2008: 242). A phenomenon such as Israel's extended ban on performances of Wagner may be viewed in this category (Taruskin 1992: 25). Indeed, the censorship of opera—ranging from intrusive influence over the formation of libretti to outright bans on performance—have more often been propelled by political considerations than for reasons of decorum. The most notorious cases make this clear: Da Ponte's modifications of Beaumarchais's play in the drafting of the libretto to *Le nozze di Figaro* in order to placate concerns of the Austrian monarchy, Verdi's frustrations with official pressure placed upon the opera houses of Naples, Rome, and La Fenice in the genesis of *Un ballo in maschera* and *Rigoletto*, and Stalin's aforementioned vitriolic response to *Lady Macbeth of the Mtsensk District* (Weisstein 2001; Budden 1984; Parker 2007). More recently, specific operatic stagings have elicited interdictions from state-sponsored and/or political agencies, such as the Deutsche Oper Berlin's decision to cancel a staging of Mozart's *Idomeneo* by Hans Neuenfels depicting the decapitated head of the Prophet Muhammad out of concerns for retribution from religious fundamentalists, and the Chinese authorities' ban on Zhang Huan's mounting of Handel's *Semele* at the Beijing Festival owing to its employment of costumes and film evoking contemporary China (Bhat 2006; Jacobs 2010).

An opera might also be seen to bear the traces of a political and cultural ideology as understood in the broadest sense of the term, even if it be that of the apolitical "l'art pour l'art" movement, as in Debussy's *Pelléas et Mélisande*, the pervasive orientalism of Saint-Saëns's *Samson et Dalila* (Lindenberger 1998: 140; Locke 1991: 262–263, 266–271, 274–302), the subtly anti-Semitic dimensions of Berg's *Wozzeck* (Gilman 1996: 145–171), or the glorification of the bohemian in Puccini's *La bohème*. And there has been no shortage of interest in the "sexual politics" of opera, manifested in the "queering" of specific operatic works, such as Britten's *Peter Grimes*, say (Brett 2006: 20–33, 36–39, 42–53), or of both performers and their roles (Koestenbaum 1993: 218–219; Castle 1995: 200–238) in Lacanian readings of the function of the sexual within the symbolic orders of the legal and political systems as reflected in works of diverse composers, most of all, Wagner (Žižek 2002: 121–149), and in feminist interpretations of a host of canonical warhorses, from Verdi's *La traviata* to Bizet's *Carmen* and beyond (Clément 1989: 47–53; McClary 1992: 30–43). Finally, within the past twenty-five years or so the political nature of operatic staging, of specific productions, has emerged as a subject of interest in its own right (Nattiez 1992; Spotts 1994: vii–viii, 185–188, 209–211, 282, 286; Levin 2007: 61, 143–144, 151).

The degree to which a given discussion of opera includes consideration of politics is often an indication of the nature of the methodology employed. Broadly speaking, studies of opera prior to the late 1970s tended to mention the politics of the age, of the composer, and of the libretto's machinations only in passing (Grout 1960: 509–511, 524, 595–617). Most, though by no means all, of this kind of work was undertaken by musicologists, and indeed it was not until the advent of such journals as *19th-Century Music* (inaugurated 1977) and subsequent publications, which welcomed scholars from a host of other disciplines, and the influx into musicology of diverse theoretical models already widely represented in various other fields within the humanities, that the role of politics within the study of opera assumed greater importance, and came to be seen from a host of vantage points.

The least overtly concerned with political and even ideological matters have been scholars who drew upon deconstruction, with its attention to the semiotic properties of music (Abbate 1991: passim, especially 16–27) and post-structuralism, with its emphasis on discourse analysis (Nattiez 1990: 48, 74–77, 119–122, 171–176, 217–229). Far more manifestly attuned to the role that politics played in the formation of a given operatic work were those scholars of literature and history who came to be identified in the 1980s as "New Historicists," involved both with the cultural and historical context of an aesthetic construct and with the work as a reflection of cultural and intellectual history, which of course includes the political sphere. Critics such as these viewed their investigations as falling within the "history of ideas" (Lindenberger 1984; Robinson 1985; Gilman 1988). An instance of this kind of study is John Bokina's exemplary comparison of Machiavelli's *The Prince* with Monteverdi's characterization of various elevated operatic figures: Orfeo, Ulysses, and Nerone (Bokina 1997: 15–40). The advent of "Culture Studies," in both its British and American manifestations, went hand in hand with these developments; their proponents were far more involved with the work of the Frankfurt School, and therefore with *Ideologiekritik*, than were those methodologically more closely affiliated with deconstruction and post-structuralism. Foremost among such practitioners is Rose Rosengard Subotnik, who may be credited with having essentially introduced to her field the work of Theodor W. Adorno, initially in her analyses of the theorist's writings on music in general, and his work on Beethoven's late style in particular (Subotnik 1991: 15–56), and subsequently in her examination of passages from *Die Zauberflöte*, which are characterized by a close interrogation of the aesthetic minutiae of Mozart's music with a view toward uncovering its ideological operations (Subotnik 1996: 1–38).

But this is not to say that studies of opera have formed and emerged from competing camps characterized by methodological dogmatism, as was far more the case in literary studies from the 1970s through the 1990s. A characteristic feature of the emerging field of "opera studies" has been precisely its inter- and multidisciplinarity, and hence its heterogeneity of approaches to the subject of opera and politics, as made manifest in a host of essay collections: *Music and the Politics of Culture* (Norris 1989), *The Work of Opera: Genre, Nationhood, and Sexual Difference* (Dellamora and Fischlin 1997), *Music and German National Identity* (Applegate and Potter 2002), *Opera and Society in Italy and France from Monteverdi to Bourdieu* (Johnson, Fulcher, and Ertman 2007), and others still.

Such heterogeneity is reflected in the diverse understandings of the notion of "political music" in opera. Herbert Lindenberger, for example, discerns a correlation between the musical idiom of diverse works and the sociopolitical contexts for which they were composed, as heard in the difference between the music of Monteverdi's *L'Orfeo* of 1607, and that of his last work for the stage, *L'incoronazione di Poppea* of 1643, the former written for the court of Mantua, and the latter, the first opera successful as a commercial venture without royal patronage, for a non-aristocratic public that attended its premiere in the Teatro SS. Giovanni e Paolo, a popular theater in Venice (Lindenberger 1984: 211). Paul Robinson identifies a political dimension in the kinds of voices demanded by the music Verdi composed during the Risorgimento, and therefore discerns a link between Verdi's aesthetic decisions and nineteenth-century *Realpolitik*, arguing that different voices are suited to the expression of politics in opera to differing degrees; he writes that some "convey a sense of power" and claims that "[t]he high baritone is the political voice par excellence" (Robinson 1985: 168, 172). On the other hand, Anthony Arblaster's understanding of the phenomenon is altogether different, as is made clear in his discussion of Cherubini's "rescue opera" *Les deux journées*, in which he argues that "[t]he music is in a suitably democratic or populist vein.... There are only two solo numbers. Otherwise it consists of ensembles [...]" (Arblaster 1992: 48; apparently he believes that the more arias a work has, the less egalitarian its aesthetic form, implying that a truly populist opera would consist solely of choruses). For Lydia Goehr, the "political" in music is essentially an empty category that devolves into ideology the moment it takes on the contours of a given specific political affiliation (Goehr 1998: 37–38). With so many different conceptualizations of what is involved when we speak of "opera and politics," it is no wonder that scholars can be seen at times to be speaking at cross purposes, which may account for why there have been so few, and so few successful, comprehensive, and influential examinations of the subject.

That being the case, it is difficult to find a single object of inquiry that may serve to highlight, or make manifest, the diverse approaches just outlined. For how can the "discourse" of a given work both obviate ideological criticism *and* lend itself to an inquiry concerning traces of the power relations discernible in its composer's time, life, writings, and other works? What kinds of exegesis best reveal commonalities between the historical, political, and ideological forces of the period of composition, or of that of its reception, and the aesthetic makeup—be it textual, visual, or musical—of a given dramatic composition that encompasses a text intended to be sung? Clearly, the wider the net of approaches involved, the greater the potential for critical insight.

Richard Wagner's Political Aesthetics

A number of the concerns just outlined can be explicated through a discussion of the works of Richard Wagner, certainly one of the most ideologically laden composers ever to have set pen to paper, and one whose works have been thoroughly examined with an eye (and an ear) toward the political affiliations they evince, explicitly or by implication only. This interest has had at least a fourfold impetus: (1) the overwhelming prominence of productions of Wagner's works throughout the last century; (2) the political dimensions of many of his librettos; (3) the composer's involvement with a wide range of political issues throughout his life: his participation in the failed, mid-nineteenth century revolution in Dresden and subsequent flight and extended exile from Germany; his close association with the Bavarian monarchy in the personage of King Ludwig II; and his (tenuous and opportunistic, to be sure, but documented) enthusiasm for the unification of Germany following the Franco-Prussian war; and finally; (4) the aforementioned association of Wagner's works with National Socialism in the 1930s and 1940s.

The Wagnerian work most overtly concerned with the political machinations of a specific historical moment and setting is *Rienzi, der Letzte der Tribunen* (1842), later associated with diverse political figures, from Theodor Herzl, the founder of Zionism, to Adolf Hitler, who claimed that it was during a performance of *Rienzi* in his youth that he first conceived of his political future (Kubizek 1954: 64–66; for this reason Syberberg [1977] created a scene in his seven-and-one-half-hour film, *Hitler: Ein Film aus Deutschland*, in which the Führer rises out of a grave marked "RW" wearing a Roman toga, an image the director may also have taken from the final paragraph of Ludwig Marcuse's biography [1973: 312] of the composer, *Das denkwürdige Leben des Richard Wagner*).

Another is *Tannhäuser und der Sängerkrieg auf Wartburg* (composed 1842–1844, premiered 1845; revised and premiered 1861), much of which takes place in the thirteenth-century court of Count (*Landgraf*) Hermann of Thuringia, whose dubious role in the conflict between Philipp of Swabia and Otto IV is nowhere to be found in the music drama. Still, the setting is specific enough to allow its audience to place it in a given historical moment within Germany's monarchical and literary past. Yet another is *Lohengrin* (composed 1845–1848, premiered 1850), set in tenth-century Antwerp during its conflict with the Hungarians, "des Ostens Horden" ("the hordes of the East"). The Swan Knight is hailed by King Heinrich der Vogeler and the people of Brabant, Saxony, and Thuringia as the warrior who will lead them against the invading army. He prophesizes victory (in the ensuing, but unnamed battle of Unstrut in 933), yet his departure at the end is seen not only as a tragedy for his wife, Elsa, but more to the point, as a loss for the military security of the realm, and with it, by implication, as a danger to the continuation of Heinrich's royal line within the German monarchy.

The work that has been most assiduously interrogated with a view toward its political content and implications is *Der Ring des Nibelungen*. George Bernard Shaw, in his notorious, influential, and witty socialist reading of the cycle, *The Perfect Wagnerite: A Commentary on the Niblung's Ring* ([1923] 1967), was not the first to recognize the contemporary political critique at its center. Friedrich Nietzsche, that most astute and scathing critic of late nineteenth-century Germany, in his *Case of Wagner* (1888), had already characterized the age of Wagner as one that posterity will call one day, with awed respect, "*the classical age of war*" (Nietzsche [1888] 1967: 180).

Nonetheless, it is the subtlety of their portrayal of political concerns that make Wagner's music dramas of particular interest in the current context. For in his post-revolutionary works, Wagner actually strove to *mask* his analogy to European society and politics by subsuming it under the trappings of myth and legend. His belief that camouflage would make his arguments all the more forceful renders an investigation of the political dimensions of a post-revolutionary Wagnerian work particularly intriguing (the obvious exception to this aesthetic program being the tub-thumping German nationalism and xenophobia of *Die Meistersinger von Nürnberg*). In an often-cited letter from January 25–26, 1854 to his friend and former fellow revolutionary, August Röckel, Wagner explained the role of politics in his new aesthetic theory by making clear that his conception of the *Ring* cycle, then in progress, was based on the notion that the superior artwork *must never explicitly state* [emphasis mine] its message, but must necessarily be enigmatic. He had sent Röckel a draft for his *Ring* project, to which his friend had responded by expressing his disappointment over an apparent absence of political content. Wagner countered that such content was by no means missing, but embedded in a work that was not intended to convey its meaning too overtly:

> I believe I've managed, with a fairly accurate instinct, to stave off the urge to make everything too obvious, because it has become clear to me that too overt a disclosure of one's intention may well disturb a correct understanding.... This, then, distinguishes my poetic material from the political material that seems to be the only kind of material known these days. (Wagner 2004: VI: 59)

Though he probably had in mind, specifically, the all-but-defunct movement of "Das junge Deutschland," with its ethos of a literature in the service of social and political liberalism (Cohen 2008: 47), this passage is typical of Wagner's many and repeated characterizations of his own mature artistic program in at least two respects: first, he celebrates his own superior aesthetic by denigrating a purportedly inferior artistic paradigm (usually labeled elsewhere as Jewish); and second, he emphasizes that, for him, that inferior paradigm forms the basis for works that contain—and are limited to—a concrete, literal content—in this case, the overtly political material (Weiner 1996: 59–68, 83). As such, they are different from the more enigmatic and superior work of art, namely, Wagner's. He does not state that he has abandoned his political agenda, nor that his desire for the transformation of social and political dimensions was one thing, and his artistic compositions another. On the contrary, they are intimately connected. But in dramatic form his political ideas were to be conveyed obliquely, through suggestion, thereby resonating, he believed, all the more powerfully with an audience and in a far more provocative manner than they would have had they been more emphatically and overtly stated. It is precisely the opacity of politics couched in myth that has made the *Ring* in particular so enigmatic and endlessly fascinating, and that has allowed it to be seen as representative of a wide spectrum of political affiliations—from Communist, to Socialist (Shaw [1923] 1967), to Social Democratic, to Pan-Germanic (Nietzsche [1888] 1967: 180), to National Socialist (McGrath 1974: 79, 88, 91, 182–191, 202–203, 210, 214–219, 240–243, 245–248).

The Post-Revolutionary Wagner: *Tristan und Isolde*

Two models of thought involving the relationship between his revolutionary concerns and aesthetic projects following the flight from Dresden pervade scholarship on Wagner. On the one hand, there is a consensus of opinion that the music dramas composed following the failed revolution constitute a continuation, albeit in aesthetic form, of the interests that had informed the composer's participation leading up to and during that most political event of his life (Mayer 1981: 55–86; Krohn 1992: 165). If one takes Wagner's own interpretation of his aesthetic project seriously, this would seem to be true, at least as far as the composer's intentions are concerned. He clearly understood his Nibelung cycle not as unrelated to contemporary forces, but as a veiled portrayal of political issues, both abstract and, given his experience with his fellow revolutionary and friend Röckel, contemporary.

On the other hand, most Wagner scholars agree that political machinations are manifestly greater in the first two-thirds of the *Ring* than in the tale of the doomed Cornish and Irish lovers, *Tristan und Isolde* (composed 1857–1859, premiere 1865), the first work Wagner composed during the twelve-year hiatus from the cycle.[1] Indeed, this is the manner in which *Tristan* is usually seen, as though it were the most rapturous expression of an ineffable, otherworldly experience imaginable, and therefore, of all of Wagner's works for the stage, the one farthest removed from the quotidian existence the composer faced as a disappointed political reformer and impecunious exile. The cliché about *Tristan* is that it differs from his other works in part because it constituted a sublimation of Wagner's infatuation with Mathilde Wesendonck, the wife of his wealthy patron, Otto Wesendonck. The discovery of the affair necessitated Wagner's flight to Venice, where he completed the composition of the first act, while recording reflections on love and aesthetics which he intended to give to his "ferne Geliebte" at some future date. In the scholarship on *Tristan* there is neither much discussion of its political content, nor of the politics of its reception; ever since the appearance of Kurth's *Romantische Harmonik und ihre Krise in Wagners 'Tristan'* in 1920, most analyses and popular discussions have concerned the novelty and innovation of its music (Kurth [1920] 1968; Vogel 1962; Gregor-Dellin 1983: 427–429; Gutman 1990: 374; Dahlhaus and Deathridge 1990: 155–157; Chafe 2004; Dreyfus 2010: 101–110), its literary and philosophical sources (Borchmeyer 1991: 326–367), and the means by which its conflation of love and death influenced the decadent movement (Koppen 1974: 165–213). Typical in this regard is Carl Schorske's understanding of the work:

> *Tristan und Isolde* was conceived in [a] mood of postpolitical, ontic despair in which only the claims of libido have life. The communal eros has become confined to the personal and the sexual. One can feel the birth of depth psychology out of the spirit of frustrated populist idealism [...]. The state appears not as unjust or corrupt, as in

> *Lohengrin* or *Siegfried*, but as a symbol of eternal social restraint upon our emotional life [...]. Psyche and society are in hopeless disjuncture, in absolute opposition. In the music, the dissolution of political and moral obligation is expressed in the partial dissolution of tonality in a vastly expanded chromaticism. Wagner's political abnegation thus issued in musical innovation. (Schorske 1988: 178)

John Deathridge, one of the very few scholars who views the work differently, makes clear just how iconoclastic it is to recognize in *Tristan* a concern for nineteenth-century German politics:

> Forget the myth about the former revolutionary, now resigned, full of renunciation, wrestling with his inner demon, and suffering from a bad case of withdrawal from life. *Tristan* clearly represents a flight from the private into the public realm, not the reverse [...]. Nearly all the dissections of the famous musical passages in *Tristan und Isolde* avoid—almost suspiciously so—the extra-musical altogether. (Deathridge 2008: 125, 136)

Deathridge's primary interest here is with the juxtaposition of the private and public spheres in Wagner's thinking of the 1850s in general. But his observations also underscore the consensus of opinion that, of all of Wagner's music dramas, *Tristan und Isolde* is the work furthest removed from his contemporary world, meaning from the politics of the composer's time. Moreover, in a discussion of Isolde's *Liebestod*, Deathridge makes an apposite observation: "[...] of all the moments in Wagner's works, this is probably the least likely to be associated with anything mundane like politics, though the extra-musical allusions built into its musical fabric in the name of the absolute do not by any means exonerate it from reality [...]" (Deathridge 2008: 150).

So which view is justified? Is *Tristan* a kind of sentimental and philosophical intermission in the work of a composer in whose life specific and disparate hegemonic structures of power (liberalism, monarchism, enlightened despotism), institutions, and ideological beliefs played a considerable role in the conceptualization of both his social theories and mature art works? Is *Tristan* an aberration, an exception to a lifelong aesthetic project conceived of as a theater of contemporary social problems and future ideals? Hardly—its genesis at a key point in the development of European political history is integral to an understanding of its ideological operations. *Tristan* was conceived during the historical and political transition from the collapse of the Metternich regime to a period of greater autonomy, laissez-faire capitalism, and the slow development of both liberalism and nationalism, and it was over the course of this transition that Wagner revised his conceptualization of the monarch in the modern world. The music drama reflects both his earlier image of the ruler and his newer understanding of the figure of the politician. But, as was the case with the *Ring*, so too in *Tristan* have political issues not so much disappeared as receded into the background. That much is underscored by the fact that Wagner, in the same letter to Röckel in which he discussed his aestheticization of politics (see above), also mentioned—for the first time—his plans for the new dramatic project (Deathridge 2008: 118). In other words, the aesthetic program that masks political issues behind more universal concerns at the heart of the *Ring* is even *more* in force here, where the political dimension infuses the entire music drama, but it does so even more covertly than in those that had preceded it.

Tristan and the Politics of History

Tristan und Isolde unfolds before a background concerning the specific power relations between two realms, Ireland and Cornwall, which have undergone a fundamental transmutation before the drama begins. Without knowledge of this history, the machinations, psychological conditions, motivations, and relationships of the protagonists would make little sense. Indeed, it is only through the gradual revelation of information concerning this specific backstory that their powerful, emotionally charged states gain intelligibility, credibility, and depth. In other words, by subjecting the text of *Tristan* to a close reading in conjunction with a discussion of Wagner's aesthetic theory, biography, and historical moment, we may discern evidence of "opera and politics" in this, allegedly, least likely of places.

In the course of Act I we are given information of a political nature that, bit by bit, accounts for Isolde's shifting affective development from indignation to sorrow, from resentment to nostalgic reflection, to hurt and suffering, and finally, to unbridled hatred. Her fury is the result of her former status as princess of the royal house of Ireland, and of both the former and current official agreements between her country and that of Tristan. Cornwall, we learn, was long a subservient realm—presumably one among many fiefdoms—that swore allegiance, and paid tribute, to Ireland. This tribute took the form of an annual tax levied by the Irish king, and it was in response to King Marke's sudden refusal to pay it (owing, we may assume, to Tristan's maturation into the most formidable knight of the realm) that the Irish warrior Morold (to whom Isolde was betrothed) sailed to Cornwall to extract the levy, and presumably to punish the miscreants as well. Tristan challenged Morold to combat and slew him, whereupon he severed the warrior's head and sent it to Ireland in lieu of the expected reparation, an action that led to the composition of ballads deriding Ireland and praising Tristan as the hero who freed Cornwall. Morold's sword was poisoned, however, and Tristan, having been wounded in combat, sailed to Ireland in hope of finding an antidote from the source that brewed the poison.

As in other Wagnerian dramas set in the Middle Ages, one's most prized possession in *Tristan* is honor (one thinks in this context of the eponymous Tannhäuser, of Telramund [*Lohengrin*], and of the unnamed squires of Montsalvat [*Parsifal*], who long to retrieve the holy spear, and with it, renown; see Chafe 2004: 68–84). The daughter of a heretofore powerful and revered royal house who had blessed her betrothed's weapons, Isolde was publicly humiliated by Tristan's celebrated deed, something she baldly states to the Cornish hero:

> Had Morold lived, / who would ever have dared, / to offer us such shame?... / Betrothed he was to me, / the shining Irish hero; / I had consecrated his weapons, / for me he went into battle. / When he fell, fell, too, my honor. (Wagner 2004: VII: 21–22)

To the end of the work she has nothing but contempt for Cornwall, a realm she has always held in low regard. Throughout the music drama she refers to her lover as a "vassal" (*Vasallen*), and even calls him (to his face) a "servant" (*Knecht*), and a "traitor" (*Verräter*); in Act I she identifies herself as "booty" (*Schatz*) in every sense of the word a "trophy wife." Such epithets are the result of the former power relations of their respective realms that make Isolde's merciful treatment of the wounded man she knows only (incredibly) as "Tantris," as well as the secret fealty he swears to her thereafter, all the more poignant. What is overlooked in discussions of the music drama is the fact that the love between Tristan and Isolde was already forbidden and kept secret from the moment she allowed him to live, long before they boarded ship for Cornwall. The political relationship between their countries, and their codes of honor, would have demanded his death had he been discovered. Both this and the official dynamics between their two lands explain Isolde's furious indignation when the Cornish knight returns to bring her to his king as bride, and make the extent of her humiliation all the more palpable when the Cornish sailors mock her by singing one of the aforementioned ballads (see Figure 32.1):

> Herr Morold took / to the seas / to get tax in Cornwall. / An island swims / on the desolate sea, / there he lies buried: / Yet his head hangs / in Irenland, / paid as tax / from Engeland. / Hurrah! Our hero Tristan! / How he can pay taxes! (Wagner 2004 VII: 8–9)[2]

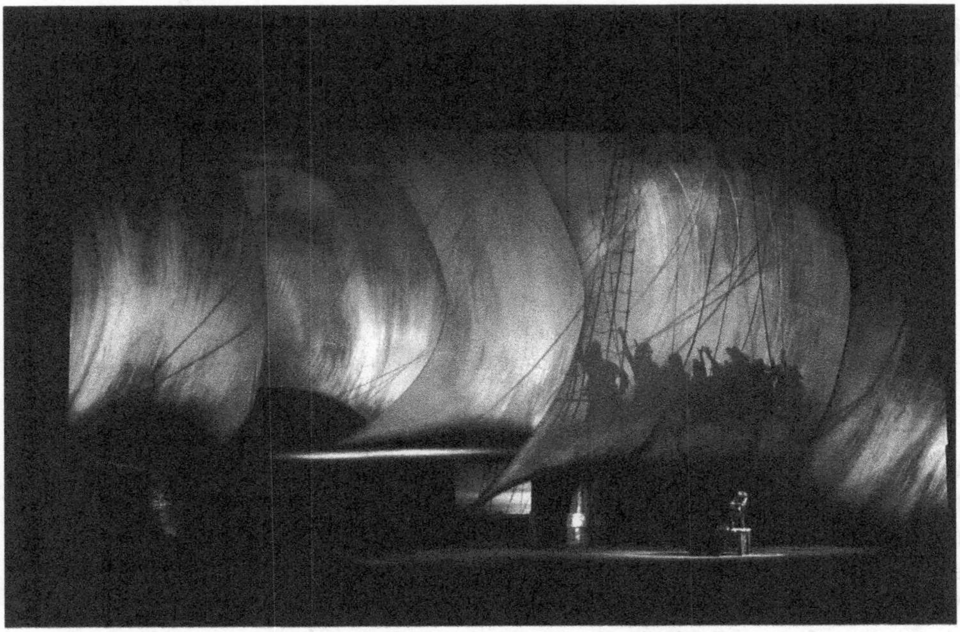

FIGURE 32.1 During a journey to Cornwall, the Irish princess Isolde (Birgit Nilsson) broods on her betrayal by the Cornish knight Tristan, while the sailors mock her. *Tristan und Isolde*, Metropolitan Opera, 1971, set design by Günther Schneider-Siemssen. Photo: Frank Dunand / © the Metropolitan Opera Guild.

Through a number of oblique and subtle references, the attentive audience comes to learn that Tristan had volunteered to bring Isolde to King Marke in response to internecine intrigues within the Cornish court. Undoubtedly, Tristan also undertook the deed as an act of self-flagellation for his forbidden love of a former enemy, something he attempts to stifle within himself by publicly extolling the virtues of the Irish princess and by urging his king to marry her, and thus make her the future Cornish queen. In his extended monologue in Act II, King Marke makes clear that he had groomed his nephew for succession to the throne, a plan that fostered jealousy among the courtiers, foremost among them Tristan's purported friend Melot, who—we learn at the end of the act—goaded Tristan into initiating a plan for a royal match that would test his honor. To Isolde, Tristan says of him:

> For my honor and renown / he was concerned like no one else. / To wanton arrogance / he drove my heart: / the pack he led, / that hounded me / to increase my honor and renown / by marrying you to the king. (Wagner 2004: VII: 55–56)

After all, Tristan's reputation is that of a selfless, devoted, and fearless champion of his king, with his ruler's and his country's welfare his greatest concern; had he hesitated in endorsing the plan put forth by the courtiers, he would have risked appearing to covet the Cornish crown for himself (Gutman 1990: 250). Following the death of Morold, the political relationship between the two realms was destabilized, and war threatened. When Tristan returns to Ireland under his own name, he extends King Marke's offer of a peace treaty between the two royal houses, to be made manifest and secured through the marriage of Isolde to the Cornish king. At a public ceremony the feud is annulled, the Irish princess is given over to the foreign entourage, and with her maid Brangäne she boards the ship, captained by Tristan, for the journey to her husband-to-be. Act I begins less than an hour before the ship comes in sight of land.

Love and Procreation under Absolute Rule

The theme of love within the purview of kingship as threatened by, and inferior to, love that lies beyond socially sanctioned limits is, like their similar aesthetic programs, a feature that *Tristan und Isolde* has in common with the *Ring*. Let us recall that in *Siegfried* (the composition of which Wagner interrupted when he turned to his *Tristan* project), the superhero shares much with his slain father, Siegmund, insofar as the young Volsung's love is shown to be spontaneous, impetuous even, natural, irrepressible, and above all, unfettered by the institutions with which the emotion is configured within civilized society. As Slavoj Žižek has pointed out in a discussion of both *Tristan* and the *Ring*, Wagner's fascination with the figure of the renegade who subverts society's institutions (marriage) and systems of power (law, monarchical government) always had a political dimension that can be identified within the composer's specific historical moment:

> [...] Wotan concocts the figure of the hero not bound by any symbolic bond and thereby free to deliver the fallen universe of contracts. This aspect of Wagner is to be located within the great ideologico-political crisis of the late nineteenth century, which turned around the malfunctioning of investiture, of assuming and performing the paternal mandate of symbolic authority. (Žižek 2002: 137)

Such heroes would also include Siegmund, a man raised as an un-, or even anti-civilized warrior, who was supposed to be "free of divine protection, / loosened from gods' law" and therefore a figure so removed from the institutions secured through contractual law (Wotan's source of authority and power, and the basis of marriage) that he could function as the king of the gods' instrument in regaining the ring. The form his love takes—incest—is championed by Wotan as natural, but vilified as repugnant and insulting by his wife, Fricka, the goddess of marriage, who represents the interests of the State:

> WOTAN: What did the couple do that was so terrible, / whom spring lovingly united? / The magic of love/enraptured them: / whom do I punish for the power of love?
>
> FRICKA: How foolish and deaf you pretend to be, / as if you truly didn't know, / that I demand restitution for the holy vow of marriage, / the sorely aggrieved!
>
> WOTAN: Unholy / I hold the vow / that unites the unloving. (Wagner 2004: VI: 26)

Because the composer viewed such unions as antithetical to nature, and free love as natural (always the realm of wonder and beauty for Wagner the romantic), nearly all of the marriages in his works for the stage produce no offspring: neither Wotan and Fricka, nor Hunding and Sieglinde, nor King Marke and Isolde give forth issue (which is also the case, technically, with Günther and Brünnhilde, and Siegfried and Gutrune, though the plots of their dramas hardly give them the time to do so). It is unlikely that King Marke would have sired any future children anyway: Isolde refers to him in Act I as "Kornwalls müden König"—"Cornwall's tired king." Marke makes clear in his Act II monologue that he has never dared "approach" her ["der mein Wille nie zu nahen wagte, / der mein Wunsch erfurchtscheu entsagte"]; theirs has been a white marriage (Wagner 2004: VII: 11, 54). Institutional, contractual unions are inferior, while "free love" is emancipating by being insurrectionary: it is an emotion of revolution, and therefore, it is only consistent that the union of the Volsung siblings Siegmund and Sieglinde produces the amoral and revolutionary Siegfried.

It is but a short step from Wagner's criticism of the institution of marriage to his denigration of political power as equally antithetical to man as a natural being; indeed, as this passage demonstrates, love is always portrayed in his works as imperiled by the lust for power—the central theme of the *Ring*. In his theoretical writings this is most clearly stated in *Oper und Drama*, in his discussion of the myth of Antigone, who sacrifices herself out of love for her brother, Eteocles, and in so doing redeems the loveless state ruled by Creon (Rather 1979: 51–54). She is the model for Wagner's Valkyrie-heroine,

Brünnhilde, whose sacrifice at the conclusion of the tetralogy washes away the last vestiges of Wotan's corrupt rule. At the conclusion to *Tristan*, no such redemption is provided by Isolde, and the insecurity of the world and the realm she leaves at the end of the drama remains. In other words, both the *Ring* and *Tristan* concern the theme of politics, but the resolution provided in the tetralogy is missing at the close of the lovers' drama.

Wagner's Conception of Power

In order to better contextualize the politics of *Tristan*, it will be useful to reflect upon Wagner's shifting conceptions of the function of the ruler over the course of a mere decade—from 1848 to the beginning of Wagner's work on *Tristan* in 1857—that began with the optimism of the revolution and closed in an age of greater despair (for former revolutionaries) over its failed aspirations. Within that decade, the composer came to distinguish between the figure of the monarch and that of the politician. To the Wagner of 1848, Germany's rulers were the guarantors, surprisingly, of a future, potentially more egalitarian and enfranchised social order. This appears to be a contradiction not only to more modern readers, but was already so to Wagner's contemporaries, for his fellow former insurrectionaries were puzzled by his concomitant endorsement of the revolution's ideals and support of the monarchical system. In contradistinction to his thoughts on the function of the nobility, by the late 1850s the figure of the politician came to constitute in Wagner's mind a hallmark of the age of modernity, which he always viewed with disdain. The success of the counterrevolution in Vienna, of Russia and Austria's efforts against German unification under Prussia in 1850, the unfolding of the Russo-Turkish War in 1853, and the machinations of *Realpolitik* under Napoleon III (and later, Bismarck) all led Wagner to give up that earlier understanding of the role of the ruler as the sympathetic steward of his people and to replace it with a far more cynical view of the actor on the contemporary European political stage.

Already in anticipation of the impending revolution, Wagner had penned an essay in 1848 ("How Do Republican Movements Relate to Kingship?" [Wagner 2004: XII: 218–226]),[3] in which he expressed his vision of an ideal relationship between a feudal lord and his *Volk* in the modern age. While he rejected communism as mechanistic and materialistic, he sought to reconcile republicanism and kingship by viewing their relationship as one of reciprocity, in which the German prince is essentially an enlightened despot, representing the needs and desires of the people and governing in a benevolent manner, a figure reminiscent of Mozart's patron and champion of Enlightenment principles, Emperor Joseph II of Austria.

Seven years later, this vision is still discernible in *Tristan*, not as one might expect in the figure of King Marke, but in the eponymous hero himself. Indeed, the only thing we know about the king's feelings for his subjects is his resistance to the court's urging him to take a bride and, with her, to secure his lineage and the continuity of the established monarchy vouchsafed by familial succession. Though he ultimately relents at Tristan's insistence that he take a bride, he does so reluctantly. We are given more information about the hero, who, although he left his fiefdom in Brittany and relinquished his feudal rights to sail to Cornwall, was so beloved by his subjects that they kept his lands in good stead, awaiting (and therefore presumably hoping for) his return. This is made clear in an exchange between the knight's loyal servant, Kurwenal, and Tristan as he regains consciousness in the opening of Act III and asks where he is:

> KURWENAL: Kareol, Sire. / Do you not know the fortress / of your fathers?
> TRISTAN: My fathers?
> KURWENAL: Just look around!
> TRISTAN: What did I hear?
> KURWENAL: The shepherd's tune, / you heard it once again; / on the hillside he's tending your flocks.
> TRISTAN: My flocks?
> KURWENAL: Sire, I should say so! / Yours the house, / court, and castle. / The folk, true / to its dear lord, / tended house and hearth / as best it could, / when once he gave / to people and folk / inheritance and possessions, / when he left/for foreign lands. (Wagner 2004: VII: 59–60)

This vision of a beloved and magnanimous ruler (in whom King Ludwig II of Bavaria, Wagner's patron and enthusiastic admirer of the music drama, doubtless saw himself) is cast into greater relief when juxtaposed with that of the more modern politician, representative of Wagner's growing skepticism regarding political matters in the late 1850s. Most useful to understanding Wagner's conception of the contemporary actor on the modern political stage is a brief and illuminating passage in the same letter to Röckel (see above) in which Wagner discusses Robespierre, the purportedly idealistic goals of the Reign of Terror, and the mechanisms used to achieve them:

> He knew of no lofty goal that compelled him to turn to evil means; rather, owing to the lack of such a goal, in order to cover up its actual lack of content, he turned to the horrific apparatus of the guillotine, for it has been proven that the "terreur" was employed as nothing other than an apparatus for ruling and governing, without any real conviction, solely for political—that is, ambitious and self-indulgent—reasons. Thus, this extremely lofty man—who ultimately could only come up with his tasteless "vertu"—had a goal only in the means, and so it is with all of these purely political heroes, who with complete justification must perish through this kind of inability, so that hopefully this entire species [*Gattung*] will soon completely vanish from history. (Wagner 2004: VI: 66)

Wagner's Robespierre is thus an agent of vintage nineteenth-century *Realpolitik* (as well as, of course, a product of the composer's hatred of all things French), and it is precisely with this understanding of "The Ruler" that he conceived of the power relations of his post-revolutionary dramas. It is not that idealism has vanished from the Wagnerian universe, far from it; rather that idealism is now tarnished by and counterpoised to the realm of the politics of modernity. In other words, this short passage suggests that, for Wagner, even the most elevated goals of social and political emancipation, such as those of the revolution (here of 1789, and by implication those of 1848–1849 as well), were compromised the moment they assumed concrete form in the world of modern life experience.

This figure of the nefarious politician as power-hungry schemer may be discerned in *Tristan* as well. After all, the successful negotiations between Cornwall and Ireland that led to a peace treaty and the symbolic union of the realms through the marriage of Isolde and King Marke are, in Wagner's hands, a kind of ruthless intrigue not unlike that found in the *Ring*, and that here, too, places power and finance over private contentment and individual emotional fulfillment. As we have seen, this state of affairs also informs the court of Cornwall, in which calculation, intrigue, and ambition propel governmental actions that serve to annul private desires.

Wagner's intellectual shift from a conception of monarchy as paternalistic to a view of all figures in the modern political arena as suspect was itself symptomatic of his own historical moment: he witnessed the gradual emergence of the bourgeoisie as a dominating force in European politics, which left its mark on post-revolutionary aesthetic projects in general, and on *Tristan und Isolde* in particular in its depiction of disrupted patriarchal procession and power within the realms of both protagonists.[4] In the universe of the drama, the reign of Ireland was to pass from the king and queen to their issue, the princess Isolde, and to her husband, the knightly nobleman Morold. With his murder the fate of the Irish crown becomes unclear. Similarly, the hereditary transfer of the Cornish crown is disrupted with the death of Marke's first queen, who "vanished childless," leaving the king to invest a favored, noble knight—his nephew Tristan—as king, even at the cost of his royal line. Structurally, then (if not legally or morally), Tristan's union with the queen thus constitutes a symbolic retention of his place as heir to the Cornish throne, as well as the place of Morold, who would have been heir to the throne of Ireland. In other words, Tristan and Morold are not only similar as two knights in love with Isolde, but are also comparable as two noblemen, both of whom were at one time destined to assume the kingship of their respective realms. Therefore, at the end of the drama the fate of both royal houses remains open. Following the deaths of Morold and Tristan, Isolde dies, and with her the possibility for royal issue that could have merged the Irish and Cornish crowns in a new and noble line to be perpetuated through patriarchal succession. The stable system of monarchy seems at an end, even as a new, Machiavellian political sensibility may be discerned in the wings, to be waiting for the death of the king. Though Melot, a political schemer as well as Tristan's betrayer and rival (for both Isolde and Marke's favor), is dead by the end of the drama, we may assume that another Cornish courtier will emerge with political aspirations.

Sounds of Power

Two radically different conceptualizations of the ruler may be discerned within the musical makeup of the work as well. Though one usually thinks of the more chromatic music of *Tristan* as the hallmark of night, passion, and intoxication, and the more tonally unambiguous passages as representing day, reason, honor, and duty, the signifying function of Wagner's music is more subtle than this black-and-white (or night-and-day) opposition might suggest. For the notion (for the revolutionary Wagner) of the ideal monarch as the steward of his people takes sonic form in an idealized music of state, which sounds both stable and sincere. This is the music of the naïve and trusting Kurwenal, and like him, of the sailors, loyal subjects of their liege who hail their king in a forthright C major as the ship finally reaches Cornwall at the conclusion to Act I. That such music functions as a kind of official marker, or sonic coat of arms, is underscored by its citation when Isolde sings of Morold in the passage quoted earlier; at the final syllable of "Irenheld" ("Irish hero"), the restless, far more destabilized musical idiom of her confrontation with Tristan gives way to a march in the woodwinds (clarinets, bassoons, and oboe), horns, and drum that almost sounds like music from *Lohengrin* (Music Example 32.1).

This is official music, royal and stolid in its stately progression, a component of a public image of power. To a modern ear it almost sounds like Elgar's "Pomp and Circumstance." Therefore, it is only consistent that this comparatively staid and stable, diatonic, tonal idiom also underpins the characterization of Tristan as the beloved leader of the people of Kareol—which is hardly surprising, given the fact that it is from Kurwenal himself that this image emerges in another passage previously cited, set to the same instruments found in the Act I march (minus the timpani), reinforced here by the strings. To emphasize Kurwenal's enthusiastic devotion to Tristan, Wagner even adds to the servant's quaint tune a trill in the bassoon (Music Example 32.2). These are the sounds of a leader upon whom a people can rely for guidance and protection.

Tristan's remarks concerning the Machiavellian Melot, however, are informed by a far more unstable and chromatic musical idiom. His are the sounds of scheming enmity and the envy of the courtier—for Wagner, the medieval counterpart to the modern politician. This is the idiom that characterizes Melot's first words to Marke ("Das sollst du, Herr, mir sagen, ob ich ihn recht verklagt? Das dir zum Pfand ich gab, ob ich mein Haupt gewahrt?"), and that Tristan adopts when he describes his betrayer to Isolde at the close of Act II (noted earlier). His account of Melot is accompanied by rising and descending figures, many of them triplets, which—especially in their chromatic form—convey a slithery destabilization, menace, and maneuvering. Dotted triplets (marked *staccato*) also hammer away on a single note, a subset of figurations characterized by increasingly diminutive and hurried note-values, eighth, sixteenth, and thirty-second, suggesting obsession, nervous excitement, and urgency of purpose. Wagner's choice of instruments emphasizes the somber image—the darker sounds of the strings (violas, cellos, and double basses) and woodwinds (the lower registers of the oboe, clarinet, and English horn, together with bass clarinet and bassoons), as well as horns—convey, both literally and metaphorically, a pervasive gloom (Music Example 32.3).

Another feature that serves to convey Melot's constant and evasive movement is the propensity of his music to suggest various keys that seldom resolve to a tonic; as such,

MUSIC EXAMPLE 32.1 Richard Wagner, *Tristan und Isolde*, Act I, scene 5. Isolde: "…seine Waffen hatt' ich geweiht…"

it resembles sounds that function elsewhere in the drama as the hallmark of eroticism. That is, while the more chromatic music that signifies the destabilization of social norms is most often understood to be the sonic symbol of sexuality, it can also be heard as downright slimy, signifying another kind of malignancy that undermines social stability, in this case that of political intrigue undertaken for personal gain. Tonally unambiguous

MUSIC EXAMPLE 32.2 Richard Wagner, *Tristan und Isolde*, Act III, scene 1. Kurwenal: "Das Volk, getreu dem trauten Herrn…"

MUSIC EXAMPLE 32.3 Richard Wagner, *Tristan und Isolde*. Act II, scene 3. Tristan: "Mein Freund war der . . . die mich gedrängt."

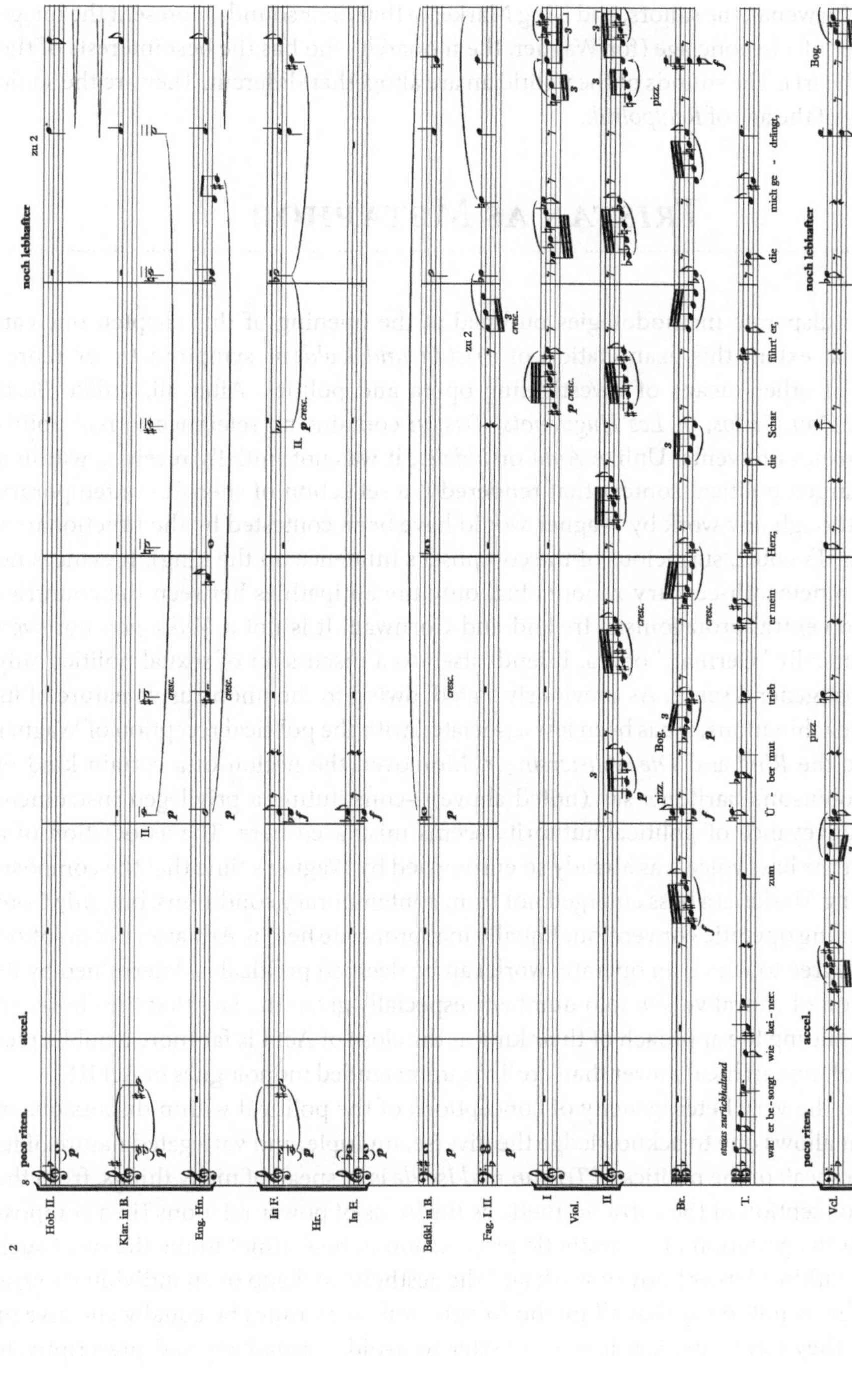
poco riten.
accel.
noch lebhafter
zu 2
Hob. II.
Klar. in B.
Engl. Hn.
In F.
Hr.
In E.
Baßkl. in B.
Fag. I. II.
Viol.
Br.
T.
Vcl.
K.B.
etwas zurückhaltend
war er be - sorgt wie kei - ner. Ü - ber mut trieb er mein Herz, die Schar führt' er, die mich ge - drängt.
pizz.
Bog.
cresc.
2

music is the domain of the ruler concerned for the well-being of his people, while tonal ambiguity is the realm of opportunism and calculation.

Understood in this context, there is something rather wistful and nostalgic in the music of Kurwenal, the sailors, and King Marke, in that their sounds represent the image of the ruler of a bygone age (for Wagner, the monarch who has the best interests of the people at heart). The sounds of the politician are altogether different. They are the sonic signatures of the age of *Realpolitik*.

Tristan as Metaphor

Given the disparate methodologies outlined at the opening of this chapter, one can ask to what extent this examination of *Tristan und Isolde* is symptomatic or representative of other means of investigating opera and politics. After all, unlike *Boris Godunov*, *Don Carlos*, or *Les Huguenots*, *Tristan* contains no reference to real political personages or events. Unlike *Aida* or *Fidelio*, it was not initially received within a highly charged political context that rendered it a reflection of specific contemporary issues (although any work by Wagner would have been contested by the functionaries of Ludwig II's court, suspicious of the composer's influence on the king). It evinces no traces of nineteenth-century xenophobia, only the antipathies between the countries of the two central protagonists, Ireland and Cornwall. It is not a *Volksoper*, not even an emphatically "German" opera. It lends itself to a discussion of sexual politics only in the most general sense. As previously stated, owing to the unobtrusive nature of its political machinations, it has been less associated with the political reception of Wagner than have the *Ring* and *Die Meistersinger*. Moreover, the notion of a certain kind of voice—Robinson's baritone, say (noted above)—constituting a privileged instrument for the conveyance of political authority seems misplaced here. The association of a ruler with the bass voice was already so entrenched by Wagner's time that the composition of King Marke as a bass emerged not from contemporary conditions, but only from long-standing operatic convention. Equally inappropriate here is Arblaster's contention that the degree to which an operatic work can be deemed political is determined by its distribution of choral versus solo numbers, especially given the fact that the chorus of sailors heralding the approach of their king at the close of Act I is far more a public recognition of monarchical power than are Tristan's extended monologues in Act III.

But it is the very heterogeneity of conceptions of the political within discussions of opera that allows one to acknowledge the diverse, multiple, and variegated nature of its traces. To speak of the politics of *Tristan und Isolde* is to speak of many things, from the general conception of the extra-aesthetic as the locus of power relations (in a composer's life, in the gestation of an aesthetic project, and in one's time) to the theme of such relations within a larger body of work and the aesthetic makeup of an individual music drama. This is not to say that all methodologies will at all times be equally effective or valid, for they never are. But it is also better to avoid normatively and prescriptively privileging one method of inquiry over all others, lest one become deaf and blind to the highly complex affective dimensions of works that voice something always ineffable and difficult to define, determined both by the nature of its specific aesthetic makeup and by the sociopolitical worlds in which it first took shape and is later received. We should view the plethora of attempts to consider the political in opera as itself symptomatic of the bewildering power this art form has always had on the emotions and minds of its audience. But then, is that not also a dimension of the political?

See also: Opera between the Ancients and the Moderns, Censorship, Gender, Audiences

Notes

1. Wagner began the musical composition of the *Ring* in 1853, but interrupted it in 1857 after completing *Das Rheingold*, *Die Walküre*, and the first two acts of *Siegfried*, only returning to the cycle in 1869 after having composed both *Tristan* and *Die Meistersinger von Nürnberg*. The only exceptions are the draft and fair copy of the full score to Act II of *Siegfried* that he finished in 1864–1865 (Dalhaus and Deathridge 1990: 170).
2. There is an acoustic pun in the libretto, in that "Iren-land" can be heard as, that is, confused with, "Irrenland," or "country of the insane." That is why Wagner changed "Irland" to "Irenland," which led to the shift from "England" to "Engeland," or "land of angels."
3. "Wie verhalten sich republikanische Bestrebungen dem Königthume gegenüber?"
4. This is, moreover, a concern in the work that followed *Tristan*, *Die Meistersinger von Nürnberg*, in which the young and impecunious nobleman, Walther von Stolzing, longs to be accepted into the middle-class guild of the Meistersinger, and thereby to woo the goldsmith's daughter, Eva.

Bibliography

Abbate, Carolyn. 1991. *Unsung Voices: Opera and Musical Narrative in the Nineteenth Century*. Princeton, NJ: Princeton University Press.

Adorno, Theodor W. [1952] 2005. *In Search of Wagner*, translated by Rodney Livingston. London: New Left Books.

——. [1959] 1994. "Bourgeois Opera." [Translated by David J. Levin]. In *Opera Through Other Eyes*, edited by David Levin, 25–43. Stanford, CA: Stanford University Press.

Applegate, Celia, and Pamela Potter, eds. 2002. *Music and German National Identity*. Chicago: University of Chicago Press.

Arblaster, Anthony. 1992. *Viva la Libertà! Politics in Opera*. New York: Verso.

Attali, Jacques. 1985. *Noise: The Political Economy of Music*, translated by Brian Massumi. Minneapolis: University of Minnesota Press.

Bhat, Deviha. 2006. "Opera Reignites Islam Row after Cancelling Production." *The Times* (September 26). Online. Available: Http:/www/religionnewsblog.com/16064/idomeneo-opera-2 (accessed February 6, 2014).

Bokina, John. 1997. *Opera and Politics: From Monteverdi to Henze*. New Haven: Yale University Press.

——. 1987. "Wagner and Marxist Aesthetics." In *Wagner in Retrospect*, edited by Leroy Shaw, Nancy R. Cirillo, and Marion S. Miller, 138–151. Amsterdam: Rodopi.

Borchmeyer, Dieter. 1992. "The Question of Anti-Semitism." [Translated by Stewart Spencer.] In Müller and Wapnewski 1992, 166–185.

——. 1991. *Richard Wagner: Theory and Theatre*, translated by Stewart Spencer. Oxford: Clarendon Press.

Brett, Phillip. 2006. *Music and Sexuality in Britten: Selected Essays*, edited by George E. Haggerty. Berkeley and Los Angeles: University of California Press.

——. 1983. "Britten and Grimes." In *Benjamin Britten: 'Peter Grimes,'* edited by Philip Brett. Cambridge Opera Handbooks, 180–189. Cambridge: Cambridge University Press.

Budden, Julian. 1984. '*Un ballo in maschera.*' In *The Operas of Verdi*. 3 vols. II: 360–423. London: Cassell.

Carr, Jonathan. 2008. "Politics and Music." In *The Oxford Companion to Music*, edited by Alison Latham. *Oxford Music Online*. Available: http://www.oxfordmusiconline.com/subscriber/article/opr/t114/e5263 (accessed August 18, 2012).

——. 2007. *The Wagner Clan: The Saga of Germany's Most Illustrious and Infamous Family*. New York: Atlantic Monthly Press.

Castle, Terry. 1995. *The Apparitional Lesbian*. New York: Columbia University Press.

Chafe, Eric. 2004. *The Tragic and the Ecstatic: The Musical Revolution of Wagner's Tristan und Isolde*. New York: Oxford University Press.

Clément, Catherine. 1989. *Opera, or the Undoing of Women*, translated by Betsy Wing. Minneapolis: University of Minnesota Press.

Cohen, Mitchell. 2008. "To the Dresden Barricades: The Genesis of Wagner's Political Ideas." In Grey 2008, 47–63.

Dahlhaus, Carl, and John Deathridge. 1990. *The New Grove Wagner*. London: Macmillan.

Deathridge, John. 2008. *Wagner: Beyond Good and Evil*. Berkeley and Los Angeles: University of California Press.

Dellamora, Richard, and Daniel Fischlin, eds. 1997. *The Work of Opera: Genre, Nationhood, and Sexual Difference*. New York: Columbia University Press.

Dreyfus, Laurence. 2010. *Wagner and the Erotic Impulse*. Cambridge, MA: Harvard University Press.

Edelman, Murray. 1995. *From Art to Politics: How Artistic Creations Shape Political Conceptions*. Chicago: Chicago University Press.

Friedländer, Saul, and Jörn Rüsen, eds. 2000. *Richard Wagner und das dritte Reich: Ein Schloss Elmau-Simposion*. Munich: Beck.

Fulcher, Jane F. 2002. *The Nation's Image: French Grand Opera as Politics and Politicized Art*. Cambridge: Cambridge University Press.

Gilman, Sander. 1996. *Smart Jews*. Lincoln: University of Nebraska Press.

——. 1988. "Strauss, the Pervert, and Avant Garde Opera of the Fin de Siècle." *New German Critique* 43 (special issue on Austria): 35–68.

Goehr, Lydia. 2003. "Art and Politics." In *The Oxford Handbook of Aesthetics*, edited by Jerrold Levinson, 471–485. New York: Oxford University Press.

——. 1998. *The Quest for Voice: On Music, Politics, and the Limits of Philosophy*. Oxford: Clarendon Press.

Gramit, David. 2002. *Cultivating Music: The Aspirations, Interests, and Limits of German Musical Culture, 1770–1948*. Berkeley and Los Angeles: University of California Press.

Gregor-Dellin, Martin. 1990. *Richard Wagner: Sein Leben, Sein Werk, Sein Jahrhundert.* Munich: Wilhelm Goldmann.
Grey, Thomas S., ed. 2008. *The Cambridge Companion to Wagner.* Cambridge: Cambridge University Press.
Grout, Donald Jay. 1960. *A History of Western Music.* New York: W. W. Norton.
Gutman, Robert W. 1990. *Richard Wagner: The Man, His Mind, and His Music.* New York: Harcourt Brace Jovanovich.
Hamman, Brigitta. 2002. *Winifred Wagner oder Hitler's Bayreuth.* Munich: Piper.
Hanisch, Ernst. 1992. "The Political Influence and Appropriation of Wagner," translated by Paul Knight. In Müller and Wapnewski 1992, 186–201.
Hunt, Lynn, ed. 1991. *Eroticism and the Body Politic.* Baltimore: Johns Hopkins University Press.
Jacobs, Andrew. 2010. "Lustful Opera, Censored, Befuddles Chinese." *New York Times* (October 25): A10.
Johnson, Victoria, Jane F. Fulcher, and Thomas Ertman, eds. 2007. *Opera and Society in Italy and France from Monteverdi to Bourdieu.* Cambridge: Cambridge University Press.
Koestenbaum, Wayne. 1993. *The Queen's Throat: Opera, Homosexuality, and the Mystery of Desire.* New York: Poseidon Press.
Koppen, Erwin. 1974. *Dekadenter Wagnerismus: Studien zur europäischen Literatur des Fin de Siècle.* Berlin: de Gruyter.
Köhler, Joachim. 2000. *Wagner's Hitler: The Prophet and His Disciple,* translated by Ronald Taylor. Malden, MA: Blackwell Publishers.
Krohn, Rüdiger. 1992. "The Revolutionary of 1848–49." [Translated by Paul Knight.] In Müller and Wapnewski 1992, 156–165.
Kubizek, August. 1954. *Adolf Hitler: The Story of Our Friendship,* translated by E. V. Anderson. London: Allan Wingate.
Kurth, Ernst. [1920] 1968. *Romantische Harmonik und ihre Krise in Wagners 'Tristan.'* Hildesheim: G. Olms. Reprographic facsimile of 2nd ed. [1923], Berlin.
Levin, David, ed. 2007. *Unsettling Opera: Staging Mozart, Verdi, Wagner, and Zemlinsky.* Chicago: University of Chicago Press.
Lindenberger, Herbert. 1998. *Opera in History: From Monteverdi to Cage.* Stanford, CA: Stanford University Press.
——. 1984. *Opera: The Extravagant Art.* Ithaca, NY: Cornell University Press.
Locke, Ralph. 1991. "Constructing the Oriental 'Other': Saint-Saëns's *Samson et Dalila.*" *Cambridge Opera Journal* 3/3: 261–302.
Marcuse, Ludwig. 1973. *Das denkwürdige Leben des Richard Wagner.* Zurich: Diogenes.
Mayer, Hans. 1981. *Versuche über die Oper.* Frankfurt: Suhrkamp.
McClary, Susan. 1992. *George Bizet, 'Carmen.'* Cambridge Opera Handbooks. Cambridge: Cambridge University Press
——. 1985. "Afterword." In Jacques Attali, *Noise: The Political Economy of Music,* 149–158. Minneapolis: University of Minnesota Press.
McGrath, William J. 1974. *Dionysian Art and Populist Politics in Austria.* New Haven: Yale University Press.
Müller, Ulrich, and Peter Wapnewski, eds. 1992. *Wagner Handbook,* translation edited by John Deathridge. Cambridge, MA: Harvard University Press.
Naegele, Verena. 1995. *Parsifals Mission: Der Einfluß Richard Wagners auf Ludwig II. und seine Politik.* Cologne: Dittrich-Verlag.

Nattiez, Jean-Jacques. 1992. "'Fidelity' to Wagner: Reflections on the Centenary *Ring*." In *Wagner in Performance*, edited by Barry Millington and Stewart Spencer, 75–98. New Haven: Yale University Press.
——. 1990. *Music and Discourse: Toward a Semiology of Music*, translated by Carolyn Abbate. Princeton, NJ: Princeton University Press.
——. 1980. "Chereau's Treachery." *October* 14: 71–100.
Nietzsche, Friedrich. [1888] 1967. *The Birth of Tragedy and The Case of Wagner*, translated by Walter Kaufmann. New York: Random House.
Norris, Christopher, ed. 1989. *Music and the Politics of Culture*. New York: St. Martin's Press.
Parker, Roger. 2007. *The New Grove Guide to Verdi and His Operas*. New York: Oxford University Press.
Potter, Pamela M. 2008. "Wagner and the Third Reich: Myths and Realities." In Grey 2008, 235–245.
Rather, L. J. 1979. *The Dream of Self-Destruction: Wagner's Ring and the Modern World*. Baton Rouge: Louisiana State University Press.
Riezler, Walter. 1971. *Beethoven*. Zurich: Atlantis.
Robinson, Paul. 1985. *Opera and Ideas: From Mozart to Strauss*. New York: Harper & Row.
Rüsen, Jörn. 2000. "'Wagner im dritten Reich': Von der Schwierigkeit, einen historischen Zusammenhang in den Blick zu nehmen." In *Richard Wagner und das dritte Reich: Ein Schloss Elmau-Simposion*, edited by Saul Friedländer and Jörn Rüsen, 15–23. Munich: Beck.
Said, Edward. 1994. *Culture and Imperialism*. New York: Vintage.
Schorske, Carl E. 1988. "Wagner and Germany's Cultures in the Nineteenth Century." In *The Mirror of History: Essays in Honor of Fritz Fellner*, edited by Solomon Wank, Heinrun Maschl, Brigitte Mazohl-Wallnig, and Reinhold Wagnleitner, 171–180. Oxford: Clio Press.
Shaw, George Bernard. [1923] 1967. *The Perfect Wagnerite: A Commentary on the Niblung's Ring*. Reprint. New York: Dover.
Spotts, Friedrich. 1994. *Bayreuth: A History of the Wagner Festival*. New Haven: Yale University Press.
Steinberg, Michael. 2004. *Listening to Reason: Culture, Subjectivity, and Nineteenth-Century Music*. Princeton, NJ: Princeton University Press.
Stern, Fritz. 1974. *The Politics of Cultural Despair*. Berkeley and Los Angeles: University of California Press.
Subotnik, Rose Rosengard. 1996. *Deconstructive Variations: Music and Reason in Western Society*. Minneapolis: University of Minnesota Press.
——. 1991. *Developing Variations: Style and Ideology in Western Music*. Minneapolis: University of Minnesota Press.
Syberberg, Hans Jürgen. 1977. *Hitler: Ein Film aus Deutschland*. Facets Video, 2007. DVD.
Taruskin, Richard. 1992. "Only Time Will Cover the Taint." *New York Times* (January 26): section 2, p. 25, col. 5.
Taylor-Jay, Claire. 2004. *The Artist-Operas of Pfitzner, Krenek and Hindemith: Politics and the Ideology of the Artist*. Aldershot, UK: Ashgate.
Vogel, Martin. 1962. *Der Tristan Akkord und die Krise der modernen Harmonielehre*. Düsseldorf: Gesellschaft zur Förderung der systematischen Musikwissenschaft.
Wagner, Gottfried. 1999. *Twilight of the Wagners: The Unveiling of a Family's Legacy*, translated by Della Couling. New York: Picador.
Wagner, Richard. 2004. *Richard Wagner: Werke, Schriften und Briefe*, edited by Sven Friedrich. Berlin: Directmedia. Digitale Bibliothek 107. (*Sämtliche Schriften und Dichtungen* = 16 vols.;

Briefe = 14 vols.; *Autobiographien*; Cosima Wagner, *Tagebücher*; Biographien: Carl Friedrich Glasenapp and Martin Gregor-Dellin.)

Weiner, Marc A. 2009. *Undertones of Insurrection: Music and Cultural Politics in the Modern German Narrative*. Rochester, NY: Transaction.

——. 1996. "Reading the Ideal." *New German Critique* 69: 53–83.

——. 1995. *Richard Wagner and the Anti-Semitic Imagination*. Lincoln: University of Nebraska Press.

Weisstein, Ulrich. 2001. "Böse Menschen singen keine Arien: Prolegomena zu einer ungeschriebenen Geschichte der Opernzensur." In *Zensur und Selbstzensur in der Literatur*, edited by Peter Brockmeier and Gerhard Kaiser, 49–73. Würzburg: Königshausen und Neumann.

Windell, George G. 1991. "Hitler, National Socialism, and Richard Wagner." In *Penetrating Wagner's Ring: An Anthology*, edited by John Louis DiGaetani, 219–238. New York: Da Capo.

Žižek, Slavoj, and Mladen Dolar. 2002. *Opera's Second Death*. New York: Routledge.

CHAPTER 33

RELIGION

JESSE ROSENBERG

Is Opera Secular by Definition?

Questions surrounding religion go to the heart of the definition of the operatic genre, as may be verified by any casual survey of published histories of opera, which divide into two groups: some locate the genesis of opera in the humanistic culture of late sixteenth- and early-seventeenth-century Italy, while others begin the narrative earlier. Examples of the first group include Romain Rolland, who begins with the *madrigal dramatique* of the sixteenth century (Rolland 1895: 36ff.), Oskar Bie, who begins with Caccini (Bie 1913: 38ff.), and Edward Dent, who doesn't bother with anything prior to Monteverdi's *L'Orfeo* (Dent [1949] 1978: 28ff.). The second group includes writers (Grout and Williams 2003: 13ff.; Orrey 1972: 11–19; Gregor 1950: 31–33; Blareau 1921: 48–59; Dumesnil 1953: 4–6) who start at least as far back as the liturgical and para-liturgical drama of the Middle Ages, characterizing it as an early example of opera or as a close precursor, if not still earlier (Greek tragedy, with its strong musical component).

Why this split in scholarly attitude toward the genesis of opera? The notion of "liturgical drama" as entirely disjunct from opera—analogous but nothing more—stems from an *a priori* assumption regarding subject matter: since opera is the exclusive product of secular culture, religion is essentially foreign to it. Even when not stated explicitly, this assumption is implied in many writings on opera. Thus, for example, Arthur Elson, an early authority, categorically denies that there is anything "to be found resembling opera" between Greek tragedy and modern times, observing that while the "so-called miracle and mystery plays were undoubtedly operatic in the sense of possessing music, [...] they exerted no influence on secular composers" (Elson 1901: 12)—as though such influence alone constituted a sufficient criterion for making the determination.

Scholarly division on the subject has continued through recent decades. Christopher Headington, Roy Westbrook, and Terry Barfoot (1987: 14–16) talk about Greek and Roman theater in their first chapter, but bring the section to a close with a discussion of liturgical drama; likewise the latest revision of Grout's standard work continues to speak of liturgical drama as a significant early phase of the genre. On the other side, medievalist Robin Wallace (1984) approaches the claim with considerable skepticism, though for reasons strongly contrasting with those of secular scholars like Dent, whose study seems marked by indifference, if not outright hostility, to religion. Wallace (1984: 228) argues that the music for such works is "anti-dramatic" rather than dramatic, and thus underscores an artistic discontinuity between liturgical drama and opera. But it is difficult to accept this judgment in the face of such theatrically compelling musical dramas as the anonymous early-thirteenth-century *Play of Daniel* and Hildegard von Bingen's twelfth-century *Ordo Virtutum*, both of which have aroused enthusiasm among audiences in non-liturgical circumstances. Similarly, Carolyn Abbate and Roger Parker, though clearly anxious to problematize common assumptions about "the birth of opera," nevertheless begin their original survey in late Renaissance Florence, firmly privileging secular culture as the matrix of the genre (Abbate and Parker 2012: 37–44).

The problem extends to the terms "opera" and "oratorio," used variously for the same works depending on the commentator. Abbate and Parker do not mention one of the first surviving examples of a complete staged action set to music, Emilio de' Cavalieri's *Rappresentatione di Anima, et di Corpo* (1600), which contains a thoroughly religious text conceived for the Oratorio di S. Maria in Vallicella in Rome. Other staged musical dramas of the first half of the seventeenth century—Stefano Landi's *Sant'Alessio* (1632) and the various sacred operas for the papal court with librettos by Rospigliosi (the future Pope Clement IX) likewise undermine the notion of opera as inherently and/or preeminently secular. Scholars of the oratorio such as Franz Hadamowsky (1955: 110–115) and Howard Smither (1978–1980: passim), moreover, have documented the expanded meaning of the word "oratorio" that appears from the mid-eighteenth century onward, referring to both staged and unstaged performances, thus erasing the crucial distinction between "opera" and "oratorio" in common parlance. The two genres, as Don Neville (1998: 598–606) has established in the case of Metastasio, have so much in common that it becomes almost a distortion to insist on the differences between them. Even *Grove Music Online* (*GMO*) shows little consistency as to whether a staged work on a biblical subject should be considered an opera. Thus, for example, *GMO* lists Donizetti's *Il diluvio universale* (on Noah and the flood) as an opera, but both Zingarelli's *Saulle* and Mayr's *Atalia* as "sacred works." Composers themselves sometimes express the same ambiguity: a sheet bound together with the autograph score of *Mosè in Egitto* bears a clear reference to the work, in Rossini's hand, as an "opera," while Rossini himself regularly referred to it as an "oratorio" in his private correspondence (Brauner 2004: xxi, xxii, xxx–xxxi). Mayr himself weighed in on the matter in his unpublished treatise on the history of the oratorio (Mayr 1843), downplaying the one distinction traditionally considered paramount (staged opera vs. unstaged oratorio) to focus on whether the poetry and music are truly inspired by religious sentiment. To Mayr, Rossini's *Mosè*, Donizetti's *Il diluvio universale*, and his own *Atalia* all evidently count as "oratorios" because they are religiously sincere (Mayr 1843: 74r). When using the term "oratorio" in these cases, both Mayr and Rossini clearly have in mind a sub-genre of opera rather than a non-operatic work.

Nevertheless, works continue to be assigned to this or that genre on the basis of circular reasoning. When Smither refers to "the tendency in the late eighteenth century to stage oratorios in Lent as if they were operas, especially in Naples but occasionally elsewhere" (Smither 2000: 614), he clearly assumes *a priori* that they weren't operas at all. But he offers no real support for this assumption or for his belief that such works as Méhul's *Joseph* and Rossini's *Mosè in Egitto* should be designated "staged oratorios" (Smither 2000: 509)—effectively excluding them from opera. Other writers (Dubowy 1995; Morgenstern 2007) display a similar inclination to categorize (without supporting evidence) as oratorios works that may be taken, with equal justification, as operas on religious subjects.

None of this is to say that historians of oratorio have no business exploring operatic works that are clearly related to it, but a good deal more circumspection is needed. Daniel Ortuño-Stühring included a fascinating chapter on Anton Rubinstein's "sacred opera" *Christus* in a book about oratorios on the life of Jesus, but took care to call the chapter an "excursis" (Ortuño-Stühring 2011: 227–287), thus clarifying that it does not altogether fit into the generic framework of his study. He also has performance practice on his side: Rubinstein encountered enormous difficulties in getting his sacred operas staged, so that *Das verlorene Paradies, Christus, Der Thurm zu Babel,* and *Moses* were actually premiered in concert form, and the latter two works were never staged at all. But overall, the situation would seem to justify a more assertive policy of reclaiming for opera works that have been arrogated by scholars of oratorio. Franco Piperno has shown the way in his magisterial series of publications on late-eighteenth- and early-nineteenth-century sacred musical works for the Italian stage (Piperno 1991, 1993, 1994a, 1994b, 2002); he makes no bones about calling such works biblical *operas*, and is happy to explode persistent myths about their character and context, including a supposed ban on operatic performance in Naples during Lent.

Opera and Pagan Religion

The foregoing considerations all relate to the Judeo-Christian religious tradition of Europe, as an element in opera. The issues are further complicated by the many opera plots derived from Greek and Roman antiquity, which include pagan religious figures and references. On the surface, all operas that feature pagan deities as characters could automatically be seen as having something to do with "religion" in a straightforward sense, but they were typically viewed in a different light altogether. Obviously, neither Rinuccini nor the composers who set his *Orfeo* libretto (Caccini and Peri) were polytheists who believed in the existence of deities such as Orpheus or Venus; they were no more adherents of pagan religion than Dante, who invoked Apollo in the first canto of his *Paradiso*. Instead, the mythic elements of these early operas were understood in the spirit of Christian humanism, allegorized and brought into conformity with (or at least lifted out of outright contradiction to) orthodox religious belief. As Robert Donington points out, such pagan elements "had been and continued to be endorsed as premonitions and intimations, attained by reason or by intuition, of Christian revelation and Christian doctrine" (Donington 1981: 25). Thus seventeenth-century operas derived from pagan mythology drew on a long tradition of humanist reinterpretations of the pagan poets and the religious elements of their creations, a rationalizing approach to myth that dates back to late antiquity (Seznec 1940: passim). Pierre Bersuire's fourteenth-century "moralized Ovid" was among the most widely circulated works in this tradition, while the logically contradictory series of arguments offered by Boccaccio in Book XIV of *Genealogie deorum gentilium* (ca. 1370) indicates how far early humanists were willing to stretch their interpretations in order to safeguard the study of Greek and Roman literature. The pagan poets, Boccaccio says, wise as they were, must have known that there was only one God; their references to "the gods" were, therefore, ways of indicating various aspects of God. Boccaccio also found evidence of a monotheistic bent in the writings of ancient authors, including the references in Plato's *Republic* to the Good which is the source of all good things, or Aeneas's prayer to "omnipotent Jove" (the qualifier "omnipotent" being applied to no other deity in pagan literature) in Book V of Virgil's *Aeneid*. Besides, Boccaccio concludes, to the extent that pagans may indeed have been polytheists, they can hardly be blamed for this; at that time divine revelation had been vouchsafed exclusively to the Hebrews, who refused to share it with other nations (Boccaccio 1963: VII: 1443). Such defenses of pagan religious reference are highly relevant to an understanding of the operatic literature itself and continue to echo down to writers of the present day. Michael Ewans devotes a section of his book to the "theodicy" of Monteverdi's *Il ritorno d'Ulisse in patria*, observing that by making Jove both omnipotent and merciful, Monteverdi and his librettist Badoaro were substituting their own Christian outlook for the very different worldview of Homer's *Odyssey*, where Zeus simply ensures "that due recompense is given for both offence and favour" (Ewans 2007: 12–16). A similarly uncharacteristic gesture of mercy is given by the god Apollo at the end of Gluck's *Alceste*. With regard to another Gluck opera, one scholar notes that when Agamemnon prays to Diana in Gluck's *Iphigénie en Aulide*, he calls her "Creator of Light" and "Beneficent God" (as opposed to *a* god or goddess), indicating that Agamemnon has "gone over the head of the spiteful lesser deity and appealed to a god more absolute even than Zeus" (Edgecomb 2005: 57).

In other operas pagan deities are simply treated as false and therefore powerless. The beginning of Purcell's *King Arthur* shows the Saxons making sacrifices to Wode, Freya, and Thor, but they are defeated by the Britons nevertheless, thanks to the protection of St. George, honored in the final chorus; the Venus who sings the patriotic "Fairest Isle," on the other hand, is strictly figurative. Likewise, the Philistines' celebration of their god Dagon in Saint-Saëns' *Samson et Dalila* is entirely in vain, as their final destruction makes clear.

How positively pagan religion is depicted in opera depends on various factors. In the Greek mythological subjects mentioned above, paganism is confined to an ancient period preceding the advent of Christianity, so that there is no conflict between polytheistic and monotheistic parties. But when subjects are drawn from later historical periods, the situation in this respect is altered. The German Romantic interest in the folk culture of the Middle Ages reached back to a period not only characterized by religious faith, but faith of a particular urgency, locked in struggle against surviving pagan beliefs. Weber's *Der Freischütz* may lack a medieval setting, but the Caspar/Samiel pair clearly draws on elements of medieval (and older) folk beliefs, presented both musically and dramatically as intrinsically evil, and justly routed by the Christianity embodied by the pious Agathe and the benevolent hermit.

A similar confrontation between pagan and Christian is evident in the Romantic operas of Wagner. In *Tannhäuser* Wagner juxtaposes representatives of Christian morality with Venus, a symbol of sensuality. In *Lohengrin* the dividing line between the two realms is sharply dramatized because the conflict between pagan and Christian no longer centers on a vacillating character unable to decide between them, but is separated into opposing characters. The resulting divide is made particularly vivid in the ways in which the respective deities are invoked in prayer. Elsa's prayers express her innocence at the outset; her first monologue *refers* to her prayers and the vision they lead to, and when no champion will come forth to defend her against Telramund's accusations, she kneels and prays (joined by the chorus). King Henry's prayer "Mein Herr und Gott" invokes God's assistance in determining the outcome, and God Himself apparently plays a significant role in the proceedings, since He guarantees the victory of the right side. The prayer in Act II, by contrast, is Ortrud's passionate invocation of the gods Wodan and Freia to bless her deceit and treachery, set to music stylistically opposed to the prayers previously heard. In the great encounter between Ortrud and Elsa that follows, the latter's response to Ortrud's cunningly worded invitations to doubt is an attempt to show Ortrud the meaning of faith by converting her to Christianity.

When pagan religion is non-Western, we can expect a disposition to present it in a negative light, as in "orientalist" operas set in more recent historical periods. In Delibes's *Lakmé* it is personified by the Brahmin Nilakantha, a grotesque Hindu caricature. But it is important to avoid overly broad generalizations about this. Act IV of Meyerbeer's *L'Africaine* indeed depicts the Indian priests as bloodthirsty, but this is balanced by the negative profile of an intolerant Grand Inquisitor in Act I; clearly, the point is to criticize the extremist religious temperament rather than one particular manifestation of it. Another noteworthy exception is Graun's *Montezuma* (1755), in which the Aztec king is far more humane than the Christians invading the New World; the dialogue in recitative between Montezuma and Cortes in Act II is cast as a religious dispute, pitting the high ethics of Montezuma against the cruel duplicity of the Spanish forces. But *Montezuma*, with its libretto by Giampietro Tagliazucchi, based on an Enlightenment-inspired prose outline by Frederick the Great, is atypical.

If, however, an opera with both Western and non-Western characters presents Islam as the religion of the latter group, a negative representation is to be expected as a matter of course, whether handled comically or seriously. In the Act II duet between Osmin and Pedrillo in Mozart's *Die Entführung aus dem Serail*, for example, Pedrillo makes "comic" references to Allah and Mohammed and their probable disapproval of Osmin's consumption of alcohol. In *L'Italiana in Algeri*, librettist Angelo Agnelli occasionally forgets that the story takes place in Algiers rather than Turkey; here, too, Islamic culture is reduced to a joke, with Taddeo hailed by a chorus of eunuchs as "Protector of the Muslims," and Mustafà's nonsensical elevation to the title of Pappataci. On the other hand, the contrasting presence of sympathetic Westerners is not strictly required for representations of Muslim characters to be inherently laughable, as demonstrated by Cherubini's *Ali Baba*. And even in a comic opera such as Cornelius's *Der Barbier von Bagdad*, Islamic references are not invariably intended to be humorous, as, for example, the incandescently beautiful call to the mosque of the three Muezzin in Act II. On the serious side, James Parakilas has drawn attention to an important but generally overlooked element of religious difference in Verdi's *Otello*, exemplified by the Christian Cypriots' fear of the hostile Muslim world that threatens their island (Parakilas 1997: 371ff.).

Religion and Censorship in Opera

One reason that opera and religion are often viewed as inherently at loggerheads lies in the practice of censorship because censors were highly sensitive to religious characters and themes, often to the point of banning them altogether. On the surface there is something counterintuitive about this. Censors working for states with established churches might be expected to take the opposite approach, that is, to encourage religious manifestations on the stage—provided, of course, that they were appropriately orthodox. Why would censors in Naples object to Donizetti's *Poliuto*—forbidding it outright—when that opera is such an inspiring advertisement for Christianity, with admirable characters who willingly face martyrdom rather than renounce the one true faith? If Marian devotion is commendable, as censors undoubtedly believed, then what could have disturbed them about the scene in Verdi's *I Lombardi alla prima crociata* in which the heroine prays to Mary?

One explanation is that to put such characters and sentiments on the operatic (or any other) stage was a kind of profanation. Once opera had come to be seen as predominantly secular—sensually appealing, with stories of passion, intrigue, and murder—it could not possibly come into contact with the sacred without sullying it. If sacred and secular were particularly close (as, for example, in De Luna's attempt to abduct Leonora as she is about to enter a convent in Act II of *Il trovatore*), the scandal increased proportionally. Sacred and profane concerns, in other words, could be permitted to reign supreme only in distinctly separate spheres. By this logic, a religious scene set within an opera is as blasphemously incongruous as a secular love song in the middle of a church service; in fact, the long history of attempts to eradicate secular musical influences from worship mirrors censors' efforts to limit religious representation in the theater. Indeed, for all the censors' sensitivity to questions of politics or sexual morals, religion seems to have been the primary preoccupation during certain periods (Parker 2007: 29). The artistic results could be dire. The directive issued by the imperial authorities in Vienna in November 1850 regarding the censorship of theatrical works specified a ban on anything offensive to "public decency, modesty, morals or religion," not only in the verbal text of the work in question, but in its staging as well; thus the awful fate of Verdi's *Stiffelio* in its first performances in Trieste, with all religious references removed, including the Gothic church setting of the final scene (Ascari 1987; Hansell 2003: xxiii–xxvi; Gossett 2006: 158–160). The situation is greatly complicated by the varying preoccupations of censors in different places and at different times. All substantive research on operatic censorship (including religious censorship) has been location-specific (Spada 1989; Giger 1999; Marvin 2001), for the simple reason that censors in Protestant London, for example, were motivated by different concerns—including religious ones such as the propriety of oaths (Ipson 2011) or references to scripture (Marvin 2001: 589–596)—from those that preoccupied censors in, say, the Kingdom of the Two Sicilies. It can hardly be accidental that the earliest example of a Christian prayer in an opera, in Act III of Étienne-Nicholas Méhul's *Mélidor et Phrosine* (1794), was a product of revolutionary France, where religious censorship had been banished along with other clerical privileges. (It is a fascinating paradox that it was the extreme secularization of European culture that made possible the reception of such religious works as Poulenc's anti-revolutionary *Dialogues des Carmélites* and Messiaen's *Saint François d'Assise*.) But one of the most interesting recent studies of operatic censorship points to entirely different factors to explain the varieties of censorship in practice. Francesco Izzo takes note of two very different cases of religious censorship faced respectively by Verdi's *I Lombardi alla prima crociata* and *Giovanna d'Arco* in the same city (Milan) just a few years apart. The censors found the Marian prayer "Ave Maria" objectionable, but eventually backed down, content with a slight change in wording for the opening salutation ("Ave Maria" became "Salve Maria"). The Marian prayer in *Giovanna d'Arco*, on the other hand, found the censors far more adamant and less willing to compromise (Izzo 2007). Izzo's conclusion—that the Marian prayer in *Giovanna d'Arco* was more alarming to the censors because it was more threatening politically—is of great significance for an understanding of the vexed relationship between religion and opera. So long as religious reference and identity were compatible with the ethos of the *ancien régime*, the only objections to religion in opera were about the encroachment of the sacred realm upon the secular or vice versa. But the increasing association of operatic prayers with what could be seen as characters representing progressive political movements made religious scenes far more disturbing to the censors. In Act III of Auber's *La muette de Portici*, for example, Masaniello exhorts his rebel followers to prayer immediately after the death of a Spanish soldier who tries to disarm Masaniello, and just before they rush off to attack the viceroy's palace. The prayer sung by Hedwige in Act IV of *Guillaume Tell*, invoking God specifically as "the hope of the weak," asks God to protect William Tell and to "punish the crime" of the Austrian occupiers of Switzerland. God was no longer to be counted on as siding with mighty empires or established churches, but rather took the side of the downtrodden, and of rebels struggling for a more equitable political dispensation. Faced with this liberation theology *avant la lettre*, it is no wonder that censors grew nervous.

The effect of distance must also be kept in mind. An onstage prayer can pose problems standing wholly apart from an association with political subversiveness or the profanation of mixing sacred elements with a secular story or characters. Praying, after all, is supposed to be something that we do, not something that we witness being done by someone else, which immediately distances us from the act. When the "someone else" is an opera singer playing a role on a theatrical stage, that distance is commensurately greater. It may not be possible to determine if it was the secularization of European culture that led to such "distancing" of operatic prayers or the operatic prayers themselves that promoted the secularization, but it is difficult to see the two processes as anything but mutually implicated (on the act of kneeling in prayer and its relation to operatic conventions and the study of gesture, see Smart 2004: 132–162).

Does "Religion" Always Mean Religion?

Is it misleading to treat religion in opera as a distinct area of inquiry, rather than something subsumed under other categories—political, ethical, or moral? Elsa's prayer from Act I of *Lohengrin*, as noted, serves as a conventional sign of innocence or sincerity. Micaëla's plea for God's protection in her Act III aria in *Carmen* locates her at an important juncture of the unfolding story. Anna Amalie Abert's dismissal of most nineteenth-century operatic prayers as religious kitsch thus falls rather wide of the mark (Abert 1971). In some cases it is easy enough to determine whether an operatic prayer reflects a genuine religious element or simply provides a characteristic color, as in a barcarolle or a soldiers' chorus. There can be, moreover, an underlying secular meaning to a religious element, as in Verdi's *Nabucco*, in which Hebrew exiles, longing to return to the Holy Land, have long been recognized as expressing the sentiments of Italians who yearn for political autonomy. Messiaen, whose *Saint François d'Assise* is just as obviously a genuine expression of his faith, consciously constructed a web of motifs charged with religious significance (Sholl 2011: 175–186). But to a large extent, the presence of sincere religious sentiment in a given operatic situation is in the eye of the beholder, and it becomes difficult to adjudicate conflicting interpretations. Andrew Thomson, in his monograph on Vincent d'Indy, takes the traditional Catholicism of the composer's *La légende de Saint Christophe* at face value (Thomson 1996: 183–188). By contrast, certain scholars view this opera as a political document, a theatrical expression of the composer's anti-Enlightenment, anti-democratic, and anti-Dreyfussard sentiments, strongly implying that the religious elements of the work (the focus on a Christian saint, the utilization of Gregorian chant) are little more than a thin veneer—a religious way of conveying an essentially secular ideology (Fulcher 2005: 97–105; Huebner 1999: 306–307). Another recent writer charts a middle path through these views, considering the religious elements of *Saint Christophe* as genuinely significant while also closely bound up with political meanings (Giocanti 2006: 257–260).

Prayer in Opera

Typologies of prayers in opera generally begin with a division into public versus private contexts, and there are many famous examples clearly belonging to one or the other category. But at times the distinction seems arbitrary. Norma's "Casta Diva" is a prayer at once embedded in a public ritual of the Druid community of Gaul, chafing under Roman occupation, and a private reflection by the heroine on her inner turmoil over Pollione's betrayal. Desdemona's "Ave Maria" in Verdi's *Otello*, a setting of a thoroughly reworked Italian adaptation of the standard Latin "Ave Maria" text, is supposed to be sung (according to the stage directions and *disposizione scenica*) while kneeling at the *prie-dieu* in her bedroom (see Smart 2004 for other women who kneel), but as Parakilas reminds us, the "Ave Maria" was also a communal prayer that received strong institutional encouragement from the church, lending quasi-public overtones to an ostensibly private religious moment (Parakilas 1995: 385). Even if we reject as unpersuasive Parakilas's further arguments that the accompanying strings function as a symbolic chorus, they nevertheless suggest that the public/private dichotomy in operatic prayer is not always obvious. A related typology of operatic prayer (Lippmann 1990) combines consideration of performing forces with dramatic movement (static vs. active). Edgecomb (2005) proceeds differently, setting forth a typology of prayer in opera on the basis of various forms of ancient Roman religious ritual (*preces*, *deprecationes*, etc.), finding in Virgil and Horace the original sources of operatic prayer types such as petition and thanksgiving. But a superficial rhetorical similarity between ancient Roman antecedents and operatic examples can also lead us astray, particularly when the straightforward definition of prayer (addressed directly to God) is obfuscated by the inclusion of essentially different phenomena. It is not easy to agree with Edgecomb that the Bridal chorus in Act III of Wagner's *Lohengrin* should be located within the tradition of operatic prayer on the grounds that it is a "rubric" chorus and therefore akin to the instructions issued by the Levite priests to the temple virgins in Act I of *Nabucco*, and even harder to go along with the same logic when applied to the women's chorus "Braid the Raven Hair" from Gilbert and Sullivan's *The Mikado* (Edgecomb 2005: 52).

Moreover, a typology of operatic prayer based on verbal rhetoric rather than musical style can lead us to gloss over other important features. Prayers that are joyful, exuberant, or extroverted constitute a clear minority; most of the numbers with titles such as "preghiera," "prière," or "Gebet" are calm and meditative. This undoubtedly reflects traditional notions about God as situated far above the world of human passion; in opera as in life, it is typically in order to still human passions that a deity is invoked in the first place. "Spargi in terra," Bellini's Norma asks the moon-goddess, "quella pace che regnar tu fai nel ciel" ("spread on earth the peace that you cause to reign in Heaven"). The rhetorical and musical equation of divinity with impassive serenity plays out both in pagan contexts, such as the preceding example from *Norma* or the priestesses' hymn to Diana in Gluck's *Iphigénie en Tauride*, and in Christian ones, such as Agathe's prayer in

Der Freischütz. Indeed, the adapters of Donizetti's *Poliuto*, in preparing a sacred *rifacimento* of the opera to serve as a sacred cantata in 1854, thought nothing of converting the priests' chorus "Celeste un'aura" into a Christian hymn to God; the religious equation of divinity with serenity allowed this problem-free change (Rosenberg 2004: 295). To worship such an impassive God, passions must naturally be left at the door. For this reason, an operatic prayer is likely to be a moment of repose, a calm before or after the storm that provides affective contrast to the more spirited parts of the score. Musical reasons for introducing a prayer scene may thus be at least as important as dramatic ones. But a slow, solemn tempo is only one of the typical characteristics of prayers in opera. Others are the obvious timbral signs of organ or bells (called for in church scenes such as Act IV of Gounod's *Faust* and Act I of *Tosca* but not limited to them), harps employed for biblical or angelic associations, and hymn-like textures. Deliberate archaisms (4–3 suspensions at cadences, modal inflections, points of imitation) may be understood in various ways: as realistic evocations of the conservatism of much liturgical music, as a deliberate contrast to the more "secular" passages of an opera, or as a reflection of an unconscious assumption that religion is properly understood as belonging to the world of long ago.

Catholicism as Normative

Frequently overlooked in considerations of religion in opera is the pride of place occupied by Italy as the cradle of the genre and the country with the longest continuing tradition of opera performance, as well as the most successful importer of native operatic talent to other lands. This phenomenon alone would suffice to assign Roman Catholicism a defining role in the representation of religion on the operatic stage. Italy, together with France (and especially Paris, generally regarded as the center of opera during the early nineteenth century, and the capital of a country which, though drastically secularized, nevertheless remained deeply imprinted by Catholicism) and the political and artistic prestige of predominantly Catholic Austria (Vienna, in particular), effectively established Roman Catholic practices as normative in the representation of religion in opera. Opera in those Protestant lands where Pietism held sway (England and parts of Germany during much of the seventeenth century) faced relentless ecclesiastical criticism in any case (Flaherty 1978: 20–23). As for operas from historically Catholic lands that included Protestant characters—Meyerbeer's *Les Huguenots* and *Le Prophète*, or Verdi's *Stiffelio*—they constitute a small minority. From this follows an assumption of celibacy for those who answer the religious vocation, which will automatically spell trouble for any sensually tempted priests, monks, or nuns (or such obvious stand-ins as the vestal virgins of Spontini's *La vestale* or Bellini's Druid priestess Norma). The resulting situation for many religious characters is comparable to what has been termed the whore-madonna complex, except that it is not restricted to females. For such characters, the choice is stark indeed: One either succumbs to the sexual impulse or entirely renounces it, no middle ground being possible. It is this assumption of a strict polarity between the immoral and the celibate life that plays out in Massenet's *Thaïs*. It is inconceivable that the lascivious courtesan can reform herself by settling down to a life of controlled sexuality within the bonds of marriage; nothing but a life of harsh penance in a desert convent will suffice for her to atone for her sins. But Athanaël's alternatives are equally extreme. It is precisely his vow of chastity that turns his attraction for Thaïs into a crisis, for which the only possible resolution is what we find in Acts III and IV of the opera: an exchange of religious vocation by which Thaïs enters a convent and Athanaël foresakes his monastery. Claire Rowden has observed that the change is rendered audible by music that "corresponds to Thaïs's point of view and state of mind" in two very different duets in the opera, one in Act II (based on seduction) and the other in Act III, when the heroine's "thoughts are directed to God" (Rowden 2004: 251). The first of these duets takes on a musical intensity scarcely imaginable in a more "Protestant" (or Jewish) religious setting, while the second is marked by a regular style that portrays "a serene and converted Thaïs" (Rowden 2004: 251). In short, the more we find the religious impulse associated with clerical vocations in which chastity is mandatory, the higher the stakes are raised both dramatically and musically when sensual desire enters the picture. As for the sensuality of the music itself, the same writer offers a strong defense of the "Méditation" for violin solo and orchestra, played between the two scenes of Act II, against the strictures of Camille Bellaigue, who found its grace and elegance an inappropriate representation of the conversion to Christ of a sinner: Thaïs's "appreciation of the beauty in life is merely transferred from the physical to the spiritual plane" (Rowden 2004: 229–230). An important corollary to this idea is that the tradition of clerical celibacy can lend a peculiar moral authority to operatic characters such as the Padre Guardiano in *La forza del destino*, whose compassion for the suffering protagonists derives its strength from the transcendence of earthly passions symbolized by his vow to remain chaste.

The strongly Catholic underpinnings of many representations of religion in opera have further implications for a proper understanding of the subject. In addition to the usual sense of the word "religious," which may refer to any person of religious conviction, Roman Catholic usage also employs the term specifically to refer to an ordained member of a holy order. There is therefore a risk of confusing the two definitions. In the case of Verdi's *Don Carlos*, it may be erroneous to regard the Grand Inquisitor—a member of a holy order and a powerful official of the Church—as "religious" in the ordinary sense. In her exposition of the strong parallels between the Inquisitor's confrontation with King Philip and the confrontation of La Zia Principessa and her niece in Puccini's *Suor Angelica*, Helen Greenwald shows that it is actually the *non-clerical* Zia Principessa who corresponds to the clerical Inquisitor through certain shared attributes (age, infirmity, and above all, hypocrisy), while her niece, who *has* taken holy orders, corresponds to the victim of the Inquisition (Greenwald 1994: 223–226). The character David in Mascagni's *L'amico Fritz* has received a different sort of ordination, but the opera presents him in a manner virtually shorn of all distinguishing religious qualities, despite the fact that he is a rabbi (Rosenberg 2008). In brief, the presence on stage of a religiously ordained character is not necessarily a sign of religious content.

Religious Attitudes of Composer and Librettist

Is it possible to determine composers' or librettists' attitudes toward religion from the way in which religious themes are treated in the operas they create? The extremely varied interpretations proceeding from such an assumption would suggest that this is a highly risky business. *Lohengrin* may seem at first glance a celebration of Catholic religiosity, but Wagner took great pains in his essay "A Communication to My Friends" to demonstrate the falsity of this view (Wagner [1851] 1896). On the contrary, he confessed that at first the Lohengrin myth filled him with "repugnance with which we look upon the carved and painted saints and martyrs, on the highways, or in the churches, of Catholic lands" (Wagner [1851] 1896: 333) Only upon later reflection did he come to see the deeper human significance of the poem—the universal need for unconditional love—which he found prefigured in the myth of Zeus and Semele. With Wagner we have at least the advantage of a body of critical writings to help point us in certain interpretative directions (though this, too, can be risky), and other composers similarly help us out with more or less direct testimony. Britten declared in a 1963 interview that he was "certainly a dedicated Christian," but one influenced by radical theologians such as Dietrich Bonhoeffer—a promising point of entry into the study of the series of sacred operas on which he was about to embark, such as *The Burning Fiery Furnace* (1966) and *The Prodigal Son* (1968) (Carpenter 1992: 421). But with someone like Verdi, as tight-lipped about his convictions as Wagner was garrulous, we confront a situation in which an artist often regarded as a non-believer was able to present, time and again, religious scenes of powerful effect. Here, too, many commentators construct from these powerful scenes a picture of Verdi as believer, but have shown little concern for establishing the legitimacy of their methods. "It seems clear to me," said Luigi Floris Ammannati at the second international Verdi conference in 1969, "that to speak of the religiosity in Verdi's *Don Carlos* means to speak of the religiosity of Verdi." But what solid evidence for the rest of us lies beneath what "seems clear" to him (Ammannati 1971: 76)? Decades earlier, Gino Roncaglia acknowledged that while it is unnecessary to be a criminal in order to depict one artistically, it may likewise be possible for an atheist to write convincing religious music. But he immediately contradicted himself by insisting that "the evident fervor and intimacy of the religious scenes in Verdi's operas effectively rule any such interpretation out of the question" (Roncaglia 1940: 45). Giulio Confalonieri presented what may be considered a classic formulation of the argument:

> No man could have intoned death in the majestic rhythm in which it is intoned by the poet of Violetta, of Leonora, of Aida, if this man had considered death to be a simple biological event—the most trivial of all, in fact, because lacking in any tomorrow. As Gluck said, "music does not know how to lie." The ecstasy of Gilda and Radamès in their final hour cannot merely signify abandon at the close of physical life; it presages a rebirth and anticipates a new harmony, (p. 744)

> delivered from the anguish and injustice of earthly existence. The choral prayers of *I Lombardi* and the solitary prayer of Desdemona cannot be addressed to an illusory entity; the terror of Rigoletto and his obscure expectation of a tremendous punishment presuppose the certainty of a judge. (Confalonieri [1950] 2008: 2, quoted in Abbiati 1959: II: 575)

Other commentators have relied on external evidence to argue the direct opposite. Josef Loschelder is merely one of many critics to seize upon an 1883 letter by Verdi's friend Clara Maffei about the composer's lack of religious belief and his convictions regarding the ultimate meaninglessness of life, as providing a conclusive summary of Verdi's views, although he goes further than most in assuming that Iago's cynical "Credo" speaks directly for Verdi (Loschelder 1938: 17). Two often-quoted letters from Verdi's wife Giuseppina Strepponi, both dating from 1872, have been plausibly interpreted to mean that Verdi was a non-believer (Di Ascoli 1974: 282–283; Luzio 1947: IV: 286). Other biographical details, such as Verdi's regular attendance at Mass during his last years at his Sant'Agata estate, or his cordial relations with the chaplain at the Casa di Riposo, the retirement home for musicians which Verdi founded, point to a different conclusion. "Internal" (musical) evidence is hardly likely to settle the issue. Between Gilda, who, in the closing duet of *Rigoletto*, sings confidently of joining her mother in heaven, and the agonized title character, who is clearly having none of it, Verdi's music does not take sides in any way that we can regard as definitive. Gilles de Van is undoubtedly correct, moreover, in observing that the *Requiem* and other sacred works by Verdi are inconclusive as well, since they may be heard as questioning or wrestling with religion rather than embracing it faithfully (de Van 1998: 343–344).

The attitudes of composers and librettists toward religion are also highly relevant to the modest number of operas that treat Jewish religious themes. Fromental Halévy's decision to compose the music for *La Juive*, in which the Jewish-raised character Rachel (though ethnically of Gentile background) proudly chooses martyrdom as a Jew over conversion to Christianity, must have been prompted at least in part by his own strong identification with the Jewish people. However, he was willing to overlook certain religious oddities of Scribe's libretto, particularly in the Passover Seder scene (with its absurd misunderstanding of the significance of *matzoh* in the ritual meal), not to mention the lingering anti-Semitic stereotypes unrelated to Judaism (Hallman 2002: 231–254). Scribe's liberal and anti-clerical tendencies also find strong expression in the grand operas he wrote with another Jewish composer, Meyerbeer, and for reasons not altogether dissimilar to Halévy's. *Les Huguenots*, *Le Prophète*, and *L'Africaine*, though lacking Jewish characters or themes, speak directly to areas of Jewish concern within European society, with their strongly implied critiques of narrow sectarianism and religious intolerance (Letellier 2005: 65–79).

In the case of operas based on stories from the Old Testament, the question of whether the composer or librettist of a given work is of Jewish background is well-nigh inescapable if we are to come to a true understanding of it in religious terms. The issue is greatly complicated by the fact that Judaism, the specifically religious aspect of Jewish identity, is often impossible to disentangle (assuming that it is right to do so) from non-religious components of that identity such as nationhood or race, not to mention certain personal attributes or patterns of behavior perceived by Gentiles as characteristic. Here, too, we are faced with the difficult question of whether religious references in opera are to be accepted as such or rather subsumed under some other concern. Klara Móricz, in her article on Ernest Bloch's incomplete biblical opera *Jézabel*, admirably brings out the subtle complexities of this issue, since Bloch himself over the years issued a number of public and private pronouncements indicating a purely racial identification with Jewish peoplehood, in contradistinction to cultural ties or religious conviction (Móricz 2001: 439–447). Indeed, a composer's specific notion of Jewishness will often determine important aspects of musical style in an Old Testament opera, including the projected *Jézabel* just cited, such as whether or not to employ an orientalist-exotic idiom for Hebrew characters (Móricz 2001: 462–476). It has been pointed out that in Saint-Saën's *Samson et Dalila*, it is the heathen Philistines rather than the Hebrews who receive an exotic musical representation; Ralph Locke argues on this basis that this is a case where the Hebrews are accepted straightforwardly as "proto-Christians" with whom a predominantly Christian audience can readily identify (Locke 1991: 282). The related case of Verdi's *Nabucco* (Hebrews interpreted as stand-ins for Italians in their desire to win political autonomy) has already been mentioned. Rossini's *Mosé in Egitto*, however, illustrates the confusion that can result from conflicting perceptions of Jewish identity. Stendhal, in the sixth chapter of his famous *Life of Rossini*, claimed to hear in a Hebrew chorus in this opera an example of deliberate musical exoticism "reminiscent of the Jewish synagogue" (as opposed, one gathers, to some other kind of synagogue), an observation made by no one else in the entire primary or secondary literature (Stendhal [1824] 1957: 113), demonstrating that even if Old Testament operas are created with the expectation that a Christian audience will identify with Hebrews, there is no guarantee that all members of the audience will do so. More recent biblical operas present a similarly mixed picture. While Darius Milhaud's *David* (1954, with a concert premiere in Jerusalem) or Mario Castelnuovo-Tedesco's *Saul* may safely be presumed to be proud identifications with the Jewish religious tradition, a somewhat controversial secondary literature has grown up around Schoenberg's *Moses und Aron*. Some scholars (Fubini 1994: 127–137; Batnitzky 2001: passim), taking Schoenberg's own pronouncements regarding the Jewish nature of the opera as a point of departure, have emphasized the religious aspects of this opera. These elements range from the obvious (the covenant, the ban on idols) to the speculative, such as the perceived correspondence between monotheism and the construction of a large-scale work on a single twelve-tone row, or the suggestive similarity between an opera left incomplete and *En Sof* ("the One Without End," the term in Caballah for the infinite God) (Ringer 1993: 72, 81, 186). On the other side, Herbert Lindenberger's skeptical survey of the putatively religious elements of the opera is marked by concern that these only obscure the more important personal, political, and aesthetic meanings in the work (Lindenberger 1989: 65–75). Bluma Goldstein has gone further, showing how in many respects the opera actually undermines or runs counter to normative Jewish interpretations of the Exodus (Goldstein 2000: passim), while Malcolm MacDonald minimizes the specifically Jewish religious sense of the opera by insisting that it "transcends sectarian boundaries." To MacDonald the opera belongs with those works by Schoenberg that testify to his concern for "the relation of the individual to the inner and outer worlds—to the spirit and to the collective, to humanity at large and, beyond that, to the yet larger, eternal world of religious conviction and speculation" (MacDonald 2008: 293).

Such conflicting interpretations serve as a helpful reminder of the risk of overstating the importance of composers' and librettists' beliefs when interpreting the religious scenes of their operas. Roncaglia's reminder of how unnecessary it is that an artist be a criminal in order to depict one is worth remembering, even if he himself forgot it when considering religion in Verdi's operas. Few would conclude that Musorgsky sympathized with the Old Believers' opposition to reforming the Orthodox liturgy in the seventeenth century simply because he wrote such moving music for them in *Khovanschchina*; the consideration is essentially irrelevant. Nor is it necessary for composers to believe in angels in order to write such glorious music as that for the ballet that closes Act II of Humperdinck's *Hänsel und Gretel*, or the angelic dictation of the *Missa Papae Marcelli* in the climactic scene of Act I of Pfitzner's *Palestrina*. It is vastly more important for composers (and audiences) to be able to enter into the spirit of such beliefs than actually to share them.

Religion in Massenet's *Manon*

A detailed examination of the St. Sulpice scene (Act III, scene 2) in Massenet's popular opera *Manon* may help to clarify some of the preceding points, and to show how the presentation of religion in an opera can illuminate attitudes toward religion at a given historical moment.[1] It will be useful to begin by reviewing the religious references in the opera preceding the St. Sulpice scene. Religion first appears in Manon's opening lines, when she explains that she is now supposed to enter a convent; she makes the remarkable admission that she had temporarily forgotten all about her destination amid her excitement over the trip she made to Amiens. The convent reference strikes a discordant note amid an extended solo number of considerable exuberance, despite her physical fatigue. One senses from the outset how regrettable it is to force someone of such irrepressible spirits to enter a convent. Later in the act, after Manon's brother asks her to await his return, she refers once more to her convent in a regretful manner in a melancholy B minor ("Voyons, Manon," 78); this time, too, the reflection on her fate comes directly on the heels of an expression of youthful exuberance (her admiration for the fashionable ladies Poussette, Javotte, and Rosette). This reinforces the central point that holy orders for Manon, far from being a vocation, are something imposed, part discipline and part punishment. Once she meets and falls in love with Des Grieux, she tells him where she is bound—but only after admitting that she has been accused by her family of loving pleasure too much; he passionately disapproves. Although she says that it is the will of God, to which she is resigned, her resistance to his blandishments is weak and rapidly overcome. In sum, each time in Act I that we hear of the convent that Manon is supposed to enter, it is in the context of a clear indication that it is not her choice (89–91).

As for Des Grieux, there is no indication in the entire first act of a religious inclination or temperament on his part, much less a vocation. Act II lacks any reference at all to religion, and in Act III, religion is brought into the drama as an incongruous element, the sharpest possible contrast to the bustle and worldly excitement of the opening scene, the fashionable Cour de Reine: Manon overhears the Count refer to his son with the religious title "Abbé." Religion here re-enters this *opéra comique* in the subtlest manner imaginable, a *spoken* conversation between De Bretigny (for whom she had abandoned Des Grieux) and the Count. The spoken lines are accompanied by the orchestral motive frequently given during passages associated with Des Grieux, as the count explains that his son is now completing his studies at the seminary of St. Sulpice and preparing for holy orders (218–219). De Bretigny's ironic comment on Des Grieux's new religious vocation seems entirely justified; nothing preceding this announcement could have prepared him (or the audience) for it. Manon timidly questions the Count in a *parlante* passage over the graceful minuet-like theme that has been weaving in and out of the score since the *entr'acte* leading into Act III. Religious reference is then canceled out as abruptly as it had been brought in, as the series of ballet *divertissements* commences. Manon's decision to surprise Des Grieux at St. Sulpice, and to dissuade him from pursuing the religious life, reverses the situation of Act I, though she seems motivated mainly by egotism, finding it intolerable that Des Grieux has now forgotten her, as his father has now assured her.

The change from scene 1 to scene 2 of Act III—from the Cour de Reine to the seminary of St. Sulpice—represents a shift from a secular space to a sacred one, fully in line with the traditional view that some spaces are more sacred than others. The St. Sulpice scene opens with sustained chords played on the organ, in which the modal harmonic coloring, as well as the 4–3 suspensions, both connote an environment removed from worldly concerns (246). In addition to setting the scene, the organ solo also has a more strictly diegetic function as a postlude following a devotional service during which Des Grieux has given an impressive sermon. The strings then enter with another archaism, a brief fugal exposition in a quasi-Bachian style. Featuring a "tonal" (intervallically adjusted) answer to the G major subject, it is as adroitly executed as other eighteenth-century styles that Massenet drew upon for his score and could easily have come straight from one of the textbook exemplars he used in his counterpoint classes at the Paris Conservatory. The curtain rises on the St. Sulpice reception room, and we see and hear the arrival of the "aristocratic and bourgeois women" after hearing Des Grieux's sermon in the seminary chapel (246–248). The churchly musical style established at the beginning of the scene disappears during the ladies' exclamations over the eloquence and learning of the young man who preached; their enthusiasm, effectively expressed in brightly rushing sixteenth notes, strongly suggests that Des Grieux's appeal for them is more than a strictly spiritual one. The suspicion is reinforced by their references to the sweetness of his voice and the passion of his delivery, and will be further confirmed when the arrival of Manon later in the scene is accompanied by an agitated version of what is recognizably the same bubbly music heard during the women's chorus that directly precedes it. Even in the passage for the ladies, however, there are brief and intermittent musical recurrences of two ecclesiastical signifiers heard earlier (suspensions and imitative counterpoint), as though they were temporarily collecting themselves in an attempt to resume a more proper attitude (248, 250). Once Des Grieux enters the reception room from the seminary chapel, the orchestra brings back the Bachian passage played near the beginning of the scene, as the ladies respectfully greet the young seminarian. The organ postlude is heard once more (253), bringing a perfect arch form to a close.

The dialogue between Des Grieux and his father, in which the Count attempts to dissuade his son from taking his priestly vows, provides the one instance in the libretto of a religious scene that approaches genuine theological reflection. At first the dialogue is spoken, accompanied by gently sustained chords, save for the brief recurrence of the love music theme familiar from the previous two acts, now heard fleetingly during Des Grieux's remark that he has found only bitterness in the world (253). But the Count's heartfelt appeal for Des Grieux to return to the world and take a wife is marked by a return to singing (254). The father's plea is also couched in explicitly religious language: heaven itself imposes the duty of marriage. The Count stands here on firm doctrinal grounds; in Roman Catholic teaching, marriage is no less a sacrament than holy orders. The dichotomy between "religion" (conceived as renunciation) and the everyday world is thus exposed as essentially false, but Des Grieux cannot or will not consider this argument. Clinging to the dichotomy, he insists—in speech, not song—that he will carry out his religious vows, and the affectionate farewell between father and son, including the Count's announcement of the inheritance that will now be placed at the disposal of his son, is also spoken.

Des Grieux's "Ah, fuyez, douce image" (Ah, flee sweet image) has long been one of the most beloved tenor arias in the repertoire. It opens with an impassioned recitative in which Des Grieux discloses both his motivation and the nature of his theological understanding: there is nothing he wants more than the "sacred repose" of religious faith and to place God "between the world" and himself (258). During the lyrical portion of the aria ("Ah, fuyez"), he is obviously thinking of Manon, but the rhetorical setup is oblique; strictly speaking, his words are not addressed to the absent Manon but rather to his fervid memory (symbolized by anguished recurrences of the love theme) of her "sweet image," which inhibits his resolve to proceed to ordination (258–260).

Whether by design or by a happy coincidence of meaning and musical form, in the same way that Des Grieux calls upon God to stand "between the world and myself," a prayer is inserted into the middle of the aria. This prayer marks one of those instances where the very popularity of an aria as a detached "highlight" grossly distorts the sense of a passage. We hear a shortened version of the same organ prelude (261) played at the beginning of the St. Sulpice scene. But when the aria is included in a solo vocal recital (or a recording bearing a title like "Jussi Björling Sings Beloved Tenor Encores"), the organ solo becomes the first musical indication of a churchly environment; the effect is that Des Grieux's prayer is a sudden and unaccountable switch of gears, rather than a reminder of the ambience previously established in the scene. Still more important is what immediately precedes the prayer portion of the aria in a complete presentation of the scene: a brief exchange between the porter of the seminary, who enters to announce that the celebration of the Divine Office (presumably a Vespers service) is about to commence, and Des Grieux, who responds that he will come shortly. The prayer is thus prompted by a dramatic moment of singular urgency, as he pleads with God to "purify his soul" (261). Des Grieux returns to apostrophize Manon's haunting image in a second "Ah, fuyez" section in abbreviated form and with a coda, now with two further timbral signifiers not present the first time around, a harp and an offstage church bell of obviously diegetic function, as Des Grieux exits the stage.

It is inconceivable that Massenet was unaware that his orchestral accompaniment to the agitated entrance of Manon (263–264), though now in C minor and presented at a faster tempo, is thematically identical to the music of the ladies who had expressed their admiration for Des Grieux's sermon at the beginning of the scene. After another reminiscence of the love theme, this time slowly mournful and played by the solo oboe (264), Manon speaks her sentiments while an organ-accompanied *Magnificat*, developing the same Bachian textures and motives heard earlier, sounds within the chapel. During an interval in the choral *Magnificat*, itself a sharp departure from propriety but poetically apt for the expressive opportunity it affords the soprano, Manon bursts out with her plea for God to return to her the affections of Des Grieux (266–268). The religious content has grown increasingly concentrated; Massenet nested Des Grieux's prayer into his aria and embedded Manon's prayer to be reunited with her former lover within a choral setting of the Virgin's response to the Annunciation.

The duet for the lovers which brings the act to a close does not refer musically to religion (save for the church bell heard toward the end), but does so textually: Des Grieux's declaration that it was God's will for their love to be short-lived, his desperate prayer to God to sustain him, his cry that it is blasphemous for her to speak of their love in a holy space, and his insistence that he must depart for the church service when he hears the tolling of the bell. But the musical style tells us otherwise, making it clear that Des Grieux's love for Manon has won out over his priestly vocation well before he arrives at the point of stating this verbally. In a straightforward sense, religion will now exit the stage, never to reappear during the final two acts, at least insofar as explicit scenic or musical references are concerned. In the end, however, the lovers find redemption through their mutual love, now shorn of all youthful folly by their shared suffering: Des Grieux through the deep compassion he feels for Manon and Manon through her sincere penitence for having contributed to Des Grieux's ruin. Des Grieux, who never becomes a priest after all, exceeds his authority when he cries to Manon that not only he but "Heaven itself" forgives her (373). This may well be a sop to a sentimental audience grateful for the reassurance that the lovers' violations of conventional morality are now erased. The lovers are forgiven their sensual indulgence, and three hours of music of the utmost sensual appeal is likewise validated. It is not so much a matter of transferring a sense of beauty "from the physical to the spiritual plane," as described in Rowden's perceptive analysis of the *Méditation* in Massenet's *Thaïs*, cited above. Here the breakthrough is nothing less than theological. Thanks to Manon, Des Grieux transcends the conceptual dichotomy of his encounter with his father in Act III, recognizing that God is present within human love, not only in the renunciation of it.

See also: Censorship, Operatorio? Operatic Images

Note

1. All page references are to the Schirmer piano-vocal score (Massenet [1884] 1940) included in the bibliography.

Bibliography

Abbate, Carolyn, and Roger Parker. 2012. *A History of Opera: The Last Four Hundred Years*. New York: W.W. Norton.

Abbiati, Franco. 1959. *Giuseppe Verdi*. 4 vols. Milan: Ricordi.

Abert, Anna Amalie. 1971. "Darstellung des Gebets in der Oper." *Triviale Zonen in der religiösen Kunst des 19. Jahrhunderts*. Studien zur Philosophie und Literatur des neunzehnten Jahrhunderts 15, 148–157. Frankfurt: V. Klosterman.

Ammannati, Luigi Floris. 1971. "Nota sulla religiosità nel 'Don Carlos' di Verdi." *Atti del II° congresso internazionale di studi verdiani*, 76–79. Parma: Istituto nazionale di studi verdiani.

Ascari, Diana Dionisi. 1987. "Da *Stiffelio* a *Guglielmo Wellingrode*: gli interventi della censura." In *Tornando a Stiffelio*, edited by Giovanni Morelli, 129–139. Florence: Olschki.

Batnitzky, Leora. 2001. "Schoenberg's *Moses und Aron* and the Judaic Ban on Images." *Journal for the Study of the Old Testament* 92: 81–98.

Bie, Oskar. 1913. *Die Oper*. Berlin: S. Fischer.

Blareau, Ludovic. 1921. *Histoire de la création et du développement du drame musical*. Brussels: Lamertin.

Boccaccio, Giovanni. [1370] 1963. *Genealogie deorum gentilium. Tutte le opere di Giovanni Boccaccio*. Vols. 7–8, edited by Vittore Branca. Milan: A. Mondadori.

Boll, André. 1963. *L'opéra: spectacle intégral*. Paris: Olivier Perrin Éditeur.

Brauner, Charles. 2004. "Introduction." Gioachino Rossini, *Mosè in Egitto*, edited by Charles Brauner. *Edizione critica delle opere di Gioachino Rossini*. Sez. I: 24, xxxi–xlii. Pesaro: Fondazione Rossini.

Carpenter, Humphrey. 1992. *Benjamin Britten: A Biography*. New York: Charles Scribner's Sons.

Confalonieri, Giulio. [1950] 2008. "Religiosità di Giuseppe Verdi (a 50 anni dalla sua morte)." *Rassegna musicale delle edizioni Curci* 3 nn. 5–6 (ottobre–dicembre): 1–2. Reprint. *Rassegna musicale Curci* 41 (January): 6–9.

Dent, Edward J. [1949] 1978. *Opera*. Harmondsworth, UK: Penguin Books. Reprint. Westport, CT: Greenwood Press.

Di Ascoli, Arturo. 1974. *Quartetto Milanese Ottocentesco: Lettere di G. Verdi, G. Strepponi, C. Maffei, C. Tenca e di altri personaggi del mondo politico e artistico dell'epoca*. Rome: Archivi Edizioni.

Donington, Robert. 1981. *The Rise of Opera*. New York: Charles Scribner's Sons.

Dubowy, Norbert. 1995. "Mayr und das Oratorium: das Beispiel "Samuele." *Beiträge des 1. internationalen Simon-Mayr-Symposions vom 2. bis 4. Oktober 1992 in Ingolstadt*, edited by Karl Batz, 111–160. Ingoldstadt: Donaukurier.

Edgecomb, Rodney Stenning. 2005. "Conventions of Prayer in Some 19th-Century Operas." *Musical Times* 1893: 45–60.
Ellis, William Ashton, ed. and trans. 1892–1899. *Richard Wagner's Prose Works.* 8 vols. London: Kegan Paul.
Elson, Arthur. 1901. *A Critical History of Opera*. London: Seeley & Co.
Ewans, Michael. 2007. *Opera from the Greek: Studies in the Poetics of Appropriation.* Aldershot, UK: Ashgate.
Flaherty, Gloria. 1978. *Opera in the Development of German Critical Thought.* Princeton, NJ: Princeton University Press.
Fubini, Enrico. 1994. *La musica nella tradizione ebraica*. Turin: Einaudi.
Fulcher, Jane F. 2005. *The Composer as Intellectual: Music and Ideology in France 1914–1940*. New York: Oxford University Press.
Giger, Andreas. 1999. "Social Control and the Censorship of Giuseppe Verdi's Operas in Rome (1844–1859)." *Cambridge Opera Journal* 11/3: 233–265.
Giocanti, Stéphane. 2006. "Vincent d'Indy est-il un compositeur religieux?" In *Vincent d'Indy et son temps*, edited by Manuela Schwartz, 255–262. Sprimont, Belgium: Mardaga.
Goldstein, Bluma. 2000. "Schoenberg's *Moses und Aron*: A Vanishing Biblical Nation." In *Political and Religious Ideas in the Works of Arnold Schoenberg*, edited by Charlotte M. Cross and Russell A. Berman, 159–192. New York: Garland.
Gossett, Philip. 2006. *Divas and Scholars: Performing Italian Opera.* Chicago: University of Chicago Press.
Greenwald, Helen M. 1994. "Verdi's Patriarch and Puccini's Matriarch: Through the Looking-Glass and What Puccini Found There." *19th-Century Music* 17/3: 220–236.
Gregor, Joseph. 1950. *Kulturgeschichte der Oper.* Vienna/Zurich: Gallus VerlagWien/Scientia Verlag Zürich.
Grout, Donald Jay, and Hermine Weigel Williams. 2003. *A Short History of Opera.* 4th ed. New York: Columbia University Press.
Hadamowsky, Franz. 1955. "Barocktheater am Wiener Kaiserhof: mit einem Spielplan (1625–1740)." *Jahrbuch der Gesellschaft für Wiener Theaterforschung* 1951/1952: 7–117.
Hallman, Diana R. 2002. *Opera, Liberalism, and Antisemitism in Nineteenth-Century France: The Politics of Halévy's 'La Juive.'* Cambridge: Cambridge University Press.
Hansell, Kathleen Kuzmick. 2003. "Introduction." Giuseppe Verdi, *Stiffelio*, edited by Kathleen Kuzmick Hansell. *The Works of Giuseppe Verdi*. Ser. I: 16, xi–xxxix. Chicago: University of Chicago Press; Milan: Ricordi.
Headington, Christopher, Roy Westbrook, and Terry Barfoot. 1987. *Opera, A History.* New York: St. Martin's Press.
Huebner, Steven. 1999. *French Opera at the Fin de Siècle: Wagnerism, Nationalism, and Style.* New York: Oxford University Press.
Ipson, Douglas. 2011. "Giuriamo per la Patria: The Operatic Oath Scene in Revolutionary Rome, 1846–1849." PhD diss., University of Chicago.
Izzo, Francesco. 2007. "Verdi, the Virgin, and the Censor: The Politics of the Cult of Mary in *I Lombardi alla prima crociata* and *Giovanna d'Arco*." *Journal of the American Musicological Society* 60/3: 557–597.
Kinderman, William. 1985. "Wagner's *Parsifal*: Musical Form and the Drama of Redemption." *Journal of Musicology* 4/4: 431–446.
Kretzschmar, Herman. 1919. *Geschichte der Oper.* Leipzig: Breitkopf & Härtel.

Letellier, Robert Ignatius. 2005. *Meyerbeer Studies: A Series of Lectures, Essays, and Articles on the Life and Work of Giacomo Meyerbeer*. Rutherford, NJ: Fairleigh Dickenson University Press.

Lindenberger, Herbert. 1989. "Arnold Schoenberg's *Der Biblische Weg* and *Moses und Aron*: On the Transactions of Aesthetics and Politics." *Modern Judaism* 9/1: 55–70.

Lippmann, Friedrich. 1990. "Casta Diva: La preghiera nell'opera italiana della prima metà dell'Ottocento." *Recercare: Rivista per lo studio e la pratica della musica antica* 2: 173–209.

Locke, Ralph. 1991. "Constructing the Oriental 'Other': Saint-Saëns's *Samson et Dalila*." *Cambridge Opera Journal* 3/3: 261–302.

Loschelder, Josef. 1938. *Das Todesproblem in Verdis Opernschaffen*. Köln/Stuttgart: Petrarca-Haus/Kommissionsverlag Deutsche Verlagsanstalt.

Lösel, Steffen. 2009. "'May Such Great Effort Not Be in Vain': Mozart on Divine Love, Judgment, and Retribution." *The Journal of Religion* 89/3: 361–400.

Luzio, Alessandro. 1935–1947. *Carteggi verdiani*. 4 vols. Rome: Reale accademia d'Italia.

Marvin, Roberta Montemorra. 2001. "The Censorship of Verdi's Operas in Victorian London." *Music & Letters* 82/4: 582–610.

Massenet, Jules. [1884] 1940. *Manon*. Opera in Five Acts. Piano-vocal score. New York: G. Schirmer.

Mayr, Johann Simon. 1843. "Cenni storici intorno all'oratorio." *Zibaldone* [collection of notebooks]. Vol. 13. Bergamo, Biblioteca Civica A. Mai, Bergamo, 64v–84v.

Morgenstern, Anja. 2007. *Die Oratorien von Johann Simon Mayr (1763–1845): Studien zu Biographik, Quellen und Rezeption*. Mayr-Studien 6. Munich/Salzburg: Musikverlag Katzbichler.

Móricz, Klara. 2001. "Sensuous pagans and righteous Jews: Changing Concepts of Jewish Identity in Ernest Bloch's *Jézabel* and *Schelomo*." *Journal of the American Musicological Society* 54/3: 439–491.

Murata, Margaret. 1981. *Operas for the Papal Court 1631–1668*. Ann Arbor, MI: UMI Research Press.

Neville, Don. 1998. "Opera or Oratorio?: Metastasio's Sacred 'Opere serie.'" *Early Music* 26/4: 596–607.

Orrey, Leslie. 1972. *A Concise History of Opera*. London: Thames and Hudson.

Ortuño-Stühring, Daniel. 2011. *Musik als Bekenntnis: Christus-Oratorien im 19. Jahrhundert*. Weimarer Liszt-Studien, im Auftrag der Deutsche Liszt-Gesellschaft, herausgegeben von Detlef Altenburg, 6. Laaber: Laaber-Verlag.

Parakilas, James. 1997. "Religion and Difference in Verdi's *Otello*." *Musical Quarterly* 81/3: 371–392.

Parker, Roger. 2007. *The New Grove Guide to Verdi and His Operas*. New York: Oxford University Press.

Piperno, Franco. 2002. "Rossini (vero e falso), il 'Quinto Fabio' di Nicolini (Roma 1918) e 'L'Atalia' di Mayr (Napoli 1822)." In *Pensieri per un maestro: Studi in onore di Pierluigi Petroblli*, edited by Stefano La Via and Roger Parker, 171–192. Turin: EDT.

——. 1994a. "'Effetto Mosè': Fortuna e recezione del *Mosè in Egitto* a Napoli e in Italia (1818–1830)." In *La recezione di Rossini ieri e oggi. Atti dei Convegni Lincei 110*, 165–194. Rome: Accademia Nazionale dei Lincei.

——. 1994b. "Il *Mosè in Egitto* e la tradizione napoletana di opere bibliche." In *Gioachino Rossini, 1792–1992. Il testo e la scena. Atti del Convegno 1992*, edited by Paolo Fabbri, 255–271. Pesaro: Fondazione Rossini.

———. 1993. "'Stellati sogli' e 'immagini portentose': Opere bibliche e stagioni quaresimali a Napoli prima del *Mosè*." In *Napoli e il teatro musicale in Europa tra Sette e Ottocento: Studi in onore di Friedrich Lippmann*, edited by Bianca Marina Antolini and Wolfgang Witzenmann, 267–298. Florence: Olschki.

———. 1991. "Drammi sacri in teatro (1750–1820). In *Mozart, Padova, e la 'Betulia liberata.'* Quaderni della Rivista italiana di musicologia 24, 289–316. Florence: Olschki.

Ringer, Alexander. 1990. *The Composer as Jew*. Oxford: Clarendon Press.

Rolland, Romain. 1895. *L'Histoire de l'opéra en Europe avant Lully et Scarlatti*. Paris: Ernest Thorin.

Roncaglia, Gino. 1940. *L'ascensione creatrice di Giuseppe Verdi*. Florence: G. S. Sansoni.

Rosenberg, Jesse. 2008. "An Operatic Rabbi: David Sichel and Mascagni's *L'amico Fritz*." In *D'une scène à l'autre: L'opéra italien en Europe*. 2 vols., edited by Damien Colas and Alessandro di Profio, II: 407–424. Wavre: Mardaga.

———. 2004. "Rifacimenti sacri della musica operistica di Donizetti: questioni tipologiche e valutative." In *Il Teatro di Donizetti: Atti dei convegni delle celebrazioni 1797/1997–1848/1998, II: Percorsi e proposte di ricerca. Venezia 22 14 maggio 1997*, edited by Paolo Cecchi and Luca Zoppelli, 293–303. Bergamo: Fondazione Donizetti.

Rowden, Claire. 2004. *Republican Morality and Catholic Tradition in the Opera: Massenet's 'Hérodiade' and 'Thaïs.'* Weinsberg, Germany: Lucie Galland.

Sholl, Robert. 2011. "The Shock of the Positive: Olivier Messiaen, St. Francis, and Redemption through Modernity." In *Resonant Witness: Conversations between Music and Theology*, edited by Jeremy S. Begbie and Steven R. Guthrie, 162–189. Grand Rapids, MI, and Cambridge, UK: William B. Eerdmans.

Smart, Mary Ann. 2004. *Mimomania: Music and Gesture in Nineteenth-Century Opera*. Berkeley and Los Angeles: University of California Press.

Smither, Howard E. 1979–1980. "Oratorio and Sacred Opera, 1700–1825: Terminology and Genre Distinction." *Proceedings of the Royal Musical Association* 106: 88–104.

———. 1977–2000. *A History of the Oratorio*. 4 vols. Chapel Hill: University of North Carolina Press.

Spada, Marco. 1989. "*Ernani* e la censura napoletana." *Studi verdiani* 5: 11–34.

Stendhal [Henri Beyle]. [1824] 1957. *Life of Rossini*, translated by Richard N. Coe. New York: Criterion Books.

Sternfeld, F. W. 1993. *The Birth of Opera*. Oxford: Clarendon Press.

Taylor, Philip S. 2007. *Anton Rubinstein: A Life in Music*. Bloomington: Indiana University Press.

Thomson, Andrew. 1996. *Vincent d'Indy and His World*. Oxford: Clarendon Press.

Van, Gilles de. 1998. *Verdi's Theater: Creating Drama through Music*, translated by Gilda Roberts. Chicago: University of Chicago Press.

Wagner, Richard. [1851] 1896. "Eine Mitteilung an meine Freunde." In *Sämtliche Schriften und Dichtungen*, edited by Hans von Wolzogen and Richard Sternfeld. 16 vols. Leipzig: Breitkopf & Härtel. IV: 230–344. In Ellis 1896 [as "A Communication to My Friends"], I: 267–392.

Wallace, Robin. 1984. "The Role of Music in Liturgical Drama: A Revaluation." *Music & Letters* 65: 219–228.

CHAPTER 34

RACE AND RACISM

JOHN GRAZIANO

THE topic of race and racism in the history of opera is multifaceted and complicated. It is observed in a large number of contexts and can be discussed from a number of perspectives, depending on a music historian's interests. Certain aspects of the topic have generated significant interest in the scholarly community, including, for example, issues of the representation of non-Western characters and stereotypes; of religious intolerance; and of the personal beliefs of composers and librettists. The definition of race is somewhat amorphous; it can be defined as "a family, tribe, people, or nation belonging to the same stock" (Merriam-Webster 2012). Racism is defined as "a belief that race is the primary determinant of human traits and capacities and that racial differences produce an inherent superiority of a particular race" (Merriam-Webster 2012). The combination and interaction of these two related definitions give rise to studies that may only be superficially connected to the issue. For example, is the "blacking up" of a white singer who is singing Otello racist? How does one negotiate case studies where the issues overlap, where the boundaries among various kinds of intolerance—the line between racism and anti-Semitism, for example—are not always clear? In what context, then, does one examine the question of religious intolerance in Wagner's *Die Meistersinger von Nürnberg*? The character of Beckmesser, an officious city clerk, has been viewed by some scholars, such as Barry Millington (1991), as representing a Jewish pedant, akin to Grimm's "Jew in the Brambles," who gets his just deserts in the opera at the hands of the Christian cobbler, Hans Sachs (Millington 1991; others, like Hans Rudolf Vaget [1995], argue against the Wagner-Grimm connection). In the context of Wagner's well-known anti-Semitism, and his antipathy to the music critic Eduard Hanslick, of whom Beckmesser may be a parody, not to mention the appropriation of Wagner's music by the Third Reich, the complexity of the question of racial and religious intolerance is quite difficult to unpack (see, for example, Botstein 2009; Millington 1991; Weiner 1997; Levin 1996). As Millington has noted:

> The work may also be regarded [...] as the artistic component in Wagner's ideological crusade of the 1860s: a crusade to revive the 'German spirit' and purge it

> of alien elements, chief among which were the Jews. It can further be argued that anti-Semitism is woven into the ideological fabric of the work and that the representation of Beckmesser carries, at the very least, overtones of anti-Semitic sentiment. (Millington 1992)

Another area of inquiry on race that has attracted a number of studies is the examination of exoticism in opera scores and librettos. Scholars have detailed the use of the exotic "Other" (i.e., representatives of a non-Western group of people—a tribe or nation) in librettos, which have appeared almost from the birth of the genre. Either as characters in disguise or as residents of distant countries, these dramatic representations have offered composers and librettists an opportunity to use non-European characters to define their cultures, behaviors, and, sometimes, musics. In a recent book, for example, Ralph P. Locke examines how Handel set librettos that feature Muslim monarchs without attempting to illustrate their "otherness" musically (Locke 2009: 87–95). In some librettos, the "Other" is a person whose social or cultural norms differ from those of the West. Two well-known examples— Mozart's *Die Entführung aus dem Serail* and Rossini's *L'Italiana in Algeri*—are comedies, where cultural clashes resolve themselves in a light-hearted happy ending. In works such as Giacomo Meyerbeer's last opera, *L'Africaine* (1865), Leo Delibes's *Lakmé* (1883), and Giacomo Puccini's *Madama Butterfly* (1904), however, cultural disparities ultimately lead the exotic character to a tragic end.

Differences in cultural norms do not always serve as the basis for the depiction of the "Other." Delineation of black characters can depict an overt racism. For example, the character of the Moor, Monostatos, in Mozart's *Die Zauberflöte* can be viewed as the archetypal depiction of a black servant who is base, evil, and has animalistic predilections toward the white (virgin) maiden, Pamina, who lies asleep as his captive. As Julian Rushton has noted, "Monostatos, the untrustworthy servant, represents ordinary nature going bad... he chooses evil and seeks power (over Pamina, by misused sexuality and by joining the Queen [of the Night])" (Rushton 1992). But, as Naomi André posits, defining racism in opera is not always a clear-cut case:

> When Verdi's Otello dies, he is treated heroically in the opera [...]. He pays for his jealousy [...] but is ennobled by his death [...]. Yet there is another, racialized, way of looking at Otello: he is an exoticized Moor whose civilized demeanor might have been more of a shock when he does *not* fulfill the stereotype of the wild savage. (André 2012: 23)

At the turn of the twentieth century, many composers were drawn to librettos that dramatized the Otherness of non-white ethnicities. Popular Broadway comic operas, such as Sidney Jones's *The Geisha* (1896), which concerns the love of an English naval officer and a geisha at a teahouse, responded to the public's interest in the exotic in terms of both the story and the music. This interest was also seen in works destined for the opera house. Mascagni's *Iris* (1898), set to a libretto by Luigi Illica, tells of a Japanese love triangle, though the composer did not attempt to write exotic music to match his libretto. Victor Herbert's *Natoma* (1911), with Mary Garden in the title role, was the most well received of several American operas on Native American and Spanish themes; it portrays a love story between a servant girl, an "Indian," as Herbert referred to the character—"the last of her race"—and a white naval officer. Herbert undoubtedly knew the harmonized transcriptions of Native American melodies collected by Alice Cunningham Fletcher (1838–1923) and Francis La Flesche (1857–1937), but instead of quoting them exactly, he combined various fragments to construct his own versions of the music. (Pisani 2005: chapter 8).

Historians have also documented how composers and librettists characterize various ethnic groups, sometimes defined as "races," in their works. Halévy's *La Juive*, for example, is an exposition of religious intolerance and the Jewish-Christian conflict in France, which was of major importance during the nineteenth-century July Monarchy (Hallman 2002: especially 253–296). Delius's *Koanga* (1898) views race in personal terms: the opera relates, through the use of a flashback, the story of a West African tribal chief who is brought to the New World to work as a plantation slave. The emotional entanglements among a newly enslaved African man, a female "quadroon" slave, and a Spanish owner, his wife, and overseer, lead to the use of vodun spells and curses, and ultimately, to death for many of the protagonists. The librettist, Charles Keary, made no attempt to portray the races realistically, nor was Delius evidently interested in that kind of portrayal. According to Eric Saylor,

> *Koanga* is far from a realistic portrayal of black life in the United States, and was most certainly not meant to be. More likely, Delius was inspired by the story's exoticism [...] and was more concerned with capturing a mood than faithfully re-creating a culture. (Saylor 2012: 82)

A related aspect of this type of study is the characterizations of the ethnicities of various composers. For example, Giacomo Meyerbeer, a German Jew, whose birth name was Jacob Liebmann Meyer Beer, faced discrimination in France, particularly during the July Monarchy, in spite of being given honorary French citizenship. Critics viewed him through stereotypes then current in France, complaining that he lacked a French national identity (Murphy 2001).

Operas that deal with race, racism, and non-white culture have been written in the twentieth century as well. Ernst Krenek's *Zeitoper*, *Jonny spielt auf* follows the escapades of an African-American jazz violinist and his relationships with white women in 1920s Germany. Because of its delineation of interracial relationships, even within a comedic context, the opera caused controversies in Europe and America. According to W. E. Yates, the Viennese premiere in 1927 "was the occasion of virulent objections by Austrian Nazis to allegedly malign Jewish and black influence, with a big anti-semitic protest meeting organized in a hall in the third district" (Yates 1996: 213). Jonathan O. Wipplinger notes that several conservative critics viewed the opera as the "triumph of black over white culture" (Wipplinger 2012: 246).

Lisa Barg (2000) discusses a different aspect of the color issue by way of Virgil Thomson's *Four Saints in Three Acts*, showing that Thomson's eclectic score and Stein's libretto have "no overt connection to themes associated with African American life and culture" (Barg 2000: 233). Yet the New York premiere (February 20, 1934) with an all-black cast has given it a special place in the history of opera. There are numerous interpretations of its possible meanings, from a compendium of nineteenth-century Americana (Baptist hymns, sentimental ballads, marches, etc.) to avant-garde musical language to Dadaism and postmodernism, and stylized tableaux that coexisted with African-American tropes of the 1920s.

Racism in Opera Productions and Performance

Significantly fewer investigations have been undertaken of the history of racism and its effects on the production and performance of opera during the past century and a half. Although this is a topic that has strongly affected the American opera scene until recently, only a few scholars have addressed the historical and social issues that limited the participation of African-American and Asian singers in opera companies until the 1950s. Most articles and books on African-American singers' attempts to join mainstream white opera companies do not approach the issue directly. Instead, through biographical narratives, readers must tease out the lack of opportunity that non-white opera singers faced in trying to establish a viable career. An important offshoot of that issue is the question of the value of "blind casting" and its effect on opera production in the twenty-first century. The remainder of this chapter will be devoted to exploring the lives of a select group of African-American and Asian singers, their individual encounters with operatic institutions, resources for further study, and relevant performance issues, including color-blind casting.

Resources

A key problem that researchers face when attempting to investigate the lives and careers of earlier African-American singers is the lack of primary sources; for most of the singers active in the nineteenth century, the information necessary to construct a chronology of their training, concerts, and the critical reception they received is, more often than not, anecdotal. Given this lack of primary source material, where does the researcher find information on these "invisible" performers, the venues in which they appeared, the music that they performed, and the qualities and ranges of their voices? Resources vary depending on the period under consideration. For the ante- and postbellum periods, when African-American singers were largely "invisible" to the majority population, for example, James M. Trotter's *Music and Some Highly Musical People* (1881) is an essential source. Newspapers, where they are still extant, can also provide the researcher with evidence of specific performances and repertory. Unfortunately, some conservative black newspapers did not report on cultural events because of their opposition to performances of secular music by African-Americans. For information on singers active during the late-nineteenth- and early-twentieth-century periods, Maud Cuney-Hare's *Negro Musicians and Their Music* (1936) is another key source. Many more newspapers from this period survive, such as the *New York Age* and *The Freeman*, which devote extensive columns to the burgeoning number of performers and performances, both popular and classical. Many later sources tend to reiterate the materials presented in Trotter and Cuney-Hare.

Antebellum Years

Although he evidently had access to many of the performers about whom he writes, Trotter's survey does not generally focus on the details of their careers. A good example of his approach is his narrative on Elizabeth Taylor Greenfield (d. 1876), perhaps the first African-American singer to appear in a public concert. Trotter states that she was born in 1809, but 1817 and 1824 have also been proposed. Each date has a different meaning for understanding her career. For example, there is documentary evidence that she was singing at private parties in the early 1840s, but if she had been born in 1824, she would have still been in her teens. On the other hand, if 1809 is correct, she would have been a mature artist.

In October 1851, Greenfield sang before the Buffalo Musical Association and then at a public concert. Over the next two years, as her reputation grew, Trotter notes that she was compared to Jenny Lind (1820–1887) and Teresa Parodi (1827–after 1878), and was referred to as the "Black Swan." (This type of sobriquet was given to many black singers of the nineteenth century, who were "honored" by comparisons to well-known singers.) Reviews from Greenfield's concerts (as reported in Trotter 1881: 73–78), indicate that she was a contralto, with a range of thirty-one notes, from G^2 to E^5. The reviews of her concerts are in general agreement:

> She has a voice of great sweetness and power [...] and her control of it is beyond example for a new and untaught voice. (*Buffalo Express* undated review, quoted in Trotter 1881: 72)
>
> [...] and we heard but one expression in regard to the new vocalist, and that was wonder and astonishment at the extraordinary power and compass of her voice, and the ease with which she passed from the highest to the lowest notes seemed without an effort. Her first notes of "Where are now the hopes I cherished?" ["In mia alfin tu sei" from Bellini's *Norma*] startled the whole audience, and the interchange of glances, succeeded by thunders of applause at the end of the first verse, showed that her success was complete. She was loudly encored, and in response sang the baritone, "When stars are in the quiet sky," [Edward Bulwer-Lytton] which took down the house. (Unidentified Buffalo newspaper, quoted in Trotter 1881: 73)

> She possesses a truly wonderful voice; and, considering the poverty of her advantages, she uses it with surprising taste and effect. In sweetness, power, compass, and flexibility, [her voice] nearly equals any of the foreign vocalists who have visited our country, and it needs only the training and education theirs have received to outstrip them all. (*The Daily State Register*, Albany, January 19, 1852, quoted in Trotter 1881: 75).

The critic for *The Globe* (Toronto, May 12–15, 1852) reflected the public's initial skepticism:

> Anyone who went to the concert of Miss Greenfield [...] expecting to find that he had been deceived by the puffs of the American newspapers, must have found himself most agreeably disappointed [...] [Greenfield] advanced calmly to the front of the platform.... There was a moment of pause, and the assembly anxiously listened for the first notes. They were quite sufficient. The amazing power of her voice, the flexibility, and the ease of execution, took the hearers by surprise; and the singer was hardly allowed to finish the verse, ere she was greeted with the most enthusiastic plaudits, which continued for some time. The higher passages of the air were given with clearness and fullness, indicating a soprano [*sic*] voice of great power. The song was encored; and Miss Greenfield came back, took her seat at the piano, and began, to the astonishment of the audience, a different air in a deep and very clear bass or baritone voice, which she maintained throughout, without any great appearance of effort, or without any breaking. She can, in fact, go as low as [the bass, Luigi] Lablache [1794–1858], and as high as [soprano] Jenny Lind [1820–1887]—a power of voice perfectly astonishing. It is said she can strike thirty-one full, clear notes; and we could readily believe it. (Trotter 1881: 77–78)

Following concerts in nearly all the free states, Greenfield traveled to England in 1853 to perfect her technique. According to Trotter, she sang in private concerts with British artists; many of these concerts were sung under the patronage of English royalty, including the Duchess of Sutherland, the Duchess of Norfolk, and the Earl and Countess of Shaftsbury. At an after-dinner concert at Stafford House, she sang two verses of "Old Folks at Home"—the first verse as a soprano and the second, most likely an octave lower, as a tenor. Trotter notes that the highlight of her trip was undoubtedly a command performance at Buckingham Palace on May 10, 1854, before Queen Victoria, accompanied by the eminent Sir George Smart. On her return to the United States, Greenfield continued to concertize from time to time, but devoted most of her time to teaching and occasionally producing concerts that, according to some sources, included operatic excerpts.

While Trotter's biography gives us somewhat more than a thumbnail sketch, he does not address questions concerning Greenfield's musical studies and repertory: Did she have any professional training in vocal techniques? Was the compass of her voice evenly produced, or did she have distinct register breaks? Based on the reviews of her singing, it is apparent that Greenfield had a natural voice that probably matured during her teens. Her lessons, given initially by her owner/mistress, in voice, piano, guitar, and Irish harp undoubtedly developed her musicianship. But it is not clear that she ever had lessons in vocal technique. While she was sent to England to "study," according to some of the sources, we do not yet know if she achieved that goal. It is unfortunate that the reviews Trotter reprints do not specify Greenfield's repertory in greater detail. From the few numbers mentioned earlier and several others, such as "I Know That My Redeemer Liveth" from *Messiah* and the "Cradle Song" by William Vincent Wallace (1814–1865), we can posit that she was *coached* on the standard classical pieces from opera and oratorio, as well as the popular ballads by American and British composers. In London, the sources note that she received some additional coaching from George Smart. It is doubtful that she was ever given the opportunity to learn an entire operatic role. A researcher can also deduce that she was probably subjected to intermittent racism during her stay in London. At one concert, Lord Shaftsbury felt the need to comment, "I consider the use of these halls for the encouragement of an outcast race, a *consecration*. This is the true use of wealth and splendor when it is employed to raise up and encourage the despised and forgotten" (Trotter 1881: 83). A thorough investigation of British and American papers would undoubtedly shed more light on how this African-American pioneer singer was received by the different social strata in America and Great Britain.

Soon after Greenfield settled in Philadelphia, she gave a concert with a young tenor, Thomas J. Bowers, who was introduced as her student although he had not studied with her. Bowers (1826–1885), the son of a church warden, had been musically trained along with his brother and sisters. His tenor voice was compared to that of Giovanni Mario di Candia (1810–1883), the famous Sardinian tenor, who toured the United States in 1854 with his wife, Giulia Grisi (1811–1869). Bowers and Greenfield were engaged by a Colonel Wood to embark on a concert tour of New York State and part of Canada. Bowers said his appearances as a concert singer were not so much to show off his voice as "to show to the world that colored men and women could sing classical music as well as the members of the other race by whom they had been so terribly vilified" (Trotter 1881: 134). The extent of his repertory has not been researched. Trotter mentions two arias: "Spirito gentil" from *La favorita*, and "How So Fair" ("M'appari") from Flotow's *Martha*. It is probable that he also sang duets, such as "Ah! I Have Sighed" ("Ah, che la morte ognora") from *Il trovatore* (also cited in Trotter 1881: 134), with Greenfield and later with his sister, the soprano Sarah Sedgwick [Bowers] (dates unknown), who founded the Sedgwick Concert Company. There has been no investigation of this company, its repertory, and the length of its existence.

The Luca family was also active during the antebellum period. Trotter notes that John C. Luca was born a free black in Milford, Connecticut, in 1805. A shoemaker by trade, he learned to read music at a local music school. After moving to New Haven, he married and had four sons, Simeon, John (Jr.), Cleveland, and Alexander. The family, including Mrs. Luca, a soprano, and later her sister, the soprano Diana Lewis, toured many of the Northern states and in 1859 joined with the Hutchinson Family Singers, a group of four performers—John, Asa, Judson, and Abby—for a series of interracial concerts. The Hutchinsons toured the United States and England in the 1840s and 1850s and took up various causes, such as abolitionism, women's rights, segregation of the races, and temperance (Hutchinson 1896). Given their known repertory, operatic excerpts were not programmed on these concerts. In the Luca family's own concerts, however, they are known to have performed a "Fantasia from Lucia," which may have included all or part of the tenor-baritone duet, "Qui del padre ancor respira." After the Civil war, the Luca family disbanded, though John Luca, Jr. (ca. 1832–1910) continued to sing as a member of the Hyers Sisters company, to be discussed below.

These African-American musical pioneers were important as role models for the next generation of classical performers. Performing for mixed audiences during the time of slavery, they were viewed by some as exotic, though reviews indicate that after they performed, at least some audience members accepted their ability to sing professionally. Touring black artists faced numerous problems with lodging and the rental of theaters or performing spaces, as well as segregation of the audience, even in Northern U.S. and Canadian cities. That they persevered in spite of the racism prevalent in the United States is a testament to their desire to demonstrate that African-Americans were capable of singing Western art music as well as sentimental and folk songs and spirituals. Further research into their performances of operatic excerpts is necessary before the extent of their repertories can be truly assessed.

Postbellum Years

After the Civil War, African-American performers were still viewed by the dominant white population as exotic and cultural novelties. A black minstrel troupe, the Georgia Minstrels, was formed before the 1870s; they toured the Northern states and ventured into the territories of the Midwest and the West. The Fisk Jubilee Singers, created to raise money for their college, concertized in the United States and England with great success. Another troupe, which included two sisters from California, together with a few other singers, formed the Hyers Sisters Concert Company. Our knowledge of the sisters' early life, recounted by Trotter, is sketchy; the elder, Anna Madah, was born in 1853, and the younger, Emma Louise, in 1855. Since they made a joint debut in 1867, when Emma was only twelve years old, their training as singers is not known. Did they study with their father? Did he teach them operatic excerpts? According to a review in the *San Francisco Chronicle*:

> Their musical power is acknowledged; and those who heard them last evening were unanimous in their praises, saying that rare natural gifts would insure for them a leading position among the prime donne of the age.
>
> Miss [Anna] Madah has a pure, sweet soprano voice, very true, even, and flexible, of remarkable compass and smoothness. Her rendition of "Casta Diva," [from Bellini's *Norma*] and her soprano in the tower scene from "Il Trovatore," and Verdi's "Forse e' lui che l'anima," [from *La traviata*] as also in the ballad, "The Rhine Maidens," [Henry Smart, "The Rhine Maiden"] was almost faultless, and thoroughly established her claims to the universal commendation she has received from all the connoisseurs in melody who have heard her.

> Miss [Emma] Louise is a natural wonder, being a fine alto-singer, and also the possessor of a pure tenor-voice. Her tenor is of wonderful range; and, in listening to her singing, it is difficult to believe that one is not hearing a talented young man instead of the voice of a young girl [. . .]. (quoted in Trotter 1881: 162–163)

That Anna was able to sing one of the most difficult arias of the soprano repertory, receiving a positive review from a white critic, is significant. A more thorough search of California newspapers could, perhaps, document more fully how these young singers were brought up. Trotter notes that after they had been taught by their parents (who appear to have been musically trained, though not professional musicians), the sisters were given Italian and German lessons, and studied voice with a German musician, Hugo Sank, and with the contralto Josephine d'Ormy, a Hungarian who had appeared as Maffio Orsini in Donizetti's *Lucrezia Borgia* at New York's Castle Garden with Jenny Lind.

In 1871, the teenage sisters embarked on a transcontinental tour, a highlight of which was their appearance at Patrick S. Gilmore's 1872 World Peace Jubilee in Boston, where they were well received. As is clear from the *Chronicle* review, from the beginning of their careers, the sisters were heard in operatic excerpts. In Salt Lake City, they performed portions of two scenes from the first and second acts of Donizetti's *Linda di Chamounix*: "Ah, tardai troppo, e al nostro favorito" and "Qui pria della partenza" (Act I, no. 4), and an excerpt from Act II. With their father, they also sang a trio, "The Magic-wove Scarf," from the English composer John Barnett's 1834 popular opera, *The Mountain Sylph,* which called for coloratura passages that "were delivered by [Anna] smoothly and distinctly." Also heard on the program were Count di Luna's aria "Brighter Than Stars Soft Gleaming" ("Il balen del suo sorriso") from *Il trovatore*, sung by Emma, and "See, 'Tis the Hour: How Sinks the Sun!" ("Regnava nel silenzio") from Donizetti's *Lucia di Lammermoor*, sung by Anna. With baritone John Luca, Jr. (1832–1910), and tenor Wallace King (ca. 1840–1903), they sang "Greeting to Spring," a vocal arrangement of Johann Strauss II's *Blue Danube* waltz. Reviewers everywhere, not least from *The Springfield Republican*, were impressed by the sisters' vocal talents:

> The voice of [Anna Hyers] is beautiful pure and liquid in its higher range; and she sings notes far above the staff with the utmost ease, where most sopranos gasp and shriek. So easily, indeed, does she sing them, that few persons are aware of the dizzy vocal heights which she scales. (Quoted in Trotter 1881: 176)

Because they were not able to appear with any of the white opera companies that traversed the country, beginning in 1876, and during the next fifteen years, the sisters traveled with their own company, the Hyers Sisters Concert Company, which was organized by their father. Although scholars have been able to trace some of their peregrinations, significant investigation is still needed to trace the length and breadth of the travels of these important African-American artists. During the early 1880s, they produced and performed in at least six plays with music, including *Out of Bondage*, by Joseph Bradford, a white Bostonian playwright, and E. S. Getchell's *Urlina, the African*

Princess (Graziano [2002] 2008). Though scholars know little about some of these musical plays, a few appear to have been centered on racial themes. In each of the shows for which programs have been discovered, we can document that they interpolated operatic arias and ensembles. During the late 1880s, the name of the company was changed to the Hyers Sisters Comic Opera Company, probably to reflect the repertory that they were performing, and they continued to travel across the country for another decade. Further studies of the Hyers sisters' contributions to the cultural history of nineteenth-century America are needed to determine the extent of their tours, the racial mix of their audiences, and the artistic and financial success of their efforts.

While the Hyers family was able to sustain a professional concert troupe successfully for almost two decades, another troupe, the Colored Opera Company, probably composed mostly of amateur singers, was organized in February 1873 as a way to raise funds for St. Augustine's Church, a black congregation in Washington, D.C. In an attempt to capitalize on the enormous popularity of Julius Eichberg's comic opera, *The Doctor of Alcantara* (1862, revised 1879), the Portuguese-American conductor and composer John Esputa (1832–1882) was chosen as the musical director. The singers, though probably not of the caliber of the Hyers, Luca, or Bowers families, were adequate for the demands of Eichberg's opera. Their choice of repertory gives evidence that soon after the Civil War, during Reconstruction, there was an educated community of free African-Americans who were able to plan and perform in a recent musical work of the white community for charity. They gave performances in Washington and Philadelphia, raised $75,000 for the church fund, and then disbanded.

Although the singers discussed above were known to the public at large, audiences, both black and white, still thought of them as exotic. Attendance at their performances served different purposes: Black audiences came to see African-Americans on the stage, even if they did not fully embrace opera and concert music. White audiences came to satisfy or reinforce their doubts that African-Americans had progressed beyond their "savage" origins—to check out if these alleged singers could actually perform these operatic arias and ensembles, sentimental songs, and parlor songs. If reviews are any indication of the white audiences' general skepticism, then one can begin to grasp the enormous difficulty black singers had to overcome to convince an audience of their artistry. For example, the Washington *Daily Chronicle* noted that for the performance of the Colored Opera Company, "[q]uite a third of the audience was composed of white ladies and gentlemen, largely attracted, perhaps, by the novelty of the affair" (quoted in Cuney-Hare [1936] 1974: 208).

During the 1880s, as Reconstruction was winding down and a small black middle class was developing, several female soloists came to prominence. The most prominent among them were Marie Smith [Williams] (1849–1937), Flora Batson Bergen (1864–1906), and Matilda S. Joyner Jones (1868–1933). While scholars have a general knowledge of Williams and Batson, there has been no detailed study of their lives and careers. A few biographical details are known. Smith was born in Natchez, Mississippi, but was taken to Cincinnati as an infant; after early studies with local teachers, she journeyed to San Francisco and Boston, where she was sponsored by the Boston socialite Mrs. Frances

Bailey Gaskin, and then went to London to study voice. She sometimes appeared with her husband, Sampson Williams, who was known as Signor Veloski, the Hawaiian tenor. Smith's renown was such that on November 13, 1878, at the age of twenty-nine, she gave a private concert for Rutherford B. Hayes and his guests in the Green Room of the White House, where her repertory included "Ernani, involami" (*Washington Post*, November 14, quoted in Haggard 2010: xl). A review in the *New York Times* of May 8, 1879, mentions, in conjunction with a recital given at Steinway Hall, that Smith, whose stage name was Selika—after the heroine of Meyerbeer's last opera, *L'Africaine*—"has come [...] from the West with the favorable notices of several prominent journals and of Messrs. Max and Maurice Strakosch." It continues,

> Mme. Selika has a voice of considerable power and of musical quality, and showed in her performance last evening that she has given study and attention to the art of singing... Her rendering of the *cabaletta* ["Sempre libera"] from "Traviata" was her best performance, to which she added in response to an encore "The Last Rose of Summer," which was well sung and deserved the applause it received. (Selika 1879)

Of her concert appearance in Paris during a European tour from 1882 to 1885, *Le Figaro*'s critic noted, "Marie Selika sang in great style. She has a very strong voice, of depth and compass, rising with perfect ease from C to C, and she trills like a feathered songster. Her range is marvelous and her execution and style of rendition show perfect cultivation. Her 'Echo Song' [by Carl Eckert] cannot be surpassed. It was beyond any criticism. It was an artistic triumph" (quoted in Cuney-Hare [1936] 1974: 223). In Berlin, the *Tageblatt* critic confirmed the opinions of his Parisian colleague, "after her first aria, she was twice recalled, and could quiet the wild applause only by rendering a selection with orchestral accompaniment... she is endowed with a voice of surpassing sweetness and extraordinary compass" (quoted in Cuney-Hare [1936] 1974: 223). In 1883, while studying in London, she gave a command performance for Queen Victoria. Further research into Selika's repertory, as well as the extent of her European tour, and when and where the Strakosches heard her, would begin to amplify the scattered comments that are now known.

An equivalent case can be made for Flora Batson, whose career was similar to Selika's. From the information available at the present, she appears to have had a range of more than three octaves, though it may have had a register split, since she was known as the "Double-Voiced Queen of Song." Flora Batson grew up in Providence, where she began her studies. She made her public debut as a teenager. Batson was the *prima donna* of the Bergen Star Concert Company, which was organized and managed by a white entrepreneur, John Bergen, who became her husband in 1887. Batson was known worldwide; on her three world tours, she sang before many royal heads of state, including Queen Victoria, Pope Leo XIII, the Royal Family of New Zealand, and Queen Liliuokalani of Hawaii. Although her main repertory consisted mainly of sentimental ballads and art songs, she also performed operatic excerpts. In spite of her worldwide fame, Batson gave many concerts at local churches in the black community across the country; she would be joined by local amateurs, who eagerly appeared with her before an audience of their friends and relatives. Further research on her career and audacious decision to travel in the United States with her white husband would significantly increase our understanding of white reaction to her marriage and to African-American social issues at the turn of the twentieth century.

Matilda S. Jones, known as Sissieretta (the "Black Patti"), has received the most attention among nineteenth-century African-American vocalists. I have surveyed her life, from her birth in Virginia to her progress as a star performer elsewhere (Graziano 2000), and will summarize here. Born in Virginia in 1868, Matilda Joyner moved with her mother to Providence as a child and studied music there. She married Richard Jones in 1884 and over the next four years embarked on a career that was unmatched by her black contemporaries. While black singers up to this time sang before mixed race audiences, Jones, who used Sissieretta as her given name and was known to the public by the sobriquet "Black Patti"—a reference to the most famous soprano of the second half of the nineteenth century, Adelina Patti—had an unparalleled career as a superstar in white venues. After a very successful eight-month concert tour to the Caribbean in a company of black singers, she was so well known to the Providence white community that she was asked in March 1889 to sing at a fundraising event organized by the city's Irish community to raise money for the defense of the Irish member of the British Parliament, Charles Stewart Parnell. After a year-long tour, managed by her husband, of several islands in the Caribbean as well as a few Central and South American countries, Jones was given a contract at $150 a week by the American Lecture and Musical Agency, owned by Major James B. Pond, to star with the white virtuoso cornetist, Jules Levy (1838–1903), and his band, in the Black Patti-Levy Concert Company. They appeared together in a variety of venues attended mostly by white audiences that often numbered in the thousands. During the summer of 1892, the Black Patti appeared at concerts in Saratoga Springs, New York, and Asbury Park, New Jersey. Her August 5 appearance in Saratoga attracted so many people that she was invited back for an additional three-day residency in the middle of the month, and yet another two-day engagement at the end of the month. The *Daily Saratogian* of August 16, 1892, commented:

> The interest manifested in the "Black Patti" was shown by the great crush of people who began pouring into the park an hour before the beginning of the concert. Both entrances were used and the rush did not cease for an hour and one half. Every chair, bench or seat of any kind, or anything that could be used as a seat was taken and still sixty percent of the people stood during the entire program [...] the pavilion [...] was surrounded on all sides by the crowd of between five and six thousand people who were attracted by the phenomenal singer they were anxious to hear. (Quoted in Graziano 2000: 571)

She was the first black performer to regularly tour with several otherwise all white ensembles; her appearance during the early 1890s as the soloist at a charity concert with Antonin Dvořák, in his arrangement of "Old Folks at Home" for soprano and tenor soloists—the latter part sung by the African-American Harry Burleigh (1866–1949)—and mixed chorus and orchestra—brought her to national attention. The concert was seen and positively reviewed in great detail by most of the New York critics. In addition to the Dvořák premiere, Jones also sang the "Inflammatus" from Rossini's *Stabat Mater*. On January 24, 1894 (10), the *New York Herald* reported:

> Mme. Jones was an enormous success with the audience. To those who had heard her for the first time she came in the light revelation, singing high C's with as little apparent effort as her namesake, the white [Adelina] Patti. (Quoted in Graziano 2000: 580)

After organizing another company in which she was the only black artist, Jones traveled to Europe, where she appeared in London, Paris, Milan, Copenhagen, St. Petersburg, Berlin, and other German cities. Before her trip to the "Old World," Jones studied various operatic arias with Louise Cappiani. She programmed such numbers as "Sempre libera" (*La traviata*), "Caro nome" (*Rigoletto*), and "Robert, toi que j'aime," from Meyerbeer's *Robert le diable*, as well as the "Lullaby" from Jacobowski's *Erminie*, Luigi Arditi's "Ecstasy," Sir Henry Bishop's "Bobolink" song, and Gounod's "Ariette" waltz (written for Adelina Patti), all virtuoso pieces that were programmed by prominent concert soloists of the period.

Early in 1896, in spite of her successful foray into the world of white concert giving, Jones decided to abandon that career trajectory to star in an all black company, the Black Patti Troubadours. In the troupe's minstrel/vaudeville/concert shows, she only appeared in the final segment, where she and other members of the cast sang—in appropriate costumes and with a variety of sets—opera and operetta excerpts from *Carmen*, Donizetti's *La fille du régiment*, the quartet from *Rigoletto*, the sextet from *Lucia di Lammermoor*, and the Act I one finale from John Philip Sousa's *El Capitan*. The Troubadours, a company of fifty, toured successfully for more than fifteen years, usually forty-four weeks each season; their travels took them to the Deep South, where they were one of the few black troupes to schedule performances, as well as on four transcontinental tours. They traveled in their own train coaches to deal with the problems of segregated hotels across the country.

Of all the African-American singers who were active before the turn of the twentieth century, Jones had the best chance of joining a white opera company. Although she probably never learned a complete role, her musical abilities were well schooled and she would have had little trouble, if any, in participating in a first-class white company. There was opportunity, however, for Jones to sing complete performances, though joining the African-American opera company organized by Theodore Drury (see below) would have meant giving up, at least for a month or so, her Troubadours salary, reputed to be $500 per week. While the second part of her career as the operatic star of an all-black variety show, has yet to be documented in detail, there is sufficient information about her early career to allow historians to begin to construct a contextual environment around it.

Additional research will give American historians a fuller picture of these three major artists, who found alternative ways to sustain successful careers in a segregated country where a lack of opportunity to perform with or join mainstream musical organizations limited their options. Unfortunately, although many singers were recorded at the beginning of the twentieth century, Sissieretta Jones and Selika Williams apparently were not invited to do so; thus, our knowledge is limited to the reviews that discuss the quality and extent of their voices (Brooks 2004).

The Twentieth Century

With the rise of a black middle class, and in spite of "Jim Crow" laws that were enacted in the late 1890s, African-American singers continued to pursue alternative careers in the performance of opera. The baritone Theodore Drury (ca. 1860s–1940s) was an important presence in these attempts. Although much more research into his company and career is necessary to provide a fuller picture of his efforts, a few facts are known. Drury, who attended the National Conservatory of Music in the 1890s when Dvořák was its head, first organized a company in 1889. A notice in the African-American newspaper *New York Age*, announces a performance of his company in an excerpt from *Il trovatore* at Clarendon Hall in Manhattan. This company was not financially successful; in 1900, he formed a new company, which presented complete operas with an orchestra. A racist review in the *New York Times* (May 29, 1906) regarded a performance of *Aida* with great irony. After a condescending description of the various segments of the mostly black audience—"In the rear of the house there was a large gathering of serious-faced negro men who were dressed in the height of fashion. They wore red fezes, on the fronts of which were emblazoned in gold the design of a secret society. They marched into the house in a body"—the reviewer, quoting a member of the audience, comments on the differences in color of the performers who were chosen to portray the Ethiopians (light in color) and the Egyptians (much darker), with "one or two exceptions." He then dismisses the inadequacy of the scenery in Act III (there is no mention of the scenery in the other acts). When he finally discusses the performers, once again he is descriptive of their physical appearance. Mme. Estelle Clough (ca. 1860s–1930s), who sang Aida, was "short and stout," her Radames (James Wortham) "short and very stout," Amneris (the white contralto Genevieve Motley) "a tall, lithe figure" and a foot taller than her father, the King. Drury sang the part of Amonasro, whose "skillful rolling of the whites of his eyes when made a captive showed admirably his state of mind [...]. [H]e made a figure that aroused the deep sympathy of the audience for his captive state." Only one passing reference is made to the performance itself; the reviewer notes that Clough "frequently won applause with her high notes, her eyes being fixed at such times upon the [white] Director, Eugene Salvatore." In spite of the negativity of the white press, Drury's company continued intermittently at least through the 1920s, though the details of the operas performed, the cities and theaters in which they appeared, and the singers he hired still need to be researched.

While racial discrimination and prejudice were prevalent in the United States through much of the first half of the twentieth century, several African-American singers, mostly women, had more opportunities to perform with white companies—in Europe. African-American males had less success with white companies both here and abroad; a few of the more famous performers, such as the bass Paul Robeson (1898–1976) and the tenor Roland Hayes (1887–1977), have received scholarly attention (see Robeson, Jr. 2001, 2010; Hayden 1989). For Todd Duncan (1903–1998), who is known primarily as the first portrayer of Porgy in Gershwin's *Porgy and Bess*, and who was the first African-American opera singer to join a white company (the New York City Opera) in 1945, no full-length biography exists, though his papers are available for scholarly research at the University of Michigan's Bentley Historical Library. Jules Bledsoe (1897–1943), who created the role of Joe in Jerome Kern's *Show Boat*, appeared with a number of white opera companies during the 1930s, in both the United States and Europe. In addition to singing the role of Amonasro with companies in Cleveland and Chicago, he sang the title role in the 1934 European premiere in Amsterdam of Louis Gruenberg's *The Emperor Jones*, which he repeated in other European cities (Cuney-Hare [1936] 1974: 360–361), and the title role in Musorgsky's *Boris Godunov* (Nettles 2003: 16). An examination of the reviews of his historic performances with white companies, especially in the European performances of *The Emperor Jones*, as well as the remainder of his abbreviated career on Broadway and in film, is lacking.

Many recent specialized studies of African-American female singers have brief surveys of these otherwise unknown performers (see Smith 1994; Story 1986). Similarly, the careers of Lillian Evanti (née Evans) (1890–1967) and Catarina Jarboro (Katherine Lee Yarborough) (1903–1986), for example, are outlined in Hill and Hatch 2003, but there is little detail on the reception of their performances, on their repertory, and on the extent of their careers in the context of the operatic scene of the 1920s and 1930s. For example, Hill and Hatch note that Evanti "reportedly knew some twenty-four operas" (181), but this information has not been expanded upon. Aside from the title role in *Lakmé*, which, as the first African-American to sing with a European company, she performed in Nice (in 1927) and Paris, and Violetta in *La traviata*, which she sang with several European companies and with the National Negro Opera Company in Washington, D.C. (her only performances of a complete staged opera in the United States), our knowledge of the rest of her career is virtually nonexistent. According to one source (Logan and Winston 1982), she auditioned for the Metropolitan Opera in 1932, but was not asked to join the company. Further study of her life is needed to illuminate both the triumphs and challenges she faced in the course of her career.

Jarboro, who appeared as a member of the chorus of Sissle and Blake's *Shuffle Along* (1921) when she was still in her teens, studied voice in New York and traveled to Europe in 1926 to continue her education. She made her debut as Aida at the Puccini Theater in Milan in 1930, and then appeared at still undetermined opera houses in other European cities. In 1932, when she returned to the United States, she again sang Aida, during the final season of the Chicago Civic Opera, and then appeared as Selika at the New York Hippodrome. In the fall of 1933, Jarboro became the first African-American woman to sing a complete opera, Meyerbeer's *L'Africaine*, probably in the Italian version, in an otherwise all-white company run by the innovative impresario Alfredo Salmaggi (1886–1975). Unable to secure other contracts in the United States, Jarboro returned to Europe. In a tantalizing article in the *California Eagle*, an African-American newspaper, the composer William Grant Still reports that, after returning from a concert tour in Lithuania, Jarboro

> found awaiting her numerous contracts—one of them a formal request for her to sing the role of "Tosca" [...] A report from the Brussels performance of [Carl Goldmark's] "The Queen of Sheba" at the Theatre de la Monnaie [...] states "We have saved for last the excellence of the interpretation. Mme. Jarboro is, it goes without saying, the heroine of the composition: a veritable reincarnation of the celebrated sovereign whose queenly ardors were a little savage, and yet like those of the eternal woman. It was not the first time that the public of Brussels has applauded this woman's wonderful artistry, her rich voice and her dramatic instinct." (Still 1937: 5)

Jarboro returned to the United States in 1941 at the start of World War II. Her European, as well as her later American, career still needs to be documented; she is an important link in the process that led to the opportunities given to the following generation of African-American singers. Following Marian Anderson's long anticipated and overdue debut at the Metropolitan Opera as Ulrica in *Un ballo in maschera* (January 7, 1955), Rudolf Bing capitalized on his artistic and sociocultural success by engaging two young African-American sopranos. In 1956, Mattiwilda Dobbs (b. 1925) was the first black artist to be offered a long-term (eight-year) contract. A coloratura soprano, she sang the roles of Zerbinetta (*Ariadne auf Naxos*), Zerlina (*Don Giovanni*), Olympia (*Les contes d'Hoffmann*), Lucia (*Lucia di Lammermoor*), and Oscar (*Un ballo in maschera*). In 1958, Gloria Davy (1931–2012) joined the company; she became the Met's first black Aida. During the following three seasons, she was heard as Pamina (*Die Zauberflöte*), Nedda (*Pagliacci*), and Leonora (*Il trovatore*). To some extent, their ground-breaking presence in the company was overshadowed by the enormous success of Leontyne Price, whose debut in January 1961 with tenor Franco Corelli in *Il trovatore* signaled the wide acceptance of African-American singers in American opera companies.

Asian Singers

Asian singers during the first half of the twentieth century faced different issues in trying to join white companies. Discrimination against Asians by white companies has been tied to the lack of knowledge and singing techniques that may differ from those in the West. Tamaki Miura (1884–1946) was a pioneer who studied Western art music, and sang, in 1915, with Vladimir Rosing's company in London and with the San Carlo Opera Company in the United States; she was limited, however, to such roles as Cio-Cio-San in *Madame Butterfly*, and the title roles in *Iris* (1898) by Mascagni and *Madame Chrysanthème* (1893) by André Messager. The history of her vicissitudes, as well as of those Asian singers who followed in her footsteps, has been documented by Mari Yoshihara (2007).

In spite of the progress that has taken place during the past half century, racism in opera is still present, though not to the same extent as earlier. As Yoshihara notes,

> Most roles in the standard opera repertoire are white, and in the cultural climate in which white performers playing non-white roles have been hailed for their ability to bridge the cultural gap through their artistry whereas non-white performers playing white roles were often seen as unbelievable. (Yoshihara 2007: 210)

In 1981, Leona Mitchell noted that "there is prejudice against Black *men*, tenors especially—the lovemaking parts where Black men really get close to White women. This disturbs some people" (Heymont 1981: 33). It was noted once more by Harolyn Blackwell ten years later: "It's still considered a risk today to cast Black males in romantic roles" (Ebony 1991: 76). Some discussion revolves around the concept of what might be acceptable as "dramatically credible" when the romantic leads are of different races. The African-American tenor George Shirley has raised the issue several times, at a 1978 meeting of the Central Opera Service's National Conference, and in two later interviews. In 1990, in a wide-ranging discussion with Wallace Cheatham, he posits three reasons why black males singers may have difficulty in reaching "superstar status":power between singer and manager of different races; acceptance of black males in traditional romantic roles opposite white females; and the black performer's physical looks (the darker in complexion the performer, the more difficult it is for whites to accept that person in costume and makeup playing a 'white role,' such as Rodolfo or Des Grieux. There is less of a problem with white artists playing ethnic personalities: Aida, Otello, or Cio-Cio-San) (Cheatham and Shirley 1990: 102). Amplifying on this last point, Shirley responds to those who complain that blacks or Asians should not play white roles: "But if you want people to *look* the part, that means you can't hire an Italian tenor to do 'Othello' because he doesn't look the part. That means if you do 'Aida' you can't hire a White soprano because she's not Ethiopian" (Heymont 1981: 33; see also Shirley 2012). More recently, Lawrence Brownlee has commented on this same issue in several interviews, noting that while he feels very fortunate in his career, race undoubtedly interfered with his being hired. He does say, however, that he believes things are changing (Brownlee 2012). Asian singers face some of the same problems: in a recent *New York Times* interview (February 20, 2011), the Korean bass Kwangchul Youn notes that "[i]t takes courage to cast a short Korean in parts [King Marke in Wagner's *Tristan und Isolde*] where people expect a tall, blond European" (Gurewitsch 2011).

In 1981 Leontyne Price described her feelings after Rudolf Bing chose her to star in the opening production at the new Metropolitan Opera house: "I was never so reminded that I was Black as I was during this particular responsibility. There were crank calls, anonymous letters, threats of bombing. I don't think anybody else would have stood what I did to open that house [...]. To people in the music business it was a plum; it was the greatest honor for any living singer. But I really paid for the responsibility and the honor—paid in full" (Heymont 1981: 33). Ten years later, however, *Ebony* celebrated the superstar status of Jessye Norman in opera houses around the world, and praised the general public's acceptance of "about 20 Black American women [who] are recognized throughout the world as being among the finest classical singers of the day" (Ebony 1991: 76).

Blind Casting

Blind casting in traditional productions is another option for opera companies and directors to pursue. The recent production of Rossini's *Armida* at the Metropolitan opera with Lawrence Brownlee in the role of Rinaldo is an example of such casting. But in operas where race portrayal is intrinsic to the plot, such an approach can be problematic. A company that chooses to cast the roles of Otello and Iago with a white and black singer, respectively, in a traditional production without special makeup, would undoubtedly face a "credibility" issue, both with audiences and, especially, in the press.

While *Otello* falls into a somewhat ambiguous category in that there are only a few tenors at any given time who are capable of singing the title role, some operas *require* racial casting. One cannot, for example, imagine a performance of *Porgy and Bess* with a white cast, or even a white performer in one of the starring roles. A small but significant number of twentieth-century operas likewise fall into this category, including Scott Joplin's *Treemonisha* (1914); Louis Gruenberg's *The Emperor Jones* (1933); Clarence Cameron White's *Ouanga* (1934); William Grant Still's *Troubled Island* (1939); T. J. Anderson's *Soldier Boy, Soldier* (1982); and Anthony Davis's *The Life and Times of Malcolm X* (1986) and *Amistad* (1997). Yet that casting concept has not yet been fully addressed in operas that portray Asian characters; at the recent premiere of Tan Dun's *The First Emperor* (2011), for example, though some of the roles were sung by Asians, the role of Emperor Qin was sung by Plácido Domingo.

In an earlier time, when opera was seen primarily in the opera house, the use of makeup and lighting generally blurred the racial identities of singers; audiences at these live performances, even when opera glasses were utilized, were generally too far away from the performers to see them clearly (for more on the contemporary opera scene, see Tommasini 2012). Today, with the advent of DVDs and HD broadcasts in theaters, the close-ups that audiences see do not allow the masking of the races of cast members. Perhaps the issue of race and racism, which has so long been an unspoken part of opera performances in the United States and elsewhere, has been resolved by technological advances and a more tolerant society. The racism that pervaded American culture through the nineteenth and first half of the twentieth centuries has been eliminated in opera houses, but it remains to be seen how the issues raised by blind casting will be answered over the next few decades.

See also: Exoticism, Religion, Gender

Bibliography

André, Naomi. 2012. "From Otello to Porgy: Blackness, Masculinity, and Morality in Opera." In André et al. 2012, 11–31.

——, Karen M. Bryan, and Eric Saylor, eds. 2012. *Blackness in Opera*. Urbana: University of Illinois Press.

Barg, Lisa. 2000. "Black Voices/White Sounds: Race and Representation in Virgil Thomson's *Four Saints in Three Acts*." *American Music* 18/2: 121–161.

Botstein, Leon. 2009. "German Jews and Wagner." In *Richard Wagner and His World*, edited by Thomas S. Grey, 151–200. Princeton, NJ: Princeton University Press.

Brooks, Tim. 2004. *Lost Sounds: Blacks and the Birth of the Recording Industry 1890–1919*. Urbana: University of Illinois Press.

Brownlee, Lawrence. 2010. "An Interview with Lawrence Brownlee: The American Tenor Talks by email to Margarida Mota-Bull." Online. Available:http://www.musicweb-international.com/SandH/2010/Jan-Jun10/brownlee_interview.htm (accessed August 7, 2012).

Cheatham, Wallace, and George Shirley 1990. "Conversation with George Shirley: A Renowned Divo Speaks." *The Black Perspective in Music* 18/1–2: 141–178.

Chybowski, Julia J. 2014. "Becoming the 'Black Swan' in Mid-Nineteenth-Century America: Elizabeth Taylor Greenfield's Early Life and Debut Concert Tour." *Journal of the American Musicological Society* 67/1: 125–165.

Cuney-Hare, Maud. [1936] 1974. *Negro Musicians and Their Music*. New York: Da Capo Press.

Ebony. 1991. "The Age of the Black Diva." [unsigned essay]. *Ebony* 46/10: 74, 76.

Foner, Philip S. 1978. *Paul Robeson Speaks: Writings, Speeches, Interviews, 1918–1974*. Larchmont, NY: Brunner/Mazel.

Foster, Mel. 2002. "The African American Operatic Tenor: Coping with Discrimination." *Journal of Singing* 58: 203–214.

Graziano, John. [2002] 2008. "Images of African Americans: African-American Musical Theatre, *Show Boat* and *Porgy and Bess*. In *The Cambridge Companion to the Musical*. 2nd ed., edited by William A. Everett and Paul R. Laird, 89–102. Cambridge: Cambridge University Press.

——. 2000. "The Early Life and Career of the 'Black Patti': The Odyssey of an African American Singer in the Late Nineteenth Century." *Journal of the American Musicological Society* 53/3: 543–596.

Gurewitsch, Matthew. 2011. "Standing Small, Singing Big, All Sulfur and Zest." *New York Times*. February 7, 2011. Online. Available: http://www.nytimes.com/2011/02/20/arts/music/20youn.html?_r=1 (accessed August 7, 2012).

Haggard, Dixie Ray, ed. 2010. *African Americans in the Nineteenth Century: People and Perspectives*. Santa Barbara, CA: ABC-CLIO, LLC.

Hallman, Diana R. 2002. *Opera, Liberalism, and Antisemitism in Nineteenth-Century France: The Politics of Halevy's 'La Juive.'* Cambridge: Cambridge University Press.

Hayden, Robert C. 1995. *Singing for All People: Roland Hayes, A Biography*. Boston: Select Publications.

Heymont, George. 1981. "Blacks in Opera." *Ebony* 37/1: 32–36.

Hill, Errol G., and James V. Hatch. 2003. *A History of African American Theatre*. Cambridge: Cambridge University Press

___. 1993. "The Hyers Sisters: Pioneers in Black Musical Comedy." In *The American Stage: Social and Economic Issues from the Colonial Period to the Present*, edited by Ron Engle and Tice L. Miller, 115–130. Cambridge: Cambridge University Press..

Hutchinson, John Wallace. 1896. *Story of the Hutchinsons (Tribe of Jesse)*. Boston: Lee and Shepard.

Lee, Maureen D. 2012. *Sissieretta Jones: The Greatest Singer of Her Race, 1868–1933*. Columbia: University of South Carolina Press.

Levin, David J. 1996. "Reading Beckmesser Reading: Antisemitism and Aesthetic Practice in *The Mastersingers of Nuremberg*." *New German Critique* 23/3: 127–146.

Locke, Ralph P. 2009. *Musical Exoticism: Images and Reflections*. Cambridge: Cambridge University Press.

Logan, Rayford Whittingham, and Michael R. Winston. 1982. *Dictionary of American Negro Biography*. New York: W. W. Norton.

Merriam-Webster. 2012. "Race" and "Racism." Online. Available: http://www.merriam-webster.com/dictionary/race http://www.merriam-webster.com/dictionary/racism (accessed August 6, 2012).

Millington, Barry. 1992. "*Meistersinger von Nürnberg, Die*." In *The New Grove Dictionary of Opera. Grove Music Online. Oxford Music Online*/Available: http://www.oxfordmusiconline.com/subscriber/article/grove/music/O003512 (accessed August 6, 2012).

——. 1991. "Nuremberg Trial: Is There Anti-semitism in *Die Meistersinger*?" *Cambridge Opera Journal* 3/3: 247–360.

Murphy, Kerry R. 2001. "Meyerbeer, Judaism and French Music Criticism of the 1830s." *Context* 22: 1–18.

Nettles, Darryl Glenn. 2003. *African American Concert Singers before 1950*. Jefferson, NC: McFarland.

Pisani, Michael V. 2005. *Imagining Native America in Music*. New Haven: Yale University Press.

Robeson, Paul, Jr. 2010. *The Undiscovered Paul Robeson, Quest for Freedom, 1939–1976*. New York: Wiley.

——. 2001. *The Undiscovered Paul Robeson, An Artist's Journey, 1898–1939*. New York: Wiley.

Rose, Paul Lawrence. 1996. *Wagner: Race and Revolution*. New Haven: Yale University Press.

Rushton, Julian. 1992. "*Zauberflöte, Die*." In *The New Grove Dictionary of Opera. Grove Music Online. Oxford Music Online*. Available: http://www.oxfordmusiconline.com/subscriber/article/grove/music/O907810 (accessed August 6, 2012).

Saylor, Eric. 2012. "Race, 'Realism,' and Fate in Frederick Delius's *Koanga*." In André et al. 2012, 78–100.

Selika. 1879. "Amusements; Mme Selika's Concert." *New York Times* (May 8). Online. Available: http://query.nytimes.com/mem/archive-ree/pdf?res=F30A11FF385A137B93CA A9178ED85F4D8784F9 (accessed August 7, 2012).

Shirley, George 2012. "Il Rodolfo Nero, or The Masque of Blackness." In André et al. 2012, 260–274.

Smith, Eric Ledell 1994. *Blacks in Opera: An Encyclopedia of People and Companies, 1873–1993*. Jefferson, NC: McFarland.

Still, William Grant. 1937. "Jarboro Asked to Sing Role of Tosca in Italy." *The California Eagle* (November 11): 5.

Story, Rosalyn M. 1986. *And So I Sing: African American Divas of Opera and Concert*. Westport, CT: Greenwood Press.

Tommasini, Anthony. 2012. "Colorblind Casting Widens Opera's Options." *New York Times* (December 21). Online. Available: http://www.nytimes.com/2012/12/23/arts/music/operas-colorblind-casting-at-glimmerglass-and-the-met.html?pagewanted=all&_r=0 (accessed May 25, 2013).

Trotter, James M. 1878. *Music and Some Highly Musical People*. Boston: Lee and Shepard.

Vaget, Hans Rudolf. 1995. "Sixtus Beckmesser—A 'Jew in the Brambles'"? *Opera Quarterly* 12/1: 35–45.

Weiner, Marc A. 1997. *Wagner and the Anti-Semitic Imagination*. Lincoln: University of Nebraska Press.

Wipplinger, Jonathan O. 2012. "Performing Race in Ernst Krenek's *Jonny spielt auf*." In André et al. 2012, 236–259.

Yates, W. E. 1996. *Theatre in Vienna: A Critical History, 1776–1995*. Cambridge: Cambridge University Press.

Yoshihara, Mari. 2007. *Musicians from a Different Shore: Asians and Asian-Americans in Classical Music*. Philadelphia: Temple University Press.

CHAPTER 35

GENDER

ALEXANDRA WILSON

Gender Studies in Opera: From Characterization to Reception

The impact of literary feminism upon the nascent New Musicology of the 1980s led scholars in the first instance to an exploration of the representation of women in operas—female characters as constructed musically and dramatically, for the most part, by men. The provocative and still widely read work of Catherine Clément (1989) uncovered patriarchal agendas encoded in much-loved operas to which the beauty of the music supposedly deafens us: the core tragic nineteenth-century repertory offered particularly rich pickings in this regard. But Clément's thesis was widely critiqued for functioning purely at the level of plot and for ignoring the power granted to women on the operatic stage by their vocal virtuosity. Musicologists responded by grappling with the thorny question, in Mary Ann Smart's words, of "how to draw operatic *music* into feminist interpretation" (Smart 2000: 5), exploring ever more subtle ways of analyzing the potent contribution of music, words, gesture, body, costume, and staging to the depiction of gender on the operatic stage.

The results—imaginative, often celebratory, and spanning an ever increasing range of repertories—illuminate the fact that gender studies in opera is much more than a monolithic account of the fantasized suppression of women by male composers. Wendy Heller, in her study of the operatic mythologization of "exceptional women" in seventeenth-century Venice (2003), and Bonnie Gordon (2004), in her discussion of the ways in which the female performers of Monteverdi's operas used their voices and bodies as vehicles through which to express their "unruliness," both reveal the operatic sphere as a liberated realm for women at moments in history when their freedoms were otherwise heavily circumscribed. Carolyn Abbate, in her contribution to Ruth Solie's pioneering *Musicology and Difference*, has also contested the archetype of the tormented nineteenth-century opera heroine, reading opera as an unusual art form that has empowered women by defying the "conventional opposition of male (speaking) subject and female (observed) object" (1993: 228–229).

Opera is also a particularly rich medium through which to consider the socially constructed, inherently performative nature of gender itself. Throughout its history the art form has repeatedly challenged received notions of "masculinity" and "femininity," notably through character types such as the travesty role (see Blackmer and Smith 1995). Conventional modern gender models are particularly inadequate for the consideration of operatic repertories and performing traditions that pre-date the nineteenth century, as evidenced by the extensive work on the castrato, a figure whom Roger Freitas (2009) positions as occupying an "eroticized middle ground" in his detailed case study exploring the career of an individual singer of the seventeenth century. But what we might call "blurred" gender types also lived on in later repertories: Naomi André (2006), for instance, has opened our eyes to the existence of a range of "hybrid" female voice types in early nineteenth-century Italian opera that maintained "heroic" stylistic characteristics previously associated with the castrati.

It will be apparent from such diverse examples that the field today encompasses a vast range of topics, including not only musical constructions of gender on the operatic stage, but performance and reception issues, opera's contribution to wider social debates, its voicing of political messages, and its uses as a didactic tool. Opera studies has drawn fruitfully in its methodologies from the broader field of feminist music criticism, notably the groundbreaking work by Marcia J. Citron (1993) on the musical canon and Susan McClary (1991) on the musical semiotics of gender, gendered metaphors in music theory and musical narrative (whether in texted or non-texted music), and the gendered discourses that surround musical performers. Other disciplines, moreover, including sociology, film studies, anthropology, literary theory, and even the sciences, have contributed much in terms of theoretical richness to the field. Linda and Michael Hutcheon (2000), for instance, have drawn upon their perspectives as, respectively, a literary theorist and a medical doctor in order to explore the impact of the body—physical health, size, norms of beauty—on the singer's performance, the physicality of our responses to opera, and the expression of bodily preoccupations within the operatic repertory itself. And while the literature on women in opera still dominates the field to date, scholars are increasingly turning their attention to operatic masculinities (see, for example, Brett 2006; Henson 2007; and Purvis 2013), as we begin to comprehend that there is no more one fixed model of operatic masculinity than there is of operatic femininity.

Performance studies relating to gender now range across a wide variety of topics, from voice types to the intersection of voice and body. Historians have explored the training and career patterns of singers from the past, both well known and long forgotten, examining not only how they sang (and in so doing often made a vital contribution to the creation of operatic texts), but how they acted, and even their gestures, facial mannerisms, and style of dress. Susan Rutherford (2006) has addressed such questions with the aim of rescuing prima donnas from the typically sensationalist hype that surrounds them as a collective entity. The marketing mechanisms used to promote singers and the ways in which they have shaped their own public image have also been the subject of recent scrutiny, together with their representation in literature and on screen, their place within broader celebrity culture, and the transformation of their role in the age of recording (Cowgill and Poriss 2012; Grover-Friedlander 2005).

Subjective responses inflected by gender and sexuality to particular singers and performances have also attracted scholars' attention, opening up a rich terrain of investigation that intersects with interdisciplinary theories of fandom and stardom and with queer theory. Some of the literature in this area has adopted an intensely personal approach while simultaneously illuminating a set of global questions. Terry Castle (1995), for instance, uses her self-professed "infatuation" with Brigitte Fassbaender as a point of entry for a broader discussion of the phenomenon of diva-worship in historical context and the erotic appeal of operatic voices. This latter point is discussed more extensively by Wayne Koestenbaum in *The Queen's Throat* (1993), in which he explores his own sexuality by analyzing his operatic preferences and fantasies, at the same time finding analogies between singing and sexuality.

Questions of "masculinity" and "femininity" have also coalesced in unexpected ways under the broad umbrella of opera reception studies. Reception historians are increasingly attentive to the impact of gendered concerns and subjectivities upon responses to opera past and present, and here gender becomes inseparable from other social concerns. Gender has frequently been used as a political weapon, a particularly sharp blade in the critic's toolbox, employed with varying degrees of violence to denigrate singers, works, or entire repertories—even the very genre of opera itself. Femininity has historically all too often been routinely positioned as masculinity's negative Other, in opera criticism as in so many areas of cultural life, as critics demean male composers by labeling their music "feminine" or "effeminate."

As I have discussed elsewhere (Wilson 2007b), Giacomo Puccini, notably, fell victim to such an attack with the publication in 1912 of a book entitled *Giacomo Puccini e l'opera internazionale*, whose author, Fausto Torrefranca, sought to undermine Puccini's status as Italy's preeminent national composer. Torrefranca's insults took inspiration from a plethora of generalized nineteenth-century and *fin-de-siècle* clichés about female creativity, and more specifically the misogynistic ideas of such writers as Pierre-Joseph Proudhon, Otto Weininger, Cesare Lombroso, and Paolo Mantegazza, in such a way as to depict the composer's music as weak, derivative, and decadent. Torrefranca's line of reasoning was a deliberate inversion of the exaggerated celebratory rhetoric of heroic masculinity that had been applied to Puccini by his supporters, which positioned him variously as a classical statue, an athlete, a warrior, and the descendant of an ancient race.

Yet Torrefranca expressed disdain for the genre in which Puccini wrote as much as for the man himself, castigating popular Italian opera as decadent and effete. That an Italian critic should attack his own nation's school of opera in such terms may seem surprising, but Torrefranca wanted to reinvent Italian music via a two-pronged approach—by reviving early Italian instrumental music on the one hand, and acting as an advocate of contemporary, modernist Italian music on the other. Here we can see an interesting parallel with the gendering of various other, non-operatic musical genres. As Jeffrey Kallberg (1996) has demonstrated, Chopin's contemporaries labeled him as "effeminate" merely by dint of the fact that he specialized in small-scale piano works intended for performance in intimate domestic settings, which were often performed by women.

Perhaps unsurprisingly, the impulse to characterize opera in negative gendered terms has tended to be particularly pronounced in nations whose relationship with the art form has been complex. The remainder of this chapter will form a case study of the convergence of opera, politics, and gendered rhetoric in one such nation, Britain, at a fascinating yet often neglected moment in its musical history. Opera promoted considerable anxiety in early-twentieth-century Britain, both among members of the musical establishment and the population at large. During the interwar period, long-standing arguments intensified in the pages of the press about whether opera ought to be performed in English, about the training and careers of British opera singers, and about the prospect of government subsidy for opera. Furthermore, new operatic problems presented themselves at this time: about how—indeed whether—opera ought to be broadcast, and how it ought to be categorized according to new cultural classifications that were emerging in the 1920s. Underpinning all of these questions about performance, dissemination, funding, and cultural status, however, was a more fundamental and enduring public debate about whether Britain was constitutionally "an operatic nation" at all, and this was where gendered rhetorics could be fruitfully invoked.

Such tactics were often highly defensive in motivation. Gender, opera, and politics converged bluntly, for instance, in a 1911 book entitled *Music and Nationalism* by Cecil Forsyth, a staunch advocate of English opera. Forsyth sought to account for England's relatively weak indigenous operatic tradition in past centuries via implicit gendered criticism of more operatically productive nations. The English, Forsyth argued, had been historically poor at writing operas but good at fighting wars; the reverse, he claimed, applied to the Italians. The slight upon Italians' masculinity was barely disguised. A decade and a half later, however, the British conductor Thomas Beecham adopted a very different gendered strategy—one that is more interesting than Forsyth's xenophobic knee-jerk reaction. Rather than "feminizing" opera in an attempt to justify Britain's lack of prominence in the genre, Beecham conversely sought to "masculinize" the art form so as to promote opera to the British people. Here I shall focus in detail upon Beecham's late 1920s "Imperial League of Opera" and its symbolically titled journal, *MILO* (Member of the Imperial League of Opera), placing them into their wider cultural contexts in order to demonstrate how opera became enmeshed in extra-musical debates wherein gender was inextricably bound up with concerns of imperialism and national identity.

The Imperial League of Opera and Its Contexts

During the years following World War I, many members of the British musical establishment believed London to have lost its lead as an international operatic center. A number of nationalistically inspired initiatives were therefore launched to promote opera, either through theatrical performance or recordings. Particularly significant was the foundation in 1927 by the conductor Thomas Beecham of the grandly titled "Imperial League of Opera." The League was conceived as a financial venture to put British operatic performance on a firmer footing; nevertheless, its motivations were also ideological. Beecham and his circle wanted to build an audience for opera, believing that the art form could "improve" people, that it offered the key to creating a civilized society, and that it had a role to play in supporting the by then waning British imperial "mission."

This case study explores what the language used by opera propagandists of the inter-war period can tell us about early-twentieth-century Britons' complicated relationship with the operatic art form. In *MILO*, opera became part of a nexus of ideas about masculinity, militarism, classicism, imperialism, physical strength, national vigor, and civilization. The strategy Beecham was employing in order to advance opera's cause was to rescue it from the sorts of "feminine" clichés evoked by Forsyth. The promotion of opera by the League was thus framed explicitly as a military campaign, and one being waged on two fronts: against Britain's foreign cultural rivals (predominantly Germany but increasingly the United States) on the one hand, and against perceived British philistinism on the other.

Before turning in detail to the highly charged gendered rhetoric surrounding the Imperial League of Opera, some historical context seems necessary in order to illuminate why the need for an opera propaganda machine in early-twentieth-century Britain was so acute. During the later Victorian period, opera had been enjoyed in Britain by members of all classes, thanks to performances by touring opera companies and excerpts played by brass bands and in music halls. In the early decades of the twentieth century, however, opera's patterns of dissemination began to change. Competing leisure activities—cinema, spectator sports, operetta—tempted away a portion of the audience, while opportunities to encounter live opera diminished, most notably due to the decline of the touring opera companies (Russell 1997: 81, 230, 294–295).

Moreover, opera's social signification also began to change in the early decades of the twentieth century. During the 1920s in particular, a stricter codification of the distinction between "high" and "low" culture was beginning to be conceived, as intellectual elites strove to defend their position as guardians of culture in the face of the accelerating expansion of mass entertainment. Opera's place in such discussions was a vexed one. It could certainly not be straightforwardly labeled as "high" culture, and many members of the musical establishment were quick to dismiss it as a bastardized art form that one critic described as "only completely satisfactory to undeveloped artistic tastes" (Salmon 1920: 520). Nevertheless, opera in Britain indisputably underwent a certain repositioning as "art" during this period as its "entertainment" status declined—mirroring similar developments in the United States (see Levine 1988)—and with this shift came gendered implications. The operatic institutions that remained most visible were those such as Covent Garden, which catered to an elite audience largely perceived by the general public as effete, whereas the most "manly" dissemination of operatic music—through the brass band repertory—began to recede from view.

Operatic culture suffered a general decline in Britain during this period, even in its most prestigious manifestations. London had been a preeminent operatic center during the late Victorian and Edwardian eras, with opportunities for audiences to hear the world's most celebrated singers. From the vantage point of the late 1920s, the composer Isidore De Lara reflected that "at that time [the Victorian era] there were great singers, public favourites, who by their vocal power alone could draw large audiences; and we had in those days a season of international opera greater than you could hear abroad" (De Lara 1928: 277). While provincial operatic activity continued much as before during World War I, Covent Garden closed (Rodmell 2013: 118–119). By the 1920s, opera in Britain was a distinctly haphazard, hit and miss affair, something that many people who cared about opera felt to be a national embarrassment. Herman Klein wrote an article for the *Musical Times* entitled "Our Lost Operatic Lead" (1922), in which he looked back nostalgically to the glory days at Covent Garden of the late nineteenth century. Klein concluded that Britons had "lost the habit" for opera before the war and probably wouldn't be able to afford to resume the habit even if they wanted to. Money to fund opera during the interwar period was certainly in short supply. Opera seasons were presented on a sporadic basis and were regularly canceled. The touring companies were on hard times, limiting opportunities for audiences in the regions, while by the early 1930s even the most elite of operatic institutions, the Royal Opera House at Covent Garden, came within a whisker of being knocked down.

Throughout the first four decades of the century, schemes were frequently devised to put opera on a surer footing, but many of them failed to come to fruition. In 1924 De Lara launched a "National Opera Scheme," backed by the newly established *Gramophone* magazine, which had proposed asking two million people to give £1 each to raise funds to build a permanent home for opera in Britain, which would have seats within the financial reach of all sectors of society. He expressed a fervent belief that "among the middle and even . . . the labouring classes there is a great thirst for musical art" and that "[t]here is an ever-growing need for culture. The minds of the great masses have been opened, and their brains are demanding food of a higher quality" (De Lara 1928: 276–277). *Gramophone* appealed for funds for De Lara's venture throughout 1925, but by 1926 was hinting that it was struggling, finally admitting in early March 1927 that it had handed the money received back to the donors (*Gramophone* 1927: 429).

Undeterred by the failure of De Lara's scheme, Thomas Beecham stepped into the fray that same year with the launch of his Imperial League of Opera (henceforth ILO). Like De Lara, Beecham (1927) argued that the old aristocratic patronage of opera was impossible, that it was hopeless to expect support from the state. The answer was to turn to the nation's opera lovers. And since De Lara (1928: 276) had noted the decline of interest in opera patronage since the turn of the century by "the great ladies of the land," Beecham (himself the son of a highly successful businessman) saw an opportunity to "masculinize" opera propaganda so as to appeal to a new breed of male, upper middle-class philanthropists. He calculated that he could attract 150,000 members around the country, each of whom he would charge 10 shillings a year and encourage to take out a five-year subscription. With the proceeds raised, he estimated that he would be able to mount an annual London opera season of five to six months per year, plus shorter seasons in the provinces: *The Times* reported promised seasons in Manchester, Liverpool, Birmingham, Leeds, Edinburgh, and Glasgow (*The Times* 1927a). A new orchestra was planned, which was to have a vast new theater as its regular base. The proposed first season would introduce British audiences to then unfamiliar repertory, to include works by Rossini (*The Italian Girl in Algiers* and *The Thieving Magpie*), Berlioz (*The Damnation of Faust* and *The Trojans*), Smetana (*The Bartered Bride*), Borodin (*Prince Igor*), and a particular Beecham favorite, Delius (*A Village Romeo and Juliet*) (Lucas 2008: 190). Beecham received strong support for his scheme from *The Times* and from *Gramophone*. A manifesto for the scheme appeared in the former entitled "Opera: Yes or No" (*The Times* 1927d), while both periodicals published regular updates on the appeal's progress. For a time, at least, the money poured in.

But Beecham was not just interested in raising funds; his underlying aim was to raise taste. As he said in November 1927, following a rush of large donations, "I now want not only the money; I want an audience for opera. Twenty millionaires don't make an audience" (*The Times* 1927b). Beecham's endeavors to attract members of the League included giving widely reported speeches the length and breadth of the nation about the poor state of operatic culture; putting on concerts; soliciting the support of the Royal Philharmonic Society; and embarking on a twenty-three-town "Operatic Party Tour" (discussed in further detail in Lucas 2008: 174–191). As a manifesto for the League, Beecham launched in 1929 a periodical, *MILO*, edited by the composer and former editor of *The Sackbut*, Philip Heseltine (who worked largely under the pseudonym Peter Warlock), from offices on London's New Bond Street. *MILO*'s aim was "to combat musical apathy, especially operatic apathy" (cited in *The Times* 1929). It was sent free of charge to all members of the ILO, with copies available for non-members to purchase for 6d (sixpence in the old UK system used until 1970), and served several functions: to update members on the League's progress; to attract new members; and "to interest and educate the public generally in all matters pertaining to opera" (Anon. 1929b). While the League, its financial ambitions, its successes, and its eventual setbacks have been documented elsewhere (Lucas 2008; Blackwood 1994), no detailed attention has thus far been paid to its organ, *MILO*.

MILO followed in the footsteps of a slightly earlier magazine: *Opera*, published in 1923–1924 by the British National Opera Company (a troupe that emerged after the demise of Beecham's opera company of the 1910s and used many of the same singers). The impulse to establish periodicals about opera at this time would have been inspired by the flourishing of literary and cultural magazines in London during the 1920s. *MILO* drew the support of important figures from across the arts, including the painter Augustus John and the director and theater designer Edward Gordon Craig, as well as the composers Ernst Krenek and Constant Lambert. Other proposed contributors included the baritone Frederic Austin, the theatrical manager C. B. Cochran, the academic Edward Dent, the poet and playwright Robert Nichols, the organist and musicologist Richard Terry, and the critics Francis Toye and W. J. Turner (Anon. 1929a).

Despite the support of such prestigious figures, the magazine was ultimately to be short-lived. Only three issues appeared—in October, November, and December 1929—with the journal being forced to fold in January 1930, together with the Imperial League of Opera itself, when the effects of the US stock market crash began to be felt in Britain (Smith 1994: 266). Yet, despite its brief existence, the journal stands as an important cultural document. An analysis of the rhetorical strategies used in its pages and in the ILO's publicity more generally is highly revealing of the ideologies that shaped the promotion of opera in interwar Britain.

MILO and Classical Masculinity

MILO's title was symbolic. Although it was, at the simplest level, merely an acronym for "Member of the Imperial League of Opera," the designation also had a significant double meaning. Milo of Croton was a great athlete from the ancient world and many times Olympic victor. He had led a successful military campaign in 510 B.C. by the citizens of Croton in southern Italy against the neighboring Sybarites, a race renowned for its luxury and decadence. Warlock mapped Milo's vanquishing of the Sybarites directly onto the athlete's namesake magazine, writing in the inaugural issue:

> The modern descendants of the Sybarites are those who are indifferent to the claims of art and beauty. A vigorous offensive that shall rouse them from this condition is being launched, and it is suggested that each member of the Imperial League of Opera should be a modern "Milo" and a soldier in the great army of intellectual progress. (Warlock 1929)

The references to Milo of Croton associated Beecham's operatic "army" with a highly idealized vision of masculinity. Milo was a wrestler of colossal proportions, capable of feats of extreme strength, including carrying a marble statue or a bull; bursting a band around his forehead simply with the pressure in his temples; and even, according to some accounts, of saving the life of the mathematician Pythagoras by supporting a collapsing building upon his shoulders. In a career spanning over twenty years, his sporting victories were numerous: he won six times at Olympia, as well as being awarded numerous crowns at Delphi, the Isthmus, and Nemea. Moreover, his military triumph against the Sybarites was the stuff of legend. The account by Diodorus Siculus states that the Croton army numbered one hundred thousand but faced a Sybarite army boasting three times as many men. Milo allegedly led his men into battle wearing his sporting regalia—his Olympic crowns, lion skin, and club (Poliakoff 1987: 8, 117–119).

That this nexus of athleticism, militarism, and raw masculinity should be associated with opera is somewhat surprising, for music had often been posited in Victorian and Edwardian Britain as an effeminate pursuit associated principally with foreigners. This was a period when many male musicians struggled with the conflict between their desire for social esteem as "gentlemen" and popular conceptions of their employment as a less-than-manly pursuit. As Corissa Gould has argued (2005: 170), "the male composers of the Victorian and early Edwardian eras, aware of the ambiguous status of music and its potential impact on their profession, took various steps that can be read as attempts to masculinize composition, thereby legitimizing it as suitable for a 'man.'" Forsyth's argument, cited earlier, demonstrates that opera was regarded as a particularly "feminine" branch of music; to find opera-going and athleticism being evoked in the same breath was highly unexpected, since the two pursuits were more often constructed as polar opposites. In 1928, for instance, the composer turned journalist Francesco Berger wrote in *The Times*:

> The average Briton has hitherto shown himself supremely indifferent about opera, neither rejoicing when he had it nor grieving when he had it not. Given the option of hearing an opera or attending a football or cricket match, he will certainly select the latter. (Berger 1928: 10)

Beecham and Warlock, together with their exclusively male team of projected contributors, clearly hoped to increase public support for opera by reversing this gendered coding, seeking to associate the art form in their written propaganda with athleticism, military victory, and imperialism. Moreover, the proposed performance of Berlioz's *The Trojans* by the company of the Imperial League of Opera, had it ever come to fruition, would have offered them a particularly rich vehicle through which to perform their ideals of classical masculinity on the operatic stage.

Milo embodied the ideal of the "sportsman soldier," one that would have had particular resonance for an elite readership who had attended British public schools (the paradoxically named fee-paying institutions that trained the nation's future leaders) during the Edwardian era. At such schools, sport was elevated to a cult, associated with ideals of courage and heroism, and regarded as essential training for those destined to become men of empire. As J. A. Mangan writes, "For many Victorians and Edwardians there was an obvious link between the development of endurance, toughness and courage on English playing fields and pioneering in Australia, preaching in Africa and soldiering in Burma" (1981: 138). Although Beecham claimed to have been a reluctant sportsman at school, playing sports "with a well-calculated absence of zeal" in order to concentrate on music (1944: 29), he knew the enthusiasm athletics could be calculated to engender in his peers.

A knowledge of the ancient world was also part and parcel of a privileged education in early-twentieth-century Britain. Both Beecham, who attended Rossall School in Lancashire, and Warlock, an alumnus of Eton, were of a social class for whom classical references were a normal part of everyday conversation. Indeed, Beecham's 1944 autobiography is peppered with them to the extent that it becomes impenetrable to the non-initiated. When, for instance, he recounts his realization that he was never to become a great opera composer, he remarks that he might have become a reasonably successful composer of songs and small-scale works, adding, "But at that time I was unmindful of the sound Daedelian maxim that middle flights are safest for tyros, and as it seemed a case of 'Aut Caesar aut nihil' I chose the latter alternative" (Beecham 1944: 74).

In couching *MILO* in terms of seemingly obscure classical references, Beecham and Warlock might appear to have been aiming their campaign at a select few, many doubtless already opera habitués. The matter is more complicated, however, for the reverence for classical athleticism that underpinned the *MILO* venture had a wider social reach than one might at first imagine. In the early decades of the twentieth century, the public-school ethos was very effectively disseminated through juvenile literature to a large audience of British boys who had never had the benefit of such an education. Furthermore, by the 1920s, the public at large was becoming increasingly familiar with the strongmen of the ancient world via the mass media. Classical references ceased to be the sole preserve of highbrow literature, theater, and art and increasingly permeated the domain of popular culture, including popular novels, circus acts, and advertising.

Numerous early films celebrated classical musclemen, bestowing upon them not only physical force and military might but civilizing powers. Famous examples include: Enrico Guazzoni's 1912 *Quo Vadis*, which featured a Milo-esque wrestling slave, Ursus; Giovanni Pastrone's 1914 *Cabiria*, whose hero, Maciste, spawned numerous subsequent films; and Fred Niblo's 1925 *Ben Hur*. In the early-twentieth century, wrestlers and musclemen appealed primarily to a working-class, male audience, and the classical strongman who became an archetype of early-twentieth-century cinema was a decidedly populist figure (Wyke 1997: 44). This phenomenon was exemplified most obviously by Maciste (played by a former stevedore, Bartolomeo Pagano), of whose films Alan Mallach writes: "No other form of art, or entertainment, had ever offered Italy's working-class audience a figure who was so clearly one of their own, and with whom they could so readily identify" (2007: 360). There are close resonances here with Milo who, unlike most ancient athletes, was of humble rather than aristocratic origins (Poliakoff 1987: 118).

While the Imperial League of Opera was hardly a populist movement, it did aspire to expand the audience for opera. The ILO's stated aim was "to popularise opera and make it accessible to the greatest number of music lovers" (Bishop 1930: 9), while the inaugural issue of *MILO* announced its intention "to interest and educate the public generally in all matters pertaining to opera" (Anon. 1929b). Beecham may have made gaffes about "the general public" and provincial audiences (Lucas 2008: 185), but he was committed to providing an alternative to the fashionable and exclusive "Season" at Covent Garden and believed that there would be genuine opera lovers in the regions if only they had a chance to hear good opera performed well. To some extent, at least, Beecham must have envisaged that his "great army" would contain foot soldiers as well as an officer corps.

The Times newspaper, which acted at this time as a mouthpiece for Beecham's initiative, argued in 1927 that "[t]he most difficult part of the explainer's task is to banish the prevalent idea that opera is an extravagant luxury which no one but the idle rich can afford to enjoy" (*The Times* 1927c). That *MILO* was successful to a certain degree in extending its reach beyond a narrow elite of established opera-goers is demonstrated by the fact that its launch was reported in *The Era*. *The Era* was a popular weekly theatrical newspaper straddling highbrow-lowbrow boundaries, covering plays, variety performances, pantomime, brass bands, dance music, and light music, and that profiled novelty acts such as performing lions and the "Wild West" nightclub and variety theater entertainer Tex McLeod.

Masculinity and Empire

I should like to turn now to the connection between ideals of classical masculinity and popular imperialism. The iconography of Greek and Roman athleticism was used regularly in the interwar period in the cause of jingoistic nation building, as emblematized most famously by Mussolini's conscious cultivation of a proto-classical self-image (see Mack Smith 1983). In Italy, muscles and the classical body were appropriated into the nation-building project via a variety of media. As Maria Wyke writes, "The musculature of the classical body displayed on the screen became a site on which could be constructed the emerging patriotic consciousness of 1920s Italy, while its very classicism helped legitimate the forms that national identity took" (1999: 364). Such rhetoric and imagery even made its way into discussions of composers. As noted above, Puccini's promoters appropriated such classicizing, nation-building references in constructing his popular reputation (Wilson 2007b).

The leaders of the Imperial League of Opera appear to have been employing a similar strategy, yet the impulse that prompted such rhetoric was a defensive one. By the late 1920s there was a widespread awareness that the British Empire had passed its heyday and that international power was shifting away from Britain (Dawson 1994: 153). Political decline was mirrored by fear of cultural decline: Herman Klein (1922) had noted that Britain was becoming an operatic backwater, as talented European singers were now "skipping" London and going straight to the United States. In reality, the United States had its own share of operatic problems during the 1920s. Although opera was flourishing at the New York Metropolitan Opera and in Chicago during this decade, the number of touring companies was falling, just as it was in the United Kingdom, and opera was in decline in many major American cities, including San Francisco (Dizikes 1993: 413). Nevertheless, the question was one of perception. Beecham wrote in the inaugural issue of *MILO* that "I have read in an American paper an opinion that England seems to be becoming more and more content with the position of nursery to other more grown-up and musically appreciative countries" (Beecham 1929b: 6).

In the pages of *MILO* and in speeches he made up and down the country, Beecham voiced his anxiety about Britain's artistic inferiority to other nations and his ambition to use culture—opera in particular—to reassert Britain's standing on the international stage and to support the nation's by then waning imperial "mission." He was particularly troubled by the fact that Britain had no permanent opera house, telling *The Times* in 1928 that Germany had 135 opera houses (not to mention 210 permanent orchestras), Italy 70 opera houses, and France 5 in Paris alone (*The Times* 1928). Beecham wanted to help the nation to shake off its sense of cultural inadequacy, announcing at a dinner for the Musicians' Club in May 1928 that "[t]here is in this country an inferiority complex.

For goodness' sake let us get it out of ourselves, and 24 months after the foundation of this opera scheme I will undertake to provide out of British resources, an establishment equal to any in the world" (*The Era* 1928).

Predictably, *MILO* and the broader publicity surrounding the Imperial League of Opera is suffused with imperial ambition. What is more surprising—because it confounds the ingrained British stereotype of opera as an "elite" art form (as discussed further in Wilson 2007a)—is that the language and imagery used by the ILO was that of *popular* imperialism, at a time when notions of imperialism were changing and being critiqued by the intellectual community. In the 1920s the term "imperial" did not, of course, evoke the negative resonances it does today, and the use of a certain amount of celebratory imperial rhetoric would not have surprised a contemporary audience. "Imperial" was a tag used by the owners of hotels, theaters, and music halls in an attempt to bestow an air of grandeur on their premises. (A prime example is the lavishly ornate Imperial Hotel in Russell Square, London, constructed between 1905 and 1911. For photographs of this now demolished building, see Stamp 2010: 61.)

The term was also used by numerous organizations, whether explicitly promoting imperialist ideals (such as the propagandist British Empire Union) or simply exploiting the imperial label to bestow credibility upon themselves. Occasionally the designation carried more sinister overtones, as in the Imperial Fascist League established by Arnold Leese in 1929. Beecham's use of the term "imperial" was, at one level, simply following an established convention of associating the term with the theatrical arts, as exemplified by the "British Empire Shakespeare Society," a troupe active during the late 1920s, whose activities were regularly reported in the pages of *The Era*. De Lara had planned an "Imperial Opera House" (1928: 278), while in 1902, as a young man, Beecham had himself conducted operas on a tour given by an outfit that John Lucas calls the "decidedly ramshackle Imperial Grand Opera Company" (2008: 20).

But imperialism was becoming a contentious phenomenon by the late 1920s. While it has now been comprehensively demonstrated by historians that imperialist sentiment did not founder in the aftermath of World War I, as has often been asserted, the tone of imperialism changed. The acceptable face of empire was now more about international cooperation and mutual economic benefit than about conquest and exploitation (Porter 2004: 274). While in 1900, according to Beecham, "The sense of security was universal, and no man in his senses doubted for a moment that the British Empire, which was then about one hundred and fifty years old, was destined to remain just where it stood for another thousand or two at least" (1944: 43), such certainty about the empire's longevity was, by the 1920s, beginning to waver.

As high culture and popular culture increasingly diverged in the interwar period, so too did ideas about empire. High culture set itself apart from popular ideals of empire, yet the public at large remained oblivious to contemporary intellectual critiques of the imperial project. What Jeffrey Richards calls "the common culture of the country," on the other hand, was defined by a patriotism that embraced militarism, conservatism, imperialism, and racialism (1986: 143). This brand of empire, which is strongly evoked in *MILO*, recalls the older, Edwardian model, based on ideals of sporting prowess, militarism, and derring-do. References to the colonial adventures of heroic British soldiers had been ubiquitous in the Edwardian period. Such references continued to be promoted in much the same terms after the war via popular journalism, children's adventure stories, school textbooks, memorabilia, and commercial advertising (especially postcards and cigarette cards), and found a new outlet through the medium of film (Mackenzie 1984: 10, 17, 26). Moreover, the 1920s was a decade that saw the rise of explicitly imperialist organizations and events: The Empire Marketing Board ran from 1926 to 1933 (for further reading, see Constantine 1986); the Imperial Institute in South Kensington was reaching the peak of its propagandist outreach in the late 1920s (Mackenzie 1984: 130); and an extravagant Empire Exhibition was held at Wembley in 1924 and 1925.

The daily press at this time constantly asserted the need for more opera in English by British composers. Beecham realized that he was going to have to respond to such demands, but was aware that such an ideal would be difficult to achieve (Beecham 1944: 87–88). Nevertheless, he hoped that the singers performing in ILO productions would be drawn exclusively from the Empire (Beecham 1927: 10). Here he was tapping into a strong vein of xenophobic hostility toward foreign "celebrity" singers that prevailed in the British press throughout the 1920s. Reporters frequently lamented that audiences were paying a lot of money to hear such singers, which might have been better spent supporting local musicians. (I discuss this cultural protectionism further in Wilson 2012.)

At times, an even more chauvinistic side of "old-style" imperialism—an ethos that was being questioned in almost all quarters of the press by the late 1920s (Bingham 2004: 183)—is also evoked in the ILO literature and surrounding discourses. *MILO* established a dichotomy between the "barbarism" of modern British society and an idealized civilized state. References to savages and barbarians might seem to evoke the simplistic jingoism of the Edwardian classroom. Indeed, *MILO* did at one point use a schoolboy as a mouthpiece for its ideals. The magazine ran an essay competition for the boys of King Edward's School, Birmingham, and printed the winning entry, whose young author held forth that:

> There is no getting out of the fact that our national form of entertainment has risen no higher than the cinema. To put it frankly, it is a crime. All countries are agreed that such things as opera cannot be left out of the programme of a civilized nation. (Craig 1929: 35)

Rather immature as such rhetoric may seem, Beecham used very similar language himself, hoping to shame the nation (and particularly what he positioned as the uncultivated hinterland of its provinces) by comparing it to regions untouched by British imperial rule, as imagined in the crudest terms. Chiming with extensive debates then current in the press about whether Britain was constitutionally an operatic nation, Beecham lamented in the inaugural issue of *MILO* that "[t]he State of England has never taken one step in the way of forming or elevating the taste of the people. It has ever shown a singular indifference to things intellectual and spiritual, worthy only of a great barbarian country" (Beecham 1929b: 6). In the next issue he went further, writing in a capital-centric article entitled "London and the League" that "[i]n many parts of the Kingdom I have discovered less knowledge of the subject than I should expect to find in the middle of Africa" (Beecham 1929a: 2).

Typical references to "purifying" people's musical tastes and to the nation's "spiritual welfare" suggest an overt sense of "mission." Such comments were part of the wider lexicon of early twentieth-century opera discourse. Upon her retirement from the stage in 1926, Nellie Melba wrote a letter to the *Musical Times* expressing her delight at noting a recent "quickening in musical appreciation" among British audiences. This she attributed to "broadcasting and the gramophone," which she called "the two most eloquent missionaries to the musical heathen in our midst" (1926). De Lara used similar language, calling these same technological developments "the apostles... of dramatic music in England" (1925). Moreover, opera and missionary zeal came together in concrete form during the mid-1920s in a church in Battersea, South London (as discussed by De Lara 1925). The priest, a certain Reverend Green, inspired by the spirit of "rational recreation" promoted by the Christian Socialist reformers of the late nineteenth century, had set up an "opera club." A group of young parishioners—poor and previously unacquainted with classical music—gathered each Sunday after evensong and, with the aid of gramophone records, would go through the story and music of an opera.

Although Beecham went nowhere near as far as Reverend Green in engaging directly with what Melba had called the "musical heathens," he managed to surround himself with the aura of a zealous missionary. According to *The Era*, "like Peter the hermit, Sir Thomas Beecham continued to preach upon the highway... and compel the people to come in" (Henderson Williams 1930a: 7). Nevertheless, in the same article (a summary of the musical events of 1929), the newspaper reported that concert halls stood half empty, long-established music societies were sending round the begging hat, and music critics were out of work. As for opera, the periodical opined that "[f]rom time to time the Press felt the pulse of the Imperial League of Opera—and shook its head." Yet, further down the same page, it was reported that "[t]he summer season at Covent Garden proceeded on the usual lines: it was, perhaps, harder than ever for those of little wealth to hear opera" (Henderson Williams 1930b: 7).

In the autumn of 1929, upon launching *MILO*, Beecham bullishly announced that the League was "already more than four times as large as any other musical organization in the world," offering England's best chance of "redeeming her musical reputation in the eyes of the world" (Henderson Williams 1929: 5). A few months later, the League was struggling and *MILO* had folded. By the end of the year, Peter Warlock would be dead: a presumed suicide. A history of manic depression and difficult personal circumstances may both have contributed to Warlock's actions. (His illegitimate son, the art critic Brian Sewell, speculates that the cause was Warlock's inability to cope with the prospect of a child and its mother's refusal to have an abortion [Sewell 2011: 17–23].) According to a contemporary account by the critic Cecil Gray, however, "the more lucrative sources of [Warlock's] income had dried up entirely, and the subsequent collapse of *Milo* and the indefinite suspension of the opera scheme had given the final blow" (Gray 1934: 289).

Attempts to revive the flagging ILO dragged on into the 1930s. Throughout the summer of 1932 and the spring of 1933, a dedicated trio of distinguished ILO supporters, Sir Hugh Allen (Heather Professor at Oxford and Principal of the Royal College of Music), Oliver Sylvain Baliol Brett (3rd Viscount Esher), and Reginald McKenna (Chairman of the Midland Bank and former Liberal Chancellor of the Exchequer and Home Secretary), drafted and redrafted an appeal to the donors who had originally contributed to the scheme. These donors had been told that they would be entitled to a reimbursement of their donations should the scheme fail to raise adequate funds; now, however, the ILO's organizers appealed to members for permission to retain the donations in order to relaunch the scheme. Few were to be persuaded, however, and by the summer of 1934, the ILO was instructed by the High Court of Chancery to return the donations to the contributors forthwith (Allen 1934).

That *MILO* folded was perhaps unsurprising. Rather than attempting to enthuse a broad readership about opera, the magazine was primarily obsessed with the ILO's own activities. Its tone was unremittingly defensive and propagandistic; typical article titles were "Opera: A Vindication," "The British Public and Opera," and "The Need for Opera in England." Beecham and his supporters could not be said to have been successful in confronting either of their sworn enemies. However, the fact that this and other schemes to promote opera during the interwar period were ultimately unsuccessful is beside the point. What is interesting for the purposes of this chapter is the language used and the agendas that were at stake.

British Opera Needs You

The jingoistic tone of the League is summed up in an advertisement for the League itself that appeared several times in *MILO*, presumably aimed at readers who had bought or been given a single copy without yet subscribing (see Figure 35.1). The advertisement asks the reader a serious of blunt and increasingly patriotically inspired questions, all prefaced by the words "DO YOU." These progress from the simple "Do you want more opera?" and "Do you want better opera?" to questions that play on the inferiority of British operatic culture and the plight of British singers forced to seek out a living overseas ("Do you want Britain to cease to be the only country in Europe without an established Opera?" "Do you want to bring home the great British singers who are now compelled to earn their living abroad?"). The appeal concludes with the question "Do you want to redeem and maintain our reputation as a great musical nation?" If the answer is yes—and it could hardly be no, given the emotive terms in which the questions are put—the reader is urged to join the ILO today in order to "materially help to raise the British musical and theatrical professions out of their present depressed condition."

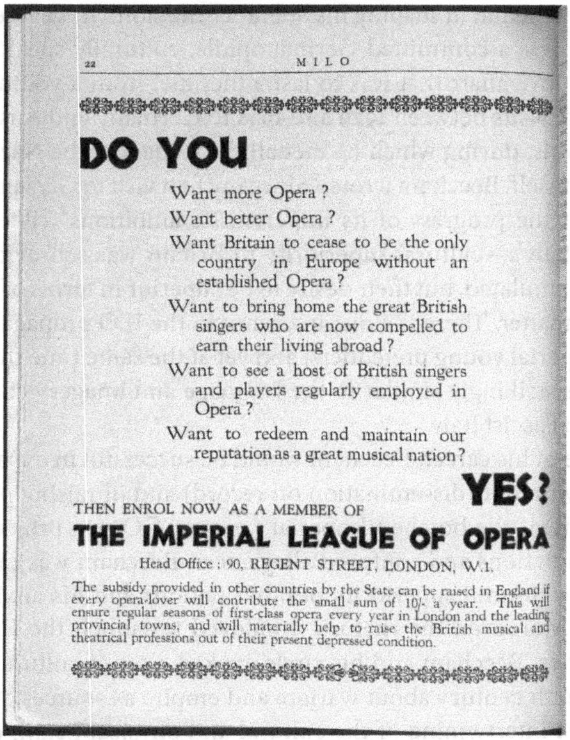

FIGURE 35.1 Imperial League of Opera advertisement. *MILO* 1, no. 2 (November 1929), British Library shelfmark P.433/36. © The British Library Board.

In its call to arms, the advertisement is reminiscent of a series of famous and highly effective World War I military recruitment posters in which Secretary of State for War Lord Kitchener is depicted, finger outstretched to the reader, declaring that "[y]our country needs you." (The poster inspired numerous imitations, such as the American Uncle Sam poster of 1917 bearing the words "I Want You for US Army.") The fact that Beecham had been mightily impressed by Kitchener's no-nonsense campaign is well documented. In his autobiography he praises Kitchener, "the most popular and successful of English soldiers," for his "trumpet-blast of reality, blowing away forever into the air the theories and arguments of economists, politicians, philosophers and novelists," concluding: "Here was talking, as they say in my county of Lancashire: this was real war with a vengeance" (Beecham 1944: 150–151). Beecham describes Kitchener's poster campaign as an "appeal […] for a mighty army of volunteers" and evidently hoped to enlist a similar "mighty army" to the operatic cause.

Sources such as the *MILO* advertisement make manifest the fact that the ILO endeavor and its gendered subtexts were underpinned by an uneasy relationship with foreign rivals. Just as Kitchener wanted to enlist young men to fight against Germany, so too—metaphorically—did Beecham. Beecham's relationship with Germany was a complex one, fundamental in shaping his operatic "mission." It is evident from his autobiography that he was a committed Germanophile, culturally speaking at least, from his teens. It was a love affair that was to last a lifetime, from a youthful pilgrimage to Bayreuth to annual visits between 1929 and 1938 to Germany and Austria to conduct at major music festivals, during which he met all the leaders of the Nazi party, including Hess and Hitler himself. Beecham wrote, "Since my first visit to Germany, I had followed with keen interest the progress of its imperialistic ambitions" (Beecham 1944: 130). Germany's—and Italy's—cultural superiority to Britain was self-evident to Beecham, and a model to be emulated, but their desire to be superior in terms of global power was a more troubling matter. There is a distinct sense in the ILO propaganda of a desire to "see off" these imperial young pretenders, and yet at the same time the rhetoric of classical athleticism is strikingly similar to the language and imagery contemporaneously being employed in Fascist Italy.

Over the course of his career, Beecham would be successful in expanding the British operatic repertory (and its dissemination on record) and in raising performance standards. At the heart of the botched Imperial League of Opera project, however, lay a network of contradictions and confused allegiances. Beecham was caught between his admiration for the cultural superiority of other nations and his anxiety about British imperial decline. Moreover, the rhetoric employed to launch the ILO speaks of further vexed identities. Beecham and his circle evoked a set of cultural ideas developed in the late nineteenth century about warfare and empire as sources of moral regeneration and about the intertwining of the cultural and physical health of the nation. Yet such ideas were often confused and outdated. In Beecham's fantasy, idealized masculinities from the distant and recent past converge. He might, however, have paused to consider the fact that alongside Milo the heroic strongman existed another, ultimately more vulnerable, Milo. Attempting to rend a tree asunder as a show of strength in later life, the athlete's hands became trapped and he was set upon by a pack of wolves. Indeed, it was Milo's demise rather than his triumphs that lived on in later cultural representations (sometimes with lions substituted for wolves). Milo's final moments captured the imagination of many seventeenth- and eighteenth-century artists, including the sculptors Pierre Puget and Etienne-Maurice Falconet and the painters Charles Meynier and Joseph-Benoît Suvée, as well as the unknown nineteenth-century sculptor of the bronze depicted in Figure 35.2.

Similarly, the heroic brand of masculinity that surrounds Beecham and Warlock's *MILO* campaign, replete with stereotypes of romance and adventure, had, ironically, been dealt a severe blow by World War I, with its horrors of mangled and disfigured male bodies (see Bourke 1996), while even a more everyday conception of "traditional" masculinity was coming under threat by the mid-1920s from mass unemployment (Bingham 2004: 229).

Beecham wrote in the first issue of *MILO*, "It is an indisputable fact that in a country where operatic life and culture are wanting, there is no sound health in the whole musical body of it. But the Imperial League of Opera is not intended only for the propagation of opera. It is intended to be a rallying point for all the musical culture of this country,

FIGURE 35.2 Nineteenth-century bronze of Milo of Croton, sculptor unknown, Holland Park, London. Photograph © Alexandra Wilson.

and finally of the Empire" (1929b: 4). Beecham had big ambitions for his League, then, which extended far beyond the pragmatic business of raising money to build an opera house. The short-lived *MILO* and the broader ILO campaign, with their panoply of references to health, corporeality, and masculinity, held up a mirror to much broader debates, the bold, assertive imagery scarcely concealing an aching anxiety about imperial decline and perceived artistic inadequacy. Opera may have been Britain's artistic *bête-noire* during the 1920s, ridiculed by self-styled "serious" musicians and the popular press alike, but the pages of *MILO* reveal that the art form had the capacity to resonate with many of the deepest conflicts of national, cultural, and gendered identity that confronted the British nation between the wars.

See also: Castrato Acts, Politics, Patronage, Audiences

Bibliography

Abbate, Carolyn. 1993. "Opera; or, the Envoicing of Women." In Solie 1993, 225–258.

Allen, Hugh. 1934. Letter to Lord Esher (July 27). Oxford New College Archives, Hugh Allen Papers, PA/ALL 1/14/4.

André, Naomi. 2006. *Voicing Gender: Castrati, Travesti, and the Second Woman in Early-Nineteenth-Century Italian Opera*. Bloomington: Indiana University Press.

Beecham, Thomas. 1944. *A Mingled Chime: Leaves from an Autobiography*. London: Hutchinson and Co.

——. 1929a. "London and the League." *MILO* 1 (November): 2–3, 2.

——. 1929b. "A Message From Thomas Beecham." *MILO* 1 (October): 4–6.

——. 1927. "The Future of Opera." *The Times* (November 5): 10.

Berger, Francesco. 1928. "Opera in England: The Native Form." *The Times* (October 6): 10.

Bingham, Adrian. 2004. *Gender, Modernity, and the Popular Press in Inter-War Britain*. Oxford: Clarendon Press.

Bishop, G. W. 1930. "Sir Thomas Beecham Answers his Critics." *The Era* 94 (October 8): 9.

Blackmer, Corinne E., and Patricia Juliana Smith, eds. 1995. *En Travesti: Women, Gender Subversion, Opera*. New York: Columbia University Press.

Blackwood, Alan. 1994. *Thomas Beecham: The Man and His Music*. London: Ebury Press.

Bourke, Joanna. 1996. *Dismembering the Male: Men's Bodies, Britain and the Great War*. London: Reaktion Books.

Brett, Philip. 2006. *Music and Sexuality in Britten: Selected Essays*. Berkeley and Los Angeles: University of California Press.

Castle, Terry. 1995. "In Praise of Brigitte Fassbaender: Reflections on Diva Worship." In Blackmer and Smith 1995, 20–58.

Citron, Marcia. 1993. *Gender and the Musical Canon*. Cambridge: Cambridge University Press.

Clément, Catherine. 1989. *Opera, or the Undoing of Women*, translated by Betsy Wing. Minneapolis: University of Minnesota Press.

Constantine, Stephen. 1986. "'Bringing the Empire Alive': The Empire Marketing Board and Imperial Propaganda, 1926–33." In MacKenzie 1986, 192–231.

Cowgill, Rachel, and Hilary Poriss, eds. 2012. *The Arts of the Prima Donna in the Long Nineteenth Century*. New York: Oxford University Press.

Craig, N. J. F. 1929. "The Need for Opera in England (The Prize Essay on Sir Thomas Beecham's Recent Address to the Boys of King Edward's School, Birmingham)." *MILO* 1 (Christmas): 34–35.

Dawson, Graham. 1994. *Soldier Heroes: British Adventure, Empire and the Imagining of Masculinities*. London: Routledge.

De Lara, Isidore. 1928. Many Tales of Many Cities. London: Hutchinson.

——. 1925. "An Imperial and Permanent Opera House." *Gramophone* 2 (April): 419. Find this resource:

Dizikes, John. 1993. *Opera in America: A Cultural History*. New Haven: Yale University Press.

The Era. 1928. "British Music and Musicians. Sir Thomas Beecham and Lack of Opportunity." *The Era* 91 (May 23): 9.

Forsyth, Cecil. 1911. *Music and Nationalism: A Study of English Opera*. London: Macmillan.

Freitas, Roger. 2009. *Portrait of a Castrato: Politics, Patronage, and Music in the Life of Atto Melani*. Cambridge: Cambridge University Press.

Gordon, Bonnie. 2004. *Monteverdi's Unruly Women: The Power of Song in Early Modern Italy*. Cambridge: Cambridge University Press.

Gould, Corissa. 2005. "Aspiring to Manliness: Edward Elgar and the Pressures of Hegemonic Masculinity." In *Masculinity and Western Musical Practice*, edited by Ian Biddle and Kirsten Gibson, 161–181. Farnham, UK: Ashgate.

Gramophone. 1927. "Trade Winds and Idle Zephyrs." *Gramophone* 4 (March): 429.

Gramophone. 1925. "An Imperial Opera House." *Gramophone* 2 (February): 331.
Gray, Cecil. 1934. *Peter Warlock: A Memoir of Philip Heseltine*. London: Jonathan Cape.
Grover-Friedlander, Michal. 2005. "The Afterlife of Maria Callas's Voice." *Musical Quarterly* 88/1: 35–62.
Heller, Wendy. 2003. *Emblems of Eloquence: Opera and Women's Voices in Seventeenth-Century Venice*. Berkeley and Los Angeles: University of California Press.
Henderson Williams, L. 1930a. "Music in 1929." *The Era* 93 (January 1): 7.
——. 1930b. "Opera." *The Era* 93 (January 1): 7.
——. 1929. "Milo." *The Era* 93 (October 30): 5.
Henson, Karen. 2007. "Verdi, Victor Maurel and *Fin-de-Siècle* Operatic Performance." *Cambridge Opera Journal* 19/1: 59–84.
Hutcheon, Linda, and Michael Hutcheon. 2000. *Bodily Charm: Living Opera*. Lincoln: University of Nebraska Press.
——. 1996. *Opera: Desire, Disease, Death*. Lincoln: University of Nebraska Press.
Kallberg, Jeffrey. 1996. *Chopin at the Boundaries: Sex, History, and Musical Genre*. Cambridge, MA: Harvard University Press.
Klein, Herman. 1922. "Our Lost Operatic Lead." *Musical Times* 63: 20–21.
Koestenbaum, Wayne. 1994. *The Queen's Throat: Opera, Homosexuality, and the Mystery of Desire*. New York: Vintage.
Levine, Lawrence. 1988. *Highbrow/Lowbrow: The Emergence of Cultural Hierarchy in America*. Cambridge, MA: Harvard University Press.
Lucas, John. 2008. *Thomas Beecham: An Obsession with Music*. Woodbridge: The Boydell Press.
Mack Smith, Denis. 1983. *Mussolini il Duce: Quattrocento immagini della vita di un uomo e di vent'anni di storia italiana*. Milan: Fabbri.
MacKenzie, John M., ed. 1986. *Imperialism and Popular Culture*. Manchester: Manchester University Press.
MacKenzie, John M. 1984. *Propaganda and Empire: The Manipulation of British Public Opinion, 1880–1960*. Manchester: Manchester University Press.
Mallach, Alan. 2007. *The Autumn of Italian Opera: From Verismo to Modernism, 1890–1915*. Boston: Northeastern University Press.
Mangan, J. A. 1981. *Athleticism in the Victorian and Edwardian Public School: The Emergence and Consolidation of an Educational Ideology*. Cambridge: Cambridge University Press.
McClary, Susan. 1991. *Feminine Endings: Music, Gender, and Sexuality*. Minneapolis: University of Minnesota Press.
Melba, Nellie. 1926. "A Musical Renascence." *Musical Times* 67: 259.
Poliakoff, Michael B. 1987. *Combat Sports in the Ancient World: Competition, Violence, and Culture*. New Haven: Yale University Press.
Porter, Bernard. 2004. *The Absent-Minded Imperialists: Empire, Society, and Culture in Britain*. New York: Oxford University Press.
Purvis, Philip, ed. 2013. *Masculinity in Opera*. New York: Routledge.
Richards, Jeffrey. 1986. "Boys' Own Empire: Feature Films and Imperialism in the 1930s." In MacKenzie 1986, 140–164.
Robinson, Paul. 2002. *Opera, Sex, and Other Vital Matters*. Chicago: University of Chicago Press.
Rodmell, Paul. 2013. *Opera in the British Isles, 1875-1918*. Farnham, UK: Ashgate.
Russell, Dave. 1997. *Popular Music in England, 1840–1914: A Social History*. 2nd ed. Manchester: Manchester University Press.

Rutherford, Susan. 2013. *Verdi, Opera, Women*. Cambridge: Cambridge University Press.

——. 2006. *The Prima Donna and Opera, 1815–1930*. Cambridge: Cambridge University Press.

Salmon, Arthur L. 1920. "The Artistic Values in Opera." *Musical Times* 61: 519–520.

Senici, Emanuele. 2005. *Landscape and Gender in Italian Opera: The Alpine Virgin from Bellini to Puccini*. Cambridge: Cambridge University Press.

Sewell, Brian. 2011. *Outsider. Always Almost: Never Quite*. London: Quartet Books.

Smart, Mary Ann, ed. 2000. *Siren Songs: Representations of Gender and Sexuality in Opera*. Princeton, NJ: Princeton University Press.

Smith, Barry. 1994. *Peter Warlock: The Life of Philip Heseltine*. New York: Oxford University Press.

Solie, Ruth. 1993. *Musicology and Difference*. Berkeley and Los Angeles: University of California Press.

Stamp, Gavin. 2010. *Lost Victorian Britain: How the Twentieth Century Destroyed the Nineteenth Century's Architectural Masterpieces*. London: Aurum Press.

The Times. 1929. "Imperial League of Opera: New Musical Periodical." *The Times* (October 10): 12.

The Times. 1928. "Music in England: Sir Thomas Beecham's Criticism." *The Times* (October 2): 11.

The Times. 1927a. "Imperial League of Opera: Big Initial Response." *The Times* (November 17): 12.

The Times. 1927b. "Imperial League of Opera: Response to Sir Thomas Beecham's Appeal." *The Times* (November 23): 14.

The Times. 1927c. "Opera: 'But' and 'If'. Explainers Wanted." *The Times* (November 26): 12.

The Times. 1927d. "Opera: Yes or No. Sir Thomas Beecham's Question." *The Times* (November 19): 12.

Warlock, Peter. 1929. "Editorial." *MILO* 1 (October): 2.

Wilson, Alexandra. 2012. "Galli-Curci Comes to Town: The Prima Donna's Presence in the Age of Mechanical Reproduction." In Cowgill and Poriss 2012, 328–347.

——. 2007a. "Killing Time: Contemporary Representations of Opera in British Culture." *Cambridge Opera Journal* 19/3: 249–270.

——. 2007b. *The Puccini Problem: Opera, Nationalism, and Modernity*. Cambridge: Cambridge University Press.

Wyke, Maria. 1999. "Herculean Muscle!: The Classicizing Rhetoric of Bodybuilding." In *Constructions of the Classical Body*, edited by James I. Porter, 355–379. Ann Arbor: University of Michigan Press.

——. 1997. *Projecting the Past: Ancient Rome, Cinema, and History*. New York and London: Routledge.

CHAPTER 36

EXOTICISM

W. ANTHONY SHEPPARD

OPERATIC exoticism is a form of representation that has appeared throughout the history of the genre. This representational system has included the beliefs, customs, styles of dance and music, physical appearance, and so on, of peoples and places deemed different and distant, either geographically or temporally, from the daily experience of the intended audience and/or the composer, librettist, director, and performers. Such representation may be achieved through stereotypical devices of plot, character type, stage and costume design, poetic style, choreography, and music. Exoticism may or may not involve direct or indirect forms of cross-cultural influence and encounter, which occur along a very broad spectrum of possibilities never entirely removed from the imaginary. Many of the most popular operas in history involve some degree of exotic representation.

The foregoing definition may seem reasonable and fairly complete. However, as with any viable "-ism," the application of "exoticism" as a critical term in operatic scholarship has inspired debate. At issue is whether exoticism necessarily involves elements of both representation and influence or whether either can occur independently of the other. Nor is it entirely clear what qualifies as a form of exotic representation and of exotic influence. Must exotic representation result from authorial intention, or should our investigations focus on audience reception of these operas? Behind much of this discussion has been an attempt to determine the extent to which Edward Said's concepts of orientalism are applicable to the interpretation of exoticism in opera (Said 1978, 1993). To what extent did opera participate in European imperialist projects? To what extent has opera served a didactic function in shaping its audience's understanding of various exotic cultures? Equally pressing is the determination of just how essential techniques of exotic representation were to the creation and experience of these operas and the position of these operas within operatic history more generally.

Definitions in the Mind of the Beholder

Although the "exotic" attribute may eventually be internalized by the subaltern, it otherwise exists entirely in the mind of the beholder. Thus, it is impossible to establish precisely the boundaries of its domain. Moreover, the extraordinary has been standard fare for opera from the start. As Mark Everist has noted, "nearly all subjects for the libretti of serious opera lay outside everyday experience of composers, librettists and audiences" (Everist 1996: 231). Given the large number of operatic characters who suffer extreme mental states such as madness or violent bouts of jealousy, or who possess magical powers, or whose divinity or royalty remove them from the common lives of most audience members, opera itself might well seem an exotic entertainment, as Samuel Johnson averred.

In operatic scholarship the term "exotic" normally refers specifically to the representation of cultural or historical difference. Until recently, the assumption has been that the creators of operatic exoticism are white (predominately male) Euro-Americans and that the others being represented are of the "non-Western" category: Mozart representing Turks; the India of Hasse or Delibes and the Japan or China of Puccini; Verdi and Bizet composing in "Gypsy style"; the representation and influence of African-Americans and jazz in German *Zeitoper*; the Native Americans of Rameau, Cadman, and Adams; the portrayal of Montezuma by Graun, Sessions, or Rihm. Critics have tended not to include representations of the "folk" inspired by nationalist sentiments in their discussion of operatic exoticism, despite the frequently clear overlap in representational techniques. Along these lines, Jonathan Bellman has pointed to the ascertainment of a composer's representational intentions as being crucial for determining differences between exoticism and nationalism (Bellman 1998: ix). Carl Dahlhaus explicitly linked his discussion of exoticism with nationalism in his study of nineteenth-century music (Dahlhaus [1980] 1989: 304; see also Locke 2009: 72–79). Ralph Locke has argued that operatic exoticism requires reference, however inaccurate, to an actual place and group of people (Locke 2000: 269). This requirement seems sensible, until one considers an opera such as Britten's *Death in Venice*, in which stylistic features inspired by the composer's encounter with Indonesian gamelan correspond with the representation of homosexual desire, rather than with a specific exotic setting or people. While Venice itself may have retained its semi-exotic status in the northern European imagination well into the twentieth century, and Tadzio's Polishness could be framed as exotic, neither Indonesia nor Indonesians are referenced in the opera, and yet exoticism certainly seems to be in play in this work. Of course, Monteverdi's use of the *regal* for the representation of Charon at the shores of the river Styx in *Orfeo* would also not qualify as an instance of operatic musical exoticism in this view. Exoticism's rampant run throughout operatic history makes any attempt at definitional precision a quixotic venture.

Attempting to define exoticism necessarily also involves consideration of its relationship to other representational categories, in addition to nationalism. Strictly speaking, the most proximate such categories—orientalism and primitivism—should be viewed as subspecies of exoticism. However, "orientalism" is often employed as a roughly equivalent term that more clearly points to the political implications of exoticism and specifically to the work of Said. (For a far more restricted use of the term "orientalism" for operatic criticism, see Everist 1996.) This, in turn, raises the question of why these various forms of exoticism have been so pervasive in opera history. Numerous scholars, including this author, have followed Said's lead in assuming that exoticism has repeatedly offered justification and even inspiration for political imperialism, racist policies, and other ill-founded public perceptions, without making extensive attempts to establish causal relations. Clearly, the enticements of exotic difference also offered enhanced entertainment options for the creators of opera, and some audiences appear still to revel in the bipolar experience of desire and repulsion when encountering the exotic in the opera house. More practically, operatic exoticism allows for the exploration of issues and desires that could not be shown in a domestic setting without violating serious social taboos. In this sense, exoticism in opera functions allegorically to point back to the self, rather than to a specific exotic other. The implications of this view of the dynamics of exoticism are far-reaching, as Locke has noted: "the realisation that European subjectivity may persist behind these dark-skinned masks, that—to change the metaphor—the Orient may often be a blank screen for projecting Western concerns about itself, can change in important ways the listener's or critic's response to the work" (Locke 1991: 285). Locke has called for equal attention to be paid to how these operas function to shape Western perceptions of the East *and* to how these operas explore Western concerns in a setting without direct relevance to East/West relations (Locke 2000: 281 and Locke 1993: 61). Ultimately, exoticism might be said to function in large part to define the self, to have defined "whiteness" through contrast with the other.

Does Exoticism Persuade?

Given our general assumptions that exotic representation in opera has historically played a role in shaping public perception, policy, and political actions toward the exotic other, it is now necessary to substantiate this claim more carefully. Head (2003) has taken musicologists to task for not fully considering the political ramifications of orientalist representation. We need to ask the extent to which exotic representation may be ignored by an audience in favor of a less focused consumption of the musical and visual spectacle. Conversely, could orientalist opera function cathartically, playing out desires, fears, and even cultural hostility in an artistic form rather than in life? Perhaps extreme emotions experienced in the opera house stay in the opera house and one leaves less, rather than more, likely to commit murder, adultery, suicide, or racist-driven conquest after having experienced their dramatic presentation onstage. Our critique of operatic exoticism has tended to emphasize the possible negative ramifications of such representation, and rightly so. Yet, it is also possible that certain orientalist operas served a more positive educational function by bringing their audiences to the point of appreciation of another culture (however fantastically represented), instilling positive impressions and empathy (albeit for reasons of dubious morality and of clear condescension), and, perhaps, even offering critiques of imperialism itself (see Locke 2005 for a relevant discussion of *Aida*). Furthermore, although our primary focus in such interpretive endeavors should be on how audiences received these works, we may well ask whether a given composer actively sought to portray an exotic people in a certain way or whether the composer was chiefly interested in matching the exoticism of the libretto and stage design or in capitalizing on a fad for exotic spectacle.

This more skeptical position on the impact of operatic exoticism needs to be addressed, but it, in turn, raises the question of the potential power of subliminal impressions. Perhaps the more elaborate and detailed the musical and visual exotic display, the more powerfully the representation comes across and the more likely it will be received as authentic, along with the work's perspectives on exotic peoples. It is important to recall that for the majority of audience members, orientalist operas and other artistic forms offering exotic representations (such as film today) have long served a didactic role as a primary or even singular source of information about other cultures.

A relatively recent concern has centered on how (and even whether) orientalist operas from the past should be staged now. Is it possible to create new productions that undermine orientalist representation through parody or to engage in cross-cultural influence and representation of the exotic without trading in orientalism? Numerous productions in recent decades have attempted to distance old operas from their modes of representation. One may set *The Mikado* without visual representation of "old Japan," as did Jonathan Miller in his 1986 ENO production, and yet the verbal and musical *japonisme* remains (see Beckerman 1989). Other productions and new operas have flamboyantly reveled in exotic representation in the spirit of camp or parody. The costumes, body makeup, and general color scheme of Richard Hudson's designs for the 1998 production of *Samson et Dalila* at the Metropolitan Opera are relevant here, as is Menotti's 1963 *The Last Savage*, the Turkish Embassy scene in Corigliano's 1987/1991 *The Ghosts of Versailles*, and David McVicar's 2005 Glyndebourne Festival production of Handel's *Giulio Cesare*. Again, the question remains whether any parody is perceived in such cases, or whether the audience experiences the production as straight orientalist spectacle. These questions take a particularly complex form when the creators of opera and of operatic productions are themselves deemed exotic from a white Western perspective, for example, Joplin's *Treemonisha*, Still's *Troubled Island*, and Tan Dun's *The First Emperor*. This would also lead us to consider the participation of the "exotic other" in its own exoticizing, as in the appearance of Japanese sopranos as Butterfly and African-Americans in *Aida* or *Porgy and Bess*.

Evolving Approaches to Exoticism

Scholars of operatic exoticism have been interested in tracking which exotic peoples and locales have been referenced in opera, in which periods, and for what reasons, and in determining which national traditions and composers have engaged most frequently in such forms of representation. A long-term focus of such scholarship has been to identify the techniques, musical signs, and stylistic features employed in this representation, their relationship (if any) to actual exotic musical models, and the extent to which specific composers changed their styles and techniques to accomplish exotic representation. Important to this investigation is comparative study with non-operatic musical genres and consideration of why exotic musical representation has flourished particularly in opera. More recently, scholars have investigated the ways in which political context may have predetermined operatic exoticism, and how operatic exoticism itself may have shaped public opinion and political action in different periods. Given the large number of prominent orientalist operas, the potential for rich interdisciplinary and comparative study between operatic, balletic, and cinematic exoticism, and the possible broader social relevance of such works, it should not come as a surprise that exoticism has recently developed into a major field in operatic scholarship.

Studies of operatic exoticism were produced throughout the twentieth century, yet it is only in the past twenty years that the field has grown dramatically. Just under two dozen scholarly works on operatic exoticism appeared in the 1970s, and a similar number were published in the 1980s. The number of writings increased nearly sixfold in the 1990s (as musicology itself expanded), and a similar rate of production held for the first decade of the twenty-first century. The timing of this increase may be understood in part as a delayed musicological response to the 1978 publication of Said's *Orientalism*. Given the focus of much of this scholarship on the role of exoticism in the representation of gender and sexuality in opera, the rise of feminist musicology during this period may also account for the growth of the field. Furthermore, it is likely that the contemporary compositional focus on cross-cultural fusions and the market success of World Beat in the 1980s and 1990s inspired some of this scholarly interest in operatic exoticism. Tracking the evolving historical interests of musicology more generally, earlier scholarship focused particularly on the *alla turca* style of the late eighteenth century. As the field developed, attention turned primarily to examples from the nineteenth century and to the relevant operas of Puccini. More recently, scholars have considered examples from both the first and most recent centuries in operatic history. Many of these studies have focused on individual works, and yet operatic exoticism has not entirely lacked for broad surveys (for example, Gradenwitz 1977; Lindenberger 1998; Scott 1998; and Locke 2009).

The first major studies to engage with Said's arguments as they relate to opera were Said's own 1987 investigation of *Aida*, Ralph Locke's 1991 essay on *Samson et Dalila*, Susan McClary's 1992 focus on the relationship between exoticism, race, and gender representation in *Carmen*, and Richard Taruskin's 1992 contribution on Russian operatic orientalism. Although, as Everist notes, Said himself seemed less eager to apply his critical perspectives and conclusions on orientalism in general to orientalist operas in particular than have numerous musicologists (Everist 1996: 224 n. 26). Locke's article proved particularly seminal, and his substantial subsequent work has placed him at the center of this field. With his wide-ranging 2009 monograph, *Musical Exoticism: Images and Reflections*, Locke produced a capstone to his decades-long scholarship on exoticism. Locke has repeatedly called for a "new paradigm" for approaching operatic exoticism, one that would include consideration of an opera's entire score and production, and not only those passages containing clear exotic signals (an argument Locke has made in numerous articles; see Locke 2000, 2005, 2007a, 2007b, 2008). I have also argued for a broader view of musical exoticism: "[in exoticism] the musical component may reveal no stylistic influence at all, or may exhibit influence from an exotic source different from that involved in the genesis of the work's other elements" (Sheppard 2001: 13).

The common approach to the study of operatic exoticism has been to focus on sections displaying deliberate features of musical difference in the service of exotic representation. This approach is exemplified by Bellman's definition of exoticism: "the borrowing or use of musical materials that evoke distant locales or alien frames of reference" (Bellman 1998: ix). Such definitions tend to place less emphasis on issues of representation and more on the analysis of influence. A focus on influence led James Parakilas, for example, to label both the duet of Lakmé and Mallika and the entrance of Butterfly as non-exotic (Parakilas 1994: I: 47, II: 51). Such narrower definitions of musical exoticism tend to focus particularly on issues of mode and harmony at the expense of other musical elements. However, Parakilas is in line with Locke when he describes an example "lacking any definable Eastern color" as still functioning as a form of musical exoticism (Parakilas 1994: II: 44). Parakilas also notes an absence of exotic musical markers for Carmen throughout much of her opera and offers the intriguing idea that the disappearance of her exotic musical signals at the opera's midpoint reflects Don José's "disenchantment once the reality of life with Carmen destroys the tantalizing dream" (Parakilas 1994: I: 47). Of course, a less interesting explanation for the falling away of exotic musical signals during the course of an orientalist opera is that once a composer clearly identifies certain characters as exotic near the opera's opening, he or she may feel little need to keep this up. Exotic markers may be dropped in an opera in order to bring an exotic character closer to the audience, as during much of Butterfly's love scene with Pinkerton, and they may recur to reassert that character's otherness, as at the moment of Butterfly's suicide. (On the relationship between Butterfly's suicide scene and the web of Japanese markers in Puccini's opera, see Greenwald 2000.) Locke's own attempts in his analysis of *Samson et Dalila* to interpret the striking shift in musical style for the representation of the Philistines from stereotypically exotic in the opera's first act to mainstream Western in the last may have set the stage for his call for a wider focus. Locke rightly has also argued for a broader approach that includes discussion of music's role in exotic representation in cases when no exotic musical model is involved and even in operas where the music seems to lack all deliberate markers signaling cultural difference. He has emphasized how music works in league with the visual and verbal elements of opera to create exotic representations but has recently tended not to emphasize the lasting power of musical stereotypes previously established in the service of such representations. Less persuasive is Locke's suggestion that dance and other visual theatrical elements function more straightforwardly in exotic representations (Locke 2000: 272).

Periodization

Concomitant with the attempt to define the boundaries of operatic exoticism are efforts to establish its periodization. This project requires the recognition of both differences and continuities throughout this history. To date, difference has been emphasized and divisions in the chronology of operatic exoticism have been noted between operas composed before the late eighteenth century, works composed between the late eighteenth and early twentieth centuries, and operas composed since the early twentieth century. In her summary of early operatic exoticism, Miriam K. Whaples stated that "the composer might—and most often did—ignore the problem [of exotic representation] entirely and leave the establishment of exotic atmosphere to the librettist, the scenic designer, and the costumer" (1958: 261). She also noted:

> In the absence of conventions of exoticism comparable to those governing other kinds of tone-painting (*Affektenlehre*), each composer was left to his own resources of musical characterization . . . devices which, while they do have non-European application, are also found within European styles without exotic connotation. *We have found no instance of musical exoticism before 1800 which uses non-European devices not also found in the European vocabulary.* [Italics in original] (Whaples 1958: 263)

Locke's call for the investigation of "all music in context" in studies of operatic exoticism is, in part, motivated by a desire to discuss pre-1750 operatic exoticism in terms similar to those employed for nineteenth-century works. Locke himself has pointed to 1750 as marking a shift in compositional practice where exotic representation began to overlap with cross-cultural influence in the *alla turca* style (Locke 2007a: 490). At the moment, the investigation of early operatic exoticism offers one frontier in this scholarly field (for instance, see Bloechl 2008).

A more contentious periodization question centers on the relationship between earlier orientalist operas and twentieth- and twenty-first-century operatic representation of the exotic. Initially, examples from the past hundred years may well seem quite different from nineteenth-century operatic exoticism. The common separation between passages featuring clear exotic signifiers and a "normal/unmarked" style—that is, a perceptual division between figure and ground in the musical discourse—breaks down in many cases in the twentieth century for those composers whose "normal style" would itself be deemed exotic by most audience members. In addition, numerous composers have experienced a more sustained engagement with the music of other cultures and have attempted to avoid the use of inherited musical stereotypes in their representations of the other. And yet, as I have argued elsewhere, "a difference in level of expertise and encounter does not necessarily result in a difference in the actual use of the exotic" (Sheppard 2001: 12), or, as Matthew Head has put it, "the distinction between orientalist representation and a multicultural fusion of idioms cannot be made purely on the basis of the text and its formal properties" (Head 2003: 211–212). Similar motivations and techniques of exotic representation are evident in both nineteenth-century examples and in more recent "postcolonial" operas and in operas created by composers, librettists, and directors whose own origins would conventionally place them in the "exotic" category themselves. I argue that cross-cultural influence necessarily involves some degree of exotic representation, at least in a work's reception and assuming that the influence has been announced in some way or is not entirely submerged. Pure or neutral forms of influence, devoid of all exotic signification, remain elusive.

To Ignore or Investigate "Influence"?

One currently held assumption in the study of operatic exoticism is that there are few dividends to be gained through detailed comparison between works of exotic representation and their possible exotic musical models. In fact, such investigation—more prevalent in the past, as noted above—is often viewed with critical suspicion as an outmoded approach to these works that ignores pressing political concerns. To oversimplify, following the moment in the academy in the 1980s when multicultural perspectives encouraged an intellectual move beyond Eurocentric confines, postcolonial theory suggested that liberal multiculturalism too easily elided into new forms of orientalism and that the goals of multiculturalism were utopian at best. The revisionary perspective on the study of operatic exoticism is itself not new. Dahlhaus, for one, dismissed the cross-cultural comparative approach most forcefully before the field of exotic representation in opera fully took off, declaring:

> it is wrong to judge exoticism by the criteria of descriptive anthropology.... The crucial point is not the degree to which exoticism is "genuine," but rather the function it serves as a legitimate departure from the aesthetic and compositional norms of European music in the context of an opera or a symphonic poem. It is not so much the original context as the new, artificial context which we should examine if we want our analysis to be historical—that is, to pursue the aesthetic and compositional significance of the phenomenon in the nineteenth century. To do otherwise is to lose ourselves in comparative anthropology, which can do nothing more than establish various degrees of corruption in the music or style quoted. In a word, musical exoticism is a question of function, not of substance. (Dahlhaus [1980] 1989: 302)

This stark and compelling position on the value of comparative study and clarion call for focus on the function of musical exoticism has been influential over the past several decades. Building on Dahlhaus, Head has made the important point that even if a literal inclusion of the exotic other had been possible in orientalist opera, the audiences for these works would still have received this music as a form of exotic representation (Head 2003: 211–212).

Given the frequency of statements against analytical investigation of potential cross-cultural influence in these operas, it is worth pausing to consider what we might be missing and to what extent this dismissal represents a form of intellectual expedience. Certainly, in many cases there seems to be little to discuss in these terms. And yet, our understanding of Saint-Säens's approach to exoticism and his attempts to exceed the exotic modal character of his musical models would be the poorer had not Locke identified and detailed the influence of the *hijaz maqam* in *Samson et Dalila*. McClary's interpretation of Bizet's construction of "Spanishness" relies in part on knowledge of the Cuban origins of the Habanera dance. Noting the traces of Janissary instrumentation and *usul* rhythmic patterns in *alla turca* operas allowed Mary Hunter (1998) and Head (2000), among others, to detail the reception of such exotic topoi and to consider the audience's encounters and associations with these musical features beyond the opera house. Taruskin's analysis of Musorgsky's *Boris Godunov* is the richer for his tracing of the history of "cultural appropriation" of Russian folk song—but here, I suppose, we slip from exoticism to nationalism (Taruskin 1993: 300–312).

Clearly, some consideration of the relationship between the musical "original context" and the operatic "artificial context" has proven revelatory in the study of operatic exoticism. At minimum, such detailed comparative analysis reveals something crucial about the composers of certain orientalist operas and their approach to exotic cultures. Exhaustive attempts to trace individual melodies back to exotic sources without a broader consideration of other musical elements and efforts to adjudicate "authenticity" or "degrees of corruption" are indeed misguided for our understanding of the dynamics of exotic influence. However, the studies mentioned here, as well as numerous others, have demonstrated the potential value of a carefully framed analytical and comparative approach to exotic representation and influence in opera. If we offer no commentary in our discussion of these operas on the relationship between exotic models and specific acts of exotic musical representation, we have turned a deaf ear to a key aspect of compositional process in exoticism. We have also silenced the sources of influence and have allowed the operatic creation to stand fully in their place for our readers.

Modernism and the Exoticist Impulse

Bellman has observed that exoticist works are often denigrated by critics and scholars in terms of their lack of authenticity and their unsavory political implications, that such operas have been designated "as inhabiting a lower plane than other varieties of music"

(Bellman 1998: xiii). There is certainly a good deal of validity to this claim, at least for older scholarship. In the standard analytical accounts of the development of European music from the nineteenth through twentieth centuries, orientalist operas have rarely been referenced. It could be argued that significant features of stylistic and technical development in the first decades of the twentieth century—particularly in terms of timbral, rhythmic, and modal exploration—can be traced back to passages of high exoticism in nineteenth-century opera. Could it be that these "peripheral" operas, these works that have been considered somewhat exotic themselves in terms of the operatic tradition, infiltrated European music in ways rarely acknowledged? Was operatic exoticism actually a significant catalyst for stylistic and technical change more generally? The influence of late-nineteenth-century Russian orientalist opera on Stravinsky, as detailed by Taruskin (1996), and studies of Puccini's *Turandot* (Wilson 2007: 185–220) that point to its strains of musical modernism, may be cited here in support of this supposition. Of course, support for this hypothesis may also be found in statements made by certain modernist composers themselves.

In a retrospective (some might say, revisionary) mode late in his career (1942), Strauss discussed the "advanced" style of his *Salome* and noted that he had long faulted exoticist operas for lacking "true oriental colour and scorching sun." He claimed that the plot inspired him to create "truly exotic harmonies, which sparkled like taffeta particularly in the strange cadences" and that his indulgence in bitonality in this work should be considered "a unique experiment with a peculiar subject, but it cannot be recommended to imitators" (Strauss [1949] 1953: 150). Here Strauss directly blames the impulses of exotic representation for the harmonic audacity that many of his contemporaries heard as a declaration that the musical future had arrived. Analytical scholarship that might champion the progressive musical influence of the exoticist impulse runs the risk of being charged with political naïveté or of willfully ignoring the social implications of exotic representation. And yet such an approach could help to bridge the conceptual gulf between the nineteenth and twentieth centuries in European music that some of our histories continue to reinforce. By noting the debts of certain modernist composers to the traditions of orientalist opera, we might be led more readily to observe other strands of continuity.

Strauss's attempts to distance himself from musical modernism by pointing to the circumstantial and temporary influences of exoticism on his work ironically dovetail with attempts by avowed modernists to distance their own works from discussions of exotic representation. Numerous scholars have followed the lead of these composers in assuming that a chasm exists between nineteenth-century orientalist opera and modernist cross-cultural or "transcultural" composition. For instance, Locke has referred to the "discouraging impact of musical modernism on overt explorations of the musically exotic" (Locke 1998: 105) and has recently attempted to tease out differences between "overt exoticism," "submerged exoticism," and "transcultural composing" while also acknowledging connections across these categories (Locke 2009: 214–247). In actuality, modernism had a discouraging impact on operatic composition in general and, rather than being banished or entirely submerged, the exoticist impulse (both in new and in conventional forms) proved central to the development of modernist opera and music theater and was frequently inspired by long-standing motivations. A broader conception of both "opera" and "exoticism" reveals that exotic representation and exotic influence were intertwined and continued to play out on a continuum, rather than categorically, in the twentieth century. As Gilles de Van has aptly put it: "The increasingly exact knowledge of the other goes hand in hand with its retrieval as a metaphor for our own longings" (de Van 1995: 92). And yet, modernist and postmodernist composers have certainly felt the full weight of the history of operatic exoticism and have pondered their relationship to that history. In the balance of this chapter, I consider a few twentieth-century operas that referenced the tradition of musical exoticism itself as a model and, in some cases, attempted to display that tradition at some remove through parody.[1]

The Golden Calf and an Aztec King

The Germanic strain of modernism and serialist operas would appear to be an unpromising point of entry for this investigation, and Arnold Schoenberg is certainly not the first figure who comes to mind in considering twentieth-century musical exoticism. In fact, Schoenberg publicly disparaged those modernist composers interested in forms of cross-cultural influence and exotic representation. And yet, his *Moses und Aron* contains one of the most aggressively exotic scenes in all of opera. Although the Bible devotes but one verse to the Israelites' construction and worship of the Golden Calf, Act II, scene 3 proves the longest in Schoenberg's opera. The violence, sexual intensity, and stilted style of the scenario resemble the expressionist theater of Kokoschka and of Schoenberg's own *Die glückliche Hand*, and the wave upon wave of wantonness points back to Wagner's Bacchanal in the Venusberg in *Tannhäuser*. Schoenberg represents the Israelites as bestial, ultra-exotic others engaged in mass hysteria. Rather than inviting charges of anti-Semitic representation, as have been leveled against Strauss's *Salome*, this scene suggests that any group is susceptible to "going primitive" under certain conditions. The musical representation of this exotic hysteria deviates sharply from the rest of the opera and from Schoenberg's norms. In attempting to represent exotic rituals of human sacrifice and debauchery in a twelve-tone opera, Schoenberg placed an uncharacteristic emphasis on the percussion section and composed layers of intense ostinati for the uninhibited dancing. Having no specific exotic model in mind as a source of influence, Schoenberg turned to certain forms and specific composers of European modernist music itself for inspiration in composing this scene. At the altar of the Golden Calf we have found a new source of exotic music, and he is Stravinsky.[2]

Roger Sessions had Schoenberg's *Moses und Aron* very much in mind as he composed his own exoticist opera involving ritual sacrifice, *Montezuma* (1963). (Olmstead [1985b: 127] has suggested a parallel between the two pairs of principal male characters in these operas.) Like Schoenberg, Sessions turned to Stravinsky's *Rite of Spring* ostinati and perhaps to Strauss's *Elektra* and to Schoenberg's own Golden Calf scene as models of exoticist representation. In his portrayal of the Spanish and Aztec characters and their historic encounter, Sessions intended to depict "the futility of conquest" (Olmstead 1985b: 85) and to emphasize the similarities between these two groups. He also set out to suggest clear parallels between the Aztec sacrifice in the second tableau of Act II and the Spanish *auto-da-fé* in Act III. However, Montezuma has fewer lines than the other major characters, and the music for the Aztec sacrifice stands apart from the main body of the opera in its emphasis on percussion instruments. Moreover, Sessions gestured toward exotic authenticity by calling for an Aztec Teponaxtli slit drum, but also included numerous other percussion instruments, including those of Chinese origin. In contrast, the Spanish *auto-da-fé* appears to be devoid of exotic musical signals. Jürgen Maehder has asserted that in this opera, musical exoticism does not mesh well with serialism and that the attempt to transport nineteenth-century exoticism into a modernist idiom proved "unsuccessful" (Maehder 1992: 276). Ultimately, despite a new liberal perspective on imperialism and exotic representation, *Montezuma* remains within the tradition of operatic orientalism.

A more recent music theater treatment of the encounter between Cortez and Montezuma again reveals the persistence of techniques of exotic representation, despite the creators' protestations against exoticism. Wolfgang Rihm's 1991 *Die Eroberung von Mexico* is based primarily on a dramatic outline by Artaud (*The Conquest of Mexico*, 1933) and displays an aesthetic that is in line with early-twentieth-century expressionist theater. The work also employs a poem by Octavio Paz ("Root of Man," 1937) and an anonymous Aztec song text, both literary sources intended, perhaps, to offer a degree of exotic authenticity (on Rihm's literary sources for this work, see Williams 2004: 244). As with Sessions, Artaud's scenario is critical of Western imperialism. Alastair Williams has argued that the work's psychological sophistication moves it "beyond the confines of nineteenth-century orientalism," despite numerous musical features borrowed from that tradition (Williams 2004: 249). Extending the common gendered binaries of orientalism, Montezuma is portrayed in the opera by a soprano and by two other accompanying female voices, while Cortez is played by a baritone with accompanying male voices. Given Rihm's statement that Montezuma remains a male character despite his female vocal representation, Williams claims that the opera moves "beyond any simple dualism of male colonizers and female colonized" (Williams 2004: 261). Williams also remarks that Montezuma "ceases to be a human subject" (2004: 263–264). The Aztec female translator Malinche is cast as a mute dancer. In this opera, the subaltern does not speak much.

The exotic setting in *Die Eroberung von Mexico* is established musically at the start with percussion representing native drums; Montezuma's music features tritones and open fifths and is accompanied by bowed antique cymbals. Williams (2004) notes these features, but claims that the work is involved in "negotiating and engaging orientalist tropes rather than merely deploying them" (250), that Cortez himself is represented as "other" (256), and that Cortez and Montezuma "achieve a degree of intersubjectivity" in their final duet (270). Williams states that "Rihm and Artaud are concerned primarily neither with the history of Mexico nor with its politics as a modern nation; rather they are preoccupied with the location as an environment in which to play out the discovery self makes of the Other in more general terms" (2004: 249). Thus, as Williams himself notes, in this work the exotic other and setting once again offer the opportunity for the West to "play out" its own concerns. As new works proclaim their attempts to move beyond the tradition of operatic exoticism their creators (and defenders) appear to presuppose an audience sophisticated enough to see through or ignore the clear signs of orientalist representation.

"Almost a Satire": A Bearded Lady and a Belly Dancer

Other twentieth-century operas engaged in the parody of exoticism itself as a way of coming to terms with the operatic past. Two particularly prominent operas offered cameo appearances of eighteenth-century *alla turca* and comic "Turkish" characters. Baba the Turk in Stravinsky's *The Rake's Progress* (1951) is doubly framed as an impersonation of the exotic (Figure 36.1). As a bearded lady, she is a sideshow star who wears her "Turkishness" rather lightly. Joseph Kerman referred to her as "the un-exotic Baba" (Kerman 1988: 195). Indeed, Stravinsky does not draw on any of the obvious exotic musical stereotypes for her portrayal. Just before Nick first mentions her to Tom in Act II, scene 1, we twice hear a thirty-second note flourish in the harpsichord that features two successive tritones. However, this gesture in the opera points to Nick's diabolical plans, rather than Baba's exotic qualities. Baba's own melodic lines occasionally feature tritones and frequently involve awkward leaps, particularly the "jackass heehaw" effect of minor ninths. In an opera of awkward vocal contours, her disjunct lines still stand out. As in *opera buffa*, these intervals and overblown *seria* stylistic features undermine and brand her as a pompous character, but do not necessarily signal an exotic status. And yet, Baba embodies many of the attributes of the exotic operatic other, and we may assume that any musical bearding or exoticizing would prove rather superfluous. In fact, Baba's exoticism, like Handel's exotic tyrants, demands Locke's broader paradigm for its full appreciation. She is simultaneously repulsive and enticing, irrational and passionate, and her very presence is a performance of ambiguous gender and even sexual deviance. Numerous critics have considered her character a "homosexual joke" perpetrated by the work's librettists Auden and Kallman on Stravinsky. For example, Taruskin refers to Baba as "a madcap gay inversion of the conventional 'trouser role'" and as "Auden and Kallman's catty little joke at the expense of the elderly, conventionally homophobic and decidedly unhip composer" (Taruskin 2009: 110). She is a collector of exotic oddities and is nearly auctioned off as an exotic object herself. Her entrances and exits are all staged and even inspire applause from her onstage audiences. Like a wind-up doll, Baba suggests that the exotic figure may now be turned off and then wound up again at whim for the purposes of representational play.

FIGURE 36.1 Cindy Sadler as Baba the Turk in the Princeton Festival 2011 production of Igor Stravinsky's *The Rake's Progress*. Reproduced with the permission of the Princeton Festival.

In the famous Act I finale of John Corigliano's *The Ghosts of Versailles* (1991)—one of the more successful operas of the late twentieth century—eighteenth-century operatic *alla turca* is again doubly framed. We watch as the titular aristocratic French ghosts watch a performance of a fictitious opera by Beaumarchais, which abruptly leaps to a scene set in the Turkish embassy at the time of the French Revolution. In the original production, the Turkish Pasha was visually represented by a gigantic mechanical doll, and he is musically signaled in the score by a highly melismatic, augmented second-laden vocal line, with crotale punctuations marking his speech, and accompanied by an onstage "Turkish" band including a *dumbec* and low drum with repeated drum patterns and a sinuous oboe. As the British ambassador arrives, the onstage Turkish band plays an exotically twisted version of "God Save the King," thus perpetrating the time-honored joke about the East attempting to imitate the West musically.

An "Egyptian singer" named Samira (originally played triumphantly by Marilyn Horne) performs in a style that embraces high camp and the stereotypical signs of musical orientalism while it simultaneously gestures toward exotic authenticity (see Figure 36.2). Anne Shreffler suggests that Horne was "got up to look like a female impersonator. At the very least, Samira evokes the same kind of cross-gender fascination as Stravinsky and Auden's Baba the Turk" (Shreffler 2001: 130). In preparation for her

FIGURE 36.2 Marilyn Horne as Samira in the Metropolitan Opera premiere production of John Corigliano's *The Ghosts of Versailles*. Reproduced with the permission of the Metropolitan Opera Archives.

performance, Horne studied videos of belly dance and was provided with recordings of Middle Eastern vocalists by Corigliano. Samira's highly melismatic line is infested with the augmented second sonority and leads to a clear *wazn*-like rhythmic pattern in the ensuing dance. In the original production of the opera, Samira was accompanied by an onstage violist (Midhat Serbagi, a classical European violist of Lebanese heritage) who adopted Arabic bowed string techniques and who suddenly burst into an Arabic-style vocalization. In the lineup of exotic dancing girls who eventually perform with Samira we spy the character Figaro, dressed in drag as a bearded exotic woman and musically veiled with an outrageous falsetto voice mocking the history of the castrati. Ultimately over a hundred performers filled the stage in this finale, including a marching band of masked kazoo players intended to represent an ensemble of the North African double-reed *rheita*.

What and who are we laughing at as we revel in Corigliano's over-the-top Act I "Turkish" finale? Is the history of orientalist representation the target of this satire or are "we" (the intended audience) still laughing at the exotic other? Does Figaro in his exotic drag parody Samira/Horne as Samira/Horne parodies Middle Eastern female performers and perhaps European divas who have portrayed them in orientalist operas? Corigliano appears simultaneously to poke fun at operatic exoticism and to draw on aspects of cross-cultural influence. In this scene, all the major elements of orientalist representation are flamboyantly present: irrationality, excessively ornamented and decorative staged performance, bold female sexual display, gender ambiguity, stereotypes of musical exoticism, cultural cross-dressing, and so on. We likewise encounter a claim of exotic authenticity, for as did Saint-Saëns, Corigliano had traveled to North Africa and had heard performances on the *rheita* in Marrakech in 1966. This influence and its comic potential was also present in Corigliano's "Rheita Dance," the fifth movement of his 1975 *Concerto for Oboe* in which the soloist is called upon to employ an embouchure that produces a piercing timbre and flexible pitch approximating that of the *rheita*. Just as Samira rolls her eyes as the onstage exotic violist briefly usurps her role as soloist, so too the oboe soloist and orchestra in the concerto attempt to wrest back control from the principal orchestral oboist who "continues unperturbed" in an intrusive solo of his or her own. In fact, one of the principal musical gestures in Samira's scene was taken by Corigliano straight from his *Concerto for Oboe*. Corigliano has stated in his program notes that the concerto movement itself included, in addition to the rough *rheita* imitations, "a kind of refined, perfumed Stravinskian *orientale*, almost a satire on orientalisms-via-Paris."

Tangled Critical and Operatic History

Is it possible to parody orientalism without simultaneously perpetuating it? Not every critic has heard a parody of the orientalist operatic past in this scene. In a 1992 review of *The Ghosts of Versailles*, Said pointed particularly to the Act I finale:

> Here we get Marilyn Horne as Samira, the Ottoman pasha's favorite singer, who disports herself in a disgracefully idiotic caricature of not Turkish but Arabic music, with poorly written and pronounced Arabic words as her text. The scene serves no dramatic or musical purpose but that of sanctioned tastelessness: The Arab/Islamic world, quite bad enough in its present morass, is degraded still further by this utterly silly and confusing scene. Why a great singer like Horne should agree to perform such trash is rather bewildering. (Said [1992] 2008: 141)

Said clearly did not allow for the possibility that Corigliano and Hoffman (his librettist) intended to caricature European orientalist representation rather than Turkish or Arabic culture.

At least one critic, Herbert Lindenberger, has even stepped forward to defend operatic orientalism itself against the "gross caricature" and "crude parody of both the eighteenth- and nineteenth-century versions of orientalism" exhibited in this scene (Lindenberger 1998: 175). However, in his attempt to distance recent opera from the orientalist tradition, Lindenberger's discussion becomes quite tangled. He appears determined from the outset to declare that operatic orientalism is over, claiming that "it is clear that the operatic Orient visible in recent works is scarcely orientalist in any earlier sense," and yet his evidence and examples suggest the opposite conclusion (1998: 175). Although operatic orientalism includes both the experience of attraction and revulsion in encountering the exotic, Lindenberger proclaims that Glass's *Satyagraha* offers a form of "reverse orientalism," by which he means a positive celebration of Eastern thought (1998: 175). He also deems *Satyagraha* "more genuinely a product of Eastern influence," and thus removed from orientalism given Glass's studies of Indian classical music (1998: 176–177), although he later acknowledges that composers of orientalism have long sought exotic authenticity and, like Glass, have consulted experts (1998: 178).

Also in this vein, Lindenberger claims that in *The Death of Klinghoffer* Adams treats both the Western Jewish characters and the Eastern Arabs in "as evenhanded a way as is conceivable" (1998: 177). However, he then notes that although the chorus of Jews at the opening of the opera has "no trace of local color in its music," the Arab chorus features melismatic lines that audiences recognize as exotic markers (1998: 178). He cites Adams as saying that he wanted to depict "otherness" in his musical representation of the Arabs and that he turned to the music of a Syrian composer for inspiration. The parallels with Saint-Saëns's *Samson et Dalila*, in which the Jewish chorus is differentiated from the music of the Philistines in the same way, seem clear, as does the implication for the target audience's identification with one group of characters over the other. Lindenberger attempts to save *Klinghoffer* from the "orientalist" label by arguing that the "Near Eastern coloring of this music [...] never suggests the sexuality or the glamour of nineteenth-century orientalist opera, nor does Adams [employ it] [...] to suggest threats of violence," and he concludes that "Adams's is an orientalism stripped of its traditional meaning, if indeed we can call it an orientalism at all" (1998: 178; for more on exoticism in the operas of John Adams, including *The Death of Klinghoffer*, see Sheppard 2013). Again, as in the case of Rihm's representation of the Aztecs, although orientalist representational techniques and musical stereotypes are present, we are asked to consider them as having lost all of their referential meaning. This suggests a modernist and postmodernist "emancipation of orientalist signs." However, as with early atonality, in which dissonance continued to have its traditional associations even in the hands of the very composers proclaiming its emancipation, this "emancipation" is rather utopian.

Past Postmodernism?

The parody of operatic exoticism featured in such postmodern works as *The Ghosts of Versailles* might suggest that exoticism itself has run its course. However, this conclusion would be premature, for the framing and parody of exoticism within opera has its own history. Both Corigliano and Hoffman have cited Rossini's *L'Italiana in Algeri* (a major opera in Horne's career) and *Il Turco in Italia* as models—operas that in various ways twisted the norms of *alla turca* while also indulging in the representational form. As Alex Ross has put it in reference to *The Ghosts of Versailles*, "Isn't there something utterly redundant about staging a satire of Rossini?" (Ross 1992: 32). Just as Corigliano and Hoffman cite and allude to Mozart and Rossini, Rossini himself referenced Mozart and other orientalist opera. The Act I finale of *Ghosts* was inspired by the Act I finale of *L'Italiana*, which, as the music turns the characters into clockwork automatons, seems to reference the effect of Papageno's magic bells on Monostatos in *The Magic Flute*. Rossini clearly echoed the Janissary chorus and overture from Mozart's *Abduction from the Seraglio* in his Act II "Kaimakan" chorus in *L'Italiana* and, as would Corigliano in *Ghosts*, quoted the Commendatore's declaration to Don Giovanni near the end of Mozart's opera in his *Il Turco* (Betzwieser 1994: 114). Mustafà's famous sneezes in *L'Italiana* likely suggested the Pasha's crucial sneeze in the Act I finale of *Ghosts*. Although Rossini only rarely engages elements of the *alla turca* style directly, Locke's "broader paradigm" would surely lead us to note how music nonetheless characterizes the exotic in these operas. As Osborne observes: "Mustaf[à], arrogant and domineering, is caricatured at the opera's outset, rendered ridiculous in the introduzione by grotesque intervals and elaborate coloratura" (Osborne 2007: 212). Most crucially for our purposes, Osborne concludes that in *Il Turco*, Rossini "gently mocks the vogue for all things Turkish whilst smiling wryly at the operatic procedures and conventions that give it life" (2007: 218).

An archeological investigation of *The Ghosts of Versailles* and Rossini's *alla turca* operas, to take but one comparative example, reveals multiple layers of inter-exoticist influence. Rather than quenching opera's thirst for exoticism, parody repeatedly rekindles the embers of exotic representation. Indeed, a parody may well leave its audience craving the original form all the more. As would multiple twentieth-century composers of operatic exoticism, Rossini appears both to engage in orientalist representation and comically and critically to frame it within his operas. This conceptual move did not need to wait for modernist or postmodernist perspectives. Rather, the particular centrality of exoticism in operatic history has long been acknowledged within opera itself.

See also: Race and Racism, Gender, What Is Opera? Politics

Notes

1. My discussion and juxtaposition of Schoenberg's *Moses und Aron* with *Montezuma* by Sessions and Stravinsky's *The Rake's Progress* with Corigliano's *The Ghosts of Versailles* derives, in part, from a presentation I delivered in a graduate seminar on operatic orientalism led by Carolyn Abbate at Princeton University in the spring of 1993. I am grateful for comments made by Abbate and by my fellow students on that occasion.
2. I am certainly not alone in noting the several references to the music of Stravinsky in this scene. For a brief discussion of the representation of human sacrifice in modernist music,

focusing on Schoenberg and Stravinsky and touching on works by Rihm and Henze, see Schultz 2000: 153–160. Daniel Albright has heard references to Strauss's *Elektra* in this scene, but points more to stylistic elements of jazz that lead him to suggest that in the Dance of the Butchers "Schoenberg may have intended [...] a parody of pop music" (Albright 2008: 441–454).

Bibliography

Abbate, Carolyn. 1993. "Opera; or, the Envoicing of Women." In *Musicology and Difference*, edited by Ruth Solie, 225–258. Berkeley and Los Angeles: University of California Press.

Albright, Daniel. 2008. "Butchering Moses." *Opera Quarterly* 23/4: 441–454.

Ashbrook, William, and Harold Powers. 1991. *Puccini's 'Turandot': The End of the Great Tradition*. Princeton, NJ: Princeton University Press.

Becker, Heinz. 1976. *Die 'Couleur locale' in der Oper des 19. Jahrhunderts*. Regensburg: Gustav Bosse.

Beckerman, Michael. 1989. "The Sword on the Wall: Japanese Elements and Their Significance in *The Mikado*." *Musical Quarterly* 73/3: 303–319.

Bellman, Jonathan, ed. 1998. *The Exotic in Western Music*. Boston: Northeastern University Press.

Betzwieser, Thomas. 1994. "A Propos de L'Exotisme Musical de Rossini." In *Gioachino Rossini, 1792–1992. Il testo e la scena. Atti del Convegno 1992*, edited by Paolo Fabbri, 105–126. Pesaro: Fondazione Rossini.

——, and Michael Stegemann. 1995. "Exotismus." In *Die Musik in Geschichte und Gegenwart*, III: 225–243. Kassel: Bärenreiter.

Bhabha, Homi K. 1983. "The Other Question—the Stereotype and Colonial Discourse." *Screen* 24/6: 18–36.

Bloechl, Olivia A. 2008. *Native American Song at the Frontiers of Early Modern Music*. Cambridge: Cambridge University Press.

Born, Georgina, and David Hesmondhalgh, eds. 2000. *Western Music and Its Others: Difference, Representation, and Appropriation in Music*. Berkeley and Los Angeles: University of California Press.

Brett, Philip. 1994. "Eros and Orientalism in Britten's Operas." In *Queering the Pitch: The New Gay and Lesbian Musicology*, edited by Philip Brett, Elizabeth Wood, and Gary C. Thomas, 235–256. New York: Routledge.

Clark, Caryl. 2009. *Haydn's Jews: Representation and Reception on the Operatic Stage*. Cambridge: Cambridge University Press.

Cook, Susan C. 1988. *Opera for a New Republic: The Zeitopern of Krenek, Weill, and Hindemith*. Ann Arbor, MI: UMI Research Press.

Cooke, Mervyn. 1998. *Britten and the Far East: Asian Influences in the Music of Benjamin Britten*. Woodbridge: Boydell Press.

Dahlhaus, Carl. [1980] 1989. *Nineteenth-Century Music*, translated by J. Bradford Robinson. Berkeley and Los Angeles: University of California Press.

Everist, Mark. 1996. "Meyerbeer's *Il crociato in Egitto: Mélodrame*, Opera, Orientalism." *Cambridge Opera Journal* 8/3: 215–250.

Fauser, Annegret. 2005. *Musical Encounters at the 1889 Paris World's Fair*. Rochester, NY: University of Rochester Press.

Gilman, Sander L. 1988. "Strauss and the Pervert." In *Reading Opera*, edited by Arthur Groos and Roger Parker, 306–327. Princeton, NJ: Princeton University Press.

Girardi, Michele. 2000. *Puccini: His International Art*, translated by Laura Basini. Chicago: University of Chicago Press.

Gradenwitz, Peter. 1977. *Musik zwischen Orient und Okzident: Eine Kulturgeschichte der Wechselbeziehungen*. Wihelmshaven and Hamburg: Heinrichshofen.

Greenwald, Helen M. 2000. "Picturing Cio-Cio-San: House, Screen, and Ceremony in Puccini's *Madama Butterfly*." *Cambridge Opera Journal* 12/3: 237–259.

Groos, Arthur, and Virgilio Bernardoni, eds. 2008. *Madama Butterfly: l'orientalismo di fine secolo, l'approccio pucciniano, la ricezione*. Florence: Olschki.

Harrison, Frank L. 1985. "Observation, Elucidation, Utilization: Western Attitudes to Eastern Musics, ca. 1600–ca. 1830." In *Slavonic and Western Music: Essays for Gerald Abraham*, edited by Malcolm H. Brown and Roland J. Wiley, 5–31. New York: Oxford University Press.

Head, Matthew. 2003. "Musicology on Safari: Orientalism and the Spectre of Postcolonial Theory." *Music Analysis* 22: 211–230.

——. 2000. *Orientalism, Masquerade and Mozart's Turkish Music*. London: Royal Musical Association.

Hunter, Mary. 1998. "The *Alla Turca* Style in the late Eighteenth Century: Race and Gender in the Symphony and the Seraglio." In Bellman 1998, 43–73.

Kerman, Joseph. [1956] 1988. *Opera as Drama*. Rev. ed. Berkeley and Los Angeles: University of California Press.

Kramer, Lawrence. 1990. "Culture and Musical Hermeneutics: The Salome Complex." *Cambridge Opera Journal* 2/3: 269–294.

Lancefield, Robert Charles. 2004. "Hearing Orientality in (White) America, 1900–1930." PhD diss., Wesleyan University.

Lindenberger, Herbert. 1998. *Opera in History: From Monteverdi to Cage*. Stanford, CA: Stanford University Press.

Locke, Ralph P. 2009. *Musical Exoticism: Images and Reflections*. Cambridge: Cambridge University Press.

——. 2008. "Doing the Impossible: On the Musically Exotic." *Journal of Musicological Research* 27/4: 334–358.

——. 2007a. "A Broader View of Musical Exoticism." *Journal of Musicology* 24/4: 477–521.

——. 2007b. "Unacknowledged Exoticism in Debussy: The Incidental Music for *Le martyre de saint Sébastien* (1911)." *Musical Quarterly* 90/3–4: 371–415.

——. 2006. "Aida and Nine Readings of Empire." *Nineteenth-Century Music Review* 3/1: 45–72.

——. 2005. "Beyond the Exotic: How 'Eastern' Is Aida?" *Cambridge Opera Journal* 17/2: 105–139.

——. 2000. "Exoticism and Orientalism in Music: Problems for the Worldly Critic." In *Edward Said and the Work of the Critic: Speaking Truth to Power*, edited by Paul A. Bové, 257–281. Durham, NC: Duke University Press.

——. 1998. "Cutthroats and Casbah Dancers, Muezzins and Timeless Sands: Musical Images of the Middle East." In Bellman 1998, 104–136.

——. 1993. "Reflections on Orientalism in Opera and Musical Theater." *Opera Quarterly* 10/1: 48–64.

——. 1991. "Constructing the Oriental 'Other': Saint-Saëns's *Samson et Dalila*." *Cambridge Opera Journal* 3/3: 261–302.

Maehder, Jürgen. 1993. "Cristóbal Colón, Montecuzoma II. Xocoyotzin and Hernán Cortés on the Opera Stage: A Study in Comparative Libretto History." *Revista de musicologia* 16/1: 146–184.

——. 1992. "The Representation of the 'Discovery' on the Opera Stage." In *Musical Repercussions of 1492*, edited by Carol E. Robertson, 257–287. Washington: Smithsonian Institution Press.
——. 1985. *Esotismo e colore locale nell'opera di Puccini*. Pisa: Giardini Editori e Stampatori.
McClary, Susan. 1992. *Georges Bizet: 'Carmen.'* Cambridge Opera Handbooks. Cambridge: Cambridge University Press.
Olmstead, Andrea. 1985a. "The Plum'd Serpent: Antonio Borgese and Roger Sessions's *Montezuma*." *Tempo* 152: 13–22.
——. 1985b. *Roger Sessions and His Music*. Ann Arbor, MI: UMI Research Press.
Osborne, Richard. 2007. *Rossini: His Life and Works*. 2nd ed. New York: Oxford University Press.
Parakilas, James. 1994. "The Soldier and the Exotic: Operatic Variations on a Theme of Racial Encounter: Part I and II." *Opera Quarterly* 10/2: 33–56 and 10/3: 43–69.
Parker, D. C. 1917. "Exoticism in Music in Retrospect." *Musical Quarterly* 3/1: 134–161.
Pisani, Michael V. 2005. *Imagining Native America in Music*. New Haven: Yale University Press.
Ross, Alex. 1992. "The Ghosts of the Met." *The New Republic* (March): 29–33.
Said, Edward W. [1992] 2008. "Uncertainties of Style." In *Music at the Limits*, 140–148. New York: Columbia University Press.
——. 1993. *Culture and Imperialism*. New York: Knopf.
——. 1987. "The Imperial Spectacle." *Grand Street* 6: 82–104.
——. 1978. *Orientalism*. New York: Pantheon Books.
Schultz, Wolfgang-Andreas. 2000. "Menschenopfer und Moderne–ein fiktives Interview." In *Musik–nicht ohne Worte*, edited by Manfred Stahnke, 153–160. Hamburg: Bockel.
Scott, Derek B. 1998. "Orientalism and Musical Style." *Musical Quarterly* 82/2: 309–335.
Sheppard, W. Anthony. 2013. "The Persistence of Orientalism in the Postmodern Operas of Adams and Sellars." In *Representation in Western Music*, edited by Joshua Walden, 267–286. Cambridge: Cambridge University Press.
——. 2009. "Blurring the Boundaries: Tan Dun's *Tinte* and *The First Emperor*." *Journal of Musicology* 26/3: 285–326.
——. 2005. "Cinematic Realism, Reflexivity and the American 'Madame Butterfly' Narratives." *Cambridge Opera Journal* 17/1: 59–93.
——. 2001. *Revealing Masks: Exotic Influences and Ritualized Performance in Modernist Music Theater*. Berkeley and Los Angeles: University of California Press.
Shreffler, Anne. 2001. "Phantoms at the Opera: *The Ghosts of Versailles* by John Corigliano and William Hoffman." *Contemporary Music Review* 20/4: 117–135.
Strauss, Richard. [1949] 1953. "Reminiscences of the First Performance of My Operas" [1942]. In *Recollections and Reflections*, edited by Willi Schuh and translated by L. J. Lawrence. London: Boosey and Hawkes.
Taruskin, Richard. 2009. "In *The Rake's Progress*, Love Conquers (Almost) All." *The Danger of Music and Other Anti-Utopian Essays*, 109–117. Berkeley and Los Angeles: University of California Press [Originally published in the *New York Times*, November 16, 1997].
——. 1996. *Stravinsky and the Russian Traditions*. Berkeley and Los Angeles: University of California Press.
——. 1993. *Musorgsky: Eight Essays and an Epilogue*. Princeton, NJ: Princeton University Press.
——. 1992. "'Entoiling the Falconet': Russian Musical Orientalism in Context." *Cambridge Opera Journal* 4/3: 253–280.
Taylor, Timothy D. 2007. *Beyond Exoticism: Western Music and the World*. Durham, NC: Duke University Press.
Van, Gilles de. 1995. "Fin de siècle Exoticism and the Meaning of the Far Away." [Translated by William Ashbrook]. *Opera Quarterly* 11/ 3: 77–94.

Weiner, Marc. 1997. *Richard Wagner and the Anti-Semitic Imagination*. Lincoln: University of Nebraska Press.
Whaples, Miriam K. 1998. "Early Exoticism Revisited." In Bellman 1998, 3–25.
——. 1958. "Exoticism in Dramatic Music, 1600–1800." PhD diss., Indiana University.
Williams, Alastair. 2004. "Voices of the Other: Wolfgang Rihm's Music Drama *Die Eroberung von Mexico*." *Journal of the Royal Musical Association* 139/2: 240–271.
Wilson, Alexandra. 2007. *The Puccini Problem: Opera, Nationalism, and Modernity*. Cambridge: Cambridge University Press.

CHAPTER 37

CENSORSHIP

FRANCESCO IZZO

On October 6, 1600, a selected audience at Palazzo Pitti in Florence attended the performance of *Euridice*, the first opera whose score has survived in its entirety. Ottavio Rinuccini's poetry, set to music for the occasion by Jacopo Peri, tells the tale of Orpheus and Eurydice, drawing on Book 10 of Ovid's *Metamorphoses*. Anyone who knew, even superficially, this literary text, must have realized that Rinuccini's poetry departed from it in numerous ways. The most notable difference was the ending: Orpheus does not lose his bride (and consequently himself), but returns victorious from the gates of hell, where he has succeeded in snatching his beloved from the underworld deities; an all-too-benevolent, music-loving Pluto has handed back Eurydice unconditionally upon hearing his heartfelt song. The justification for this finale is self-evident: *Euridice* was produced in the context of the festivities for the wedding of Maria de' Medici to Henry IV of France. A tale in which a groom loses his bride as he surrenders to his passions is hardly suitable for such a celebration, and Rinuccini must have taken this into account in preparing his text. But was he fully persuaded of this change? Or did he diverge from Ovid only because a happy ending was vital in order to make the work performable in the context where it originated? Did he create his finale autonomously, or did other agents (the patron, Jacopo Corsi, or the Medici themselves) influence or instruct him so as to obtain poetry that was suitable for that context?

No documentary evidence shows under what pressures Rinuccini diverged from Ovid, and we can be content with the obvious explanation that the original ending was unfit for a wedding celebration. In fact, there is no need to assume that such documentary evidence ever existed. On grounds of dramatic effectiveness, the "occasional" ending of *Euridice* is one of the essential points for which many an opera lover would unhesitatingly favor Monteverdi's *L'Orfeo* (and its libretto, written by Alessandro Striggio) over Rinuccini and Peri's work. This case reminds us that since the very beginnings of opera, when a literary work becomes the source for a libretto, changes in structure and contents are often not merely the autonomous authorial response to the demands imposed by the different expressive media or to other artistic concerns;

they are also the reflection of external factors that could become determinant during the creative process of a new opera. Individual and collective agents—such as patrons, impresarios, performers, publishers, and political and religious authorities—as well as circumstantial factors, including local and international politics, cultural and religious climate, and occasional matters, could bear a substantial influence on an opera's shape and contents.

I begin with *Euridice* not for the sake of chronological progression, nor because I consider it an especially important case of what we might wish to call censorship. Rather, I take this consequential work as my starting point because it confronts us with the need and the difficulty to define censorship, both as a general concept and as it can be understood in the context of operatic production and circulation. On the one hand, it is difficult to imagine a reason other than occasion and expectations of the patron that would prompt the concoction of an otherwise indefensible happy ending for the mythical pair of lovers; in order to be performable at a wedding, the libretto of *Euridice* had to meet those expectations. On the other hand, strictly speaking (if one, for example, wanted to adhere to a basic dictionary definition [i.e., the *Oxford Dictionary Online*], and use "censorship" merely to describe "the practice of *officially* examining books, movies, etc., and *suppressing* unacceptable parts"; emphasis mine), one might well argue that *Euridice* (along with countless other operas), was never "censored," in the sense that it was never subjected to *official* examination or to *suppression* of its contents.

Both lines of reasoning are perfectly legitimate, and each should be followed closely in the attempt to understand operatic censorship as an integral aspect of the production and circulation of opera—one that, manifesting itself in a variety of ways, encompasses the entire history of the genre. Rather than unidimensionally embracing one of these two extremes (the idea that any form of conditioning can be referred to as censorship *or* the notion that only the official suppression of parts or all of a text qualifies as censorship), it is by grasping the tension and the continuum that exist between these extremes that we can begin to contemplate the complexity and the diversity of operatic censorship.

Conjectural Evidence

One paradigm that has remained constant through the history of opera is that its creation and production is a complex and costly affair, involving numerous individual and institutional agents. Those who have supported it have had the power and felt the necessity to orient, coerce, or censure authorial intent at different levels and at different points of the creative and productive process. Thus, the case of *Euridice* is hardly unique. It is plausibly the first of countless instances in which an opera seems to express the tastes, expectations, and will of the patrons as much as—or, perhaps, more than—those of the authors. There are numerous documented instances of patrons, rulers, or other political authorities weighing in on matters arising very early in the creative process of a new opera. Well into the nineteenth century, for example, "King Charles Felix of Sardinia chose subjects, approved libretti, and even demanded fewer arias and more concerted pieces" (noted by Rosselli 1984: 82). And it is a known fact that even today, managers, trustees, and boards of directors are often crucial in determining the repertory to be performed by opera companies. While their choices are typically dictated by matters of taste or financial concerns (*Die Zauberflöte* or *La bohème* attract more corporate sponsors and produce greater box office revenue than *La clemenza di Tito* or *Le villi*, not to mention operas by lesser known composers) rather than political, religious, or moral issues, there are sociopolitical contexts in which sensitive subject matter may pose a serious obstacle to the performance of specific operas. (While opera is becoming increasingly present in various Islamic countries, it seems unlikely that an opera house in the Arab Emirates would be allowed or agree to produce Rossini's *L'Italiana in Algeri* or Verdi's *I Lombardi alla prima crociata*.)

Euridice is also one of countless instances in which the reader or spectator, four centuries ago as well as today, may be called to form an opinion on the relationship between the opera "as we know it" on one hand, and the opera "as it would or could have been" in the absence of the external influences that can be regarded as censorship. The opera "as we know it" is preserved and transmitted through a variety of written documents (scores and librettos) and, more recently, through audio and video recordings. The opera "as it would have been" in the absence of censorship can sometimes be reconstructed with extreme precision through a comparative study of different manuscript and printed scores and librettos as well as correspondence, legal documents, and archival records—thus becoming a viable alternative to the opera "as we know it." A well-known example is found at the beginning of Act III of Giuseppe Verdi's *Rigoletto*. The Venetian censors demanded that the Duke of Mantua, upon his arrival at Sparafucile's inn, should request Sparafucile to provide "una stanza e del vino ("a room and some wine") instead of the original "tua sorella e del vino ("your sister and some wine"). It is only the latter, uncensored line that justifies Rigoletto's reaction, "Son questi i suoi costumi ("These are his customs")], and textual work on Verdi's autograph score conducted by Martin Chusid (Verdi 1983) for the critical edition of the opera has restored the original poetry. The uncensored version of the passage is available in print and heard often (albeit not consistently) in recent recordings and in live performances, and has thus become part of *Rigoletto* "as we know it."

Documentary evidence, however, does not always come to our aid so readily. As in the case of *Euridice*, it is reasonable to assume that the circumstances of the creation of other operas produced for an individual patron, court, or other closely circumscribed context (such as a commercial opera house under the tight control of its impresario or owners) would have a significant impact on the choice of the subject matter or on the treatment of specific aspects or passages. Preventive measures were commonly taken to fulfill the expectations, needs, or demands of those whose backing made opera possible, leading to the production of texts in which censorship may be present but is difficult to detect: What has been left is often only sources produced, as it were, *post facto* and containing no trace of the censorial process. Mauro Calcagno has explained this clearly in relation to seventeenth-century opera in Venice:

> Venice saw the publication of its first opera librettos in 1637. Soon thereafter, the city became the European capital of *dramma per musica*. It is difficult to assess the effect of censorship on [them] [...] Opera patrons, however, must have imposed forms of preventive censorship during the production process—"patrons" meaning anyone who had power over a librettist, from impresarios to theater owners. (Calcagno 2006: 356)

Drawing on Tommaso Accetto's treatise *Della dissimulazione onesta* (On Honest Dissimulation; 1641), Calcagno shows how readers at the time could be expected—and even explicitly invited—to read "between the lines" of a published text. To be sure, Accetto refers to his own treatise as a "small book," and invites his readers to reconstruct the "large book" that would have existed in the absence of censorship; Calcagno suggests that drawing on Accetto's methodology, today's reader, too, may identify what he calls "conjectural evidence" of censorship in seventeenth-century opera librettos. His discussion of the case of *Eliogabalo*, a libretto by Aurelio Aureli set to music by Giovanni Antonio Boretti and performed during the 1667–1668 season at the Teatro SS. Giovanni e Paolo in Venice draws on more than the poetry itself (the words that were not only printed in the libretto, but also presumably sung and heard in performance). It also takes into account "what modern literary critics describe as the privileged space of transaction between author and public, or the paratextual elements—in this case, the illustrated frontispiece, the title page, the dedication, the letter to the reader, and the plot summary" (Calcagno 2006: 357). In the letter to the reader printed in the 1667–1668 libretto, Aureli warned the reader that the poetry was the "last-minute replacement of an earlier version set to music by Francesco Cavalli that had been unexpectedly forbidden. As Calcagno shows, this was due to the brothers Grimani, owners of the theater, who fired impresario Marco Faustini and Cavalli shortly before the production of the latter's *Eliogabalo* and prompted the revision of Aureli's libretto and its new musical setting by Boretti. In his revised text, Aureli was able to eliminate or radically modify some of the scenes that had seemed morally or politically questionable to the Grimanis (namely, the slaying of the emperor-tyrant Heliogabalus at the end of the opera and an audacious passage in which the lascivious emperor appoints prostitutes to the Roman senate), while also providing elements—which Calcagno, drawing on Gérard Genette's theories of trans-textuality (Genette 1997a, 1997b), defines as "paratextual"—that would render alternative versions of those same scenes readable "between the lines."

Calcagno's excellent discussion of *Eliogabalo* develops on solid premises, since this is a case of censorship at the hand of specific individuals, documented thanks to the survival of Cavalli's unperformed setting and of several librettos, which include not only the version published in Venice in 1667–1668, but also those printed for revivals in other cities as well as in Venice in 1687. The "conjectural" work in this case concerns not the act itself of censorship, but rather the motives lurking behind it. The importance of Calcagno's study, in fact, lies in its methodology: This particular instance of operatic censorship provides a key to interpret other cases where the change or elimination of unwelcome scenes, concepts, or messages, or the treatment of sensitive subject matter, may have originated under circumstances analogous to those of *Eliogabalo*, and that may be understood, at least conjecturally, as censorship. This, of course, need not apply only to opera in seventeenth-century Venice. If anything, it should serve as a stimulus to look for evidence of audiences "reading between the lines" and of authors who produced texts that were publishable and performable (subjecting them to censorship), while at the same time engaging their audiences with decipherable hints of their true intentions.

All too often we have worried about censorship exclusively insofar as authors voiced their frustration about it and attempted to resist it, and the fact is that not many librettists or composers have done so overtly. Even Giuseppe Verdi—often unproblematically depicted as a quintessential Romantic artist gifted with exceptional integrity who rejected compromise—engaged in fierce confrontations with the censors only after he became firmly established and financially secure. *Rigoletto* (1851) and *Un ballo in maschera* (1859), whose original subject matter in different ways deals with the theme of regicide (not surprisingly a taboo in the authoritarian states of pre-unification Italy), provide excellent examples of a composer who compromised with the authorities only after engaging in intense negotiations with them and obtained that at least some conditions that he deemed essential were met. *Un ballo in maschera*, whose censorship has been studied in detail by David Rosen (1999–2000), reached the stage only after its libretto went through various radical transformations, changing locale no fewer than five times (Stockholm, Stettin, Florence, Göteborg, and Boston), and its proposed protagonist, King Gustav III of Sweden, was demoted to governor of a North American colony (not unlike the King of France in *Rigoletto*, transformed into the Duke of Mantua). While *Un ballo in maschera* was originally intended for Naples, negotiations with the local authorities fell through, and the opera finally saw the light of day in Rome. The censorship of *Rigoletto* and *Ballo* is thoroughly documented in correspondence and other sources and is widely discussed in published literature (Chusid 1998; Lavagetto 2010). Arguably, the composer's vociferous opposition to the censors during the second decade of his career has earned him a great deal of critical attention, including the honor of the only entry devoted to an opera composer in the monumental *Censorship: A World Encyclopaedia*, edited by Derek Jones (2002), perhaps the most ambitious and vastly comprehensive reference tool on censorship to date. But the patent cases of Verdi and of works such as *Rigoletto* and *Un ballo in maschera* have sometimes obscured how censorship was present also where no ostensible resistance was staged against it. Thus, Jones's *Encyclopedia*, emblematically, contains no entry on opera *tout court*. And John Rosselli, in a vastly admirable discussion of opera in mid-nineteenth-century Italy, argued that "[c]ensorship was one, but only one means of interference; it did not become an acute problem until the last decade before Italian unity, when governments severely shaken by the 1848 revolutions met with the full tide of literary romanticism" (Rosselli 1984: 82). This argument is reasonable if one interprets the term "censorship" in the twofold sense of official suppression of subject matter and verbal content *and* authorial resistance to that suppression. But if it is intended more broadly, to include also the concern with the possible intervention of the censors (be they patrons, government officials, or other agents) and the pragmatic willingness to subject to, or even to prevent such intervention, censorship was arguably not only "an acute problem," but perhaps also more powerful and pervasive when no visible effort was made to counter its power.

Self-Censorship and Legislation

On September 19, 1840, Bartolomeo Merelli, impresario at La Scala, wrote the following to the *Direzione* of the Milanese theaters:

> The undersigned would like to produce as soon as possible the opera *La figlia del reggimento* by Signor Maestro Donizetti, and for that reason submits the related libretto, already preventively adjusted according to the views of the Imperial Royal Censorship, for its definitive approval, and offers his profoundest regards.[1]

The preventive adjustments to which Merelli alluded must have satisfied the censors of the Austrian government in Milan, and no further modifications were apparently required. This allowed the Italian premiere of Donizetti's *opéra comique* to take place less than two weeks later, on October 2, 1840. The adjustments concerned primarily a change of locale from the Austrian Tyrol to neutral Switzerland: It must have seemed obvious to the impresario that the Milanese censors would have objected to an opera (albeit a comic one) that described the French invasion of a territory of the Austrian empire (Izzo 2004). Aside from the specific information it conveys on one of Donizetti's most successful works, Merelli's letter is important, for it shows that even in the world of commercial opera and in contexts where authoritarian rule exerted its influence on the publication and performance of opera, the process of censorship was not necessarily one that began with the submission of an uncensored text that was then modified or outright suppressed according to the views of the authorities. On the contrary, it began before such submission took place, and if the prevention was successful, this made the work of the censors much simpler, sometimes reducing it to the mechanical task of apposing their seal of approval without further ado. If no other modifications were required, the process was straightforward—and fast. Merelli made it clear that he wished to produce *La figlia del reggimento* "as soon as possible," and thought it appropriate to let the Direzione know that he was aware of "the views" of the censors, and that by way of Calisto Bassi, who prepared the first Italian translation of *La fille du régiment*, he had modified the text accordingly. Of course, any delays caused by the censors would have had an adverse impact on the fall season at La Scala, resulting in financial loss or other complications, and from the perspective of the impresario prevention was certainly a lesser evil.

There is a substantial difference between this instance of preventive intervention, which we might call self-censorship, and the efforts of Peri and Rinuccini to fulfill the expectations of their patron. In the former case, the intervention was deliberately aimed at avoiding an official act of repressive censorship, and the explicit language used by Merelli indicates a level of awareness and confidence that was essential in order to deal effectively with official censorship in the nineteenth century. Impresarios, librettists, composers, and performers had to understand and adapt to the limits of what was acceptable in the theater in terms of content, verbal expression, and visual elements and action.

To be sure, the requirements imposed by censorial bodies changed substantially depending on location and political climate. The situation in mid-nineteenth-century Italy was particularly complex due to political fragmentation (between the Restoration and 1861 the peninsula was divided into several political entities, mostly controlled by the Austrian Empire, the Catholic Church, or the Bourbons) and political turmoil. But other parts of Europe were certainly not exempt from censorship. In France, the Restoration monarchy imposed a strict control on theatrical activities, and the "no censorship" promises that followed the July revolution were short-lived. According to several authors, the ability of a poet like Eugène Scribe to navigate successfully through different political climates is directly connected with his prompt perception of what was expected and his mastery of self-censorship (Hallman 2002: 144). In a speech delivered in 1836, Scribe went so far as to praise preventive censorship as it was exercised in Paris at the time, regarding it as more acceptable and constructive than earlier forms of repressive censorship (such as those that in 1832 had led to the ban of Victor Hugo's *Le roi s'amuse*; Hallman 2002: 59–60). In Victorian England, all theatrical texts, including opera librettos, had to be approved by the Office of the Lord Chamberlain prior to performance. As the Comptroller to the Lord Chamberlain explained in 1866, the aim was "principally to exclude any scriptural subject, or plays in which highway men or immorality are exalted, and any personal, or personally political questions" (cited in Marvin 2001: 584) And while Roberta M. Marvin (2001) has offered a good overview of the censorship of Verdi's operas in Victorian London, we know depressingly little about whether and how the texts of operas composed or translated into English were preventively adapted (or self-censored) along the lines of the Comptroller's expectations during this and other periods of English history. Censorship was no less pervasive in Russia, involving both operas composed locally and those presented in translation (Zidaric 2004). The case of Nikolai Rimsky-Korsakov's last opera, *The Golden Cockerel* (1907, performed posthumously in 1909) is a telling one; it reveals how the authorities could be both extremely strict and remarkably inconsistent, requiring for example that specific passages be altered in performance but allowing them to survive intact in the printed score (Abraham 1971: 46). Here, too, there is certainly much to be learned on the practice of self-censorship, and the investigation could easily be extended into other areas of Europe, thus far under-represented in studies of opera and censorship, including Spain, Portugal, and most of central and northern Europe.

An important study by Philip Gossett (1990b) discusses the difference between censorship (which he labels "external") and self-censorship (which he labels "internal"), and explores the implications of these concepts in regard to editorial work conducted on the operas of Giuseppe Verdi. Gossett shows that it is not always possible to separate clearly between the two. To return to the example from *Rigoletto* mentioned earlier in this chapter: While what prompted the change of the Duke's line "Tua sorella e del vino!" seems clear enough (a concern with a morally offensive passage), it is more complicated to determine *who* prompted it. It could have been external intervention, of course (i.e., a censor demanding that "tua sorella" be changed to "una stanza" lest he deny permission to perform the opera); it could have been Verdi and/or Piave reaching this decision internally; or, finally, it could have been the management of La Fenice suggesting the alteration, possibly to avoid the danger of a single problematic passage providing a pretext for the censors to prohibit the performance of the entire opera (Gossett 1990b: 251). If the alteration was requested by the management, then the latter, just like Merelli in the case of *La figlia del reggimento*, is in a hybrid position, external in relation to Verdi and Piave, but internal in relation to the censors.

Censorship versus Prohibition

Thus far I have presented reasons and instances that should encourage us to think about operatic censorship beyond the limits of official intervention. Despite all the preventive ("internal") care taken by authors and other agents to comply with the expectations and requirements of political authorities and funding agents and to minimize the restrictive or repressive intervention of government officials or other authorities, acts and legislation aimed at controlling operatic activities constitute a fundamental reality in the world of opera. Opposition to opera as a genre and as a musical and cultural practice on moral or religious grounds is encountered frequently, and especially in its early days it was not uncommon to read about it in treatises and pamphlets. In some extreme instances, the control comes to the point of outright prohibition of opera per se, rather than of individual works or aspects. A recent extreme instance is the ban on all music performance and listening (including ownership of musical instruments and equipment for the reproduction of sound) imposed by the Taliban regime in Afghanistan from 1998 until its fall in 2001, where the exclusion of opera fell under a dramatically wider umbrella restricting freedom of expression on a number of levels. And at several points in seventeenth- and eighteenth-century Papal Rome, the performance of opera and other forms of staged musical entertainments was forbidden, as it was deemed morally offensive. And even when opera was in fact allowed in the city, it is worth remembering that women could not appear onstage, and male performers ordinarily took up female roles through the eighteenth century (an unusual kind of official restriction that did not affect the verbal text of an opera but rather its sonic and visual form in performance).

Some instances of outright prohibition are intriguing, such as the ban on the performance of opera imposed by Pope Clement XI between 1703 and 1708. In that case the prohibition was not strictly based on moral grounds, but came as an *ex-voto* of sorts offered for the fact that a powerful earthquake that shook central Italy in 1703 had mostly spared the city of Rome. During those five years, various musical entertainments were created in Rome (including cantatas and oratorios) that, while not operas proper, adopted the musical idiom and dramatic strategies of opera. Cecilia Bartoli (2005) has explored some of that repertoire in her album *Opera Proibita*, which includes dazzling extracts from cantatas and oratorios by Alessandro Scarlatti, Handel, and Caldara; "opera proibita," however, is as captivating an expression as it is misleading, for it might be taken to refer to operatic repertoire that had been prohibited, whereas it is music created in lieu of opera during the period of its prohibition in Rome. It is possible to argue that Handel's oratorio *La Resurrezione* (1708), performed in semi-staged form at the palace of the Ruspoli family with a female singer (Margherita Durastanti) in the role of Mary Magdalene, was a substitute for opera—indeed, even to the point of coming across as an act of provocation and thus incurring the pope's wrath—but not that it actually was an opera.

But the ban of opera *tout court* only falls under the umbrella of censorship in its broadest sense, and is perhaps best referred to as prohibition. Censorship, by contrast, even at its strictest, has to do with the suppression or alteration of individual works or (far more commonly) specific passages or aspects deemed offensive or threatening in one or more of three fundamental areas—religion, morals, and politics. This is, of course, a form of restriction, but one that ultimately aims at making the show go on, albeit within limits determined by the political and social status quo. Nowhere is this more extensively documented than in nineteenth-century Italy, where these areas are sometimes enumerated explicitly in legislative acts. A document issued in 1849 by the Reale Soprintendenza of the Neapolitan theaters (transcribed and translated in Black 1984) begins as follows: "Any theatrical work the subject of which directly offends Religion, Politics or Morality shall be rejected." (It is worth pointing out that censorship here is specifically aimed at the *subject*, and that musical content is not a stated concern.) In the wake of the failed revolutions of 1848–1849, censorship in the Italian states became increasingly strict and the Neapolitan authorities here clearly stated that they were concerned with all three aspects, but different governments could prioritize one kind of censorship over another, depending on their own agenda or allegiances. Linda Fairtile (1997) offers an insightful discussion of two censored librettos for Verdi's *Attila* (1846), one printed in Rome in 1847 and the other (with the title of *Gli Unni e i Romani*) in Palermo in 1855, showing how the Roman censors intervened mainly on matters of religion, whereas radical changes in Palermo eliminated the theme of regicide and other politically charged aspects of *Attila*. And Chusid (1998) surveys how the censors of various states in pre-unification Italy altered the librettos of *Rigoletto* and *Les vêpres siciliennes* differently, depending on location and on changing political, moral, and religious agendas. It goes without saying that these three types of censorship often overlap: Religious matters commonly bear moral implications, and can sometimes have political ramifications as well, as the treatment of religious themes (in particular, references to the Virgin Mary and their censorship) in Verdi's *Giovanna d'Arco* (1845) indicates (Izzo 2007).

The wording of the Neapolitan document from 1849 is deliberately strong, calling for the "rejection" of entire "works." In the reality of mid-nineteenth-century Italy, however, instances in which whole operas were rejected, officially or *de facto*, are relatively uncommon, and therefore quite famous. The prohibition of Donizetti's *Maria Stuarda* (1834) just before its planned premiere in Naples is a case in point: the execution of a Catholic sovereign didn't sit well with King Ferdinand. And the subject of *La battaglia di Legnano* (1849), Verdi's contribution to the cause of the Roman republic in 1849, became unthinkable in Italy in the aftermath of the failed revolutions, and the opera circulated during the 1850s in a version with a completely different setting (*L'assedio di Arlem*). Verdi himself, even before *La battaglia* received its premiere in Rome, was well aware that the revolutions in most of Italy were failing, and on September 24, 1848, wrote to his librettist, Salvadore Cammarano, from Paris: "In the event that the censors were not to permit it, do you believe that by changing the title, the locale, etc., we'll be able to retain all or most of the poetry?"[2] (Mossa 2001: 51)—very much a pragmatic and productive response to a repressive climate.

More commonly, however, operas were altered relatively little, so as to make their performance possible in a restrictive political climate. Changes sometimes concerned only individual words that were mechanically replaced: "patria" (homeland) became "gloria" (glory), "libertà" (freedom) became "lealtà (loyalty), and "Dio" (God) became "cielo" (heaven)—to mention only a few notorious examples. A well-known anecdote concerning Verdi's *I Lombardi alla prima crociata* tells how the Milanese archbishop was deeply concerned about the abundance of religious references and imagery in the opera, including the onstage depiction of sacred places and of a sacrament, whereas the chief of police, supposedly out of sympathy for the young composer, allowed the premiere of the opera at La Scala in 1843, demanding only that the opening of Giselda's prayer be changed from "Ave Maria" to "Salve Maria" (Pougin 1881: 48). When the opera was produced in other Italian theaters, however, local censors sometimes demanded more substantial changes (Izzo 2007).

One of the finest discussions of how a censorial system could be not unidimensionally repressive, but also permissive, is Andreas Giger's 1999 study "Social Control and the Censorship of Giuseppe Verdi's Operas in Rome (1844–1859)," which shows how censors working in a highly restrictive context could modify their standard criteria and seek to achieve compromises with other agents in an effort to make "difficult" works performable while minimizing the threat they posed to the *status quo*. In Giger's words:

> We might compare this system [of censorship] with modern politics, where a political decision represents not necessarily the best or most logical solution, but one that is influenced by competing lobbies—in this case the *Civiltà Cattolica*, the audience, the impresario, and the Deputation. The papal government stood somewhere in between: on the one hand, it had to provide the upper classes (aristocracy and rich bourgeoisie) with their most important social and cultural pleasure; on the other hand, it needed the censorial system to avoid serious violations of religious, political, and moral ethics. (Giger 1999: 264)

To be sure, the prestige of its operatic institutions was a fundamental element in the cultural politics of Papal Rome, and if that prestige was to be maintained, the active participation of an influential composer like Verdi in the musical life of the city, and especially the opportunity to present new operas by the composer, was deemed essential. And,

Giger continues, Verdi's new operas for Rome "unavoidably led to some violations of the church's and the state's ethical codes, but the Roman government had to accept them if operatic life was to continue" (Giger 1999: 264–265). The combination of censorial pressure and willingness to compromise explains how Verdi's operas for Rome, from *I due Foscari* (1844) to *Un ballo in maschera* (1859), could reach the stage (Rosen 1999–2000 shows in detail the process that gradually made the subject of *Un ballo in maschera* acceptable for the Roman authorities). Thus, the work of the censors involved, but was certainly not limited to, repression. Rather, it offered guidance, contributed to reshaping aspects of texts that were deemed unacceptable, and even turned a blind eye where compromise had to be reached in order to grant the performance of a new opera by a prestigious composer. While Giger refrains from inductively extending the findings of his case study beyond the chronological and geographical boundaries of mid-nineteenth-century Rome, his work is all the more significant, for it confronts us with the fundamental fact, frequently observed in recent times by critical theorists but rarely spelled out by opera scholars, that the visible, authoritarian, repressive side of censorship often conceals another, less visible but equally important, productive side. Beyond its power of silencing authorial voices in the name of political, moral, or religious propriety, censorship can therefore be understood as having itself an authorial voice of sorts.

Opera (Un)Censored: *La lega lombarda*

Not all operas submitted to the censors in mid-nineteenth-century Rome received the same privileged treatment as Verdi's works, however. Giger's study provides an excellent context within which to explore the censorship of *La lega lombarda*, a *dramma lirico* in a prologue and three acts by Filippo Meucci set to music by Antonio Buzzi, submitted to the papal authorities in 1846 and met with outright rejection. In order to be performed in Rome, the libretto had to be recast, its subject removed from twelfth-century Lombardy, and its title changed to *Gusmano di Medina* (Giger [1999: 243] mentions the manuscript libretto for *Gusmano di Medina*, which was approved by the Roman censors, but not its censored source). The tale of this opera is discussed in detail in Douglas Ipson's admirable study of operatic oath scenes in mid-nineteenth-century Rome (Ipson 2011: 2) and resembles that of many other works whose librettos had to be fully rewritten (with a radically different plot and context) in order to rescue the music. Indeed, the censorship of *La lega lombarda* could be archived rapidly if it were not for three important reasons: first, the plot centers on the same historical events described three years later in Verdi's *La battaglia di Legnano*; second, the libretto appeared in print in Paris (Meucci 1846), prefaced by a long and fiery letter by the author ("Lettera dell'autore ad un amico che serve di prefazione") dated September 21, 1846, which among other things illustrates the circumstances under which the opera was prohibited; third, the forbidden opera did not fall into oblivion, but was rescued and performed at key locations and moments during the final phases of the Italian Risorgimento.

The action of *La lega lombarda* takes place in the second half of the twelfth century. Its prologue refers vaguely to Frederick I Barbarossa's second campaign in Italy (1158), which ended with the defeat of Milan, whereas the main body of the opera (Acts I–III) describes the formation of the Lombard league and its victory against the Emperor's army at Legnano in 1176. In the prologue, the people of Milan have surrendered to Barbarossa. Their first consul, Manfredo, declares defeat. His daughter, Matilde, is in love with Oberto (head of the city of Lodi), whom Manfredo blames for having given his allegiance to Frederick. Manfredo plans to flee to the Holy Land with Matilde, but she is led away by Oberto instead. When Manfredo sees her at Oberto's side, leading Frederick to the throne, he curses her. In Act I, several years later, Matilde finds Manfredo hiding in a monastery. She tells him that Oberto is ready to lead the people of Lodi in battle against Barbarossa. In Act II, a league of twenty Lombard cities is formed in Pontida and declares war on Barbarossa under Manfredo's leadership. In Act III, the Lombards defeat Barbarossa's army at Legnano. Manfredo is mortally wounded and dies in Matilde's arms as the Lombard people praise his patriotic courage. (The points of comparison with *La battaglia di Legnano*—especially the contents and structure of the final act—are obvious, and the relationship between the two librettos, albeit beyond the scope of the present discussion, deserves careful examination.)

In his introductory letter, Meucci indicated that the authorities had initially approved the libretto, and that the political censor had apposed his signature on the text: "the revising commission [*giunta di revisione*] could not condemn it, as you will see from the signature apposed by the political censor"[3] (Meucci 1846: v). It was the "ordine diplomatico" ("the diplomacy") that regarded the text with suspicion, Meucci explains:

> The weakness and the insecure conscience of a theatrical deputy pushed the drama to the tribunal of Monsignor Pietro Marini, Governor of Rome. His verdict was inexorable: *La lega lombarda* had to be rejected as a work that could have displeased the high will of the royal family of Austria. I turned at once to the Secretary of State, His Eminence Pasquale Gizzi, and to the excellent ruler, Pope Pius IX. Same answer: *La lega lombarda* could displease the most august House of Austria.[4] (Meucci 1846: v–vi)

Meucci spells out the problem clearly: an analogy could be drawn between the medieval tale of Lombard cities uniting against Federico Barbarossa and the reality of mid-nineteenth-century Italy, where brewing hostility toward the Austrian Empire and its hold over several states in northern and central Italy (most notably Lombardy-Venetia) might (and soon would) have resulted in upheavals and revolutions. From the viewpoint of the papal authorities (remarkably including, according to Meucci, the pope himself), the libretto of *La lega lombarda* contained allusions to the contemporaneous political scenario, or at least lent itself to be read in this sense. Meucci, however, goes on forcefully to question such a metaphorical reading:

> Whoever wanted to believe that Ferdinand of Austria is depicted as Frederick I Barbarossa would infamously bring slander against me. And when will such shameful suspicion of allusions ever cease? There is no historical episode that may not [be

> seen to] relate to our times: everything can be twisted and misconstrued; one can fear malice and conspiracy in everything: and thus one would have to leave all stories untouched, because with the force of cavils, all can be compared. Wretched [is] that government that believes all garments to be tailored to itself![5] (Meucci 1846: vi)

We may take Meucci's passionate statement at face value or read it as an exercise in irony. (In favor of the latter goes the rather cynical mention of the Austrian emperor, Ferdinand I, famously feebleminded and unfit for political life; a body of counselors controlled the government of the empire, and Ferdinand finally abdicated in 1848.[6]) Regardless of the approach we choose to take, the poet clearly concentrates on the subject of the opera rather than on individual scenes, passages of poetry, or verbal expressions. If one chooses to read the libretto closely, expressions of patriotism abound, drawing on imagery and language encountered frequently in pre-1848 Italian poetry and opera librettos. The following *a due* passage that concludes the Matilde-Manfredo duet in Act I is a case in point:

Quella voce ai vinti in core
  Di speranza avviva il raggio
  È scintilla di coraggio
  Che un incendio desterà.
Starà l'ira del Signore
  Degli oppressi in sulle spade,
  E nell'Itale contrade
  Lo stranier divorerà. (Meucci 1846: 17)

> [That voice enlivens the ray of hope in the heart of the defeated; it is a spark of courage that will ignite a fire. The wrath of the Lord will be in the swords of the oppressed, and will destroy the foreigner on the Italian soil.]

Analogously, the chorus that seals the oath of the Lombards at the end of Act II contains religious imagery:

Guerra guerra! invitto è il braccio
  Che difende il suol natio,
  E l'altare del suo Dio
  Da profani salvo fa.
Guerra guerra! eterno ghiaccio
  Stringe il sangue al masnadiero,
  Quando l'italo guerriero
  Ridestato in campo sta. (Meucci 1846: 23)

> [War, war! Undefeated is the arm that defends his native soil, and saves the altar of his God from the profane. War, war! Eternal frost takes hold of the bandits' blood when the Italian warrior is reawakened on the battlefield.]

Particularly meaningful in both passages is the combination of the patriotic theme with the idea of a divine mission, an approach that recurs frequently not only in oath scenes (discussed widely in Ipson 2011), but in a variety of dramatic contexts in opera of the time. Most of Temistocle Solera's librettos for Verdi exemplify this approach perfectly. Indeed, in *La lega lombarda*, Matilde and Manfredo sing their words in response to a chorus of monks who warn that God has the power to restore destroyed cities to their former splendor—a reminder that those who fight for their homeland are also standing up for their own religious faith.

In the absence of Meucci's letter, the reader might be led to believe that this sort of rhetoric, as well as, more generally, the frequent references to religion and the presence of a monastery scene in Act I should have worried the Roman authorities more than the ostensible metaphorical allusion to the Italian struggle against the Austrian Empire. And, of course, it is perfectly possible that in his prefatory letter Meucci, well known for his liberal views, for which he was arrested on one occasion in 1832, chose to pursue a liberal political agenda by exaggerating the scope and motives of the papal censorship. *La lega lombarda* may well be his first attempt to address the theme of Italian nationalism in the more permissive climate that followed the election of Pope Pius IX in June 1846, and the opera was soon followed by various works and speeches in which Meucci overtly supported the idea of a united and independent Italy. He was no extremist, however, and in the introductory letter to the Paris edition of *La lega lombarda* he stated clearly that he did not support military action as a way toward Italian unification and liberation. He publicly endorsed Massimo D'Azeglio's moderate views, which also rejected recourse to violence (Bergamaschi 2011). As soon as the upheavals of 1848 began, however, he authored the text of an *Inno guerriero italiano*, a thoroughly explicit call to arms set to music by Gaetano Magazzari, performed in Rome in March 1848 and published by Ricordi (Gossett 2005). He was then actively involved in the Roman Republic (he briefly became chief of police), and this made him unwelcome once the Republic failed and the pope returned. Meucci was expelled from the Papal States and spent the rest of his life in the Kingdom of Sardinia and then in the newly formed Kingdom of Italy. He died in Pisa in 1865, some five years before the temporal power of the pope collapsed and the Stato Pontificio was annexed to the Kingdom of Italy.

Regardless of his motives, Meucci's prefatory remarks to the Parisian edition of *La lega lombarda* called the reader's attention to the question of censorship in real time, clarifying that already before the revolutions of 1848–1849 there was a serious concern with the subject matter of operas that potentially alluded to the contemporaneous political scenario, in particular with references or analogies to the Austrian rule over various Italian states. His words suggest a corrective to John Rosselli's claim that censorship in Italy "did not become an "acute problem" in Italy until the last decade before Italian unity" (Rosselli 1984: 82). Moreover, they indicate that such a concern was present not only in the states where the Austrian Empire exerted direct control, but also in the Stato Pontificio, where we have hitherto believed that the censors were mostly concerned with religious or moral matters. The political censorship of *La lega lombarda* had to do not with a direct offense or threat to the local status quo, but with the fear that the performance of an opera based on this subject could have caused a negative response from Austrian authorities whose support was deemed essential in Papal Rome.

But the vicissitudes of *La lega lombarda* do not end with its prohibition in Rome and the publication of its libretto in Paris. Indeed, the opera reached the stage with its original poetry (albeit with a few modifications not attributable to censorship) in the wake of the failed revolutions of 1848–1849, just when censorship in most Italian states became even stricter and particularly attentive to references to nationalism, patriotism, and rebellion against foreign rule contained in opera librettos. To be sure, most authoritarian governments in Italy would have rejected *La lega lombarda* just as firmly as they opposed Verdi's *La battaglia di Legnano*. The opera, however, was granted a premiere in Barcelona in 1850, followed, more significantly, by productions at the Teatro Carignano in Turin on September 14, 1850, and the Teatro Civico in Sassari in October 1851. It is no coincidence that the two latter cities were in the Kingdom of Sardinia, which after the failed revolutions stood out as the one power in the Italian peninsula that could oppose the Austrian Empire. Just as the Teatro Carlo Felice in Genoa had hosted an uncensored production of *La battaglia di Legnano* in the spring of 1850, Turin and Sassari paid similar homage to an episode in Italian history that had been and continued to be off limits as subject matter in most of Italy during the Risorgimento. The opera was well received at both venues: A review of the Turin production in *L'Italia musicale* (September 18, 1850) describes in detail the favorable response to each individual number, and in particular to Act II: "The scene of the oath moved the audience to the liveliest manifestations of enthusiasm. At the end of the act, the principal singers and the composer had to appear onstage amidst the most general acclaim"[7] (*LIM* 1850). And according to a concise review (November 8, 1851) in the same journal in Sassari, the opera was performed numerous times: "Each piece was followed by applause, and especially the death of Manfredi in the *terzetto* is such a piece that would animate even the coldest artist in performance and excite every audience"[8] (*LIM* 1851: 357). It is no surprise that although these productions in the Kingdom of Sardinia were rather successful, *La lega lombarda* never made it to other parts of Italy; even an attempt to produce the censored version of the opera, *Gusmano di Medina*, at the Teatro della Canobbiana in Milan in 1851, failed, probably for political reasons (Ipson 2011: 259–260).

La lega lombarda took to the stage again a decade later, just as soon as censorial agencies began to crumble in various parts of the Italian peninsula in the wake of the second war of Italian independence, which saw the Kingdom of Sardinia victorious over the Austrians and which resulted rapidly in the formation of the Kingdom of Italy. At that point, the opera appeared in Bologna on November 26, 1859, to great acclaim: an unsigned review (November 28) in *Teatri arti e letteratura* gave a concise history of the work, remarking, "The music of this *Lega lombarda* was written already in 1848 [*sic*] and was well liked then in Turin, but it was not produced again elsewhere, for hatred of its title"[9] (*TAL* 1859: 210). During the following Carnival season, finally, it made its way into the former Austrian domain of Lombardy-Venetia, at the Teatro della Concordia in Cremona and the Teatro Carcano in Milan. Its performance at the latter venue, curiously enough, came in the wake of an equally timely production of Verdi's *La battaglia di Legnano* the previous summer. The management of the theater must have valued the opportunity to present to the public of liberated Milan two different renditions of a subject that at that point had become a Risorgimento staple (Fubini 1971; Ipson 2011: 212–244). The *Gazzetta musicale di Milano*, which resumed publication on January 1, 1860, after the political events of 1859, was quick to point out that the opera was not a new work but one "tried and forgotten for many years, and now galvanized in a new and artificial existence for the attraction of its title and subject"[10] (*GMM* 1860: 11). The review praised the performance but criticized the music as lacking in originality, claiming that it was stylistically indebted to Verdi's early operas. As the changed political scenario allowed the Ricordi firm to distribute again *La battaglia di Legnano* in its original, uncensored version, it should not surprise that their journal's response to a potential direct competitor was lukewarm at best. It is a concise note in *Teatri arti e letteratura* (January 5, 1860) that spells out the public response in unequivocal terms: "Furor [...] There were 23 curtain calls for the maestro and the performers"[11] (*TAL* 1860: 238).

Of course, we cannot be sure whether, in absence of censorship and without Meucci's denouncement in the Parisian edition, this opera would have received the attention it did in 1850–1851 and in 1859–1860. What seems clear is that the tale of *La lega lombarda* is a tale in which censorship, drawing on terminology employed by Richard Burt (1998), not only *removed* and *replaced* Meucci's text in the reality of pre-1848 Rome, but also *displaced* that text to Paris, where, we might presume, it never would have been printed, had the Roman authorities allowed its performance. The displacement was not only geographical, but also chronological. Denied the opportunity to circulate in the 1850s "for hatred of its title" (and subject matter), in 1859–1860 the piece earned recognition (albeit short-lived) in united Italy at the side of other operatic monuments to the Risorgimento, including Verdi's *La battaglia di Legnano*. A discussion of the censorship of this opera would not be complete if it were circumscribed to the events of 1846, since the impact of those events reverberated not only through the restrictive political climate of the 1850s, but also, more visibly, in the more permissive (and celebratory) context of the liberation of most of northern Italy.

Conclusion

If the censorship of *La lega lombarda* only succeeded in displacing its text to other locations and moments in time, it follows that even when it sought to suppress and replace, censorship could have an important, albeit unintentional, productive outcome, placing a censored work on a fast track to the stage as soon as political circumstances changed. Indeed, the suggestion that the *raison d'être* for the later productions of *La lega lombarda* may lie precisely in the opera's having been censored in the first place is based on a cautious, deductive approach; a more adventurous, inductive approach may lead us to open up new scenarios for a consideration of the question of operatic censorship at large. An opportunity comes from Martha Feldman's excellent case study of the transformation of

Antonio Sografi and Niccolò Zingarelli's *La morte di Mitridate* in the context of the fall of the Venetian republic in 1797 (Feldman 2007: 404–430). Feldman illustrates how Sografi revised his own libretto, written the previous year for settings performed in Vicenza and Trieste, to offer a depiction of an evil sovereign and of his death, completely at odds with the tenets of *opera seria* and its conventional support of absolute rulers. She shows how Sografi himself altered key parts of the libretto, emphasizing the negative connotations of Mitridate, modifying the roles of submissive characters subjected to a tyrant's authority into "self-determining citizens," and providing a text well suited to represent the Francophile ideologies that permeated the cultural life of the city during the short-lived Napoleonic domination of the city. Zingarelli consequently altered portions of his score, initially composed to the 1796 version of the poetry. There is no reason to believe that Sografi (or, for that matter, Zingarelli) would have resisted the changes, or even that the latter were imposed on them by political officials. In fact, Sografi himself certainly welcomed the opportunity to depict the death of an evil tyrant in the new climate of the city. The shape of his text as it was printed and heard at La Fenice in Venice in 1797, then, is neither the result of suppressive requests from a censor nor the reversal of previous censorial interventions in a new permissive climate. It is, strictly speaking, merely a transformation. But if *opera seria* at large, including of course earlier works that focused on the tale of Mitridate, was the product of a culture of subservience to absolute rulers (where rulers themselves were typically responsible for the selection and the approval of subject matter for operas performed in their own court theaters), wouldn't it be reasonable to claim that without being censored, its texts are, broadly viewed, products of censorship? If so, the 1797 *La morte di Mitridate* can rightfully be read as an uncensored *opera seria* of sorts, not unlike *La lega lombarda*. Both texts told a tale as some (authorities, intellectuals, members of the audience) had long wanted to hear it, their will denied in one instance by the authoritarian intervention of political authorities, in another by the presence of censorship as an agent that determines not what is forbidden, but what is acceptable as subject matter.

Before closing, we must be aware that there are numerous aspects of operatic censorship that remain at the margin of the present discussion. For one thing, at the risk of seeming unfashionable, this chapter confronts us with the enormous relevance of the verbal component of opera. Indeed, whether or not the textual content is intelligible when sung in performance, the attention the censors devote to it in different periods and contexts suggests a preoccupation with what members of the audience understood of that content. But there are instances in which the target of the authorities seems to be the music itself, as in the case of Shostakovich's opera *Lady Macbeth of the Mtsensk District* (1934), famously censured in *Pravda*, the official newspaper of the Soviet regime, following the hostile response of Stalin to a performance in January 1936, and subsequently modified by the composer and performed again only after Stalin's death with the title of *Katerina Izmaylova*. According to Laurel Fay (1992), in the Soviet Union the revised version of the opera was accepted as the definitive one "at face value" (indicating a fundamental unawareness or disregard of the circumstance that led the composer to modify his score). In other parts of the world, however, it is the original, "uncensored" version that has recently earned a prominent place in the repertoire. In this case, too, the original opera (the musical text) was not merely *suppressed* and *replaced*, but also *displaced*.

A great deal of the present discussion of censorship is evidently indebted to important critical theories on the subject, first and foremost Michel Foucault's *Power/Knowledge* (1980), which contains a passionate call to "escape from the limited field of juridical sovereignty and State institutions, and instead base our analysis of power on the study of techniques and tactics of domination" (1980: 102). The awareness of those techniques can provide far more than an explanation for those instances in which texts were suppressed, but also for the productive mechanisms of censorship. While the ban of *La lega lombarda* in 1846 Rome is the immediately visible aspect of censorship, its subsequent reintroduction is as much a product of censorship as its prohibition. To borrow the words of Judith Butler (in an acute discussion of the regulation of the term "homosexual" in recent American history), "the effort to constrain [the opera] culminates in its very proliferation—an unintended rhetorical effect of legal discourse" (Butler 1997: 131). Butler herself goes on to suggest that "censorship is a productive form of power: it is not merely privative, but formative as well." And she indicates that "the question is not whether certain kinds of speech uttered by a subject are censored, but how a certain operation of censorship determines who will be a subject depending on whether the speech of such a candidate for subjecthood obeys certain norms of what is speakable and what is not" (1997: 133). A shift in political climate, as in Venice in 1797 or in post-unification Italy, had the power not only to change those norms, but also to define what was acceptable or desirable by drawing a fairly simple equation with what had been previously suppressed.

Much of what we have learned through the years about the censorship of opera is directly related to the close investigation of source materials (librettos, scores, legislative acts) that document specific interventions of government officials and other authorities. This kind of research is crucial both for its textual ramifications and for its cultural significance, and deserves to be pursued with unrelenting commitment. At the same time, we can follow in the footsteps of some of the more innovative studies in this field (Giger 1999; Calcagno 2006), drawing on theoretical discussions of censorship, such as those of Foucault, Butler, and Post (to mention only a few), and using the ever-increasing documentary information at our disposal to consider more closely how censorship as a phenomenon shaped and continues to shape the culture of opera. We may reach the twofold conclusion that censorship is more pervasive than we may believe (is any opera completely free of censorship?), as well as never completely effective as a form of suppression. On this note, it may be apt to conclude with an amusing anecdote concerning one of the leading baritones of the nineteenth century, Giorgio Ronconi, and his perception of censorship. Like most baritones who performed Bellini's *I puritani* in Risorgimento Italy, Ronconi was required to sing the duet that concludes Act II in a censored version that involved the replacement of the expression "gridando libertà [crying liberty]" with "gridando lealtà [crying loyalty]," and of "amor di patria [love of the homeland]" with "amor di gloria [love of glory]." In an unidentified opera house in the Kingdom of Sardinia, the singer supposedly did not comply, and was sent to prison for three days as a result.

He took his revenge a few nights later, according to Giovanni Ruffini's autobiographical novel, *Lorenzo Benoni, or Passages in the Life of an Italian* (1853):

> Not long afterwards, the following verse, in allusion to a peasant who had enlisted, occurring in Signor Ronconi's part in the Elisir d'Amore, *Vendè la libertà, si fé soldato* (he sold his liberty and became a soldier), Signor Ronconi, like a clever wag as he was, altered the text into *Vendè la lealtà, si fé soldato* (he sold his *loyalty*, and became a soldier). This variation was received by the public, to whom everything in the shape of opposition was welcome, with enthusiasm. ([Ruffini] 1853: 158)

Ruffini was a patriot and an exile, and in 1843 had earned a place in the operatic firmament by co-authoring the libretto for Donizetti's *Don Pasquale*. The authenticity of the anecdote may be difficult to prove, but its appearance in print in 1853 is again testimony to the public exposure of operatic censorship at the time, in this instance through a playful transformation of an unproblematic passage in *L'elisir d'amore* into a hypertextual reference to the censored *Puritani*. And Ruffini's reference to the audience—especially the suggestion that the public was both aware of and opposed to censorship—is fascinating. Scholars who privilege a traditionalist approach to the study of the Risorgimento can be thoroughly pleased with anecdotes such as this one. But can one argue (not necessarily in relation to this specific anecdote or context) that opera censorship worked not against the audience, but in their favor, protecting them against unwelcome content? Such a question may be difficult to answer but deserves close consideration in the next generation of studies of this subject.

See also: Politics, Patronage, What Is Opera? Audiences

Notes

1. "Il sottoscritto vorrebbe produrre al più presto l'opera La figlia del Regimento [sic] del S.r Maestro Donizetti, e perciò ne rimette il relativo libretto, già in prevenzione regolato secondo le viste dell'I.R. Censura per la sua definitiva ammissione, e si rassegna il più profondo rispetto (I-Mt, Spettacoli Pubblici 19/6)."
2. "Caso mai le Censure nol permettessero credete voi che si potrà cambiando titolo, località etc.... ritenere tutta o quasi tutta la verseggiatura?"
3. "[L]a giunta di revisione non ha potuto condannarla, come potrai vedere dall'apposta firma del censore politico."
4. "La debolezza e la mal sicura coscienza di un deputato teatrale spinsero il dramma al tribunale di Mons. Gover. di Roma Pietro Marini: il suo giudizio fu inesorabile: la Lega Lombarda dovea essere respinta, come opera che potea dispiacere all'alta volontà della regnante famiglia d'Austria./Mi volsi ad un tempo stesso al Segretario di Stato Emin. Pasquale Gizzi, ed all'ottimo regnante Pontefice Pio IX. La stessa risposta: la Lega Lombarda può dispiacere all'augustissima Casa d'Austria."
5. "Chi volesse credere raffigurarsi Ferdinando d'Austria in Federigo Barbarossa, mi apporrebbe turpemente una calunnia. E quando cesserà mai così vergognoso sospetto di allusioni? Non è brano di storia, che non possa riferirsi a' tempi nostri: tutto si può estorcere

e travisare; in tutto temersi malizia e disegno: e così bisognerebbe lasciare intatte tutte le storie, perché tutte a forza di cavilli posson mettersi a paragone. Misero quel governo che tutte le vesti crede tagliate per la sua persona!"

6. Many thanks to Claudio Vellutini for this suggestion.
7. "La scena del giuramento scosse il pubblico alle più vive dimostrazioni di entusiasmo. Finito l'atto, gli artisti principali ed il maestro dovettero comparire al proscenio fra le più generali acclamazioni."
8. "Ogni pezzo fu seguito da applausi, e specialmente la morte di Manfredi nel terzetto è tal brano da animare nell'esecuzione il più freddo artista ed entusiasmare ogni pubblico."
9. "La musica di questa *Lega lombarda* fu scritta fin dal 1848 e piacque allora a Torino, né altrove fu poscia riprodotta, in odio del titolo."
10. "[...] da molti anni provato e dimenticato, ed ora galvanizzato a nuova e posticcia esistenza per l'attrattiva del titolo e del soggetto."
11. "Furore... Le chiamate al maestro ed agli artisti furono 23."

Bibliography

Abraham, Gerald. 1971. "Satire and Symbolism in *The Golden Cockerel*." *Music & Letters* 52: 46–54.

Antolini, Bianca Maria, Arnaldo Morelli, and Vera Vita Spagnuolo, eds. 1994. *La musica a Roma attraverso le fonti d'archivio: Atti del convegno internazionale Roma 4–7 giugno 1992*. Lucca: Libreria musicale italiana.

Banti, Alberto M. 2000. *La nazione del Risorgimento: Parentela, santità e onore alle origini dell'Italia unita*. Turin: Einaudi.

Bartlet, M. Elizabeth C. 1992. "On the Freedom of the Theatre and Censorship: The Adrien Controversy (1792)." In *1789–1989: Musique, histoire, démocratie*. 3 vols., edited by Antoine Hennion. I: 15–30. Paris: Maison des Sciences de l'Homme.

Bartoli, Cecilia. 2005. *Opera Proibita*. Decca 475 7029.

Bergamaschi, M. T. "Meucci, Filippo." *Dizionario biografico degli Italiani*. Online. Available: http://www.treccani.it/enciclopedia/ricerca/Meucci,-Filippo/Dizionario_Biografico/ (accessed February 6, 2014).

Black, John. 1984. "Code of Instructions for the Censorship of Theatrical Works: Naples 1849." *Journal of the Donizetti Society* 5: 147–150.

Brindicci, Monica. 2000. "L'incertezza dell'opera: Censure, revisioni, adattamenti, collages." In *Donizetti, Napoli, l'Europa: Atti del convegno di studi, Napoli, 11–13 dicembre 1997*, edited by Franco Carmelo Greco and Renato Di Benedetto, 103–107. Naples: Edizioni scientifiche italiane.

Buia, Anna. 1990. *Un così eroico amore: Genesi e diffusione censurata del libretto de 'La Traviata.'* Milan: Associazione Amici della Scala.

Burt, Richard. 1998. "(Un)Censoring in Detail: The Fetish of Censorship in the Early Modern Past and the Postmodern Present." In *Censorship and Silencing: Practices of Cultural Regulation*, edited by Robert C. Post, 17–41. Los Angeles: The Getty Research Institute Publications and Exhibitions Programs.

Butler, Judith. 1997. *Excitable Speech: A Politics of the Performative*. New York: Routledge.

Calcagno, Mauro. 2006. "Censoring *Eliogabalo* in Seventeenth-Century Venice." *Journal of Interdisciplinary History* 36/3: 355–377.

——. 2000. "Staging Musical Discourses in Seventeenth-Century Venice: Francesco Cavalli's *Eliogabalo* (1667)." PhD diss., Yale University.

Calzolari, Monica. 1994. "La censura nella Roma pontificia dell'Ottocento: Il ruolo predominante della Direzione Generale di Polizia." In Antolini et al. 1994, 287–298.

Cataldi, Renata. 1994. "La censura sugli spettacoli nella Roma pontificia dell'Ottocento: Le licenze del cardinal vicario." In Antolini et al. 1994, 299–320.

Chusid, Martin. 1998. "On Censored Performances of *Les vêpres siciliennes* and *Rigoletto*: Evidence from the Verdi Archive at New York University." *Verdi Newsletter* 25: 3–19.

Commons, Jeremy. 1983. "Un contributo ad uno studio su Donizetti e la censura napoletana." In *Atti del 1 convegno internazionale donizettiano*. 2 vols., edited by Pieralberto Cattaneo, I: 65–106. Bergamo: Azienda Autonomo di Turismo.

Degrada, Francesco. 1984. "A Note on Censorship." In *Verdi's 'Macbeth': A Sourcebook*, edited by David Rosen and Andrew Porter, 56–58. New York: W. W. Norton.

Di Stefano, Carlo. 1964. *La censura teatrale in Italia*. Rocca San Casciano: Cappelli.

Fairtile, Linda B. 1997. "Censorship in Verdi's *Attila*: Two Case Studies." *Verdi Newsletter* 24: 5–7.

Fay, Laurel. 1992. "*Lady Macbeth of the Mtsensk District*." *New Grove Dictionary of Opera* Online. Available: http://www.oxfordmusiconline.com/subscriber/article/grove/music/O002507 (accessed February 6, 2014).

Feldman, Martha. 2007. *Opera and Sovereignty: Transforming Myths in Eighteenth-Century Italy*. Chicago: University of Chicago Press.

Foucault, Michel. 1992. *The Use of Pleasure: History of Sexuality*. Vol. 2. London: Penguin.

——. 1980. *Power/Knowledge: Selected Interviews and Other Writings 1972–1977*, edited by Colin Gordon. New York: Pantheon Books.

Fubini, Mario. 1971. "Un mito del Risorgimento: *La Lega lombarda*." In *Romanticismo italiano: Saggi di storia della critica e della letteratura*, 157–188. Bari: Edizioni Laterza.

Fulcher, Jane. 1987. *The Nation's Image: French Grand Opera as Politics and Politicized Art*. Cambridge: Cambridge University Press.

Genette, Gérard. 1997a. *Palimpsests: Literature in the Second Degree*, translated by Channa Newman and Claude Doubinsky. Lincoln: University of Nebraska Press.

——. 1997b. *Paratexts: Thresholds of Interpretation*, translated by Jane E. Lewin. Cambridge: Cambridge University Press.

Giger, Andreas. 2010. "Behind the Police Chief's Closed Doors: The Unofficial Censors of Verdi in Rome." *Nineteenth-Century Music Review* 7/2: 63–99.

——. 1999. "Social Control and the Censorship of Giuseppe Verdi's Operas in Rome (1844–1859)." *Cambridge Opera Journal* 11/3: 233–265.

GMM. 1860. "Teatro Carcano: *La lega lombarda*: Musica del Maestro Buzzi." *Gazzetta musicale di Milano* 19 (January 9): 11–12.

Goodman, Andrew. 1983. *Gilbert and Sullivan at Law*. London: Associated University Presses.

Gossett, Philip. 2006. *Divas and Scholars: Performing Italian Opera*. Chicago: University of Chicago Press.

——. 2005. "Le 'edizioni distrutte' e il significato dei cori operistici nel Risorgimento." *Saggiatore musicale* 12: 339–387. English version in Johnson et al. 2007 [as "'Edizioni distrutte' and the Significance of Operatic Choruses during the Risorgimento"], 181–242.

——. 1990a. "Becoming a Citizen: The Chorus in *Risorgimento* Opera." *Cambridge Opera Journal* 2/1: 41–64.

——. 1990b. "Censorship and Self-Censorship: Problems in Editing the Operas of Giuseppe Verdi." In *Essays in Musicology: A Tribute to Alvin Johnson*, edited by Lewis Lockwood and Edward Roesner, 247–257. Philadelphia: American Musicological Society.

Grantaliano, Elvira. 1994. "La censura nella Roma pontificia dell'ottocento: Tipologie ed esempi." In Antolini et al. 1994, 321–336.

Hallman, Diana. 2002. *Opera, Liberalism, and Antisemitism in Nineteenth-Century France: The Politics of Halévy's 'La Juive.'* Cambridge: Cambridge University Press.

Heidlberger, Frank. 2003. "Halévys *Jüdin* in Wien: Zur Rezeptionsgeschichte einer Oper zwischen Zensur und Antisemitismus." In *Actes de colloque Fromental Halévy: Paris, novembre 2000*, edited by Francis Claudon, Gilles de Van, and Karl Leich-Galland, 244–266. Weisenberg: Musik-Edition Lucie Galland.

Ipson, Douglas Leon. 2011. "'Giuriamo per la patria': The Operatic Oath Scene in Revolutionary Rome, 1846–1849." PhD diss., University of Chicago.

Izzo, Francesco. 2007. "Verdi, the Virgin, and the Censor: The Politics of the Cult of Mary in *I Lombardi alla prima crociata and Giovanna d'Arco*." *Journal of the American Musicological Society* 60/3: 557–597.

——. 2004. "Comedy between Two Revolutions: Opera Buffa and the Risorgimento, 1831–1848." *Journal of Musicology* 21/1: 127–174.

Johnson, Victoria, Jane F. Fulcher, and Thomas Ertman, eds. 2007. *Opera and Society in Italy and France from Monteverdi to Bourdieu*. Cambridge: Cambridge University Press.

Jones, Derek. 2001. *Censorship: A World Encyclopaedia*, 4 vols. London: Routledge.

Kimbell, David R. B. 1981. *Verdi in the Age of Italian Romanticism*. Cambridge: Cambridge University Press.

Krakovitch, Odile. 1997. "L'Opéra-Comique et la censure." In *Die Opéra comique und ihr Einfluß auf das europäische Musiktheater im 19. Jahrhundert: Bericht uber den Internationalen Kongress Frankfurt 1994*, edited by Herbert Schneider and Nicole Wild, 211–234. Hildesheim: Olms.

——. 1985. *Hugo censuré: La liberté au théâtre au XIXe siècle*. Paris: Calmann-Lévy.

Lavagetto, Mario. 2010. *Un caso di censura: Il 'Rigoletto.'* 2nd ed. Milan: Mondadori.

LIM. 1851. "Teatri e notizie diverse: Sassari." *L'Italia musicale* 3 (November 8): 357–358.

LIM. 1850. "Teatri: Torino." *L'Italia musicale* 2 (September 18): 265.

Marvin, Roberta M. 2001. "The Censorship of Verdi's Operas in Victorian London." *Music & Letters* 82/4: 582–610.

——. 1991. "Il libretto di Berio per l'*Otello* di Rossini." *Bollettino del Centro Rossiniani di Studi* 31: 55–76.

Meucci, Filippo. 1846. *La lega lombarda nel secolo XII: Dramma lirico*. Paris: n.p.

Morrison, Simon. 1998. "Sergei Prokofiev's *Semyon Kotko* as a Representative Example of Socialist Realism." *Musik als Text: Bericht über den internationalen musikwissenschaftlichen Kongreß der Gesellschaft für Musikforschung*. 2 vols., edited by Hermann Danuser and Tobias Plebuch, I: 494–497. Kassel: Bärenreiter.

Mossa, Carlo Matteo, ed. 2001. *Carteggio Verdi-Cammarano (1843–1852)*. Parma: Istituto nazionale di studi verdiani.

Mugayar Kuhl, Pablo. 1998. "Censura y autocensura: G. Martinelli y la ópera en Portugal en el siglo XVIII." *La abolición del arte*, edited by Alberto Dallal, 317–337. Mexico City: Universidad Nacional Autónoma de México (Instituto de Investigaciones Estéticas).

Neef, Sigrid. 1990. "Verdrängung, Sublimierung und Projektionen: Zu Opern und Operngeschichtsschreibung der DDR.'" *Musik und Gesellschaft* 40: 544–551.

Pancino, Livia. 1994. "*Arsilda regina di Ponto*: Per una ricostruzione della versione primitiva." *Informazioni e studi vivaldiani* 15: 51–74.

Ponzo, Giovanni. 1980. *Le origini della libertà di stampa in Italia (1846–1852)*. Rome: Giuffré Editore.

Pospísil, Milan. 2007. "Österreichische Opernzensur in Prag: *Gustave III* und *La Juive*." *Eugène Scribe und das europäische Musiktheater*, edited by Sebastian Werr, 122–152. Berlin: Lit.

Pougin, Arthur. 1881. *Giuseppe Verdi: Vita aneddotica*. With notes and additions by Folchetto [Giacomo Caponi]. Milan: Ricordi.

Raffaelli, Renato, ed. 1996. *Otello*. I libretti di Rossini 3. Pesaro: Fondazione Rossini.

Ringer, Alexander L. 1971. "The Political Uses of Opera in Revolutionary France." *Bericht über den internationalen musikwissenschaftlichen Kongress Bonn 1970*, 237–242. Kassel: Bärenreiter.

Rizzuti, Alberto. 2001. "Music for a Risorgimento Myth: Joan of Arc 1789–1849." PhD diss., University of Chicago.

Rosen, David B. 2010. "A Tale of Three Libretti: *La muette de Portici* in Italy." *L'immaginario scenografico e la realizzazione musicale: Atti del convegno in onore di Mercedes Viale Ferrero, Torino, Teatro Regio, 5–6 febbraio 2009, Venezia, Fondazione Giorgio Cini, 5–6 marzo 2009*, edited by Maria Ida Biggi and Paolo Gallarati, 167–179. Turin: Edizioni dell'Orso.

——. 2007. "'Si ridesti ~~il Leon di Castiglia~~ la fiamma sopita': Ricordi's Censored Libretto of *Ernani* and Some Vicissitudes of the Conspiracy Scene." *Verdi Forum* 34: 9–27.

——. 1999–2000. "A Tale of Five Cities: The Peregrinations of Somma's and Verdi's *Gustavo III (and Una vendetta in dominò and Un ballo in maschera)* at the Hands of the Neapolitan and Roman Censorship." *Verdi Forum* 26–27: 53–66.

Rosselli, John. 1984. *The Opera Industry in Italy from Cimarosa to Verdi: The Role of the Impresario*. Cambridge: Cambridge University Press.

Rubsamen, Walter H. 1946. "Political and Ideological Censorship of Opera." *Papers of the American Musicological Society*, edited by Otto Kinkeldey and Gustave Reese, 30–42. Philadelphia: American Musicological Society.

[Ruffini, Giovanni]. 1853. *Lorenzo Benoni, or Passages in the Life of an Italian*. Edinburgh: Th. Constable & Co.

TAL. 1860. Note on *La lega Lombarda*. *Teatri arti e letteratura* (January 5): 238.

TAL. 1859. Article on *La lega Lombarda*. *Teatri arti e letteratura* (November 28): 210.

Taruskin, Richard. 2009. *The Danger of Music and Other Anti-Utopian Essays*. Berkeley and Los Angeles: University of California Press.

Verdi, Giuseppe. 1983. *Rigoletto*, edited by Martin Chusid. *The Works of Giuseppe Verdi*. Series I: 17. Chicago: University of Chicago Press; Milan: Ricordi.

Werr, Sebastian. 2008. "'Tutta immorale, ed orrenda': Hugo, Romani, Donizetti e la censura italiana." In *D'une scène à l'autre. L'opéra italien en Europe*. 2 vols., edited by Damien Colas and Alessandro di Profio, II: 273–278. Wavre: Mardaga.

Zidaric, Walter. 2004. "Traduction/adaptation des livrets d'opéras: Le rôle de la censure en Russie aux XIXe et XXe siècles." *La traduction des livrets: Aspects théoriques, historiques et pragmatiques*, 495–504. Paris: Presses de l'Université de Paris-Sorbonne.

PART V

TRANSMISSION AND RECEPTION

CHAPTER 38

HOW OPERA TRAVELED

LOUISE K. STEIN

> Sig. [Gaetano] Martinelli, poet...is now about to depart. But since he fears the sea very much, particularly in the current season, he has therefore decided to make the trip by land. If he goes from here [Ludwigsburg] to Strasbourg, and from there by successive and continuous carriages that run regularly from place to place through all of France, he hopes to be at Barcelona within a few days. Then, from Barcelona he will cross Spain by the best and fastest method that he can and arrive there [Lisbon] with the greatest possible haste, without stopping anywhere...Sig. Martinelli will bring with him my promised music together with my most respectful esteem [...].
>
> (Letter from composer Niccolò Jommelli to Pedro José da Silva Bottelho, at the Portuguese royal theater, January 27, 1769, translated in McClymonds 1980: 486)

An Itinerant Genre

By land or by sea, however arduous and fraught with delays, travel was essential to opera's development from the early years of its history. The travels of the genre and of individual operas, productions, texts, scores, singers, composers, librettists, patrons, audiences, producers, stage architects, and impresarios all contributed to the early modern expansion of opera's domain. But in its first two centuries, opera did not merely "spread" like a fog or a virus throughout Italy and Europe, and then somehow to distant or resistant places such as Lisbon, St. Petersburg, Lima, or Mexico City. Opera reached new venues and audiences thanks to the wealth, power, and considerable motivation of those who carried it, invited it, financed it, or carefully prepared the way. Whereas most studies of opera in the early modern period have focused on the fundamental work of composers and librettists, this essay focuses on the activity of producers, patrons, and performers, especially the mechanisms that brought them into contact with each other across political, linguistic, and geographical boundaries.

I propose here to bring to the fore the motivations and mechanisms behind opera's trajectory. Here the "prime movers" in the history of opera production are the aristocratic producers or patrons of opera, supported by their concrete connections with each other and with traveling colleagues, agents, singers, and composers. The sponsors of opera in the early modern period were not uniformly invested in producing the same kind of opera, nor were they all solely interested in opera as a display of oppressive power.

In spite of its expense and complexity as a performance medium, opera became an essentially flexible and itinerant phenomenon in the early modern period, even in an age in which musical life was primarily controlled by stodgy administrative structures and rigid hierarchies of social class or ecclesiastical position. As far as is known, the first public operatic performance was given in Venice in 1637 by a traveling company put together by the creative team of impresario, composer, and theorbo player Benedetto Ferrari and librettist and singer Francesco Manelli, thanks to the invitation and financial backing of the patrician Tron family. The Tron brothers' interest in opera was both a matter of civic pride and financial investment in their newly renovated Teatro San Cassiano. When other patrician families and theater owners followed their example, Venice became the launching site for the growth of opera as a business (Rosand 1991: 66–81; Glixon and Glixon 2006: 3–6, 66–71).

Members of the Venetian patriciate had first experienced opera in nearby Padua when they attended the 1636 performance of *Ermiona*, a spectacular sung entertainment organized by the marquis degli Obizzi that sparked their interest in producing visually spectacular musical theater. The mixed character of Venetian opera, with its combination of the serious and the comic, the lyrical and the farcical, is a reminder that when Ferrari and his company of "Febiarmonici" began to bring opera to new sites in northern Italy in the 1640s, they adapted the genre to the familiar model of the traveling *commedia dell'arte* troupe, transforming it even as their travels transmitted it (Bianconi and Walker 1975: 380–382). Itinerant troupes from Rome and Venice traveled to other cities and courts within Italy at the invitation of aristocratic sponsors whose own desire to produce opera was fueled both by social competition and the experience of attending operas during the Venetian carnival. When companies that had already succeeded in Venice, or that formed there especially to travel, forged arrangements with local impresarios beyond the lagoon, the Venetian model of the *dramma per musica* grew to become an exportable "prototype" that assured its own survival, renovation, and relevance, because it was adaptable and shaped by an easily reproduced set of conventions (Bianconi 1987: 180–186, 190–198).

In a sense, the rigid social bonds and hierarchies that characterized the early modern experience contributed to the spread of opera. Within a decade of its metamorphosis into a commercial entertainment, opera traveled well beyond Venice in a constantly expanding itinerary—a "mobile professional force" from Venice supported by "seigneurial patronage" even performed the first Italian opera heard at the French court, thanks to the persistent efforts of the powerful statesman Cardinal Giulio Mazzarini (Jules Mazarin) (Murata 1995: 87–105). Though his original intention was to bring a Roman production to Paris, when that effort failed, the French ambassador to the Venetian Republic and assorted French aristocrats in Venice assured Mazarin that there was "nothing in the world more regal nor more worthy" than a Venetian production (Murata 1995: 102). In the end, the first Italian opera produced in France (albeit with spoken dialogue) was *La finta pazza*, with libretto by Giulio Strozzi and music by Francesco Sacrati, performed in December 1645 at the Petit Bourbon with dazzling changes of scene and machinery by Giacomo Torelli. The choreographer and director Giovan Battista Balbi and his troupe had performed the opera in Florence in 1644 and were invited to France by the queen (the Spanish-born Anne of Austria). Balbi and Torelli "and not any composer or singer, served as the catalysts that finally brought grand opera, as it were, to Paris" (Murata 1995: 103).

La finta pazza is exemplary of the fact that, in the hands of determined patrons and traveling companies, seventeenth-century operas were not limited to one production or even to a small cluster of performances, despite the fact that the same opera was unlikely to be presented in consecutive seasons in the same city. Operas were not composed or performed as closed musical "works"; every new production necessarily involved adaptation and improvisation of several kinds. The well-documented performance history of *Il Giasone* by Francesco Cavalli, probably the best traveled of Venetian operas, illustrates this point—a plethora of printed libretti and manuscript scores witness *Giasone*'s history and the extent to which it was adapted or revised in different productions. Between its Venetian premiere and the end of the century, *Giasone* was produced in Milan, Florence, Lucca, Naples, Bologna, Milan, Piacenza, Palermo, Livorno, Vicenza, Ferrara, Genoa, Ancona, Siena, Brescia, Reggio Emilia, and Rome, as well as in smaller *commedia dell'arte* performances that spoofed the opera (Bianconi 1987: 196). It is hardly surprising that *Giasone* was among the first operas to be produced in Naples under the Spanish viceroys, given that Spanish *comedias* were among the librettist Giacinto Andrea Cicognini's unacknowledged sources (see Tedesco 2006: 221–245). *Giasone* was performed "in Palazzo dalla compagnia de Fedel Armonici" in 1652 and 1653 at the viceroy's invitation, though it had already been performed "many other times," according to a report sent to the secretary of the Tuscan grand duke by Vincenzo Medici (I-Fas, Mediceo del Principato, f. 4115; see also D'Alessandro 1984: 414–441). Thus an opera designed for Venice and its more heterogeneous publics became a staple after it was introduced at the palace of the Spanish viceroy, Iñigo Vélez de Guevara y Tassis, eighth count of Oñate y Villamediana, in the very different social and political environment in Naples. Presumably, Oñate had experienced Italian opera for the first time during his tenure as Spanish ambassador in Rome (July 1646–February 1648; Bianconi and Walker 1995: 380–382). But he had long demonstrated a passion for the theater and for the *comedia española*: before his journey to Italy, he rented one of the most expensive private boxes or *aposentos* in Madrid's public Corral del Príncipe in 1642 (Shergold 1967: 534; Varey and Shergold 1971: 122), and while in Rome he was among a small but influential group of devotees who attended informal performances of Spanish *comedias* in Italian translation (Teodoro Ameyden's translations of Lope de Vega's *Los melindres de Belisa* and Calderón de la Barca's *La dama duende*, noted in Profeti 1996: 33–37). Oñate was one of the richest of the Spanish Grandees and spent lavishly on art, architecture, and urban reform during his short reign in Naples, making it easy for the Neapolitan nobility to "admire" his power, as they enjoyed the newly created spacious avenues and magnificent vistas he financed (Minguito Palomares 2001: 966–969). Opera fit within his plan for the renovation of public spaces and public life in Naples—its performances further accentuated his *grandeza*. The *Giasone* performances he offered to the nobility in Naples were staged by the Venetian theatrical engineer Giovan Battista Balbi, to whom Oñate may have been a kind of Maecenas (Minguito Palomares 2001: 969; concerning Balbi and the travels of *Giasone*, see Michelassi 2003, 2010; and Tedesco 2005). Most of the operas in the first series financed by Oñate (whose planning began in September 1650 with preparations for the October premiere of *Didone, ovvero L'incendio di Troia*) were by Francesco Cavalli, the leading Venetian composer of the moment, thus bringing the very best of the genre to Naples. If Oñate celebrated "the victory over Masaniello with a kind of spectacle as yet unknown in Naples" (Fabris 2007: 154), it is also clear that these productions had little or no intrinsic political relevance to the Neapolitan situation, in plot or musical style, though three of the Cavalli operas produced in Naples in the 1650s almost certainly included music by the local composer Francesco Provenzale as well (Fabris 2007: 155–159). The December 1652 Neapolitan production of Cavalli's *La Veremonda* for the Queen of Spain's birthday may have been an exception—this premiere "per ordine di Sua Eccellenza" in the Sala Grande of the Palazzo Reale was an overtly political event (Bianconi and Walker 1975; Heller 2005: 147–164). *Veremonda* was the first performance of an opera specifically composed for Naples (though its libretto was a reworking of an earlier Cicognini libretto). The viceroy's sponsorship was crucial: although the "comici forastieri italiani, chiamati Febi armonici, che rappresentano in musica" did not have any permanent position at Oñate's court, they stayed on after their Neapolitan debut in 1650 with his financial support to prepare for subsequent seasons (Prota-Giurleo 2002: 15–16; Bianconi and Walker 1975: 381–382; Michelassi 2010 reexamines Balbi's essential contribution[1]).

Importing Opera

The practical problems that Viceroy Oñate confronted when he introduced opera in Naples expose some of the typically adverse conditions that opera encountered in its early travels to new cities and courts. Lacking experienced opera composers and stage designers, and because the singers in the Neapolitan royal chapel were not permitted to perform onstage, Viceroy Oñate was compelled to import opera as a complete package, with artistic values and performers from outside Naples whom he supported financially (though it is unclear to what extent he drew on his personal or household accounts in place of or together with funds assigned to him by Madrid). Further, since Naples did not have a dedicated opera theater at this early date, performances were staged in a temporary theater erected in the Gioco della Pilotta, a kind of tennis court attached to the viceroy's palace (also known as the Teatro del Reale Parco or the Pallonetto), and later in a redecorated salon. Some of the performances were open to the paying public (Bianconi and Walker 1975: 379), with the result that Oñate effectively launched opera as a commercial enterprise right from the site of royal authority, the *palazzo reale*. In so doing, not surprisingly, he was following a Spanish precedent: productions first seen only by the royal family and invited members of the nobility at the Coliseo theater in the Buen Retiro palace in Madrid were routinely opened to the public, with ticket holders entering through a side door to the royal theater that faced away from the sovereign's private quarters and administrative spaces (the influence of many Spanish conventions and attitudes in Neapolitan productions is explored in Stein 2009, 2012, 2014).

Opera's introduction at Naples underlines the extent to which the decisions of patrons and producers could enhance or negate the self-promotion or "marketing" of composers and librettists. If it seems obvious that Balbi and Cavalli (whether as a team or in separate initiatives) successfully offered *Veremonda* as a new opera as well as a series of older Cavalli operas to Oñate, it is also clear that another viceroy might well have settled for less. Spanish viceroys and governors in Naples and Milan were essential agents in the larger history of seventeenth-century opera, even if their short residencies and foreign expectations render them difficult for modern scholars to assess as producers. Oñate's investment at Naples left an important legacy, though opera as a commercial venture there began to be fully operative only after he was recalled to Madrid at the end of 1653. On his orders, the Teatro di San Bartolomeo had been reconditioned to become an opera theater. Subsequently, with the investment of its owners and following the Spanish model, the Santa Casa degl'Incurabili (the administrators of the lunatic asylum) became a public theater run by impresarios but whose proceeds supported charities and the hospitals (Bianconi and Walker 1984: 265; Stein 2009; Cotticelli and Maione 1993: 145–175). Commercial performances in Naples did not replace the private ones so important to the social life of the court and the Neapolitan nobility (Stein 2012)—rather, the impresarios were still obliged to and supported in some way by the viceroy. In 1657–1659, for example, a collection of singers who called themselves the Accademia degli Armonici performed at the Teatro di San Bartolomeo, but their contract with the impresario Gregorio delle Chiave obligated them to perform at the Palazzo Reale as well (Prota-Giurleo 2002: 24–28).

Exporting Opera: *Partenope's* Italian Travel

When opera was introduced at a new location, it did not necessarily enjoy immediate stability or a consistent level of quality in successive productions, as the Neapolitan situation demonstrates. In Naples, a relatively stable mechanism for opera production was established only later, toward the end of the seventeenth century, thanks to the investment of two other opera-loving Spanish viceroys (Gaspar de Haro y Guzmán, marquis del Carpio, and Luis de la Cerda, duke of Medinaceli). They transformed Naples from a way-post on the operatic itinerary into an operatic proving ground with high standards (Stein 2012). Some of the most widely traveled operas of the early eighteenth century were created initially for Naples. *Partenope*, a libretto by the Roman poet Silvio Stampiglia (a founding member of the Arcadian Academy) set first for Naples by Luigi Mancia in 1699, is a well-known example. The siren Partenope of ancient Greek myth and Homer's *Odyssey* is recast in the libretto as a shipwrecked queen who is washed up onto the beach at Naples, where she gratefully founds a city in her name. In early modern times, the mermaid-siren was a common symbol of Naples, or "Partenopeia," as founded by the ancient Greeks. From Naples, the Stampiglia libretto traveled widely into the third decade of the eighteenth century, adapted to new performance circumstances and in musical settings by several composers. By 1720, over a dozen different *Partenope* operas had been produced in theaters scattered across what is now the Italian geography, though the libretti reveal that just about every production involved several kinds of revision to Stampiglia's original (see Freeman 1968: 356–385, though he does not include the Mexico City libretto).

Partenope traveled in a continual process of reinvention. Among the most significant but common revisions were the substitute arias. The Ferrara 1709 and Bologna 1710 productions of *Partenope* involved seventeen and sixteen aria substitutions, while the Florence 1701 and Rimini 1715 productions included only two substitutions. The Modena 1720 performance required a total of twenty-two substitute arias. The travels of the *Partenope* libretto (and, possibly, some of Mancia's music) serve as an important reminder of the extent to which seventeenth- and eighteenth-century operas were designed as vehicles for performance, rather than closed masterworks. An opera based on a widely circulated and popular libretto might very well be performed as a composite with arias from different earlier productions, in the manner of an unacknowledged *pasticcio* (serious or comic), without a significant quantity of new music from any single composer (Freeman 1968: 384; Walker 1952: 369–383). Individual operas, libretti, and traveling productions were revised and adapted, usually to please new patrons or audiences, but also for new casts or special effects from the stage designers. Scenes were cut or reordered, roles were expanded, attenuated, or deleted altogether; recitative passages (almost an afterthought in the compositional process) were dispensable and even recomposed after the start of a production; and arias were added, recomposed, deleted, substituted, and appended more often than not. Substitute arias were introduced, sometimes at the request of singers who wanted to perform the signature pieces they were already famous for. Singers also borrowed arias from each other in open competition. But substitute arias and revisions were also sometimes introduced by poets and composers who worked to "improve" an opera or to impress a particular patron or client. This is arguably the case in some of the revised or recomposed versions of Venetian operas made by composers who served the Spanish viceroys in Naples, notably Alessandro

Scarlatti in the service of Viceroy del Carpio in the 1680s. Travel, exchange, and collaboration among singers, composers, patrons, and producers both depended on and facilitated the flexibility of Baroque opera, and surely also contributed to the spontaneity and frequently disruptive behavior of opera audiences whose expectations were easily raised, satisfied, surprised, or disappointed at the theater.

Precisely because its plot was highly improbable, entertaining, and adaptable, *Partenope* not only returned to be staged again in Naples in 1722, but was composed anew by two important Neapolitan composers of a younger generation (Domenico Sarro in 1722 and Leonardo Vinci for Rome in 1724). The libretto was also produced as a comic opera by Handel for the Royal Academy in London in 1730. Handel's opera even maps some of the libretto's previous travels, for it "contains substitute aria texts introduced earlier in the productions of Venice, Bologna, and Modena . . . but also shares eighteen aria texts with the Naples original of 1699" (Freeman 1968: 384). Handel's 1730 cast included three singers who had already performed in the Ferrara 1709 and Naples 1722 *Partenope* productions, though not in the roles they were assigned in Handel's score, which was, in any case, free of musical borrowings from earlier musical settings, as far as is known. London's Covent Garden theater provided a very new climate and audience for a *Partenope* reborn in Handel's music, but Handel's interest in the libretto most likely came about through his contact with singers who knew the earlier settings by other composers (Dean 2006: 154–155).

Partenope: Naples to Mexico

If connections among singers and composers help to explain the performance history of the *Partenope* libretto, they do not easily explain how *Partenope* reached the distant American shores of the Atlantic world. *Partenope* seems to have been the first opera ever performed in Mexico and in North America, most likely thanks again to a strong web of connections among Spanish aristocrats enamored of Italian opera. An undated *Partenope* libretto published in Mexico City indicates that a performance there sometime around 1710 reproduced the 1699 Neapolitan model quite faithfully. This "Fiesta, performed in the Royal Palace at Mexico City" for King Philip V's name-day either presented a musical setting of the libretto in Italian (with very few changes), or in Spanish translation—the Mexico City libretto offers the Italian text by Stampiglia with the unsigned Spanish translation on facing pages (Stampiglia n.d.).[2] *Partenope* arrived in the Atlantic world with her strongly Neapolitan identity intact, but open to Spanish translation. The Mexico City libretto does not name composer or translator, and no score has been found, but scholars have surmised that the translator and arranger or composer was Manuel Zumaya (also Sumaya), a *criollo* musician and scholar who served as a singer, organist, and later chapel master at the Cathedral in Mexico City.

Among the versions of Stampiglia's *Partenope* in circulation in the early eighteenth century, the text of the Mexico City libretto is closest to the version composed by Mancia for Naples in 1699, though it is not an exact replica (Stampiglia 1699).[3] This close identification with Naples provides a clue to the opera's performance date in Mexico and the path it traveled to get there. Most likely, the libretto (and perhaps a musical score or a collection of arias from the Neapolitan *Partenope*) reached Mexico City thanks to relationships among Spanish aristocrats—the same network that launched the voyage of other operas to other far-flung Spanish territories, along with all manner of books, paintings, and luxury goods. The dedicatee of the 1699 Naples libretto was María de Girón y Sandoval, duchess of Medinaceli, the wife of the Neapolitan viceroy Luis Francisco de la Cerda y Aragón, duke of Medinaceli. His sister, Juana de la Cerda y Aragón, was married to Francisco Fernández de la Cueva, tenth duke of Alburquerque and marquis de Cuellar, who served as viceroy of New Spain through January 1711. It is likely that Fernández de la Cueva initiated the project of producing *La Partenope* so that his wife and his court would be regaled with the same kind and level of entertainment as his sister and powerful brother-in-law famously enjoyed in Naples. Letters from this period among Spanish nobles attest to the importance of this kind of emulation and competition as the motivation for sharing libretti and musical scores (Stein 2001: 87–91). Zumaya's *La Partenope* was most likely produced between 1700 and January 1711 when Fernández de Cueva's term as viceroy of New Spain ended.[4]

Mechanisms of Recruitment and Adaptation

The political responsibilities, travel itineraries, and family obligations of Spanish viceroys prompted them to introduce and cultivate opera at courts that lacked an operatic infrastructure (Naples in the mid-seventeenth century and Mexico in the early eighteenth century). But the Spaniards were hardly alone in this regard. Without an opera producer and specially trained singers, the de facto ruler of France in the 1640s, Cardinal Mazarin, was forced to relinquish his initial plan to import a Roman opera to Paris, though he at least managed to bring *La finta pazza*, thanks to the availability of Torelli, Balbi, and the Febiarmonici. Similar plans for the importation of opera were also modified in London and elsewhere on the Continent in the late seventeenth century, when the travels of German and English aristocrats or their agents similarly contributed to the internationalization of opera. Duke Johann Friedrich of Brunswick-Lüneburg's frequent sojourns in Venice, for example, were the inspiration for his efforts to bring opera to Hanover. The duke hired the composer Antonio Sartorio to direct his Roman Catholic Hofkapelle (before 1666), but spent considerable time in Venice and allowed Sartorio to do so as well. The best singers from the ducal chapel in Hanover were hired by eager impresarios at the Venetian theaters in successive seasons, and the duke encouraged them to perform there annually at carnival. The duke's influence in

Venice and in the world of opera grew to be considerable, which in turn enhanced his political reputation for sophistication and liberality. The duke's hiring of Sartorio and his other dealings with singers and theaters were effected through his contacts within the Venetian aristocracy, including the librettist Pietro Dolfin, whose own reputation was strengthened by this mutually beneficial relationship (Vavoulis 2003: 556–609). Approximately thirty Venetian libretti were dedicated to the duke or to members of his family between 1654 and 1688. The first opera known to have been produced in Hanover, however, was Antonio Cesti's *Orontea*, a well-traveled opera by a Venetian composer that was most likely first composed for another northern destination, the Hapsburg court at Innsbruck. In Hanover, *Orontea* was presented at a temporary theater in the ducal castle. Perhaps because Duke Johann Friedrich preferred to travel to Venice rather than build an opera theater at home, Hanover lacked a purpose-built theater for opera. Friedrich's successor, Duke Ernst August, oversaw the completion of the Grosses Schlosstheater in the Leineschloss, which opened in January 1689 with a performance of Agostino Steffani's *Henrico Leone*.

In London, royal and aristocratic support was likewise essential in roughly the same period as a foundation for the development of both venues and mechanisms for the production of Italian opera. As is well known, King Charles II in 1683 sent the English actor and impresario Thomas Betterton to France to hire an opera company for the English court that would "represent something at least like an Opera in England for his Majesty's diversion" (quotations from the diplomatic correspondence are explicated in Winn 1992: 254). In Paris, Betterton likely attended a public performance or performances of Lully's *Phaëton*. His contact with musicians there was facilitated by British aristocrats eager to be of service to the royal errand. Betterton carried with him a letter of introduction from the Earl of Sunderland to Viscount Preston, the British ambassador to Louis XIV. Though he was unsuccessful in this misguided attempt to hire an entire French production or a complete Lully opera package for his king, Betterton recruited the composer Louis Grabu (a Spaniard who had worked in England previously but had sought and recently failed to obtain a French court position). Grabu, the "would-be Frenchman," was "afforded considerable preferment upon his return" (Price 1984: 13), and in collaboration with the poet John Dryden composed *Albion and Albanius* for the British court. His score shows traces of French influence, and the music for one prominent scene was clearly modeled on the scene of Proteus' transformation from Lully's *Phaëton* (White 2002: 410–427). It is also likely that the staging of *Albion and Albanius* was heavily influenced by what Betterton and Grabu witnessed at the Paris opera. In this way, even if a full production did not cross the English Channel in 1689, operatic ideas and specific, immediately relevant artistic models traveled to the British court. The text of *Albion and Albanius* started out as a prologue to a larger Dryden project (probably what became *King Arthur, or The British Worthy*) but was reworked into *Albion and Albanius*, a stand-alone opera with French-flavored music by Grabu. Henry Purcell's setting of Dryden's *King Arthur*, as an English "dramatick opera" or semi-opera, also contains French dances and the imprint of French formal structures.

Within two decades of Betterton's trip to France, the British aristocracy's wholesale investment in Italian opera and feverish pursuit of flashy Italian singers were inspired by their visits to Italy on the Grand Tour (see especially Hume 1984; Price 1978; Gibson 1987; Hume 1988; Dean and Knapp 1987: 140–150; and McGeary 2007). In addition to the firsthand impressions and memories of Italian productions that these men brought to London, which others read about in their letters and journals, the travel of virtuoso Italian singers to London in the first two decades of the eighteenth century was crucial. The Neapolitan castrato Nicolo Grimaldi, known as Nicolini, was the most successful among the first wave of Italian singers to sing publicly in London. The Nicolini phenomenon was the brainchild of Sir John Vanbrugh, architect and owner of the new Queen's Theatre in the Haymarket, at whose insistence a highly placed intermediary—the earl of Manchester, then the British Ambassador Extraordinary to Venice—negotiated with Nicolini and offered generous financial incentives (Roach 1976). The details of his recruitment show just the kind of behind-the-scenes intervention by aristocratic intermediaries that promoted opera's early travels in the several diasporic waves that brought opera and its creative forces (singers and composers) to non-Italian theaters in Europe and beyond.

Nicolini arrived in England in 1708 with the homecoming of the earl of Manchester's entourage. Motivated by the glitter of potential profits, the theater manager Owen Swiney promoted Nicolini's London debut in Alessandro Scarlatti's *Pirro e Demetrio* in Nicola Haym's arrangement; thus, both the opera and its star singer were Neapolitan, though the London version of *Pirro* was considerably revised and truncated. Of course, Nicolini was no stranger to travel. Though he was trained in Naples and made his early career there (his stage debut had taken place at the San Bartolomeo theatre thanks to a discerning early patron, Viceroy marquis del Carpio), he was on the road for most of the decade preceding his departure for London, singing primarily in theaters in the north of Italy (Rome, Parma, Bologna, Genoa, Reggio nell'Emilia, Rovigo, Vicenza, Ferrara, and Venice). Handel most likely first heard Nicolini not in London, but in Venice, in the role of Arsace in Antonio Caldara's setting of *Partenope* in 1708 (Dean and Knapp 1987: 81). The singer later created two Handel roles with enormous success in London (*Rinaldo*, 1711, and *Amadigi*, 1715) before returning to Italy.

As I have outlined here, Italian opera and its music (whether on the Venetian model in the mid- to late-seventeenth century, or following trends that originated in Naples in the early eighteenth century) were well received at many foreign destinations. In London, the very different activities of Grabu and Nicolini brought about strikingly contrasting results in the decades on either side of 1700. But both cases demonstrate just how entirely dependent was the introduction of opera in London on the expertise and diplomatic placement of English nobles stationed abroad, together with the financial and entrepreneurial support of the English aristocracy. Of course, expert singers and experienced composers were crucial to the eventual establishment of opera in London, just as they were in other places where opera, musical idioms, and performance conventions were introduced successfully or brought lasting results.

Opera in the Spanish Orbit

When opera arrived at new sites without the direct influence or even presence of an operatic composer or trained singers, it traveled not as a packaged production or even as a firm set of conventions, but rather as an ideal concept, untethered to any direct influence or secure conduit of musical style. The introduction of opera to the Spanish court in Madrid early in the reign of Philip IV provides a case study of this rare phenomenon (Whitaker 1984: 43–66; Stein 1993: 191–205; Profeti 1999). *La selva sin amor*, the first Spanish opera, was produced when Florentine diplomats attached to the Tuscan embassy in Madrid decided to produce a fully-sung opera for the Spanish royal family. Their plan was especially to showcase the talents of Cosimo Lotti (a stage architect on loan from the Medici court who sought a court appointment) and to impress the young Philip IV, a lover of both music and theater. Lotti recently had traveled to Madrid with the entourage of the duke of Pastrana when the duke returned from Rome after his years as Spanish ambassador to the Holy See. The project of producing a fully-sung opera in Madrid in 1627 was daunting—indeed, it may be that the newly arrived Lotti, the duke of Pastrana, and the Tuscan diplomats themselves were the only people in Madrid who had ever seen or heard an opera. Lotti produced a visually spectacular "eclogue" in seven scenes, *La selva sin amor*, with a text by the prolific and esteemed Spanish poet and dramatist, Félix Lope de Vega Carpio (1630b; a little-known manuscript libretto is found in E-Mn, MS 3661, fol. 53, "La Selva sin Amor selva de Amores," 1630a). It is likely that Lope de Vega had studied an earlier Florentine libretto, since *La Dafne* and *L'Euridice* by Ottavio Rinuccini both circulated in print. His libretto for *La selva sin amor* is entirely in Italianate poetic forms, aside from a few ensemble songs (*coros*) assigned traditional octosyllabic Spanish meter. Because none of the Spanish court composers had any experience with opera or even with the *cantar recitando* of Italian accompanied monody, the Florentine diplomats drafted the Bolognese lute player Filippo Piccinini (who was among the king's favorite musicians) as their composer. Piccinini was reluctant to try his hand at opera and begged considerable assistance from an amateur musician named Bernardo Monanni, a secretary at the Tuscan delegation. The opera project is described in letters to the grand duke's secretary in Florence as "an embassy undertaking," and the play as a "little machine play in the Florentine manner." The flurry of activity on behalf of this little *favola in musica* had distinctly political purposes beyond its benevolent cover of cultural enrichment. *La selva sin amor* (whose music has not been recovered) indeed attracted the king's attention—it was enormously useful to its highly placed advocates and illustrates just how an opera production might open the path toward diplomatic or political negotiations. But this opera's utter failure to set a trend in Madrid is a glaring example of how difficult it was for opera to succeed when it was unveiled in new venues without the talents of trained and expert singers and composers. When he dedicated his libretto to the Almirante de Castilla a few years later (fol. 103–4 in his 1630 collection), Lope de

Vega reported that he had experienced "rapture" when he heard his verses performed in song. Notwithstanding his self-congratulatory recollection that the "music itself expressed admirations, complaints, love, anger, and all of the other affects," *La selva sin amor* seems to have been a flop. The usually vociferous critics at the court of Philip IV were notably silent, offering neither polemic nor panegyric about the performance or the new genre. Cosimo Lotti's remarkable scenic effects were apparently the only part of the experiment that bore repetition, and no further attempts to produce fully-sung opera were launched at the Spanish court before 1659.

La selva sin amor was a unique attempt by a few politically well-placed foreign amateurs to produce a non-Spanish kind of opera in Madrid in the seventeenth century. Later, opera was produced successfully by Spaniards in several cities within the Spanish dominions (beginning with the Italian operas sponsored by the count of Oñate in Naples in 1650–1653). A pair of operas in Spanish—*La púrpura de la rosa* and *Celos aun del aire matan*—were staged in Madrid in 1660–1661 to celebrate momentous political events, namely the Peace of the Pyrenees and the marriage of the Infanta María Teresa to Louis XIV of France. *La púrpura de la rosa* was performed January 17, 1660, though it may have received its premiere in the last months of 1659; the date of the premiere of *Celos aun del aire matan* has usually been given as December 5, 1660, but the more likely date is June 7, 1661 (Stein 1993: 219–220, confirmed by Montoya 2004: 287–289). Aside from the Italianate staging designed by the visiting engineer Antonio Maria Antonozzi, these were wholly Spanish productions with polymetric Spanish texts by Pedro Calderón de la Barca and music by the court composer and harpist Juan Hidalgo (Stein 1993: 205–257; Stein 1991: 126–167). The two operas were produced by a brilliant courtier and patron of art, Gaspar de Haro y Guzmán, marquis de Heliche y del Carpio, the son of the king's chief minister and the aristocrat entrusted with arranging court theatrical productions. He is the same seventh marquis del Carpio, who later served as viceroy of Naples in the 1680s and brought Alessandro Scarlatti there (see Stein 2002: 226–235; Stein 2001, 2012, and 2014). *Celos aun del aire matan*, the only one of the two operas whose Madrid score survives, also illustrates just how Spanish theatrical and musical conventions shaped the unusual genre of fully-sung opera in Madrid at this time. Most Spanish musical plays were partly sung rather than strictly operatic, given the *comedia*'s emphasis on verisimilitude (Stein 1993).

The genre of fully-sung opera was chosen for the celebrations of 1660–1661, but no Italian composer or singers were brought to Madrid for these productions, though Antonozzi designed the scenic and visual effects. The very idea of singing while acting, so essential to fully-sung opera, was initially a hard sell in Madrid, according to the earlier comments of the stage engineer Baccio di Bianco, who reported in 1652 that the papal nuncio at the Spanish court, Giulio Rospigliosi (opera librettist and prime mover in the history of opera in Rome) was "eager to introduce the recitative style, but only little by little, because one cannot get it into the heads of these gentlemen that one can speak singing, so he hopes that with patience he will win them over, and make them like what they berate so much without having seen or heard it" (Stein 1993: 136–137). The Madrid operas, partly-sung semi-operas, and *zarzuelas* were all produced for the royal court but performed by the same acting companies that offered spoken *comedias* in the public theaters. Thus, when the marquis de Heliche produced the operas of 1660–1661, the Spanish actresses who played and sang all of the serious solo roles in the operas had already performed sung roles in the *zarzuelas* and semi-operas he had produced in the 1650s. To facilitate their work as actress-singers, the composer Juan Hidalgo had answered the challenge posed by fully-sung dialogue by employing easily memorized strophic *coplas* and flexible, tuneful *recitado* whose combination of declamation with lyrical conjunct melodies is derived from the native tradition of the sung *romance* (Stein 2003). With, arguably, the busiest seasons of spoken theater and the richest theatrical culture in Europe, as well as an abundance of native musical types, Spanish patrons, dramatists, and composers did not feel the need to import foreign performers just for opera, and they did not travel to Italy to learn a foreign musical idiom.

Both of these Spanish operas traveled outside Spain, and they were revived at the Madrid court for special political occasions or royal commemorations in subsequent decades. The score of *Celos aun del aire matan* was sent to the imperial court in Vienna, in answer to repeated requests from the Empress Margarita (daughter of Philip IV), though it is unclear whether the opera or excerpts from it were ever performed there. A production of *Celos aun del aire matan* (in Spanish) was presented in Naples in 1682 by Giovanni Battista Ludovisi, prince of Piombino, in his apartments in the Castel Nuovo. The production was given on successive evenings for a crowded but "invited" audience that included (but was not limited to) the Neapolitan nobility. These performances honored the wedding of his sister, Lavinia Ludovisi, to the duke of Atri. The cast seems to have involved both Spanish and Italian singers. In mid-October 1681, the prince was already preparing the *comedia in musica.* He reportedly angered the viceroy (marquis de los Vélez) by recruiting one of the singers needed for the official opera the latter was planning for the king's birthday (November 6), paying the unnamed singer "a kingly sum" (Stein 2009).

The Naples 1682 libretto of *Celos aun del aire matan* is a fancy, commemorative edition of Calderón's text, including a unique *loa* or prologue (Calderón de la Barca 1682). It was most likely printed privately, rather than offered for sale, since it carries no printer's name or mark. The title page does not name a composer, but the phrase "Fiesta que se representó a sus magestades en el Coliseo del Buen Retiro. Y repetida en Napoles... En la occasion del Despossorio de la Excelentisima Señora mi Señora D. Lavinia Ludovisio, con el Excelentisimo Señor Duque de Atri" suggests that this *fiesta cantada* performed in Naples was identical to the one given previously in Madrid—in other words, that the same music was used in both the Madrid and Neapolitan productions. (Hidalgo's music is preserved in two manuscript sources; see Stein 1993: 219 and passim, and Stein's critical edition [Hidalgo 2014].) The production in Naples "pleased the audience more for the beauty of the costumes and sets than for the quality of the musical performance and composition,"[5] probably because the Spanish music composed by Hidalgo just over twenty years earlier seemed old-fashioned and musically tame in 1682 Naples. But the prince of Piombino seems to have chosen this aged and rarely performed work because of its overt political associations. Placing his sister Lavinia in a marriage beneficial to the Spanish political cause had been a difficult and protracted undertaking, and, as a reward for her agreement to marry the duke of Atri, the bride was promised an especially lavish set of celebrations (Stein 2009 and 2012). Neapolitans clucked that the events surrounding Lavinia's marriage cost "spese quasi reale" (Confuorto 1930: 79).

Celos aun del aire matan was, quite literally, a royal opera, since it had been created in 1660 to honor the Spanish royal wedding of the century, and was only revived at the royal Alcázar palace in Madrid (in 1679, and then again in 1684 and 1697). It cannot have been coincidental, however, that the opera was first performed to celebrate a royal marriage in which the Spanish royal succession hung in the balance, given that the Naples 1682 production celebrated a nuptial contract that resolved another dynastic crisis—the problem of the Ludovisi succession, so crucial to the survival of this leading "Spanish family" in Italy (Stein 2009). In Naples in 1682, just as in Madrid in 1660–1661, *Celos aun del aire matan* carried a strong encouragement toward marital fidelity and procreative activity on behalf of the Spanish cause, a message as appropriate to Lavinia Ludovisi's marriage as it had been to the Infanta María Teresa's marriage twenty years earlier (Stein 1993: 210–257; Stein 1991; Stein 2002: 186–193).

The travels of *Celos aun del aire matan* to Vienna and Naples were facilitated by the same kind of dynastic and political ties that brought the libretto (and possibly a score) of the Naples *Partenope* to Mexico City around 1710. But what is especially striking about the choice of *Celos* for the 1682 Naples wedding is the fact that the opera itself was politically emblematic. The performance history of its companion opera from 1660, *La púrpura de la rosa*, reveals that this opera also carried a striking set of political associations, even far away from the strictly European context. Hidalgo's setting of *La púrpura de la rosa* was revived at the Spanish royal court in 1680 within the celebrations that honored the marriage of Carlos II and Marie-Louise of Orléans. Later, in 1701, *La púrpura de la rosa* became the first opera of the Americas when it was performed in Lima, Peru, as composed, revised, or compiled by the Lima cathedral chapel master, Tomás de Torrejón y Velasco, a Spaniard who had moved to Peru at a very young age and became the most noted composer in the New World in his day (Stein 1999). Calderón's aged libretto and much of Hidalgo's music from the Madrid version made their American debut as the culminating event in a series of celebrations dedicated to Philip V's accession as the first Bourbon king of Spain—another Spanish-French alliance that resulted, in fact, from the royal wedding and treaty of 1659–1660 (Stein 2006: 433–458). Here again, a Spanish opera was revived in a far-away territory in celebration of a dynastic occasion within a web of familial connections. Philippe d'Anjou was the grandson of the union between Louis XIV and María Teresa of Spain. He was proclaimed Philip V, king of Spain, in Madrid on November 24, 1700, and in Lima in October 1701. The opera was performed at the viceroy's palace in Lima in December 1701 and January 1702 to honor his eighteenth birthday. The Calderón libretto was chosen most likely for its strong royal and pro-French associations and its pacifist message—in 1659–1660 the opera celebrated peace between Spain and France, and its argument for peace was just as relevant in 1701 after the accession of the first Bourbon king to the Spanish throne amidst the outbreak of the War of the Spanish Succession. The score is entirely Hispanic, full of *tonos* and *tonadas* with their *coplas* and *estribillos*, and repeating Hispanic dance patterns ready for improvised variations or *diferencias*. Whether Torrejón's Lima score was newly composed in 1701 or based on Hidalgo's score from 1660, it is self-consciously Hispanic in its musical content.

Opera sailed to the New World thanks to leading Spanish aristocrats whose families served successive monarchs, in a series of connections and motivations typical of the Spanish tradition. It is quite probable that the viceroy, Melchor Portocarrero Lasso de la Vega, count of Monclova, and the composer, Tomás de Torrejón y Velasco, had heard *La púrpura de la rosa* when it was first performed at court in Madrid in 1659–1660. The text and music of *La púrpura de la rosa* reached Lima most likely in the luggage of the viceroy or through the hands of a court official related to him by blood or other alliance. A less likely explanation is that the composer Torrejón brought a copy of Hidalgo's score with him when he sailed to the New World years earlier, as a page in the retinue of a previous viceroy, the count of Lemos. Whatever the precise itinerary of the manuscript score now preserved in Lima, it is clear that the Spanish viceroy who sponsored the Lima performances produced it because of the political significance to be drawn from the associations the opera carried from Madrid. By 1701, Monclova had served in the colonies longer than any other colonial viceroy. In his letters from Peru, he lamented the dearth of his kind of culture in Lima, and noted that the colonies were still "at the edge of the world" (Stein 2001: 88).

Monclova's letters reveal his homesickness, nostalgia, and desire to maintain his ties with Madrid by replicating in Lima something of the court culture that his long service in the colonies had deprived him of. What's more, his letters point to precisely the kinds of relationships that facilitated the travels of opera, theater, and theatrical music from Europe to the New World. Familial relationships and obligations among the nobles who governed the Spanish Empire made for a web of aristocrats, linked or opposed by family obligations, debts of honor, political alliances, and so forth. This tightly connected group supported the Spanish cause in every colonial outpost, and controlled the flow of cultural materials to and from the New World and among the Spanish possessions in Italy, the Spanish embassies at other European courts (especially those of the Habsburg cousins before 1700), and other points in the Spanish orbit.

Opera and Diplomacy

The travels of opera both supported and were fueled by the practice of early modern diplomacy. Though it has often been stated that early opera represented the politics of power and exclusively served to glorify or legitimize monarchs and other absolute rulers, the personal motivations, preferences, and networks of its sponsors have been too little known to modern scholars, though they shed light on the precise mechanisms behind opera's geography and the conduits through which it traveled. Opera's spread within the

Italian geography in the early modern period was facilitated primarily by impresarios or the heads of traveling troupes, such as Giovan Battista Balbi, and agents in the employ of noble patrons. Here the hands-on activity of the Spanish viceroys in Naples stands out as a clear instance of how foreign diplomats and representatives with particular personal, social, and sometimes political objectives were instrumental in opera's history during a formative period, and how their "foreign" expectations and assumptions shaped productions, local practices, and conventions. Opera's travel and reception beyond Italy were especially dependent on the personal motivations, political needs, and tastes of individual sovereigns or their representatives. Taken as a group, for example, it is clear that the Florentine diplomats in Madrid in 1627, Mazarin in Paris in 1645, Charles II in London in 1683, the count of Monclova in Lima in 1701, the duke of Alburquerque in Mexico around 1710, and the directors of the Royal Academy in London in Handel's time did not share the same reasons for importing opera and investing in operatic production. When opera succeeded or failed in far-flung locations with new audiences and untutored potential patrons, its musical style and aesthetic values were rarely the crux of the issue, though they were sometimes the excuse for pamphlet wars or polemic. Opera adapted to foreign climates and diverse economies of production, and it accommodated a range of musical types and sub-genres. It should be abundantly clear as well that the primary agents behind the travels of opera in the early modern period were rarely the opera composers themselves.

See also: Patronage, Politics, Audiences

Notes

1. I thank Nicola Michelassi for graciously sharing a section of his typescript with me in advance of its publication.
2. There are two copies of this undated libretto, one at the National Library in Mexico City and the other at the John Carter Brown Library at Brown University. My thanks to Drs. Emma Julieta Barreiro, Aurelio Tello, Craig Russell, Ken Ward, and Michael Hamerly for their assistance in verifying these sources.
3. Many thanks to Dinko Fabris for kindly sharing his copy of the Mancia score.
4. The title page states in contradictory fashion that the opera was performed "el día de San Felipe por los años del Rey nuestro Señor" ("the day of Saint Philip for the birthday of the King our Lord"). Saint Philip was celebrated at the beginning of May in this period (May 1), though the reference to the "birthday of our King" points to Philip V's birthday (December 19) as the date of performance. The publication date is also unsure; scholars have assumed 1711 because it is suggested in Beristáin de Souza 1898: III: 325. The publishing house named on the title page, "Herederos de la Viuda de Miguel de Ribera," was especially active in the period 1714–1732, according to Ken Ward of the John Carter Brown Library at Brown University, whose advice I gratefully acknowledge.
5. "[...] La comedia del Sr. Principe di Piombino è riuscita di sodisfazione più in riguardo della vaghezza degli habiti, e scena che della musica e compositione"; February 10, 1682, Giovanni Pietro Cella (I-Fas, Mediceo del Principato, f. 4122).

BIBLIOGRAPHY

Beristáin de Souza, J. M. 1898. *Biblioteca hispano americana setentrional.* 5 vols. Mexico: Herederos de la Viuda de Miguel de Ribera.

Bianconi, Lorenzo. 1987. *Music in the Seventeenth Century*, translated by David Bryant. Cambridge: Cambridge University Press.

Bianconi, Lorenzo, and Thomas Walker. 1984. "Production, Consumption, and Political Function of Seventeenth-Century Opera." *Early Music History* 4: 209–296.

——. 1975. "Dalla *Finta pazza* alla *Veremonda*: Storie di Febiarmonici." *Rivista italiana di musicologia* 10: 379–454.

Calderón de la Barca, Pedro. 1682. *La gran comedia Zelos aun del ayre matan… Fiesta que se representó a sus magestades en el Coliseo del Buen Retiro. Y repetida en Napoles por el Excelentiss. Señor Prinzipe de Pomblin, y de Venosa, &c. En la occasion del Despossorio de la Excelentis. Señora mi Señora D. Lavinia Ludovisio, con el Excelentis. Señor Duque de Atri, &c. Napoles 1682* (I-Rbc, Comm. 487/4).

Cella, Giovanni Pietro. 1682. Letter of 10 February. I-Fas, Mediceo del Principato, f. 4122.

Confuorto, Domenico. 1930. *Giornali di Napoli dal 1679 al 1690*, edited by N. Nicolini. Vol. 1. Naples: Lubrano.

Cotticelli, Francesco, and Paologiovanni Maione. 1993. *Le istituzioni musicali a Napoli durante il Viceregno Austriaco (1707–1734)*. Naples: Luciano.

D'Alessandro, Domenico Antonio. 1984. "L'opera in musica a Napoli dal 1650 al 1670." In *Seicento napoletano: Arte, costume, e ambiente*, edited by Roberto Pane, 409–430. Milan: Edizioni di comunità.

Dean, Winton. 2006. *Handel's Operas 1726–1741*. London: Boydell Press.

——, and John Merrill Knapp. 1987. *Handel's Operas 1704–1726*. Oxford: Clarendon Press.

Fabris, Dinko. 2007. *Music in Seventeenth-Century Naples: Francesco Provenzale (1624–1704)*. Aldershot, UK: Ashgate.

Freeman, Robert. 1968. "The Travels of Partenope." In *Studies in Music History, Essays for Oliver Strunk*, edited by Harold Powers, 356–385. Princeton, NJ: Princeton University Press.

Gibson, Elizabeth. 1987. "The Royal Academy of Music (1719–28) and Its Directors." In *Handel Tercentenary Collection*, edited by Stanley Sadie and Anthony Hicks, 138–164. Basingstoke, Hampshire: Macmillan Press.

Glixon, Jonathan E., and Beth L. Glixon. 2006. *Inventing the Business of Opera: The Impresario and His World in Seventeenth-Century Venice.* AMS Studies in Music. New York: Oxford University Press.

Heller, Wendy. 2005. "Amazons, Astrology and the House of Aragon: *Veremonda* tra Venezia e Napoli." In *Francesco Cavalli e la circolazione dell'opera veneziana nel Seicento*, edited by Dinko Fabris, 147–164. Naples: Turchini Edizioni.

Hidalgo, Juan. 2014. *Celos aun del aire mata:* fiesta cantada *(Opera in Three Acts) with Text by Pedro Calderón de la Barca*, edited by Louise K. Stein. Recent Researches in the Music of the Baroque Era. Middleton, WI: A-R Editions.

Hume, Robert D. 1988. "The Sponsorship of Opera in London, 1704–1720." *Modern Philology* 85: 420–432.

——. 1984. "Opera in London, 1695–1706." In *British Theatre and the Other Arts, 1660–1800*, edited by Shirley Strum Kenny, 67–91. Washington: Folger Shakespeare Library.

McClymonds, Marita P. 1980. *Niccolò Jommelli, the Last Years, 1769–1774*. Ann Arbor, MI: UMI Research Press.

McGeary, Thomas. 2007. “Farinelli’s Journey to England.” In *Il Farinelli e gli evirati cantori*, edited by Luigi Verdi, 97–109. Lucca: Libreria musicale italiana.

Michelassi, Nicola. 2010. *La doppia Finta pazza: Un drama veneziano in viaggio nell’Europa del Seicento*. 2 vols. Florence: Olschki.

——. 2003. “Musici di Fortuna. I Mondi Teatrali di Giovan Battista Balbi e ‘La Finta pazz’ tra Venezia e l’Europa 1637–1654.” PhD diss., Università degli Studi di Firenze.

Minguito Palomares, Ana. 2001. “La política cultural del VIII conde de Oñate en Nápoles 1648–1653.” In *Calderón de la Barca y la España del Barroco*. 2 vols., edited by José Alcalá-Zamora and Ernest Belenguer, 957–974. Madrid: Centro de Estudios Políticos y Constitucionales.

Montoya, María Teresa Chaves. 2004. *El espectáculo teatral en la corte de Felipe IV*. Madrid: Ayuntamiento de Madrid.

Murata, Margaret. 1995. “Why the First Opera Given in Paris Wasn’t Roman.” *Cambridge Opera Journal* 7/2: 87–105.

Price, Curtis. 1984. *Henry Purcell and the London Stage*. Cambridge: Cambridge University Press.

——. 1978. “The Critical Decade for English Music Drama, 1700–1710.” *Harvard Library Bulletin* 26: 38–76.

Profeti, Maria Grazia, ed. 1999. *La selva sin amor*. Lope de Vega Carpio. Florence: Alinea.

——. 1996. *Materiali, variazioni, invenzioni*. Florence: Alinea.

Prota-Giurleo, Ulisse. 2002. *I Teatri di Napoli nel secolo XVII*, edited by Ermanno Bellucci and Giorgio Mancini. 3 vols. Naples: Il Quartiere Edizioni.

Roach, Joseph R. 1976. “Cavaliere Nicolini: London’s First Opera Star.” *Educational Theatre Journal* 28: 189–205.

Rosand, Ellen. 1991. *Opera in Seventeenth-Century Venice: The Creation of a Genre*. Berkeley and Los Angeles: University of California Press.

Shergold, Norman D. 1967. *A History of the Spanish Stage from Medieval Times until the End of the Seventeenth Century*. Oxford: Clarendon Press.

Stampiglia, Silvio. 1699. *La Partenope drama per musica di Silvio Stampiglia tra gl’Arcadi Palemone Licurio dedicato all’illustriss. & eccell. signora la signora D. Maria de Giron, y Sandoval, duchessa di Medina-Coeli, e vice-Regina di Napoli*. Naples: Domenico Antonio Parrino e Michele Luigi Mutio.

——. N.d. *La Partenope Fiesta, que se hizo en el Real Palacio de México el día de San Phelipe, por los años del Rey nuestro Señor Don Phelipe V (que Dios guarde)*... Mexico: Herederos de la Viuda de Miguel de Ribera.

Stein, Louise K. 2014. “Three Spaniards Meet Italian Opera in the Age of Spanish Imperialism.” In *Passaggio in Italia: Music on the Grand Tour in the Seventeenth Century*, edited by Dinko Fabris and Margaret Murata 229–245. Turnhout: Brepols.

——. 2012. “A Viceroy Behind the Scenes: Opera, Production, Politics, and Financing in 1680s Naples.” In *Structures of Feeling in Seventeenth-Century Cultural Expression*, edited by Susan McClary, 227–268. Toronto: University of Toronto Press.

——. 2009. “Opera and the Spanish Family: Private and Public Opera in Naples in the 1680s.” In *España y Nápoles. Coleccionismo y mecenazgo artístico de los virreyes en el siglo XVII*, edited by José Luis Colomer, 223–243. Madrid: Centro de Estudios Europa Hispánica.

——. 2006. “The First Opera of the Americas and Its Contexts.” *Opera Quarterly* 22/3–4: 433–458.

——. 2003. “The Origins and Character of *Recitado*.” Collected in the proceedings of the International Conference on Early Opera and Monody, *In Armonia Favellare*, University of Illinois, Urbana-Champaign. *Journal of Seventeenth-Century Music* 9.1. Online. Available: http://www.sscm-jscm.org/jscm/ (accessed August 23, 2012).

——. 2002. "Three Paintings, a Double Lyre, Opera, and Eliche's Venus: Velázquez and Music at the Royal Court in Madrid." In *The Cambridge Companion to Velázquez*, edited by Suzanne Stratton-Pruitt, 170–293. Cambridge: Cambridge University Press.

——. 2001. "De la contera del mundo: Las navegaciones de la ópera entre dos mundos y varias culturas." In *La ópera en España e Hispanoamérica*, edited by Emilio Casares and Alvaro Torrente, 79–94. Madrid: Fundación Autor.

——. 1999. Tomás de Torrejón y Velasco/Juan Hidalgo and Pedro Calderón de la Barca. *La púrpura de la rosa*, edited by Louise K. Stein. Madrid: Fundación Autor.

——. 1993. *Songs of Mortals, Dialogues of the Gods: Music and Theatre in Seventeenth-Century Spain*. Oxford: Clarendon Press.

——. 1991. "Opera and the Spanish Political Agenda." *Acta Musicologica* 63/2: 126–167.

Tedesco, Anna. 2006. "'Scrivere a gusti del popolo': *L'Arte Nuevo* di Lope de Vega nell'Italia del Seicento." *Il saggiatore musicale* 13: 221–245.

——. 2005. "Francesco Cavalli e l'opera veneziana a Palermo dal *Giasone* (1655) alla nascità del Teatro Santa Cecilia (1693)." In *Francesco Cavalli e la circolazione dell'opera veneziana nel Seicento*, edited by Dinko Fabris, 205–238. Naples: Turchini Edizioni.

Varey, John E., and Norman D. Shergold. 1971. *Teatros y comedias en Madrid: 1600–1650. Estudio y Documentos*. London: Tamesis Books.

Vavoulis, Vassilis. 2003. "A Venetian World in Letters: The Massi Correspondence at the Hauptstaatsarchiv in Hannover." *Notes* 59/3: 556–609.

Vega Carpio, Lope Félix de. 1630a. *Laurel de Apolo, con otras rimas*. Madrid: Juan González. [E-Mn, R-177].

——. 1630b. "La Selva sin Amor selva de Amores." E-Mn, MS 3661, fol. 53.

Walker, Frank. 1952. "*Orazio*: The History of a *Pasticcio*." *Musical Quarterly* 38/3: 369–383.

Whitaker, Shirley B. 1984. "Florentine Opera Comes to Spain: Lope de Vega's *La selva sin amor*." *Journal of Hispanic Philology* 9: 43–66.

White, Bryan. 2002. "Grabu's *Albion and Albanius* and the Operas of Lully: '... Acquainted with All the Performances of the French Operas.'" *Early Music* 30/3: 410–427.

Winn, James Anderson. 1992. *Love and the Arts in the Age of Dryden*. Ann Arbor: University of Michigan Press.

CHAPTER 39

THE OPERATIC CANON

JAMES PARAKILAS

A System of Cultural Upbringing

Though the opera houses of the world have a remarkably uniform standard repertory, the operatic canon is not just a list of the works in that repertory. Opera itself is a canonic art form. It provides a cultural standard against which other art forms (and more than art forms) are measured. That standard can be found operating whenever the word *opera* is used, even parodistically, to name art forms remote from opera (and each other) in origin, nature, or status: rock opera and soap opera are examples. It can be found operating when a theater critic uses the word *operatic*, as Ben Brantley did in the *New York Times* (April 16, 2009) to describe Tom Kitt and Brian Yorkey's new Broadway show, *Next to Normal*, as "a feel-everything musical, which asks you, with operatic force, to discover the liberation in knowing where it hurts." Within the wider culture, opera stands for intense dramatic expression and extravagant visual, choreographic, instrumental, and, above all, vocal spectacle. It is not only because it is so seldom performed that Satie's austere *Socrate* can scarcely count as part of the operatic canon.

To say that opera is a canonic art form is also to say that within that art form the entire system of production and consumption, not just the repertory, is canonic. The canonic repertory fits, for example, with the canonic opera house. That oversized theater with its oversized spaces (auditorium, pit, stage, and backstage) and oversized performing forces (the full orchestra, the large chorus and ballet corps, along with the stentorian soloists) is made for the characteristically grandiose scenes in the standard repertory—the Triumphal Scene, the Prize Song Competition, the Coronation Scene—and not for the sights and sounds of early opera or the traditional Broadway show or almost any spoken drama. Likewise, the canonic repertory, performed in its canonic home, demands and relies on a canonic style of vocal production. A singer possessed of that vocal production can plausibly appear in a Broadway show (Ezio Pinza in the original production of *South Pacific*, Paulo Szot in a recent revival) only by taking a role marked apart from the others as European, cultivated—operatic. The experience of the opera-goers is a correspondingly canonic affair. They know the high C is coming at the end of "Di quella pira," and they respond according to how it compares to others they remember. The most knowing among them even know that that note does not appear in the canonic score of *Il trovatore*, but they rejoice in it as a gift from the canonic performing tradition.

The operatic canon, then, is among other things a system of cultural upbringing for opera-goers and performers alike. Opera-goers see and hear canonic operas in canonic productions and learn to think about them in canonic ways. Each composer and each work come to represent a distinct kind of emotional experience, a distinct perspective on life—all articulated by the plentiful literature of program notes, histories, biographies, and magazine and website articles provided to opera-goers. Performers learn these canonic attitudes in the same ways that opera-goers do, but they also meet them as a pedagogical system: in their training, individual numbers and whole roles are arranged in a graded set of challenges, each hallowed by long experience as a distinct and necessary step in the mastery of their art, whether that is singing or playing or conducting. For singers, one of the first steps is to master some of the *Arie antiche*, the arias from the first two centuries of Italian opera that Alessandro Parisotti published in three volumes in 1885 and that have been republished in various editions, with some additions, ever since (Parisotti 1885). These arias teach students the classic singing technique for opera, even though the arias have been stripped of any association with the stage, if they come from opera at all (not clear in the case of the favorite "Caro mio ben"). Even Cecilia Bartoli's recording of these *Arie antiche* (1992) does nothing to reconnect them to the stage; rather, it makes a loving tribute to what so many singers share as the experience of learning to sing. And in that sense, these arias surely count as among the most canonic works in the operatic repertory.

But the performer's training does not end in graduating from school to stage. Regional and touring opera companies provide the next step in the training of many young singers (as well as players, conductors, and other artists). Those companies give singers the opportunity to try out their roles, learn new roles, deepen their skills, and gain confidence before audiences as they seek places on the rosters of major companies. And the working of this system, too, depends on the canonic repertory. It would hardly serve an ambitious singer, after all, to perfect the roles of Mimì and Cio-Cio-San and Liù in her days in a touring company if Puccini were not as central to the repertories of the major companies as of the minor ones. In that sense, the training-ground function of the minor companies limits the repertorial adventurousness of both kinds of company.

Opera did not develop a canonic repertory quickly. But as the foregoing suggests, learning how that repertory eventually developed requires asking more than how and why opera houses stopped producing seasons of new works and started producing seasons of old ones. It requires asking how opera evolved as a business, a system of training, a popular entertainment, a cultural touchstone, and an object of study. It also requires noticing that what counts as an operatic canon—in particular, what kinds of "text" count as canonic—changes from one point in the history of opera to another. This chapter therefore treats the operatic canon not as a single development unfolding in history, but as a series of canonic systems, presented here in roughly chronological stages because each became an issue at a different time in the four-century history of opera.

Recyclings

If, for instance, we presume that the canonic texts in opera are the scores, then we will have to move very far forward in that history before we can find anyone treating a text as canonic. It is not that a canonic score was an inconceivable idea in Europe at the time that opera began. The plainchant of the Catholic Church was a canonic corpus of musical texts, and hymnals served a comparably canonic role (even if they were not comparably time-tested) in the Protestant churches. Furthermore, many of the earliest operas—those of the first decades of the seventeenth century—were published, often in handsome editions, sometimes giving fairly full indications of the instrumental parts, sometimes prefaced by dedicatory essays explaining the composer's concept of the operatic genre. These publications may be construed as canonizing in one sense: they asserted the importance of the new genre and of each of the published works in the development of that genre. That is, they contributed to the discourse about opera. But they did not serve the canonizing purpose of keeping the works alive in performance (see Macnutt 1992b: III: 1155–1156).

In fact, by 1640, when opera had moved from its phase as a courtly experiment to its longer life as a commercial as well as courtly institution, the publication of opera scores essentially ended on the Italian peninsula for well over a century. But in that period Italian opera scores were endlessly copied by hand, so that a work that was successful in one city could be staged in other cities, not only throughout Italy but across Europe. Operatic works—and their scores—were products in an enterprise of fashion, and every time a score was copied for a new opera house, it was tailored anew to fit the needs and tastes of the latest purchaser. Then, after the fashion for that work was past in one season or more, the score was put on the shelf.

Librettos were another story. The literary text of an opera was the one element that had the power to connect the work—and the new genre of opera—to an established canon: Greek and Roman literature. For the earliest operas, librettos were published, sometimes with elaborate dedications or justifying essays or *argomenti*, citing the sources of the story in classical literature and history. After opera became commercial, librettos continued to be published, but now they were "usually pocket sized, printed on cheap paper, sewn into wrappers and rife with typographical errors: ephemeral objects, quickly redundant" (Macnutt 1992a: II: 1185). This doesn't sound like a description of a canonic (or canonizing) text. But the librettos of classical-themed operas continued to include *argomenti* that placed the work in the classical tradition. We can even imagine a characteristic transition in the minds of opera-goers, who bought the libretto on or just before the opening night of an opera and engaged the production for the first time with the classical context fresh in their minds, then set the libretto aside and developed a more familiar relationship to the show as they returned to it again and again. The "ephemeral object" with its classical learning did not totally control the opera-goers' evolving experience of the work, but it colored that experience at a crucial moment.

Meanwhile, librettos rather than scores were the vehicles of another form of canonic renewal: the remake. The very first Florentine opera librettos, Rinuccini's *Dafne* and *Euridice*, were both given two separate musical settings (*Dafne* by Peri and Corsi in 1598 and by Gagliano in 1608; *Euridice* by Peri in 1600 and by Giulio Caccini in 1602). This set a pattern for opera composition into the nineteenth century. Not only were certain classical and Renaissance stories made the subjects of opera after opera, but certain librettos on those subjects, suitably adapted for new conditions of performance and reception, were recomposed, often more than once. This industry of remakes reached its climax in the work of the poet Pietro Metastasio (1698–1782), most of whose twenty-seven *opera seria* librettos were given dozens of musical settings (and in one case, *Artaserse*, nearly ninety) over the course of a century; each of those settings might in turn be produced in several cities. Appointed Caesarian court poet by the Hapsburg emperor early in his career and favorably compared to the Greek tragedians by contemporaries like Voltaire, Metastasio lent far more prestige to the operatic genre in the eighteenth century than any composer. His librettos were not just printed up in flimsy format for reading at the opera house; they were collected in over forty editions in his lifetime, some of them luxurious collector's editions with appreciative introductory essays and illustrations of scenes (Neville 1992). In the eighteenth century the librettos of Metastasio could be said to constitute the canon of Italian opera.

In France—not the only country outside Italy to create its own opera industry and repertory in the seventeenth century, but the only one to sustain it in the face of the Italian opera juggernaut in the eighteenth—things unfolded differently. Unlike Italy, where operatic activity like political power was widely dispersed, France was a single nation where the monarchy worked at concentrating cultural as well as political power in its own hands. It not only sponsored the creation of a French form of opera, but issued a monopoly for the direction of the royal opera company and the composition of works by that company. Lully acquired that monopoly in 1672 and held it until his death fifteen years later. In that time he created a repertory of French opera by composing one new opera virtually every year. Since he was the only musician permitted to compose French operas and since Italian operas were not performed at his opera house, he achieved a varied repertory each season by reviving earlier works of his alongside his new opera. By the time of his death, Paris had a repertory of Lully operas that, unlike Italian operas anywhere, stayed in production and in the public consciousness. Even after his death, when other composers were creating new works at the Paris Opéra, Lully's operas continued to be produced there—at least one every year—until a century after he took up his operatic monopoly. Like any canonic works, the Lully operas provided a touchstone for newer creations.

The touchstone effect was made remarkably explicit in 1777, when Gluck, then the reigning composer of the Paris Opéra, composed a new setting of the libretto that Philippe Quinault had written for Lully's *Armide* of 1686. This might seem no different in principle from a composer being the last in a long line to set a given Metastasio libretto. The difference is that Lully's setting of *Armide*, unlike any single previous setting of the Metastasio text, was central to the operatic upbringing of the audience. For Gluck to set that libretto was to challenge Lully for a place in the French operatic canon.

Domestication and Discourse

A canon is not the same thing as a repertory (see Kerman 1983), and the canonic life of the Lully operas depended on far more than their repeated production in Paris and elsewhere. It depended in the first place on the publication of scores of various sorts: whole operas, single numbers from them, and arrangements and contrafacta of those numbers. These publications domesticated the music that people heard in the theater, keeping alive the memory of what they heard and saw there, transforming it in their consciousness as they recreated it with their own voices and hands and imagined themselves in their favorite roles (see Parakilas 1995). Their domestic performances even extended the audience of the music to include their friends and servants who never heard it in the theater at all, so that it was described at the time as having entered the national consciousness (see Le Cerf de la Viéville [1705] 1950: 498–499). And when these domestic performers returned to see the opera again, they were bonded with others like themselves by a communal internalization of the individual roles. It was often reported, in fact, that during certain airs in the Lully operas, spectators in the parterre sang along so loudly that it was impossible to hear the singers onstage (see Schneider 1982: 303).

Another development that contributed to the canonization of the Lully operas was the creation of a public discourse about them. The inventors of opera, in Florence and other Italian cities, had published plenty of treatises and prefaces justifying their ideas and practices, but once their enterprise was launched, the publication of critical and theoretical writings on opera became sporadic in Italy. The production of the earliest operas in French occasioned a comparable flurry of publications—writings largely by literary figures concerned with the questions of whether singing could be a medium for serious drama and whether and how the French language could support it. But in France the public debates never let up (see Cowart 1981). Lully's death, in fact, only heated them up, as the question of how far French musicians dared to stray from his canonic model (a question usually posed as a competition between Italian and French styles of music) was passionately disputed in print throughout the eighteenth century. One particularly significant round in this ongoing debate was the exchange of 1753–1754 (see Dill 1994) between Rousseau and Rameau over the merits of Lully's setting of Armide's great monologue of murderous indecision in the second act of *Armide* (1686), "Enfin, il est en ma puissance." This scene was already widely praised in the critical writings of earlier decades as one of the great vehicles for dramatic expression in all of Lully's output. What distinguished this new exchange, and especially the contribution of Rameau—the greatest theorist of tonal music as well as Lully's greatest successor in opera composition—was that it put the tools of musical analysis at the service of canonic judgment in opera.

Oddly absent from this range of publications that contributed to the canonization of Lully's operas was much writing about the history of opera. To be sure, in those eighteenth-century general histories of music (notably, those of Burney and Hawkins) whose coverage reaches as far as the seventeenth century, the founding and development of opera has its place. But hardly anyone seems to have considered the history of opera a subject in itself until well into the nineteenth century: [Henry] Sutherland Edwards's *History of the Opera: From Monteverde to Donizetti*, published in 1862, offered a very modest early step in that direction.

Aside from that lacuna, the crucial means of creating an operatic canon were all in use by the beginning of the nineteenth century. But the repertories that had so far served as canonic in opera, notably the librettos of Metastasio and the operas of Lully, were discarded or were on their way to being discarded by then, and almost all the works that constitute the standard repertory of the great opera houses today had not even been composed. The nineteenth century was momentous for the operatic canon: it was the period when opera houses turned from changing-fashion houses to fixed-repertory houses and yet—in the face of the concomitant drying-up of demand for new works—it was also the period in which the great majority of the works that now constitute that fixed repertory were created. It is not a simple matter to explain how that came about.

The Repertory House

The question of how opera houses turned into repertory houses has not yet been investigated as an international phenomenon the way William Weber has investigated the comparable question about the repertory of concert halls (Weber 2008). Instead, it has been taken up country by country. John Rosselli, for instance, dates this transformation in Italian opera houses to the period from the 1840s to the 1870s. He connects it with political upheaval, the channeling of artistic creativity into other genres, and above all "the spread of a new kind of opera house, large, unsubsidized, bringing opera and ballet at low prices to a wider public" (Rosselli 1984: 171). In other words, he understands the change primarily in terms of the targeting of a new and larger market. But he does not make clear why a new, larger, and socially more diverse audience would be drawn to an unchanging repertory of older works rather than a constantly changing repertory of new ones, or why new, larger opera houses would be used largely for the production of older works that were originally created for smaller opera houses, rather than for recent works composed for just such large houses. Another scholar, Matthew Ringel, studying the changing repertory of London opera houses, has pointed to the effect of the nineteenth-century copyright laws, which gave opera houses an inducement to perform older works that did not have copyright protection (Ringel 1996: 142–155). That consideration presumably did not apply equally in Italy, where publishers of new works had a large say in the repertory choices of opera houses.

Such studies of the economics of opera production need to be joined with other studies that consider the effects of changes in government regulation and subsidy (such as Toelle 2007 and Ellis 2009) and the social makeup of opera audiences and the forces that reshaped their ideologies of taste (such as Ther 2006 and Hall-Witt 2007). All of these can be reinforced by the larger number of studies devoted to the turn toward canonic ideology and programming in the nineteenth-century concert hall (such as Johnson 1995; Gramit 2002; and Weber 2008). The comparison calls for caution in that concert music was often held up at the time as a more uplifting object of attention than opera. But it is striking that what Weber identifies as the period when "classical music achieves hegemony" in the European concert hall, 1848–1875, is exactly the same as that which Rosselli identifies with the rise of the repertory opera house in Italy. And if opera houses now found themselves competing with concert halls for prestige, that competition—that grasping for prestige—should have something to tell us about the rise of the operatic canon.

Scholars of the changing repertory and taste in both the opera house and the concert hall focus on the confluence of two cultural forces. The first was the rise of a class of expert tastemakers—critics and educators—who campaigned for audiences to give serious attention to the work rather than mere adulation to the performer. The second was a new relationship between two components of the audience: the aristocratic class, feeling increasingly self-conscious about its behavior as its place in the house grew less and less dominant, and the middle class, eager to earn a place for itself in these temples of cultural prestige. It is easy at least to discover some of the means by which the tastemakers played on the nervousness that each of these classes within the audience prompted in the other. In mid-nineteenth-century England, for instance, just as John Ella provided analytical program notes for his concerts of chamber music (Bashford 2007), Davidson's "Musical Libretto-Books" provided opera-goers with histories of the operas and musical examples from the scores, along with the texts of the operas and facing translations (see Macnutt 1992a: II: 1189). It was not new, we have seen, for opera audiences to be expected to read before the show began, but now they were being asked to read about an established opera as a serious work of art rather than—as in the previous centuries—about the classical story that gave cultural legitimacy to a new opera. The public was being trained to regard operas as musical classics.

In considering the combination of all these economic, social, and cultural forces, one can begin to understand how a fixed repertory of classic works could have complemented other developments in nineteenth-century opera. It begins to make sense, for instance, that the imperial opera house that opened in Vienna in 1869 was inaugurated with a performance of *Don Giovanni*, an opera from the previous century. The national pride that sustained the construction of the opera house dictated that the building be inaugurated not with a new work, but with what was by then regarded as the masterpiece of Austria's greatest native son.

The Power of Publicity

But how exactly did the nineteenth-century operatic canon get developed? How did it come to include Mozart operas from the 1780s, Rossini and Weber operas from the 1810s and 1820s, Meyerbeer and Donizetti from the 1830s, and eventually Verdi and Wagner from later decades? How did operas from so many countries, in so many languages, get to be part of the same canon, often translated as they crossed borders, so that they could share the stage all over the Western world? The answers are not the same for every component of the canonic repertory.

The fact that Mozart's operas did not disappear from the stage in the decades after his death, but gained an undying hold on audiences and critics, points to what now seems a growing social consciousness of a divide between the "highbrow" and the "lowbrow"—to use Lawrence Levine's distinction (1988)—in the taste of that day. But the route to determining what was highbrow in Mozart was circuitous. The canonization of Mozart owed much to writings published in those first decades after his death, both works of the imagination—by Hoffmann (1989), Mörike ([1856] 2003), and Kierkegaard ([1843] 1987)—and works of biography and criticism, by Rochlitz ([1798–1801] 1991), Oulibicheff (1843), and Jahn (1856–1859) (see Gruber 1994). To all of these writers, the operas were paramount among Mozart's creations, yet the operas they singled out were on the whole not the obviously highbrow works—the ones on classical themes—but the earthier comedies. Furthermore, the productions of their day, those on which they could have based their appreciation of his genius, were often by today's standards disrespectful of the composer's texts. In the case of Rossini, the works, especially the serious Italian operas, seem to many people today a curious compound of the highbrow and the lowbrow—the most relentlessly showy vocal stunts poured into powerfully ordered musical scenes that serve dramas of high seriousness. We can only suppose that this compound suited the sensibility of an operatic public that was still negotiating the highbrow-lowbrow divide, since those operas held sway across the continent for half a century, as hardly any operas by a single composer have done before or since.

It was not surprising that operas like Mozart's and Rossini's that would hold the stage throughout Europe for decades would be Italian operas, that is, operas written for Italian singers, since Italian singers continued to dominate the operatic scene across Europe in the nineteenth century, as they had done since the birth of the genre. What is more surprising is that with the creation of grand opera in Paris by 1830, French opera became equally international in its reach—equally capable of advancing candidates for the operatic canon—and it became so without French singers going abroad to the extent that Italian singers did. French opera had its own system for making its products irresistible to opera houses and audiences across Europe. That begins with the products themselves. French grand opera of the middle third of the nineteenth century offered more stage spectacle than Italian opera of the same period: grander sets and more splendid costumes, both often designed to recreate specific historical times and geographical locations with unmatched specificity, lit with breathtaking and innovative lighting effects (including the famous sunrise in *Le Prophète*, 1849, the first use anywhere of electricity in stage lighting; Bergman 1977: 278). These visual effects were complemented at the Opéra by musical effects created to test the capacities of the largest and best-trained orchestra and chorus of any opera house in the world, working with an expansive rehearsal schedule that no other house could match. Only in the vocal challenges it posed to its solo singers did French opera of the period not outdo Italian opera. Finally, the political and social climate in Paris allowed the creators of grand opera to tackle subjects that would have been considered too subversive of the political order or offensive to religious authority and morals to be introduced on the stage elsewhere: the history of intolerance in the Christian Church, the suppression of nationalist movements by monarchs, the debauchery of clergy and nuns, the devil himself onstage.

All in all, it would appear that Parisian grand opera presented such obstacles to production outside Paris that it must have been condemned to stay confined to its own house. In fact, the most successful grand operas—and those were the grandest and most scandalous—made their way quickly to every corner of the operatic world. Everyone wanted to see and hear *Robert le diable*, *Guillaume Tell*, *La Juive*, and *Les Huguenots*, and opera houses obliged. This is above all a story about the power of publicity. Premieres at the Paris Opéra were prepared by publicity campaigns and attended by reviews to an extent that no artistic productions in any medium had ever been before. Not just the columns of the numerous Paris newspapers were filled with gossip and comment about the Opéra, but so were those of newspapers and journals across Europe, written by their own correspondents (Heinrich Heine and Richard Wagner among them), paid to report on operatic doings in Paris. Once the appetites of audiences from Lisbon to St. Petersburg were whetted, the overcoming of obstacles could begin. The plots of French operas were rewritten to make the works less objectionable to church and government censors elsewhere. Permission might be denied for a while: *Les Huguenots*, even bowdlerized, was thought too troubling to Protestant sensibilities to be played in many cities where Protestants were a significant part of the population (Walter 1987: 17; Becker and Becker [1983] 1989: 77). But sooner or later it proved less troublesome to let a work be produced than to keep turning it away. By that time, in any case, the work was somewhat dated... not as shocking as it had been... and was on its way to becoming canonical.

Meanwhile, there were still the production difficulties to be overcome. Other opera houses simply lacked the human and material resources to put on Parisian grand operas, but the audiences elsewhere wanted to see them and wanted to see them badly enough that their opera houses eventually assembled the resources for the job. Publicity created the desire, and Paris was happy to teach other cities the secrets. When operas were composed for opera houses elsewhere, only the vocal score and arrangements of individual numbers were published; if another opera house wanted to perform the work, it would have to pay for the composer's autograph score and the parts from the original opera house to be copied by hand. But works composed for the Paris Opéra were generally published in full score with parts, so that any other opera house could easily acquire the complete musical materials. Furthermore, the production manual (*livret de mise en scène*) of many a Parisian grand opera was published, giving descriptions of the sets and costumes of the original Paris production, along with painstaking, almost line-by-line representations of the blocking in that production, for the staff of any other opera house to ape.

The published full score not only facilitated widespread production of the Paris operas, but proved a stepping-stone to canonization, since it stabilized and idealized one version of the music (even though that was often not quite what had been performed at the premiere in Paris). By contrast, the practice in Italian opera of generating copies from the composer's autograph full score allowed either the composer or performers beyond his control to keep adapting the score to the exigencies of each new performing situation—the capacities of this or that house, the tastes and strengths or weaknesses of this or that soloist—for some time after the initial production. The Italian practice, lasting through most of Verdi's career before yielding at last to the Paris model, was responsive and communal rather than stable or ideal or authoritative, and it has immensely complicated the canonic task of preparing critical editions of the operas of Rossini or Donizetti or even Verdi (see Gossett 2006; Poriss 2009).

The publication of Paris production manuals, meanwhile, expanded the definition of the score—the canonizable content of the work—to include the original staging of a work, and likewise expanded the definition of the author of an opera to include the set and costume designers and stage director as well as the librettist and composer. Those definitions have not lasted. Today no stage director or designer feels bound to honor the original production manual of any opera as canonic, the way the conductor feels bound to honor the score (Latham and Parker 2001). But at the time, those production manuals evidently taught the production staffs at many opera houses how, with the right resources, they could turn out productions of Parisian operas that looked as well as sounded Parisian.

The Parisian model of publishing full scores and production manuals was no doubt considered by the business people who ran the Opéra as an aid to their enterprise, since it provided immediate and short-term promotion of specific works, as well as of the idea of the Opéra as a source of operatic fashion. But those same publications would have gotten composers thinking in the longer term. Meyerbeer and his contemporaries, asked to publish an authoritative version of their score—even while the world-premiere production for which they were composing it was subjecting that score to new changes at every rehearsal—must have found themselves, almost against their will, thinking of their job as composing for the canon. Brought up in a Rossinian culture in which highbrow and lowbrow blended with ease, Meyerbeer helped inaugurate the new Paris system, including its systems of publications and publicity, and he had difficulty—as his ever-slower production of works attests—coming to terms with what an opera needed to be in order to become canonic now: a purely highbrow work. By contrast, Wagner, who grew up with the Paris systems of publicity and publication as his model, embraced the concept of writing for the canon early on. In fact, there could be no clearer example of striving for the canonic than the Bayreuth Festspielhaus. A composer who has an opera house built for the performance of one of his works is not imagining that that work will soon have had its day.

By the last third of the nineteenth century, the opera houses of the Western world were quickly developing not just a canonic repertory, diverse in its sources—from Mozart to Verdi and Wagner—but also a canonic system for presenting it. In fact, that system introduced a uniformity of production that somewhat counteracted the diversity of the repertory. Thus the Imperial Viennese Opera house that opened in 1869, seating thousands, was designed to stage works on the scale of Parisian grand operas, but *Don Giovanni*, the work performed to inaugurate that opera house, had been created for a house that seated a few hundred. Accordingly, in its new home *Don Giovanni* was staged as if it were a Parisian grand opera (see illustration 7 in *New Grove Dictionary of Opera*, "Vienna").

Not that this new standard repertory, however canonic, was itself either uniform or static. It had local emphases: the Glinka operas were standard fare in Russian opera houses and nowhere else (a situation almost as true today as then). New works were eagerly added to the repertory and the canon. In some cases these were works of such consistently high tone that they were designed, as it were, for the canon: *Otello* and *Parsifal*, the latter of which in effect joined the canon before it joined the repertory, since the Wagner estate kept the work off all stages except Bayreuth for its first three decades. In other cases a process of elevation had to occur before the work could be canonized. An example was *Carmen*, which was as earthy and as much of a generic hybrid as *Don Giovanni*, without the excuse of having been written by Mozart, but was nevertheless assumed into the canon, at the height of the Victorian age, just as quickly as its unseemly spoken dialogue could be replaced with dignified recitative.

A Prestige Gap

The critical and scholarly literature about music, meanwhile, failed to support the creation of the operatic canon in the way it supported that of the instrumental canon. In fact, the ideology that canonized concert music in the nineteenth century did so in part by decanonizing and dismissing opera. It is worth recalling that music analysis, one branch of that literature, had been a powerful system of operatic criticism in the hands of Rameau. In his reply to Rousseau he had examined every melodic interval, every chord change, every rhythmic turn of Armide's great recitative in the light of her uncertain resolve, fluctuating rhetoric, and unsteady gestures. Nineteenth-century music theorists from Marx to Tovey, by contrast, turned away from the analysis of opera, and in particular from such close analysis of the relationship of notes to words in operatic speech, to the project of making music without texts intelligible (whether it was the symphonies of Beethoven or the program music of Berlioz) and hence of reinforcing the prestige of that music. Even an exception like Rudolf Westphal's *Elements of Musical Rhythm, with Special Regard to Our Operatic Music* (1872) turns out to be not such an exception when we realize that his operatic examples almost all come from the one opera revered as standing above its not-altogether-prestigious genre: *Don Giovanni*. Through most of the twentieth century, too, most music theorists gave precious little attention to opera or other vocal music, and the exceptions, like Alfred Lorenz in his monumental study of Wagner's music dramas (1924–1933), often turn out to treat operas more like instrumental music than like stage works with sung words. Not until late in the twentieth century did musical analysts in any number undertake to bring words, notes, and action together when they analyzed long-canonized operas or canonized relatively recent ones like *Wozzeck*. Even today, few operatic numbers find their way into music theory textbooks, and the two that do regularly appear there are orchestral, not vocal excerpts: the prelude to *Tristan und Isolde* and the two tintinnabular chords from the Coronation Scene of *Boris Godunov*.

In musicological scholarship, too, the promotion of instrumental music often relied on the demotion of opera, which had been both the most socially prestigious and the most artistically forward-looking genre of music for centuries. Those great canonizing projects of nineteenth-century musicology, the complete-works editions of the masters, were by and large lavished on important opera composers (Handel and Mozart, for example) only when they were also masters of instrumental and sacred music; Rossini and Verdi and even Gluck, to say nothing of Lully, had to wait. (The extraordinary tradition of musicology in Belgium seems responsible for the Grétry edition begun in 1884.) By 1924 the imbalance in prestige had grown so severe that Hugo Leichtentritt in his biography of Handel would think to lift one of the greatest of Handel's arias, Cleopatra's "Se pietà di me non senti," out of the oblivion and contempt into which his operas as a whole had fallen with this sentence: "It would not be overreaching to consider this aria worthy of being placed beside the renowned Preludes in E-flat minor and B-flat minor from the Well-Tempered Clavier, with which its gripping expression of desperate beseeching and its refinement of harmony have much in common" (Leichtentritt 1924: 668). Two centuries earlier, when both works were new and uncanonic, music lovers across Europe would have been dumbfounded at the idea of the leading aria for the leading lady in the latest Handel opera to sweep London off its feet stooping to share a sentence with a couple of little keyboard ditties by some church musician in Leipzig.

Technology and the Modern Canon

The twentieth century may seem to have been a time when the operatic canon pretty much stayed the same. Opera houses worldwide performed a repertory largely of nineteenth-century works at the end of the twentieth century, as they had done at its beginning. But, even beyond the addition of some twentieth-century works, the standard repertory at the end of the century was different in many respects from what it had been a century earlier. More to the point, the operatic canon in all other senses besides the performing repertory changed vastly in the course of the twentieth century. It changed as a cultural touchstone, a system of cultural upbringing and discourse, a system of production and consumption. And in all those changes, the constant evolution of technology played a driving role.

The capacity of opera to serve, for instance, as a cultural touchstone today depends not only on its centuries-old status as an upper-class, high-cultural musical spectacle, but also on the experience of opera—however limited and distorted—that new technologies gave to people of every class and every country in the twentieth century. Right at the beginning of the century, when open-air performances in places like the Roman arena of Verona (starting in 1913) were bringing opera to thousands at one time, recordings were bringing its sound to millions, all the time. When Caruso died in 1921, masses of fans of his recordings around the world who had never been close to an opera house mourned him—and the sound of opera that his voice represented to them—as an intimate part of their lives.

By then, radio broadcasts of opera were just beginning, soon to become a regular part of listeners' lives: Saturday matinee broadcasts began at the Metropolitan in 1931. Opera excerpts on recording and whole operas on the radio not only gave an enormous public an introduction to opera, but also gave experienced opera-goers and neophytes alike a novel mode of perceiving opera. The most spectacular form of theater was stripped of its visual spectacle and removed from the public world of the theater to any number of settings, including the most solitary, so that the listener's attention was focused entirely on the aural splendor and what it could evoke. Opera became a canon of sound-worlds, each of which carried listeners in their imaginations to the operatic stage, where the staging would carry them in their imaginations to the world that that work depicted.

The introduction of the long-playing recording in 1948 made the recording of complete operas commercially feasible, with many effects on the operatic canon. Like radio broadcast, the recorded opera gave listeners an entirely aural experience of opera, but the recording could be experienced at will, rather than on the schedule of the opera house and network. One result was that the sound of opera, sung by international stars with great orchestras, could be summoned up in the classroom. Teachers of singing, music history, and music appreciation no longer had to rely on their classroom pianos, their own wobbly voices and those of their students to convey the enchantment of opera. Operas naturally assumed a larger place in those courses, courses devoted exclusively to the history of opera began to appear, and opera could take a greater, more canonic place in the upbringing of musicians and students in general. The introduction of video recordings in the 1980s only intensified that trend, no doubt throwing more classroom emphasis on the drama of an opera, perhaps at the cost of attention to musical processes.

A second effect of the long-playing record (likewise seconded by the video recording) was to increase the number of operas that listeners could come to know. While most opera companies stayed largely within the confines of the standard repertory, any company might occasionally stage a new opera or a neglected older work, and from that production a recording might ensue, which then could be sold around the world, in some cases creating sufficient enthusiasm to prompt more and more productions, until the work became indisputably canonic. Furthermore the canonicity of composers like Donizetti and Massenet has come to depend not just on the incessant production of their few warhorses, but also to an extent on the availability of sound and video recordings of much of the rest of their operatic output, which cannot all become standard repertory. Meanwhile, newly commissioned works are often given a boost toward canonization by a publicity campaign that revolves around sales of a DVD. In the case of Adams's *The Death of Klinghoffer* (1991), a movie version of the opera (2003) kept its march to canonic status moving forward at a time when the political sensitivity of the opera's subject made productions in the opera house scarce.

For almost the entire corpus of opera before Gluck and Mozart, the importance of sound and video recordings is especially great because those operas—requiring specialized performers, instruments, staging, and houses to make their optimal effect—are not produced regularly by major opera companies. Operas from the first century and a half of the history of the medium tend to be produced largely at specialized festivals; sound and video recordings of these productions are then produced and sold, and by this means the canon of opera has been extended backward to include masterpieces of Monteverdi and Cavalli, Lully and Rameau, Vivaldi and Handel. In this case it is not just individual works or composers who have been canonized, but an entire era of operatic history that has been brought back to life. Thanks in large part to the technologies of recording, Mozart's operas have gone from being at the beginning of the operatic canon to being at its midpoint.

By comparison to audio media and video recording, movies and television have played a rather small role in the life of the operatic canon. Movies, with their huge impact on popular culture from the beginning of the twentieth century, always used some operatic music in their scores, but without identifying it to the unknowing parts of the public. Some of the movies most important in purveying opera to the masses were parodies, like the Marx Brothers' *A Night at the Opera* (1935) and the Warner Brothers cartoon *What's Opera, Doc?* (1957). Unlike opera parodies of earlier centuries, such as *Il teatro alla moda* (1720) or *The Beggar's Opera* (1728), these movies mocked something that relatively few in their audiences had actually experienced, and for that reason they were all the more powerful in creating an image and a consciousness of opera in the public at large. Serious films of canonic operas may have reached somewhat smaller audiences, but presumably have done more to draw audiences into the opera house. Even so, the directors of those films have often made true film narratives out of the operas they filmed, giving the works meanings inconceivable in stage productions (see Citron 2000).

Opera began to be broadcast on television in the 1930s, and within a few decades new operas were being commissioned expressly for television broadcast (just as operas were commissioned for radio broadcast). It would be hard, though, to discern anything like a separate canon of broadcast operas; the most successful of them, like Menotti's *Amahl and the Night Visitors* (1951), soon made their way to the stage. Video transmission of live opera performances to movie theaters has been carried out by the Metropolitan Opera since 2007. It remains to be seen what effect this medium, a cross between the live radio or television broadcast and the showing of a movie in a theater, will have on the experience of opera, the opera audience, and the operatic canon.

The opera house itself might be regarded as remarkably resistant to technologies of the electrical and computer age. In most cases, amplification is still discouraged there or is used discreetly, and a live prompter still works from the prompter's box. But at least one technological innovation in the opera house has had a profound impact on the way opera is performed and the way it is apprehended in the opera house and consequently on the operatic canon. That is the supertitle, introduced by the Canadian Opera Company in 1983. One impact has been to canonize the original language as the standard for the performance of the canonic repertory. The move away from opera in translation actually got well under way soon after World War II, when singers—who were being trained more consistently to sing outside their own language—were not only crossing national boundaries more frequently than ever before, but crossing linguistic boundaries in their repertories more frequently as well. Still, there continued to be a lively debate between advocates of opera in its original language and of opera in the language of the audience. The appearance of supertitles in the opera house (and, almost concurrently, of opera videos, with their subtitles) resolved the question in favor of the original language, leaving the international opera world with perhaps a more unified idea of the sound of any canonic opera, along with perhaps a diminished capacity to focus on the relationship of sound to meaning.

There can be hardly any doubt that the comprehensibility that supertitles and subtitles give to opera has contributed mightily to the upsurge of interest in opera, live and on video, in the last few decades, at a time when the interest in classical instrumental music, live and on recording, has slumped. The status of opera has consequently been boosted immeasurably within the overall canon of classical music. Furthermore, it can be argued that supertitles and subtitles have contributed to specific changes in the makeup of the operatic canon. In particular, these technologies appeared almost simultaneously with the breakup of the Communist bloc around 1989, so that just when individual singers and whole opera companies from Eastern Europe, deeply experienced in the performance of Slavic operas, became far freer than before to travel to the opera houses of the world, opera audiences outside Eastern Europe, accustomed to thinking that Slavic opera began with *Boris Godunov* and ended with *The Queen of Spades*, suddenly had the means to listen intelligently to operas in Russian or Czech or Polish. The result has been that Janáček has been established internationally as a central composer in the operatic canon, that Prokofiev and Rimsky-Korsakov are not far behind him, and that Smetana is now widely known to have composed *The Bartered Bride* in Czech.

Scholarship Meets Performance

Over the course of the twentieth century, innovations in technology played their part in boosting opera into a central position within the canon of classical music, but so did the work of scholars and performers, and the ways the two developments nourished each other are complex and not always easy to discern.

The work of scholars took many forms. The history of the genre, barely considered a subject in previous centuries, was given serious treatment by writers in several languages in the twentieth, starting with Hermann Kretzschmar's *Geschichte der Oper*, published in 1919. Many of these are canonic histories—historical surveys of the canonic works, as defined by opera-house repertory, supplemented (especially for the early centuries of opera) by scholarly tradition. This genre of history leaves some room for advocacy by the author of each new history. Donald Grout, for instance, in *A Short History of Opera* (1947), applied the full rhetoric of canonization to promote his judgment of *Les Troyens*, then neglected in the repertory: "in a country properly appreciative of its cultural monuments it would seem that *Les Troyens* ought to be produced regularly at state expense until singers, conductors, and public are brought to realize its greatness" (Grout 1947: 319). By contrast, the realized volumes of Lorenzo Bianconi and Giorgio Pestelli's incomplete collection *The History of Italian Opera* ([1987–1988] 1998–2003) constitute an Annales-school history of opera as a set of systems. This work is pathbreaking in its methodology by virtue of uncovering the cultural, economic, and aesthetic evolutions that produced and sustained an operatic canon—the first and foremost among national operatic canons—and thereby showing how that canon can be studied as a history, rather than a standard.

Practically contemporary with Grout's midcentury *Short History* was a canonic work of another kind, Joseph Kerman's critical survey of operatic masterpieces, *Opera as Drama* ([1956] 1988). That he chose to begin his analysis with the final scene of Verdi's *Otello* suggests a motivation in this book to lift opera as a whole to a position of intellectual prestige comparable to that of the greatest classical instrumental music. To begin with a scene of Mozart or Wagner, after all, would not have served the purpose, since those were composers whose prestige separated them from the operatic crowd. But Verdi, despite his unassailable centrality in the performing repertory, was readily dismissed at the time as merely operatic, and so to introduce the book with Verdi—in fact with an opera of Verdi derived from Shakespeare, a comparison that Kerman did not shrink from making—was to insist that *operatic* could mean dramatic or artistic in the highest sense.

The second half of the twentieth century—after Grout's and Kerman's books were published—witnessed an extraordinary outpouring of musicological scholarship on opera that continues today: scholarly editions, research into performance and reception history, critical studies, new opera journals and dictionaries.

Much of that scholarship has focused on works that have long been fixtures of the operatic canon, providing insights for fresh performance and fresh hearing of those works. One such study, Wye Allanbrook's *Rhythmic Gesture in Mozart* (1983), on the role of dance rhythms in the musical language of Mozart's operas, initiated a topical mode of musical criticism that others have extended to the whole operatic canon and beyond that to classical music in general; in that sense it helped give opera studies a new status as a driving force in musicology. Other studies, done by critics outside the field of music, from the feminist psychologist Catherine Clément (1988) to the psycho/cultural theorist Slavoj Žižek (2002), were able to raise the profile of opera in general cultural discourses precisely because they concentrated on what distinguishes opera from the rest of the classical music canon: its words and action. In that sense, these writers are continuing the tradition of discourse about opera by literary figures in sixteenth-century Florence and seventeenth-century Paris. The new contexts that these writers give to canonic operas are sometimes paralleled in the work of contemporary stage directors and designers, who have taken advantage of the largely fixed operatic repertory (and of some new stage technologies) to render the classic works new, often tearing them out of their historical settings and connecting them, at least visually, to a world closer to the audience's own, thereby both defamiliarizing and refamiliarizing the canonic (see Hunter 2008: 214–226).

Meanwhile, another part of the work of opera scholars has been to serve up neglected scores, along with knowledge and questions about them, for revival and renewed canonic consideration. That connection of scholarship and performance has characterized in particular the renewed interest in opera from the seventeenth and eighteenth centuries. It was apparent already at the beginning of the twentieth century in Vincent d'Indy's editions and productions of operas of Monteverdi and Rameau. After the midpoint of the century, the symbiotic efforts of scholars and performers were directed at reviving not just historic works, but also historically informed ways of performing them. The effect of those efforts was felt first in historicist approaches to singing and playing the music. Nikolaus Harnoncourt was one of the leaders at this stage, focusing like d'Indy on Monteverdi and Rameau. Later in the century, dance and theater historians were brought into the effort, to investigate and direct performers and designers in historicist gesture, movement, dance, costuming, and scenery. By the beginning of the twenty-first century the productions of Lully's stage works by Benjamin Lazar, Vincent Dumestre, and their collaborators (Lully 2008, for example) were including candle lighting and seventeenth-century pronunciation of French in their historicizing reach. In effect, they and others were building on the nineteenth-century practice of publishing the production manual of an opera; that is, they too were extending the inclusiveness of the canonic "text." And here technology plays an ironic role: new arts of supplementary lighting have to be added to the candlelight to make that re-canonized old technology workable, especially on the new medium of the DVD.

See also: How Opera Traveled, Patronage, Politics, Historically Informed Performance, Censorship, Autographs, Memorabilia, and the Aesthetics of Collecting, Writing the History of Opera, After the Canon, Visual Media.

Bibliography

Adams, John. 2003. *The Death of Klinghoffer*. Dir. Penny Woolcock. London: Decca; New York: Universal Music and Video Distribution DVD.

Allanbrook, Wye Jamison. 1983. *Rhythmic Gesture in Mozart: 'Le nozze di Figaro' and 'Don Giovanni.'* Chicago: University of Chicago Press.

Bartoli, Cecilia. 1992. *Se tu m'ami: Arie antiche*. New York: London. 436 267–2 CD.

Bashford, Christina. 2007. *The Pursuit of High Culture: John Ella and Chamber Music in Victorian London*. Woodbridge, UK: Boydell.

Becker, Heinz, and Gudrun Becker. [1983] 1989. *Giacomo Meyerbeer: A Life in Letters*, translated by Mark Violette. Portland, OR: Amadeus Press.

Bergman, Gösta M. 1977. *Lighting in the Theatre*. Stockholm: Almqvist & Wiksell International; Totowa, NJ: Rowman and Littlefield.

Bianconi, Lorenzo, and Giorgio Pestelli, eds. [1987–1988] 1998–2003. *The History of Italian Opera*. 3 vols. Various translators. Chicago: University of Chicago Press.

Citron, Marcia. 2000. *Opera on Screen*. New Haven: Yale University Press.

Clément, Catherine. [1979] 1988. *Opera, or the Undoing of Women*, translated by Betsy Wing. Minneapolis: University of Minnesota Press.

Cowart, Georgia. 1981. *The Origins of Modern Musical Criticism: French and Italian Music, 1600–1750*. Ann Arbor, MI: UMI Research Press.

Dill, Charles. 1994. "Rameau Reading Lully: Meaning and System in Rameau's Recitative Tradition." *Cambridge Opera Journal* 6/1: 1–17.

Edwards, H. Sutherland. 1862. *History of the Opera: From Monteverde to Donizetti*. 2 vols. London: W. H. Allen.

Ellis, Katharine. 2009. "Systems Failure in Operatic Paris: The Acid Test of the Théâtre-Lyrique." In *Music, Theater, and Cultural Transfer: Paris, 1830–1914*, edited by Mark Everist and Annegret Fauser, 49–71. Chicago: University of Chicago Press.

Gossett, Philip. 2006. *Divas and Scholars: Performing Italian Opera*. Chicago: University of Chicago Press.

Gramit, David. 2002. *Cultivating Music: The Aspirations, Interests, and Limits of German Musical Culture, 1770–1848*. Berkeley and Los Angeles: University of California Press.

Grout, Donald Jay. 1947. *A Short History of Opera*. New York: Columbia University Press.

Gruber, Gernot. 1994. *Mozart and Posterity*, translated by R. S. Furness. Boston: Northeastern University Press.

Hall-Witt, Jennifer. 2007. *Fashionable Acts: Opera and Elite Culture in London, 1780–1880*. Durham: University of New Hampshire Press.

Hoffmann, E. T. A. 1989. *E.T.A. Hoffmann's Musical Writings: 'Kreisleriana,' 'The Poet and the Composer,' Music Criticism*, edited by David Charlton and translated by Martyn Clarke. Cambridge: Cambridge University Press.

Hunter, Mary. 2008. *Mozart's Operas: A Companion*. New Haven: Yale University Press.

Jahn, Otto. 1856–1859. *W. A. Mozart*. Leipzig: Breitkopf & Härtel.

Johnson, James. 1995. *Listening in Paris: A Cultural History*. Berkeley and Los Angeles: University of California Press.

Kerman, Joseph. [1956] 1988. *Opera as Drama*. Rev. ed. Berkeley and Los Angeles: University of California Press.

——. 1983. "A Few Canonic Variations." *Critical Inquiry* 10/1: 107–125.

Kierkegaard, Søren. [1843] 1987. *Either/Or*, edited and translated by Howard V. Hong and Edna H. Hong. Princeton, NJ: Princeton University Press.

Kretzschmar, Hermann. 1919. *Geschichte der Oper*. Leipzig: Breitkopf & Härtel.

Latham, Alison, and Roger Parker, eds. 2001. *Verdi in Performance*. New York: Oxford University Press.

Le Cerf de La Viéville, Jean Laurent. [1705] 1950. *Comparaison de la musique italienne et de la musique française*. Partial English translation by Oliver Strunk in *Source Readings in Music History: From Classical Antiquity to the Romantic Era*. New York: W. W. Norton.

Leichtentritt, Hugo. 1924. *Händel*. Stuttgart: Deutsche Verlags-Anstalt.
Levine, Lawrence. 1988. *Highbrow/Lowbrow: The Emergence of Cultural Hierarchy in America*. Cambridge, MA: Harvard University Press.
Lorenz, Alfred. 1924–1933. *Das Geheimnis der Form bei Richard Wagner*. 4 vols. Berlin: M. Hesse.
Lully, Jean-Baptiste. 2008. *Cadmus et Hermione*. Dir. Benjamin Lazar. Paris: Alpha DVD.
Macnutt, Richard. 1992a. "Libretto (i)." *New Grove Dictionary of Opera*. II: 1185–1191.
——. 1992b. "Publishing." *New Grove Dictionary of Opera*. III: 1154–1166.
Mörike, Eduard. [1856] 2003. *Mozart's Journey to Prague and a Selection of Poems*, translated by David Luke. London: Penguin.
Neville, Don. 1992. "Mestastasio, Pietro." *New Grove Dictionary of Opera*. III: 351–361.
Oulibicheff, Alexandre. 1843. *Nouvelle Biographie de Mozart*. 3 vols. Moscow: A. Semen.
Parakilas, James. 1995. "The Power of Domestication in the Lives of Musical Canons." *repercussions* 4/1: 5–24.
Parisotti, Alessandro, ed. 1885. *Arie antiche*. 3 vols. Milan: G. Ricordi.
Poriss, Hilary. 2009. *Changing the Score: Arias, Prima Donnas, and the Authority of Performance*. AMS Studies in Music. New York: Oxford University Press.
Ringel, Matthew. 1996. "Opera in 'the Donizettian Dark Ages': Management, Competition and Artistic Policy in London, 1861–70." PhD diss., University of London.
Rochlitz, Friedrich. [1798–1801] 1991. "Verbürgte Anekdoten aus Wolfgang Gottlieb Mozarts Leben." English translation. In *Mozart Studies*, edited by Cliff Eisen. Oxford: Clarendon Press.
Rosselli, John. 1984. *The Opera Industry in Italy from Cimarosa to Verdi: The Role of the Impresario*. Cambridge: Cambridge University Press.
Schneider, Herbert. 1982. *Die Rezeption der Opern Lullys im Frankreich des Ancien Regime*. Tutzing: Hans Schneider.
Simeone, Nigel. 2001. "Programme Note." *Grove Music Online. Oxford Music Online*. Available: www.oxfordmusiconline.com/subscriber/article/grove/music/51278 (accessed August 24, 2012).
Ther, Philipp. 2006. *In der Mitte der Gesellschaft: Operntheater in Zentraleuropa, 1815–1914*. Vienna and Munich: Oldenbourg.
Toelle, Jutta. 2007. *Oper als Geschäft: Impresari an italienischen Opernhäusern, 1860–1900*. Kassel: Bärenreiter.
Walter, Michael. 1987. *Hugenotten-Studien*. Frankfurt: Peter Lang.
Weber, William. 2008. *The Great Transformation of Musical Taste: Concert Programming from Haydn to Brahms*. Cambridge: Cambridge University Press.
——. 1999. "The History of Musical Canon." In *Rethinking Music*, edited by Nicholas Cook and Mark Everist, 336–355. New York: Oxford University Press.
Westphal, Rudolf. 1872. *Elemente des musikalischen Rhythmus mit besonderer Rücksicht auf unsere Opern-Musik*. Jena: H. Costenoble.
Žižek, Slavoj, and Mladen Dolar. 2002. *Opera's Second Death*. New York and London: Routledge.

CHAPTER 40

CRITICS

PAUL WATT

OPERA has long exercised the minds of critics of various persuasions. As a potent mix of music and drama that engages extremes of human emotions—and excites, bores, or infuriates those who listen and watch—opera provides an especially tantalizing subject on which to write. As Craig Calhoun (2007: xxi) has observed, "Opera critics delight in provoking clashes over whether celebrity singers are past their prime, whether theatrical spectacle has triumphed regrettably over music, and whether restaging old favorites is driving out innovation." For many writers throughout opera's history, criticism was both a labor of love as well as a professional duty, and they sometimes took up a particular cause or crusade. Such was the case with Ernest Newman (1868–1959), who not only revеled in going to the opera, but devoted much of his life to discussing it, principally in the *Sunday Times* (1920–1958). Newman's criticism of opera was not confined to journalism, however; he wrote biographies of opera composers, such as *Gluck and the Opera* (1895), and books on opera appreciation, including *Opera Nights* (1943). On the other hand, critics such as Johann Christoph Gottsched (1700–1776) apparently found opera dull (Birke 1960); and Hector Berlioz, who frequently expressed his misfortune at having to be a critic, especially disliked *opéra comique*, but wrote reviews of it, and other genres, to help pay the bills (Murphy 1988: 91–111).

The beginning of professional music criticism is commonly associated with the establishment of the *Allgemeine musikalische Zeitung* in 1798 (Taruskin 2010: 291). This periodical described itself as a "musical newspaper for the general public," which was also the claim of a large number of music periodicals that were to follow in its path the world over. As the entry on musical periodicals in the *New Grove Dictionary* (Fellinger et al. 2003) attests, the types of music journals that pioneered musical criticism in many countries were extremely diverse, covering reviews, opinion pieces, and essays on organology and aesthetics. Contributors to these journals did not merely report the musical news or prescribe which composers and works were worth hearing or not; their agendas were more critical and political, a stance that has been a mainstay of musical criticism from the late eighteenth century to the present. While many critics were (or are) mere hacks, journalists, or writers of *belles lettres*, others have advocated for musical progress and reform, using their positions to effect change.

Especially apposite are the two earliest musical newspapers in Italy, the *Foglio periodico e ragguaglio de' spettacoli musicali* (1808–1809) and the *Indice, o sia Catalogo dei teatrali spettacoli italiani di tutta L'Europa* (1764–1823), both of which dealt exclusively with opera. Later, the *Gazzetta musicale di Milano*, first produced in 1842 by the entrepreneur Giovanni Ricordi (publisher to Rossini, Bellini, Donizetti, and Verdi), became the leading critical voice for new Italian opera (Jensen 1989). But most major music periodicals of the late eighteenth to the nineteenth century, including the *Neue Zeitschrift für Musik* in Leipzig (first published 1833), *La Revue et Gazette musicale de Paris* (1834), *Dwight's Journal of Music* in Boston (1852), and the *Musical Courier* in New York (1880, also published in London in the 1890s), covered an array of topics. Moreover, some of them also included translations of criticism from other continents. For example, between June and August of 1855, *Dwight's Journal of Music* published in English translation various essays by A. B. Marx and featured regular reports of performances of Italian opera from London.

Some of the most prominent critics in the first century of music criticism were composer-critics such as Berlioz (*La Revue et Gazette musicale de Paris* and other journals), Schumann (*Neue Zeitschrift für Musik*), and Weber (*Leipziger Neue Zeitung*); they had "insider" status, and thus brought to these journals a deeper authority on music. However, the composer-critic was not solely a European phenomenon, as it was also a hallmark of much music criticism in nineteenth-century North America. As Mark N. Grant notes, this "pedigree" [of composer-critic in North America] was "as impeccable as that of the better-known European line of Berlioz, Schumann, Debussy [...]" (1998: 194). North American composers to whom Grant attributes this lineage included William Henry Fry and, later, Virgil Thomson, both of whom worked for the *New York Herald Tribune*. Indeed, by the time Fry's career was underway in the 1850s, music criticism had moved beyond specialist musical periodicals and into generalist newspapers, which is still the case today. Music and opera critics from a variety of backgrounds pervaded the press, and the authority of the composer-critic gradually declined.

With the decline of the composer-critic came writers and journalists from various literary, intellectual, and musical backgrounds. Examples in the United Kingdom include, in the late nineteenth and early twentieth centuries, Rosa Newmarch, who wrote extensively on Russian music, and George Bernard Shaw, whose criticism in *The World* and other journals was renowned for its wit. In the United States, James Huneker in New York is considered one of the most outward-looking critics of his generation of the late nineteenth century (Schwab 1963: vii). At the mid-twentieth-century mark, Briton Neville Cardus continued his career in Melbourne and Sydney as both an expert cricket and music critic, while Claudia Cassidy earned a reputation in Chicago for the fiercely uncompromising criticism that earned her the nickname "Acidy Cassidy" as well as allegations of abuse of power (Grant 1998: 257–260). Today, most music critics work in the general periodical press; some of them achieve international fame, including Norman Lebrecht (former writer for the *Daily Telegraph* and *Evening Standard* in London) and Alex Ross of the *New Yorker*, who also maintains the blog "The Rest Is Noise."

This essay explores the ways that opera criticism, throughout its history, has taken on a variety of forms, often in unexpected places, and exerted surprising impact. One good example of the latter came from the literary critic John M. Robertson (1856–1933), who wrote only one article on opera in his life. Yet that single work is valuable for the light it casts on the state of musical criticism in late Victorian England. Moreover, since the rise of the "essay" genre in nineteenth-century Europe, writings about opera reached far beyond the mere reporting of news. Established in the early nineteenth century, the reviews genre—represented in England, for example, by such august publications as the *Fortnightly Review* and *Contemporary Review*—published extremely long critiques that ran to many thousands of words, addressing substantial issues such as reception, taste, and influence, and debating aesthetics, history, and nationalism.

Unfortunately, there is no authoritative history of musical criticism, much less opera criticism, in any language (Max Graf's 1947 book, *Composer and Critic: Two Hundred Years of Musical Criticism*, is too personal, general, and brief to be considered authoritative). The *Cambridge Opera Journal*, the flagship periodical of opera scholarship, has yet to publish an article dealing explicitly with an opera critic. But in some ways, that is not surprising, for we live in an age that no longer worships great men (and the majority of critics, past and present, have been male). What we have in abundance, however, are interdisciplinary studies of opera, a point much celebrated in the first issue of *Cambridge Opera Journal*, where founding editors Arthur Groos and Roger Parker observed that "[t]he fact that the five contributors to this first issue include an economic historian, a musicologist, a literary critic, an opera scholar unfettered by academic ties and a philosopher seems to us a matter of encouragement" (1989: i).

More recently, scholars have turned their attention to the subject with several new studies of nineteenth-century French critics, including Katharine Ellis's (1995) work on the *Revue et Gazette musicale de Paris*. While Ellis is concerned with writings that address all kinds of music in the period 1834–1880, she devotes her final chapters to opera, followed by studies of Wagner and Berlioz. Opera criticism as a conduit for larger questions about social issues and the nature of discourse itself can be found in Parker and Smart (2001). This collection takes in ballet as well as opera, generally avoiding reception studies of works and composer to "read" (i.e. analyze and compare) the critics as individuals. A good example is Ellis's discussion of Julien-Louis Geoffroy (1800–1814), who apparently knew little about music, let alone opera. Ellis reads Geoffroy's dilettantish ruminations not as an inferior literature but as a larger "creative force" evident in the style of other writers, many of them literary critics and novelists, that continued well into the 1830s (Ellis 2001: 68; see also Ellis 1995).

Parker sees *Reading Critics Reading* as dealing with a tranche of literature—"most of it journalistic"—that he claims was "undervalued" and "insufficiently thought about" (Parker and Smart 2001: 1). The distinction between criticism and journalism is, however, to quote Kerry Murphy, "pedantic and messy" (1988: vi). Moreover, it is sometimes difficult to demarcate journalism from criticism (or "higher criticism" from mere "reviewing," as both species of criticism are sometimes referred to) without imposing judgment on the value of different approaches to critical functions and reader responses in which a hierarchy of writers, readers, and periodicals would have to be situated. I prefer instead to advocate for a more egalitarian approach to the problem, treating criticism and reviewing as complementary and related discourses, especially when a critic wrote in both registers in the same newspaper on the same page (as did Ernest Newman in his *Sunday Times* columns). The audiences for such literatures are not always mutually exclusive, and imposing a divide between reviews and criticism is often unhelpful. Nonetheless, as Parker notes, some periods of criticism have fallen under the radar (Parker and Smart 2001: 1). In this chapter, I go to the margins of the field by discussing four British critics whose work has not been studied or "read" in much detail before. Nor have the periodicals for which they wrote been the subject of much scholarly investigation.

Looking to opera criticism of the past tells us a great many plainly observable things about performance practice, taste, and audience behavior. But it does not so readily tell us about the meaning of a critic's use of language or rhetorical devices (see Murphy 1988). Also not always apparent is the ideological stance of the critic or the editorial bias of newspapers or periodicals for which they write. I am interested in looking at opera criticism in the context of the conditions that give rise to it, and take my cue, in part, from Ian Small (1991). As Small explains, his approach to the study of criticism explores the "changes in the epistemologies underlying nineteenth-century political economy, historiography, sociology, and psychology" (1991: vii). He advocates a "sociology of knowledge" that "address[es] the wider intellectual context of the past, because it was these issues that were instrumental in determining the forms which criticism took" (1991: 5). The following case studies examine some of these wider intellectual issues in opera criticism and points of reference. The case studies do not suggest issues particular to the British context; rather, they explore themes (historical and contemporary) that will be familiar to critics, audiences, and policy makers in other countries where opera is a highly prized and contested institution.

A "Critical Breakdown": 1884 and 1986 Compared

On November 10 and 15, 1884, *Parsifal* was premiered in England at the Royal Albert Hall. It was received warmly and enthusiastically by audiences, according to the unsigned review of the opera in the *Musical Times* on December 1. Even though the reviewer conceded that parts of *Parsifal* were "less satisfactorily realised" (especially the singing by the flower maidens), he was nevertheless impressed by the opera's artistic direction and offered "unqualified praise" for the soloists (*MT* 1884: 694).

Equally satisfied by this staging of *Parsifal* was John M. Robertson, a fledging literary critic and undecided Wagnerian. What interested Robertson most about the opera was not so much the music as its critical reception. Robertson was perplexed by what the critics wrote about this performance, because the enthusiasm shown for *Parsifal* in the *Musical Times* was far from unanimous in other quarters of the press, and he decided to write an article on the matter. He called his essay "The Music of the Future" and published it in the December 1884 volume of *Progress* (Robertson 1884). Robertson told his readers that he was not going to talk about the technical side of the performance because he was not a musician, and would, rather, address what he would term a "crisis" in local musical criticism.

"The Music of the Future" is a reflective and provocative essay that does not address opera per se, but comments on the standard of criticism in London, and engages with Wagnerian-inspired debates about the evolution of music and the arts in general and the function of the music-drama in a post-symphonic age in particular. Robertson seems enamored enough of *Parsifal*—he admits to being transported by parts of it, especially "the greater part of the Third Act"—but devotes the bulk of his essay to its critical reception. He believes the local critics had made "an exhibition" of themselves in their extreme judgments of the performance, exclaiming, "[a] more abject critical breakdown has seldom been witnessed, even in the London press." And he fails to see how one critic (whom he does not name) could describe *Parsifal* as "Wagner at his worst, and sheer denial of melody from beginning to end." Robertson was embarrassed by this critical reception: "When such criticisms can appear in a leading London Journal—and something equivalent appeared in several—there is little to be said for the condition of musical culture in England as compared with what we find on the Continent" (all quotes Robertson 1884: 278). In the remainder of the article, Robertson engages with current thinking on aspects of evolutionary theory in literature and music and ends by speculating that instrumental music would in fact be "the music of the future," and that *Parsifal* performed without words was clear evidence of an evolutionary step in the right direction.

Fast forward to 1986: The scene is still London, and under attack from the critics are *Parsifal* (produced by Joachim Herz for the English National Opera) and *Der fliegende Holländer* (produced by Mike Ashman at the Royal Opera House, Covent Garden). On this occasion the writer is *Musical Times* critic Barry Millington (1986), who was dismayed by the polarized critical reception of these two operas. Although Millington cites material from critics whom he deems "fools" (1986: 333), he is careful not to name anyone in particular. Whereas Robertson had made some concessions toward incompetent critics—believing that in a soon-to-be-realized age of improved standards in journalism, the world would be rid of fatuous reviewing—Millington begins his essay ever-mindful that critics in both the nineteenth and twentieth centuries had served Wagner rather badly:

> There have been earlier periods of musical history when narrow-minded, conservative opera critics have made fools of themselves. Wagner's implacable adversary Eduard Hanslick resolutely maintained his opposition to the principle of music drama right to the end of Wagner's life; by that time even the notorious *Times* critic J. W. Davison had turned. One wonders whether posterity will view the present critical consensus that rages at so-called "directorial intervention" with the same amusement. (Millington 1986: 333)

Millington then goes on to complain about the poor reviewing of the two operas in the London press. He quotes an unnamed reviewer who claimed that "to an unprecedented extent *Parsifal* is the score. The well-shaped (if protracted) action is obscure and indeed fishy in detail. As a fairy-tale it isn't up to much, but stage attempts to fix a clearer grown-up sense upon it are exceedingly risky: better to leave Deeper Interpretation to the programme-book." To which Millington asks, rhetorically of course, "Are we seriously being invited to switch our brains off, along with our electronic alarm signals, on entering the opera house?" (Millington 1986: 33). Millington accuses the critics of *Der fliegende Holländer* of lacking "curiosity or imagination," but cites no one in support of this claim and devotes the rest of the article to historical reactions to Wagner's operas and arguments pertaining to the relationship between music and drama (Millington 1986: 334). He also discusses, generally, the politics of staging operas with modern sets and costumes, a much debated issue in today's press. After weighing the pros and cons of the aesthetic and psychological import of what he terms "avant-garde" productions, Millington concludes pragmatically by acknowledging that modern productions in fact "are, at their best, conscientious attempts to engage our minds as well as our emotions with the realities that preoccupied the composer. They may, of course, be successful, partially successful, or a dismal failure" (Millington 1986: 335).

The similarities in the essays by Robertson and Millington, written 102 years apart, are clear: Both were dissatisfied with contemporary musical criticism in London; both essays ended up traversing issues in aesthetics and reception; and both essays can be described as meta-criticism, or criticism about criticism. A cynic may say that nothing has changed in 102 years, despite the efforts of Stainer (1881), Calvocoressi (1923), and Walker (1966) to regulate criticism to overcome personal bias. But much criticism, especially in the popular press, relies on sensationalism, wit, and rabble-rousing for good reading; without these techniques, criticism can all too easily lose its punch. Still, Robertson and Millington favored an intellectual approach to opera criticism that became the hallmark of Ernest Newman's writings about opera and aesthetics in the 1890s.

Opera Criticism as Aesthetic Discourse: Ernest Newman in the 1890s

Ernest Newman was one of the most significant Anglophone music critics of the twentieth century. His sixty-five-year career (1893–1958) was preoccupied with writing about opera. In his teens Newman had attempted to write an opera based on Shelley's *Prometheus Unbound*, which provided him with insight into the process of composing opera, a skill that very few critics (apart from the rare composer-critic such as Wagner) possessed. He was the author of many books on opera, including *Gluck and the Opera: A Study of Musical History* (1895), *Opera Nights* (1943), and his *Life of Wagner* in four volumes (1933–1947), as well as thousands of articles on music and opera in a variety of periodicals from the 1890s including the *National Reformer*, *Contemporary Review*, the *Birmingham Daily Post* (1906–1919), and most well-known of all, the *Sunday Times* (1920–1958). Newman's work reached a global audience, not only through the *Sunday Times*, but also the international markets where his books were sold and articles syndicated. Unlike many critics, Newman was sometimes given the opportunity to interact with the public: the editors of two journals for which he wrote, the *National Reformer* and the *Sunday Times*, permitted him to reply to readers' questions and letters of complaint, as well as to write on topics suggested by his correspondents.

Newman, mentored in his early career by John M. Robertson, complained about the poor standard of musical criticism in England at every opportunity. He grew up sharing his mentor's aim to establish principles for criticism in order to rid it of bias. This was a noble positivist cause, but it was ultimately untenable, and Newman never managed to articulate a convincing theory or method of criticism. Much of the content of his early criticism is derivative, and despite his quest for impartial criticism, Newman was prone to emotional and sometimes hysterical outbursts, which completely undermined his simplistic aspiration for objectivity (Watt 2009: 76–108). However, some of his early opera criticism is worth examining because it demonstrates not only the ways in which the criticism of opera can intersect with the history of ideas and aesthetics, but how criticism can sometimes emerge by accident rather than design, from a seemingly unlikely set of circumstances.

The *National Reformer* (published 1860–1893) was, in the 1890s, the official organ of a group of far-left intellectuals called the "academic freethinkers." This group comprised secularists, humanists, rationalists, and atheists, whose many interests included republicanism, Darwinism, the advocacy of the rights of women, and the provision of education for all classes of society. As a rule, the *National Reformer* did not publish articles on music, because its editor believed that music should be enjoyed rather than intellectualized. But this position changed when Newman began writing for it in 1892 as an opera critic. His actual work in this periodical had little do with reporting on opera performances, however; he was more interested in Wagnerian aesthetics, and exploring the idea of the comparative method, using the parlance of biology and evolutionary theory to support his ideas. Newman wrote on opera for the *National Reformer* only because he weighed into a debate about aesthetics that Robertson started with his readers.

Although Robertson never wrote at length on music, he made two passing references about the subject in an article entitled "Tennyson" that outraged his readers so much that he was swamped with letters of complaint (Robertson 1892). His first comment was to do with a remark about Herbert Spencer on music; the second was an enthusiastic (some of his readers would term it over-enthusiastic) appraisal of Wagner. Robertson printed the exchanges (even when they became spiteful), and gave Newman, his apprentice critic, freedom to write at length on the subject and to reply to his own opponents. In the same spirit, respondents to Newman were given due space to air their points of view. Untroubled by censorship or tight editorial control, opera criticism in the *National Reformer* came into being.

In relation to Herbert Spencer and the notion of development and progress in music Robertson wrote:

> But one cannot help recurring to the suggestion of Mr. Spencer, that of all the arts which has the greatest development before it is music. That alone has the mysterious virtues of leading itself to and giving birth to all emotions in turn without stamping on itself any doctrine, seeming the most profoundly sympathetic because the most utterly undefined. (Robertson 1892: 242)

Robertson's second comment pertained to Wagner:

> But the new men [i.e., select Classical and Romantic composers] come with their new treasures; Chopin lifts unexpected veils; all the world goes round to Wagner—for a time; and still the new generations of wonder-workers arise. (1892: 242)

A correspondent named H. D. (who was clearly an anti-Wagnerian), in a piece entitled "Poetry and Music" published on October 23, argued that Beethoven, and not Wagner, was the pinnacle of progress in music and suggested that Robertson ought to be more scientific (and less metaphysical) in criticizing music. H. D. further accused Robertson of being too quick to declare Wagner a genius, believing that at least another fifty years was required to pass in order for such a proclamation to be made objectively (H. D. 1892).

Within a fortnight, Newman had weighed into the debate. On October 30, Newman contributed a short article by the same title, "Poetry and Music," in which he agreed with Robertson on Wagner's preeminence (Newman 1892a). Although Newman was to qualify his praise for Wagner's philosophical writings in his 1899 biography of the composer (Newman 1899), for the moment, he waxed lyrical on the genius of Wagner, claiming him to be "not only the deepest and clearest thinker, but also the most consummate and potent artist that ever expressed himself in music," principally because of Wagner's unique ability to balance poetry and music in his music-dramas (Newman 1892a: 277).

Newman then engaged in a fuller discussion of Wagner's aesthetic and drew on *Parsifal* to illustrate his points:

> In Wagner, there was an extraordinary balance between them [poetry and music]; he intersuffused them, consubstantiated them, and his extraordinary power in opera is due to this fact, that he took, unconsciously of course, every element in music that tended towards poetry and every element in poetry that tended towards music, and by uniting these achieved the only genuine creation of opera, the highest expression of it being the last act of "Parsifal." Opera, as an art composed of two materials, can only be successfully achieved by a compromise between them. (Newman 1892a: 277)

Yet Newman also emphasized that poetry and music were discrete entities, and in reference to biology and evolutionary theory wrote that:

> Poetry *per se* and music *per se* exist separately, each working in its own sphere. As soon as they are properly combined, individual distinctions must disappear;

> each must sacrifice something if it is to become one with the other; and the true musical-dramatic expression must come from the mental mood that is a compromise between these two diverse ways of looking at life. This mood of compromise Wagner alone has achieved, and that through a lucky hit of Nature. It may be ages before such a mind comes again. Thus, supreme as Wagner is, the future course of opera will not go on the lines laid down by him. It will have to begin its development afresh. (Newman 1892a: 277)

After debate over text-music relationships, Newman explained in a further article, "Wagner and the Music Drama," how an ideal opera should be conceived and why absolute music appeared to him to be the artwork of the future:

> Thus two things are necessary for the writing of a perfect opera—a balance in the composer between the poetical and the musical sides of his intelligence, and a complete unanimity of concept between librettist and composer. Wagner solved the latter problem by being his own librettist; and it is not too much to say that this is the one great obstacle in the way of opera, that librettist and musician will always be at variance. Whatever they have produced or ever will produce in concert is, viewed organically, a lamentable abortion. Thus I had analytical reasons for saying that opera will always be floundering about in this way, while absolute music, existing purely in one sphere, will have a less impeded development [...] If operatic music would only attempt the treatment of other subjects than love, and would try to express, for instance, some of the emotions Wagner gave voice to, its power and interest would be greater. (Newman 1892b: 375)

Newman's deliberations read like the musings of a dilettante or armchair philosopher. But to dwell on his amateur reading of aesthetics is a secondary concern: what is important is that Newman's criticism of opera in 1892 was a product of an enormous interest in Wagner and ideas of progress that obsessed many European writers in the late nineteenth century. Later, in the 1930s, the impetus behind Newman's opera criticism was entirely different: he wrote at length on opera's infrastructure, rather than musical qualities (to which we will return, shortly), but this line of attack had been started in the 1890s by W. G. Galloway in the *Speaker*.

Opera Problems: W. J. Galloway and *The Speaker*, 1890–1902

Questions of authenticity, musical infrastructure, and the expertise of the singers are never far away in the criticism of opera. Often, however, these questions of artistic function and musical capital are not mutually exclusive problems. The writings of W. Johnson Galloway (1866–1931) are a good example of how these issues and problems interrelate. Galloway was a British businessman and parliamentarian, as well as a newspaper critic and an author of two books, *The Operatic Problem* (1902) and *Musical England* (1910).

From 1890 to 1899, readers of the *Speaker*, a liberal newspaper, became well acquainted with Galloway's personal tastes and public causes through his opera criticism, some of which were articulated in more detail in *The Operatic Problem*. Like Newman, his opera criticism traversed genres; he wrote for consumers of newspapers and books.

The Speaker (published 1890–1907) was launched with a clear political cause. According to the historian Simon Nowell-Smith (1958: 161–162), the *Speaker*'s role was to reflect "the great principles which are common to all sections of the Liberal party." Initially, most of the articles in the *Speaker* were unsigned, including the opera criticism, but this practice changed in late 1899 when its new series partially abandoned anonymous criticism. By 1900 the initials "W. G." appeared at the foot of the opera criticism for the first time, which strongly suggests the author was Galloway. The style and tone of W. G. in 1900 bears a striking resemblance to that of the unsigned writer in the *Speaker* from 1890 to 1899, suggesting that Galloway was likely the author of both sets of criticism.

The *Speaker*'s opera criticism varied in function. In addition to reviewing an opera performance, which often included a history of its production, Galloway used his columns to peddle particular agendas. For example, one of his biggest concerns was the singing of operas in languages other than that in which the libretto was originally written, and he complained regularly about this practice at the Royal Opera House, Covent Garden.

Galloway's personal preference was for opera to be staged in the language in which the libretto was written, but this was rarely the case at the Royal Italian Opera at Covent Garden in the early 1890s. When, in 1890, the impresario of the Royal Italian Opera, Sir Augustus Harris, announced a season of French opera that would be sung in French, and not in Italian translation, Galloway took the opportunity to praise this foresight, writing on June 21, 1890, that

> Mr. Augustus Harris seems now disposed to throw over Italian as the exclusive language of opera; and the time, it may be hoped, will come when we will find it possible to play Wagner in German, even as he has played Gounod in French. No composer loses more than Wagner—writer of his own opera book—by his music being sung to other words than those to which the music was originally fitted. (Galloway 1890b: 678–679)

But Harris's reform was short-lived, and Galloway was far from impressed, writing a few weeks later, on July 19:

> That such works as Gounod's *Romèo et Juliette*, Gounod's *Faust*, and Meyerbeer's *Prophète*, should be played, even at the Italian Opera House, in the French language, is justifiable, and indeed commendable, since we have thus the advantage of having the music sung to the words which first inspired it. It is difficult, however, to understand why *Esmeralda*, composed by Mr. Goring Thomas to an English libretto, should be produced to-night at the Royal Italian Opera in a French version. The simple explanation is that a French translation of *Esmeralda* exists, whereas an Italian

> translation of it does not. Mr. Thomas's opera was translated into French some few years ago, with a view to production in Brussels [...]. (Galloway 1890a: 73)

This blending of languages in performances of opera was commonplace. On July 2, 1892, for example, Galloway bemoaned that *Lohengrin* had been sung in French and Italian but on one particular night a part of it had been sung in French, and a part in German, according to the languages the singers knew (Galloway 1892c: 18). Galloway was appalled that English operatic establishments did not insist that soloists learn their parts in the language of the libretto. This offended Galloway, and in his review Galloway wrote that: "Wagner sung in Italian is like a photograph made from a negative in which the salient parts have been painted out" (1892c: 18). Moreover, he felt that an opera of Wagner's, even if not quite so well sung, is more effective when sung by German singers with their German intonation. "It has been reserved for our own time to witness the representation of an opera in two strange tongues, neither of them the original language of the work performed" (Galloway 1892c: 18).

Galloway was not only embarrassed by English operatic practices; he was also embarrassed more by the lack of domestic infrastructure for opera and began to explain its deficits and to apportion blame, as Newman later did in the 1930s. He started by blaming audiences. On January 23, 1892, for example, he wrote "London audiences have no appreciation of style in music" (Galloway 1892a: 110), but by April 9 had shifted the blame to the educational system:

> It is, perhaps, more curious still that, with four schools for operatic music, we have not one theatre for operatic representations. Contrast this with the remarkable fact that, while there are a score of ordinary dramatic theatres in London, there is not one training school for actors and actresses [...]. To maintain four operatic schools in view of a non-existent Opera seems, at first sight, about as reasonable as to keep up in Switzerland a like number of naval schools in view of a necessarily non-existent marine. (Galloway 1892b: 435)

By December 22, 1894, Galloway was blaming English composers for their "dullness" (Galloway 1894: 673). Yet he nevertheless believed that the establishment of a national opera would provide the impetus for composers of British opera. He saw nothing but dark clouds on the horizon for such a scheme on October 19, 1895:

> Nothing could be more difficult than to devise a system of English operatic performances which would not, from some point of view, been open to hostile criticism. A scheme of English opera in which no place is reserved for works by English composers—and, above all, English composers of the present day—will be condemned by many. No opera, however, by a living English composer has proved sufficiently attractive to repay he cost of production. Operas by Balfe, Wallace and Benedict draw large audiences, but they are too familiar, and too much out of fashion for any manager to produce them in connection with a novel and ambitious enterprise. (Galloway 1895: 417–418)

Within five years of writing the above view, Galloway attributed the "cultural cringe" as the principal factor for excluding British composers from their local establishments. As he wrote on February 11, 1899:

> We ransack Europe for the latest developments in music; new blood, so it be Continental, is eagerly welcomed; our concert-halls and our opera-houses are open to the modern men, to Russians, Bohemians, Scandinavians, to France, to young Italy. Among ourselves alone we sedulously repress revolt from old-fashioned forms, holding out to our young composer no better prospect than our cold commendation should he succeed in writing works as nearly as possible indistinguishable from those of some long dead master. While refusing to listen to the evidence, we record our judgment: that he has nothing original to say that is worth saying. For this strange inversion of patriotism public opinion is in the main responsible. (Galloway 1899: 174)

Galloway was always optimistic that opera could flourish in Britain, which was the impetus for his book *The Operatic Problem*. This project argued for the establishment of a national opera "for the people" and the "higher education of the community" (Galloway 1902: 5–6), which harked back to nineteenth-century ideals of art as rational recreation, which held that high art stood as a remedy to emancipate the working classes from their vulgar leisure interests. Galloway argued that opera had been considered "the highest form of theatrical pastime" since its origin and that this virtue had been recognized in many countries, except England (Galloway 1902: 7). Moreover, Galloway complained that England had become a "happy dumping ground" for Italian opera but also assured his readers, perhaps sarcastically, that the English had a "dramatic instinct in music" (Galloway 1902: 12). After comparing the governance and subsidies of opera in Italy, Germany, and France, Galloway established a five-point plan for the creation of an English national opera, complete with a cost-benefit analysis of opera's value to the British economy.

Galloway clearly felt he had a public mission to reform opera and was given free rein to do so by his editor, and his method was to publicly shame the management of the Royal Opera House. Almost twenty years later, Ernest Newman was to pursue similar campaigns in the *Sunday Times*, but taking a very different approach to opera criticism from his work of the 1890s. Newman's especial interest in singing, his dislike of Italian opera, and his socialist ideology all had a bearing on his opera criticism. Like Galloway, he used ridicule and scorn as his chief weapons.

More Opera Problems: Newman, 1920–1930

As a critic, Newman was a product of the late nineteenth century. His obsession in pursuing a scientific basis for the practice of criticism was rooted in nineteenth-century positivism, and even later in his life, when the pursuit of such thinking in literary circles was well and truly outdated, Newman was still preoccupied with this dream of objective criticism. His musical taste was fairly conservative, too. A lifelong fan of the Romantics, he was hostile toward most works by Debussy, Schoenberg, and Stravinsky, and hated jazz, and he was a late convert to Mozart, especially the operas. All of these outlooks are reflected in the *Sunday Times*, where Newman held a unique and privileged position. As chief music critic, he was allowed two columns a week instead of the usual one. In "The World of Music" column, Newman was given free rein to write an essay on any musical topic he chose and his word limit was about two thousand words, although this was shortened during wartime owing to paper shortages. He was also allocated a shorter column, positioned either below or beside the essay, to write a brief concert review.

Newman's opera criticism for the *Sunday Times* in the 1930s was largely concerned with operatic reform on all fronts: from better quality singing to more sophisticated dramaturgy (Steane 1982). Newman considered himself an expert on vocal music in general and on opera in particular. In the early 1900s he had been employed as a singing teacher at the Midland Institute in Birmingham under the direction of Granville Bantock, although there is no evidence that Newman himself ever took singing lessons or worked as a singer. In 1912, Newman commenced work on English translations to the librettos of some Wagner operas, beginning with *The Flying Dutchman*. In addition to these works, he also edited an edition of songs by Wolf (1909) and at the time of his appointment to the *Sunday Times* had commenced editing *Modern Russian Songs* (two vols., 1921). He had therefore, by 1920, established himself as an authority on select vocal repertory.

Newman's appointment to the *Sunday Times* was announced in that paper on February 29, 1920, describing its new recruit as one of the leading music critics of his time, declaring that his previous work for papers such as the *Manchester Guardian* was well received by the public because of its literary import. Newman wrote about many opera problems. He tended to paint a gloomy portrait of local operatic culture, but sometimes saw some signs of hope in audience appreciation (but blind spots in some impresarios), such as the reception of John Gay's *The Beggar's Opera*. Newman wrote a review of a performance of it on June 13, 1920, just a few months into his job at the *Sunday Times*: "When one sees *The Beggar's Opera* received so uproariously as it was at the Lyric Theatre last Saturday, one wonders why this joyous, delightful work should ever have been dropped from the repertory" (Newman 1920b: 6).

The bulk of Newman's opera criticism in the 1920s and 1930s dealt largely with explaining why he believed opera had failed in Britain. First, Newman blamed the singers. On December 3, 1922 he wrote that grand opera could never succeed in England because the English singers were "not up to it" (Newman, 1922: 7). Reasons for this included the lack of an understanding of voice-placement. He also believed that the standards of singing were falling (June 17, 1923), a view shared by Thomas Beecham, so Newman claimed. He wrote often that British singers were not being trained properly, and on March 28, 1926, called for more attention to be given to vocal production and direction. A few years later, in 1931, Newman revisited the topic of pedagogy for opera singers over two weeks (May 10 and 17, 1931), asserting that separate training was required to teach opera singers how to act. Clearly, his early singing teaching skills were informing his musical criticism.

One of the biggest opera problems for Newman was acting; in his opinion, women were inferior actors in comparison to men. But he was inconsistent on the matter. In his column for May 7, 1933, entitled "Acting in Opera: The Eternal Feminine," he believed that "female singers [are] unable to move fully into character" because they are "too feminine"; that tragic and pathetic roles, as he termed them, are "outside the realism of their everyday experience" (Newman 1933a: 7). This stance contradicts somewhat his very first article for the *Sunday Times*, when he claimed that women had an easier time of acting in opera because their parts "are purely convention" (Newman 1920b: 7). Newman's view did not abate; by June 23, 1935, he continued to write that female opera singers had it easier than men because women found it more natural to gesture than their male counterparts. He raised once more the issue of pedagogy of British singers, arguing that proper training would rescue singers from acting to formula.

In Newman's estimation, by far the biggest problem confronting opera in England, which he termed "the problem of opera," was its lack of infrastructure and support, and here, once more, are echoes of Galloway's work of twenty years before. Newman also bemoaned the lack of public interest in opera. Writing in June 11, 1933, in an article entitled "Ecrasons l'infâme!" Newman wrote that "the very worst of all is the audience: I make bold to say that we shall never have a real opera in London until there is a drastic improvement in this department. It is an audience largely without traditions of taste, and with little musical culture of its own. The devotees of the German season are not so bad" (Newman 1933b: 7). Specifically, Newman blamed the public's attraction to Italian opera, particularly the support shown to it by Covent Garden, for this lack of taste. As Newman continued, in the same article:

> [T]he bulk of the audience is made up of people who are not used to music as musicians understand the term, and who therefore can hardly be expected to be particularly discriminating in their tastes. I am not insulting them, in arrogant high-brow fashion: I am merely stating the most obvious of facts [...] they have no standards whatsoever [...]. A present-day season at Covent Garden, and especially the Italian part of it, is in large part not a service but a menace to the cause of music in England, for so long as the listeners' mentality that makes these things not merely possible but rapturously admired persists, no progress is possible. But what is the remedy? This I shall try to outline in a following article. (Newman 1933b: 7)

And he did, in an extremely vitriolic tone:

> Covent Garden is a dead weight on the shoulders of opera. It has almost ceased to be an artistic institution and become a mere routine, and a routine of a dangerous kind. The repertoire has sunk into a Byzantine stagnation [...] let us get this Covent Garden poison out of our British operatic system once and for all [...] Covent Garden has long been an anachronism and is now a menace. (Newman 1933b: 7)

There are echoes of Galloway's "name, shame, and humiliate" approach here, but Newman found an operatic messiah in Thomas Beecham, describing him in the June 11, 1933, article as "the only person in Britain who is fit to have the destinies of British opera in his hands, [he] should before long create a standard of taste that would make Covent Garden seem, in retrospect, merely the bad dream of bad indigestion" (Newman 1933b: 7).

In 1929, Beecham established the Imperial League of Opera, which Newman reported on May 5, 1929, boasted forty thousand subscribers, though he noted cynically that not even the safety of numbers could deliver British opera from what he termed its state of "inertia" (Newman 1929: 7). At the root of that inertia, according to Newman, writing the following year on July 6, 1930, was the public's seemingly insatiable demand for Italian opera, which Newman himself disliked and saw as being an outmoded form:

> In many respects Covent Garden is still living in the eighteen-nineties or the first decade of the twentieth century. It labours under the pathetic delusion that there are enough great Italian singers in the world to keep an Italian season going in London for several weeks. There are not. (Newman 1933c: 7)

Like Galloway, Newman had much to say about public subsidies. In the 1920s and 1930s there was considerable support for subsidies in order to underwrite opera. Yet the two critics maintained a crucial difference in this regard. Where Galloway was elitist, Newman—a one-time freethinker, republican, and champion of educational opportunities for the working classes—could never countenance public money being used for opera, an elite and London-centric concern. Newman argued that using London as a base for a national opera project deprived people from the provinces of their right to musical facilities in their own major cities. In his article of November 29, 1925, Newman made this point explicitly and suggested that if the trustees of the National Opera Trust successfully argued for a London home for any type of national opera project, then Londoners should fund that project. Newman argued that ten cities around the United Kingdom could be home to their own opera house but asked, "Who will live to see it realized?" (Newman 1925: 7).

Singers, British and Italian opera, public taste (or rather the lack of it), and state subsidies for opera all came under examination during Newman's tenure on the *Sunday Times*. His critiques remain a valuable, if untapped, resource for understanding the evolution of opera in Britain in the early twentieth century. Toward the end of his lifetime Newman was often accused of being a "soured old cynic" (Vera Newman 1963: vii). Given his long battle to improve opera for Britons, one perhaps can understand why.

At the beginning of this chapter I quoted Craig Calhoun: "Opera critics delight in provoking clashes over whether celebrity singers are past their prime, whether theatrical spectacle has triumphed regrettably over music, and whether restaging old favorites is driving out innovation" (2007: xxi). Yet there is much more to opera criticism, and the conditions that give rise to it, than this pithy quote implies. For Robertson, Millington, Newman, and Galloway, the very act of criticism was not so much about reporting the operatic news but rather was a forum for canvassing much bigger questions.

By "reading criticism" is meant an active engagement with an entire range of issues: intellectual, social, and national. And does it matter that a dilettante or someone who knows little about music writes some operatic criticism? The answer is "no," for all criticism—essays, journalism, even letters to the editor—reveals a variety of attitudes toward music and opera, which change over time. Newman is a good case in point: in the 1930s Newman had different reasons for writing about opera than he did in the 1890s.

Over the last two hundred years there have been some mainstays in the historiography of opera criticism. The shadow of Wagner often still looms large for some audiences, and his operas are the benchmark against which all subsequent opera is judged; for others, Wagner is persona non grata. In the 2000s, debates still continue over whether the state should underwrite symphony orchestras and opera houses that run at a loss. Arguments as to the efficacy of classical music as an improver of the human condition—and opera is sometimes seen as the ultimate expression of this—persist in program notes, college textbooks, and the popular imagination. The criticism of opera is thus borne of many factors—intellectual, social, economic, and populist and reader responses—and is not always contingent on a performance.

Critics leave to posterity a kaleidoscopic insight into the many conditions that inspired them to put pen to paper. Reading these documents, or regarding them as meta-criticism, casts not only a spotlight on the meaning of opera in a certain place at a certain time, but its reception across the generations, some of which, over time, does not appear to change very much at all.

See also: The Operatic Canon, Gender

Bibliography

Birke, Joachim. 1960. "Gottsched's Opera Criticism and Its Literary Sources." *Acta Musicologica* 32/4: 194–200.

Bullock, Phillip Ross. 2009. *Rosa Newmarch and Russian Music in Late Nineteenth- and Early Twentieth-Century England*. Aldershot, UK: Ashgate.

Calhoun, Craig. 2007. "Foreword." In *Opera and Society in Italy and France from Monteverdi to Bourdieu*, edited by Victoria Johnson, Jane F. Fulcher, and Thomas Ertman, xxi–xxxi. Cambridge: Cambridge University Press.

Calvocoressi, Michel-Dmitri. 1923. *The Principles and Methods of Musical Criticism*. London: Oxford University Press.

Cardus, Neville. 1947. *Autobiography*. London: Collins.

Cassidy, Claudia. 1949. *Europe—on the Aisle*. New York: Random House.

Ellis, Katharine. 2001. "A Dilettante at the Opera: Issues in the Criticism of Julien-Louis Geoffroy, 1800–1814." In Parker and Smart 2001, 46–68.

——. 1995. *Music Criticism in Nineteenth-Century France: La Revue et Gazette musicale de Paris, 1834–1880*. Cambridge: Cambridge University Press.

Fellinger, Imogen, et al. 2003. "Periodicals." In *Grove Music Online. Oxford Music Online*. Available: http://www.oxfordmusiconline.com.ezproxy.lib.monash.edu.au/subscriber/article/grove/music/21338pg71 (accessed March 2, 2012).

Galloway, W. Johnson. 1910. *Musical England*. New York: John Lane.

——. 1902. *The Operatic Problem*. London: John Long.
——. 1899. "Bias of Anti-Patriotism in Music." *Speaker* (February 11): 173–174.
——. 1895. "English Opera at Covent Garden." *Speaker* (October 19): 417–418.
——. 1894. "Tunefulness of Delibes." *Speaker* (December 22): 673.
——. 1892a. "Music." *Speaker* (January 23): 110.
——. 1892b. "Operatic Trials." *Speaker* (April 9): 435.
——. 1892c. "Royal Italian Opera Activities." *Speaker* (July 2): 18.
——. 1890a. "Goring Thomas's Esmeralda." *Speaker* (July 19): 73.
——. 1890b. "The Italian Opera Season." *Speaker* (June 21): 678–679.
Graf, Max. 1947. *Composer and Critic: Two Hundred Years of Musical Criticism*. London: Chapman & Hall.
Grant, Mark N. 1998. *Maestros of the Pen: A History of Classical Music Criticism in America*. Boston: Northeastern University Press.
Griffiths, Paul. 1986. "Opera in London: Fantasy Lacking in True Magic." *The Times* (17 March).
Groos, Arthur, and Roger Parker. 1989. "Editorial." *Cambridge Opera Journal* 1/1: i.
Hanslick, Eduard. [1871] 1986. *On the Musically Beautiful: A Contribution towards the Revision of the Aesthetics of Music*, translated by Geoffrey Payzant. Indianapolis, IN: Hackett.
H. D. 1892. "Poetry and Music." *National Reformer* (October 23): 70.
Heyworth, Peter. 1986. "A Tale of Two Missed Chances." *Observer* (March 23): 23.
Jensen, Luke. 1989. *Giuseppe Verdi & Giovanni Ricordi with Notes on Francesco Lucca: from 'Oberto' to 'La traviata.'* New York: Garland.
Kolodin, Irving, ed. 1968. *The Critical Composer: The Musical Writings of Berlioz, Wagner, Schumann, Tchaikovsky, and Others*. Port Washington, NY: Kennikat Press.
Kostelanetz, Richard, ed. 2002. *Virgil Thomson: A Reader—Selected Writings, 1924–1984*. New York: Routledge.
Laurence, Dan H., ed. 1981. *Shaw's Music: The Complete Musical Criticism of Bernard Shaw*. 3 vols. 2nd rev. ed. London: The Bodley Head.
McColl, Sandra. 1996. *Music Criticism in Vienna, 1896–1897: Critically Moving Forms*. Oxford: Clarendon Press.
Millington, Barry. 1986. "Saucepans of Spaghetti: A Semiology of Opera Criticism." *Musical Times* 1719 (June): 333–335.
Morrow, Mary Sue. 2007. *German Music Criticism in the late Eighteenth Century: Aesthetic Issues in Instrumental Music*. Cambridge: Cambridge University Press.
MT. 1884. "Parsifal at the Albert Hall." Unsigned review. *Musical Times* (December 1): 693–694.
Murphy, Kerry. 1988. *Hector Berlioz and the Development of French Music Criticism*. Ann Arbor, MI: UMI Press.
Newman, Ernest. 1943. *Opera Nights*. New York: Putnam.
——. 1933–1947. *The Life of Richard Wagner*. 4 vols. New York: Alfred A. Knopf.
——. 1935. "Acting in Opera: How It Might be Improved." *Sunday Times* (June 23): 7.
——. 1933a. "Acting in Opera: The Eternal Feminine." *Sunday Times* (May 7): 7.
——. 1933b. "Écrasons l'infâme!" *Sunday Times* (June 11): 7.
——. 1933c. "The Sins of Covent Garden: repentance and salvation." *Sunday Times* (June 18): 7.
——. 1931a. "Acting in Opera." *Sunday Times* (May 10): 7.
——. 1931b. "Miming in Opera." *Sunday Times* (May 17): 5.
——. 1930. "Some Covent Garden errors." *Sunday Times* (July 6): 7.
——. 1929. "The Last Lap." *Sunday Times* (May 5): 7.
——. 1926. "Science, Sensation and Singing." *Sunday Times* (March 28): 7.

——. 1925. "The Opera Problem." *Sunday Times* (November 29): 7.
——. 1923. "Pessimism and Progress." *Sunday Times* (June 17): 6.
——. 1922. "English Opera and English Singers." *Sunday Times* (December 3): 7.
——, ed. 1921. *Modern Russian Songs*. New York: Oliver Ditson.
Newman, Ernest. 1920a. "Actors and Actresses in Opera." *Sunday Times* (March 7): 7.
——. 1920b. "The Beggar's Opera." *Sunday Times* (June 13): 6.
——. 1912. *The Flying Dutchman*. [Translation from the German of the libretto]. Leipzig: Breitkopf & Härtel.
——, ed. 1909. *Fifty Songs by Hugo Wolf*. New York: Oliver Ditson.
Newman, Ernest. 1907. *Hugo Wolf*. London: Methuen.
——. 1899. *A Study of Wagner*. London: Bertram Dobell.
——. 1895. *Gluck and the Opera: A Study in Musical History*. London: Bertram Dobell.
——. 1892a. "Poetry and Music." *National Reformer* (October 30): 277.
——. 1892b. "Poetry and Music: A Reply." *National Reformer* (December 4): 373–375.
Newman, Vera. 1963. *Ernest Newman: A Memoir*. London: Putnam.
Nowell-Smith, Simon. 1958. *The House of Cassell, 1848–1958*. London: Cassell.
Parker, Roger, and Mary Ann Smart, eds. 2001. *Reading Critics Reading: Opera and Ballet Criticism in France from the Revolution to 1848*. New York: Oxford University Press.
Plantinga, Leon A. 1967. *Schumann as Critic*. New Haven: Yale University Press.
Pleasants, Henry, ed. 1970. *Hanslick's Music Criticisms*. New York: Dover.
Robertson, John M. 1892. "Tennyson." *National Reformer* (October 16): 241–242.
——. 1884. "The Music of the Future." *Progress* 4 (December): 278–284.
Ross, Alex. "The Rest Is Noise." Online. Available: www.therestisnoise.com (accessed August 24, 2012).
Schwab, Arnold T. 1963. *James Gibbons Huneker: Critic of the Seven Arts*. Stanford, CA: Stanford University Press.
Small, Ian. 1991. *Conditions for Criticism: Authority, Knowledge, and Literature in the Late Nineteenth Century*. Oxford: Clarendon Press.
Stainer, John. 1880–1881. "The Principles of Musical Criticism." *Proceedings of the Royal Musical Association* (7th session): 35–52.
Steane, John. 1982. "Newman of the 'Sunday Times'." *Opera* (February): 126–131; (April): 369–375; and (June): 582–589. Reprinted in Steane, John. 1992. *Voices, Singers and Critics*, 220–240. London: Duckworth.
Taruskin, Richard. 2010. *Music in the Nineteenth Century*. Vol. 3 of *The Oxford History of Western Music*. New York: Oxford University Press.
Walker, Alan. 1966. *An Anatomy of Musical Criticism*. Philadelphia: Chilton Books.
Watt, Paul. 2009. "The Intellectual Life of Ernest Newman in the 1890s." PhD diss., University of Sydney.
Wilson, Alexandra. 2010. "Music, Letters and National Identity: Reading the 1890s Italian Music Press." *Nineteenth-Century Music Review* 7/2: 99–116.

CHAPTER 41

SOUNDINGS OFFSTAGE

THOMAS CHRISTENSEN

On July 20, 1848, at Her Majesty's Theatre in London, Meyerbeer's grand opera *Les Huguenots* received a triumphant performance in an Italian version entitled *Gli Ugonotti*. Shortly thereafter, the following announcement appeared in numerous London newspapers advertising the current offerings of a popular music publisher:

> LES HUGUENOTS.—The Pianista, No. 96 and 97, 2s each, contains:—Adolphe Adam's splendid arrangements of this Opera, which is the best piano arrangement extant. Also, Meyerbeer's "Prophete" in the Pianista, 117 and 118, 2s. each; "Roberto," in 82, 2s. Also, Donizetti's "Lucia," in Nos. 98, 99 2s. each, "Sonnambula," "Don Pasquale," "Puritani," "Lucrezia," "Barbiere," and 40 other Operas, note for note as performed at the Italian Theatres, with Overtures complete, 2s. each, full music size. Post free, 30 stamps; or three Nos., 6s. 6d. in stamps.—Pianista Offices, 16A Argyll-street, Oxford-street; and 67 Paternoster-row. (*The Daily News*, Wednesday, August 15, 1848; Cited in Lockhart 2012: 95)

For just two shillings, the interested musician could take home a piano arrangement of Meyerbeer's score (or one of another forty-odd opera scores, as noted). But had the interested reader looked further, she or he would have discovered an entire library of various kinds of transcription drawing from *Les Huguenots* that could be purchased for even less money: dozens of simplified arrangements of individual airs, dances, and choruses for various configurations of instruments; numerous piano potpourris (or "melodic revues") of themes from the opera strung together in a single movement; virtuosic fantasies (paraphrases or *Réminiscences*) on "motives" from the opera composed by the likes of Liszt or Thalberg. Indeed, so saturated was the music publishing market with arrangements of music from hit operas such as *Les Huguenots*, one might deduce that as many musicians knew their operatic repertoire through the medium of the piano as from staged performance. And this deduction would not be unfounded.

Piano arrangements were indispensable and ubiquitous means in the nineteenth century for the dissemination and consumption of opera music. Composers and producers used them to help publicize and popularize their wares; at the same time, there was a seemingly insatiable demand for these popularizations by a growing bourgeois class of enthusiasts who wanted to hear this music outside the opera house, and perhaps to play some of it themselves at home on their own piano-fortes. Above all, music publishers relied on transcriptions for their livelihood; they were the most profitable wares in their publishing catalogues.[1]

The configurations and functions of a keyboard transcription can take many forms. There is, of course, direct replication, in which an arrangement tries to be as faithful as possible to the original score of the music. (The note for note piano-vocal scores described in the *Pianista* advertisement above are usually thought of as unmediated representations.) But most adaptations for the piano tend to move in two other, opposing directions: reduction or augmentation. In the reduction, selected excerpts from the opera are extracted and radically simplified to accommodate the fingers of beginning pianists. In the augmentation, a composer or performer elaborates a given operatic melody with virtuosic embellishments and passage work, or perhaps in a free adaptation.

For the most part, both of these kinds of keyboard adaptations stand today under a cloud of disrepute. The first is seen as ephemeral remnants of a bygone culture of musical amateurism in which operatic music was trivialized to be within the compass (and taste) of beginning pianists and singers. The second kind of arranging has suffered perhaps even greater opprobrium. The many salon adaptations of operatic music by nineteenth-century piano virtuosi have rarely been treated in more recent times with much respect, more often being dismissed by critics as ostentatious displays of the performer's technical prowess rather than musical works possessing any real artistic merit.

As disreputable as both of these traditions of transcription are today, they constitute critical agents in the history of opera. Indeed, it is not too far-fetched to say that operatic music heard outside the theater in the guise of these domestic and salon arrangements for piano was as important a part of operatic history as that experienced during a staged live performance. For it was through such secondary media that the majority of musicians for some two centuries arguably got to know their operatic repertoire. Today, of course, there are CDs, iPods, the Internet, and (still!) phonograph recordings. But before the age of mechanical reproduction, it was the piano that provided most music lovers the means to reproduce or hear operatic music. It is my aim in this chapter, if not to rehabilitate this much maligned transcriptional culture, at least to place it in a more sympathetic historical frame.

Transcriptions in the Marketplace

Perhaps the first thing to emphasize about the keyboard transcription is that it was driven almost exclusively by commercial forces—by composers and producers seeking to promote their wares, by amateur musicians seeking simplified excerpts of opera music that could be performed at home on the keyboard, and by professional virtuosi capitalizing on the popularity of a given opera. With only intermittent fluctuation, this commercial market was sustained throughout the entire eighteenth and nineteenth centuries. Of course, opera was not the first genre of music that was subjected to keyboard translations. (Since the middle of the fourteenth century, we have surviving in notation keyboard intabulations of popular songs and dance music.) Yet it was operatic music that soon became most closely associated with the transcriptional marketplace and the keyboard arrangement in particular.

Perhaps no other place and period in music history can better illustrate the market forces that drove opera transcription than England during the early eighteenth century. I select this moment, not simply because England was one of the first countries in which we find a commercially thriving operatic culture, but because with the rise of English theater music after the Restoration, we find conditions that ideally met the minimal criteria for the transcriptional marketplace: (1) a relatively stabilized repertoire of songs from commercially successful musical productions; (2) musically literate consumers desiring—and capable—of reproducing this music at home on domestic instruments; and (3) a mature printing and marketing culture by which transcriptions of the music could be produced and sold.

We can see these conditions already coalescing in the collections of popular theater songs and "ayres" published in 1673 "for one voice to sing to a theorbo-lute, or bass-viol, being most of the newest songs sung at court and at the publick Theatres" issued by the music entrepreneur John Playford (Spink 1989). As Playford's title suggests, these collections included selections of stage music (including much by Henry Purcell) that could now be performed by musicians in their own homes. All one needed was the ability to sing the notated melody line and find someone to play the accompanying bass part on a string or plucked instrument. Later title pages from the 1680s, such as Playford's *The Banquet of Music* (Figure 41.1), allowed for the harpsichord or organ to play the accompaniment as a "thorow-bass." Properly speaking, this first generation of theater songs was not operatic, since the songs were sung largely as intermezzi or additions to spoken plays. But, as Italian opera gained a foothold in England by the turn of the eighteenth century, the pattern had already been set. Henry Playford *fils* and later the indefatigable John Walsh issued in ever increasing numbers collections of "favourite songs" or "choice ayres" from the popular operas that began to be heard on London stages in the eighteenth century—by both English as well as Italian composers. (Ironically, it was only in London that a large number of Italian operas from the eighteenth century were ever printed.) Typically, these operatic "scores" were engraved in large folio editions. The edition from which Figure 41.2 is drawn, for example, is entitled *Songs in the New Opera of Camilla by Seigniour Bononcini as they are perform'd at the Theatre Royall.* Many of these collections were printed as bifolia such that individual songs could be detached and sold separately for a penny or two. As seen in Figure 41.2, the typical Walsh arrangement of an opera "song" consisted of a vocal part (a radically simplified version of the embellished melody that one would presumably hear in the theater) accompanied by an unrealized basso continuo. Often a separate violin or flute part that doubled the vocal line was printed at the bottom of the song. Presumably the flute could substitute for the

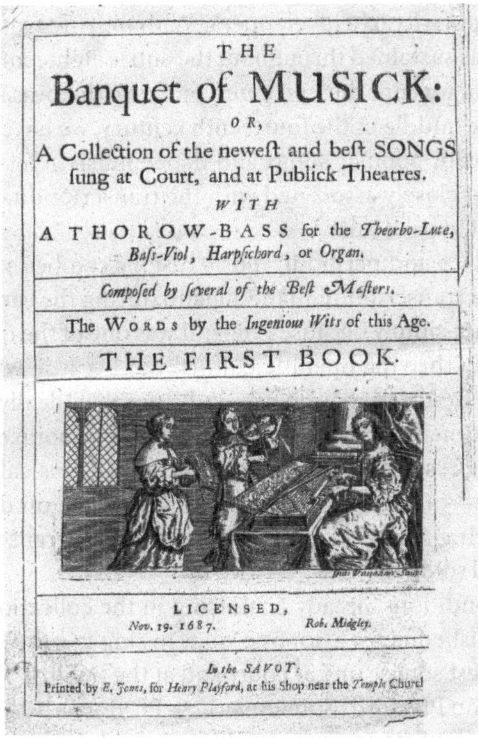

THE
Banquet of MUSICK:
OR,
A Collection of the neweſt and beſt SONGS
ſung at Court, and at Publick Theatres.
WITH
A THOROW-BASS for the Theorbo-Lute,
Baſs-Viol, Harpſichord, or Organ.

Compoſed by ſeveral of the Beſt Maſters.

The WORDS by the Ingenious Wits of this Age.

THE FIRST BOOK.

LICENSED,
Nov. 19. 1687. Rob. Midgley.

In the SAVOY:
Printed by E. Jones, for Henry Playford, at his Shop near the Temple Church

FIGURE 41.1 Title page to Henry Playford's *The Banquet of Music* (1687). Reproduction courtesy of the Newberry Library.

voice, thus creating a little flute sonata with basso continuo. But there was no reason the flutist could not simply perform the tune as a solo; it was common enough to find such solo renditions of opera melodies for instrumentalists well into the nineteenth century (Leopold 1992: 123–136).

All this was unapologetically *Hausmusik*, as the Germans would later call it: music for domestic performance by a growing class of musical amateurs. As Walsh—and his many competitors—soon discovered, there was an almost insatiable appetite for such renditions of opera music. Thousands upon thousands of such song engravings were churned out by busy English printers (often in unauthorized, pirated editions) throughout the eighteenth century (Hunter [1997] has identified 198 separate publications of such opera transcriptions comprising over two thousand separate songs published between 1703 and 1726 in England). But it was not just the printers who gained from these publications. Without the promise of both the income as well as the promotional advertising generated by the sales of this sheet music, English composers and producers (who depended less than their Continental counterparts upon royal patronage) would not have been able to mount the productions of comic operas that they did with such alarming frequency throughout the century (Girdham 1997: 83).

FIGURE 41.2 Song from Bononcini's *Camilla* (1707). Reproduction courtesy of the Newberry Library.

To illustrate the extent of this commerce, we might take the example of a single English opera: Handel's *Giulio Cesare*, premiered at the Haymarket in 1724 (see Smith 1970: 30–35). For the publication of his opera, Handel turned to the firm of John Cluer rather than his regular publisher John Walsh, since Cluer specialized in cheaper quarto (or "pocket") editions that had greater market appeal. Cluer printed in quick succession five abridged editions of the opera's arias in reduced format (*The Favourite Songs in the Opera of Julius Caesar*, shown in Figure 41.3). But piracy was a constant thorn in the side of English publishers of all kinds of literature throughout the eighteenth century (Johns 2010), and savvy pirate printers, knowing the market value of a Handel commodity, were never far off. Another dozen or so unauthorized reprints of Cluer's collection followed over the next few years (the title page simply saying something like "Printed and Sold at the Musick Shops").

In addition, Cluer (and once again, John Walsh) spun off single sheet publications of individual arias and "symphonies" from the opera. The result was that, within ten years, English consumers had no fewer than twenty-seven separate publications available to them for purchase containing music from this single Handel opera. And this number does not take into account any of the subsequent anthologies, song collections,

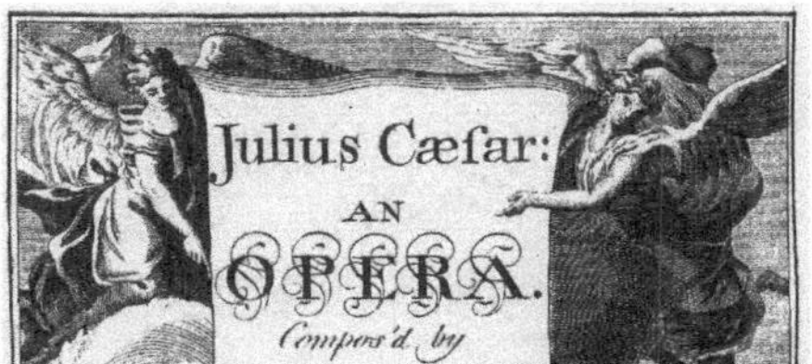

FIGURE 41.3 Title page to Cluer's "Pocket" edition of Handel's *Julius Caesar* (1724). Reproduction courtesy of the Newberry Library.

and gentlemen's magazines published through the century in which individual songs continued to be excerpted.[2]

These many collections of song transcriptions had first and foremost an obvious practical value by reducing the bulky folio editions of operatic music (when they existed) to more manageable formats, such as the quarto, instituted by Cluer. But they were quickly imitated by other English and continental publishers. Indeed, the possibility of carrying around a collection of opera songs in one's own pocket was cited repeatedly by publishers as one of the true virtues of these publications. As Cluer boasted:

> As all things of this nature that have appear'd in the world have been generally of a size more adapted to a Library, than to accompany one abroad, we flatter ourselves with the hopes of a favourable reception for this collection, the manner of introducing it being entirely new etc. To give the airs all possible advantages, they are correctly engraved on copper plates figur'd for the harpsichord, and also transpos'd for the flute by a careful and judicious master; and may be carried with the greatest ease in the pockets of Gentlemen and Ladies. (Cluer 1724, n.p.)

But there was another more profound consequence of this culture of musical transcription that can scarcely be exaggerated: through these transcriptions, music that was conceived and premiered in the public sphere of the opera house is now miniaturized and made available for mass domestic consumption.[3] The opera song had become a saleable commodity.

Music for the Court and the Home

The commercial marketplace for operatic music pioneered by English publishers in the late seventeenth century was only partially emulated on the continent, where differing musical traditions and social conditions shaped the nature of the transcriptional economy. The French experience is a good case in point. Opera in the *ancien régime*, as we know, developed in a more insular fashion than elsewhere in Europe, partly due to indigenous French dramaturgical traditions as well as factors of royal patronage. The great *tragédies en musique* produced by Lully and his successors in the late seventeenth century were manifestly regal genres used for the publicity of the king and his court, and their dramatic structure and emphasis on vocal declamation did not translate easily into keyboard renditions. Still, there developed the same desire among French musicians to "domesticate" court opera, if on a more modest scale. But it was the instrumental music of opera that seemed to receive the most interest.

Beginning in the last quarter of the seventeenth century (and lasting well into the eighteenth century), we find selected overtures and ballet movements of Lully's stage works transcribed into relatively simple *clavecin* textures playable by any amateur with modest skills. As harpsichord renditions, they proved to be some of the most popular music of the entire century. Indeed, Bruce Gustafson has made the astonishing observation that during this period, there were "more than twice the number of harpsichord transcriptions of selections from Lully's operas than original harpsichord pieces by any composer" (Gustafson 1995: 132). Most of these transcriptions remain in manuscript today, although a few were published.

As an example of the latter, we might consider a print by Jean Henri d'Anglebert (1635–1691), who actually established his name as the major *clavecinist* before Couperin partly due to the success of his transcriptions of Lully's music. His *Pièces de clavecin* (1689) consisted of four original suites interspersed with arrangements of several of Lully's overtures, entrées, and other ballet music. Like an exquisitely etched cameo of some massive canvas, d'Anglebert reduces some of Lully's most monumental music to the intimacy of the harpsichord. As seen in Figure 41.4, the solemnity and pomp of Lully's "Chaconne" from *Phaeton* becomes delicate *galanterie* through the reduction of texture and lightening of the medium, not to mention the taming of the dotted rhythms through the incorporation of d'Anglebert's celebrated *style brisé*.

But if the harpsichord was the preferred medium of transcription for operatic music in the early eighteenth century, it was hardly the only one. We find transcriptions of individual dance music from Lully's operas also for lute, theorbo, and guitar. Arrangements of his full scores for a small chamber ensemble of string

FIGURE 41.4 Transcription for harpsichord of the *Chaconne de Phaeton de Mr. de Lully*, in d'Anglebert, *Pièces de clavecin* (1689). Collection of Thomas Christensen.

instrumentalists were also common under the rubrics *partition réduite* or *partition en trio* (Ranum 1990). These various reductions of Lully's music for smaller performing forces suggest once again the primary commercial motive driving the transcription trade that promoted the domestication of music designed for the public sphere. Music heard at court or in the grand *palais royale* is now brought into the inner sanctuary of the home to be played by an amateur on the harpsichord or with a small group of instrumentalists.

It is obvious that the delicate harpsichord renditions of d'Anglebert cannot convey the same sense of gravitas of the original *tragédie en musique* given the vastly differing sonic effect and social settings. But that was obviously not the intent. These operatic reductions, as one of Ballard's own promotional advertisements stated, were meant to "make these incomparable works much more accessible than they have been until now... the variety of these editions will satisfy the different needs of all who would wish to make music" (cited in Christensen 2000: 73). D'Anglebert, too, conceded that his arrangements possessed a "different character" from that of the original. But he argued that the public would nonetheless be grateful to him for making "the works of this incomparable man" accessible on the harpsichord.

Despite the obvious popularity of Lully's ballet music for French audiences, the vocal music of his operas was hardly neglected. We must remember that Lully was the first composer to have virtually his complete stage works printed in "full" scores. But these large folio editions printed in Ballard's movable type were not very practical for home use. (One admirer of Lully's music, who in 1676 asked how he could get to hear some of the composer's most celebrated tunes, was simply told to find someone who sang well! [Rose 2005: 70]).

When Foucault broke Ballard's monopoly on music printing in France in 1702, it meant that there could then be a means to satisfy Lully's fans who wanted to get to know his music better. Following the lead of their English counterparts, French printers such as Baussen, Le Clerc, and Foucault began to issue beautifully engraved "reduced" scores of Lully's operas that thinned the normal five-part textures to a simple basso continuo/treble polarity. Equally popular were the many *recueils*, or collections of opera music in reduced textures and formats. All manner of arias, duets, and "symphonies" found their way into simplified transcriptions for the enjoyment of French amateurs. The range of music published is surprisingly broad given the notoriously insular tastes of the French. While excerpts from comic operas and ballets were the most popular, even the odd aria from an *opera seria* made its way through the French transcription mill.

The Forte-Piano and the Triumph of Amateurism

In 1784, the French publisher Le Roy announced the imminent appearance of a *Pot-pourri d'airs choises tirés des plus jolis opera comiques & arrangés pour la harpe ou forte-piano avec accompagnement de violon ad libitum*. There are two things that are of interest about this announcement. First, there is the novel title of the work, which introduces the genre of the "potpourri" in which various tunes—or more commonly, parts of tunes—from an opera are intermingled within a single work. We will return to this in a moment. For now, though, I want to draw attention to a second word found in the title: the "forte-piano."

By the last quarter of the eighteenth century, the piano had almost fully eclipsed the harpsichord as the favored domestic keyboard instrument. (Although, as Le Roy's full title reminds us, the harp also gave the piano a run for the money, at least for a little while.) And there were good reasons for this. Among other things, the piano proved to be an ideal instrument for vocal accompaniment and perforce, the opera transcription. Softer in tone and touch than the harpsichord, it was a more congenial partner to the voice, able to mimic orchestral nuances of texture, dynamic, and articulation with greater subtlety. Charles Burney was only one of many observers who contrasted the new instrument favorably to the noisy racket of the harpsichord. Speaking disdainfully of the composer William Babel (1690–1723), who had dabbled in a number of early harpsichord variations based on Handel's operatic themes, Burney noted the liberating effect Johann Christian Bach's arrival in London had on the operatic transcriptions:

> [Babel] seems to have been the first, in this country at least, who thinned, simplified, and divested the Music of keyed-instruments of the crowded and complicated harmony, and which from the convenience of the clavier, and passion for full and elaborate Music, it had been embarrassed from its earliest cultivation. This author acquired great celebrity by wire-drawing the favourite songs of the opera of Rinaldo, and others of the same period, into showy and brilliant lessons, which by mere rapidity of finger in playing single sounds, without assistance of taste, espression, harmony, or modulation, enable the performer to astonish ignorance, and acquire the reputation of a great player at a small expence. There is no instrument so favourable to such frothy and unmeaning Music as the harpsichord [...]. At length, on the arrival of the late Mr. (Christian) Bach, and construction of piano-fortes in this country, the performers on keyed-instruments were obliged wholly to change their ground; and instead of surprising by the seeming labour and dexterity of execution, had the real and more useful difficulties of taste, expression, and light and shade, to encounter. (Burney [1789] 1957: 996–997)

The typical piano accompaniment for opera airs at the end of the eighteenth century was as simple as had been the harpsichord transcriptions earlier in the century. It usually consisted of the outer voices filled in with a simple harmony that could be played with the right hand. On occasion, slightly more elaborate figurations in the left hand might be called for. (No more, we should note, were keyboardists expected to understand and realize the figured bass.) We can see a typical example composed and published by Johann Adam Hiller. Taking the music from one of his own *Singspiels*, *Die Liebe auf dem Lande* (a genre that offers yet another sign of growing middle-class influence on changing operatic tastes), Hiller offered his readers a transcription of a duet playable by a single pianist. While a few instrumental cues are indicated in the score by the use of a smaller type face (an innovation of Breitkopf), the overall instrumental sonority is rendered in the monochromatic tone of the piano-forte.

This transcription stands to the *Singspiel* aria as does that of a small black and white engraving to the larger painted canvas that it attempts to reproduce. Indeed, more than once, these piano transcriptions were described by contemporaries as kinds of engravings: each takes a large work and reduces it for mass reproduction by washing away the colors and instrumental timbres. Most important, both the engraving and the piano transcription serve a utilitarian function of bringing the artwork from the glare of the public sphere into the intimate confines of the parlor and dressing room.

There is one other observation to make about Figure 41.5. The aria transcribed actually is part of a larger vocal score of Hiller's complete *Singspiel*; it was not a part of some collection of individual "favorite songs." "Ha, deiner Liebe droht" comes from a *Klavier-Auszug* that constitutes the complete work in piano transcription; all arias, duets, and choruses, the overture, and if there are any, even dance and incidental music, are included. (About the only thing left out of these full scores are the recitatives, which were rare in the genre of the *Singspiel* in any case.) This marks a

FIGURE 41.5 Excerpt of Johann Adam Hiller's "Ha, deiner Liebe droht" from *Die Liebe auf dem Lande* (1768). Reproduction courtesy of the Newberry Library.

major new commodity of music printing that would henceforth become all too familiar thereafter: the piano-vocal score, called *partition* in French or *spartito* in Italian (see Hansemann 1943; Christensen 2000). While the piano vocal score certainly had a use for domestic, amateur performance, it had another more utilitarian function: it became an indispensable aid for studying and rehearsing the opera for singers and producers. Indeed, for many operas well into the nineteenth century, it would have been the only printed record of the music, given that full orchestral scores were rarely published due to their extravagant expense and low demand. While Hiller may not be the inventor of the piano vocal score (Baussen's engraved folios of Lully's operas arguably deserve that honor), Hiller's editions are certainly the first practical vocal scores in their compact, oblong quarto format. And Hiller was the first to recognize the democraticizing virtues of the piano in the domestication of opera.

Yet even the poor *Klavier-Auszug* was more than what most amateur musicians needed, however simplified it might be to play. More often than not, consumers only wanted to play select "hits" from a given opera. For them, publishers continued to offer the usual song collections or individual excerpts for purchase. As we scan publication lists starting in the early nineteenth century, the number of such collections reaches mind-numbing quantities. A colorful assortment of "operatic gems," "choice ayres," and "pearls from the opera" poured forth from European publishers attempting to keep up with the seemingly insatiable demand by amateur pianists who wished to know and play the latest stage music.

Arthur Loesser has casually surmised that piano pieces based on operatic themes constituted "the largest fraction" of music published for piano between 1825 and 1875 (Loesser 1954: 361). William Lockhart has recently verified this supposition through a systematic analysis of entries in Friedrich Hofmeister's massive catalogues of nineteenth-century musical publications. Lockhart has calculated that fully 30 percent of unaccompanied piano music published between 1829 and 1900 consisted of arrangements—the vast majority drawn from the operatic repertoire (Lockhart 2012: 97–105). A peak of sorts was reached in the mid-1830s, when 47 percent of all publications for the piano consisted of such arrangements. But the percentage never dropped below 20 percent, even at the end of the century.

This is an astonishing quantity of music, consisting of thousands upon thousands of individual publications that, for the most part, are completely unknown to us today. Yet its importance for the representation and popularization of the opera can scarcely be exaggerated. That last point was certainly understood well enough in the nineteenth century. A reviewer for the *Quarterly Musical Magazine and Review* in 1822 noted with some bewilderment—but also guarded appreciation—the mania for opera arrangements:

> Arrangements are now so abundant, that it becomes necessary for us at least to announce the appearance of those principally worthy [of] notice, although little can be said of them. To those who are acquainted with the operas of MOZART and ROSSINI (and who is not?) their contents need no recommendation. It belongs to us therefore only to name the various forms in which they appear, and the amateur will select those adaptations which may best suit his taste or fall in with his instrument. They are presented to him in all shapes, as duets, with or without accompaniments for the harp, piano forte, flute, violin and violoncello. We believe MOZART's operas have been arranged in almost every possible way, and for all instruments. ROSSINI's works are now undergoing the same processes. The passion for arrangement is, we think, a little run mad—It however has its benefits: it extends very widely the knowledge of the greatest composers, for there are many persons, in the provinces especially, who have few other chances of becoming acquainted with their works. (*QMMR* 1822: 228–229)

Perhaps the most representative genre of this growing amateur culture in regard to the opera transcription was the "potpourri." We have already noted that the title was used by the French publisher Le Roy in 1784. While the potpourri has a long pedigree in music history as a genre, by the end of the eighteenth century—as suggested by Le Roy's publication—it became almost exclusively associated with opera music. Written most typically for a solo keyboardist, the potpourri became defined as a continuous mélange (a "medley") of tunes or "motives" from a single opera. By stringing together the major airs, duos, dances, and choruses of a given opera in one continuous fantasy, the potpourri became, in effect, a kind of "pocket opera" for home consumption. Little, though, would Le Roy have suspected how popular the operatic potpourri would soon become as a genre.

By the second quarter of the nineteenth century, the opera potpourri had grown into the most popular genre of opera transcription for amateur pianists. Such potpourris (sometimes also called "Souvenirs," "Reminiscences," or "Melodic Revues") continued to pour out of the printing shop, filling the piano benches of generations of amateur pianists and keeping an army of transcribers busy across Europe. Moreover, many of these potpourris were written for piano duet, one of the favorite configurations of the transcription industry. The duet offered a double advantage: Not only was the music divided up into parts, making the performance all the easier for amateur pianists, it also offered a social opportunity for performance (discussed in Christensen 1999).

Johann André of Offenbach started by publishing some of the earliest operatic potpourris for piano in the nineteenth century, a tradition it continued thanks to the efforts of transcribers such as Henri Cramer, who was able to toss off over two hundred such arrangements for its catalogue. The rival publishing enterprise of Schott produced its many versions of operatic potpourris in *volkstümlichen Einheitspreis* (popular unit price) using arrangers such as Sidney Smith, Georges Bell, Georg Kleinmichel, and Ferdinand Beyer. But undoubtedly the most prolific arranger of these piano potpourris during the entire nineteenth century was the mysterious "G. W. Marks," whose some five hundred publications in this vein were issued by the Hamburg publisher August Cranz (see Figure 41.6). (We know in fact that the name is just a pseudonym for a platoon of real-life transcribers who did the actual hack work, including the likes of the young Johannes Brahms.) But whether opera tunes appeared strung together in potpourris or

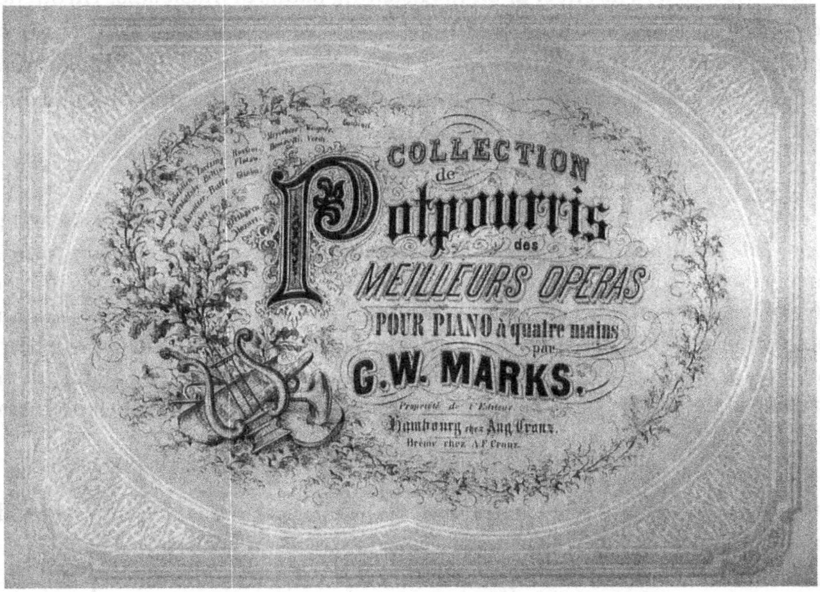

FIGURE 41.6 Title page of an opera potpourri for four hands by "G. W. Marks" (ca. 1860). Collection of Thomas Christensen.

were issued in single excerpts, amateur musicians could now replicate operatic music—and perhaps something of the opera experience—in their own homes.

Betrayal and Redemption of the Copy

But at what price? Reducing several hours of stage music to a miniaturized mélange of hit tunes lasting a few minutes could perhaps be seen as the first symptom (or even catalyst?) of a type of fetishism and distracted listening that received such scorn by critics such as Adorno in the twentieth century (for a classic statement of Adorno's position here, see Adorno 1982). Yet these dangers were already clear to more conservative pedagogues in the nineteenth century. As early as 1835, the music lexicographer, Gustav Schilling, warned piano teachers of the perils of the opera potpourri:

> Music teachers should be wary of giving these works too frequently to their students, because the purpose of the potpourri can only ever be to aid the passing of time and as pleasant amusement for the dilettantes, and musical education is never improved by them. (Schilling 1835: 207; cited in Lockhart 2012: 72)

The potpourri, Schilling concluded, was merely a "colourful mishmash with no artistic unity." It is no wonder, then, that Busoni later referred disparagingly to the genre as the "plebejischen Potpourri" (Busoni [1910] 2006: 55).

It was not just Schilling or Busoni who expressed some anxiety about the cult of the opera transcription and its effect upon the listening habits of musicians. Throughout the nineteenth century, opera transcription was subjected to searing ridicule and censorious reprobation by dyspeptic critics across Europe as deformations of the original. For every writer who applauded the democratizing potential of the potpourri or *air choisi*, there were at least two who would deplore its corruption of musical values. Wrote one exasperated Viennese critic from 1847:

> Far too many contemporary operas—or at least those originating from beyond the Rhine—die at the hands of piano arrangers before they even reach the Rubicon [...]. Scarcely has its feeble germination begun than the transcription vampires immediately descend upon the sweet, defenseless body and begin to suck out with their gluttonous snouts the few inventive and fresh ideas offered by such products in order to send into the world etudes, quadrilles, transcriptions, souvenir themes, and *airs varies* arranged for ten, twenty, sixty, or more fingers of every kind of proficiency or lack thereof. [4] (*AWMZ* 1847: 435)

For many, it was not the specific genre of the potpourri or *airs varies* that aroused ire as much as the piano washing away the colors and textures of the original music. Another Austrian critic summarized this argument succinctly in a review from 1841:

> There are so many examples where the effect can only be obtained by the instruments for which it was written, for example, the trio in the fifth act of Sibellinen

> [Les Huguenots], where the clarinet alone works indescribable magic; or the original, if somewhat odd, C minor song of Marzell [Marcel] in the first act accompanied by piccolo, bassoon, and bass drum. How empty this would all sound on the piano. Consider, too, the oboe solo in Lindpaintner's overture to Vampyr, and the English horn solo in Rossini's William Tell, the frightening effect of the horns, tremolo violins and violas with pizzicato basses in the second act finale of Weber's Der Freischütz, not to mention those effects which the poor disappearing basset horn is capable of, and countless others.[5] (*AWMZ* 1841: 411)

Yet for all that the piano was an etiolating instrument—bleaching the instrumental colors and vocal sonorities of the opera score into a bland black and white rendition—it did have an obvious utilitarian value in making music available to a vast number of amateur performers who otherwise would never have had a chance to hear this music sung in a live performance. For all that the piano transcription could be portrayed as a mass commodification of the aesthetic experience, the fact was that it *did* offer a musical experience of sorts to its consumers. Could there then have been some redemptive value to these poor, maligned facsimiles?

For a number of observers, the answer was clearly affirmative. The piano reduction, for all its obvious drawbacks, nonetheless provided a kind of musical education to vast numbers of musicians that would simply not have been possible by any other means. George Bernard Shaw was only one voice among many who noted with obvious approval the importance of the piano as an agent of musical literacy:

> One of the truest practical things Wagner ever said was that the masterpieces of music are kept alive, not at the theaters and concert-halls, but at the pianofortes of lovers of music. It is the young people who hammer away at Meyerbeer and Verdi just as other young people read Dumas and Victor Hugo; who get their knowledge of the Bible from Handel and Bach much as Marlborough got his knowledge of history from Shakespeare; who, having learnt from Mozart how to appreciate Molière, arrive at the level of epic poetry and Greek tragedy through Wagner, all with the aid of a Bord pianette and a cheap library of Peters editions [...]. The fact remains that nobody, not even a critic, can acquire more than a fragmentary musical culture from public performances alone. You may find a veteran who has heard every soprano from Pasta to Calvé, every tenor from Rubini to Van Dyk, every Don Giovanni from Ambrogetti to Maurel, every pianist from Cramer to Paderewski, and yet he may know less of the great composers than the playgoer who never reads knows of Shakespeare. (Shaw 1931: 146–147)

Might we push Shaw's argument a bit further and ask if this culture of transcription did more than just impart musical *Bildung* to the masses? Might it have itself been a positive agent for shaping the reception of music among its many practitioners? It is not out of the question. For by domesticating the operatic experience as bourgeois *Hausmusik*, the popular transcription may well have changed the nature of what opera "meant" to many listeners. After all, as we are reminded by Roger Chartier, the leading historian of reading and the book today, "when the 'same' text is apprehended through very different mechanisms of representation, it is no longer the same. Each of its forms obeys specific conventions that mold and shape the work according to the laws of that form and connect it, in differing ways, with other arts, other genres, and other texts" (Chartier 1995: 2).

What might be some of the genres and forms that the opera transcription would connect to? For amateur musicians, they could be many of the sentimental songs or lyrical piano pieces already contained in the benches of most pianists. The reception of opera music in the home parlor or drawing room (played, let us not forget, typically by female pianists) offers a radically differing aesthetic frame for the opera. And it cannot be doubted that many of the bourgeois values of sentimentality and Romanticism instilled by domestic performances of this music could well have affected the audience in the opera itself, many of whom likely got to know this music by first playing it—and hearing it—in a keyboard transcription. It could even be that the attentiveness and rapt absorption newly exhibited by concert audiences in the second quarter of the nineteenth century, which has been acutely discussed by cultural historians such as James Johnson, may have actually been developed through the cultivation of *Hausmusik*—and specifically the many replications of opera music through simplified piano transcriptions (Christensen 2000: 87; Petrat 1986: 29–55, passim).

Cults of Virtuosity

Of course operatic transcriptions were not just the province of amateurs reproducing this music in simplified arrangements in domestic settings. As I pointed out at the beginning of this chapter, there was a counter genre of operatic transcriptions performed by virtuosi—particularly piano virtuosi—that we might also consider here. It is hardly surprising that the great piano virtuosi of the nineteenth century would be drawn to opera music; after all, the first widely celebrated music virtuosi in music history were opera singers. Yet in almost every way, the virtuosic piano transcription of opera music stands as a dialectical opposite of the amateur transcription culture we have considered up to now. Rather than private, intimate music, the virtuosic transcription is patently public music for the salon and concert stage. Rather than music simplified and pruned for beginning fingers, the virtuosic transcription was complicated and demanding, beyond the capacities of all but the most accomplished pianists; it is music written by—and usually performed by—professionals. And needless to say, it inverts the gender identity; whereas the majority of domestic pianists performing the opera parlor gems in the nineteenth century could be presumed to be female, the pianists performing the virtuosic transcriptions were almost exclusively male.

We can see the beginning of the culture of the piano virtuoso already in the late eighteenth century with the genre of the variation. Tethered to the rise of the piano-forte and the genre of the potpourri, the variation became a favored staple of both domestic music culture and the more public venues of the salon and drawing room. And not surprisingly, opera themes were preferred fodder for the variation mill. Haydn indulged in the genre, while Mozart published a number of variation sets on themes by composers such as B. Schack, Gluck, Paisiello, Dezède, Salieri, and Grétry. (In the generation following his death, the favor was returned as composers drew from his operatic patrimony themes for their sets of variations; tunes from his *Zauberflöte* became some of the most popular sources for this purpose.)

By the turn of the century, composers such as Daniel Steibelt, Henri Herz, J. G. Müthel, and Joseph Gelinek were able to make virtual careers out of their many piano variations on popular opera themes. Indeed, Gelinek, a Bohemian composer active in Vienna, wrote at least 120 sets of variations, the majority on opera themes.[6] To be sure, the difficulty of Gelinek's variations rarely exceeded the capacity of an accomplished amateur pianist. At most, his typical set of variations—usually a simply transcribed opera tune in binary structure followed by a half dozen or more variations—offered formulaic embellishments or passage work on the thematic material, culminating in one or two variations in the *style brilliant*. Little by little, though, the level of technical competence demanded of the pianist in many of these opera variations increased. In many of the variations on opera themes published after the turn of the century by pianists such as Hummel, Czerny, Kalkbrenner, and—let us not forget—Beethoven, we have clear evidence that the genre was evolving from a largely amateur culture to a professional one, from the home parlors into the public space of the salon and—eventually—the concert hall.

Technically speaking, of course, such variation sets are not so much transcriptions as they are elaborations and interpretations. Yet as a means of representing and propagating operatic music outside the opera house (however transformed) they must be considered as part of the transcription culture I have been describing in this chapter. And in many ways, actually, they can be said to evince closer fidelity to the character of operatic performance than do the more prosaic transcriptions. Not only does the genre of the variation partake of the same displays of melodic embellishment and performance virtuosity that would have been familiar to anyone who had attended an opera, we might say that the performer of these variations takes on something of the persona of the operatic singer. Certainly in terms of fame and fortune, the top instrumental virtuosi of the nineteenth century competed on equal footing with any operatic diva.

There is perhaps no more paradigmatic figure to consider in this history than Paganini. As the first bona fide instrumental virtuoso to storm the entire European continent in the nineteenth century, Paganini relied on the genre of the opera variation for much of his concert successes. Paganini penned a number of celebrated variation sets on opera themes to play in his concerts, including a set on the cavatina "Di tanti palpiti" from Rossini's *Tancredi* and "Dal tuo stellato soglio" from the same composer's "biblical" opera, *Mosè*, in 1819. (This last aria, incidentally, often called the "Moses Prayer," became one of the favorite themes for composers to treat in variation sets during the nineteenth century. Still, no one but Paganini would have dared to write a variation set in which the violin soloist is restricted to a single G string!) Paganini's opera variations really became small operatic *scene* in their own right, complete with cantabile introductions, recitative-like transitions, and the cabaletta theme laden with hair-raising passage work (unplayable in his day by any but Paganini), rivaling the vocal prowess of a Pasta or Malibran. And as we well know, his variations were the inspiration for a young pianist named Franz Liszt, whose earliest compositions included a set of variations on a theme of Rossini in the style of Paganini (*Variations brillantes sur un thème de G. Rossini*, ca. 1824, S. 149).

As ubiquitous as variations sets were at the beginning of the nineteenth century, they were soon overtaken in popularity by another genre: the opera paraphrase. Much like the opera potpourri that we earlier looked at, the paraphrase takes several themes from a given opera and treats them freely in a kind of fantasy. In the virtuosic paraphrase, though, the material is radically transformed—and augmented—beyond that of the amateur medley that constituted the publications of G. W. Marks and his like (Suttoni 1973).

The most celebrated pianist of the opera paraphrase was certainly the Viennese pianist Sigismund Thalberg (1812–1871). Of his eighty-two published works, the majority were operatic paraphrases that he would take on his numerous European tours and perform to astounded audiences. (Thalberg was most famous, perhaps, for a special keyboard technique he developed that allowed him to play the operatic melody in an inner voice with his thumbs while his other fingers would provide dazzling harmonic figurations and embellishments in the outer voices, thus suggesting what was termed by his contemporaries as a "three-handed" technique of performance.) But Thalberg was only one of dozens of piano virtuosi who flocked to European stages performing operatic variations and paraphrases (Hamilton 2008). And let us not overlook the other instrumental virtuosi who also proliferated in the middle of the nineteenth century; virtually every orchestral instrument had a famous virtuoso or two, who could be counted on to perform their own brilliant variations and paraphrases of operatic material. It was a rare concert, indeed, in which some kind of operatic music was not heard on a program, whether as a piano paraphrase, a singer performing a few choice arias with accompaniment, or an orchestra playing a favorite overture. And all of these, we should keep in mind, would normally occur on the very same program, such being the eclectic nature of the nineteenth-century concert.

With Franz Liszt, the genre of the paraphrase ascended to its greatest artistic merit. In fifty-seven solo piano publications composed on operatic themes (and called, variously, "Réminiscences," "Fantasies," "Paraphrases," "Illustrations," or "Divertissements"), Liszt elevated the paraphrase beyond the typical mélange of operatic themes into works of unprecedented artistic imagination. Of course, there were always the virtuosic finger pyrotechnics in these works for which he—and the genre— was so celebrated. But Liszt also seemed intent to add his own compositional imprint in these many concert adaptations, particularly after 1840, when he began rethinking the virtuosic paraphrase and considering ways to make the genre have more artistic integrity (Kregor 2010). The result was a paraphrase that did not attempt to provide a parade of themes in the vein of the potpourri merely to display the pianist's technical skills, but rather to take selective thematic ideas deliberately from the opera and meld them into a coherent musical composition.

A good case in point is the *Réminiscences de 'Norma'*, composed in 1841. With unprecedented verve and imagery, Liszt's fantasy presents us a dramatic psychological portrait of the opera's eponymous heroine. In just sixteen minutes, Liszt is able to convey musically the epic struggle Norma faces between her duty as devoted mother and Druid high priestess and her thwarted passion for Pollione, a Roman soldier. Themes from the opening of the opera are freely developed and juxtaposed in ever closer contiguity with music drawn from the tragic finale of the opera. This ultimately culminates in furious climax in which the tragic conflict of duty and passion is brilliantly rendered through a contrapuntal tour de force in which discrete thematic materials are now merged—or better put, set on a course of tragic collision. In compositional ingenuity, Liszt's *Réminiscences de 'Norma'* is a dazzling, penetrating study of the dreadful forces tugging at Norma's psyche, one that is perhaps only conveyable in performance by a solo pianist.

Not all of Liszt's adaptations, of course, are quite so free. His transcriptions of much of Wagner's music, for example, are surprisingly faithful. That is to say, while there are certainly the pianistic challenges we have come to expect in anything by Liszt, his transcriptions still track the score with relative fidelity. For all its fearsome difficulties, his rendition of the *Tannhäuser* overture (1848) is a remarkable facsimile of the original. (Liszt is even able to convey a range of instrumental sonorities and colors by means of voicing, articulation, and pedaling; see Rehding 2010.) His transcription of *Parsifal*, on the other hand, is all the more astounding for its austere simplicity. In all cases, though, Liszt approaches the transcription as a *pianistic* genre. That is to say, his aim is never rendition, rather, a "transcription of the spirit" that exploits the sonic capabilities of the piano as a technological medium—and ultimately as a "universal" musical utterance (Gooley 2010).

We have seen how, through the transcription and its many sub-genres, operatic music enjoyed a vibrant life for over two centuries outside the opera house—a life that in many ways was as important to the reception and meaning of opera as that which took place on the stage. By allowing musicians of differing social levels, of varying performing abilities, and working over vast geographical and cultural distances to hear this music, the operatic transcription radically extended the circulatory system of opera in society.

One final point as a closing thought: unlike the passive consumption of music through recordings that so characterizes contemporary listening, transcription culture was an active one in which pianists themselves (whether amateurs in their own homes or professionals on the concert stage) enacted the music. Transcription allows—and in fact demands—that the pianist not only become invested in the performance, but *part* of the performance. By the early twentieth century, of course, passive listening encouraged by mechanical media became the primary means by which operatic music (or any music, for that matter) was experienced in the home. It is thus not a coincidence that the ascendance of the phonograph (and later the radio) marks in almost inverse proportion the decline of the opera transcription as part of the greater operatic experience of its many fans. (Virtually the only stage music reproduced anymore for home performance comes from the Broadway musical.) But what price have we paid for this transformation? As we still very much live in this age of "mechanical reproduction" of the work of art (alluding to Benjamin's famous diagnosis; Benjamin 1968), a glance backwards to a time when musicians had a greater personal investment in the music they heard offers us a melancholic reminder of one of the costs we have paid for our technological triumphs.

See also: Sources, Rehearsal Practices, Autographs, Memorabilia, and the Aesthetics of Collecting, The Operatic Canon

Notes

1. Actually, "transcriptions" might not be the most appropriate term to describe these publications, as there was a wide spectrum of latitude in how freely operatic music was appropriated and reworked by musicians. Properly speaking, a "trans-scription" is a literal "writing down" of some performance in notation. A more precise word here may be "arrangement" (or perhaps "adaptation" or "paraphrase"). But as the forms and varieties of these arrangements were so numerous, I will take some liberty with my nomenclature and follow current usage by grouping them all together within a general "culture of transcription" (Schröder 1994).
2. There were other spin-offs, and here, once again, Cluer paved the way by issuing packs of playing cards in which each card was adorned with a single song melody (see Kidson et al. 2001).
3. Not that this was the first time public music migrated to a more intimate, private sphere. Over a century and a half earlier, English Catholics, suffering under the repression of Tudor Protestants, appropriated much of their sacred repertoire, originally written to be sung by choruses within the great cavernous vaults of English cathedrals, and sang them secretively as intimate chamber music in the privacy of their homes (see Milsom 1995: 161–179).
4. "Gar viele der modernen Opern wenigstens jene von überrheinischem Ursprunge sterben durch die Clavier-Arrangeurs ab, noch ehe sie den Rubikon überschreiten [...]. Kaum hat es seine armliche Vegetation begonnen, flugs hangen sich die arrangierenden Vampyre an das zarte schwächliche Wesen, und saugen mit gierigem Rüssel, die wenigen gesunden und frischen Gedanken, die ein solches Produkt bringt, auf, um sie als Etuden, Quadrillen, Transcriptionen, Souvenirs Themes und Airs variés für 10, 20, 60, oder mehr Finger von jeder Fertigkeit, oder auch Unfertigkeit arrangirt, in die Welt zu senden."
5. "Es gibt der Beispiele so viele, so die Wirkung nur durch das Instrument, für welches geschrieben ward, erzielt werden kann, z. B. das Terzett im fünften Acte der Sibellinen, wo die Clarinette allein einem unbeschreiblichen Zauber hat, der originelle, wenn auch bizarre Chanson des Marzell im ersten Acte sein C-minore, mit Piccolo, Fagott, und Grand-Tambour; wie mank ist er schon auf dem Piano. Das Oboesolo in Lindpaintner's Ouverture zum "Vampyr," jenes für's englische Horn, in Rossini's "Tell," schauerliche Wirkung der Hörner, der tremilirenden Violinenen und Violen mit pizzikirenden Bassen im Finale des zweiten Actes von Weber's "Freischütz," jener Effecte nicht zu gedenken, welche die leider verschwindenden Bassenhörner nach sich ziehen und so unzählige andere."
6. One set of Gelinek's variations on the cavatina "Nel cor più non mi sento" from Paisiello's opera *L'amor contrastato* was reprinted in no less than eight differing editions (see Hader 2006: preface, n.p.).

BIBLIOGRAPHY

Adorno, Theodor W. 1982. “On the Fetish-Character in Music and the Regression of Listening.” In *The Essential Frankfurt School Reader*, edited by Andrew Arato and Eike Gebhardt, 270–299. New York: Continuum.

d’Anglebert, Jean-Henry. [1689] 1965. *Pièces de Clavecin*. Monuments of Music and Music Literature in Facsimile. New York: Broude Brothers.

AWMZ. 1847. “Aus Brünn.” *Allgemeine Wiener Musik-Zeitung* 108 (September 4): 435–436.

——. 1841. “Über das Arrangieren.” *Allgemeine Wiener Musik-Zeitung* 97 (August 14): 411.

Benjamin, Walter, 1968. “The Work of Art in the Age of Mechanical Reproduction.” In *Illuminations*, edited and translated by Hannah Arendt, 217–252. New York: Harcourt, Brace, and World.

Burney, Charles. [1776–1789] 1957. *A General History of Music from the Earliest Ages to the Present Period*. 2 vols. Re-edition with critical and historical notes by Frank Mercer. New York: Dover.

Busoni, Ferruccio. [1910] 2006. “Wert der Bearbeitung.” In *Von der Einheit der Musik*, edited by Martina Weindel. Wilhelmshaven: Florian Noetzel.

Chartier, Roger. 1995. *Forms and Meanings: Texts, Performances, and Audiences from Codex to Computer*. Philadelphia: University of Pennsylvania Press.

Christensen, Thomas. 2000. “Public Music in Private Spaces: Piano-Vocal Scores and the Domestication of Opera.” In *Music and the Cultures of Print*, edited by Kate van Orden, 67–93. New York: Garland Press.

——. 1999. “Four-Hand Piano Transcription and Geographies of Nineteenth-Century Musical Reception.” *Journal of the American Musicological Society* 52/2: 275–292.

Chung, David. 2004. *Jean-Baptiste Lully: 27 brani d’opera trascritti per tastiera nei secc. XVII e XVIII*. Bologna: Ut Orpheus Edizioni.

——. 1996. “Keyboard Arrangements of Lully’s Music and Their Significance for French Harpsichord Music.” PhD diss., University of Cambridge.

Cluer, John. 1724. *A Pocket Companion for Gentlemen and Ladies: Being a Collection of the Finest Opera Songs & Airs in English and Italian. A Work Never Before Attempted. Carefully Corrected & Also Figured for the Organ, Harpsichord and Spinet by Mr. Richard Neale*. London: Cluer’s Printing Office.

Girdham, Jane. 1997. *English Opera in Late Eighteenth-Century London: Stephen Storace at Drury Lane*. Oxford: Clarendon Press.

Gooley, Dana. 2010. “Stormy Weather: Liszt and the Noisiness of Pianistic Mediation.” *Musik Theorie: Zeitschrift für Musikwissenschaft* 25/3: 223–245.

Gustafson, Bruce. 1995. “France.” In *Keyboard Music before 1700*, edited by Alexander Silbiger, 90–146. New York: Schirmer Books.

——, and David Fuller. 1990. *A Catalogue of French Harpsichord Music 1699–1780*. New York: Oxford University Press.

Hader, Wolfram, ed. 2006. *Joseph Gelinek, Sechs variation über die Cavatina “Nel cor più non mi sento” von Giovanni Paisiello für Klavier*. Frankfurt: Laurentius-Musikverlag.

Hamilton, Kenneth. 2008. *After the Golden Age: Romantic Pianism and Modern Performance*. New York: Oxford University Press.

Hansemann, Marlise. 1943. *Der Klavier-Auszug von den Anfangen bis Weber*. Leipzig: Helmut Meyen.

Hiller, Johann Adam. 1768. *Die Liebe auf dem Lande*. Leipzig: Breitkopf.
Hunter, David. 1997. *Opera and Song Books Published in England 1703–1726: A Descriptive Bibliography*. London: Bibliographical Society.
Johns, Adrian. 1998.*The Nature of the Book: Print and Knowledge in the Making*. Chicago: University of Chicago Press.
Kidson, Frank, et al. 2001. "Cluer, John." In *Grove Music Online. Oxford Music Online*. Available: http://www.oxfordmusiconline.com/subscriber/article/grove/music/05989 (accessed February 6, 2014).
Kregor, Jonathan. 2010. *Liszt as Transcriber*. Cambridge: Cambridge University Press.
Leopold, Silke. 1992. *Musikalische Metamorphosen: Formen und Geschichte der Bearbeitung*. Kassel: Bärenreiter.
Lockhart, William. 2012. "Listening to the Domestic Music Machine: Keyboard Arrangement in the Nineteenth Century." PhD diss., Humboldt-Universität zu Berlin.
Loesser, Arthur. 1954. *Men, Women and Pianos: A Social History*. New York: Simon and Schuster.
Milsom, John. 1995. "Sacred Songs in the Chamber." In *English Choral Practice 1400–1650*, edited by John Morehen, 161–179. Cambridge: Cambridge University Press.
Petrat, Nicolai. 1986. *Hausmusik des Biedermeier im Blickpunkt der zeitgenössischen musikalischen Fachpresse (1815–1848)*. Hamburg: Karl Dieter Wagner.
Presser, Diether. 1955. "Die Opernbearbeitung des 19. Jahrhunderts." *Archiv für Musikwissenschaft* 12/3: 228–245.
QMMR. 1822. "New Arrangements." *Quarterly Musical Magazine and Review* 4: 228–229.
Ranum, Patricia M. 1990. "'Mr de Lully en trio': Etienne Loulié, the Foucaults, and the Transcription of the Works of Jean-Baptiste Lully (1673–1702)." In *Jean-Baptiste Lully: Actes du colloque Saint-Germain-en-Laye—Heidelberg 1987*, edited by Jérôme de la Gorce and Herbert Schneider, 309–330. Laaber: Laaber.
Rehding, Alexander. 2010. "Domestizierte Virtuosität: Zu Klavierbearbeitungen von Wagners *Tannhäuser*." *Musik Theorie: Zeitschrift für Musikwissenschaft* 25/3: 199–221.
Répertoire International des Sources Musicales [RISM]. *Recueils imprimés xviiie Siècle*. 1964. Series B2. Munich: Henle.
Rose, Stephen. 2005. "Music in the Marketplace." In *The Cambridge History of Seventeenth-Century Music*, edited by Tim Carter and John Butt, 55–87. Cambridge: Cambridge University Press.
Schilling, Gustav 1835. "Potpourri." *Encyclopädie der gesammten musikalischen Wissenschaften oder Universal-Lexicon der Tonkunst*. Stuttgart: Franz Heinrich Köhler.
Schröder, Gesine. 1994. "Bearbeitung." In *Die Musik in Geschichte und Gegenwart*. I: 1321–1337. Kassel: Bärenreiter.
Shaw, George Bernard. 1931. *Music in London, 1890–94*. Vol. 1 of *The Collected Works of Bernard Shaw*, edited by Ayot St. Lawrence. New York: Wm. H. Wise.
Smith, William C. 1970. *Handel: A Descriptive Catalogue of the Early Editions*. 2nd ed. Oxford: Basil Blackwell.
Spink, Ian, ed. 1989. *Choice Ayres, Songs & Dialogues to Sing to One Theorbo-lute or Bass-viol. Being Most of the Newest Ayres and Songs, Sung at Court and at the Publick Theatres… Newly Re-printed with Large Additions*. 1676. London: John Playford. Reprinted in *Music for London Entertainment 1660–1800*. Series A: Vol. 5A. London: Stainer and Bell.
Suttoni, Charles. 1973. "Piano and Opera: A Study of the Piano Fantasies Written on Opera Themes in the Romantic Era." PhD diss., New York University.

CHAPTER 42

VISUAL MEDIA

MARCIA J. CITRON

In a review of the recent collection *Wagner and Cinema*, W. Anthony Sheppard questions the meaning of "and" in the volume's title (Sheppard 2011: 444; Joe and Gilman 2010). He is riffing on the legendary philosophizing of Tristan and Isolde in their Act II duet, where "and" purportedly unlocks the nature of their relationship and leads to Schopenhauerian insights on love beyond death. For Sheppard, "and" becomes the starting point of an extended discussion of the ways in which Wagner is associated with cinema and how the collection plays out the relationships.

The little connective holds comparable significance in the broader arena of opera's relationship with film. Since the start of critical inquiry twenty-five years ago (Tambling 1987), a fundamental question has concerned the nature of the relationship. Is it one of equality? Does opera take precedence? Is it inevitably so because of the preexistent status of opera and its rhetorical force? Interestingly, the first response, by Tambling, was a strong attempt to criticize opera and what it represents. According to Tambling, most films of operas promote a regressive social agenda because opera is reactionary and culturally harmful. The most successful opera-films work against the opera or its music and use it for leftist political critique—for example, Joseph Losey's *Don Giovanni* (1978). Beyond its pointed ideology, Tambling's book introduced the idea that the opera/film intersection should not place opera in a favored position. It also set the stage for the critical notion that the combination creates an independent work that is larger than and different from the sum of its parts. Meanwhile, the growth in media studies and its components—cinema, television, technology, sound, spectatorship, and film music—has provided fertile ground for subsequent work. Most research has shifted to the domain of musicology from other fields (Tambling, for example, is in comparative literature). The move is unthinkable without musicology's own expansion into new areas, especially film music and popular music, and its attraction to interdisciplinarity and criticism in the wake of Kerman's (1985) challenge to the field.

The subject of opera and film is much more than "opera-film" and demonstrates the complexity of the connective. Opera is not an infrequent participant in mainstream film, that is, a film that is not entirely made up of an opera. Sometimes opera appears as part of a diegetic performance in the fiction. Not only does this illuminate contemporary views of opera and its rituals, but it shows opera's ability to contribute something central to the filmic story and comment on it. In the Marx Brothers' *A Night at the Opera* (1935), the opera scene forms a "site of anarchy" (Koch 1986: 25–26) that encapsulates the comedic and narrative turns of the story while it mocks the genre's pretense (Grover-Friedlander 2005: 33–50; Kramer 2002: 133–144). Other visits assume a larger narrative role. *Moonstruck* (1987) may be extreme in this respect, but no one would deny that it is one of the most beloved movies of any genre (Citron 2010b: 173–211). The performance of *La bohème* at the Metropolitan Opera that is attended by the lead couple seals their romance and bonds the skeptical Loretta (Cher) to the opera-obsessed Ronny (Nicolas Cage), the poetic baker. But it also is the culmination of the wacky operatic tone of the screenplay (which won an Oscar for John Patrick Shanley) and the many excerpts from *Bohème* on the soundtrack. Like the most successful films that engage opera, *Moonstruck* is much more than a wonderful movie: It ends up telling us a great deal about Puccini's opera and affects our view of the work when we encounter it on the stage.

Another kind of link reverses the terms and reframes the connection. In this ontological variation, a film takes on the qualities of opera to the point where it can be called operatic. Perhaps the most well-known example is Coppola's *Godfather* trilogy (Citron 2010b: 19–57). As in most recent work in opera and film, it is not easy to characterize the main theoretical underpinnings of the study. Across the field, most scholars start with the film and see where its musical and narrative elements lead, which usually involves multifaceted observations and newly constructed theories to fit the work. Put a bit differently, scholarship on opera and film operates in a fluid playing field drawn from many disciplines and resists a definable body of theoretical perspectives. It trades in diversity. This is all to the good. It leads to flexible, musically informed interpretations that proceed from the characteristics of the particular opera, film, medium, and director. Thus it makes most sense in the present forum to discuss the main approaches in terms of specific films (and authors) instead of specific theories. That having been said, I will mention a few issues and approaches that have attracted attention under the categories of media, music, and technology. These set the stage for the case studies that occupy the second half of the chapter.

Media

While the ontological question is largely settled for opera-film—the opera/film intersection operates as an independent work—it is still not clear-cut across the wider swath of opera's interaction with visual media. Opera in medial form is a product of the general societal trend toward media convergence, whether as televised shows streamed to a laptop or iPad, or PowerPoint presentations with integrated music and video. In this fast-changing environment, there are potentially unlimited possibilities for opera's involvement with visual media, and categorization of opera's status and participation thus becomes challenging. Semiotics offers a promising path for dealing with the combinations under the rubric of intermediality, which has been used productively in a few studies (Kuhn 2005; Citron 2010b). The theory of intermediality exists in several forms, including those proposed by Wolf (1999) and Rajewsky (2002). Wolf's open-ended system for denoting the relative contribution of the medial components is particularly helpful when considering the role and style of the music, as it leaves ample room for interpretive judgment. Wolf offers two large categories—overt intermediality and covert intermediality. In an overt encounter, the dominant signifiers of each medium are present and there is a sense of a real hybrid. In a covert situation, the main signifiers of only one medium are present. A common example of covert intermediality occurs when opera music in a mainstream film acts as underscoring and thus falls under the purview of film (as film-score music), not opera. Viewer knowledge can play a major role in the determination. An opera-informed viewer might continue to perceive the music as opera, while a general viewer would hear it as part of the film's soundtrack. This suggests that the semiotic grid needs to be tempered with the realities of spectatorship, knowledge, and other factors of the receiving experience.

While we cannot know what the future will bring, many imaginative examples of media convergence in opera and film already exist. The 1987 film *Aria* comes from a time when big-budget opera-films experienced broad distribution and MTV rose to international fame (Joe 1999; Citron 2010b: 58–93). Producer Don Boyd's project represents an interesting response to the two movements. It consists of ten pop-infused segments from diverse operas by diverse film directors (most unknown figures). While the experiment did not alter the course of opera and film and seems dated despite its avant-garde aims, it demonstrates the potential for imaginative takes on visually reproduced opera and offers a few magnificent segments that seriously affect our view of the source opera. Particularly memorable is Franc Roddam's "Liebestod," an explicitly sensual visualization of Wagner's charged music. Cartoons have also stuck their noses into opera. Who can forget the hilarious Bugs Bunny animation *What's Opera, Doc?* (1957) and its cry of "Kill the wabbit" sung to the Ride of the Valkyries. A more recent example of media convergence is Bill Viola's *Tristan Project* video (Kramer 2010; Joe 2010a, 2010b).

From the side of staged opera, more and more productions include film and video projections, while directors use cinematic principles to integrate their concepts with the sets. This "new" approach follows from famous historical examples. For example, in *Parsifal*, the landscape backdrop that moves sideways during the Transformation Music in Act I reverses direction in Act III. And in *Lulu*, the impact of the upstart filmic medium appears in a real film complete with Berg's "Film Music," composed for the purpose. More recently, the convergence of opera with stage and mediated processes appears with stunning impact in the Metropolitan Opera's popular HD broadcasts in movie theaters (Sheppard 2007). Other houses have followed suit. In an interesting variation, the Glyndebourne Festival has begun to offer live streaming of productions on their Internet site, including their celebrated production of *Die Meistersinger*, aired in the summer of 2011.

The move toward convergence floats in fascinating tension with the recognition of difference by dint of the multiplicity of visual media and their individual characteristics. Television has been theorized as a separate entity from cinema (Ellis 1992). It has its own flow, place of consumption, conditions of viewership, physical scale, and cultural role. The televised relay broadcast from the opera house is an important element in the history of opera and film (Citron 2000: 40–50). The studio film tailored for television flourished in Europe in the 1970s and 1980s and preserved important work of figures such as Götz Friedrich and Jean-Pierre Ponnelle. But with the advent of large-screen TV and the fact that much viewing takes place as video playback or on a personal device, the aesthetic differences between television and cinema have blurred. This is not to say that television and cinema have converged into some amorphous "film" middle ground. It just means that the theorized characteristics of the two should be tempered and not considered as determining of the final product. For example, the breakneck montage of contemporary cinema has infiltrated television editing, and televisual style has informed many cinematic works. As the relay has transferred (mostly) to the cinema screen and the economic interests behind TV studio films have waned, the impact of television *qua* television has receded of its own accord. Most recent work in opera and film has skirted the issue altogether—not in any intentional way, but because it doesn't loom large in what is significant about a particular medial treatment.

If we scroll back a bit, Walter Benjamin's famous ideas about mediated art are worth remembering (Benjamin 2008). While most scholars are comfortable enough with the loss of aura that Benjamin ascribes to reproduced opera, tension lurks in some quarters of the broader musical community. Many singers are skeptical toward mediated opera because it counters the vitality and physical embodiment of live opera—a position argued by Abel (1996). But even the live relay, whether on television or in the movie theater, is mediated to some degree. Benjamin's loss of aura is less certain. Moreover, as Sheppard notes, a new kind of aura takes hold for those in the movie theater (Sheppard 2007: 383–386). We are not physically at the Met, but a short aesthetic distance away. This "sense of occasion" (Citron 2000: 49) is critical and lures people back for more HD productions. In any event, the live/mediated issue does not amount to an either/or choice, or shouldn't. Each type of presentation has something important to offer. It is critical that both continue full force, even as the two idioms come closer together and spark creative responses to the other.

Music

In most films, the style of the operatic music has a direct bearing on how the film turns out—its choices in key elements such as setting, montage, narrative, pacing, meaning, and relationship with other film music (if there is any). Thus opera studies supply an important resource for scholars of opera and film. This can range from traditional studies of a composer's operas, as in the Cambridge Opera Handbooks, to newer takes on the repertoire, for instance those devoted to narrative, performativity, or a more sophisticated representational apparatus. I mention this obvious cache because the field runs the risk of overstressing filmic aspects and overlooking the import of the particular opera music in the filmic product. This musical perspective works hand in hand with film-music issues. Gorbman's (1987) seminal categories of diegetic and non-diegetic have provided the base for inquiry into opera and film. Although the discursive makeup of opera-film does not lend itself readily to these concepts, they play an important role in mainstream film that involves opera. Yet, recent film-music studies have shown that they often prove inadequate in conveying a sense of what is happening in a particular place (see, for example, Stilwell 2007; Neumeyer 2009; and Winters 2010). Witt (2006) offers one suggestive variation for opera and film—the notion of psychodiegetic music, which refers to a character's internal state expressed in the music. Thus, for example, when Loretta is "moonstruck" with a burst of Puccini's music as she kicks a can down the street, she doesn't literally hear the music but internalizes it psychodiegetically as she bonds with her lover, who is blasting it from afar on the phonograph. The moment also demonstrates the usefulness of Chion's notion of the *acousmêtre*: heard music without the presence of a visible source (Chion 1994: 71–73, 126–131). Abbate ([1991] 1996) helped to popularize the concept in musicology as she allied it with the narratological idea of ventriloquism. Ventriloquism characterizes the workings of most opera-films, as they rely on playback and dubbing to render the operatic music, substituting "dumb vessels" for emoting bodies. In the larger picture, the many ways in which operatic music appears in film fall under the purview of the soundtrack and what it does in visually recorded media (Joe 2013).

The operatic voice in film is key to the work of Grover-Friedlander (2005, 2011). In many films the voice stages its own death or its afterlife. Nowhere is this more apparent than in two films centered on Maria Callas. Fellini's *E la nave va* (1983) concerns a dead opera diva, one Edmea Tutua, whose ashes are carried out to sea for a ceremonial spreading attended by adoring fans and colleagues (Grover-Friedlander 2005: 131–152). During the emotional journey the voice of Tutua is heard wafting on records: the aural remains of a vanished singer who lives on in the recorded voice. Tutua, of course, represents Callas—not only by way of the media circus that attended her death, but her name. "Edmea," Tutua's first name, is an anagram of a famous filmic part Callas played, the title role in Pasolini's *Medea* (1969). In Zeffirelli's cinematic *hommage* to his idol, *Callas Forever* (2002), Fanny Ardant is the singer herself, now near the end of her life. Callas's recorded voice from her prime is resuscitated for the soundtrack of an opera-film, and the aging star is to lip-synch to her earlier voice. Visual and aural death/life intersect powerfully in Zeffirelli's film. Grover-Friedlander persuasively interrogates the vocal meanings in real and mediated opera and their connection with living icons and their reproduced vocal remains (Grover-Friedlander 2011: 45–75).

Technology

Technological mediation has resonance beyond the voice, and in many films opera is emitted from some kind of apparatus. The phonograph has proved an attractive vehicle. For example, Stilwell (2006), discussing teeny-bopper films, shows how the phonograph carves out a masculine sphere for a lead character. While this is a far cry from opera, the connection between masculinity and technology can also be seen in *Moonstruck*. Thus, as Ronny controls the phonograph space where *Bohème* is played, he thereby controls the sexual dynamic with Loretta. In other films opera-on-the-phonograph has different associations. Werner Herzog's *Fitzcarraldo* (1982) tells the story of an opera-obsessed European (Klaus Kinski) around 1900 who is determined to build an opera house in the Amazon jungle (Leppert 2007). Facing enormous practical difficulties in negotiating the ship on water and over land, the crazed protagonist cranks up opera on the phonograph as he sails the river. The device stands for cultural mastery and psychological fanaticism. He never reaches his goal, but the heady days of listening to arias in a white linen suit capture the impossible idealism of his quest. In *The Shawshank Redemption*, opera wafts over the loudspeaker in a prison after an inmate (Tim Robbins) breaks into the warden's office and puts an LP of *The Marriage of Figaro* on the turntable (Hunter 2002). As the men stand transfixed by the glorious sounds of the "Letter" duet, the phonograph (by way of further sound mediation) becomes the means to spiritual liberation through opera. The phonograph also assumes narrative force in *Sunday, Bloody Sunday* (1971) (Citron 2010b: 212–245). In John Schlesinger's groundbreaking movie of a bisexual love triangle, the stunning trio "Soave sia il vento" from *Così fan tutte* occurs several times on the soundtrack. It is introduced by way of the phonograph. In a highly ritualized scene, the camera scans the tasteful cultural space of fifty-something Daniel (Peter Finch), a London physician. It comes in close to track the needle dropping on the disk. Then we hear "Soave." The apparatus not only marks Daniel as a refined aesthete, but sets up "Soave" as a diegetic element. When it is heard several times later, always without the phonographic anchor, the piece takes on a near-diegetic status or some complicated position vis-à-vis the fiction because the phonograph defined it inside the story the first time it appeared. And in the famous scene in Jonathan Demme's *Philadelphia* (1993) when AIDS patient Andy (Tom Hanks) listens to Callas's voice, the phonograph becomes the means to phantasmagoric pleasure and escape from the diseased body (Weiner 2002)—a sphere of control in an otherwise powerless life.

Opera music also hooks up with other reproducing technologies inside film. In an unusual case, the television relay of an opera forms a central role in Claude Chabrol's 1995 masterpiece *La Cérémonie* (Citron 2010b: 136–172). As *Don Giovanni* is emitted from a telecast from the Salzburg Festival, the well-heeled Lelièvres are gunned down execution-style by their resentful maid and her crazy girlfriend. Here the broadcast medium, television, is indicted for its role in bourgeois complicity, an idea thematized throughout the film. But the opera music itself is not called into question. In fact, it remains in aural form on a tape recorder that the police recover, and may lead to the capture of the killers. It creates the impression, *pace* Grover-Friedlander, that aural traces of the voice and music of opera are what's important. It may also suggest a desire to return to an era before television and the reign of the visual: an ironic comment on Chabrol's own visual enterprise of film.

Sound forms a focal point in many studies. Reflecting research into cinema and media more broadly, sound has emerged as a hot area of inquiry, in part as a response to Chion's call for greater attention to this element. Altman (2000), greatly influenced by Chion's work, argues against the tyranny of image in film work and proposes that *mise-en-bande*, the aural makeup of a film, be accorded as much weight as *mise-en-scène*. On the operatic side, Poizat posits suggestive aural elements for opera in film in his explorations of the "cry" in opera (Poizat 1992: 40–92). In another helpful move, media studies is starting to theorize the very quality of the sound world in film: what has been dubbed the sound design or sound landscape (Buhler, Neumeyer, and Deemer 2011: 23). This is promising for opera and film. What is the quality of the musical sound? Resonant? Dry? Does it vary in the film? What are the expressive and semiotic implications of the sound quality at a given moment, and how do they affect the meaning of the opera music? Another useful element in the consideration of sound involves the relationship between noise and the opera music. Opera-films run the gamut in the extent to which noise appears on the soundtrack; as Altman has noted, "soundtrack" indicates much more than music, although the term is commonly used as a synonym for the music. On one end stands Francesco Rosi's *Bizet's Carmen* (1983), where everyday noises meld so seamlessly with the music that the result is a "musicalization of the noise track" that asserts film's realism instead of opera's illusion (Leicester 1994: 269). At the other extreme are films such as Hans-Jürgen Syberberg's *Parsifal* (1982), where virtually no noise intrudes to assert reality. Most opera-films lie somewhere in between. In mainstream film, opera's relationship with simultaneous noise works to calibrate the operatic-ness of the moment and to control the balance between illusion and reality. The use of dialogue works in a similar way. Intermedial theory, especially Wolf's open-ended system, has the ability to assess the impact of noise on the medial combination, and should do so whenever it is pertinent to the situation.

Puccini

In his review of *Wagner and Cinema*, Sheppard also asks the question, "Why Wagner?" He observes that "other composers (notably Puccini) could fruitfully be considered in relation to film [...]" (Sheppard 2011: 445). While no volume to date is devoted to Puccini and film, his operas have been discussed in terms of cinema. Wilson concludes that a productive path for future work on the composer lies along filmic lines (Wilson 2007: 224–228), but doesn't advocate for exploration of specific films as much as for the idea that the interpretive strategies developed for film studies could benefit analysis of the cinematic construction of the operas. Over a decade earlier, Franklin pointed out the "proto-cinematic" character of Puccini's works and described *Tosca* as a film score in everything but name (Franklin 1994; reworked in Franklin 2011: 42–47). In between, Greenwald (2001) looked into two films of *Madama Butterfly*—by Ponnelle (1973) and Frédéric Mitterrand (1995)—in a discussion of *Japonisme* in the opera. Other operas appear in mainstream film. *Turandot's* "Nessun dorma" becomes the focal point of Ken Russell's imaginative visualization for *Aria*. A highlight of the pastiche, it offers a death-and-resurrection tale that follows the "Liebestod" in an unforgettable narrative progression (Citron 2010b: 58–76). *Gianni Schicchi* figures in the soundtrack and plot of John Huston's black comedy *Prizzi's Honor* (1985), with Puccini's early sigh motive as recurring underscore and "Oh mio babbino caro" in a striking diegetic turn (Hunter 2002). And in *Moonstruck*, the populist disposition of *Bohème* persuades us to rethink the opera's cultural relationship to kitsch (Citron 2010b: 173–211).

Two recent films of *Tosca* engage many of the major themes of opera's intersection with visual media. Giuseppe Patroni Griffi's Tosca (conceived and produced by Andrea Andermann) bears the unusual title of a "live film." In July 1992, a live performance was beamed by satellite from the places in Rome where the action takes place and at the designated times of the day. Act I was broadcast at noon from Sant'Andrea della Valle, Act II at 8:00 PM from the Palazzo Farnese, and Act III at 6:00 AM the next morning from Castel Sant'Angelo. Almost a decade later comes Benoît Jacquot's exciting movie *Tosca* (2001), one of the most imaginative opera-films ever made. Both films break down the components of the opera and reassign them with respect to media. Medial experimentation lies at the heart of the treatments and leads to a hyper-real conception in each that is utterly appropriate to Puccini's melodramatic opera. In the process, the films negotiate the meaning of realism, artifice, and theatricality in operatic transposition, and their relationship to mediated representation of *Tosca*. Yet they do it in very different ways, and at first blush may seem like opposites. The more one looks, however, the more one sees some amazing similarities at the macro level. Just as importantly, both are vividly successful versions of *Tosca* in a media-saturated age.

Griffi's "Live Film" *Tosca* (1992)

The moniker "live film" is of course contradictory. Film denotes the camera capturing something that is then replayed, and hence isn't live, an ambiguity that Griffi plays out in his film. Liveness is "real" in some ways but manufactured or undercut in many others, complicating the ontological status of the work. When the production was first aired it was beamed live to Europe, but not, for example, the United States, where it was only first seen in 1993 in one continuous broadcast. So much for liveness. At that point the Griffi *Tosca* became a copy, and liveness was transformed from a medial signifier into a stylistic marker or mere curiosity. The video released the same year confirmed the new status of the work. Most people know the Griffi *Tosca* through video, and so the inherent contradiction of "live film" only grows with its reproduced transmission.

Another aspect of liveness in the Griffi involves currentness. At the start of the film (I take the liberty of calling it that) we see Rome below us as the sound of a helicopter fills our ears. We are whirring above the city, in a way that White (1994) likens to "reportage." Soon messages in multiple languages and alphabets stream across the screen. The images and sounds convey a sense of global optimism: a utopian vision for political unity in the wake of the newly formed European Union and its promise for the planet. The reportage goes hand in hand with liveness. We share in the optimism of the moment, of the Europe-wide transmission, and of the celebration of European culture at a seminal font, Rome. With the stress on liveness comes an emphasis on cutting-edge technology. This devolves to the very project of "live film" and what the production team is attempting to achieve with this unusual setup. Liveness foregrounds technology, which suggests reportage, which signifies technology, and so on, in a loop that is conveyed in the logo of a satellite circling around the word "Tosca" that appears before each act. Paradoxically, just as in all technologically focused entities, the new technology brandished by the transmission begins to look clunky and outdated rather quickly, an issue for this *Tosca*. Does the dated technology compromise the validity and quality of the production, or become a curious sideshow to the main event? I see it as the latter: take away the novelty, and this is still a filmic *Tosca* to be reckoned with.

Catherine Malfitano (Tosca), Plácido Domingo (Cavaradossi), and Ruggero Raimondi (Scarpia) star in a compelling rendition of the opera. In her role debut, Malfitano is suitably theatrical as the tempestuous opera diva, a quality that suffuses the medial arrangement. Although the "sets" are the actual locations, realism is challenged by the ultra-theatrical lighting that foregrounds melodrama and reasserts opera-as-theater. At the same time, we see very deep focus into the magnificent physical spaces—the visual clarity into far recesses that cinematographer Gregg Toland of *Citizen Kane* fame developed. The cavernous magnificence of Sant'Andrea della Valle is a feast for the eye as the singers perform. Equally satisfying is the sense of the Palazzo Farnese as a real building with windows in an adjoining room to the outside. In affirming the spatial depth of real places, the "film" aspect of Griffi's project comes to the fore. The camera has tremendous freedom of movement, an unlimited 360-degree perspective to capture the characters and the setting—something found in mainstream film and of course opera-film. But the combination of cinematic camerawork and live singing, as opposed to opera-film's playback, is unusual and possibly unique in visually mediated opera. Whether seen as a live broadcast or on video, it makes for an exhilarating experience.

Act I in the church (Figure 42.1) is bathed in sunlight, real and artificial, but Act II unfolds in the dark confines of a warren of rooms at night (Figure 42.2). Cinematographer Vittorio Storario ratchets up the melodrama with lurid lighting that plays up Scarpia's evil and the staginess of what happens in the Act. Some interesting and anachronistic effects are created by the claustrophobic camerawork. Often handheld, the camera frequently follows characters as if directly behind them or comes in very close to their heads. Sometimes these shots are angled from below, imparting the feel of an off-kilter emotional stance. While brilliantly capturing the horror of the plot, they have a surprising effect on modern viewers, or at least this contemporary viewer. More to the point, they remind me of a reality show. The camera "snoops" in an intruding manner, prying in a voyeuristic way from below, behind, right-in-the-eyes in front. I call it anachronistic, for reality shows did not exist in 1992. In earlier times it might have been described as a mix of soap-opera and documentary style—or what's been dubbed "docu-soap" in television studies (Langford 2005: 29). In opera-film, Peter Sellars's video updatings of the Mozart–Da Ponte operas (1991) come closest to this style (Citron 2000: 205–248), but as they still imply a "fourth wall," they are not really comparable.

FIGURE 42.1 Griffi's *Tosca*, Act I in Sant'Andrea Della Valle, with Plácido Domingo. © Rada Films.

FIGURE 42.2 Griffi's *Tosca*, Act II in Palazzo Farnese, with Ruggero Raimondi and Catherine Malfitano. © Rada Films.

Captured live, the performance in this *Tosca* does not entail playback of previously recorded singing. This avoids the problems of coordination that arise with lip-synching. Real singerly physicality is foregrounded. In its many close-ups, the camera does not shy away from vibrating lips, tongues, and throats. There are no ghostly vessels here, *pace* the charge hurled at early film and some opera-films, and no ventriloquism. Opera as embodied performance is emphasized, not some indirect process filtered through technology. But technology is engaged in the practical matter of coordinating the voices with the orchestra, which, in a real feat, plays simultaneously from a location almost a mile away. The venues are connected via microwave, and at the start of each act, when Zubin Mehta ascends the podium in front of the orchestra, we glimpse the television monitors he watches for coordinating with the singers at another location. Interestingly, he and the players are decked out in tuxedoes, a curious imposition of the "sense of occasion" that comes with opera in the opera house. Yet the vague black background creates a disembodied orchestra that contrasts boldly with the embodied vocal performance and its location. Singerly embodiment does not equate with comfort, however. The original broadcast at the original times means that the singers stayed up all night and performed at dawn, a difficult hour, to say the least. The project was saturated by strain. Although that may have enervated the mood at the start of Act III (Figure 42.3), it also dents some of opera's illusion. Or perhaps it reinforces it by showing that a constructed reality is needed for performing opera, and when conventional realism intrudes, the need for the constructedness becomes more apparent.

The tensions in "live film" also affect the sound design. The different locations yield different acoustic conditions, which Malfitano discussed in an interview before the live broadcast (Kozinn 1992). The problem is most noticeable atop Castel Sant'Angelo in

FIGURE 42.3 Griffi's *Tosca*, Act III atop Castel Sant'Angelo, with Domingo. © Rada Films.

Act III, where the open air created a strangely dry sound environment. The voices lack warmth and resonance, and there is a mismatch between the fully sonorous envelope of the orchestra, at an interior location, and the unfocused quality emitted outdoors. As a whole, the sound quality of the production was improved for the video release, and I found it to be excellent, even in the analog format of VHS. The process of post-production might be seen as a means of transitioning from the vagaries of liveness to the constructedness of film, which is essentially what the production became in video format. Another element in the transformation involved a few places where some flaw in the broadcast was replaced by pre-taped footage or edited out, for example, Domingo's "live" accidental fall in Act I. Hence liveness is nigh impossible to meld with film from a practical perspective. Nonetheless, just as with *Aria* a few years before, Griffi's experiment represents a landmark in the mediatization of opera and signals innovative projects to come.

Jacquot's *Tosca* (2001)

None is more innovative than Jacquot's *Tosca*. The widely distributed movie is one of the most innovative and complex opera-films in its range of expressive devices, visual techniques, and narrative strategies. While strongly cinematic, the film also emphasizes theater and hence opera, although many conventions of opera-film are burst. Jacquot's essay in "more is more" thus renegotiates meanings of real and artificial in filmic and operatic terms (Vincent 2011), and most powerfully with respect to the traditions of opera-film.

Unlike Griffi's straining towards authenticity, which amounts to a move toward unity, Jacquot fragments the components of opera-film. In an interview (Riding 2002), the director speaks of the decor as "quotations," but this turns out to be an apt metaphor for the whole enterprise. Music, performance, image, place, time, story, coordination, singer, character, orchestra, conductor, and star are all isolated and reworked in a fabulous mash-up that works surprisingly well. Producer Daniel Toscan du Plantier, who was also behind Losey's *Don Giovanni* and Rosi's *Bizet's Carmen*, sees the "vivisection"—the removal of some of opera's heat—as a way to make opera, especially one as "inflated" as *Tosca*, work on the screen (Riding 2002). By cooling down, *Tosca*'s "heat" has a chance to stand out even more. The passion does not get smothered under the excesses of melodrama that attend the opera, and the glorious performances of Angela Gheorghiu, Roberto Alagna, and (once again) Raimondi are suitably over the top yet held in check cinematically.

The film gives us three discursive modes: the fiction proper, excerpts from the recording session (rendered in washed-out black-and-white; see Figure 42.4), and grainy color shots of real places or locations mentioned in the text. The three intermingle during the film, sometimes in close proximity and sometimes widely spaced. The semiotic field of *Tosca* thus expands to much more than the fiction, as it takes in the producing and performing of the music track, its relationship to what becomes the film *Tosca*, and the configuration of place and its myriad connections to the work.

FIGURE 42.4 Jacquot's *Tosca*, black-and-white cutaway to recording studio in Act I, with Antonio Pappano, conductor, and Orchestra & Chorus of the Royal Opera House, Covent Garden. © Avatar Films.

The movie was filmed in a studio in Cologne, and the sets consist of "faux" versions of the real locations, bypassing authenticity as these "quotations" of real places are surrounded by a black void. In Act I the "real" elements of Sant'Andrea della Valle—its heavy pillars, floor pattern, and gilt gate leading to a chapel—are juxtaposed against the black void from which characters emerge. Tosca enters and exits in long-shot from blackness in the background (Figure 42.5). Scarpia also enters from darkness and barely leaves the nihilistic space as his black coat blends into it. Angelotti's and Cavaradossi's passings through the side chapel end in an enveloping black void, with only the gilt gate as reference point. Tosca's journey from darkness amid the grand churchly space is especially theatrical as the fixed camera captures her long walk onto the "stage set" from the constructed blackness in the rear. Diva indeed! In Act II two big elements define the room in the Palazzo Farnese: a large fireplace and Scarpia's desk. All else is black. With space barely defined it is not a theatrical concept so much as a psychological one, where the void expresses an absence of sanity and morality. Act III atop Castel San'Angelo shows a big black void around the "stage" that is the deck. The effect comes to a head at the musical climax of the lovers in "Trionfal di nova speme," where they sing in unaccompanied octaves of the triumph of hope. Jacquot gives us an extraordinary bird's-eye view of the couple as the camera pulls back with a crane shot (Figure 42.6). More and more blackness enfolds the structure. In medial terms, this stresses theater by way of the constructed artifice, but also affirms cinema and its ability to craft images in imaginative ways. The effect is quite different from the comparable place in the Griffi, where the beauty of the dawning day affirms the project's realism and its mission of liveness.

Grainy footage occurs in a few places in the film. In Act I it visualizes descriptive words in the text. For example, when Tosca sings to her lover of their "casetta" we see a jumpy handheld sequence of their house in highly stylized graininess (Figure 42.7).

FIGURE 42.5 Jacquot's *Tosca*, entrance of Tosca in Act I, with Angela Gheorghiu. © Avatar Films.

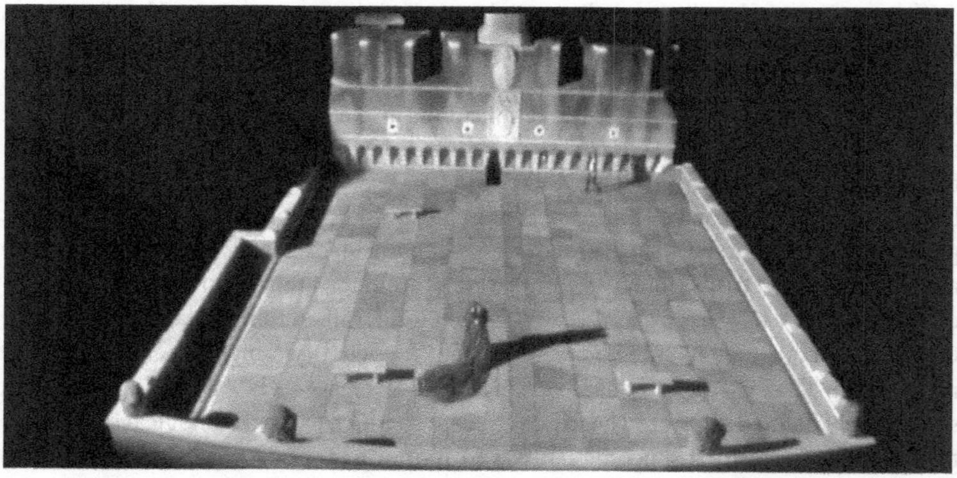

FIGURE 42.6 Jacquot's *Tosca*, "Trionfal di nova speme" in Act III, with Roberto Alagna and Gheorghiu. © Avatar Films.

A bit later, Cavaradossi tells Angelotti of the well with the concealed room where he can hide, and visual word-painting pictorializes the place in an exaggerated grainy texture. Perhaps the most mannered use of grainy film occurs in the "Te Deum." As Scarpia expresses his madness through Puccini's obsessive music, defined by an ostinato bass, Jacquot repeatedly spins the camera a full 360 degrees in a point-of-view shot around the malevolent figure. Into the whirl comes grainy footage of the real church ceiling and its now-hazy frescoed designs. Of course, it is not Scarpia who is literally turning,

FIGURE 42.7 Jacquot's *Tosca*, grainy shot of "casetta" in Act I. © Avatar Films.

but the camera that is stepping in to represent him. As in the black-on-black scheme of Scarpia in his environment, the distorted vision of iconic art sketches inner psychology and demonstrates cinema's power in opera-film to limn the inner life as well as what's on the surface.

Act II has hardly any cutaways from the fiction. Near the start, though, we see grainy footage of what appears to be the real interior of the Palazzo Farnese. Although it has many more objects than the minimal version to appear in the fiction, it takes on a ghostly quality by virtue of the film's texture. Authenticity of place seems to be defined, as in the Griffi, but Jacquot's version resembles the sort of "evocation" he mentions as a guiding principle of the film—an evocation as in a dream, one that avoids "illustration" (Riding 2002). The other extra-fictional moments devolve to the sort of text-painting seen in Act II. When Scarpia orders that the window be opened so the "cantata" can be heard, we get a grainy look at the exterior of the Palazzo Farnese, but when he has it shut, we see it against a loud closing noise that marks the onset of the terror about to unfold.

The start of Act III presents many grainy exterior shots of Castel Sant'Angelo and one of the top of St. Peter's from the Castel's parapet. This place in the film features the most intercutting of alternative discourses. Jacquot's narrative arrangement makes sense because the plot is "on hold" for a long time, and the extended stretch of instrumental music needs something visual to make it work in film. Here, the shots of Roman places become signs of cultural memory—they are not reinforcing authenticity, as in the Griffi, but memory, as filtered through grief, torture, and horror. Culture is stained, twisted. Not surprisingly, this is also the portion of *Tosca* that recapitulates earlier musical themes, motives, and story elements. In particular, recognition of the past in "E lucevan le stelle" crystallizes this invocation of memory. Before the aria, Jacquot introduces a startling effect that amounts to a fourth discourse. He repeats earlier filmic sequences, in the church and Palazzo Farnese, but shows them in reverse, literally playing the film backward. Except for a brief respooling with human puppets in Powell and Pressburger's *Tales of Hoffmann* (1951), I cannot recall such an effect in opera-film. While Jacquot captures *Tosca's* recapitulative impulse and emphasis on memory, I find it a bit contrived and consider it the weakest aspect of the film. It is as if he ran out of ideas. On the other hand, it demonstrates the constructedness of filmic narrative and the rendering of opera on film—the unnaturalness of opera-film itself.

Constructedness looms large in Jacquot's third discursive device in the film, the black-and-white sequences in the recording studio. These appear frequently in Acts I and III, and are missing from Act II until the final two chords after the fiction has ended. As in the rest of the film, the black and white is tonally inflected by a bleached look that both heightens and dulls the images, as it contrasts the look of the fiction with the grainy interruptions. The movie starts and ends in the studio: the source of everything, it seems to say. Unlike Griffi's dressed-up orchestra and conductor, everyone here is in ordinary clothes. This glimpse into daily work exposes the labor and physicality involved in producing music by singers and players. While no other opera-film breaks in as often, I'm reminded of a couple of movies that allude to the process. Syberberg's *Parsifal* briefly shows the conductor, Armin Jordan, superimposed on the fictional story during the Good Friday music, and Bergman's *Magic Flute* breaks the fiction with views of the singers before they enter the stage and during intermission. In the Jacquot, however, the making-of element attains a significance that approaches that of the fiction. In fact, it is such an integral element of the film that it redefines what "fiction" means for this *Tosca*.

In Act I most of the characters are introduced in a kind of visual "cavatina" by way of the recording studio. When they utter their first word or are mentioned by someone, we get a black-and-white close-up of them in the process of recording. Among the memorable moments are the first words of Angelotti, and the sudden cutaway from the church to Raimondi in the studio (in black!) when Cavaradossi mentions "Scarpia" as the purveyor of evil and torture. Or just before Scarpia appears in the story, we see Raimondi rise behind the mike as he prepares to sing (Figure 42.8). After no singerly cut-ins during the claustrophobic horrors of Act II, the third act brings back the narrative device of introduction via the studio. Cavaradossi has not been seen for a long time, and now Alagna appears in a studio exchange with the guard. This lasts for a while and fits into Jacquot's approach in the first half of Act III that compensates for the dearth of plot with an array of alternative discourses. The stint with Alagna holds our interest and segues seamlessly into his aria, which is confined to the fiction proper.

The discursive element of the studio has a suggestive relationship with playback. It becomes a literalization of this staple of opera-film as it discloses how the music on the soundtrack comes into being. At the same time, it stages a fascinating duet between the two modes of presentation. Sometimes this occurs in close succession: we see a character lip-synching in the fiction and, shortly after, the singer physically emitting the music in the studio. While Gheorghiu appears to be "singing" *sotto voce* in the fiction because we see vibrating tongue and throat, the other singers are not: the "dummy" phenomenon that is characteristic of opera-film and contrasts boldly with the Griffi. In the Jacquot,

FIGURE 42.8 Jacquot's *Tosca*, black-and-white cutaway to Ruggero Raimondi in Act I. © Avatar Films.

the lively interaction between the modes highlights the distinctiveness of character and singer as two separate personas. This is emphasized even more when the studio shots of singers show them gesturing broadly as they might at a vocal coaching. It captures their immersion in musical production per se and underscores the contrast with the restrained acting style when they are "in role" in the fiction. Yet both modes evince an "operatic" sort of exaggeration. In this way, the opera singer and the opera character come closer together, which is especially apt in an opera whose title character is an opera singer. Another interesting arrangement of playback occurs inside the fiction when added speech accompanies the playback singing. A memorable example is during the love duet in Act I. As Cavaradossi's music at "Quale occhio al mondo" begins and Tosca responds, the singers do not lip-synch the soundtrack but speak the very words we are hearing sung. It is not clear if the characters hear that sung music. Regardless of whether they do, the multiplication of sonorous discourses replicates the visual proliferation in the film. As the number continues the whole becomes internalized: heard music with no speech or moving lips. Such "interior singing" appears several times in the movie, for example, in Sant'Andrea della Valle as Scarpia plots his next move.

Jacquot reportedly wanted live singing to a pre-recorded orchestra track, but the film company rejected the plan because of the costs of sound-proofing a film studio (Riding 2002). The insertion of the recording session, which the director captured on video, seems to be a compromise solution. Liveness interrupts, comments on, and amplifies the story and exposes opera and its filmic representation as a construction built on real singers and instrumentalists. Although the Griffi trades in live singing and foregrounds it as a demanding physical act, its position inside the fiction minimizes its force *qua* music-making as it blends with the acting-out of the story. Jacquot's separation isolates music-making and underlines its specialness. But the embodied performing act never overwhelms *Tosca*. In Jacquot's skilled hands it intensifies the trope of "operaticness"—of performance itself—that lay behind this hyper-theatrical work of Puccini.

Coda

The hyper-realism that attends these extraordinary films plays out in a recent incarnation of *Tosca* inside film. *Quantum of Solace* (2008), a recent installment of the James Bond franchise, includes a striking visit to *Tosca* at the Bregenz Festival (Citron 2011). Here the "Te Deum" and the F sharp minor instrumental music of Act II form a thrilling backdrop to a micro-second montage and a refiguring of the scopic dynamics surrounding opera. *Tosca* is further separated into its component parts, with little intact except its extraordinary ability to limn narrative and function as a film score in a highly unlikely place. It demonstrates that opera is a versatile tool in film. From the other side, opera benefits enormously from wider exposure through such mediated treatments. History suggests that new technologies will continue to broaden the scope for the transmission and reinterpretation of opera.

See also: Operatic Images, The Operatic Canon, Voice

Bibliography

Abbate, Carolyn. 1991 [1996]. *Unsung Voices: Opera and Musical Narrative in the Nineteenth Century*. Princeton, NJ: Princeton University Press.

Abel, Sam. 1996. *Opera in the Flesh: Sexuality in Opera Performance*. Boulder, CO: Westview Press. Find this resource:

Altman, Rick, with McGraw Jones and Sonia Tatroe. 2000. "Inventing the Cinema Soundtrack: Hollywood's Multiplane Sound System." In *Music and Cinema*, edited by James Buhler, Caryl Flinn, and David Neumeyer, 339–359. Hannover, NH: Wesleyan University Press.

Benjamin, Walter. 2008. "The Work of Art in the Age of Its Technological Reproducibility: Second Version." In *The Work of Art in the Age of Its Technological Reproducibility and Other Writings on Media*, by Walter Benjamin, edited by Michael W. Jennings, Brigid Doherty, and Thomas Y. Levin, translated by Edmund Jephcott, Rodney Livingstone, Howard Eiland, et al., 19–55. Cambridge, MA: Harvard University Press.

Brèque, Jean-Michel, and Alain Duault, eds. 1987. *Cinéma et Opéra*. Joint Issue of *L'Avant-Scène Opéra* 98 and *L'Avant-Scène Cinéma* 360.

Buhler, James, David Neumeyer, and Rob Deemer. 2010. *Hearing the Movies: Music and Sound in Film History*. New York: Oxford University Press.

Chion, Michel. 1994. *Audio-Vision: Sound on Screen*, translated by Claudia Gorbman. New York: Columbia University Press.

Citron, Marcia J. 2011. "The Operatics of Detachment: *Tosca* in the James Bond Film *Quantum of Solace*." *19th-Century Music* 34/3: 316–340.

——. 2010a. "'Soll ich lauschen?': Love-Death in *Humoresque*." In Joe and Gilman 2010, 167–185.

——. 2010b. *When Opera Meets Film*. Cambridge Studies in Opera. Cambridge: Cambridge University Press.

——. 2000. *Opera on Screen*. New Haven: Yale University Press.

Cook, Nicholas. 1998. *Analysing Musical Multimedia*. Oxford: Clarendon Press.

Csobádi, Peter, Gernot Gruber, Jürgen Kühnel, Ulrich Müller, et al., eds. 2001. *Das Musiktheater in den Audiovisuellen Medien: Vorträge und Gespräche des Salzburger Symposions 1999*. Anif/Salzburg: Verlag Mueller-Speiser.

Ellis, John. 1992. *Visible Fictions: Cinema, Television, Radio*. London: Routledge.

Franklin, Peter. 2011. *Seeing Through Music: Gender and Modernism in Classic Hollywood Film Scores*. New York: Oxford University Press.

——. 1994. "Movies as Opera (Behind the Great Divide)." In *A Night in at the Opera: Media Representations of Opera*, edited by Jeremy Tambling, 77–112. London: John Libbey.

Goldmark, Daniel, Lawrence Kramer, and Richard Leppert, eds. 2007. *Beyond the Soundtrack: Representing Music in Cinema*. Berkeley and Los Angeles: University of California Press.

Gorbman, Claudia. 1987. *Unheard Melodies: Narrative Film Music*. Bloomington: Indiana University Press.

Greenwald, Helen M. 2001. "Issues of Authenticity in Two Films of *Madama Butterfly:* Ponnelle (1974) and Mitterrand (1995)." In Csobádi et al. 2001, 295–305.

Grover-Friedlander, Michal. 2011. *Operatic Afterlives*. New York: Zone Books.

——. 2005. *Vocal Apparitions: The Attraction of Cinema to Opera*. Princeton, NJ: Princeton University Press.

Hunter, Mary. 2002. "Opera *in* Film—Sentiment and Wit, Feeling and Knowing: *The Shawshank Redemption* and *Prizzi's Honor*." In Joe and Theresa 2002, 93–120.

Joe, Jeongwon. 2013. *Opera as Soundtrack*. Aldershot, UK: Ashgate.

——. 2010a. "Interview with Bill Viola." In Joe and Gilman 2010, 431–440.

——. 2010b. "*The Tristan Project:* Time in Wagner and Viola." In Joe and Gilman 2010, 358–380.

——. 1999. "Don Boyd's *Aria:* A Narrative Polyphony between Music and Image." *Journal of Musicological Research* 18/4: 347–369.

——. 1998. "Opera on Film, Film in Opera: Postmodern Implications of the Cinematic Influence on Opera." PhD diss., Northwestern University.

——, and Sander Gilman, eds. 2010. *Wagner and Cinema*. Bloomington: Indiana University Press.

Joe, Jeongwon, and Rose Theresa, eds. 2002. *Between Opera and Cinema*. New York: Routledge.

Kerman, Joseph. 1985. *Contemplating Music: Challenges to Musicology*. Cambridge, MA: Harvard University Press.

Koch, Gerhard R. 1986. "Vom Nutzen des Grenzgängerishen: Wie sich Oper und Film befruchten." In *Oper-Film-Rockmusik: Veränderungen in der Alltagskultur*, edited by Hans-Klaus Jungenheinrich, 18–27. Kassel: Bärenreiter.

Kozinn, Allan. 1992. "Music Notes: Complex Production, Even for Opera." *New York Times* (July 6).

Kramer, Lawrence. 2010. "'The Threshold of the Visible World': Wagner, Bill Viola, and *Tristan*." In Joe and Gilman 2010, 381–407.

——. 2002. *Musical Meaning: Toward a Critical History*. Berkeley and Los Angeles: University of California Press.

Kuhn, Bernhard. 2005. *Die Oper im italienischen Film*. Essen: Die blaue Eule.

Langford, Barry. 2005. "'Our Usual Impasse': The Episodic Situation Comedy Revisited." In *Popular Television Drama: Critical Perspectives*, edited by Jonathan Bignell and Stephen Lacey, 15–33. Manchester: Manchester University Press.

Leicester, H. Marshall. 1994. "Discourse and the Film Text: Four Readings of *Carmen*." *Cambridge Opera Journal* 6/3: 245–282.

Leppert, Richard. 2007. "Opera, Aesthetic Violence, and the Imposition of Modernity: *Fitzcarraldo*." In Goldmark et al. 2007, 99–119.

Neumeyer, David. 2009. "Diegetic/Nondiegetic: A Theoretical Model." *Music and the Moving Image* 2/1. Online. Available: http://www.jstor.org/action/showPublication?journalCode=musimoviimag (accessed February 6, 2014).

Poizat, Michel. 1992. *The Angel's Cry: Beyond the Pleasure Principle in Opera*, translated by Arthur Denner. Ithaca, NY: Cornell University Press.

Rajewsky, Irina. 2002. *Intermedialität*. Tübingen: Francke.

Riding, Alan. 2002. "Film: A 'Tosca' That Wants You to Know It's a Movie." *New York Times* (July 14).

Sheppard, W. Anthony. 2011. Review of *Wagner and Cinema*, edited by Joe and Gilman (2010). *Journal of the American Musicological Society* 64/2: 444–455.

——. 2007. "Review of the Metropolitan Opera's New HD Movie Theater Broadcasts." *American Music* 25/3: 383–387.

Stilwell, Robynn. 2007. "The Fantastical Gap between Diegetic and Nondiegetic." In Goldmark et al. 2007, 184–204.

Tambling, Jeremy, ed. 1994. *A Night in at the Opera: Media Representations of Opera*. London: John Libbey.

——. 1987. *Opera, Ideology and Film*. New York: St. Martin's Press.

Vincent, Delphine. 2011. "Deconstruction of the Illusion of Reality and Identification in Jacquot's *Tosca*." Unpublished paper delivered at "Music and the Moving Image Conference," New York University (May 20).

Weiner, Marc A. 2002. "Why Does Hollywood Like Opera?" In Joe and Theresa, 75–92.

White, Jonathan. 1994. "Opera, Politics, and Television: *Bel canto* by Satellite." In Tambling 1994, 267–296.

Wilson, Alexandra. 2007. *The Puccini Problem: Opera, Nationalism, and Modernity*. Cambridge: Cambridge University Press.

Winters, Ben. 2010. "The Non-Diegetic Fallacy: Film, Music, and Narrative Space." *Music & Letters* 91/2: 224–244.

Witt, Alexis L. 2006. "*Amadeus*, Opera, and the Music of the Mind." Unpublished paper for Rice University course "Opera on Film."

Wlaschin, Ken. 2004. *Encyclopedia of Opera on Screen: A Guide to More Than 100 Years of Opera Films, Videos, and DVDs*. New Haven: Yale University Press.

Wolf, Werner. 1999. *The Musicalization of Fiction: A Study in the Theory and History of Intermediality*. Amsterdam: Rodopi.

CHAPTER 43

OPERATIC IMAGES

HELEN M. GREENWALD

> It might be better to begin by thinking of images as a far-flung family which has migrated in time and space and undergone profound mutations in the process.
>
> (Mitchell 1986: 9)
>
> "I'll have what she's having."
>
> (Ephron [Crystal] 1989)

Opera as "Placed" Product: The Family of Operatic Images

The line in the 1989 film *When Harry Met Sally*—"I'll have what she's having"—may be one of the most memorable and apposite reactions on record to an image, and not least a theatrical one. Sally (Meg Ryan) is, after all, acting—demonstrating to Harry (Billy Crystal) how well she can fake an orgasm and fool a man (the screenplay was written by Nora Ephron [1989], but according to Keyser [1989], the line was first suggested by Billy Crystal). Fakery or not, the image represents something intensely desirable, and that is confirmed by an onlooker's response. The scene might have unfolded differently and far less piquantly if more words had been spoken; it might have played this way: Woman customer, seeing Sally gesturing in ecstasy, says to waiter: "What is that woman over there having?" Waiter (business as usual): "She's having xx [looks like it could be a turkey sandwich]. Woman: "I'll have the same." Fortunately for us, the filmmakers understood well that theater in all of its forms depends on observation, reaction, and above all, pacing.

Sometimes, opera itself is the image—the desired object—a phenomenon illustrated most successfully in the one medium where it often serves a diegetic function: film (see Citron 2000, 2010). Here are three examples: the first is Kenneth Lonergan's 2011 *Margaret*, in which the deeply troubled teenager Lisa Cohen (Anna Paquin) reconnects with her mother (J. Smith-Cameron) in the Metropolitan Opera House as Offenbach's

"Barcarolle" (from *Les contes d'Hoffmann*, performed by Renée Fleming and Susan Graham) brings the young girl's emotions to the surface. In *Pretty Woman*, Edward (Richard Gere) takes Vivian (Julia Roberts) to see *La traviata*, which parallels, at least to a point, the life the pair are living at that moment. Opera gives the film dimension, the character of Edward depth and the kind of sensitivity that we might not suspect lives in the heart of a Wall Street predator. Moreover, when Edward arrives at Vivian's apartment to declare his commitment to her, we hear the strains of "Amami, Alfredo" in the background (Lawton 1990). Similarly, in Norman Jewison's 1987 Moonstruck, Ronny Cammareri (Nicolas Cage) wants to take Loretta Castorini (Cher) to the opera so that he will have at the same time the two things he loves the most—opera and Loretta—and he promises to let her go afterward. It's hardly a farewell performance, though; post-operatic passion leads to the bedroom (Shanley 1987; see Citron 2008, 2010). As a diegetic phenomenon in film or on stage (consider the play-within-a-play), an operatic performance can be a "placed product," an advertisement for itself. In the cited examples, opera is a type of cure-all: the catalyst for happy endings and conflict resolution, an "elixir" of love. A rational response? "I'll have what she's having."

Film is only one branch of an extended family of images that embraces opera's artistic, often comical, frequently commercial, and sprawling complex of composers, poets, works, performers, designers, costumers, artists, journalists, fans, and profiteers. Opera mirrors the tastes, trends, and desires of those it wishes to entertain and persuade. Operatic images, especially in live performance, exemplify old adages—"actions speak louder than words," "a picture is worth a thousand words"—with the added dimension of sound.

One of the most fertile grounds for discussing the visual aspects of opera is the phenomenon of *Regietheater* (Director's theater), the single element of modern operatic production that has raised the ire of so many in so short a time, as impresarios and theaters struggle to present something new to a public that craves novelty and innovation. A common complaint against *Regietheater* is that what is seen and what is heard are contradictory, as the inescapable historicity of musical style sometimes clashes with updated settings or symbols whose meanings can be elusive (the dead rabbits in Christoph Schlingensief's 2004 *Parsifal* at Bayreuth come to mind here). But even the most radical and puzzling of stagings rely on how well the audience can search its visual memory banks for clues to unlock the meaning of what is shown. Opera, like nearly every art form, thus depends on communal experience and recognition—of character, place, and time, but also archetypes, allusions, icons, and symbols. As theater historian Marvin Carlson observes, "The theatre more than any other art deals in things that are like other things" (Carlson 1989: 3).

This chapter addresses the remarkable nexus of high art and commercial enterprise in which the visual materials of opera—inside the opera house and outside the opera house—reflect not only its devoted audiences, but also a larger segment of the public that may experience opera simply through everyday encounters with books, newspapers, and advertising. Some questions to be considered are: How did composers and librettists engage a culture's visual history and use those images to transmit their message? What did the audience expect to see and what would they have understood that modern viewers cannot or do not any longer comprehend? How might the modern scholar unlock those issues? How does opera sell itself or other products? How do music and image work together in ways that are specifically "operatic"?

I begin with instrumental music and follow with popular images—caricatures, cartoons, and advertisements—that express the way we disseminate and receive what we see and hear or want others to see and hear. The final portion of the chapter is about stagecraft and ideology—costumes, makeup, cultural icons, and especially the role that revered works of art might play in opera. I then turn to Verdi's 1846 *Attila* to show how Verdi used imagery to tailor his opera for its Venetian audience and to project a timely and meaningful political message.

Instrumental Music and the Operatic Imagination

Operatic instrumental music, like incidental music (an ancestor of the movie score), can paint a picture, mimic the speed and intensity of the action, define time and place, and add emotional depth to the dramatic situation. When the curtain is closed and there is nothing to look at, opera composers employ instrumental music to create atmosphere or stimulate the imagination (as in the entr'acte, intermezzo [see Morris 2002], overture, and opening curtain [see Greenwald 1991]). Historically, the overture was an expected "first" gesture that did not intrude on the "real" drama, which began with the curtain (Greenwald 1991: 5). By the early years of the nineteenth century, overtures and preludes had not yet connected routinely or substantively with the operas they introduced: Rossini, for example, thought nothing of recycling the overture to *Aureliano in Palmira* (1813) in both *Elisabetta, regina d'Inghilterra* (1815) and *Il barbiere di Siviglia* (1816). For at least one nineteenth-century critic, Berlioz, the traditional overture produced little more than a yawn; he noted in his memoirs after attending the opera in Rome that the overture was still "a kind of noise which theatre orchestras produce for the rise of the curtain, and to which no one pays any attention" (Berlioz [1865] 2002: 171; see also Greenwald 1991: 4). But eighteenth-century critics and composers (see Algarotti's *Saggio sopra l'opera in musica* and the Gluck/Calzabigi "Dedication" to *Alceste*, cited in Greenwald 1991: 3) had already begun to object to this "all-purpose exordium," as Mozart tested the dramatic efficacy of a tonally open and thematically prescient overture in *Don Giovanni*. Composers had begun to rethink the combined visual and musical first impressions that they wished to convey, and by the late nineteenth century many had abandoned the independent overture altogether as the "number" structure in opera disintegrated in favor of continuous music (see, for example, Verdi's *Otello* and *Falstaff*). Puccini was surely the most resourceful of his colleagues when it came to these matters, as he designed a "boutique" opening for each new work. Among many noteworthy examples are *Manon Lescaut*, in which he raises the curtain during the prelude (Greenwald 1991: 11–12 and passim), and *Il tabarro*, where he withholds the music until after the curtain has risen. As Greenwald (1991: 9) observes about the latter, "[t]he silence comes as a surprise, thwarts our expectations of hearing music at the beginning of the opera, and diverts our attention to a more precise and realistic visual impression. At least momentarily, it subordinates sound to sight, and as a result, we are nowhere more keenly aware of the musical downbeat than here." But if, as Julian Budden (1987: 332) has asserted, Puccini was "Wagner's best Italian pupil," then the composer studied his "teacher's" expository methodologies closely. Puccini's model, and particularly for the opening of *La fanciulla del West*, may well have been *Das Rheingold*, where Wagner "created an entirely musical illusion, as he began in the depths of the Rhine river (and in the depths of the orchestra) and increased the range and density of his sound gradually until the aural and visual image is changed by the [sound and sight of the] Rhinemaidens" (Greenwald 1991: 14–15). The "pictures" that open *Fanciulla* are similarly "primal": the natural setting of the high Sierras dissolves into manmade abodes, as the continuous music of the prelude follows the seamless visual transformation from outdoors to indoors, from sunset to artificial light (Greenwald 1991: 16, 175ff.; see also Senici 2005).

Composers also used instrumental music within their works to underscore a dumbshow (or pantomime). Butterfly's vigil in Puccini's *Madama Butterfly* (1904) is a particularly interesting example, because the stage picture is silent, the voices now heard from unseen precincts, along with the orchestra, in a musical rendition of the passage of night into day (Greenwald 2000). Puccini, however, was following a long line of opera composers who wrote pictorial music, often engaging common musical tropes to accompany natural phenomena. A good example is the "liberty" sunrise that Verdi underscored in *Attila* (1846) with a Haydnesque crescendo that had already become an essential audio element of contemporary light shows (Greenwald 2009a). Moreover, as Gundula Kreuzer (2012) observes, even the visual materials of the modern industrial age became associated with Wagner's *Ring* and its social contexts in critical commentary that extended to "all manner of vapor—steam, fog, fumes" (2012: 179).

Music defines the gesture—whether it is falling to one's death (Greenwald 2012) or to one's knees (Smart 2003, 2004)—and underscores the dance. As Wye Jamison Allanbrook (1983) demonstrates, Mozart used dance in his operas not only for simple accompaniment, but to represent social strata or even create chaos, as in the Act I finale of *Don Giovanni* (1787). Verdi learned well from Mozart, and dance music became a tool for irony in the "conspiracy" duet between two "ugly" men in *Rigoletto* (1851), where the hunchback Rigoletto and the assassin Sparafucile "dance" around each other in a tradition-defying sweet major mode.

Illustration: Caricatures, Cartoons, Composers, and Critters

Singers are probably the most "imaged" figures in all of opera, and not always for the better, as Thomas Rowlandson (1756–1827) shows in his drawing *John Bull at the Italian Opera* (1811; Figure 43.1 and on the cover of this volume). The overtly earnest performer

FIGURE 43.1 Thomas Rowlandson, *John Bull at the Italian Opera*. Print (London, October 2, 1811). Hand-colored etching, ink and wash on paper. Harry Beard Collection, Victoria and Albert Museum, S.4652-2009. © Victoria and Albert Museum, London.

clutches his (or is it her?) breast and leans forward at the edge of the stage in a futile effort to move the audience, who recoil, gasp, and scowl in disapproval, or pay no attention at all. John Bull, a character first developed in the early eighteenth century by John Arbuthnot and adopted by others (including Rowlandson) as the archetypal no-nonsense Briton—portly and proud, conservatively dressed—sits in the second balcony, clutching the railing, deeply displeased. Cynical in perpetuity, the pit musicians look bored, while the continuo player strains to make eye contact with his charge in an attempt to restore musical order. Two centuries later, Rowlandson's cartoon is still fresh and relevant, as it captures the "risk" of going to the opera—the possibility that despite heroic efforts, singers will miss notes, sing out of tune, forget lines, and cause us pain—both physical and spiritual. And it is those superhuman efforts and their failures in particular that have incited caricaturists and cartoonists to mischief.

But caricaturists also capture the joy of opera. Nearly three generations of opera lovers and theater-goers delighted in Al Hirschfeld's (1903–2003) drawings of actors, composers, and musicians, which appeared regularly in the Arts and Leisure section of the Sunday *New York Times*. Hirschfeld sketched Luciano Pavarotti on a number of occasions, always emphasizing his girth, good humor, and bravado. In Figure 43.2,

FIGURE 43.2 Al Hirschfeld, *Pavarotti*, drawing. © AL HIRSCHFELD. Reproduced by arrangement with Hirschfeld's exclusive representative, The MARGOT FEIDEN GALLERIES LTD., NEW YORK. WWW.ALHIRSCHFELD.COM.

Hirschfeld shows Pavarotti's mouth open in a big toothy grin: there is just something so smart about Hirschfeld's rendering of Pavarotti; it not only goes to the generosity and ebullience of his subject, but also to the splendidly absurd girth of opera itself.

One provocative figure who lives on in contemporary conversation and media is the castrato Carlo Broschi, known as "Farinelli" or "Farinello." According to Daniel Heartz, Farinelli inspired so many portraits in his lifetime that it is even possible to track his career through evolving imagery. Artists, such as Jacopo Amigoni, in his 1735 "Farinelli Crowned by Music," deified him, while others, such as Leone Ghezzi, caricatured him with gleeful cruelty, showing the singer in female dress, turned in profile to emphasize his most obvious physical flaw, "a protruding upper lip" (Heartz 2004: 118–119). Much later, the "divine monster" Angelica Catalani was lampooned in the media, frequently depicted as overtly sexual, an icon of the "loose singer" (see Figure 17.1 in Chapter 17). Singers later suffered at the hands of animators, who portrayed them as oversized, arrogant, loud, and annoying animals—rabbits, birds, and even whales. This anthropomorphic turn has continued to delight fans of Warner Brothers' hilarious "The Rabbit of Seville" (Jones 1949) and "What's Opera Doc?" (Jones 1957), as well as Disney's soulful "The Whale Who Wanted to Sing at the Met" (Geronimi and Luske 1946. The singing whale is advertised within the cartoon as "The biggest thing to hit the Met"; see Grover-Friedlander 2011: 197–206). And let us not forget Clara Cluck, the *bel canto* chicken, who debuted in 1934 and appeared numerous times alongside other Disney inventions from Mickey Mouse to Roger Rabbit.

Caricatures, cartoons, and comic strips depend on the kind of mass familiarity that enables parody. The original target must have a strong profile: Brünnhilde, with her horned helmet, is the *sine qua non* of a camera-ready object for satire, and her ongoing role in popular culture suggests that opera, or at the very least, an archetypal Wagnerian image, has been absorbed into the public consciousness (whether it is understood or not). One example with a long run is Dik Browne's (1917–1989) internationally syndicated comic strip "Hägar the Horrible" (begun in 1973 and continued by the artist's son Chris Browne), which features the beleaguered Hägar's nagging wife, Helga, a Brünnhilde with blonde braids and Viking horns. Another contemporary example is Russell Myers's comic strip "Broom-Hilda" (launched 1970), whose title is a play on words that actually has nothing to do with the eponymous heroine, a green-skinned witch, who otherwise bears no resemblance at all to her would-be namesake.

In Wagner's own time, however, it was not Brünnhilde, but the composer himself who dominated print caricatures. John Grand-Carteret (1892) assembled one of the earliest collections of cartoons aimed at Wagner, an iconographic history (until 1891) of the composer, beginning with chapters on his penmanship and signature, his music hand, and extant portraits. Grand-Carteret ruminates in his introduction on the nature of caricature, noting that lampooned subjects invariably possess a revolutionary character of extreme degree and a near-obsessive faith in their own beliefs, the common currency of what may be one of the oldest forms of editorializing, the political cartoon. Like the political cartoon, opera caricature must be timely, often linked to performance, just as Hirschfeld's portraits were advance notice for the week ahead in New York.

Not surprisingly, the nineteenth-century spike in newspaper production yielded an enormous number of cartoons and caricatures of musical figures. Artists, such as André Gill, whose works were published from 1865 to 1876 in two Parisian newspapers, *La Lune* and *L'Éclipse*, made a career out of caricaturing composers (Rossini, Auber, and Offenbach, in addition to Wagner) and singers such as Patti and Nilsson (Breckenbill 2009). Sometimes a single high-profile work was pummeled relentlessly by journalists. As Clair Rowden (2009) demonstrates, the subject of Massenet's *Thaïs* (1894)—cleric attempts to convert exotic courtesan; lustful motivation is revealed—generated a furor in the press. The visual legacy of that onslaught, moreover, reveals a nexus of political, social, and artistic trends, as soprano Sybil Sanderson, who sang the title role, also came under fire.

The culture of illustration flourished at the end of the nineteenth and beginning of the twentieth centuries as translations of Grimm, Andersen, and the *Arabian Nights* surfaced (see Tatar 2002). Wagner's operatic stories were absorbed into that traffic in the drawings and watercolors that followed soon thereafter. Especially noteworthy here is Arthur Rackham (1867–1939), whose magnificently illustrated edition of the text of Wagner's *Ring* ([1910–1911] 1976) reimagined it as a fairy tale. Rackham, who created romantic and rarefied environments for the Rhinemaidens and gods, was part of the "Golden Age" of British book illustrators and contemporary British Wagnerism. Rackham's younger colleague Aubrey Beardsley (1872–1898) began, but never finished, illustrating his "The Comedy of the Rhinegold," after Wagner's opera (see Sutton 2002). The increased popularity of illustration also encouraged growth of the graphic novel (traceable to the eighteenth century) and the comic book, media for which Wagner's *Ring of the Nibelung* seemed to be tailor-made (Thomas et al. 1989–1990). But in all of these graphic efforts, singing is rarely if ever represented, as the pictures serve only to tell the story in the kind of frozen dramatic moments that eventually became the province of poster art.

A contemporary and direct union of the illustrative arts and opera may be found in the work of Maurice Sendak (1928–2012), best known as an imaginative illustrator and writer of children's books. But Sendak also maintained a lifelong interest in opera and a rich professional relationship with director Frank Corsaro, who was greatly inspired by him (Corsaro 2013). Sendak contributed to productions of Prokofiev's *The Love for Three Oranges*, Ravel's *L'heure espagnole* and *L'enfant et les sortilèges*, Mozart's *The Magic Flute*, Janáček's *The Cunning Little Vixen*, and Stravinsky's *Renard*, to name only a few (Corsaro 2013). In addition, Sendak became an illustrator of opera in the manner of Rackham when he provided the images for playwright Tony Kushner's picture-book adaptation of Hans Krása and Adolf Hoffmeister's 1938 *Brundibár* (Kushner 2003). In what could be a unique circumstance, Sendak became librettist and designer for two operas by Oliver Knussen, who found inspiration in Sendak's picture books *Where the Wild Things Are* (book 1963; opera 1979–1983) and *Higglety Pigglety Pop!* (book 1967; opera 1985–1985, rev. 1999).

The Art of Persuasion: Advertising

Some of the best evidence of what the general public wants and expects may be gleaned from advertising. The artists and writers who represent the creative side of this industry have maintained a shrewd understanding of the viewing public, and most especially its propensity to self-romanticize. As Richard Leppert has noted, "It is lost on no one that a significant portion of our conscious and unconscious understandings of ourselves and our immediate world is framed by the imagery of advertising" (Leppert 1996: 3).

I begin here with video—television commercials that use opera to sell something other than opera. Since these mini-films must get their messages across in thirty seconds, instant recognition is critical, and music often does the job. Advertisers sometimes take a familiar operatic melody and refit it with a new rhythmically compatible text, as, for example, "Spa-ti-ni spaghetti sauce" instead of "La donna è mobile" (viewable at Spatini n.d.) More commonly, television commercials use opera as an absurd counterpoint to the featured product, playing into aural memory and even the sound of common experience. A good example is singing in the shower, used by Kohler plumbing in its 2012 television commercial for a shower head: A man scrubs away and sings along with a radio broadcast of Bellini's "Finì... Me Lassa!" from *I puritani* (view at Kohler 2012). The payoff at the end of the commercial is a comic trifecta for those in the know: he's a plumber who sings opera (feeding on the Ronny Cammareri-the-baker phenomenon); he's a Goldilocks, having commandeered someone else's home to take a shower (here under the pretense of "legitimately" testing the equipment); and he's singing passionately in a venue least like a gilded opera house (Woody Allen used the same joke in his 2012 *To Rome with Love*).

Opera posters tell us a lot about programming—who sang what and where. The advertising for the Venetian premiere of Verdi's *Attila* at the Teatro La Fenice on March 17, 1846, does precisely that and little more (viewable at Fenice 1846). The most interesting social aspect of the poster is the ticket pricing. The stated currency, Austrian lire, attests to ongoing foreign presence in Venice, and scaled prices show that soldiers and children would be admitted for half price (two Austrian lire). Posters often reveal political motivation as well as information. Jérôme de la Gorce (1987) has shown, for example, that the advertisement for the first performance of Lully's *Fêtes de l'Amour et de Bacchus* (1672) opens a window on public safety and politics in its warning that no one, including members of the nobility and lower echelons of the community, will be admitted without a ticket. While profit seems to be the first concern, the powers behind the production also wanted to bar political opportunists looking to distribute pamphlets. The classical decorations on the poster—allegorical figures of Euterpe and Thalia—place both opera and composer in the best possible intellectual light in another attempt to preempt would-be critics (La Gorce 1987: 311–312).

Poster culture flourished in Italy in the late nineteenth century and especially in the Ricordi workshop, which included set and costume designer Adolfo Hohenstein (known for his work on the first Italian performances, in 1889, of Wagner's *Die Meistersinger von Nürnberg* and the premiere performances of Puccini's *La bohème* and *Tosca*). Hohenstein, together with his student Leopoldo Metlicovitz (who designed the poster for Giovanni Pastrone's 1914 silent film *Cabiria*), followed the style and detail of book illustration, now used to seduce and sell as well as delight. Their posters fired the imagination by capturing a defining point in the drama. Thus, for example, Hohenstein, in his *Tosca* poster (1899), embeds the scene of Tosca standing over Scarpia's body in a blood-red field that creeps irregularly throughout the tableau, contained only by the shadowy borders cast by the candelabra flanking the corpse. The opera's title, *Tosca*, stands firmly against the red field; circling through the letter "o" is what appears to be an asp—no doubt symbolizing the reptilian Chief of Police who, even in death, exerts a stranglehold on the heroine. The only other printed information on the illustration names the librettists, author of the original literary source (Sardou), composer, and publisher in darker colors (the poster is widely available for viewing online).

Opera and Art

The stage tableau can often refer directly to an iconic pose or historical moment, perhaps even one captured multiple times by artists wishing to reinterpret the past or revive it for political or didactic purposes. For example, we can trace the visual roots of Rossini's 1822 opera *Zelmira* to illustrations and paintings that inspired the opera's literary source, Dormont de Belloy's 1770 play, *Zelmire*. Dormont drew his plot from the legend of Pero and Cimon, in which a courageous wife and mother demonstrates her "filial devotion" by keeping her imprisoned father alive with her own breast milk. The story was retold graphically under the rubric of "Roman Charity" or "Filial Devotion" on canvases from at least the seventeenth century (Rubens 1612, for example), enjoying a revival in Dormont's own time through the work of Jean-Jacques Bachelier (1764), Louis Jean François Lagrenée (1765), and Jean-Baptiste Greuze (1767), to name only a few. Rossini's take on filial devotion, moreover, also engages ideas explored in the "rescue operas" of the late eighteenth and early nineteenth centuries that focused on familial as opposed to sexual love (*Fidelio* the most famous of them; see Greenwald 2005 and 2009b).

Sometimes the relationship between the operatic tableau and a cultural icon is less a matter of direct imitation than of social panorama. For example, the Japanese woodcuts that began to trickle into Europe from the late eighteenth century and attained vastly new importance with the opening of Japan in 1854 and the early Meiji period (beginning 1868) influenced a generation of artists, writers, composers, and librettists in a vogue for the exotic. Puccini's *Madama Butterfly* stands out among them, and not least for the composer's risky decision to situate the entirety of his work on the single set of Cio-Cio San's home, rejecting for the middle act the proposed contrasting venue of the American Consulate, which would have clearly juxtaposed East and West (Groos 1997). By tying his heroine to her home for the duration of the opera, Puccini drew on the Japanese perception of the home as the center of the life cycle that could not be abandoned except in death (Greenwald 2001), which has its own iconographic and musical traditions.

Generally speaking, the death of a character is reserved for the final curtain, in a familiar choreography where the heroine (less commonly, the hero) falls to the floor as a tonic chord pounds loudly enough to raise the audience to its feet (as in both *La traviata* and *Madama Butterfly*). But what iconic prescription for death does Puccini follow in *La bohème*, where Mimì passes away without notice, much less a lover by her side or a tonic chord in the background, and surrenders the curtain—and the cadence—to Rodolfo? Certainly not those numerous images of the "good" death depicted in Renaissance representations of the dying Virgin surrounded by apostles that served as archetypes for the countless deathbed scenes that proliferated thereafter, including Benjamin West's 1770 *The Death of General Wolfe*, Jacques-Louis David's 1787 *The Death of Socrates*, and the famous engraving of Abraham Lincoln on his deathbed that appeared in *Harper's Weekly* (1865). Rather, Puccini and his librettists tapped into an evolving modernist perception of death and its representation that promoted a more interior style of acting (think Duse as opposed to Bernhardt) and shifted the emphasis to the living grief-stricken rather than the victim (see, for example, Edvard Munch's 1895 *Death in the Sickroom*; Greenwald 2012a).

The relationship between sight and sound in such examples is often complexly layered, and I offer in conclusion to this brief overview the figure of Satan, whose attempts at seduction, ultimately realized in a crude image and voice, converged in the music and illustrations of Hildegarde von Bingen's *Ordo Virtutum* (twelfth century) and evolved by the nineteenth century into the humanized mirror image of man's foolishness, adopting both his physique and voice in operas by Spohr and Gounod and contemporary artworks by Fuseli and Doré (Greenwald 2007).

"Stagecraft as Ideology": Toward Verdi's *Attila*

Costumes

What is intended for one audience may completely escape the understanding of another, as images,[1] to reiterate the words of W. J. T. Mitchell that head this chapter, "migrat[e] in time and space." A good case for study is the 2008 production of Beethoven's *Fidelio* at the Hungarian State Opera, directed by Bálasz Kovalik and designed by Kovalik and Angelika Höckner, with costumes by Mari Benedek. Beethoven's paradigms of family, imprisonment, liberty, and revolution are so well known and strongly articulated in both text and music as to guarantee their immunity to the radical impulses of modern directors, including those of Kovalik in Budapest. The production eschewed traditional sets and furnishings to play out on a series of bare, white steps, a "blank" space that allowed for a widely disparate array of visuals, including body doubles and Christ figures. The opera's finale, a hymn to enlightenment, justice, and marriage, was clothed as a 1960s "rainbow gathering" (see *Fidelio* 2008 for an image of the finale). This carnivalesque aspect of the production, however, was balanced by costume designer Benedek's systematic use of green, white, and red for the principal characters. While the color coding may have puzzled some spectators, it seems likely that the local Budapest audience, for whom Hungary's revolutionary history survives in recent memory, may well have seen in Benedek's choices a clear reference to the Hungarian flag: horizontal stripes of (reading upward) green, white, and red. The same production holds forth on other aspects of surface impression, as the part of "Fidelio," that is, Leonore in her male disguise, is mimed by a dancer, while "Leonore" dressed in a glamorous red gown, sings the role from the side of the stage.

But such sexual confusion has been common currency on the opera stage from its inception. Comprehension always hinges on accepted vocal traditions or audience perception that a character is doing something contrary to his or her real gender, as in *Le nozze di Figaro* where Susanna and the Countess disguise Cherubino (sung by woman) as a girl to dupe the Count.

Faces: Anna Nicole to Attila

Operas based on the exploits of historical figures can bear the same burden as the "biopic," that is, how to dress and make up characters whose faces are well known. In the case of singer-subjects or public orators, there is the additional problem of sound: Joaquin Phoenix had to learn to sing in the style of Johnny Cash (*Walk the Line* 2005), just as Jamie Foxx had to learn Ray Charles a year earlier (*Ray* 2004). But how does opera cope, if at all? Opera films, such as *The Great Caruso* (1951), generally employed photogenic singers such as Mario Lanza, who were able to offer a credible aural portrayal while making the subject a good deal more physically attractive than he actually was. But in film, beauty has almost always trumped sound, and lip-synching solved the problem when it was not possible to cast a role with a singer like Lanza (of course, this is a central problem of filmed musicals as well). Clemente Fracassi envisioned a slam dunk feat in casting his 1953 *Aida* with Sophia Loren lip-synching Renata Tebaldi. Until fairly recently, it was rare that an opera would treat a contemporary subject, not least one with a character still alive in communal memory (Verdi's *La traviata* is a notable exception). But that has changed with operas about Richard Nixon and Anna Nicole Smith, strongly "operatic" personalities whose faces and gestures have become iconic. Thus, in Mark-Anthony Turnage's *Anna Nicole* (2011), soprano Eva-Maria Westbroek was submerged under a platinum blonde wig and large breasts (presumably a padded body suit).

But what of the many figures of ancient history whose images exist only as descriptions recorded by witnesses? How are we to understand a series of evolving likenesses, one extrapolated from the last and modified for contemporary use in a game of visual "telephone"? Here I turn to Attila the Hun, whose final days Verdi inscribed into his 1846 opera *Attila*, based on Zacharias Werner's *Attila, König der Hunnen* (1808), and premiered in 1846 at La Fenice in Venice. The opera tells a familiar story of oppression, liberation, and revenge: Attila attacks Aquileia, embattled citizens flee across the lagoon and found the city of Venice. The Hun plans to attack Rome, but in an encounter with a Christian priest, he experiences a religious vision, retreats, and vows to lead a better life, but is killed on his wedding night by a vengeful wife (curtain).

The earliest account of Attila the Hun dates from the fifth-century Roman diplomat and historian Priscus, who described him thus: "he was short with a broad chest and a large head; his eyes were small, his beard sparse and flecked with gray, his nose was flat, and his complexion dark" (Kelly 2009: 171). Other descriptions and pictorial representations of Attila typically include a beard, a sword, and a scourge, as shown in Hartman Schedel's fifteenth-century illustration for the Nuremberg Chronicle (see Attila 1493 for a link to this image). Attila's beard, sword, and scourge survived for at least two more centuries, classified, for example, as "moral emblems" in the 1758 Hertel edition of Cesare Ripa's 1603 *Iconologia*, where, according to the caption, the figure of Attila "represents God" (image 71 of Ripa [1758–1760] 1971).

A little more than a century later, Aurelio Bianchi-Giovini wrote a capsule history of Attila and Venice in the October 13, 1847, issue of *L'Italia musicale* that was intended as publicity for current productions of Verdi's opera (Bianchi-Giovini 1847). Bianchi-Giovini painted quite a different picture of Attila: he was small and deformed; he had the flat, wide snout, nostrils, and low brow of a dog, sparkling eyes, cheeks scarred with a hot iron, a row of white teeth covered with thin lips, and an awkward gait that made him seem like a beast who stood upright on two legs. Unfortunately, no illustration accompanied the article, although one can imagine what a police sketch artist could do with such a detailed description. Today, our perception of Attila, at least the operatic one, is quite different, shaped by performances in the 1980s and 1990s by bass Samuel Ramey, whose costume and makeup drew on mid-twentieth-century "sword and sandal" films, and inspired one critic to label him a "stud muffin" (Super-Conductor 2012; the image may be seen at Ramey 2012).

A Context for *Attila*: Popular Histories, Madame de Staël, and Zacharias Werner

Verdi's *Attila* resonates deeply with a wide range of historical and cultural phenomena, including early Christianity and the liturgical cycles, art history and iconography, popular histories, Venetian civic pride, and the rapidly developing technologies of optical entertainments and stagecraft. Italians of the 1840s, moreover, were experiencing a type of modern renaissance in which ancient history, particularly as it defined identity and reflected religious beliefs, infused the cultural landscape. We should keep in mind Basevi's remarks about theology and culture in 1840s Italy when considering *Attila*, as well as works with more overtly religious themes, such as *I Lombardi alla prima crociata* and *Giovanna d'Arco*:

> It is worth remembering that at that time the religious ideal was spreading like a fashion, so much so that the reigning philosophy was altogether identified with it. Theology had invaded every order of knowledge, and Christianity, defended as the foundation of civilization, had acquired a dazzling splendor under the pen of very illustrious writers. (Basevi 1859: 21; trans. Izzo 2007: 557)

Even though, as Francesco Izzo has shown, the church presence in *primo ottocento* Italy was distinctly anti-progressive, religious themes fascinated writers, composers, and poets, who used them "to enhance the local color or the emotional intensity of paintings, poems, literary works, and operatic scenes" (Izzo 2007: 558). And, while most overtly Christian references were notably purged by censors from opera texts, including *Attila*'s, the figure of the Hun, an enlightened infidel linked to both Venetian history and the Easter season, did not, as a rule, incur draconian reaction from censors.

In all likelihood, Verdi first encountered Werner's drama by way of Madame de Staël's discussion of it in her expansive study of German culture, *De l'Allemagne* ([1813] 1968). Verdi spoke about *De l'Allemagne* in letters and even urged his friend and colleague Francesco Maria Piave to read it (see Greenwald 2012 for relevant correspondence and more on the genesis of the *Attila* libretto). Perhaps Verdi saw in Attila another Nabucco (a tyrant brought to his senses by heavenly forces, i.e., a thunderbolt), and with him yet another opportunity to explore human relations through an epic lens. Moreover, as Carlotta Sorba (2009) has pointed out, Verdi's choice of subject was completely in accord with the "cultural climate of the age, and confirmed the composer's readiness to gather and rework the great themes of his time for a large public" (Sorba 2009: 241). The early Middle Ages were a common point of reference for the *primo ottocento* population, who looked to the "great migrations" of the fourth and fifth centuries to find their roots and therein construct their own identities. There was a veritable onslaught of texts on the subject, as well as theatrical productions, including Alessandro Manzoni's *Adelchi* (1822), which concerned the fall of the Lombards (Sorba 2009: 342). As Sorba observes, "[...] some of the key issues of the age stood at the centre of this national reclamation of the Middle Ages: social conflict, the democratization of the political system, and the degree to which the monarchy was to have a role in it" (2009: 243). Attila figured prominently in these volumes as one of the "new barbarians," whose exploits were perpetually chronicled and rewritten (Lendvai 2003: 25). The earliest accounts of him were far less than heroic. According to Paul Lendvai,

> The Magyars were claimed to be descendants of the hideous Asiatic Scythians of legend, half men and half apes, a witches' brood begotten by devils [...] identified with the Huns, who are remembered only too well in Europe. Attila had, after all, become in Western eyes the embodiment of barbarism, the anti-Christ, and at the time of the Renaissance he already appeared in Italian legends as king of the Hungarians, constantly hatching plots, and depicted with dog ears, the bestial offspring of a greyhound and a princess locked up in a tower. (Lendvai 2003: 25)

The 1840s, in particular, saw mass market production and dissemination of medieval histories, among the most popular of which was the major work of the Swiss historian Sismondo de' Sismondi, *Storia della caduta dell'Impero Romano e della decadenza della civiltà dall'anno 250 al 1000*, which had first appeared in 1836 and included a chapter on the Huns' invasion of Aquileia (Sorba 2009: 246). The subject of Attila's exploits, particularly in Italy, had already been set by other composers (among them, Handel, Jommelli, and Galuppi) before Friedrich Ludwig Zacharias Werner wrote *Attila, König der Hunnen* (1808), the play that would become the literary source for Verdi's opera (for more on other "Attila" operas, see Engelhardt 1992; for a detailed comparison of Werner's play and Solera's libretto, see Unfer Lukoschik 2002: 71–89).

In his play, Werner celebrates the triumph of Christianity over the pagan through a vision, but also the machinations of a Judith (who seduced Holofernes and beheaded him when he passed out in a drunken stupor; Odabella in the opera, Hildegunde in the play). Werner achieved fame by way of de Staël's *De l'Allemagne*, which reflected and stimulated continued pan-European fascination in the land wars of the early Middle Ages (Sorba 2009), and as Pierluigi Petrobelli has noted, "gave life to the romantic movement" (2002: 157). It became required reading, as Sorba shows, and exerted enormous influence, especially in Italy, where figures such as Giacomo Leopardi and Giuseppe Mazzini later reflected upon its importance (Sorba 2009: 345; see also Gerhard 2009, 2010; Mazzini 1910: VII: 203–236; Gerhard and Candoni 2007).

Madame de Staël was something of a force of nature to which many of Germany's brightest were drawn. Schiller, Lord Byron, Schlegel, and Sismondi visited her at Coppet, her home in Switzerland, as did Werner, whom she considered the successor to Goethe (de Staël [1813] 1968: I: 369). Madame de Staël was impressed enough by him to devote an entire chapter of *De l'Allemagne* to his dramatic works, and especially *Attila*,

FIGURE 43.3 Raphael, *The Meeting of Leo the Great and Attila* (1514). Photo: Vatican Museums.

König der Hunnen, which elucidated the relationship between love and religion, what would become an extremely potent elixir for Verdi, who inevitably also found a political context for it.

De Staël considers the high point of Werner's play to be the encounter between Leo the Great (Leone, an "old Roman" in the opera) and Attila, an event iconicized by Raphael's 1514 fresco in the Vatican, *The Meeting of Leo the Great and Attila* (Figure 43.3).[2] She describes both the fresco and Werner's dramatic rendering of it in his play and accords it much mystical significance. (The actual meeting, however, took place outside Mantua on the banks of the river Mincio, a far less useful venue for the purposes of propaganda, politics, religion, and legend-building.) In the play, the Hun retreats from Rome after seeing a vision of St. Peter, a tableau of spiritual conversion, as de Staël observes: "From this moment the Christian religion stirs the soul of Attila, despite the beliefs of his ancestors, and he orders his army to distance themselves from Rome"[3] (de Staël [1813] 1968: 377).

Verdi had already composed a scene of a tyrant experiencing an epiphany in *Nabucco*, and his renewed attraction to the idea, particularly as it served metaphorically in revolutionary Italy, is not surprising. Moreover, in *Attila*, the stage image would be understood immediately by his culturally literate audience; if Werner was unknown, Raphael was a superstar. As Douglas Ipson (2009) has shown, the fresco was already an international attraction in the 1840s, described in numerous travel guides, including Octavian

Blewitt's *A Hand-book for Travellers in Central Italy Including the Papal States, Rome, and the Cities of Etruria* and the *New Guide of Rome and the Environs according to Vasi and Nibby* (Ipson 2009: 349).

Not surprisingly, Verdi eventually asked Temistocle Solera to write the libretto; he was a frequent collaborator with a well-practiced epic style realized in *Nabucco*, *I Lombardi alla prima crociata*, and *Giovanna d'arco*. Together they made a number of interconnected changes and additions to Werner's play. The most important revision is that of Attila's religious vision-cum-Werner, and the most significant addition is the scene of the birth of Venice at the end of the Prologue, which Pierluigi Petrobelli calls "a crucial moment in the evolution of Verdi's dramatic conception" (Petrobelli 2002: 159).

The Sunrise, the City, and the Holy Season

The Venetians were delighted with the scene of the founding of their city. Tommaso Locatelli, writing for the March 18 issue of the *Gazetta privilegiata di Venezia*, lauded the composer for it (Locatelli 1846: 225–227), while the Milanese Luigi Casamorata was far more skeptical; he deemed the tableau extraneous to the story and claimed that it was added solely to flatter the Venetians, for whom the opera was written (Casamorata 1847: 18). Casamorata was right: Verdi most certainly tailored *Attila* for a local audience, and in a scene that is visually and musically spectacular, he drew on seasonal festivities and invoked existing icons that stimulated civic pride. For modern consumers, the scene is a bird's-eye view of the union of technology and ideology in 1840s Italy (Greenwald 2009a).

Verdi was not only intent on having such a scene, but also on ensuring its proper realization on the stage. As he wrote to impresario Francesco Lanari (who then quoted the passage to President of La Fenice Giuseppe Berti in his letter of September 29, 1845), "What I would like to be sublime is the second part of Scene VI, which is the founding of Venice: the sunrise should be well done, because I want to express it in the music [...]"[4] (Conati 1983: 159). The sets were designed by Giuseppe Bertoja, whose sketches became a model for future productions, especially those designed by Romolo Liverani for Fano (1850) and Cesena (1851) (Jesurum 1996, 2006; Viale Ferrero 2002: passim and plates 44–47; Giovagnoli 1998). The scene was illuminated by the new gas lighting at La Fenice (Baker 2013: 179–181; Baker 1998: 209–240; Capra 1996: 230–264). Publisher Francesco Lucca, enormously proud of the accomplishments of the Venetian premiere of *Attila*, but also intent on furthering his own interests by keeping the opera before the public as well as ensuring (or attempting to ensure) continuity in performance, printed Bertoja's sketches in *L'Italia musicale* (1847: 117). An inscription at the top of Bertoja's sketch for the scene of the lagoon confirms Verdi's attention to sound and sight: "As written in the opera by M. Verdi, all buildings were [constructed] in separate pieces and the background of the sky changed from stormy to calm with the rising of the sun."[5] Two articles accompanied the illustration, Bianchi-Giovini's history of Attila in Italy (see above) and a detailed description of the coordination of lighting and music, using projections and a transparent curtain, as lamps simulated the flickering embers of the decimated landscape. A crescendo of light corresponded precisely to Verdi's scoring (see *LIM* 1847: 113 and Greenwald 2009a and 2012: xviii for a complete translation of the description).

The addition of the sunrise scene was actually neither far-fetched nor gratuitous, since Attila's siege of Aquileia has been irrevocably linked to the founding of Venice, celebrated annually on March 25, the Feast of the Annunciation, the day on which the angel Gabriel was sent to Nazareth to inform Mary of her virgin conception of the baby Jesus (exactly nine months before December 25). Moreover, the sunrise was a vital icon for both creation and liberation, following earlier works that evoked such imagery, including Haydn's *Creation*, Rossini's *Guillaume Tell*, and Félicien David's symphonic ode *Le désert* (Greenwald 2009a). As David Rosand has shown, the Venetians enjoyed a long history of mythologizing their genesis and defining themselves as "the first republic of the new era, born in Christian liberty, hence a true historical successor to pagan Rome" (Rosand 2001: 6). The enactment of the founding of Venice thus had deep relevance for the citizens of the lagoon, who tied the birth of their city to the birth of the Christian savior, as well as to the vernal equinox. The king of the Huns had also played a real part in the event and retained a symbolic role as one in a multitude of humbled pagans in numerous allegories of the triumph of Christianity over the heathen. The date of March 25, as Edward Muir notes, was thus also

> mystically conjoined with the founding of Rome [...] the beginning of the Christian era, the annual rebirth of nature [...] [and] permanently bound the destiny of Venice to the veiled will of God, the harmony of nature, and the imperial authority of Rome. (Muir 1981: 71; see also Brusegan 2007: 21–24)

The festivals commemorating the founding of Venice and the Annunciation were described in many of the histories that proliferated in early-nineteenth-century Italy, including the *Origine delle feste veneziane* (1817–1829), the remarkable discourse on the union of the religious, historical, and civic aspects of Venice and its festivals by noblewoman Giustina Renier Michiel (1755–1832), who devoted the first volume to the founding of the city. Renier Michiel's work was in wide circulation and, according to Muir, "[t]he most extensive exposition of Venice's myths and public rituals ever written [...]" (Muir 1981: 61).

Attila himself attained a quasi-sacred status in Venice, according to Renier Michiel; he claimed to possess the sword of Mars (the god of war), and with this unique favor bestowed by such a powerful entity, he commanded such devotion and adulation among his followers that they "became accustomed to saying that their eyes could not bear the majestic splendor of the King of the Huns"[6] (Renier Michiel 1817–1829: I: 12–13). Leo's confrontation with him outside the gates of Rome was thus all the more religiously and politically potent. As Muir observes, Attila

> ...became part of the modern European mythical heritage [...] and survived even the republic: during the Austrian occupation of Venice in the nineteenth century, Verdi chose the Attila legend for an opera that slipped *Risorgimento* propaganda past the censors of the modern 'Huns.' (Muir 1981: 68–69)

While many other barbarian intruders breached the areas surrounding Venice, notably Padova, the Attila legend provided a convenient point of reference for the civic-minded Venetians, and the Hun became a cultural icon.

The Venetians undoubtedly understood very well the abundance of "local color" in Verdi's opera. In 1846, moreover, the carnival season at La Fenice mirrored the church calendar, beginning St. Stephen's day (December 26), the day after Christmas, encompassing pre-Lenten festivities, much of Lent itself, and ending on March 24, as the community looked towards Easter, the climax of the cycle of birth, resurrection, and rebirth, observed in 1846 on April 12 (for more on what was originally considered a "normal" season, see Rosselli 1984: 61). The rescheduling of the premiere of *Attila* from January to March, because of Verdi's illness, seems in retrospect serendipitous, as the opera closed the season on March 24, the day before the Feast of the Annunciation. While religious subjects were common enough in operas performed during Lent (*Giovanna d'Arco* comes to mind here), few, if any, have the time-place specificity of *Attila*.

Raphael's Fresco, Attila's Vision

Verdi had been quite ill throughout the composition of *Attila*, and one of the first things he did in February 1846 when he felt well enough to return to work was to ask his friend Vincenzo Luccardi to go to the Vatican and write a detailed description of Raphael's fresco *The Meeting of Leo the Great and Attila*:

> I know that in the Vatican, either in the tapestries or in the Raphael frescoes, there must be the meeting of Attila with Saint Leo. I need a description of the figure of Attila: draw me a few strokes with your pen, then explain to me with words and numbers the colors of his outfit: I particularly need information about his hairstyle. If you will do this favor for me, I will give you my saintly benediction. (Gaetano and Luzio 1913: 441; trans. Gossett 2006: 465)

Verdi surely knew the fresco well enough, and needed Luccardi to remind him of the details of its colors and costumes.

The fresco is but one of the many accounts—visual and verbal—of Attila's 452 A.D. meeting with Leo the Great that began to circulate as early as 455 A.D. At the heart of these narratives is the mystery behind Attila's sudden decision not to attack Rome. Modern historians posit that money and/or the Emperor Valentinian's sister, Honoria, were exchanged for peace. But much longer lived is the allegory that Raphael tells in his fresco: Attila, a superstitious man, seized by a vision of Saints Peter and Paul, retreats in fear. The fresco is an "action" scene staged against a landscape of familiar images, the coliseum in the central distance and an obelisk; the surrounding area is aflame. There is a confrontation: the papal entourage stands to the left and Attila's troops to the right. The principal players as well as the opposing forces are shaded in an opposition of light and dark: Leo is dressed in gold and white bishop's costume and headdress and is seated on a white horse. The bearded Attila, nearly dead center, dressed in hues of grey and brown, is seated on a black horse; he twists his body as his head remains riveted to the spectacle above. He swings both arms in the opposite direction of his body and raises his palms to stop the flood of his army pouring in from the right at the signal of the trumpeters, also facing right. The sudden movement of the Hun king initiates chaos in a distinct counterpoint to the stately papal envoy. The soldiers point to the sky, where sword-wielding images of Saints Peter and Paul hover above the scene. In addition to his sword, Saint Peter holds the iconic papal keys. Both figures are bearded, and their eyes are directed at Attila. Their simple drapery, classical and windswept, is common currency in Renaissance depictions of mystical or mythological characters, evading literal interpretation, and allowing, as artist Marianne Ryan explains, "allusion and illusion to take over from pure representation" (Ryan 1999: 38, quoted in Doy 2002: 184). The motif of light and dark bisects the scene, as the saints hover in a clear sky above the pope, while Attila and his troops are shrouded in the smoky clouds of war. The religious message is clear in the fresco, but the political one is even stronger. As art historian Ingrid Rowland points out: "The repulse of Attila served as a warning to all prospective invaders of Italy" (2005: 114). Attila's surrender to Leo was thus a potent addition to the litanies of oppressed nations as well as a miraculous story that served a powerful religious institution.

Raphael painted the fresco in partial fulfillment of Julius II's 1507 commission to redecorate his new apartments in the Vatican (he commissioned Michelangelo to paint the Sistine Chapel around the same time; see Nesselrath 1993 for details of the genesis of the fresco). The artist worked on the rooms until his death in 1520, after which Leo X supervised as Raphael's students completed them. Altogether, Raphael and his studio produced a series of four rooms that became known as the *Stanze di Raffaello* (Raphael Rooms). All of the rooms are thematic, reflecting Christian history and doctrine, and most important, the triumph of the Catholic Church over Paganism. The Attila fresco appears in the Stanza di Eliodoro (Room of Heliodorus), where, as Rowland notes, "[Raphael] presented four examples of the Church in action, in keeping with the traditional contrast between the active and the contemplative Christian life" (2005: 115). More specifically, according to Arnold Nesselrath (2012), Raphael, following Julius's mandate, created a series of scenes in which God intervenes to "save his people." All of the frescoes in the Stanza di Eliodoro thus illustrate not only a triumph over the infidel, but the ways in which the church defends its people as well as itself. The room's namesake, Heliodorus, appears in the Apocrypha, Maccabees II (3: 1–40), and like Attila, is brought down—in front of witnesses—by the power of God, revealed through a vision. Heliodorus, sent by Seleucus to empty the treasury of the Temple of Jerusalem, is attacked by three apparitions, all young and strong: a horse and rider armed with a mace and two young men wielding switches who "scourged him continually, and gave him many sore stripes" (Maccabees II: 3:27). He was brutalized within an inch of his life until he "acknowledged the power of God" and was spared. Julius II also appears in the painting, on a litter carried by Raphael himself (making eye contact with the viewer) and his students. The pope is bearded, having sworn in 1510 that he would not shave until "he had expelled the French from the Italian peninsula" (Rowland 2005: 112; see also, Ipson

2009: 349). In *The Liberation of Saint Peter*, under a moonlit sky, Peter is miraculously freed by an angel from his confinement in the Mamertine Prison. The imprisoned saint was likely understood in this context as yet another metaphor for occupied Italy, and he is shown both behind bars and outside the prison, where the guards are asleep. *The Mass of Bolsena* depicts a German priest who doubts the validity of transubstantiation, but witnesses the miracle of the bleeding host during Mass.

The legendary meeting of Leo and Attila became the centerpiece of Act IV of Werner's play, and the Act I finale of Verdi's opera. Werner, who had led an undisciplined life as a young man, renounced his dissolute ways, converted to Catholicism, and gained a reputation as a playwright and charismatic preacher; his *Attila* reflects certain aspects of his apparent religious zealotry in the ecstatic moments the playwright offers both Attila and the character of Leo. Both composer and playwright created scenes that correspond directly to the basic design of the fresco, that is, a tableau showing two processions of opposing clergy and barbarians. But play and opera part ways, particularly on matters of costume, in the important moment of the central character's religious vision, the entity that causes Attila to change his mind. Moreover, whatever it is that Attila sees in the sky is not physically staged in play or opera, but rather imagined by the audience through verbal cues given by Attila himself, and accompanied by music appropriate to the image. Of course, a modern high-tech production could very well bring such a vision to life in any number of ways, but neither Werner in 1808 nor Verdi in 1846 gave any indication that the images should be displayed during performance. What is important for now is that the divergent details of play and opera pit institutional song against arioso, while distinguishing portrait from illustration and exposing ways in which fiction can be more powerful than fact.

Let us consider the play first: Werner's text makes clear that instead of Raphael's classically draped figures, the Hun really sees a single image, which audiences could have understood only as a realistic and modern portrait of Saint Peter as Bishop of Rome. As a religiously enrapt chorus of onlookers sings the Latin hymn "Veni creator spiritus," presumably in its original form, Werner's Attila describes his vision to his squire:

> Edecon! Do you not see up there a giant of horrifying countenance [...]? ... He wears a temple of gold bejeweled with pearls on his silver head, and while he wields a flaming sword in his right hand, he raises his rose-bedecked left hand with two gleaming keys of ore that he has stolen from the hands of Wotan, as if to close the gates of Valhalla.[7] (Werner 1808: Act IV, scene 3, 195–196)

Werner has conflated various iconographies, including a reference to Raphael's fresco, but not an exact duplication of it. The crown that Werner's "giant" wears and the two keys in his hand belong to the official papal regalia, the *triregnum* (a three-tiered headdress) and the "Keys to the Kingdom of Heaven," the insignia and coat of arms of Vatican City, as depicted commonly in papal portraits, for example, *Saint Peter on his Throne* by a contemporary of Raphael, Vasco Fernandes (1506, Viseu, Portugal, Grão Vasco Museum; widely available on the Internet). The flaming sword has multiple symbolic meanings, the most basic of which is its role in Genesis 3:24, where it guards the Tree of Life after Adam and Eve are banished from Eden. Werner's Attila, moreover, sees and understands the image on his own terms—his god, Wotan, and his heaven, Valhalla—against a Christian adversary, who threatens that belief. That belief is supported and amplified by the singing of the familiar hymn, "Veni creator spiritus."

Verdi tells the same story, avoiding, however, Werner's institutional liturgy and emblems to capture the spirituality of the moment as well as the detail of Raphael's allegory. Verdi was barred from quoting "Veni creator spiritus," as was originally proposed (see Berti's letter to Lanari of August 18, 1845, in Conati 1983: 156), and substituted instead a freshly composed unaccompanied four-part chorus for women and children with nearly the same text, "Come visit our minds, O Spirit of Creation"[8] (Solera 1846: 16; Verdi [1846] 2012: Act I, n. 9, mm. 63–70). But Attila's music is neither song nor hymn, his text a deeply personal revelation and a capitulation to forces beyond earthly matters:

> This is not a dream which now invades my soul! There are two giants who fill the sky... their eyes burning and their swords aflame... their burning points reach me. Halt spirits! Here man withdraws... before the gods the king prostrates himself![9] (Solera 1846: 17; Verdi [1846] 2012: Act I, n. 9, mm. 111–127)

Verdi and the *Tableau Vivant*

The long-lived history of the visual depiction of historical and/or didactic events developed out of need, a way to instruct a society that could not read, but also a way of providing evidence of madness or delusion, as Verdi had already done before *Attila*, in *Nabucco*, and after, in *Macbeth*. Long after literacy, however, the pictures not only sustained their instructive value, but became absorbed into the cultural consciousness.

In "staging" Raphael, Verdi also constructed a species of *tableau vivant*, which Philip Gossett has compared to the Act I finale of Stephen Sondheim and James Lapine's musical, *Sunday in the Park with George* (1984), where protagonist Georges Seurat assembles his characters into a freeze frame of his most famous painting, *A Sunday Afternoon on the Island of La Grande Jatte* (1884; Gossett 2006: 465). The tradition of the *tableau vivant* stems from the Middle Ages, however, and in particular, according to Lucien Rimels (1961), the "festival of the Resurrection, in which they reproduced evangelical scenes for the purpose of enlightening the viewers." All of the frescoes in Raphael's Stanza di Eliodoro perform the same role as frozen moments of biblical events, miracles, and most important, scenes originally presented live in medieval liturgical drama. Those scenes were also part of festival pageantry, where they were set up on platforms and carried in processions, especially during carnival season. They were enjoyed widely in Italy, not least in Venice, and well into the nineteenth century, as Renier Michiel attests. The practice evolved over time into an important dramatic tool and even a parlor entertainment, reported by the likes of Mendelssohn, Goethe, and also Madame de Staël, an ardent practitioner of *tableaux vivants*, who delighted visitors with her costumed portrayals (Frantz 1998: 174–175).

Such reenactments—especially in the early nineteenth century—as Maurice Samuels observes, reflect the "increased importance of historical illustration [...]" (2004: 65), which, when theatricalized, "mimicked the gestural configurations of paintings and engravings [...] familiar to audiences at the time" (124). These flesh and blood tapestries thus permitted the community, now "united against a common enemy," to witness for itself the fall of a tyrant (Samuels 2004: 131), heretic, or pagan—events portrayed in nearly every picture in the Stanze di Raffaello and every narration in corresponding scripture. In fact, the words of the assembled choristers in *Attila* tell us as much when they declare Attila's fall a moral victory of canonic import:

> Behold the might of the Eternal! / By a shepherd boy was Goliath defeated/by a humble girl was mankind saved / by an unknown people was the faith spread/before a devout and pious assembly / Now withdraws the king of the heathens!"[10] (Solera 1846: 17)

See also: Visual Media, Castrato Acts, Divas and Divos, *Regietheater*/Director's Theater, What is Opera? Politics, Production Aesthetics and Materials

Notes

1. The section heading quotes John Rockwell's subtitle in his *New York Times* essay on Wagnerian stagings (Rockwell 1989).
2. My sincere thanks to Professor Arnold Nesselrath, deputy to the director for the curatorial and conservational departments, Vatican Museums, for sharing so generously his time and vast knowledge of the Raphael Rooms in the Vatican Museums.
3. "Dès cet instant la religion chrétienne agit sur l'âme d'Attila, malgré les croyances de ses ancêtres, et il ordonne à son armée de s'éloigner de Rome."
4. "[...] quelle che desidererei sublime è la Seconda alla Scena VI. che è il principio della Città di Venezia: Sina ben fatto l'alzare del Sole, che io voglio espremere colla Musica [...]."
5. The complete inscription reads: "[Rio Alto sulle Lagune Adriatiche Attila—Gran Teatro la Fenice/[toward centre:] 1845 [toward right:] E53 / Quando l'opera fu scritta dal M Verdi tutti i fabbricati erano in spezzati staccati e il fondo di cielo / cambiava dal temporale al sereno e con lo spuntare del sole [right]." My thanks to Daniela Macchione for her generous help with the transcription.
6. "Da quel momento questo favorito del Dio della guerra acquistò un carattere sacro, ed i suoi cortigiani sia per divozione, o piuttosto per adulazione, solevano dire, [p. v.1, 12] che i loro occhi non potevano sostenere lo splendore maestoso del re degli Unni."
7. "Edecon! Siehst du in jenen Höhen nicht einen Riesen, schrecklich anzusehen [...] Ein Tempel von Gold, mit Perlen geschmükket, er trägt ihn auf silberumlocketem Haupt, und, während die Rechte das Flammenschwert zükket, erhebet die Linke mit Rosen umlaubt, zwei Schlüssel von Erz, die Strahlen ergießen, / Also ob sie, die Thore Walhallas zu schließen, der Riese den Händen des Wodan geraubt!"
8. "Vieni—Le menti visita, / O spirto creator..."
9. "No!... non è sogno—ch' or l'alma invade! Sono due gigantic—che investon l'etra... / Le ardenti punte—giungono a me. / Spirti fermte.—Que l'uom si arretra; / Dinanzi ai numi—prostrasi il re!"

10. "Oh dell'Eterno—mira virtute! / Da un pastorello—vinto è Golia, / Da umil fanciulla—l'umo ha salute, / Da gente ignota—sparsa è la fè . . . / dinanzi a turba—devota e pia / Ora degli empi-s'arretra il re!"

BIBLIOGRAPHY

Allanbrook, Wye Jamison. 1983. *Rhythmic Gesture in Mozart: 'Le nozze di Figaro' and 'Don Giovanni.'* Chicago: University of Chicago Press.

Attila. 1493. Image of Attila the Hun in the *Nuremberg Chronicle* of 1493. Online. Available: http://brandeisspecialcollections.blogspot.com/2010/09/nuremberg-chronicle-liber-chronicarum.html (accessed July 22, 2012).

Baker, Evan. 2013. *From the Score to the Stage: An Illustrated History of Continental Opera Production and Staging.* Chicago: University of Chicago Press.

——. 1998. "Verdi's Operas and Giuseppe Bertoja's Designs at the Gran Teatro la Fenice, Venice." In Radice 1998, 209–240.

Basevi, Abramo. 1859. *Studio sulle opere di Giuseppe Verdi.* Florence: Tofani.

Berlioz, Hector. [1865] 1969. *The Memoirs of Hector Berlioz*, translated and edited by David Cairns. New York: Alfred A. Knopf.

Bianchi-Giovini, Aurelio. 1847. "Storia: Attila e i primordi di Venezia." *L'Italia musicale* 1/15 (October 13): 113–115.

Breckenbill, Anita. 2009. "André Gill and Musicians in Paris in the 1860s and 1870s: Caricatures in *La Lune* and *L'Éclipse.*" *Music in Art: International Journal for Music Iconography* 34/1–2: 215–228.

Brusegan, Marcello, with Francesca Scarrica. 2007. *Miti e leggende di Venezia: le origini, I simboli, le storie e I personaggi di una città sospesa tra l'acqua e il cielo.* Rome: Newton Compton.

Budden, Julian. 1987. "Wagnerian Tendencies in Italian Opera." In *Music and Theatre: Essays in Honor of Winton Dean*, edited by Nigel Fortune, 299–332. Cambridge: Cambridge University Press.

Capra, Marco. 1996. "L'Illuminazione sulla scena verdiana ovvero l'arco voltaico non acceca la luna?" In Petrobelli and Della Seta 1996, 230–264.

Carlson, Marvin. 1989. "The Iconic Stage." *Journal of Dramatic Theory and Criticism* 3/2: 3–18.

Casamorata, Luigi. 1847. "*Attila*, Melodramma di T. Solera, Musica del Maestro Giuseppe Verdi." *Gazetta musicale di Milano* VI/3 (January 17): 17–19.

Cesari, Gaetano, and Alessandro Luzio, eds. 1913. *I copialettere di Giuseppe Verdi.* Milan: Stucchi Ceretti.

Citron, Marcia J. 2010. *When Opera Meets Film.* Cambridge Studies in Opera. Cambridge: Cambridge University Press.

——. 2008. "'An Honest Contrivance': Opera and Desire in *Moonstruck.*" *Music & Letters* 89/1: 56–83.

——. 2000. *Opera on Screen.* New Haven: Yale University Press.

Conati, Marcello. 1983. *La bottega della musica. Verdi e La Fenice.* Milan: Il Saggiatore.

Corsaro, Frank. 2013. "On Stage: Theater, Opera, and Ballet: M & M (Maurice and Me)." In *Maurice Sendak: A Celebration of the Artist and His Work*, exhibition catalogue (Society of Illustrators, New York, June 2013), curated by Justin G. Schiller and Dennis M. V. David, and edited by Leonard S. Marcus, 133–149. New York: Abrams.

de Staël, Germaine. [1813] 1968. *De l'Allemagne*. 2. vols., edited by Simone Balayé. Paris: Garnier-Flammarion.Find this resource:

Doy, Gen. 2002. *Drapery: Classicism and Barbarism in Visual Culture*. London: I. B. Tauris.

Engelhardt, Markus. 1992. *Verdi und andere. 'Un giorno di regno', 'Ernani', 'Attila', 'Il corsaro' in Mehrfachvertonungen*. Parma: Istituto nazionale di studi verdiani.

Ephron, Nora. 1989. *When Harry Met Sally*. Directed by Rob Reiner. Columbia Pictures.

Fenice. 1846. Poster for premiere of Verdi's *Attila*. Online. Available: http://www.archiviostorico-lafenice.org/ArcFenice/ImageView.ashx?id=67474&multimediaType=Poster&fullTextSearch=Attila (accessed July 26, 2012).

Fidelio. 2008. "Adam Fischer Started his First New Production with "Fidelio" at the Hungarian State Opera." Online. Available: http://haydnphil.org/en/newsletter/report08.htm (accessed July 22, 2012).

Folena, Daniela Goldin, Wolfgang Osthoff, and Rainer Franke, eds. 2002. *Verdi und die deutsche Literatur/Verdi e la letteratura tedesca*. Laaber: Laaber.

Frantz, Pierre. 1998. *L'esthétique du tableau dans le théâtre du XVIIIe siècle*. Paris: Presses universitaires de France.

Gerhard, Anselm. 2010. "Politische Aussagen in neuem Licht: *Attila* und die Bedeutung des 'chiaroscuro' für Verdis musikalische Dramaturgie." *Schweizer Jahrbuch für Musikwissenschaft*. Neue Folge 28/29, edited by Luca Zopelli, 151–170. Bern: Peter Lang.

——. 2009. "Verdi's *Attila*: A Study in Chiaroscuro." *Cambridge Opera Journal* 21/3: 379–389.

——, and Jean-François Candoni. 2007. "De la tragédie romantique allemande à l'opéra italien: '*Attila*' de Verdi, entre discours patriotique et internationalisation de l'opéra." In *A travers l'Opéra. Parcours anthropologiques et transferts dramaturgiques sur la scène théâtrale européenne du XVIIIe au XXe siècle. Études en l'honneur de Gilles de Van*, edited by Siro Ferrone und Andrea Fabiano, 241–261. Paris: L'Harmattan.

Geronimi, Clyde, and Hamilton Luske (directors). 1946. "The Whale Who Wanted to Sing at the Met [Willie the Operatic Whale]. Burbank, CA: Walt Disney Productions. Online. (Partially) Available: http://www.youtube.com/watch?v=Gcu-B6EhjFE (accessed June 23, 2012).

Giovagnoli, Attilio. 1988. "Due bozzetti di Romolo Liverani per l'opera *Attila* di Verdi al Teatro Comunale Provvisorio di Fano." *Nuovi studi fanesi* 3: 165–72.

Gossett, Philip. 2006. *Divas and Scholars: Performing Italian Opera*. Chicago: University of Chicago Press.

Grand-Carteret, John. [1892]. *Richard Wagner en Caricatures*. Paris: Larousse.

Greenwald, Helen. 2012a. "*Ars moriendi*: Reflections on the Death of Mimì." In *The Arts of the Prima Donna in the Long Nineteenth Century*, edited by Rachel Cowgill and Hilary Poriss, 167–185. New York: Oxford University Press.

——. 2012b. "Introduction" to *Attila*. In Verdi [1846] 2012, xi–xxviii.

——. 2009a. "*Son et lumière*: Verdi, *Attila*, and the Sunrise over the Lagoon." *Cambridge Opera Journal* 21/3: 267–277.

——. 2009b. "*Zelmire/Zelmira*: de Belloy, Tottola, Rossini, and 'Les Genres des Tragédies.' " In *D'une scène à l'autre. L'opéra italien en Europe*. 2 vols. Edited by Damien Colas and Alessandro di Profio, II: 239–253. Wavre: Mardaga.

——. 2007. "Staging Satan: Spohr's *Faust* and Weber's *Der Freischütz*." *Die Schaubühne in der Epoche des 'Freischütz: Theater und Musiktheater der Romantik*, Vorträge und Gespräche des Salzburger Symposions 2007. Wort und Musik: Salzburger Akademische Beiträge 70, edited by Jürgen Kühnel, Ulrich Müller, Oswald Panagl, et al., 226–238. Salzburg: Verlag Mueller-Speiser.

——. 2005. "Historical Introduction" to Gioachino Rossini, *Zelmira*, edited by Helen M. Greenwald and Kathleen Kuzmick Hansell. *Edizione Critica delle Opere di Gioachino Rossini.* 4 vols. Sez. I: 33. Pesaro: Fondazione Rossini.

——. 2000. "Picturing Cio-Cio San: House, Screen, and Ceremony in Puccini's *Madama Butterfly*." *Cambridge Opera Journal* 12/3: 237–259.

——. 1998. "Realism on the Opera Stage: Belasco, Puccini, and the California Sunset." In Radice 1998, 279–296.

——. 1991. "Dramatic Exposition and Musical Structure in Puccini's Operas." PhD diss., City University of New York.

Groos, Arthur. 1997. "*Madama Butterfly*: Il perduto atto del consolato americano." In *Giacomo Puccini: L'uomo, il musicista, il panorama europeo. Atti del Convegno internazionale di studi su Giacomo Puccini nel 70o anniversario della morte (Lucca, 25–29 novembre 1994)*, edited by Gabriella Biagi Ravenni and Carolyn Gianturco, 147–158. Lucca: Libreria musicale italiana.

Grover-Friedlander, Michal. 2011. *Operatic Afterlives*. New York: Zone Books.

Heartz, Daniel. 2004. "Farinelli Revisited: From the Sublime to the Ridiculous." In Daniel Heartz, *From Garrick to Gluck: Essays on Opera in the Age of Enlightenment*, edited by John A. Rice, 113–132. New York: Pendragon.

Ipson, Douglas. 2009. "*Attila* Takes Rome: The Reception of Verdi's Opera on the Eve of Revolution." *Cambridge Opera Journal* 21/3: 249–256.

Izzo, Francesco. 2007. "Verdi, the Virgin, and the Censor: The Politics of the Cult of Mary in *I Lombardi alla prima crociata and Giovanna d'Arco*." *Journal of the American Musicological Society* 60/3: 557–598.

Jesurum, Olga. 2006. "Set Designs for Italian Opera by Romolo and Tancredi Liverani." *Music in Art: International Journal for Music Iconography* 31/1–2: 51–62.

——. 1996. "Le prime opere di Verdi nella interpretazione scenografica di Romolo Liverani." *Studi verdiani* 11: 222–240.

Jones, Chuck (director). 1957. *What's Opera Doc?* Burbank, CA: Warner Brothers Cartoons.

——. 1949. *The Rabbit of Seville*. Burbank, CA: Warner Brothers Cartoons.

Kelly, Christopher. 2009. *End of Empire: Attila the Hun and the Fall of Rome*. New York: W. W. Norton.

Keyser, Lucy. 1989. "It's Love at the Box Office for *Harry Met Sally*…" *Washington Times* (July 25).

Kohler. 2012. Video of Kohler television commercial using Bellini's "Finì… Me lassa!" [*I puritani*]. Online. Available: http://www.youtube.com/watch?v=wyrqog7oQsU (accessed July 22, 2012).

Kreuzer, Gundula. 2012. "*Wagner-Dampf*: Steam in *Der Ring des Nibelungen* and Operatic Production." *Opera Quarterly* 27/2–3: 179–218.

Kushner, Tony. 2003. *Brundibár*. [Adapted from the libretto by Adolf Hoffmeister.] Illustrated by Maurice Sendak. New York: Hyperion.

La Gorce, Jérôme 1987. "Lully's First Opera: A Rediscovered Poster for *Les fêtes de l'Amour et Bacchus*." *Early Music* 15/3: 308–314.

Lawton, J. F. 1990. *Pretty Woman*. Directed by Garry Marshall. Touchstone Pictures.

Lendvai, Paul. 2003. *The Hungarians: A Thousand Years of Victory in Defeat*, translated by Ann Major. Princeton, NJ: Princeton University Press.

Leppert, Richard. 1996. *Art and the Committed Eye: The Cultural Functions of Imagery*. Boulder, CO, and Oxford: Westview Press.

LIM. 1847. Description of Lighting for Verdi's *Attila* and Bertoja's sketch for Prologue. *L'Italia musicale* I/15 (October 13): 113–117.

Locatelli, Tommaso. 1846. "Bulletino degli spettacoli di quaresima—Gran Teatro la Fenice—Attila, *dramma lirico di* Temistocle Solera; *messo in musica dal M.* Verdi." *Gazzetta di Venezia* (March 18). Reprinted in *L'Appendice della Gazzetta di Venezia, prose scelte di Tommaso Locatelli* [1877]. 16 vols. IX: 225–227. Venice: Co'tipi del gondoliere.

Mazzini, Giuseppe. 1910. Translation of and introduction to Werner: *Der 24. Februar*. In *Scritti editi ed inediti*. VII: 203–236. Imola: P. Galeati.

Mitchell, W. J. Thomas. 1986. *Iconology: Image, Text, Ideology*. Chicago: University of Chicago Press.

Morris, Christopher. 2002. *Reading Opera between the Lines: Orchestral Interludes and Cultural Meaning from Wagner to Berg*. Cambridge: Cambridge University Press.

Muir, Edward. 1981. *Civic Ritual in Renaissance Venice*. Princeton, NJ: Princeton University Press.

Muraro, Maria Teresa. 1996. "Nuovi significati delle scene dei Bertoja alla Fenice di Venezia." In Petrobelli and Della Seta 1996, 83–108.

Music in Art: International Journal for Music Iconography. 1998–. Journal website. Online. Available: http://rcmi.gc.cuny.edu/?page_id=331 (accessed July 22, 2012).

Nesselrath, Arnold. 2012. "Verdi di Fronte a Raffaello." *Teatro di Rome*: '*Attila*' Program book for performances of Verdi's *Attila* May–June 2012, 108–111. Rome: Teatro di Roma.

——. 1993. "La stanza d'Eliodoro." In *Raffaello nell'appartamento di Giulio II e Leone X: monumenti, musei, gallerie ponteficie*, curated by the Direzione Musei Vaticani, 202–245. Milan: Electa.

Osthoff, Wolfgang. 2002. "Caratteri, poesia, passione—Zur Musik von Verdis *Attila*." In Folena et al. 2002, 91–116.

Petrobelli, Pierluigi. 2002. "Verdi e Madame de Staël." In Folena et al. 2002, 153–164.

——, and Fabrizio Della Seta, eds. 1996. *La realizzazione scenica dello spettacolo verdiano. Atti del congresso internazionale di studi. Parma, Teatro Regio-Conservatorio di musica 'A. Boito.' 28–30 settembre 1994*. Parma: Istituto nazionale di studi verdiani.

Petrobelli, Pierluigi, Olga Jesurum, and Marisa Di Gregorio Casati, eds. 1994. *'Sorgete! Ombre serene!' L'aspetto visivo dello spettacolo verdiano*. Parma: Istituto nazionale di studi verdiani.

Rackham, Arthur. [1911] 1976. *Siegfried and The Twilight of the Gods by Richard Wagner with illustrations by Arthur Rackham*, [Wagner text] translated by Margaret Armour. London: William Heinemann; New York: Doubleday. Reprint. New York: Abaris Books.

——. [1910] 1976. *The Rhinegold and The Valkyrie by Richard Wagner with illustrations by Arthur Rackham*, [Wagner text] translated by Margaret Armour. London: William Heinemann; New York: Doubleday. Reprint. New York: Abaris Books.

Radice, Mark A., ed. 1998. *Opera in Context: Essays on Historical Staging from the Late Renaissance to the Time of Puccini*. Portland, OR: Amadeus Press.

Ramey, Samuel. 2012. Photo of Ramey as Verdi's Attila. Online. Available: http://www.samuelramey.com/attilapopup.html (accessed June 23, 2012).

Renier Michiel, Giulia. 1817–1829. *Origine delle feste veneziane*. 5 vols. Venice: Avisopoli.

Rimels, Lucien. 1961. "Quadro vivente." In *Enciclopedia dello spettacolo*, edited by Silvio D'Amico, 613–614. Rome: Le Maschere.

Ripa. [1758–1760] 1971. *Cesare Ripa: Baroque and Rococo Pictorial Imagery. The 1758–60 Hertel Edition of Ripa's 'Iconologia' with 200 Engraved Illustrations*, edited by Edward A. Maser. Image 71 = "The Scourge of God." Reprint. Toronto: Dover. Online. Available: http://books.google.com/books (accessed July 22, 2012).

Rockwell, John. 1989. "Wagner's 'Ring': Stagecraft as Ideology." *New York Times* (March 26). Online. Available: http://www.nytimes.com/1989/03/26/arts/wagner-s-ring-stagecraft-as-ideology.html?pagewanted=all&src=pm (accessed June 23, 2012).

Rosand, David. 2001. *Myths of Venice: The Figuration of a State.* Chapel Hill: University of North Carolina Press.

Rosselli, John. 1984. *The Opera Industry in Italy from Cimarosa to Verdi.* Cambridge: Cambridge University Press.

Rossi, Francesco, Anthony P. Graziano, et al. 1993. *Michelangelo and Raphael with Botticelli-Perugino Signorelli-Ghirlandaio and Rosselli in the Vatican: All the Sistine Chapel, the Stanzas, and the Loggias.* Vatican City: Musei vaticani.

Rowden, Claire. 2009. "Opera and Caricature in the French Fin-de-siècle Press: Massenet's *Thaïs*, a Case Study." *Music in Art: International Journal for Music Iconography* 34/1–2: 274–290.

Rowland, Ingrid D. 2005. "The Vatican Stanze." In *The Cambridge Handbook to Raphael*, edited by Marcia B. Hall, 95–119. Cambridge: Cambridge University Press.

Ryan, Marianne. 1999. *Textures of Memory: The Poetics of Cloth.* Exhibition catalogue. Nottingham: Angel and Rowe Gallery.

Shanley, John Patrick. 1987. *Moonstruck*. Directed by Norman Jewison. Metro-Goldwyn-Mayer.

Samuels, Maurice. 2004. *The Spectacular Past: Popular History and the Novel in Nineteenth-Century France.* Ithaca, NY: Cornell University Press.

Senici, Emanuele. 2005. *Landscape and Gender in Italian Opera: The Alpine Virgin from Bellini to Puccini.* Cambridge: Cambridge University Press.

Smart, Mary Ann. 2004. *Mimomania: Music and Gesture in Nineteenth-Century Opera*. Berkeley and Los Angeles: University of California Press.

——. 2003. "'*Cadere in ginocchio*': Melodrama and Transcendence in Middle-Period Verdi." In *Verdi 2001: Atti del Convegno internazionale—Parma-New York-New Haven (24 January–1 February 2001)*. 2 vols., edited by Fabrizio Della Seta, Roberta Montemorra Marvin, and Marco Marica, II: 855–878. Florence: Olschki.

Solera, Temistocle. 1846. *Attila: Dramma lirico in un Prologo e tre Atti.* Libretto to Verdi's *Attila*. Venice: Molinari.

Sorba, Carlotta. 2009. "*Attila* and Verdi's Historical Imagination." *Cambridge Opera Journal* 21/3: 341–348.

Spatini. n.d. Spaghetti sauce commercial. Online. Available: http://www.youtube.com/watch?v=hhBrziu5QdI (accessed September 27, 2012).

Super-Conductor. 2012. Review of Verdi's *Attila* at La Scala (2003). Online: http://super-conductor.blogspot.com/2010/03/dvd-review-attila-at-la-scala.html (accessed February 24, 2012). The review is no longer available.

Sutton, Emma. 2002. *Aubrey Beardsley and British Wagnerism in the 1890s.* New York: Oxford University Press.

Tatar, Maria. 2002. *The Annotated Classic Fairy Tales.* New York: W.W. Norton.

Thomas, Roy, Gil Kane, Jim Woodring, and John Costanza. 1989–1990. *The Ring of the Nibelung*. Graphic novels. 4 vols. New York: DC Comics.
Unfer Lukoschik, Rita. 2002. "L'*Attila* di Zacharias Werner ed il libretto per Verdi." In Folena et al. 2002, 71–90.
Verdi, Giuseppe. [1846] 2012. *Attila. Dramma lirico in a Prologue and Three Acts*, edited by Helen M. Greenwald. *The Works of Giuseppe Verdi*. Ser. I: 9. Chicago: University of Chicago Press. Milan: Ricordi.
Viale Ferrero, Mercedes. 2002. "Stage and Set." In *Opera on Stage*, edited by Lorenzo Bianconi and Giorgio Pestelli and translated by Kate Singleton. *The History of Italian Opera* 5: 1–24. Chicago: University of Chicago Press.
Werner, Friedrich Ludwig Zacharias. 1808. *Attila, König der Hunnen*. Berlin: Realschulbuchhandlung.

Resources for the Study of Music Iconography

Erenstein, Robert. 1999. "Theatre Iconography: Traditions, Techniques, and Trends." In Heck 1999, 136–149.
Heck, Thomas F. 1999. *Picturing Performance: The Iconography of the Performing Arts in Concept and Practice*. Rochester, NY: University of Rochester Press.
Panofsky, Erwin. 1939. *Studies in Iconology: Humanist Themes in the Art of the Renaissance*. Oxford: Oxford University Press.
Peeters, Frank. 1999. "Scenography, Iconography, and Semiotics: toward an Analytical Framework." In Heck 1999, 150–162.
RIdIM/RCMI Inventories of Musical Iconography. 1987–. Project description and list of publications. Online. Available: http://rcmi.gc.cuny.edu/?page_id=317 (accessed July 22, 2012).
Seebass, Tilman. 2012. "Iconography." In *Grove Music Online. Oxford Music Online*, http://www.oxfordmusiconline.com/subscriber/article/grove/music/13698 (accessed July 22, 2012).
Winternitz, Emmanuel. 1967. *Music Instruments and Their Symbolism in Western Art: Studies in Musical Iconology*. New Haven: Yale University Press.

CHAPTER 44

SOURCES

LINDA B. FAIRTILE

In the broadest sense, sources document a musical work's creation and performance history. Scholars who engage in source study may be seeking to establish a text, trace a work's genesis, or separate the strands of its performing tradition. Focusing on the sources of a single composer can illuminate the development of a personal aesthetic as well as expose the degree to which outside forces may have influenced his decisions. Studying the sources for a single work may reveal multiple texts and interpretations, only some of which originated during the composer's lifetime. Regardless of the goal, source studies encourage us to confront issues of authorship, chronology, and tradition.

Sources of instrumental music and of non-dramatic vocal music are generally understood to include preliminary sketches and drafts, manuscript and printed scores, performing parts, and, in the latter case, materials related to the choice or development of the vocal text. Letters, diaries, administrative papers, and even journalistic reviews can also be considered sources. Opera, as a collaborative fusion of music and drama, expands this list to include such materials as set and costume designs, staging manuals, lighting plots, and prop lists. Technology has further augmented the inventory, first with still photographs, and later with audio and video recordings. This chapter will concentrate on documents as sources.

The skills that are needed to study opera sources are many and varied, but they share a common prerequisite: the researcher must be acutely aware of the context(s) in which these materials were created and utilized. In most cases, this presumes an understanding of opera as a business as well as an artistic endeavor. The preparation of scores and other performing materials, whether through hand copying, mechanical printing, or computerized note-setting, consumes money and time, and a composer's working method may be influenced as much by the practical needs of a theater or a publisher as by his own habits and predilections. Factors as diverse as the availability of a singer, the dimensions of a stage, or the political atmosphere of a city may profoundly influence the creation or re-creation of an opera, leaving their mark, in turn, on supporting documents. Occasionally, sources bear witness to the *im*practicality of a tradition, as musical or theatrical styles outpace accepted methods of production. In such cases, the gradual introduction of new methods may overlap with older processes, challenging our understanding of performance practice.

It goes without saying that the researcher should be familiar with a composer's work habits before undertaking a study of his or her sources in order to give the various types of materials their proper emphasis. Some composers' working librettos for example, yield comparatively little information about their compositional choices, while others' contain detailed annotations that are central to their emerging musical conceptions (Bailey 1979; Jones 2007; Carter 2010). Understanding how a composer customarily progressed from preliminary ideas to a finished score can help to compensate for missing documents, allowing established behaviors to inform speculation about the content of a lost source. At the same time, knowledge of personal compositional practices may forestall a fruitless search for materials that never existed in the first place.

In any field of study, the researcher must be disciplined and persistent in tracking down sources. Owing to particular traditions of production and distribution, operatic materials can be especially widely dispersed. While some documents are in publicly accessible libraries and archives, others may be in the hands of publishers, theaters, or individual collectors. Guides to locating these materials include thematic catalogues, critical editions, monographic series such as *Cambridge Opera Handbooks* and Garland/ Routledge's *Composer Resource Manuals* (later called *Routledge Music Bibliographies*), and websites of organizations dedicated to individual composers. (Among the more informative websites devoted to composers of opera are those of the Arnold Schoenberg Institute, the Britten-Pears Foundation, and the Kurt Weill Foundation for Music [see bibliography]. Each provides detailed information about its composer's manuscripts and other source materials.) Increasingly, researchers are creating their own tools to monitor the whereabouts of primary sources. The University of Chicago's *OperaCat*, which tracks materials related to five Italian opera composers (Rossini, Donizetti, Bellini, Verdi, and Puccini) as they appear in sale catalogues from the nineteenth century to the present, could be a model for further such collaborations between scholars and technologists.

This chapter addresses some of the issues that arise from the study of operatic sources, specifically, librettos, sketches, drafts, autograph scores, performing parts, and other production materials. Whether focusing on a composer, a work, or a repertoire, the scholar typically confronts questions about the relationships embodied in these sources: composer and performer, physical structure and content, and original and revision, among others. While the number of surviving documents for any opera depends on a variety of factors, works from the nineteenth century generally have the largest quantity of accessible materials and, correspondingly, the greatest representation in the literature on source studies. For this reason, this chapter is weighted toward operas from that period. As the pace of technological development accelerated through the twentieth century, the means of creating and reproducing operas was correspondingly transformed; thus the special challenges of studying the sources of contemporary opera will also be addressed.

Librettos

The documentary evidence of a libretto's genesis typically consists of correspondence, drafts, and fair copies, at times revealing that the composer played an active part in its creation. His participation in the process may be recorded in letters to his librettist, as well as notations made directly on the evolving text. From some of the most storied collaborations—Verdi and Boito, Scribe and Meyerbeer, Strauss and Hofmannsthal—we learn about musical and dramatic values, in addition to the genesis of specific works. In other cases, the availability and, indeed, the awareness of documentary sources varies greatly, since the working papers of librettists tend to receive less attention than those of composers. Recent scholarly interest in the process of libretto-making, however, has resulted in the publication of preliminary materials such as those for Puccini's *La bohème* (Bernardoni 2008), *Tosca* (Ravenni 2009), and *Madama Butterfly* (Groos et al. 2005).

Relatively few opera librettos are based on original stories. Many are derived from existing literary works, and a good number are adaptations of earlier librettos. The first stage in creating a libretto consists of plotting out its macrostructure, overlaying the basic storyline with scenic divisions, large-scale musical forms, and opportunities for dialogue; Italians call such an outline the *selva* or *programma* (Della Seta 2004: 69). While it is not always possible to trace every aspect of a libretto's lineage, surviving sources can sometimes suggest the content of documents that no longer exist. After examining the autograph score of Handel's *Rodelinda*, as well as the printed libretto by Nicola Haym and the earlier libretto by Antonio Salvi that served as Haym's source, Andrew V. Jones proposed what the opera's "pre-compositional" libretto may have looked like before Handel adapted it to his musical needs (Jones 2007: 74, 76–77).

As usual, Richard Wagner presents a special case. As the sole author of both the text and music of his stage works, he had no need to correspond with a librettist, eliminating a potential source of information about his operas' genesis. But because Wagner was such an influential figure, both in his own estimation and that of the culture that surrounded him, he left behind a wealth of documentary evidence illuminating his creative process. Wagner typically fashioned his librettos in a four-phase method consisting of a cursory prose sketch, a more detailed prose draft, a verse draft, and a fair copy of the complete text (Darcy 1992a: 196). Fortunately, many examples of these documents survive, together with supplementary manuscripts, to reveal rejected scenes, actions, and conversations that differ significantly from the final librettos. At the same time, these preliminary materials disclose the relatively late development of fundamental dramatic concepts, such as Wotan's spear and Loge's dominion over fire, which are present in neither the prose sketch nor the prose draft of *Das Rheingold* (Darcy 1992a: 199–200). The peculiar language of the *Ring* operas, with their alliteration and protracted narratives, presents additional challenges that often surface in Wagner's verse drafts.

A creative work in its own right, with its own documentary history, a libretto is nonetheless typically studied for the sake of its musical setting. In addition to supplying the opera's text, sometimes in unique versions, printed librettos frequently contain information about performers and production staff, additional works on the program, and advertisements of upcoming performances or publications. When a score does not survive, the corresponding libretto may be the only evidence of an opera's existence. While the content of a published libretto can differ significantly from the text that the composer has set to music, it nonetheless represents the "official" wording provided for the audience to read and contemplate at their leisure. For this reason, the avoidance of controversy—with or without its creators' approval—has been a primary concern throughout the history of the published libretto.

Censored librettos are a potent source of information about operas that were modified against their authors' wishes. An especially rich trove is the Censors' Bureau collection at the Archives Nationales in Paris, which contains copies of librettos submitted by statute prior to a work's premiere. These dated documents, originating during a new opera's rehearsal period, can help sort out layers of revision, or even recover lost versions that are missing from other sources. The value of censors' librettos is illustrated in Lesley A. Wright's account of the fortunes of *Carmen* (Wright 1978), which establishes that many of the revisions to Bizet's autograph score date from the rehearsal period.

Librettos with composers' annotations fall into a special category by virtue of their intimate association with the creative process. While many composers mark a libretto as they plan musical structures and delineate characters, Richard Strauss's annotations are extraordinary in both quantity and content. Strauss's working librettos for *Ariadne auf Naxos* (Erwin 1981) and *Elektra* (Gilliam 1991), both typical of his practice, include a basic tonal framework, meter and tempo markings, brief thematic ideas, and miscellaneous verbal cues pertaining to vocal and instrumental detail. These documents offer a unique perspective, recording the composer's mental processes as he read, and serving to remind him of these early choices throughout the composition phase. Annotated librettos resulting from Strauss's collaboration with Hugo von Hofmannsthal also include the poet's handwritten recommendations about text setting and other aspects of the word-music relationship (Erwin 1976: 494).

For a composer-librettist, the presence of musical jottings in predominantly textual sources raises additional questions of primacy and chronology. The popular view that Wagner conceived words and music concurrently, at times notating both in the same document, is not easily proven by surviving sources. Musical notation can be found in both the fair copies and first printing of the *Ring* libretto, but due to the interrelationship of the four constituent music dramas, as well as Wagner's tendency to write untexted vocal sketches, linking musical fragments to words on the basis of physical proximity is often inconclusive (Darcy 1992a: 204–206, 217).

Sketches

In common parlance, the term "sketch" is often applied to a wide range of preliminary compositional materials at various stages of development. At the same time, many music scholars reserve the word for the earliest phases of creation. The following discussion is concerned principally with the latter interpretation.

Sketches—the private jottings of composers testing the potential of their ideas—are often the most challenging musical sources to interpret. Deprived of their contexts, and frequently their texts as well, operatic sketches can be especially enigmatic; for example, among Hector Berlioz's sketches for *Les Troyens* are leaves on which he experimented with modal scales and chord progressions (Holoman 1980: 127). At the same time, sketches can be exceptionally revealing for a composer like Wagner, whose myth-making prose tends to obscure the origins of his creations. The well-known "La Spezia vision," the dreamlike (or perhaps merely dyspeptic) state in which Wagner claimed to have received, fully formed, the iconic E-flat major opening of *Das Rheingold*, is refuted by sketches predating the alleged reverie (Darcy 1993 draws on the composer's sketches to reconstruct the labored genesis of the *Rheingold* opening).

Wagner left behind an unusually large number of musical manuscripts: for *Der Ring des Nibelungen* alone, over 3,700 pages survive (Deathridge 1977b: 383). For decades the study of these documents was hampered by inadequate analytical vocabularies, such as the categories of sketch materials defined by Otto Strobel (Strobel, 1929), the first director of the Wagner Archive at Wahnfried. The limitations of Strobel's taxonomy have both practical and ideological roots, as it fails to account for changes in Wagner's working method over the course of his lifetime and shrouds the composer's habits in a fog of hagiography (Deathridge 1974–1975: 75). With the publication of the *Wagner Werk-Verzeichnis* (Deathridge, Geck, and Voss 1986), a more flexible terminology has emerged to describe the various sketches and drafts, both textual and musical, which precede Wagner's completed stage works.

Writing not long after the surge of interest in sketch studies occasioned by the Beethoven bicentennial, Douglas Johnson famously argued that preliminary manuscripts are incapable of yielding significant analytical insight about the completed works that they anticipate (Johnson 1978: 13). Yet in her monograph on Alban Berg's *Lulu* manuscripts, Patricia Hall observes that "sketches are most helpful for [music that employs] highly defined theoretical systems, which, because of their complexity or unapparent relationships, we do not yet fully understand" (Hall 1996: 11–12). She notes that Berg's row charts and form tables are indispensable analytical tools, and the graphically separated motives in his sketches illuminate the tangled layers of the finished score. Hall also finds dramatic clues in Berg's *Lulu* sketches that support the existence of an underlying plan governing the double and triple assignment of roles to singers.

A subset of operatic sketch studies explores works left incomplete at their composers' deaths, resulting in preliminary materials without a concrete realization, as well as the tantalizing prospect of posthumous collaboration. In most cases, these joint efforts are rooted in fertile soil: Friedrich Cerha based his completion of the third act of *Lulu* on a virtually finished short score together with fully orchestrated passages from Berg's *Lulu Suite* (Cerha 1981: 543), while Arturo Toscanini's performing version of Arrigo Boito's *Nerone* drew upon a piano-vocal draft with abundant orchestral cues (Del Nero 1995: 169). Less common are unfinished operas based on little more than fragmentary sketches, requiring composition as well as painstaking scholarship. *Die drei Pintos* is one such example, which Mahler based on Carl Maria von Weber's sketches for seven numbers—some no more than single-line fragments—as well as other unpublished music by the deceased composer (Zychowicz 2000: x–xi).

Among the best-known leaves of operatic manuscript are those that Puccini left for his unfinished *Turandot*. Nearly half of these thirty-six pages constitute a virtually continuous draft, lacking only its orchestration. The remaining sketches, however, are so fragmentary that their relationship to the unset portion of the libretto may never be determined (Maehder 1984). The air of mystery surrounding Puccini's *Turandot* sketches is intensified by the fact that they have never been published in their entirety, either in facsimile or transcription, and access to the original manuscripts is strictly controlled. Despite these precautions, however, there have been several unauthorized completions, in addition to those commissioned from Franco Alfano shortly after Puccini's death (Fairtile 2004) and from Luciano Berio in recent years (Uvietta 2004).

Drafts

Many opera composers draft extended musical passages in short-score format—typically, vocal parts, bass line, and one or more staves of instrumental material—before progressing to a fully orchestrated score. A continuity draft (also called a *particella* or *Particell*) may be created in a single pass, or a series of shorter preliminary drafts may precede a continuous draft of a larger unit, such as a complete act. The purpose of a draft is to lay out the structure of a musical unit while also capturing its most prominent features. Drafting is the essence of composition, and an operatic draft is, in a sense, a finished work, even though it does not contain the complete musical texture. For this reason, it has long been common to prepare singers' vocal scores directly from the composer's drafts rather than waiting for him to orchestrate the opera fully.

As with non-dramatic music, studies of operatic drafts often focus on ultimately rejected settings, the "road not taken" eclipsed by the reading that we know today. Typically, the composer's judgment is vindicated, as the final version is demonstrated to be more effective and imaginative than earlier efforts. Linda Tyler's consideration of a draft for "Da schlägt die Abschiedsstunde," from Mozart's *Der Schauspieldirektor*, reveals it to be less expressive than the final version, in part because it does not participate in the web of metrical and dramatic connections that she detects throughout the opera (Tyler 1990: 263–264). In his study of singers' influence on Mozart's compositional method, Ian Woodfield cites the evidence of ink colors to suggest that the composer habitually left his aria drafts incomplete until he could consult with the singers who would be performing them. Woodfield compares the pedestrian climax of "Per pietà" (*Così fan tutte*), first notated in the aria's draft, with the florid replacement that immediately follows it, positing that the soprano Adriana Ferrarese might have requested the latter to show off her high notes (Woodfield 2003: 40–41).

Sometimes a draft is the only source for an instrumental passage that was part of an opera's compositional history, but is absent from the finished score. For the first production of *Peter Grimes*, the director Eric Crozier asked Britten to extend the first act's "Storm Interlude" in order to cover a scene change. Britten expanded the interlude's rondo structure, and the appearance of the draft suggests that he worked in uncharacteristic haste (Reed 1996: 100–101). This passage does not appear in any score of *Peter Grimes*, and it is not certain whether it was ever performed. Although the decision to compose the additional music did not originate with Britten, he was nonetheless persuaded to do so for practical reasons, a scenario that repeats itself throughout operatic history.

A more extreme example that illustrates the usefulness of a draft in recovering lost music is Verdi's *Una vendetta in dominò*, an early version of *Un ballo in maschera* that was effectively smothered in its cradle by censorship. Verdi prepared a nearly complete draft of *Una vendetta*, as well as a "skeleton score"—bass line, vocals, and prominent instrumental parts copied onto the paper that would become the autograph score—before learning that censors forbade its performance due to fears of political unrest. Eventually, he succeeded in refashioning the opera as *Un ballo in maschera*, incorporating most of *Una vendetta*'s skeleton score into the new work. The original draft, however, preserves the essence of *Una vendetta* virtually intact. Using these two documents, together with an even earlier version of the libretto called *Gustavo III*, Philip Gossett and Ilaria Narici created a "hypothetical" reconstruction of Verdi's original concept for *Un ballo in maschera* (Gossett 2008: 421 and Gossett 2006: 489–513).

At times, a compositional draft turns out to be both less and more than meets the eye. Carl Maria von Weber, by all accounts a swift and fluent composer, left relatively few preliminary manuscripts: *Euryanthe* and *Oberon*, in the collection of the Deutsche Staatsbibliothek in Berlin, are his only surviving drafts for completed operas. The *Euryanthe* draft is so orderly that it resembles a fair copy, seemingly devoid of the typical compositional struggles, and yet closer examination reveals erasures and overwriting that obscure earlier layers of notation (Tusa 1991: 145). While Weber's first drafts for portions of these operas are available, allowing examination of his earliest recorded ideas in selected passages, it is not possible to trace the genesis of either *Euryanthe* or *Oberon* in full. In recent years, however, technology has come to the aid of scholarship: photographically enhanced reproductions of Weber's drafts reveal the content of the erased layers, facilitating a more thorough study of these operas (Tusa 1991: 148).

It is unusual to find a foreign hand in preliminary musical materials, especially those of a composer whose artistic creed brooked no collaborators. Yet Wagner's pencil drafts for all four *Ring* operas, as well as *Tristan und Isolde*, were traced over in ink after he completed them. Whether inking may have made the drafts easier to read during the composition phase (Bailey 1979: 293), or simply preserved them for posterity (Darcy 1992a: 218), these non-autograph interventions complicate the study of Wagner's manuscripts. The hand of his paramour, Mathilde Wesendonck, appears in *Das Rheingold*, *Die Walküre*, half of *Siegfried*, and most of *Tristan und Isolde*, while the writing in the remaining drafts is unknown. It can be difficult to trace the drafts' development, and even to discern their final layer, since Wagner tended not to cross out the readings that he replaced, and Wesendonck subsequently inked nearly everything that she saw (Darcy 1993: 21). Over time, Wagner's pencil markings have faded, rendering microfilms of the drafts virtually useless. Once again, technology comes to the rescue: the ability to manipulate digital photographs of manuscripts, temporarily changing their color and contrast, often reveals notations that are no longer visible to the naked eye.

Autograph Scores

Depending on the circumstances, an autograph score can be the most awe-inspiring, informative, or controversial of musical sources. Autographs have historically been valued as the locus of "the composer's intentions," although both that assumption and the validity of the phrase are no longer taken for granted. Given the collaborative nature of opera—not only the typical division of labor between composer and librettist, but also the contributions of performers, production staff, and even audiences—privileging the autograph score over other sources may at times seem arbitrary, giving undue emphasis to one moment in the opera's life. In some cases, the autograph cannot even be counted on to supply the composer's own realized vision, when markings made at other times, or by other hands, vie with earlier layers of notation. Nonetheless, the autograph score provides indispensable evidence of the composer's developing ideals, and in many cases serves as the starting point to investigate the influence of external forces.

Like all manuscripts, operatic autographs can become lost, and because they are typically bound in multiple volumes, individual acts have on occasion been separated from one another. The near worship of Mozart's *Don Giovanni* autograph by its onetime owner, Pauline Viardot, was hardly the norm in past centuries (Everist 2001–2002: 168–169). Occasionally the backstory of an autograph's disappearance is itself worthy of operatic treatment: Charles Gounod's *Polyeucte* fell victim to a custody dispute between the composer and an ex-lover who scrawled her name across every page. While awaiting the score's return, Gounod rewrote the entire opera from memory (Huebner 1990: 87–90). The lost fourth act of Puccini's *Edgar*, cut after the opera's second production, was dramatically rediscovered by his granddaughter shortly before it was to have been performed from a reconstructed edition based on published sources. (Fairtile 2008: 27).

While World War II and its turbulent aftermath consumed music manuscripts of all genres, the consequences for opera seem especially acute. Wagner's fair copies of *Das Rheingold* and *Die Walküre*, presented to Adolf Hitler by the German government, are presumed to have perished in 1945. The autograph of Puccini's *La rondine*, the only one of his operas not published by the Ricordi firm, is also lost. The manuscript holdings of the Prussian State Library, including the complete autograph of *Die Zauberflöte* and portions of *Così fan tutte, Idomeneo, Die Entführung aus dem Serail*, and *Le nozze di Figaro*, were evacuated to the countryside for safekeeping, but postwar border changes trapped them behind the Iron Curtain. It was not until 1977 that the Polish government returned *Die Zauberflöte* to Germany, although the Jagiellonian University in Kraków continues to hold the remaining scores (several of these are now available in facsimile edition; see Mozart 2006–2009). In 2002 a score containing most of Vivaldi's lost opera, *Motezuma*, was discovered among the treasures that departing Soviet soldiers had stolen from the Berlin Sing-Akademie in 1945 and deposited in the Kiev Conservatory.

Sometimes it is the composer himself who is responsible for the loss of an autograph score. Verdi, whose operas were frequent victims of censorship, grew frustrated with the alterations imposed on *Stiffelio*, and after several years he withdrew the score to adapt its music to a less controversial text. The new opera, *Aroldo*, is literally built on the foundations of the old, since Verdi removed seven musical numbers from the *Stiffelio* autograph and incorporated them, to varying degrees, into the new score (Gossett 1993: 201–203). The fate of the remaining pages of the *Stiffelio* autograph remained a mystery until 1992, when it was revealed that they had passed, virtually complete, to Verdi's heirs, who briefly made them available for the purpose of creating a critical edition edited by Kathleen Kuzmick Hansell (Verdi [1850] 2003). Although the autograph of *Stiffelio* no longer exists, it has nonetheless managed to fulfill one of the scholarly functions traditionally associated with sources of this type.

During the rehearsal period, operas may undergo changes both subtle and extensive. To be sure, the long-standing practice of altering a work at this stage often benefits the composer, as he is able to experience and evaluate what had heretofore existed only in his imagination. At the same time, composers sometimes face pressure from singers, conductors, and others who urge their own modifications to the score. Without supporting documentation, it can be nearly impossible to determine whether an alteration was desired by the composer or imposed upon him. While Berlioz scribbled sarcastic descriptions of the cuts forced on *Les Troyens* directly into his autograph score (Lacombe 2001: 23), such vivid protestations are rare in musical sources. Correspondence, memoirs, or newspaper reports may disclose the circumstances behind a particular revision, but the autograph will typically reveal only what was changed, remaining silent about why.

Scores can sometimes be coaxed to give up their secrets when compared with a contemporaneous libretto. The autograph of Gounod's *Faust* contains only a fraction of the opera's original text. Where the missing words should appear, gaps are instead visible in the manuscript's folio structure, indicating that Gounod had likely set the entire text to music, but then removed pages from the score during rehearsals (Huebner 1990: 119n). While the censor exacted his predictable toll, other parts of the opera fell victim to the demands of Marie Miolan-Carvalho, Gounod's first Marguerite and, not coincidentally, the wife of the Théâtre Lyrique's director, Léon Carvalho. By studying the surviving fragments that Gounod had removed from the autograph, as well as correspondence, newspaper accounts, and early editions, Steven Huebner has convincingly reconstructed the original *Faust*, thus broadening our understanding of the opera's characters and its genre (Huebner 1990: 120).

Although intentional cuts may account for most of the gaps in an autograph score, the work habits of certain composers raise the possibility of alternate explanations. Rossini and Bellini, two composers who did not prepare drafts of their operas, could not anticipate how many score pages an orchestrated musical number would require; therefore, they wrote on loose bifolios meant to be bound consecutively in the finished autograph (see Tyson 1987: 17 for a description of a prototypical "late operatic score" by Mozart that presents a similar arrangement). In such an arrangement, an individual bifolio could easily become detached and lost, without indicating a deliberate modification to the score (Gossett 2006: 58). Missing score pages can also distort our understanding of the orchestration of operas from the late eighteenth and early nineteenth centuries. The use of oblong manuscript paper at a time when orchestral forces were beginning to expand beyond the paper's vertical capacity required certain accommodations: one solution was to insert loose pages, collectively called a *spartitino* by Italians, to contain the "overflow" instruments, typically brass and percussion. These inserted pages, too, are easily lost, which can give the false impression of a thinner orchestral texture (Gossett 2006: 54).

Owing to particular traditions of composition and production, it is not unusual to discover multiple hands in the autograph score of an opera. Identifying the foreign notations, when possible, may elucidate why they are present and how their interventions might have affected the composer's own contribution. In some cases it is simply a matter of expediency. Benjamin Britten often asked his copyist, Imogen Holst, to transfer vocal lines from his composition draft into his autograph score; Britten then penciled the orchestral texture into the latter himself. In the case of *The Turn of the Screw*, Holst eventually inked over Britten's notation as well, since the composer needed to conduct from this score in a poorly illuminated orchestra pit (Evans 1985: 65).

Perhaps the most complex autograph manuscripts, in terms of the number and type of interventions, are those of Gioachino Rossini. At times pressured to create an opera, quite literally, in a matter of weeks, Rossini might ask other musicians to contribute not only *secco* recitative, but sometimes also entire musical numbers, albeit ones of lesser significance. Contributions such as Michele Carafa's to *Mosé in Egitto*, Giovanni Pacini's to *Matilde di Shabran*, and Luca Agolini's to *La Cenerentola* are identifiable not only by their composer's hands, but also by their "working" appearance in the midst of Rossini's fair copy (Gossett 2004: 83). In addition to these higher profile interventions, Rossini's scores also contain passages in which his own orchestral accompaniments support vocal melodies supplied by his copyists. To add to the complexity, Rossini lost possession of some of his autographs, which were at times altered by performers. The end result is that portions of Rossini's autograph manuscripts can actually be less authentic than copyists' manuscripts containing his corrections, or those that were used in productions that he supervised (Cagli et al. 1974: 43).

Some autograph scores also contain annotations by copyists or editors. Rehearsal numbers, pagination, and formatting marks are not uncommon in scores that were used as exemplars for manuscript or printed copies. Puccini's *Edgar*, his second opera, goes a step further, since it contains an ongoing dialogue between the young composer and a member of the editorial staff of his publisher, Ricordi. Scattered throughout *Edgar*'s autograph score are the editor's questions, notational clarifications, and even corrections, all geared toward producing a usable copy of the manuscript. The score also contains Puccini's responses as he answers the editor's queries, accepts or rejects his suggestions, and asks questions of his own. Apparently, the *Edgar* autograph repeatedly traveled between Puccini and Ricordi as the copyist's manuscript was being prepared. The result is a remarkable conversation between a young composer and a presumably more experienced editor, as the former moved closer to the accomplished orchestrator that he would soon become.

Performing Scores and Parts

The survival of performing scores and parts, like autograph materials, can be threatened by war and other disasters. But lacking the cultural significance of composers' autographs, performing materials are not always moved to safety when their surroundings are endangered. Ricordi's extensive rental archive was destroyed in a bombing raid during World War II, taking with it invaluable evidence of performing traditions dating back over a century. Fortunately, similar materials are often discovered in theater archives throughout the Western world, either because duplicate scores and parts were prepared locally, or the originals were never returned to the publisher. Composer-centered archives such as the American Institute for Verdi Studies (see bibliography) hold microfilmed copies of performing materials obtained throughout Europe and the United States.

Performing scores and parts can furnish essential evidence of not only the practices of a particular place and time, but also modifications to individual operas. They must, however, be approached with an understanding of their origins, not the least because regional differences in duplication practices influence the relative reliability of manuscript materials. In Italy, throughout the eighteenth and much of the nineteenth century, a handwritten copy was made from the autograph, and this, in turn, served as both the exemplar for instrumental parts and as the performing score that was loaned to theaters. Additional scores and parts were often prepared by local copyists at these theaters, and they, in turn, sold or rented their materials—of variable quality and accuracy—on what was essentially a black market. If nothing more than a vocal score could be obtained, an enterprising copyist would often prepare his own orchestration for sale or for rent. Such illicit activity persisted even after Bellini and Donizetti made distribution agreements with Ricordi, their publisher, and both composers' correspondence is rife with complaints about performances from unauthorized copies (Gossett 2006: 82–83). These materials, often inaccurate at best, may furnish evidence of local performing traditions, but they should not be trusted as authoritative texts. In France, by contrast, performing materials for provincial theaters were centrally produced directly from the autograph score. As a result, these parts exhibit a higher degree of fidelity to their source (Gossett 2006: 79).

Performing materials can be an indispensable resource for tracing an opera's development beyond the autograph score. Certain types of revisions, especially those whose utility becomes apparent only when the work is staged, are more likely to appear in scores and parts used in the theater. Ian Woodfield's study of manuscript materials for *Così fan tutte* reveals that during the opera's rehearsal period, Mozart marked cuts and other changes in the copyist's score from which he led performances, rather than in his own autograph (Woodfield 2008: 152; Edge 2001). These alterations, in turn, were transferred to a "reference score" used to create subsequent copies. Like all changes made while preparing a performance, Mozart's in *Così fan tutte* may represent accommodations to specific circumstances rather than abstractly conceived improvements. Nonetheless, their presence in a score intended to serve as an exemplar confirms their significance, while also challenging the autograph's traditional position as the principal source of the composer's intentions.

In addition to cutting material, composers sometimes create additional music during the rehearsal period. To sustain dramatic interest and also to cover any backstage noises resulting from set changes, it is common to place instrumental interludes between scenes of an act, but it is often difficult to predict the amount of time that might be needed for these passages in the theater. Leoš Janáček composed interludes to link the scenes of *Kát'a Kabanová* during rehearsals for the opera's second production, and he lengthened them some six years later after observing additional performances. Because theaters ransacked Universal Edition's rental archive during World War II, the only complete sources for the interludes are two sets of instrumental parts originating at the National Theater in Brno (Straková 1982: 134, 142). Similar compositional circumstances compelled Claude Debussy to extend the interludes in *Pelléas et Mélisande*, but in this case, because André Messager conducted from the composer's autograph, the revised interludes appear in that score. Messager maintained that Debussy composed the extended interludes during rehearsals, while Henri Büsser, who conducted the remaining performances in the initial run, insisted that they originated several months after the premiere. Evidence seems to favor Messager's recollection (Grayson 1988: 76–78).

Printed scores, though a relatively recent means of transmission, may also contain important details about an opera's genesis. In the last decades of the nineteenth century, engraved full scores began to supplant the manuscript copies that were rented to theaters. At first, publishers only printed scores, which because of anticipated demand and textual stability would likely recoup the initial costs, such as Ricordi's rental editions of *La traviata*, *Otello*, *Falstaff*, and *Aida*. Similar changes also occurred in France, where Choudens circulated manuscript scores of Bizet's commercially risky *Les pêcheurs de perles* (Lacombe 2001: 312) and *Carmen* (Wright 1978: 61) before engraving full scores in the 1890s. Publishers' reluctance to commit money and time to uncertain ventures persisted into the twentieth century, as Ricordi waited some three years to engrave a full score of Puccini's repeatedly revised *Madama Butterfly*.

The printed score of Verdi's *Falstaff*, engraved in the months before the opera's 1893 premiere, seems, in a sense, to have assumed the role of the autograph manuscript. James Hepokoski surmises that Verdi checked and corrected proof copies of the printed score and orchestral parts (Hepokoski 1992: 31). But while the composer typically annotated his autographs to produce "definitive" sources that reflected subsequent modifications, some of the changes in the engraved *Falstaff* score do not appears in the autograph. Thus Hepokoski argues that the autograph, while a precious artifact of the creative process, is merely an "initiator text," and should not be considered the opera's principal source. For Hepokoski, the 1893 printed score assumes that role, by virtue of its more recent, composer-sanctioned readings.

Certain aspects of performance practice, such as vocal ornamentation, are amply illustrated in scores that were used or owned by singers. In distinguishing between "salon-style" and "theater-style" ornamentation in Rossini's vocal numbers, Damien Colas confirms that ordinary published scores are unreliable sources of actual practice (Colas 2004: 121). Rossini's handwritten ornamentation survives in both singers' personal scores and in performing materials retained by theaters. Singers, however, tended to record their own preferred ornaments only in rapid tempos, relying on improvisation in *cantabile* passages (Colas 2004: 122). Even if they bear no connection to the composer, the performing scores of prominent singers have become treasured artifacts, transmitting personal interpretations and establishing traditions that are sometimes at odds with the composer's own wishes.

Recent Developments

Scholars of the twentieth century and beyond must inevitably confront the decline in written communication occasioned by the use of the telephone, as well as by the greater ease with which people now travel to speak face to face. The recent adoption of e-mail only partially mitigates the gradual disappearance of the letter as a medium of communication. Those who study the music of the recent past face a similar collection of rewards and challenges. While technology has given us audio and video recordings of performances, digital photography of manuscripts, and online catalogues of archival collections, the personal computer threatens to eliminate many of the documents that have traditionally enabled the study of an opera's genesis. Where composers once drafted an aria on manuscript paper, many now enter musical ideas into a computer, deleting notes and overwriting old files without a trace. John Adams involves computers in the compositional process itself, describing his recent practice as a combination of handwritten sketching and computer-assisted drafting:

> I don't go through a whole piece making a pencil "rough draft" in the way that, for instance, Mahler did a "short score." Instead, I keep several spiral-bound manuscript books, and I only use them when I need to figure out something that is not clear in my mind. I might sit at the piano or I might just scribble in the book until I've understood something and seen how it works, and then I go back to the "sequencer" program, and I'll enter it into the MIDI file so that it plays back in real time. I create exceptionally long and complex sequences with the software. They play a whole bank of samples that I have stored in several hard drives. I've collected these samples over ten years, so I have a lot of them, and I update them periodically. I have two hefty

> computers that I run in tandem when I'm making a MIDI sketch of a big orchestra piece or an opera. (May 2006: 20–21)

Some contemporary composers, mindful of scholarly interest in their work processes, make a special effort to preserve paper copies of their computer-generated materials. Daron Hagen retains and prints successive drafts of his operas so that every change is documented, and he communicates with his collaborators by e-mail rather than over the telephone (telephone conversation with the author, May 27, 2009). Like many composers today, Hagen self-publishes his works. His method of distributing performance materials to the cast of *Amelia*, premiered by the Seattle Opera in 2010, illustrates a benefit of working in an online environment: the opera's principal singers were given access to a password-protected website on which Hagen placed pdf files of *Amelia*'s vocal score. When he modified a scene, he simply uploaded an edited file, and an automatically generated message informed the cast of the change.

Production Materials

Numerous types of non-musical sources contribute to our knowledge of individual operas and to our understanding of broader issues affecting their creation and performance. The *libroni*, or internal ledgers, of the publisher Ricordi establish the date that a score could be assigned to copyists or engravers. Theater rosters, pay records, and the like have long been consulted to determine the activities of a singer or the makeup of an orchestra. Sergio Durante uses the evidence of a contract, especially its reference to specific set designs, to revise the accepted compositional chronology of Mozart's *La clemenza di Tito* (Durante 1999: 573). In each of these cases, documents created in order to facilitate operatic productions serve the additional purpose of giving testimony about those productions. Many of these materials continue to reside in the archives of theaters or publishers (see, for example, the historical archive of Venice's Teatro La Fenice, the web address for which is noted in the bibliography as Fenice 2014), while some can now be found in library collections.

In recent decades, increased attention has been paid to staging manuals (*livrets de mises en scènes* in French, *disposizioni sceniche* in Italian) that describe scenery, blocking, gesture, props, and other visual aspects of opera production. Although these documents might appear to serve similar purposes in French and Italian opera, they actually represent two different traditions. The *livrets de mises en scènes*, brought to scholarly attention largely through the efforts of H. Robert Cohen, are best known from a series of some two hundred volumes published by Louis Palianti, the assistant stage manager of the Opéra Comique from 1836 to 1872 (Lacombe 2001: 58). The staging manuals in Palianti's collection (*Collection de mises en scènes de grands opéras et d'opéras-comiques publiées par M. L[ouis]Palianti*; modern editions of *livrets de mises en scènes* include Cohen 1990 and Cohen 1998), as well as countless others, were circulated among provincial theaters so that they could model their performances on those produced in Paris. As Arnold Jacobshagen has observed, however, these manuals did not necessarily depict the operas' original productions, and were often full of cuts, text changes, and other modifications (Jacobshagen 2001: 251).

Italian *disposizioni sceniche*, by contrast, incline more toward control than illustration. The best-known examples, for seven of Verdi's later operas, were issued by, and in some cases authored by, Giulio Ricordi, head of the firm that published Verdi's music (Ricordi has issued modern editions of the *disposizioni sceniche* for four operas: Verdi's *Un ballo in maschera*, *Simon Boccanegra*, and *Otello*, as well as Boito's *Mefistofele*). Although the Italian staging manuals were likely inspired by their French counterparts, Ricordi clearly indicated that his were prescriptive rather than descriptive. The *disposizione scenica* for *Otello* (Hepokoski and Viale Ferrero 1990) is the final known volume for a Verdi opera (Ricordi's *libroni* contain an entry for a *disposizione scenica* dedicated to *Falstaff*, but no copy has ever been located). It is breathtakingly detailed, often giving line-by-line interpretations that include movements, motivations, and facial expressions (Gossett 2006: 460).

The visual elements of opera production are also preserved in designs for sets, costumes, and entire theaters. While these materials often reside in libraries and archives, they are sometimes reproduced in exhibition catalogues and secondary literature. In his analysis of what appear to be the original sets for Bizet's *Carmen*, Evan Baker details various formats in which set and costume designs were transmitted throughout nineteenth-century France, and suggests locations where they can be studied today (Baker 1990: 230–231). Olga Jesurum's exploration of stage sets created by Romolo and Tancredi Liverani for Italian operas of the early nineteenth century identifies entire albums of watercolor designs in both Italy and New York (Jesurum 2006). The influence of performance space on the production of French Baroque opera has been studied by Barbara Coeyman, who uses seventeenth-century architectural plans to help visualize stage works by Lully and Lalande (Coeyman 1990).

The wide variety of source materials that survive for many operas reinforces the genre's fundamentally collaborative and fluid nature. Even documents that originate with the composer frequently reveal the influence, if not outright intervention, of multiple creators. The notion of a fixed, definitive text crumbles in the presence of rehearsal revisions, substitute arias, and reactions to criticism. From Mozart's reworkings of *Così fan tutte* to Daron Hagen's updated pdfs of pages from *Amelia*, composers themselves call attention to the ongoing development of countless operas.

See also: Editing Opera, Reconstructions, Production Aesthetics and Materials, Autographs, Memorabilia, and the Aesthetics of Collecting

Bibliography

Abbate, Carolyn. 1983. "The Parisian 'Vénus' and the 'Paris' *Tannhäuser*." *Journal of the American Musicological Society* 36/1: 73–123.

American Institute for Verdi Studies. Online. Available: http://www.nyu.edu/projects/verdi/ (accessed June 17, 2014).

Arnold Schoenberg Institute. Online. Available: www.schoenberg.at (accessed January 11, 2014).

Ashbrook, William, and Harold Powers. 1991. *Puccini's Turandot: The End of the Great Tradition*. Princeton, NJ: Princeton University Press.

Bailey, Robert. 1979. "The Method of Composition." In *The Wagner Companion*, edited by Peter Burbidge and Richard Sutton, 269–338. New York: Cambridge University Press.

——. 1969. "The Genesis of *Tristan und Isolde* and a Study of Wagner's Sketches and Drafts for the First Act." PhD diss., Princeton University.

Baker, Evan. 2013. *From the Score to the Stage: An Illustrated History of Continental Opera Production and Staging*. Chicago: University of Chicago Press.

——. 1990. "The Scene Designs for the First Performances of Bizet's *Carmen*." *19th-Century Music* 13/3: 230–242.

Bernardoni, Virgilio, ed. 2008. *Verso 'Bohème': Gli abbozzi del libretto negli archivi di Giuseppe Giacosa e Luigi Illica*. Florence: Olschki.

Brauner, Patricia B. 1999. "Le edizioni critiche di opera italiana dell'Ottocento: scope, fonti, metodi e futuro." *Fonti musicali Italiane* 4: 207–218.

Britten-Pears Foundation. Online. Available: www.brittenpears.org (accessed August 25, 2012).

Brown, Bruce Alan. 2001. "Die Wiederverwendung Der Autograph- Und Aufführungspartituren Von Mozarts *Idomeneo*." In *Mozarts 'Idomeneo' und die Musik in München zur Zeit Karl Theodors. Bericht über das Symposion der Gesellschaft für Bayerische Musikgeschichte und der Musikhistorischen Kommission der Bayerischen Akademie der Wissenschaften, München, 7.–9. Juli 1999*, edited by Theodor Göllner and Stephan Hörner, 69–75. Munich: C. H. Beck.

——. 1995. *W. A. Mozart. 'Così fan tutte.'* Cambridge Opera Handbooks. New York: Cambridge University Press.

Cagli, Bruno, Philip Gossett, and Alberto Zedda, 1974. "Criteri per l'edizione critica di tutte le opere di Gioachino Rossini." *Bolletino del centro rossiniano di studi* 14/1: 1–61.

Carter, Chandler. 2010. "*The Rake's Progress* and Stravinsky's Return: The Evolving Approach to Setting Text." *Journal of the American Musicological Society* 63/3: 553–640.

Cerha, Friedrich. 1981. "Zum III. Akt der Oper *Lulu*." *Österreichische Musikzeitschrift* 36/10–11: 541–550.

Cesari, Francesco, and Guido Paduano, eds. 2010. *'Edgar': Musset, Fontana, Puccini*. Pisa: Pisa University Press.

Coeyman, Barbara. 1990. "Theatres for Opera and Ballet during the Reigns of Louis XIV and Louis XV." *Early Music* 18/1: 22–37.

Cohen, H. Robert, ed. 1998. *The Original Staging Manuals for Ten Parisian Operatic Premières, 1824–1843*. Stuyvesant, NY: Pendragon.

——. 1990. *The Original Staging Manuals for Twelve Parisian Operatic Premières*. Stuyvesant, NY: Pendragon.

——, and Marie-Odile Gigou, eds. 1986. *Cent ans de mise en scène lyrique en France (env. 1830–1930): Catalogue descriptif des livrets de mise en scène, des libretti annotés et des partitions annotées dans la Bibliothèque de l'Association de la régie théâtrale (Paris)*. New York: Pendragon Press.

Colas, Damien. 2004. "Melody and Ornamentation." [Translated by Cormac Newark]. In Senici 2004, 104–123.

Conati, Marcello. 2000. "La disposizione scenica dell'*Adriana Lecouvreur* di Cilea." In *Francesco Cilea e il suo tempo: Atti del Convegno Internazionale di Studi*, edited by Gaetano Pitarresi, 51–62. Calabria: Edizioni del Conservatorio di Musica F. Cilea.

Cummings, Graham. 1998. "Handel's Compositional Methods in His London Operas of the 1730s, and the Unusual Case of *Poro, Re dell'Indie* (1731)." *Music & Letters* 79/3: 346–367.

Danko, Larisa. 1992. "Prokofjews Opernskizzen." In *Bericht über das Internationale Symposion 'Sergej Prokofjew: Aspekte seines Werkes und der Biographie,'* edited by Silke Schloen, 165–171. Regensburg: Gustav Bosse.

Darcy, Warren. 1993. *Wagner's 'Das Rheingold.'* Oxford: Clarendon Press.

——. 1992a. "Autograph Manuscripts." In Millington 1992, 196–221.

——. 1992b. "Compositional Process." In Millington 1992, 244–248.

Deathridge, John. 1974–1975. "The Nomenclature of Wagner's Sketches." *Proceedings of the Royal Musical Association* 101: 75–83.

Deathridge, John. 1977a. *Wagner's* 'Rienzi': *A Reappraisal Based on a Study of the Sketches and Drafts.* New York: Oxford University Press.

——. 1977b. "Wagner's Sketches for the *Ring*: Some Recent Studies." *Musical Times* 118/1611: 383–389.

——, Martin Geck, and Egon Voss, eds. 1986. *Wagner Werk-Verzeichnis* (WWV). *Verzeichnis der musikalischen Werke Richard Wagners und ihrer Quellen.* Mainz, London, and New York: Schott.

Della Seta, Fabrizio. 2004. "New Currents in the Libretto." In *The Cambridge Companion to Verdi*, edited by Scott L. Balthazar, 69–87. Cambridge: Cambridge University Press.

Durante, Sergio. 1999. "The Chronology of Mozart's *La clemenza di Tito* Reconsidered." *Music & Letters* 80/4: 560–594.

Edge, Dexter. 2001. "Mozart's Viennese Copyists." PhD diss., University of Southern California.

Erwin, Charlotte E. 1981. "Presketch Planning for *Ariadne auf Naxos*." *Musical Quarterly* 67/3: 348–365.

——. 1976. Review of *The 'Ariadne auf Naxos' of Hugo von Hofmannsthal and Richard Strauss* by Donald G. Daviau and George J. Buelow. *Journal of the American Musicological Society* 29/3: 492–496.

Evans, John. 1985. "The Sketches: Chronology and Analysis." In *Benjamin Britten. 'The Turn of the Screw,'* edited by Patricia Howard, 63–71. Cambridge Opera Handbooks. New York: Cambridge University Press.

Everist, Mark. 2001–2002. "Enshrining Mozart: *Don Giovanni* and the Viardot Circle." *19th-Century Music* 25/2–3: 165–189.

Fagone, Vittorio, and Vittoria Crespi Morbio, eds. 2003. *La scena di Puccini.* Lucca: Fondazione Ragghianti.

Fairtile, Linda B. 2008. "Ricostruzione dell'*Edgar* 'originale'." House program, Teatro Regio di Torino (25 June): 27–32.

——. 2004. "*Duetto a tre*: Franco Alfano's Completion of *Turandot*." *Cambridge Opera Journal* 16/2: 163–186.

——. 1996a. "Giacomo Puccini's Operatic Revisions as Manifestations of His Compositional Priorities." PhD diss., New York University.

——. 1996b. "Verdi's First 'Willow Song': New Sketches and Drafts for *Otello*." *19th-Century Music* 19/3: 213–230.

Fenice. 2014. Archivio storico Teatro La Fenice Venezia. Online. Available: http://www.archivistoricolafenice.org/ArcFenice/index.aspx (accessed 17 January 2014).

Gilliam, Bryan. 1991. *Richard Strauss's 'Elektra.'* Oxford: Clarendon Press.

Giroud, Vincent. 2002. "*Pelléas et Mélisande*: Le manuscrit Koch de l'Université Yale." *Revue musicale de Suisse Romande* 55/2: 42–51.

Gossett, Philip. 2008. "The Skeleton Score of Verdi's *Una vendetta in dominò*: Two Surviving Fragments." *Notes* 64/3: 417–434.

——. 2006. *Divas and Scholars: Performing Italian Opera.* Chicago: University of Chicago Press.
——. 2004. "Compositional Methods." In Senici 2004, 68–84.
——. 1993. "New Sources for *Stiffelio*: A Preliminary Report." *Cambridge Opera Journal* 5/3: 199–222.
Grayson, David A. 1986. *The Genesis of Debussy's 'Pelléas et Mélisande.'* Ann Arbor, MI: UMI Research Press.
Groos, Arthur. 2000. "Luigi Illica's Libretto for *Madama Butterfly* (1901)." *Studi pucciniani* 2: 91–196.
——, et al., eds. 2005. *'Madama Butterfly': Fonti e documenti della genesi.* Lucca: Maria Pacini Fazzi, 2005.
Hall, Patricia. 2004. "A Tale of Two Sketchbooks: Reconstructing and Deciphering Alban Berg's Sketchbooks for *Wozzeck*." In *A Handbook to Twentieth-Century Musical Sketches*, edited by Patricia Hall and Friedemann Sallis, 102–113. Cambridge: Cambridge University Press.
——. 1999–2000. "The Making of an Electronic Facsimile: Berg's Sketches for *Wozzeck*." *Computing in Musicology* 12: 275–282.
——. 1996. *A View of Berg's 'Lulu' through the Autograph Sources.* Berkeley and Los Angeles: University of California Press.
Hepokoski, James A. 1992. "Overriding the Autograph Score: The Problem of Textual Authority in Verdi's *Falstaff*." *Studi verdiani* 8: 13–51.
——, and Mercedes Viale Ferrero, eds. 1990. *'Otello' di Giuseppe Verdi*. Milan: Ricordi.
Holoman, D. Kern. 1984. "The Berlioz Sketchbook Recovered." *19th-Century Music* 7/3: 282–317.
——. 1980. *The Creative Process in the Autograph Musical Documents of Hector Berlioz, c. 1818–1840*. Ann Arbor, MI: UMI Research Press.
Huebner, Steven. 1990. *The Operas of Charles Gounod*. Oxford: Clarendon Press.
Jacobshagen, Arnold. 2001. "Staging at the Opéra-Comique in Nineteenth-Century Paris: Auber's *Fra Diavolo* and the *livrets de mise-en-scène*." [Translated by Mary Hunter]. *Cambridge Opera Journal* 13/3: 239–260.
Jesurum, Olga. 2006. "Set Designs for Italian Operas by Romolo and Tancredi Liverani." *Music in Art: International Journal for Music Iconography* 31/1–2: 51–62.
Johnson, Douglas. 1978. "Beethoven Scholars and Beethoven's Sketches." *19th-Century Music* 2/1: 3–17.
Jones, Andrew V. 2007. "The Composer as Dramatist: Handel's Contribution to the Libretto of *Rodelinda*." *Music & Letters* 88/1: 49–77.
Kinderman, William. 2005. "The Third-Act Prelude of Wagner's *Parsifal*: Genesis, Form, and Dramatic Meaning." *19th-Century Music* 29/2: 161–84.
Kopf, Stephan. 1994. "Das Autograph gibt Auskunft: Zur Entstehung der Oper *Der Kaiser von Atlantis* von Viktor Ullmann." *mr-Mitteilungen* 9: 1–6.
Kurt Weill Foundation for Music. Online. Available: www.kwf.org (accessed August 25, 2012).
Lacombe, Hervé. 2001. *The Keys to French Opera in the Nineteenth Century*, translated by Edward Schneider. Berkeley and Los Angeles: University of California Press.
Leafstedt, Carl S. 2000. "Pelléas Revealed: The Original Ending of Bartók's Opera, *Duke Bluebeard's Castle*." In *Bartók Perspectives: Man, Composer and Ethnomusicologist*, edited by Elliott Antokoletz et al., 226–244. New York: Oxford University Press.
Maehder, Jürgen. 1984. "Studien zum Fragmentcharakter von Giacomo Puccinis Turandot." *Analecta musicologica* 22: 298–379.
May, Thomas. 2006. "John Adams Reflects on His Career." In *The John Adams Reader: Essential Writings on an American Composer*, edited by Thomas May, 2–28. Pompton Plains, NJ: Amadeus Press.

Millington, Barry, ed. 1992. *The Wagner Compendium*. New York: Schirmer Books.

Mozart, Wolfgang. 2006–2009. *Così fan tutte, ossia, La scuola degli amanti*, K. 588. 3 vols. Facsimile of the Autograph Score, Staatsbibliothek zu Berlin-Preussischer Kulturbesitz, Biblioteka Jagiellońska Kraków (Mus. ms. autogr. W. A. Mozart 588), Stadt—und Universitätsbibliothek Frankfurt am Main (Mus. Hs. 2350). Introductory Essay by Norbert Miller. Musicological Introduction by John A. Rice. Palo Alto, CA: Packard Humanities Institute.

——. 2006–2009. *Die Entführung aus dem Serail*, K. 384. 2 vols. Facsimile of the Autograph Score, Staatsbibliothek zu Berlin-Preussischer Kulturbesitz, Biblioteka Jagiellońska Kraków (Mus. ms. autogr. W.A. Mozart 384). Introductory Essay by Heinrich Birus. Musicological Introduction by Ulrich Konrad. Palo Alto, CA: Packard Humanities Institute.

——. 2006–2009. *Don Giovanni*, K. 527. Facsimile of the Autograph Score. Bibliothèque nationale de France, Paris, Département de la Musique (Ms. 1548). Introductory Essay by Hans Joachim Kreutzer. Musicological Introduction by Wolfgang Rehm. Palo Alto, CA: Packard Humanities Institute.

——. 2006–2009. *Le nozze di Figaro*, K. 492. Facsimile of the Autograph Score. Staatsbibliothek zu Berlin-Preussischer Kulturbesitz, Biblioteka Jagiellońska Kraków (Mus. ms. autogr. W.A. Mozart 492). Introductory Essay by Norbert Miller. Musicological Introduction by Dexter Edge. Palo Alto, CA: Packard Humanities Institute.

——. 2006–2009. *Die Zauberflöte*, K. 520. 3 vols. Staatsbibliothek zu Berlin-Preussischer Kulturbesitz (Mus. ms autogr. Mozart 620). Introductory Essay by Hans Joachim Kreutzer. Musicological Introduction by Christoph Wolff. Palo Alto, CA: Packard Humanities Institute.

Nero, Domenico Del. 1995. *Arrigo Boito: Un artista europeo*. Florence: Le Lettere.

Newsom, Jon, and Alfred Mann, eds. 2000. *The Rosaleen Moldenhauer Memorial: Music History from Primary Sources: A Guide to the Moldenhauer Archives*. Washington, DC: Library of Congress.

Radice, Mark A., ed. 1998. *Opera in Context: Essays on Historical Staging from the Late Renaissance to the Time of Puccini*. Portland, OR: Amadeus Press.

Ravenni, Gabriella, ed. 2009. *'Tosca' di Giacomo Puccini: Facsimile della copia di lavoro del libretto*. Florence: Olschki.

Reed, Philip. 1996. "Finding the Right Notes." In *The Making of 'Peter Grimes': Notes and Commentaries*, edited by Paul Banks, 79–115. Woodbridge: Boydell Press.

Rosen, David. 2001. "On Staging That Matters." *Verdi in Performance*, edited by Alison Latham and Roger Parker, 28–33. New York: Oxford University Press.

Schickling, Dieter. 1998. "Puccini's 'Work in Progress': The So-Called Versions of *Madama Butterfly*." *Music & Letters* 79/4: 527–537.

Senici, Emanuele, ed. 2004. *The Cambridge Companion to Rossini*. Cambridge: Cambridge University Press.

Straková, Theodora. 1982. "The Interludes." In *Leoš Janáček: 'Káťa Kabanová,'* edited by John Tyrrell, 134–143. Cambridge Opera Handbooks. Cambridge: Cambridge University Press.

Strobel, Otto. 1929. "Richard Wagner als Arbeitsgenie." *Allgemeine Musikzeitung* 56: 525, 543–544, 563.

Tusa, Michael C. 1996. "Beethoven and Opera: The Grave-Digging Duet in *Leonore* (1805)." *Beethoven Forum* 5: 1–63.

——. 1991. *'Euryanthe' and Carl Maria von Weber's Dramaturgy of German Opera*. Oxford: Clarendon Press, 1991.

Tyler, Linda. 1990. "Aria as Drama: A Sketch from Mozart's *Der Schauspieldirektor*." *Cambridge Opera Journal* 2/3: 251–267.

Tyson, Alan. 1987. *Mozart: Studies of the Autograph Scores*. Cambridge, MA: Harvard University Press.
Uvietta, Marco. 2004. "'È l'ora della prova': Berio's Finale for Puccini's *Turandot*." *Cambridge Opera Journal* 16/2: 187–238.
Verdi, Giuseppe. [1850] 2003. *Stiffelio*, edited by Kathleen Kuzmick Hansell. *The Works of Giuseppe Verdi*. Series 1: 16. Chicago: University of Chicago Press; Milan: Ricordi.
Voss, Steffen. 2004. "Die Partitur von Vivaldis Oper *Motezuma* (1733)." *Studi vivaldiani* 4: 53–73.
Woodfield, Ian. 2008. *'Così fan tutte': A Compositional History*. Woodbridge: Boydell Press.
——. 2003. "Mozart's Compositional Methods: Writing for His Singers." In *The Cambridge Companion to Mozart*, edited by Simon P. Keefe, 35–47. Cambridge: Cambridge University Press.
Wright, Lesley A. 2000. "Looking at the Sources and Editions of Bizet's *Carmen*." In *'Carmen': A Performance Guide*, edited by Mary Dibbern, ix–xxi. Hillsdale, NY: Pendragon Press.
——. 1978. "A New Source for *Carmen*." *19th-Century Music* 2/1: 61–71.
Zychowicz, James L. 2000. "Introduction." In *Die drei Pintos [by] Gustav Mahler, Based on Sketches and Original Music of Carl Maria von Weber*, ix–xx. Madison, WI: A-R Editions.

CHAPTER 45

RECONSTRUCTIONS

CHARLES S. BRAUNER

WHAT constitutes an opera reconstruction? First, what constitutes an opera? As Roger Parker puts it, " [...] what is the relation between the score (the musical trace) and its various performances? and in which does the work reside?" (Parker 2006: 6). An opera is a text, a musical score, sets, costumes, singing, acting, conducting, orchestral playing.

> [...] music intended for the theatre [...] requires the theatre. The costumes, the sets, the acting, or, to express it in more realistic terms, the gestures and movements of the singers, even the co-ordination of the performance and the particular style set by the director, are all extremely important, conditioning elements. (Baldini [1970] 1980: 77–78)

Since musical notation is only a suggestion or an approximation of how a musical work will sound, a score is a skeleton, incomplete without its realization. Every performance is different, and every performance is therefore a reconstruction. Or perhaps there is no such thing as an opera reconstruction since there is no original to reconstruct. Even a performance that duplicates every aspect of an opera's first performance, should such a thing be possible (and clearly it is not), would not be a reconstruction, since the attempt itself makes the performance something different from the unselfconscious original, much as the *Don Quixote* of Jorge Luis Borges's fictional Pierre Menard is different from that of Cervantes (and "infinitely richer" [*infinitamente más rico*]; Borges 1939). At any rate, extremely few opera productions attempt to duplicate even a fraction of the elements of the opera's first production.

Or an opera is the score with its text; its realization in a particular production with a particular set of participants is extrinsic to the work itself. In this view, reconstruction is possible, that is, reconstruction of a score and its text. If we take the word "reconstruction" in its narrowest sense, we could define an opera reconstruction as the recovery of a work that once existed but no longer does. This narrow definition is not without its problems. "Recovery" implies that nothing has been added, but as every editor knows, you cannot produce an edition of an opera without an editor's additions. Even in a photographic reproduction of the composer's autograph score, the editor has in a sense added the decision to leave it at that, with the inevitable mistakes, inconsistencies, and ambiguities. Anything beyond that—correcting mistakes, reconciling inconsistencies, resolving ambiguities—takes us beyond recovery. Then any edition is a reconstruction—perhaps a reconstruction of a hypothetical version that represents the composer's intention (with all the problems that this loaded word brings forth). Realizing this allows us to open the category of reconstruction to a broader array of issues than recovery of a lost work, which in turn affords us the opportunity to discuss diverse aspects of the opera scholar's craft.

While many operas have been lost, very few have been or can be reconstructed in the narrowest sense. One example is Rossini's *Il viaggio a Reims*, an opera—a *pièce d'occasion* (the occasion being the coronation of Charles X as king of France in 1825)—whose existence was known (among other things, the original published libretto survives), but which was thought to have been irrecoverably dismembered after its four and only performances. No complete score of the opera was thought to survive, and indeed no complete score of the opera has been found (the following discussion is based on Gossett 2006: 152–158; for the reconstructed score, see Rossini 1999).

The stages in the reconstruction may be summarized as follows:

1. 1970: Recognition in Philip Gossett's dissertation that about half of *Viaggio* was reused three years later in *Le comte Ory* and which pieces were so reused (Gossett 1970: 515–520).
2. 1974: Discovery by M. Elizabeth C. Bartlet among uncatalogued manuscripts in the Bibliothèque nationale of parts labeled "Il viaggio a Reims" or "Andremo a Parigi?" The latter was an adaptation of *Viaggio* for the Théâtre Italien in 1848. The parts, however, were incomplete.
3. 1977: Discovery by Gossett (with the help of librarian Emilia Zanetti) of uncatalogued manuscript pages in the library of the Accademia Santa Cecilia in Rome of the autograph score of almost all the music from *Viaggio* that had not been reused in *Comte Ory*.
4. 1983: Discovery by Gossett in the Österreiches Nationalbibliothek in Vienna of parts for *Il viaggio a Vienna*, an adaptation of Rossini's opera made for the wedding of Emperor Franz Joseph in 1854.
5. Realization (or surmise) by Gossett that the music for the one piece still missing, a chorus, was a contrafact of a chorus from *Maometto II*.

Even this procession of discoveries and surmises oversimplifies the story. For example, the chorus mentioned in no. 5 is for women only in *Maometto* but (probably) for mixed voices in *Viaggio*, so the music had to be adapted for its new medium. More complicated is the "Gran pezzo concertato," an ensemble of fourteen soloists in *Viaggio* that was reduced to seven soloists plus chorus in the score of *Comte Ory* printed by the Parisian publisher Troupenas and ten plus chorus in *Andremo a Parigi?* The vocal lines in the *Viaggio* edition were based on the parts for *Viaggio* for some characters and those for *Andremo a Parigi?* for others and reconstructed from incomplete hints for one. The edition took the instrumental parts, on the other hand, from the Troupenas score of *Le comte Ory*. (For details on this number, see Rossini 1999 Commento critico: 159–162.) Other passages remain uncertain, and one stretch of recitative had to be composed anew. Of course, "One never knows [...] where another manuscript might appear" (Gossett 2006: 157) and therefore change some of the readings, especially in the above examples; in fact, in a manuscript copy of *Le comte Ory* in Paris, not consulted for the edition of *Viaggio*, the piece derived from the "Gran pezzo concertato" has thirteen soloists and five-part chorus. Nevertheless, the reconstruction of *Il viaggio a Reims* is reasonably definitive. Another such opera was Verdi's *Stiffelio* (Gossett 2006: 158–164; Verdi 2003).

Conflations

A somewhat different case is that of Monteverdi's *L'incoronazione di Poppea*. Two manuscript copies of this opera survive, one in Venice and one in Naples, neither the composer's autograph and neither containing the opera as it was presented in its original production in Venice in 1643; both were probably prepared in conjunction with a revival of the opera in Naples in 1651 (Rosand 2007: 88–91). In addition, we have a printed scenario connected to the opera's premiere, two printed libretti—one from the Naples 1651 performance, the other included in the works of the librettist, Francesco Busenello, 1656—and seven manuscript libretti (Rosand 2007: 62; Rosand believes that Busenello's published libretto was substantially the same as the libretto he gave Monteverdi some thirteen years earlier—see 64–65). The two manuscript scores differ substantially from one another, and all the libretti are different from each other as well. It is, of course, possible to perform one or the other of the manuscript versions (e.g., the recording of the Venice version by the City of London Baroque Sinfonia led by Richard Hickox), although it is unlikely any seventeenth-century performance agreed entirely with either manuscript. However, the temptation to reconstruct the composer's (or composers') original version, or the version performed at its premiere (they are not necessarily the same thing), by conflating the two manuscripts has proved great, as in Alan Curtis's edition (Monteverdi 1989).

Until 1993, conflating the two surviving manuscripts with the idea of reconstructing a hypothetical original was largely a speculative task that depended on the reconstructor's ideas of the composer's style and judgments about quality. That some or even all of the opera might not be by Monteverdi only complicated the task. (The extent of Monteverdi's involvement in the composition of this opera—he died the year of its premiere—is under dispute. See, for example, Curtis 1989. Rosand [2007: 23–38, 61–68, 88–128] discusses the issue without coming to a definite conclusion, although she accepts Monteverdi's authorship for most of the opera.) Unlike most operas from the seventeenth until well into the nineteenth century, no libretto seems to have been published in connection with the premiere; at least, none has survived. The discovery in

Table 45.1 Three versions of *L'incoronazione di Poppea.*

Version	Score used as basis	Adding from the other score, and subtracting, according to
Autograph	Venice, restoring crossed-out passages	Busenello's published libretto (hence eliminating "Pur to miro")
Venice premiere	Venice	scenario and Udine libretto
Naples revival	Naples	Naples libretto (hence eliminating Seneca and his followers)

1993 of a manuscript libretto in the Biblioteca comunale of Udine that closely matches the 1643 scenario, and that is the only libretto bearing Monteverdi's name, has clarified the situation (Fabbri 1993: 19–23; the libretto was published in Busenello 1997). Perhaps most notable is the presence in this libretto of the disputed final duet, "Pur ti miro, pur ti godo," which suggests that it was part of the opera's premiere, whoever wrote the music. The peripatetic text of this duet appeared both before *Poppea*, in the second production of Benedetto Ferrari's *Il pastor regio* (Bologna, 1641), and after, in Filiberto Laurenzi's *Il trionfo della fatica* (Rome, 1647) (Bianconi 1987: 195; unfortunately, the music for Ferrari's opera does not survive. Curtis [1989: 43–50] has suggested on stylistic grounds Francesco Sacrati as the possible composer, but it is possible that Monteverdi set the text anew—see Rosand 2007: 36–38).

Rosand distinguishes among three versions of the opera to reconstruct (2007: 127–128; see Table 45.1). Still, numerous problems remain, including passages of text with no music in either score, instrumental passages that conflict between the two scores, and the apparent transposition of the role of Ottone, creating harmonic conflicts present in both scores (on the role of Ottone, see Rosand 2007: 118–121).

Several lessons may be learned from the situation of *Poppea*.

1. Libretti are important documents. Until at least the late nineteenth century, libretti were published in conjunction with specific performances, and so they enable us to trace the history of an opera as it changes over time. Although *Poppea* is unusual in that no printed libretto from the premiere survives (the same is true of Monteverdi's other Venetian operas), we do have the manuscript libretto from Udine that is almost certainly derived from the score as it existed at the premiere. The printed libretto from Naples is probably a better indication of the opera as it was performed there in 1651 than either of the surviving scores.
2. The original state of the composer's autograph and the state of the opera at its premiere are not necessarily the same thing. If Rosand is correct that Busenello's published libretto contains the text of Monteverdi's lost autograph score, the latter was quite different from the score as it existed at the premiere, and some or all of the differences may well reflect the work of a composer or composers other than Monteverdi.

3. There are limits to what a libretto can tell us. It cannot tell us precisely what music was performed to the text. It cannot tell us whether the "Pur ti miro" of *Poppea* was the same as that sung in Ferrari's opera or a new composition. It cannot tell us what the original state of Ottone's music was.
4. There is a difference between reconstructing an opera for a critical edition and reconstructing it for performance. A critical edition must choose what state of the opera to present, if different states are recoverable—different states such as the composer's original conception, the work at its premiere, the work as revised by the composer for the final time—although the edition will normally also present alternative possibilities in appendices. The performers may then choose from these possibilities, even mixing and matching as they desire.
5. Different choices about what to perform can result in very different works. An opera that ends with "Pur ti miro," with the two amoral lovers luxuriating in their sexuality, is different from an opera that ends with a formal ceremony of coronation that is more about power than about sexuality.

In the case of *Poppea*, conflating the two musical sources as Rosand suggests seems a logical, even a desirable, step given the surviving material. Other conflations are more problematic. At least two operas in the standard repertory—Mozart's *Don Giovanni* and Beethoven's *Fidelio*—are commonly presented in inauthentic conflated versions. In the case of *Fidelio*, the frequent practice has been to insert the "Leonore no. 3" overture before the final scene, perhaps because the overture is a fine piece whose omission seems a pity or perhaps because the opera would seem rather short without it. This insertion seems harmless enough, and we might add to our justification the fact that Beethoven manifestly struggled with this opera (so why not help him along?) and that the final version is itself a conflation of music from two very different periods of Beethoven's career: 1805–1806 and 1814. Such reasoning, however, leads to the possibility of creating other conflations. We might, for example, feel that Beethoven was occasionally too harsh in his pruning of the 1805 version and therefore prefer the longer version of some pieces, for example, "O namenlose Freude," which Beethoven reduced from 213 measures in 1805 to 124 in 1806 and 1814 (Beethoven 1967, 1970, 1870; reverting to the 1805 version of the opera itself involves reconstruction in some cases, such as Florestan's Scene und Arie—see Tusa 1993).

We might decide that tampering with a great composer's final thoughts is illegitimate and that we should simply use the version of 1814, leaving "Leonore no. 3" for orchestral concerts. This line of reasoning, however, leads to the problem of Mozart's *Don Giovanni*. In transplanting the opera from Prague (1787) to Vienna the following year, Mozart replaced the tenor's aria "Il mio tesoro" with a new one, "Dalla sua pace," moving it from the second act to the first; to the now shortened second act he added a scene for Leporello and Zerlina and a *scena ed aria* for Donna Elvira. Leporello's escape aria in Act II was replaced by a recitative (Rushton 1981: 53–57; see also Mozart 1968). As the opera is normally given today, Ottavio sings *both* arias, Elvira sings her added scene, Leporello sings his aria, and the Zerlina-Leporello scene is omitted. Hardly anybody does the composer's final version, and nobody to my knowledge has argued that the final version is preferable (although Rushton 1981: 57 argues for its viability).

In addition to these changes, Mozart "tried out various options and experimented with the score" (Rehm 2009: 15–16). These experiments included several small cuts and, most notably, the finale. The autograph (Mozart 2009: 2: 548–557) shows a large cut in the final scene (mm. 689–749 in Mozart 1969), replaced by a ten-measure transition; the Viennese libretto omits the final scene entirely and ends with Don Giovanni's death (the libretti for both the Prague and Vienna productions are reproduced in Mozart 2009: 3: 63–108; see Rehm 2009: 24–29 for further discussion). None of these options is regularly adopted in the opera house today.

A good case can be made for restoring the first version as dramatically tighter, while the conflation lacks "authenticity and sense" and Elvira's aria "is often, and understandably, considered an excrescence" (Rushton 1981: 57, 101). Here, however, we confront the realities of the opera house. It is hard to imagine an Elvira, one capable of meeting the considerable demands of the role, agreeing to forgo her big scene, and most Ottavios would likely object as well. We do want a first-class Elvira, don't we? Ottavios probably have less leverage, but I would argue that "Dalla sua pace" is too lovely to omit. But if "Dalla sua pace" is too lovely to omit, we must accept either the final version, which few find desirable, or a conflation. We need not accept the usual conflation, but it has proved hard to escape.

What is the principle here? There are conflicting forces: original version, final version, an authentic version whether original or intermediate or final (I use the term "authentic" here in a restricted sense, meaning a version in which the composer had a hand, the "hand" ranging from direct involvement to acquiesence in the work of others), singers' preferences, the director's or conductor's or some musicologist's aesthetic judgment. It is tempting for a musicologist to argue for the last, and I will have more to say about this later, but the fundamental point is that no absolute position seems satisfactory to all individual examples.

Completions

A number of operas have been left incomplete upon the death of the composer. Two works of the twentieth century illustrate opposite approaches to this issue: Alban Berg's *Lulu* and Arnold Schoenberg's *Moses und Aron*. By his death in 1935, Berg had essentially completed *Lulu* in short score and had orchestrated the first two acts and the beginning of the third; in addition, a piano-vocal score of the third act had been prepared in manuscript and partially engraved, and Berg had arranged a set of orchestral pieces derived from *Lulu* (*Symphonische Stücke aus 'Lulu'*), two from the third act. For many years the composer's widow refused to allow the completion of the opera, for reasons that nobody can quite explain. The opera was performed in a two-act version, with the third act as a pantomime accompanied by the music of the *Symphonic Pieces*. After Helene Berg's death in 1976, the publisher brought out a completed version by composer Friedrich Cerha. Cerha faced the inevitable problem of reconstructing Berg's orchestrations, and the short score had some gaps. However, precisely because of the tightly knit structure of the work, particularly the relationship between the third act and the previous two, completion proved relatively unproblematic (on the vicissitudes of the opera, see Clements 1992: 93–94; see also Perle 1964 and 1979).

Moses und Aron was left incomplete not by the composer's death (in 1951) but rather by his inability to find an appropriate musical setting. Schoenberg had completed the text and music of the first two acts and the text of the third by 1932 (like Berg, he had written his own libretto), but he seems not to have composed any music for the third act beyond a few fragments, although he long yearned to complete the opera (Cherlin 2007: 231–234). Opinion has divided over whether the two completed acts can stand alone or the opera should be performed with the third act text spoken (Cherlin 2007: 234, fn 7 on 369); in a letter to Francesco Siciliani, director of the Maggio Musicale Fiorentino (November 27, 1950), Schoenberg himself offered both possibilities (Schoenberg 1965: 285). No doubt the fact that it ends with Moses saying "O Wort, du Wort das mir fehlt!" helps give the fragment a sense of completion, or rather that incompletion is a logical way to conclude the work.

Reversions

Many operas underwent revisions at the hands of the composer—Puccini, for one, was a compulsive reviser (Schickling 1998: 527; see also Fairtile 1996)—and one object of musicology has been the recovery of the original version of operas that have come to be known in revised versions. A central question surrounds these efforts: Why did the composer revise the opera? In the eighteenth century, the reasons often had to do with the need to supply new material for a new production, since audiences and especially singers expected something different from what had been produced elsewhere or earlier. We often assume, then, that the original version represents a more unified realization of the drama, and we tend to favor the original over the revision in the works of Handel and Mozart, for example, as may be seen by the furor over Cecilia Bartoli's substitution of "Al desio di chi t'adora" for "Deh vieni, non tardar" in *Le nozze di Figaro* (Tommasini 1998; see above for a discussion of the problems of the idea of the "original" version with regard to *L'incoronazione di Poppea*). We tend to believe that by the mid-nineteenth century revisions result not from the external pressures of the opera house but from the composer's dissatisfaction. But then, while the final versions of such works as *La traviata* and *Madama Butterfly* are preferred to the originals, the reconstruction of the originals allows us to explore a composer's development and aesthetic choices.[1]

A particularly interesting example of such a reconstruction is *Un ballo in maschera* (the following account is based on Gossett 2006: 492–511 et passim). Censorship was a constant problem in nineteenth-century Italy (Gossett 2006: 60, 158; Giger 1999), and Verdi seems to have suffered from it more than earlier composers, the result of the increasing conservatism of the Catholic Church under Pius IX (pope from 1846 to 1878), the revolutions of 1848, and the desperation of old regimes, particularly that of the Kingdom of Two Sicilies, to hold on as the Risorgimento flowered. *Un ballo in maschera* began as *Gustavo III*, based on Eugène Scribe's French libretto set by Daniel Auber in 1833 about the assassination of Swedish King Gustaf III at a masked ball in 1792. It was then transferred to Pomerania and called *Una vendetta in dominò*, losing the king as the victim, which version Verdi completed in draft. Further censorship moved the setting out of Europe to colonial Boston, notwithstanding the unlikelihood of masked balls ever having occurred in the center of New England Puritanism. "*Un ballo in maschera* has not ceased to be a problem ever since" (Gossett 2006: 494). The Boston setting is unhistorical and not what Verdi had conceived when he wrote most of the music, but simply changing the setting back to Sweden has its problems as well (Gossett 2006: 495–496).

The recovery of *Gustavo III/Una vendetta in dominò* exploits Verdi's practice of starting with a continuity draft in which he "traces in detail the shape and melodic content of the score" (Gossett 2006: 496). Surviving is Verdi's continuity draft for Act I with the text of the original *Gustavo III* and from the finale of Act II through Act III with the text of *Una vendetta* as well as some fragmentary sketches of the missing parts of Act II. Verdi would then make a skeleton score consisting of the vocal parts and bass line plus other important instrumental parts, on which he then filled in the orchestration. In the autograph score of *Ballo*, one can see earlier layers that go back to the skeleton score of *Una vendetta*, but Verdi also replaced parts of the score (about 25 percent) with new ones for *Ballo* alone, most notably a completely different aria for the baritone in Act III. The recovery of the earlier opera then involved using the continuity draft, the skeleton score, some inferences about that 25 percent of the autograph (many of the replacements seem to have been transpositions) and a certain amount of creativity, particularly in orchestration, the biggest task of which was the need to orchestrate the original baritone aria of Act III. This reconstruction (by Philip Gossett and Ilaria Narici) was performed at the Gothenburg, Sweden, Opera in 2002. We should note that because of the interruptions to Verdi's work, the recovery of *Una vendetta in dominò* is the reconstruction of an opera that never existed.

Sometimes the original version of an opera is not recoverable, for example, Rossini's *Mosè in Egitto*. In its first production (Naples, 1818), the third act was poorly received. Although at least part of the blame could be placed on the production, which did not adequately depict the parting of the Red Sea, Rossini recomposed the entire act to a new text. The music of the original third act is lost (Rossini 2004: xxiv–xxvii). It would have been entirely characteristic of Rossini to reuse the discarded music in another opera, as he did with *Viaggio* and numerous other works, but he seems not to have done so. At least, no such reuse has been identified. So unless the music turns up in some unsuspected library, we will not be able to reconstruct the opera's 1818 version without composing a great deal more music than is normally acceptable in a reconstruction.

Lost music does occasionally turn up, in fact, but is sometimes not complete. For the second production of his *Tancredi* (Ferrara, 1813), Rossini wrote a new ending, closer to the tragic ending of the Voltaire play on which the libretto was based than was the happy ending of the first production (Venice, 1813). This new ending was rediscovered in 1976, but it was missing a few lines of *recitativo secco*, which therefore had to be composed anew (Gossett 2006: 149–152). Sometimes, however, much more extensive composition is required. How much composing is acceptable before we leave the realm of reconstruction and enter that of a new work?

Construction or Reconstruction? Puccini's *Turandot*

Probably the most famous example of opera completion—and one that continues to vex scholars—is Puccini's *Turandot*. It is also the operatic completion most frequently performed. Like *Lulu*, *Turandot*—libretto based on the eighteenth-century play by Carlo Gozzi (English translation in Gozzi 1989)—was left incomplete by the composer's death, but also, like *Moses und Aron*, by the composer's difficulty in finding an appropriate musical setting. Puccini had finished Acts I and II and the first part of Act III, through the death of Liù. He left twenty-three folios of drafts and sketches for the remainder, leaving the final version of the libretto unsettled as well. (The sketches have been most extensively studied in Maehder 1984a, 1984b, 1985; I will refer to the last in this chapter. See also the summary in Fairtile 2004: 167.) In the surviving material we may distinguish two continuity drafts presenting substantial continuous passages in short score with text. One, fifty-seven measures, Calaf's "Principessa di morte!" follows immediately where the completed score ends and breaks off where he seizes and kisses Turandot. The other, twenty-three measures, picks up after the kiss with "Oh mio fiore matutino." The remaining sketches are more fragmentary, some without text; the composer's intentions for their use are often unclear. (On the distinction between continuity drafts and sketch fragments, see Ashbrook and Powers 1991: 132.)

In addition to the sketches, we have several indications of what Puccini had in mind. One is negative: although "during the last eight months of his life Puccini focused exclusively on the opera's conclusion" (Fairtile 2004: 163), he never managed to get very far. He was dissatisfied with the libretto and, beginning as early as 1921, repeatedly asked librettists Giuseppe Adami and Renato Simoni for rewrites: "I think the central nub is the duet. And the duet as it is doesn't seem to me what is wanted"[2] (Letter to Adami, [October? 1921], Puccini 1928: 272). An important detail appears in a letter of July 9, 1822: "I would like Turandot's iciness to melt in the course of the duet [...] and to finish in ecstasy, in jubilation, in sunlit glory"[3] (Puccini 1928: 279; trans. Girardi 2000: 449).

The struggle continues in a series of letters to Adami beginning September 7, 1924, and ending on November 16:

> Toscanini has just left here [...]. The duet was discussed and it does not please him much. What to do? I don't know. Perhaps Toscanini will summon you [Adami] and Simoni to Salso [maggiore]. I will come too, and we shall see if there is some way to remedy the situation.[4] (September 7, 1924. Puccini 1928: 297. The meeting never occurred.)
>
> There has been much discussion about our duet and I am a little perplexed [...]. I have some ideas about the heart of the duet. The beginning I am not changing unless something better is suggested to me.[5] (September 14, 1924. Puccini 1928: 298)
>
> At last I have received the lines from Simoni. They are truly beautiful and they complete and justify the duet. There is just one word: *slender* as a flower, that must be changed.[6] (October 8, 1924. Puccini 1928: 298)

This seems to settle the issue, but then:

> There was so little left to do to put together the famous duet for good. Come on, dear Adamino, please me, make a great effort and dedicate two or three hours to me and send me the verses that I need. But do this little bit of work in such a way that it is definitive, so that we don't have to go back to it.[7] (October 10, 1924. Puccini 1928: 300)
>
> Simoni's verses are good and seem to be just what are wanted and what I had dreamed of. All the rest of Liù's address to Turandot were things that did not connect up well, and you rightly said: the duet is complete like this. Perhaps Turandot speaks too much in this segment. We'll see.[8] (October 22, 1924. Puccini 1928: 300–301)
>
> It must be a grand duet. The two almost otherworldly beings enter among humans through love and this love must at the end invade everyone on stage in an orchestral peroration. Now make an effort.[9] (November 16, 1924. Puccini 1928: 301)

In October, in the midst of all this, Puccini reportedly said, "The opera will be performed incomplete, and then someone will come on stage and tell the audience: 'At this point Maestro Puccini died'" (Fraccaroli 1957: 212, reported in Girardi 2000: 438), which is exactly what Toscanini did at the first performance.

All of this suggests not only problems with the libretto as late as two weeks before Puccini's death on November 29, but also with the entire dramatic conception of the denouement: "the inhuman Princess's conversion to humanity" (Ashbrook and Powers 1991: 132). Still more arguable, to my mind, is Calaf, who continues to love Turandot after he has witnessed the torture and suicide of Liù and his father's pathetic pleadings, and even after he has rightly called Turandot "Principessa di morte!" As Julian Budden concludes, "Clearly the man who can persist in his wooing of a woman of whom he knows nothing, and whom he has every reason to dislike, immediately after a slave-girl has killed herself for his sake, is bound to forfeit our sympathy" (Budden 1992: 838–839. Puccini seems to have thought that the death of Liù would help motivate the "thawing" [*sgelamento*] of Turandot [letter to Adami, November 3, 1922. Puccini 1928: 282; trans. Ashbrook and Powers 1991: 80]. This seems to me a considerable miscalculation.).

Another clue to Puccini's thinking is his association of the opera with Wagner's *Tristan und Isolde*. One of the sketch fragments (f. 17r) bears the phrase "poi Tristano" at the bottom (facsimile in Maehder 1985: 91, and Maguire 1990: 337). Another (f. 22r) has "Tris" in its eighth measure (facsimile in Maguire 1990: 340); this has been (plausibly, given the contents of the fragment) taken as a reference to *Tristan* (Uvietta 2004: 194, including a transcription of the first nine measures of the sixteen-measure fragment. The facsimile shows the ninth measure, and the fifteenth, crossed out. For some reason, Berio regarded mm. 1–9 and 10–16 as separate fragments, even though they are continuous on the page, perhaps because of a change of meter to 9/8 at m. 10.). A final reference to *Tristan* is in a letter from critic Leonardo Pinzauti to Luciano Berio (December 29, 2001) in which Pinzauti recounts a meeting between one Salvatore Orlando and Puccini:

> During a holiday some time around 1923, the young Salvatore went to visit Puccini [...] and it was there (he said with tears in his eyes) that the Maestro played him the finale of *Turandot* on the piano. 'Salvatorino,' said Puccini, 'I'm going to play you the last scene: it's a finale like that of *Tristan*.' Orlando remembered that the last bars were *pianissimo*. (Uvietta 2004: 195, fn. 18).[10]

This *Tristan*-like pianissimo ending seems closer to the transfiguring orchestral postlude described in November 1924 than the "ecstasy, jubilation, sun-lit glory" of July 1922.

Turandot was completed for its initial production by Franco Alfano, but Alfano's original completion was rejected. His second attempt, made at the insistence of Toscanini—largely cutting some passages and replacing others with ones derived from the sketches, most notably eight measures at Calaf's "Il mio mistero?" (Fairtile 2004: 180–182)—has been widely adopted by opera houses, although Alfano's original version has recently gained some favor. (Ricordi published a piano-vocal score of the opera with Alfano's original completion in 1926 [Puccini 1926a] and later with the revised completion [Puccini 1926b]. The scores are identical through the second system of p. 354, up to rehearsal n. 36 of Act III. Alfano's contribution begins on p. 353 at rehearsal 35.) Several writers have suggested a conflation of Alfano's two completions (Maehder 1985: 127–128; Ashbrook and Powers 1991: 180–181, fn 16; Fairtile 2004: 183–184).

Since Alfano, there have been at least three later completions. A completion by Janet Maguire seems never to have been published or performed (Maguire 1990). Another has been recently made by Chinese composer Hao Weiya (Delli 2008). The only one widely available is by Luciano Berio (Berio 2001), first performed in concert at the Canary Islands Music Festival in January 2002 and staged in Los Angeles, Amsterdam, and Salzburg later that year (a DVD of the Salzburg production has been issued by TDK; for detailed examinations see Uvietta 2004 and Parker 2006: 99–120; see also Tommasini 2002 and Wang 2002). I will focus on Berio's completion in comparison to Alfano's. Berio uses somewhat more of Puccini's sketch fragments than Alfano had, but my interest here is not Berio's cleverness in creating a "montage" (Uvietta's word: 2004: 192) of Puccini's themes nor which composer is more faithful to Puccini's intended use of these ideas, the latter question being entirely speculative, but rather the different results achieved by the two completions.

I see three questions as crucial:

1. What should follow Calaf's kiss? (Ashbrook and Powers [1991: 132] recognize here Puccini's "universally valid method for thawing the icy Princess: a passionate kiss, in short, sex.") As mentioned above, the first continuity draft breaks off at the point (f. 11v; facsimile in Maguire 1990: 326) where Calaf kisses Turandot, rehearsal 38+10 in Alfano's revised edition. The libretto then contained three lines of text:

Turandot:	Che fai di me?... Che fai di me?... ["Che è mai di me!" in Alfano]
	Qual brivido!... Perduta!...
	Lasciami!... No!...
Calaf:	Mio fiore;

(For the libretto, see Maehder 1985: 141–148; Maguire 1990: 354–359; Uvietta 2004: 232–237; Maehder shows how Alfano modified the libretto, Uvietta how Berio did so.) Alfano originally gave this text twenty-one measures of music (the first eleven orchestral); this was reduced to seven in the revised version, omitting "Qual brivido!" and "Lasciami! No!" Most commentators feel that this interlude is crucial for making Turandot's change of heart convincing and that Alfano's version, at least the second one, is simply inadequate (e.g., Carner 1958: 468–469; Uvietta 2004: 191). Berio (2001: 17–27); while suppressing the above text entirely, inserts an extended orchestral interlude, fifty-seven measures (about 2:45), beginning with a deceptive cadence and incorporating several of Puccini's fragments as well as quotations from Wagner's *Tristan und Isolde*, Mahler's Symphony no. 7, and Schoenberg's *Gurrelieder* (Uvietta 2004: 192–195, 205–206; see also 233).[11] These quotations and more *Tristan*-like chromaticism, perhaps suggesting the emotional uncertainty and turmoil Turandot is feeling, are followed by a diatonic passage involving the "superposition of the motif of recognition from Act I, 'O padre, sì, ti ritrovo' [...] on to a fragment of 'Nessun dorma' [...]" (Uvietta 2004: 207; the symbolic significance of the return of "O padre [...]", here and in the final postlude, escapes me).

2. How can Turandot's solo "Del primo pianto" function dramatically? Puccini left only the beginning (starting at rehearsal 42 in Alfano's revised version; a facsimile of this sketch has not been published, but the transcription in Uvietta 2004: 225 shows five complete measures and the beginning of a sixth). As Ashbrook and Powers observe:

> Alfano's first composition [...] ran to 105 measures; they were cut down to 64 measures for the second composition by hacking out a half-dozen chunks of from 3 to 13 measures each. It was butcher-work on what is a crucial piece dramatically, for only here is there any real remnant in the opera of Gozzi's original plausible preparation for Turandot's otherwise implausible conversion: she was affected as she had never been before by her first sight of the Prince, and his heroic bearing thereafter [...] "Del primo pianto" needs all the time and emphasis it can get, and if the opera is to be done with Alfano's completion at all, for this piece the longer version should be used [...]. (Ashbrook and Powers 1991: 138–139)

After the beginning, Alfano's work is mostly his own, although one phrase (at rehearsal 43) somewhat resembles a fragment, f. 15v (Fairtile 2004: 175–176; the phrase is a return of rehearsal 41 + 1. Facsimile in Maguire 1990: 332). Berio (2001: 35–40) alters the opening measures that Puccini had left in draft, then continues with a passage from "In questa reggia" and ends with a quotation of the first notes of the opera (Uvietta 2004: 201 and 234; the first twelve measures of Berio's work are found on 226–227). Berio's solo is only twenty-six measures (40–45 seconds), and he also severely shortens the text. Rather than an important passage of introspection and self-realization, Turandot's solo becomes just a stage in the passage climaxing in Calaf's revelation of his name.

3. What should happen at the very end? In Alfano's revised version, Turandot addresses her father ("Padre Augusto, conosco il nome del straniero! Il suo nome è Amor!" five measures), followed by a brief transition (five measures), and the chorus loudly proclaims "O sole! Vita! Eternità," etc., to the main tune from "Nessun dorma" (thirteen measures). This is slightly contracted from the first version, and there are differences in detail, but in both versions the ending is triumphant but also perfunctory.

Berio's ending (Berio 2001: 55–58) also quotes "Nessun dorma," but it is otherwise completely different from Alfano's (see Uvietta 2004: 237; ten measures of this "orchestral coda" are printed on 229–230). The closing chorus is gone; in the twenty-measure instrumental postlude there are quotations from other parts of the opera as well: the riddle scene of Act II, "O padre, sì, ti ritrovo" from Act I, and at the end a phrase from Liù's "Tu che di gel sei cinta" where she sings "l'amerai anche tu." The ending is *pianissimo*, as suggested in the letter quoted above (see Music Example 45.1).

Instead of Alfano's "inopportune triumph of love" (Uvietta 2004: 189), we get, in Berio's own words, "no longer a 'happy end' but a more open and reticent conclusion" (quoted in Parker 2006: 100). "'Amore' remains the last word, [...] but moral judgment is explicitly suspended: love is capable of pushing human beings to commit acts of sublime immorality [...]" (Uvietta 2004: 190. Note that Alfano's "Amore" is part of a cadential passage while Berio's is dissonant and tonally ambiguous). We might interpret Berio's quotation of "Tu che di gel" as a reminder of Liù's suffering or, especially as the dissonances are resolved to the final E flat chord, a fulfillment of her prophecy ("You too will love him"). Whichever, Berio's ending is more in keeping with the *Tristan* references, while Alfano's are closer to "ecstasy, jubilation, sun-lit glory." Whether any of the endings overcomes the problem of motivation (and therefore achieves psychological plausibility) may be debated.

MUSIC EXAMPLE 45.1 Reduction of final four measures of Luciano Berio, *Turandot: completamento* (del terzo atto), Milan: Ricordi. © Casa Ricordi—Milano.

In effect, any completion becomes a commentary on the opera, a reflection of what the completer thinks the opera is or should be about, the more so in Berio's completion whose harmonic style, quite different from Puccini's, serves to separate the ending from the rest. Other choices besides Alfano's and Berio's are possible. An ending might focus more overtly on Liù, bringing back more of the music of her death scene as a rejection of Turandot and Calaf's immorality. Or it might resort more to the Gozzi play, labeled "tragicommedia" but aside from the death of Turandot's latest suitor in Act I essentially a comedy.

Or we might follow Toscanini's lead and put down our metaphorical batons after the death of Liù, in short, treating the fragment Puccini left as a fragment. This was the opinion of Claudio Sartori (1958: 28, quoted in Fairtile 2004: 179): "The opera must not be concluded in any way. It must remain a document of unreachable aspirations unrealised by a maestro who was killed by the error of having believed in a dream too vast for his possibilities." Fairtile (2004: 183), on the contrary, asserts, "*Turandot* needs some sort of conclusion in order to deliver what he valued above all, namely, a satisfying evening of musical theatre."

An important question remains: How obligated is the collaborator to try to decipher the composer's intentions, at best ambiguous, and to incorporate the material he left?

RECAPITULATION: OFFENBACH'S *LES CONTES D'HOFFMANN*

Jacques Offenbach (1819–1880) died before he had quite completed the opera, and its early history is one of unraveling and accretion:

- The Giulietta act omitted at the premiere, later placed between Olympia and Antonia.
- Pieces composed by Offenbach but cut or never used, chiefly: a scene for the Muse in the Prologue and Epilogue, the Muse thus reduced to a brief speaking role in the Epilogue; a trio for Nicklausse, Hoffmann, and Coppélius and a duet for Hoffmann and Nicklausse in the Olympia act; a romance for Nicklausse in the Antonia act (according to Michael Kaye [private e-mail], this last was abandoned by Offenbach himself, as were several other pieces).
- Recitatives by Ernest Guiraud (the same composer who wrote the recitatives for Bizet's *Carmen*) added to replace spoken dialogue. (Offenbach originally wanted recitative but was forced to substitute spoken dialogue when the proposed venue changed from the Théâtre de la Gaîté-Lyrique to the Opéra-Comique after the former's bankruptcy. Some recitative passages composed by Offenbach were included at the Opéra-Comique.)
- The chanson "Tourne, tourne miroir où se prend l'alouette !" taken from Dapertutto (Giulietta act) and given to Coppélius (Olympia act) with the text "J'ai des yeux, de vrais yeux." Dapertutto compensated with the chanson "Scintille, diamant," with a melody originally from Offenbach's *Le voyage dans la lune* of 1875.

- The so-called Septet (really a sextet with chorus), "Hélas! mon cœur s'égare encore !" (originally "Hélas je vais encore la suivre") added to the Giulietta act.

(Succinct summaries of the early vicissitudes of the opera, traceable in the editions published by Choudens from 1881 to 1907, may be found in MacDonald 1980 and in Kaye 1992 and 1996.)

Thus, the opera as generations have come to know it, reflecting a production in Monte Carlo in 1904 (published as Offenbach 1907, hereafter the Choudens version), is an amalgam of music Offenbach wrote for it, music he wrote for another opera (Offenbach himself reused music from earlier operas, including the famous Barcarolle), music by Guiraud (including many of the recitatives), and music by someone else (André Bloch, according to Michael Kaye [private communication]). The arrangement of the acts is certainly not the one Offenbach intended: Prologue-Olympia-Antonia-Giulietta-Epilogue. The Giulietta act and Epilogue are much shorter than they once were or might have been.

There survive hundreds of pages of music scattered in Europe and America, pieces the composer had abandoned, material unfinished at the composer's death, and pages removed from the score when cuts and alterations were made for the early performances—drafts, sketches, piano-vocal-score, and full-score pages, entirely or partially in Offenbach's hand. Some 1660 pages in the possession of Offenbach's heirs, recovered by conductor and Offenbach scholar Antonio de Almeida, formed the basis of a new edition by Fritz Oeser, published in 1977 (Offenbach [1977] 1982: ix; Kaye and Keck 2009: viii gives the figure as 1,250 pages). Oeser's version restored the order of the acts, retrieved omitted numbers, returned "Tourne, tourne" to Dapertutto and removed his "Scintille, diamant" and the following Septet. Oeser's self-description was, "While the new versions of Acts I–III at least come close to an 'Urtext' edition, Acts IV and V are an arrangement by the editor" (Offenbach [1977] 1982: xv; see also Oeser 1981). This is certainly true of Acts IV and V, which are fleshed out extensively with music taken from Offenbach's *Die Rheinnixen* used to set passages from drafts of the libretto, but it understates the editor's interventions in all the acts: transpositions, rewriting of the text, passages written or orchestrated by Oeser himself. While he restored pieces that are authentically Offenbach, the end result is a version that is as much an editorial construct as the Choudens. (See reviews by MacDonald 1980; Winter 1983; and Schneider 1984. A commercial recording was issued, conducted by Sylvain Cambreling.)

Oeser's interventions have been made unnecessary by the discoveries of Michael Kaye,[12] the first version of whose edition (now co-edited with Jean-Christophe Keck) became available for rental in 1988, although the full score has not yet been made available for sale (Offenbach forthcoming).[13] In 1984, more than three hundred additional pages emerged, mostly autograph but orchestrated by Guiraud. This was followed by the discovery of the so-called Censor Libretto, which Léon Carvalho (director of the Opéra-Comique) submitted to the Parisian censor on January 5, 1881. These materials formed the basis of the first Kaye version. Then in 1993, Jean-Christoph Keck unearthed the autograph (again orchestrated by Guiraud) of the finale of Act IV, very likely the last piece Offenbach wrote before his death, the text identical to that in the Censor Libretto (Kaye and Keck 2009: viii). Two commercial recordings based on the Kaye version were issued, one conducted by Jeffrey Tate (1992, with spoken dialogue) and one by Kent Nagano (1996, with Guiraud's recitatives), both before the Act IV finale had become available.

The Kaye-Keck edition, too, restores Offenbach's order of the acts and the omitted and misassigned pieces, without Oeser's recompositions. As might be expected, its principal innovations are encountered in Acts IV and V. In Act IV, it adds a chorus and a chanson for Giulietta, restores the authentic gambling/seduction scene, places the reprise of the Barcarolle before the duet, and—instead of ending the act with this reprise, during which Giulietta goes off in a gondola with Pitichinaccio (as in the Choudens version)—ends with everyone mocking Hoffmann for the loss of his reflection, Hoffmann's denunciation of Giulietta, and his blindly stabbing and killing Pitichinaccio. (Kaye has constructed an alternative ending in which Giulietta is poisoned by a drink that Dapertutto intended for Hoffmann, the music "based on fully orchestrated manuscripts apparently rehearsed at the Opéra-Comique before the Giulietta Act was omitted"—the music recapitulates melodies from earlier in the act—the text taken from the Barbier and Carré play that was the basis of the libretto.)

While Acts I–IV can be, and have been, reconstructed to a state that, we can say with some confidence, closely matches Offenbach's conception, the Epilogue remains uncertain. The problem stems from the Censor Libretto. Through Act IV, this source provides, if not an infallible, a reliable guide to the structure of the opera, and it can be used as a template in which to fit the pages that the composer left behind, as the Kaye-Keck edition has done. In Act V, however, the libretto's content is minimal: some dialogue, a chorus "Folie! Oublie tes douleurs!" and an additional strophe of Hoffmann's "Kleinzach" song of Act I. Since Offenbach left many more pieces than this, the task of the editor has been to try to divine his intentions and assemble these pieces in a logical order. In doing so, Kaye was aided primarily by five libretto drafts in the hand of the librettist, Jules Barbier, and by a libretto published in 1881 in conjunction with the premiere and which itself has two versions of the last act, reflecting changes made by Barbier and Guiraud after Offenbach's death. Kaye also had the editions of the opera published by Choudens, useful primarily for Guiraud's recitatives, as well as the manuscripts documenting the alterations and versions performed at the Opéra-Comique (Kaye, private communication).

A summary of the result, omitting the spoken dialogue and Guiraud's recitatives, may be seen in Table 45.2. (Note that Kaye's reconstruction differs here from the Kaye-Keck edition, which includes in the main text only the two pieces in the Censor Libretto and the finale *Apothéose*, "Des cendres de ton cœur.")

Table 45.2 Michael Kaye's reconstruction of *Les contes d'Hoffmann*, Act V.

	Source
Chorus: "Folie! oublie tes douleurs!"	Censor libretto/Barbier draft
Chœur des Ésprits "Glou, glou" (reprise from Act I)	Barbier draft
Chœur des Étudiants "À nous ton vin!" (reprise from Act I)*	Chorus "Vidons les tonneaux" in 1881 libretto contains much of this text
Hoffmann, "Pour le cœur de Phryné": additional strophe of Act I "Kleinzach" song	Censor libretto/Barbier draft
Chorus, "Jusqu'au matin remplis, remplis mon verre" (reprise from Act I)	1881 libretto
La Muse "Ingrat! Et moi?…moi, la fidèle amie" (melodrama) and "Des cendres de ton cœur" (air)	Barbier draft/1881 libretto

*Kaye inserts here an option for Stella to rebuke Hoffmann, based on an autograph fragment but without a direct source in the libretti. This editorial denouement also provides for Hoffmann's attempted suicide that Barbier indicated in his autograph libretti.

Most crucially, the libretto sources provide several different endings for the opera:

- The "Kleinzach" song (Censor Libretto and Barbier draft no. 5);
- A Drinking Chorus "Luther! Luther! Tison d'enfer," a reprise from Act I (1881 libretto);
- "Des cendres de ton cœur"
    - For the Muse (*appears enveloped by a luminous aura*) (Barbier draft no. 1; also in 1881 libretto but earlier in the act),

      May cinders of your heart reignite your genius!
      In serenity smile at your sorrows!
      The muse will soothe your holy suffering!
      We are made great by love and greater by tears![14]
    - For the Muse with a second strophe for Stella, "Adieu! je t'abandonne" (Barbier draft no. 4),
    - For Hoffmann ("Des cendres de mon cœur") with second strophe for Stella (Barbier draft no. 3).

The Kaye-Keck edition brings *Hoffmann* as close to the form that Offenbach intended as we can currently get. While like Puccini, Offenbach's intentions with regard to the Epilogue are uncertain, at least Offenbach certainly composed the ending Kaye chose. So *Hoffmann* becomes more like *Il viaggio a Reims* than *Turandot*, an opera that can be recovered almost completely. Anyone who wishes to perform *Offenbach's* opera must use the Kaye-Keck edition.

However, *Hoffmann* differs from *Viaggio* in one important respect: it has a long performing tradition in an inauthentic version. The Choudens version has persisted in the opera house, for a variety of reasons: inertia (many singers and conductors do not want to relearn a score), performers' preferences (as with retaining Donna Elvira's "Mi tradì quell'alma ingrata," many baritones would insist on singing "Scintille, diamant"), expense (renting a new score and parts rather than reusing ones already present in the opera house library and in the public domain; also, new editions earn royalties for editors); and familiarity (both audiences and performers learned to love the opera in its traditional form). But there are also aesthetic issues, involving the order of the acts and the pieces resurrected.

One critic, for example, has asserted, "the Giulietta act is drastically weaker, theatrically and musically, than the 'corrupt' old version." He disliked Giulietta's aria, among other things, and laments the loss of "the two knockout numbers—the 'diamond aria' and the climactic septet—that, along with the Barcarolle and Hoffmann's aria, make the scene live."

> [...] The musicological message to the audience sometimes seems to be, 'That's how he wrote it; eat your peas.' This is not acceptable, first because death denied Offenbach his own opportunity to trim, reshape and improve, and second because abdication of artistic judgment in deference to the enshrined ideal of the composer's intentions is bad policy. (Crutchfield 1988)

One may certainly dispute Crutchfield's judgments, and he did not know the authentic finale to this act, which had not yet resurfaced. Moreover, whatever one thinks of Giulietta's aria (the Kaye-Keck edition will publish three versions of it), it necessitates that she be a high soprano, not the traditional mezzo, and so the same singer can sing all the roles of Hoffmann's *innamorate*, as Offenbach intended, making them consistent with the other doublings: Lindorf-Coppélius-Miracle-Dapertutto, La Muse-Nicklausse, Andrès-Cochenille-Frantz-Pitichinaccio. Of course, we cannot know what Offenbach would have done to "trim, reshape and improve." Still, the question of theatrical effectiveness versus the composer's intentions remains.

As it does with the order of the acts. It used to be argued that the traditional arrangement, with Giulietta before Antonia, was superior because it showed a progression of Hoffmann's beloveds from automaton to uncaring courtesan to fully emotional woman, and therefore to increasingly tragic consequences, reasoning that has been rejected (Offenbach [1977] 1982: xiv–xv; Winter 1983: 938). Although I find it more cogent than some, perhaps a better argument for the traditional order may be made through the music, as follows: The musical highpoint of the opera is the trio "Chère enfant! que j'appelle comme autre fois" in the finale to the Antonia act. When it follows this number, the Giulietta act risks becoming anticlimactic, the beauties of the Barcarolle and the shock of Pitichinaccio's murder notwithstanding. Having the Antonia act last might also argue for a shorter version of the Epilogue so as not to dissipate the energy of the trio.

More important than this opinion is the recognition that, like *Turandot*, *Hoffmann* becomes a quite different work in the new completion. Having the same singer sing all the beloveds makes them manifestations of Hoffmann's ill-conceived ideal (as Nicklausse says in some versions of the Epilogue) rather than separate individuals. The murder of Pitichinaccio makes the action more violent, and placing Giulietta after Antonia makes Hoffmann seem increasingly crazed rather than tragic. Ending with the so-called apotheosis of the Muse makes us take Hoffmann more seriously; a drinking chorus makes him more comical.

As with other operas, one can imagine a conflation of the Choudens and Kaye versions. In fact, the Kaye-Keck edition makes it possible to perform "Scintille, diamant" and the Septet (as on the Nagano recording); Guiraud is unavoidable if we are to do the recitatives. But this compromise obscures the larger issue: Because of the state in which Offenbach left it at his death, *Les contes d'Hoffmann* invites treatment as an open text. As Parker says in concluding his discussion of Berio's *Turandot*, " [...] why not rethink the music? [...] Is nothing to be gained by opening these scripts to more radical metamorphoses [...]?" (Parker 2006: 119). To which one might reply, are we not justifiably reluctant to replace the conception of a great composer with posthumous accretions? A musical performance is, among many other things, an opportunity for the listener to engage with the mind of a great artist, which is why we remain so interested in opera reconstructions.

See also: Editing Opera, Sources, Autographs, Memorabilia, and the Aesthetics of Collecting

Notes

1. On *La traviata*, see Verdi 1997 and reviews: Fairtile 1999 and Kowals 1999. No critical edition of *Madama Butterfly* has been published. On the revisions, see Schickling 1998: 527–537. Concerning the difference between the score as initially completed and as presented at the premiere, see Schickling 1998: 529–530, 536. On problems in editing Puccini, particularly *Madama Butterfly*, see Gossett 2013: 118–125.
2. "Penso che il grande nocciolo sia il duetto. E questo duetto così com'è non mi pare sia quello che ci vuole."
3. "vorrei che Turandot sciogliesse il suo ghiaccio nel corso del duetto [...] e finire in estasi, in tripudio, in gloria solare."
4. " È partito or ora di qui Toscanini [...]. Si è parlato del duetto che non piace molto. Come si fa? Io non so. Forse Toscanini convocherà Simoni e voi a Salso. Verrò anch'io e si vedrà se c'è verso di migliorare la situazione."
5. "Si discute molto sul nostro duetto ed io sono un po' perplesso! [...] Ho delle idee in cuore duetto. L'attacco non lo cambio se non mi si propone di meglio."
6. "Finalmente ho ricevuto i versi di Simoni. Sono veramente belli e completano e giustificano il duetto. C'è una parola: *esile* come un fiore, che bisogna cambiare."
7. "C'era tanto poco da fare per mettere insieme per bene il famoso duetto! Via, via, caro Adamino, fatemi il piacere, fate il grande sforzo di dedicarmi due o tre ore e mandatemi i versi che mi occorrono. Ma fate questo piccolo lavoro in modo che sia definitivo e da non ritornaci più."
8. "I versi di Simoni sono buoni e mi pare che fosse quello che ci voleva e che io avevo sognato. Tutto il resto dell'invocazione di Liù a Turandot, erano cose che non attaccano e bene avete detto voi: così il duetto è completo. Forse Turandot in quello squarcio parla troppo. Vedremo."
9. "Deve essere un gran duetto. I due esseri quasi fuori del mondo entrano fra gli ultimi per l'amore e questo amore alla fine deve invadere tutti sulla scena in una perorazione orchestrale. E allora fate uno sforzo."
10. Uvietta accepts this testimony without question as "historically credible" even though reported second hand seventy-eight years after the event, and even though there is no

evidence that Puccini had even begun the finale by 1923 and certainly hadn't finished it. Still, the possibility is intriguing.

11. Parker provides the passage in piano-vocal reduction (107–110). Wagner is especially prominent. Ashbrook and Powers (1991: 136–138) suggest some of the same fragments for this interlude. Their transcription of the fragments (137) is slightly different from Uvietta's (193).
12. I am deeply indebted to Michael Kaye for sharing material about his new edition of *Les contes d'Hoffmann* prior to its publication. This section is heavily dependent on this work.
13. I will distinguish here between the Kaye *version*, representing Kaye's goal to come as close as now possible to Offenbach's final intentions, and the Kaye-Keck *edition*, which includes alternate versions of some pieces, pieces abandoned by Offenbach, and the inauthentic pieces from the Giulietta act. According to the publisher (in a private email, January 16, 2014), the edition is not yet finished, although a preliminary piano-vocal score is available for sale. The *Vorwort*, signed by the editors and dated 2009, contains a chart showing the contents of the edition in its current state (see Kaye and Keck 2009: xi–xv).
14. "Des cendres de ton cœur réchauffe ton génie" ! / Dans la sérénité souris à tes douleurs ! / La muse apaisera ta souffrance bénie ! / On est grand par l'amour et plus grand par les pleurs !"

Bibliography

Ashbrook, William, and Harold Powers. 1991. *Puccini's* Turandot: *The End of the Great Tradition*. Princeton, NJ: Princeton University Press.

Baldini, Gabriele. 1970. *Abitare la battaglia. La storia di Giuseppe Verdi*, edited by Fedele D'Amico. Milan: Garzanti. Translated into English (1980) by Roger Parker as *The Story of Giuseppe Verdi: 'Oberto' to 'Un ballo in maschera.'* Cambridge: Cambridge University Press.

Beethoven, Ludwig van. 1970. *Leonore*. 1806 version, edited by Willy Hess. Wiesbaden: Breitkopf & Härtel.

——. 1967. *Leonore*. 1805 version, edited by Willy Hess. Wiesbaden: Breitkopf & Härtel.

——. 1870. *Fidelio*. Leipzig: C. F. Peters.

Berio, Luciano. 2001. *Turandot: Completamento (del terzo atto)*. Milan: Ricordi.

Bianconi, Lorenzo. 1987. *Music in the Seventeenth Century*, translated by David Bryant. Cambridge: Cambridge University Press.

Borges, Jorge Luis. 1939. "Pierre Menard, autor del *Quijote*." Spanish text. Online. Available: http://www.literatura.us/borges/pierre.html (accessed February 24, 2010).

Budden, Julian. 1992. "*Turandot*, ii." *New Grove Dictionary of Opera*, IV: 838–839. London: Macmillan.

Busenello, Francesco. 1997. *L'incoronazione di Poppea* [Udine libretto]. In *Libretti d'opera italiani dal seicento al novecento*, edited by Giovanna Gronda and Paolo Fabbri, 54–105. Milan: Arnoldo Mondadori.

Carner, Mosco. 1958. *Puccini: A Critical Biography*. London: Duckworth.

Chadwick, Nick. 1988. Review of Berg/Cerha, *Lulu*. *Musical Times* 129: 249.

Cherlin, Michael. 2007. *Schoenberg's Musical Imagination*. Cambridge: Cambridge University Press.

Clements, Andrew. 1992. "*Lulu*, ii." *New Grove Dictionary of Opera*, III: 93–96. London: Macmillan.

Crutchfield, Will. 1988. "A Revised 'Hoffmann.'" (Review of performance in Los Angeles). *New York Times* (October 20). Online. Available: http://query.nytimes.com/gst/fullpage.html?res=940DE6DA1439F933A15753C1A96E948260&scp=3&sq=crutchfield%20hoffmann&st=cse (accessed August 1, 2012).

Curtis, Alan. 1989. "La Poppea Impasticciata or, Who Wrote the Music to *L'incoronazione* (1643)?" *Journal of the American Musicological Society* 42/1: 23–54.

Delli, Maddalena. 2008. In suite101.com. (March 28).Online. Available: http://italian-opera.suite101.com/article.cfm/new_finale_for_puccinis_turandot (accessed July 1, 2008).

Fabbri, Paolo. 1993. "New Sources for 'Poppea.'" [Translated by Tim Carter.] *Music & Letters* 74/1: 16–23.

Fairtile, Linda B. 2004. "*Duetto a tre*: Franco Alfano's completion of *Turandot*." *Cambridge Opera Journal* 16/2: 163–185.

——. 1999. Review of *Giuseppe Verdi: 'La traviata,'* edited by Fabrizio Della Seta. *Music & Letters* 80/2: 335–338.

——. 1996. "Giacomo Puccini's Operatic Revisions as Manifestations of His Compositional Priorities." PhD diss., New York University.

Fraccaroli, Arnaldo. 1957. *Giacomo Puccini si confida e racconta*. Milan: Ricordi.

Giger, Andreas. 1999. "Social Control and the Censorship of Giuseppe Verdi's operas in Rome (1844–1859)." *Cambridge Opera Journal* 11/3: 233–265.

Girardi, Michele. 2000. *Puccini: His International Art*, translated by Laura Basini. Chicago: University of Chicago Press.

Gossett, Philip. 2013. "Some Thoughts on the Use of Autograph Manuscripts in Editing the Works of Verdi and Puccini." *Journal of the American Musicological Society* 66/1: 103–128.

——. 2006. *Divas and Scholars: Performing Italian Opera*. Chicago: University of Chicago Press.

——. 1970. "The Operas of Rossini: Problems of Textual Criticism in Nineteenth-Century Opera." PhD diss., Princeton University.

Gozzi, Carlo. 1989. "Turandot: A Tragicomic Tale of China for the Theatre in Five Acts." In *Five Tales for the Theatre*, edited and translated by Albert Bermel and Ted Emery, 128–183. Chicago: University of Chicago Press.

Kaye, Michael. 1996. "An Appreciation of the Early Sources." Program booklet to Erato recording of Offenbach, *Les Contes d'Hoffmann*, 21–35. Erato 0630-14330-2.

——. 1992. "'Hoffmann' after Offenbach." Program booklet to Philips recording of Offenbach, *Les Contes d'Hoffmann*, 31–44. Philips 422374.

——, and Jean-Christoph Keck. 2009. *Vorwort* to Offenbach forthcoming. Online. Available: http://www.schott-music.com/shop/resources/694158.pdf (accessed January 16, 2014).

Kowals, Rebecca. 1999. Review of Verdi, *La traviata*, edited by Fabrizio Della Seta. *Music Library Association Notes* 55: 991–994.

Lamb, Andrew. 1992. "*Contes d'Hoffmann*." *New Grove Dictionary of Opera*. I: 923–925. London: Macmillan.

MacDonald, Hugh. 1980. "Hoffmann's Melancholy Tale." *Musical Times* 121: 622–624.

Maehder, Jürgen. 1985. "Studi sul carattere di frammento della 'Turandot' di Giacomo Puccini." Italian translation of 1984b. *Quaderni pucciniani* 2: 79–163.

——. 1984a. "Puccini's *Turandot*: A Fragment." Abridged English translation of 1984b. *English National Opera Guide* 27: 35–53.

——. 1984b. "Studien zum Fragmentcharakter von Giacomo Puccinis *Turandot*." *Analecta musicologica* 22: 298–379.

Maguire, Janet. 1990. "Puccini's Version of the Duet and Final Scene of *Turandot*." *Musical Quarterly* 74/3: 319–359.

Monteverdi, Claudio. 1989. *L'incoronazione di Poppea*, edited by Alan Curtis. London: Novello.

Mozart, W. A. 2009. *Il dissoluto punito, ossia il Don Giovanni, K527, 540a, 540c*. Facsimile of the Autograph Score, Bibliothèque nationale de France, Paris, Département de la Musique (MS 1548). 3 vols. Introductory Essay by Hans Joachim Kreutzer. Musicological Introduction by Wolfgang Rehm. Translated by J. Bradford Robinson. Los Angeles: The Packard Humanities Institute.

——. 1968. *Don Giovanni*, edited by Wolfgang Plath and Wolfgang Rehm. *Neue Mozart Ausgabe*. II: 5: 17. Kassel: Bärenreiter.

Oeser, Fritz. 1981. Vorlagenbericht [critical commentary] to Offenbach, *Les contes d'Hoffmann*, edited by Fritz Oeser. Kassel: Alkor-Edition.

Offenbach, Jacques. Forthcoming. *Les contes d'Hoffmann*, edited by Michael Kaye and Jean-Christophe Keck. Mainz: Schott Musik International, in collaboration with Boosey and Hawkes (Berlin and London) and Bote & Bock (Berlin). [See also Kaye and Keck 2009].

——. [1977] 1982. *Les contes d'Hoffmann*, edited by Fritz Oeser. Piano-vocal score with English preface and translation. Kassel: Alkor-Edition.

——. 1907. *Les contes d'Hoffmann*. Partition Chant et Piano. Paris: Choudens.

Parker, Roger. 2006. *Remaking the Song: Operatic Visions and Revisions from Handel to Berio*. Berkeley and Los Angeles: University of California Press.

Perle, George. 1979. "The Complete 'Lulu'." *Musical Times* 120: 115–120.

——. 1964. "'Lulu': The Formal Design." *Journal of the American Musicological Society* 17/2: 179–192.

Puccini, Giacomo. 1974. *Letters of Giacomo Puccini, Mainly Connected with the Composition and Production of His Operas*, edited by Giuseppe Adami and translated by Ena Makin. New edition revised and introduced by Mosco Carner. London: Harrap.

——. 1928. *Epistolario*, edited by Giuseppe Adami. Milan: A. Mondadori.

——. 1926a. *Turandot*. Piano-vocal score. Milan: Ricordi. With Alfano's original completion (plate no. 119772. NB: some scores with this plate number have the revised ending).

——. 1926b. *Turandot*. Piano-vocal score [see 1926a].With the revised completion (plate no. 121329).

Rehm, Wolfgang. 2009. "Musicological Introduction" to Mozart 2009, III: 13–30.

Rosand, Ellen. 2007. *Monteverdi's Last Operas: A Venetian Trilogy*. Berkeley and Los Angeles: University of California Press.

Rossini, Gioachino. 2004. *Mosè in Egitto*, edited by Charles S. Brauner. *Edizione critica delle opere di Gioachino Rossini*. Sez. I: 24. Pesaro: Fondazione Rossini.

——. 1999. *Il viaggio a Reims, ossia l'Albergo del Giglio d'Oro*, edited by Janet L. Johnson. *Edizione critica delle opere di Gioachino Rossini*. Sez. I: 35. Pesaro: Fondazione Rossini.

Rushton, Julian. 1981. *W. A. Mozart, 'Don Giovanni.'* Cambridge Opera Handbooks. Cambridge: Cambridge University Press.

Sartori, Claudio. 1958. *Puccini*. Milan: Nuova Accademia Editrice.

Schickling, Dieter. 1998. "Puccini's 'Work in Progress': The So-Called Versions of 'Madama Butterfly.'" [Translated by Robert Vilain.] *Music & Letters* 79/4: 527–537.

Schneider, Herbert. 1984. Review of Offenbach, *Les contes d'Hoffmann*, edited by Fritz Oeser. *Die Musikforschung* 37: 87–90.

Schoenberg, Arnold. 1965. *Letters*, edited by Erwin Stein and translated by Eithne Wilkins and Ernst Kaiser. New York: St. Martin's Press.

Tommasini, Anthony. 2002. "Critic's Notebook: Updating 'Turandot,' Berio Style." *New York Times* (August 22). Online. Available: http://query.nytimes.com/gst/fullpage.html?res=9Eo

DE0DD163CF931A1575BC0A9649C8B63&sec=&spon=&pagewanted=1 (accessed August 1, 2012).

——. 1998. "Critic's Notebook; an Imbroglio for 'Figaro,' its Director and Bartoli." *New York Times* (November 9). Online. Available: http://query.nytimes.com/gst/fullpage.html?res=9A07E5DF103EF93AA35752C1A96E958260 (accessed August 1, 2012).

Tusa, Michael C. 1993. "The Unknown Florestan: The 1805 Version of 'In des Lebens Frühlingstagen.'" *Journal of the American Musicological Society* 46/2: 175–220.

Uvietta, Marco. 2004. "'È l'ora della prova': Berio's Finale for Puccini's *Turandot*." [Translated by Cormac Newark and Arman Schwartz.] *Cambridge Opera Journal* 16/2: 187–238.

Verdi, Giuseppe. 2003. *Stiffelio*, edited by Kathleen Kuzmick Hansell. *The Works of Giuseppe Verdi* [WGV]. Series I: 16. Chicago: University of Chicago Press; Milan: Ricordi.

——. 1997. *La traviata*, edited by Fabrizio Della Seta. *The Works of Giuseppe Verdi* [WGV]. Series I: 19. Chicago: University of Chicago Press; Milan: Ricordi.

Wang, Truman C. 2002. "Berio's Brilliant Solution to the Turandot Riddle" [review of the Los Angeles 2002 performance]. *Classical Voice* (June 4). Online. Available: www.classicalvoice.org/articles/RV_turandot_060402_laopera.htm (accessed July 1, 2008).

Winter, Robert. 1983. Review of Offenbach, *Les contes d'Hoffmann*, edited by Fritz Oeser. *Music Library Association Notes* 39: 937–939.

Recordings

Monteverdi, Claudio. 1994. CD. Monteverdi, *L'incoronazione di Poppea*.Venice version. City of London Baroque Sinfonia led by Richard Hickox Virgin Classics 061783.

Offenbach, Jacques. 1996. CD. *Les contes d'Hoffmann*, edited by Michael Kaye and conducted by Kent Nagano (with Guiraud's recitatives). Erato 0630-14330-2.

——. 1992. CD. *Les contes d'Hoffmann*, edited by Michael Kaye and conducted by Jeffrey Tate (with spoken dialogue). Philips 422374.

——. 1988. CD. *Les contes d'Hoffmann*, edited by Fritz Oeser and conducted by Sylvain Cambreling. EMI CDC 7 49642 2.

Puccini, Giacomo. 2002. DVD. *Turandot*, completed by Luciano Berio and conducted by Valery Gergiev. TDK DVUS-OPTURSFR.

CHAPTER 46

EDITING OPERA

PATRICIA B. BRAUNER

> The fact is that until an editor has done his work, and done it properly, no performer can safely play old music, no analyst can safely analyse it, and no historian or critic can safely assess it.
>
> (Emery 1957: 14)

Theories of Editing

Several approaches to editing, or textual criticism, developed over the nineteenth and twentieth centuries. The so-called classical approach (first applied by scholars seeking to reconstruct the original text of biblical and classical works for which there is no author's text) collates all the available sources of the text, and the editor selects from among the variant readings to create a text.

Copy-text editing contrasts with this in that the editor chooses a single source to be a base text and emends its reading when it appears defective, choosing among the variants found in the other sources. This approach—the term was defined by Ronald McKerrow (1904) in his edition of the works of Thomas Nashe (1567–ca. 1601) as "the text used in each particular case as the basis of mine" (xi)—was also espoused by Joseph Bédier (1928). How to identify the "best available" source, however, remained a problem; editors disagreed over whether the oldest source or the one judged most "reliable"—perhaps even containing emendations made by the author—should be the copy-text, and over how much the copy-text should be emended. As Helen Greenwald (2009) has noted, the impetus for modern critical editions of music, although rooted in "contemporary ideals of authenticity and methodology," does make a "baseline score [...] the platform for all editorial decisions."

Clearly these approaches are open to bias, conscious or unconscious. A more rigorous method, "stemmatics," generally associated with the name of Karl Lachmann (1816), attempts to organize the sources into a family tree (*stemma*) by tracing commonality of variants, with the premise that commonality of variants indicates a common origin. Analogously, the ordering of relationships among plant and animal species based on variants in DNA results in a type of family tree that diagrams the order of evolutionary branching in a species (*cladogram*). Richard Dawkins (2004: 123–127) explains how the process works in evolutionary biology. The premise for devising the tree is that of parsimony, or "economy of explanation": the parsimonious cladogram is the one with the fewest evolutionary changes necessary for all sequences to derive from a common ancestor. In this methodology, as used by textual critics for mapping the relationship among manuscripts by studying textual variants (127–133)—Dawkins's model is The Canterbury Tales Project (TCTP n.d.)[1]—not all variants carry equal weight, since scribal tendencies toward individualized spelling and punctuation give no real clue about the scribe's source text. In texts, it is possible for a variant to be changed in a later copy and thus revert accidentally to the original text, a possibility not allowed by the biological model. Furthermore, whereas in a cladogram only the order of branching is indicated, in a tree called a *phylogram*, the length of the branches represents quantity of change, and, according to Dawkins,

> [b]ased upon a simple count of the number of changes, parsimony erroneously groups together the termini of especially long branches. [... T]he more text we look at, the more erroneous similarities we find, and the stronger our conviction in the wrong answer. (Dawkins 2004: 131)

An alternative, likelihood analysis, seeks to determine which is the "best," or most likely tree. As Dawkins notes, "we can't look at all possible trees, but there are computational shortcuts and they work pretty well" (2004: 132).

That a work of art, literary or musical, is a social phenomenon, involving not only the author's intention but also the communication of that intention to the performer and hence to the audience (see Grier 1996: 16 and footnote 43 for sources), was proposed by literary critic Jerome McGann (1983), which led musicologist James Grier to state that "[t]he piece [...] resides equally in the score and in the performing conventions that govern its interpretation at any particular historic moment [...]. The work exists in a potentially infinite number of states, whether in writing (the score) or in sound (performance) [...]" (Grier 1996: 22–23).

Grier's work (required reading for all would-be music editors) is strongly influenced by literary textual criticism. His goals are "to examine the nature of editorial mediation" and "to show how the editor's critical engagement plays an active role in every aspect of editing" (Grier 1996: 4–5). As D. C. Greetham points out in his foreword to the paperback edition of McGann:

> one of the criticisms leveled by intentionalist critics against McGann has been that his theories do not result in different editorial procedures and do not produce different editions from those constructed in "critical" editions. (Greetham 1992: x)

However, Grier emphasizes that operatic "source materials are often related to specific performances, whose historical circumstances, therefore, affect the nature and evaluation of the source evidence" (Grier 1996: 206). It is perhaps just this availability, selection, and use of source material that makes the greatest difference between one edition of an opera and another.

Editing and Technology

The editions of The Canterbury Tales Project are digital, each tale published on a separate CD-ROM. Digital images of all the extant fifteenth-century witnesses are included, along with transcriptions of all their texts (in the case of "The Nun's Priest's Tale," these comprise fifty-one manuscripts and four incunabula). Clicking any word in the edition brings up a window displaying a list of all variants for that point in the text, along with a "variant map" indicating which sources have each variant. There are links to collations and to manuscript descriptions and even more possibilities to explore the textual transmission.[2] All the materials available to the editor are thus presented to the user, along with computational analysis of the variants.

Lamenting that musicology has "lagged considerably behind textual scholarship in matters pertaining to textual criticism," Ted Dumitrescu states that "this reluctance of musical scholarship to engage with modern text-critical approaches is not purely a matter of reasoned conservatism, but is also predicated upon technological working conditions" (Dumitrescu 2009: 59). To this end, he and his colleagues are developing software for encoding and analyzing the variants in mensural notation (musical notation being inherently more complicated than verbal texts) as well as an online database of transcriptions and commentaries (Computerized Mensural Music Editing Project; see CMME n.d.). To counter the tendency of textual critics to attempt to recover an authoritative original text while disregarding the conditions under which the work was created and its subsequent transmission, Dumitrescu reports a project in which

> widely disseminated Mass settings by Josquin and Mouton, edited digitally for online publication, will serve as a test case for a concrete comparative assessment of various computational and post-Lachmannian stemmatic techniques. Among the most significant consequences of the study is the development of a new stemmatological framework specifically tailored to notated musical material. (Dumitrescu 2009: 60).

The project "OPERA—Spektrum des europäischen Musiktheaters in Einzeleditionen" begun in 2009 at the University of Bayreuth under the sponsorship of the Academy of Sciences and Literature in Mainz, is producing critical editions of selected works from the seventeenth to the twentieth centuries. The twenty-one works in the plan of publication are divided into six modules, each representing different editorial challenges, as, for example, the issue of authorship in pastiches and parodies or works that underwent a long and complex creative process. The form of the editions is hybrid: the score will be presented in print, while the commentary and libretto are published in electronic form, using software developed by Edirom Digitale Musikedition, which makes it possible to illustrate complex source situations. Thus "OPERA" seeks to investigate issues relevant to opera editing and to develop specific and potentially extendable concepts for each individual case.[3]

The form in which an opera has been transmitted depends in part on the period in which it was composed, each period presenting different conditions for the performance of an opera and for the preservation and transmission of its text. For example, Monteverdi's late operas are preserved in very few sources, most of which disagree with each other. The emergence of new sources over more than a century and the scholarly debate provoked by each new discovery resulted in a series of editions, ranging from Hugo Goldschmidt's *L'incoronazione di Poppea* in 1904 to Alan Curtis's *Il ritorno d'Ulisse in patria* of 2002 (see Rosand 2007: 23–38, especially 29). The critical edition *Francesco Cavalli—Opere*, under the general editorship of Ellen Rosand, finds multiple librettos but few musical sources for many works. Believing that "the textual edition can often reflect more about the reception of the opera than the score does...each individual opera will have a text editor as well as a music editor" (Cavalli 2012). The Cavalli edition also provides materials that enable modern performers who are not specialists to express the conventions of the Baroque scores. Friedrich Chrysander's edition of Handel's *Tolomeo* (1878) was largely based only on the autograph, whereas Michael Pacholke's 2000 edition used eight sources, most of them unknown to Chrysander (Strohm 2003: 981). Rossini's and Verdi's operas generally survive as autograph scores, multiple manuscript copies, some performing materials, printed piano-vocal reductions, and some printed full scores, yet Rossini had nothing to do with the production of printed editions of his work other than the sale of publication rights, whereas Verdi was actively involved with Ricordi in preparing the printed editions. Puccini's continual revisions led to changes in the published versions from one printing to the next. Sources for Offenbach's *Les contes d'Hoffman* were, at the time of his death, in disarray and became further scattered (a performing edition by Michael Kaye is discussed in Brauner, Chapter 45 of this volume). Sources continue to appear in libraries as they update their catalogues, in auctions, and in the property of heirs; scholars must reevaluate the known sources—and types of sources—in the light of the new.

Rarely does even the composer's score exist as a unique source, complete and unmodified. There may be sketches, changes to the content of the opera, revisions resulting from revivals in other theaters or with other casts, all of these sources relating to one or another state of the work. To cite examples from living composers, John Harbison reworked *The Great Gatsby* after its premiere at the Metropolitan Opera on December 20, 1999. He later said:

> My corrections of the piece were almost entirely based on one experience, which was the first time I heard it all the way through at dress rehearsal.... Some changes were made for the Chicago performances [2000] and there were a few more I was not able to work out to my satisfaction at that point and have since. This is so much more difficult than composing, to figure this kind of thing out. But most of what I've done is based on that original perception. (Harbison 2002)

Lewis Spratlan's remarks in a panel discussion before the world premiere on July 24, 2010 of his 1978 opera *Life Is a Dream* were summarized by Anthony Tommasini:

> [O]n re-examining this score after decades, he thought the music fitted the story and made only minor adjustments. The most significant one came last year during a workshop in Santa Fe. He felt that the final encounter between Rosaura and Segismundo, which hewed close to Calderón, was too curt, he said. So he asked [the librettist James] Maraniss for additional lines and added 12 pages of music. (Tommasini 2010)

If the composer's score does not exist, the editor must approach the surviving sources differently. Editions that are based on one source present only a single state of the work, since the evidence of the other witnesses is lacking (and, if the source bears modifications and the editor is not meticulous, may not even present a state in which the opera had ever been performed). A critical edition should present all the material created by the author as part of that "work," as represented in all available sources, and it should account for non-authorial interventions. It should incorporate current scholarship, new bibliographical sources, and new documentary resources. Any edition should be as accurate as possible, not transmitting errors from earlier editions. Beyond that, it should consider the work within the framework of its historical, social, and cultural milieu, helping performers to interpret the notation as the composer expected.

Must the editor remove herself as much as possible from personal choice? As Walter Greg observed:

> It is impossible to exclude individual judgement from editorial procedure: it operates of necessity in the all-important matter of the choice of copy-text and in the minor one of deciding what readings are possible and what not; why, therefore, should the choice between possible readings be withdrawn from its competence? Uniformity of result at the hands of different editors is worth little if it means only uniformity in error; and it may not be too optimistic a belief that the judgement of an editor, fallible as it must necessarily be, is likely to bring us closer to what the author wrote than the enforcement of an arbitrary rule. (Greg 1950: 26)

Bringing the edition "closer to what the author wrote" was and is a common goal of editors. As Maria Caraci Vela wrote in her introduction to *La critica del testo musicale*,

> Philology [...] has as its subject a text as a cultural document and as its goal the restitution of that text in the form as close as possible to that which it had when the author considered it finished, or, in the case of a text that the author never completed and that he continued correcting, in the most advanced form that the work attained.[4] (Caraci Vela 1995: 6)

A decade later, Caraci Vela called this statement a classic description of musical textual criticism but suggested a broader definition in keeping with current concepts:

> [...] reflection on a musical text with the aim of restoring it critically, evaluating both its relationship to its author and that with those who have used it and transmitted it and, in so doing, have interpreted it each time.[5] (Caraci Vela 2005: 18)

The Case of Rossini's *Il barbiere di Siviglia*

Editing with an Autograph Score

Operas whose sources are in disarray or whose text is in some way incomplete are the subject of Chapter 45 ("Reconstructions") of this volume. In this chapter we will consider an opera for which the composer's autograph survives, Rossini's *Il barbiere di Siviglia* (1816). The musical numbers (omitting the *secco* recitatives) in Rossini's autograph score, confirmed by the libretto published in Rome in 1816, are listed in Table 46.1.

The autograph score of *Barbiere* (I-Bc UU2[1, 2]), which became the property of the impresario of the Roman Teatro Argentina that commissioned it, has been preserved since 1862 in the Museo internazionale e biblioteca della musica di Bologna, formerly the Civico museo bibliografica musicale and before that the Liceo musicale (see Gossett 1993 for a full-color facsimile and detailed description of the manuscript). All the closed numbers in the opera are written in Rossini's own hand, although much of the guitar accompaniment to the Canzone Conte (N. 3) is in another hand. Most of the *secco*

TABLE 46.1 Musical numbers in *Il barbiere di Siviglia*.

	Overture
	Act I
N. 1	Introduction "Piano pianissimo senza parlar"
N. 2	Cavatina Figaro "La ran la lera, la ran la là"
N. 3	Canzone Conte "Se il mio nome saper voi bramate"
N. 4	Duet Conte – Figaro "All'idea di quel metallo"
N. 5	Cavatina Rosina "Una voce poco fa"
N. 6	Aria Basilio "La calunnia è un venticello"
N. 7	Duet Rosina – Figaro "Dunque io son... tu non m'inganni..."
N. 8	Aria Bartolo "A un Dottor della mia sorte"
N. 9	Finale [Primo] "Ehi di casa... buona gente..."
	Act II
N. 10	Duet Conte – Bartolo "Pace e gioia sia con voi."
N. 11	Aria Rosina "Contro un cor che accende amore"
N. 12	Arietta Bartolo "Quando mi sei vicina, amabile Rosina..."
N. 13	Quintet "Don Basilio!... – (Cosa veggo!)"
N. 14	Aria Berta "Il vecchiotto cerca moglie"
N. 15	Temporale
N. 16	Trio "Ah qual colpo inaspettato!"
N. 17	Accompanied Recitative "Il Conte!...ah che mai sento!..." and Aria Conte "Cessa di più resistere"
N. 18	Finaletto Secondo "Di sì felice innesto"

recitatives, as was common at the time, were composed by another musician, possibly Luigi Zamboni, the first Figaro, himself. Two recitatives, those before and after the Aria Berta (N. 14), are in the hand of a second collaborator, as yet unknown, while Rossini himself wrote the brief passage of recitative within the Canzone Conte (N. 3). The autograph is complete except for the absence of a full score of the Sinfonia, which Rossini borrowed from his opera *Aureliano in Palmira* (Milan, Teatro alla Scala, December 26, 1813) and which is represented in the score of *Barbiere* by a bass part in a copyist's hand (see below). Our knowledge of the opera as Rossini prepared it in January and February of 1816, and thus of its original version, would seem to be unproblematic.

Bärenreiter-Verlag published the critical edition, edited by the present author under the direction of Philip Gossett (Rossini 2008), in the series *Works of Gioachino Rossini* (WGR). Two volumes incorporate the full score (with preface, facsimiles, and libretto) and an extensive critical commentary (420 pages). Editors must, of course, present a work in a form as close as possible to what in their best judgment Rossini meant when he wrote down the score and handed it on to the copyists and performers. Rossini composed by first drafting a skeleton score consisting of the bass line, the vocal parts, and the first violin or other prominent melody part, so that singers' parts could be copied, and they could begin learning them. Only later did he orchestrate the numbers. Anecdotal reports of the speed at which Rossini composed *Barbiere* abound, but in fact, since a scenario for the opera was drawn up and signed by the librettist, Cesare Sterbini, on January 17, 1816, and the premiere was on February 20,[6] his work was certainly not leisurely.

While Rossini's method of composition was convenient for production in the opera house, it produced inconsistencies in the autograph score. Frequently the dynamic signs in the bass line are different from those in the other instruments. Knowing that the bass line would have been written first can suggest either that Rossini was more precise in writing the dynamic signs there, *or* that his intentions are clarified by the signs in the parts added later. Articulations and expressive markings may appear only in the first measure or two of an accompanimental passage or only in the first statement of a theme. The editor must justify any extensions of such markings to other occurrences of the figuration or passage. In Figaro's cavatina (N. 2), on the other hand, Rossini did not write staccatos for the first and second statements of "La ran la là" etc. (mm. 48–49, 56–57), but he did write every staccato in the repetitions at 77–78 and 85–86. Had staccatos appeared in the first passage rather than the second, we might have believed that Rossini meant them as an example to be followed in the repetition, but we suggest instead that he intended a crisper expression of the refrain in the repetition (where the orchestration is derived "Come Sopra" from the instrumental introduction at 1–15).

Editorial Interpretation and Errors

A problem of rhythmic interpretation occurs in the first Finale, where the police force arrives and the Officer (Ufficiale) tries to arrest the drunken soldier (Almaviva in disguise). Measures 393–395 are unaccompanied. The lowest vocal staff is Basilio, and

Rossini wrote the part of the Ufficiale on the same staff. The five other soloists end with a half note and two quarter rests (omitted from Bartolo, above Basilio, because Rossini's indication "Ufiziale" interferes). As the autograph clearly shows (Music Example 46.1), Basilio originally ended with a quarter note. Presumably Rossini wrote out this part before the other vocal lines, making the transition from Basilio to the Ufficiale. However, the Ufficiale has the equivalent of seven eighth notes (including the eighth rest creating the necessary pickup note), which would have been one eighth too many even in the first version. The older Ricordi edition, reprinted by Kalmus (Music Example 46.2), properly made the Ufficiale enter on the pickup to the third beat, reducing the quarter note to an eighth, but wrote the text incorrectly: "Oh inteso" instead of "ho inteso" ("I have understood"); there is no difference in pronunciation.

Ricordi's edition of 1969, edited by Zedda (Music Example 46.3), shifts the entrance back to the pickup to the second beat, a weak beat, thereby disturbing the declamation. It keeps the quarter note and makes the next eighth note a quarter note so that the rhythm matches the repetition of the statement. It only partially emends the text, an

MUSIC EXAMPLE 46.1 *Il barbiere di Siviglia*, autograph, Finale Primo, mm. 394–395.

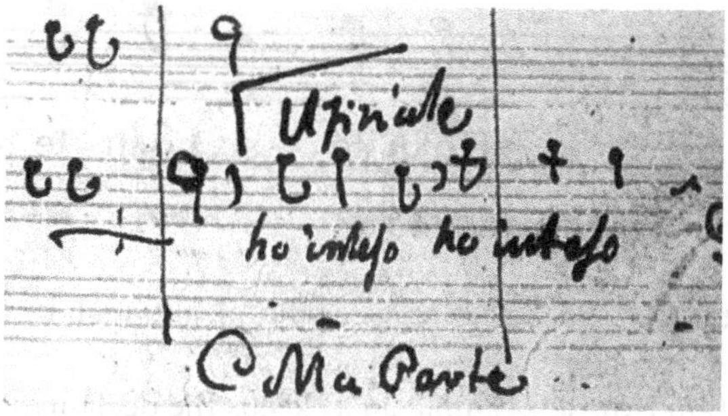

MUSIC EXAMPLE 46.2 *Il barbiere di Siviglia* (Ricordi/Kalmus, n.d.).

MUSIC EXAMPLE 46.3 *Il barbiere di Siviglia*, ed. Zedda (Ricordi, 1969).

MUSIC EXAMPLE 46.4 *Il barbiere di Siviglia*, ed. Brauner (Bärenreiter, 2008).

error that is corrected in Zedda's 2010 revised edition, although he maintains his rhythmic interpretation.

Bärenreiter's edition (Music Example 46.4) keeps the declamation correct by eliminating the eighth rest between the two phrases, since the part is *a piacere*—Rossini marked the score "Colla Parte" at 394. WGR also fully restores Rossini's text.

One should note that early printed editions show a variety of attempts at emending this faulty measure, introducing various elements of the three solutions illustrated here, while manuscript copies often follow the autograph literally.

Who Wrote What When, *ossia* The Barber and His Guitar

Figaro's famous "Largo al factotum" (N. 2) and the Count's canzone to Rosina, "Se il mio nome saper voi bramate" (N. 3) present puzzles of a different sort, ones that are not a problem of interpretation of ambiguous notation but rather ask what Rossini intended his performers to do. Nine out of nineteen manuscript copies of N. 2 lack Figaro's offstage singing (mm. 20–33) at the beginning of piece. There seem to be only two plausible explanations: either the absence is an oversight by one copyist, reproduced in sources derived from his manuscript, or Rossini added the vocal part after at least one copy had been made. Determining the former would require attempting to create a *stemma* for the known copies; the latter would require a minute examination of the autograph, perhaps involving microscopic or chemical analysis of the ink, since the part is present in the autograph and is not obviously a later addition. In either case, the manuscripts lacking the vocal part in those measures are somehow related. The edition includes the part, since it is in the autograph and in the libretto, but notes the common variant.

The second puzzle is the guitar accompaniment in the Count's canzone (N. 3). For Almaviva's extravagantly staged serenade in the Introduction, "Ecco ridente in cielo," Rossini wrote the guitar part in full. In the canzone, however, where the guitar is the sole accompaniment, he wrote only a group of chords near the end of the first strophe (from m. 14, third beat, through 16), designed to ensure the modulation from A minor to C major; the rest of the part he left blank. Geltrude Righetti-Giorgi, the first Rosina, reported that Manuel García (the Count) accompanied himself ([1823] 1956: 32–33). The recitative before the canzone requires the Count to play the guitar, which is handed to him by Figaro. The barber says, "Here's the guitar: quickly, let's go"; the Count's line "Well then, let's try" is followed by the stage direction "he takes the guitar and sings, accompanying himself"[7] (Sterbini 1816: 16). At some point, another hand sketched an accompaniment on the blank staff in the autograph (not García, surely, for he was a composer in his own right and would not have made the mistakes that are present). Copies representing the early state of the score lack this added accompaniment. Although ten manuscripts (as well as many printed vocal scores) omit the entire canzone, the complete accompaniment as in the autograph is present in two manuscripts (one with an additional six-measure introduction); two others share a different accompaniment for guitar, modifying even Rossini's own chords; and one substitutes an accompaniment for harp. Bärenreiter prints the accompaniment of the autograph, noting and correcting its errors.

Editing without an Autograph: The Overture

When an autograph is lacking, the collation of all available sources becomes absolutely necessary. In the *Barbiere* autograph, the music for the overture, which is the overture to Rossini's *Aureliano in Palmira* (Milan, 1813), consists only of a bass part (staves for cello and double bass) in the hand of a copyist. The manuscript copies of *Il barbiere di Siviglia* present confused testimony. Eight have no overture at all. In some it has been removed, while in others it was never present (one manuscript exists only as Act II). Two copies use the version of the *Aureliano* overture as Rossini had significantly reworked it for *Elisabetta, regina d'Inghilterra* a few months earlier (Naples, October 1815). Three use the overture to *Il Turco in Italia*. Seven copies do use the *Aureliano* overture but make no adjustments for the smaller orchestra in the rest of the *Barbiere* score.

There is no doubt that *Barbiere* reused the *Aureliano* overture. Gossett (1993) points out that early commentators who mention the overture knew that it was borrowed from *Aureliano in Palmira* and that the tale of a different, discarded overture became popular only in the middle of the nineteenth century (Gossett 1993: 23–24). It may even have been Rossini himself who initiated the rumor. In 1866 Rossini in Paris asked his friend Domenico Liverani to look for the "original" overture (it is likely that the autograph score was with the copyist Bonoris Zappi in Bologna by 1818 and that Rossini had known it [Rossini 1992–: IIIa: 323]), but he may not have realized that it had at some point passed into the ownership of Rinaldo Bajetti, a member of the Accademia Filarmonica of Bologna, and that Bajetti's will left it to the Conservatory in Bologna in 1862 (Rossini 2008b: 11). The composer wrote to Liverani on June 12, 1866:

> [...] here am I to thank you for the trouble you went to in trying to locate (in my so-called autograph of *Barbiere*) the original of my overture and of the concerted piece for the Lesson. Who could own them now? Patience—Escudier wanted, as a pendant to the *Don Giovanni*, to do a complete edition of *Barbiere* according to my original, and he hoped that I could help him by obtaining the replaced pieces. But it will have to be less because fate wants it that way.[8] (2008a: xx)

Did Escudier possess a source in which the overture to *Aureliano in Palmira* had been removed or replaced, along with "Contro un cor"? The two manuscripts of *Il barbiere di Siviglia* preserved in the Bibliothèque nationale in Paris suggest this possibility, although we have no evidence connecting them to Escudier. Both lack an aria for Rosina in the lesson scene, while one has the overture to *Turco* and the other has the version for *Elisabetta, regina d'Inghilterra*. Since Rossini still had in his possession the autograph of *Elisabetta*, the *Barbiere* overture clearly must have differed.

To edit the overture, therefore, it was necessary to bring in the witnesses for *Aureliano in Palmira*, whose autograph, unfortunately, is lost. To the seven *Barbiere* manuscripts that contain the unaltered *Aureliano* overture (and one manuscript of the overture alone, which has the indication "Nel Barbiere di Siviglia" in a later hand and therefore could have been copied from an *Aureliano* source), we added the fifteen known copies of *Aureliano in Palmira*. All twenty-three manuscripts of the overture were examined. Contemporary copyists generally replaced idiomatic Rossinian notational signs (closed crescendos or closed accents, long staccatos, unusual beamings) with conventional ones. To the extent that the sources provide any evidence of these signs, then, they can be grouped within a stemma and possibly placed closer to the lost autograph than copies that do not reproduce those signs.

A survey of all the *Aureliano* manuscripts led us to choose as the base or primary text a manuscript in the Biblioteca estense universitaria of Modena (I-MOe Ms. F. 998). This copy has the complete orchestration (many copies lack the percussion parts, which were probably copied in a separate *spartitino*—a short score containing low instrumental parts—that became lost), and it is relatively rich in dynamics and articulation, reducing the amount of editorial intervention in the score. The readings of the base source were compared with those of all other *Aureliano* witnesses and the eight relevant *Barbiere* sources. The readings of the base text were not always chosen for the edition, but all instances of variants taken from other sources are fully collated in the critical commentary. The chosen readings were then compared to the autograph of the *Elisabetta* overture wherever there were equivalent passages; while its readings were not allowed to supplant those of the *Aureliano*/*Barbiere* sources, they occasionally served to reinforce the choice of Rossinian signs rather than less characteristic ones.

We wished to provide a version of the orchestra that accords with the instrumentation of the rest of the opera, however, because the ensemble scraped together for *Barbiere* was smaller than that for *Aureliano*, having only one flutist (who doubled piccolo), one oboist (who doubled flute and piccolo), and one percussionist (*Barbiere* has no timpani). Even though in a modern production it is highly unlikely that an orchestra would hire an oboist who would double both flute and piccolo, we provided an arrangement of the flute and oboe parts for one instrument on each part, seeking to present a useful compendium of the four notated parts. The original *Aureliano* musical lines for two flutes, two oboes, and timpani are included in the score in smaller type. The edition is definitely not a presentation of a particular text for the overture. While we hope that it approximates the way Rossini might have arranged it, we have no evidence of what happened during the rehearsals of *Barbiere*. The eclectic approach in this case does, we believe, present the work in a useful and not inauthentic form for the twenty-first century.

The Later Tradition and Its Place in the Edition

Il barbiere di Siviglia has, unlike most of Rossini's works, remained continuously in the repertory. After a list of performances of *Barbiere* in almost every year from the premiere on February 20, 1816, to 1895 (exceptions are 1883, 1885, 1891), the biographer Giuseppe Radiciotti remarks: "After this point, we do not enumerate the performances of this opera"[9] (1927–1929: III: 214). The inaugural run of *Barbiere* was limited to seven performances, since the beginning of Lent on February 28 closed the Roman theaters. The opera was first revived only a few months later: in Bologna in August and in Florence in the autumn. In September 1819 it was staged in Vienna at the Theater an der Wien, then in Paris (October 26, 1819), where Manuel García, the original Count Almaviva, had made its production a condition of his contract with the Théâtre Italien (Radiciotti 1927–1929: I: 204). *Barbiere* was performed in Brussels, Munich, Breslau, and Amsterdam (all 1821), and in 1826 García brought it with his company to New York, where his daughter Maria Malibran sang Rosina to her father's Almaviva and the Figaro of Manuel García, Jr., who had been a boy when the opera premiered ten years earlier.

Manuscripts and librettos surviving from the early nineteenth century show how quickly the original Roman *Barbiere* underwent changes. We know of no revivals with which Rossini was directly involved; the metamorphoses were at the hands of performers and impresarios. (During the spring of 1818, Rossini supervised a revival of *La gazza ladra* to inaugurate the Teatro Nuovo [now Teatro Rossini] of Pesaro, intending to follow that production with a revival of *Barbiere*, but he fell ill after the first performance of *La gazza ladra*. There is no evidence that he supervised the two performances of *Barbiere*.) The first known revival, in Bologna, opened on August 10, 1816. Rossini, in Naples at that time, may have heard of it from his parents, living in Bologna. He wrote to his mother on August 27:

> My *Barbiere di Siviglia* will surely be booed in Bologna since [Andrea] Verni [Figaro], [Amerigo] Sbigoli [Almaviva], La Giorgi, etc. cannot perform this [opera] without offending good sense.[10] (Rossini 1992–: 3a: 140–142)

Geltrude Righetti-Giorgi was the only singer who had been in the original cast. Perhaps Rossini included her as one who would offend good sense because in the Bologna revival she appropriated for herself Almaviva's Act II aria "Cessa di più resistere" (N. 17) and replaced Rosina's lesson scene aria "Contro un cor" (N. 11) with one of her own choice, "La mia pace, la mia calma." The composer of the substituted aria is unknown, but it must have been made for this production rather than borrowed from another opera, because it uses the *tempo di mezzo* (mm. 28–52) of Rossini's original aria, in which Rosina and the disguised Almaviva have a furtive conversation. "La mia pace" appears as the lesson scene aria in four manuscript copies and a number of printed vocal scores. Because of its historical importance, and even more because of the way it incorporates the original *tempo di mezzo* to maintain the dramatic situation, WGR prints an edition of "La mia pace" as an appendix. In the revival in Florence, Righetti-Giorgi substituted a more elaborate piece, "Perché non puoi calmar" (probably by Stefano Pavesi), and she omitted "Cessa di più resistere" entirely. The practice of replacing the aria in the lesson scene quickly spread and by the late nineteenth century led in some cases to the equivalent of a mini-recital for the prima donna.[11] (For a sympathetic discussion of the custom, see "*Che vuol cantare?* The Lesson Scene of *Il barbiere di Siviglia*," chapter 5 in Poriss 2009: 135–168.)

The Florentine revival of 1816 made another important contribution to the transformation of Rossini's opera. The grand *buffo* aria "A un Dottor della mia sorte" (N. 8) for Bartolo (sung in Florence by Paolo Rosich) was replaced by "Manca un foglio," by the Teatro della Pergola's resident composer Pietro Romani. The Romani aria, simpler than Rossini's, was also soon widely performed and is found in about half of the manuscript copies consulted. In her memoirs Righetti-Giorgi ([1823] 1956: 37) suggested that Rossini was aware of this substitution and not displeased by it, but there is no evidence from Rossini himself. Because it became so firmly attached to the performing and textual tradition of *Il barbiere di Siviglia*, WGR prints this aria, too, as an appendix.

The twenty surviving manuscript sources examined for the Bärenreiter critical edition of *Il barbiere di Siviglia* are copies produced for theaters or individuals and now reside in libraries around the world (for a complete description, see Rossini 2008b: 11–65, 70–74). Their content varies: the Count's little self-accompanied canzone (N. 3) in Act I is missing from ten and marked to be cut in another. "Manca un foglio" replaces "A un Dottor" in eight, with Bartolo's aria missing completely in three more and placed at the beginning of Act II in another.

The lesson scene (N. 11) shows the greatest variety of solutions: Rossini's "Contro un cor" is found in only six of the manuscripts; "La mia pace," substituted by Geltrude Righetti-Giorgi in Bologna in 1816, is in four, and five have no aria (this does not necessarily mean that the aria was omitted, but only that a substitute was not inserted into the score). One copy contains a scena, "Ohimè che orror! qual tetro carcere tenebroso," and aria, "Pietà del mio dolore"; this piece has not yet been identified, although parts of it seem like a parody of Rossini's prison scene for Amenaide in the second act of *Tancredi*. Another has in the lesson scene the concluding aria from Rossini's *Elisabetta, regina d'Inghilterra*, slightly modified and lacking the chorus. A manuscript in Weimar, entirely in German, reflects the first Vienna production at the Theater an der Wien, September 28, 1819. It contains (though marked to be cut) a "Bolleros" [sic] for Rosina, "Ein Quell der Freuden ist treue Liebe" (attributed in an edition printed by H. A. Probst of Leipzig in the 1830s to one Grünbaum).[12] This copy also demonstrates another way the sources manipulate the text of the work: in the Trio (N. 16) and the Finaletto Secondo (N. 18), the part of Rosina—and at one point that of the Count—is rewritten to cope with a soprano prima donna rather than a contralto.

The group of nine manuscripts that lack an offstage "La ran la lera, la ran la là" before Figaro enters the scene with "Largo al factotum" (N. 2) share other characteristics, but unfortunately, the surviving manuscripts that we have located must represent a much larger body of sources, and they must reflect some local choices of content, because it is impossible to group them clearly into a family with distinct "species." A unique manuscript replaces all the recitatives with spoken dialogue, and Bartolo's is in Neapolitan dialect. It lacks an aria for Bartolo—perhaps the *buffo* inserted a well-known Neapolitan song—and in general corresponds to the version of the opera performed in small theaters in Naples from 1818 on.

Three full scores were published in Rossini's lifetime: a French version by Castil-Blaze (Paris, 1821), an Italian score by Ratti and Cencetti (Rome, 1828), and a late score published by Guidi (Florence, 1864) based on the autograph, which had recently been donated to the library of the Liceo musicale of Bologna. The Castil-Blaze score has the text in French and in Italian, but since French performances used spoken dialogue, it lacks all the recitatives. Several numbers are rearranged or omitted entirely, and in the lesson scene Rosina sings "Di tanti palpiti" from *Tancredi* instead of "Contro un cor." Ratti and Cencetti, copyists (Cencetti was in fact the copyist for the Teatro Argentina in 1816) and publishers, printed a score under the title *Almaviva, o sia Il barbiere di Siviglia*, in 1828 (the title of the opera as printed in the libretto for Rome in 1816 was *Almaviva o sia l'inutile precauzione*, but it was always called *Il barbiere di Siviglia* in later librettos, in all the copies, and by Rossini himself in his letters). The printed score is not based directly on the autograph but rather reflects the readings of manuscript copies prepared by the firm. While it may be historically close to Rossini's score and does present the entire opera in its original form (including the recitatives), the print has a large number of incorrect and modified notes and a thoroughly unsatisfactory treatment of articulation and dynamic indications.

Manipulations of the original content of *Barbiere*, as seen in librettos from revivals and in manuscript copies of the opera, are naturally reflected in printed vocal scores, which carry the transformation even farther. For example, in the score published by Mechetti (Vienna, 1820), the beginning of Act II has an orchestral "Intermezzo" of fifty-four measures derived from themes in the second Finale, followed by Romani's aria for Bartolo with German text only ("Hier fehlt mir ein halber Bogen"). This Intermezzo and German aria for Bartolo also appear in the Breitkopf & Härtel edition, as does Grünbaum's aria for Rosina found in the Weimar manuscript described above. Another aria for Rosina is interpolated after Bartolo's arietta in the lesson scene; it is "Cara adorata immagine," from Giovanni Pacini's *Il barone di Dolsheim* (Milan, 1818). The aria "Cessa di più resistere," transposed up a fifth, is given to Rosina, as in the 1816 revival in Bologna. This form of the opera is essentially followed by the Paris edition of Boïeldieu (1821–1822), which proclaimed "the proofs have been revised and corrected, for the words, by M. Louis Balochi [later the librettist of *Il viaggio a Reims*], and for the music, by several composers,"[13] and by the editions of Marquerie Frères (1839) and Veuve Launer (1844). Other Parisian piano-vocal scores (Carli, 1820–1821, and Pacini, 1822–1823) present the opera closer to its original form, although they all omit the Count's canzone and either omit his aria (N. 17) or transpose it for Rosina.

An essential part of nineteenth-century performance was vocal ornamentation, and composers and audiences expected singers to embellish their parts. Popular performers prompted publication of single musical numbers from operas, such as, for example, an early print of N. 7, the Duet for Rosina and Figaro (Paris, Carli, c. 1821), the title page of which reads: "Duo / sung by M.[me] Fodor and M.[r] Pellegrini / in the *Barber of Seville*. Music by Rossini / with all the ornaments these two singers introduce there, written by themselves."[14] Manuscript copies and printed scores alike may have ornamentation added by their users, and published instruction manuals relevant to this period include one by Manuel García, Jr. (Paris, 1847). Ornamentation is also found in transcriptions of operatic pieces for piano or piano and solo instrument. Rossini himself wrote a number of variations for Rosinas, whom he unfortunately failed to identify on three of the five known manuscripts. It would be remiss of an editor not to help performers to understand what Rossini's expectations were and what individual singers' styles might have been, so WGR publishes editions of all the known autograph variants for *Barbiere* in an appendix. It further includes an appendix prepared by Will Crutchfield that presents a broad selection of ornamentation for *Barbiere* and analyzes the style of ornamentation used by singers who worked with Rossini or who studied with those singers. He points out that

> ornamental notation is inherently variable and flexible. [...] Since, for the vast majority of sources, we do not have multiple drafts to compare, we must be ready to imagine the many possibilities of non-literalism, of incompleteness, and even of confusion in the notation as we find it. (Rossini 2008b: 370)

The variants are presented in the order of their appearance in the score, with ornamentation of the same passage from different sources aligned for comparison.

In 1969, more than one hundred years after Guidi's edition based on the autograph of *Il barbiere di Siviglia*, Ricordi published an edition by Alberto Zedda that again returned to the composer's manuscript. In a review in *MLA Notes*, Marvin Tartak wrote that "this new edition from Ricordi can inspire confidence in future scholars; it is an exemplary work of its kind, and I have no hesitation in recommending it as a reliable source for nineteenth-century research" (Tartak 1971: 795).

At that time, Zedda's edition was unusual in the world of nineteenth-century Italian opera, and his use of some secondary sources as well as the autograph was seen by Tartak as remarkable. Nevertheless, in a paper presented to the Major Orchestra Librarians' Association (MOLA) in 1999, Clinton Nieweg, then Principal Librarian of the Philadelphia Orchestra, and Robert Sutherland, then Associate Chief Librarian of the Metropolitan Opera, wrote:

> It is curious that in this day of trends towards accurately reproducing the composer's "ink," the celebrated and much used "critical" edition of [*Il*] *barbiere di Siviglia*, by Alberto Zedda has done exactly the opposite, mirroring more closely the editorial style, now much maligned, which occurred at the turn of the century. He has notated the articulations and ornaments which most knowledgeable musicians and coaches would have automatically brought to their work. (Nieweg and Sutherland 1999: 4)

As for the Bärenreiter edition, Crutchfield commented:

> Why a *new* critical edition a few decades after Zedda's? The short answer: much has been learned since *Barbiere* helped get the ball rolling forty-odd years ago. The Zedda score did inestimable service in alerting everyone to what had been going on for so long, and in bringing those who used it far closer to Rossini's opera. But in the intervening years of research and labor, editors have developed far more tools for figuring out how to handle the sources, how to resolve ambiguities in a composer's score, how to present the information to the musicians who use it, and so on. (Crutchfield 2008: n.p.)

And how does it all play out, once the scholarship and editing is done, and the critical edition is available for performance? The orchestra librarians Nieweg and Sutherland observe:

> Conductors sometimes base their decision on which edition to use on what they know, what they own, what they were told was "best," on publisher pedigree or advertising, and occasionally on knowledge of the differences between the available editions. [...] Many conductors have the "only" correct insight into how a piece should be performed and which is the most appropriate edition to achieve the performance. (Nieweg and Sutherland 1999: 4)

Joyce DiDonato, who sang Rosina in the first production using the Bärenreiter edition, wrote on her blog, "It's a huge challenge to retrain your brain after so many performances! There are a number of articulation marks either added or deleted, etc, and some other big text changes. But overall, it's still 'Barbiere'!" (DiDonato 2008).

See also: Reconstructions, Sources

Notes

1. The Canterbury Tales Project, now housed at the Institute for Textual Scholarship and Electronic Editing at the University of Birmingham, describes its methodology on its website (see TCTP n.d.): "We compare all the manuscripts, creating a record of their agreements and disagreements with a computer collation program (*Collate*). We use computer-based methods, some drawn from evolutionary biology, to help reconstruct the history of the text from this record of agreements and disagreements."
2. See TCTP n.d. For a description and a link to an interactive sample of the edition of "The Nun's Priest's Tale," see SDE n.d.
3. "[...] den jeweiligen Objekten neue, gegenstandsspezifische und einzelfachübergreifende Editionskonzepte entwickelt." (OPERA 2009)
4. "La filologia... ha per oggetto un testo quale documento di cultura e per scopo la restituzione del testo medesimo nella forma più vicina possibile a quella che esso aveva quando l'autore lo considerò compiuto, o, nel caso di un testo che l'autore non arrivò mai a considerare tale e sul quale esercitò la sua attività correttoria, nella forma che attesta l'opera al livello più avanzato in quella direzione."
5. "[...] la riflessione su di un testo musicale allo scopo di procurarne la restituzione critica, valutandone sia il rapporto con l'autore sia quello con chi nel tempo ne ha usufruito e lo ha tramandato e, così facendo, lo ha di volta in volta interpretato."
6. Although in a letter to his mother dated February 22, Rossini wrote (1992–: IIIa: 119), "Yesterday evening my opera opened [...]." The likelihood is that Rossini was mistaken in dating his letter. Saverio Lamacchia points out that the date of February 21 "would imply 7 consecutive performances until the 27th, without even one day of rest for the singers," when the company had already had thirty-two performances of *L'Italiana in Algeri*, also in Teatro Argentina's season (January 13–February 19), not to mention rehearsals (Lamacchia 2008: 40).
7. "[E]cco la chitarra[:] presto andiamo. [...] Ebben, proviamo." and "(prende la chitarra, e canta accompagnandosi)."
8. "[...] eccomi dunque a ringraziarvi per le premure datevi onde rinvennire (nel così detto mio autografo del *Barbiere*) l'originale mia Sinfonia, e il pezzo concertato della lezione, chi ne sarà mai il possessore? Pazienza... L'Escudier voleva fare, come pendent del Don Giovanni una edizione completa secondo il mio originale del *Barbiere* e sperava ch'io l'avessi messo in misura procurandole i pezzi rimpiazzati, ne sarà di meno poiché il destino lo vuol così."
9. "Da questo punto le rappresentazioni di quest'opera non si contano più."
10. "Il mio *Barbiere di Siviglia* sarà sicuramente fischiato in Bologna mentre Verni, Sbigoli, La Giorgi, etc non possono rappresentare questa [azione] senza urtare il buon senso."
11. In a production at the Metropolitan Opera of New York that opened on February 19, 1954, Roberta Peters sang "Contro un cor," and the Metropolitan archive specifies "From this date onward, until 1/23/71, the selection sung by Rosina in the Lesson Scene was Contro un cor, the aria originally written by Rossini for this episode" (Metropolitan Opera n.d.).
12. The tenor Johann Christoff Grünbaum (1785–1870) was married to the soprano Therese Müller (1791–1876), daughter of the composer Wenzel Müller, who was his daughter's teacher. It is not impossible that Therese, who in 1819 sang Desdemona in the first Viennese performance of Rossini's *Otello*, was herself the composer of this aria for Rosina.

13. "Les Epreuves ont été revues et corrigées, pour les Paroles, par M.r Louis Balochi, et pour la Musique, par plusieurs Compositeurs."
14. Duo / Chanté par M.me Fodor et M.r Pellegrini / dans le Barbier de Séville / Musique de Rossini / avec tous les agrémens que ces deux chanteurs y font, écrits par eux mêmes.

Bibliography

Aversano, Luca. 2004. "La produzione di musica a stampa in Italia nell'Ottocento." In Fiore 2004, 341–362.

Bédier, Joseph. 1928. "La tradition manuscrite du *Lai de l'ombre*: Réflexions sur l'art d'éditer les anciens textes." *Romania* 54: 161–196, 321–356.

Beghelli, Marco. 2004. "Il libretto d'opera." In Fiore 2004, 277–314.

Canettieri, Paolo, Vittorio Loreto, Marta Rovetta, and Giovanna Santini. 2005. "Ecdotics and Information Theory." *Rivista di filologia cognitiva*. Online. Available: http://w3.uniroma1.it/cogfil/ecdotica.html (accessed January 13, 2014).

Caraci Vela, Maria. 2005. *La filologia musicale. Istituzioni, storia, strumenti critici.* Vol. I: *Fondamenti storici e metodologici della filologia musicale*. [Cremona]: Libreria musicale italiana.

——. 1995. "Introduzione." In *La critica del testo musicale. Metodi e problemi della filologia musicale*, edited by Maria Caraci Vela. [3]–35. Studi e testi musicali: Nuova serie, 4. Cremona: Libreria musicale italiana.

Cavalli. 2012. *Francesco Cavalli (1602–1676)—Opere*. Publisher's project description. Kassel: Bärenreiter. Online. Available: https://www.baerenreiter.com/en/program/complete-editions-and-editions-of-selected-works/francesco-cavalli-opere/ (accessed January 13, 2014).

CMME. n.d. The Computerized Mensural Music Editing Project. Online. Available: http://www.cmme.org (accessed January 13, 2014).

Crutchfield, Will. 2008. "About *Il barbiere di Siviglia*." In *Caramoor. 2008 International Music Festival. Il barbiere di Siviglia* (program booklet).

Dawkins, Richard. 2004. "The Gibbon's Tale." In *The Ancestor's Tale: A Pilgrimage to the Dawn of Evolution*, 123–136. Boston and New York: Houghton Mifflin.

Devriès-Lesure, Anik. 2004. "Un commercio in espansione: L'editoria musicale in Francia nel Settecento. Pratiche editoriali." In Fiore 2004, 263–276.

DiDonato, Joyce. 2008. Comment, February 10, 2008, 11:09 pm. Online. Available: http://www.joycedidonato.com/2008/02/07/gratitude-day-63/ (accessed January 13, 2014).

Dumitrescu, Ted. 2009. "In the Editor's Workshop: Sixteenth-Century Transmission and Twenty-first-Century Textual Criticism." Paper given November 13, 2009, American Musicological Society annual meeting, Philadelphia, PA. *Programs and Abstracts of Papers Read at the American Musicological Society. Seventy-fifth Annual Meeting*, 59–60.

Edirom Digitale Musikedition. Online. Available: www.edirom.de (accessed January 13, 2014).

Emery, Walter. 1957. *Editions and Musicians: A Survey of the Duties of Practical Musicians & Editors towards the Classics*. London: Novello.

Fiore, Carlo, ed. 2004. *Il libro di musica: Per una storia materiale delle fonti musicali in Europa*. Palermo: L'EPOS.

Gossett, Philip. 2008. "Who Needs a New Critical Edition of *Il barbiere di Siviglia?*" *[t]akte: Das Bärenreiter-Magazin*. Online. Available: http://takte-online.de/index.php?id=524&L=1&tx_ttnews[tt_news]=74&tx_ttnews[backPid]=464&cHash=58foafo1f3 (accessed January 13, 2014).

——. 2006. *Divas and Scholars: Performing Italian Opera*. Chicago: University of Chicago Press.

——. 1993. Introduction to the facsimile edition of *Il barbiere di Siviglia. L'arte armonica*. Ser. I: 2. Rome: Accademia Nazionale di Santa Cecilia.

——. 1970. "The Operas of Rossini: Problems of Textual Criticism in Nineteenth-Century Opera." PhD diss., Princeton University.

Greenwald, Helen. 2009. "Greenwald Opera Edition Staged." *New England Conservatory* (July 23). Online. Available: http://necmusic.edu/greenwald-opera-edition-staged (accessed January 13, 2014).

Greetham, D. C. 1992. "Foreword." In Jerome J. McGann, *A Critique of Modern Textual Criticism*. Charlottesville and London: University Press of Virginia.

Greg, Walter W. 1950. "The Rationale of Copy-Text." *Studies in Bibliography* 3: 19–36.

Grier, James. 1996. *The Critical Editing of Music: History, Method, and Practice*. Cambridge, Cambridge University Press.

Harbison, John. 2002. Interview "An Opera Composer in Search of An Opera House" by Robert Wilder Blue. Online. http://www.usoperaweb.com/2002/april/harbison.htm (accessed September 20, 2009).

Lachmann, Karl. 1816. *Sextus Aurelius Propertius: Carmina*, edited with notes by Karl Lachmann. Leipzig: Gerhardt Fleischer.

Lamacchia, Saverio. 2008. *Il vero Figaro o sia il falso factotum. Riesame del "Barbiere" di Rossini*. Turin: De Sono Associazione per la Musica.

Lewis, David. 2009. "Representation, Encoding and Critical Editions." In *09051 Abstracts Collection: Knowledge Representation for Intelligent Music Processing*. Dagstuhl Seminar, 25–30 January 2009. [23]–24. Online. Available: http://drops.dagstuhl.de/opus/volltexte/2009/1972/pdf/09051_abstracts_collection.1972.pdf (accessed January 13, 2014).

MacNutt, Richard. 2006. "The Early Vocal Scores of Rossini's *Il barbiere di Siviglia*: A Can of Bibliographical Worms." In *Festschrift Otto Biba zum 60. Geburtstag*, edited by Ingrid Fuchs, 705–725. Tutzing: H. Schneider.

McGann, Jerome J. 1983. *A Critique of Modern Textual Criticism*. Chicago: University of Chicago Press.

McKerrow, Ronald B. 1904. "Note on the Treatment of the Text Adopted in This Edition." In *The Works of Thomas Nashe*. Vol. 1. London: A. H. Bullen.

Metropolitan Opera. n.d. Online. Available: http://archives.metoperafamily.org/archives/frame.htm [Met Performance] CID:164950 [Keyword Search>Performance Date>19 February 1954] (accessed January 13, 2014).

Nieweg, Clinton, and Robert Sutherland. 1999. "A Discussion of Various Editorial Trends and How a Conductor's Decision to Use a Particular Edition May Impact the Librarian." Major Orchestra Librarians' Association. Online. Available for download: http://mola-inc.org/m/files/view/Editions-Paper-1999 (accessed January 13, 2014).

OPERA. 2009. OPERA—Spektrum des europäischen Musiktheaters in Einzeleditionen. Online. Available: http://www.opera.adwmainz.de (accessed January 13, 2014).

Poriss, Hilary. 2009. *Changing the Score: Arias, Prima Donnas, and the Authority of Performance*. AMS Studies in Music. New York: Oxford University Press.

Radiciotti, Giuseppe. 1927–1929. *Gioacchino Rossini: Vita documentata, opere ed influenza su l'arte*. 3 vols. Tivoli: Arti Grafiche Majella di Aldo Chicca.

Righetti-Giorgi, Geltrude. [1823] 1956. *Cenni di una donna già cantante sopra il maestro Rossini, in risposta a ciò che ne scrisse nella [e]state dell'anno 1822 il giornalista inglese in Parigi e fu riportato in una gazzetta di Milano dello stesso anno*. Bologna: Sassi. Reprint in Rognoni, Luigi. 1956. *Rossini*.Turin: ERI.

Rosand, Ellen. 2007. *Monteverdi's Last Operas: A Venetian Trilogy*. Berkeley and Los Angeles: University of California Press.

——, Stanley Sadie, and Roger Parker. 1992. "Editing." *The New Grove Dictionary of Opera*. Online. Available: http://www.oxfordmusiconline.com/subscriber/article/grove/music/O005746 (accessed January 18, 2014).

Rossini, Gioachino. 2009. II barbiere di Siviglia (Almaviva o sia L'inutile precauzione), edited by Alberto Zedda. *Edizione critica delle opere di Gioachino Rossini*. Sez. I: 17. Pesaro: Fondazione Rossini-Ricordi.

——. 2008a. *Il barbiere di Siviglia* [*Almaviva o sia L'inutile precauzione*], edited by Patricia B. Brauner. *Works of Gioachino Rossini* [WGR]. Kassel: Bärenreiter.

——. 2008b. Critical Commentary to Rossini 2008a.

——. 1993. *Il barbiere di Siviglia: Facsimile dell'autografo*. L'arte armonica. Ser. I: 2. Rome: Accademia Nazionale di Santa Cecilia.

——. 1992–. *Lettere e documenti*, edited by Bruno Cagli and Sergio Ragni. 4 vols. Pesaro: Fondazione Rossini.

——. 1969. *Il barbiere di Siviglia*, edited by Alberto Zedda. Milan: Ricordi.

Rot, Michael. 2009. "Zurück zur Handschrift." *[t]akte* 1/2009: 24. English translation online. Available: http://www.takte-online.de/en/search-result/article/browse/1/artikel/zurueck-zur-handschrift-giuseppe-verdis-falstaff-in-einer-wissenschaftlich-kritischen-neuausg/Michael%20Rot/index.htm?tx_ttnews%5BbackPid%5D=588&cHash=766168cdc001bdf624af77e5670b3616 (accessed January 13, 2014).

SDE. n.d. Scholarly Digital Editions. "The Nun's Priest's Tale." Online. Available: http://www.sd-editions.com/NP/index.html (accessed January 18, 2014).

Seckerson, Edward. 2009. "Rossini, *Il barbiere di Siviglia*, Royal Opera House, London." *The Independent*. Online. Available: http://www.independent.co.uk/arts-entertainment/classical/reviews/rossini-il-barbiere-di-siviglia-royal-opera-house-london-1732407.html (accessed January 13, 2014).

Sterbini, Cesare. 1816. *Almaviva o sia L'inutile precauzione*. Rome: Puccinelli.

Strohm, Reinhard. 2003. Review of Georg Friedrich Händel, *Tolomeo, re d'Egitto*, edited by Michael Pacholke. *Hallische Händel-Ausgabe* (2000). *Music Library Association Notes* 59/4: 980–983.

Tartak, Marvin. 1971. Review of *Il barbiere di Siviglia*, edited by Alberto Zedda. *Music Library Association Notes* 27/4: 794–795.

TCTP. n.d. The Canterbury Tales Project. Online. Available: http://www.canterburytalesproject.org/ (accessed January 13, 2014).

Tommasini, Anthony. 2010. "Overdue Debut for Composer and Exiled Prince." *New York Times* (July 25) Online. Available: http://www.nytimes.com/2010/07/26/arts/music/26dream.html?scp=50&sq=opera&st=nyt (accessed January 13, 2014).

Toscani, Claudio. 2004. "L'opera italiana dell'Ottocento: le fonti manoscritte." In Fiore 2004, 315–340.

CHAPTER 47

WRITING THE HISTORY OF OPERA

PHILIP GOSSETT

What Is Opera?

There are many ways to define "opera." In the most restrictive sense the term refers exclusively to those works commonly done in opera houses, theaters constructed for the purpose of providing venues for a certain kind of opera, those from the time of Mozart in the 1780s to the death of Puccini in 1924, with an occasional side glance at earlier works (particularly those of Georg Friedrich Handel) and later ones (in particular, the operas of Benjamin Britten). No matter how one conceives the details of this period—and some of the problems (e.g., to become operas, acceptable in this category by being sung throughout; works conceived as *opéras comiques*, with spoken dialogue, such as Gounod's *Faust* or Bizet's *Carmen*, were supplied with poor recitatives so that they would be sung throughout)—it was certainly a great one in Europe, and (as Carolyn Abbate and Roger Parker 2012 make clear in their *A History of Opera*) it is over. If we intend by "opera" this restrictive sense of the word, we cannot expect to find a lively, modern version of the conception. Were we to allow a less restrictive definition, on the other hand, the situation is somewhat different. A definition that embraces more works from the late seventeenth century to today would allow us to include works written for princely courts in the earliest period (works like the *Euridice* of Jacopo Peri or the *Orfeo* of Claudio Monteverdi), works with spoken dialogue (written in Paris as *opéras comiques* or for Germany as *melodramas* by composers such as André Modeste Grétry or Georg Anton Benda), and many works of today written by composers such as Philip Glass or Azio Corghi. Without looking for compositions that have already been accepted in today's opera houses, but allowing a more flexible—and inclusive—definition of what opera might mean, one already increases the number of acceptable works and sees a very different picture of the genre today. Finally, one might think in entirely different terms of opera (which in general terms means simply "work") as referring to any work that attempts to join together music and theater, that uses music to enhance the theatrical experience: this definition would allow us to include Greek drama (see the collection of essays published in Brown and Ograjenšek 2010) or Broadway musicals (see, for example, Carter 2007, Mordden 1999, Stempel 2010, or Greenspan 2006), and would convey a much more comprehensive sense of what opera could mean. Under those circumstances, to speak of the end of opera would be faintly ridiculous: we live in a world where music in stage presentations or even in motion pictures plays an ever more crucial role in defining dramatic values. We could speak of new or older forms of the interaction between music and theater, but not of an end to the search for just this kind of interaction.

Analysis versus Biography: A False Dichotomy

Even were we to restrict ourselves to the narrowest vision of the nature of opera, we would find that there are prejudices that must be overcome when we write a history of the genre. The advent of the so-called New Criticism in literature (Richards 1929) sparked similar interest in music among generations of critics. Even when our colleagues in literature had long since given up this false dichotomy, musicologists labored under the notion that somehow there was a difference between analysis and biography. To accept this position, we would have to assume that by analysis we refer basically to a kind of Schenkerian model in which the writer tries to demonstrate that a given work can be treated as part of a set of similar pieces; what analysis does is to show just how that particular work is put together (I am well aware that this definition does not cover all the writings of such an eminent scholar as Joseph Kerman, whose *Opera as Drama* of 1956 defined a particular way of looking at criticism of opera). Thus, in literature an analysis attempts to demonstrate the inner workings of a poem or a play, whereas in music everything not part of an ideal work is relegated to a different realm of thought. According to this view, we cannot expect to learn anything significant about a work by considering its sketches, since these are interesting only as part of biography, whether of a particular composition or of its author, not of a true analytic vision. Thus did Douglas Johnson (a student of Kerman) reject all analytic work with sketches in an infamous article about Beethoven published in 1978, which had a negative influence on study of the Beethoven sketchbooks for an entire generation. This viewpoint also created a situation in which entire genres of music, for which the concept of an analyzable work did not function effectively, such as virtuoso music for keyboard or opera, for that matter, would need either to be excluded altogether, or else a single vision of a complex history would have to be accepted as the work (this is my principal complaint about a lovely book by Goehr 1992). And yet, we know full well—and new editions of these so-called works clarify just how important this differentiation could be—that even Wagner, in his *Tristan und Isolde*, was more than willing to have modifications introduced in performance to suit the needs of successive casts (see the list of variants in Wagner 1992). But where should such flexibility stop? And, despite this evidence, can we continue to speak of a single *Tristan*, as an analyzable work? I think not. There may well be elements of it that can be analyzed in harmonic or other terms, but the opera as a whole resists easy categorization.

Biography does not have a good reputation in musicological circles. Going back to Guido Adler's description of the important elements in a musicological discussion, biography per se was relegated to an inferior position (Adler 1885, 1911). The situation has not improved since Kerman contemplated it as a "positivistic" way of dealing with history (see Kerman 1985, whatever positivism might mean in this context). And yet, when we contemplate intellectual work on opera or any element of musical theater we wish to study and its creators (and, yes, I believe that the composer *is* the "creator" of such a work, not the singers, not the librettists, not the directors—no matter how significant their impact might be on the initial and final outcome), we are constantly faced with puzzles that can only be addressed through biographical studies. Many scholars, such as Poriss (2009), Rutherford (2006), and Smart (1994), have argued for the importance in the operatic world of the past two hundred years of collaborations between performers and composers. Whereas in other disciplines there is a flourishing discussion of the nature of biography, fueled mainly by eminent biographers, such as Leon Edel, whose work on Henry James is well known (see Edel 1984), or Hermione Lee (2009), who has written extensively on Virginia Woolf, in music serious contemplation of the field has been very limited (but see Pekacz 2006).

Can We Separate a Work from Its Creator?

What can we say of intelligence about Rossini's operatic career, without considering his decade-long sojourn in Naples, not to mention his decision after *Guillaume Tell* of 1829 to abandon the operatic stage? What can we say about Wagner without knowing of his dreadful experiences in Paris, both as a young man knocking in vain on the door of the Opéra with a libretto prepared for what Louis Dietsch would ultimately compose as *Le vaisseau fantôme, ou le maudit des mers* (1842), and as a mature composer attempting to produce *Tannhäuser* at the same theater in the early 1860s (for a necessary corrective to inherited views on the history of *Le vaisseau fantôme*, see Millington 1986), not to mention the support he obtained from King Ludwig of Bavaria? If we do not differentiate Monteverdi's operas for princely courts after 1600 from his operas written for the Venetian public theaters around 1640, how can we expect to account for the differences between these works? (Someone who understands the significance of this difference in the life and works of Monteverdi is Ellen Rosand: see Rosand 1991 and 2007.) And unless we know about Verdi's experiences with the theaters in Italy during the first part of his career (through *Un ballo in maschera* of 1859), how can we judge his later works, none of which was written for an Italian theater, until *Otello* of 1887? (As I have tried to point out in Gossett 2009, the expression *anni di galera* does not refer to Verdi's operas of the 1840s, but rather to all his operatic composition for Italy through 1858.) Unless we know of Donizetti's truly terrible experiences in Naples, with *Maria Stuarda* in 1834 (these are described in the preface to the critical edition of the opera; see Donizetti 1992), then with *Poliuto* in 1838, we cannot appreciate the changes in his compositional style for Paris and Vienna that occurred after he left Italy for points north. In short, the history of even the most restricted view of opera mentioned above cannot help but be tormented by the complicated state of each individual composition.

What is Puccini's *Manon Lescaut*, first performed in 1893, but revised continually by performers and by the maestro himself for thirty years, until Toscanini conducted a revival of it on the opera's thirtieth anniversary in 1923 and introduced changes approved by Puccini? Even so, as Suzanne Scherr Steger (2013) has clearly demonstrated, were we to examine the score as published today by Puccini's original publisher, Ricordi of Milan, we would find many changes that were never authorized by the composer. Some of these changes might be part of the socialization of the score, to use in musical terms the idea introduced during the 1980s by Jerome J. McGann in his analysis of the poems by Byron, but some of them are more substantive (for his most important contribution to textual studies, see McGann 1983). And what should we think of as Puccini's *Edgar*, which the composer himself modified at least twice, including the removal of the fourth act, which was restored for the first modern performance of the original version in Turin (2008). The editor, Linda Fairtile, was to have reconstructed the opera's fourth act on the basis of the vocal score, since the composer's autograph had been presumed lost. Quite unexpectedly (I have been told), the owner of the missing manuscript produced it in late 2007, in time to use Puccini's original orchestration for the performances (see Puccini forthcoming). Indeed, the more work that has been done on individual operas, using the term in its most restrictive sense, the less able are we to write a history based on the work concept: Hilary Poriss (2001) has shown the extent to which moments we may today consider quintessential to any particular piece, such as the mad scene in Donizetti's *Lucia di Lammermoor*, were in fact rejected by early viewers of the opera and by early singers who replaced this scene regularly with another piece from the same composer's *Fausta*. How can we pretend that Maria Callas, singing Rossini's *Turco in Italia* under the direction of Gianandrea Gavazzeni (this performance is preserved in a recording still available), would have allowed the conductor to cut her principal aria, "Squallida veste," from the score had she known it existed? She must not have known of it, for it makes Fiorilla a much more complex character than might otherwise appear. And the situation is not helped by the antics of Beverly Sills, who sang the part at the New York City Opera in 1977 and pretended that this aria was a fake mad-scene. I will never forget her interpretation, throwing herself on the stage at the end of the piece, lifting her head off the floor, and winking at the audience. The audience loved her, of course, but Rossini's complicated opera was forgotten in the process.

Thus, even writing a history of opera in its most restrictive sense, we find ourselves constantly facing up to the fact that it is our ignorance of this past that allows us to write a simplistic narrative of the genre, one that accepts all too easily the ways that these compositions have been habitually manhandled. I am not referring to those places where *prima donnas* or *primo uomos* might have made changes in the score, but rather to those places where we simply accept what contemporary censorship required of composers. So, as Francesco Izzo (2007) has so brilliantly demonstrated, how can we permit an opera like Giuseppe Verdi's *Giovanna d'Arco* to be known today in a form that transforms a vision of the Virgin Mary as a warrior, endowing Joan of Arc with a shield and a sword, into La Pia (the Pious One) simply because an image of Mary supporting a war against a foreign oppressor was not permissible to the Austrians, who cared more about a perceived threat to the fate of their rule over Milan than they did about the nature of Verdi's opera? We still hear "Salve Maria" in Verdi's *I Lombardi*, even though the letters "*S*" and "*l*" were added in a foreign hand to Verdi's original "Ave Maria," by censors who did not want the text of the Marian prayer enunciated on stage. In fact, when Verdi revised the opera for Paris in 1847 as *Jérusalem*, he used the original words for Hélène's prayer, "Ave Maria." At least it is difficult to hear a performance today of Verdi's *Rigoletto* in which the tenor's response to Sparafucile's demands in the third act is that he wants two things right away: "Una stanza e del vino" ("A room and some wine"). Everyone seems to know that the words "Una stanza" were added to Verdi's autograph by another hand, replacing the offensive "Tua sorella" ("Your sister"). What, Verdi asked in a famous letter, would the Duke be doing in an inn at the edge of the city were it not that he had an assignation there?

How can we allow *Un ballo in maschera* to be brought back to its Swedish origins, as the story of the assassination of King Gustave III in 1792, while maintaining the words Verdi was obliged to use after 1858 when he was forced to move the opera from that original site in Stockholm? (As Verdi wrote to his librettist Antonio Somma on July 8, 1858, "The Censors will permit the characters and situations, etc., but they want to transfer the place away from Europe. What would you say to America at the time of the English domination? If not America, elsewhere, perhaps in the Caucasus"; see Ricciardi 2003: 280). And so we still picture Ulrica, the soothsayer, described by Oscar (in an infamous line), as being black ("Dell'immondo sangue dei negri" ["of the foul blood of the negroes"]), even when she becomes a Swede, in whose country black faces were unknown, even though we know that the original words were "Ulrica, la sibilla" ("Ulrica, the sibyl"). How can we permit Ulrica to describe the Satan she raises in the second scene as having the "torch of the future" in his right hand, when we know that Verdi wanted Satan to have "the keys to the future" in his right hand, keys which in Rome (whose censors were responsible for prohibiting many of Verdi's best verses), were the exclusive property of Saint Peter? It is all too easy to envision how we permit such stupidities: it is more important for a modern opera house to make it possible for singers who do not know that these are stupidities to join the cast of an opera with no rehearsal at all, than it is to get these matters right.

New Sources, New Views: *Il viaggio a Reims*, *Le comte Ory*, and *La gazzetta*

There are many pieces for which it is only the discovery of important sources that makes possible a very different view of a composition. Here are two Rossinian examples, one pertaining to two works of the 1820s, *Il viaggio a Reims* and *Le comte Ory*, the other pertaining to the only comic opera he composed for Naples, *La gazzetta* of 1816.

For many years, we knew nothing at all (except the words) of an opera Rossini wrote for the Théâtre Italien of Paris in 1825, his first completed work for Paris, *Il viaggio a Reims*, the only one written to Italian words. Only when the eagle-eyed M. Elizabeth C. Bartlet, in the mid-1970s, spotted some manuscripts derived from it (they were used in 1848 for a parody of the opera given in that year at the Théâtre Italien, *Andremo a Parigi?*) did we begin to be able to reconstruct the opera. And yet, it was a crucial work for understanding the history of opera in the 1800s, since it was the last opera in Italian to be written by Rossini and it was enormously successful in Paris (for further information about *Il viaggio a Reims*, see the critical edition of the opera, Rossini 1999). Yet the composer withdrew it from circulation, since he believed correctly that, as an occasional work written for the coronation of a king (Charles X), it could not hold the stage beyond that moment in history. There was such an outcry by Parisian critics, who wanted to hear the opera again, that Rossini decided to reuse much of the score (but only those parts of it that could find a happy home elsewhere) in his third French opera, *Le comte Ory* of 1828.

But what constituted *Le comte Ory*? Until the proximate publication of the critical edition of the opera (Rossini 2013), we will not know for certain. But we already know that Rossini conceived it much more like *Il viaggio a Reims* than what later remained, not least because he was obliged to shorten it to permit the Opéra to stage a full-length ballet the same evening as *Ory*, which had no internal ballets. In fact, examination of the records of the Opéra makes clear that *Le comte Ory* was never performed alone. We know the opera thus far exclusively from a poor copy printed in 1828 by Rossini's Parisian publisher, Eugène Troupenas, a copy that facilitated the opera's circulation in the French provinces. And so, whereas the first-act finale is borrowed from the "Gran pezzo concertato" for fourteen solo voices in *Il viaggio a Reims*, the Troupenas edition of *Le comte Ory* reduces it to seven solo voices and chorus, a far cry from Rossini's original conception of the piece. We know, too, that the newly composed finale of the opera, which seems very short, *is* indeed short, for Rossini originally composed some fifty additional measures, which were cut early in the rehearsals of *Le comte Ory* so as to keep its length modest. How can we hope to write the history of French opera of the nineteenth century without this kind of information?

The situation is quite different for *La gazzetta*. This comic opera was composed by Rossini in 1816 as one of the first works he wrote for Naples. As such, it borrows extensively from earlier works; Rossini often introduced himself to a new venue with pieces that were unknown to that public (but later he did relatively little borrowing; this is true both for Naples and Paris). For many years we believed that he may not even have composed the (heretofore missing) quintet in the middle of the first act, for which we had the words, but not the music. And yet, if we were to make any sense of the plot, which is, after all, based on a comedy by Carlo Goldoni, *Il matrimonio per concorso*, at least some of that material needs to be heard. We could not sanction performances of the drama without the moment in which the second pair of lovers, Alberto and Doralice, decide that they are meant for one another. This occurs in the recitative preceding the missing quintet. And so, we reluctantly published the critical edition of the opera with only a minimum amount of composition, done by myself, entirely of recitative (Rossini 2002). This was not so outrageous an enterprise, for, in fact, none of the recitative in the entire opera is by Rossini: it is all in the hand of collaborators on the score; my intervention, therefore, had no sense of *lèse majesté* associated with it.

But neither the autograph manuscript of the opera nor any secondary source pertaining to the opera, including vocal scores purporting to present complete versions of the opera, had a hint of the recitative scenes (not even of the Alberto-Doralice scene, which I was forced to set to music for the critical edition) or of the missing quintet. Indeed, Marco Mauceri, a fine scholar who had studied the opera, wondered aloud whether Rossini had ever composed it (Mauceri 1993: 129). Yet no one was content to perform *La gazzetta* without something in this place. We knew that one-act *farse* by Rossini all featured a major ensemble in the middle, while in many two-act comic operas (including *Il Turco in Italia* and *La Cenerentola*) there is an ensemble at this point, in addition to the big finale of the first act. The absence of the quintet in *La gazzetta*, in short, was palpable. At the Rossini Opera Festival in Pesaro, Dario Fo, the stage director, had the text of the libretto declaimed rhythmically by members of the cast, while the continuo group played the melody of a Rossini song, "La danza" from the *Soirées musicales* in the background. The German Rossini Society went Fo one better; for their performance of the opera in Bad Wildbad during their annual summer festival of 2007, they commissioned Stefano Piana to compose a quintet based on Rossini's music (for a description, see Piana 2007). That he simply did not have enough information to do this effectively did not stop them.

Well, the autograph of this quintet turned up last year in the Conservatory of Palermo (see Gossett 2012). We do not know how it got there, but it is present, and it had a good many surprises. To take just one example, the last section of the quintet is derived from the final section of the *Finale Primo* of *Il barbiere di Siviglia*. We could tell that already from the text in the printed libretto (both pieces share the text "Mi par d'esser con la testa / In un'orrida fucina"), but the finale of *Il barbiere* has the peculiarity of beginning its reprise in a key (E flat major) different from the C major with which the section begins. But this does not happen in *La gazzetta*, where the finale of the quintet begins properly in C major. On the other hand, the reprise is not identical, since in *La gazzetta* a counterpoint is added to the initial idea for the reprise, a counterpoint not present in *Il barbiere di Siviglia*. We realized soon that neither of the solutions adopted in the past (to assume the quintet had not been composed or to provide a new composition) was acceptable. Furthermore, it was crucial to know the entire opera or one could not make intelligent observations about its place in the history of the genre. That is a continual problem. We know many operas, even of the so-called standard repertory, in texts that are in many respects imperfect. How can we write the history of a genre without knowing better the works belonging to that genre? And by this I mean not only the text as it has come to be known in the repertory regularly performed today, but of the various stages in its performing history.

Knowing the *Complete* History of a Work

I have often wondered how the editors of the Donizetti edition, Gabriele Dotto and Roger Parker, could justify, on other than the most banal practical grounds, omitting consideration of *completed* operas, such as *Buondelmonte* (actually performed in place of the banned *Maria Stuarda* in Naples in 1834) or of *L'ange de Nisida* (the first version of *La favorite*), never performed because the theater for which it was written, the Théâtre de la Renaissance, closed (see Everist 2005). It is all well and good to know that Donizetti modified these texts for practical reasons, but how can we understand the history of the genre without knowing these earlier works on which the operas in the current repertory were based?

Writing the history of opera, even in the most restrictive form of that concept, without understanding the history of each opera, seems to me a thankless task. Certainly Rossini composed his *Semiramide* (1823) originally to conclude with the silent death of the queen by the hand of her son, Arsace, and we must be aware of that conclusion if we wish to discuss the use of a tragic ending in Italian opera of the first half of the nineteenth century. But we must also know the version of the opera that Rossini prepared for Paris, in which the queen, though dying, remains able to take her leave and provide a blessing for her son, Arsace, and his future wife, Azema. And how can we pretend to know *Zelmira* (1822) without knowing that the original conclusion, which is dramaturgically poor, was modified extensively by the composer for a Parisian revival of the opera in 1826 (reconstructed by Helen Greenwald for the critical edition of the opera; see Rossini 2005)? It is true that much of this revised version, although by no means all of it, was derived from an earlier opera that had not appealed to Rossini's contemporaries, *Ermione* of 1819. That both these revised versions have found favor in opera houses in recent years reflects an awareness of the flexibility with which composers treated their scores during the course of the nineteenth century and an understanding that the sanctioned versions are by no means always to be trusted.

There is a wonderful Verdian example, his *La forza del destino.* It is an opera generally known in the version the composer himself prepared in 1869, first performed at Milan's

Teatro alla Scala. It is not an easy opera to comprehend, because Verdi insisted on treating it differently from a simple *melodrama*. It is not, and should never be confused with, *Il trovatore*. Verdi, very much in the spirit of the original drama by the Duke di Rivas in Spain, sought to establish in it a "slice of life." Interestingly, although Verdi was often asked to eliminate or reduce the part of the comic priest, Fra Melitone, he was never willing to do so, just as he did not modify in any significant fashion the contents of two scenes crucial to the shape of the work, the Scena dell'Osteria (Scene at the Inn) of Act II and the Accampamento (military encampment) of Act III. But we know the composer's motivation for some of the poorer changes he introduced into the opera he had originally written in 1861–1862 for what is today the Mariinsky Theater in St. Petersburg. In revising the work for Milan in 1869, Verdi paid close attention to some of the problems that were considered by the critics to have accompanied the project from early in its history. Certain changes were improvements, and I would not want to be without the revised music for Leonora in her scene in Act I with Don Alvaro, but others are not. For example, Act III originally had the following shape: we are in Italy fighting the Germanic invaders. Don Alvaro, the tenor hero of the opera, and Don Carlo, a baritone, son of the Marchese who was killed unintentionally by Don Alvaro in the first act of the opera, are both present in the wars under false names. They form a strong friendship, threatened when Don Alvaro is badly wounded in combat. Don Alvaro grants Don Carlo, whose identity he does not know, the key to his private papers, in which there is a portrait of Don Carlo's sister, Don Alvaro's beloved Leonora. Thinking that Don Alvaro will die, Don Carlo is torn as to whether to open the "Urna fatale del mio destino" ("Fatal urn of my destiny") or not. He decides that he has not promised to avoid any contact with Don Alvaro's papers, only not to open the lock unless Don Alvaro dies. So he opens the urn and finds the picture of Leonora. Now he learns that the bullet has been removed, so that Don Alvaro's life has been saved. Don Carlo is overjoyed. If Don Alvaro will live, I can kill him, he sings in a great cabaletta, "Egli è salvo! o gioia immensa" ("He is safe! Oh immense joy").

In the 1862 opera, at this point falls the Accampamento scene, which shows life in the military camp. It lasts almost a half hour and provides an opportunity for the audience to gain psychological distance between Don Alvaro's surgery and his recovery. After the Accampamento there was a duet for Don Carlo and Don Alvaro, in which the former asks the latter if he has now recovered enough to fight a duel. With the Accampamento scene in its original position, there is sufficient time between this scene and the preceding Don Carlo aria to permit the characters to adopt their new positions. They fight the duel and Don Alvaro believes, incorrectly, that he has killed Don Carlo. He returns to the stage, horrified at what he has done and concludes the act with a great aria, "Quel sangue sparsi!" ("What blood have I spilled!"), which ends with the tenor Tamberlick's trademark, a sustained high C (Enrico Tamberlick premiered the role in 1862). For a reprise of the opera in early 1863 in Madrid, Verdi transposed the aria down a full step, because, as he told Ricordi in a letter of April 1863, "De Bassini [who sang the part of Fra Melitone] will give you a manuscript in which you'll find the cabaletta of the tenor Aria in the third act. I've lowered it by a tone and orchestrated it anew because no one could perform it as it was written for Tamberlick" (Ricordi Archive/Istituto nazionale di studi verdiani Parma: letter 175).[1]

Now, in Milan in 1869, it was considered inappropriate to end the act of an opera in this way: It smacked too much of earlier practices (think of the end of Act III of *Il trovatore*, with the tenor's cabaletta "Di quella pira" ["Of that pyre"] and the oft-interpolated high C beloved of many tenors). And so, Verdi felt constrained to remove the aria from *La forza del destino*. But, trying to decide how to conclude the act, he thought of nothing better than to use the Accampamento scene, which ends with the much-loved "Rataplan" for Preziosilla and the chorus. Switching that piece to the end of the act, though, required Verdi to place the entire Accampamento at the conclusion of the third act, and therefore to create a dramaturgical problem: How does one permit the audience and the characters of the opera to have sufficient time to grasp that Don Alvaro is now well enough to fight the famous duel? For this purpose Verdi composed for 1869 a very brief choral passage, "Compagni, sostiamo" ("Companions, let us remain here"), which doesn't have nearly the heft of the original Accampamento scene. But now, Verdi has found a new ending for the act, and the dramaturgy be damned. How can we write about the history of opera unless we know that this is the case? Performers know the difference and have often in recent years tried to compensate for Verdi's error, for an error it was.

I would not say that Bellini had a similar problem in *I puritani* (1835), because the result is so successful, but originally the opera did not divide the second and third acts: There was a single act, and the Scena d'Elvira, now in Act II, was followed immediately with a Scena d'Arturo, now in Act III. Still, Bellini found that the duet he had written for two secondary characters, Riccardo and Giorgio, which concluded with the famous "Suoni la tromba" ("Sound the trumpet"), a piece he considered too liberal for Italian tastes, especially in Naples, would do well in Paris as a close to a new Act II. And so for Paris, but *not* for Naples, he divided the opera into three acts, with the second act concluding with "Suoni la tromba," which he knew would be an audience favorite. How can we write a history of opera assuming only the Parisian version of the work?

Verdi had many problems with his *Un ballo in maschera* (1859), some of which have already been discussed (for some of the documents discussed here, see Ricciardi 2003). As is well known, he had originally planned this opera to be about the assassination at a masked ball of Gustave III, king of Sweden, but—after Verdi refused a disastrous revision of the opera in Naples, for which city the composition was originally written, as *Adelia degli Adimari* (which he contemptuously referred to as "Adelia degli Animali" [for Verdi's annotations of the libretto see Luzio 1935: I: 251])—he was forced by Roman censors to move the site and to remove all references to the death of a king. And so *Ballo* ended up in Boston, about which Verdi was notoriously ignorant (masked balls in a Puritan stronghold in the United States at the end of the seventeenth century?), just as ignorant as Puccini was about New Orleans in his *Manon Lescaut*. (Did you know there was a desert, in which Manon could die, near New Orleans? No one in the United States knows of this geographical peculiarity.) All of this is fine so long as we are content to play the opera in Boston, but many stage directors today want to bring it back to its original venue, in Sweden. And so we get "Del'immondo sangue dei negri" even in Sweden.

I will never forget a performance of *Ballo* in Parma, at the Teatro Regio, in which the Ulrica was white, indeed, but the Amelia was a black soprano (a wonderful singer, to be sure, but one whose physical attributes seemed inappropriate for the wife of Gustave's one-time friend, Ankastrom).

The issues I have raised here are of significance not only for the nineteenth century in Italy, the period and the works I tend to know best. Despite the best work of great scholars such as Nino Pirrotta, Ellen Rosand, and Howard Brown, we know relatively little about the earliest period in the less restrictive history of opera, the sixteenth and seventeenth centuries. We have much more information about Venice than we do about Rome or other centers of operatic activity in Italy. This is in part a function of the scholars who have sought out Venice such as Ellen Rosand (1993) and Beth and Jonathan Glixon (2005). But it does not necessarily tell the entire story, as has been effectively demonstrated by Margaret Murata (1981), Valeria De Lucca (2011), and Louise Stein (1993), among others. Likewise, the eighteenth century remains *terra incognita*, despite the efforts of scholars such as Ellen Harris (who has worked extensively on the music and biography of George Frideric Handel) and Daniel Heartz (whose efforts were particularly praised by Richard Taruskin in Chapter 8, "The Comic Style," in Volume 2 of his *History of Western Music*, where he writes, "Heartz accounted for the notorious void [our knowledge of the eighteenth century] by noting the fact—which many at the time found maddening to acknowledge—that the historiography of eighteenth-century music 'has been done largely by, for, and about Germans'" [Taruskin 2010: 400]). And, although everyone knows the contributions of Kurt Weill, with his *Dreigroschenoper* (1928), a contemporary vision of John Gay's *The Beggar's Opera* (1728), and his *Aufstieg und Fall der Stadt Mahagonny* (1930), both written in collaboration with Bertolt Brecht and both widely performed in today's opera houses, we had to wait until 2012 before a scholar took seriously the works Weill wrote for the Broadway stage after he was forced to emigrate from Germany (Hinton 2012). There have been important productions of Francis Poulenc's *Dialogues des Carmélites* (1957) and of Olivier Messiaen's *Saint François d'Assise* (first performed in 1983), but the operas and musical dramatic works by others in France, Germany, and England remain little known today. It is as if we expected each and every work performed to be a masterpiece: They weren't in the seventeenth, eighteenth, and nineteenth centuries, and we need to accept the notion that many works will not outlive their first performances.

What Is Opera?

Today's world is one in which previous distinctions between high art and more popular styles are ever less significant. Tim Carter's work (2007) on versions of Rodgers and Hammerstein's *Oklahoma* stands in a lonely position, but we know that Leonard Bernstein's *Candide* continues to be performed in a version that the composer sanctioned, to be sure, but that ruins some of his finest music, too identified in the composer's mind with the Broadway origins of the work. Yet to pretend we know something about the expanded sense of the term "opera" without this material is risible.

In fact, to write reasonably about Kurt Weill, one needs to know not only the history of opera in the most restricted use of the term, but also the way it has been transformed by the Broadway musical and by films in recent years (on the subject of opera and film, see Citron 2010). Yet, among opera scholars there is considerable resistance to defining the form in a way that would accommodate these manifestations of the desire to fuse together music and drama. Still, to pretend knowledge of the use of music to define the theatrical experience and to ignore pieces such as Jerome Kern's 1927 *Show Boat* (performed in 2012 at Lyric Opera of Chicago), Irving Berlin's 1946 *Annie Get Your Gun* (performed in 2012 at Glimmerglass Opera), or *Candide* (performed at the Teatro alla Scala, Milan, in 2007), all compositions that have found their way into opera houses over the past decade—sometimes to the horror of those who favor a restricted sense of the term—seems decidedly wrongheaded. And it would be equally wrongheaded to refuse to recognize that for many in the modern world, pieces such as Andrew Lloyd Webber's *Evita* (1976), *Cats* (1981), or *The Phantom of the Opera* (1986), not to mention Claude-Michel Schönberg's *Les Misérables* (1980/1989) in its Broadway evocation, are examples of how music and the theatrical experience can be seen as one. Nor are we required to like each and every work that needs to be recognized in our expanded history.

What sense, after all, would it make to refer to the successes of the films of Charlie Chaplin, and not only the silent films, or of Alfred Hitchcock, without speaking of the way the music of Chaplin himself or of Bernard Hermann has been fundamental to the success of these endeavors? Similarly, Nino Rota has received a great deal of attention by Italian musicologists in recent years, but it was in the films of Federico Fellini that he first came to be widely known. How can we write the history of music and theater without paying attention to that world? There are those who are trying to draw serious attention to the use of music in films (see Rosar, ed., *The Journal of Film Music*), but because the commercial elements of film music are so strong and because composers in that genre are not allowed to work out their own desires, but are dependent on their interaction with directors of the films, they are not granted the same kind of attention that was demanded by composers such as Verdi and Wagner in the nineteenth century, both of whom believed that the composer alone should define each work, and that all others were ancillary to their fundamental positions. And yet, we know that both Verdi and Wagner were compelled by the circumstances of theatrical life to compromise their beliefs. This is simply the reality for composers who seek to create an amalgam of the arts, and we must not refuse it.

Writing the history of opera demands attention to all the different ways in which music and theater or film can interact. We cannot restrict ourselves sensibly to the form of opera whose day has probably passed, despite some valiant efforts in the twentieth century, after the death of Puccini in 1924, to grant it new life. The broader our definition of what constitutes "opera," the more likely we are to celebrate its continuity in today's world.

See also: What Is Opera? Musical Theater(s), Divas and Divos, Censorship, Patronage, How Opera Traveled, Editing Opera, Reconstructions, Sources

Note

1. "De Bassini ti consegnerà un rotolo in cui vi è dentro la cabaletta dell'aria del Tenore del Terzo atto. L'ho abbassata d'un tono ed istromentata di nuovo perché nissuno potrebbe eseguire quella che fu scritta per Tamberlich. Ti prego però di farla mettere in tutti li spartiti che noleggerai e di mandarla subito a Londra da Arditi. Addio, addio." Ricordi says in a letter of April 23 that he has received V's missive and will do exactly as he asks.

Bibliography

Abbate, Carolyn, and Roger Parker. 2012. *A History of Opera*. New York: W. W. Norton.

Adler, Guido. 1911. *Der Stil in der Musik:* Prinzipien und Arten des musikalischen Stil. Leipzig: Breitkopf & Härtel.

——. 1885. "Umfang, Methode und Ziel der Musikwissenschaft." *Vierteljahrsschrift für Musikwissenschaft* 1: 5–20.

Brown, Howard Mayer. 1976. *Music in the Renaissance*. Englewood Cliffs, NJ: Prentice Hall [with many later reprints, including contributions by Ellen Harris and Louise Stein].

Brown, Peter, and Suzana Ograjenšek, eds. 2010. *Ancient Drama in Music for the Modern Stage*. New York: Oxford University Press.

Carter, Tim. 2007. *Oklahoma! The Making of an American Musical*. New Haven: Yale University Press.

Citron, Marcia. 2010. *When Opera Meets Film*. Cambridge Studies in Opera. Cambridge: Cambridge University Press.

De Lucca, Valeria. 2011. "L'Alcasta and the Emergence of Collective Patronage in Mid-Seventeenth-Century Rome." *The Journal of Musicology* 28/2: 195–230.

Donizetti, Gaetano. 1992. *Maria Stuarda*. 3 vols., edited by Anders Wiklund. *Edizione Critica delle Opere di Gaetano Donizetti*. Milan: Ricordi.

Edel, Leon. 1984. *Writing Lives: Principia Biographica*. 2nd ed. New York: W. W. Norton.

Everist, Mark. 2005. *Giacomo Meyerbeer and Music Drama in Nineteenth-Century Paris*. Aldershot, UK: Ashgate.

France, Peter, and William St. Clair, eds. 2002. *Mapping Lives: The Uses of Biography*. New York: Oxford University Press.

Glixon, Beth L., and Jonathan Glixon. 2005. *Inventing the Business of Opera: The Impresario and His World in Seventeenth-Century Venice*. AMS Studies in Music. New York: Oxford University Press.

Goehr, Lydia. 1992. *The Imaginary Museum of Musical Works: An Essay in the Philosophy of Music*. Oxford: Clarendon Press.

Gossett, Philip. 2012. "Das neu endeckte Quintett aus Rossinis *La gazzetta*." *La Gazzetta* [Zeitschrift der deutschen Rossini Gesellschaft] 22: 2–10.

——. 2009. "Introduction" to "An *Attila* Symposium." *Cambridge Opera Journal* 21/3: 237–240.

Greenspan, Charlotte. 2006. *"Pick Yourself Up": Dorothy Fields and the American Musical*. New York: Oxford University Press.

Hamilton, Nigel. 2007. *Biography: A Brief History*. Cambridge, MA: Harvard University Press.

Harris, Ellen. 2001. *Handel as Orpheus: Voice and Desire in the Chamber Cantatas*. Cambridge, MA: Harvard University Press.

Heartz, Daniel. 2003. *Music in European Capitals: The Galant Style 1720–1780*. New York: W. W. Norton.

——. 1993. *Haydn, Mozart, and the Viennese School 1740–1780*. New York: W. W. Norton.

——. 1990. *Mozart's Operas*, edited, with contributing essays, by Thomas Bauman. Berkeley and Los Angeles: University of California Press.

Hinton, Stephen. 2012. *Weill's Musical Theater: Stages of Reform*. Berkeley and Los Angeles: University of California Press.

Izzo, Francesco. 2007. "Verdi, the Virgin, and the Censor: The Politics of the Cult of Mary in *I Lombardi alla prima crociata* and *Giovanna d'Arco*." *Journal of the American Musicological Society* 60/3: 557–597.

Johnson, Douglas. 1978. "Beethoven Scholars and Beethoven Sketches." *19th-Century Music* 2/1: 3–17.

Kerman, Joseph. 1985. *Contemplating Music: Challenges to Musicology*. Cambridge, MA: Harvard University Press.

——. 1956. *Opera as Drama*. New York: Alfred A. Knopf.

Lee, Hermione. 2009. *Biography: A Very Short Introduction*. New York: Oxford University Press.

Luzio, Alessandro, ed. 1935[–1947]. *Carteggi verdiani*. 4 vols. Rome: Reale Accademia d'Italia.

Mauceri, Marco. 1993. "*La gazzetta* di Gioachino Rossini: Fonti del libretto e autoimprestito musicale." In *Ottocento e oltre. Scritti in onore di Raoul Meloncelli*, edited by Francesco Izzo and Johannes Streicher, 115–149. Rome: Pantheon.

McGann, Jerome J. 1983. *A Critique of Modern Textual Theory*. Chicago: University of Chicago Press.

Millington, Barry. 1986. "*The Flying Dutchman, Le vaisseau fantôme* and other Nautical Yarns." *The Musical Times* 127/1717: 131–135.

Mordden, Ethan. 1999. *Beautiful Mornin': The Broadway Musical in the 1940s*. New York: Oxford University Press.

Murata, Margaret. 1981. *Operas for the Papal Court, 1631–1668*. Ann Arbor, MI: University Microfilms.

Pekacz, Jolanta T., ed. 2006. *Musical Biography: Towards New Paradigms*. Aldershot, UK: Ashgate.

Piana, Stefano. 2007. "Auf der Suche nach dem verlorenen Quintett. Anmerkungen zur Rekonstruktion der Szenen VI, VII und VIII im ersten Akt von Rossinis *La gazzetta*." *La Gazzetta* [Zeitschrift der deutschen Rossini Gesellschaft] 17: 7–22.

Pirrotta, Nino. 1982. *Music and Theatre from Poliziano to Monteverdi*. Cambridge: Cambridge University Press. English translation of *Li due Orfei: Da Poliziano a Monteverdi*. Milan: Einaudi, 1965 [with many later reprints, some with an essay on scenography by Elena Povoledo].

Poriss, Hilary. 2009. *Changing the Score: Arias, Prima Donnas, and the Authority of Performance*. New York: Oxford University Press.

——. 2001. "A Madwoman's Choice: Aria Substitution in *Lucia di Lammermoor*." *Cambridge Opera Journal* 13/1: 1–28.

Puccini, Giacomo. Forthcoming. *Edgar*. 2 vols., edited by Linda Fairtile. *Edizione critica delle opere di Giacomo Puccini*. Milan: Ricordi.

Ricciardi, Simonetta, ed. 2003. *Carteggio Verdi-Somma*. Parma: Istituto nazionale di studi verdiani.

Richards, I. A. 1929. *Practical Criticism: A Study of Literary Judgment*. London: Kegan Paul.

Rosand, Ellen. 2007. *Monteverdi's Last Operas: A Venetian Trilogy*. Berkeley and Los Angeles: University of California Press.

——. 1991. *Opera in Seventeenth-Century Venice: The Creation of a Genre*. Berkeley and Los Angeles: University of California Press.

Rosar, William H., ed. 2008. *The Journal of Film Music*.

Rossini, Gioachino. 2014. *Le comte Ory*, edited by Damien Colas. *Works of Gioachino Rossini* [WGR]. Kassel: Bärenreiter-Verlag.

——. 2005. *Zelmira*. 4 vols., edited by Helen M. Greenwald and Kathleen Kuzmick Hansell. *Edizione Critica delle Opere di Gioachino Rossini*. Sez. I: 33. Pesaro: Fondazione Rossini.

——. 2002. *La gazzetta*. 3 vols., edited by Philip Gossett and Fabrizio Scipioni. *Edizione Critica delle Opere di Gioachino Rossini*. Sez. I: 18. Pesaro: Fondazione Rossini.

——. 1999. *Il viaggio a Reims*. 3 vols., edited by Janet L. Johnson. *Edizione Critica delle Opere di Gioachino Rossini*. Sez. I: 35. Pesaro: Fondazione Rossini.

Rutherford, Susan. 2006. *The Prima Donna and Opera, 1815–1930*. *Cambridge Studies in Opera*. Cambridge: Cambridge University Press.

Smart, Mary Ann. 1994. "The Lost Voice of Rosine Stoltz." *Cambridge Opera Journal* 6/1: 31–50.

Steger, Suzanne Scherr. 2013. "Puccini's *Manon Lescaut*: Compositional Process, Stylistic Revisions, and Editorial Problems." PhD diss., University of Chicago.

Stein, Louise. 1993. *Songs of Mortals, Dialogues of the Gods: Music and Theatre in Seventeenth-Century Spain*. Oxford: Clarendon Press.

Stempel, Larry. 2010. *Showtime: A History of the Broadway Musical Theater*. New York: W. W. Norton.

Taruskin, Richard. 2010. *Music in the Seventeenth and Eighteenth Centuries*. Vol. 2 of *The Oxford History of Western Music*. 5 vols. New York: Oxford University Press.

Wagner, Richard. 1992. *Tristan und Isolde*, edited by Isolde Vetter and Egon Voss. Richard Wagner, Complete Works: 8. Mainz: Schott.

PART VI

OPERA ON THE EDGE

CHAPTER 48

1900–1945

JOY H. CALICO

WAGNER, MODERNISM, AND POLITICS

WAGNER, modernism, politics: these are the tangled red threads running through the labyrinth of recent scholarship devoted to opera in the period 1900–1945. Operas are analyzed as responses to the continuing and often overwhelming presence of Richard Wagner; as various incarnations of modernism or resistance to it; and as cultural products ineluctably linked to the politics of their day. Some scholars expand the notion of modernism, challenging what they perceive as a narrative of modernist hegemony, acknowledging and legitimizing instead the works of composers who hewed more closely to the conventions they had inherited from their respective traditions. Still others note the importance of the revival of early opera, whose musico-dramatic style was so alien to twentieth-century audiences that it might as well have been brand new (Rameau in France, Handel in Germany, Monteverdi in Italy). This wide range of new, and seemingly new, works commingled with the canon to produce an operatic culture virtually unparalleled in its variety. Perhaps most significant, these forty-five years are defined by war, authoritarian regimes, and the nearly unfathomable destruction they wrought: economic crises, dislocation, persecution, and loss of life. Such political events and power structures influenced every aspect of daily life, including the quantity, style, performance, and reception of opera. In many cases, the choices musicians made under those dire circumstances directly determined responses to their work and posthumous reputations.

The three themes of Wagner, modernism, and politics are relevant to the entire period, but each one corresponds most strongly to a particular chronological subunit, and this chapter is divided accordingly: Wagner figures most prominently between 1900–ca. 1920 (end of World War I, demise of the Russian Empire and emergence of the Soviet Union); modernism is the burning question ca. 1920–1933 (the period between the end of World War I and the rise of Hitler, during which time Mussolini and Stalin came to power in their respective countries); and politics defines the period 1933–1945 (increasing unrest followed by hostilities in 1937, declaration of World War II in 1939). Finally, it will come as no surprise that the specter of nationalism looms throughout.

Defining Opera after 1900

First, however, it is worth considering a fundamental question of definition: What, precisely, *is* opera in this period? How does one tell an opera from a *Lehrstück* from the myriad other music-theater permutations that emerged at this time? Nigel Simeone's "A Chronology of Twentieth-Century Opera Premieres" provides a useful point of departure (Simeone 2005). His list features many works explicitly identified by their composers as some kind of opera: Karol Szymanowski's *Król Roger* is an "opera in three acts," as is Aarre Merikanto's *Juha*; Ethel Smyth's *The Wreckers* is a "lyrical drama;" Virgil Thomson's *Four Saints in Three Acts* is an "opera to be sung." A composer invokes a recognizable genre to link his or her work to an extant operatic tradition, and this was more common than one might expect, given the scholarly emphasis on innovation in this period (Calico 2008:19). Simeone's list also includes a large number of pieces explicitly identified by their composers as something *other* than opera, however: Kurt Weill's *Mahagonny Songspiel* and Paul Hindemith's *Lehrstück*, two works whose very titles contain generic designations that identify them as non-, if not anti-, operas; and Arthur Honegger's *Le roi David*, incidental music for a play that was later rescored as a *psaume symphonique*. Igor Stravinsky's *Histoire du soldat* is there, despite the fact that it lacks both singing *and* an actual genre designation (described by its composer simply as "to be read, played, and danced"), while his *Pulcinella*, a "ballet with song," is not.

Simeone's assimilation of non-operas into his opera list may have been determined by performance and reception conventions that have accrued to the works over time, but the hybridization and experimentation that gave rise to alternative genres reveal much about the state of opera in the first half of the twentieth century. Numerous social and stylistic conventions once considered inviolable were challenged, including venue, medium, form, duration, and style (Sheppard 2001). Ever since the demise of private noble theaters, opera had been ensconced in the opera house, but radio operas, such as Gian Carlo Menotti's *The Old Maid and the Thief* or Bohuslav Martinů's *Veselohra na mostě* (*Comedy on the Bridge*), circumvented the standard venue and its socioeconomic infrastructure. Radio was widely viewed as a democratizing medium, so these works defied the audience class-structure of staged opera as well as its assumed theatricality.

Canonical operas tended to consist of two to five acts, suggesting conventions of dramaturgy and of intermission socializing; the new prevalence of one-acts signals reconsideration of both aspects, and of the assumption that a work must achieve a minimal critical mass of duration before it can be designated as an opera. One-acts appealed especially to German composers (Hindemith wrote four, Ernst Krenek five, and Richard Strauss and Weill six each), but not exclusively; examples can be found across the spectrum of musical and dramatic styles, including Joseph-Maurice Ravel's

L'heure espagnole and *L'enfant et les sortilèges*, Béla Bartók's *A Kékszakállú herceg vára* (*Bluebeard's Castle*), Luigi Dallapiccola's *Il prigioniero*, and Dmitri Shostakovich's *Nos* (*The Nose*), to cite just a few (Kirsch and Döhring 1991). Some freestanding one-acts are so abbreviated as to be miniatures: Arnold Schoenberg's *Die glückliche Hand*, a "drama with music," lasts about twenty minutes and features minimal singing, even within that short duration; Hindemith's *Hin und zurück* is an "operatic sketch" twelve minutes in length; Slavko Osterc's *Salome* is a "minute opera parody" that clocks in at eleven. Richard Wagner's *Ring* (and, later, Karlheinz Stockhausen's *Licht*) notwithstanding, most operas had existed as discrete pieces, but the penchant for one-acts also gave rise to brief works in sets (Gian Francesco Malipiero's *Sette canzoni*, Darius Milhaud's three *Opéra-Minutes*). And regardless of duration, many featured closed arias in the style of number opera, frequently with spoken dialogue between songs (Stravinsky's *Mavra*, Weill's *Dreigroschenoper*) instead of the continuous, large-scale forms favored by the late Romantics. Finally, even a kind of "art-music" style could no longer be taken for granted as an essential characteristic, as twentieth-century vernaculars became part of opera's vocabulary (George Antheil's *Transatlantic*, Krenek's *Jonny spielt auf*, George Gershwin's *Porgy and Bess*).

Wagner

So much genre-bending, and the attendant challenges to conventions of venue, medium, form, scope and style, often stemmed from composers' efforts to cope with Wagner. Compositional responses to his music and aesthetic principles ran the gamut: emulation, adaptation, assimilation, rejection, and negation—but there was no escaping him altogether (Deathridge 2005). Even the normative opera-going experience was the one Wagner had endorsed: darkened house, humble silence, theatricality. Lawrence Kramer observes that "Wagner becomes both central and radically extrinsic to the institution of Opera, both its primary model and its primary antagonist, its authentic self, beyond emulation, and its monstrous Other" (Kramer 2004: 16). Chromatic harmony, extended forms, and endless melody signaled allegiance to Wagner/Opera, as might the appropriate venue (opera house) and audience (knowledgeable and reverent); the inverse was also true, in that the absence of these features signaled resistance to, even outright defiance of, Wagner/Opera. The most vehement rejection of Wagner as the "monstrous Other" came from Ferruccio Busoni, whose "new classicality" was demonstrated in his operas (*Die Brautwahl, Arlecchino, Turandot, Doktor Faustus*) and inspired his student Weill to conduct his own operatic experiments in the 1920s (Riethmüller and Shin 2004). At the opposite end of the spectrum was Hans Pfitzner's idealization of Wagner, which reached its apex in *Palestrina*, a three-act *musikalische Legende* designed to demonstrate the sustained superiority of German culture, even under the duress of wartime (Taylor-Jay 2004). Most works occupied a kind of middle, synthetic ground. Franz Schreker's operas ran the gamut from Wagner-inspired (*Der Schatzgräber*) to a highly individual, heady mix of timbre, nonfunctional harmony, and sexuality (*Der ferne Klang*), and staked his claim to a different modernism (Hailey 2002). Still less clear is the place of Strauss's formidable oeuvre, particularly *Salome* and *Elektra*, in which one can trace both the outermost trajectory of Wagnerian harmony and instrumentation as well as modernism (Steinberg 2006: 633–634). Bryan Gilliam argues that Strauss's fifteen operas are the result of "his initial engagement with the various Wagnerisms of his day and his ultimate rejection of all of them beyond musical technique" (Gilliam 2014: 17).

Anxiety over Wagner's influence was certainly not limited to Germany, and scholars often view developments in other operatic traditions by the extent to which Wagner had made inroads into them. Concerns about German invasion via his music informed the composition of new operas, discourse about national opera traditions, and even high politics in other countries, and perhaps nowhere more so than in France (Fauser and Schwartz 1999; Huebner 2006). Pro- and anti-Wagner factions that coalesced after the Franco-Prussian War persisted past the *fin de siècle*, and emerged with renewed fervor after World War I. In France, Wagner stood in for Opera as well as for Germany. Efforts to keep his operas off the stage during World War I came to naught because he was too popular, and in the 1920s d'Indy defended him with the claim that the German had "'saved' French music from the Jews, who had invaded 19th-century opera, rerouting it from its own national tradition" (see d'Indy 1930: 13 and Fulcher 2005: 135). Scholars have parsed Debussy's complex engagement with Wagner, as well as the musical and political significance of applying the adjective "Wagnerian" to *Pelléas et Mélisande* (Pasler 1987; Kelly 2008).

Wagner may have been less politically charged in Italy than in Germany and France, but he was no less present. Allan Mallach describes some works of Pietro Mascagni, Italo Montemezzi, and Riccardo Zandonai as "*Tristan*'s Children" (Mallach 2007: 311). More crucially for consideration of the canon, Julian Budden asserts that "Wagner's best Italian pupil was Puccini" (Budden 1987: 332). Alexandra Wilson has shown that domestic reception of Puccini's operas was filtered through contemporaneous debates over Wagner, and despite "certain aspects of his compositional process [that] bear a Wagnerian influence," these were not enough to sway pro-Wagner critics (Wilson 2007: 45; 40–46 passim). Among those technical devices was a sophisticated use of motifs. Puccini was "alone among his Italian contemporaries" in taking the recurring motif as the primary dramatic and musical structuring device, although he never allowed it to upstage the primacy of the voice (Budden 2005: 478).

Given the German Wagner's status as stand-in for all of Opera, it is perhaps inevitable that he also figures in recent research that reconsiders the use of "nationalism" as a category. Such categorization can be a facile means of marginalizing non–Italian-French-German operas. Richard Taruskin has noted that "however admiringly it is apparently done, casting a composer as a 'nationalist' is preeminently a means of exclusion from the critical and academic canon (though not, obviously, from the performing repertoire)" (Taruskin 2000: 48). Much new research seeks to admit contemporaneous Russian, Hungarian, and Czech opera into the larger continental discourse, and, as has been shown, engagement with Wagner was central to that operatic conversation. Brian S. Locke takes this approach in his work on a group of younger Czech composers—Otakar Ostrčil, Vítězslav Novák, and Josef Foerster—who aligned themselves with musicologist Zdeněk Nejedlý in opposition to the Wagnerism then being taught at the Prague Conservatory (Locke 2006). Locke does not attempt to legitimize Czech opera by assimilating it into or measuring it against the Western operatic canon; instead, he identifies significant points of contact, overlap, and rejection.

Modernism

The dearth of scholarship that treats modernist opera as a specific subgenre is surprising. After all, opera "played a vital role in the birth of musical modernity" (consider *Erwartung*, *Wozzeck*, *Pelléas et Mélisande*, and *Bluebeard's Castle*), even if the genre is "barely mentioned" in general accounts of musical modernism (Timms 2009: 23). In a rare attempt to define modernist opera, historian Michael P. Steinberg writes that it "seeks emancipation from the hold of Wagner, Wagnerism, and its nationalist mythology" (Steinberg 2006: 632). The rejection of Wagner as a definitive feature of most modernisms is standard, but for Steinberg modernist opera does not just reject *German* nationalism; it defies nationalist categorization altogether. He situates modernist opera as a "subcategory of *fin de siècle* European modernism" that ended in 1933 (for reasons that will be discussed in the next section on politics):

> Operatic modernism fits within a paradigm widespread in the history of modernism but not in the history of opera. The suggestion is that operatic modernism after Wagner might be understood as postnational rather than national—in other words, that the desire for an authentically French, Hungarian, or Czech opera not be understood to mimic the desires and claims of (German) music drama or musical-dramatic nationalism. Though the operas of Béla Bartók, Antonín Dvořák, and—most impressively and systematically in recent years—Leoš Janáček have entered the canon and the repertory of opera houses, they still tend to inspire and submit to rhetoric of the national, the folk, and the ethnic. (Steinberg 2006: 632)

Likewise, historian Lawrence Wolff dismisses "nationalist" as an inaccurate descriptor for Janáček's modernist operas, but he does not favor a post-national view. Instead, Wolff considers the multiple, overlapping identities brought to bear on the citizens of the reconfigured region known as Central Europe after World War I (local, municipal, regional, provincial, and imperial) and privileges the provincial Moravian over the national when assessing Janáček's modernism:

> Yet, though modernism in some spheres exemplified cosmopolitan transnational values, the fundamental provincialism of Moravia was, by definition, anything but cosmopolitan, contrasting with nationalism in a different fashion. Janáček's operas

> suggest that modernism had a prenational as well as a postnational component: provincialism could be as modernist as cosmopolitanism was. (Wolff 2006: 690)

Derek Katz also takes a nuanced view of overlapping identities, finding varying degrees of synthesis and emphasis across Janáček's late operas (Katz 2009).

Despite Steinberg's identification of post-nationalism as a feature of modernist opera, this section nevertheless groups the works by language and country of origin so that the approach is consistent throughout the chapter. This treatment is also consistent with the manner in which most opera scholars pursue their work, which reflects their training as much as their personal predilections. There remains no shortage of literature on German modernist opera, but it is worth remembering that the German-language opera stage was virtually dominated by the works of Strauss, the "ambivalent modernist" (Robinson 2002). In the 1910s and 1920s, Schreker, Pfitzner, Korngold, and Zemlinsky enjoyed tremendous success with German operas as well. Their work has received increased scholarly attention in recent years as a pluralist notion of modernism has emerged, thereby expanding the canon of works that qualify as modernist and more accurately reflecting the full range of operatic culture in the period (Hailey 2002). Taylor-Jay refutes the notion that a single, monolithic modernism was uncontested at the time, and reminds that its dominance was not inevitable: "While the Schoenbergian and Adornian army may have won the battle, it was not the only participant" (Taylor-Jay 2004: 22). She interprets the artist-operas of Pfitzner, Krenek, and Hindemith as alternatives to, rather than different strands of, modernism.

Scholars of Italian modernist opera have tended to focus on the postwar period and the extraordinary works of Sylvano Bussotti, Luigi Dallapiccola, and Luigi Nono. Among those who focus on the early twentieth century, Berghaus has shown that Futurism, which repudiated operatic *verismo* in Francesco Pratella's definitive *Manifesto dei musicisti futuristi* of 1911, and *verismo* had more in common than advocates of either would have admitted (Berghaus 1998); this relationship may bear comparison to that which German modernists had with Wagner. The next generation, led by Ildebrando Pizzetti, Gian Francesco Malipiero, Franco Alfano, Ottorino Respighi, and Alfredo Casella, ran the stylistic and political gamut, as will be discussed in the section on politics below. Of these, Malipiero and Casella are most often cited as exhibiting modernist tendencies (Waterhouse 1994, 1999). Generally speaking, however, all is overshadowed by Puccini. The title *Puccini's 'Turandot': The End of the Great Tradition* (Ashbrook and Powers 1991) implies that *Turandot* was not just the end of a particular style but the end of Italian opera *sui generis*, while Mallach's *The Autumn of Italian Opera: From Verismo to Modernism 1890–1915* (2007) portrays a genre in decline nearly a decade before Puccini's death prevented his completion of *Turandot*. As part of the movement toward modernist pluralities, however, a major reconsideration of Puccini as modernist is underway, and that may have repercussions for all the Italian composers cited above. In *The Puccini Problem*, Wilson recounts the controversies that surrounded the composer in his own day, stemming primarily from efforts to reconcile Italian-ness with some kind of modernity. Her agenda is to reconstruct the social and political contexts in which Puccini was received in his own day and to situate him as "a profoundly modern figure" rather than "an insignificant throwback to the nineteenth century" (Wilson 2007: 7).

If the literature on Italian opera in this period is dominated by Puccini's oeuvre, the literature on French opera is dominated by a single opera: Debussy's symbolist *Pelléas et Mélisande* (1902), the first and quintessential French modernist opera. Barbara Kelly traces the process whereby *Pelléas*—a highly unusual, "potentially isolated" work—had come to stand in for and be definitive of French music by the time the composer died in 1918 (Kelly 2008: 58). Jann Pasler's social history of the Apaches, that group of artists, writers, and musicians who bonded over the premiere of *Pelléas* and found common cause in its defense, is a valuable contribution to our understanding of these controversies and their place in larger Parisian society (Pasler 2007). There is little sense that opera played a role in French musical modernism otherwise; consider the title of an essay by sociologist Antoine Hennion: "Rewriting History from the Losers' Point of View: French Grand Opera and Modernity" (Hennion 2007). The decade after *Pelléas* produced just a handful of operas generally construed as modernist. Paul Dukas followed Debussy's lead with his own symbolist opera, *Ariane et Barb-bleue*, based on a Maeterlinck libretto, and Ravel's *L'heure espagnole* was a modernist parody of Wagnerian and symbolist excess in the form of an *opera buffa* (Huebner 2006). The notion of Fauré as modernist is given credence in a study of his single completed opera, *Pénélope* (Sobaskie 2003).

Stravinsky's *conte lyrique, Le rossignol*, premiered in Paris in 1914, and was a harbinger of things to come in that city; its brief, three-act, hybrid theatricality (pantomime-ballet-pageant) reflects the composer's ambivalence about the operatic genre and presages the variety of French music theater experimentation to come after World War I, often in league with leading cultural figures such as Jean Cocteau, Pablo Picasso, and Paul Claudel. Darius Milhaud wrote everything from miniature chamber operas, as in the cycle of three ten-minute operas known as *Opéra-Minutes*, to the outsized, ambitious *Christophe Colomb* in two acts with twenty-seven scenes (Kelly 2003). W. Anthony Sheppard's work on French manifestations of "total theater" and resistance to it, as well as the role of exoticism in this repertoire, is particularly revealing (Sheppard 2001). More recently, Jane Fulcher has posited the category of the French "opera of ideas" as a phenomenon of the 1920s, asserting that "this apparently insignificant decade in French opera is indeed seminal in terms of the genre's changing function, its evolving intellectual and political role" (Fulcher 2005: 115).

Politics

Italian Fascism and German Nazism are usually described as two manifestations of Fascism, ideologies that privilege nation and/or race above the individual and are characterized by a "centralized, autocratic government headed by a dictatorial leader, severe economic and social regimentation, and forcible suppression of opposition" (Merriam Webster). Steinberg has noted the unusual relationship between opera and these two states ("In a still underexplored historical case of a dog that did not bark, opera did not serve these regimes," according to Steinberg 2006: 634–635), but the regimes did police and censor operas, their artists and institutions. Jeremy Tambling traces the link between opera and what he calls "the culture of Fascism" deep into the nineteenth century, especially (but not exclusively) to Wagnerism, and posits Fascism as the dark side of modernity (Tambling 1996). Where Tambling's argument is abstract and philosophical, Erik Levi focuses on the bureaucratic apparatuses and new operas composed under the Fascist regimes in Italy (1922–1945 under Mussolini) and Germany (1933–1945 under Hitler), but does not consider the occupied territories or the appropriation of extant opera for political purposes (Levi 1996). Opera under Italian Fascism has received comparatively little scholarly attention. Documented ties to Il Duce appear to have affected the study of operas by Respighi, Casella, Alfano, and Mascagni, although the collection *Italian Music during the Fascist Period* (Illiano 2004) represents first steps toward addressing that lacuna. Luigi Dallapiccola's Italianate, lyrical brand of dodecaphony appeals to the operatically inclined, while his retreat from Fascism makes him more palatable than some of his contemporaries. Ben Earle's analysis of Dallapiccola's masterpiece *Il prigioniero* in its original Cold War context, however, challenges facile readings of this work, standard since the 1950s, as mere twelve-tone music of commitment (Earle 2007).

While Puccini's *Turandot* is frequently invoked to demarcate the end of an era, some interpret it less as opera's apotheosis than its capitulation: *Turandot* delivers opera to spectacle, and this "is also its delivery to fascism, to its aesthetic of power through spectacle." They are particularly critical of its brutal, forced happy ending. "In this sense, the opera *Turandot*, as distinct from the intentions of its creators [...] and its producers [...] emerges as a fascist work" (Steinberg and Stewart-Steinberg 2007: 276). A tipping point was reached in 1934 when Respighi, Zandonai, Pizzetti, and other conservatives repudiated the modernism of Casella and Malipiero by publicly calling for a revival of the nineteenth-century tradition. Levi notes that the opera scene in Mussolini's Italy was not nearly as isolationist as that in contemporary Germany, however; works by Bartók, Hindemith, Berg, and Stravinsky were staged in Italy "long after their work had been proscribed by the Nazis" (Levi 1996: 273).

Opera during the Third Reich tends to elicit attempts to identify "Nazi Music," meaning music that "upheld the tenets of a central ideology and were artistically inferior" (Potter 2005b: 439–440). Such efforts are futile because the regime had no consistent aesthetic policy for opera or any other music, and was far more interested in the reach of popular entertainment such as operetta and radio (Heldt 2005: 158). Furthermore, "staging the Nazi movement itself, common in film and drama, was frowned upon in opera"; instead, newly composed operas tended to be based on folk tales, fairy tales, and classic subjects (Heldt 2005: 159). In terms of acceptable musical style, the most consistent feature was inconsistency. Despite the crusade against Degenerate Music there were "stark inconsistencies between the pronouncements against 'degeneracy' and the new operatic works that thrived—and even won Hitler's praise—in the Third Reich, despite their atonal and jazz-inspired scores that were noticeably reminiscent of works by Schoenberg, Krenek, and Weill" (Potter 2005b: 440). Some speculate about "operas that might have been," thanks to the mass emigration of composers with prior success in the genre who relocated and then retooled: Goldschmidt, Hindemith, Korngold, Krenek, Schoenberg, Toch, Weill, Wellesz, Wolpe, and Zemlinsky (Heldt 2005: 158; Taylor-Jay 2004). Of course, those hypothetical losses are negligible compared to the losses incurred by those who were unable to emigrate, such as the prisoners at the so-called model camp of Terezín. Viktor Ullmann's *Der Kaiser von Atlantis* and Hans Krása's children's opera *Brundibár* were both composed there and have garnered much recent attention in conjunction with Holocaust Studies (Laux 2005; Schultz 2007).

Pursuing research on opera during the Third Reich also leads down the rabbit hole of Wagner's operas, his descendants, Bayreuth, and the Führer (Friedländer and Rüsen 2000). Pamela Potter traces the roots of the controversy to Adorno's 1937 essay "In Search of Wagner," in which Adorno explicitly identified anti-Semitism "not only in Wagner's prose but also in several of his musical works" (Potter 2005: 752); interest, both scholarly and prurient, shows no sign of abating. Another perennially problematic figure is Richard Strauss, arguably the most famous German musician of his day, whose entanglement with the Party apparatus has been interpreted variously as naive, apolitical, and opportunistic (Potter 1992). The operas he wrote between 1933 and 1945 remain less well known than his earlier works, although Zychowicz submits that this should not be attributed to the political context but to an artistic one, since Strauss produced these works when he was no longer "the rebel, innovator, and Wunderkind," and while working without his longtime librettist Hofmannsthal (Zychowicz 2003: 286).

There was considerable musical-theater experimentation in the 1920s and early 1930s in the Soviet Union as well. In fact, this period could be considered a high point in Russian operatic life because of the wide array of operas being staged and the theatrical innovation on display in those productions (Bartlett 2008). There is little published on these forays into appropriately Soviet opera, however, save Ivan Dzerzhinsky's song opera *Tikhiy Don* (*Quiet Flows the Don*), which is assured a place in Soviet opera history as the ostensible role model against which Shostakovich's *Lady Macbeth of the Mtsensk District* was measured and found wanting (Taruskin 2000). *Lady Macbeth* has come to symbolize the artistic casualties of Stalin's purges. Marina Frolova-Walker outlines the policy ramifications of the *Lady Macbeth* affair, which resulted in a Stalinist Soviet opera project so beset by contradictions that no new work could meet bureaucratic expectations, and it was discontinued in 1946 (Frolova-Walker 2005).

Biography of a City: *Aufstieg und Fall der Stadt Mahagonny*

Few works better demonstrate the convergence of this welter of Wagner, modernism, and politics—not to mention genre—than Brecht and Weill's *Aufstieg und Fall der Stadt*

Mahagonny (1927–1929). Mahagonny is a fictional city in the United States, and the characters in the opera have distinctly Americanized names. This reflects a common trope of Weimar-era literature in which German authors formulated fantastical notions of that country derived from film and fiction, part land of opportunity and part land of capitalist exploitation and misery. The score features some musical Americana, as well, mostly in the form of pieces coopted from their 1927 *Mahagonny-Songspiel*, such as the famous "Alabama Song." Overall, however, Weill's score for *Aufstieg und Fall der Stadt Mahagonny* is far more opera than song, as indicated by its deliberate generic designation as an opera (this is discussed further below). As for the libretto, Americans may be struck by the artistic license taken with geography, since three fugitives found a pleasure city close enough to Alaska to attract men returning from mining and lumberjack work, yet close enough to Pensacola for that city to be described as "nearby." In fact, Mahagonny could be Las Vegas, if it were not for the great natural disaster of Act I: an approaching hurricane. The pleasures on offer there include eating, sex, fighting, and drinking, all available as long as one has the money. Overindulgence leads to death, however, and poverty is a capital offense. The male lead, Jim Mahoney, is brought up on a variety of charges, but he is ultimately executed because he has run out of money. The opera ends in chaos, with the citizens in disarray, the city on fire in the background, and the words "Nothing will help him or us or you now."

Brecht and Weill's brief, famously problematic yet highly productive partnership was a result of the cultural maelstrom that was Berlin during the Weimar Republic. The Greater Berlin Act of 1920 incorporated the surrounding areas into the city proper for the first time, and the capital was suddenly a sprawling metropolis with four million inhabitants. The modern city inspired all manner of art, even if only as model dystopia, as in Fritz Lang's silent film *Metropolis* (1927). Urban life as experienced in Berlin in the 1920s—a city known for its social and political agitation, cutting-edge art, and decadence—left its mark on five of Brecht and Weill's six musical theater collaborations. *Mahagonny-Songspiel, Die Dreigroschenoper, Happy End, Aufstieg und Fall der Stadt Mahagonny*, and *Die sieben Todsünden* treat the mostly negative effects of the modern city on the human condition (only *Der Jasager* does not). In fact, Stephen Hinton argues persuasively that the main character of *Aufstieg und Fall der Stadt Mahagonny* is actually the city of Mahagonny itself, and not any of the colorful characters who inhabit it. This is evident in the title as well as in the composer's plot synopsis, in which Weill identifies just one character by name (Jim Mahoney), and mentions him only twice. By comparison, Weill refers to the city fourteen times, and states explicitly that "the main character of the piece is the city, which emerges from people's needs" (Hinton 2012: 148–149). Of course, this was not the first time that a city had been important in an opera's plot; but while Paris is vital to *La traviata*, it does not vie with Violetta for center stage. Mahagonny is the star, and, just as the title promises, the opera is its biography. The city is the quintessentially modernist subject for an opera.

The list of Brecht and Weill's musical theater collaborations above can be taken as a representative sampling of the genre experimentation underway during this period. Their first version of the city of Mahagonny appeared onstage in *Mahagonny-Songspiel*, a twenty-five-minute work commissioned for the Deutsche Kammermusik Festival Baden-Baden in 1927. The generic designation is clearly intended as a play on the word *Singspiel* to signal retention of the format of numbers connected by spoken dialogue, with a nod toward its American-style songs. It was staged in a boxing ring. That material then formed the basis for *Aufstieg und Fall der Stadt Mahagonny*, a work written between 1927 and 1929 and explicitly designated as an opera. During this time, Brecht and Weill also completed *Die Dreigroschenoper* ("play with music in a prologue and three acts," 1928—and described by both as "the prototype of opera"), *Happy End* ("comedy with music in three acts," 1929), and *Der Jasager* ("Schuloper in two acts," 1930). Their last collaboration was the "sung ballet" *Die sieben Todsünden* (1933). To this list could be added the Lehrstück *Lindberghflug* (1929), a participatory piece in which the listener at home was meant to sing the title role while the work was broadcast on the radio. Both Weill and Hindemith contributed to the score.

As noted, much genre-bending represented artists' quest for alternatives to Wagner, and the same is true for Brecht and Weill. By the time the playwright met the composer, the former had recovered from his youthful, ardent dalliance with Wagner's operas. When Brecht derided opera writ large, he was actually complaining about the *Gesamtkunstwerk*, which he took as representative of the opera genre and all its problems: musical, theatrical, institutional, and social. He quite admired the operas of Mozart, so it was not as if he deemed the entire genre unsalvageable—just its most excessively Romantic version, and the narcotic effect he believed its continuous music had on the audience. Brecht opposed the Wagnerian theatricality that had become standard in German theaters, operatic or not, and approached the issue from the perspective of audience experience (Calico 2008). Weill was a protégée of the composer Ferruccio Busoni, who advocated alternatives to Wagner in aesthetics, form, and style. Each came to the partnership with his own idea for a type of "epic opera" that might provide a foil to the *Gesamtkunstwerk*. They found common ground in *Die Dreigroschenoper*, when Brecht seemed to think that eliminating the continuous musical score in favor of discrete numbers would render the music less effective. Weill, on the other hand, relished the return to a form of number opera. The songs from *Die Dreigroschenoper* became wildly popular as independent hits extracted from the show, a development that undermined Brecht's theory about the limited potency of music in that format.

All the while, they collaborated on the *Mahagonny* opera. Weill had considerable input into the libretto, even telling his publisher in November 1927 that "I have been working daily with Brecht on the libretto, which is being formed completely in accordance with my directions. This type of collaboration, on the basis of which a libretto is actually structured from a purely musical point of view, opens up whole new possibilities." The foreword he prepared in December 1929 for the publisher, Universal Edition, contains this unequivocal statement: "The subject matter of the opera *Aufstieg und Fall der Stadt Mahagonny* made possible a structure based purely on musical laws" (cited in Hinton 2012: 141). The commercial success of the *Dreigroschenoper* songs, coupled with Weill's public assertion that music was the most important element in the epic opera project, provoked a response from Brecht that is equal parts manifesto for epic theater and death certificate for opera ("Notes on the Opera 'Mahagonny'"). This statement accompanied his publication of the opera libretto in 1930, but it should be noted that the libretto he published was not the version Weill had composed. (Brecht frequently published revised versions of his texts. This has led to considerable miscommunication between musicologists and literary scholars, since the latter tend to focus on the final version of a text, while musicologists focus on the version set to music, which is usually early.) Brecht's heated and often theoretically oriented rhetoric can be confusing. Hinton draws a distinction between two components of Brecht's theory: epic structure and epic effect. The former is "a theory of creation, a poietics," and the latter is "a philosophy of performance and reception, an aesthetics" (Hinton 2012: 147). Pragmatically speaking, the collaborators parted ways because Weill advocated a return to a Mozartean structure akin to number opera, and Brecht, who could not abide the supremacy of music in that formulation, gave up the genre as beyond rehabilitation. Their notions of what would make an opera epic, which is essentially anti-Wagnerian, were no longer sufficiently compatible. Brecht would not complete another work designated as an opera until 1951, when he and Paul Dessau produced *Die Verurteilung des Lukullus* in what was by that time East Berlin. As Matthew W. Smith has shown, however, this did not prevent Brecht from assimilating the totalizing aspect of the *Gesamtkunstwerk* experience into his theories of epic theater (Smith: 2007).

As for its modernist credentials, *Aufstieg und Fall der Stadt Mahagonny* falls within Steinberg's parameters as laid out above by virtue of its date of composition and its reckoning with Wagner. Steinberg asserts that "[M]odernist opera is European, international, and emancipatory where its leading historical and political referents are German, nationalistic, and hegemonic" (Steinberg 2006: 631–632). This raises the question of whether it is even possible for a German opera to qualify as modernist, since its German identity is also its historical and political referent and, as laid out in this binary, the opposite of the essential modernist feature "European." Apparently the answer is "yes," since Steinberg goes on to discuss Strauss's *Salome* and *Elektra*, but these date from the first decade of the twentieth century, and he is largely silent on matters of German opera as he nears his cut-off date of 1933. Interestingly enough, Weill is not mentioned at all, an omission that may reflect persistent disciplinary differences between history and musicology. By contrast, literary scholar Herbert Lindenberger follows musicologist Alexander Ringer in his assessment that Schoenberg's *Moses und Aron* and *Aufstieg und Fall der Stadt Mahagonny* were the two pillars of the future of opera; Lindenberger positions them as antitheses, equally significant polar opposites (Lindenberger 1998).

For Steinberg, modernist opera is characterized by a post-nationalist style that challenges German hegemony in the form of Wagner's Opera as stand-in for all opera, and rejects Wagnerism's national mythology. Challenges to Wagner are abundant in *Aufstieg und Fall der Stadt Mahagonny*, although the extent to which they may be construed as post-nationalist is debatable. The first published vocal score plainly states that the names of characters can be changed to reflect the country of any given performance, since "the city of Mahagonny is in every sense international" (although in practice that rarely happens). Weill's effort to re-establish number opera as the definitive operatic structure and Brecht's attempts to undermine the anaesthetizing effects of continuous music both challenge the notion of Wagner as Opera, as does the use of projected inscriptions. Number opera is the basic form of *opera seria*, with its self-contained da capo arias joined by recitative, and it is also the basic formula for the musical, in which songs are linked by spoken dialogue. On both counts, Weill eschews Wagnerism. Nevertheless, the opera features continuous music with recitative and significant orchestral segments. Furthermore, it features numerous allusions to works from the operatic canon (Mozart's *Zauberflöte*, Beethoven's *Fidelio*, Verdi's *Il trovatore*, and Wagner's *Tristan und Isolde*), as well as demonstrations of considerable craft in the arts of the neo-Baroque: counterpoint, as in the musical rendering of the hurricane, and cantilena, in the ethereal "Crane Duet" (Hinton 2012: 151–152). On the other hand, the score also includes contemporary dance rhythms, the song form and song style he had cultivated in previous works, and traces of the "austere classicism" he had undertaken for *Der Jasager* (Hinton 2012: 101). Hinton astutely compares this marriage of styles to that found in late Mozart, wherein "the 'learned style' (*stile antico*) is played off against the more modern and more obviously popular 'gallant style'" (Hinton 2012: 151). Ultimately, Weill was committed to the perpetuation of the opera species. He did so by preserving those elements of the tradition he found most useful and combining them with the Weimar-Republic equivalent of the galant style. In terms of musical style, then, *Aufstieg und Fall der Stadt Mahagonny* does pose a challenge to German hegemony in the sense that said German hegemony was Wagner as stand-in for Opera, but its DNA is still recognizably Austro-German. "German" as historical and political referent was perhaps unavoidable, but the other pre-modernist vices, "nationalist" and "hegemonic," are conspicuously absent.

Nazi politics shaped the fate of *Aufstieg und Fall der Stadt Mahagonny* from its first performance, which took place at Leipzig's Neues Theater on March 9, 1930. It was supposed to have premiered in Berlin. Otto Klemperer had agreed to give the first performance at the Kroll Oper, but he (like the publishers) balked at the libretto, and other arrangements had to be made. The Nazi party was making significant political inroads by this time, and they instigated protests against the Jewish Weill at the Leipzig performance. Weill's wife Lotte Lenya was with him that night, and recalled the scene as follows:

> I have been told that the square around the opera house was filled with Nazi Brown Shirts, carrying placards protesting at the "Mahagonny" performance. But I had come to Leipzig the day of the performance, and I could see, hear, think nothing but "Mahagonny"; Kurt's parents and I were in our seats, and the performance well underway, before I was startled out of my absorption by the electric tension around us, something strange and ugly. As the opera swept toward its close, the demonstrations started, whistles and boos; by the time the last scene was reached, fist fights had broken out in the aisles, the theatre was a screaming mass of people; soon the riot had spread to the stage, panicky spectators were trying to claw their way out, and only the arrival of a large police force finally cleared the theatre. (Lenya 1959: 8)

Subsequent performances in Braunschweig and Kassel could go on only after the artists had agreed to make cuts that would render the opera less offensive, although these sanitized versions elicited protests as well; a performance in Frankfurt in October 1930 was likewise disrupted by Nazi demonstrations. In December 1931 the impresario Ernst Joseph Aufricht finally got a performance onstage in Berlin, at the Theater am Kurfürstendamm. This version was severely reduced and truncated to accommodate the performers, who were mostly singing actors known to Weill and Brecht from *Die Dreigroschenoper*.

Nazi politics also shaped the fate of the opera's creators. A Jewish composer and a Marxist playwright were easy targets for the regime, and their works were suppressed until 1945. Both fled Germany, and, like so many other European intellectuals in this period, went to the United States. Weill emigrated with Lenya in 1935, became an American citizen, and took New York by storm, ruling Broadway for the last several years of his life; he died in 1950 at age 50. Brecht finally landed at the port of Los Angeles in 1941, where he eked out a living until he was called to testify before the House Committee on Un-American Activities (HUAC) during the Red Scare of 1947; he fled to Europe before he could be further detained. He died in 1956, having spent his last years in East Germany at the helm of his dedicated theater, the Berliner Ensemble. The two scarcely communicated while both were in the United States.

See also: Politics, The Language of National Style, Critics

Bibliography

Ashbrook, William, and Harold Powers. 1991. *Puccini's 'Turandot': The End of the Great Tradition*. Princeton, NJ: Princeton University Press.

Bartlett, Rosamund. 2008. "Shostakovich as an Opera Composer." In *The Cambridge Companion to Shostakovich*, edited by Pauline Fairclough and David Fanning, 179–197. Cambridge: Cambridge University Press.

Berghaus, Günter. 1998. *Italian Futurist Theatre, 1909–1944*. New York: Oxford University Press.

Budden, Julian. 2005. *Puccini: His Life and Works*. New York: Oxford University Press.

——. 1987. "Wagnerian Tendencies in Italian Opera." In *Music and Theatre: Essays in Honour of Winton Dean*, edited by Nigel Fortune, 299–332. Cambridge: Cambridge University Press.

Calico, Joy H. 2008. *Brecht at the Opera*. Berkeley and Los Angeles: University of California Press.

Cooke, Mervyn, ed. 2005. *The Cambridge Companion to Twentieth-Century Music*. Cambridge: Cambridge University Press.

Deathridge, John. 2005. "Wagner and Beyond." In Cooke 2005, 14–25.

d'Indy, Vincent. 1930. *Richard Wagner et son influence sur l'art musical français*. Paris: Delagrave.

Earle, Ben. 2007. "Dallapiccola and the Politics of Commitment: Re-reading *Il prigioniero*." *Radical Musicology* 2. Online. Available: http://www.radical-musicology.org.uk/2007/earle.htm (accessed August 22, 2012).

Fauser, Annegret, and Manuela Schwartz. 1999. *Von Wagner zum Wagnérisme: Musik, Literatur, Kunst, Politik*. Leipzig: Leipziger Universitätsverlag.

Friedländer, Saul, and Jörn Rüsen, eds. 2000. *Richard Wagner im Dritten Reich: ein Schloss Elmau-Symposion*. Munich: Beck.

Frolova-Walker, Marina. 2005. "Russian Opera: Between Modernism and Romanticism." In Cooke 2005, 181–196.

Fulcher, Jane F. 2005. *The Composer as Intellectual: Music and Ideology in France 1914–1940*. New York: Oxford University Press.

Gilliam, Bryan. 2014. *Rounding Wagner's Mountain: Richard Strauss and Modern German Opera*. Cambridge: Cambridge University Press.

Hailey, Christopher. 2002. "Franz Schreker and the Pluralities of Modernism." *Tempo* 219: 2–7.

Heldt, Guido. 2005. "Austria and Germany, 1918–1960." In Cooke 2005, 146–164.

Hennion, Antoine. 2007. "Rewriting History from the Losers' Point of View: French Grand Opera and Modernity," translated by Sarah Boittin. In Johnson et al. 2007, 330–350.

Hinton, Stephen. 2012. *Weill's Musical Theater: Stages of Reform*. Berkeley and Los Angeles: University of California Press.

Huebner, Steven. 2006. *French Opera at the Fin de Siècle: Wagnerism, Nationalism, and Style*. New York: Oxford University Press.

Illiano, Roberto, ed. 2004. *Italian Music during the Fascist Period*. Turnhout: Brepols.

Johnson, Victoria, Jane F. Fulcher, and Thomas Ertman, eds. 2007. *Opera and Society in Italy and France from Monteverdi to Bourdieu*. Cambridge: Cambridge University Press.

Katz, Derek. 2009. *Janáček: Beyond the Borders*. Rochester, NY: University of Rochester Press.

Kelly, Barbara L. 2008. "Debussy and the Making of a *musicien français: Pelléas*, the Press, and World War I." In *French Music, Culture, and National Identity, 1870–1939*, edited by Barbara L. Kelly, 58–76. Rochester, NY: University of Rochester Press.

——. 2003. *Tradition and Style in the Works of Darius Milhaud, 1912–1939*. Aldershot, UK: Ashgate.

Kirsch, Winfried, and Sieghart Döhring, eds. 1991. *Geschichte und Dramaturgie des Opernakters*. Laaber: Laaber-Verlag.

Kramer, Lawrence. 2004. *Opera and Modern Culture: Wagner and Strauss*. Berkeley and Los Angeles: University of California Press.

Lenya, Lotte. 1959. "I Remember Mahagonny." *Philips Music Herald* 4/1: 6–9.

Levi, Erik. 1996. "Toward an Aesthetic of Fascist Opera." In *Fascism and Theatre: Comparative Studies on the Aesthetics and Politics of Performance in Europe, 1925–1945*, edited by Günter Berghaus, 260–276. Oxford: Berghahn.

Lindenberger, Herbert. 1998. *Opera in History: From Monteverdi to Cage*. Stanford, CA: Stanford University Press.

Locke, Brian S. 2006. *Opera and Ideology in Prague: Polemics and Practice at the National Theater, 1900–1938*. Rochester, NY: University of Rochester Press.

Mallach, Alan. 2007. *The Autumn of Italian Opera: From Verismo to Modernism, 1890–1915*. Lebanon, NH: Northeastern University Press.

Pasler, Jann. 2007. "A Sociology of the Apaches: Sacred Battalion for *Pelléas*." In *Berlioz and Debussy: Sources, Contexts, and Legacies: Essays in Honour of François Lesure*, edited by Barbara L. Kelly and Kerry Murphy, 149–166. Aldershot, UK: Ashgate.

——. 1987. "*Pelléas* and Power: Forces behind the Reception of Debussy's Opera." *19th-Century Music* 10: 243–264.

Potter, Pamela. 2005a. "Wagner, Richard." In *Antisemitism: A Historical Encyclopedia of Prejudice and Persecution*, edited by Richard S. Levy. Santa Barbara, CA: ABC-Clio.

——. 2005b. "What is Nazi Music?" *Musical Quarterly* 88/3: 428–455.

——. 1992. "Strauss and the National Socialists: The Debate and its Relevance." In *Richard Strauss: New Perspectives on the Composer and His Work*, edited by Bryan Gilliam, 93–113. Durham, NC: Duke University Press.

Riethmüller, Albrecht, and Hyesu Shin, eds. 2004. *Busoni in Berlin: Facetten eines kosmopolitischen Komponisten*. Stuttgart: F. Steiner.

Robinson, Paul. 2002. *Opera, Sex, and Other Vital Matters*. Chicago: University of Chicago Press.

Sheppard, W. Anthony. 2001. *Revealing Masks: Exotic Influences and Ritualized Performance in Modernist Music Theater*. Berkeley and Los Angeles: University of California Press.

Simeone, Nigel. 2005. "A Chronology of Twentieth-Century Operatic Premieres." In Cooke 2005, xviii–xlvii.

Smith, Mathew Wilson. 2007. *The Total Work of Art: From Bayreuth to Cyberspace*. New York: Routledge.

Sobaskie, James William. 2003. *La modernité et l'humanité de 'Pénélope' de Gabriel Fauré*. Nantes: Université de Nantes.

Steinberg, Michael P. 2006. "The Politics and Aesthetics of Operatic Modernism." *Journal of Interdisciplinary History* 36/4: 629–648.

——, and Suzanne Stewart-Steinberg. 2007. "Fascism and the Operatic Unconscious." In Johnson et al. 2007, 267–289.

Tambling, Jeremy. 1997. *Opera and the Culture of Fascism*. Oxford: Clarendon Press.

Taruskin, Richard. 2000. *Defining Russia Musically: Historical and Hermeneutical Essays*. Princeton, NJ: Princeton University Press.

Taylor-Jay, Claire. 2004. *The Artist-Operas of Pfitzner, Krenek, and Hindemith: Politics and the Ideology of the Artist*. Alsderhot, UK: Ashgate.

Timms, Andrew. 2009. "Modernism's Moment of Plenitude." In *The Modernist Legacy: Essays on New Music*, edited by Björn Heile, 13–24. Aldershot, UK: Ashgate.

Waterhouse, John C. G. 1994. "Verso la 'seconda maniera': Casella e l'avanguardi internazionale del primo Novecento." In *Alfredo Casella negli anni di apprendistato a Parigi*, edited by Giovanni Morelli, 175–186. Florence: Olschki.

——. 1999. *Gian Francesco Malipiero 1882–1973: The Life, Times, and Music of a Wayward Genius*. Amsterdam: Harwood Academic.

Weill, Kurt. 1958. *Aufstieg und Fall der Stadt Mahagonny*. LP recording. Columbia K3L 243.

Wilson, Alexandra. 2007. *The Puccini Problem*. Cambridge: Cambridge University Press.

Wolff, Lawrence. 2006. "Commentary: The Operatic Tragedy of Central Europe." *Journal of Interdisciplinary History* 36/4: 683–695.

Zychowicz, James L. 2003. "The Late Operas of Richard Strauss." In *The Richard Strauss Companion*, edited by Mark-Daniel Schmid, 285–299. Westport, CT: Praeger.

CHAPTER 49

AFTER THE CANON

ROBERT FINK

> But opera, with its traditional audience, has cut itself off from time and change. It lives in a ghetto. Opera can only be compared to a church where the parishioners' highest desire is to keep on singing their 18th-century cantatas. I have no desire to liberate the people who voluntarily suffocate themselves in the ghetto—I have no objection to that type of suicide.
>
> (Boulez 1967)

> Do words not matter in opera? It's not something I'd thought about, because opera is so often in a foreign language, which discourages close reading. But I began to wonder whether opera follows different rules: Because words are sung, do they transcend any bombastic triviality, any wounding awfulness?
>
> (Rosenbaum 2008)

Blow Up the Opera Houses!

In the early morning hours of November 2, 2001, conductor Pierre Boulez was detained by Swiss security forces, whose cross-check of hotel registries against a list of those known to have made "terroristic" statements in the past turned up the name of a famous composer and modernist musical intellectual. Evidently a malicious critic had once phoned in a complaint to the Swiss authorities that Boulez had threatened to "blow him up" after a bad review; the accusation went unchallenged, and, correlated with a record of Boulez's own incendiary comments about opera in a 1967 interview with the German weekly *Der Spiegel*, formed enough of a pattern to justify the temporary confiscation of his passport and some pointed questions before he headed off to the airport.

The interview had been published under the provocative title "Blow Up the Opera Houses! ("Sprengt die Opernhaüser in die Luft!"), something that Boulez had indeed said, and though the Swiss took a fair amount of ribbing for their literal-mindedness, the rhetorical violence of Boulez's rejection of the postwar operatic scene remains striking. The call to blow up opera houses was in fact one of the milder moments of the conversation, presented ironically as an "elegant, if costly" solution to a proliferation of outmoded designs that prevented even the newest of German concert halls from embracing technical advances in staging. No aspect of postwar operatic culture escaped the revolutionary's wrath: the opera world was a self-segregating "ghetto" for intellectual suicides; the typical opera house was a "musty closet," a "music museum"; the one he knew best, in Paris, was badly maintained, full of "dust and shit," fit only for musical "tourists" whose taste he found "sickening." Boulez's prescription for this sclerotic opera culture was a therapeutic "bloodletting" along Maoist lines, complete with imported cadres of Red Guards to crack heads (Boulez 1967).

A savage attack on decrepit musical institutions is always news, as the editors of *Der Spiegel* were well aware; harder to accept, perhaps, was Boulez's categorical disinterest in the last thirty years of contemporary opera: "I stand by that: Since Alban Berg's *Wozzeck* and *Lulu* not a single opera worthy of discussion has been composed." Boulez was brutally dismissive of new works by Henze ("a hairdresser flogging superficial modernism") and Blacher ("movie set music"), and was completely unimpressed by the number of operatic commissions handed out to young composers by the German authorities: "I don't think you can commission a new movement into life. It's like saying that an obstetrician is sufficient to bring a child into the world. There's something else that needs to happen first." Nor was he himself interested in reforming or saving contemporary opera from its devotees, who seemed to him perfectly happy in their eighteenth-century intellectual ghetto.

Boulez spoke to *Der Spiegel* as a composer-*provocateur*, the antithesis of a disinterested cultural critic, but his blanket dismissal of opera after 1945 as aesthetically and ideologically irrelevant cannot be ignored. The second half of the twentieth century presents a strange series of paradoxes to the historian of opera. New opera houses and companies proliferated in the boom years of the 1950s and 1960s across Europe and America; and yet, in the large houses, the core operatic repertory focused ever more tightly on a small (and shrinking) number of nineteenth-century works, while the Continental triumph of *Regietheater*, or "director's opera," underscored the desire to make the increasingly old seem new (Chaikin 2010: 132–171). Advances in recording technology and the advent of inexpensive long-playing records made diverse performances of a wide range of operatic literature available for the first time to a mass public (Day 2000: 101–102); but the 1950s saw the final collapse of the touring companies that had once brought metropolitan opera to provincial audiences (Horowitz 2005: 494–495). Cold War cultural politics targeted new music for state support, and operatic commissions were no exception, but Boulez was right: few of the new works produced on either side of the Iron Curtain would outlive their propaganda value.

Perhaps most complex and paradoxical was the relationship in the late twentieth century between compositional technique and the demands of public theater. It is a broad but supportable generalization that, since the birth of monody, most technical advances in Western musical composition and performance have been driven by the spectacular expressive needs—and grandiose budgets—of serious opera. The linkage is clearest, perhaps, at the center of the nineteenth-century repertory, studded with avant-garde populists (Rossini, Meyerbeer) who developed elaborately "modern" techniques of harmony and orchestration to impress ever broader swathes of the new bourgeois public. In the music dramas of Wagner, this fusion of technical sophistication and mass stage appeal found definitive expression, setting the terms upon which Western art music would "progress" into the new century. But by the late 1960s, it was arguable that Berg's two intricate, sensational operatic masterpieces had indeed "finished off that chapter" (Boulez 1967). All the important postwar technical innovations in musical composition—total serialism, indeterminacy and chance, the turn to electronics and computers—were defiantly hermetic and abstract, with advanced composers like Boulez, Babbitt, and Stockhausen making a cardinal virtue out of their post-Fascist reluctance to move the masses. A few members of the avant-garde did continue with opera as a public art. Some tried to "out-Berg" Berg (Zimmermann, *Die Soldaten*, 1964; Ligeti, *Le grand macabre*, 1974–1977); others stoically thematized the fear that their work was anachronistic (Britten, *Death in Venice*, 1973); some refused to call their stage works "operas," preferring the less loaded and more politically up-to-date term "action," as in "musical action" (Berio, *Un re in ascolto*, 1979–1983), "theatrical action" (Nono, *Prometeo*, 1984), or "actions for music" (Henze, *We Come to the River*, 1976). The controversial Henze was a logical target for Boulez's hauteur; after working along the neoclassical lines of Stravinsky's *The Rake's Progress* with Auden and Kallmann on *Elegy for Young Lovers* (1961), Henze went on to proclaim in 1963 that "[e]verything [in music] tends towards theatre, and returns again from it" (Henze 1982: 131). As a gay man with a taste for operatic display, Henze's personal and professional isolation in avant-garde circles had made the German musical scene claustrophobic for him (he decamped to Italy in 1953). For self-consciously avant-garde composers, Henze's interest in the opera house as a setting for raw emotion and political spectacle could only be seen as aesthetically retrograde, its crowd-assembling-and-pleasing social function better served by popular music and Hollywood movies (Taruskin 2010: Chapter 5).

In a development that Boulez would never have anticipated, it was the collapse of the avant-garde for which he spoke that returned twentieth-century opera to the forefront of classical music consciousness. The most significant development in late-twentieth-century opera may well have been its transformative alliance with a growing trend inside post-Cage musical experimentalism that Michael Nyman dubbed in 1974 the "new determinacy" (Nyman [1974] 2002: 139–171). Repetitive music, or "minimalism," as it later became generally known, was originally just another species of postwar formalism, as rigid and impersonal in its demands as the integral serialism advocated by Boulez and his followers. But by the 1980s, in the hands of composers like Philip Glass and John Adams, operatic minimalism had unexpectedly developed into the prime musical example of a postmodernist "trans-avant-garde," invested more in sensuality and the expressive techniques of the past than avant-garde purity of purpose (Oliva 1993). With minimalist repetition in opera came a return to regular rhythm and affective tonal relationships as the organizing force behind staged spectacle. (The 1975 choral piece in which Glass worked out the musical language for his breakthrough *Einstein on the Beach* [1976] was titled, programmatically, *Another Look at Harmony.*)

The fact that Glass's first "opera" had its North American premiere at New York's Metropolitan Opera House was a fluke: it was late summer, the house was dark, and thus available for enterprising avant-gardists to rent, no aesthetic questions asked. *Einstein on the Beach* was an opera in name only, a five-hour abstraction with no plot, no characters, no arias, no trained singers, no orchestra, and no intermissions. But the technical and sonic demands of the staged production meant that *Einstein* toured through the opera houses of Europe, catching the attention of the same intendants whose commissions Boulez had found so sterile a decade before. As Glass recalls it, his second big stage work, *Satyagraha* (1980), was a response to Hans de Roo's post-*Einstein* request for "a *real* opera," one that used "[the Netherlands Opera] orchestra, chorus and soloists, people trained and practiced in the singing of traditional operas" (Glass 1987: 87). The result was a "grave, formal, lyrical and beautiful" work for which the postwar self-absorption in compositional technique was definitively set aside: "No one could listen to the *Satyagraha* score without realizing that the music is about more than its sounds, structures, figurations, and procedures" (Porter 1981: 97–98).

By the end of the twentieth century, opera, allying itself with the most vibrant strand of the musical trans-avant-garde, seemed to have recaptured Wagner's synthesis of the technically new and the socially relevant. Glass returned to the Met in 1992 through the front door, with *The Voyage*, an opera commissioned to commemorate the 500th anniversary of the discovery of America. John Adams and director Peter Sellars combined the expansive tonal language of minimalism with other trans-avant-gardist tricks like stylistic pastiche and high-low fusion to create the blockbuster success *Nixon in China* (1987), a self-conscious updating of *Boris Godunov* for the age of media simulation (Kamuf 1993). Boulez, it appeared, had gotten it all wrong.

Opera and Drama at the Twilight of the Canon

In fact, not only had opera escaped the ghetto to which Boulez consigned it; for some critics, the continued vitality of opera as a public art was the only piece of good news about classical music itself. The story of opera at the turn of the twenty-first century took place under the gathering gloom of an extended twilight of Western art music, in which the fate of opera was caught up in the larger question of whether classical music itself was "dying" (Fink 1998; Kramer 2007b). Joseph Kerman, whose *Opera as Drama* ([1956] 1988) had set the parameters of postwar American operatic criticism, was, on behalf of the operas he loved, openly impatient with arguments to "the morbidity of classical music," which he labeled a metaphor gone bad, "a tired, vacuous concept that will not die" (Kerman 2008: 7). Kerman's determined optimism was rooted in his belief that the tradition of operatic classicism could still be vital *as drama:* "to the most damaging charge that the culture levels at classical music, its inability to renew itself, opera gives the lie. Music must generate an expanded repertory that will arouse critics and attract audiences; opera is doing this" (Kerman 2008: 15). In fact, for Kerman, opera, not the symphony, was the lifeline of classical music, a hardy species of musical theater whose total disappearance, unlike instrumental concert music, was inconceivable. Opera, he claimed, had "world history" on its side (Kerman 2008: 19).

This idea has a long pedigree. Early-seventeenth-century opera was the first secular style to challenge church music as serious public art, justifying itself by explicit recourse to the civic theater of ancient Greece (the original "Classics"). As it spread across Europe, lyric tragedy thus made non-liturgical music intellectually respectable, giving vocal melody an important new job (the imitation of emotionally heightened speech), and linking the craft of musical composition to newly revalued classical ideals of rhetoric and ethics. For much of Western music history, composing an operatic tragedy was a serious endeavor, while instrumental music, however carefully crafted, was considered frivolous, a mere "playing with sensations," as Immanuel Kant famously remarked ("[Musik]... bloß mit Empfindungen spielt..."; [1790] 1908: V: 329). Sonatas and concertos had little to do with deep thought or big ideas; they were agreeable space and time fillers, more likely to fade into the background than challenge the mind. It was only when the mercantile bourgeoisie became the main supporters and consumers of opera that aristocrats and musical intellectuals deployed transcendental idealism (and German symphonies) to fight the *nouveaux-riches* and their taste for expensive spectacle (Weber 2008: 85–121). From the operatic perspective, the entire "uplifting" discourse of classical music is based in anti-theatrical prejudice and class resentment. Why then should opera stoop to save classical music, when the very idea of musical "classicism" had been hijacked to cordon off its unwelcome fans?

Some of the highest-profile operatic ventures in the post-classical world of the early twenty-first century have foundered on just this contradiction between the inclusive values of opera and the self-reflexive ideology of classical music. Simply put, it was not possible at the turn of the twenty-first century for serious opera to *save* classical music without, in some sense *being* classical music; and if opera was to be classical music, then its sense of itself as "serious" could hardly escape being infected by the solipsistic value system of the Western musical canon, where art music would rather languish alone than cede its hard-won independence from language and drama. *Prima la musica e poi le parole* has been the canonical slogan as far back as 1786, when a burlesque of that title by G. B. Casti (with music by court composer Salieri) was staged opposite Mozart's *Der Schauspieldirektor* in the cavernous *orangerie* of Vienna's Schönbrunn Palace: first the music, and [only] then the words. If, as Kerman has argued, opera's saving essence is the bond between cultivated art music and the endlessly renewable vitality of theater (Kerman 2008: 19), its greatest threat may well be decaying fallout from the nineteenth-century explosion of "absolute" instrumental music.

It will be useful to consider a specific case study, an eagerly awaited contemporary opera on perhaps the definitive postwar subject, the making and deployment of the atomic bomb. The critical reception of John Adams's and Peter Sellars's *Doctor Atomic* (2005) is a particularly good test of the staying power of traditionally staged opera as public drama, given the extraordinary expectations attendant on this much-hyped premiere from the creative team responsible for both the most successful political opera of the postwar era, *Nixon in China*, and one of its most notorious failures, *The Death of Klinghoffer* (1991). Crucially, those two previous operas had verse libretti composed in pungent English vernacular by poet Alice Goodman; in this they differ from Philip Glass's operatic trilogy, where the verbal drama takes a back seat to surrealistic stage pageantry. The Adams-Sellars-Goodman operas conformed, unlike almost anything around them in the postwar era, to Kerman's ideal of opera as drama, drawing equally on the power of words and music. But *Doctor Atomic*, thanks to power imbalances in its creative team, entered the world without a librettist. The music came first and last, and the creative team, just as in Salieri and Casti's little farce, tried to adapt preexisting poetry and prose to the expediencies of musical drama. The general disappointment in the result shows what happens when a contemporary composer and director presume hubristically on continued patience with *prima la musica, e poi le parole* outside a small coterie of classical music devotees. No opera houses were detonated; but the mystique of sung drama did suffer some serious collateral damage.

A Faustian Bargain

The impulse to create a new opera on the subject of J. Robert Oppenheimer and the Manhattan Project did not come from John Adams, nor did it spring, like many new operatic ventures, from a desire to annex the popularity of a preexisting movie, play, or novel.[1] The idea occurred to Pamela Rosenberg, the ambitious general director of the San Francisco Opera, who imagined Oppenheimer as "an American Faust." Here was a commission, thought Rosenberg, whose dramatic armature could draw on perhaps the most powerful theatrical trope of modernity, the Faustian "quest for ultimate knowledge" (Gurewitsch 2005).

Goethe's *Faust* as the inspiration for a grand opera prioritizes the German perspective on "serious" music that looks away from the opera house and back to the concert hall. Yes, Busoni tried to write a Faust opera (*Doktor Faust*, 1924), and Gounod's saccharine 1859 version is still a mainstay of the *théâtre lyrique*. But truly serious treatments of the Faust legend have occurred mostly in symphonic guise: Berlioz's rarely staged *Le damnation de Faust*, Liszt's "Faust" Symphony, or the second half of Mahler's titanic Eighth. Arguably, the most influential musical readings of Goethe's *Faust* are still the earliest, ideal ones imposed directly onto the symphonies of Beethoven by Wagner, A. B. Marx, and other nineteenth-century German critics (Fink 2004: 116–119). It is hard to escape the notion that Rosenberg was hoping to entice a modern Beethoven, the man she considered the "greatest composer alive," back into her house by offering him a Faustian theme worthy of symphonic *Sturm und Drang*. Approached in early 2000,

Adams initially demurred, saying he "had no more operas in him," but eventually he succumbed to his desire to "say something immensely important, yet also reach a lot of people" (Ross 2005: 63). In this same interview, Adams disavowed that his work actually was the American *Faust* that Rosenberg wanted: "I didn't want this opera to come into the world loaded with that baggage." But the trope appears, nonetheless, in almost every review (Tommasini 2005).

Adams took on the commission in 2002; at some point before September of the next year, librettist Alice Goodman withdrew from the project.[2] Rather than find a replacement, Adams and Sellars chose to assemble the opera's text themselves from preexisting material, as they had done with the Bible stories and political poetry that made up Adams's Nativity oratorio, *El Niño* (2000). Abandoning the wide-angle view of the original libretto, which would have followed Oppenheimer into the 1950s and his battle with Edward Teller over the hydrogen bomb, Sellars immersed himself in the historical minutiae of Los Alamos: transcripts of wartime meetings and military orders; memoirs, interviews, and letters written by the participants; detailed diagrams and photos of the spherical "Gadget" itself, dripping with wires, destined to be the centerpiece of the stage set; and, most sensationally, reams of newly declassified documents from the Manhattan Project. The chronology of the opera shrank to just the few days before the first atomic test on July 16, 1945, and the goal became to create a documentary mosaic of journalistic immediacy within which, as *The New Yorker* admiringly reported, "almost every line could be checked against a source" (Ross 2005: 62).

The final libretto was assembled, not composed: Sellars's research provided a ready stream of urgent, rat-a-tat recitative; the collaborators fashioned lyrical arias from contemplative poetry, favoring passages from authors whose words the hyper-literate Oppenheimer habitually used in writing and conversation (Donne, Baudelaire, the Bhagavad Gita). The liberal use of declassified documents allowed Sellars to designate the radically pruned story as a moral fable, even though it shied away from representing either the "sin" of Hiroshima or the eventual downfall of its Faustian scientific protagonists. As Sellars glossed it during a workshop preview of the opera eleven months before its premiere, his libretto sought to provide an abstract yet powerful vehicle for healing through recovered memory.

> And [now we] ask these artists to go into an area of such deep toxicity, and out of that bring something of beauty—of lasting beauty—which is why the libretto consists of classified documents that were meant to be buried alive forever. And now that very thing that President Truman was not allowed to read—because the security apparatus kept it away from the President of the United States—is being sung in the clear light of day by chorus and orchestra . . . which again offers some hope for the world. (Sellars 2004)[3]

The creation of a "memory space" around a holocaust-like event, rather than direct engagement through representational storytelling, was a change in strategy strongly validated by the 2003 Pulitzer Prize awarded to Adams for his multimedia composition *On the Transmigration of Souls* (2002). Written to commemorate the attacks of September 11, 2001, this work for chorus and orchestra avoids all but the most symbolic representation of that day's events, and like Sellars's libretto for *Doctor Atomic,* assembles its "found" texts into an abstract meditation on transgression and loss.

It was thus clear by 2004, as Adams began to compose, inspired sonically by the bombast of 1950s science fiction soundtracks and the craggy modernism of Edgard Varèse, that *Doctor Atomic* was, to put it in slightly crass terms, going to be a tough sell. Audiences would not get operatic tragedy in the full-blooded mode of *Faust*: They would *not* hear the hubristic Oppenheimer exult, "I am become Death, destroyer of worlds" (Freed 1965); they would *not* see the bomb drop on innocent civilians; they would *not* watch with mounting pity and terror as nemesis, in the form of Edward Teller and the twin furies of anti-communism and the arms race, drove Doctor Atomic to his final disgrace. Sellars's static, foreshortened libretto was elliptical to a fault: he refused on aesthetic principle to represent the devastating reality of an atomic blast, a theatrical coup Adams also flinched away from, agreeing that it would have been "clichéd on arrival" (Tommasini 2005). Pamela Rosenberg's dream of a blockbuster opera, the new American *Faust,* was turning into a dissonant symphonic poem harnessed to a documentary work of experimental theater. A trenchant critical observer once usefully summed up the history of classical concert promotion in America as the perennial struggle between commercialized "ballyhoo" and quasi-religious "uplift" (Horowitz 1994: 17–42); given the grim, abstract tone of *Doctor Atomic,* selling it to the traditional opera public with the usual ballyhoo was not an obvious option.

Certainly no effort or expense was spared to create an explosion of publicity, a "cultural chain reaction," around *Doctor Atomic* (Winn 2005a); as one jaded critic noted, "new operas are always big events, but the hype surrounding this one went off the scale" (Swed 2005). What was needed was uplift *as* ballyhoo, a concerted attempt to embed the premiere(s) in a general outpouring of intellectualized excitement. In San Francisco, the opera was positioned as part of an interdisciplinary consideration of history, science, morality, and aesthetics, and its launch was accompanied by a flotilla of ancillary cultural events involving the Bay Area's major universities, the San Francisco Exploratorium, the Pacific Film Archive, the Berkeley Art Museum, the Metanexus Institute, the Left Coast Ensemble, and the American Physical Society. The *Doctor Atomic* push in New York was even stronger, a veritable Manhattan Project of arts management built around a new production by Penny Woolcock, the British director who had made a controversial 2002 film of Adams's *The Death of Klinghoffer*. As *The New Yorker*'s online blog somewhat ambivalently noted, Peter Gelb, general director of the Met, "promoted the heck out of" *Doctor Atomic,* using Sloan Foundation money to put a bevy of academic humanists, physicists, and playwrights at the Graduate Center of the City University of New York in dialogue with the creative team, cast, and director of the production, veterans of the A-bomb project, political historians, and other public intellectuals at Lincoln Center ("They're promoting the heck out of it"; see Platt 2008). Sometimes ballyhoo led to strangely insensitive juxtapositions: the fact that Met conductor Alan Gilbert was of

Japanese-American heritage was grist for the publicity mill, motivating a presentation to the Japan Society of New York, an audience that one might assume would be particularly allergic to Hiroshima-inspired hype.

With the release of Sellars's DVD version of the original San Francisco production of *Doctor Atomic* in the summer of 2008, and the Metropolitan Opera premiere that fall, Adams, who often worried in interviews about the relevance of contemporary classical music to the mass audience of late capitalism, came as close to cultural ubiquity as any twenty-first-century opera composer could get. This important premiere deserved the largest possible audience, so Gelb's Metropolitan put the full force of its national media connections behind *Doctor Atomic*. The opera was broadcast four times over the XM/Sirius satellite radio network and streamed over the Internet from the Metropolitan's website; on Saturday, November 8, a matinee performance of *Doctor Atomic* was simulcast in High Definition video to movie theaters in major cities around the globe. Back at the Met, in a gesture that Gelb hailed as a blow struck on behalf of "the democratization of art," wealthy opera patrons Karl Leichtman and Agnes Varis bought up $500,000 dollars worth of premium orchestra seats and announced they would resell them to the public for just $30 (Michaels 2008). Call it uplift or ballyhoo—no expense would be spared to spread *Doctor Atomic*'s fallout as broadly as possible across the landscape of American arts, letters, and science.

The opera's critical reception between 2005 and 2008 thus affords an optimal set of data with which to test the Kerman hypothesis: Would *Doctor Atomic*, transforming the Manhattan Project into a quasi-Faustian meditation on apocalypse with music by America's most famous living composer (and the canny backing of America's most powerful cultural institutions), justify the inheritance of nineteenth-century classical music to the educated bourgeois audience of the twenty-first century? Would the Gadget actually go off?

A Three-Hour Symphony of Dread

The San Francisco premiere of *Doctor Atomic* was an international cultural event, covered across the United States and Western Europe; subsequent premieres in Chicago and Amsterdam received less attention, but the New York premiere inspired another massive burst of press coverage (see the bibliography for a listing of key notices and reviews, 2002–2009). The overall tenor of its reception justifies David Patrick Stearns's retrospective observation that "few major operas enter the world with so little critical consensus as *Doctor Atomic*" (Stearns 2008). In fact, collective analysis of the opera's strengths and weaknesses has remained relatively consistent over the years. But except for a few unequivocal admirers who persistently acclaimed *Doctor Atomic* as a total success (Swed 2008), critics could not agree on whether their admiration for Adams's music or distaste for Sellars's libretto should be decisive (Gereben 2005). Partisans of contemporary art music, predisposed to admire Adams's development as a composer, tended to render a positive judgment on the opera as a whole. *The San Francisco Chronicle*'s Joshua

Kosman, a long-time supporter, hardly hedged his bet, anointing *Doctor Atomic* "some kind of masterpiece" (Kosman 2005b); Mark Swed's original review in the *Los Angeles Times,* while noting intimations of backstage disarray, hastened to assure his readers that the opera was "a magnificent achievement" filled with "music of unearthly splendor and gorgeous lushness" (Swed 2005). Adams was lauded for definitively "transcending" his minimalist roots (Brug 2005), and for manipulating a post-Wagnerian orchestra and generous admixtures of dissonance to overwhelming effect (Fleming 2005). But an odd disconnect shadowed this praise; although a few critics imagined the massive orchestra as a force for dramatic characterization, most responded to the thermonuclear power of instrumental sound wielded for its own sake:

> Whole spans of the orchestral and choral music tremble with textural density. Stacked-up clusters and polytonal harmonies have stunning bite and pungency. Skittish instrumental lines come close to sounding like riffs from a serialist score… When he needs to propel the music forward, Mr. Adams, true to form, creates a din of pummeling rhythms, fractured meters and jolting repeated figures: call it atomic Minimalism. (Tommasini 2005)

In a significant mistaking of the part for the whole, critics of *Doctor Atomic* referred to Adams's "music" when they were almost always speaking exclusively about his *orchestral* music, imagined as a force of nature operating at the sub-atomic level; the vocal lines, which in a traditional opera would be the most direct musical link to the human story acted out on stage, did not often figure into these critical judgments. In this vein, Alex Ross inadvertently revealed a general ideological predilection when he described *Doctor Atomic* just before its San Francisco premiere as "a three-hour symphony of dread" (Ross 2005: 65). In the world of the classical canon, there can be no higher praise for an opera than mistaking it for a symphony, as conductor Robert Spano later did, evoking that most canonical symphonist of all as inspiration for his concert performances of *Doctor Atomic* with the Atlanta Symphony: "The formal structures are so big that 'Doctor Atomic' is almost Beethovenian in that way. All the small parts refer back to the big overarching idea. The structure is always right there" (Ruhe 2008).

A Libretto Is Not a Program Note

Doctor Atomic is indeed very carefully put together. But, according to the Kerman hypothesis, the enduring cultural vitality of opera will derive not from well-wrought musical structures, but from its continued ability to involve audiences in the emotional spectacle of a well-staged drama. On these terms, the new opera was almost universally deemed a failure. Disappointed critics, well aware that the text was the work of a controversial director moonlighting as a writer, attacked Sellars's literary shortcomings at every level, deploring the libretto's ideological preachiness, its lack of sustained character development or structural tension, and especially its long stretches of lumpy, prosaic borrowed language. Many recoiled from the perceived "banality and pretension" (Canning 2008) of Sellars's "lethally self-conscious" anti-nuclear symbolism (Reed 2009), in which, as one exasperated critic summed it up, "Motherhood = good; nuclear weapons = bad. Hey, thanks, man!" (Page 2005; the reference is to the stage design of Act II, in which a life-size replica of the atomic device dangles menacingly over a baby's crib). Scientists and historians complained that this moral calculus was oversimplified, discounting the real human losses anticipated during an Allied invasion of Japan; *Die Welt* remarked acidly that, as Iraq and North Korea flirted anew with nuclear destruction, "what might have been a critical report from the concert hall... proved only professionally stale, percussion-peppered political correctness" (Brug 2005).

Even sympathetic critics found Sellars's libretto for *Doctor Atomic* strangely "antitheatrical" (Stearns 2005), making for "an opera that is not conventionally dramatic in any way" (Kosman 2005b). Many found the "metaphor and high-flown imagery" of the collaged libretto non-operatic, and its central characters unreadable (Clements 2005). Several, noting its "lofty, dullish" (Harvey 2005) avoidance of stage action and the focus on issues of power and responsibility, likened the result to eighteenth-century *opera seria* (Sutcliffe 2005). Structural problems were worst in the second act, a long decrescendo of action that made many reviewers impatient; waiting for the bomb to go off, at least one missed the presence of a real writer who could have advocated for opera as drama: "I wonder if Act II would be so becalmed dramatically... if Sellars had taken up the creative writer's responsibility for finding a narrative dynamic that Adams's previous librettist Alice Goodman so wonderfully exercised in *Nixon* and *Klinghoffer*" (Sutcliffe 2005).

Nowhere was the lack of a professional hand more keenly felt than in the actual language of the opera's text: The critical consensus was that Sellars had failed as a practical poet whose first job should have been to provide patterns of crisp, singable verse for the composer to set. True, a distinct minority *liked* the fact that scientific equations, bureaucratic memoranda, and weather reports were sung in grand operatic style: Dennis Overbye, award-winning author of *Einstein in Love*, saw *Doctor Atomic*'s singing physicists as figures of a new, secular epic: "To hear the chorus of khaki-clad scientists and engineers sing of such matters is to have the gritty details of engineering and science raised to liturgy. It re-mythologized the atomic project for me in a way I had not thought possible" (Overbye 2005). But the consensus view of Sellars's wordsmithing was strongly negative. Critics fell over each other bashing the "verbal flabbiness" (Clements 2005) of his libretto: "it is alarmingly, sometimes ludicrously intrusive, veering between extremes of technobabble opacity and the purplest of poetic hyperbole" (Reed 2009).

Perhaps the most devastating appraisal came not from a professional critic, but a rival. Mark Adamo, whose 1998 opera *Little Women* had been one of the very few American works to match the genuine popular success of Adams's *Nixon in China*, came away bitterly disappointed from *Doctor Atomic*, blaming the composer for letting loyalty to an old friend blind him to the fact that the text collage he had accepted in place of a real libretto doomed the work to dramatic nullity: "Nothing is shaped: nothing develops; so there's nothing to compose into. Sellars seemed more committed to an anti-dramatic method of creating a text than to exploring the story and the issues. Didn't Adams hear what was missing? If he did, didn't he care?" Adamo, a strong partisan of sung drama, scolded his more famous, more "symphonic" colleague for not taking the practical exigencies of the theater seriously. An opera shouldn't be a three-hour symphony composed to illustrate, rather than set, its texts. "A libretto," he snapped, "is not a program note" (Adamo 2008).

THE *SPINAL TAP* OF OPERA

Adamo's dismissal might itself be dismissed as professional jealousy—but much harder to ignore are the incredulous responses to *Doctor Atomic* from non-musical intellectuals drawn in to see it by the intimation of a "capital-I Important" intellectual event (Winn 2005b) with ramifications far beyond the clubby world of contemporary music composition. For at least one of these opera-house neophytes, the experience was shocking to the point of complete disillusion:

> I found myself sitting stunned in the well-dressed opening-night crowd. Rarely an operagoer myself (I prefer poetry and drama without orchestral distractions), I'd nonetheless always respected operagoers for what I presumed to be their sophisticated taste. What amazed me was the respectful, reverent, awed look on the faces of the crowd around me... *Doctor Atomic* began to seem like the *Spinal Tap* of opera [...]. (Rosenbaum 2008)

Ron Rosenbaum, long-time essayist for *The Village Voice* and other intellectual periodicals, and the author of two well-received books of cultural journalism (*Explaining Hitler* and *The Shakespeare Wars*), announced defiantly in the online magazine *Slate* that he had fled the Met's *Doctor Atomic*, the *Spinal Tap* of opera, at the first intermission. Rosenbaum's extended dissection of the opera's failings, entitled "The Opera's New Clothes: Why I Walked Out of *Doctor Atomic*," echoes many of the critical opinions surveyed above: he found the opera's "dorm-room poster" moralizing pretentious, and its characters opaque and wooden. As a professional writer, he saved his harshest vitriol for Sellars's use of language, which he found, even by what he understood to be the low intellectual standard of opera librettos, "pedestrian, speechifying, and [in the love scenes] embarrassingly schlocky" (Rosenbaum 2008).

It's not clear from Rosenbaum's denunciation whether he realized that some of those "schlocky" passages in Act I were translations of Baudelaire's *Fleurs du mal*, or whether he recalled from the opera's program booklet that the pedestrian speechifying was assembled from the actual words of historical figures in the Los Alamos drama. But—and this is where things get interesting for prognosticators about classical music's future—it's not likely that either point would have mattered to him. Rosenbaum, less attuned perhaps than a composer like Mark Adamo to the politics of operatic collaboration, did not complain that the libretto of *Doctor Atomic* was unusually amateurish and poor because no real poet or playwright had worked on it; he decided, rather, that opera librettos must always have been this amateurish and poor, and he just hadn't known it. The fact that the libretto of this new work was in English, and terrible, clotted bureaucratic English at that, ripped the veil of mystification from opera *itself* as a dramatic form, suddenly revealed parading across the stage of Lincoln Center with no aesthetic covering for its naked absurdity:

> "Singing" relentlessly dull prose does not raise it to the level of art. Instead it makes everything sound—forgive me—bombastic. Imagine, if you will, starting at the top of this column and "singing" it, intoning it with a tuneless, stentorian, pompous affect.
>
> Come on, try! Give it your best mock operatic treatment:
> Does this ever happen to you:
> You discover key forgotten elements
> In over familiar fables...
>
> Now imagine these (admittedly pedestrian) words being performed on what looks like a multimillion-dollar set by a male chorus making dreadfully hammy gestures at one another. (Rosenbaum 2008)

Rosenbaum was not the only observer who found that a contemporary opera in everyday English disclosed serious literary problems with the form; this was a position taken by a number of non-musicians who, caught up in the cultural hype around the premiere, felt moved to write about *Doctor Atomic*. New York novelist Carl Watson found the text-setting awkward ("words seemed to have been stuffed into a musical phrase that was just fine without it"), but admitted this might be because the foreign texts of most operas let him sidestep the enabling fiction that, in opera, the *singers* are actually supposed to be *speaking*: "I have never been a fan of English-language operas, and this is because I can understand them. Opera lyrics tend to be pretty corny, even downright dumb, and they have a lot more power if they are lost without translation, becoming part of the music" (Watson 2009).

This may seem like philistinism, but it has a long and honorable history, especially in the English-speaking world. It was in 1711 that Joseph Addison famously remarked how "nothing has more startled our English audience than the Italian *recitativo* at its first entrance upon the stage. People were wonderfully surprised to hear generals singing the word of command and ladies delivering messages in music" (Addison 1711: 1). To a student of Western art music, it is remarkable that people are once again capable of being surprised by recitative, the most well-worn convention of the operatic stage. Rosenbaum's twenty-first-century indictment—that opera turns the trivial meaninglessly bombastic—finds its clear precedent in the seventeenth-century verdict handed down by the erudite Charles de Saint-Évremond in what musicological anthologist Edward Lippman characterized as his "notorious" letter on opera addressed to George Villiers, the 2nd Lord Buckingham, in 1677:

> There is another Thing in Operas so contrary to Nature, that I cannot be reconciled to it; and that is the singing of the whole Piece, from beginning to end, as if the Persons

> represented were ridiculously match'd, and had agreed to treat in Musick both the most common, and most important Affairs of Life. Is it to be imagin'd that a Master calls his Servant, or sends him on an errand, singing; that one Friend imparts a secret to another, singing; That Men deliberate in Council, singing; That Orders in time of Battle are given, singing; and That Men are melodiously killed with Sward and Darts? (Lippman 1992: 48ff)

We seem to have misplaced about two centuries of aesthetic arguments in favor of *melos* on the dramatic stage. Many music critics found the libretto of *Doctor Atomic* too much a literary conceit, fundamentally *un*-operatic; but for the literary Rosenbaum, the strange musical burden of the operatic mode, the fatal need to "sing" everything, foreclosed any emotional insight a character drama about the atomic bomb might try to provide: "Who wouldn't give anything for a brilliant artist trying to imagine what was going through Oppenheimer's head at such a time? But the operatic mode distances and dehumanizes those bombastically announcing their inner thoughts" (Rosenbaum 2008).

Rosenbaum even rejected on literary grounds the one moment in the Adams-Sellars collaboration that had achieved general critical acclaim, Oppenheimer's tense neo-Baroque aria at the end of Act I, fashioned from John Donne's Holy Sonnet 14 ("Batter my heart, three person'd God") in a nod to "Trinity," Oppenheimer's literary code name for the Alamogordo test site. Kosman (2005b) thought Donne's dense poetic language inspired Adams to an equally "compact" setting, like the "fissile core" that powers a nuclear weapon (or a three-hour opera). But Rosenbaum could not get past the violence done to Donne:

> For me, the breaking point may have been the segment of the libretto most celebrated by critics, the appropriation of John Donne's "Holy Sonnet About the Trinity" ("Batter my heart, three-person'd God..."). I found the attempt to "enhance" it by unnecessarily repeating words in its sung version evidence of a fundamental lack of understanding of the poem, the mechanics of which are as intricate as the internal dynamics of a nuclear chain reaction. (Rosenbaum 2008)

Rosenbaum's New Critical respect for the tensile strength of complex grammatical constructions is admirable. Upon reflection, one does see how repeating individual words and phrases could be understood to derail the measured rhetorical progression of Donne's elaborate poetic conceits.[4] But in practical terms, this level of literary purism puts the composer of opera in an old-fashioned aesthetic double bind whose effect is to make serious music drama well-nigh impossible. If the libretto is verbose and prosaic, then intoning its banalities is tediously absurd; if the libretto is condensed and lyrical, then the inevitable repetitions of text (did Rosenbaum think that this was a mannerism unique to Adams?) will be equally absurd, in the manner so entertainingly burlesqued by Mr. Jonathan Swift in his *Cantata* of 1746: *Prima le parole, e non poi la musica, per favore!* (See Figure 49.1).

The recrudescence of seventeenth-century aesthetic positions in the postmodern present is fascinating to a musicologist, who experiences something like the naïve scientific wonderment of the paleontologists faced with living dinosaurs in Michael

FIGURE 49.1 Jonathan Swift, *A Cantata. The Works of Jonathan Swift, Dean of St. Patrick's, Dublin*, edited by John Hawkesworth (London: 1754), VII: 435.

Crichton's *Jurassic Park*. But such reactionary reception is discouraging if one is counting on new operas to throw out the lifeline to Western art music. Yes, the example of *Doctor Atomic* shows that opera still has provisional access to a mythic register that can, given the right subject and enough money, be marketed to the educated public at large; it can indeed try to be music "for the man who enjoys *Hamlet*," to paraphrase the title of a famous midcentury musical appreciation text that has, ironically, less to do with music theater than the German instrumental canon, although it does make an exception for Mozart's *Magic Flute* (Haggin 1944). But the recent reception of *Doctor Atomic* shows the riskiness of enticing novice audiences unfamiliar with classical music into the opera house, primed for a scintillating new drama of ideas. Opera's time-hallowed conventions of text and setting can appear silly, even anti-intellectual to newcomers, especially for contemporary stories, where recognizable characters sing in vernacular language about still-controversial issues. Long-resolved debates about the aesthetic value of music itself may be reopened; audiences may be repulsed, not attracted by opera's garish spectacle; cultural ground may be lost, rather than gained.

Go Ask Alice

Given the general dissatisfaction with the collage of found texts Adams and Sellars used in place of a libretto, it is surprising that few music journalists tried to find their ex-collaborator Alice Goodman, the poet and dramatist originally asked to provide one. When Tom Service of *The Guardian* did get Goodman on record just before the San Francisco premiere, her explanation for the failure of the *Doctor Atomic* collaboration was distractingly sensational: "I found that the structure John and Peter had got together with me was really anti-Semitic, with Oppenheimer as the good blue-eyed Jew and Edward Teller as the bad limping one with the greasy hair, and a host of virtuous native Americans pitted against the refugee physicists out in the New Mexico desert. I couldn't see how it could be anything but deeply offensive" (Service 2005). In the wake of *The Death of Klinghoffer*, which had been attacked, perhaps wrongly, by many New York critics as both offensive and anti-Semitic (Fink 2005), this was an incendiary charge which Adams could only dismiss angrily in the same article as "preposterous." (It would indeed have seemed strange to those who later saw the opera, since Sellars's truncated scenario for *Doctor Atomic* eliminated "good Jew" Oppenheimer's infamous betrayal by "bad Jew" Teller on the House Committee on Un-American Activities [HUAC] witness stand in 1953, at the height of the anti-Semitic anti-communist hysteria that put Julius and Ethel Rosenberg in the electric chair.)[5] Adams himself aggressively defended Sellars, finding dramatic cohesion in his work that few others could see: "He did a brilliant job of solving the challenge. I think that the dialogue in *Doctor Atomic*, particularly in the first act, virtually crackles with the high energy of human interaction. It's every bit as involving and as realistic as anything I've seen in any other opera libretto" (Adams in May 2006: 223).

Goodman's accusation of anti-Semitism in the original scenario is a distraction from the real problem, which, it seems to me, has much more to do with chauvinism, both masculine and musical, on the part of her collaborators. Many commentators found the finished opera's gendered division of moral labor, where men have the power to make the bomb, and women only the powerlessness to feel guilty about it, not only historically inaccurate (by all accounts, Kitty Oppenheimer was a spouse both acute and ambitious) but dramatically shallow. It is hard to imagine an empowered female librettist allowing her male colleagues to get away with transposing the most retrograde aspect of Goethe's *Faust*, its antique gender politics, into an opera about American modernity. She might have weaned them of condescending faux-chivalry like this, from Adams, in an interview just before the premiere: "I use Goethe's term *das ewig Weibliche*, the Eternal Feminine [because] I think that women have a moral awareness that men have perhaps not achieved" (Adams in Gurewitsch 2005).

But can we really blame Adams, the dominant force in this collaboration, for treating his librettist as callously as famous composers treated librettists just as soon they could get away with it, that is, when operas by Wagner and Verdi were allowed (provisionally) into the classical music canon, with its fundamental(ist) belief in the primacy of "abstract" music? Rosenbaum (2008) insinuates in his review that music critics, who "felt the music was all that mattered," had deliberately covered up the "emptiness" where *Doctor Atomic*'s libretto should have been. He had a point, given the kind of special pleading that sometimes leached through even the most positive notices, like Stearns's claim that "a libretto's success is ultimately judged by the music it inspires" (2005) or Gurewitsch's prediction that "in opera, it is music that has the last word, and in the long run it is on the music that the mythic claims of the Adams triptych will rest" (2005). A more thorough-going betrayal of Kerman's capacious view of opera as drama could hardly be imagined; one might as easily claim "mythic" status for all the Rossini operas whose jaunty overtures are the only thing we now play in the concert hall.

In early 2004, well in advance of the publicity blitz around *Doctor Atomic*, an enterprising reporter had already traveled to the north of England to research an unrelated human interest story on why a once-famous poet and opera librettist would step away from the international spotlight to minister to the provincial poor. The resulting article had more to do with Alice Goodman's own life choices than with the failure of her long working relationship with Adams and Sellars—anti-Semitism was not mentioned at all—but the new curate of Kidderminster did eventually unburden herself on how her relationship with the mercurial young composer of *Nixon in China* had recently changed:

> John... always trusted me to do what was right. We had what I would call a polyphonic collaboration where we were thinking/feeling/doing things that weren't quite *ad idem* and didn't have to be. I wasn't there just to put John's ideas into words. Now, I feel my role has diminished, the parameters have narrowed. And it's not unconnected with the fact that John is now the most famous, most performed living composer in the world... and I'm a curate in Kidderminster. (White 2004)

Adams later observed with a certain amount of smugness that Goodman had been "a literary person working in what's fundamentally a musical world, opera, always feeling that her value was never quite appreciated" (Adams in May 2006: 220). One can hardly blame him—this is how real composers are *supposed* to talk—but there may be, at the twilight of the classical music canon, something a little Faustian, something overreaching, in the figure of the "great" composer who arrogates to himself all the responsibility for the operatic collaboration. Busoni, after all, died without ever finishing the Faust opera whose unwieldy libretto he had written himself.

Prima la musica, e poi le parole. The twentieth century is littered with operas doomed to irrelevance by composers who thought they no longer needed librettists, from Arnold Schoenberg to Pulitzer Prize–winner John Harbison, whose faux-modest account casts himself as poet in the role of his own overworked and overmatched literary factotum: "*The Great Gatsby* is a music-driven opera in which the composer bullied the librettist as they worked together. Every choice was in favor of musical opportunities; Fitzgerald's novel was 'respected' only insofar as it furthered the musical design" (Harbison 2000: 1). But *la musica* doesn't always get the last word, as lukewarm reviews of *The Great Gatsby* reveal: "The more purely dramatic scenes were uneven and often went on too long, as if the composer were unwilling to cut short the writer. Often the inventive orchestral conversation was more interesting than the vocal lines going on above" (Stevens 1999). Like Harbison and Harbison's *Great Gatsby*, Adams's and Sellars's *Doctor Atomic* failed to hold the stage, and thus will ultimately fail to fulfill Joseph Kerman's criterion for classical music as a living culture—"[it] must generate an expanded repertory that will arouse critics and attract audiences."

(They Do Not Move)

Back in 1967, *Der Spiegel*, surveying the devastation of the contemporary opera scene as depicted by Boulez, posed the obvious follow-up question. "People say Pierre Boulez himself wants to write an opera . . . how would yours be different from, let's say, the works of Henze?" (Boulez 1967). The composer's first thought was not of the music, but the words. He had no interest in setting a preexisting text ("Literature set to music is sterile"); in fact, the whole idea of "setting to music" (*Vertonung*) bored him. Boulez sought the musical transformation (*Verwendung*) of words into theater: "I'd like to try an experiment where words and music were conceived simultaneously. In other words, I'd like to work with a writer who feels, with every word that he puts down, that music appears, that the text is only capable of existing in conjunction with music" (Boulez 1967). In a visionary moment, Boulez evoked transcendence of the dichotomy at the root of *prima la musica, e poi le parole,* imagining an ideal collaboration where *neither* music nor words would take artistic priority, but would arise together from a single creative impulse. The model appears to have been the revolutionary stage works of Jean Genet, but as Boulez noted, one would have to postulate a cultural revolution in order to realize anything like them on the postwar operatic stage. Thus, perhaps, the rare flash of humility when asked whether he would be composing any operas: "I'd like to—whether I will is uncertain."

As of this writing, forty-five years have passed since Pierre Boulez proposed dynamiting the opera houses of Europe to clear space for his vision of a truly modern music theater. The opera houses are, of course, still standing upright, and, although he has conducted operas by Wagner, Debussy, and Berg at Bayreuth and elsewhere, Boulez himself never got around to writing one. The most recent swirl of rumors say the octogenarian composer might be planning a premiere in 2015 at the historic Teatro alla Scala in Milan (Service 2010). The subject has been the cause of some journalistic ironizing, given the extraordinary delay such a long-awaited debut would represent: Boulez, it is reported, may well finish his composing career with an operatic setting of a preexisting literary classic, Samuel Beckett's 1953 play *Waiting for Godot.*

Needless to say, there has been no mention of a librettist.

(*Silence.*)
ESTRAGON: Sing something.
VLADIMIR: No no! (*Reflects.*) We could start all over again perhaps.
ESTRAGON: That should be easy.
VLADIMIR: It's the start that's difficult.
ESTRAGON: You can start from anything.
VLADIMIR: Yes, but you have to decide.
ESTRAGON: True.
(*Silence.*)[6]

See also: 1900–1945, Versification, Musical Dramaturgy, Politics

NOTES

1. From the works of F. Scott Fitzgerald (Harbison, *The Great Gatsby*, 1999) to Tennessee Williams (Previn, *A Streetcar Named Desire*, 1998) and Grahame Greene (Heggie, *The End of the Affair*, 2004); from director Elia Kazan, who directed *Streetcar*, to John Ford (Gordon, *The Grapes of Wrath*, 2007) and all the way to horror auteur David Cronenberg (Howard Shore, *The Fly*, 2008), the subjects of recent American operas have often been sold to impresarios and audiences as "instant masterpieces," musical treatments of stories and characters so familiar and successful that the operas based on them couldn't miss. On such derivative works and the desire to produce "The Great American Opera," see Kramer (2007b).
2. A timeline of the first *Doctor Atomic* production can be found at the San Francisco Opera's www.doctor-atomic.com, although as an official, *ex post facto* account, it passes over many details of great interest to critical posterity that must be sourced from journalistic accounts. Adams and Goodman were both listed, along with Peter Sellars and conductor Donald Runnicles, when the commission was announced to the press in December 2002. See, for instance, van Gelder 2002.
3. Gurewitsch (2005) reports a working copy of the libretto in which every line was literally footnoted. Peter Sellars's remarks are from a transcript of the San Francisco Opera's *Doctor Atomic* Workshop, October 30, 2005. According to Ross (2005: 62), Sellars took as his model Kenzaburo Oe's novel *A Personal Matter*, in which "the word 'Hiroshima' occurs once." (The same is true of *Doctor Atomic*.) Sellars implies that a documentary-collage style is uniquely suited to subjects like Hiroshima and the Holocaust because the bathetic failure of representational artifice is an unacceptable risk; see Wlodarski 2010 for a critique of what Holocaust scholars call "secondary witness" in Steve Reich's *Different Trains*, another musical memory space that attempted to avoid bathos with a documentary approach.
4. Close reading of the works of John Donne was foundational to the advent of New Criticism in American literary studies, in particular as demonstrated by Brooks (1947), who begins with an extended analysis of Donne's "The Canonization" along the lines Rosenbaum adumbrates. The approach has had a long life in the Yale English Department, where Brooks taught from 1947 to 1975 and Rosenbaum earned his B.A. in English Literature in 1968.
5. How much Goodman actually worked on *Doctor Atomic* is not clear. Ongoing scholarship on the opera's compositional history promises to shed quite a bit more light on the troubled genesis of the libretto; in particular, a hand-written scenario in three (!) acts, the product of the initial planning meetings between Adams, Sellars, and Goodman, has recently been brought to light by musicologist Alice Miller Cotter (personal communication with the author).
6. Samuel Beckett, *Waiting for Godot*, Act II: 1798–1805, in Bloom 2008: 56–57.

BIBLIOGRAPHY

Adams, John, and Peter Sellars. 2005. *Doctor Atomic*. London: Boosey & Hawkes.

Addison, Joseph. 1711. *The Spectator* 129 (April 3): 1.

Bloom, Harold, ed. 2008. *Samuel Beckett's 'Waiting for Godot.' Bloom's Modern Critical Interpretations*. New York: Bloom's Literary Interpretations.

——. 2004. *Literature of the Holocaust*. Philadelphia: Chelsea House.
Brooks, Cleanth. 1947. *The Well Wrought Urn: Studies in the Structure of Poetry*. New York: Harcourt, Brace, Jovanovich.
Boulez, Pierre. 1967 "Sprengt die Opernhaüser in die Luft!" *Der Spiegel* 40 (September 25).
Chaikin, Paul M. 2010. "Circling Opera in Berlin." PhD diss., Brown University.
Day, Timothy. 2000. *A Century of Recorded Music*. New Haven: Yale University Press.
Fink, Robert. 2005. "*Klinghoffer* in Brooklyn Heights: Opera, Anti-Semitism, and the Politics of Representation." *Cambridge Opera Journal* 17/2: 173–213.
——. 2004. "Beethoven Antihero." In *Beyond Structural Listening? Postmodern Modes of Hearing*, edited by Andrew Dell'Antonio, 109–153. Berkeley and Los Angeles: University of California Press.
——. 1998. "Elvis Everywhere: Musicology and Popular Music Studies at the Twilight of the Canon." *American Music* 16/2: 135–179.
Freed, Fred. 1965. *The Decision to Drop the Bomb*. NBC White Paper (documentary film).
Glass, Philip. 1987. *Music by Philip Glass*. New York: Harper & Row.
Goehr, Lydia. 2007. *The Imaginary Museum of Musical Works: An Essay in the Philosophy of Music*. New York: Oxford University Press.
Haggin, B. F. 1944. *Music for the Man Who Enjoys Hamlet*. New York: Alfred A. Knopf.
Harbison, John. 2000. "Composer's Note." Publisher's brochure for *The Great Gatsby*. Online. Available: www.schirmer.com (accessed January 20, 2012).
Henze, Hans Werner. 1982. *Music and Politics: Collected Writings, 1953–81*, translated by Peter Labanyi. Ithaca, NY: Cornell University Press.
Horowitz, Joseph. 2005. *Classical Music in America: A History of Its Rise and Fall*. New York: W. W. Norton.
——. 1994. *Understanding Toscanini: A Social History of American Concert Life*. Berkeley and Los Angeles: University of California Press.
Kamuf, Peggy. 1993. "The Replay's the Thing." In *Opera Through Other Eyes*, edited by David J. Levin, 79–105. Stanford, CA: Stanford University Press.
Kant, Immanuel. [1790] 1908. *Critique of Judgment. Gesammelte Schriften*. II § 53. Akademie-Ausgabe. Berlin: George Reimer.
Kerman, Joseph. 2008. "Opera and the Morbidity of Music." In *Opera and the Morbidity of Music. A New York Review Collection*, 7–20. New York: New York Review of Books.
——. 1998. *Write All These Down*. Berkeley and Los Angeles: University of California Press.
——. [1956] 1988. *Opera as Drama*. Rev. ed. Berkeley and Los Angeles: University of California Press.
Kramer, Lawrence. 2007a. "The Great American Opera: *Klinghoffer, Streetcar*, and the Exception." *Opera Quarterly* 23/1: 66–80.
——. 2007b. *Why Classical Music Still Matters*. Berkeley and Los Angeles: University of California Press.
Lebrecht, Norman. 1997. *Who Killed Classical Music? Maestros, Managers, and Corporate Politics*. New York: Birch Lane Press.
Levine, Lawrence. 1990. *Highbrow/Lowbrow: The Emergence of Cultural Hierarchy in America*. Cambridge, MA: Harvard University Press.
Lippman, Edward. 1992. *History of Western Musical Aesthetics*. Lincoln: University of Nebraska Press.
May, Thomas. 2006. *The John Adams Reader*. New York: Amadeus Press.
Nyman, Michael. [1974] 2002. *Experimental Music: Cage and Beyond*. 2nd ed. Cambridge: Cambridge University Press.

Oliva, Achille Bonito. 1993. "The International Trans-Avant-Garde (1981)." In *Postmodernism: A Reader*, edited by Thomas Docherty, 257–262. New York: Columbia University Press.

Porter, Andrew. 1981. "Gospel of Peace" [review of Philip Glass, *Satyagraha*]. *The New Yorker* (August 17): 97–103.

Sellars, Peter. Comments on *Doctor Atomic*. San Francisco Opera, *Doctor Atomic* Workshop, October 30, 2004. Online. Available: http://www.doctor-atomic.com/interview_sellars.html (accessed January 20, 2012).

Service, Tom. 2010. "Pierre Boulez to Write an Opera of Waiting for Godot—Maybe." Entry in *OnClassical* weblog (July 9). Online. Available: http://www.guardian.co.uk/music/tomserviceblog/2010/jul/09/pierre-boulez-opera-waiting-for-godot (accessed January 20, 2012).

Stevens, David. 1999. "Harbison Mixes Up a Great 'Gatsby'." *New York Times* (December 29).

Swift, Jonathan. 1754. *A Cantata* (1746). In *The Works of Jonathan Swift, D. D., Dean of St. Patrick's, Dublin*. VII: 432–435. London: C. Davis et al.

Taruskin, Richard. 2010. *Music in the Late Twentieth Century*. New York: Oxford University Press.

Thelen, David, Richard H. Kohn, et al. 1995. "History and the Public: What Can We Handle? A Round Table about History after the *Enola Gay* Controversy." *The Journal of American History* 82/3: 1029–1144.

Weber, William. 2008. *The Great Transformation of Musical Taste: Concert Programs from Haydn to Brahms*. Cambridge: Cambridge University Press.

Wlodarski, Amy. 2010. "The Testimonial Aesthetics of *Different Trains*." *Journal of the American Musicological Society* 63/1: 99–141.

Reporting on and Critical Reception of *Doctor Atomic*, 2002–2009

Adamo, Mark. 2008. "John, Atoms." Weblog (October 14). www.markadamo.com/journal (accessed March 9, 2009).

Brown, Geoff. 2008. "Netherlands Opera: Doctor Atomic (DVD)." *Times of London (Online)* (August 1).

——. 2007. Review of Adams, 'Doctor Atomic' Symphony. *Times of London (Online)* (August 23).

Brug, Manuel. 2005. "(K)ein amerikanischer Faust: 'Doctor Atomic' von John Adams und Peter Sellars in San Francisco." *Die Welt* (October 4).

Canning, Hugh. 2008. "Doctor Atomic—the Sunday Times Review." *The Sunday Times (online)* (October 19).

Clements, Andrew. 2005. "Doctor Atomic at San Francisco Opera." *The Guardian* (October 5).

Eichler, Jeremy. 2005. "An Opera That Hovers on Threshold of the Nuclear Age." *Boston Globe* (October 6).

Fleming, John. 2005. "Explosive Opera." *St. Petersburg (Florida) Times* (October 21).

Gereben, Janos. 2005. "'Doctor Atomic' Batters Heart, Mind." *San Diego Magazine* (October 1).

Gurewitsch, Matthew. 2005. "The Opera That Chooses the Nuclear Option." *New York Times* (September 25).

Harvey, Daniel. 2005. "'Doctor Atomic' in SF." *Variety* (October 4).

Kevles, Daniel J. 2005. "*Dr. Atomic*: An Opera about the Moral Complexities of Hiroshima." *Slate* (October 19).
Kosman, Joshua. 2005a. "S.F. Opera to Premiere Work by John Adams in New Season—Handel, Bellini Also in Lineup." *San Francisco Chronicle* (January 13).
——. 2005b. "Using a Trinity of Unconventional Drama, Haunting Score, and Poetry, S. F. Opera Confronts Our Age's Most Terrifying Topic." *San Francisco Chronicle* (October 3).
Maxwell, Dominic. 2007. "A Legend Out of His Own Time." *The Times of London (Online)* (January 26).
Michaels, Sean. 2008. "Opera Sponsors Buy £250,000 Worth of Tickets." *The Guardian* (October 9).
Morrison, Richard 2009. "The man who put a bomb under opera. He gave us Nixon and Mao, and terrorism at sea. Now John Adams goes nuclear with *Doctor Atomic*. Richard Morrison meets a composer re-inventing opera." *The Times of London* (February 14).
Overbye, Dennis. 2005. "'Dr Atomic': Unthinkable Yet Immortal." *New York Times* (October 18).
Page, Tim. 2005. "'Doctor Atomic': Unleashing Powerful Forces." *Washington Post* (October 3).
Platt, Russell. 2008. "New Paths." Entry in *Going Places* weblog. *The New Yorker* (October 3). Online. Available: http://www.newyorker.com/online/blogs/goingson/2008/10/new-paths-metci.html (accessed January 15, 2012).
Reed, Peter. 2009. "ENO Delivers with a Bang; Or How I Learned to Love an Opera about a Bomb." *The Sunday Telegraph* (March 8).
Rosenbaum, Ron. 2008. "The Opera's New Clothes: Why I Walked Out of *Doctor Atomic*." *Slate* (October 24).
Ross, Alex. 2005. "Countdown: John Adams and Peter Sellars Create an Atomic Opera." *The New Yorker* (October 3): 60–71.
Ruhe, Pierre. 2008. "'Atomic' Emperor of Opera." [Interview with Robert Spano]. *Atlanta Journal-Constitution* (November 16).
Service, Tom. 2005. "'This Was the Start of a New Epoch in Human History.'" *The Guardian* (September 29).
Stearns, David Patrick. 2008. "'Doctor Atomic': The Met's Manhattan Project." *The Philadelphia Inquirer* (October 16).
——. 2005. "Heroic A-bomb Opera Will Create Fallout." *The Philadelphia Enquirer* (October 5).
Sutcliffe, Tom. 2005. "Doctor Atomic [in SF]." *The Times of London (Online)* (October 4).
Swed, Mark. 2008. "In Opera, Print Takes a Tragic Turn." *Los Angeles Times* (December 7).
——. 2005. "An Explosive Premiere." *Los Angeles Times* (October 3).
Tommasini, Anthony. 2005. "Countdown to the Eve of Destruction." *New York Times* (October 2).
van Gelder, Lawrence. 2002. "Footlights." *New York Times* (December 24).
Waleson, Heidi. 2005. "All About the Bomb." *The Wall Street Journal* (October 4).
Watson, Carl. 2009. "A Review of the Opera, Dr. Atomic." *A Gathering of the Tribes* (January 21). Online. Available: http://www.tribes.org/web/2009/01/21/a-review-of-the-opera-doctor-atomic/ (accessed January 20, 2012).
White, Michael. 2004. "God's Opera Writer." [Interview with Alice Goodman]. *The Telegraph* (February 8).
Winn, Steven. 2005a. "'Atomic' Sets Off Cultural Chain Reaction." *San Francisco Chronicle* (September 29).
——. 2005b. "The Bomb May Be Too Big Even for Art to Grasp." *San Francisco Chronicle* (October 6).

EPILOGUE

CHAPTER 50

COMPOSING OPERA

JAKE HEGGIE

The First Act

Work on *Le nozze di Figaro* has been interrupted and Mozart is at court to persuade the emperor to allow his new opera to be staged. The emperor thinks it's a bad idea because Beaumarchais's banned play incites class struggle. Mozart's entreaties, including descriptions of his astounding ensembles, are fruitless. But when he acts out the opening scene of the opera, down on his hands and knees, his sense of theater wins the day: the emperor has visible evidence of how this might work. He is suddenly intrigued, engaged, and delighted.

This is more than a deftly crafted scene from *Amadeus* by the playwright and screenwriter Peter Shaffer. Any theater composer will tell you it is part of the job. In addition to acting it out in our own heads as we compose, we have to make it live for others—especially the producers—long before the curtain rises for the first time. Today, instead of emperors, we have an opera company's general director, artistic director, board of directors, and donors. These are the producers who must feel the confidence, courage, and enthusiasm to fund a project, to be engaged, intrigued, and delighted—and by doing so, to create possibility and connection for many others. This is not necessarily the first step in the creation of a new opera, but it is an early and critical one.

Composing opera is a delicate enterprise, fraught with challenge. "Like growing orchids in Alaska," says playwright Terrence McNally (in the 2001 PBS Documentary *And Then One Night: The Making of Dead Man Walking*). It requires an enormous amount of passion, talent, faith, patience, and time on the part of everyone involved. It also requires a lot of money. A lot. Whether it's *La bohème* or a world premiere, the financial stakes in opera are high. But with all the considerable unknowns of a new work, the stakes are even higher. For in addition to the financial stakes, there is a fear factor within the traditional opera-going audience, suspicious and wary of new work.

The request for this chapter came to me as one of the fortunate and grateful few who compose opera as part of a remarkable life in music theater. I'm an American composer (*Moby-Dick, Dead Man Walking, Three Decembers*), so this piece takes a mostly American perspective on composing opera in the early years of the twenty-first century; it takes into consideration my own experiences as well as those of a few distinguished colleagues, each of whom was kind enough to answer questions by e-mail or phone: Mark Adamo (*The Gospel of Mary Magdalene, Little Women, Lysistrata*), John Adams (*Doctor Atomic, Nixon in China, The Death of Klinghoffer*), Philip Glass (*Satyagraha, Appomattox, Galileo Galilei*), Stewart Wallace (*Hopper's Wife, Harvey Milk, The Bonesetter's Daughter*), and the late Daniel Catán (*Il Postino, Rappaccini's Daughter, Florencia en el Amazonas*).[1]

The Theater

The particular challenge with opera is that it is theater, and therefore it only truly exists when it is being performed. Because of the enormity of forces involved, a creative team can speculate on success, but frankly, you don't really know what you've got until it's up and running in front of an audience.

A new grand opera at a major opera house can cost millions of dollars and a staggering number of hours to develop and produce. The overall budget, including commission fees, costs of production, marketing, union, cast, crew, orchestra, chorus, staff expenses, ushers, front of house expenses, and theater rental for multiple performances for my opera *Moby-Dick* (2010) at the Dallas Opera was $2.5 million, and the projected budget for my next opera there, *Great Scott* (2015), is nearly $3 million (figures provided by the Dallas Opera, based on five performances of the new opera). The San Francisco Opera world premieres of Adams's *Doctor Atomic* (2005), Philip Glass's *Appomattox* (2007), Wallace's *The Bonesetter's Daughter* (2008), Christopher Theofanidis's *Heart of a Soldier* (2011), and Adamo's *The Gospel of Mary Magdalene* (2013) have price tags that range between $4.5 million and $6 million (figures provided by the San Francisco Opera, based on six to eight performances). Even a smaller-scale production, such as Nico Muhly's *Dark Sisters* (2011) with seven singers and an orchestra of thirteen players, had a budget of $1 million (a co-commission and co-production of Gotham Chamber Opera, Music-Theatre Group, Opera Company of Philadelphia; the $1 million figure also includes two workshops, one invited preview, and six performances).

New works in the "for-profit" world of musical theater, or Broadway, also take countless hours and might also cost millions. But a major new musical will usually be given several weeks of run-throughs and tryouts to see if it works. The creative team will have the ability to make changes every day: Is the storytelling clear? Does it play for the audience? Is this really the right cast? Expensive, but the producers and creators insist upon this process. They want to be sure the piece is really ready to open, because you get one shot at an opening, and the hope is that it will run a long time and everybody will make a profit. The same happens with major motion pictures: They are screened for test audiences to determine if any changes are needed in advance of the official premiere.

In the not-for-profit world of opera, however, there is only speculation on the parts of the creative team and the opera company. There might be a private workshop early on to give it a listen and anticipate any issues with dramaturgy (storytelling), structure, or musical matters. There might be more than one workshop. Then, before the opening, there are a few precious weeks of rehearsal to put it all together. But, the first chance to see if a major new opera works, if it plays for the audience, is when it is shot out of a cannon on opening night. Yes, opening night.

Because the forces are so large, it is too costly to preview a large new opera even once in front of a test audience. So the electrifying moment of truth—an opera's first preview performance—is the world premiere. This is also the performance that is reviewed, written about, discussed, and broadcast all over the world in seconds. Years of labor, hopes, and dreams rest on that first precarious performance when all elements finally come together... hopefully. Everyone knows the number of performances is limited. There is no chance for an extended or open-ended run as there sometimes is on Broadway. The most an opera company can hope for is a sold-out run, possibly an added performance, and the exciting possibility that another company might choose to produce it. But realistically, after the first complete run of perhaps three to eight performances, will there be an opportunity to make changes and try again? Perhaps, but it is rare.

According to OPERA America (a nonprofit, national service organization for opera, located in New York City, created in 1970 to serve and strengthen the field through programs and resources designed to enhance the creation, presentation, and enjoyment of opera), during the eleven complete opera seasons from 2000–2001 through 2010–2011, there were 329 world premieres of varying sizes: this accounted for approximately 14.5 percent of the total repertoire produced. That is, in fact, an impressive number. But of those 329 new operas, just 33 received a second production. (The figures provided include OPERA America's professional company members, associate producing members, and educational producing associate members. This membership includes companies from the United States, Canada, Europe, Australia, and Asia. It should be noted that a few of these companies are devoted entirely to the creation of new works, which skews the percentage higher.)

Opera is not a profit-making venture. Aside from its heyday in the nineteenth century, when the audience was hungry for new operas and it was a popular art form that might actually turn a profit, it has required sponsors and donors who do not expect a financial return on their investment. OPERA America reports that in fiscal year 2010, ticket sales accounted for only 30.7 percent of revenues for a Level One opera company (a company with annual expenses greater than $10 million); the remaining 69.3 percent was income from investments, other earned sources (such as equipment rentals), and contributions (OPERA America 2011 annual report).

New works are supported with the goal of enlarging and enriching the repertoire—not just to curate the classics, but to keep the art form alive by creating new, timely, and meaningful works that will intrigue, engage, delight, and connect with a contemporary audience. They require us to participate, show up, pay attention, reflect, and take a chance. Against considerable odds, our passion still compels us to do this.

The Story

Fifty percent of the success of a new opera lies in finding the right story to tell. The age-old question is: "What comes first, the music or the words?" Before either, there is the story. The right story will inspire action, scenes, situations, characters, their journeys and transformations. Those will inspire words and, ultimately, music. I know when a story is right for me because I immediately start to hear musical textures in my head: orchestral and vocal textures, colors and dramatic possibilities. If this doesn't happen from the first suggestion of a story, I know it's probably not the right story for me.

Throughout history, composers and librettists have relied upon stories that are in some way familiar to the audience. In the seventeenth and eighteenth centuries, these were primarily well-known legends and myths about struggles between gods, heroes, nobles, and mortals. Often, the same libretto would be set by several composers; certainly the same stories were set numerous times. From the late eighteenth century onward, an opera might be based on a popular play or novel. In the twentieth century, we turned additionally to movies, documentaries, newspaper serials, biographies, political events, short stories, television, and so on.

The common thread is instant connection with the public. Why does this matter? It matters because, whether seeking outright entertainment or something much deeper, an audience yearns for connection. And in general, the audience is less resistant to something with which it has some sense of familiarity—especially for a new opera. You're already asking an audience to absorb several thousand measures of new music on a single hearing. Add to that an unknown story, and you have the potential for one overwhelmed audience.

Theater composers have learned through experience: people see more than they hear. When attending a new opera, the first thing audience members will do is to take in all the visuals: the theater itself, the set, lights, costumes, and so on. If the opera is in their own language, they will try to understand every single word and endeavor to make sense of the characters, the situations, and the story. I don't know if there is evidence to prove it, but I believe that for *most* of the general public, the very last thing they will absorb on first hearing is the music. If there is confusion or frustration in understanding language or story, the audience member might shut down and not pay attention to any of it. Even if there is no confusion at all, the audience will generally walk away with, at most, an "impression" of the music. How else can one explain early critical reactions to Bizet's *Carmen* (1875), such as the *Boston Gazette* review of January 5, 1879: "The composer of *Carmen* is nowhere deep; his passionateness [*sic*] is all on the surface, and the general effect of the work is artificial and insincere. Of melody, as the term is generally understood, there is but little. The air of the Toreador is the only bit of 'tune' in the opera, and this [. . .] scarcely rises above the vulgarity of Offenbach."

So, whatever the time period, composers and librettists have learned to seek out stories that open the audience to a musical telling. Operas, generally, are not about solving complex mysteries or telling complex stories. This is why some opera plots can seem almost simplistic, and why overly complicated plots are confusing. Operas are about finding the hot emotional core of a situation and exploring it to its fullest through music. High stakes sweeten the pot dramaturgically and musically. The only way a listener can truly be open to that experience is if she or he doesn't have to focus on everything else.

Consider this: when discussing a new film, immediate questions include "What's it about?" (meaning: tell me in ten words or less) and "Who's in it?" Tell people you're writing a new opera and they'll ask the same question: "What's the story?" If there's no recognition, the next question will likely be "Who's in it?" If there's still no recognition, there's usually a blank look, a shrug of the shoulders, and a muttered "Oh."

That person is seeking a connection, an anchor—something familiar to hang on to and excite the imagination so as not to be quite so unsure of this big unknown entity. If there is no connection, that person will likely feel distance from the project even before a word or a note has been written.

The Creative Team

A great story alone, of course, won't make a meaningful opera. That story has to be an inspiration to a composer and librettist who are in agreement about how they want to tell this story. Opera requires passion, and it has to start with the energy a creative team brings in wanting—*needing*—to tell the story as an opera. They will have to dedicate several years of their lives to do this. The composers I spoke with suggested that it takes, on average, two to four years for a major project from initiation to completion. That is my experience, as well.

This being the case, it's important that the composer and librettist respect each other, appreciate working together, enjoy being together, and share a common vision for the piece. They are virtually moving into a house together for several years. Both of them must be flexible and recognize that their work is always in the service of the drama. Several colleagues have commented on this process, including Daniel Catán, who said, "Many changes to the libretto come up as the music is composed. . . . I need the help and understanding of the librettist." Stewart Wallace looks "for chemistry. A good collaborator." He also adds that he "will never work on a preexisting libretto because it's important that the libretto is driven by the musical needs and the things that inspire a specific composer."

A fine librettist is hard to come by. Opera librettos are not plays or poems, nor are they novels or scripts. They are a peculiar cross section, and it takes a very skilled writer with stage and music savvy to craft one successfully. The librettist has to write something in which music can take care of details that don't need to be spoken; he or she must compellingly distill the story to bare essentials, often cutting, rearranging, or rewriting famous parts of an existing story; he must set up scenes for solos and ensembles where the connecting material is brief; it takes much longer to sing words than to recite them, so he must find the few words that express the poetic core of each scene. And yet, we need to follow the journey of each character so that the threads of the story are clearly delineated.

Glass, who has composed more than twenty-five operas, is adamant about what he doesn't want: "No poets and no novelists. I find that the best collaborators are film writers and playwrights. They know how things work on the stage and are used to quick changes and rewrites." Adamo always crafts his own libretti, as did Carlisle Floyd and Richard Wagner, among others. But it seems the majority of composers like to collaborate with a writer rather than tackle the entire thing themselves. "I look for someone who demands as high a standard in words as I consider myself to have in music," says Adams.

My first opera collaboration was *Dead Man Walking* with Terrence McNally as librettist. Early on, McNally told me that he is not a poet, but a playwright; he would write a play and try to set up situations and language that would inspire music. He advised that if the music was taking off and I needed different words, I should let him know or write temporary words myself. The music has to lead. That policy has served me well with subsequent librettists, especially Gene Scheer, with whom I work every step of the way in the creation of the libretto. There are months of back-and-forth discussions and drafts until, ultimately, the libretto inspires music. Even then, the libretto may change because music will give us information about the character that we didn't have before. In my operas, the libretto is finished when the opera is finished. But it has to be quite far along when I start to compose.

Glass describes a different approach: "Before I go to the librettist, I create my own scene- by-scene outline based on what I visualize and the kind of music I want to write. Then I give the librettist all of my reference materials. I need writers who are able to conform to theatrical ideas that may not be their own." Adamo makes several successive scenarios and drafts of the piece, but adds, "The acting comes first. Knowing how you would physically play that scene in space." In the end "the first draft of the libretto is the first draft of the score because there are musical needs that pre-shape the language."

Essential to the creative team are, of course, the conductor and director. I always work with both from the start. It's very easy for a composer and librettist to get too close to their work, and these members of the team will give invaluable perspective.

The Theater Composer

Everything has to be in service of the drama, including the music. This is why opera also requires a particular type of composer: the theater composer—a flexible composer who writes music that serves and leads a drama, who loves the voice, whose first impulse in telling a story is to write for the voice, and who is willing to listen to others and to use that information to make cuts, rewrite, and revise the score so it will work as theater.

There are many kinds of music, of course, but in the "classical" or "concert" field, I think there are basically two kinds of composers: abstract composers, essentially solo artists who excel in symphonic work, chamber music, solo instrumentals, and so on, where they are in total command of the situation and call all the shots; and theater composers, collaborative artists who are storytellers, creating music that serves and leads a drama.

Of course, there are the rare and miraculous few who have done all of it extremely well: Mozart, Britten, Janáček, Prokofiev, Tchaikovsky, Dvořák, to name a few familiar dead ones. There are also abstract composers who write very theatrically, but who don't really write for the stage.

My firm belief is that if the composer of a new opera is not truly a theater composer—with an innate ability to serve drama with music—a new opera likely will not work. It may contain extraordinary music, but as theater it will probably fall short. An exciting aspect of the new works being commissioned by opera companies today is that they seem willing to give opportunities to composers from many backgrounds: film composers, Broadway composers, pop/rock/jazz artists, and more.

Since 1974, Houston Grand Opera has accrued a rather stunning history of commissioned world premieres, more than forty-five new operas, large and small. Several of the more recent works were developed by HGOco, the company's arm for community engagement. Its Song of Houston project commits to composers and librettists who tell stories from the many immigrant communities in Houston. Recent operas have included *Cruzar la Cara de la Luna* (2010), a "mariachi" opera by José Martínez and Leonard Foglia about the Mexican immigrant experience; Jack Perla and Eugenie Chan's *Courtside* (2011), an opera set in the Chinese community of Houston; and Gregory Spears and Farnoosh Moshiri's *The Bricklayer* (2012), about the Iranian experience in Houston.

New opera development programs are also under way at Fort Worth Opera, Washington National Opera, Philadelphia Opera, and New York's Metropolitan Opera in conjunction with Lincoln Center Theater. OPERA America has seen interest in new works grow steadily and in 2011 initiated the New Works Forum. The goal? To identify, support, and give opportunities to a new generation of true theater composers and librettists.

News

Most new operas are written on commission from an opera company or a consortium of several companies when they decide that being curators of the established art form is not enough. They are ready to take the plunge. Sometimes the composer makes the initial approach, but most often the company decides it is ready to commission a new work and seeks out a composer. That composer, in consultation with the opera company, decides on a librettist. Together, they look for the right story.

Occasionally, although rarely, an opera company will accept a new, completed work that was created entirely on speculation. However, this is definitely the exception. A commission means that a company can participate actively during the two or three years of the opera's creation. The composer and librettist can assist in efforts to raise funds and awareness, engage the community, and also reassure a nervous board of directors.

For more than thirty years, the performing arts have had, at best, a tenuous place in the core curriculum of public schools in the United States. As a result, a majority of people under age thirty have virtually no connection to opera, and most young people don't see why it matters at all. Opera has become so marginalized that it has almost no presence in popular culture except as parody in television commercials. Audience saturation with the core repertoire has led companies to explore unusual, bold, and creative productions, and still the audience must be lured in. Productions of popular favorites aren't guaranteed to sell out. Economic crisis can cause companies to close their doors forever, moving the art form even further away from the audience. Keeping opera alive and newsworthy means that there must be news.

The commission of a new opera is news. It can be a means of getting the attention of the media and the community, it can have resonance in local schools and community groups, reaching the prized younger audience, and it can be a means of initiating a dialogue within the community. In other words, the audience can participate. The opera company feels more connected and essential to the community. Even better, a new work can get a new crowd into the opera house. And if they enter the door once, perhaps they'll do it again. (Unless, of course, they don't like the experience and never come back! There's a lot riding on the perceived "success" of a new opera.)

The interest and enthusiasm of the community can help to generate philanthropy for the project, which is critical in a business that requires a great deal of money to work well.

Composing Opera

So, hypothetically, an opera company wants to commission a new opera with producers who are willing to support the project. A composer has been engaged and has chosen an excellent librettist; together they have found an intriguing, meaningful, powerful story to tell on the opera stage. Rights have been secured. The librettist and composer have spent time together talking about the story to decide what the major roles will be, how the story will be distilled, and what will happen. They have found an excellent conductor and director to be primary collaborators from the start. The basic forces have been determined: the size and scope of the opera, number of principal roles, chorus or no chorus, size of orchestra, production budget, and so on. The creative team has thought about who would be ideal in the roles, and the company wastes no time in attempting to cast them.

Casting is everything. You can eliminate everything else, but if you don't have singers, you don't have opera—and not just singers, but great singing actors. New operas especially must be produced at the highest level possible if they stand the slightest chance for success. Fine opera singers are rare, busy, and expensive. They have to be booked years in advance. Their interest must be piqued. A composer and librettist will write roles based on the characters, but they will be dressed on the original cast: their confidence, participation, enthusiasm, and commitment is essential. A single recognizable star can give the project the extra credibility that can be of enormous help in exciting donors and the opera-going public. The composer, librettist, conductor, and director will all make suggestions for casting, but the final decision usually rests with the opera company. As Glass observes, "The opera house is the composer's house. Early on in the process, I'll even walk the stage and orchestra pit with the conductor to see what size orchestra we can manage, as well as chorus, etc."

Everything happens years in advance. The season for the new opera is planned and a date is decided. And before a note or a word has been written, an announcement of the project is made to the media to start a buzz about the new opera. Fundraising and speculation begin right away.

A delivery schedule is decided for the libretto and score: when a complete first draft of the libretto will be submitted and approved; when a piano score will be submitted; when the finished score and parts will be delivered. At all stages, the opera company usually retains the right to make suggestions and give approval. Throughout the process, the composer will likely be asked to make presentations to the opera company, its board of directors, donors, etc. The general director is the principal in initiating and facilitating every part of the project, the creative team's primary champion, contact, and liaison.

So, years in advance of the premiere, this massive ship leaves the dock, slowly making its way to deeper waters. Now, at last, it's time to write—the part the creative team lives for.

First, the libretto—from this all-important foundation, the opera is given its scaffolding, architecture, and sense of flow. The characters are identified by their actions, conflicts, and the language they use. The story is distilled to bare essence. Places for arias, ensembles, choruses, etc., are identified. All of this information—including voice types, possible casting, and so forth—must ignite and inspire the composer's imagination. The libretto isn't ready until it provides the ultimate goal of inspiring music. The story itself might have already provided inspiration for music, but the libretto is the composer's bible for the project. This is another reason a librettist has to be an extremely flexible writer, and why the composer/librettist relationship is so important. Many operas have been held up for ages while the libretto is crafted.

The composer works closely with the librettist in shaping the work. Most of us like to have a complete draft of the libretto before starting to compose. With this information, the composer identifies a musical universe for the opera: a sound world in which characters will emerge, revealing themselves and their journeys. The composer makes essential decisions about pacing and tempo as well as the use of orchestral color. And all of the composers I spoke with acknowledge that the libretto continues to change as the music is composed. A composer has to be a dramatist as well, not just somebody who sets words.

How a composer writes is, of course, extremely subjective. It is impossible to predict where and how inspiration will strike. This is another reason the process starts years in advance with a story that resonates musically for the composer. Most composers have a routine that includes "going to work" every day. When I write, I go to my studio to work: sometimes a couple of hours, sometimes ten hours in a day. Some composers, including Glass, Adams, Wallace, and myself, like to start writing from the beginning of the libretto and move through it organically; although sometimes that is not possible because of schedule, and when and where inspiration strikes.

Some composers begin by writing out of order, creating moments such as arias and ensembles first then composing connecting material. Adamo likes to compose the structural pillars of the opera first to find material he will use and develop throughout. Catán would start in the middle of the first act and then move both ways from there; as he once said, "The final moment of the opera and the beginning are the very last things I do." In any event, by the time these particular composers started their work, they had been thinking about and living with the idea of the opera for a long time. From the initial idea to a first draft of the libretto will likely be a year or more.

Methods of orchestration also differ. Glass writes the full score from the start, leaving the task of creating a piano reduction to somebody else. Earlier in their careers Adams, Wallace, and Adamo began the process by writing piano-vocal scores first, but later found their ways to writing directly to full score. Adams recalls, "I used to do a very rough piano-vocal first, so that the singers could begin learning, and then I would go back and do the orchestration. I did that up through *El Niño*. But for *Doctor Atomic* and *A Flowering Tree*, I composed straight through to full score." Wallace takes a different approach: "For *The Bonesetter's Daughter*, I composed directly to full score because I wanted to focus on texture and timbre as a way to make this very American opera and score feel like China. Having done that, I think I will continue to work this way in the future."

Catán and I like to create a comprehensive piano-vocal score first, and then flesh it out to a full orchestral score after being sure the piece works. I work with what is known as a short score—three or four lines with indications for orchestration—and only write out the complete score after a full workshop and further discussions with the creative team. Composers frequently write directly to computer now, but there are still some holdouts who notate the entire score by hand, including Glass and myself. We write everything by hand and send it off to a copyist. Adams starts with paper and pencil, and then moves to the computer.

The process of composition is a very private time for the composer. It can go swiftly or agonizingly slowly. Glass allows only six months to compose the entire score, finishing as rehearsals begin! *Dead Man Walking* and *Moby-Dick* both took me two and half years, but *The End of the Affair* had to be written in an agonizing ten months because the libretto came very late. Adams, too, usually requires about two years to compose, but notes one important exception: "*A Flowering Tree* was created in an impossibly short period—nine months—including writing the libretto. I had to meet a short deadline, but it nearly destroyed my health, so I wouldn't recommend that!"

The Finale

When is the opera finished? Verdi, Puccini, Mozart, and Rossini made different versions of their operas based on watching and listening to performances of their work, while taking into account the specific gifts of the singers involved, the cultural demands of a certain time period, and so on. Some of their scores exist in several versions. Thanks to the vast recorded archive of operas that goes back more than one hundred years (and new critical editions), we have the opportunity to hear how some of these scores differ.

With a new opera, the first version heard on opening night might be the only version ever heard. Perhaps, by some remarkable stroke of good luck, it will be the finished product. If a recording is going to be made, it will likely be of the premiere. Today, a recording means the piece exists. It is the composer's calling card, engraved for the future. And yet, it doesn't allow for changes. Recordings have become so essential and taken for granted that I've actually had people ask me for a complete recording of an opera that hasn't even been performed!

Was the new opera successful? It all depends on the measuring stick for success. We often think of this in financial or critical terms, but to me, the bigger question is: Has the work found an audience—large or small—for which it resonates?

For most new operas, the premiere is another beginning. The creative team learns from watching their work performed live in front of an audience. Changes and new ideas will be incorporated, and perhaps there will be another chance to see them at work. This process will continue until the composer and librettist decide, at last, that the new opera is finished.

Composing *Moby-Dick*

In February 2005, a little more than four years after the premiere of *Dead Man Walking*, Terrence McNally and I were together in New York to create a one-woman scene for soprano (*At the Statue of Venus*) when a call came from Jonathan Pell, artistic director of the Dallas Opera: Would we be interested in creating a new grand opera for the company's 2009–2010 season? Not just any season, mind you: the inaugural season in the dazzling Winspear Opera House, still under construction at that point. Thrilled to be asked, and honored at the prospect of being part of the first season in a bold new American opera house, Terrence looked at me and said, "There's only one opera I'm interested in writing: *Moby-Dick*."

He had hinted at this before, but the reality of it suddenly seemed terrifying: too big, too vast, too difficult, too dense, too … much. Then I took a breath, and in his eye I saw a real sparkle. And I knew that if he, one of the great men of the theater, felt in his heart that it was possible, then it must be so. I did some research, read the book, dug deep inside, and realized I was indeed terrified by it, challenged, but also hugely inspired by the musical and dramatic possibilities. Melville's language is ravishingly beautiful, his characters fascinating, tough, and psychologically complex. There is a great sense of adventure throughout, much is at stake, and the overall story fits into what I have found works consistently in grand opera: a vast, inevitable landscape that looms over intimate, transformative human journeys.

So, I called Jonathan and said, "We want to do *Moby-Dick*." Silence. "Anything else?" was the reply. "Nope. *Moby-Dick*. Ben Heppner is Ahab. The entire story takes place at sea. Two acts. Under three hours, including an intermission. I want Patrick Summers to conduct." After a couple of months of back and forth about how the project could work, the people at the Dallas Opera accepted and embraced this as the story we all really wanted to do. It was a huge leap of faith for the company, but it fit with the bold idea they had for a new opera house and for taking the entire community on a big adventure.

As we proceeded, it became ever clearer how brilliant Terrence's idea was: in addition to the innately operatic qualities of Melville's book, it also has the invaluable quality of instant name recognition. Most people, even though they might not have read the book, have certainly heard of it, and have a basic idea of what it's about. There's no need to go on and on explaining the story. So the question isn't "*What* is that?"—it is "*How on earth* are you going to *do* that?" That is a great place to start a big project.

I read the book one more time, underlined passages I loved, language I wanted to use, highlighted characteristics of the different people in the story, then put it away. Terrence and I were more than a year into the project when, for personal reasons, he felt he had to withdraw. Generously, he encouraged me to find a new writing partner and to use anything he and I had already discussed. It was a huge decision: to start fresh with *Moby-Dick*, or start over with another project? By this time, the Dallas Opera had found enthusiastic co-producers for the new opera, and this decision would affect all of them deeply.

In 2005, I had begun collaborating with Gene Scheer. By this time, he had written librettos for two operas by Tobias Picker (*An American Tragedy* and *Thérèse Raquin*), as well as numerous songs for great singers like Renée Fleming, Denyce Graves, Stephanie Blythe, and Nathan Gunn. We started by writing songs together and found we had excellent creative chemistry, liked each other, and most important, saw eye-to-eye on the goal: serve the drama. By this time, we were already working on a chamber opera called *Three Decembers* (based on an original story by McNally), starring mezzo-soprano Frederica von Stade, for the Houston Grand Opera and San Francisco Opera. So it felt right and natural to ask Gene about *Moby-Dick*. He had the same open-mouthed, terrified response that I'd had, and asked for some time to re-read the book and consider what he might be getting into. A week later, he called and said, "I'm in."

Indeed, he jumped in quickly and we met frequently in New York, or communicated by phone or e-mail. The major breakthrough in terms of storytelling was the decision to end with the famous line "Call me Ishmael" rather than begin with it. Opera is theater and it requires action on stage. What is more moving than to see people make decisions in real time? Gene's excellent example of this is in *La bohème*: we watch Mimì and Rodolfo fall in love in Act I. How much better this is than if they only recounted to us the story of how they fell in love!

So, by putting Ishmael's famous line at the end of the opera—by really earning that line—we could tell the story actively, in real time. And the character who is transformed through the journey, who survives to call himself Ishmael, is the one who will go on to write the novel years later. (It is interesting to note that Melville's line is "Call me Ishmael" and not "My name is Ishmael." It implies that this is not his given name, but a name he has chosen.) This was incredibly liberating because we wouldn't be bound to a narrator and could distill events in the novel to a line or even a gesture: something that would inspire a budding author to write at length later in his life.

The Dallas Opera announced the commission in January 2008 to its board of directors, major donors, and subscribers at a big event at the Dallas Aquarium. There were gasps over the subject, and roars of approval for the news that Ben Heppner had indeed signed on to sing Ahab before a single word or note had been written. The one big request I received that night which still resonates was from a board member who asked: "Please, let us be part of this. Keep us involved. Let us hear what you're doing. Let us participate." I was very moved and empowered by that request.

With five committed co-commissioners (Dallas Opera, San Francisco Opera, San Diego Opera, Calgary Opera, and State Opera of South Australia) plus commitments from conductor Patrick Summers and tenor Ben Heppner, Gene and I felt incredible confidence and support. The Houston Grand Opera had even rescheduled its 2010 production of *Lohengrin* so that Maestro Summers could be in Dallas to conduct *Moby-Dick*. Shortly after the announcement, Leonard (Lenny) Foglia agreed to join us as dramaturg and director. A gifted and busy Broadway director, he had by then directed the national touring production of *Dead Man Walking*, as well as the premieres of my operas *The End of the Affair* and *Three Decembers*. With him on board, the core creative team was complete. Now we just had to create the thing.

The commission agreement (signed in September 2007) specified the following delivery schedule for the opera:

- Scenario of characters (for casting) and general outline: December 28, 2007
- First draft of libretto for Act I: May 1, 2008
- First draft of libretto for Act II: October 1, 2008
- Piano score for Act I: January 1, 2009
- Piano score for the entire opera: August 1, 2009
- Workshop: September/October 2009
- Full score: December 1, 2009

- Orchestra parts: January 31, 2010
- First performance: April 30, 2010

After *Three Decembers* opened in Houston (February 29, 2008) Gene and I dug into *Moby-Dick.* In early April, we met on Nantucket Island for four days to work on the libretto in earnest. We toured the whaling museum, met with the leadership of the Nantucket Historical Association, walked the historic streets, and had the astounding good fortune to meet Nathaniel Philbrick, the acclaimed author of the prize-winning book, *In The Heart of the Sea: The Tragedy of the Whaleship Essex.* It tells the story of the Essex, rammed and sunk by a sperm whale in 1820; it was this very story that had inflamed Melville's imagination. This book, more than any other source, made *Moby-Dick* come to life for me. Philbrick was a stalwart friend to the project from our initial meeting.

Gene and I talked at length about characters: Who are they are and what do they want? What motivates them and drives them on? What parts of their journeys are essential to the opera? How do they talk? How do they sing? We decided on two primary parallel relationships: (1) Captain Ahab and First Mate Starbuck; (2) the first-time (or "greenhorn") sailor, Ishmael, and the first harpooneer, Queequeg. Ahab and Starbuck are in charge of all decisions that affect the physical well-being of everybody on board, and Starbuck is the only one who sees the destructive madness of Ahab's obsession with the white whale. Ishmael and Queequeg are on a journey of the heart and soul, with Queequeg as the spiritual center of the ship and Ishmael as the everyman who seeks a sense of connection and belonging in the world.

We had already identified Ahab as a heldentenor: His voice must sail over everything to inspire and energize the crew. His language would feature the great, noble poetry given him by Melville. Starbuck, by contrast, would be a big lyric baritone, his language beautiful but simpler. Ishmael, innocent and lost in the world, would be a tenor. His language would become more poetic as he grew, and his journey became more defined. Queequeg, the most grounded, would be a bass-baritone, anchored by a prayer in his native tongue. Another pair, Flask and Stubb, who provide comic relief, would be a character tenor and character baritone. Pip, the fourteen-year-old cabin boy who is the innocent vulnerable child of the ship, would be sung by a high soprano in a trouser role; the offstage voice of Captain Gardiner would be a baritone. The male choristers are all whalemen, of course, with several small solo roles from within the choir. We decided on key scenes in the opera that moved us both and seemed essential to the storytelling. By early May, Gene did indeed present me with a first draft of Act I. And then, at last, I was alone with a blank page of manuscript paper.

Just after the Nantucket trip, I caught a very bad cold and my right eardrum ruptured. During the six months it took my eardrum to heal completely, I worked to find the musical universe of *Moby-Dick*. Gene found a prayer in Samoan, and through that language, I composed Queequeg's chant (Music Example 50.1).

I also found a restless rhythmic figure of flowing arpeggiated sixteenth notes that appears in the first measures of the Prelude (see Figure 50.1).

MUSIC EXAMPLE 50.1 Jake Heggie, *Moby-Dick*: Queequeg's Chant (Act I, mm. 131–136).

I found a rhythmic figure in 8/8 to represent Ahab's awkward walk (Figure 50.2). The stage directions read, "The light has changed. It is just before dawn. Ahab paces and exits. We hear the sailors asleep below deck. Queequeg is chanting to his idol. Nearby in a bunk or hammock, Ishmael sleeps fitfully."

But overall, I was completely stuck. All that incredible buildup and support, and there I sat in my studio making slow, awkward, unsatisfying progress. I took walks and naps, sat at the piano, avoided the piano, cleaned my studio, avoided the studio. I slogged along rather terrified for months. Gene delivered his first draft of Act II on schedule. I felt panic.

By December 2008, I had sixty so-so pages of music. And then I realized that I was missing the keystone: Ahab. I hadn't found him musically. I understood all of the other characters, but Ahab still eluded me. As I mentioned earlier, I like to start at the beginning of the opera and move through organically. But I was getting stuck over and over again, unable to break through the brick wall. That's when I discovered a place in the middle of Act I where I had an inkling about some music for Ahab. At last, I got smart, took the path of least resistance, and wrote the aria and scene that begins with Ahab

FIGURE 50.1 Jake Heggie, *Moby-Dick*, first page of Prelude. The composer's autograph score.

singing "I Leave a White and Turbid Wake." Suddenly, it was as if the old captain himself stood before me. There he was, the aching human, the great leader, aware of the terrible path he was going down, but unable to stop himself. The music is turbulent but lyrical and aching; vocal melismas give a sense of yearning and anguish.

FIGURE 50.2 Jake Heggie, *Moby-Dick*, Ahab's Walk (Act I, scene 1, mm. 1–10). The composer's autograph score.

In that scene, the core harmonic progression for the entire opera suddenly emerged: E minor–C major (first inversion)–C minor[9] (first inversion)–C minor (first inversion)–E minor, out of which almost all material would be drawn. The following excerpt from my manuscript copy of the Prelude accompanies the stage direction, "Ahab stands alone on the deck of the *Pequod*. He is very still as he stares over the ocean and the sky. Everything seems to be revolving—stars, planets, the world." The musical indication is "Flowing," and the opera begins with the recurring arpeggiated sixteenth notes. The essential harmonies make their first appearance in mm. 11–15 (see Figure 50.1).

It was as if the musical world for this opera suddenly cracked open, and I was allowed to listen. I threw out the sixty pages I had written, keeping only Queequeg's chant. And in January 2009—when the Act I piano score was due—I began Act I. By March, I had the complete act. By the end of July, I had all of Act II. I had never had such a terrifying buildup, and never such a gratifying, wondrous period of creation. I felt on fire with the opera, as though I knew the characters personally; all I had to do was listen to them and take dictation.

During these months, Gene and Lenny would come to my studio in San Francisco, or I would meet them in New York, and together we would go over what I had written. We worked on every corner of the opera. Lenny, as dramaturg and director, made sure the dramatic through-line was clear for each character and each part of the story, and that something vital was at stake in each and every scene. Each moment had to be essential to the storytelling, or out it went. We found places for rewrites, places for more information, places where there was too much information. For example, we rewrote the

"Coffin Scene" (Act II, scene 5) several times. It is a scene where Ishmael contemplates Queequeg's coffin: at first it was purely instrumental, with Ishmael watching the coffin being constructed; then it was a solo for Ishmael with all other characters heard from offstage through; and eventually it was a solo for Ishmael with offstage chorus at the end. Our work was always about a search for clarity, essence, and momentum. Many times, Gene and I worried about how Lenny would manage to stage certain moments: The whale hunts? The wreck of the *Pequod*? But he assured us, if the scene is right and it belongs in the opera: "I will find a way to stage it effectively."

By this time, the opera had been completely cast, and Lenny had started to meet with designer Robert Brill. But, though they were in discussions about a possible look for the opera, they wanted first to hear the score. I finished the piano-vocal score just in time for a workshop hosted by the San Francisco Opera in early August 2009. For five days, a generous group of singers worked with conductor Patrick Summers, me, Gene, and Lenny, to rehearse the new opera. We cut, rearranged, and tried scenes in different orders. For example, in Act I, scene 4, Ahab sings his aria "I Leave a White and Turbid Wake," then a duet between Queequeg and Ishmael emerges, and finally Starbuck enters to create a big quartet. During the workshop, we rearranged the sequence so that the duet was first, followed by the Ahab solo, and then the quartet. After hearing it both ways, we went back to the initial form. We also made the big choice to change Ishmael's name to "Greenhorn" for the entire opera. He had been referred to as "greenhorn" or "greenie" throughout the libretto, which is historically correct for the period (a first-time whaleman was called a greenhorn). It also enhanced his search for identity; he tells Queequeg in their Act II duet, "together we will find a name for me."

On the fifth day of the workshop, there was a complete read-through: eight singers, two pianos, an invited group of people from the producing companies, and the entire creative team, including designers. I am here to tell you: if an opera comes off the page and works for an audience with singers sitting in metal chairs, using scores on music stands, with piano accompaniment, you know you might be on to something.

After the reading, I met with Gene, Lenny, and Patrick to discuss the additional changes needed to the score. Overall, we felt we were in pretty good shape, but the first act still seemed long to me at ninety-six minutes. I wanted to cut it down to ninety minutes. I trimmed some of Starbuck's and Queequeg's first arias (Act I, scene 3) so that the drama and momentum of the opera did not stop, tightened the quartet in scene 4, and found some "invisible" cuts in other parts of the act (a measure here or there). Those changes, along with some rewrites to Act II, were completed in September, and by early October 2009 a complete piano-vocal score was sent to the cast and crew of *Moby-Dick*: 5,312 measures of music in a 587-page score. Then a chorus score was created so that the men of the Dallas Opera Chorus could begin their work. Around this time, I took a trip to New York to see what Lenny and his design team had come up with. Gene and I were blown away by their presentation, for it seemed completely unified with the libretto and score.

With the bones of the opera set, I started to orchestrate. During this period, I made several trips to Dallas to play music from the score at events for subscribers, donors, and board members. I remember one particular event where an elderly woman raised her hand right at the beginning and asked, "Will I like it?" "No," I replied. "You'll love it."

By early February 2010, I was finished. Bear in mind that I still write everything by hand. All along, I'd been sending pages to my copyist, Bill Holab, in New York. He is something of a wizard at his craft, able to read a composer's rapid handwriting and put everything into the computer at a remarkably fast pace. *Moby-Dick* has a cast that includes eight solo roles (seven men and a soprano for the trouser role of Pip) plus a large male chorus; the orchestration includes three flutes, three oboes (one doubling English horn), three clarinets (one doubling bass clarinet), three bassoons (one doubling contra-bassoon), four horns, three trumpets, three trombones, three percussionists playing a battery of instruments, harp, and a large string section. My copyist had to find a way to negotiate all of that into a legible large-scale format (so the conductor would actually be able to use it!), then generate parts, put in musical cues for the players, print and bind scores and parts and get them to the Dallas Opera before rehearsals began in late March 2010. All of this had to be proofread by several pairs of eyes, too. String parts were generated first so the music librarian in Dallas could put in bowings indicated by the principal string players, then the percussion parts so they could configure and divide up the percussion section, and finally the winds and brass.

Somehow, all of this came together in a timely fashion, and rehearsals began on schedule in late March: five intense weeks of work as we barreled toward opening night. Between staging and musical rehearsals, there were many public forums, fundraising and press events, seminars, and more to build enthusiasm and community awareness of the April 30 premiere. The set arrived just two weeks before the premiere and technical rehearsals began for lighting, set changes, and Elaine McCarthy's stunning projections of the sea, sky, waves, storms, and the ocean. Additionally, highly stylized computer graphics gave us a starry voyage through the universe, whaleboats on the raked wall of the stage (Figure 50.3), and the wreck of the *Pequod*.

This particular opera also requires acrobats and climbers to ascend rigging and ladders to the top of the proscenium. The cast, too, had to learn to negotiate the difficult production—some of them singing from twenty-five feet above the stage (Figure 50.4). It was thrilling.

With each rehearsal in the theater, we began to see and hear the opera come together. At the final dress rehearsal, the second act had yet to be completely lit, and projections had not been finished. Finally, on Friday, April 30, at 5:30 PM, the technical crew was told they had to vacate so the theater could be prepared for the 7:30 PM opening. Minutes later, the entire computer system crashed. Fortunately, I was not aware of any of this. The professional crew kicked into high gear and somehow solved the problems and averted a catastrophe. Shortly after 7 PM, the doors opened, and at 7:30 PM, Patrick Summers indicated the downbeat of *Moby-Dick*.

Why do I love this art form? Because it demands the very best of every single person involved, including the audience. Opera raises the bar very high and tests our limits. The cast, orchestra, chorus, and crew have to perform at the peak of their abilities; they must move and breathe as one in the same moment, as indicated by the conductor's baton.

FIGURE 50.3 Whaleboats against a starry sky. © Karen Almond, Dallas Opera.

FIGURE 50.4 The *Pequod* with sailors in the rigging. © Karen Almond, Dallas Opera.

Even better: they are all eager to do this. And when it all comes together, it can be emotionally shattering and thrilling. It can transform one's heart and soul. It can have that much power.

We were very fortunate with *Moby-Dick*. Somehow, the force was with us, and all went well beyond our wildest imaginings on opening night. We were also incredibly fortunate to know that because of the commission consortium, we had four assured productions ahead of us: State Opera of South Australia, Calgary Opera, San Diego Opera, and finally San Francisco Opera. From the start, we knew we'd be able to work on the piece after the premiere and see the changes up on the stage. In the second production (South Australia), I was able to cut a few measures toward the end of the opera and alter a few word settings; the design team was able to refine and finish the physical production. In the third production (Calgary), we saw the finished production and learned how a smaller, more regional company would be able to handle the opera.

Two years before the Dallas world premiere of *Moby-Dick*, my right eardrum ruptured from a cold. One month after that premiere, my left eardrum ruptured from another cold. The circle is complete. Both have healed wonderfully, and I'm listening again.

Note

1. Comments from Mark Adamo, John Adams, Daniel Catán, and Stewart Wallace were via e-mail exchanges in February and March 2009. Philip Glass's comments are from a phone conversation on March 10, 2009.

Index of Musical Works

The following list of operas, musicals, operettas, oratorios, cantatas, ballets, and songs (and a handful of instrumental works) is alphabetized by composer's last name. Some titles are listed in English translation as well as the original language, according to contributors' use. Works that are regularly credited to a team (e.g., Rodgers and Hammerstein) list the composer first. Page numbers followed by *f*, *t* and n indicate figures, tables and notes, respectively. Numbers in *italics* indicate music examples.

General Index

Page numbers followed by *f*, *t* and n indicate figures, tables and notes, respectively. Numbers in *italics* indicate music examples.
For musical works, please see the **Index of Musical Works.**